Contemporary
Literary Criticism

Guide to Gale Literary Criticism Series

For criticism on	Consult these Gale series
Authors now living or who died after December 31, 1999	*CONTEMPORARY LITERARY CRITICISM (CLC)*
Authors who died between 1900 and 1999	*TWENTIETH-CENTURY LITERARY CRITICISM (TCLC)*
Authors who died between 1800 and 1899	*NINETEENTH-CENTURY LITERATURE CRITICISM (NCLC)*
Authors who died between 1400 and 1799	*LITERATURE CRITICISM FROM 1400 TO 1800 (LC)* *SHAKESPEAREAN CRITICISM (SC)*
Authors who died before 1400	*CLASSICAL AND MEDIEVAL LITERATURE CRITICISM (CMLC)*
Authors of books for children and young adults	*CHILDREN'S LITERATURE REVIEW (CLR)*
Dramatists	*DRAMA CRITICISM (DC)*
Poets	*POETRY CRITICISM (PC)*
Short story writers	*SHORT STORY CRITICISM (SSC)*
Literary topics and movements	*HARLEM RENAISSANCE: A GALE CRITICAL COMPANION (HR)* *THE BEAT GENERATION: A GALE CRITICAL COMPANION (BG)*
Asian American writers of the last two hundred years	*ASIAN AMERICAN LITERATURE (AAL)*
Black writers of the past two hundred years	*BLACK LITERATURE CRITICISM (BLC)* *BLACK LITERATURE CRITICISM SUPPLEMENT (BLCS)*
Hispanic writers of the late nineteenth and twentieth centuries	*HISPANIC LITERATURE CRITICISM (HLC)* *HISPANIC LITERATURE CRITICISM SUPPLEMENT (HLCS)*
Native North American writers and orators of the eighteenth, nineteenth, and twentieth centuries	*NATIVE NORTH AMERICAN LITERATURE (NNAL)*
Major authors from the Renaissance to the present	*WORLD LITERATURE CRITICISM, 1500 TO THE PRESENT (WLC)* *WORLD LITERATURE CRITICISM SUPPLEMENT (WLCS)*

ISSN 0091-3421

Volume 179

Contemporary Literary Criticism

Criticism of the Works
of Today's Novelists, Poets, Playwrights,
Short Story Writers, Scriptwriters, and
Other Creative Writers

Janet Witalec
PROJECT EDITOR

GALE®

THOMSON

GALE

Detroit • New York • San Diego • San Francisco • Cleveland • New Haven, Conn. • Waterville, Maine • London • Munich

THOMSON

★

GALE™

Contemporary Literary Criticism, Vol. 179

Project Editor
Janet Witalec

Editorial
Tom Burns, Jenny Cromie, Kathy D. Darrow,
Jeffrey W. Hunter, Justin Karr, Lemma Shomali

Indexing Services
Laurie Andriot

Rights Acquisition & Management
Margaret Chamberlain, Mari Masalin-Cooper,
Lori Hines

Imaging and Multimedia
Lezlie Light, Dave Oblender, Kelly A. Quin,
Denay Wilding

Composition and Electronic Capture
Kathy Sauer

Manufacturing
Stacy L. Melson

LIBRARY OF CONGRESS CATALOG CARD NUMBER 76-46132

ISBN 0-7876-6752-8
ISSN 0091-3421

Printed in the United States of America
10 9 8 7 6 5 4 3 2 1

Contents

Preface vii

Acknowledgments xi

Literary Criticism Series Advisory Board xiii

Preface

Named "one of the twenty-five most distinguished reference titles published during the past twenty-five years" by *Reference Quarterly,* the *Contemporary Literary Criticism* (*CLC*) series provides readers with critical commentary and general information on more than 2,000 authors now living or who died after December 31, 1999. Volumes published from 1973 through 1999 include authors who died after December 31, 1959. Previous to the publication of the first volume of *CLC* in 1973, there was no ongoing digest monitoring scholarly and popular sources of critical opinion and explication of modern literature. *CLC,* therefore, has fulfilled an essential need, particularly since the complexity and variety of contemporary literature makes the function of criticism especially important to today's reader.

Scope of the Series

CLC provides significant passages from published criticism of works by creative writers. Since many of the authors covered in *CLC* inspire continual critical commentary, writers are often represented in more than one volume. There is, of course, no duplication of reprinted criticism.

Authors are selected for inclusion for a variety of reasons, among them the publication or dramatic production of a critically acclaimed new work, the reception of a major literary award, revival of interest in past writings, or the adaptation of a literary work to film or television.

Attention is also given to several other groups of writers—authors of considerable public interest—about whose work criticism is often difficult to locate. These include mystery and science fiction writers, literary and social critics, foreign authors, and authors who represent particular ethnic groups.

Each *CLC* volume contains individual essays and reviews taken from hundreds of book review periodicals, general magazines, scholarly journals, monographs, and books. Entries include critical evaluations spanning from the beginning of an author's career to the most current commentary. Interviews, feature articles, and other published writings that offer insight into the author's works are also presented. Students, teachers, librarians, and researchers will find that the general critical and biographical material in *CLC* provides them with vital information required to write a term paper, analyze a poem, or lead a book discussion group. In addition, complete biographical citations note the original source and all of the information necessary for a term paper footnote or bibliography.

Organization of the Book

A *CLC* entry consists of the following elements:

- The **Author Heading** cites the name under which the author most commonly wrote, followed by birth and death dates. Also located here are any name variations under which an author wrote, including transliterated forms for authors whose native languages use nonroman alphabets. If the author wrote consistently under a pseudonym, the pseudonym will be listed in the author heading and the author's actual name given in parenthesis on the first line of the biographical and critical information. Uncertain birth or death dates are indicated by question marks. Single-work entries are preceded by a heading that consists of the most common form of the title in English translation (if applicable) and the original date of composition.

- A **Portrait of the Author** is included when available.

- The **Introduction** contains background information that introduces the reader to the author, work, or topic that is the subject of the entry.

- The list of **Principal Works** is ordered chronologically by date of first publication and lists the most important works by the author. The genre and publication date of each work is given. In the case of foreign authors whose works have been translated into English, the English-language version of the title follows in brackets. Unless otherwise indicated, dramas are dated by first performance, not first publication.

- Reprinted **Criticism** is arranged chronologically in each entry to provide a useful perspective on changes in critical evaluation over time. The critic's name and the date of composition or publication of the critical work are given at the beginning of each piece of criticism. Unsigned criticism is preceded by the title of the source in which it appeared. All titles by the author featured in the text are printed in boldface type. Footnotes are reprinted at the end of each essay or excerpt. In the case of excerpted criticism, only those footnotes that pertain to the excerpted texts are included.

- A complete **Bibliographical Citation** of the original essay or book precedes each piece of criticism. Source citations in the Literary Criticism Series follow University of Chicago Press style, as outlined in *The Chicago Manual of Style,* 14th ed. (Chicago: The University of Chicago Press, 1993).

- Critical essays are prefaced by brief **Annotations** explicating each piece.

- Whenever possible, a recent **Author Interview** accompanies each entry.

- An annotated bibliography of **Further Reading** appears at the end of each entry and suggests resources for additional study. In some cases, significant essays for which the editors could not obtain reprint rights are included here. Boxed material following the further reading list provides references to other biographical and critical sources on the author in series published by Gale.

Indexes

A **Cumulative Author Index** lists all of the authors that appear in a wide variety of reference sources published by the Gale Group, including *CLC*. A complete list of these sources is found facing the first page of the Author Index. The index also includes birth and death dates and cross references between pseudonyms and actual names.

A **Cumulative Nationality Index** lists all authors featured in *CLC* by nationality, followed by the number of the *CLC* volume in which their entry appears.

A **Cumulative Topic Index** lists the literary themes and topics treated in the series as well as in *Literature Criticism from 1400 to 1800, Nineteenth-Century Literature Criticism, Twentieth-Century Literary Criticism,* and the *Contemporary Literary Criticism* Yearbook, which was discontinued in 1998.

An alphabetical **Title Index** accompanies each volume of *CLC*. Listings of titles by authors covered in the given volume are followed by the author's name and the corresponding page numbers where the titles are discussed. English translations of foreign titles and variations of titles are cross-referenced to the title under which a work was originally published. Titles of novels, dramas, nonfiction books, and poetry, short story, or essay collections are printed in italics, while individual poems, short stories, and essays are printed in roman type within quotation marks.

In response to numerous suggestions from librarians, Gale also produces an annual cumulative title index that alphabetically lists all titles reviewed in *CLC* and is available to all customers. Additional copies of this index are available upon request. Librarians and patrons will welcome this separate index; it saves shelf space, is easy to use, and is recyclable upon receipt of the next edition.

Citing *Contemporary Literary Criticism*

When citing criticism reprinted in the Literary Criticism Series, students should provide complete bibliographic information so that the cited essay can be located in the original print or electronic source. Students who quote directly from reprinted criticism may use any accepted bibliographic format, such as University of Chicago Press style or Modern Language Association (MLA) style. Both the MLA and the University of Chicago formats are acceptable and recognized as being the current standards for citations. It is important, however, to choose one format for all citations; do not mix the two formats within a list of citations.

The examples below follow recommendations for preparing a bibliography set forth in *The Chicago Manual of Style,* 14th ed. (Chicago: The University of Chicago Press, 1993); the first example pertains to material drawn from periodicals, the second to material reprinted from books:

Morrison, Jago. "Narration and Unease in Ian McEwan's Later Fiction." *Critique* 42, no. 3 (spring 2001): 253-68. Reprinted in *Contemporary Literary Criticism.* Vol. 169, edited by Janet Witalec, 212-20. Detroit: Gale, 2003.

Brossard, Nicole. "Poetic Politics." In *The Politics of Poetic Form: Poetry and Public Policy,* edited by Charles Bernstein, 73-82. New York: Roof Books, 1990. Reprinted in *Contemporary Literary Criticism.* Vol. 169, edited by Janet Witalec, 3-8. Detroit: Gale, 2003.

The examples below follow recommendations for preparing a works cited list set forth in the *MLA Handbook for Writers of Research Papers,* 5th ed. (New York: The Modern Language Association of America, 1999); the first example pertains to material drawn from periodicals, the second to material reprinted from books:

Morrison, Jago. "Narration and Unease in Ian McEwan's Later Fiction." *Critique* 42.3 (spring 2001): 253-68. Reprinted in *Contemporary Literary Criticism.* Ed. Janet Witalec. Vol. 169. Detroit: Gale, 2003. 212-20.

Brossard, Nicole. "Poetic Politics." *The Politics of Poetic Form: Poetry and Public Policy.* Ed. Charles Bernstein. New York: Roof Books, 1990. 73-82. Reprinted in *Contemporary Literary Criticism.* Ed. Janet Witalec. Vol. 169. Detroit: Gale, 2003. 3-8.

Suggestions are Welcome

Readers who wish to suggest new features, topics, or authors to appear in future volumes, or who have other suggestions or comments are cordially invited to call, write, or fax the Project Editor:

Project Editor, Literary Criticism Series
The Gale Group
27500 Drake Road
Farmington Hills, MI 48331-3535
1-800-347-4253 (GALE)
Fax: 248-699-8054

Acknowledgments

The editors wish to thank the copyright holders of the criticism included in this volume and the permissions managers of many book and magazine publishing companies for assisting us in securing reproduction rights. We are also grateful to the staffs of the Detroit Public Library, the Library of Congress, the University of Detroit Mercy Library, Wayne State University Purdy/Kresge Library Complex, and the University of Michigan Libraries for making their resources available to us. Following is a list of the copyright holders who have granted us permission to reproduce material in this volume of *CLC*. Every effort has been made to trace copyright, but if omissions have been made, please let us know.

COPYRIGHTED MATERIAL IN *CLC*, VOLUME 179, WAS REPRODUCED FROM THE FOLLOWING PERIODICALS:

American Drama, v. 2, Fall, 1992. Copyright 1992 by *American Drama.* Reproduced by permission.—*Antioch Review,* v. 57, Winter, 1999. Copyright 1999, by *Antioch Review.* Reproduced by permission.—*Artforum,* v. 39, October, 2000. Copyright 2000, by *Artforum.* Reproduced by permission.—*Belles Lettres,* v. 4, Fall, 1988; v. 10, Fall, 1994. Reproduced by permission.—*Books & Culture,* v. 7, November-December, 2001. Copyright 2001 by *Books & Culture.* Reproduced by permission.—*Christian Science Monitor,* v. 86, June 3, 1994; v. 92, November 9, 2000. © 1994, 2000. Christian Science Publishing Society. All rights reserved. Reproduced by permission from *The Christian Science Monitor.*/v. 85, July 2, 1993 for "Review of *A River Sutra,* " by Merle Rubin; v. 92, November 2, 2000, for "A Perfect Genetic Future" by Merle Rubin. © 1993, 2000 The Christian Science Publishing Society. All rights reserved. Reproduced by permission of the respective authors.—*CLA Journal,* v. 37, September, 1993. Copyright, 1993 by The College Language Association. Used by permission of The College Language Association.—*Commentary,* v. 102, December, 1996, for "Out of Africa" by Peter L. Berger. Copyright © 1996 by the American Jewish Committee. All rights reserved. Reproduced by permission of the publisher and the author.—*Contemporary Review,* v. 255, October, 1989; v. 270, April, 1997. Copyright 1989, 1997 by *Contemporary Review.* Reproduced by the permission of Contemporary Review Ltd.—*English Journal,* v. 85, September, 1996 for "Dairy Farm Tragedy" by Carol J. Pierce. Copyright © 1996 by the National Council of Teachers of English. Reproduced by permission of the publisher and the author.—*The Explicator,* v. 45, Winter, 1987; v. 53, Summer, 1995; v. 60, Spring, 2002. Copyright © 1987, 1995, 2002 Helen Dwight Reid Educational Foundation. Reproduced with permission of the Helen Dwight Reid Educational Foundation, published by Heldref Publications, 1319 18th Street, NW, Washington, DC, 20036-1802.—*The French Review,* v. 73, March, 2000; v. 74, October, 2000; v. 76, February, 2003. Copyright 2000, 2003 by the American Association of Teachers of French. Reproduced by permission.—*The Georgia Review,* v. 49, Spring, 1995. Copyright, 1995, by the University of Georgia. Reproduced by permission.—*The Hudson Review,* v. 54, Summer, 2001. Copyright 2001, by *The Hudson Review.* Reproduced by permission.—*Human Rights Review,* v. 2, October-December, 2002, for "Gesture without Motion? Poetry and Politics in Africa" by Elizabeth Heger Boyle. Copyright 2000 by Human Rights Review. Reprinted by permission.—*Journal of American Culture,* v. 17, Summer, 1994. Copyright 1994 by *Journal of American Culture.* Reproduced by permission.—*Journal of Commonwealth Literature,* v. 25, August, 1990. Copyright 1990 by *Journal of Commonwealth Literature.* Reproduced by permission.—*Journal of Evolutionary Psychology,* August, 2002. Reproduced by permission.—*Journal of Modern African Studies,* v. 28, September, 1990; v. 36, December, 1998. Copyright 1990, 1998 by Journal of Modern African Studies. Reprinted with permission of Cambridge University Press.—*Journal of Narrative Theory,* v. 31, Summer, 2001. Copyright 2001 by *JNT: Journal of Narrative Theory.* Reproduced by permission.—*Literature & Theology,* v. 12, June, 1998 for "Song of the Unsung Antihero: How Arthur Miller's *Death of a Salesman* Flatters Us," by Jonathan Witt. Copyright 1998 by Oxford University Press. Reproduced by permission of publisher and author.—*Literary Criterion,* v. 29, 1994. Copyright 1994 by *Literary Criterion.* Reproduced by permission.—*Los Angeles Times Book Review,* April 9, 1989; July 11, 1993; June 5, 1994; March 29, 1998; October 15, 2000. Copyright, 1989, 1993, 1994, 1998, 2000 *Los Angeles Times.* Reproduced by permission.—*Michigan Quarterly Review,* v. 37, Fall, 1998 for "*Death of a Salesman*: A Playwrights' Forum" by Philip C. Kolin, and others; v. 37, Fall, 1998 for "Willy Loman: Icon of Business Culture" by Brenda Murphy. Copyright © The University of Michigan, 1998. All rights reserved. Reproduced by permission of the respective authors.—*MLN,* v. 115, September, 2000. © The Johns Hopkins University Press. Reproduced by permission.—*Modern Drama,* v. 31, June, 1988; v. 41, Winter, 1998; v. 43, Spring, 2000. Copyright © 1988, 1998, 2000 University of Toronto, Graduate Centre for Study of Drama. Reproduced by permission.—*Modern Fiction Studies,* v. 37, Autumn, 1991. Copyright © 1991 by Purdue Research Foundation, West Lafayette, IN, 47907. All rights reserved. Reproduced by permission of The Johns Hopkins University.—*National Women's Studies Association Journal,* v. 11, Spring, 1999. Copyright 1999, by National Women's Studies Association Journal. Reproduced by permission by Indiana University Press.—*New Leader,* v. 83, November-December,

PHOTOGRAPHS AND ILLUSTRATIONS APPEARING IN *CLC,* VOLUME 179, WERE RECEIVED FROM THE FOLLOWING SOURCES:

Literary Criticism Series Advisory Board

The members of the Gale Group Literary Criticism Series Advisory Board—reference librarians and subject specialists from public, academic, and school library systems—represent a cross-section of our customer base and offer a variety of informed perspectives on both the presentation and content of our literature criticism products. Advisory board members assess and define such quality issues as the relevance, currency, and usefulness of the author coverage, critical content, and literary topics included in our series; evaluate the layout, presentation, and general quality of our printed volumes; provide feedback on the criteria used for selecting authors and topics covered in our series; provide suggestions for potential enhancements to our series; identify any gaps in our coverage of authors or literary topics, recommending authors or topics for inclusion; analyze the appropriateness of our content and presentation for various user audiences, such as high school students, undergraduates, graduate students, librarians, and educators; and offer feedback on any proposed changes/enhancements to our series. We wish to thank the following advisors for their advice throughout the year.

Jane Hamilton
1957-

American novelist and short story writer.

The following entry presents an overview of Hamilton's career through 2001.

INTRODUCTION

After winning the PEN/Hemingway Foundation Award for best first novel with *The Book of Ruth* (1988), Hamilton continued to attract both critical and popular attention for her series of novels, including *A Map of the World* (1994), *The Short History of a Prince* (1998), and *Disobedience* (2000). With astute psychological insight, Hamilton examines the subtle nuances of family dynamics in the face of tragedy, misfortune, and dysfunction, as her characters are thrust into nightmarish circumstances beyond their control. Her novels are typically set in rural or suburban areas of the American Midwest, where the claustrophobic atmosphere of family and community life often threatens to crush the spirit of the individual. In addition, much of Hamilton's fiction explores the internal lives of her characters, usually voicing their unique perspectives and personal insights through a first-person point of view. Critically acclaimed for her well-drawn characterization and evocative settings, Hamilton was widely recognized by mainstream audiences after *The Book of Ruth* and *A Map of the World* were chosen as selections for the Oprah Book Club.

BIOGRAPHICAL INFORMATION

The youngest of five children, Hamilton was born in 1957 in Oak Park, Illinois, a suburb of Chicago. Her father was an engineer for General Motors, and her mother was a theatre critic for the *Chicago Daily News*. From an early age, Hamilton's passion for reading and writing were encouraged by her grandmother—a former journalist—and her mother, whose notable poem "A Song for a Fifth Child" appeared in *Ladies Home Journal*. In 1979 Hamilton graduated from Carleton College in Northfield, Minnesota, with a B.A. in English. While at Carleton, she won the Class of 1885 Prose Award in 1977 and 1979. After graduation, Hamilton accepted an entry-level editorial job at a New York publishing company. Before she moved to New York, however, she stopped to visit a friend who was working at an apple orchard in Rochester, Wisconsin, and eventually decided to stay at the orchard rather than travel to New York. Hamilton later married Robert Willard, one of the orchards' owners, in 1982. In 1983 her first short story, "My Own Earth," was published in *Harper's* magazine. The December 1983 issue of *Harper's* published her story "Aunt Marji's Happy Ending," which was later cited as a Distinguished Short Story of 1984 and recognized in *The Best American Short Stories, 1984*. Hamilton's first novel, *The Book of Ruth,* has been awarded the PEN/Hemingway Award, the 1989 Banta Award, and the Great Lakes College Association New Writers Award. When Oprah Winfrey, the popular American television talk-show host, launched her book club in 1997, she chose *The Book of Ruth* and *A Map of the World* as early selections. Subsequently, both novels became international best-sellers. A film adaptation of *A Map of the World* was released in 1999.

MAJOR WORKS

Typically set in the Midwest, Hamilton's novels address the suffering, redemption, and resilience of the human spirit often found in contemporary American families. Inspired by a series of homicides in rural Wisconsin in 1983 when several men killed their mothers-in-law, *The Book of Ruth* is set in the fictional town of Honey Creek, Illinois. Ruth, the protagonist, is a sensitive and creative young woman who struggles to survive in her emotionally isolated and poverty-stricken community. While recounting her childhood experiences—marred by an emotionally abusive mother and a largely absent father—Ruth falls in love with and marries Ruby, an emotionally unstable man. The couple moves into Ruth's mother's small house, where the ensuing conflict between son-in-law and mother-in-law violently escalates to an inevitable conclusion. Set in the fictional town of Prairie Center, Wisconsin, which is slowly changing from a rural to a suburban area, *A Map of the World* tells the stories of Alice and Howard Goodwin and their young daughters. The local community has continued to treat the family as outsiders despite their six years of residency in Prairie Center running a dairy farm. Divided into three parts alternately narrated by Alice and Howard, the novel opens with the accidental drowning death of a neighbor's two-year-old daughter whom Alice agreed to baby-sit. Underscoring the town's suspicions of Alice's character, the tragedy snowballs into a series of false accusations that Alice has also molested local schoolchildren. Alice is subsequently arrested and sent to jail to await trial. At this point, Howard's narration begins, recounting his struggles to keep his family intact and the events of his wife's trial. Exonerated after the trial, Alice resumes her story, which includes her reconciliation with the dead two-year-old's mother and the family's eventual decision to leave the farm. In a marked departure from Hamilton's usual protagonists and themes, *The Short History of a Prince* is a coming-of-age story about a gay man who struggles to reconcile his high school fantasies with the realities of his adult life. A third-person narrative, the novel concerns Walter McCloud, whose story alternates between events during the 1970s and 1990s. The first section features fifteen-year-old Walter studying ballet—and dreaming of performing the role of Prince Siegfried in the *Nutcracker*—at the same time that his older brother is dying of Hodgkin's disease. The second section follows thirty-eight-year-old Walter as he returns to the Midwest to teach high school English and attempts to come to terms with his homosexuality after spending the intervening years working at a Manhattan dollhouse factory. Narrated in the first person, *Disobedience* centers around Henry Shaw as he remembers his coming-of-age at the age of seventeen. After prying into his mother's e-mail account, Henry discovers that she is having an extramarital affair. The rest of the narrative focuses on the effects and implications that this discovery brings to bear on Henry's relationships, particularly with his mother.

CRITICAL RECEPTION

Critics have widely praised Hamilton for her insight into the human psyche and her effective treatment of such themes as forgiveness and suffering, often favorably comparing her novels to the works of Jane Smiley and Sue Miller. Reviewers have also lauded her efforts to create characters endowed with sensitivity and endurance, particularly the protagonists of *The Book of Ruth* and *A Map of the World*. Although commentators have frequently noted the realistic portraits and evocative atmospheres of everyday Midwestern life in her novels, especially as experienced by women, some have argued that the plotting of *A Map of the World* is both predictable and mechanical. Some critics have also complained that Hamilton's novels tend to be overly sentimental and melodramatic, sometimes comparing her plots to those of television soap operas. However, Hamilton's supporters have asserted that her distinctive authorial voice, precise language, and subtly nuanced characterizations greatly outweigh any perceptions of formulaic plotting. Reviewers have also remarked that, despite the dominantly feminine perspectives of her early novels, Hamilton constructed a striking and believable male point of view in *The Short History of a Prince*. Commentators have additionally compared the stream of consciousness narration of the male protagonist in *Disobedience* to that of Holden Caulfield in J. D. Salinger's *Catcher in the Rye*.

PRINCIPAL WORKS

The Book of Ruth (novel) 1988; published in Great Britain as *The Frogs are Still Singing,* 1989
A Map of the World (novel) 1994
The Short History of a Prince: A Novel (novel) 1998
Disobedience (novel) 2000

CRITICISM

Suzanne Berne (review date fall 1988)

SOURCE: Berne, Suzanne. "Dreams of Love." *Belles Lettres* 4, no. 1 (fall 1988): 13.

[*In the following review, Berne outlines the plot of* The Book of Ruth, *highlighting its central themes in contrast with those of Elizabeth Benedict's* The Beginner's Book of Dreams.]

You would miss Honey Creek, Illinois, if you were driving through "listening to your favorite song on the radio or telling a story about your neighbor." It is one of those small, depressed towns that flick by your car window, just another collection of houses needing paint and a cow pasture. But in this town lives Ruth, a luminous spirit encased in a homely child, waiting for someone to stop and discover her.

Jane Hamilton's first novel, **The Book of Ruth,** is about the dream of happiness. It is also about the nightmare of deprivation. Ruth's favorite recollection is of the time her father, scooping ice cream at the dinner table, missed her dish and the ice cream landed on Ruth's head instead. Everyone became hilarious. "I wanted to preserve the scene," she tells us, "just as fossils do, keeping rare animals so still in stone . . .; on that July night we were actually experiencing the gladness some people feel every day, not just once in a summer." That "gladness," which many of us take for granted, is like a starving child's vivid memory of a lollipop: Insubstantial but intoxicating, the memory itself measures the depth of the craving.

Ruth was ten when her father ran away to Texas to escape the frustration and rage of her mother, May (who looks "like she went and slept face down on an oven rack"), and the drabness of Honey Creek in general. "I couldn't stand the thought of him being happier there," says Ruth of her father in Texas, "but I had sense enough to know it was true." Ruth's brother, Matt, also leaves the first chance he gets. A math whiz, as adored as Ruth is ignored, Matt goes off to MIT, becomes a scientist, gets written up in *Time,* and abandons Ruth and May to each other.

They are not a well-matched pair. Embittered by an early disappointment, May is addicted to suffering. She devotes herself to making life harsher than it already is for a family trying to get through Midwestern winters selling eggs. The only person who ever makes Ruth feel special is her Aunt Sid; they correspond throughout her childhood, allowing Ruth the tenuous pleasure of writing made-up stories about her happy family. Aunt Sid tells her she's resilient—"I liked being resilient," says Ruth, "because it sounded like a jewel glittering in the light." As life gets grimmer, she clings to the notion that "the meek are going to inherit the earth," convinced her time is coming.

It is not surprising that Ruth falls in love with someone even more deprived and dismissed than herself. It is also not surprising that the marriage is a disaster. Two famished people cannot feed each other. For a while they subsist on fantasies about independence from baleful May—with whom they live—and the perfect lives they will have someday. Ruth is waiting for her inheritance, and all the while her jewel-like resilience is ground down.

Finally, after a devastating tragedy, she realizes how she has wasted her time. "No one inherits one single thing," she says. "We're only passers-by, and all you can do is love what you have in your life. A person has to fight the meanness that sometimes comes with you when you're born." Dreams, she decides, are only useful if they foment change; and "meanness" does not have to be a birth-right.

Hamilton has written a breathtaking book, precise and beautiful in its language, full of sharp wisdom, and permeated by an appreciation of the world's ironies even in the midst of great pain. Hamilton handles incongruities like a snake charmer, coaxing all kinds of shimmies out of a sentence. May, for instance, wears an "extra-large fuzzy green sweater that looked like a bloated zucchini consuming her." A neighbor has the "shortest fattest legs in the state of Illinois. If she wasn't a person you'd laugh at the shape you saw out there in nature." And describing her cruel father-in-law, Ruth says: "He's the kind of person you could imagine biting the heads off of game birds."

The Book of Ruth is the story of poetry trapped inside ugliness, and of the spirit's revenge when love is denied. It began with a girl who was waiting to be discovered; it ends with a young woman beginning to discover herself. Along the way, the splendor of the telling illuminates the desperate story being told.

Love is not denied in *The Beginner's Book of Dreams* but it comes hobbling along, moaning and asking for handouts. Elizabeth Benedict's second novel opens with eight-year-old Esme Singer lighting candles in St. Patrick's Cathedral with her beautiful mother, Georgia. Esme is trying to decide what to pray for. Her father? "That when he comes to New York he will take her skating?" Or something with long-term benefits: "That she will not be fat?" Or with immediate benefits: "That her mother will not get drunk again the way she did last week?" By the time Esme finishes her wish list, the sad infirmities of her life have been revealed.

Georgia Singer is a woman who runs through husbands like panty-hose. "You pulled too hard, put them on in a hurry, sat too far back on a bench . . . you didn't even have to move and they ran." A tall Lauren Bacall look-alike from Redondo Beach, Georgia is also a hopeless, helpless lush who waits for a "knight in shining armor" to wake her out of sodden bad dreams. She is looking for the Holy Grail but keeps settling for glasses of Scotch and for men she does not love. "The worst thing," she tells herself, "is not having anyone to kiss on New Year's Eve."

Her ballast in life is Esme. Prematurely old, Esme is there through all the husbands, boyfriends, apartments, fights—nothing everything. Georgia is forever falling on Esme, telling her how much she loves her as she tries to walk up the stairs. Esme is determined not to be like her mother. Instead she comforts herself by imagining the time when her father, Meyer, will send her an airplane ticket to California, where he is always about to become rich. The book's title is derived from one of Meyer's schemes, a manual on how to prepare to be a winner: "A Quitter Never Wins And A Winner Never Quits," he proclaims. "Dreams are not born of indifference, laziness, or lack of ambition." Alas, dreams are not realized by schlemiels and alcoholics either.

Although Meyer sends Esme letters special delivery, the promised visits never materialize. Eventually Esme realizes her father is as much of a sham as her mother, who could have been a Hollywood starlet but is now a cosmetics saleswoman at Bonwit Teller. With energetic disgust, Esme sets about making a different life for herself.

Benedict has written a book full of the dreads and passions of childhood. We follow Esme into adulthood, watch her grow up from a dumpy, self-conscious child into a stunning, self-conscious young woman. Along the way, Benedict provides a sassy commentary on the world of New York intellectual "wannabes" of the 1960s and early 1970s. Esme's dream is to be one of them, someone who has read all the "right" books, knows the names of the right artists and photographers, has the right blend of shabby, erudite elegance in her apartment. Her dream is a world where she will never have to feel embarrassed, where her parents' irresponsibility and abandonment will never be obvious. In the attempt to keep life's humiliations at bay, Esme falls in love with her fantasy of love, rejecting the love that is actually offered to her, flawed and human though it may be. Gradually she realizes that love is what she was wishing for in St. Patrick's Cathedral so many years before, and that accepting crippled love does not have to make her a cripple.

Love and dreams are intertwined, both of these novels seem to be saying. All of us have our "book of dreams." To dream, one has to have ambition, faith, a personal definition of perfection. The belief in life's possibilities, in life's beauty, is finally the dream of love.

Judith Paterson (review date 5 February 1989)

SOURCE: Paterson, Judith. "Labors of Love and Loss." *Washington Post Book World,* 19, no. 6 (5 February 1989): 6.

[*In the following review, Paterson examines the elements of classical tragedy in* The Book of Ruth.]

In a return to be welcomed, love and God seem to be making their way back into fiction. Jane Hamilton's passionate and adroit first novel, **The Book of Ruth,** seldom shows the hand of the beginner as she unravels the tragedy of a young woman's inability to reconcile her love for her sweet, slightly deranged husband, Ruby, and her loyalty to her mother, May, a mean-spirited woman driven half-mad by a lifetime of emotional deprivation.

Ruth Dahl's troubles begin long before she is born. May's first husband dies in World War II, leaving his bride without hope of happiness. Fifteen years later she marries Ruth's father, Elmer, in as joyless a coupling as you are likely to find in fiction. Elmer stays until Ruth is 10 years old and her science-wizard brother is 12. As the dumb kid sister of the brother May worships in a kind of parody of her feelings for her lost love, the girl becomes little more than a servant and emotional punching bag in her mother's house.

Ruth is saved from the semi-literate banality of her peers by a librarian aunt and a blind woman who teaches her the classics of literature on tape, and by her own sacramental view of nature and human existence. Thus she gropes toward adulthood, a passive and incho-

ate young woman torn between her mother's warped views and a growing sense of herself as someone who deserves better. The internal conflict finally erupts in violence between May and Ruby—each spellbound by the evil in the other.

Tragic in the classical sense, the book leaves the heroine standing upright in a fallen world. She has lost the two people she thought she couldn't live without and gained the right to her own life and the love of her infant son.

Jane Hamilton's ambitious and satisfying first novel asks one of literature's biggest questions: what is the meaning of human suffering? In the end, she gives the old answer—to expose the truth and teach forgiveness.

Jay Parini (review date 24 November 1989)

SOURCE: Parini, Jay. "Into the Nether Regions." *Times Literary Supplement,* no. 4521 (24 November 1989): 1313.

[*In the following review, Parini focuses on Hamilton's characterization in* The Frogs are Still Singing, *the title under which* The Book of Ruth *was published in Great Britain. He compares the novel's preoccupation with poverty and isolation to Carolyn Chute's* Letourneau's Used Auto Parts *and Susan Richards Shreve's* A Country of Strangers.]

Perhaps because of the obvious and painful contrast between the rich and poor of their country, American writers from Steinbeck and James T. Farrell to Raymond Carver and Bobbie Ann Mason have been drawn to the nether regions of poverty and isolation. This vein—which contrasts with the flashier school of Yuppy fiction that has had more attention recently—continues to draw younger writers, with varying results. Carolyn Chute arrived on the scene with a bestselling first novel, *The Beans of Egypt, Maine,* casting the coldest possible eye on a small New England town where incest and other kinds of family violence occurred with chilling matter-of-factness. The veracity of her portrait was reinforced by an astonishing grasp of the local dialect. She returns to rural Maine with her second novel, *Letourneau's Used Auto Parts.* It is as depressing as one might expect, though a streak of optimism tints her portrait of Big Lucien Letourneau, himself the "miracle" of Miracle City. He is one of those men who "always lets his heart of gold get the better of him"; girlfriends, runaways, wives and ex-wives, hippies and ex-hippies, dogs, small children and miscellaneous hangers-on cling to Big Lucien, who has mastered Freud's art of "polymorphous perversity". He runs the Used Auto Parts Business of the title, and it is about the only successful operation in town; indeed, everything and everyone else is a failure.

Chute is an acute sociologist, supplying an up-to-date anthology of slang words, brand names and lower class-specific habits:

Lillian and Junie both fix their hair the modern way . . . root and perms, they are called, the shaggy raggedy look . . . and both use gold clips or old bandannas to tie up their shaggy raggedy hair into frenzied ponytails. The bandannas are often red to match their lookalike red sweaters with white lambs across the chest.

She writes with off-hand poetic grace ("It is a warm mint-color evening which smells of wet streets and wet brakes"), though she occasionally strains for effect ("The moon rises before dark, a moon you can see through, like Kleenex"). For the most part, *Letourneau's Used Auto Parts* confirms the high promise of *The Beans.*

"What it begins with, I know finally, is the kernel of meanness in people's hearts", says Ruth Dahl, the perceptive and subtle narrator of Jane Hamilton's first novel, *The Frogs are Still Singing,* in which Ruth explores the full-blown "meanness" lurking in the soul of Honey Creek, a town that straddles the lonely border region of northern Illinois and Wisconsin. "I want to be like Charles Dickens and write about all the good and strange people", Ruth says at one point. She also wants to write a "fiction book" in which the characters and events in her life meet with better ends than reality is willing to provide. Life, so far, has gone rather badly for Ruth.

Deeply tangled in a family web only partially self-spun, she is seen by everyone around her as a failure, especially compared to her brilliant older brother, Matt, who is able to use his intelligence to contrive a way out of the circle of poverty. Ruth cannot separate from Honey Creek; she clings pathetically to her unstable, bitter, and often cruel mother, May (a Dickensian figure, to be sure); later, she cannot separate from Ruby, her idle and abusive husband.

We follow Ruth's own story in clear, almost heartbreakingly hopeful language as she marries Ruby (whose main interest is smoking marijuana while he watches the re-runs of old television comedies) and occupies her days at the Trim 'N Tidy Dry Cleaners. Much of the plot turns on Ruth's role as ineffectual mediator between May and Ruby, who seem to have been predestined to hate each other. *The Frogs are Still Singing* is a well drawn, often tender portrait of a young woman caught in a situation of bleak cultural and material deprivation.

Susan Richards Shreve's sixth novel, *A Country of Strangers,* follows quickly on *Queen of Hearts,* which was widely admired for its lyrical style and copiously peopled story: qualities apparent here as well. Set in desolate farm country on the swamplands outside Washington DC, the novel recreates the dismal aura of hatred and anger that marked post-slavery southern life in the not-so-deep south just after the Depression. The story centres on Charley Fletcher, a young journalist who takes a job in the Office of Censorship established in the wake of Pearl Harbor. A determined liberal, he finds himself in a situation that tests his loudly professed idealism when he buys a small farm with an imposing Palladian manor house called Elm Grove, unwittingly dispossessing a powerful and extremely bitter black man called Moses Bellows, who may (we soon learn) have killed the previous owner before simply moving into Elm Grove himself—a bold move for a black man in the days when Klan violence was often unchecked.

The novel moves through the spring of 1942 into the winter of 1943, the plot turning through cycles of violence towards a sensitively and imaginatively conceived climax. A key figure in the plot is Bellows's niece, who bears the unlikely name of Prudential Dargon (she was named after the insurance company); she "was thirteen, high-tempered and bone-thin with a gentle round belly that was a baby growing into its sixth month of incubation". Her mother has sent her to be "tamed" by her strong uncle and affectionate aunt; as it happens, it is Prudential who tames everyone else. By the end of the novel, she has taught everyone under the aegis of Elm Grove a lesson in humanity.

Suzanne L. MacLachlan (review date 3 June 1994)

SOURCE: MacLachlan, Suzanne L. "One Woman's Map of a Troubled World." *Christian Science Monitor* 86, no. 133 (3 June 1994): 13.

[*In the following review, MacLachlan assesses the themes and plot of* A Map of the World.]

Jane Hamilton, author of *The Book of Ruth,* for which she received the PEN/Hemingway Foundation Award for best first novel, has written another engrossing, powerful book that should attract some much-deserved attention.

A Map of the World is not an easy or light read; indeed, it takes on some of the toughest issues of modern life. But the writer's skill in describing a community and a way of life, as well as her insight into the hearts of her characters, render this story difficult to forget.

The title refers to a map of the world that the main character labored over after the death of her mother. As a girl, she would sit before the map, imagining herself "in an ideal country, alone and at peace."

By tackling such major themes as motherhood, death, love, and child abuse. Hamilton draws us her own map of the world, one devoid of safe havens. What we are left with, however, is a better understanding of the strength of the human heart and the power to rise above calamity.

Alice and Howard Goodwin live and work with their two young daughters. Emma and Claire, on the last dairy farm in Prairie Center, Wis., on the outskirts of Racine. Most of the tightknit community keeps its distance from the family, regarding them as displaced urban hippies.

Although he suspects that the family farm will soon be obsolete, Howard is unable to imagine any other way of life. "I had wanted to spend my life caring for land, being a steward, and raising food. . . . Alice once said that most men must secretly want a barn, even city-dwelling men."

Alice, who strives to be a proper farm wife and live up to Howard's expectations, constantly fears that she doesn't have the right instincts to be a good mother. Sometimes, when she leaves the girls with her best friend, Theresa, she runs home, ignores the ruin of her housekeeping and Howard's calls for assistance, and dances with abandon to Hungarian music in her bedroom with the shades drawn. Afterward, she can peacefully go out to pull weeds, drive the tractor, or make the family dinner.

One hot summer day, when it is Alice's turn to baby-sit for Theresa's two daughters, she becomes distracted looking over her map of the world. She is upstairs just long enough for Theresa's youngest child, Lizzy, to wander out to the farm's pond and drown.

While still reeling under the weight of guilt and grief, Alice is accused by another mother of having sexually abused her son. The vindictive woman expertly takes advantage of Alice's outcast status after Lizzy's death.

Soon, events spin out of control: Alice lingers in jail awaiting trial on charges of sexual abuse because Howard cannot raise bail; he and his daughters are shunned by the townspeople and lose all sense of normalcy in their lives; Theresa, struggling to come to grips with the death of her young child, is the only one able to rally around the sinking family.

"Sometimes people get so confused by how fast everything's moving they have to throw somebody out, to make them feel better. It could have been anyone, really," Alice realizes. Although Howard was always the stronger and more stable of the two, raised to work hard and keep in motion, it is Alice who learns about the durability of the human spirit in the stillness and tedium of jail.

Hamilton writes eloquently about land, nature, and the human heart. Yet a sense of spirituality pervades *A Map of the World.* Alice and Howard found shelter, love, and benevolence in a farmhouse; when their home was gone, they had to look higher to find forgiveness and understanding.

Richard Eder (review date 5 June 1994)

SOURCE: Eder, Richard. "Some Things are Unforgivable." *Los Angeles Times Book Review* (5 June 1994): 5, 15.

[*In the following review, Eder describes the principal characters of* A Map of the World *in the context of the novel's narrative structure and themes.*]

In a patch of Wisconsin woods, late on a summer afternoon, two women stand a few feet apart, each leaning her back against a tree and swatting mosquitoes. They face the same direction; neither looks at the other. They were best friends but Alice had a moment of distraction while minding Theresa's baby, Lizzie, and the child wandered off and drowned in the farm pond. Now, days later, Alice is almost mute while Theresa talks wildly, trivially, unstoppably: a frozen swimmer and a thrashing swimmer in a pond of bottomless pain.

Still thrashing, Theresa relates her visit to a former priest who was her high school teacher and whom she once had a crush on. Albert—married, divorced and grown fat—took her to a luncheonette for Cherry Cokes. Insistently, he made her tell the entire story of her 2-year-old daughter's life, and write down each of the 57 words she had mastered. By the time Theresa finished, she realized that what Lizzie had was not a fragment of a life but an entire one, though short. She and Albert—now weeping for the child he has helped make real—began to rock "just hard enough so that one edge of the booth came up like a swing set will you know, that isn't grounded in cement?"

Still frozen, Alice thinks: "Theresa was going to talk at high speed through the seasons, through the rain and sleet and snow, until she was briny and then moss covered."

It is not the Job-like accumulation of scourges upon Alice Goodwin and her farmer husband, Howard, that makes Jane Hamilton's second novel [*A Map of the World*] remarkable. Not that the scourges are trivial. There could be no more terrible combination of agony and shame than to know that a moment of absent-mindedness has allowed the death of a friend's child. Or than to be arrested and charged immediately afterward—as Alice is—with sexually abusing children at the school where she works as a nurse.

Indeed, the accumulation—the neighbors turn bitterly vindictive, the Goodwins' children are traumatized and Howard loses the farm that has been his life's dream—is as melodramatic and arbitrary as a soap opera. But then, so was Job's story (*boils,* yet?). It is not the particular blows of providence that exalt the Old Testament story, but a man's voice protesting the pain of our cosmic vulnerability. In *A Map of the World,* it is not the buildup of the two tragedies that is most distinctive—the events are told with brilliant horror but their sequence and linkages can be awkward—it is the different calligraphies they inscribe on Alice, Howard and Theresa.

Some of the same horror is at the root of Sue Miller's *The Good Mother* (a woman's lover is accused of sexually abusing her daughter) and Rosellen Brown's *Before and After* (a family is shattered when a teenage son is charged with murder). All three show how the outside world—society, the law—can make our privacies public and unrecognizable to ourselves. Or as Howard muses at one point: "I was dazed by the equation that overnight made Alice's troubles into everyone's troubles."

The difference is the voices. Theresa's out of the circle of trees: wandering, coming apart and coming together to relate a remarkable deliverance by a fat man in a luncheonette booth; remarkable, among other things, for being both a near-miracle and entirely natural. Alice's, frozen in shame as well as grief—and in her own knotted nature—raging at Theresa's. This is only one example; throughout, *A Map of the World* will suddenly alter its light, revealing beneath the fabric of its characters' lives, thoughts and emotions a kind of X-ray of their souls.

The story is told alternately by Alice and Howard. Alice begins with an account of a precarious idyll. She and Howard, former hippies, more or less, have bought a farm in a transitional area. Suburbs are encroaching; the old-style rural community of Howard's dreams no longer quite exists. Instead of helping with the haying, the neighbors are more likely to get up petitions about the farm's noise, smells and effect on property values.

For Howard, a dairy farm is heaven, down to its most menial and exhausting jobs. "I always thought that work was as common and fine as air," he will say. Alice can't quite submerge in his Arcadian dream; there is tension under the determinedly upbeat account of their life that starts the book off. Tension becomes horror the day Theresa leaves Lizzie with her. Hamilton slows the narrative to nightmare speed: Suddenly Lizzie is no longer in the room with her older sister and Alice's two children. She thinks of the pond, runs there on suddenly heavy legs, her bare feet "like two pink erasers." A pink gingham bottom bobs on the water's surface, 15 feet out.

Days of breakdown follow. Alice's account of her paralysis—she can't take care of the children, endure the funeral, visit Theresa or do much besides sleep; and Howard's patience turns to despair—is another nightmare. It ends, oddly enough, and she goes from lethargy to hyperactivity, when the second horror falls upon the first.

The police come and arrest her. A 9-year-old schoolboy, a problem child who at one point goaded her into slapping him, has reported that she fondled him. The account seems inspired and promoted by his dysfunctional, promiscuous mother; but a communal hysteria sets in. There are other complaints, a formal charge, months in prison—until Howard sells the farm to pay the exorbitant bail—and finally a trial that frees her into a life of utterly changed and uncertain prospects.

Some of the story limps a bit. The courtroom scenes are compellingly taut, but not especially distinctive. Alice's eccentric lawyer is a grotesque that doesn't quite come off. He serves, though, to parody the processes of the law, and as part of Hamilton's questioning of the nature of present-day society. The dream of community is no longer viable; people live by fashion and slogans. The mere mention of abuse—in the absence of social ties and the ground-knowledge that they instill—is enough to set off a conflagration.

Such questions, though provocative, are no more the real heart of the book than the plot is, or the accomplished set scenes, among them a vivid account of Alice's time in jail, and of the brutal and sometimes compassionate social order set up by the inmates. Alice's harsh, illuminating vision—released from jail, she and Howard pass a wedding and she notes: "The bride had some teeth missing. Maybe she'll be covered by her husband's dental plan. Maybe she'll be able to get them fixed"—is a poetry of despair that turns, in a stunning final passage, into something like a chorale.

Howard's account of his time alone with the children as he struggles to keep his farm going, is only seemingly matter-of-fact. It is another kind of poetry, bucolic and sad. Theresa, passionate but purposeful—she and Howard fall in love and relinquish it in one single, powerfully erotic and entirely chaste movement—is a child of light. Her poetry is of a third order; like Eric Rohmer's films, its magic takes form from what is random, commonplace and disconnected.

Moureen Coulter (review date fall 1994)

SOURCE: Coulter, Moureen. "After the Fall." *Belles Lettres* 10, no. 1 (fall 1994): 25, 27.

[*In the following review, Coulter summarizes the central themes of* A Map of the World, *noting that Hamilton's examination of the power of forgiveness is "remarkable."*]

What does it mean to fall from grace, and where do the fallen go? Are they forever banished from their former blessedness, or can they hope to regain its heights?

These theological questions have structured many a catechism over the years, but even children who learn the answers "by heart" can later have trouble applying them to the unforeseen messiness of their adult lives. Alice Goodwin, the protagonist of Jane Hamilton's remarkable new novel, *A Map of the World,* confesses to just such bewilderment at the beginning of her narrative:

> *I used to think if you fell from grace it was more likely than not the result of one stupendous error, or else an unfortunate accident. I hadn't learned that it can happen so gradually you don't lose your stomach or hurt yourself in the landing. You don't necessarily sense the motion. I've found it takes at least two and generally three things to alter the course of a life: You slip around the truth once, and then again, and one more time, and there you are, feeling, for a moment, that it was sudden, your arrival at the bottom of the heap.*

Alice's fall does seem to be literally the result of "an unfortunate accident": the death of her neighbor and best friend's two-year-old daughter Lizzy one summer morning when the child and her older sister have been left in Alice's charge. Her "stupendous error" is allowing herself to be distracted, while changing for a swim, by the rediscovery in a dresser drawer of the maps of a fictional world she had invented during her childhood. "My maps had taken over my life for months at a time," Alice recalls wonderingly. But by the time she finishes dressing, Lizzy has left the house and made her way unaccompanied to a nearby pond, where she drowns.

"When I am forced to see those ten minutes as they actually were, when I look clearly, without the scrim of half-uttered prayers and fanciful endings, I am there, tall and gangly and clumsy and slow, crying out unintelligibly, splashing through the water to Lizzy," Alice reports, but no amount of retrospection, however clear-sighted, can alter the outcome. The lives of Alice and her husband, Howard; of Lizzy's parents, Theresa and Dan; of both couples' other children and relatives are irrevocably and decisively altered by both the fact and the circumstances of the child's death. No one, least of all Alice, can escape the conclusion that she is to blame.

If there can be any greater torment for a woman than the loss of her own child, it may be the knowledge that she is responsible for, or at least implicated in, the loss of another. It is to Hamilton's credit that she is able to convey the paralyzing confusion of Alice's thoughts and feelings in the months that follow Lizzy's death in language that is so clear and credible. Alice's guilt isolates her by erasing the familiar patterns of communication with Howard and Theresa that had helped to demarcate her adult "map of the world." It also renders her vulnerable to attack by people outside the boundaries drawn by marriage and close friendship, so that before the fateful summer is over Alice finds herself

jailed on unrelated charges of child abuse and threatened with the loss of her own daughters. Falling from grace does indeed turn out to be a more protracted experience than she had imagined, with more hands ready to push her off of the precipice than to pull her back.

The novel ends with Alice's legal exoneration and her reconstituted family's move to a new house in a new city. The grace that she seems to have regained might best be described as a restored sense of herself and of her place in the world, her bearings according to the compass of the heart. Its source is not judgment but forgiveness: Alice's forgiveness of others, especially Howard, as much as theirs of her. This, too, is a theological truth, but one usually taught by parable rather than catechism, and that is how Alice and Howard learn it and how they teach it to us. "I had that marvelous clarity for an instant," says Alice, "and so I understood that the forgiveness itself was strong, durable, like strands of a web, weaving around us, holding us." Thus are the fallen raised.

Jean Hanff Korelitz (review date 20 January 1995)

SOURCE: Korelitz, Jean Hanff. "Slouching to Suburbia." *Times Literary Supplement,* no. 4790 (20 January 1995): 20.

[*In the following review, Korelitz praises* A Map of the World *for its skillful evocation of rural Midwestern life.*]

Jane Hamilton's tense novel [*A Map of the World*] opens with the accidental drowning of a two-year-old girl. While her two daughters and her best friend's two daughters, whom she is minding, are all playing downstairs, the narrator, Alice Goodwin, dashes upstairs to look for a bathing-suit, happens on the long-forgotten map of the world she had drawn the summer of her mother's early death, and pauses over it for one breathless, elastic moment. Long enough. In just that blink of time, Lizzie Collins disappears, finds the glorious, bucolic pond on the Goodwin farm, and is lost.

You would think that would be agony enough, but the accident merely marks the onset of troubles for the Goodwin family. In the aftermath of the drowning, Alice spins into a cataclysmic depression—powerfully evoked by Hamilton—neglecting her own most basic needs and utterly incapable of caring for her family:

> I was naked except for my socks. I had forgotten the order of things. I was a mother, and mothers were supposed to rise to the occasion because they had children to care for; they were to cook the stew in a crisis because there was no alternative to nourishment other than death. We were not to die until youngest child

graduated from college. . . . How can I cook the stew when I don't know what clothes to put on next? I wanted to ask. Maybe it was better if the children died first because then a person could relax, stop worrying, and just take up grief.

Then, even at the moment she begins to pull herself together again—bolstered by the unexpected forgiveness of the dead girl's mother—the unthinkable happens: Alice is accused of sexually abusing a student at the school where she works as a nurse, is manacled and taken away. In her absence, her husband Howard takes over the narrative and the family, struggling to work the farm and care for the children, as the enormity of their trouble sinks in and the small Midwestern community on whose social outskirts they have lived rushes to shun them further: "We had always been satisfied with our circumscribed life. We had been proud, I think, to know that we could get by with so little." Now, their few acquaintances coldly turn away and strangers openly condemn them.

As with many outrageous injustices, there is a kernel of truth in the charges against Alice. In the recent long-running sex-abuse case in a North Carolina day-care centre (which Hamilton says inspired her), the hysteria of children and parents alike and the ultimate, outrageous conviction and imprisonment of several teachers was traceable to one slap, delivered by a teacher to a misbehaving child. And Alice raised her hand to Robbie Mackessey, a sullen, damaged six-year-old whose staring unnerved her. When Robbie comes forward with his accusation and a second wave of students begin to accuse the school nurse of various perversities, Howard, sees before his wife does, that, whatever the trial brings, their life in Prairie Center, Wisconsin, is over.

It is in Hamilton's descriptions of that life that her literary gifts are most in evidence. She captures the rhythms of farming, the peculiar insanity required to undertake an endeavour so unlikely to provide security, financial or otherwise, the unspeakable beauty that changes through the seasons: "In May, when the grass was so green it hurt to look at it, the air so overpoweringly sweet you had to go in and turn on the television to dull your senses." This particular farming centre is slouching towards suburbia, its farms steadily being carved up into residential subdivisions. When, in the midst of all this determined progress, the Goodwins arrived, pilgrims from the city with a dream of farming, they were marked as outsiders from the start.

American reviewers have been comparing *A Map of the World* to Sue Miller's *The Good Mother* and Rosellen Brown's *Before and After,* those two fictional celebrations of maternal agony. It isn't difficult to see why. The novel is relentlessly painful, even with the promise of redemption which we suspect may lurk in

its final pages. But Hamilton's prose offers rewards, and Alice, though never entirely likeable, earns our esteem as we watch her claw her way out of the maw.

Carol J. Pierce (review date September 1996)

SOURCE: Pierce, Carol J. "Dairy Farm Tragedy." *English Journal* 85, no. 5 (September 1996): 109-10.

[*In the following review, Pierce highlights the realistic portrayal of daily life on Midwestern farms for women in* A Map of the World, *drawing thematic and character comparisons to classical tragedy.*]

Books take us to lands and times we can only imagine and let us encounter characters who people a culture or an era much different from our own. This is a message we impress on our students daily. However, lately, it seems more of us are interested in the people and places of what we term the "real world."

The recent popularity and exploding fame of Robert Waller's *The Bridges of Madison County* let those of us in Iowa know that people out there want to glimpse what life is like on a rural farm. But the life of lonely Francesca Johnson is not the reality of life for a woman on a farm not far away in rural, fictional Wisconsin. We can imagine for Waller fans, the fantasy of *Bridges* is hard to beat. But those of us who would like a more in-depth look at a modern farm woman's life should open the cover of Jane Hamilton's *A Map of the World* and meet the very real Alice Goodwin.

Alice Goodwin's life consists of chasing her active pre-schoolers, dealing with an extremely hot Wisconsin summer without the comfort of central air conditioning, and supporting her starry-eyed husband in his dream to own, operate, and even scrape out a living on one of the area's last operating dairy farms.

Alice begins by telling her own story. How will she ever face potty training Claire? Why does little Emma react so violently to not being able to pour her own milk on her cereal? When will she have a minute to do what needs to be done so that her household is as efficient and homey as that of her best friend Theresa? Alice introduces us to her life, and we can immediately relate to the everyday misfortunes and struggles that readily parallel the not-so-funny aspects of our own mundane struggles.

On this particular day, though, Alice's life will change forever. She is about to have everything that is harrying her become a minor trifle in the face of great human tragedy. To say what specifically happens would be to take away from this haunting narrative but, trust Hamilton, the plot never lets the reader go in this guaranteed page-turner. We are sucked into the life of Alice and her family the way Midwestern farm buildings can be sucked into a twisting tornado, sometimes dropped gently somewhere else, but always in an altered state—recognizable after their trip, but never the way they once were. Alice, Howard, their daughters, and their friends are about to have a similar experience. The reader stays tuned to this book for much the same reason an ancient Greek theater-goer stayed glued to a tragedy by Sophocles. There is a need for us to see how the main character will handle herself in the face of life's most challenging turmoil.

Alice screams silently, "I DON'T KNOW WHAT TO DO." Her husband's solution is to "keep in motion." This she does, comparing herself to a Biblical Job and his all-too-familiar trials. What she does to face her days creates an amazingly tenable story with a lesson we know to be true, but would rather ignore. In our seemingly secure and simple lives, there lurks the possibility for all of us that what happens to Alice and Howard Goodwin could also happen to us or someone we love: this book is the stuff of which headlines are made in a dozen local papers every morning.

I read *A Map of the World* while on vacation in Wisconsin. Reading a St. Paul newspaper that week, I found at least four stories in the real news to parallel the events of Hamilton's compelling novel. Though it might be more pleasant to think of life in terms of Waller's farm wife and her knight in shining armor, many will prefer this fiction with a more formidable edge. Alice and Howard Goodwin, though far from perfect, have the stuff of real-every-day-down-in-the-mud-and-grit-of-life heroes. A reader will not soon forget their story and their struggle to "keep moving."

Jane Hamilton and Sybil Steinberg (interview date 2 February 1998)

SOURCE: Hamilton, Jane, and Sybil Steinberg. "Jane Hamilton: A Kinship with Society's Outcasts." *Publishers Weekly* 245, no. 5 (2 February 1998): 68-9.

[*In the following interview, Hamilton discusses the inspiration for the characters and themes of her novels through* The Short History of a Prince.]

A young man coming of age in suburban Illinois in the 1970s, obsessed with ballet, literature and classical music, aware that he's gay but determined to remain closeted. The protagonist of a novel by David Leavitt, Alan Gurganus or Dale Peck? Not this time. While these gay male writers would seem to own the territory, it's a female novelist praised for her depiction of women who has dared to trespass in an area generally reserved for men who have lived the experience.

The Short History of a Prince, Jane Hamilton's third novel, out soon from Random House isn't the first time this author, who claims apologetically to have had "a very ordinary life," has so effectively imagined herself into the mind of a character thrown to its fringes. Talking with *PW* during a recent visit from her Wisconsin home to her publisher's Manhattan offices, Hamilton declares a spiritual kinship with the troubled central characters of her three novels: Ruth, the emotionally abused but brave and resilient protagonist of *The Book of Ruth* (1988), whose dreams of domesticity vanish in an eruption of violence; Alice, the restless, self-destructive heroine of *A Map of the World* (1994), who is responsible for the death of a child and spends time in jail falsely accused of sexual abuse; and, now, dreamy, aesthetic Walter, whose lonely, unfulfilled life is defined by the secret he dares not share. "I spent my entire youth being in love with gay men because they were the most interesting and compassionate people I knew," Hamilton says. "For me, writing Walter didn't feel like a stretch."

In *The Short History of a Prince,* teenager Walter McCloud's passion for ballet is not sanctified by talent. Despite his artistic aspirations and his absorption in classical technique, he is awkward and ungainly. His desire to dance the role of Prince Siegfried in a production of *The Nutcracker* is granted in an ironic manner that shames him, and this dark fulfillment is followed by the crucifying experience of his life, when he's discovered wearing a ballerina's tutu and is sadistically humiliated by the ballet master and mocked by the young man he loves.

Though Hamilton herself was never publicly embarrassed, she keenly remembers her own adolescent despair at failing to become a graceful dancer. "My legs were big; my derriere was big; I had no turnout; my feet were flat—but still I really loved it," she recalls. "What I bring to the character of Walter is my experience of dancing and of being the worst in the class. Probably most people feel that way some of the time, but I internalized the feeling. I felt I was out of the mainstream."

Inspiration came from another source as well. The character of Walter McCloud is also based on her dearest friend in high school, to whom the book is dedicated. The inscription reads: "For JMW—for Boonkie." According to Hamilton, Boonkie is "the spiritual twin" to Walter. "In some ways, Walter is the marriage of this friend and myself. I wanted the word 'prince' in the title because Walter is a prince in every way." She thinks that the characters in her previous books were "only warm-ups" for Walter, that his quiet suffering and endurance is faithful to the longings and insecurities of outsiders in society who take refuge in the spiritual solace of literature, dance and music.

Songs of Isolation

Hamilton herself projects nothing but prairie whole-someness to jaded New York eyes. She is sturdily unpretentious, with none of the professional glamour that bestselling authors generally radiate. It's not just her well-scrubbed, makeup-free complexion, her hair yanked back and anchored with an elastic band, or her comfortable outfit of baggy sweater and tights. She has a strong jaw, a clear and level gaze and a modest and candid way of talking about her problems with the creative process.

Moving in 1982 to the small rural community of Rochester, Wisc., population 1000, was a crystallizing experience of social alienation for Hamilton. "I felt I was an anthropologist in a foreign country," she says. Born in 1957, she had been raised in suburban Oak Park, Ill., the youngest of five siblings in a close-knit home where reading was a cherished pastime and writing a given. Her mother composed poetry; a verse in Jane's honor called "A Song for a Fifth Child" was published in the *Ladies' Home Journal.* Her grand-mother wrote for a feminist newspaper and tried her hand at novels. "I just assumed that if you were a girl-child you were supposed to grow up and write," she says.

Whatever her ambitions, they went underground when she graduated from Carleton College in Minnesota in 1979, and impulsively stopped off on the way to New York (and the vague offer of a job in publishing) to visit a friend who was working on a farm for the sum-mer. "They needed help; it was picking season. So I stayed a week, then I stayed two weeks, a month. I fell in love with my friend's cousin, Bob Willard, and I married him. It took me about 10 years to think I could belong there. And maybe another four years to think I wanted to belong there." Having children, a boy and a girl now 13 and 10, contributed to her acceptance in the tight-knit community. The crucial factor was her services as president of the board of the public library, a labor of love she calls "a lifesaver."

Looking back, Hamilton says she's grateful for the detour. Her applications to graduate schools had been rejected; "I felt bad about that, but I knew that I wasn't ready for a high-powered graduate program. Ultimately, it was good for me to be in this tiny town where the book review didn't come. I was in my own little fog trying to figure out the forms for myself. I wrote, but I didn't know what I had to say yet. So it was serendipi-tous that I ended up in the middle of nowhere."

Except for the four months of intense activity during apple-picking season, Hamilton had a lot of free time in which to try her hand at short fiction. "I spent basically three years writing one story," she says with a rueful

laugh. Eventually she sold it to *Harper's.* She won "a few" Wisconsin Art Board grants and an NEA grant. But she was still searching for her subject.

The inspiration came from an event that rocked Wisconsin's rural communities: in a nearby town, a man murdered his mother-in-law. Hamilton recalls feel-ing immediate empathy for the murderer's wife. She herself was living in a very small house with her husband and his aged aunt. "Even though I loved these new relations of mine, I could understand how a situa-tion could get out of hand. I was young, I was frustrated. I needed my own territory and I didn't know how I was going to get it. And so I took my frustrations and plugged them into someone entirely different from me. I wanted to see if I could slip into someone else's skin."

What she found was a strange emotional bond with her inadequately educated, culturally deprived and miser-ably poor heroine. "***The Book of Ruth*** is fueled by Ruth's voice because I felt possessed by Ruth," Hamil-ton says. It was not easy to sell such a downbeat slice of life. The agent Hamilton had used for her short stories was not interested in the novel. When a friend gave her a list of agents, Hamilton dutifully worked through the alphabet, sending out the manuscript and receiving rejection letters in return. "Finally I was at the end of the alphabet. The last name was Amanda Urban." With no idea of Urban's clout in the industry, Hamilton made her "last stab. She called me within a week and said, 'Who are you?' She sold it in another week," Hamilton reports.

Katrina Kenison at Ticknor & Fields bought **The Book of Ruth.** Reviews were good, and Hamilton didn't care that sales were modest. Before **Ruth** won the PEN/ Hemingway Foundation Award in 1989, Martha Levin at Doubleday/Anchor bought the paperback rights for a "really small sum, maybe $2000," Hamilton says with no discernible regret.

The favorable critical reception and the prestigious prize, in fact, threw Hamilton into the proverbial second book slump. She was "paralyzed," she says, by the thought that she'd now have to produce a book every two years. But as the self-imposed deadline came and went, she was relieved to find that she was again "writ-ing a book just for myself." She began what became *A Map of the World* after a child in her son's day-care center drowned in his family's swimming pool. The initial chapters, which express the almost palpable anguish of the heroine, who is responsible for the death of her best friend's daughter, were surprisingly easy to write. Problems arose when she couldn't figure out how the story would proceed after that crucial scene. Feeling adrift, she wrote three versions of the novel, each with a different middle and ending. "Those books were ter-rible, just terrible!" she groans.

Meanwhile, Hamilton had been impressed by a documentary about a couple who were falsely convicted of sexually molesting children in a day-care center. A short time later, she herself was angrily confronted by her best friend for letting their two small daughters take off their clothes on a hot summer day. Accused of unnatural behavior for something she considered perfectly normal, Hamilton was undone. "I didn't want to write another trendy novel about sexual molestation," she says, but the subject seemed inescapable.

Placing the book was not a sure thing. Kenison had left Ticknor & Fields, and the imprint was soon to fold. According to Hamilton, Binky Urban again found the editor with the appropriate sensibility—Deb Futter at Doubleday. (Hamilton followed Futter, whom she calls her "soul mate," when she later went to Random House.)

Even before Futter saw *A Map of the World,* however, Hamilton had the help of another kind of editor: Steven Shahan, a lawyer in upstate New York who is married to Elizabeth Weinstein, Hamilton's college roommate, and still the first reader of her work. (*A Map of the World* is dedicated to both of them.) Shahan led Hamilton through the legal process of a trial. He was "absolutely indispensable," she says.

Critics remarked on the stunningly accurate portrayal of Alice's cell mates, most of them black and victimized by life. Though quite different in their histories, the women share an admiration of Oprah Winfrey. Hamilton had never seen the show when, in 1988, one of the producers called and invited her to lunch as a surprise for Oprah, who had loved *The Book of Ruth.* At that time, Oprah was not yet established as a messianic force in the publishing world, and Hamilton was amazed that Oprah quoted lines from the book from memory.

Several years later, when Oprah announced the formation of her TV book club, *The Book of Ruth* was her third choice. Immediately, sales of the paperback edition, which had been selling well (to the tune of 75,000 copies), soared; the current net figure is well over a million. Given the often finicky market for midlist fiction, Hamilton says, "Oprah does what God couldn't do."

The reference to the deity is only half jocular. Like all of her protagonists, who search for meaning in a world seemingly devoid of solace, Hamilton has only a marginal adherence to conventional Christian faith. "I've always broken out in hives when I go into any organized religious situation," she says. All three of her protagonists find that biblical injunctions mock the truth of their lives, and yet each of them arrives at a moment of understanding. Transcendence comes to Walter just when he is about to lose his family's three-generational homestead, the one element that's "essential to his having any faith at all in life," Hamilton says.

"I think of my characters being extremely Christian in the way they lead their lives," she adds. Maybe my books have a lot of religious grappling because I'm still trying to figure it out for myself."

Having experienced the disapproval of some of Rochester's churchgoing ladies over *The Book of Ruth,* she is bracing herself for another negative reaction, this time for placing a gay hero in a town very much like Rochester. Yet she feels she is a writer with a mission: "I want to express something important here. I really love Walter and I want other people to love him, too. He has a special place in my heart."

Richard Eder (review date 29 March 1998)

SOURCE: Eder, Richard. "The Dollhouse." *Los Angeles Times Book Review* (29 March 1998): 2.

[*In the following review, Eder offers a positive assessment of* The Short History of a Prince, *praising the novel's "sympathy and nerve."*]

If you are William and the world won't accept you as William and you have to keep fighting so that it will, then what do you call yourself once it does? The question stirs uneasily within what is conveniently known as gay fiction; it is one that Jane Hamilton—married to an apple grower and mother of two—explores with sympathy and nerve.

Hamilton, author of *The Book of Ruth* and *A Map of the World,* writes hard novels beautifully. In *The Short History of a Prince,* she tries to see beyond what, in the first full literary generation, has tended understandably to show itself as a kind of gay exceptionalism.

Her valiant and precarious protagonist, Walter McCloud, graduates from his short history as a gay prince into a long future as a human commoner. His identity is in no way blurred. It simply undergoes the fate of all identities: to be one among those elements that make up our common lot and that bump, bruise and abrade each other to become parts of a whole, that is defined less by what it is than by where it goes. Gay is the route that some of us must take to arrive at being human.

The Short History of a Prince places Walter, waif-like, in the bosom of a large and ebullient Midwestern clan that gathers to spend summers and holidays in a rambling Victorian house on a Wisconsin lake. The ingathering goes back several generations. Its ritual swimming, sailing, meals and the confection of a special lard cake are tribal rites conducted with varying degrees of insistence and skepticism by Walter's two aunts and his mother.

Champagne bottles from decades of celebration are labeled and preserved; so is a wall-sized Pegboard hung with framed family photographs. When it falls over and smashes—one of the three sisters is suspected of having taken a hand, or rather a foot—this may or may not be understood as a whiff of subversion.

Hamilton's novel goes back and forth between the early '70s, when Walter was in his teens, to the mid-'90s. It charts his difficult journey partly in terms of his changing relationship over the years to the summer house and the family that gathers there and partly in terms of the changes in his regular life.

As a teenager, he is a passionate, but no more than competent, ballet student, commuting to class from his Chicago suburb along with two more gifted friends. Mitch, beautiful but lazy, will eventually give up dance; Susan, brilliant and dedicated, will go on to join the New York City Ballet, leave it after the death of George Balanchine, marry and move to Miami to dance with the local company.

Walter, Mitch and Susan form a tight triangle—isosceles, like most such triangles. Mitch and Susan are a couple; Walter, their necessary audience, wit and didactic authority on all things musical and balletic. He half-suppresses, half-conceals his passion for Mitch, allowing himself, for a time, no more than the fantasy of putting on a tutu and dancing as his ballerina partner.

Ripe with artistic intensity and erotic implication, the trio is a tiny hothouse kingdom in the bland Chicago suburbs. Walter, as adolescents can do, converts the role of odd man out into that of little lame prince. The world presses in on such principalities, though, and inevitably there is a breach. Dan, Walter's older brother, is stricken with cancer, and their parents exhaust their time and attention in long hospital vigils. Much worse, Susan falls in love with the sick boy and helps their mother to nurse him.

Walter's triangular realm collapses. Susan has opened its gates to the enemy: the family ties and obligations it was meant to be free of. In the wreckage, Walter and the rejected Mitch begin to have clandestine sex. For Mitch, basically heterosexual, it is simply a brute release; for Walter, it is romantic ecstasy.

Until the night, that is, when his parents come home unexpectedly. While Mitch hides under the bed, Walter's mother sits on top of it to tell him that Dan is about to die. It is the book's pivot: life and death upon the bed; beneath, the remains of a fantasy that cannot withstand them.

Short History does not work the pivot all at once. Hamilton is adept at climactic moments, but her true quality lies in weaving them into the long procession of time and human contradictions. Shuttling between past and present, she depicts by increments Walter's growth out of fantasy into reality. There is pain in both.

The fantasy lies not in her protagonist's sexual orientation and desires but in his walling them off from other parts of his nature that are at least as profound, perhaps more so. He is an American of the Midwest; as the years go by, its values tug more and more strongly, and so do his ties with his extensive and turbulently human family.

From stormy adolescent rejection, the book has him take a calmer distance with a move to New York. He lives an untrammeled gay life there until his friends begin to die. But there is something else: After casting about professionally, he finds odd satisfaction working for an artisan who makes elaborately detailed dollhouses for the very rich.

Dollhouses—while a thousand miles to the northwest is the full-sized lakeside exemplar that he has fled and cannot manage to lose. Hamilton wields her symbols with audacity; mostly she wields them with great skill. They are her sheep dogs, sinuously herding along a story whose strength and weakness both lie in the same thing: a radiant didacticism.

Walter escapes from his escape: He returns to the Midwest to take up a job teaching English in a dreary Wisconsin town. He deals with cloddish students, a white-bread community to whom the notion of a gay lifestyle is unimaginable and with no cultural life at all. He accepts loneliness and isolation; all because, however difficult, it is better to teach children than to make dollhouses.

Hamilton portrays his new life with vivid skill. It is a delicately detailed frost-bound picture with one or two signs of a spring—a responsive student, a promising school musical, his discovery of his talent for teaching—that will never be particularly lush. The lakeside family reunions, with their muted turbulence, are drawn well, though they are too long and sometimes fall flat. They are handsomely adorned vehicles without much gasoline.

As the years go by, not only does Walter change, so does his perception of his family. He begins to recognize the individuality in what had seemed an oppressive solidity. The two aunts emerge with splendid particularity, and his mother and a seemingly conventional younger sister turn out to be the most unexpected and engaging characters in the book.

Hamilton's admirable affection for Walter leads her, near the end, to shower him with rewards that it is beyond even an author's power to bestow. Occasionally there seem to be too many sheep dogs nuzzling him toward maturity. Still, it is an admirable maturity, one that accepts the harsh friction and bitter frustration of bringing together the sexual side of himself with the familial and communal. At the end, he retains the hope of finding a lover—out of town for any foreseeable future—and makes plans to stay on over the years.

"It might take a few years but eventually with the staging of the right musical comedy, with the success of a student or two, the people of Otten would begin to see him. In the meantime, they might feel the vibration, the sound of his own quiet voice echoing out into the town, the words he'd been saying since the beginning: I am among you."

Touching words, and they will not convince some. Still, a book's function is not only to convince. Sometimes it is to encourage.

Jane Hamilton and Judith Strasser (interview date May-June 1998)

SOURCE: Hamilton, Jane, and Judith Strasser. "Daily Harvest: At Work with Novelist Jane Hamilton." *Poets & Writers* 26, no. 3 (May-June 1998): 32-45.

[*In the following interview, Hamilton discusses her family and career during two meetings with Strasser—one at a public reading, the other at Hamilton's home—detailing the effects of* The Book of Ruth *on both areas of Hamilton's life.*]

Awards and royalties, rave reviews and *Oprah* aside, practical Jane Hamilton follows a self-prescribed diet of daily doggedness when it comes to writing. She says she starts by sitting in her study, which overlooks her family's orchard, and "committing bad words to paper." What she winds up with, as is once again confirmed by her just-published third novel, *The Short History of a Prince,* is a highly polished work of art.

My college-age son and I arrive at the Harry Schwartz Bookshop in Brookfield, Wisconsin, 20 minutes before novelist Jane Hamilton is scheduled to speak. More than one hundred folding chairs have been set out in rows. We look for a place to sit, but all the chairs are either filled with bodies, or draped with jackets and coats. A bookshop staff member says she expects two hundred people to show. Jed and I take up positions on the floor, leaning back against the hardcover fiction shelves. By the time the staff member introduces Jane— "Here, straight from *The Oprah Winfrey Show*"—a standing-room-only crowd, too large to count, stretches beyond the chairs, past the shelves, into the center of the store.

"This is my neighborhood bookstore," Jane tells us. She's wearing a long velour dress, a dark blue-green, simply cut. (Later, when I watch a tape of Jane on *Oprah,* I see the same dress. Maybe she bought it for the show.) Although she's in her thirties, she looks like a graduate student. She wears no makeup. Her long brown hair sweeps back from a high forehead and falls gracefully forward over one shoulder and breast. She tells the audience she had to reread *The Book of Ruth* before she appeared on *Oprah;* she hadn't looked at it since the Anchor Books paperback came out eight years before, in 1989. (Ticknor & Fields published the hardcover in 1988.) "It was an odd experience—as if I was meeting a long-lost dead relative who'd come back to life. I wanted to say, You're dead! Go away!" Her voice fills with mock irritation and she makes a shooing gesture with her hands.

Everyone laughs—a couple hundred middle-aged women and ten (I counted) men.

Jane Hamilton tries not to think about whether she's a "woman's writer." "I hate it!" she says. "You go into bookstores, and everything's divided: gay and lesbian, black, Hispanic. Why can't everybody be all together? We're all writing fiction." But Hamilton's first two books feature female protagonists who struggle with problems that ring true to many flesh-and-blood American women. Ruth Dahl, who narrates her own life in *The Book of Ruth,* suffers from a severe case of low self-esteem, brought on by poverty and physical and emotional abuse. In *A Map of the World* (Doubleday, 1994), Alice Goodwin's life falls apart— she suffers, as she puts it, "a fall from grace"—following the kind of momentary lapse of attention that afflicts every harried mother of young children. Women empathize with Ruth and Alice. And women buy more novels than men. Maybe for those reasons—or maybe because Oprah Winfrey's book club has just featured *The Book of Ruth* and Oprah's audience is predominantly female—many more women than men have braved the slick roads and bitter January night to meet Jane Hamilton at a bookstore in a suburban Milwaukee mall.

Jane reads a short passage from the end of *The Book of Ruth,* a paragraph or two. "Perhaps Ruby was sick," the novel's narrator says about the husband who nearly killed her. The room falls completely still. "I'm sure I wasn't a perfect specimen either. . . . A person has to fight the meanness that sometimes comes with you when you're born, sometimes grows if you aren't in lucky surroundings. . . . The Bible is right on one score: it doesn't do one bit of good to render evil for evil." When Jane finishes, she says she was stunned, on rereading, to find these words. She'd forgotten that Ruth was so compassionate. And then she tells her admirers that she'll be happy to answer their questions. At first, no hands go up. There's long, awkward silence. "But if you don't want to do that," she jokes, "we could all sing 'Kumbaya.'"

Funny, plain-spoken, without any illusions about fame, Hamilton still shows up at the Madison Farmer's Market to sell Macoun and Lodi apples and apple cider from the Ela Orchard stand. She and her husband, Bob Willard, live at the orchard in Rochester, on land that has been in Willard's family since his great-great-grandfather settled in southeastern Wisconsin before the Civil War. *The Book of Ruth* is set in a rural community much like Jane's; the novel, Jane tells a questioner, is "extremely loosely based" on an incident that occurred in the neighborhood. A man killed his mother-in-law. The people had been orchard customers, people Bob's Aunt Mary knew.

Six weeks after Jane's bookstore appearance, I head east on U.S. 12 to drive the 80 miles from Madison to Rochester. It's foggy, a gray and brown landscape caught between winter and spring. Withered leaves on ragged corn stubble wave like flags in the wind. Dirty snowbanks line the road; ice crusts low-lying fields. But the willows are greening. Some fields have been plowed. I follow Jane's directions past the leafless orchard to the white clapboard house that faces a barn, an old stone silo, a windmill in the front yard. Jane greets me warmly and welcomes me into her house, all white walls and wood, recently remodeled. The construction project, begun the year after *A Map of the World* hit the *New York Times* best-seller list, seems a tangible manifestation of Jane's success. It transformed a tiny, dark farmhouse that Jane says was "falling to pieces" into a home with a modern kitchen and spacious rooms flooded with natural light. There's nothing ostentatious or fancy about the place. It reflects Jane's practical, down-to-earth nature.

I ask her how the family coped with the disruption of such a big construction project. "We had men working in the house for nine months," she says, "but it was so hopeful, I refused to let myself go crazy." Upstairs, she has a room of her own, a long, narrow studio with bookshelves lining the walls. When she looks up from her computer, she sees the apple tree that bears the fort in which her son and daughter play, and the rolling hills and orchard beyond.

She feeds me homemade cornbread and black bean soup in the big, airy farmhouse kitchen. I sit on a chair; she pulls up a rough-hewn bench, "an Ela family relic" that belonged to Bob's great-great-grandfather. I tell her that I was surprised, after reading her books, that she didn't start out with an autobiographical novel, as many young novelists do. She laughs. "Some people have had really dramatic and interesting lives by the time they're twenty-five," she explains, "and I hadn't, particularly.

I'd exhausted the drama in four stories. But also I look at *Ruth* and I know full well why I wrote that. I was living across the road in the big orchard house, in a tiny downstairs apartment with an eighty-year-old woman [Bob's Aunt Mary] and my husband-to-be." Aunt Mary ran the orchard with her brother Ben; Ben, his wife, and their children also lived in the house. "And I loved them, they were wonderful, interesting, generous people, and still—" Jane pauses. The older generation, she explains, had a Depression mentality. "You didn't drive to town [Burlington, six miles away] unless there was a whole carful of people with a month's worth of errands." It took only 50 minutes to drive to Milwaukee, but Jane couldn't just go there to visit a bookstore. Her life was full of love and rewarding work—and still she felt stifled. "I didn't have anywhere to go or be. I wanted to explore how and why and when and where you explode because you don't have your own territory."

Jane's own story may not be dramatic, but it is the stuff of writerly fantasy: a young woman with no formal training applies herself to her craft, wins prizes, makes the best-seller list. She grew up in Oak Park, Illinois, a middle-class suburb of Chicago, famous for its liberal politics, integrated housing, and Frank Lloyd Wright architecture. Her father, an engineer, worked as a stress analyst for General Motors; her mother, Ruth, was a freelance journalist and theater critic for the *Chicago Daily News,* and a sometime poet. In 1957, *The Ladies' Home Journal* published "A Song for the Fifth Child," a poem Ruth Hamilton wrote to honor Jane's birth. The piece was later reprinted in several anthologies, and was appropriated (without permission) for nursery needlepoint kits.

As the last of five children—and the youngest by five years—Jane recalls that "there was really no need for me to talk. I was in a family of great talkers. I had really funny brothers." She had trouble competing. "I felt comfortable expressing myself on paper, and I felt I could be clever [on paper] in a way that I couldn't be verbally." Jane's grandmother and mother had both been writers; it seemed a natural path to take. But Jane had only modest expectations for herself. At Carleton College, in Minnesota, she majored in English and wrote a couple of short stories when she took the English department's two "Craft of Writing" classes. One day, she was in the basement of the English building, and she heard a voice drifting down the stairwell from the third floor. It was a professor she admired, telling someone that Jane would write a novel some day. "And I was completely shocked, because I had written one or two ten-page-stories, and I thought I had said everything that was in me. And the fact that he thought I would do that was just staggering."

The summer after she graduated, she set out for New York to become a writer. She'd lined up a job "reading slush in the children's books department at Dell." On the way east, she stopped at the Ela Orchard to visit a college friend. The friend turned out to have a cousin. They needed help with the apple harvest. Jane pitched in for a few weeks. She liked the life, she fell in love, and she gave up the idea of going to New York. "I knew I didn't really have editorial skills," she says. "I was completely unprepared for the real world. I wanted to be somewhere with nice people whom I could cook with, and catch my breath after college. It was very fortuitous."

In her early years at the orchard, Jane lived in the big house with Bob and his extended family. She spent summers and falls doing hard, physical labor. "And then I had winter and spring to kind of fumble along [with the writing] and figure it out." She wrote for her own pleasure. "I assumed I'd never be published because people had told me it was impossible." She thinks she continued to write because she *didn't* go to New York. "It was a great thing to be here [at the orchard], just working at the forms by myself, and not talking about it, not reading *The New York Times Book Review* every week, and not worrying about who was doing what down the block."

Still, Jane felt she was "missing out on something crucial" because she didn't have any formal training in writing. She applied to the Iowa Writers' Workshop; she was rejected. "I knew I wasn't ready for it. I wasn't confident enough to withstand that kind of scrutiny." Nonetheless, the rejection stung.

Then, in 1980, a summer intern at *Harper's* pulled one of Jane's stories out of the slush. "I don't know who that was. I wish I did," Jane says. "That person really launched me." *Harper's* fiction editor, Helen Rogan, called on Jane's birthday, offering to buy the story and apologizing that she could only pay $500 for it. The money seemed a fortune to Jane, but the greater fortune was less tangible. "It was a rough story, and she helped me shape it. She gave me the gift of a great editor. She spent a lot of time with me, and that made me think I could spend time on my writing."

Not long after, Jane spent two months at Ragdale, a writing retreat in Lake Forest, Illinois. There she met several writers who had graduated from Iowa. "It was like being in the same litter. You hook up with people who share your sensibilities and can maybe be constructive critics. So I got that, without having to go into debt or go through the rigors of a [graduate] program I wasn't ready for."

The Book of Ruth began as a 10-page short story that Jane describes as "the book, condensed." She worked on it for a year and a half. "Then someone said, 'It's too intense to be a story.'" She spent another year turn-

ing it into a novel, finishing the first draft in 1984 just as her son Ben was born. After two more years of work on revisions, Jane began her search for a publisher. She worked through a list of agents, but found no one willing to take on the book. Then she sent the manuscript to a friend's editor at Harper & Row. He passed it on to someone else. A year later, that editor called to say she thought **Ruth** would be a good young adult novel; it just needed some cutting and changing. Jane disagreed, and took the manuscript back. She started to work through a new list of agents, given to her by a friend who had taken a workshop with fiction writer David Leavitt (*Arkansas: Three Novellas,* Houghton Mifflin, 1997; *Family Dancing,* Warner Books, 1991). She chose a name from the list at random, and sent the manuscript out. Two weeks later, Amanda Urban called to say she had sold the book. Jane mailed the completed manuscript to Ticknor & Fields just before the birth of her daughter, Hannah, in 1987.

Readers love *The Book of Ruth* because they love Ruth, the impoverished, uneducated young woman who narrates the story of her life with an abusive mother, a husband who's both emotionally damaged and mentally slow, and an infant son. Ruth retains her dignity and compassion under extraordinarily difficult circumstances. Oprah Winfrey read *The Book of Ruth* when it first came out, in 1988. "I was overwhelmed," she told her TV book club in 1997. "I would wake up in the morning, wondering what Ruth was doing."

Jane did the same, during the five or six years she worked on the book. "I had the Ruth channel going all the time as I lived my life," she tells her Brookfield bookstore audience. Creating the character, she says, was an act of imagination. "I think some people have the idea that all you need to do is write from life. But I don't know anybody, really, like Ruth. And I'm not Ruth. She has a gift that I don't have—always seeing the good in things."

Still, the portrait of Ruth clearly draws on Jane's experience as a young mother. The scenes in which Ruth talks about Justy, her infant son, are among the most tender and convincing in the novel. "If I ever have the chance to go back and live my days over," Ruth says, "the first months with Justy are the ones I'd choose. It was like real life, how I always imagined it was supposed to be. . . . I kept asking myself, Am I a real live woman? Is my body actually making the milk in my breasts? Is this truly my husband who's handing me the talcum powder so I can make our baby clean and dry? I asked questions constantly, to make sure it all wasn't one magic cream puff."

Jane grew so attached to Ruth that she cried as she drove home from the post office, after sending the book off to Ticknor & Fields. "I remember . . . saying, 'I love you, Ruth,'" she told Oprah. "'I hope you have kind treatment. And I hope people love you as much as I do.'"

And people did. *The Book of Ruth* won the PEN/Ernest Hemingway Foundation Award for best first novel of 1988. Oprah Winfrey loved the book so much that her producer invited Jane to the studio for lunch with the star. This was nearly a decade before Winfrey launched her famous book club, and Jane had never watched *Oprah,* never even heard of her. "I asked my publicist, 'Do I have to do this?'" she laughs. "The publicist said yes."

Jane left her two preschool-age children at home and went to Chicago. The producer had planned the lunch as a surprise for Oprah: a special meet-the-author treat. Jane remembers sitting in the waiting room, reading Simone de Beauvoir's feminist treatise, *The Second Sex,* while Oprah taped back-to-back shows, one about fathers and daughters who can't communicate and another about battered wives. After the taping, the producer ushered Jane into "the Oprah empire" backstage. Oprah spent the meal quoting her favorite parts of the book from memory.

Looking back, it's clear that by 1989, Jane's career was well launched. Back then, it was not so obvious. Even after *The Book of Ruth* was published, Jane says, she was frustrated and irritable. She slices two oranges and hands me a plate of homemade chocolate chip cookies. "I don't know what young women think now. But my generation was the first that was told we could do everything. And that is really a lie." In the late 1980s, she and Bob had no money for day care. They shared the computer on which Bob kept orchard accounts and "were always having a standoff" over who could use it at night. Jane worked in their bedroom "with laundry everywhere." After Hannah's birth, she could only find time to write in two-hour chunks every other day, "which meant I was always losing my thread."

Fellowships from the Wisconsin Arts Board and the National Endowment for the Arts were "critical," Jane says. They came at a time when money was scarce, and made it possible for her to pay for day care, buy her own computer, and rent a small office in town. "I was in the mall, between the plumber and the travel agent." The walls were thin, and she could hear the travel agents fielding their calls. "I thought of us as engaged in the same enterprise, travel of some sort." It was in this storefront office, behind a plate glass window screened with curtains Bob's Aunt Mary had batiked, that Jane began to write *A Map of the World.*

Jane's mother had reported how much her friends admired *The Book of Ruth.* "They kept saying, 'It will be so hard to top this one,'" Jane says. She believed

them. Working on the second novel, Jane had to learn to silence the critics, external and internal. She also had to learn how to plot a work of fiction.

"There's no plot in *The Book of Ruth,*" Jane insists. Ruth's story came to her "all in a stream." But in *A Map of the World,* plotting was essential. And Jane had never learned how to create a plot. "All I had to go by was what I learned in seventh grade from Mrs. Driggs, which was the old Aristotle diagram, the inverted check mark. Build-build-build to your conflict, then you have it, and then there's resolution."

The story begins as Alice Goodwin, a school nurse and farmer's wife, is watching a neighbor's child. The child wanders off and drowns in the farm's small pond. Jane spent several years trying to figure out what happened next. She says that she really wrote four distinct novels before she arrived at *A Map of the World.* In each draft, the child drowns and Alice gets in trouble. In the first version, she goes to a Sufi community in upstate New York to try to sort things out. In the second, she goes to visit her husband's aunt. In the third, she seeks comfort from her own "sort of deranged aunt." Finally, Jane realized that Alice had to work out her own problems in her own community, and that the novel was about her community and her marriage. "And then I got it." In the fourth, and final, version, Alice fights charges of child abuse, as well as an enveloping grief that sours her relationships with her own husband and children. It took Jane five years to get the plot. "It was not a fun process, I have to say."

The process may have been painful, but it was ultimately successful. Reviewers called *A Map of the World* "a spectacularly taut drama," and both the Book-of-the-Month Club and the Quality Paperback Book Club chose it as an alternate selection. But what kept Jane writing, during those difficult years?

"I knew I had to get Alice out of the trouble," she says. "I'd gotten her into this mess. I felt compelled by her."

Ironically, although Alice is, like Jane, a farm wife and an essentially middle-class professional person, she was more difficult to write than Ruth. "I didn't always like Alice. She irritated me sometimes, and I worried about her being irritating to readers. There's a rawness to her. She's very judgmental."

Jane also struggled with the question of who should narrate this second novel. She remembered that John Cheever said a writer has to earn the privilege of writing in first person by learning to write in the third person. "I'd only written one story in my life in the third person, and I thought, Okay, now I have to learn to do this." Jane tried to write the first two or three versions of *Map* in the third person. She says they were "very stiff." Finally she realized that the story belonged to Alice and her husband, Howard, and she permitted Alice to narrate the first and last sections of the book and Howard, the middle third.

Someone in the Brookfield audience wonders whether Jane has to work at writing, "or does it all just well up and come out?" Jane shakes her head. "I work at it every day. It's actually fairly plodding work." Over lunch, she tells me that she learned an artist's discipline as a child. She was a very serious ballet student for five years, commuting into downtown Chicago for lessons every day. But her legs were not set properly in her hips for classical ballet, and as a result, she had trouble with her feet. A doctor insisted that she stop dancing when she was 11. But the ballet training has served her well. "Ballet is very, very hard, and it hurts. The teachers were harsh and demanding, and we worked. I think about my writing, and think that a lot of people have a lot of talent and end up not doing anything with it because they don't have that discipline. I have dogged, methodical ways of working rather than unbridled talent. I'm in there every day and just have my nose to it."

Jane's "methodical ways of working" involve multiple drafts and many years on a single project. She says that the beauty of working on a book for a long time is that "*it* teaches *you*. Writing one draft—what fun would that be?"

The hardest part of the process is getting the first draft out, "committing bad words to paper and knowing it's not going to be very good. Trying to find the form of it." When she's completed one draft, she goes back to the beginning and rewrites the entire manuscript. Then, when she's "pretty sure of it," she reads it aloud, first to herself, and then to her husband. "Bob has an unerring instinct. He'll say, 'An eleven-year-old would never say that,' and he's right. He doesn't say much, but what he says is always right."

Jane says reading the work aloud is extremely important, because it's so different in the ear and on the page. She listens for rhythm, for the credibility of dialogue, for word placement and repetition. "It's everything," she says. "It's really about getting to know it, and know it as well as I possibly can." And when she reads it to Bob, "it sounds totally different hearing through his ears." Finally, when the manuscript is ready for line-editing, she sends it to Deb Futter, her editor at Random House.

Futter raves about Jane, calling her "a heartbox, one of the most delightful, down-to-earth people I've ever worked with. Dealing with her is like reading her books, the level of human compassion is so high." Jane worked on her third novel, *The Short History of a Prince,* for three years before she felt she could show it to Futter. "She rewrote the book many times. We faxed back and forth a lot. It's a very personal book for her; I knew she wanted to get it right."

Jane feels that the new book, which Random House just published, is something of a departure. It is, finally, written in the third person. Instead of a woman with problems, the protagonist is a gay man named Walter McCloud. And the setting has moved away from farm country. "Walter does end up being a high school English teacher in a small town," Jane says, "but he's a very urban person." She describes him somewhat disparagingly as a "dilettante . . . a boy who wants to be a ballet dancer and has no talent." In the book Walter only gets to dance the Prince in *The Nutcracker* because "there were no older boys in Miss Amy's school."

The Short History of a Prince leaps effortlessly back and forth between 1972-73, Walter's sophomore year in high school, and 1995-96, his first year as an English teacher. Fifteen-year-old Walter discovers his sexuality at the same time that his brother, a high school senior, is dying of Hodgkin's disease. As an adult nearing 40, he wrestles with questions of family continuity while he tries to come to terms with life as a gay man in a small, conservative, Midwestern town. Hamilton tells us just enough of the in-between years to let us know that Walter frittered away his twenties and most of his thirties in New York, selling doll house furniture and searching for love among other aficionados of the opera and ballet.

Despite Jane's sense that the new book differs from her earlier work, in many ways *The Short History of a Prince* offers readers more of the same fine writing they have come to expect from her. As in *The Book of Ruth* and *A Map of the World,* Hamilton's close attention to domestic detail and to the nuances of language shine through. Her wry humor does, too. When Walter's mother camps out at the hospital, for example, the short description of her absence deftly conveys an abandoned child's sense of loss and dangerous opportunity, tough-guy belligerence and despair. Walter and his best friend come home from school day after day to find the house empty of all life but his dying brother's dog, Duke. The boys "fixed themselves bowls of Kix. They added miniature marshmallows . . . along with raisins, peanuts, bananas and chocolate sauce—anything they could find. . . . Walter made popcorn, and once they poured melted unsweetened chocolate over the kernels. The bitterness surprised them, and so they added sugar and, for balance, a dash of salt. Duke ate the mess from the trash later that night and early the next morning he puked outside Walter's bedroom door. It was nothing less than a personal vendetta, Walter knew. The dog, although stupid in most ways, had a talent for vengeance."

By the end of the book, it's clear that Walter—warts and all—truly is a prince, and that Jane feels as much empathy for him as she does for her first two protagonists, Ruth Dahl and Alice Goodwin. In her acceptance of Walter—who, like Ruth and Alice, fits awkwardly into society—Jane offers her readers another lesson about humanity written with the author's characteristically light and deft hand.

What makes *Prince* most different from *Ruth* and *Map,* Jane thinks, is its tone. "It's the happiest thing I've written," she says. Perhaps the book reflects Jane's growing satisfaction with her own life. Like most women in two-career families, she is stressed by demands on her time. She regrets that she has not been the mother she imagined she'd be, "this great earth mother type who sewed dolly clothes and made Play-Doh from scratch." But Hannah and Ben—now 10 and 13—are well past the stage where they must be watched every minute they're not asleep. Jane has full days to write while they are in school. And her books have done well financially. Oprah's book club invitation did not—as many suspect—make Jane a millionaire; she must split royalties from Doubleday's paperback sales of *The Book of Ruth* with Ticknor & Fields, the hardcover publisher. But after being supported by her husband, after many years of money worries, Jane now has enough savings to carry her family through several years.

As we talk, the sun finally pierces the fog. Shafts of light stream into the big farm kitchen. Bob comes through the back door, carrying a sheaf of invoices. He tells us how beautiful the orchard was in the morning, while he was pruning the apple trees. He saw skeins of geese heading north; heard the cries of sandhill cranes. He disappears into his office to do orchard paperwork. I ask Jane if she misses working with the apples.

"I miss being involved in something in a physical way, something that's not exercise for the sake of exercise," she says. I recall her years of ballet. But she adds, "I'm really happy in my current job. What better thing than to spend your day staring out the window and looking up words in the dictionary? It feels like a great luxury."

Rosellen Brown (review date June 1998)

SOURCE: Brown, Rosellen. "Something Completely Different." *Women's Review of Books* 15, no. 9 (June 1998): 6-7.

[*In the following review, Brown focuses on the dual passions of Walter, the protagonist in* The Short History of a Prince, *noting his key differences from Hamilton's previous protagonists.*]

Although readers may turn to us for guidance, book reviewers infrequently have a chance to think much, or at least long, about the work at hand. Film, drama and music critics have far shorter deadlines, but still we rarely have the leisure to let a book settle in our minds, let alone sink below consciousness level. That's a pity, because fiction works differently over time than it does when we must snap to and deliver an instant response.

All of which is an appropriately slow introduction to Jane Hamilton's leisurely *Short History of a Prince.* This is an odd book which, perhaps because it seemed exasperatingly random, took me some time to appreciate but which has lingered in my memory in much the way an encounter with a real person persists when he or she has eluded easy categorizing. This novel lives as a voice (slightly loopy), as detail (infinitely trivial), as moment (mostly small, with a few huge and moving show-stoppers narrated in the same offhand and off-center tone). Original and quirky. *The Short History of a Prince* is the very opposite of "high concept."

Jane Hamilton is the author of two highly acclaimed novels, *The Book of Ruth* (winner of the PEN/ Hemingway Award) and the bestselling *A Map of the World,* quite dissimilar stories set in small mid-western towns. When Oprah anointed Ruth a useful heroine in her laudable pantheon of Discoveries for the Reader in Need of a Push Into New Waters, Hamilton gained a large audience. While Ruth is a humble and sympathetic narrator and Alice of *A Map of the World* an astringently intelligent and sophisticated one, readers may have a bit more trouble falling into line behind Walter McCloud, who's the woefully inadequate, if game, prince of Hamilton's new book. But (with an exemption for homophobes), given time Walter will likely charm them as he charmed me.

We see Walter, the younger of two sons in a fairly ordinary suburban Chicago family, in alternating sections as a teenager in 1972 and almost 25 years later as the adult he has become, a high school English teacher slightly more eccentric than his small Wisconsin town is accustomed to. In high school Walter desperately wants to be a ballet dancer—his fierce, independent and probably lesbian aunt Sue Rawson introduced him to the *Nutcracker* early and he took off from there—but, not to put too fine a point on it, he just doesn't have the stuff. His best friends, Susan and Mitch, have it (as well as, for a while, each other), but what Walter has instead is the inflamed and self-absorbed consciousness of beauty, wit and longing that will make his head far more interesting to live inside than either of theirs, though Susan is complex and challenging early and late.

Walter, who's not in love with Susan but with Mitch, is already, at sixteen, both sabotaged and saved by his sense of humor and gay sensibility. Dancing, in the first movement of *Serenade,* he

> threw himself into the wind of the large fan on the dining-room table and struck a pose. He buffeted back and forth, in and out of the steady push of air. If only he had on one of the blue chiffon costumes that Balanchine's dancers wore, a gown that would flutter and billow after him. He was going full tilt—no one could say that he did not have enough feeling for the entire ensemble of twenty-eight girls.

> (p. 12)

Inspired, he runs upstairs and returns in a brocaded velvet coat, "a genuine piece from Liberace's Mr. Showmanship Collection, an item he had found on a day God blessed him for fifteen dollars at a yard sale. . . . As he came back into the room it dawned on him that Liberace, Tchaikovsky and Balanchine were really after the same aesthetic." Hamilton lampoons Walter's passion even as she honors it:

> He was thinking, as he moved, that there was surely a place between the hootchy-kootchy, the watusi, well beyond the hokey pokey, but running neck and neck with the gavotte, the galliard, the courante, and with all due respect to the cha-cha, the fandango, the monkey and the mambo—a place where those forms would meld into something very like what he thought he was doing with his hips at the moment.

> (p. 13)

Walter suffers spectacularly well-described shame when he finally grows old enough to hope to dance in his Chicago ballet school's *Nutcracker* alongside Susan and Mitch, only to be exiled to a humiliating farm team production in Rockford, where, among other embarrassments, his partner is heavy enough to be nearly unliftable: so much for Walter's short history as a prince.

Later, in one of the novel's most devastating scenes, his ballet teacher, disgusted to find him gotten up as a swan—"He rose on his pointes and with the tentativeness of a first flight he wobbled and fluttered his arms"—punishes him brutally by sending him out into the street in his beautiful disguise, bloody feet crammed into a woman's toe shoes, not so much a cross-dresser but a boy in love with glorious illusion. Walter is foolish and brave, dignified and absurd, and (given enough time and distance) he knows and does not even regret it.

The other passion at the center of *The Short History,* which forces Walter to confront his narcissistic self-absorption, is the illness and death by cancer of his older brother, the sweet and courageous Daniel. Needless to say, everything shifts in his family; when he appears to go about his business as if nothing of much moment were happening, Susan, who loves Dan, demonstrates to Walter how blinkered his vision has

become. But Hamilton plays these scenes from a peculiar perspective: she concentrates on many non-tragic scenes, like Walter's and Mitch's vengeance on an irritating neighbor, on Walter's obsession with ballet and on his love for his friend—"the smell of him, the sharp body odor . . . Mitch. One name. That single word"—who indulges him with what turns out to be painful casualness, the kind of adolescent boy-boy sex that often passes and leaves little trace. Groping each other, they never speak or see or, afterwards, acknowledge what they have done. Mitch, when last seen in the nineties, is married and living in California.

The obliqueness with which so much of this is played out is one of the engaging qualities of this quirky book that took me some time to get used to. Neither death nor sex stands precisely at its center, at least not definitively. With the notable exception of the painful *Swan Lake* scene (in which, he later thinks, "he had been punished . . . for his shameful relations with Mitch, his hateful feelings toward Susan, his indifference to his brother . . . forty lashes for every one of his lapses, his hostilities, his perversity"), Walter as a teenager hardly seems to suffer the guilt, questioning, doubt and self-disgust we have come to associate with gay characters discovering their sexuality. When we meet him he has already acknowledged and seemingly accepted who he is; there is no angst-ridden Coming Out drama.

That's refreshing, but it may also be unrealistic. The adult Walter pays one small retrospective obeisance to what he suffered as a young man, but we don't see it much as it's happening: "My major secret, liking boys, was not only shameful, but I didn't know how I was going to carry it forward into adulthood. I sometimes figured I'd live with my mother, both of us like old ladies eating rump roast on Sunday afternoons, buttoning up and taking a walk in the park."

And Walter, as an adult, does turn out to be lonely, insufficiently loved, confused by his future, but this, too, is given us only as a kind of retrospective hearsay. Returned to Wisconsin from working in New York at a dollhouse shop, he speaks ruefully of the short season in which he flourished: "I spent my twenties indulging myself, believing it was good and right to be happy, sexy . . . to give in to everything beautiful and sunny, to have rich friends, to make sure I got an invitation to the Hamptons on the weekends. I was Lily Bart, minus the face, the figure and the hats." (Also, fortunately, minus the suicide.) What saves him, finally, from disillusionment and disarray, is that he comes to respect his place as a literate, energetic, slightly peculiar teacher and as the recipient of his aunt's and his parents' faith and affection when they plot to leave the family's Wisconsin house on the lake to him: the legacy and history of his particular people. It is an intimate and redemptive gift.

The success of any book depends on whether we are looking in the right place for the principle that moves it. Jane Hamilton's intention seems to be to demonstrate the many kinds of love and responsibility we bear each other in addition to the complex duties and pleasures of friendship: the aesthetic, the familial, the erotic. Sue Miller's *For Love* did this, a few seasons back, love (chiefly heterosexual) again experienced through its tiniest, most intricate and petty gestures, as if to say the larger the ambition the more modest the execution.

What's most admirable about this novel, aside from how funny it is just under the surface of its serious events, is that Hamilton has dared to imagine a character so wholly different from those in her previous books (except that all of them turn out, ultimately, to be earnest and dignified good citizens in their ways) and that she has framed her story off center and surrounded it with good talk and good stories detailed the way a novelist shows *her* love, with patience and precision. She has made it a fructifying take on real life lived by real people, though this one's a little too scattered in its effects to show up on *Oprah*. Looking back on it from this distance I'm not sure why I didn't trust it in the first place. But second place will do.

Jane E. Gordon (review date winter 1999)

SOURCE: Gordon, Jane E. Review of *The Short History of a Prince*, by Jane Hamilton. *Antioch Review* 57, no. 1 (winter 1999): 115.

[*In the following review, Gordon examines the disparity between the protagonist's extraordinary dreams and his ordinary life in* The Short History of a Prince.]

This story [*The Short History of a Prince*] is about the transformative power of ordinariness, coming to terms with death, and acceptance of real life. One might say it is about the death of fantasy, and the acceptance of ordinary reality. Told in a style that juxtaposes the present and past of Walter McCloud, a Midwestern English teacher in the present, gay adolescent in the past, it is a story of a person eventually coming to terms with the loss of his brother to cancer, the loss of his own dreams of being a ballet star, the acceptance of his homosexuality (not very well worked out), and the realization that he is going to settle for an ordinary life.

Walter is a younger brother to Daniel, an athlete, liked by many, and his parents' favorite. Walter, who has been tagging along as second in line, has been cultivating an identity as a ballet dancer, attending a ballet school with his friends Susan and Mitch. Mitch and Susan are a couple, and Walter has an unrequited crush on Mitch. Susan and Mitch are much better dancers,

with promise of careers, than Walter, who desires the aura of fame and grandeur. When Daniel's cancer is discovered, the household begins to revolve around him. Walter is left on his own, to whirl in an almost airless cocoon of denial and desire. He begins an affair with Mitch, and Susan begins an affair with Daniel. In a sense, Daniel's eventual death sets the three teenagers free from the web they have created around themselves. However, the Walter of the present must still step into life and claim his reality. The short history of a prince ends with the long beginning of an ordinary life.

Amy Levin (essay date spring 1999)

SOURCE: Levin, Amy. "Familiar Terrain: Domestic Ideology and Farm Policy in Three Women's Novels about the 1980s." *NWSA Journal* 11, no. 1 (spring 1999): 21-43.

[*In the following essay, Levin traces the influence of 1980s myths about family life on the heroines of* A Map of the World, *Jane Smiley's* A Thousand Acres, *and Bharati Mukherjee's* Jasmine, *explicating each novel's perspective on "family" in terms of a specifically Midwestern American identity and the interaction between global farming policies and political ideology.*]

During the 1980s, Republican administrations glorified nostalgic visions of family life. These visions coexisted with social and fiscal policies that had negative ramifications for small farms, families, and women. This paper analyzes three contemporary novels—*Jasmine* by Bharati Mukherjee (1989), *A Thousand Acres* by Jane Smiley (1991), and *A Map of the World* by Jane Hamilton (1994)—in which the heroines' lives on their farms are influenced by contemporary myths. Like some of their predecessors, today's novelists express nostalgia for a harmonious homestead; however, they reveal the flawed nature of such visions and question their public acceptance. Ultimately, the heroines leave their farms for anonymous lives in town, indicating some resignation to the power of dominant ideologies. At the same time, the three novels offer distinct perspectives on region and narrative, as well as more specifically on what it means to be a Midwesterner. These perspectives complicate the connections among farming, families, and ideology, throwing into relief global events such as the surge in undocumented immigrants, as well as questions of identity.

* * *

During the 1980s, the American press documented hardships experienced by rural families as a result of shifts in public policy and attitudes. More recently, women novelists have provided another record of these events, focusing on the interrelated effects of government regulations and domestic ideology on the lives of farm women. Specifically, three novels—Jane Smiley's *A Thousand Acres* (1991), Jane Hamilton's **A Map of the World** (1994), and Bharati Mukherjee's *Jasmine* (1989)—use first person narratives to comment ironically on the farm woman as popular icon. Yet, even as the authors offer a critique of social and political values, their heroines remain enmeshed in powerful ideologies regulating gender, sexuality, and the family. The novels reflect on the nature of literary regionalism as well, illustrating how it may give voice to some of those neglected by the dominant discourse, while it may silence still others.

In *The Land before Her: Fantasy and Experience of the American Frontiers, 1630-1860,* Annette Kolodny has traced the existence of connections between social ideology and domestic fiction back to novels written prior to the Civil War. She indicates the ways in which some nineteenth-century women's novels about the West perpetuated nostalgic visions of the American home, and she outlines how several authors reinforced contemporary ideals of frontier farms and ranches. Such portraits of farm life, accompanied by pastoral imagery, were opposed to views of corrupt, dirty towns and cities. Kolodny links this theme in fiction to nineteenth-century conceptions of women's roles, indicating how novels at once supported and subverted popular values. Carol Fairbanks (1986) expands on Kolodny's theory, writing about later authors. Fairbanks suggests that these women, like some of those described by Kolodny, "wanted to undermine or, at a minimum, modify the public's image of the lives of women on the frontier" (1986, 25). Works about farming in the Midwest during the turbulent 1980s suggest that these points apply to contemporary literature as well.

In their edited collection of articles, Sherrie Inness and Diana Royer go beyond Kolodny and Fairbanks, arguing that regionalism "offers a forum for social protest" (1987, 1). Yet even protest is complicated because of women's liminal status as community insiders and outsiders: "As regional writers present their communities, real and imagined, they engage in multiple discourses born out of those communities, discourses that embody cultural conflict and reflect social tension even as they seek to resolve those very issues" (3). They emphasize that protest arises out of women's need to construct their own identities. Thus, by definition, such regionalist works address issues of difference and in particular of "how foreignness is constituted" (10), literally and figuratively. By implication, they are "essential to understanding how the United States constitutes itself" (1). The importance of this concept is evident when one considers the historical context of the novels to be discussed.

During the 1980s, the Reagan and Bush administrations, spurred on by the Moral Majority and other conservative coalitions, glorified visions of family life, even though—or perhaps because—many Americans were convinced that the family as they knew it was rapidly disintegrating. Magazines such as *Newsweek* devoted special issues to the plight of the family, including articles such as one wondering, "What Happened to the Family," which lamented, "marriage is a fragile institution," and the "irony here is that the traditional family is something of an anomaly" (Footlick 1990, 16).

At the same time, farms were portrayed as a refuge from the forces pulling families apart, as well as from isolating and corrupting aspects of urban survival. For many, the Midwest remained a metonym for rural living, and farms took on metaphorical associations with a prelapsarian America, where families enjoyed prosperity, togetherness, and a certain moral certitude. In this almost mythical realm, women kept impeccable houses and baked bread, and people of color were virtually invisible.

In the first half of the decade, country was, quite literally, the fashion. In 1979, *Mademoiselle* featured an article entitled "Barn Makeover," offering readers advice on purchasing items necessary to replicate the effect (198). In 1985, *Vogue* chronicled socialite Robin Duke's conversion of a barn on Long Island into a "haven for simple pleasures after decades of globe-trotting" and a "dream house, a pleasingly rustic, French-accented country retreat" (Talley 1985, 258-260). Never mind that the old horse stall separating the dining and living areas was probably as close as the socialite and her guests would get to farming, or that the homes on most Midwestern farms lacked imported French antiques. What such texts recorded was an enduring fantasy of mythic proportions.[1]

Idealized visions coexisted with increasingly conservative social and fiscal policies that had negative ramifications for small farms, families, and women. The same week that *Time* magazine reviewed the film *Witness*, noting the "tone of civilized irreconcilability" between the heroine's rural, Amish life and the hero's spiritually starved urban existence as a policeman (Schickel 1985, 91), its cover stories recorded the crisis facing America's farms.[2] Popular magazines throughout the year ran articles about the farm bill, the administration's attitudes toward price supports and credit, and their negative effects on family operations.

Specialized magazines, such as *Successful Farming*, recorded similar circumstances as the decade progressed. The April and May 1979 issues of *Successful Farming* hinted at trouble with articles entitled "Loan Request Denied" (Kellum 1979, 28) and "He Sold His Cow

Herd in the Face of Rising Prices" (Kruse and Baxter 1979, 13). Yet, such troubles seemed scattered and remediable; the farmer who had to relinquish his cow, for instance, turned to raising corn. An article by Carol Tevis, who reported on women and families, was optimistically entitled "Mom Is the Key," and noted the importance of women to successful farm transfers and keeping the family together (Tevis 1979, 34-35).

Thus, in the first part of the decade, farming and general interest magazines revealed that for many the vitality of the Midwestern farm belt was associated with and perceived as a reflection of the condition of the American family. Any threat to the farm represented a potential assault on the family, as well as on the moral values in which the family was grounded. The government crackdown on farm credit and price supports met bitter anger, having provoked in farmers a sense that their way of life was under attack, with "partisans . . . waging the battle with nearly religious intensity" (Church 1985, 25).

Ironically, these perceptions of a direct relationship between the fate of the family and of the farm, between moral and economic stability, may have facilitated the administration's pursuit of its agricultural policy. In the middle of the decade, public personages such as David Stockman and Agriculture Secretary John Block presented farmers as irresponsible financial managers who failed to provide for their families and thus undercut the stability of the nation. Concomitantly, what had been portrayed as valuable, fertile "real estate" (to use a category proposed by Carol Fairbanks) was increasingly referred to as a kind of "waste land,"[3] over cultivated or left fallow in crop rotation plans designed to yield maximum federal subsidies (1986, 68). The 1985 issue of *Time* on farming prominently featured Stockman's reproach: "For the life of me, I cannot figure out why taxpayers of this country have the responsibility to go in and refinance bad debt that was willingly incurred by consenting adults who went out and bought farmland when the price was going up" (Church 1985, 24). Through such rhetoric, politicians were able to weaken popular nostalgia surrounding agricultural life. This strategy made policies hostile to farming interests more palatable to taxpayers in towns and cities, who felt they had something to gain—morally and financially—with the elimination of easy credit and price supports for their neighbors. Farmers themselves blamed the "greed" of their colleagues (Tevis 1992, 16), as well as the government and bankers, but not their own practices.

By the end of the decade, *Successful Farming* testified to the devastating effects of the 1980s on farms and their families. In "Diminished Expectations," Carol Tevis (1992) compared 1974 and 1991 surveys of thousands of families. The results were discouraging.

Federal policies were frequently blamed for the desperate plight of farms; the author reported that "A strong sense of disillusionment prevails regarding government" (15). More specifically, said a woman from Kentucky, "I believe the government wants the family farm out" (10). Respondents also linked government policies to the collapse of the family: "Many farm men and women point to the increase in off-farm employment [necessitated by the economy] as a factor behind the erosion of social relationships, and the decline in neighboring in their communities" (15). Not only did the survey indicate that "[t]he feeling that family life is threatened is more pronounced," (1992, 14) but it cited a farmer who took a stab at earlier rosy pictures of rural life: "I hate the way farm magazines glorify the farm with all the sentimental slop" (16). In light of such disgruntlement, it is not surprising that in the 1991 survey, only 63 percent of the respondents thought the family farm would survive (9).

Similarly, sociological and anthropological studies of women in rural America have noted increasing anxiety and tension, which they locate historically and contemporaneously. Their methodologies include large samples, as well as interviews and case studies, and some of them take an explicitly feminist perspective. For instance, Deborah Fink traces the history of the myth that "farm people were happier, healthier, and more virtuous than city people" back to Jeffersonian idealism (1992, 2), entrenching perceptions of rural America in the political ideology of the new Republic. Fink further argues that visions of the "frontier West as a place where women could shake free" (4) are feminist reconstructions of the past, whereas many farm women have lived and continue to live in virtual isolation. She indicates that "the organization of labor within the nuclear family undermined its liberating potential" (10) and permitted the elision of women from study, as well as the neglect of farm women's troubles (189-196). Her work chronicles "subtle acts of sabotage" (xv), or women's modes of resistance, in contrast to the portraits of united families in popular farm publications.

In *Open Country, Iowa: Rural Women, Tradition, and Change,* Fink (1986) takes a feminist anthropological perspective in focusing on women since World War II. In this work, Fink emphasizes the importance of economics in farm country, in particular in such changes as increased mechanization and women's difficulties in finding adequately paying off-farm jobs that might reduce their dependence on men (161-197). She also identifies land transfers (203) and a lack of social services to help with domestic violence, child care, and other needs (208) as difficulties for farm women. And, unlike the reporters in popular farm publications, she contends that the patriarchy itself is a major source of tension and unhappiness in farm life (209). To the extent that other social and political structures support the patriarchy, she finds them complicit as well.[4] Thus, while farmers in the public press blamed many of their problems on external forces, and the government accused farmers of fiscal irresponsibility, scholarly researchers noted internal family tensions as well.

These connections between the health of the family and of the farm, between political policy and domestic ideology, which researchers such as Kolodny documented in nineteenth-century novels, are central in *Jasmine, A Thousand Acres,* and **A Map of the World.** Smiley's novel is set in 1979, and Hamilton's at the end of the 1980s or beginning of the 1990s. Mukherjee's focuses primarily the middle of the 1980s. The novels thus span the decade and offer a retrospective on its events. At the same time, the three texts provide distinct perspectives on the region and what it means to be a Midwesterner: the heroine of Smiley's work is born and bred in Iowa, the family in Hamilton's book has chosen to farm in Wisconsin, and Mukherjee's protagonist arrives in Iowa after a long odyssey that began in Punjab. These different temporal and spatial removes complicate the connections among farming, families, and ideology, throwing into relief global events, such as the return of Vietnam war veterans or the surge in undocumented aliens, as well as questions of national and regional identity.

The effects of these various removes are particularly significant, because they exemplify theories developed by contemporary scholars on regionalism in literature. First, these novelists contest the idea of a single, monologic definition of a region, instead "[v]iewing geography as a two- or three-tiered field, as a combination or dialectic of what there is and what people believe or imagine there is" (Loriggio 1994, 6). Every one of these texts supports Marjorie Pryse's assertion that the region that is experienced by marginalized individuals, including women, minorities, and ideological "outsiders," is very different from the Midwest experienced by members of the dominant population (1994, 48). This difference generates conflict and plot (Loriggio 1994, 12-13).

Second, these novels illustrate a distinction made by Marjorie Pryse between regionalist literature, written or narrated by insiders, and regional literature, which is written or narrated by outsiders and captures "local color" (1994, 48). The literature of insiders tends to elicit "empathy" (Fetterley and Pryse, 1992, xv) and to express an "implicit pedagogy" (Pryse 1994, 48), while outsiders maintain an ironic remove. While all three novels include characters whose perspectives exemplify this duality, Mukherjee's text ultimately challenges and collapses the distinction.

Third, the novels enact various, contested views of region by presenting conflict not only among differing factions in the local population, but also between inhabitants and government outsiders, or between long-term residents and newcomers. Thus, just as the article from *Vogue* (Talley 1985) cited above offers a view of farming that differs from the representations in *Successful Farming,* these novels contain myriad perspectives on farms and their owners. At their best, these novels are about the (re)possession of space, and of memories or myths of that space, which inhabit it and affect individual constructions of it.

Specifically, in all three novels, the heroines' lives on their farms are influenced by myths of "an idyllic rural life" (Hardigg 1994, 82). Moreover, the ultimate collapse (or near collapse) of their families and modes of living is directly related to economic policy, government farming regulations, and social ideologies that offer oppositional views of their efforts. Because citizens of neighboring towns represent or carry out government threats, the distinctions between farm and town life become critical.

Within the novels, these issues are embedded in contemporary discourse pertaining to sexuality and sex crimes. Just as the fate of the family farm is directly related to who holds political and financial control, so is the fate of the protagonist's body. The heroine of Smiley's book finds herself deeply affected by her experiences as an incest victim; Hamilton's protagonist is accused of molesting children; Mukherjee's Jasmine is raped (and her husband is crippled by an angry farmer). Ultimately, the novels might be considered maps of a world, charts not only of the limited acreage the heroines possess and are possessed by, but also topographical surveys of an important segment of American society and reflections on the forces that shape and dominate regions. As Mukherjee's heroine notes repeatedly, the Midwest has much in common with Punjab, a reference to the presence of violence and factionalism, as well as to agrarian life.

In *A Thousand Acres,* Smiley, too, signals that she is chronicling more than the story of a single family. In her first chapter, she locates the heroine's farm geographically: "No globe or map fully convinced me that Zebulon County was not the center of the universe" (1991, 3). This sense of significance, even portentousness, is underscored by the obvious resemblances between Smiley's plot and *King Lear.*

Nevertheless, initially the Cook farm appears to be a placid, well-managed thousand acre spread, tended by Larry Cook and his sons-in-law Ty and Pete. Ginny, the narrator, fulfills traditional models of wifely and daughterly excellence in her attention to the quotidian. Like the authors in the domestic fictions described by Kolodny, Ginny intersperses information about farming with accounts of important events, to educate the uninitiated:

On a farm, no matter how careful you are about taking off boots and overalls, the dirt just drifts through anyway. Dirt is the least of it. There's oil and blood and muck, too. I knew women with linoleum in every room, and proud of the way it looked "just like parquet". . . . But mostly, farm women are proud of the fact that they can keep the house looking as though the farm stays outside.

(120)

Such apparent digressions add to the impression that the novel's intent goes beyond telling a family story; moreover, this particular description indicates that little has changed since the nineteenth century. The house and kitchen garden remain the wife's domain, from which she banishes the "dirt" of the "outside." The farmhouse, with floors "like parquet," is a replica of the neat town houses of Easterners, rather than a pivotal space between domestic and natural realms.

This equivalence extends to the ground itself; Smiley "sees an inescapable link between the exploitation of the land and that of woman" (Duffy 1991, 92). Smiley herself has commented in interviews that "[w]omen, just like nature or the land, have been seen as something to be used" (quoted in Duffy 1991, 92), arguing that "men equate women with nature and that nature is evil, something to be controlled" (quoted in Walter 1992, 63). In fact, exploitation is a central theme of this novel that appears to hark back to a more innocent and generous mode of life. Smiley attacks the pernicious and insidious ways society has long condoned the exploitation of women and nature.

The propriety of the farm home (and family) is little more than an illusion for the judging chorus of townsfolk (Bakerman 1992, 128)—and, as often as not, the evil is perpetrated by men. Prim white curtains screen out Pete's abuse of Ginny's sister Rose. Rich crops are fed by polluted ground water, which may be responsible for Ginny's miscarriages, as well as for her sister's cancer. Ginny's absorption in small chores anesthetizes her, while her preoccupation with caring for her father masks years of control and sexual abuse on his part. Smiley thus builds a delicate set of images that allude to the moral and physical status of the family.

The central events in Smiley's plot are also directly related to political occurrences, and particularly to domestic policy. The return of Jess Clark, the prodigal son who eventually has affairs with both Ginny and Rose, records the community's increasing tolerance for Vietnam War draft evaders. Jess is accepted because he has returned to the family, for in the world of *A Thousand Acres,* keeping the family together, no matter how cruel it may be, is a primary value. Smiley's complex portrait of Clark implicitly criticizes this social value. Initially, Jess appears a sexy rebel-hero, returning

to regenerate the community with his organic farming. Yet Jess's decision to seduce Ginny at the old dump suggests he is just another male who uses women for his pleasure. The dump is a version of Eden after the fall; its snakes may be harmless, but poisons reside in the indigenous plants.[5] When Jess turns from Ginny to her sister Rose, Ginny's romantic fantasies are revealed to be as false as her idealized pictures of the farm.

Smiley debunks another farming myth as well: the dream of the growing family farm, shored up with loans and modern technology until it becomes an enormous, gleaming, corporate enterprise, a gem of real estate. When Larry Cook decides to relinquish the reins of the farm to his two eldest daughters (Caroline, the youngest, refuses to participate), their husbands concoct plans to engage in a vast hog farming enterprise, a significant portion of which revolves around the disposal of waste as manure. The failure of these plans occupies a major portion of the plot.

The new hog buildings are financed with loans from Marv Carson, the local banker. Marv Carson is a health fanatic, constantly worrying about ridding his body of "toxins" (29). This preoccupation with waste among the men is emblematic of their stance toward nature and anticipates (or echoes, given that the novel was published in 1991) political rhetoric of the 1980s. In a 1985 *U.S. News & World Report,* Secretary of Agriculture John Block is quoted saying, "We in agriculture built our own trap . . . expanded too much and too fast" (63). The obsession with profligacy, refuse, and its disposal reflects the falsity of the farm enterprise, for the men are constantly trying to make waste less apparent.

More importantly perhaps, as Jess Clark's return indicates, the enterprise is dependent on the family's togetherness as much as it is on credit. When cracks begin to appear in the fabric of the family, and Caroline and Larry sue for the return of the farm, Marv Carson, together with the lawyer, Ken LaSalle, stop work on construction (263). As the court date approaches, Ginny and Rose are urged to pay attention to the impressions they create because,

[m]ost issues on a farm return to the issue of keeping up appearances. Farmers extrapolate quickly from the farm to the farmer. . . . What his farm looks like boils down to questions of character. . . . A good farmer (a savvy manager, someone with talent for animals and machines, a man willing to work all the time who's raised his children to work the same way) will have a good farm. A poor-looking farm diagrams the farmer's personal failures.

(199)

One's ability at farming translates into moral "goodness." Character, credit, and judgment are inextricably connected to appearances. What Ginny learns is that just as the farm's expansion is built on credit rather than assets, and its fertility is built on a sheet of poisoned water, so her family's apparent closeness rests on false versions of the past. When the secrets are aired, the family cannot hold together any more than the farm can succeed when the tenuousness of the connections among its managers are exposed.

Yet the family does not fail in a vacuum; it fails because it is exposed to the neighboring community, which rushes to judgment. Ginny is as concerned about the responses of local townsfolk as she is about the verdict of the jury. Thus, the town becomes an extension of the "outside," the world of government and banking that dooms the family itself, as well as its farm. Conversely, governmental and financial institutions are not presented as dark, anonymous forces; they have representatives in the community, which is set in contradistinction to the farm.

At the end of the novel, Ginny leaves the farm for an anonymous waitressing job near an interstate outside Minneapolis-St. Paul. Everything is sold when Rose dies. The main purchaser is the Heartland Corporation (368), whose name suggests the Midwest has become so dissociated from feeling that even matters of the heart are incorporated. Ginny's husband moves to Texas, and she fashions a family for herself by raising Rose's daughters.

Instead of inheriting the land and livestock, Ginny's legacy is "regret" and "solitude." She must pay for the sins and silences of the past, even as she acknowledges that she will always carry with her "molecules of topsoil and atrazine and paraquat and anhydrous ammonia" (368-369), the poisons of her previous existence. These linger in the memory of her father, "the gleaming obsidian shard I safeguard above all the others" (371).

The reference to the "shard" in the novel's closing line is as ambiguous as the conclusion itself. This chip of darkness, a fragment of the evil at the heart of her family, is a memento she will carry forever. It is not immediately clear, however, why Ginny must "safeguard" it. The chip is important because it is hard and tangible. It is the past rendered solid. The obsidian prevents Ginny from idealizing the family and its past once again. Nevertheless, Ginny chooses not to tell all the truths to her surviving sister, Caroline. To the end, then, she colludes in some ways with the community, which would have her maintain a false view of her father's actions.

In a revision of the cultural myth that inscribes the land as female, Smiley closes her novel with the image of a community of women creating a new life in an urban environment. Yet the family at the end of the novel lacks "faith." It is isolated and poor; what truth there is

has diminished them. The characters are detached from nature and the earth that has sustained them. One of Ginny's nieces is interested in "vertical food conglomerates" (369), while Ginny serves food to strangers regardless of whether it is in season. Wastes disappear to an invisible sewage plant. Ginny's life seems oddly impersonal. If she has purged much of the pain of farm life, she has done so at the cost of its individual quality. In retrospect then, the earliest parts of the novel take on an elegiac tone, not for the family as it really was, but as it appeared. Readers find themselves longing for a world where Ginny would whip up a batch of muffins or hang the laundry to dry in the sun. And one could argue that this tone ultimately reinforces a certain ideal of family life.

In sum, Smiley offers no satisfying resolution. The cleanness in Ginny's life is purchased at the cost of connection and an accompanying loss of detail. What readers must lose in the end are their own illusions and nostalgia. If the resulting world is bleaker, it is also a realm where women can exist independently, and that is its victory. The information about land costs, the historical descriptions of the farmhouse, the loving pictures of Ginny cooking, all of these overlay pain and abuse. Smiley's book resembles the novels Kolodny analyzes because it, too, functions in some ways as a manual, offering useful facts. But it is not the manual it appears to be. The advice we are supposed to listen to was embedded in the novel from the earliest pages, as in, "perhaps there is a distance that is the optimum distance for seeing one's father" (20).

In reading Smiley's novel, it is not initially apparent that the details about farming are linked to the advice about families, that Smiley's descriptions of farm conditions, such as the pollution of groundwater, bear metaphorical as well as literal significance. Smiley's concern for women and the environment seems to be at odds with many Reagan-Bush era government policies. Yet, while she attacks myths of families and farms, she echoes criticism of farming as wasteful and exploitative, a way of life built on empty credit and dropping values. Her critique is similar to the government's, it just comes from a different direction. Thus, it could be argued that, like several of the texts cited by Kolodny, Smiley's novel ultimately supports some of the very ideas it appears to subvert. At the same time, the text poses a dilemma for those who would take a bio-regionalist perspective, highlighting its nostalgia for "the lost potential of American places" (Kowalewski 1994, 38). Instead of offering hope for renewal in the land, Smiley's characters seek solace near the city.[6]

Jane Hamilton, too, focuses on issues of ideology, power, and memory in her construction of a region.[7] Her second novel, *A Map of the World* (1994), exposes the harmful effects of governmental involvement in social and farm policy, yet it diverges from *A Thousand Acres* in several significant ways. First, **A Map of the World** is set about ten years later. Sex crimes have come into public discourse instead of remaining hidden. The community is more suburban than agrarian; one of the characters is creating a "Dairy Shrine," to "commemorate" a passing way of life (Hamilton 1994, 21). Second, the heroine and her husband have *chosen* to farm. They resemble the Ericsons, a family whose farm fails early in Smiley's novel. Third, Alice has never acquired household management skills. It is all she can do to contain the household chaos, be patient with her daughters, and seem caring in her part-time job as a nurse.

Despite these dissimilarities, Hamilton's work resonates with many of the themes found in Smiley's fiction. Initially, the farm of Alice and Howard Goodwin (an ironic choice of surname), is described as "a self made paradise," studded with a pond and an orchard. The rich, almost sensual, details build a careful picture of the locale, where Alice does her "best to be a good farm wife" (Hamilton 1994, 13), and her husband throws himself into local history. As in *A Thousand Acres* and the works studied by Kolodny, some of the details instruct, such as when Alice notes that she "made butter in the food processor" (12) or when Howard states, "It is a rule of nature that taking a day off on a farm sets a person back at least a week" (157). Other details document information for historical reasons as when Alice explains the workings of their hay baler (13).

These facts must be recorded because a "dream of a Midwest Arcadia is destroyed" (Kent 1994, 26) by the novel's central events. Yet, from the beginning, the "dream" is as deceptive as the Cook family enterprise in *A Thousand Acres*. The presence of an old orchard suggests that this Eden contains evil as well as good, that it exists after the creation of labor: "the tedium of work and love—all of it was my savior," says Alice (Hamilton 1994, 5). Even as they face the "usual problems that came with farming in what was becoming suburbia" (12), Alice notes that the Goodwins are "labeled from the first as that hippie couple" (13), existing "[o]utside the bounds of the collective imagination" (4).

The Goodwins' neighbors, "very few [of whom] seemed to make the connection between the sustaining white liquid they poured on their breakfast cereal and Howard's clattering, stinking enterprise across the way" (12), cannot face what they have left. They are so distant from nature that their streets bear the names of other states and connect through fake covered bridges (15). Instead of owning livestock, they possess refrigerators "with juice spigots hanging down like goat tits" (17). Given the way the townspeople have abandoned

farming, they offer a vision of what might have occurred to the inhabitants of Zebulon County in Smiley's novel within ten years of the book's events.

Political and economic policy are visible in the townsfolk's decision to leave farming, as well as in the transformation of the landscape into neatly separated subdivisions. Moreover, the Goodwins are heavily in debt, and the young couple must constantly borrow from Howard's mother. Families have been disrupted as well. Alice lost her mother while she was young, as did Ginny in *A Thousand Acres,* and the absence of mother seems correlated to a growing alienation from "Mother Nature." Significantly, Alice's friend Teresa, who is in many ways the moral center of the novel, works as a therapist, helping to keep or bring other families together.

The Goodwins' fall is precipitated by two crises: first, one of Teresa's daughters drowns while Alice is supposed to be watching her, and second, Alice is accused of molesting boys at the elementary school where she works as a nurse. Alice's guilt over the drowning incapacitates her. While public opinion supported Larry Cook against allegations that he committed sexual abuse, it is not so kind to Alice Goodwin. Indeed, the accusations confirm her scapegoating and throw the family into emotional and financial crisis. As in the household in *A Thousand Acres,* family roles have been rigidly distinguished. Howard does not know how to manage the farm while tending the children. Further economic hardship is created by Alice's legal expenses. As in *A Thousand Acres,* the heroine's family finds itself feverishly trying to create an impression of "normalcy" for a community that is reinforced by predatory governmental agencies: "If we let ourselves fall apart, the neighbors, or the police, might descend upon us and pick our bones clean" (167).

If the Cook farm floats on pesticide-laced water as well as on its hidden past, Prairie Center in **A Map of the World** is contaminated solely by spiritual pollutants. While Smiley seems to cast blame primarily on the men in the community, Hamilton distributes blame equally, noting the importance of another mother in accusing Alice. At the elementary school, values are so skewed that instead of being seen as a healer, the nurse is perceived as a criminal who gives children shots and molests them. A single mother whose sexual acts are witnessed by her son paints herself as a martyr to virtue. Instead of being innocents, boys spread vile rumors of a sexual nature.

In contrast to Smiley's novel, where the family colludes to keep secrets from the community (and the community chooses not to see these secrets), the town in *Map of the World* is the source of malicious gossip. Innuendo becomes a means of asserting power, ideology a crushing machine. Howard argues, "Lawyers, people in the system, politicians, were so crippled by bureaucracy and jargon they no longer had common sense" (133). A domestic policy that finally begins to attend to sex crimes becomes an agency of power against the very people it was designed to help when social service employees attempt to deprive Howard and Alice of their children.

Ironically, Alice finds a kind of peace and redemption in prison, a community of women created and regulated by the state, so marginalized that it bears no regional markers. Bill Kent is critical of Alice's "ennobling but unconvincing jailhouse epiphany" (1994, 26), yet it seems necessary because Alice believes her incarceration compensates for the girl's drowning. When she is attacked by another inmate, Alice "took it, like a sponge" (Hamilton 1994, 302).

More importantly, Alice finds herself in a community that is not built on illusions of righteousness or truth. Even though prison life is highly regimented, the prisoners find ways to subvert the system. Cruelty and violence are out in the open, and the inmates acknowledge that truths may be varied, multiple, and anarchic:

> Jail is one of the last holdouts on earth, a place where there is still an oral tradition. Sometimes I think the inmates made trouble not only so there'd be a story to tell, but so there'd be five stories to tell, each rendition becoming funnier or more grotesque or outlandish. There were stories to tell certainly, but there were also stories to tell about the telling of the stories. Although I long ago lost faith in the idea of Truth, I knew that once I spoke, the stories would take on their own shape, their own truth.
>
> (274)

Alice's neighbors gain tremendous satisfaction in telling stories, too. The difference is that the women in jail do not—and cannot—exert power over others by insisting their accounts are the "legal" versions. Their marginality resembles the isolation of Ginny and Rose's daughters at the end of *A Thousand Acres*.

The scars left by the community's stories are indelible. The accusations that cause Alice's incarceration are designed to protect the children of the community, but disrupt her family irremediably. Howard and Teresa seek solace together temporarily, creating guilt and discomfort. Later, Howard must sell the farm in exchange for a sterile, minuscule townhouse: "The whole place was deceptive. Here, it seemed to squeak and stink, is the American dream. Except that everything we were supposed to want, everything that looked so good, was too small or too flimsy for use" (263). When Alice is freed, the family is reunited, but, as in *A Thousand Acres,* the victory, if one could call it that, is small. The farm is lost and becomes a retreat for urban

Boy Scouts. The Goodwins have become separated from the land, from the myth of regionalism that sustained them.

The tone of the ending is muted. If Smiley's novel is a manual on family relations, Hamilton's book tells us that even Arcadia contains ponds that may be dangerous. Alice observes: "the terrible thing is that there is so much good, and gradually it slips away from you. I had not believed until last summer that loss is determined, charted" (387). The map Alice made as a child was of a dream world, where she sat, "imagining myself in an ideal country, alone and at peace" (382). Now her family remains alone, even though they are "outcasts making a perfect circle" of forgiveness (382).

Like Smiley's heroine, Alice must carry the scars of the past in her mind and on her body. The conclusion of this novel provides more resolution, though it, too, connects the downfall of the family farm with corruption in the country's moral fiber. In locating the corruption primarily outside the family, Hamilton does not ultimately condemn farmers or families themselves. Perhaps this is because she depicts a universe after the farm crisis of 1985. The Goodwins, who were not born farmers, have tried to insert themselves in a story about the Midwest that is already over. Their farm has always been a zoo (literally and figuratively), so it is appropriate that Howard ends up working in one.

Moreover, like Ginny, Alice invokes the various and deceptive faces "truth" can wear. While Ginny challenges public perceptions of *wife* and *daughter,* Alice throws into question the ideological agendas implicit in definitions of such terms as *mother* and *nurse*. Alice is perceived as a failure in the community, even as a force of evil, because she embodies alternate visions of these common occupations. Even though her idealized existence is shattered by her experiences, her story exists, a small nub embedded in the fabric of society. Howard is pessimistic, however, about its permanence: "She would be the great-great-grandmother who spent several months in jail. The ancestor who abused the boy. . . . It seemed cruel that her afterlife was already determined" (230). She will be silenced by the weight of others' versions of events, which reflect larger social beliefs.

The question of whether and how much difference is tolerated by the community is even more pronounced in Mukherjee's *Jasmine,* another novel concerning a woman's attempts at self-definition. Even though the novel was not written by a Midwesterner, *Jasmine* offers significant variations on the themes developed in Hamilton's and Smiley's texts. Beginning in India and ending with a journey to California, Mukherjee's text presents a "map of the world" that is embedded in a regional setting even more explicitly than *A Thousand Acres* or *A Map of the World* itself.

Moreover, *Jasmine* invokes the distinction between regional and regionalist texts or characters only to throw it into question. On one level, *Jasmine* renders the very distinction moot, because the heroine takes different perspectives during various points in her life. On another level, the novel offers both regional and regionalist perspectives simultaneously. *Jasmine* is a regional work in the sense that it is written and narrated by an outsider with critical distance from the milieu. At the same time, it offers a regionalist perspective, giving voice to the increasing numbers of Asian immigrants in the Midwest, individuals who may be marginalized on the basis of linguistic, racial, and cultural differences. Most importantly, the novel draws attention to the fact that distinctions between insiders/outsiders are questionable, because they are based on discriminations made by those empowered and rendered visible by their status as members of the majority.

These distinctions between insiders and outsiders come into play as Jasmine travels around the world, adopting different personas. She is given various names—Jyoti, Jasmine, Jase, and Jane—to indicate the shifting phases of her existence. Having emigrated to the United States and served as a nanny in New York for several years, Jasmine chooses exile in Elsa County, Iowa, because it is the birthplace of Duff, the adopted little girl she looked after. The money from the adoption covered Duff's mother's college tuition, and the opportunity to be her nanny offers Jasmine an escape from the stifling Indian community in Flushing. Consequently, Jasmine decides, "Iowa was a state where miracles still happened" (Mukherjee 1989, 175). For Jasmine, Duff—and, by extension, the county of her birth—initially represents openness, acceptance, freedom, and caring.

Once again, the Midwest—with the community of Baden—is presented as an idyllic environment. Jasmine is offered a job as a teller and rapidly enters a relationship with Bud Ripplemayer, the bank's manager and "secular god of Baden" (174). The breakup of Bud's first marriage causes a stir, but as Jasmine and Bud adopt Du, a Vietnamese child, and Jasmine becomes pregnant, they appear to blend back into the community of families.

Like Smiley's Ginny, Jasmine offers advice about understanding the Midwest and farmers' lives. She explains that unfed hogs sound like abused children and that farmers need to get away from their responsibilities in winter. Additional information is reported, often originating with Bud or his ex-wife Karin: "Bud always says, of young farmers or the middle-aged ones with shaky operations, Look out for drinking" (19). In this community, too, character and the success of a farm are inextricably linked: "The First Bank of Baden has survived in harsh times because Bud can read people's characters. Out here, it's character that pays the bills or

doesn't, because everything else is just about equal" (20). This determination of character exists as part of a network of gossip, which is communicated over the telephone and at events such as quilt sales.

Community gossip reveals danger under the town's bucolic veneer. In contrast to the towns in the other two novels, in Elsa, violence is so frequent as to seem almost banal. "Over by Osage a man beat his wife with a spade, then hanged himself in his machine shed" (138), comments Jasmine flatly. Bud is shot and paralyzed by Harlan Kroener, "a disturbed and violent farmer" (170), and Darrel Lutz, the owner of a neighboring farm, adopts the rhetoric of hate groups and eventually commits suicide.

The violence is driven both by a literal drought and the drying up of credit, which in turn is caused by government policy. Whereas Bud "used to welcome" the state inspectors' visits,

> it's become impersonal. Cranky bureaucrats, men with itchy collars and high-pitched voices, suggesting that *this* looks like a bad loan, and this and this, saying in pained voices that a banker who cosigns his neighbor's loan . . . is getting that farmer in a tougher spot.
>
> (188)

In the communities in Smiley's and Hamilton's books, bankers are associated with the external forces destroying farms; here "[e]ven a banker is still a farmer at heart" (171). The enemies are functionaries enforcing policies that trap farmers in debt and despair, tearing apart their families.

A few farmers are able to leave for winter or to negotiate loans to develop and sell their land. Others are rooted like crops in the soil. As Karin comments bitterly (and somewhat comically), "I won a Purple ribbon in a 4H state fair with my How-to-Pack-a-Suitcase demo . . . but I never got to travel" (181). Yet economics alone do not determine who will go. Karin notes that "She could have [left], but she chose to stay" (203). What really traps local residents is an inability to conceptualize other parts of the world as distinct: "In Baden, the farmers are afraid to suggest I'm different. . . . They want to make me familiar" (29). Bud never questions Jasmine about India because "it scares him" (9); to the extent that he recognizes her past, he does so in clichéd terms that cast Asia as Other, unknown: "Bud courts me because I am alien. I am darkness, mystery, inscrutability" (178). "The family's only other encounter with Asia" (14) was when Bud's brother Vern was killed in Korea, adding to the aura of danger and silence surrounding the continent. Torn between ignoring difference and fearing its perils, the inhabitants of Elsa County have no compelling reason to leave home.

Even Jasmine denies difference. Of Florida, she says, "The landscape was not unfamiliar: monsoon season in Punjab" (97). Iowa is flat like Punjab (4), and the farmers there remind Jasmine of the ones she "grew up with" (8). The Indians in Flushing "had kept a certain kind of Punjab alive, even if that Punjab no longer existed" (143), so that after a while, Jasmine notices that "I had come to America and lost my English" (143). Unlike the inhabitants of Elsa County, however, Jasmine is repulsed by such similarities, especially since the greatest resemblance is in the area of regional or factional prejudice.

To the extent that Midwestern characters acknowledge the existence of otherness, they do so only to tame or domesticate it. Asia and Africa provide the women of Baden and Elsa County multiple opportunities for charitable events, such as quilt sales. These allow the women to socialize and trade news. At a fair to raise funds for starving Ethiopians, the women seem oblivious to the fact that "[e]very quilt auctioned, every jar of apple butter licked clean had helped somebody like me [Jasmine]" (179). The merchandise consists of little more than cast-offs from local families. Instead of representing genuine compassion for the sufferings of others, the objects seem designed to elide any sign of difference or exoticism:

> There was a model tractor commemorating John Deere's fortieth anniversary. All the dolls had yellow hair. It had been a simpler America. The toys weren't unusual or valuable; they were shabby, an ordinary family's cared-for memorabilia. Bud's generic past crowded in display tables. I felt too exotic, too alien.
>
> (180)

The surface of Baden, with its deliberate and continual references to a "simpler America," obscures violence and difference in the same way that the apparent fertility of the farm in *A Thousand Acres* hides subterranean pollution. As in *Map of the World,* the locals blame outsiders for the violence, but like Alice, Jasmine shows repeatedly that it is inherent in the community. Moreover, even though Jasmine remarks, "Every night the frontier creeps a little closer" (16), immigrants remain invisible. At the hospital, Asian doctors treat women, but one has to "poke around" (27) to find them. The stories of people like Jasmine and Du remain undocumented, outside the law and the "official" versions of the television newscasts (23). The silencing of foreignness exemplifies the "conservative, nostalgic" qualities of regionalism described by Warren Johnson, who notes that "[r]egionalism would seem to be the converse of exoticism. The depiction of the foreign and exotic frequently seeks to evoke what is repressed in the dominant culture for being extreme or excessive" (1994, 105) and is thus perceived as threatening.

Despite its international flavor, then, Mukherjee's novel insists on fragmentation and regional conflict in a way that the other two works do not. From the beginning, for instance, Jasmine specifies that Baden is neither Danish or Swedish, but German (8). The early sections of the novel show the effects of Sikh separatism and of a terrorist attack that kills Jasmine's first husband. Not only does the murderer reappear in Central Park, but when Darrel Lutz begins to lose his sanity, he accuses Bud of being a tool of the *Eastern* establishment (193). There is even a pecking order among immigrants; Du, who is from urban Saigon, looks down on the Hmong émigrés (130). Ironically, even though such prejudices constantly invoke difference, they ultimately render it impossible to distinguish between insiders and outsiders; the policies that create have and have-nots also spawn endless numbers of factions, and factions within factions.

Rather than embracing such fragmentation, Jasmine leaves Bud for the "perfectly American" Taylor (151), choosing a myth of nationality over the actuality of factionalism, a fiction of self-development over a narrative of entrapment. Jasmine's departure echoes Ginny's abandonment of the farm in Smiley's novel. Jasmine has changed with her names from the timid Indian widow who wanted to immolate herself to the self-sufficient Iowa farm woman tending a handicapped husband. Her ability to transform herself, gained through years of traveling and suffering, distinguishes her from the rooted Iowa women: "The world is divided between those who stay and those who leave" (203).[8]

In much canonical literature, the quest is presented as a male prerogative, while females remain at home. One could therefore argue that much regional literature is gendered as female because "characters in regional fiction are rooted" (Fetterley and Pryse 1992, xvii), too. In her discussions of some of the nineteenth-century texts she analyzes, Kolodny (1984) supports these assertions, tracing the historical efforts of pioneer women to cultivate their environment, rendering it homelike and familiar. Yet, even as these three novels about farming in the 1980s question ideological and social traditions, they break with literary convention by presenting female characters who choose, or are forced, to journey. Their itinerancy is instigated by the devastation of the land and the accompanying cruelty of its owners. Women such as Ginny in *A Thousand Acres* and Alice in *A Map of the World* ultimately must forge urban existences, contradicting stereotypes that gender the earth as female and portray it as freer and somehow purer than the city. Similarly, Jasmine is a traveler leaving behind natives and other migrants who have walled themselves in: "the frontier is pushing indoors through uncaulked windows" (Mukherjee 1989, 214).

With its reference to the frontier and "uncaulked windows" of makeshift abodes, the conclusion of Mukherjee's novel reinscribes itself within the lore of

America's past, reinforcing a notion that anything is possible for someone with the correct spirit. Indeed, Jasmine constitutes a female version of the myth of the self-made American: "We murder who we were so we can rebirth ourselves in the images of dreams" (1989, 25). If, as she claims, the people of Elsa County are "puritans," then Jasmine is one of the Elect (1989, 204), protected by the trinity of Brahma, Vishnu, and Shiva.

Jasmine's "Rescuer" (1989, 187), the man who encourages her to escape from Iowa, is Taylor. Yet Jasmine's decision to follow Taylor is ambiguous. Jasmine presents the choice as liberatory: "I am not choosing between men. I am caught between the promise of America and old world dutifulness." The America she claims for herself is one where "Adventure, risk, [and] transformation" are possible. Taylor is not taking her back to New York but to the Western edge of the country—California—which is also Du's new home. The novel concludes with the heroine "reckless from hope" (1989, 214) like a male adventurer in a nineteenth-century novel.

But what has Jasmine chosen? She is initially attracted to Taylor because he seems "entirely American": "I fell in love with what he represented to me, a professor who served biscuits to a servant, smiled at her, and admitted her to the broad democracy of his joking, even when she didn't understand it" (1989, 148). This statement makes an essentialist equation between being an upper middle class intellectual and being American, as if to be a banker/farmer in the Midwest were somehow less American (a comment that reverses many stereotypes, even as it colludes with 1980s political rhetoric against farmers). Although Jasmine denies being a "gold digger" (1989, 174), one cannot help wondering about Taylor's increased attraction after Bud is paralyzed and his bank is increasingly controlled by outsiders, given the importance of financial success in the myth of the self-made American. Similarly, Jasmine's astoundingly rapid acquisition of knowledge of literary classics such as *Jane Eyre,* together with her ready acceptance outside the immigrant world, obscures the realities and prejudice in American society.

The world Jasmine chooses, then, is not free of the ideological illusions surrounding the Midwest of the 1980s. Like the heroines in Smiley's and Hamilton's works, one could argue that Jasmine has chosen a diminished realm and a fractured or weakened family. Taylor offers not wholeness but an "unorthodox family" (1989, 212), appropriately, as he is a physicist specializing in subatomic particles. Moreover, Jasmine's departure leaves traditional family structures and roles intact; although Jasmine claims that she is relinquishing her role as a "caregiver" (1989, 214), she initially met Taylor when she was his child's nurse, and she will continue to tend Duff. It is questionable, therefore,

whether the move is truly liberatory, or whether her narrative merely reinscribes conventional gender and power relations: "As exotic caregiver, homemaker, and temptress, Jane is the model immigrant woman who says and does nothing to challenge the authority or ethnocentrism of the white American male" (Grewal 1993 191). If this is the case, the manual embedded in the text is not so much a guide to the Midwest as a revision of Benjamin Franklin's autobiography, another work that equates character and worldly success.

To the extent that Jasmine has learned about America, she has familiarized herself with a 1980s ideology that lays claim to classlessness but looks down on farmers, that values technology and money over the vagaries of crops, livestock, and the weather. Even though Jasmine bears the psychic and physical effects of rape, she seems reborn after killing her attacker and slicing her tongue, effectively silencing herself. The effects of this violence do not seem indelibly written on her body, although Bud is permanently crippled and can only father a child with the assistance of technology. The novel seemingly liberates Jasmine, but fails to challenge a system that traps and oppresses many Midwesterners. Similarly, the novel elides the fates of most immigrants, who continue their undocumented existences on the margins of the American economy. By leaving such social and political structures in place—and suppressing alternative stories—Jasmine bows to their power. The book gestures toward a regionalist perspective that "speaks for us, the new Americans from nontraditional immigrant countries" (Mukherjee 1988, 1), but ultimately settles for a critical distance from the newly reconstituted Midwest.

Taken together with *A Thousand Acres* and *A Map of the World, Jasmine* demonstrates that fiction continues to document the complicated effects of social beliefs and economic trends on individuals, as well as the silencing of women, immigrants, and the otherwise marginalized. Like their predecessors, today's novelists express nostalgia for a more harmonious form of life; however, they reveal the flawed nature of earlier social visions and question the public's acceptance of them. In the end, the heroines leave their farms for lives in town, indicating a certain resignation among the authors to the overwhelming power of dominant ideologies concerning women, farming, and family in 1980s America.

Ultimately, the ambiguous endings of all three novels, including the heroines' mixed success at finding a more liberated existence, have significant implications for our readings of contemporary women's regionalist fiction. While this fiction succeeds in giving voice to the unheard and offering a critique of agrarian idealism, the authors are unable to conceive of a world where women can extricate themselves from powerful discourses pertaining to gender, social policy, and politics. The protagonists offer readers advice, but the advice is not what it seems, outdated, or useless. The strength of regionalist fiction—that it comments from inside the region rather than from outside—is also its weakness, for it cannot rise above community structures and social ideology. For women heroines, this means that their narratives must express nostalgia for a past that never was and dream of future unity that may never be.

Notes

1. Together with these pieces on interior design, country music enjoyed a swell in popularity, promoted by such films as *Urban Cowboy* (1980) and *Coal Miner's Daughter* (1980).

2. Three 1985 films—*Country, Places in the Heart,* and *The River*—depicted greedy bankers. They portrayed the struggles of families to stay together and remain solvent. A fourth film, *Sweet Dreams,* offered an escape from the hardships of rural living, depicting Patsy Cline as a nearly saintly figure.

3. In analyzing women's perceptions of the prairie, Fairbanks provides examples of "four broad categories: Prairie as Garden, Prairie as Wilderness, Prairie as Real Estate, and Prairie as Wasteland" (1986, 68). When discussing texts about the 1980s, the last two categories seem particularly apposite.

4. "Interaction in Farm Families: Tension and Stress," by Rosenblatt and Anderson (1981), cites similar factors, such as intergenerational land transfers and struggles for control.

5. More than that, the dump evokes femininity and particular features of female anatomy. Situated "at the back of the farm, in a cleft behind a wild rose thicket," nature there is "untamed" (Smiley, 1991, 123). "The 'shade tree . . . [which] sported thick, needle like thorns" (122) echo the image of the *vagina dentata,* emblem of men's fear of uncontrolled women. It is no wonder, then, that only the rebellious Jess will risk sexual encounters in the place. Nevertheless, like the others, he "used it for refuse" (122), since he late betrays Ginny.

6. A consideration of some of Smiley's other works reveals a certain consistency. In *The All-True Travels and Adventures of Lidie Newton* (1998), Smiley offers the narrative of a nineteenth-century woman in the Kansas Territory. A selection from Catherine Beecher's manual for women precedes each chapter which comments ironically upon the advice. In the novella *Good Will* young family attempts to create a self-sufficient farm. For a while, their "kind of paradise" (1989, 173) blooms literally and figuratively. Yet prejudice surfaces when their son torments an African-American girl (in an inversion of stereotypes, she and her mother represent urban middle class success). *Ordinary Love* (in the same volume as *Good Will*) reflects the powerlessness women against laws that keep them in cold marriages or deprive them of their children. Moreover, like *A Thousand Acres,* it illustrates the force of rumor and the perception that the federal government has run amuck.

7. Hamilton's first novel, *The Book of Ruth* (1990), deals with these themes indirectly, depicting a family in a small town where most of the inhabitants have given up farming for their primary source of income. Some fill menial jobs; others have resigned themselves to permanent unemployment, changing their energies into drugs, alcohol, or abusive behavior. Poverty, ignorance, and anger build until the novel's tragic denouement. Although the government is never explicitly blamed, social and fiscal policies exacerbate the family's desperate circumstances, and the ineffectual, even comical, behavior of government employees clearly contributes to the conclusion.

8. Jasmine's assertion about "those who stay and those who leave" resembles a statement in Smiley's *Ordinary Love*: "humans organize their societies in two ways—either as nomadic ones, where everyone walks thousands of miles in his lifetime, or as settlements that everyone flees and then returns to" (1989, 80-81).

References

Bakerman, Jean S. 1992. "'The Gleaming Obsidian Shard': Jane Smiley's *A Thousand Acres.*" *Midamerica* 19: 127-137.

"Barn Makeover." 1979. *Mademoiselle,* October, 198-199.

Block, John. 1985. "It Looks Pretty Bleak for a Lot of Farmers." Interview. *U.S. News & World Report,* 18 February, 63-64.

Church, George. 1985. "Real Trouble on the Farm." *Time,* 18 February, 24-31.

Duffy, Martha. 1991. "The Case for Goneril and Regan." Rev. of *A Thousand Acres,* by Jane Smiley. *Time,* 11 November, 92.

Fairbanks, Carol. 1986. *Prairie Women: Images in American and Canadian Fiction.* New Haven, CT: Yale University Press.

Fetterley, Judith, and Marjorie Pryse. 1992. Introduction. In *American Women Regionalists, 1850-1910: A Norton Anthology,* ed. Judith Fetterley and Marjorie Pryse, xi-xx. New York: W. W. Norton.

Fink, Deborah. 1986. *Open Country, Iowa: Rural Women, Tradition, and Change.* Albany: State University of New York Press.

———. 1992. *Agrarian Women: Wives and Mothers in Rural Nebraska, 1880-1940.* Chapel Hill: University of North Carolina Press.

Footlick, Jerrold K. 1990. "What Happened to the Family?" *Newsweek,* Winter/Spring, 16-20.

Grewal, Gurleen. 1993. "Born Again American: The Immigrant Consciousness in *Jasmine.*" In *Bharati Mukherjee: Critical Perspectives,* ed. Emmanuel S. Nelson, 81-196. New York: Garland.

Hamilton, Jane. 1990. *The Book of Ruth.* New York: Anchor.

———. 1994. *A Map of the World.* New York: Anchor.

———. 1998. *The Short History of a Prince.* New York: Random House.

Hardigg, Viva. 1994. "Mapping America's Heart." Rev. of *A Map of the World* by Jane Hamilton. *U.S. News & World Report,* 13 June, 82.

Inness, Sherrie A., and Diana Royer, eds. 1987. *Breaking Boundaries: New Perspectives on Regionalism.* Iowa City: Iowa University Press.

Johnson, Warren. 1994. "Regionalism and Value Structure in Erckmann-Chatrian." In *Regionalism Reconsidered: New Approaches to the Field,* ed. David Jordan, 105-118. New York: Garland.

Jordan, David, ed. 1994. *Regionalism Reconsidered: New Approaches to the Field.* New York: Garland.

Kellum, John. 1979. "Loan Request Denied." *Successful Farming,* April 28.

Kent, Bill. 1994. "Witch Hunt in Prairie Center." Rev. of *A Map of the World* by Jane Hamilton. *New York Times Book Review,* 17 July, 26.

Kolodny, Annette. 1984. *The Land before Her: Fantasy and Experience of the American Frontiers, 1630-1860.* Chapel Hill: University of North Carolina Press.

Kowalewski, Michael. 1994. "Bioregional Perspectives in American Literature." In *Regionalism Reconsidered: New Approaches to the Field,* ed. David Jordan, 29-46. New York: Garland.

Kruse, Loren, and Jim Baxter. 1979. "He Sold His Cow Herd in the Face of Rising Prices." *Successful Farming,* May, 13.

Loriggio, Francesco. 1994. "Regionalism and Theory." In *Regionalism Reconsidered: New Approaches to the Field,* ed. David Jordan, 3-27. New York: Garland.

Mukherjee, Bharati. 1988. "Writing: Give Us Your Maximalists!" *New York Times Book Review,* August 28, 28-29.

———. 1989. *Jasmine.* New York: Fawcett Crest.

Pryse, Marjorie. 1994. "Reading Regionalism." In *Regionalism Reconsidered: New Approaches to the Field,* ed. David Jordan, 47-63. New York: Garland.

Rosenblatt, Paul C., and Roxanne M. Anderson. 1981. "Interaction in Farm Families: Tension and Stress." In *The Family in Rural Society,* ed. Raymond T. Coward and William M. Smith, Jr., 147-166. Boulder, CO: Westview Press.

Schickel, Richard. 1985. "Afterimages." Rev. of *Witness,* directed by Peter Wier. 18 Feb., 91.

Smiley, Jane. 1989. *Ordinary Love and Good Will.* New York: Ivy.

———. 1991. *A Thousand Acres.* New York: Fawcett Columbine.

———. 1993. *Barn Blind.* New York: Fawcett Columbine.

———. 1995. *Moo.* New York: Alfred A. Knopf.

———. 1998. *The All-True Travels and Adventures of Lidie Newton.* New York: Alfred A. Knopf.

Talley, André L. 1985. "First Person Rural." *Vogue,* June, 258-265.

Tevis, Carol. 1992. "Diminished Expectations." *Successful Farming* Mid-March, 9-17.

———. 1979. "Mom Is the Key." *Successful Farming,* August, 34-35.

"The Twenty-First Century Family." 1990. *Newsweek,* Winter/Spring [Special Issue].

Walter, John. 1992. "Environment." Editorial on *A Thousand Acres,* by Jane Smiley. *Successful Farming,* April, 63.

Susan Salter Reynolds (review date 15 October 2000)

SOURCE: Reynolds, Susan Salter. Review of *Disobedience,* by Jane Hamilton. *Los Angeles Times Book Review* (15 October 2000): 11.

[*In the following review, Reynolds assesses the characters of* Disobedience *in light of typical family relations in modern society.*]

Henry [in ***Disobedience***] is 17, a bit of a hacker but not completely solitary. His sister Elvira is 13 and obsessed with the Civil War. In reenactments that she lives to participate in, she pretends to be a boy. Henry's mother, Beth Shaw, is a folk musician; his father, the socialist, teaches history at a high school in Chicago, where the family moved from Vermont. Henry learns by reading his mother's e-mail that she is having a passionate affair with a violin maker. For an entire year, he reads and prints her e-mails, saying nothing. He's got his own dramas to play out, a lovely girlfriend in another state named Lily, his certain-to-be-gay sister, his mother's strident book group friends who hate all men, his slightly dull good-guy dad. Not to mention another e-mail he reads in which he learns that a psychic has told his mother that in a past life she was married to her son. Hamilton's stories of family life always have a great deal of edge and ambiguity in them. She does not shrink from the lines that get crossed in family life behind closed doors, and this archeology is important work. Her characters are unusually intelligent, with all of the tools to become full and happy adults, so there is not a lot of whining and wallowing. In fact, there is a lot of laughing in serious moments, a lot of distance from the sentimental and the heavy. This may be a good thing, but it does tend to flatten the drama in Hamilton's prose and to flatten the weight of pain among various transgressions, from hurt feelings to adultery. In this, the structure of the novel resembles family life, in which normalcy and continuity prevail at all costs.

Ron Charles (review date 9 November 2000)

SOURCE: Charles, Ron. "A Family Quartet out of Tune with Itself." *Christian Science Monitor* 92, no. 245 (9 November 2000): 18.

[*In the following review, Charles analyzes the principal characters of* Disobedience *in terms of the relationship between technology and human nature.*]

Jane Hamilton has written a novel so disturbing that no one will enjoy reading it. But **Disobedience** is so provocative that you must.

Certain books capture the interaction between new technology and old human weakness at just the right moment. In *The Octopus,* Frank Norris used the sprawling railroads of 1901 to explore the ancient terror of losing control of one's destiny. In *The Great Gatsby,* F. Scott Fitzgerald plowed a flame-yellow car through a reckless fantasy of self-invention. In *2001,* Arthur Clarke programmed the world's most modern computer to remind us of the old danger of hubris.

Someday, literary historians will look back at **Disobedience** and whisper, "You've got mail." Could the ancient prophet of Galilee have anticipated the secret backup file when he warned. "There is nothing covered that shall not be revealed"?

With stunning economy, the narrator of this haunting novel, Henry Shaw, describes his senior year in high school—the year he fell in love, his sister shaved her head, and his mother committed adultery.

It's an old story, as Henry reminds us, but the latest technology has transformed it. He begins with these words: "Reading someone else's e-mail is a quiet, clean enterprise. There is no pitter-pattering around the room, no opening and closing the desk drawers, no percussive creasing as you draw the paper from the envelope and unfold it. . . . No smudge of ink, no greasy thumb print left behind. In and out of the files, no trace."

Children have been spying on their parents since the kids found Noah drunk in his tent. But the illusion of e-mail privacy alters the dangers of illicit intimacy and the possibilities for surveillance.

When Henry accidentally opens his mother's AOL account, he discovers a passionate correspondence between straight-laced Mrs. Shaw and a musician in Wisconsin. In that moment, he's entangled in a web of betrayal and sexual fantasy that he never escapes.

At a time when he should be exploring his own fresh feelings of romance, he's stained by the intimate details of his mother's affair. He eavesdrops on their adulterous correspondence for months, carefully printing out their letters and storing them in his room for further study.

Throughout the narrative, sometimes in the same paragraph, he refers to his mother with a variety of names—Mom, Liza, Mrs. Shaw, Beth, Elizabeth, the fornicatress, Liza38—reflecting the grotesquely confused nature of his relationship with her. In the most excruciating passages of this *Freudian nightmare,* we can hear echoes from her e-mail woven into his own courtship and fantasies.

Seeing his mother from the inside-out alters his relationship with his sister and father, too. Once he's started down the path of spying, he can't help treating them all as subjects of his cynical critique.

Mr. Shaw teaches history with a special emphasis on debunking romantic notions of America's heritage. Henry, who's already seen enough romantic notions debunked, is baffled by his father's "insistent joy." How, he wonders, can his father be enthusiastic about the past if he knows the ugly details of slavery, war, and betrayal. To Henry, it's the same blindness that allows him to stay married to a woman he should discern is cheating on him.

Gradually, though, he comes to appreciate his father's mysterious tolerance, largely because he sees how crucial that attitude is for his younger sister. Elvira is a confirmed tom-boy, passionately dedicated to Civil War reenacts. While Mrs. Shaw rages against Elvira's budding lesbianism, Mr. Shaw encourages her interest in history and takes pride in her courage. Ten years later, Henry feels the bitter irony of how well his strange sister turned out, while he, the perfect son, remains so disturbed.

When Henry mentions that he focused on the work of Henry James in college, the influence is clear; he's inscribed himself into his own Jamesian tale, complete with a heavy dose of Freudian allusions. Hamilton's greatest accomplishment here is this narrative voice—a psychologically astute creation that's compelling and chilling. How masterfully she creates a character who jokes he was a middle-aged teenager, but now sounds like an adolescent adult. He has the voice of a 17-year-old boy forced to grow up too fast but the perspective of a grown man arrested in boyhood by exposure to the e-primal scene.

It's surprising, but there are also comic moments in this troubling tale of dysfunction. For instance, when Elvira insists on wearing a Confederate uniform (with sword) to a cousin's wedding, we can hear all the rhythms of family tension rising into absurdity.

Disobedience is an exquisite vase teetering on the table's edge. One wrong move by Mrs. Shaw or Henry could shatter their family beyond repair. One wrong line by Hamilton could drop the story into moralism—another chauvinist classic about the damage wrought by an immoral woman. But Mrs. Shaw is no wanton monster, and Henry is no innocent victim. Managing that precarious, psychological wobble is a remarkable feat.

Twice touched by Oprah's golden wand (*The Book of Ruth* and *A Map of the World*), Hamilton has produced some of the most discussed novels of the past decade. Clearly, this is another troubling masterpiece in what's fast become a remarkable body of work.

Jane Hamilton and Pegi Taylor (interview date January 2001)

SOURCE: Hamilton, Jane, and Pegi Taylor. "Jane Hamilton: Good Writing Is in the Details." *Writer* 114, no. 1 (January 2001): 26-31.

[*In the following interview, Hamilton discusses her writing process and teaching career, her inspiration for and significance of various elements in* Disobedience, *and the roles of setting and humor in her novels.*]

Jane Hamilton has had a meteoric writing career. Her novel, **The Book of Ruth,** won the PEN/Hemingway Foundation award for best first novel in 1989. *A Map of the World,* her second novel, landed on *The New York Times* bestseller list in 1994. Both books, which feature rural women struggling to come to terms with irreparable loss, were chosen by talk-show host Oprah Winfrey for her television book club; in 1999, a film version of *A Map of the World* was released starring Sigourney Weaver.

Hamilton's third novel, *The Short History of a Prince* (1998), was a startling departure from her first two. The protagonist, Walter McCloud, is a gay man in mid-life reviewing his adolescence, when he dreamed of dancing in a production of *The Nutcracker*: His ballet teacher forces him to realize he lacked sufficient skills, and his passion for his first male lover is brutally rebuffed. At the same time, Walter's older brother becomes terminally ill.

Hamilton spoke to *The Writer* shortly before embarking on a publicity tour for her fourth novel, *Disobedience.* Her latest work chronicles a year in the life of the Shaw family, as narrated by 17-year-old Henry. The family lives in suburban Chicago, where the father, Kevin, teaches history at a progressive high school. Henry focuses his attention on his sister, 13-year-old Elvira, who takes on the persona of a boy to participate in Civil War reenactments, and their piano-playing mother, Beth, whom Henry discovers is having an affair with a violin maker. Tensions in the family come to a head on the way to a Battle of Shiloh reenactment. Hamilton explores both teenage and middle-age malaise with great sensitivity and humor.

Hamilton lives on an apple orchard in Rochester, Wis., with her husband, Bob Willard, and two teenage children, Ben and Hannah. While writing in her second-floor office at home, she looks out over rolling farmland. She may see a whooping crane, the apple trees in full blossom, or some of their sheep grazing in the pasture. Most days, whether tromping through snow or hidden by cornstalks, she takes a walk through the countryside as a break from writing.

Laughing often, Hamilton speaks with great vitality, but with equal care. She is intensely curious, asking almost as many questions as she answers. A voracious reader with a remarkable memory, she has strong opinions about contemporary fiction and even recites some poetry.

[*Taylor*]: *What would you call the most difficult part of writing?*

[Hamilton:] For me, it will probably always be the first draft. This is a quote from someone: "You have to be willing to commit bad words to paper to write anything at all." The sentences don't flow and the details aren't quite right. The first draft is sort of outline-ish, and I wouldn't want anyone to read it.

*You said in a Random House interview that "***The Book of Ruth** *was fueled by Ruth's voice," and "In* **A Map of the World,** *I felt propelled by the incidents." What fueled* **The Short History of a Prince** *and* **Disobedience***?*

Each book has a kernel that is the starting point and, in a way, its own fuel. In *The Short History of a Prince,* I was interested in capturing that whole ballet school dynamic. That was the kernel and then there were other elements that fell into the story. *The Short History,* in particular, isn't fueled by the voice or the plot. The one who carries it is Walter himself. The plot and voice hang on him. *Disobedience* is a book about voice, and everything is hung on Henry's voice.

Your ear for dialog seems at its best in **Disobedience,** *from Beth Shaw's women friends ranting about men, to Elvira's teenage friend Hilare mouthing off, to disjointed family conversations at the dinner table. How were you able to handle so many different voices with authenticity?*

I did something I'd never done before that was helpful: I read the work chapter by chapter into a tape recorder and then listened to it while driving long distances. It was a strange thing. I felt like I was a fresh reader, a fresh listener. It was probably not the best highway driving I've done. I'd think, "Oh my God, I've got to change that word," and then scribble little notes to myself. But it was very useful, and I would recommend it as a technique for anybody.

You've spoken about reading all your novels out loud to your husband. What happens when you read your books to him?

I read the work to Bob when I can go no farther. I read the end of *Disobedience* to him, which I knew wasn't right, and I couldn't quite figure it out. I read it out loud to myself, but there's something about his presence in the room and hearing the words through his ears that makes it possible to instantly identify a phrase, a sentence or a scene that doesn't work.

There's nothing like reading something you've made to a specific listener. He knows where everything comes from. It's very gratifying. He laughs and cries in just about all the right places. You can't have more of an experience with a book than that.

Disobedience *includes over a dozen e-mails as part of the text, as well as a few letters. Why did you decide to add this epistolary element to the novel?*

I knew there had to be some way for Henry to find out what his mother was up to. It is a device. I didn't suddenly in the middle of it decide to include those e-mails. They were there almost from the very start. They have to reveal what his mother, as well as the lover, is thinking and feeling. Letters can be useful as a revealing tool for all kinds of characters. The reader can understand, in a way Henry can't, what the letters mean.

What are you thinking about when you form the initial paragraph of a chapter?

Those beginnings are important because they have to take you into the body of the chapter. They have to seize the reader. Some writers write to please their readers; some writers couldn't care less. I don't write for readers—that is, I try not to worry about whether a reader will be comfortable or pleased—but I do feel it's important to have a good start and to draw the reader in. I'm aware of not having an inert first paragraph.

In your syllabus for a fiction-writing course you taught at Carleton College in 1996, you quote Willa Cather: "Art should simplify. That, indeed, is very nearly the whole of the higher artistic process; finding what conventions of form and what detail one can do without and yet preserve the spirit of the whole." Can you give an example of your own simplifying process?

I wrote a 20-page prologue for **The Short History of a Prince,** and I knew it wasn't interesting to anybody but myself. My editor said I should get rid of it, and I knew she was right. I condensed it down to about four pages. It was distilling the essence—taking the most important things and whittling it down. Sometimes you don't need to write about everything.

You plant a powerful image early on in **Disobedience.** *Henry has recently discovered his mother's affair and realizes, "To picture my mother a lover, I had at first to break her in my mind's eye, hold her ever my knee, like a stick, bust her in two." Can you remember how that image emerged?*

Well, I remember thinking that no self-respecting teenage boy would really spend much time thinking about his mother having sex. Children in general don't like to imagine their parents engaged in that activity. So then I began to think, "What does Henry have to do to think about her in that way?" which he actually does quite a bit. The "breaking" seemed like the only possible way, giving him a certain power, making him the master puppeteer.

Do you have a particular stance toward the use of metaphorical language?

People tend to use too many metaphors. I've come to this as a reader. When I read I often want to edit on the spot: "unnecessary." It's very, very rare to have a metaphor that actually works, that has the power to stun. I think just from reading enough fiction where metaphors weren't aptly used, I've cut them out myself.

You're known as a writer who does extensive revisions. Do you revise in stages, looking for certain aspects like characterization, or do you go after everything at once? Do some parts, like the opening or closing, get more attention than others?

Generally, I'll write the first couple of chapters over and over and over again until I have the momentum to go to the middle. And I'll write that, and then I'll start again at the beginning and go through the middle. And then I'll start again at the beginning and go through the middle. And then I'll take a sprint to the end. And then I'll start over, because the ending changes how the beginning is, and the middle. And then I'll go through it again, and then I'll go through it again, and then I'll go through it again. Then the ending will need attention. I'll start in the middle and go to the end, and then just work the end, the end, the end, the end, the end. And then, usually, I go through it again.

For me the pleasure is going over it, having the details fall into place and hearing it in a different way each time. I have tried to respect the amount of time it takes.

In your syllabus for the fiction-writing course, you advised students to "Look at life through your character's eyes as you eat lunch, go to sleep, wake up, brush your teeth, walk around campus." What was it like to walk around as teenage Henry for a couple of years?

Well, I had to listen to that awful music. I knew that he was funny initially, had that wry, ironic sensibility, but I didn't know how deeply sad he was going to be. I kept trying to talk him out of it. One of my pet lines is when he says in his ambivalent, wishy-washy jeans way, "In those days my heart, I guess it was, sank more or less, every day." We grew together in that element.

In a Publisher's Weekly *interview, you said the characters in your first two novels were "only warm-ups" for Walter. How were the characters in your prior three novels warm-ups for Henry?*

I could not have written this book without first writing about Walter. Walter and Henry are in many senses related. Elvira is sort of a flip side of Walter. She's not comfortable with her gender and her identity. But I think Walter had that same ironic sensibility that Henry has. I think those books are linked in a way that the other two books aren't.

The Library Journal *said your forte was "depicting adolescents left not by villainy but by circumstances on the fringes of family life while they figure out ways to raise themselves." This is true for Henry in* **Disobedience,** *too. What do you think is the source of this gift?*

I've always been interested in adolescence—that time in your life when, in many ways, you're very powerful and yet you know you're essentially powerless. It's a terrible tension, and I find it very compelling.

What do you consider most important for creating a fully realized character?

Every detail you include for the character has to be psychologically true to that character. And that's something you can only accomplish with time. You can write something and think it's terrific and really be married to the sentence—and get distracted by the fact that the detail in that lovely sentence doesn't really fit the character. So you have to be very careful. Care and time will prove to you whether those details actually work. God, I've come to agree, is in the details.

Place plays a huge role in all your novels. In **Disobedience,** *Henry contrasts his teenage years in Illinois with his early childhood in Vermont. At one point, he suddenly feels homesick for Vermont and laments, "I missed the shape in the near and far distance, of mountains, what was so grotesquely absent in the Midwest." All your other novels describe the Midwest's beauty. What did it take to turn a critical eye on this landscape?*

I was writing this book and doing a reading at a bookstore in the Midwest when the topic of landscape came up. A woman from West Virginia started talking about how much she missed the mountains and what it felt like to be without them. I was casting about for ways to think about the landscape, and I did borrow things she said that illuminated for me what it really would be like to live without mountains.

Publisher's Weekly *called* **A Map of the World** *"a piercing picture of domestic relationships under the pressure of calamitous circumstances." The husband and wife, Alice and Howard Goodwin, tell the story in* **Map.** *Henry relates the calamitous domestic circumstances in* **Disobedience.** *What opportunities or frustrations did writing about a marriage from a teenage son's point of view afford you?*

No one can know what goes on in a marriage. Children can't, although they are as close to it as anybody. I wanted to show what the marriage was as much as possible, but I couldn't do it completely because Henry's telling it. And that did represent a certain challenge. Kevin Shaw gets short shrift in the book; he's the most mysterious character. I probably did fail to have him shine through past Henry's pen. That was a frustration, and one that I was trying to figure out how to fix up to the last minute.

Both Henry and his friend Karen witness and describe a crucial scene, where Beth comes to her daughter's aid at a Shiloh reenactment. Henry and Karen evaluate the mother's actions quite differently. Why did you decide to juxtapose these two perceptions? Don't you risk the trustworthiness of Henry as narrator?

All along he's reliable in his unreliability. I first knew what he saw, and then I realized that what he saw was not complete, or that there was a different point of view.

Karen came in very handy because I didn't want to have Beth Shaw tell it. I would think the reader would still trust Henry, because what he sees is true to himself and makes sense for him. He doesn't step out of himself to tell it.

All of your novels are written in the first person except **The Short History of a Prince.** *Why did you write* **Disobedience** *in the first person?*

It's the way it came to me. I tried to write **A Map of the World** in the third person, and I strained for it, even though deep down I knew it didn't serve the book well. Eventually I ditched it and wrote it in the first person. When I wrote a story about Elvira in 1996, it was written in the first person from Henry's point of view. For some reason, I can't say precisely why, he was always the one in charge of the narrative, the filter. It happens at an intuitive level. It's one of the first things that come.

In **Disobedience,** *you write, "Through her music Beth Shaw expressed the typical sentiments of a classical pianist: beauty, the briefness of rapture, and let's not forget sadness, sorrowing, the grandeur of lost passion, lost youth." How does this list compare to what you want to express through your writing?*

I'm most interested in trouble and how people relate to each other and themselves as they get through whatever trouble is at hand, whether it's love or lost youth.

Henry says, "I got to thinking that maybe treachery is the only interesting story." How does treachery play a part in all your novels?

In order to write anything, the writer has to be in touch with the fact of the dark side. Everybody has the experience of treachery in some way or another. What's interesting is discovering what a character is made of, testing that character by letting him react to treachery that is done to others or to himself.

Your editor, Deb Futter, described **Disobedience** *as "funny, even devilish at times." Did you set out to write a funny novel, or did the characters and plot invite it?*

No, I didn't set out for it to be funny, but it was clear to me right away that Henry's sensibilities could amuse me. He looks in his wry way at his sister, so there's lots of comic possibility there. He's just standing back and looking at the whole family dynamic. He was wry from the start, but his material is rich.

What role does humor play in your writing?

Each of the books has funny bits in them—even Alice [**A Map of the World**]. I think Alice is funny. Not many people pick up on that, and I feel for her in that regard.

As I get older, I rue things that are overly earnest. There are a couple of novels I've read recently that were written by people in their 20s and they were so very, very earnest. My reaction was that if only they'd waited a few more years, they might have been able to make the books a little funny.

You've said in the past that you always know the last lines of your novels from the start. How does having a last line in mind influence your writing?

The last line is merely a beacon; it's a destination. It doesn't mean that the book is going to be didactic, or that it's the final answer, or that it's the message. It's a place to arrive at. You can get there and realize that's not really what you wanted to say after all. It is merely a marker.

What happened to short story Jane? You haven't had a short story in Harper's *since* **"Rehearsing 'The Firebird'"** *came out in June 1990.*

I really think I am a novelist. **Disobedience** began as a short story about Elvira, and for the amount of disruption that happened in 15 pages, it wasn't believable, it didn't have any weight. In the story, the parents were divorced after Beth ran off with a worker from 3M. Henry's sensibility and Elvira's quirkiness are the survivors of that story. Somewhere along the line I realized that the story could be about the marriage, instead of the divorce.

I wrote, in about 1987, a story called **"Sue Rawson's Swindle"** and then another story called **"Prince,"** basically about Walter's dog, but they were just fragments. The stories served as character sketches for **The Short History.** The stories were very small outlines, just as, I suppose, a painter makes a study for a painting. He draws only the hands or the arms and then, later, you get a painting with all the body parts of several nudes.

You told Publisher's Weekly *that you became "paralyzed" while writing* **A Map of the World.** *This wasn't an issue for your third or fourth novels. Can you imagine a situation when writer's block might strike you again?*

Sure. Any day. Each project is imbued with terror. What if you can't get through it? What if it falls apart? What if there isn't anything there? What if you can't figure out how to end it? What if the middle falls flat? What if, what if, what if? What if in the end you really don't have anything to say?

What haven't I asked you that I should have?

Oh, the title for **Disobedience**; this is one of the kernels. I got it from A. A. Milne's poem "Disobedience." [Hamilton recites from memory:]

James James
Morrison Morrison
Weatherby George Dupree
Took great
Care of his Mother,
Though he was only three.
James James
Said to his Mother,
"Mother," he said, said he:
"You must never go down to the end of the town, if
you don't go down with me."

James James
Morrison's Mother
Put on a golden gown,
James James
Morrison's Mother
Drove to the end of the town.
James James
Morrison's Mother
Said to herself, said she:
"I can get right down to the end of the town and be
back in time for tea."

I was going to put a little snippet in as an epigraph, but
I just didn't want to start the novel with a nursery
rhyme. I figured if you knew it, you knew it, and if you
didn't, it didn't matter. That poem had such meaning to
me, starting with when [my son] Ben came home from
D.A.R.E. [the drug education program] and told me I
could never have another glass of wine. The child really does not want the parent to have any kind of life
that's separate from him. That poem is so perfect.

James James
Morrison Morrison
(Commonly known as Jim)
Told his
Other relations
Not to go blaming him.
James James
Said to his Mother,
"Mother," he said, said he:
"You must never go down to the end of the town
    without consulting me."

Molly McGrann (review date 2 February 2001)

SOURCE: McGrann, Molly. Review of *Disobedience*,
by Jane Hamilton. *Times Literary Supplement*, no. 5105
(2 February 2001): 23.

[*In the following review, McGrann explores the
significance of the disconnect between past and present
in the characters of* Disobedience, *observing that the
novel's tension hinges on the relationship between
mother and son.*]

Thirty-eight-year-old Beth Shaw (Eliza) is having an affair with a Ukrainian violinist, partly conducted through
passionate daily e-mails [in ***Disobedience***]. These are
discovered by seventeen-year-old Henry Shaw when he
accidentally opens his mother's file. "I was the boy in
the family and therefore, statistically, the person most
likely to seize upon the computer culture, the child to
wire the household, tune it into our century."

The Shaw family are mostly out of step with the twenty-
first century: Beth's husband, Kevin, teaches history,
and he and their daughter, Elvira, are "living historians"
or Civil War re-enactors, spending their weekends sleeping in fields and shooting muskets. In her daily life,
thirteen-year-old Elvira prefers to be Elvirnon, a starved
drummer boy who wears a hand-stitched 11th Illinois
uniform and sleeps on a bedroll on her bedroom floor
in the family's comfortable Chicago brownstone. Beth
is a pianist with a repertoire of ritual English dancing
tunes, and the family vacations each summer at a folk-
song and dance camp. Even the technologically inclined
Henry is prematurely adult, "perfectly amiable", his
mother brags, playing ping-pong and chess with his
"lost-in-the-past" parents.

As gatekeeper to the chat rooms of his mother's infidelity, Henry discovers his own susceptibility to romantic
love. "I was seventeen and did not know very much,
although I had the weight of the world on my shoulders.
In those days my heart, I guess it was, sank more or
less every day. I was no longer a boy, not yet a man,
nowhere industrious as a dog. I had nothing in me then
but useless sorrow."

Henry's voice, which might otherwise be deemed preco-
cious, has aged ten years and gained an English degree
by the time he writes of his mother's giddy infidelity.
His perspective is additionally bolstered by sitting in
when Beth's reading group comes together to discuss
"the inviolate self", as well as by the wise words of his
close friend, the poet Karen, and by his own love
experiences, among them Lily, "light and dew, a gust of
wind", the daughter of a hurdy-gurdy player.

Despite the attention Jane Hamilton lavishes on Kevin
and Elvira's Civil War activities, Kevin remains a
distant, helpless figure. "It is always about her", Henry
admits; the fundamental tension of the novel comes
from the relationship between mother and son. Henry,
in his twenties, attends film school and for his personal
narrative films himself reading aloud his mother's correspondence. His professor wonders, "What's wrong
with this kid? Why is he so stuck?" And here is Hamilton's gift, as demonstrated already in ***The Book of Ruth***
and ***A Map of the World***: to meditate on the stalled life,
"the fresh drama of silence, exile".

Nicci Gerrard (review date 11 February 2001)

SOURCE: Gerrard, Nicci. "Truth and Deception." *Observer* (11 February 2001): 15.

[*In the following review, Gerrard focuses on the
emotional consequences of knowledge and truth on the*

narrator of Disobedience, *particularly as they affect his relationship with his mother.*]

Jane Hamilton is the chronicler of family relationships; the cartographer of the human heart. Everyday catastrophe blows apart the lives of her characters, so that pain, guilt and all the tensions and terrors of intimacy are exposed. In all her books the domestic is turned into the epic. Sorrow is a human condition. Betrayal becomes an earthquake rumbling along the fault lines of love. A depiction of one quiet tragedy becomes the map of the world. Her novels are lush, long-winded, easy to read, intense and brimming with dangerous emotions. They are melancholy blockbusters.

Disobedience tells an old story: the adulterous relationship between a woman and a man. The woman is a musician, a wife and a mother of two: Mrs. Beth Shaw. The man, Richard Poloco, is a violin player who lives in a wooden cabin, wears shabby clothes and is a seductively two-dimensional cliche, like a pen-and-ink drawing of a romantic lover.

The daughter, Elvira, is beautiful and stubborn and strange; all her adolescent passions channelled into Civil War reconstructions. She dreams not of boys but of glorious slaughter. Henry, the quieter oldest child, narrates the story of his mother's long betrayal, looking back in his late twenties, on his 17-year-old self. He discovered his mother's secret, through (a post-modern touch) her emails. He's a computer buff, amiable, shy.

On the brink of troubled adulthood, he discovers his mother isn't just Mrs Shaw. She's someone else as well, someone lyrical, rapturous and besotted: she's Liza38 (the computer name Henry gave her), sneaking off to see her lover each week, deceiving her family.

The affair is imagined by the son, who constructs it from the messages he reads. He evokes for himself his mother naked, his mother joyful. The clothes she wore, the looks she threw, the way she would have smiled, the way she must have felt. The fact that the ostensible subject of the novel—a love affair—becomes refracted in this way does not matter. The real subject of *Disobedience* is apparently obedient Henry's relationship to his mother. He looks at her, voyeuristic, when she is unaware of his gaze. He tracks her life. He follows clues she doesn't know she is leaving. He torments himself.

The shadow subject of *Disobedience* is the tricky nature of truth and knowledge. We think we know a person but we know only the face we see. Like Henry's mother, we are the objects of other people's narcissistic inventions.

Hamilton is an emotional, full-throttle writer. Not for her understatement, reticence, simple lucidity. She describes and re-describes events. She seems more interested in emotions than creatures. She loves to dwell on the meaning of betrayal, or grief—on all the psychodramas of the human soul.

Vicky Hutchings (review date 12 March 2001)

SOURCE: Hutchings, Vicky. "Boy Talk." *New Statesman* 130, no. 4528 (12 March 2001): 55-6.

[*In the following review, Hutchings emphasizes the interplay between the narrator's teenaged and adult perspectives in* Disobedience.]

Henry Shaw, the 17-year-old narrator of Jane Hamilton's *Disobedience,* is a modern-day Holden Caulfield. Using his mother's password (Liza38), he logs on to her computer and, like any teenager, is outraged to discover that she has "got mail". "What was the old girl up to?" Why, she is having an affair with a man who lives in Wisconsin, no less.

But there's a potential problem. A Holden Caulfield would not be able to penetrate the torment and torture of his mum, Beth Shaw, and her lover, Richard Pollaco. Not without help, that is. What adolescent boy would understand why his mother talks endlessly about Pollaco at home? "She wouldn't bring him up if she was deceiving my father, if she was deceiving us. Would she? Not in front of us all. Not at *dinner*," responds the prim, disapproving teenager. But then comes the mature afterthought: "She wanted to both hold his name in her mouth and say it. Say it again and again in our presence. Richard Pollaco. Pollaco, Pollaco, Richard." And what regular guy would see why his mother keeps fondly remembering—even urging her son, daughter and husband to join her in remembering—favourite family moments? At *this* moment in her life? Yet he grasps it effortlessly—she is testing the weight of the family history to see what it is worth, to see if it is worth staying.

The 17-year-old Henry is cleverly overlaid by an older Henry, musing a decade later, with adult insight, on that turbulent year in the Shaw family. But both voices are important, because Henry the man would never remember the fiddling minutiae of family life with such clarity. In slipping back and forth between the two Henries, Hamilton never hits a wrong note.

But another pitfall is Henry's gender. He knows far too much about how women think. He even knows the shocking truth about why women join book clubs. But, by a further sleight of hand, Hamilton plays with our expectations of gender, so nothing surprises any more. The wife is having an affair while her husband shops, cooks, does the washing-up and waits for things to return to normal; the daughter, Elvira, a civil war reenactor and part of a hardcore infantry unit, shaves her head to pass as a boy; and Henry lets his "unusually clean and shiny" hair fall down his back and wants to major in women's studies.

In the eccentric Shaw family, it is the absence of a television until Henry is 14—something that must surely amount to child abuse in the United States—that astonishes us most. Hamilton's off-the-wall characters, dry wit and perception into the seduction of assuming a new identity—in which Henry's mother can become "someone other than the usual and approved Beth Shaw"—make this a wonderful read.

William H. Pritchard (review date summer 2001)

SOURCE: Pritchard, William H. "Fiction Chronicle." *Hudson Review* 54, no. 2 (summer 2001): 313-19.

[*In the following review, Pritchard examines a selection of recent novels, including* Disobedience, *arguing that Hamilton's realistic portrayal of a mother-son relationship is "a solid and credible achievement."*]

William Trevor's most recent collection of short fiction has met with universal praise, an unusual consensus even for such a distinguished writer.[1] As one of the reviewers who praised it, I can't help wondering whether anything in addition to the clear merit of his work is responsible for the unanimity. It may have something to do with a related fact—that even more than with most writers, detailing the plot and describing the characters of a Trevor story is of no use in suggesting that story's feel, its texture. Mr. Trevor's sensibility is extraordinarily resistant to "ideas," while the tone and manner of the pieces, divergent in their locations (Ireland, England) and mode (lyric, ironic, comic), everywhere conceals as much as it reveals the writer. V. S. Pritchett's stories provide an analogous instance of writing so poised and in control of itself, so un-polemical, that it is unlikely to provoke readers into critical dissent.

Trevor is able to imagine and inhabit with equal convincingness the minds of men and of women, from simple and limited minds to very sophisticated ones indeed. These assertions may be tested if an interested reader will read, in succession, what struck me as the collection's three best stories: "The Mourning" (about a young Irishman in London), "Against the Odds" (a Belfast woman on the move), and "Death of a Professor" (an Oxbridge don subjected to a hoax). These belong with the best of Trevor's shorter efforts, but there isn't a single one of the twelve stories in *The Hill Bachelors* that reveals less than writerly mastery.

Trevor is the best short fictionist in England, and I would make a similar claim for John Updike in this country.[2] But consider the freedom and eagerness with which American reviewers have taken the measure of this writer's limitations, as demonstrated in his new collection. One need go no farther than Michiko Kakutani's judgments about the stories in her *New York Times* review: "superfluous and formulaic"; "desultory chronicles" that are "content to substitute charm for psychological detail, glibness for felt emotion." Clearly Updike is a writer who is fair game for being patronized and seen through. *Licks of Love: Short Stories and a Sequel* is unsatisfyingly titled after its perhaps least impressive story ("Licks of Love in the Heart of the Cold War"); the "sequel" is of course "Rabbit Remembered," a novella of nearly 200 pages revisiting the folks in Brewer, Pennsylvania, ten years after its leading citizen Harry Angstrom departed this world. A shorter version appeared in *The New Yorker,* but the full remembrance is richer, fleshed out in detail, culminating in a fine comic moment at the new millennium New Year's Eve 1999, in which Rabbit's son Nelson, on the verge of messing things up yet once more, is instead allowed a measure of success, even reward. The revisiting and, to some extent, recuperation of Nelson, especially his discovery of his half-sister Annabelle, is perhaps the most affecting thing about "Rabbit Remembered." Updike's decision not to leave him wholly at rest, forty years after he first came on the scene in *Rabbit, Run,* was a bit of inspiration.

But the revisitings in a number of stories from this volume are (contra Kakutani) not at all "superfluous"—or rather it is superfluity as style in Frost's sense of the word: "the mind skating circles round itself as it moves forward." Updike's subjects are those that have made the stuff of his fiction: his mother ("Cats"), his father ("My Father on the Verge of Disgrace"), his Pennsylvania boyhood ("Lunch Hour"), his life as imperfect father and husband in the fifties and sixties ("The Woman Who Got Away," "How Was It Really?," "New York Girl"). Who else is there—for us oldsters—to bring back what a school boiler room looked like in the 1940s:

> In front of you, across a dizzying gap, were the immense coal-burning furnaces that warmed the school. You could see the near furnace take a great sliding gulp of pea coal from its hopper, and the mica viewing-portals shudder with orange incandescence, and bundles of asbestos-wrapped steam pipes snake across the ceiling.

In "How Was it Really?," the narrator claims not to remember with any specificity or certainty just what happened in his years as married bringer-up of children. But, along with remembering Rabbit, Updike remembers everything else and makes his compelling style out of such superfluity.

Moving on to three novels of domesticity, parents and children, hometown views:[3] Shelby Hearon is a veteran, and her fifteenth book is a happy fusion of humorous observation with the slings and arrows of family trials. Its first-person narrator, Ella, has always played distinct second fiddle to her glamorous older sister Terrell, beloved by their mother, while Ella, the outcast, escapes suffocation in East Texas gentility by eloping to Louisiana with a stud named Buddy. Buddy however does not last, and Ella and her child Robin ("Birdie") keep a remote, epistolary distance from the folks back home. Then Terrell, married and mother of two boys, commences an affair and involves Ella in its concealment, pretending to visit her while visiting the guy instead. Terrell's sudden death in a plane crash precipitates Ella's eventual confrontation of her unsatisfactory relation to her mother, along with her dawning love for Terrell's husband. It sounds laborious told this way, but as conducted by Hearon's gently wised-up and also vulnerable voice, the narrative becomes a pleasure. Hearon is fully at home in the world of things, of roses, clothes, foods—as when Ella and Terrell go to a place in Texas called Central Market, "the Louvre of food":

> Feeling like a refugee, a charity case, I tagged along behind her through warehouse-size spaces heaped up with pyramids of potatoes, mountains of rare mushrooms, lettuces beyond imagining, imported cheese and butter from every corner of the earth, flavored milks thick as cream, loaves of crusty buttermilk bread, still warm scones fragrant as perfume. Meat rooms bejeweled with filets of beef and racks of lamb. Fish rooms studded with shellfish on ice, overlapped with roof tiles.

The plot-resolution of things is less interesting than the things as they occur along the way. But this is a highly agreeable book, saved by Shelby Hearon's command of irony and idiom from the clichés of sentimental romance.

Jane Hamilton is a writer new to me (this [*Disobedience*] is her fourth novel), and like Hearon has ready resources of humorous control as she tells the story—also in first person—of a seventeen-year-old boy, Henry Shaw's, coming of age in his final pre-college year. Henry lives with his family in Chicago; his father, Kevin, is a history teacher; his sister, Elvira, a fanatic Civil War buff; and his mother, Beth, a talented pianist who falls in love with a violinist named Richard Polloco. Henry discovers this by accessing his mother's e-mail letters to her friend and to Polloco confessing the situation. The discovery takes over his life, and from a later perspective he meditates intelligently about the implications of this knowledge, wondering why he didn't run away: "I could gaze all those years back and consider why I had stayed in Chicago, why I hadn't taken serious drugs or wrecked the Ming dynasty pottery in our neighbor's brownstone for attention." He admits there were reasons to finish high school and that he lacked the financial means to bring off a flight:

> The true reason, however, one I would not have acknowledged, was with me like new muscle, flexing, growing, becoming. By the force of my self, because I had to eat in the kitchen and sleep in my bed, because I moved through the house, my mother, I believed, had to stay in place.

This feeling animates the narrative as Hamilton gives us a version of a *Holden Caulfield* thrust into responsibility for his parents' future. The novel varies its landscape and characters: Henry goes north with his mother and sister to Polloco's cabin for a day visit (the excuse is music) and south to Shiloh for a disastrous re-enactment of the Civil War battle. His own erotic fortunes with a girlfriend from the East are also treated, though the book's real interest stays with the quite moving mix of feelings he expresses toward his mother. Like Shelby Hearon's, Hamilton's novel has trouble knowing how to end itself, but page by page it is a solid and credible achievement.

Amit Chaudhuri is a respected young writer, but on the basis of *A New World* I'm puzzled as to exactly why. It is a novel in which nothing happens of significance and in which the laid-back style of narration doesn't invite us to judgment and preference. A divorced professor of Economics, Jayojit Chatterjee, and his young son, Bonny, visit his parents in Calcutta for the summer. His mother feeds them rich food; Jayojit sleeps a lot and chats with his father (a retired Admiral); he goes out on errands, walks about Calcutta, observes people and places, and provides mild commentary on the passing parade. Every so often we flash back to his marriage and its cooling into divorce; these memories of life in California are again commented on in a reserved manner, with the narrowest range of tonal play. It is a novel everywhere "well written" in which nothing stands out—there is no temptation to quote from it by way of making an illustrative point. This is doubtless a strategy on Mr. Chaudhuri's part to resist easy poignance and even the slightest hint of the melodramatic. But in resisting melodrama he manages to resist drama as well, and has produced a book pretty much without inflection, its overall tone of observation an impassive one bordering on indifference. Or maybe Chaudhuri's gentle take on things, on the Bengali milieu, is too subtle for these Western ears. A novel to admire, perhaps, but not much to like.

Offhand I can't think of a novelist more unlike Amit Chauhuri than Julian Barnes, whose literary performance is as acrobatic and show-offy as Chauduri's is reserved.[4] I first became aware of Mr. Barnes about thirty years ago when he did a weekly stint of television reviewing for *The New Statesman,* invariably producing some of the funniest copy going. So if you establish yourself as a smart aleck who can do excellent stand-up comedy, it would hardly do to exclude it from your fiction. Barnes's new novel is a follow-up to *Talking It Over* of ten years ago, which introduced us to the three principal players—Stuart, Gillian, and Oliver—who dominate the new book. Stuart and Gillian were married, then Oliver came along and took her away from him; now Stuart, having exiled himself to America, remarried and divorced, is back in town, rich, and eager to concern himself with Gillian's situation. Meanwhile Oliver, always excessive, is failing at his job (he is a writer of sorts), sinking into depression, but ever more extravagant in his verbal performances, as in this reflection apropos of his meeting Stuart again:

> While quaffing and quenching with him, I did not, out of sheer tact, enquire too subcutaneously about his sojourn in the Land of the Free, but it did strike me that if the fluidity were sloshing around his calves like a Venetian flood-tide he might—to switch city-states—care to Medici some of the Moolah in my direction.

Indeed an antic disposition, yet it's possible for not only Stuart but the reader to weary of such fireworks.

As always, some of Barnes's contributions are very funny indeed. Here is Gillian, picking up on her previous remark that at night she and Oliver fall into bed and don't have sex:

> When I said we fall into bed and don't have sex, you did know it was a joke, didn't you? I should say we have sex about as often as the national average, whatever that is. As often as you do, perhaps. And some of the time, it's national average sex. I'm sure you've had it yourself.

Perfect timing, and amusing also are the short, catchy chapter titles in which one of the talking heads addresses a "you" the reader is invited to become. "Would You Rather?" begins with Oliver:

> You know that game called Would You Rather? As in, would you rather be buried up to your neck in wet mud for a week or compare all the recorded versions of the New World Symphony? Would you rather stroll down Oxford Street bollock-naked with a pineapple on your head or marry a member of the Royal Family?

These quotations will suggest the darkly playful (postmodern?) (deconstructive?) mode of the novel, in one ear and out the other but clever enough in the process to have convinced Knopf that a first printing of 40,000 copies was in order.

Since postmodern can mean anything one likes, I'll apply it to Don DeLillo's strange little book, as devoid of jokes as Julian Barnes is full of them.[5] Or rather, call *The Body Artist* one continuous sick joke, beginning when the protagonist's husband offs himself in the space between chapters one and two. His wife Lauren, "the body artist," hangs out by herself in a big rented house somewhere on "the coast" where she spends much time sanding her body with a pumice stone or improving it with emery boards, scissors, clippers, and creams. Then a very strange, wild boy is discovered in an upstairs room. Lauren calls him "Mr. Tuttle" because he reminds her of a high school science teacher of that name. "Mr. Tuttle" talks funny ("It is not able," "Is when it comes," "I am doing. This yes that. Say some words"), but the whole book talks funny:

> It was the kind of day in which you forget words and drop things and wonder what it is you came into the room to get because you are standing here for a reason and you have to tell yourself it is just a question of sooner or later before you remember because you always remember once you are here.

Compare darkest Faulkner, from *Light in August*:

> Memory believes before knowing remembers. Believes longer than recollects, longer than knowing even wonders. Knows remembers believes a corridor . . .

DeLillo's idea, I guess, is that—in the narrative language about Mr. Tuttle—"There has to be an imaginary point, a nonplace where language intersects with our perceptions of time and space, and he is a stranger at this crossing, without words or bearing." It doesn't seem to me, at this late date, a very good project for the novel. I've always had reservations about DeLillo, had trouble finishing his books, but *Underworld,* his previous one, had enough imaginative substance to make the long trip worth it. Not so with *The Body Artist.*

Of course DeLillo is Serious, all art and a yard wide, while John le Carré and Barbara Vine (a.k.a. Ruth Rendell) are popular writers working in genres just a shade inferior.[6] I fell away from le Carré after *A Perfect Spy* of fifteen years ago, so have not read his post-cold war fiction. But any page of the new novel shows how thoroughly professional and expert are his moves even if I can never quite follow the twists and turns of plot or keep up with the shifts in place. *The Constant Gardener* moves us from Kenya to Germany, from an island off the Italian coast to Saskatchewan and back. But wherever he deposits his hero, Justin Quayle, a British intelligence officer intent on bringing to book the murderers of his wife Tessa (she was killed, along with her black companion, while on an investigative mission in Kenya), the terrain, the landscape, is nameable and fully named. Quayle, attending Tessa's funeral, is firmly placed

> on a lush plateau of tall grass and red mud and flowering ornamental trees, both sad and joyful, a couple of miles from the town center and just a short step from Kibera, one of Nairobi's larger slums, a vast brown smear of smoking tin houses overhung with a pall of sickly African dust, crammed into the Nairobi river valley with a hand's width between them. The popula-

tion of Kibera is half a million and rising, and the valley is rich in deposits of sewage, plastic bags, colorful strands of old clothing, banana and orange peel, corncobs, and anything else the city cares to dump on it.

With such specification and amplification you can see, if not quite agree, that the novel must go on for 500 pages.

For all its expertise with landscape, its finely rendered infightings and treacheries among the British foreign service people, its excellent, detailed transcripts of interrogations and harassments, the book's moral center is a simple one. Reviewing it in the *New York Times Book Review,* Rand Richards Cooper pointed to the ruinous—for the novel—quality of le Carré's outraged idealism, outrage at the spectacle of ruthless drug companies trying out an insufficiently tested anti-tuberculosis drug on impoverished Kenyans. (Le Carré's Author's Note at the end of the novel testifies to his hard-working research on the "Pharma" people.) But in the course of unmasking them, the novel's hero, Justin Quayle, becomes ever more the white knight, superb and incorruptible in his quest. Ambiguity, the stock-in-trade of earlier le Carré, gets short shrift in *The Constant Gardener* and not to the novel's advantage; still, you have to marvel at the executive skill with which this very ambitious novelist continues to get things done.

Fifteen years ago, with *A Dark-Adapted Eye,* Ruth Rendell published her first novel under the name of Barbara Vine. I am not sure how much considerations of sales and the novelist's embarrassing rate of high productivity had to do with the decision. (Joyce Carol Oates has done a similar doubling in this country.) *Grasshopper* is the tenth Barbara Vine novel to appear since 1986; this of course in addition to twelve Rendell novels, five of them featuring her detective Inspector Wexford, over the same period. My sense is that under the Vine imprint, Rendell gives herself more room to explore material not classifiable as or forced into the mystery-thriller-crime-novel genre. *Grasshopper* is an instance of such exploration: its protagonist is a woman, Clodagh Brown, currently an electrician in London, looking back on her life eleven years ago with a group of odd individuals in a Maida Vale flat presided over by a young man, courtesy of his wealthy parents. Silver's flat (his real name is Michael Silverman and Clodagh falls in love with him), is a fourth-floor walkup, which suits Clodagh since she's claustrophobic, uneasily living in a basement room down the street. She has come to London after a tragic accident to her boyfriend, sustained as the two young people were climbing a pylon in Suffolk (where Clodagh's parents live). Now she is enrolled in, but scarcely attending, a technical college while spending her time with Silver and his

friends, playing grasshopper on the roofs of London. Barbara Vine's really astonishing achievement in the book is to turn those nighttime rooftop adventures into a beautiful landscape of the imagination:

> We were looking across the backs of houses, the fronts of houses, streets between, the dark tops of leafy trees and their gold-lit trunks, gardens of gloomy evergreens and pale shrubs, the faces of flowers white and shimmering, stone walls and stone tubs and urns, statuary, and in one small enclave a dark shining pool in which golden fish darted.

The topographical and architectural sweep of the city is handsomely evoked:

> London rolled away below us, to the Heath and Highgate, the towers of Somers Town and Euston, the ribbon streets of Edgware, and, like a low pyramid, Harrow-on-the-Hill. Regent's Park lay like pastoral acres of countryside or the royal hunting ground it once was, its lake a broken piece of mirror.

At 400 closely-packed pages, *Grasshopper* occasionally tests a reader's patience, but in its old-fashioned way seems to me to have more of what Henry James called "felt life" than is to be found in the artier Julian Barnes or Don DeLillo.

At the solid age of seventy-five, Gore Vidal has written finis to his seven-volume tour of American history.[7] His effort has been—in words from this book—on behalf of "an odd sort of nation whose true history might prove to be uncommonly interesting if one were ever able to excavate it from under so many other long lost nations." The period treated is 1940-1955, with a final coda set in 2000; there is a touch of irony in the title, yet since these have been Mr. Vidal's years they are treated not without affection, to put it mildly. As in its predecessors, characters in *The Golden Age* are divided between fictional and "real" ones, the strategy being to let the former interpret and speculate about the latter. It's hard to care much about the fictional ones on their own (though there are continuities with the previous *Empire*), and Vidal's serviceable prose doesn't do anything to give them poetic or metaphoric life. But the descriptions of public figures and events are terrific: "the round-faced Hoover with his Humpty Dumpty starched collar"; "Wilkie . . . dark curly hair cut in farm-boy style, one lock carefully trained to fall over his right eyebrow." Vidal was there in imagination—and indeed sometimes in fact—at the party conventions of 1940, 1944, at the election of 1948. He must have pressed his nose more than once to the window of The Brass Rail restaurant (7th Avenue and Times Square), "a feeding ground for carnivores . . . passersby could see chefs at work, slicing joints of beef, ham, turkey." And readers of this journal will be interested to note that one of the fictional characters helped to found *The Hudson Review,* an "elegant literary quarterly" that another character finds "serious if a bit too strong on what was currently being called the New Criticism." The novel's pages are full of artistic people and places—Paul Robeson, the Chelsea Hotel, Dawn Powell, Parker Tyler, Peggy Guggenheim, and many others including a flattering cameo appearance by the author himself ("Gore, Peter noticed with some pain, was still lean while he himself had never been heavier or hungrier") who gets off some Vidal-like one-liners.

He once said in an interview that the Golden Age in American history was the postwar 1946 decade (but how does Joe McCarthy fit in?) and that we proceeded to blow this great opportunity. In the novel's final, retrospective chapter a character looks ahead to the horrors of air travel in the twenty-first century as we find ourselves "trapped in a technological Calcutta":

> Crowded air terminals whose vast, confusing distances must be negotiated on foot by the anxious traveler who moves from delay to cancellation to, at the bitter end, lost baggage after a harrowing flight in a narrow ill-maintained metal cylinder, breathing virus-laden recycled air, all the while wondering anxiously if he has boarded one of the now too frequent carriers doomed to be hurled from sky to earth as overworked pilot loses his bearings, or a structural fault, known but unattended to, causes a fiery wire in the fuselage to make exciting contact with fuel supply.

Still, the novel's final word is "hope," its perspective a disillusioned, but somehow genial, even godlike, one. I can't think of a better way to explore our American past than to hole up with Gore Vidal's seven novels, from *Burr* through *The Golden Age.* Take careful notes.

Notes

1. *The Hill Bachelors,* by William Trevor. Viking. $22.95.

2. *Licks of Love: Short Stories and a Sequel,* by John Updike. Alfred A. Knopf. $25.00.

3. *Ella in Bloom,* by Shelby Hearon. Alfred A. Knopf. $23.00. *Disobedience,* by Jane Hamilton. Doubleday $24.95. *A New World,* by Amit Chaudhuri. Alfred A. Knopf. $22.00.

4. *Love, Etc.,* by Julian Barnes. Alfred A Knopf. $23.00.

5. *The Body Artist,* by Don DeLillo. Scribner. $22.00.

6. *The Constant Gardener,* by John le Carré. Scribner. $28.00. *Grasshopper,* by Barbara Vine. Harmony Books. $25.00.

7. *The Golden Age,* by Gore Vidal. Doubleday. $27.50.

FURTHER READING

Criticism

Archer, Kirstie. "A Map of the Human Heart." *Lancet* 357, no. 9260 (24 March 2001): 1968.

> Archer offers a positive assessment of *Disobedience,* noting Hamilton's ability to "make a story with themes covered so many times before resonant and compelling."

Brownrigg, Sylvia. "The Scarlet Letters." *New York Times Book Review* (19 November 2000): section 7, p. 9.

> Brownrigg acknowledges Hamilton's "warm" and "humane" portrayal of the modern American family in *Disobedience* but criticizes the novel's "inertness" and lack of immediacy.

Cassidy, Christine. Review of *The Short History of a Prince,* by Jane Hamilton. *Lambda Book Report* 6, no. 11 (June 1998): 20-2.

> Cassidy compliments Hamilton's sensitive and realistic gay protagonist in *The Short History of a Prince,* praising the novel's emphasis on family relations and humor.

Hamilton, Jane, and Michael Schumacher. "Profile of a First Novelist: The Book of Other People." *Writer's Digest* 70, no. 10 (October 1990): 28-9.

> Hamilton discusses her process of conceptualizing and writing *The Book of Ruth.*

Johnson, Greg. "In Jane Hamilton's Novel, a Farm Family Faces Nightmarish Adversity." *Chicago Tribune* (12 June 1994): section 14, p. 5.

> Johnson evaluates the success of the characters, narration, and setting of *A Map of the World* but finds the plot mechanical and at times melodramatic.

Plunket, Robert. "Teacher in Tights." *Advocate* (26 May 1998): 83.

> Plunket compliments the "very credible and sympathetic portrait" of the gay male protagonist in *The Short History of a Prince.*

Ruckenstein, Lelia. "The Boys at the Barre." *Washington Post Book World,* 28, no. 22 (31 May 1998): 7.

> Ruckenstein contrasts the protagonist, themes, and tone of *The Short History of a Prince* with Hamilton's previous efforts, highlighting the novel's subtlety.

Shields, Carol. "Consequences of a Moment." *Washington Post Book World* 24, no. 22 (29 May 1994): 5.

Shields explores the pivotal event that drives the plot of *A Map of the World,* detailing its effects on the protagonist's relationship to her husband and the community.

Additional coverage of Hamilton's life and career is contained in the following sources published by the Gale Group: *Contemporary Authors,* **Vol. 147;** *Contemporary Authors New Revision Series,* **Vol. 85; and** *Literature Resource Center.*

Michel Houellebecq
1958-

French novelist, poet, essayist, screenwriter, and critic.

The following entry presents an overview of Houellebecq's career through 2003.

INTRODUCTION

One of France's most celebrated and notorious authors, Houellebecq attracted a firestorm of controversy for his disturbing critique of contemporary society and the future of genetic engineering in *Les Particules élémentaires* (1998; *The Elementary Particles*). In this and other novels, such as *Extension du domaine de la lutte* (1994; *Whatever*) and *Plateforme: Au milieu du monde* (2001; *Platform*), Houellebecq casts a bleak, highly cynical light upon the vacuity and alienation of Western consumer culture and sexual liberation. His sordid depictions of sex and nihilism, rendered with deadpan sociological detachment, link the deterioration of late-twentieth-century Western society to the emptiness of 1960s-era liberalism and the ideals of individualism, thus raising the ire of critics on both the left and right.

BIOGRAPHICAL INFORMATION

Houellebecq was born on February 26, 1958, on the French-controlled island of La Réunion, located east of Madagascar in the Indian Ocean. His father, a mountain guide, and mother, an anesthesiologist—who were both involved in the counter-culture movement of the 1960s—eventually relinquished their parental responsibilities and, at age six, Houellebecq was sent to the Paris suburbs to live with his paternal grandmother. Houellebecq adopted his grandmother's surname and attended a boarding school near Meaux. In 1980 he earned a degree in agricultural engineering and married his first wife, with whom he had a son. After their divorce four years later, Houellebecq received treatment for depression in a psychiatric clinic and later worked for the French National Assembly. During the 1980s, he wrote poetry and befriended Michel Bulteau, editor of *Nouvelle Revue de Paris*, which published Houellebecq's early poems. In 1991 he published his first three books—*H. P. Lovecraft: contre le monde, contre la vie*, a critical study of the acclaimed American horror writer, *Rester vivant*, a volume of essays and poems, and *La poursuite du bonheur: poemes*, a poetry collection that was awarded the Prix Tristran Tzara. In 1992 Houellebecq married Marie-Pierre Gauthier. Despite condemna-

tion of his fiction from some critical circles, which resulted in his dismissal from the editorial board of the literary journal *Perpendiculaire*, Houellebecq has received several significant literary awards, including the Prix Flore for *Extension du domaine de la lutte*, the Prix Novembre for *Les Particules élémentaires*, and the Grand Prix National des Lettres Jeunes Talents for his overall body of work. Houellebecq collaborated with Philippe Harel on the screenplay for the film adaptation of *Extension du domaine de la lutte*, which was released in 1999. Houellebecq has also adapted and recorded his poetry to the experimental electronic music of Bertrand Burgalat, with whom he produced his first album, *Présence humaine*, in 2000. Houellebecq relocated to Ireland in 1999, taking residence on an island off the coast of County Cork

MAJOR WORKS

Extension du domaine de la lutte is the first-person account of an unnamed thirty-year-old computer analyst who travels to conferences to teach the use of a statistical program developed by his company for the government. At work he encounters young, egocentric corporate aspirants, and at night, he frequents local bars and discos with a feckless colleague in the hope of finding female companionship. Neither is successful in his efforts to connect with others, and their futility reflects the deleterious effects of social fragmentation and isolation in contemporary society. In the end, the narrator's colleague dies in a tragic car accident, and the narrator himself suffers a nervous breakdown. After being confined to a mental institution, the narrator observes that the patients are not sick, but merely long for physical connection. *Les Particules élémentaires* centers upon the experiences of two half-brothers: Michel, an eminent, though emotionally stunted, molecular biologist; and Bruno, an unattractive high-school teacher whose hedonistic longings are unfulfilled. The essential emptiness of both men is traced to the failure of their free-spirited hippie mother, who selfishly abandoned them to separate grandparents as children, leaving them fatherless and without maternal nurturance. The novel, which is a largely an indictment of 1960s permissiveness and hypocrisy, is finally revealed to be a retrospective account from the year 2079. From this future vantage, it is learned that the cloning techniques pioneered by Michel have facilitated the development of genetically superior human beings who are sexless and immortal, thus eliminating two of the most troubling but distinctive features of humanity—individuality and desire. In 2000 Houellebecq published *Lanzarote: et autres textes,* a novella set on the volcanic island Lanzarote in the Canary Islands. The story is told from an anonymous first-person narrator who, after becoming bored with his life in Paris, travels to Lanzarote with plans to indulge in his basest desires. However, after becoming involved with an eccentric cast of tourists and locals, including two lesbians from Germany, the narrator is consumed with depression and ennui fueled by the island's self-obsessed, overly commercial atmosphere. Houellebecq's next novel, *Plateforme,* again brings focus to the tourism industry, centering upon Michel, a disaffected forty-year-old employee of the French Ministry of Culture who travels to Thailand to escape the trauma of his father's murder. While on a package tour, he becomes enamored with Thai prostitutes and concludes that Western sexual desire and Third World economic interests are both fulfilled in sex tourism. Michel eventually helps Valerie, a sexually adventurous travel executive, develop an ambitious business plan for a sex resort in Thailand. Their scheme, as well as the intensive research and planning behind it, reveals the crassness of Western market forces and the inevitability of globalization. In the end, Islamic fundamentalists bomb the decadent Thai resort, and Valerie dies violently in the explosion. In addition to his novels, Houellebecq has composed several volumes of poetry, including *La poursuite du bonheur: poemes,*

Le sens du combat (1996), and *Poésies* (2000). In 1998 Houellebecq published *Interventions,* an assemblage of book and film reviews, interviews, and provocative essays in which he espouses his left-conservative views on a variety of topics.

CRITICAL RECEPTION

Though *Extension du domaine de la lutte* has been well received and respected for its unrelenting bleakness, *Les Particules élémentaires* has placed Houellebecq at the center of a vitriolic French national debate that became known as "L'Affaire Houellebecq." In particular, French leftists have reacted strongly against Houellebecq's suggestion that counter-cultural liberals of the late 1960s caused a social and moral catastrophe by privileging self-gratification over the needs of family and community. Others have condemned *Les Particules élémentaires* for its alleged advocacy of eugenics, the pornographic elements of the novel, and Houellebecq's apparent sympathy—or at least ambivalence—toward Stalinism in giving the novel's antihero the last name of a former Soviet official (Djerzinski). Since the novel's first publication, Houellebecq has become a *cause célèbre* in France and *Les Particules élémentaires* has become an international best-seller, translated into more than twenty languages. In Britain and America, *Les Particules élémentaires* has been widely praised, with critics lauding Houellebecq's unsettling dissection of contemporary life and his incitement of French intellectuals. Houellebecq's acerbic writing, misanthropy, and alleged fascism have caused many to compare him to Louis-Ferdinand Céline, a notorious French writer whose seminal novels were marred by the author's anti-Semitism and Nazi sympathies. Like Céline, however, the offensiveness of Houellebecq's political incorrectness has been often outweighed by the scathing humor and incisiveness of his social critique. As a novel of ideas, *Les Particules élémentaires* has also been favorably compared to Aldous Huxley's *Brave New World,* though most reviewers have found Houellebecq's book an ambitious though lesser achievement. The publication of *Plateforme* has further enhanced Houellebecq's reputation as a social provocateur—this time for his derogatory portrayal of Islam, a religion he had denounced as barbaric in other public statements. Nevertheless, Houellebecq's cynicism and dark satire has continued to be appreciated by reviewers, though many have argued that *Plateforme* has failed to match the promise of *Les Particules élémentaires.*

PRINCIPAL WORKS

H. P. Lovecraft: contre le monde, contre la vie (criticism) 1991
La poursuite du bonheur: poemes (poetry) 1991

CRITICISM

Maria Green (review date summer 1995)

SOURCE: Green, Maria. Review of *Extension du domaine de la lutte,* by Michel Houellebecq. *World Literature Today* 69, no. 3 (summer 1995): 550.

[*In the following review, Green comments on Houellebecq's depiction of modern alienation in* Extension du domaine de la lutte.]

In his fourth novel, Michel Houellebecq deals with our modern *mal du siècle,* alienation. Can we still learn anything new on this worn-out topic, depicted, described, analyzed, turned inside out by the best artists, writers, philosophers, sociologists, and psychologists of our century? It seems that the author of **Extension du domaine de la lutte** can still display a new aspect of our modern ailment when he ushers the reader into the realm of computer science.

The narrator sets out to chart his own voyage of discovery in a novel about himself. Of course, this modern novel is a far cry from the sizzling passions of *Wuthering Heights.* The genre of the novel was not invented to display indifference, dehumanization, nihilism. The narrator sees clearly that while society is moving toward the goal of being perfectly informed, transparent, and in perfect communication, meaningful individual communication is simply obliterated in our private life.

The antihero-narrator is a well-paid engineer in a company that has just developed a new program to make statistics easy for government offices. He is sent to various provincial towns with a colleague to teach the use of the new program. In his seminars he meets young, dynamic, ambitious computer experts. He sees and describes them with deft originality in terms of snakes and bulldogs—whereas he himself feels like a trapped chimpanzee. Our modern world appears to him under the rule of Mars and Venus, based on domination, money, and fear on the masculine side and on seduction on the feminine side.

Life in the office is structured, but what are you supposed to do in your free time? Should you spend it looking out for others? Our narrator is *not* interested in others. After the botched-up seminars, he and his colleague roam and stake their sensual claim in the territory of the young, in bars and discotheques. The colleague is plagued by his calvary: the young man with a froglike face and not an ounce of charm cannot get rid of his virginity. The narrator had lost his Véronique two years earlier. Now he is unable to find a new girlfriend on his own terms. The topic of sexual misery emerges, and the narrator interpolates two miniessays. The first deals with inequality, as pitiless on the sexual as on the economic level. The second is a virulent attack on psychoanalysis, another form of alienation. He bets that if you place a decent, slightly disturbed girl in the clutches of an analyst, she will quickly be turned into an antisocial, egocentric, avaricious shrew, unable to love physically or mentally. Véronique adopted Lacan's motto: "Plus vous serez ignoble, mieux ça ira!"

This bleak novel, in which the adjectives *sinistre, morose,* and *amer* abound, ends tragically. The colleague is killed on the highway after a frustrating night at a disco, and the narrator suffers a nervous breakdown. In the mental institution he suddenly understands that none of the patients is sick, they simply crave physical contact. As nobody loves them, they turn violently against themselves. Without intimate friendships, without love, the realest reality, the very tapestry of life is unraveled.

Anita Brookner (review date 2 January 1999)

SOURCE: Brookner, Anita. "Prize-Winning Novels from France." *Spectator* 282, no. 8891 (2 January 1999): 35.

[*In the following excerpt, Brookner discusses Houellebecq's controversial portrayal of sexual excesses and cloning in* Les Particules élémentaires.]

The disgusting and depraved **Les Particules élémentaires** by Michel Houellebecq led to the author being suspended from a literary journal on grounds of offences against good taste. (The publicity did him no harm at all.) I liked this, though it is undoubtedly obscene, but, more than obscene, despairing. The sexual revolution to which the protagonist, Bruno, contributes, vigorously though unappealingly, is held responsible for the disillusionment which overtakes its adherents in middle age and beyond. The answer, says Houellebecq, or his other protagonist, Michel, is genetic modification. In future reproduction will be achieved by cloning. It was the eugenic implications of this idea which so offended the authorities, so that to have admitted this novel would be seen as an act of political incorrectness. Yet what is shocking about it is not the sexual extravagance, for which the author blames both New Age philosophies and orgiastic crypto-religious cults (not perhaps adequately documented), but the morose determinism with which he pursues both the addiction and its cure, or rather antidote. Not everyone will be able to follow this writer in his diagnosis of consumer-oriented sex, but not a few will agree with him in his stoical distaste for a phenomenon which has perhaps mutated from appetite to bulimia. His book won the Prix Novembre.

Frédérique Leichter (review date summer 1999)

SOURCE: Leichter, Frédérique. Review of *Les Particules élémentaires,* by Michel Houellebecq. *World Literature Today* 73, no. 3 (summer 1999): 492.

[*In the following review, Leichter praises Houellebecq's provocative depiction of contemporary alienation and sterility in* Les Particules élémentaires.]

Les Particules élémentaires, the second novel by Michel Houellebecq, who stepped into the limelight in 1994 with *Extension du domaine de la lutte,* was the focus of much attention within Parisian literary circles last fall. Despite attacks by the media, it must be admitted that this is an original and profoundly disturbing novel whose ambition, declared almost defiantly, is to be "the chronicle of the metaphysical mutation of our occidental civilization at the dawn of the new millennium." For the author, the feelings, thoughts, and obsessions described in the book are all symptoms of "l'air du temps." In this way, *Les Particules élémentaires* defends itself from any criticism with an unassailable strategy: any attempt to contest the relevance of Houellebecq's analyses will be interpreted in terms of psychoanalytic resistance. Critics beware!

"Ce livre est avant tout l'histoire d'un homme, qui vécut la plus grande partie de sa vie en Europe occidentale, durant la seconde moitié du XXème siècle. Généralement seul, il fut cependant, de loin en loin, en relation avec d'autres hommes. Il vécut en des temps malheureux et troublés. . . . Les sentiments d'amour, de tendresse et de fraternité humaine avaient dans une large mesure disparu." The book's sociological and prophetic

ambitions are emphasized from the very first sentence: the story of Michel, a researcher in biology, and his half-brother Bruno, a high-school literature teacher, is meant to be emblematic. The novel builds on a series of revealing episodes in the lives of the two brothers—a neglected childhood, frustrated teenage years, and a lonely coming to age—which are narrated either directly or retrospectively, through their later confessions. Born of a negligent mother whom the sexual revolution had liberated from conjugal and maternal duties, the brothers embody the unbearable "mal être" of the modern human condition. In order to escape a desperate need for love, Michel, about forty years of age, takes up with his childhood girlfriend, whereas Bruno spends his holidays in "Le Lieu du Changement," a sunny New Age camp where aging hippies gather to forget their decay. But love appears only as an ever-futile strategy: "Au milieu du suicide occidental, il est clair qu'ils n'avaient aucune chance." Sex, with its accursed frustrations and delusions, takes love's place. Ultimately, Bruno ends up in a mental institution, whereas Michel discovers a scientific alternative to free mankind from sexual reproduction.

Such is the analytic grid of our contemporaries that Houellebecq offers by dissecting modern misery with a cold, almost clinical hand. For him, the world we inherited from 1968, obsessed with sexual pleasure, is a sterile one. The psychological depth of individuals has dried up. Everyone has become a "particule élémentaire." Human interactions are no longer possible. Without common values to share, our conversations are empty. Likewise, Houellebecq's writing remains cold, as if the words were indifferent to their own meanings. Caught between satiric irony and vicious complacency, the author's ideological position might well startle the reader, for *Les Particules élémentaires* reads like the manifesto of a *provocateur.* A brilliant *provocateur,* nevertheless.

Chase Madar (review date 22 October 1999)

SOURCE: Madar, Chase. Review of *Interventions,* by Michel Houellebecq. *Times Literary Supplement,* no. 5038 (22 October 1999): 36.

[*In the following review, Madar compliments Houellebecq's tone of iconoclastic "left-conservatism" in* Interventions.]

The scandal and success of Michel Houellebecq's novel *Les Particules élémentaires* (1998) has led the editors at Flammarion to deem their author's miscellaneous journalism worth assembling under a single binding. *Interventions* is a hodgepodge of book and film reviews, feuilletonistic sketches and interviews. Some items, like **"Opera Bianca"**, a male/female dialogue for a video installation, seem present only to fill space in this slim book, but most of the enthusiasms (for modern physics, Kant and silent film) and anathemas (against hippies, the Maastricht treaty and holidays; a lead-off essay called **"Jacques Prévert est un con"**) collected here are pungent and amusing. Houellebecq often expresses thoughts which seem blasphemous from a Parisian. He has no use for the practice of *écriture,* noting casually "Je m'intéresse moins au language qu'au monde." Less iconoclastic, and less interesting, is his long essay **"Approches du Désarroi",** which is mostly about the evil genius of consumer society, much of it second-hand from Régis Debray and Jean Baudrillard. Like many Western intellectuals, Houellebecq is fixated on the mass media, and grants to communications technology, such as word processors and television sets, powers that Plotinus would have blushed to give to his One.

What sets all this apart is a left-conservatism, similar to that of the Frankfurt School and of the American scholar Christopher Lasch. Houellebecq blames, as he did hyperbolically in his best-selling novel, the problems of post-war France on the generation of 1968. After that mythical year, he writes, "la machine sociale a recommencé à tourner de manière encore plus rapide, encore plus impitoyable". The author elsewhere argues that the pursuit of personal liberation has only engendered selfishness and the destruction of the family, here posited as the last breakwater against the encroaching, devouring market. Closing the book are feuilletons on topics including life on Mars, German retirees, pornography and the uselessness of male *Homo sapiens*; these miniatures are happy marriages of *l'analyse froide* and unexpected lyricism, the same marvellous combination that worked so well in *Les Particules élémentaires.*

Gretchen Rous Besser (review date March 2000)

SOURCE: Besser, Gretchen Rous. Review of *Les Particules élémentaires,* by Michel Houellebecq. *French Review* 73, no. 4 (March 2000): 763-64.

[*In the following review, Besser lauds* Les Particules élémentaires *as a "major tour de force," akin to the works of Aldous Huxley and George Orwell.*]

What could partake more of millennial fever than the apocalyptic vision encountered in Houellebecq's compelling and unsettling *Particules élémentaires*? As in the best of suspense fiction, the key to the novel's mystery—a celebratory poem inserted at the beginning—is not revealed until the "Epilogue." Only at the end do we realize the temporal perspective from which the novel's events (beginning in July 1998, proceeding in fits and starts, with prognostications of the future and flashbacks to the past) are to be viewed—the year 2079.

Until this ultimate revelation, we assume we have been reading, in antipodal counterpoint, the life stories of the eminent physicist Michel Djerzinski and his half-brother Bruno. Diametrically different in temperament, interests, and ultimate achievement, the brothers share certain similarities of background and accident: from broken homes, solitary, unloved, and fatherless, each loses the woman of his life to suicide.

Determinism marks the future of society and individual. When in his forties, Bruno reflects: "Considérant le passé, on a toujours l'impression—probablement fallacieuse—d'un certain déterminisme" (87). Similarly, for Michel: "Les conditions initiales étant données, pensait-il, le réseau des interactions initiales étant pénétré, les événements se développent dans un espace désenchanté et vide; leur déterminisme est inéluctable" (113). In line with this deterministic outlook, each of the two protagonists is the product of biological, social, historical, and psychological forces. In ontological terms, each is a "mutant"—Michel a pure intellect, devoid of emotion; Bruno a sex-driven animal.

Houellebecq anchors his narrative in the here and now with concrete, quotidian details. Michel keeps champagne in a "Bendt" refrigerator, drives a Toyota, sleeps on a "Bultex" mattress. Bruno participates in graphically described group sex. The author intersperses his narrative with scientific explanations (analyzing sexual pleasure according to "Krause corpuscles") and with sociohistorical reflections. As frames of reference, he alludes to the work of Albert Einstein, Werner Heisenberg, Niels Bohr, Aldous and Julian Huxley, Kant and Comte. Although the book may appear to ramble, we recognize in retrospect that every aspect—its self-reflection, temporal lapses, historical sketches, overviews of sexual mores, scientific emphases, orgiastic descriptions, metaphysical queries or reflections—is essential to the "thesis" which the novel illustrates and expounds.

Instances of torture, brutality, violence, as well as sexual libertinism and family fragmentation, convey a sense of progressive decline—the necessary precondition for the utopia (a word Houellebecq carefully avoids using) which Michel's work will herald. The cult of youth, legalized contraception and abortion, divorce, emphasis on the individual and fragmentation of family, growth of materialism, replacement of traditional religion by alternate forms of spiritual seeking—the endless ripples that Houellebecq decries in the current of late twentieth-century Western evolution—are dramatized in his characters' lives.

The end provides an unexpected (but, of course, predetermined) apotheosis for humanity. The proselytizing scholar Frédéric Hubczejak, during the first decades of the twenty-first century, succeeds in having Michel's theories accepted worldwide. The scientist who first cloned cows, Michel has brought about a new species of humanity, infinitely reproducible and thus immortal. By eliminating the individual and suppressing sexual difference, humankind has at last achieved the godlike dream of world peace, eternal youth, and immortality (while the multiplication of "Krause corpuscles" offers unimaginable erotic sensations). Thus, Michel's ascetic lifework and Bruno's lifelong sensual obsession—fantasies derived from opposite ends of the human spectrum—are reconciled in the asexual, fraternal composition of a new world order.

However unpalatable and improbable Houellebecq's thesis may appear to be, however confounding his appraisal of Western "erotic/publicity-driven society" (200), his book is a major *tour de force* in the lineage of Huxley and Orwell. Structurally suspenseful, succinct in purpose, clever and biting, humorous and persuasive, *Les Particules élémentaires* tells a fascinating story, with exhortatory admixtures of science and eroticism, social commentary and metaphysical inquiry. The result is a heady and exhilarating brew, intellectually challenging, emotionally disturbing, and philosophically controversial.

James Harkin (review date 22 May 2000)

SOURCE: Harkin, James. Review of *Atomised,* by Michel Houellebecq. *New Statesman* 129, no. 4487 (22 May 2000): 57.

[*In the following review, Harkin commends Houellebecq's sense of foreboding, grand themes, and cynicism in* Atomised.]

Released to a fanfare of outraged publicity in Paris nearly two years ago, *Les Particules élémentaires* quickly became a bestseller and made a minor celebrity of its author, Michel Houellebecq. Already translated into 22 languages, it is at last available in English under the title *Atomised.*

It is not hard to see why Paris was so offended. *Atomised* is a hugely ambitious novel of ideas—or, more accurately, a novel about the lack of ideas and morale in contemporary French society. It interweaves the disparate biographies of two half-brothers as they face up to their respective mid-life crises.

Bruno is a teacher whose hopes of becoming a writer have turned sour, and whose opportunistic enthusiasm for free love is never quite matched by his success with the opposite sex. Michel, on the other hand, is an otherworldly scientist who has devoted his life to a lonely programme of research into molecular biology, but who

is now on leave and reconsidering his vocation. Both their predicaments, it is implied, can be traced in part to the influence of their hippy mother, Janine, now in a hospice, whose faddish experiments in counter-culture led her to neglect her children.

Houellebecq uses these three characters to take a pop at just about everyone: New Agers, feminists, the French literary and scientific establishments and the values of a "consumer society". The mother, in particular, functions as a cipher for Houellebecq's disgust with the pitiful trajectory taken by Sixties radicalism since its heyday in 1968. In *Atomised,* Houellebecq moves towards a much more general novelistic expression of social disintegration. In his account, economic inequalities converge with sexual and biological inequalities to create an overarching mood of gloom and fatalism.

All of this might be a bore if the book were not put together so stylishly; and it is often very funny. Despite an austere prose style and little in the way of plot development, Houellebecq sustains our interest by conveying a mounting sense of foreboding, the feeling that something of world-historical importance is about to be disclosed. The philosophical disquisitions of his characters, too, are punctuated by a mordant and irreverent humour. It is his knack of weaving grand themes into the most inauspicious material that gives Houellebecq his distinctive edge.

Atomised upset the French left because of its harsh judgement of the consequences of a "permissive society", and its apparent endorsement of eugenics and the case against abortion. While the sometimes hysterical response to his book cannot have done Houellebecq any harm, much of it seems misplaced.

Houellebecq is no reactionary, and we need not take the ideas of his characters at face value. Rather, *Atomised* showcases the kind of virulent cynicism that can have come only from the pen of a disillusioned leftist, and the novel is best understood as the detritus of the manifesto for sexual liberation presented by the *soixante-huitards* themselves.

The French newspaper *Le Figaro* astutely placed Houellebecq within a new wave of French writers identified by their *deprimisme,* or depressionism. Just as in Catherine Breillat's recent film, *Romance,* there is plenty of in-your-face sexual experimentation in *Atomised*; but, instead of liberating its subjects, it degrades them. Sex becomes a powerful metaphor for decadence and perdition, and the reader watches as Bruno loses himself in an orgy of self-abasement.

The only character who emerges with any integrity is the sexless Michel, who finds redemption in a lunatic scheme to iron out base human desires through genetic manipulation. But even this, it seems, is no more than Houellebecq's final, sick joke at the expense of his contemporaries.

Chase Madar (review date 23 June 2000)

SOURCE: Madar, Chase. Review of *Atomised,* by Michel Houellebecq. *Times Literary Supplement,* no. 5513 (23 June 2000): 33.

[*In the following review, Madar commends the disturbing realism, dark humor, and occasional tenderness of* Atomised.]

Published in France two years ago as **Les Particules élémentaires,** [*Atomised*] won the Prix Novembre, and has sold hundreds of thousands of copies throughout Europe; it has also provoked charges of nearly every prejudice imaginable and fervid denunciations from readers across several generations.

Atomised tells the story of two half-brothers, each an exemplary loser: Bruno, a high school teacher, is an undersexed hedonist, while Michel is a brilliant but emotionally desiccated biochemist. Abandoned by their hippie mother when they were small, neither has ever properly recovered; all their attempts at the pursuit of happiness, whether through marriage, the study of philosophy or the consumption of pornography, merely lead to loneliness and frustration. This despair is meant to characterize not just post-war French society, but the human race in general; at the end of the novel we learn that a breed of genetically modified humanoids, designed by Michel, has supplanted a terminally unhappy human race.

As this indicates, **Atomised** is an ambitious novel of ideas, in which the characters casually comment on the decline of religion, the rise of consumerism and, most prominently, the corrosive effects of liberal individualism. What makes this tolerable, irresistible in fact, is the author's supreme talent for illustrating his Left-conservative message with vivid scenes from a wide range of social milieus. Michel Houellebecq has clearly done a considerable amount of research in order to realize his brutally realistic settings: the sterile habitat of scientific researchers, a New Age camp site for greying soixante-huitards, a naturist beach resort, a classroom full of inattentive teenagers who are supposed to be studying Proust. And the frequent scenes of bad sex between forty-somethings make for excruciating reading. While this masochistic naturalism is often surprisingly funny, it is also periodically relieved by moments of tenderness.

Atomised (the French edition of which was reviewed in the *TLS,* January 15, 1999) is an engrossing and inventive novel, moving briskly from lyricism to cold-eyed reportage, from Buddhist prayers to theories on DNA replication. The translator Frank Wynne handles these clashing linguistic registers with grace and authority. Although he has starched out some of the original's colloquialisms, he has still managed to preserve the novel's urgent, confessional tone.

Jack I. Abecassis (essay date September 2000)

SOURCE: Abecassis, Jack I. "The Eclipse of Desire: L'Affaire Houellebecq." *MLN* 115, no. 4 (September 2000): 801-26.

[*In the following essay, Abecassis contends that the outpouring of critical controversy surrounding* Les Particules élémentaires *stemmed from Houellebecq's iconoclastic assault on Western ideological, moral, and metaphysical ideals surrounding sexuality and the rights of individual self-fulfillment.*]

> Sous l'être humain, il y a la brute
> Configurée en profondeur
> Mais au fond de sa vie sans but,
> L'homme attend le deuxième sauveur.[1]

THE AFFAIRE

Paris, October 1998. The routine of *la rentrée littéraire* breaks. Instead of the usual quarrels limited to a small circle of literati, there erupts a serious and sustained public debate in literary reviews, newspapers, radio and television. After a pause of many years, perhaps dating back to the publication of *Voyage au bout de la nuit* and *L'Etranger,* Michel Houellebecq's **Les Particules élémentaires** becomes the focal point of a national public debate.[2] On this point *Le Monde*'s Van Renterghem is categorical: "Rarement un roman aura fait couler autant d'encre, suscité tant de passions, d'emballements ou de détestations, de gonflements incontrolés en débats et en polémiques."[3] At its heart, l'*Affaire Houellebecq* has little to do with literary value per se; it concerns, rather, the desecration of the regime of desire, our last idol.

Having triumphed on the economic and political level, post-1945 liberal democracy sought to expand the range of rights (and implicit duties) consistent with its underlying logic: the exponential increase in individual autonomy in all domains, including the most private and intimate. For the first time ever, the possibilities of desire availed themselves to the citizens of democracies. With its refrain—the Rolling Stones' "I Can't Get No Satisfaction"—sexual gratification became almost a form of civic duty. In this new cultural regime, rights were no longer exclusively limited to the political and economic. Libidinal potential (love, sex, orgasms), first postulated as a possible social state by Margaret Mead, then scientifically described and explained by Master and Johnson, and finally consecrated as personal epiphany in Erica Jong's *Fear of Flying,* now donned an urgent imperative aura. This urgency simply meant that orgasms, both in quantity and variety, were to become the focal point of a cultural project. Orgasms became a *must.* Obviously, except for doing away with legal barriers (i.e. laws regarding privacy), one cannot grant desire on the formally legal and political level. That is, the law may, for example, stipulate minimum wages, but the law cannot guarantee minimum sexual satisfaction. Desire nevertheless did attain the level of an implicit promise, integral to any form of genuine self-enactment. Such was, and still is perhaps, the cultural project of the post-1945 period. Yet Houellebecq's *Les Particules élémentaires* deflates desire in all its permutations, from a cultural and political project on the grand conceptual level, to the minute details of contemporary daily life on the phenomenological level. In short, Houellebecq postulates the impossibility of desire as a generalized cultural project. This polemical *roman à thèse* describes and analyzes the implosion of the sexual babble. By now we, as Westerners, have a huge investment in our libidinal and desiring selves: we cherish this libidinal babble, as demonstrated by the vehement polemics detonated by the deflationary *Les Particules élémentaires.* Houellebecq's fictional-essayistic grinder minces through our most cherished beliefs—that happiness equals sexual and romantic satisfaction, that Being equals desiring and becoming the object of desire.[4] As a genre, the novel accomplishes its principle task of grinding down to a pulp the very grains of ideological self-understanding to which its readers cling with comic tenacity.[5]

The *Affaire Houellebecq* swept through the Parisian cultural landscape. The novel was the best seller of the *rentrée* and well beyond (250,000 copies sold by June 99 in France and translations by important publishing houses in all major languages). Not only was the novel wide-ranging in its devastating critique of cherished idols, but its ideological grounding was also disorienting. A critique from the right; a critique from the left— these are moves that cultural players understand and therefore discount accordingly. But a player who seemingly mines and undermines all premises at the same time; a player who derides the very sacred grounds upon which all other players carry out their ideological rituals—that constitutes true transgression. And all the more so in France, where the worn discourses of the classical right and left still dominate most public debate. Again, *Le Monde*'s Van Rentherghem, described best this ideological ambiguity:

> Inclassable, Houellebecq dérange, divise. Quelle est la "position" de cet écrivain venu de la gauche qui rend hommage tour à tour à Staline et à la "compassion," aux "cathos traditionalistes" et à l'eugénisme? On lui reproche d'être nihiliste, "déprimiste," "antihumaniste,"

pessimiste. A gauche, on le voit "communiste utopique" (*Les Inrockuptibles*) ou au contraire "flou," proche de la pensée d'Alain de Benoist et encensé par la "lepénisation des esprits" (*Perpendiculaire*). A droite, le livre embarrasse, comme en témoigne le feuilleton contradictoire paru en divers épisodes dans le *Figaro*: d'abord dénoncé comme "interminable porno-misère," puis réhabilité comme victime d'un terrorisme intellectuel de gauche.[6]

To understand the Houellebecq phenomenon requires thinking in fluid and unconventional categories. Inasmuch as their moves are entirely predictable, the awkward pronouncements from left and right *pro et contra* Houellebecq offer little insight. Yet at least two serious French intellectuals, Alain Finkielkraut and Philippe Sollers, recognized in *Les Particules élémentaires* a conceptual and esthetic turning point of real value.[7] Another article in *Le Monde,* this time by Frédéric Badré, singles out Houellebecq's novel as being a prime representative of a new tendency in the French novel. The common theme of all these authors (Houellebecq, Darrieussecq, Gran—and I would add Masséra) is the deflation of the *regime of desire* in a style which is "sans esthétisme, sans pudeur, sans séduction particulièrement artiste."[8] In what follows I will take my cues from Finkielkraut, Sollers and Bardé, leave aside the trivial and purely sectarian aspects of the *Affaire,* and concentrate on *Les Particules élémentaires* as a polemical *roman à thèse,* thereby fleshing out the deeper fracture lines which were at the origin of this polemic. I will proceed from history to metaphysics. That is, from the exterior contingency (the world of objects, sex and public/private selves) to the interior permanence of a given consciousness (ahistorical metaphysics and idiosyncratic religious temperament). I show why and how Houellebecq's combination of cultural critique, science fiction, moral metaphysics and narrative was so potent, to the point of detonating a major *Affaire.* Beyond that, I suggest that this novel articulates, if awkwardly, a discontinuity in contemporary French fiction. Taken in the context of authors cited above, a new pattern of fiction writing is emerging, and Houellebecq is, if not its best writer, certainly its clearest thinker and therefore its most polemical advocate.

THE CRISIS

The Houellebecqian inferno of the present is the allegorical story of Michel and Bruno, exemplars of late twentieth-century nihilism and despair played in a minor key—that of the lives of French state functionaries. But, unlike his peers (Darrieussecq, Gran, Maséra), Houellebecq does not restrict himself to a description, as devastating as it might be, of the inferno of desire. He goes much further in that he puts into motion a Kierkegaardian dialectic whose only outcome could result in the ontological erasure of *Homo sapiens* and the birth of post-human clones. Structured as a hagiography (the birth, struggle, temptation and finally conversion of a Savior) recounted by a clone-narrator living in 2079 CE, the novel acquires a quasi-religious aura. Simply put, this is a novel about the erasure of humanity as we know it and the creation of a new race of immortal and asexual clones, *Homo cybernicus*. In Houellebecq, the seventeenth-century French *Moraliste* meets the nano-cyber-molecular engineer—and the human disappears. But these hagiographic-futuristic-science-fictional elements constitute only the frame within which a concrete phenomenology of the world of French suburban functionaries weaves itself. Though formally a science fictional novel, science fiction plays a very minor role in the narrative itself. Yet the juxtaposition of the banal and the sublime (and really eminent) science fiction can be jarring and therefore effective. Indeed, this combination of phenomenology of the daily, eschatological metaphysics and science fiction is the secret to the success of the narrative.

From the first page, the sinister air of an apocalyptic crisis colors the narrative. Michel, the hero of the novel, leads a life of quiet despair. "Il vécut en des temps malheureux et troublés. . . . Les sentiments d'amour, de tendresse et de fraternité humaine avaient dans une large mesure disparu; dans leurs rapports mutuels ses contemporains faisaient le plus souvent preuve d'indifférence, voire de cruauté" (*PE* [*Les Particules élémentaires*], 9). An impending radical mutation awaits, as if living in the late 1990s the reader belongs to the end of an era, hoping for an insight into a future in which he will have no part. Indeed, from the narrator's point of view, the end of the twentieth century is already the distant past. For the novel tells quite literally the story of the erasure of those miserable and sinful *Homo sapiens*—us—and our replacement by post-human sentient beings, free of all misery, free of original sin.

To hook his readers, Houellebecq paints disturbing portraits of Michel and Bruno. They are half-brothers, both abandoned by their egotistic and hedonistic mother (a sixties "hippie" of sorts), neglected by their fathers (too absorbed in pleasure and greed); one is brought up by a kind grandmother (Michel), the other in a brutal boarding school (Bruno). For obvious psychological reasons, Michel and Bruno, abandoned sons, are destined for psychological misery. In a partially autobiographical synthesis, Houellebecq repeatedly links the affective misery of their childhood to their respective sense of permanent inadequacy (this psychological determinism is perhaps the weakest part of the novel). Moreover, the perceived duty to exercise the newly-won right of being productive in the libidinal economy could only exacerbate the brothers underlying misery. The gift of sexual liberation bequeathed to Michel and Bruno by their (absent but liberated) parents is for them particularly poisonous.

OBJECTS

The space of ***Les Particules élémentaires*** is most immediately palpable as the space of the consumer object. This shared familiarity among author-reader-critic resides in the mutual recognition of a universe of objects familiar to all. This explains in part the instant appeal of the novel. The reader takes an almost sadistic pleasure in the minute, yet detached, description of suburban daily routines. Strangely, these neuter descriptions, which avoid the common pitfall of facile lampooning, remind me of the popular Internet phenomena known as the *Jennicam,* where a permanent hidden camera records all the actions of a perfectly ordinary young woman.[9] What are these Internet surfers watching and why are they watching? The answer might be the same for some aspects of ***Les Particules élémentaires*** as for the *Jennicam.* In these banal objects and gestures, the reader of the novel as well as the Internet surfer contemplates his own universe in its objectal nudity. There, in the space between the eye and the spectacle of the absolute banal, we can locate the impulse of the initial identification and transference between the reader and the text, spectator and image. But, again, why is this so fascinating? Perhaps because the contemplation of repetition qua repetition is our latest spectacle! The object per se is the linchpin here—the one secured point of contact between the author, the reader and the text, their sole indubitably shared experience. In the case of ***Les Particules élémentaires,*** this fascination resides in the absolute symmetry between the reader and the fictional character. No longer a space of the heroic or the exploratory, the difference between the reader and the fictional character has been reduced to a contemplation of the same by the same. After all, this aesthetic seems to obey a mimetic necessity. If, in fact, we live in a space of the pure consumer object, then let objects—in their shuddering banality—be our privileged objects of identification and transference, mirrors of our refractive egos.

Put differently, Houellebecq's *objet banal* represents constricted mimetic desire. Instead of a multiplicity of sites where different mimetic possibilities may exist, resulting in many varied experiences of subjectivity, here we come to the ultimate constriction of a mimetic field embodied in global name-brand consumerism. Nike shoes are desired for the same reasons everywhere. Through marketing, global celebrities (e.g. Michael Jordan) become icons for and of collective transference and fantasy, and the objects these celebrities promote become vehicles of collective desire. Without any regard to geographical location or historical experience, all desiring consumers are operating within the same logic, within the same constricted and carefully engineered global mimetic field. It is within this universe that the most easily accessible dimension of the half-brothers' story unfolds.

Michel and Bruno spend their lives in a world where personal space organizes itself around objects bought in various discount outlets: frozen ravioli dinners, cheap wine in six-pack promotions, vacation equipment, gadgets, etc. Each object is precisely described with its price and place of purchase: "[M]ichel sortit de sa poche un appareil photo Canon Prima Mini (zoom rétractable 38-105mm, 1 290 à la FNAC)" (*PE,* 318); "Juste avant de partir [Bruno] avait acheté une tente igloo à la Samaritaine (fabriquée en Chine populaire, 2 à 3 places, 449 F)" (*PE,* 123). Then comes the sorting out of junk mail where cruise ships are described as floating utopia (*PE,* 282-83), followed by the saccharine text of the catalogue *3 Suisses.* It reads: "Optimisme, générosité, complicité, harmonie font avancer le monde. DEMAIN SERA FEMININ" (*PE,* 153).

Though impressive, these detailed descriptions of the quotidian could not in themselves explain the force of the novel. For at least the past thirty-five years descriptions of various *Systèmes des objets* (Barthes, Baudrillard, Pop Art) abound.[10] Yet Houellebecq's consumer objects figure as background components of a violent critique of what he believes to constitute our ultimate myths of liberation and individuation: the myth of love, desire, seduction, writ large, available to all. Or more precisely, the false belief that these erotic experiences can become common, a thread in the fabric of the daily, another conquered territory in the march toward freedom. To the democratic man, so goes the myth, the great orgasm can be as commonly consumed and experienced as a can of Campbell's Soup. Here the narrative moves from the derisive to the disturbing; here the reader's facile identification and transference cease and the anxiety mounts; here the complicit smile turns into a blank stare. This is in fact also where the bonfire of our last hopes—the everlasting increase in the consumption of objects in order to augment our individuality, our desire and ultimately our orgasms— burns down to their elemental particles.

What makes Houellebecq's universe more disturbing than Warhol's or Baudrillard's is above all the lack of any alibi for consumption. Once the motive of an ever-increasing individuation through desire is absent or becomes debunked, all alibis for frenetic individuation disappear. Desire no longer justifies. That is precisely the origin of Houellebecq's disturbing effect on his readers and critics. Having this very alibi pulled from under our feet, we become unhinged. Take Michel, for instance. Floating in his life capsule, consumer objects do not justify themselves in any regime of sense. No longer a means to attain an end (as instruments in the maximization of freedom, individuation, and pleasure) these objects obey their own nihilistic logic, namely, being what they are for no other purpose except that of their consumption and disposal. These floating objects are not inscribed in Michel's life in any narrative which

transcends their pure banality. Michel lives alone, experiences no erotic desire, exists purely as a thinking and consuming monad. His only social interactions are with his brother, occasionally, and with the local Monoprix checkout clerks. When he is alone, he drinks himself into oblivion. An internationally recognized molecular biologist, this forty-year-old lives only in his work, forsaking all forms of community, save for strictly cordial relations with his laboratory colleagues, his caged white canary who greets him every night and for daily forays into scientific Internet sites. Michel embodies in fact the archetypal hero described in Houellebecq's first published essay: "Les héros [of a certain fantastic genre] se dépouillent de toute vie, renoncent à toute joie humaine, deviennent purs intellects, purs esprits tendus vers un seul but: la recherche de la connaissance."[11]

The clone who narrates this hagiography is categorical about Michel's sexuality: in the libidinal economy, he is unemployed—worse, he is homeless and so chronically depressed that, save for a passing fantasy, he has lost all desire. In Houellebecqian terms Michel forms part of the permanent sexual underclass: "sa bite lui servait à pisser, et c'est tout" (*PE,* 28). With Michel we know that we are definitively at the end of an era. *Don Quixote* and to a lesser extent *Madame Bovary* lived in a fictional world where every sign and object was highly invested with individuating potential. Functioning as the dynamos of the narrative, asymmetries abound between perception, imagination and desire. But in *Les Particules élémentaires,* we have the story of the Last Man who desires nothing except his own ontological erasure. Michel's life before his conversion experience is perhaps a representation of that zero through which being must pass to mutate itself; Michel's life embodies that almost completely neutral zero value through which one must pass from the negative to the positive.[12] With Michel as an allegory, a regime of sense and desire ends, and there emerges the possibility of a new posthuman regime.

Sex

If Michel gives up on individuation through desire and satisfaction, his brother Bruno seems to have invested himself completely in individuation through sex. Thus, Houellebecq plays Michel off Bruno, opposing the monk to the satyr, which allows him a great deal of tonal staccato in the narrative. But this latter-day satyr is anything but an alpha male, a Don Juan, a satisfied lover. Though a satyr in his behavior and fantasies, Bruno is driven by this quest for satisfaction to clinical insanity. Abandoned by his mother, frozen in his relations to his father, sexually abused in the most vicious manner by roommates in his high school dormitories, obsessed by the modest size of his penis, Bruno is also a loser in the libidinal economy. His destiny is masturbation; his fantasies are masochistic; his hopes for true satisfaction nil. Houellebecq describes this high school teacher masturbating throughout his life, in all places, always with the secret hope of being discovered and humiliated. The fantasy of shame and abasement plays itself out endlessly. In one of the more comic and disturbing chapters in the novel, Bruno takes a two-week vacation at a New Age camping site. There he spends his time at various workshops such as "*sensitive gestalmassage,* libération de la voix et rebirth en eau chaude, etc." (*PE,* 141, italics in original), but he is really most interested in peeping at showering thirteen-year-old girls.

> De retour à sa tente il se servit un whisky et se branla doucement en feuilletant Swing Magazine, "le droit au plaisir"; . . . Il n'envisageait pas réellement de répondre à ces différentes annonces; il ne se sentait pas à la hauteur d'un *gang bang* ou une douche de sperme. . . . Pour réellement parvenir à s'infiltrer dans le réseau porno, il avait une trop petite queue.
>
> (*PE,* 126)

Unlike his liberated mother and father, Bruno experiences the rituals of sexual liberation not as a participant, but as a voyeur hoping to be humiliated and punished. To the chagrin of some of his readers and critics, Houellebecq paints a graphic and repetitive picture of Bruno's obsessive masturbation at every stage in his life and in a variety of public places. The biographical and psychological etiology of Bruno's psychopathology are of little importance in the context of this analysis. What is important, however, is the opportunity that this theme offers Houellebecq to undermine the modern dream of integrating sexuality into the regime of liberty. For Houellebecq, sexuality remains resistant to the logic of marketing redistribution (i.e. democratization), operating within the logic of a liberalized libidinal economy. In sum, economic and political freedom cannot be extended to sexuality.

Such was indeed the principle theme of *L'Extension du domaine de la lutte,* Houellebecq's earlier novel which was turned into a movie in 1999.[13] A parody of 1980s French corporate culture recounting the utter social and sexual misery of a software engineer, this modest work has already attained in France the rank of a cult novel—"*L'Etranger* for the information generation" hails the cover of the English translation of the novel. Houellebecq's main thesis in this novel is the disturbing analogy between classical liberal economics and contemporary sexuality:

> Tout comme le libéralisme économique . . . le libéralisme sexuel produit des effets de paupérisation absolue. Certains font l'amour tous les jours; d'autre cinq ou six fois dans leur vie, ou jamais. Certains font l'amour avec des dizaines de femmes; d'autres avec aucune. C'est ce qu'on appelle la "loi du marché." Dans un

> système économique où le licenciement est prohibé, chacun réussit plus ou moins à trouver sa place. Dans un système sexuel où l'adultère est prohibé, chacun réussit plus ou moins à trouver son compagnon de lit. En système économique parfaitement libéral, certains accumulent des fortunes considérables; d'autres croupissent dans le chômage et la misère. En système sexuel parfaitement libéral, certains ont une vie érotique variée et excitante; d'autres sont réduits à la masturbation et la solitude.[14]

In short, the extension of liberty to sexuality is poisonous, for the more you extend liberty, the more you risk and eventually lose. At a certain point you must limit its extension. Within the idiosyncratic brew of Colbertiste, Gallic and Marxist understanding of (Anglo-Saxon) economic and social liberalism, liberty must necessarily lead to fundamentally agonistic modes of interaction; it creates few winners and many losers. This first novel then contains the Houellebecqian sociohistorical argument in its embryonic state: (1) liberty equals increased competition, (2) when extended to sexuality, competition equals increasing violence, (3) violence equals accelerated differentiation among winners and losers—to the detriment of the great majority. In economics as in sex, free competition ("libéralisme") must thus necessarily bring about the pauperization and alienation of the majority. Consequently, "libéralisme sexuel" returns the late twentieth century to the baboon state: it is the winner-take-all world of the alpha male, which in Houellebecq's world is the Dionysian male rock and roll star. Furthermore, the underlying question implicitly reiterated in virtually every page of *L'Extension du domaine de la lutte* is this: is there any limit to the diminished returns (to the sexual majority) in the extension of liberty? In the apparent absence of such a limitation, all we can look forward to is the acceleration of *agon,* accomplished by the fleshing out of areas at present free of market competition (family, religion, leisure, etc.). According to Houellebecq, this infinite extension of economic logic to the private domain, heretofore immune from it, has already brought about the erasure of all zones of private activities free from the violence of economic and consumer logic. There can no longer be two parallel arenas of individuation, the one economic and public, the other, affective and private. "Libéralisme," therefore, brings back to human life the all-pervasive agonistic modality of the natural state, of ambient violence; it is in harmony with nature qua aggression (that is, individuation through aggression), whence, perhaps, its power and appeal. Violent and evolutionarily rational, the end of history would resemble, then, its violent beginning. Beginnings and endings telescope into each other in the figure of the hierarchical baboon (cave man to Mick Jagger—and back). The circle is fully drawn; an impasse dawns. To advance, only a radical rupture will suffice.

This argument can seem all too familiar, having currency within the discourses of both progressive and conservative points of view in that both certain conservatives and liberals suggest that libidinal global capitalism (from Benetton to hard-core pornography) represents moral threats of various kinds. Yet Houellebecq's narrative explores these ideas in a more metaphysical and provocative mode, thereby going well beyond standard historical and sociological arguments. As we shall now see, the narrative collapses the distinction between private and public selves; it establishes a necessary link between sexual liberation and violence; it locates the root of the problem in human nature.

THE SINGLE DOMAIN

Repeatedly Houellebecq makes the claim that the distinction between public and private selves no longer holds, and that in this new *érotico-publicitaire* economy, where the desire of every agent is engineered by Eros-driven marketing, private and public selves could hardly constitute distinct universes with distinguishable logics. On the one hand, market economics, ruled by supply/demand equations, "attractiveness, novelty and price/quality ratios" form the dominant logic underlying virtually all public and economic transactions.[15] On the other, an affective system, independent of the public and economic market, as it were, operating according to private and intimate individual taste, idiosyncratic and hence apparently free of determinism, constitutes the private and erotic self. These two fields of action, however, are not insulated compartments. If purely objective criteria, operating within a competitive environment, form the economic sphere, then these same criteria and this same environment also sooner or later percolates down to the personal. This is the case since every detail of the private and personal occupies a place within an erotico-consumer sphere: shape of the body, smell of the body; each detail is labeled and thus the whole fabric of the personal becomes integrated into the generalized economy driven by erotic marketing. Collapsing in this manner the productive self and the romantic self into a single category, Houellebecq telescopes all activities into a single field of action, all obeying more or less the same rules.

> Actuellement, nous nous déplaçons dans un système à deux dimensions: l'attractivité érotique et l'argent. Le reste, le bonheur et le malheur des gens, en découle. . . . nous vivons dans une société simple, dont ces quelques phrases suffisent à donner une description complète.[16]

The individual self, which in modernity has always been distinct from the collective, becomes here generic and serial, oscillating exclusively between eroticism and money. No longer in opposition to the world, it is continuous with it since the dialectic between the interior and the exterior, between the individual and the collective, slowly disappears. As if dialed into the ruthless digital economy, to the *érotico-publicitaire* machine

which devours him, the self has once and for all lost the tension between being and appearance. The fate of the subject in the *érotico-publicitaire* society is to identify with the ideal that devours him. Once capitalism and globalization have done away with religion, family and nation, there no longer remains a space where counter-practices could successfully survive. The only grounding for Being and being, to use the Heideggerian distinction here, is the market—the capital market as well as the flesh market.

This telescoping of the private and public places **Les Particules élémentaires** outside the logic of the romanesque comedy of the authentic and the inauthentic, still the dynamo of most romanesque production up to the romantic and existential novels. To understand this environment, which Houellebecq aptly names the post-1968 *érotico-publicitaire,* is to recognize underneath its sleek appearance the thinly disguised baboon-like hierarchies and symbolic violence. Beneath the cool and democratic surface there awaits for all desiring subjects a cruel battlefield where, by definition, the vast majority is reduced either to the role of spectators (celebrity cult) and/or to the role of permanent paupers. It is a winner-take-all world, inhabited by a few alpha winners and a multitude of omega losers. Indeed, Michel and Bruno, the two paupers in the libidinal economy, two omega losers in the world of desire and satisfaction, clearly recognize their omega status. But their recognition takes different forms. While Michel completely withdraws from the libidinal, Bruno glues himself to the libidinal, only to reconfirm repeatedly its refractive and ultimately resistant nature.

If the libidinal has proven to be so resistant to conquest and long-lasting possession, it is because in it—in the erotic and the sexual—the Western will has found its most unnerving opponent. Put simply, the classical metaphysics of the scientific and democratic project revolve around a set of assumptions about the relationship between knowledge and action. To know is to take hold of something, and once a known thing is held, it yields to the will of the thinking subject.[17] Thomas Mann's rationalist, Settembrini, formulated this perfectly: "Human reason needs only to *will* more strongly than fate, and it *is* fate" (italics in the original).[18] Knowing, handling, controlling, explaining, predicting: all these concepts have been extremely productive in the conquest of nature, except for sexuality. The idea that once the scientist lifts the veil of ignorance from the face of Eros, its secrets will reveal themselves, and, therefore, erotic experience could become common currency—this was indeed the modern delusion concerning sexuality.[19] Armed with method and knowledge (i.e, psychoanalysis, the Masters and Johnson report), the individual would free himself from prior constraint, would no longer be "superstitious," "neurotic." Beyond the horizon of knowledge lay the promised land of orgasmic bliss. Here, we come to the heart of Houelle-becq's critique of the "mechanical" understanding of liberty, especially where liberty's dominion extends to sexuality, where desire becomes another step in the (almost finalized) march toward complete autonomy.

> La croyance, fondement naturel de la démocratie, d'une détermination libre et raisonnée des actions humaines, et en particulier d'une détermination libre et raisonnée des choix politiques individuels, était probablement le résultat *d'une confusion entre liberté et imprévisibilité.* Les turbulences d'un flot liquide au voisinage d'une pile de pont sont structurellement imprévisibles; nul n'aurait songé pour autant à les qualifier de libres.
>
> (*PE,* 280, my emphasis)

Considering the problem of sexuality, the democratic-scientific fallacy consisted in making a categorical mistake, based on false analogy: "Dernier mythe de l'occident, le sexe était une chose à faire; une chose possible, une chose à faire" (*PE,* 164), which would have been analogous to "la géometrie était une chose à faire," or "le système monétaire sera une chose à faire." Whereas a democratic conception of liberty in almost all other domains would be compatible with the "knowing-seizing-controlling" model of knowledge, with sexuality, Houellebecq argues that the idea of complete freedom based on knowledge and dominion is illusory. The implicit analogies between the knowledge of natural phenomena and the knowledge of sexuality were a categorical delusion to which, curiously enough, our contemporaries still cling with great, and perhaps comic, tenacity.[20] Even if one knows everything about sexuality, this knowledge does not translate into mastery. Sexuality can never be mastered. Its boundaries may be mapped, its possibilities enumerated, its field, as it were, outlined, but never shall it escape the gravitational pull of human constraints—hierarchies, domination, submission, violent differentiation, symbolic negotiations.

Houellebecq's example of the movement of water molecules at a given time-space instance is indeed il-luminating, for it points toward a different conception of liberty. Within a well-defined set of possibilities, certain movements may occur; they are neither strictly predictable, nor are they free from constraint. They are neither self-determining, nor self-enacting, nor autono-mous. But also, and most importantly, they are also not strictly determined. The molecules are "free" to move about randomly within a certain time-space configura-tion, but they cannot take off to the moon. Similarly, sexuality and eroticism inhabit a field whose boundaries are marked by hierarchies, domination, submission, violent differentiation, symbolic negotiations. And within this field there is much room for variety. Yet its boundaries form a constraint that the thinking will can-not overcome. It is not simply the ideational overcom-ing of the *Fear of Flying* which will liberate you from

the gravity of the sexual (inhibitions and taboos motivated by evolution), in the way that science defeats gravity. There is something *intransitive* in the relation between mechanical and quantum logics, and the result-ing confusion is a categorical mistake of dire conse-quences. In other words, sex is and is not at the same time a function of the will (an aspect of nurturing); it is knowable and mysterious, simultaneously. This is how and why sexuality became entangled with the "mechani-cal" metaphysics of the democratic will.

The crisis of desire points us toward the limit of the will. The democratic right cannot be extended to the realm of desire. Economic and political drives are amenable to legal and social mechanisms that can keep them in check. Yet this liberal logic is not transferable to sexuality. Once sex becomes "'accessible and right," pursued for its own ends without any legal or medical danger, the violent dialectic that it unleashes is not eas-ily amenable to constraints. Whereas liberalism was and is successful in creating wealth exponentially over a long period of time, the sexual revolution did not create an exponential increase in orgasms. In fact, it only exacerbated the underlying misery which sexuality represents for most people. This is why Houellebecq contends that the tragic onset of AIDS can be viewed as a relief, at least to the heterosexual and homosexual paupers, since the fear of AIDS gave one the perfect rational alibi to exit the unbearable regime of desire. Circa 1985, not being a libidinal success all of a sudden loses its stigma and becomes a tacit, but real, norm.[21]

THE GROSS MISCALCULATION OF THE BRAVE NEW WORLD

If indeed the late nineties represents a period of a grand ideological malaise, it is because the successive sexual liberations of the post WWII period have exacted a frightful price. Certainly, there is today much more formal liberty in virtually all domains, but Houellebecq insists that these liberties just bring into relief our generalized anxiety and feeling of inadequacy, at least for the omega majority. After all, liberal freedom means the freedom to fail, including failing at sex—an altogether unacceptable proposition for Houellebecq. This prognosis lies at the heart of Houellebecq's systematic derision of the sexual liberation of the last three decades. We surely possess at present more sexual freedom than ever before, but, paradoxically, we also endure proportionally more sexual misery than ever. Misery is a function of freedom (to fail), a function of the very thought that happiness is at hand, yet never quite realized. Michel and Bruno, as well as most characters in the novel, are formally free to participate in the great orgy, except that they are all too neurotic, too small, too poor or too old to ever be invited. Their liberation exists mostly in the domain of the formally possible and permissible, not in the domain of practice.

In fact, the alpha's apparent liberation only serves to highlight the omega's hopelessness. Confronted by the possibility of fulfillment, the "inadequate" suffer from the absence of sustained libidinal fulfillment (the *érotico-publicitaire* ideal). For most, then, sexual liberation does not lead to satisfaction, but rather to a more acute consciousness of inadequacy. "Notre malheur n'atteint son plus haut point que lorsque a été envisagé, suffisamment proche, la possibilité pratique du bonheur" (*PE,* 306). This is a feature of most liberations: scientific atheism led to an acute awareness of the obscurity and the absence of god (Pascal, Sade) rather than to a metaphysical reconciliation with the world. In other words, "liberations" rarely create a positive space. Instead, rather than having been exorcised once and for all, the archaic demons lurk in the background, repressed and latent, only to resurface sporadically as symptoms. The resurfacing of repressed material is a form of hysteria which germinates at the revolution's heart.

And this repressed material is the potential violence that is latent in sexuality, and especially in a sexual liberation. This is precisely what a sexual liberation prophet like Aldous Huxley did not recognize in the dialectic of emancipation. Naïve and optimistic, Huxley grossly miscalculated the dialectic between sex, individuation and narcissism. In an intense conversation with Bruno about Huxley, Michel asserts the following:

> L'erreur d'Huxley est d'avoir mal évalué le rapport de forces entre ces deux conséquences. Spécifiquement, son erreur est d'avoir sous-estimé l'augmentation de l'individualisme produite par une conscience accrue de la mort. De l'individualisme naissent la liberté, la sensation du moi, le besoin de se distinguer et d'être supérieur aux autres. . . . Huxley oublie de tenir compte de l'individualisme. Il n'a pas su comprendre que le sexe, une fois dissocié de la procréation, subsiste moins comme principe de plaisir que comme principe de différenciation narcissique; il en est de même du désir de richesse.
>
> (*PE,* 199-200)

Huxley's naiveté consists in believing that liberation depends on clearing out, by some smart social engineering, obstacles such as family neurosis and religious taboos. Once identified, these purely constructed and contingent obstacles become known, and therefore subject to modification or erasure, clearing the way to emancipation and happiness. For Houellebecq, on the other hand, the world of sexuality, taboos and transgression belongs to a given and almost immutable human nature which resists the "knowing-seizing-controlling" model of knowledge and action. You cannot know and modify sexuality in the way that you know and modify other natural phenomena.

But there is much more here. When sexuality is at stake, the combination of knowledge and its individuating potential, otherwise known as liberty, often degenerates into pure violence. Houellebecq here is obviously a keen reader of Sade. He understands that individualism, fueled by the consciousness of death, gives birth to erotic liberty, the space of narcissistic monstrosity. That is, erotic liberty leads to an exponential increase in the opportunity to individuate along narcissistic lines with violence always lurking at the end of the road. "[Huxley] n'a pas su comprendre que le sexe, une fois dissocié de la procréation, subsiste moins comme principe de plaisir que comme principe de différentiation narcissique; il en est de même du désir de richesse" (*PE,* 200). The insurmountable obstacle of any Utopia is the Ego, the Will to Power, fallen appetites. At the heart of desire, the Augustinian would say, is always the will to dominate and eventually harm, the *libido dominandi*; even for the young infant, let alone for the mature adult.[22] Since what is ultimately sought in pure desire is not pleasure but narcissistic domination, naked aggression emerges as taboos fall away and transgression becomes the norm.

> Un basculement subtil et définitif s'était produit dans la société occidentale en 1974-1975, se dit Bruno. . . . Ces années . . . les sociétés occidentales basculaient vers quelque chose de sombre. En cet été 1976, il était déjà évident que tout cela allait très mal finir. *La violence physique, manifestation la plus parfaite de l'individuation,* allait réapparaître en Occident à la suite du désir.
>
> (*PE,* 192, my emphasis)

The culture of desire becomes violent as the Summer of Love degenerates into a Sadean orgy; the wisp of love vanishing in the crack of the whip. As the threshold for pleasure elevates and the thirst for power though pleasure, and pleasure through power, deepens, Eros cedes to Thanatos—such is the ruthless logic of hyperindividuation. It was true for Sade; it is true for Houellebecq. Such is also the reiterated lesson we are to take away from one of the major subplots of the novel concerning the allegorical biography of the di Meola family.

Francisco di Meola is a leader of the flower children in California; late in life he decides to die in France. A beautiful physical specimen, this son of an Italian immigrant becomes a guru to the Beat generation, the Hippies and then the so-called New Age. His singular claim to fame is a short meeting with the dying Aldous Huxley. Di Meola seduces Catherine (a plastic surgeon), who also happens to be Michel and Bruno's mother. She promptly divorces, abandons her sons and moves into De Meola's Big Sur compound. To be sure, Di Meola comes off as charming enough. He is a handsome charlatan, mostly limiting himself to endless drug use, the seduction of East Coast teenage puritans in search of "IT." His son, David di Meola, is also physically perfect, rich and virile. Like his father, David seduces women in droves, including Anabelle, who is

Michel's high school sweetheart, a virgin up to that point and Michel's first, last and only amorous interest. David's desires soon expand beyond conventional sexual gratification. He moves to Southern California and becomes involved in heavy sadomasochism, thinly veiled as "satanic" ritual. Things degenerate quickly. Soon sadomasochism transgresses fantasy play, and David di Meola finally realizes his celluloid dream; only it is not as a Hollywood actor-rock-star, but as the sadistic protagonist of snuff movies. By the time the state of California indicts him for multiple murders and torture, he has produced and acted in a number of these films in which multiple victims bleed to death on camera. David has made sure his face figures prominently at the worst moments of the video. At last, he too is a star, of sorts.

As the Di Meolas's story illustrates, liberation of the libido devours its own protagonists, even in the case of the most dominant and violent of the alpha males. Accelerated differentiation within the parameters of desire's truth brings about a pagan holocaust of being. Again, this was all in Sade, but Houellebecq succeeds in an historical reiteration of the Sadean algorithm. The Sadean "truth of desire" weaves itself now within the sinuous discourse of the liberal and democratic *érotico-publicitaire,* rather than within the deconstruction of the discourse of Enlightenment.[23] The net results, however, remain the same.

If the di Meola subplot brings into relief the "hard" version of post-1945 libido, its "softer" version, experienced by the average reader and critic, might perhaps be more disturbing. "Le désir sexuel se porte essentiellement sur les corps jeunes, et l'investissement progressif du champ de la séduction par les très jeunes filles ne fut au fond qu'un retour à la normale, un retour à la vérité du désir analogue à ce retour à la vérité des prix qui suit une surchauffe boursière anormale" (*PE,* 133). If you create a cult of the body, of its strength, beauty, suppleness; if the body constitutes your ultimate measure, time condemns you to self-loathing. "Dans un monde qui ne respecte que la jeunesse, les êtres sont peu à peu dévorés" (*PE,* 139). Devoured are the beings who worship the body, for the flesh ages, regardless of the efforts of plastic surgeons (Michel's parents). To accentuate the scorn visited upon older women, Houellebecq draws minute physiological descriptions of the subdermal tissue degradation of the vagina and the breasts. The pedophilic Bruno genuinely wants to love Christianne; but at the view of her aging vagina, his contempt and loathing are unmistakable. Satiated after a number of encounters in the same evening, Christianne tells Bruno: "J'ai bien vu tout à l'heure que tu n'étais pas vraiment attiré par ma chatte; c'est déjà un peu la chatte d'une vieille femme" (*PE,* 199). Christianne, this forty-five-year-old teacher, can never measure up to the adolescents Bruno has been ogling in the public showers. Taken to its ultimate aesthetic and logical consequence, desire reverts naturally to pedophilia, witness the Calvin Klein advertising campaigns. To the middle-aged single woman only a destiny of masturbation and loneliness and self-loathing remains. Christianne says, "A partir d'un certain age, une femme a toujours la possibilité de se frotter contre des bites; mais elle n'a plus jamais la possibilité d'être aimée. Les hommes sont ainsi, voilà tout" (*PE,* 176). Time necessarily marches on, and all that ages becomes its victim. Such is the fate of the cult of youth. Moreover, even winners in the youth culture, like Michel's first love Anabelle, are shortly condemned to the same miserable fate, not of death which is inscribed in our nature, but of increasing despair over sexual invisibility. And for us, late twentieth-century consumers, sexual and ontological invisibility are one, for to be is to be seen and desired. The cult of youth is a pitiless *cul de sac*: you lose, you lose; you win, you eventually lose. Such is the truth of the body through time, if its sole value resides in youth and beauty. In the final analysis, the will cannot defeat time.

What is common to both the hard and soft versions of Desire is their affinity to natural categories. Aggression in the hard version finds its home in the pure instinct of the animal, in the logic of primate survival through domination or submission. Youth and beauty, in the softer version, are natural traits, markers for reproductive fitness. Houellebecq exhibits a double, ambivalent attitude toward the natural: he describes it perfectly well in the manner of hard-core materialist anthropology and, at the same time, he openly disdains nature in the manner of classical Christian anthropology.

But let us return to the fate of desire. What a perplexing and disturbing turn of phrase—"La vérité du désir"! Houellebecq's analogy with the stock market overheating and then returning to a "truer" valuation may prove effective. The "overheating" is the rhetorical promise of a Huxley or a Mead, that once liberated, the knowledge and exercise of pure desire would cure generalized neurosis! (Notice that Freud never shared such optimism.[24]) At this point in the cycle, investors heavily discount the promised returns on "happiness and health"; it is the cycle's "bloom on the flower" moment. But once the rhetorical bubble deflates and the promised happiness and health do not materialize, desire's true value reveals itself. *Left freely to its own dynamic, pure desire concentrates on adolescents and is exercised by the powerful in an increasingly savage manner.* Such is the slide from Saul to David; from Augustus to Tiberius to Caligula; such is the slide from Rousseau's "sentiment" and soft masochism to Sade's derision and inversion of it.[25] Should some doubts linger about this "truth of desire," a quick study of current exotic sexual tourism, for example, would cure all illusions and willful delusions. The only difference from ancient times (i.e. Tiberius in Capri) is that, like most other activities, sexual tourism has become democratic, accessible to all Western tourists in poor countries.

Faced with this truth of desire, we cannot but confront, once and for all, the most disturbing of Houellebecq's deconstructions. That we live in a world of object—that we can somehow accept and neutralize in our minds; that all mimetic desire is constrained within the parameters of "le système des objets"—*idem*; but that the entire regime of desire be emptied of its salvatory teleology—the last hope for individual secular salvation!—that is simply unacceptable sacrilege. Considering our massive investment in the Romance, not merely the Romance as a literary construct, but as a serious theology of the daily, as the supposed fabric of life, it is easy to understand the resistance to *Les Particules élémentaires*.[26] All our modern narratives bespeak of this desire of desire. Houellebecq does to post-industrial urban desire what Flaubert did to the desire of the wide-eyed bored country housewife. And its deflation is precisely the scandal. If desire no longer justifies being, then the last transcendental grounding of the modern individual has been pulled out from under his feet. Within the logic of the regime of desire, the alibi for action is univocal: I undertake such and such action because I want to be happy, that is, to be desired and desiring. The deflationary power of the novel consists precisely in undermining this often unquestioned grounding for action.

METAPHYSICS

This undermining of the ideology of desire in Houellebecq takes a decisive metaphysical turn. His arguments reach well beyond the standard parameters of cultural criticism. I suppose that this also explains the appeal of Houellebecq for the French reading public and the reason why his particular form of criticism became such a subject of public debate. In reading Houellebecq, you know that you are, at heart, in the presence of a *Moraliste* of the French Augustinian variety (Arnault, Pascal, La Rochefoucauld). His is the infernal lucidity of a thinker who has thought through his subject, and who cannot shake off his insights, for better or worse. A close reading of Houellebecq's first book on H. P. Lovecraft, the early twentieth century American mystery/horror writer, [*H. P. Lovecraft: contre le monde, contre la vie*] places the polemics and the tone of *Les Particules élémentaires* in their proper universe of metaphysical affinities. This critical essay reveals Houellebecq's modality of radical negation, if not outright contempt and hatred for the world. These "phobies Lovecraftiennes," phobias of everything but his most intimate family space, constitute indeed the background radiation, as it were, to the Houellebecqian world view:

> Aujourd'hui plus que jamais, nous pouvons faire notre cette déclaration de principe qui ouvre *Arthur Jermyn*:

> "La vie est une chose hideuse; et à l'arrière-plan, derrière ce que nous en savons, apparaissent les lueurs d'une vérité démoniaque qui nous la rendent mille fois plus hideuse.

> (*Lovecraft* [*H. P. Lovecraft: contre le monde, contre la vie*], 16)

Thus aggressively and openly Houellebecq appropriates Lovecraft's principle: life is hateful, and at the edge of what we perceive there lies the dark and hollow vortex of evil, the progressive consciousness of which renders life exponentially more hideous. Uncovering and representing this "vérité démoniaque" which lies on the surface of the banal, quotidian, here and now—such is also the ambition of *Les Particules élémentaires*. Beneath the appearance of normalcy lies a horror story; not the bone-chilling tale of the fantastic genre in Lovecraft, but, instead, the horror and absolute anguish of the here and now.

In fact, all the leitmotifs which are evident in Houellebecq's subsequent novels, interviews and poetry (the misery and comedy of sex, the evilness of existence per se, a generalized eschatology, the apocalyptic desire to destroy in order to purify), already exist in his first published critical essay on Lovecraft (1991). Houellebecq's essay is clear about the extent to which this tragic negation authorizes the narrative, grounds virtually all the arguments, generates the very mood of his subsequent novels, poetry and essays. "Une âme lasse de la vie"—this is the subjective, temperamental point of departure; perhaps independent of any particular historical circumstance.[27]

In his more recent collection of essays and interviews, Houellebecq echoes his tragic view of life:

> Avant tout, je crois, l'intuition que l'univers est basé sur la séparation, la souffrance et le mal; la décision de décrire cet état de choses, et peut-être de le dépasser. . . . L'acte initial c'est le refus radical du monde tel quel; c'est aussi l'adhésion aux notions du bien et du mal.[28]

Notice that no historical argument makes sense of this statement. Nor is it explicable in psychological terms. "La séparation, la souffrance et le mal" here do not correspond in tone to the infantile drama of being separated from the mother, forced to individuate by an authoritarian father (Proust). It is, rather—to use the standard existentialist vocabulary—a statement about the relationship between being and existence; the experience of being thrown into the world and despising it. A negation across the board of all aspects of the human mess—such is the primary postulate generating the whole logic and narrative of the novel. To negate experience per se is to become "phobic" about it, precisely the vocabulary Houellebecq employs when describing Lovecraft's misanthropic phobias. The phobic vomits the world. Not *a* world, but *the* world.

Furthermore, Houellebecq's affinities with Lovecraft go even deeper than the generic penchant toward the negation of phenomena by pure thought. They share, in fact, the same modality of negation, the identical thematic *transposition,* as it were. Without ever naming itself, their *contemptus mundi* coupled with apocalyptic teleologies flow from a common Christian source. In a flash of introspective insight, Houellebecq comments on one of Lovecraft's apocalyptic passages: "Ce texte n'est rien d'autre qu'une effrayante paraphrase de saint Paul" (*Lovecraft,* 122). Why not assert the same transposition about Houellebecq?

I would contend that, with their latent Pauline themes, the writings of Houellebecq constitute an extended commentary on Pascal's assertion "Que le Moi est haïssable." What we have here, then, is a very sophisticated grafting of the Pauline and Pascalian anthropology onto the social and cultural fabric of late twentieth-century France. This must surely be one reason why Houellebecq resonates so strongly with many readers, even if they cannot consciously articulate the connection between his latent metaphysics, Christian thematics and the reader's partial affinity to this type of Augustinian *contemptus mundi.* The *Moralistes* constitute, after all, one of the most important pillars of the French intellectual and literary tradition.

Put simply, there are but two alternatives. Either you bear your sinfulness and live in full consciousness of it by assuming the full consequences of "la séparation, la souffrance et le mal" (Pascalian option) or you negate it by pure volition (Sadian option). Abstain or destroy (and be destroyed, enslave and be enslaved). Houellebecq's logic, in the final analysis, resembles the broken dialectic of the Either/Or variety.[29]

If this Either/Or is true, then we are condemned to choose between two bleak options: repression (the Pauline regime) or self-destruction (the Sadean regime) and *nothing in between.* To the extent that Michel abstains from sex and triumphs as a scientist while Bruno destroys and self-destructs in the vortex of late twentieth-century desire, the two main protagonists in *Les Particules élémentaires* embody and then play out these options. I suppose that at some level Houellebecq recognizes that this Kierkegaardian dialectic is simply unsustainable, if for no other reason than that without faith (which Houellebecq lacks) this dialectic becomes truly broken, infernal. In other words, we face here a hard impasse, rendered all the more difficult by Houellebecq's denial both of a possibility of recovering an "unbroken" past and his denial of the possibility of constructing an ameliorated future. Regressive nostalgia or progressive utopias no longer exist as viable options. These discourses and metaphysics have entirely exhausted themselves. If there is to be a breakthrough, it will be apocalyptic or not at all. Incorrigible *Homo*

sapiens will have to cede to a race of man-made clones, the *Homines cybernici.*

BRAVE NEW WORLD

True to the universal archetype of the savior narrative, Michel will go to the desert (a remote scientific laboratory in Ireland), purify himself, recognize and know the truth, and return to save the world. Literally the Angel (of science), *Michael* will bring about "l'élément le plus nécessaire à la reconstruction d'une humanité réconciliée" (*PE,* 390). Product of a totally artificial, and therefore stable, cyber-genetic engineering, the *Homo cybernicus* represents a radical discontinuity in history. The clones, which we can already envisage today (e.g. nano technology), will replace their makers—us. *Homo sapiens* will become dispensable and then extinct (*The Matrix*). Like Christians breaking away from pagans, and like Renaissance Materialists breaking away from Christians, this science-fictional new breed will supercede all previous forms of humanity. This new life will be free from the infantile obsession with ontology ("Le besoin d'ontologie était-il une maladie infantile de l'esprit humain?" [*PE,* 373]) and free from the *moi haïssable* of the aggressively narcissistic *Homo sapiens.* The following poem, near the end of the novel, describes the state of mind of the embedded narrator, a *Homo cybernicus,* living in the true Brave New World, circa 2075 CE. Comparing himself to the early Christians and the Materialists of the modern era, he proclaims:

> De même, nous pouvons aujourd'hui écouter cette
> Histoire de l'ère matérialiste
> Comme une vieille histoire humaine.
> C'est une histoire triste, et pourtant nous ne serons
> Même pas réellement tristes
> Car nous ne ressemblons plus à ces hommes.
> Nés de leur chair et de leurs désirs, nous avons
> Rejeté leurs catégories et leurs appartenances
> Nous ne connaissons pas leurs joies, nous ne
> Connaissons pas non plus leurs souffrances,
> Nous avons écarté
> Avec indifférence
> Et sans aucun effort
> Leur univers de mort.

> (*PE,* 369)

Thus, the morbid broken dialectic of the Materialists results in the annihilation of misery and the creation of the reconciled *Homo cybernicus*—perhaps a God-like incarnation. After having mercilessly debunked desire, modernity's last foray into autonomy, *Les Particules élémentaires* postulates the seemingly unthinkable. Such is the perennial flavor of eschatology, for it foresees the erasure of its bearer as well as his witnesses.

To understand the impact of *Les Particules élémentaires* in France it would be best to analogize this novel to a number of American films. Within a single narrative, **Les Particules élémentaires** encapsulates the disturbing post-1968 chilling horror of *A Clockwork Orange,* the porno-violence of *8mm,* the nihilism and despair of *American Beauty* and the horrifying science fiction of *The Matrix.* All these threads are woven into a gripping psychological novel, a social critique and a disturbing science fiction, laced throughout with the language of a classical French *Moraliste.* Regardless of how receptive or hostile its readers and critics were, such a lethal brew necessarily had to detonate the theatrical Gallic Affaire—*L'Affaire Houellebecq.*

If anything, Houellebecq clearly articulates the *syntax,* that is, the generalized articulation, of a consciousness already implicit in a number of contemporary French fiction authors. The novel represents a moment where what is already in the air finds its crystallization in a single narrative. The texts of his contemporaries, a Darrieussecq or a Gran, consist of minutely working through the *semantics* of this rupture.[30] Shying away from all polemical abstraction, and limiting themselves to a fantastic phenomenology of the banal and the private, they articulate in a more poetically and fictionally convincing manner the Houellebecquian inferno of the present. But syntax is more menacing than semantics. And that is why it was Houellebecq and not Darrieussecq or Gran who unnerved a cultural scene that has become all too comfortable with its own ideology, with peripheral Ciceronian skirmishes within a little contested *doxa.*

Notes

1. Michel Houellebecq, *Renaissance* (Paris: Flammarion, 1999), 56.

2. Michel Houellebecq, *Les Particules élémentaires* (Paris: Flammarion, 1998), henceforth *PE.*

3. Marion Van Renterghem, "Le Procès Houellebecq," *Le Monde,* Sunday, 8 Nov. 1998. A complete and up-to-date bibliography of Houellebecq criticism can be found at *Le Site des Amis de Michel Houellebecq:* http://www.multimania.com.

4. This same point, that happiness equals sexual satisfaction, especially within Freudian thought, is made clear in a recent extensive review essay by John Updike, about David Allyn's *Make Love not War, The Sexual Revolution: An Unfettered History* (New York: Little, Brown, 2000), in *The New Yorker,* Feb. 21-28 2000, 280-290.

5. I am thinking here in particular about Robert Alter's concept of the novel in "The Mirror of Knighthood and the World of Mirrors," reprinted in Miguel de Cervantes, *Don Quixote* (New York: A Norton Critical Edition, 1981), 955-974.

6. Marion Van Renterghem, "Le Procès Houellebecq."

7. Alan Finkielkraut, weekly radio program, *Répliques,* France Culture, Nov. 1998 and Sept 1999. Philippe Sollers's position on Houellebecq is discussed during the November, 1998 program.

8. Badré, Frédéric, "Une Nouvelle Tendance en littérature," *Le Monde,* 3 Oct. 1998.

9. See http://www.jennicam.org.

10. I am thinking in particular about: Roland Barthes, *Système de la mode* (Paris: Seuil, 1966); Jean Baudrillard, *Système des objets* (Paris: Denoël-Gonthier, 1968); Andy Warhol, *The Philosophy of Andy Warhol* (New York: Harvest, 1975).

11. Michel Houellebecq, *H. P. Lovecraft: Contre le monde, contre la vie* (Monaco: Editions du Rocher, 1991), 119.

12. See Robert Kaplan, *The Nothing that Is: A Natural History of Zero* (Oxford: Oxford University Press, 1999), in particular pp. 68-79.

13. Michel Houellebecq, *L'Extension du domaine de la lutte* (Paris: Maurice Nadeau, J'ai Lu, 1994).

14. Michel Houellebecq, *L'Extension du domaine,* 98.

15. Michel Houellebecq, *Interventions* (Paris: Flammarion, 1998), 63.

16. Michel Houellebecq, *Interventions,* 41.

17. For a concise discussion of this "knowing-seizing-controlling" model of knowledge and power, see Emmanuel Lévinas, *Ethique comme philosophie première* (Paris: Editions Payot & Rivages, 1992 [1980]), 67-83.

18. Thomas Mann, *The Magic Mountain* (New York: Vintage, 1995 [1925]), 374.

19. I am using the notion of the "idol" here for obvious purposes, but also for a concrete image that I cannot shake off—the image of *La Vénus d'Ile,* of Prosper Mérimée.

20. One of the great scientific feuds in the past twenty years concerns the work of the cultural anthropologist Margaret Mead, who was perhaps the first serious academic champion of the democratization of sex. She based her assertion on her field work in Western Samoa. Mead's field work was later challenged by Derek Freeman whose criticism of Mead created one of the most important debates within academia in the past thirty years. For a succinct account of this debate see Hal Hellman, *Great Feuds in Science: Ten of the Liveliest Disputes Ever* (New York: John Wiley & Sons, 1998), 177-193.

21. On this relationship between the onset of AIDS and the end of the sexual revolution, see John Updike, *"Make Love not War."*

22. Augustine. *Confessions* (Oxford: Oxford University Press, 1991), trans. Henry Chadwick. "So the feebleness of infant limbs is innocent, not the infant's mind. I have personally watched and studied a jealous baby. He could not yet speak and, pale with jealousy and bitterness, glared at his brother sharing his mother's milk. . . . [b]ut it can hardly be innocence, when the source of milk is flowing richly and abundantly" Book I, 9.

23. See in particular Marquis de Sade, *La Philosophie dans le boudoir* (Paris: PML, 1994 [1795]).

24. Sigmund Freud, *Civilization and its Discontents* (New York: Norton, 1961 [1930]).

25. See on the Sade/Rousseau "slide" Camille Paglia, *Sexual Personae: Art and Decadence from Nefertiti to Emily Dickinson* (New York: Vintage Books, 1991), 230-247.

26. I am obviously thinking here about Denis de Rougement's *L'Amour en l'Occident* (Paris: Union Générale d'Editions, 1939).

27. Michel Houellebecq, *H. P. Lovecraft,* 17.

28. Michel Houellebecq, *Interventions,* 39.

29. See Soren Kierkegaard, *Either/Or* (Princeton: Princeton University Press, 1987 [1843]), Ed. and trans. by Howard V. Hong and Edna H. Hong.

30. I am thinking here in particular about Marie Darrieussecq, *Truisms* (Paris: P.O.L, 1996); and Iegor Gran, *Ipso Facto* (Paris: P.O.L., 1998).

Jonathan Romney (review date 4 September 2000)

SOURCE: Romney, Jonathan. "Cartoon Hell." *New Statesman* 129, no. 4502 (4 September 2000): 33.

[*In the following review, Romney discusses the depiction of cynical disaffection in the novel* Extension du domaine de la lutte *and its film adaptation.*]

The first time I saw **Extension du domaine de la lutte** (aka **Whatever**), a French film marketing officer tried to persuade me that it wasn't worth seeing. "He's such a horrible man," she said, and visibly shuddered. I asked her who she meant. Was it the director Philippe Harel, who also plays the lead role, or the character himself (referred to in the voice-over as "Our Hero")? Or did she mean Michel Houellebecq, the author of the novel on which the film is based, and whom Harel is manifestly impersonating—greasy, combed-over hair, gingerly held cigarette and all? She shrugged, as if to say that they were all pretty much of a muchness. Indeed, in Harel's film, they effectively are—at least, in the sense that Harel's, Houellebecq's and Our Hero's personae unsettlingly blur together in the story of a man with a world-class identity crisis.

Houellebecq, who collaborated with Harel on the screenplay, is a cult figure in France, especially among younger readers. Thanks, in particular, to his bestselling second novel, **Les Particules élémentaires** (published in Britain as **Atomised**), he has been variously applauded as the legitimate heir to Albert Camus and Louis-Ferdinand Céline, and attacked as a misanthropic,

right-wing nihilist. Oddly, Harel's film was not commercially successful in France, possibly because it was so faithful to the book that it offered fans too few surprises. In fact, Harel offers his own twists and, if anything, his version (despite an ambiguous happy ending) offers a darker, more sour vision than the book.

Houellebecq's overwhelming preoccupation is with the drabness and futility of modern life: yes, only in France could such a writer top the bestseller lists. Our Hero is a middle-aged, middle-management man in a computer firm, who spends much of his time addressing shiny, bureaucratic seminars. He abhors his job, but has nothing else in his life—weekends are spent sitting dolefully in his kitchen. The first of many cracks in his life's grey surface appears when he forgets where he has parked his car, and never bothers to look for it.

Our Hero is not merely bored, but affects to have a complex philosophical take on the universe ("a furtive gathering of elementary particles, a fleeting shape on the way to chaos"). He is even bored and nauseated by sex—and, in Houellebecq's universe, sex is indeed boring and nauseating. The very first scene—which gives a taste of the Mike Leigh-ish cruelty of the film's social comedy, and of Houellebecq's sour misogyny—takes place at a dull office party where a woman gets halfway through a derisory striptease, then throws in the towel.

The first part of the film provides a flat, matter-of-fact delineation of Our Hero's doleful grind, with commentary both from his own snooty, weary voice-over, and from an omniscient narrator who suggests that Our Hero, negative though he is, doesn't know the half of it. The film evokes a world suggestive of *Reginald Perrin* as rewritten by Guy Debord, the situationist prophet of social malaise. The script is spot-on about the humourlessness of French corporate culture, and is steeped in its soul-destroying, quasi-scientific jargon ("the vendor-client matrix"). But Our Hero's analysis of this world is just as inflated, self-parodically pompous in its would-be sociological rigour—the film's title refers to Our Hero's analysis of modern sexuality in Marxist, market forces terms.

In the second half of the film, Our Hero sets off on a seminar tour with his colleague Raphael Tisserand (José Garcia), an indefatigably dapper smiler, whose eagerness to have a *"sympa"* time hides his sexual despair. Harel and Garcia make a fabulously cringe-making double act, an Abbott and Costello of the soul's dark night. Harel is weary, shabby, anoraked, resembling a scruffy cousin of Charles Aznavour; Garcia is punctiliously shiny, fussy, always up for more disappointment. The social comedy becomes uncomfortably cruel whenever the two men set foot in a disco, but this is only the prelude to Our Hero's macabre manipulation of his colleague, which is where the story topples into forbiddingly black nihilism.

What the film has to say about the contemporary urban condition may seem banal and one-dimensional, like the extended whinge of an over-articulate, embittered adolescent. Indeed, it is essentially this public persona that has made Houellebecq a household name in France—a sort of middle-aged, wearily whining Jeannot Rotten who has mellowed into complacent adulthood. But Houellebecq's world-view is carried across in his books with absolute conviction, and the blackness is all the more serious for being passed off as comic fatigue and dandyishness. Harel's dry, cool, neutral wit and Gilles Henry's studiedly sleek photography serve Houellebecq well; and, even in French cinema's currently crowded market of films about existential gloom (*Seul Contre Tous, L'Ennui* and so on), this modest adaptation stands out with appropriately charmless conviction. Unlikely though it may seem, Harel makes Houellebecq's cartoon hell a compelling place to visit.

William Cloonan (essay date October 2000)

SOURCE: Cloonan, William. "Literary Scandal, *Fin du Siècle,* and the Novel in 1999." *French Review* 74, no. 1 (October 2000): 14-30.

[*In the following essay, Cloonan examines the public controversy surrounding* Les Particules élémentaires, *Houellebecq's literary celebrity and artistic merit, and how "L'Affaire Houellebecq" sheds light on the state of French letters, culture, and intellectual debate at the end of the twentieth century.*]

In Paris this summer an editor at the Editions du Seuil complained that the *rentrée* of 1998 had been dominated, and to a degree spoiled by the attention given to one novel. She was referring, of course, to Michel Houellebecq's *Les Particules élémentaires,* which was mentioned in last year's *French Review* essay. In the ensuing months a controversy emerged, provoked in large measure by Houellebecq's former collaborators at the review *Perpendiculaire*, that was rapidly christened *l'Affaire Houellebecq.* The very name given the scandal points to its central ambiguity: was the novel problematic, or was it rather the man who wrote it? Of course, probably nobody would take a literary scandal seriously if it did not have strong personal elements. The *Perpendiculaire* group obliged by offering a particularly faint form of praise when they somewhat begrudgingly allowed that Houellebecq "n'est pas nazi; il n'est même pas lépiniste" (Duchatelet et al. 16). Houellebecq was equally sparing in his compliments when he referred to one of his former collaborators at the review as "un imbécile hargneux . . . à qui je n'ai jamais caché le peu d'estime que m'inspiraient ses productions" (**"Michel Houellebecq répond à *Perpendiculaire*"** 10).[1]

If there is one area in which French intellectuals are absolutely superior to their American counterparts, it is in their interest in and use of the media. *L'Affaire* proved to be a godsend as writers of various political persuasions and artistic ability rapidly jumped into print. The birth of a new literary school was announced, the decline of morality decried, and, as tends to happen fairly frequently, humanism was once again pronounced dead. By the summer of 1999 the scandal was already on the wane, but the review *Atelier du Roman* nevertheless devoted a large portion of its June edition to *L'Affaire.*

As this essay hopes to show, *L'Affaire Houellebecq* is less interesting for the intellectual substance of the debates surrounding the author and his novel than for what it indicates about the malaise currently affecting French letters as the century ends. Whatever one thinks of *Les Particules élémentaires,* there is nothing in the novel, either thematically or descriptively, that cannot also be found in other works. To take but three examples, some people are offended by the rampant sexuality in *Les Particules,* but in fact the *partouze* has become a staple of contemporary French fiction as Alice Massat's *Le Ministère de l'intérieur* amply illustrates. As for the alleged misanthropy of Houellebecq and his work, Vincent de Swarte's *Requiem pour un sauvage,* set in the Middle Ages, tells the story of a man who spends his youth in a cave, emerges, meets people, eats several of them, participates in a Crusade, and eventually returns to his cave. In Lorette Nobécourt's *La Conversation,* the female protagonist's curiosity about what makes men tick prompts her to attempt to skin her lover alive. What emerges in *Les Particules* is an indictment of a generation, the sacrosanct generation of '68, which, the novel implies, has failed to produce a better society, a moral code superior to the earlier humanistic model, and, perhaps most tellingly, great works of art.[2]

Les Particules élémentaires was Houellebecq's second novel. His first, *Extension du domaine de la lutte* (1994), attracted serious critical attention. It deals with an extremely depressed young man struggling against loneliness and the temptation of suicide. From the perspective of *L'Affaire Houellebecq,* it is perhaps most interesting for the way it announces one of the stylistic devices the author would adopt in *Les Particules*: "La forme romanesque n'est pas conçue pour peindre l'indifférence, ni le néant; il faudrait inventer une articulation plus plate, plus concise et plus morne" (*Extension* 42).

Houellebecq was fortunate to have caught the attention of critics from the beginning of his career as a novelist. New novelists are numerous and often quickly forgotten. In 1999 there were seventy-five first novels. Frédéric Richaud published *Monsieur le jardinier,* a loving and lovely account of the life of Louis XIV's gardener, Jean-Baptiste de la Quintinie, whose reflections on his activities become a long meditation on transience. Jean-Baptiste escapes his demons by turning to the soil; the heroine of Marion Jean's *Trouée* is less fortunate. Her efforts to deal with the passage of time lead her into a world that resembles that of *The Sun Also Rises,* where broken souls move constantly about in an effort to avoid confronting the sterility of their lives. Alain Fleischer's *La Femme qui avait deux bouches* is the first venture into fiction of a man who has had a long and distinguished career in the visual arts. This book is actually a collection of short pieces, heavily influenced by Kafka. The title refers to the first story which does indeed focus on a beautiful and brilliant woman with two mouths. Given Fleischer's university background and interest in theory, it is not surprising that the mouths in question at times take on the attributes of literary texts, at once troubling and seductive, yet always fascinating. Jean-Philippe Chatrier's *Les Deux Moitiés du ciel* is an ambitious work that centers on a love triangle of a peculiar sort, a man, a woman, and a church. The man, Henri Deleuze, must choose, and it is a tribute to Chatrier's talent that his choice of Reims cathedral makes perfect sense.

This year les Editions Arléa created a special series for first novels, "1er mille.," and Arléa has also made some excellent choices. Christine Féret-Fleury's *Les Vagues sont douces comme des tigres* is the story of a twelve-year-old girl living on a farm during World War I. Although this is a third-person narration, the reader never feels or sees anything beyond what the protagonist does. The story deals with the child's loneliness, need for love, and efforts to overcome both through schooling. In *Neige* Maxence Fermine attempts to create what might be termed a "haiku-novel." This beautiful story is set in eighteenth-century Japan. The novel, wherein no chapter is longer than a page, tells the story of Yuko-Akita, whose twin passions are haiku and snow. A gifted poet, his struggle is to overcome a fascination with whiteness, and when he does so, he enhances his existence as an artist and a man.

Claude Pinganaud is the editor at Arléa who launched the collection, "1er mille." Yet as he noted "publier un premier roman est . . . moins risqué pour un éditeur que de publier le deuxième car les journalistes sont plus attentifs, plus enthousiastes et plus indulgents" (Grangeray 4). The second novel is always harder because critics await the fulfillment of the putative promise noted in the first. Michèle Desbordes certainly meets this challenge in *La Demande* which describes the last days of "un maître italien" invited to France by the king. The "maître" is certainly Leonardo Da Vinci whose final months on earth are eased by the care and love of a simple servant woman. This novel proved an unexpected popular success which, in a work containing few incidents, can perhaps be attributed to the continuous intermingling of a fading present and an uncertain future. The reader shares the artist's recogni-

tion that his genius will permit him to overcome everything but the inevitable, and nowhere is this awareness more intense than in the act of creating: "quand l'émotion est arrivée, il ne pouvait savoir si c'était ce qu'il voyait ou la mort qui maintenant sans rien dire, chaque soir à la même heure, il sentait venir" (38).

Danielle Robert-Guédon's second novel, *Le Grand Abbatoir,* draws the sad analogy between "un abbatoir" and "une maison de retraite." The decent people who run "Val Fleuri" insist that it is not "une maison de retraite, c'est un lieu de vie à taille humaine, avec un accompagnement personnalisé. Satisfaire les résidents est notre priorité" (104-05). The residents, however, are not so pleased to be there, as are not, one assumes, the cattle entering the slaughterhouse. Marianne Dubertret published her first novel in 1984 when she was a teenager. Her second, *Un Faux Frère,* is the dark love story of a boy and girl who were brought up together because Marc's parents took Ava in as an orphan. Eventually they become lovers only later to discover that among the things they share are the same father.

Last year readers discovered Iegor Gran's talent for the burlesque and the bizarre with *Ipso facto.* This year Gran offers *Acné festival,* which alludes to the first novel (172) in the process of telling the story of a man almost sixty who suffers from acne, "un symptôme de mon manque d'affection" (64). His efforts to turn this affliction into a seduction device and ultimately into a work of art is the subject of this novel.

In 1998 Iegor Gran found himself unwittingly implicated in *L'Affaire Houellebecq.* Up until October of that year *L'Affaire* had been a nasty, but localized quarrel between the editors of *Perpendiculaire* and a former collaborator, Michel Houellebecq. *Perpendiculaire* was founded in 1995, and rapidly established itself as a leftist review concerned with the relationship between literature, politics, and society. Houellebecq was an early contributor and probably its best-known writer. Excerpts from **Les Particules élémentaires** had initially appeared in the review's pages. Political differences precipitated the break between Houellebecq and the editorial staff of the journal with the editors claiming that the misanthropic, antiabortionist, reactionary views expressed in **Les Particules** are in fact those of the author. Houellebecq, who is certainly a talented *provocateur,* provided his detractors with ample ammunition. In a series of essays and interviews that appeared in various places and were collected under the title **Interventions** (1998), he opposes the Maastricht Treaty (118), maintains that May 1968 was a failure (78), and takes a position squarely against "la débauche de techniques mise en œuvre par tel ou tel 'formaliste-Minuit,'" (53). His tone is often belligerent as the title of one essay, **"Jacques Prévert est un con,"** demonstrates. During an interview with the magazine *Les Inrockuptibles* that does not appear in **Interven-**

tions, he reportedly expressed his admiration for Stalin "parce qu'il a tué plein d'anarchistes" (Van Reuterghen 17), and in a meeting with students at the FNAC, he so annoyed his young listeners that some of the audience responded with "Vous êtes un nazi qui ne s'avoue pas" (Van Reuterghen 17). Houellebecq's gift for the outrageous interview is such that Van Reuterghen, whose *Le Monde* article I have been citing, quite properly remarks that "plutôt que d'interroger l'écrivain sur son œuvre, on l'interroge sur l'interview précédente" (17).

It was Frédéric Badré who dragged Iegor Gran into the fray and by doing so gave *L'Affaire* a broader, potentially more interesting dimension. Badré works for a rival review, *Ligne de Risque,* which takes its inspiration from Lautréamont, and therefore wishes "Que la situation explose." Nevertheless this journal refuses to participate "dans la guerre sociale" (Kéchichian 8). In an article that appeared in *Le Monde* Badré rehearsed the usual complaints about the contemporary French novel, "trop narcissique, trop autarcique, trop introverti, sans nécessité, tourné vers le passé, etc." (14). He then announced the discovery of a new "school": "avec Michel Houellebecq, Marie Darrieussecq, Iegon Gran." There is "une nouvelle tendance . . . leurs livres ont un grand succès public . . . leur radicalité ne repose pas sur la face obscure et cachée des choses, mais sur la réalité commune, sur ce que tout le monde voit autour de lui" (14). Badré argued that these writers, whose "school" he baptized "postnaturaliste," nevertheless do not follow an established path, and then made the rather fabulous claim that "ils ont compris que la beauté ne peut plus être représentée parce qu'elle n'existe plus" (14). In a calmer moment Badré added that "le roman est pour eux un simple outil pour dévoiler les contradictions de la société contemporaine et montrer l'homme en situation devant l'intolérable vide" (14).

Despite the somewhat hyperbolic tone of the essay, Badré did raise some worthwhile issues. He was arguing that certain younger novelists were moving away from the sorts of literary experimentation simplistically associated with Les Editions de Minuit, and were attempting to engage in a straightforward description of the moral and social ethos of the contemporary world. Whether or not these writers were indeed trying to "renouer la littérature . . . avec un discours universel" (14) is probably less important than that they were certainly doing something different. On a social level they were more interested in describing what was wrong with the world than in changing it, and, more arguably, in terms of literary technique they were more involved in what they said than in how they said it. Finally, even though Badré links Darrieussecq and Gran with Houellebecq, it was Houellebecq who received the bulk of the attention in the essay. By virtue of Badré's article, the author of *Les Particules élémentaires* was anointed the leader of a "school" that someone else had founded.

The issue of "postnaturalism" and Houellebecq's putative involvement with it provoked a variety of predictable reactions, but *L'Affaire* took yet another bizarre turn when *Les Particules* was unceremoniously dropped from the short list of the 1998 Goncourt selection. No clear explanation was ever provided for this decision, but if nothing else it points to the nastiness and backbiting that increasingly characterizes the awarding of the major literary prizes.

Unfortunately, this year that unpleasant tendency continued. Jean Echenoz was awarded the Goncourt for *Je m'en vais.* Echenoz is undoubtedly one of France's most interesting novelists, even if some readers may be disappointed with his latest effort. *Je m'en vais,* much like his preceding *Un An,* takes place over the course of one year. Félix Ferrer, an owner of an art gallery, leaves his wife in the first sentence: "Je m'en vais" (7), gets involved in a series of improbable adventures that lead him to Alaska in search of Indian artifacts, then returns to France with his treasures, only to have them stolen. Eventually he recovers most of the loot, gets rich, and on the last page he is once again at his now ex-wife's house, where he meets an attractive young woman. He agrees to spend some time with her, but, like all his relations with women, this will prove of short duration. He makes this clear to her: "Je prends juste un verre et je m'en vais" (253). This novel reprises many of the themes of Echenoz's earlier work (travel to out-of-the-way places, the influence of American movies on contemporary life, and the unlikely made to appear normal), but, to this reader at least, *Je m'en vais* seems a bit tired, almost as if the writer is parodying himself. However, the unpleasantness surrounding the Goncourt had nothing to do with Echenoz's novel or any individual's opinion of it.

The Goncourt committee shocked the literary prize establishment by announcing the winner almost a week in advance. This unexpected timing threw the other prize committees into disarray, especially the Femina, which had Echenoz on its short list as well. The Goncourt committee apparently opted to upset the usual calendar since other committees had been doing that for years, and as a result, the Goncourt, considered to be the most prestigious, has in recent years become the last major prize awarded.

Whatever the chagrin the Femina people might have experienced at the Goncourt's conduct, it did not prevent their awarding their prize to a fine writer. Maryline Desbiolles's *Anchise* is the sad story of a man whose life ended practically before it began. Anchise lost his wife to sickness while he was away at war, and this "cinglé, ce fou, ce pauvre con d'Anchise n'avait jamais pu oublier sa femme" (42). The story begins with his death, and recounts the story of a life that would appear uneventful to most, but which was marked forever by one event.

The Médicis went to another deserving novelist. For years Christian Oster has been entertaining readers with stories that usually feature a Gallic version of J. Alfred Prufrock. Gavarine is no exception, and he recounts in Oster's latest novel the sad/funny unraveling of his life because, as he explains, he has lost the keys to *Mon Grand Appartement.*

Daniel Picouly won the Renaudot for *L'Enfant léopard* which tells of Marie-Antoinette's final twelve hours. Her one remaining wish is to see again the illegitimate child she produced with "le nègre Zamor." The child suffers from a skin disease which gives him the appearance of an "enfant léopard." Jean-Christophe Ruffin's *Les Causes perdues,* which describes a humanitarian mission in Ethiopia, received the Interallié.

However much civility may be suffering in the awarding of the major prizes, one prize tradition remains unscathed. The major prizes are pretty much the exclusive property of major publishing houses. Gallimard got the Interallié. Seuil received the Femina, and Grasset won the Renaudot. The venerable editor in chief, Jérome Lindon, probably would not wish to agree, but when his Minuit walks off with the Goncourt and the Médicis, avant-garde publishing may be moving into the mainstream.

Mathieu Lindon, the editor's son, published a novel this year with one of France's most adventurous houses, Les Editions P.O.L. *Le Procès de Jean-Marie Le Pen* has many fine qualities, notably the indictment, less of Le Pen since that would be obvious, but rather of the Left's ineptness in confronting him. The story deals with a young *lépeniste* who committed a racist crime, an act which engenders the predictable anti-Le Pen outbursts from minority groups and leftist intellectuals. The murderer, Ronald Blistier, is not particularly intelligent or eloquent, but before his absolute conviction of white supremacy and of his own role as the real victim, his opponents are at a loss to respond. The boy eventually commits suicide, but neither his life nor death seems very important in this novel. What matters for the novelist is how such hateful views could become dogma for a growing number of people. The trial of Jean-Marie Le Pen never takes place in this novel, but in a sentence Lindon captures the essence of Le Pen's strategy: "dire en public le minimum de mots pour provoquer le maximum de mal" (26).

Robert Bober's *Berg et Beck* deals with another historical issue that remains important in contemporary France. Berg and Beck are two Jewish boys forced to wear the yellow star of David in 1942. Berg survives and his friend disappears. In 1952 Berg takes a job in an orphanage for the children of *déportés.* He does his best to help these kids, to ease their transition into normal lives, but he remains himself a victim, guilty of his own survival.

Marc Lambron's *1941* treats World War II from a very different perspective. It centers on the Vichy government as viewed by a minor official who secretly works for the Resistance. The issue is the much discussed question of how decent patriotic French people ought to have reacted. Lambron provides a brilliant characterization of the mood at Vichy: the mixture of optimism, fear, occasional self-hatred, constant insecurity and self-justification: "L'esprit partisan mal placé, les activités défaitistes, l'hostilité au Maréchal, l'entrave à l'œuvre de la restauration nationale, non merci!" (103). Lebrun's descriptions of members of Pétain's entourage are particularly striking. Take, for example, the Maréchal's personal physician, Bernard Ménétral who projects: "un air de vieil enfant qui a trop applaudi au Guignol" (119). Equally memorable are his evocations of the arrogance of the Vichy intellectual elite: "l'Ecole Normale ne donne pas une éducation, elle se contente de conférer l'infaillibilité" (325). Despite the enormous differences in style, this novel reads at times like an ominous prelude to Céline's depictions of the same world in defeat that one finds in his war trilogy. Lebrun draws many conclusions about Vichy in *1941,* but none are intended as final, as his last sentences indicate: "La mèche brûle . . . Elle n'a pas fini de brûler" (412).

Alexandre Najjar's *L'Ecole de la guerre* deals with a more recent conflict, the on and off war in Lebanon. It is a series of vignettes that details the survival strategies, "en temps de guerre, la bougie est sans prix" (59), employed by people who are never really sure where the battlefield begins and ends. In his eloquent introduction Najjar claims that all "guerres se ressemblent" (11), but then in his novel he demonstrates that every war is unique for its victims.

This year's final novel centering on warfare is in some ways the strangest. Over the years Jean Vautrin has perfected the mingling of comic book characters with serious issues. His *Le Cri du peuple* is no exception. As the title suggests, it deals with the Commune of 1870-1871. The novel's cover has a comic book version of a battle around a barricade, and the author provides in the text drawings that caricature the main characters. His hero, Horace Grondin, is appropriately larger-than-life: "Cet homme aux mains d'échorcheur, à l'ossature puissante, au regard halluciné, cet homme qui faisait sa route seul au monde, paraissait tellement hors du commun" (52). Yet this novel is not easy reading. The descriptions of the brutality, the battles throughout Paris, and the ultimate defeat of the Commune are not for the fainthearted. If Vautrin's novels often seem odd to American readers, it is doubtless because we have nothing in our literary tradition that permits our taking the comic book as a serious artistic form capable of making compelling comments on the present and the past.

A similar difference in the evaluation of literary forms affects the American and French appreciation of the mystery novel. Americans have always admired certain mystery novelists as writers, Raymond Chandler and Chester Himes are obvious examples, but have tended to view the genre as a secondary one. In contrast, at least since World War II the French have given increasing importance to the *polar*. While it is true that some *nouveaux romanciers*, such as Michel Butor and Alain Robbe-Grillet, may have freighted the form with more intellectual baggage than it can bear, the mystery novel remains in France a vehicle for serious social commentary.

Last year Michel Rio interrupted his *La Mort* to decry the perceived abuses of literary theory and historical revisionism. This year Marek Halter addresses the ethnic and cultural tensions in the Middle East with *Les Mystères de Jérusalem*. This novel mingles greed for lucre and for knowledge, sex, violence, and murder in a story whose ostensible theme, the search for lost treasure, provides the basis for a bitterly ironic commentary on the absurdity of the mutual hatred between Arab and Jew.

Of course, if the French are willing to take the mystery novel seriously, they do not do so all the time. Lovers of the genre who simply appreciate its diverting qualities would be well-advised to consider Fred Vargas's *L'Homme à l'envers*. Fred Vargas is not sufficiently known in the States. A scientist by profession, she consistently supplies compelling stories of great tension and minimum violence. Her latest effort tells of a series of murders in Southern France that appear to be the work of a werewolf. The story is gripping, the ending surprising, and those who think the French undervalue the intelligence, indeed the cunning, of Canadians will have to revisit the question.

Although Michel Rio has often displayed great talent for the parodic mystery novel, he does not limit himself to his genre. His *Morgane* is the story of Morgane la Fée. More beautiful than any other woman, more intelligent than all men except perhaps Merlin, early in life she declares war on humanity, on the violence of men and the cruelty of their God. Her credo speaks for itself: "Et moi, Morgane, . . . haïssant ce Dieu-Monstre et cet homme stupide ou menteur . . . je veux être cruelle à mon tour et répondre par le mal personnel au mal universel, parce que je suis condamnée au savoir; à la peur, à la souffrance et à la mort" (33). In the *fin du siècle* climate of 1999, it is hard not to find in this retelling of the collapse of the Round Table as well as in Morgane's own solitary demise, a commentary on a civilization that has lost its bearings.

Rio explains in his introduction that *Morgane* is to a degree a spin-off from his earlier *Merlin* (1989). He is not the only prominent novelist who cannot quite escape his prior successes, but no author so illustrates that

dilemma as does Daniel Pennac. Whether he likes it or not, Pennac remains a prisoner of *la famille Malaussène*. Critics might suggest new departures, but the public cannot seem to get enough of the comic universe he has created in Belleville. *Aux fruits de la passion* will certainly please the lovers of "Further Adventures." This time Ben's sister, Thérèse the fortune-teller, embarks on an ill-advised marriage with Marie-Colbert de Robertval. The Belleville community had enough trouble trying to understand why she wanted to marry a *comptable*, but when the guy turns out to be a *comte*, not to mention the other "c" word, the dire results are all too foreseeable. After the wedding, where the Belleville guests provide for their social superiors the appropriately politically correct element, "humbles et multiculturels" (91), mayhem ensues; some characters are murdered, one explodes, and the surprise beginning is matched by a surprise ending. As with each installment of the Belleville saga, Pennac manages his unique form of social commentary. This time the deep thinking is supplied by a dog: "Julius le Chien pratiquait la politique à la française: il s'attaquait aux images pour mieux pactiser avec les personnes" (42). Pennac will decide for himself when and if he wishes to leave the nineteenth arrondissement. For the moment one can only say that *Aux fruits de la passion* is one of his better efforts.

The pressure on a writer to address certain issues and avoid others, to change locales or philosophies is simply ridiculous. What matters is what an author does with his/her materials, and such an obvious conclusion is as true for Houellebecq as it is for Pennac. The most glaring absurdity in *L'Affaire Houellebecq* is the concentration, not simply on the man, but on his most outrageous and at times Orphic utterances. In fact, in **Interventions** Houellebecq has made some clear statements about his goals as a writer and positioned his concerns in the context of contemporary French literature. He argues, for instance, that "Je ne me situe ni pour ni contre aucune avant-garde, mais je me rends compte que je me singularise par le simple fait que je m'intéresse moins au langage qu'au monde" (110-11). While one might seriously doubt that avant-garde experimentation is necessarily apolitical, what matters more is that Houellebecq believes strongly, perhaps even naively, in literature's capacity to change the world: "on souhaite dépasser le cynisme. Si quelqu'un aujourd'hui parvient à développer un discours à la fois honnête et positif, il modifiera le monde" (111). A negative view of society's current direction need not be a cynical one, and to image such an attitude in a novel like **Les Particules élémentaires** can certainly contribute to an ongoing social discourse. The pity in *L'Affaire Houellebecq* is that the author's critics too often saddle him with the very cynicism he claims he wishes to combat.

Of all the commentators on *L'Affaire*, the novelist Dominique Noguez has been the most consistently sensible. In an essay that appeared in the review *Atelier du Roman,* Noguez dismisses the rather bizarre charge that Houellebecq has no style by pointing to the self-evident: "tout écrivain, même le plus exécrable, a un style—un style exécrable, justement" (17). He then goes on to discuss various stylistic strategies that appear in Houellebecq's writing, and compares them to those of other authors. In an essay written for *Le Monde,* "La Rage de ne pas lire," Noguez takes his distance from arguments about Houellebecq's alleged place in a new literary "school," and laments the low level of the critical discussions surrounding *L'Affaire.* He seems especially saddened by the vitriol emanating from *Perpendiculaire,* since he believes that the founders of this review

> étaient partis d'un bon pas: créant avec leurs propres forces une revue originale, animant la vie littéraire parisienne avec leurs mercredis du café Les Marronniers, se donnant à l'occasion avec humour, publiant quelques bons livres, découvrant de nouveaux talents, assurant enfin à Michel Houellebecq qu'ils ont salué parmi les premiers, une reconnaissance méritée.
>
> (1)

Noguez's reference to the accomplishments of *Perpendiculaire* raises an interesting side issue. Traditionally literary reviews have been places where new writers could find outlets for their work, and where editors might discover their authors of the future. This is no longer the case in France. The importance of literary reviews has been consistently declining. The most striking illustration of this phenomenon is that the prestigious *Nouvelle Revue Française* has radically altered its publication schedule by switching from a monthly to a quarterly format (Savigneau 8). In a similar vein editors say that they rarely visit the literary reviews in search of new talent. Given this situation, one of the possibly unintended offshoots of *L'Affaire,* which pitted a relatively new review, *Perpendiculaire,* first against a former collaborator, and then against another new review, *Ligne de Risque,* was to revive interest, for however brief a time, in literary journals.

Given the declining importance of the literary review, two publishing houses have developed new strategies for showcasing young talent. Grasset subsidizes the popular magazine, *Inrockuptibles,* and once every few years, it publishes in book form excerpts from relatively unknown writers, not all of whom publish *chez* Grasset. This year *Inrockuptibles Onze* contains selections from eleven authors (thus the title). Except for Martin Winckler, the author of last year's *La Maladie de Sachs,* the writers in the current collection are largely unknown, but Grasset's initiative harbingers well for the future; in the previous volume appeared then little-known novelists such as Marie Darrieussecq and Michel Houellebecq.

Les Editions Robert Laffont is probably the most commercially savvy publishing house in France. It therefore comes as no surprise that its collection of short pieces would stay closer to home. Every year Laffont brings out a volume of stories by members of its *Ecole de Brive.* Each collection is centered on a theme, and this year's focus was on fleeting childhood memories which nevertheless constitute *L'Or du temps.*

This year les Editions Balland launched a collection of a different sort. Initially called "Le Rayon Gay," the purpose was to provide a forum for fiction concentrating on homosexuality. However, it soon became apparent to the series's editor, Guillaume Dustan, that such a perspective was too narrow, and so he broadened the focus to include the writings of and about all marginalized people. In so doing, he renamed the collection, "Rayon." Under this rubric Balland published Dustan's own, *Nicholas Pages,* the story of his relationship with a fellow gay writer. This novel provides valuable insights into the business side of literature, the literary forums, the jockeying for prestige and even understanding that are the daily fare of any professional writer. Nicholas Pages's *Je mange un œuf* also appears in "Le Rayon," and it is an account of the novelist's daily activities where practically every morning starts with a slight variation on "je me réveille, je reste au lit, je bois un café sur le balcon" (9). A less successful novel in this collection is Frédéric Huet's *Papa a tort,* which is a *fauxnaïf* version of a young boy's slow awakening to his own homosexuality.

While Balland's venture is certainly idealistic, it may prove of dubious value. There already exist, and have existed for some time, numerous venues for works dealing with homosexuality. Every year appear novels by homosexuals addressing questions of sexual identity; it is doubtful today that a text of literary value would be refused simply because of its subject matter. Jean-François Kervéan's *Vingt Fois toi et moi* is typical of many recent explorations of the theme. In this novel the characters' gayness is a given; the social impact of AIDS is explored: "Vous croyez que le triangle rose et le sida ça vaut l'étoile jaune?" (136), and the real issue is the difficulty of forging lasting relationships. Balland is trying to move marginalized groups out of the ghetto, but the publishing house might have inadvertently only created a gilded one.

Kervéan's characters live with their sexuality; they are not obsessed by it. Such cannot be said for Morgan Sportès's heterosexual extravaganza, *Rue du Japon, Paris.* This novel details vividly an affair between a middle-aged writer and a young Japanese woman. Nothing is left to the imagination, and no fantasy remains unexplored. There are numerous allusions to *Les Liaisons dangereuses,* a work that still remains more erotic than *Rue du Japon, Paris* for no better reason than that the former leaves something to the imagination. Nevertheless, *Rue du Japon* remains a fascinating novel, not so much for the descriptive sexuality, nor for the main character's alleged aesthetic dilemma which a friend cruelly yet accurately pinpoints: "Mais tu veux quoi, au bout du compte? Ton roman ou ta Jap?" (358). Lovers of Paris will be thrilled by Sportès's ability to evoke the hidden byways and charms of the eleventh, nineteenth, and twentieth arrondissements.

In *Rue du Japon* the Japanese woman was obviously the foreigner. Amélie Nothomb reverses this situation in *Stupeur et tremblements* which describes a Belgian woman's year of working for a Japanese firm in Japan. This funny novel will do little for international understanding, as it consistently sends up Nipponese social and business practices, while describing the Japanese as work-driven robots with occasional attacks of humanity. The title refers to the emotional state that is supposed to accompany a commoner when meeting the emperor. It might also, however, summarize a reader's reaction to this book.

Nothomb's Japan is a distant country, but it is hardly exotic. Readers interested in the exploration of mysterious places would be better advised to turn to either Christian Liger's *La Nuit de Faraman* or Louis Gardel's *Grand Seigneur,* which, however distant their settings are from one another, share a common tone of melancholy and renunciation. *La Nuit de Faraman* is a beautifully written novel set in Faraman, a fictional city in France whose prosperity and surface happiness hide the secret of a terrible crime, the murder, for no rational reason, of Italian laborers working there one hundred years ago. The narrative slowly unearths the diabolic tendencies that lurk just below civilization's surface, tendencies that can burst forth in a moment of communal madness and then disappear until a young man, who might be Satan himself, comes to town.

The exoticism of the world of Louis Gardel's *Grand Seigneur* is more immediately apparent than that of the placid community of Faraman. The novel concerns Soliman the Magnificent, ruler of the Ottoman Empire. It explores the final years of the most powerful man in the East whose sense of responsibility compels him to destroy or distance himself from those he loves. This is a story of a man imprisoned by power, forced to behave in cruel and dishonest ways in the interest of statecraft. The one enemy he cannot overcome is death itself, but by the novel's end, this adversary has become his only friend: "Renoncer est le plus beau mot du monde" (142).

Soliman's problems were immediate, practical, and political. His conscience was a nagging annoyance that he had little time to examine. The modern world is often quite different, a place where the psyche and its

sundry insecurities seem to rule supreme. Simon, the main character in Leslie Kaplan's *Le Psychanalyste,* is something of a ruler in this realm. He is a psychiatrist, seemingly a Lacanian, since "Oui" is his most frequent response to anything his patients say. This is a long (457 pages) novel that follows Simon through weeks of his practice. Among the people he meets is "Miss Nobody Knows," who was the main character in one of Kaplan's earlier novels. The story follows the pattern of Simon's treatments: stories succeed stories, and nothing is resolved at the end.

François, the main character in Jacques-Pierre Amette's *L'Homme du silence,* could have been one of Simon's patients. A member of the generation of '68, and a relatively successful radio commentator at the ORTF, his girlfriend's departure precipitates a crisis. He loses interest in his job, and eventually loses his job, but this apparent catastrophe leaves him unfazed. Like Liger and Gardel, Amette displays a talent for depicting melancholy. François's story is that of a life unlived, of a generation that failed to achieve its goals, if ever it knew what they were. François just floats through existence like the water which is the central image in the novel.

Whatever one makes of Simon's efforts to help his patients in *Le Psychanalyste,* he was attempting to apply new methods of treatment to old problems. A brighter version of this effort can be found in three novels engaged in literary experimentation. François Bott's *Les Etés de la vie* is really not one novel. It is, as the subtitle indicates, "cinquante-six esquisses pour un roman d'une saison." The "saison" in question is not entirely a literary one. It is the author's life, whose stages he recounts through memories of summers near and distant. Bott has his thoughts on aging and dying, but irony, rather than melancholy is his strength. In what appears to be a sly reference to ***Les Particules élémentaires,*** he notes: "L'homme était 'une passion inutile,' mais il avait bien le droit de flirter" (60).

Oliver Rolin's *Méroé* juxtaposes a story centering on the life and death of the British General Gordon, killed at Khartoum, with reflections on the role of literature in the modern world. Gordon is isolated and out of place in the Sudan; it is only through a combination of Bible reading and brandy drinking that he maintains a fragile stability while awaiting the inevitable. Rolin seems to find in this "sorte de Lawrence du siècle passé, Don Quichotte christique" (11), a hero at once tragic and comic, because he believed so desperately that force could impose order on existence. In a novel replete with literary allusions, the author appears to suggest that language alone can create the semblance of an enduring order (128), and that the only place where humanity is really the center of the universe is in the realm of art (71).

Bott and Rolin's experiments with literary form are modest in themselves, but they become even more so when compared to Antoine Volodine's *Des Anges mineurs*. Over the last few years Volodine has introduced a plethora of new literary terms, all of which he uses to give voice to "des texts post-exotiques." The postexotic universe is the world after some catastrophic event that has placed humanity in a position where it must start over again. The form best suited to depict this situation is *le narrat*: "j'appelle narrats des instantanés romanesques qui fixent une situation, des émotions, un conflit vibrant entre mémoire et réalité, entre imaginaire et souvenir" (7). Told in forty-nine short chapters, each of which has the name of a person in the title, *Des Anges mineurs* represents Will Scheidmann's efforts to supply a *narrat* for his forty-nine minor angels.

By the time the June issue of *Atelier du Roman* which contained a series of essays on *Les Particules élémentaires* appeared, *L'Affaire Houellebecq* was pretty much spent. Summer had arrived, and besides vacations those interested in literary matters were more concerned with preparing for *la rentrée littéraire*. The essays in *Atelier du Roman* reflect this change in sensibility. They are intelligent and insightful, but also a bit incredulous at the furor created around the novelist and his text. Clearly it was time to move on to other matters.

If *L'Affaire Houellebecq* contains more than a passing interest, it may be due to factors not entirely related to the author and his novel. The reaction to both may well reflect a *fin du siècle* anxiety, a perceived absence of and desire for a major French novelist, and a nostalgia for an earlier era where France's cultural dominance remained largely unquestioned. Certainly if one grossly simplifies the thematic concerns of *Les Particules élémentaires,* the result would be an ideal end-of-the-century fiction: the last hundred years, especially the latter fifty, witnessed the collapse of traditional moral, social, and aesthetic norms, and the next century promises to be safe only for emotional zombies. This has the aura of a big millennial message, the literary equivalent of the Y2K nervousness, since it is at once global and despairing. As such it could well appeal to those who never bothered to read the book, but still managed to take offense at its putative content.

It is common today to hear complaints that France has no novelist of the stature of a Proust, Céline, or Gide. That may well be true, but it is something of a worldwide phenomenon as witnessed by the Nobel Prize Committee's need in recent years to mine retirement communities to find an author on whom they can bestow a "lifetime achievement" award. The fact is that France has many fine writers, such as Jean Echenoz, Camille Laurens, Christian Oster, and Jean-Philippe Toussaint, whose reputations are steadily growing, and others,

such as Colette, Michel Tournier, J. M. G. Le Clézio, Marguerite Duras, and Patrick Modiano who have had a significant impact on twentieth-century literature. The idea that one has to manufacture a great new talent apparently just to round off the century, or that Houellebecq, the author of two novels, is the one, simply makes no sense.

The notion of somehow creating a "school" around Houellebecq and several other young writers is similarly overwrought. Schools tend to be invented by academics or publishers; in the former instance to provide neat classifications for literary history and clearer focuses for articles, and in the latter for marketing purposes. Schools do, however, confer a certain prestige. The "école de Minuit" (which was not Minuit's invention) excited great interest in the universities and the press, and briefly made the French novel the most prominent in Europe. In this respect Frédéric Badré's decision to call Houellebecq a "post-naturaliste" might also reflect a hankering after an intellectual dominance that France no longer possesses, but arguably did have in the latter portion of the nineteenth century. Nevertheless, linking Houellebecq with Zola as a novelist is as limiting and misleading as suggesting, as has been done, that Céline and Houellebecq share significantly similar social views. Such comparisons tell little about Houellebecq's fiction, or the paths of development it may take, and nothing about his politics.

And finally, what about the novel called *Les Particules élémentaires*? Anyone interested in contemporary fiction will want to read it; not because of the controversy surrounding and enriching the best-selling author, but because it is a subtle, many-layered text that confronts many of the social issues affecting France in the last fifty years. The characters, by their thoughts and acts, take positions concerning the Generation of '68, the New Age Sensibility, the potential and dangers of contemporary scientific discoveries, and the changing moral standards in the contemporary world. Ultimately the novel poses the question of how or if literature will be able to reflect and evaluate all this. *Les Particules élémentaires* marks a major advance over Houellebecq's first one; whatever his personal views on a variety of issues, as a novelist he displays a talent that continues to grow from one book to another. He is an author who at this juncture does not need to be decried or proclaimed. Rather, Michel Houellebecq is a writer to be watched.

Notes

1. For those unfamiliar with the storyline of *Les Particules élémentaires,* Michel and Boris are two half-brothers whose mother's interest in every new trend in life-styles has exposed them to many of the twentieth century's fads. As adults they move in very different directions. Boris seizes upon the sexual

liberation of May '68, and passes from one woman and one New Age movement to another. He eventually becomes physically and emotionally exhausted and winds up in an institution. Michel is the opposite. A scientist and intellectual he has almost no affect. At the novel's end he has left France for Ireland where he clones human beings deprived of emotion.

2. I would like to thank Professors Véronique Anover, Ilse Krumschmidt, and Manuela Malakooti for their help in preparing this essay.

Works Cited

Amette, Jacques-Pierre. *L'Homme du silence*. Paris: Seuil, 1999.

Badré, Frédéric. "La Nouvelle Tendance en littérature." *Le Monde* 3 octobre 1998: 14.

Bober, Robert. *Berg et Beck*. Paris: P.O.L., 1999.

Bott, François. *Les Etés de la vie*. Paris: L'Arpenteur, 1999.

Chatrier, Jean-Philippe. *Les Deux Moitiés du ciel*. Paris: Laffont, 1999.

Desbiolles, Maryline. *Anchise*. Paris: Seuil, 1999.

Desbordes, Michèle. *La Demande*. Paris: Verdier, 1999.

de Swarte, Vincent. *Requiem pour un sauvage*. Paris: Pauvert, 1999.

Dubertret, Marianne. *Un Faux Frére*. Paris: Balland, 1999.

Duchâtel, Eric et Philippe Postel. *Pandore ou l'ouvre-boîte*. Paris: Denoël, 1999.

Duchatelet, Christophe et d'autres éditeurs (*Perpendiculaire*). "Houellebecq et l'ère du flou." *Le Monde* 10 octobre 1998: 16.

Dustan, Guillaume. *Nicholas Pages*. Paris: Balland, 1999.

Echenoz, Jean. *Je m'en vais*. Paris: Minuit, 1999.

Féret-Fleury, Christine. *Les Vagues sont douces comme des tigres*. Paris: Arléa, 1999.

Fermine, Maxence. *Neige*. Paris: Arléa, 1999.

Fleischer, Alain. *La Femme qui avait deux bouches*. Paris: Seuil, 1999.

Gardel, Louis. *Grand Seigneur*. Paris: Seuil, 1999.

Gran, Iegor. *Acné festival*. Paris: P.O.L., 1999.

———. *Ipso Facto*. Paris: P.O.L., 1998.

Halter, Mark. *Les Mystères de Jérusalem*. Paris: Laffont, 1999.

Houellebecq, Michel. *Extension du domaine de la lutte*. Paris: J'ai lu, 1994.

———. *Interventions*. Paris: Flammarion, 1998.

———. "Michel Houellebecq répond à *Perpendiculaire*." *Le Monde* 18 septembre 1998: 10.

———. *Les Particules élémentaires*. Paris: Flammarion, 1998.

Huet, Frédéric. *Papa a tort*. Paris: Balland, 1999.

Jean, Marion. *Trouée*. Paris: Balland, 1999.

Jeannet, Frédéric-Yves et al., éds. *Les Inrockuptibles Onze*. Paris: Grasset, 1999.

Kaplan, Leslie. *Le Psychanalyste*. Paris: P.O.L., 1999.

Kéchichian, Patrick. "Des Revues pour l'été." *Le Monde* 10 juillet 1998: 8.

Kervéan, Jean-François. *Vingt Fois toi et moi*. Paris: Pauvert, 1999.

Lambron, Marc. *1941*. Paris: Grasset, 1999.

Ligier, Christian. *La Nuit de Faraman*. Paris: Laffont, 1999.

Lindon, Mathieu. *Le Procès de Jean-Marie Le Pen*. Paris: P.O.L. 1999.

Massat, Alice. *Le Ministère de l'intérieur*. Paris: Denoël, 1999.

Najjar, Alexandre. *L'Ecole de la guerre*. Paris: Balland, 1999.

Noguez, Dominique. "La Rage de ne pas lire." *Le Monde* 29 octobre 1998: 1.

———. "Le Style de Michel Houellebecq." *Atelier du Roman* juin 1999: 17-22.

Nobécourt, Lorette. *La Conversation*. Paris: Grasset, 1999.

Nothomb, Amélie. *Stupeur et tremblements*. Paris: Albin Michel, 1999.

Oster, Christian. *Mon Grand Appartement*. Paris: Minuit, 1999.

Pages, Nicolas. *Je mange un œuf*. Paris: Balland, 1999.

Pennac, Daniel. *Aux fruits de la passion*. Paris: Gallimard, 1999.

Peuchmaurd, Jacques, éd. *L'Or du temps*. Paris: Laffont, 1999.

Picouly, Daniel. *L'Enfant léopard*. Paris: Grasset, 1999.

Richaud, Frédéric. *Monsieur le jardinier*. Paris: Grasset, 1999.

Rio, Michel. *Morgane*. Paris: Seuil, 1999.

Robert-Guédon, Danielle. *Le Grand Abattoir.* Paris: Balland, 1999.

Rolin, Olivier. *Méroé.* Paris: Seuil, 1999.

Rufin, Jean-Christophe. *Causes perdues.* Paris: Gallimard, 1999.

Savigneau, Josyane. "*La Nouvelle Revue Française* devient trimestrielle." *Le Monde* 8 janvier 1999: 8.

Sportès, Morgan. *Rue du Japon, Paris.* Paris: Seuil, 1999.

Tillinac, Denis, directeur. *Atelier du Roman* juin 1999: 17-82. (Pages devoted to *Les Particules élémentaires*)

Van Reuterghen, Marion. "Le Procès Houellebecq." *Le Monde* 8-9 novembre 1998: 9-10.

Vargas, Fred. *L'Homme à l'envers.* Paris: Viviane Hamy, 1999.

Vautrin, Jean. *Le Cri du peuple.* Paris: Grasset, 1999.

Volodine, Antoine. *Des Anges mineurs.* Paris: Seuil, 1999.

Lee Smith (essay date October 2000)

SOURCE: Smith, Lee. "Otherwise Engaged." *Artforum* 39, no. 2 (October 2000): 45.

[*In the following essay, Smith discusses the opposing philosophical perspectives of Houellebecq and Jean-Paul Sartre and the negative reaction of leftist French intellectuals to* The Elementary Particles, *which was regarded as an assault on the ideals of individual freedom.*]

One of the more telling recent developments in French cultural life has been the sudden nostalgia for Jean-Paul Sartre coinciding with the twentieth anniversary of his death this year. No one really misses Sartre's ideas about "Being" or the Communist International, but a reconsideration of the place he filled in French culture has signaled a genuine EU-era cultural identity crisis. He was the last in a long line of engaged and very public intellectuals, a tradition that included, in the twentieth century alone, Zola, Malraux, Camus; if France is no longer turning out Voltaire-quality men of letters, then what is France? Or, put another way, why has the most gifted French writer in several generations, forty-one-year-old Michel Houellebecq, just come out with a pop CD?

Houellebecq is the author of the 1998 novel *Les Particules élémentaires,* a controversial bestseller in France, Germany, and Holland—scheduled to be published this month by Knopf as *The Elementary Particles*—that

highlighted a cultural fault line in France between the rising generation and the established left-intellectual elites, which is to say, the generation of '68. The book was praised extensively by the most influential cultural weekly in the country, *Les Inrockuptibles,* but was passed over for most of the major literary prizes, including the prestigious Prix Goncourt. The *soixante huitards* understood the book as a frontal assault on their most cherished ideals. That generation took to the barricades in the belief that the freedom of the individual was worth dying for; Houellebecq's characters—in effect the offspring of the '68ers—aren't persuaded it's enough to live for. Feminism, sexual liberation, freedom from religion, and the reorganization of the bourgeois family haven't made people freer or even happier, Houellebecq's novel seems to suggest, just lonelier, more depressed, and more dissatisfied with what culture has left to offer. Here's what happens after one character confesses to another her love of Brazilian dance.

> "Sophie," announced Bruno, "I could go on vacation to Brazil tomorrow. I'd look around a favela. The windows of the minibus would be bulletproof. In the morning, I'd go sightseeing. Check out eight-year-old murderers who dream of growing up to be gangsters; thirteen-year-old prostitutes dying of AIDS. I'd spend the afternoon at the beach surrounded by filthy-rich drug barons and pimps. I'm sure that in such a passionate, not to mention liberal, society I could shake off the malaise of Western civilization. You're right, Sophie: I'll go straight to a travel agent as soon as I get home."

How peculiarly French that the same generation which had reclaimed Céline's literary genius despite his anti-Semitism could fail to take the satirical elements in *The Elementary Particles* as anything more than a narrow harangue meant to undermine the political legacy of May '68. The book's intelligence is certainly critical, but it is also comprehensive and precise, which, together with its narrative force, is what makes *The Elementary Particles* a major achievement in contemporary fiction. It tells the story of two half brothers—Bruno, a writer, and Michel, a scientist—who muddle their way through their broken lives, alternately seeking and avoiding relationships with family and lovers, biding their time at work, and touring the French countryside and sex resorts, until they reach, quite literally, the end of man. Michel's work is responsible for a new, genetically engineered species of humans, "asexual and immortal, a species which had outgrown individuality, individuation and progress."

Houellebecq began his writing career as a poet, and his recently released album, *Présence humaine,* his first, is best seen as an extension of his poetry. The instrumental work here sounds a lot like the pretechno synthesizer stuff that passed for French rock before MC Solaar, Air, and DJ Dimitri. Though Houellebecq doesn't play an instrument himself, he handles the lyrics, speaking (not singing) in a voice that registers somewhere around Leonard Cohen's bass. If the music is pretty insipid, the lyrics, drawn from the several volumes of Houellebecq's poetry, are not half bad. This is from the seventh and longest song on the album, **"Plein été"**: "Je suis le chien blessé, le technicien de surface / Et je suis la bouée qui soutient l'enfant mort." ("I'm the wounded dog, the technician of surface / And I'm the life preserver propping up the dead child.") In contemporary French poetry, this sort of raw imagery passes for direct statement. It's as rare as rhyming quatrains, which Houellebecq also uses. To find it, you have to go back to Baudelaire, the master technician of surface.

Indeed, if Sartre's politically engaged intellectual constitutes one tradition in French letters, Baudelaire's darker, more solitary poet works the other. Skeptical of petitions to man's rational side, Baudelaire is hardly anyone's idea of an engaged intellectual, and Houellebecq is at least as suspicious. "I don't believe in democracy or rational choices," he told me recently. "I'm not interested in freedom. It's not a clear concept. Freedom is a mystery that sometimes happens to people."

If the legacy of May '68, with its universalist claims to individual freedom, has really amounted to nothing more than dysfunctional families, psychotropic drugs, and swingers' clubs (*changistes*), then maybe France really does need a Sartre to lead it out of the darkness. Houellebecq, for his part, imagines France's EU nightmare—a species without individuation, without nation. Despite his clear lack of interest in the task, Houellebecq, it seems, will once again be asked to play the engaged intellectual. With the Human Genome Project now reaping Neil Armstrong-size headlines across the world, *The Elementary Particles,* will no doubt get caught up in the inevitable swirl of debates on the ethics of genetic engineering. What sorts of limits should we set on genetic manipulation? Shouldn't mankind press ahead with scientific progress and leave the philosophy till later? "I think all my books have ethical lessons," says Houellebecq. "But ethical lessons are so simple, aren't they?" It's the sort of moment Sartre lived for.

Merle Rubin (review date 2 November 2000)

SOURCE: Rubin, Merle. "A Perfect Genetic Future." *Christian Science Monitor* 92, no. 240 (2 November 2000): 21.

[*In the following review, Rubin asserts that* The Elementary Particles *functions as a provocative "jeremiad" but finds flaws in its implausible premise and dialogue.*]

A literary sensation in France, hailed as a great novel by critics in the rest of Europe, Michel Houellebecq's *The Elementary Particles* is an odd mixture of penetrating insight and old-fashioned ineptitude.

Although critics have compared its author to Balzac, Beckett, and Camus, it is no more a literary masterpiece than Aldous Huxley's *Brave New World.* Like Huxley's social prophecy, this is a novel that tackles big, life-changing ideas. But unlike Huxley's masterfully conceived vision of a prosperous, blandly hedonistic world governed by genetic and social engineering, the vision of the future that Houellebecq presents is poorly conceived: so full of holes, you could drive several small planets through them.

The unknown narrator tells the story from the perspective of a transcendently different "new world order" that has come about in the 21st century: "What men considered a dream, perfect but remote, / We take for granted as the simplest of things," declares an unidentified poet in the book's prologue. In this respect, Houellebecq's approach is rather like Peter Ackroyd's in *The Plato Papers.* But if both books share a vision of a harried, neurotic, materialistic world giving way to a joyous spiritual realm, Houellebecq's prose has none of the poetry of Ackroyd's.

Houellebecq gives us a pair of dissimilar half-brothers, born in 1956 and 1958, to a promiscuous, proto-hippie mother who consigned each of them to the care of a different grandmother. Bruno, the older, is a sad and typical child of his era: obsessed with sex, but not attractive or charismatic enough to rate very high in the sexual marketplace. Michel, the younger, has no sex drive, but a brilliant and original scientific mind that enables him to devise a plan for a new race of genetically engineered asexual beings who will replace humans.

The specifics of Michel's plan are not disclosed until the final pages of the book, and are rather anticlimactic. In order to accept the premise that it is possible to create a new race of beings who will be morally as well as physically improved to the point of perfection by genetic engineering, it would be necessary to believe that one's genetic makeup totally determines what kind of person one will be. It also presumes that an ability to genetically produce seemingly desirable qualities of temperament or disposition—say, calmness rather than excitability, pliability rather than stubbornness—is tantamount to creating morally superior people.

The bulk of the book—and its strength—lies in its scathing jeremiad against contemporary society. The culmination of the so-called sexual liberation of the 1960s, Houellebecq argues, is a society without moral values of any kind: "Actionists, beatniks, hippies and serial killers were all pure libertarians who advanced the rights of the individual against social norms and against what they believed to be the hypocrisy of morality, sentiment, justice, and pity. . . . Having exhausted the possibilities of sexual pleasure, it was reasonable that individuals . . . should turn their attentions to the wider pleasures of cruelty." These, indeed, are words spoken by Bruno, the brother who is himself immersed in the pursuit of sexual satisfaction, and who can speak first-hand of the loneliness and emptiness that are its end results.

The story, filled with graphic portrayals of sexual excess, is not for the squeamish. But unlike some writers, Houellebecq succeeds in making it seem repellent, chilly, and sad rather than titillating. The dialogue, however, is almost comically awkward: When the brothers get together to talk, they sound as if they are reading aloud from polemical articles.

In many ways more manifesto than novel, *The Elementary Particles* is full of provocative ideas, powerfully expressed. But a great work of literature? Not likely. A book that people should read? Yes.

Paul Berman (review date 20 November 2000)

SOURCE: Berman, Paul. "Depressive Lucidity." *New Republic* 223, no. 21 (20 November 2000): 25-9.

[*In the following review, Berman explores Houellebecq's dark, unsavory cynicism and social criticism in* The Elementary Particles, *noting similarities with Honoré de Balzac's reactionary perspective.*]

The narrator of Michel Houellebecq's first novel, *Extension du domaine de la lutte,* or *Extension of the Field of Struggle,* visits a shrink, who diagnoses him with a grim-sounding condition called "depressive lucidity." In Houellebecq's second novel, *The Elementary Particles*—the book that has aroused all kinds of controversies in France in the last couple of years, and has sold hundreds of thousands of copies, and is bound to arouse its share of American controversies, too—a main character likewise visits a shrink. The same diagnosis is proposed: "depressive lucidity." There is a pattern here. Now that I have read three volumes of Houellebecq's poetry, too, plus a collection of essays and prose poems, and have listened to his CD and his rock band, I feel confident in diagnosing "depressive lucidity" as the dominant condition afflicting whole aspects of this man's very strange writings and commentaries.

Depression does not make for an attractive or even a natural theme for a novel. The narrator of *Extension du domaine de la lutte* is a hopelessly isolated sad-sack computer technician in Paris who has no girlfriends, no friends except for an unhappy priest, no congenial workmates, no enthusiasm for his job, and no ability to savor anything that comes his way. The computer company sends him on a business trip to Rouen, where he sits in a cafe. A scary German dog ruins the atmosphere. A wedding procession passes through the street. The bride and groom turn out to be old and homely. The narrator orders a pizza. It tastes bad. He attends a porno movie. The hall is full of disgusting, masturbating exhibitionists. He falls ill. No one gives a damn about getting him to the hospital.

Life is narrow, dark, and acrid. And in *The Elementary Particles* things only get worse, unto the creepiest of sci-fi calamities. The novel's two protagonists, Michel and Bruno, half-brothers, grow from childhood into middle age with opposite personalities, neither of which proves to be even remotely adapted to the rigors of life. Michel, a timid scientific nerd, finds no pleasure in sex, is barely capable of love, and customarily lives in isolation. Bruno, an abrasive literary screwball, is a man who, when his mental state sags, masturbates in public, and, when his mental state recovers a bit, finds a fleeting pleasure by hanging out in sex clubs, in spite of how bad he feels about the modest size of his penis.

People commit suicide right and left, especially women. The gates of the mental institution are always yawning open. Only the weakest of threads ties one person to the next. You have to feel sorry for everyone involved, except for the people who are too detestable for pity. And you do have to wonder how even the most talented of writers could possibly work up ingredients as thin as these into a novel of any tastiness or texture. Novelists have lavished riches of literary skill on the topic of extreme economic impoverishment, but what can be done with extreme impoverishment in the realm of emotion? Every man is a millionaire in his emotions, Isaac Bashevis Singer said. But not in the novels of Michel Houellebecq. He himself acknowledges the difficulty in *Extension du domaine de la lutte*: "This progressive effacement of human relations is not without posing certain problems for the novel."

But then, in Houellebecq's case, there is also the other half of his diagnosed depression, the "lucidity." The lucidity in question turns out to be mostly abstract—the sort of crisp clarity in reasoning that is taught in philosophy classes. He theorizes on scientific and metaphysical themes—on the rarity and the unavoidability of mutation in chemicals and in organic life. He theorizes on history. He adopts, in *The Elementary Particles,* a doctrine out of Auguste Comte, and in good Comtean fashion sketches the stages of development which mankind has had to traverse, from primitive times through Christianity to the present epoch, with intimations of the catastrophic future.

He theorizes on the rise of individualism and on its sorry meaning for sex, love, and truth. You might wonder if an analytic lucidity on airy topics such as those can possibly suit a novel any better than does his bleak landscape of depressed isolated consciousness. For what is the purpose in writing novels? Isn't it to discover a middle terrain between the low-grounds of lonely, individual awareness and the heights of pure abstraction? Shouldn't a novel go tramping instead through the leafy trails of social existence, where people are husbands and wives and brothers and friends and enemies? Where life is verdant with facts and relations? But then, as I will not be the first to observe, the novel can do many things, and in the area of lucid theorizing Houellebecq can call on some noble precedents.

His character Bruno in *The Elementary Particles* composes a couple of outrageous racist essays about the inferiority of black men, "animals with big cocks and small reptilian brains," and sends the essays to a famous novelist in Paris—who, in a bit of mischief, Houellebecq has named "Philippe Sollers," though the real Sollers cannot be held accountable for anything that Houellebecq has done to him. The famous novelist responds warmly by saying to Bruno, "You're a real reactionary, that's good. All the great writers were reactionaries: Balzac, Baudelaire, Flaubert, Dostoevsky." That is a nice set of names, and listing them shows some gumption on Houellebecq's part, as a budding literary reactionary himself. Céline, too, would appear to be one of his ancestors, due to his bitterness and self-loathing (and his loathing for entire races of other people).

But in the matter of analytic lucidity, the name that leaps up from the reactionary list is surely Balzac's. I say Balzac partly because, in Houellebecq's volume of essays and prose poems, *Rester vivant,* or *Staying Alive,* he offers a compact and mildly rueful defense of *The Human Comedy*—of the fantastic energy in Balzac's characters, and the realism within Balzac's lack of realism. "After all," says Houellebecq, "in life there remain real elements of melodrama. Above all, in the life of other people, elsewhere." But mostly Balzac seems to me apposite because—as Houellebecq himself has pointed out in the oddly titled magazine *Les Inrockuptibles,* a hip publication—Balzac made a habit of theorizing lucidly on any number of themes, and doing it in a cool, detached style, like a scientist.

Balzac's theorizing led him to divide the whole of *The Human Comedy* into dry-sounding units called "Studies"—such as "Philosophical Studies"—quite as if he had written a series of research papers instead of novels. And what did Balzac say in those scientifically lucid reveries? In one of his "Philosophical Studies," a tale called "The Search for the Absolute" (which Houellebecq doesn't mention in anything of his that I have

read, but which seems to me loosely connected to *The Elementary Particles*), Balzac manages to speculate on a range of matters—from the diminishing variety of European culture and its reflection in architecture (a Houellebecqian theme), to the superior desirability of women with physical deformities, and onward to the deepest chemical elements of all existence and the possibility of finding our way, by means of scientific experiment, to the inmost secrets of life and the universe.

And none of that takes away from Balzac's art. On the contrary, you follow his philosophizing, and you feel that you are in contact with the manias of the writer himself, and not just those of his characters. You feel the intensity that drove him forward. In Balzac's case, that intensity was a doctrine about amorous passion. He wanted to postulate a world of untrammeled passion, especially the passion of husbands and wives for each other in good Catholic union, though he was willing to consider other combinations, too. He wanted to show that untrammeled passion is always being obstructed by some odious or irritating force.

And so he looked around, and set out to catalogue all the cheapening and obstructive aspects of the life of his time—to show us how awful are the greedy peasants, and how grotesque are the appalling Jews who have come to participate in French society, and how horrible are the workings of crass social climbing in an ambition-addled place like bourgeois Paris, not to mention in the provinces, and how dreadful are the uppity women who have lost their traditional sense of a woman's properly subservient role. He wanted to say, fie upon those many horrid modern things, fie upon the French life of his own times, fie upon modernity!

He wanted to show that, in some other era, emotions were purer and the flames of passion leaped higher. It was in earlier times, in the years before the French Revolution—in the age before that most terrible of crimes took place, the beheading of the king. For if there was any one act that tamped down the natural ardor between men and women, Balzac wanted to insist, it was the tragic decapitation of Louis XVI. Regicide undid the proper hierarchy of French society, and therefore of family life. Regicide ruined a civilization in which men were men and women were women—a civilization in which women trembled in adoration and even in fear of their haughty husbands, and men responded with manly confidence and zeal, and passion burned white. Balzac was a reactionary, in sum, because he was a Romantic.

Houellebecq's lucidity and scientific tone owe quite a bit to that sort of fantasizing, in an up-to-date version. Houellebecq knows that his characters are pathetic losers. He despises them. Bruno in *The Elementary Particles* becomes a high school teacher and exposes himself to one of his students, an act than which nothing could be more contemptible. But Houellebecq has a theory of how his characters have ended up in such a sorry pass. It is owing to the dreadful evolution of modern life. Things used to be better, years ago—in the age of aristocracy and romantic love.

In the aristocratic age, he says, "a man would feel a certain affection for his spouse—though not before she'd borne his children, made a home for them, cooked, cleaned and proved herself in the bedroom." Men were faithful. They looked to their children to carry on the family name and honor. The age of romantic love was especially wonderful. Houellebecq is a brave writer, normally speaking, and shows a studied indifference to how anyone will receive him. *The New York Times Magazine* sent a reporter his way, and he does seem to have enjoyed making an ass of himself. But for some reason, in his novels he affirms his points about aristocracy and romantic love in a timid spirit, as if even he, the earnest reactionary, cannot help fretting about looking silly.

On the delicate topic of aristocracy, Houellebecq's narrator affirms that, despite the terrible things that you may have heard about inequality and oppression under feudal regimes, the humble social classes in those days were by no means denied access to the aristocracy's noble doctrine of family life: "Merchants, craftsmen and peasants also bought into the idea." The narrator concedes that, in regard to romantic love, the relation between the sexes has not always achieved an ideal balance. Arranged marriages do not attract his admiration. And when did the custom of arranging marriages come to an end? It was in the 1950s. Only, a pity, the end of arranged marriages was followed all too quickly by the onslaught of sexual liberation. And so, as a result, "it would be fair to say that the late 1950s and early 1960s were the 'golden age of romantic love'—a time we remember today through the songs of Jean Ferrat and early Françoise Hardy."

In contrast to Balzac, who postulated as his Good Old Days the many centuries of Ancien Régime before the tragic beheading of 1793, Houellebecq's Good Old Days of aristocracy and romantic love appear to have lasted about five years, from circa 1958, which happens to be the year of his own birth, to 1963 or thereabouts. He does not mean to be funny about this. But it strikes me that hardly anyone today seems capable of laying out a properly reactionary yearning for times past without hitting a slightly ridiculous note. How else to explain the comic tone, wholly unintended, that you find in a certain kind of conservative magazine today, in America as much as in France—the Allan Bloom problem, you might call it, where the author means to be a terrible scourge, only to end up thumping an indignant pinky on the table?

Houellebecq's absurdity will have to be excused, then. He does mean to be serious. And with his several ideas about aristocracy and romantic love in place, he tears into his attack. He says that modern science may have solved the problems of material well-being, but material success has only unleashed a new problem. It has unleashed the modern individual, who is driven by the fear of death and by a sense of self to assert a final impulse: "the need to feel superior to the others." The need comes out as personal competition for money and especially for sex—even though you might have supposed that, under conditions of material plenty, economic and sexual competition would, both of them, have been rendered pointless. But not at all. The knives are out.

Houellebecq, in short, is an anti-liberal. He makes the kind of argument that any number of philosophers and social critics have been making in France for fifty years now. He thinks the bonds of community have snapped. He thinks the sense of morality and good judgment has evaporated, and that people have been left in a wretched isolation, blind to the sources of their unhappiness. And what are those sources? Here Houellebecq sets himself apart. The French Marxists of long ago used to blame capitalism, and the post-structuralists used to blame the anonymous eternal structures of anthropology, and more recently a certain kind of pessimistic French liberal has chosen to blame the whole thrust of world history. *Somebody* has to be at fault. Houellebecq blames the radicals of the '60s.

He tells us that Michel and Bruno, the nerd and the sex maniac in **The Elementary Particles,** are the sons of Janine, an enthusiastic sex cultist of the 1950s and 1960s. Janine lived the ideas that came filtering into Europe from the wilder reaches of California and Esalen and the communalism of Aldous Huxley. She was friskily promiscuous in the name of spiritual depth, and took no concern for her little boys, who were brought up by their grandmothers. And this merry irresponsibility of hers, apart from being dreadful for her own children, played its part in the growth of a horrendous murder cult, in the style of Charles Manson, something truly demonic. So the brothers are victims. They grow up as wounded souls. They are the products of hippie madness. And they are furious at their mother. She lies on her deathbed, and Bruno not very prettily calls her an old whore.

On the other hand, when Houellebecq briefly awards to Bruno, the great masturbator, some small experience of love and happiness, the angel in Bruno's life turns out to be a tender hearted, middle-aged, hippie earth-mother, who responds to his troubles by saying things like, "I know what we should do. . . . We should go and have an orgy on the nudist beach at the Cap d'Agde. You get a lot of Dutch nurses and German businessmen there. . . . You need a holiday too, and you need to get off with a lot of different women." So Bruno ends up with a girl just like dear old Mom, whose spirit of sexual adventure is revealed to have its nurturing side, after all.

This is the little twist that makes Houellebecq a novelist and not a pamphleteer. But then, he does have his ideas, and the hippie earth-mother suffers a medical catastrophe in the course of getting gang-banged, and suicide is, as always, the result. So the accusatory finger remains in place, not just in *The Elementary Particles* but in nearly everything I have read by Houellebecq. He wants to show that people like dear old Mom paved the way for the hippie masses of the 1960s and 1970s. And the hippies, together with the political radicals, wreaked the horrors of modern individualism upon mankind. They did it by breaking up the old system of moral restraints and the heritage of aristocracy and romantic love, in the name of their hopeless ideal of egalitarian love and plenty for all.

Taken as a work of social criticism, then, *The Elementary Particles,* together with Houellebecq's other writings, offers a variation on what in America, at least, has become a well-known accusation. It is the conservative accusation against the '60s generation, the complaint that, in the name of high-minded ideals, the radicals of some thirty years ago ripped out the guts of simple morality, and the normal functionings of society have been a shambles ever since. This aspect of *The Elementary Particles* (together with the sex-club scenes, of course) accounts for most of the sensation that Houellebecq has made in France. Only, in Houellebecq's variation, the accusation goes even further than what the American conservatives have proposed. This is because, in France, the '60s generation is blamed for undermining sexual morality, general morality, social hierarchy, home, church, and school. And it is blamed for advocating leftist economic ideas.

But most of all it is blamed for the non-leftist market ideas of the 1980s. That decade may have been the right-wing Age of Reagan in the United States, but it was also the left-wing Age of Mitterrand in France, under a socialist government full of veterans of the student barricades of twenty years before; and in both countries, market values and consumer merchandising began to triumph over older, venerated ideas about social life. In the United States, the '60s generation is blamed for being anti-American, but in France the same generation is blamed for being "insufficiently" anti-American—sometimes even for demonstrating an unseemly appreciation for the American popular arts and for America's spirit of innovation. In France, nobody has idolized California's Silicon Valley more than the aging heroes of 1968.

And so, when Houellebecq rails against the '60s generation in France, he is making a larger, more general complaint than America's tub-thumping neoconserva-

tives like to make about the left-wing radicals in the United States. He is complaining about the whole trend of modern life, not just a single tendency. He is complaining about the triumph of the market. And he is complaining about America and its influence.

He resents the evil tone of America's feminists and of feminism generally. He resents the shadow cast by America's demonic hippies on their French counterparts. He attributes the sexual revolution in France to America's popular arts, not just from the evil '60s and '70s. In the course of his two novels he draws a distinction between the malign influence of Marilyn Monroe and that of Brigitte Bardot, who, for reasons that I cannot quite follow, strikes Houellebecq as rather more sympathetic. Janine, the evil mother, goes so far as to rename herself Jane, just to emphasize the American connection.

He complains about the rise of uniformity, which strikes him as an American trait (just as it struck Balzac as a French trait). He blames the Americans for his own obsession with the size of his penis, since the habit of measuring penises derives, in his imagining, from the manias of American pornography, which derive from what he takes to be the American mania for measuring and classifying all things. (America, land of Descartes.) He blames America for his own bad experiences on the internet. You have to laugh at Houellebecq's account, in *Rester vivant,* of how unhappy he has been, looking for sex partners on the Internet:

> Finally, ANNIE doesn't respond any more; has she attained the enchanted summits of mutual desire? So much the better for her, so much the better for her. I settle for SANDRA W. and we begin to chat gently. Everything goes well. Everything goes very well. Packets of numeralized information circulate through the optic fibers with the speed of light. . . . All is well. I think of Albert Gore, Vice President of the United States, and the initiator of an ambitious project of a multimedia network permitting the transference of 'voice, text, data, images,' throughout the American continent. When his project is working, will I be able to hear my interlocutor? Will I be able to masturbate for her in front of a video camera?

But then, having wrapped an American flag around the cheapness of his experience, he goes on, undismayed, to borrow a few bracing and strident tones from the American accusation against the '60s, and to send them ringing through his own accusation. He likes to say that the radicalism of those satanic times dealt blows to the "Judeo-Christian" culture, which has about it the sound of an American politician. ("Judeo-Christian" wasn't Charles Maurras's idea of traditional culture, or Céline's.) In *The Elementary Particles,* Houellebecq invents a California Republican named Macmillan who has written a wild tract against hippies called, in French, *Génération Meurtre,* or *Murder Generation,* arguing that Charles Manson was the truest hippie of all, and serial murderers are the hippie legacy—all of which might bring to mind a real-life right-wing California tract of a few years ago called *Destructive Generation,* which made similarly bizarre and extravagant claims (mixed with a few good points) about the political radicals of the time. It's worth bearing in mind that Houellebecq's first book, published in 1991, was a study of the American horror writer H. P. Lovecraft. So Houellebecq, the anti-American, does have his American dimension.

And then, on top of his sillier, wild-eyed views, the novel piles on a few opinions that are positively repulsive, not just in connection to the black race and the black penis. Houellebecq seems to recoil viscerally from signs of aging in women. Nothing strikes him as more horrible than a hippie chick beginning to sag around the edges. In *The Elementary Particles,* all of these views point, at last, to a sci-fi nightmare of the future. You slowly realize that the story of Michel and Bruno has been written as some sort of formal history in the futuristic aftermath of a biological cataclysm. I will not describe the cataclysm, except to note the parallel between Michel's genetic studies in *The Elementary Particles,* in collaboration with a scientist unpronounceably named Hubczejak, and the chemical studies of Balzac's hero, Balthazar, in "The Search for the Absolute," in collaboration with a scientist named Wierzchnownia. Except that, in Balzac, the efforts of Balthazar-Wierzchnownia to get at the heart of all existence come to naught, whereas in Houellebecq the efforts of Michel-Hubczejak lead to . . . but you will have to discover that for yourself.

Balzac, being a genius, knew how to keep his theorizing and his cast of characters in proper balance, and how to keep everything aloft on ebullient clouds of enthusiasm. Houellebecq, the depressive, cannot do that. *The Elementary Particles* is an ambitious novel, filled with wild ideas on the biggest of theological and historical themes. And it is built around a complicated frame, with two protagonists and a mysterious sci-fi narrator looking back on current times from a standpoint in the future, and a few hints of Catholic mysticism thrown in, for additional confusion. But the big ideas and the complicated structure are a lot to hang on Houellebecq's thin and saturnine characters. So the novel does end up as something of a pamphlet, too ponderous in its ideas and theories to succeed fully as a novel, too cranky to take seriously as a pamphlet. The translation by Frank Wynne is fluent and natural-sounding, though I notice that Wynne has now and then clouded the clarity of the cranky ideas. *Extension du domaine de la lutte,* which appeared in 1994, is a much less ambitious book—a thin novel, that only hints at larger thoughts. But the smaller ambitions are more neatly packaged.

There is something original about Houellebecq, though, even at his worst. It is obvious enough in the novels,

and in the poetry and everything else he does, too. You might suppose that, with his sexual desperation, his rage at market societies, his hatred for his parents, and his several other bleak and bitter themes, Houellebecq's poetry would race down the page in a jagged, broken-metered rant, like the young Allen Ginsberg heading for a touchdown. But not at all. Houellebecq expresses himself in formal, even antique verse forms, with a slightly hortatory tone, rather like Victor Hugo. He is not exactly a master of technique. His ear trips him up every two or three lines. Still, you can't help marveling at how Houellebecq sticks to what are supposed to be smooth and creamy verse structures, even while heaping curses on his dying father or raging about the inequalities of love—as in his book *La poursuite du bonheur,* or *The Pursuit of Happiness*:

> Dans un ciné porno, des retraités
>   poussifs
> Contemplaient, sans y croire,
> Les ébats mal filmés de deux couples
>   lascifs;
> Il n'y avait pas d'histoire.
>
> Et voilà, me disais-je, le visage de
>   l'amour,
> L'authentique visage.
> Certains séduisants; ils séduisent
>   toujours,
> Et les autres surnagent.
>
> In a porno theater, the wheezy retirees
> Were watching, without believing,
> The badly filmed frolics of lascivious
>   couples.
> There was no story.
>
> And there, I thought, is the face of love,
> The authentic face.
> Some people seductive; they always
>   seduce,
> And the others float along.

Where you do see his best is in the prose-poems and essays. The essays are short, about the length of a one-page piece in a magazine. Some of them were written, in fact, for *Les Inrockuptibles* and other magazines. They are composed in a sullen tone, which he controls more carefully and consistently than in the novels and more gracefully than in his verse. The essays express a full-scale attitude, if not quite the whole of a personality.

He is angry. He is disenchanted. He belongs to a party, though it is not exactly a political party, not even the party of the dream-filled extreme right. He disavows any ideological affiliation of that sort, for all the satisfaction he takes in his own prejudices. "Partisanship makes for happiness, and you shouldn't be happy," he says. He belongs, instead, to the gloomy, acrid party—the party of sulphur. "You are on the side of misfortune; you are the somber party." And he expresses his sulphurous attitude forcefully, even movingly.

If the world is composed of suffering it is because the world is essentially free. Suffering is the necessary consequence of the free play of the parts of the system. You should know that, and say so.

It will not be possible for you to transform suffering into the goal. Suffering *is,* and cannot by consequence become a goal.

In the wounds that it inflicts on us, life alternates between the brutal and the insidious. Know those two forms. Practice them. Acquire a complete familiarity with them. Distinguish what separates them, and what brings them together. Many contradictions will then be resolved. Your voice will gain strength and amplitude.

Due to the characteristics of the modern epoch, love can hardly be seen anymore; but the ideal of love has not gotten smaller. Being fundamentally situated out of time, like all ideals, it cannot shrink or disappear.

Thus a particularly flagrant ideal-real discordance, source of particularly rich sufferings.

Houellebecq has not wandered into unknown territory in saying these things. But there is something new in his tone. It derives from an amazing absence in his attitude. He is not ironic. He does not hold up sixteen mirrors to admire his own attitudes from ten thousand angles. He does not laugh at himself, or snicker, or even curl his lip, except sometimes. He despises irony. He despises the notion of relative truths. "Poetry is a way of establishing definitive moral truths. You should hate liberty with all your strength. Truth is scandalous, but without it, nothing has any worth." And so he wants you to discover what is true. "Your deepest mission is to dig toward the Truth. You are the gravedigger, and the corpse." He says, "An honest and naïve vision of the world is already a masterpiece."

Houellebecq seems to me honest. He is definitely naïve. Even so, he hasn't written any masterpieces. I sincerely hope that not many people will turn to him for political and sociological insights (though they will, they will). But that tone of his, his oddly lucid whine and shriek, do get under your skin. He is not pallid, he is not a shade of himself. The man is a bit demented, but he is, recognizably, a man, and of the present moment, too.

Mark Shechner (review date November-December 2000)

SOURCE: Shechner, Mark. "The Great Emetic Novel." *New Leader* 83, no. 5 (November-December 2000): 50-1.

[*In the following review, Shechner contends that* The Elementary Particles *effectively scorns and satirizes, rather than merely moralizes, the nauseating depravity it describes.*]

Two years ago Michel Houellebecq, a seasoned provocateur, became the scourge of French literary circles with the publication of his second novel, **The Elemen-** **tary Particles.** "In France," Emily Eakin wrote this past September 10 in the *New York Times Magazine,* "Houellebecq is infamous for giving Michel, his biologist antihero, the same last name—Djerzinski—as a high-ranking Stalinist official and then defending the gesture by saying Stalin wasn't such a bad guy. After all, Houellebecq told a French magazine . . . Stalin 'killed a lot of anarchists.' His antipathy for democracy ('Liberty is equivalent to suffering,' he said on French television) has caused much hand-wringing among the intelligentsia." What are the chances of a similar *succès de scandale* in the United States? French and American readers do not usually rise to the same bait, even when a literary Stalinist is chumming the waters.

The Elementary Particles is a tale of two brothers, Bruno and Michel, who occupy opposing ends of the erotic spectrum—the stalker and the celibate, respectively. It is peppered with portentous references to continental philosophers—Kant, Comte, Nietzsche, Descartes, Marx, Pascal, Sartre, Gilles Deleuze. The Stalinist is also a philosophe. The book comes hailed as a pornotopia, yet frequently bogs down in such windy digressions as: "Remember Pascal: 'We must say summarily: This is made by figure and motion, for it is true. But to say what these are, and to compose the machine, is ridiculous. But it is useless, uncertain, and painful.' Once again he's right and Descartes is wrong." What American reader, not knowing Pascal from pasta, is going to rise up in horror at that sort of thing?

Of course, even in France, you do not make a scandal by outing Descartes; every generation has been there, done that. Rather, Houellebecq takes aim at the entire late 20th-century culture of self-fulfillment and works his way—claws and scratches his way, really—into the entrails of every cow held sacred by the cultural Left, in particular the post-Esalen, pre-Prozac, feel-good Left. Insofar as his meandering tour of therapeutic fashion touches down on both sides of the Atlantic, there will be issues indeed to rile Americans, especially those who at one time or another took the supposed healing arts of the past 40 years as comprehensive guides to the perplexed.

The half-brothers, Bruno Clément and Michel Djerzinski, are gallery exhibits of what can happen when culture gets destabilized and individuals, cut loose from tradition, sign on to cults of experience and liberation. They share a mother, Janine, whose stunning Mediterranean beauty was her passport into la rive gauche, where she danced to bebop at the Tabou with Jean-Paul Sartre. After many lovers, she married Serge Clément, a medical intern about whom Bruno would later say, "You want to know what my dad was like? Give a gorilla a mobile phone and you've got the general idea."

A modern couple, Serge and Janine find the birth of son Bruno in 1956 incompatible with their personal freedom and ship him off to his maternal grandmother in Algeria.

Janine then gets pregnant by a documentary filmmaker named Marc Djerzinski and sheds her husband as quickly as a cobra sheds a skin. Leaving that baby, Michel, with Marc, Janine then takes up with Francesco di Meola, an Italian-American who boasts of big doings in California: Ginsberg and Aldous Huxley and the Esalen Institute. Michel too will wind up with a grandmother, since Marc Djerzinski disappears on a filming trip to Tibet.

These unravelings are the opening credits of the novel, setting the stage for everything that follows. But while the book develops into a gruesome comedy of sex and fashion, we are never allowed to forget that it is at bottom about parents who love recklessly, have children thoughtlessly, and trek off in search of orgasm and satori, leaving grandma up to her derrière in diapers and dishes.

We should not, however, mistake Houellebecq's bitterness, which grinds whole movements under its heel, as anything akin to the family-values piety. Behind his diatribes against feminism, environmentalism, anarchism, Marxism, body worship, nature-worship, and New Age conversations with the Angel there smolders one raging question: Where were the mothers when their children cried?

Although Michel, who grows up to be a famed molecular biologist, gives the book its title, it is Bruno, a sexual predator, whose sufferings are seen up close. An unattractive boy, he is sent to a boarding school in Meaux where he is the "omega male" and is regularly beaten, pissed on, and sodomized. In one of the most brutal scenes in a brutal book, the prefect finds him one night "curled up on the floor of the toilet in the courtyard, naked and covered in shit." From such experiences, Bruno will be marked with self-loathing: As a young man he becomes a virtuoso of humiliation, a lonely masturbator in search of orgo-redemption, which he finds in the bodies of prostitutes or young women as ungainly as himself—one of whom will throw herself out of a window after a meeting with him.

In the 1980s, as the culture of transcendence-lite takes hold, he camps out at Lieu de Changement, "a place where the principles of self-government, respect for individual freedom and true democracy could be practiced in the 'here and now.'" All Bruno really wants to do is satisfy his sexual desires here and now and spare himself 13-hour flights to Bangkok. He succeeds, but not before being exposed to the fetishes of the leisure industry: walking on hot coals, transactional analysis, sex meditation, astrology, Egyptian tarot reading, chakra manipulation, crystal healing, Tantric Zen, sensitive Gestalt massage, rebirthing in warm water, and Siberian shamanism. The last "made a remarkable debut when, in 1991, during a long initiation in a sweat lodge fired by sacred coals, an initiate died of heart failure."

Once he finally meets an undeceived woman named Christiane, he learns the truth: that his despair is normal and that everyone in the place is filled with the same self-contempt. "Men who grow old alone have it easier than older women," Christiane tells him. "They drink cheap booze and fall asleep, their breath stinks, then they wake up and start all over again; they tend to die young. Women take tranquilizers, go to yoga classes, see a shrink; they live a lot longer and suffer a lot more."

The passionless Michel, meanwhile, cloisters himself in research, where he will eventually make breakthroughs in DNA as foundational as those of Einstein, Heisenberg and Bohr in particle physics. Beloved in his youth by the beautiful Annabelle (shades of Poe here? Of Nabokov?), he cannot respond to her, and she seeks consolation in marriages, orgies and "*liaisons dangereux.*" They meet again in their 40s for a wistful reunion, during which she becomes pregnant and aborts immediately when she is discovered to have uterine cancer.

Houellebecq has a temperamental proclivity for bleakness. Annabelle will take her own life rather than die of cancer. Christiane, Bruno's initiatrix into tenderness and partner in orgies, develops a spinal disorder and, paralyzed below the waist, throws herself down a stairwell. Francesco di Meola, who had spirited Bruno and Michel's mother off to California, turns into a maker of snuff movies whose characters are tortured and killed. This is what became of the generation of '68; this is what comes of dancing with Sartre at the Tabou.

Moral tracts can make insufferable novels. But what saves *The Elementary Particles* from being mere diatribe is its schadenfreude, the delight it takes in the monstrosity it scorns. It is a novelized cousin of tabloid pornography in that regard, a cavalcade of genitals and square-ups.

Bruno, the broken child of the sexual revolution, refuses to give up the rebellious imperatives of the self that, in his mother, had brought such misery to his life. He himself is an indifferent father to a son who is being raised by his ex-wife while he is out being a pilgrim of pleasure. The high points of his existence are the nights spent with Christiane, cruising the *echangiste* clubs of Paris, where anything goes with anyone who will go with you. It is in one of these, however, that his beloved Christiane collapses in pain while being taken from behind by a stranger.

That Michel is largely offstage in *The Elementary Particles* is a blessing. As a character he is flatter than last week's soufflé, and we gather that he exists for his contribution to the novel's weird narrative device: It is being told retrospectively from about the year 2075 by one or more of the engineered creatures who have supplanted mankind as we know it and are, it seems, the products of Michel's research. Well, no orgies for those dudes. And no readers either.

The hero of the book is Bruno, whose personal journey to the end of night causes him to end his days sedated in a clinic. It is as if Houellebecq were giving us an updated version of a degeneracy myth: poor Bruno had masturbated once too often and blown his mind. Or perhaps it was the death of his beloved Christiane (what's in a name?), who died for his sins (he had refused to care for her after she was paralyzed), that thrust him over the edge. I would have found the book truer to its pornographic premises if Bruno had emerged strengthened from his afternoons of group sex on the beaches of Languedoc and his nights at the Paris clubs, but the author, in a choice between desire and nausea, finally opted for the latter.

The Elementary Particles is nasty stuff indeed. Stalinism is only the tip of the Houellebecq iceberg. In one scene, a teenage Bruno enters his mother's bedroom one morning and kneels before her vagina; then he goes out and crushes a cat's head with a rock.

In a landmark decision that affected the fate of literature back in 1933, John M. Woolsey, United States District Judge for the Southern District of New York, declared that while "the effect of *Ulysses* on the reader undoubtedly is somewhat emetic, nowhere does it tend to be an aphrodisiac." I have often pondered the good judge's use of the word "emetic" in that decision, since I have never found *Ulysses* a book to induce vomiting. Michel Houellebecq, however, has pulled out all the stops and come away, I believe, with a modest triumph in his effort to write the great emetic novel.

Mark Lilla (essay date winter 2001)

SOURCE: Lilla, Mark. "Houellebecq's Elementary Particles." *NPQ: New Perspectives Quarterly* 18, no. 1 (winter 2001): 53-60.

[*In the following essay, Lilla discusses the French critical reaction to* The Elementary Particles *and how it relates to the era of the* fin de siecle.]

Bruno and Michel—the main characters of *The Elementary Particles*—are half-brothers but did not meet until their teens. Their mother, Janine, abandoned them when they were infants, dropping them into the laps of aging grandparents. A beautiful French girl, she was too busy living her own life to be bothered with husband or children. In the late Fifties she could be seen on the

Riviera running with the crowd made famous by the films of Roger Vadim and Brigitte Bardot. In the early Sixties she was still in the avant-garde, having abandoned St. Tropez to follow a guru to California, where she changed her name to Jane. Between their abandonment and her death the sons hardly saw her.

When we meet them in their 40s Bruno and Michel are still suffering from this trauma. Bruno, the elder one, was packed off at an early age to a French boarding school where he suffered all the humiliations of *Young Torless*—beatings, torture, rape—at the hands of older students; this being the Sixties, order and discipline had completely evaporated. Bruno became a sexual obsessive, overwhelmed by feelings of physical inadequacy that were only intensified in the promiscuous atmosphere of the Seventies: masturbation, prostitutes, pornography, marriage, divorce, nudist colonies, swingers' clubs. He lives in a state of sexual frenzy that fails to mask an insatiable need for love. He finally finds it one night while being fellated in a jacuzzi under the stars by a woman whose face he cannot see. They become a couple but their happiness is short-lived. The woman suffers from a degenerative bone condition and during an orgy her back breaks, leaving her a paraplegic. Within months she commits suicide and Bruno checks himself into a psychiatric hospital, never to emerge.

Michel, the younger brother, copes by checking out of the new sexual order and withdrawing into himself. He becomes a biologist working in the then young field of genetic engineering, and although he reaches the pinnacle of professional success in Paris he derives no real pleasure from his work and eventually abandons it. He lives alone and has no one to love; the days pass, then the seasons, but nothing happens. Then, quite by chance, he runs into a woman with whom he has had a furtive adolescent relationship. At the time she loved him but he found it impossible to respond, so she eventually left. In the Seventies she got pregnant by the son of Jane's California guru, had an abortion and spent the next two decades in fruitless search for a man who would stay with her. She wants to seduce Michel and succeeds, after a fashion, but it is soon clear that both of them are shell shocked and no longer able to love. Still, she wants a child and Michel agrees to try. She does get pregnant but doctors discover she is rotten with cancer and must abort it. Unable to face the prospect of grueling radiation therapy with little hope of success, she kills herself. Michel oversees the cremation, then leaves France permanently for Ireland, where he devotes himself to quasi-mystical, quasi-scientific speculations about biology, technology and human nature. He then disappears without a trace.

As one reads a summary of Michel Houellebecq's *The Elementary Particles,* one's heart sinks under the weight of *deja vu.* The Sixties, sex and drugs, pop culture, divorce, ephemeral love—thanks to Philip Roth, Jay McInerney, *Forrest Gump* and countless other writers and movies, we have had our noses rubbed in all of this many times before. Can any of it have escaped our attention? One would think not.

Yet to just about everyone's surprise, **The Elementary Particles** provoked an enormous storm when it was published in Paris in 1998. Michel Houellebecq had already acquired a small but devoted following among the young after the publication of his short novel *Extension du domaine de la lutte* (*Extension of the Domain of the Struggle,* 1994), which has recently been translated under the unfortunate title **Whatever.** I first heard about **The Elementary Particles** from several French friends who had the book pressed upon them by their children, and these parents were puzzled that it struck such a deep chord with adolescents. The book quickly sold hundreds of thousands of copies and the author found himself under attack as nihilistic and worse from every possible political and literary quarter, including that of former friends with whom he had started a review, *Perpendiculaire,* from whose board he was purged. I cannot think of another French novel over the past two decades that has generated this much interest, debate and animosity. Yet whenever the French talk about Houellebecq, I always feel certain that they mean something else.

* * *

The French *fin de siecle* began promptly on July 14, 1989. That day marked the bicentenary of the French Revolution, which eerily foreshadowed the collapse of the Berlin Wall and the end of the Cold War. The mood was upbeat across Europe, which watched by satellite the multimedia extravaganza put on by the French government that night on the Champs-Elysees. And it was fitting that François Mitterrand should serve as host. While as president he had responded slowly and ineptly to the breakdown of the Soviet empire in Eastern Europe, he had done more than anyone else to move France into modern Europe; he had effectively buried the French Communist Party and had made peace between the French left and liberal democracy. An important book published at the time by historians François Furet, Jacques Julliard and Pierre Rosanvallon made a convincing case that Mitterrand had bridged the cultural divide over the legacy of the French Revolution, making France into a stable centrist republic and ending the centuries-long "French exception." A new age for France, in a united Europe, seemed in the offing.

But from that day forward, nothing has gone right—or so the French seem to believe. The liberal consensus in politics and economics rubbed contrary spirits the wrong way and they began to complain of the suffocating effects of *la pensee unique.* The racist radical right, led by Jean-Marie Le Pen's National Front, refused to disappear, indeed seemed to gain strength whenever the economy took a dive. In 1992 Mitterrand submitted the Maastricht Treaty providing for European union to the French voters, fully confident of victory by a wide margin, only to find himself in a dogfight with opponents of further European integration on the right, left and republican center. The treaty was ratified by the narrowest of margins. By 1993 unemployment reached 12 percent and the Socialists lost control of the National Assembly, forcing Mitterrand to spend the last two years of his term in "cohabitation" with the Gaullists. The stale perfume of *la morosite* was everywhere.

Jacques Chirac assumed the presidency in 1995, bringing into the government a moderate right-wing majority, which tried to reform the schools and trim social benefits. The response was a series of strikes throughout the public sector, including the schools, where teachers and students marched against the government arm in arm. Out of those strikes a new movement, called "the left of the left," was born. Its intellectual wing was led by the famous sociologist Pierre Bourdieu, who publishes a review and founded a small publishing house, both named *Liber,* to militate against "neoliberalism" (the European term for unfettered capitalism), the "media" elite and cultural Americanization.

After Mitterrand died in 1996, it became clear that whatever one thought of his shady manner of governing and his personal duplicity, the French political scene had lost its last masterful *homme politique,* and it was uncertain what would become of the centrist republic. Jacques Chirac has also been forced to govern in "cohabitation" with a left-wing majority in the Assembly, which helps to maintain the center but also paralyzes it. Bold government action on all the pressing issues of the day—education, social services, crime, economic integration, the Balkans—is usually impossible. The only political gesture capable of rallying the French today appears to be the bulldozing of a McDonald's by a sheep farmer.

The truth be told, the idea of a "centrist republic" was something of a myth and not a terribly popular one. Furet and his collaborators were, in my view, absolutely right to see that the myth of the eternal French Revolution had exhausted itself and was no longer adapted to the practical demands of modern liberal democracy. They were also right to proclaim the death of the Communist myth, which since 1917 had been subtly woven into the French revolutionary one. Working-class "consciousness" disappeared in the 30 years of prosperity following World War II, and France was becoming, like its European neighbors, a society of independent citizens with bourgeois aspirations. I even think Furet was right to assert that, objectively speaking, the French have adjusted to this new social and political order rather well.

But myths are not mirrors of social reality; they are projections of aspirations, which they also reshape over time. Furet hoped that a new "republican" myth would take hold in France, one in which the modest ambitions and capacities of liberal democracy would be accepted, while the centripetal forces of individualism and capitalism would be contained through a commitment to citizenship cultivated, as in the Third Republic, by the public schools.

While this aspiration is shared by many across the political spectrum, a more powerful countermyth grew up in the Nineties. It presents the French with a horrifying dystopian vision of their future in an atomized world of disconnected individuals, spinning in space without attachments to history, the nation, family or friends. It is a world dominated by relentless technological advances that threaten all that is familiar to us, from the bioengineered food we eat to the aging of our bodies. It is, above all, a world in which love and soul have been abolished. Houellebecq's *The Elementary Particles* is the first literary monument to this myth.

* * *

A sketch of this monument can be found in Houellebecq's *Extension du domaine de la lutte,* which is a tighter work of fiction and more successfully realized. It concerns a computer programmer who works in a Dilbert-style office, as it might have been painted by Edvard Munch. Alienated workers stick to their cubicles except for lunch and office parties, where the conviviality is forced and everyone leaves depressed. The unnamed protagonist spends his weekends and evenings alone in his spartan apartment, a brutal modernist bunker surrounded by threatening public spaces. The firm is self-consciously "dynamic": its directors speak the cheerful *langue du bois* of management schools while cutting one another's throats on the way to the top. The protagonist is not the competitive type and is therefore hopelessly out of sync with his times. So he is shipped off with another employee, a fat, ugly poseur who is also failing badly in the corporate jungle, and together they make client calls in dreary provincial towns.

The protagonist is obsessed with a former girlfriend, an adept of recreational psychotherapy, who has abandoned him. He sees her as part of the "sacrificed generation" of the sexual revolution, a woman who has had so many "sexual partners" that she is incapable of love and secretly fears becoming old, ugly and alone. He has come to hate her, but even more the sexual revolution

that spawned her. So while visiting a disco in Rouen on Christmas Eve with his porcine coworker he decides to take his revenge. He persuades the frustrated young man, who gets nowhere with women, to kill a black man who just left the disco with a hot young (white) thing who has given them both the brushoff. The fool follows them to the beach, where we expect him to perform *un acte gratuit* modeled on Camus' *The Stranger,* but nothing happens. He watches the girl perform fellatio, masturbate, and then leaves. That night he dies in a car crash.

Houellebecq has a discerning eye for detail. In his best passages he reminds one of Georges Perec, especially the Perec of the masterful short novel *Les choses* (1965), which describes in exhaustive thoroughness the consumption habits of a young couple in the Sixties. Houellebecq is just as meticulous, evoking the deserted pedestrian zones in small towns at night, the stench of the fast-food stands, the repulsive tan of the well-coiffed manager on the rise, the banality of corporate slogans, the comical French obsession with vacations. But he also appears to feel that the sum of such details falls short of capturing the vertigo many of the French feel in the empty vortex of their modern lives. "This progressive effacement of human relationships is not without certain problems for the novel," he remarks in an aside. "We're a long way from *Wuthering Heights,* to say the least. The novel form is not conceived for depicting indifference or nothingness; a flatter, more terse and dreamy discourse would need to be invented."

Perec was mocking the hollowness of the new consumer society before the sexual revolution. For Houellebecq, it is sex—or, more precisely, the new relationship between economic and sexual competition—that reveals what we are today, not our consumption patterns. The irony of the title, **Extension du domaine de la lutte,** may be lost on American readers. In French it sounds like a propaganda slogan put out by radical students in 1968: Take it to the streets! But the struggle Houellebecq has in mind is not the class struggle, it is the new war of all against all that has broken out of the economic sphere and invaded every other. A long passage from the novel sums up his Big Idea:

> It's a fact, I mused to myself, that in societies like ours sex truly represents a second system of differentiation, completely independent of money; and as a system of differentiation it functions just as mercilessly. The effects of these two systems are, furthermore, strictly equivalent. Just like unrestrained economic liberalism, and for similar reasons, sexual liberalism produces phenomena of *absolute pauperization.* Some men make love every day; others five or six times in their life, or never. Some make love with dozens of women; others with none. It's what's known as "the law of the market." In an economic system where unfair dismissal is prohibited, every person more or less manages to find his place. In a sexual system where adultery is

prohibited, every person more or less manages to find their bed mate. In a totally liberal economic system certain people accumulate considerable fortunes; others stagnate in unemployment and misery. In a totally liberal sexual system certain people have a varied and exciting erotic life; others are reduced to masturbation and solitude. Economic liberalism is an extension of the domain of the struggle, its extension to all ages and all classes of society. Sexual liberalism is likewise an extension of the domain of the struggle, its extension to all ages and all classes of society. . . . Certain people win on both levels; others lose on both. Businesses fight over certain young professionals; women fight over certain young men; men fight over certain young women; the trouble and strife are considerable.

The Elementary Particles is a reworking of this idea, especially through the character of Bruno. What got it more attention than the early novel was Houellebecq's wicked sendup of the *soixante-huitards,* the student rebels of 1968 who raged against the machine of capitalism and dug up "the beach below the pavement," but who turned out to be more radical individualists than their parents and bosses. Houellebecq shares a common French interpretation of the Sixties, quite different from our own and quite refreshing. While many Americans see the Sixties as a step in the steady march of democracy—the extension of the domain of struggle, so to speak—many Frenchmen have come to see the events of 1968 as marking the triumph of a new social ideal of individualism, and the snapping of the last attachments of solidarity binding French society together. The family, the Church, the republican schools, even the Communist Party suffered a crisis of legitimacy, from which they have not recovered, in the name of the individual's right to self-determination, a right that has become the sole measure of social legitimacy. Such individualism lies at the heart of Americans' self-understanding as a people but it is a new idea in Europe and it makes the French particularly uneasy.

Houellebecq knows exactly how to play off this discomfort by insinuating the existence of a world-historical process that is smashing the complex molecules of human existence into smaller and smaller particles spinning in space. That process, he seems to believe, reached its final stage in the Sixties. In one of his unguarded essays in the collection *Rester vivant,* he recounts what it was like being a 10-year-old in 1968 and thinking something important might be happening. But he now sees that "afterward, the social machine began to turn even more rapidly, pitilessly, and May '68 only served to break the few moral rules that still served to brake its voracious operation." In this machine, everything is coordinated. The forces of neoliberal economics have succeeded in breaking down the last barriers to unfettered global competition—unions, labor laws, tariffs, subsidies, national preferences, even national currencies. (Houellebecq publicly opposed the Maastricht Treaty.)

The sexual revolution has done its part by opening the couple to permanent, relentless sexual competition, aided by feminism, which has encouraged young women to enter this and every other market, while offering solace to resentful older women made redundant. Men have reveled in their new freedom but also felt the sting of competition in the new sexual marketplace, becoming obsessed with their bodies and regressing to the oral stage of sexual development. Children now grow up with parents too selfish and harried to care for them and are abandoned in the sexual jungle to look for love at an early age. Those who succeed as adolescents become slaves as adults to a regime of dieting, exercise, antidepressants, breast augmentation, penile enhancement and liposuction, in a vain effort to maintain their competitive edge. Those who fail are given boxes of condoms in school and told to keep their chins up. You can see them in any classroom: their hair dyed, their bodies pierced to enhance their ugliness. They are lonely, depressed, self-loathing.

Had Houellebecq merely wanted to exploit all France's unconscious fears in the Nineties, he could hardly have done better than writing these two novels. But when one looks to his journalism, interviews and even poetry, it becomes apparent that he sees the world much as his characters do. This has led to some confusion in France because it makes him difficult to place politically. The literary group he helped form, and which excommunicated him, *Perpendiculaire,* had left-wing proclivities, and Houellebecq was a frequent contributor to *Les Inrockuptibles,* a slick, generation-X magazine whose political line follows that of Pierre Bourdieu. *Extension du domaine de la lutte* could be admired in those circles but *The Elementary Particles* could not. The veterans of 1968 found his mocking caricatures of them unforgivable and there are passages on race in the book that made people wince. As Bruno slides into madness he begins writing Celine-like rants about how "we envy and admire the Negro because we long to regress, like him, to our animal selves; to be animals with big cocks and small reptilian brains . . ." Houellebecq then, in a brilliant touch, has Bruno submit these pamphlets to Philippe Sollers, a slick former Maoist turned literary mandarin who makes and breaks careers in France. Sollers reads them and announces warmly, *"Vous avez du talent."*

Houellebecq can appear obsessed with miscegenation. Both novels feature black sexual athletes who provoke envious rage in white men, and many of his characters have foreign-sounding names: Janine's maiden name is Ceccaldi, Michel's father is Djerzinsky, the guru is di Meola. Is France becoming a mongrel nation? Many Frenchmen fear so, but it is this fear, not race itself, that is Houellebecq's real subject. In 1991, before he turned to writing novels, he published a short study of the American master of the gothic story, H. P. Lovecraft. Like many of Lovecraft's admirers Houellebecq considers him to be a literary genius but, unlike them, he makes no attempt to hide the fact that Lovecraft was a self-avowed racist who, for a time, supported Hitler. Houellebecq surmises that it was Lovecraft's move from Providence, Rhode Island, to New York City that transformed his genteel WASP racism into "the brutal hate of a trapped animal forced to share his cage with animals of a different, threatening species." Lovecraft, like Bruno in **The Elementary Particles,** is a racist out of misanthropic fear, a fear generated by the "machine" of modern life that knows no rules but competition and the survival of the fittest. It is thanks to the triumph of neoliberalism—economic, political, cultural, sexual— that we are all racists now.

For Houellebecq, Lovecraft is a "case." But he is also something of a visionary. His creepy stories typically revolve around a decadent, deracinated Anglo-Saxon family and its encounter with inhuman forces from another dimension that can only be entered with inhuman forces from another dimension accessed through the magic arts. Science, rather than revealing the danger, blinds us to it. His famous story "The Call of Cthulhu" begins like this:

> We live on a placid island of ignorance in the midst of black seas of infinity, and it was not meant that we should voyage far. The sciences, each straining in its own direction, have hitherto harmed us little; but some day the piecing together of dissociated knowledge will open up such terrifying vistas of reality, and of our frightful position therein, that we shall either go mad from the revelation or flee from the deadly light into the peace and safety of a new dark age.

To which Houellebecq remarks:

> Humans of the 20th century now ending, this hopeless cosmos is absolutely ours. This abject universe, where fear ripples in concentric circles out to the unnamable revelation, this universe where our only imaginable destiny is to *be crushed* and *devoured*—we recognize this absolutely as our mental universe.

There is a great deal of bogus science in **The Elementary Particles,** most of it connected to Michel's work in genetics. What Houellebecq seems to be suggesting here is that there is a subtle connection between the rise of individualism and the rise of biotechnology, the first fueling the second as we seek to reshape our natures in order better to control them. The result, though, could be a Lovecraftian horror story in which we actually succeed and are forced to encounter some horrible truth about ourselves. That seems to be the point of the prologue to the novel, which speaks of a "great metaphysical mutation" taking place, and the epilogue, a dystopian fantasy about how Michel's research finally makes possible in the 21st century the decoupling of sexuality and reproduction, preparing the way for the breeding of a perfectly satisfied, posthuman species without egos or souls.

Or is it dystopian? One of the most curious scenes in Houellebecq's curious book is a conversation between Bruno and Michel about Aldous Huxley's *Brave New World.* After a few drinks Bruno insists that it actually describes a utopia and is an accurate representation of our collective unconscious wishes:

> Everyone says that *Brave New World* is supposed to be a totalitarian nightmare, a vicious indictment of society, but that's hypocritical bullshit. *Brave New World* is our idea of heaven: genetic manipulation, sexual liberation, the war against aging, the leisure society. This is precisely the world we have tried—and so far failed—to create.

In the end, Houellebecq leaves us hanging about our future—not about its shape but about its goodness. Here, too, he is playing with an important French myth, this time that of the "end of history" and the "last man," recently revived by Francis Fukuyama. In the 1930s the Russian philosopher Alexandre Kojeve taught a famous seminar on Hegel in Paris, in which he explained how Hegel's discovery of the motor of history—the struggle for equal recognition among individuals—led to the discovery that history was about to end in what Kojeve called the "homogeneous universal state." At the political level, this state would be a set of global administrative and economic institutions run by technically competent bureaucrats free from the traditional conflicts of politics. But at the social level it would mean the disappearance of most of the human characteristics that drove history hitherto, and the cultivation of perfectly satisfied individuals living for little more than consumption, erotic satisfaction and sports.

This haunting image harks back to Nietzsche, who in *Thus Spoke Zarathustra* heaped contempt on the modern, enlightened European, calling him "the last man": a hollow-chested, thoroughly domesticated being "who makes everything small." Kojeve's syncretic vision of our post-human fate was highly influential—his students included Andre Breton, Jacques Lacan, Georges Bataille, Raymond Queneau, Maurice Merleau-Ponty, and even Raymond Aron—and it continues to make up part of the mental furniture of French intellectual life. But, as a French wag remarked to me about **The Elementary Particles,** it's not only *about* the "last man," it seems to have been written by one. Houellebecq has made the mistake of granting numerous interviews about his latest book and the more he tries to explain his ideas the less coherent they become. He has also taken to the road with a band that backs him while he reads his flat-sounding poetry, and recordings of these performances can be purchased on CD. There is now the obligatory Houellebecq website (www.multimania.com/houellebecq/) and a film based on **The Elementary Particles** is said to be underway. (The film of **Extension du domaine de la lutte** has already appeared in France.)

All this conventional self-promotion seems unfortunate. Clotted with confused theoretical speculations, *The Elementary Particles* is not a distinguished literary work; but it is a very knowing evocation of the night thoughts disturbing the slumber of the French centrist republic today. It will be interesting to see what sort of echo it has in the United States. Individualism, the collapse of authority, the breakdown of the family, pop-culture decadence, globalization, the flexible workplace, genetic engineering—we have different ways of conceiving and worrying about these problems. The American left objects to some of them, the right anguishes about others, but no one sees them all connected in the way Houellebecq does, certainly no American novelist. That may reflect our equanimity and common sense. Or it may mean that Houellebecq is on to something.

Nathan Gardels (review date winter 2001)

SOURCE: Gardels, Nathan. "Cloning: Central Planning of the 21st Century?" *NPQ: New Perspectives Quarterly* 18, no. 1 (winter 2001): 56.

[*In the following review, Gardels examines Houellebecq's depiction of global capitalism and social anomie as a precursor to genetic engineering in* The Elementary Particles.]

French novelist Michel Houellebecq's *The Elementary Particles* is a book of brutal truths about the cultural upheaval that spread across Europe and America from the 1960s through the 1970s. Unlike memoirs of the Great Proletarian Cultural Revolution in China that focus on the horrors of the time, this novel is about the personal and social consequences decades later of what we might call the Great Western Cultural Revolution.

Through the lenses of his characters Bruno and Michel, half-brothers whose mother left them to live unencumbered in California, Houellebecq ponders how liberation, sexual and otherwise, smashed not only authority and a sense of responsibility, but love itself. In the name of throwing off oppressive tradition, the protracted revolt of the 60s generation as it marched through society's institutions acted as a battering ram for the unrestrained freedom of market-mediated self-interest.

As Houellebecq sees it, by dismantling any meaningful commitment to community and others the liberatory movements of the later decades of the 20th century opened the floodgates to consumerism, allowing it to invade every aspect of life and turning all those liberated individuals into aimless atoms competing with each other for recognition. Thus the title *The Elementary Particles.*

If there are any heroes in this disturbing novel, it is Bruno's wrinkled old grandmother who unglamorously raises him with unconditional love, expecting nothing in return. She is not in the market. She just cares without calculation. Suddenly she dies and there is a terrifying emptiness.

In this critique Houellebecq shares the perspective of other French critics of totalistic capitalism from Régis Debray to Jacques Delors, who condemn American-led globalization as pushing not a market economy, but a "market society," on the rest of the world. Houellebecq's notion of free individuals as elementary particles is also similar to Pope John Paul II's view that, absent divine love and a moral order, men and women today live too often in "solitude without hope." "Bowling alone" is how the American sociologist Robert Putnam has put it.

But Houellebecq's brilliance comes in asking "what next?" He answers by imagining how our liberated civilization will mesh with the genetic revolution. It is this dark vision of posthuman history that may make Houellebecq the George Orwell of our time.

Being a French intellectual, Houellebecq sees the world in dialectical motion as phenomena turn into their opposite. The radical injustice of early capitalism gave birth to the overcompensation of totalitarian communism. Closer to his theme, the Frankfurt School critical theorists famously postulated that German fascism arose not as conventionally thought because of the authoritarian character of the paternalistic German family, but the opposite: The absence of the father from the home as he went to work in the factories of the Industrial Revolution led to the yearning for a Führer to fill the gap.

Similarly, for Houellebecq, a civilization anxious and exhausted from the incessant competition of radical freedom will too easily be drawn toward the happy womb of biological conformism. This is what is suggested by Houellebecq's character, Michel, a genetic scientist whose last name is the same as the founder of the Soviet KGB, Djerzinsky.

Accustomed to the hollowness of living without love, yet still consumers obsessed with youthful mortality, won't such a civilization, asks Houellebecq, turn to the predesigned survival of the fittest through cloning, the central planning of the 21st century?

Steven Moore (review date 21-27 January 2001)

SOURCE: Moore, Steven. "Getting Physical." *Washington Post Book World* 31, no. 3 (21-27 January 2001): 7.

[*In the following review, Moore judges* The Elementary Particles *to be a "fascinating and repugnant" novel.*]

A little over a hundred years ago, Tolstoy shocked the reading public with his novella *The Kreutzer Sonata,* a brutally frank denunciation of the mating habits of the upper classes. Michel Houellebecq's **Elementary Particles,** which at one point features a character reading *The Kreutzer Sonata,* sent similar shock waves through Europe after its publication two years ago. Though undoubtedly provocative and intriguing, it is unlikely to have the same effect here. In Europe public literary controversies still exist, whereas here a novel will make the news only if there are some political ramifications (as with Rushdie's *Satanic Verses*) or a tantalizing question of authorship (as with *Primary Colors*). **The Elementary Particles** has the added disadvantage of being so extreme in its views that it will be repugnant to most readers.

The novel is an account of two half-brothers coming of age in the '70s and finding a world that has lost its sense of community, morality and purpose. Instead of regarding the '60s as a time of liberation, of the rejection of hypocrisy, repression and conformity, Houellebecq—like many reactionaries here as well as in France—considers the '60s a disaster, when community was rejected in favor of rampant individualism and morality thrown out the window along with constricting ties and bras. The legacy of the French student revolt of 1968 and hippies dancing in the mud at Woodstock is the soulless, immoral, consumer society we now live in—a thesis so ludicrous that Houellebecq needs to go to extremes to defend it.

His two half-brothers, Michel and Bruno Djerzinski, were born to a beatnik mother who was too flaky to stick with one father, and who shipped the kids off to different grandmothers so that she could fly to California and join the burgeoning hippie movement in the early '60s. Bruno was sexually molested by his fellow students in primary school and grows up to be a sexual maniac who eventually winds up in an institution. Michel, a quiet, emotionless nerd, becomes a molecular biologist who makes revolutionary discoveries in cloning and paves the way for the brave new world of eugenics portrayed in the closing pages of the novel (which are set 80 years from now). Most of the people surrounding the brothers are so unhappy with the world bequeathed to them by those irresponsible hippies that they resort to suicide.

Instead of calling for a return to pre-'60s morality, as many conservatives do, Houellebecq (pronounced well-beck) looks to the future for a paradigm shift that would do away with the inefficient mechanics of sexual reproduction and alter the genetic code to create a race of perfect beings who have overcome "the forces of egotism, cruelty and anger" that drive our current civilization. Sexuality, which plays a major part in this novel—Bruno's escapades in nudist colonies and swing-

ers' clubs are especially graphic—would be transformed into an activity divorced from reproduction. Tolstoy's solution to the sex drive was abstinence: Just say *nyet.* Houellebecq's equally naive solution is to extend the sensitivity of the genitals via genetic engineering "to cover the entirety of the epidermis, offering new and undreamed-of erotic possibilities." Sounds like something a sex-crazed hippie would come up with.

Despite its daft ideas, **The Elementary Particles** is a fascinating read, aided by an exceptionally smooth translation by Frank Wynne. Like our own Richard Powers and Rebecca Goldstein, Houellebecq makes extensive use of scientific knowledge in his fiction, often with unsettling results. The death of a character will be followed by a detailed scientific account of the putrefaction of corpses, and another character's act of aggression will inspire an aside on hierarchical structures in animal societies. In Houellebecq's view, we are not a little lower than the angels, as the Bible flatters us, but merely a little higher than the animals, and he gives enough evidence to substantiate this hard truth. In the sections dealing with Michel, there are extensive discussions of quantum physics, molecular biology and the typology of meiosis, along with casual references to such things as the EPR paradox and Griffiths's Consistent Histories. Prepare to be challenged.

Houellebecq brings impressive erudition and a gutsy willingness to offend to his attempt to re-think and re-imagine the bases for civilization, an ambitious task most novelists would shrink from and which earns our respect, no matter how sharply we might disagree with him. Like Huxley's *Brave New World,* which is cited in **The Elementary Particles** and obviously influenced it, Houellebecq's novel is equally fascinating and repugnant, the kind of mutant gene that keeps the evolution of the novel interesting.

Gerry Feehily (essay date 18 June 2001)

SOURCE: Feehily, Gerry. "A World on the Brink of Collapse." *New Statesman* 130, no. 4542 (18 June 2001): 56-8.

[*In the following essay, Feehily discusses Houellebecq's literary celebrity, personal life, and controversy surrounding* Atomised.]

In the tunnels of the Parisian metro, the poster seems innocuous at first: "Stop talking about it. Read it." However, the talking point in question, a well-known novel entitled **Les Particules élémentaires,** is already three years old, and has been read by almost a million people. This is a remarkable figure for a literary novel that is not without difficulty; but its French publishers are clearly expecting an even greater yield, and have chosen a front cover depicting its author, Michel Houellebecq, in relaxed mode, a plastic shopping bag about his wrist. It is difficult to imagine anything quite like this happening to a British author. But Houellebecq's book—translated into English as *Atomised*—is a cultural artefact all of a piece with its chain-smoking, dishevelled author, who somewhat mockingly surmises the swell of evening commuters.

Atomised is a tortured, often demented book, concerned with the fate of two half-brothers, Bruno and Michel—victims, or case histories, of the sexual revolution. Abandoned by their mother, Janine, as the Sixties start to swing, the boys are raised separately, unaware of each other's existence until adolescence. In both cases, the early damage is irreparable. While Janine, even in old age, remains on a quest for personal fulfilment, the boys, now men, are social misfits. A bioengineer, Michel is a loner afflicted by perpetual numbness, while the intellectual Bruno prowls around Parisian sex clubs, brothels and New Age nudist colonies in search of sexual gratification. In their forties, both men find soulmates, but these women are soon wrenched away from them by cancer, degenerative disease and finally suicide. Sent mad, Bruno dissolves into a never-never land in a psychiatric ward, while Michel pursues research that leads, in 2029, to the creation of the first human clone, an immortal being engineered for pleasure, incapable of violence, cruelty and despair. It is this being, we finally realise, who is our narrator. Homo sapiens, as the song goes, have outgrown their use.

For all its sci-fi fantasy, *Atomised* is rooted in fact. Born in 1958, in La Réunion, to a mountain-guide father and a hippy mother, Houellebecq was himself abandoned, and was brought up by his maternal grandmother in Crécy-en-Brie, an unprepossessing suburb to the east of Paris. Educated in the post-1968 period, Houellebecq was profoundly affected by the loosening of disciplinary restrictions in his school in nearby Meaux, leading as it did to a new regime where the boys were left to their own devices. This resulted in predictable and catastrophic results (a suicide every month was not uncommon). From early knocks such as these, *Atomised* derives its desperate sense of loss. It differs, however, from the standard accusatory novel, in that the usual villains—abusive parents or relatives—are in thrall to world historical processes, particularly extreme 1960s individualism.

Central to *Atomised* is the idea that sexual liberation destroyed the family—"the last unit separating the individual from the market". Thus isolated, a mere particle pitted against millions of others, the modern individual experiences life as a hopeless grind of solitude and frustration. *Atomised* takes graphic issue with everything the post-1968 left holds dear, from ecology to feminism. A former communist in a country where left and right are still distinct, Houellebecq has been accused of selling out to conservatism, especially after his first novel, *Extension du domaine de la lutte*—published in English with the slackerish title *Whatever*—was a politically on-side attack on globalisation and the consumer society.

But in *Atomised,* Houellebecq broke, to some extent, political ranks. An extraordinary campaign of vilification ensued, particularly in the left-wing press, with feminists, ecologists and New Age groups lining up to brand him as anything from a reactionary to a pornographer. He responded gleefully, defending and developing some of the more cranky opinions of his character Bruno. In the end, Houellebecq was arraigned before the editorial board of *Perpendiculaire,* a radical literary review to which he was a contributor. Called on to account for Bruno's racist opinions—towards the end of the novel, he writes increasingly barmy diatribes against "negro regression"—Houellebecq countered that racism was a non-issue, preferring instead to develop his own fantastical ideas about the future of cloning. He lauded the Pope for his perspicacious analysis of the west's decline, and declared tritely that ultra-Catholics were "nice". It remained only for his somewhat po-faced and less successful peers to banish him from the review on the grounds of "political irresponsibility", not before launching a hysterical press campaign, during which Houellebecq was mentioned in the same breath as the Vichy collaborator Robert Brasillach and, most extraordinarily, Hitler.

Reactions in the UK have been considerably more measured. Commentators from both sides of the political spectrum have been lavish in their praise. This may say something about the Francophile leanings of British intellectuals—when it comes to obscenity and universal theories, after all, the French rush in where Anglos fear to tread. The UK edition has been reprinted in hardback five times—which is remarkable for a foreign-language author—and the paperback is selling briskly. In Spain, Italy and, most strikingly, Germany, the novel is a bestseller. This is puzzling, because *Atomised,* as Mark Lilla wrote in the *New York Review of Books,* mythologises the night thoughts of the French republic—the queasy sense that, up against the forces of "Anglo-Saxon" capitalism, French identity is faced with extinction.

So what explains the novel's appeal? Astried Biershenk, a German journalist who has made a short film on Houellebecq, believes that *Atomised,* in its description of sexual loneliness, appeals "to a generation which is looking for love but can't face the responsibilities". Several booksellers in Paris take a darker view. "Houellebecq is a mix of shock tactics and media overkill," said one based on the Left Bank.

Narrated in a blunt, colloquial language, *Atomised* is fiction as diagnosis, using the results of scientific experiments on rats, dogs and chickens to account for Bruno and Michel's behavioural problems. Positing each character in terms of genetic inheritance and socio-economic background, Houellebecq creates a rigorously deterministic universe where free will is illusory. Not strictly fiction, it resembles the early novel in its deep conviction that it is speaking the truth.

That still does not explain why Houellebecq has been hailed as a prophet, and why he has risen so enthusiastically to the challenge of being such. An affable, though hesitant, interviewee, drinking whisky to steady his nerves and smoking so much that his fingers are tea-coloured, he impresses by his ability to quote chunks of philosophy by heart. In truth, he is less a prophet than an archetypal Parisian figure, imbued with *l'esprit de contradiction* and a set of contrary opinions designed to confound and provoke. He cultivates the status of neurotic outsider, and it is this that appeals so much to the young, for whom he is a generational figure, a rock star with a punk sensibility.

And yet Houellebecq, in his personal habits and lifestyle, embodies much of what he seeks to castigate. He may have condemned youth culture—"a world in which the young have no respect eventually devours everyone"—but he still fronts an electronic rock combo with the French artist Plastic Bertrand. Even more curious is the virulence with which *Atomised* satirises L'Espace du Possible (a New Age campsite renamed Lieu de Changement after an out-of-court settlement), where Houellebecq was a regular visitor for 15 years.

A less resilient writer than, say, Céline, to whom he is compared, Houellebecq expresses a similar despair, not just in the human condition, but in the failure of European humanism to alleviate it. Immersing himself in pornography, dirt and violence, he shows us a world on the brink of collapse, futile beyond repeal. Houellebecq brings out our secret wish to have done with, to self-destruct. No matter how flawed and intellectually questionable *Atomised* may be, its success perhaps reveals an unconscious desire to accommodate its shocks, to share its death wish—"The meekness, the resignation, perhaps even the relief of humans at their own passing away," Houellebecq writes.

Having recently remarried, Houellebecq has bought a house on an island off the Beara peninsula in fashionable County Cork, where he lives in reclusive isolation, refusing to speak English—to him, the language of globalisation. He is presently in Thailand, working on his third novel, and later this year he will tour with his band.

Conscious of his iconic status, he protests that "Sartre had an answer for everything—I don't". Whether his celebrated nihilism can survive his remarkable success remains to be seen. For the moment, he is very famous: more talked about, as the poster in the metro suggests, than read. In his Irish seclusion, however, he will undoubtedly have time to let his art breathe. Not just France, but increasingly the rest of Europe, is waiting.

Gerry Feehily (review date 10 September 2001)

SOURCE: Feehily, Gerry. "Sex Tourism." *New Statesman* 130, no. 4554 (10 September 2001): 54.

[*In the following review, Feehily argues that* Plateforme *is a disturbing, if somewhat flawed, novel whose satire and absurdity is lost on Houellebecq's detractors.*]

Michel Houellebecq is back, and his new novel, *Plateforme,* has already come under vehement attack. Since the publication of *Atomised* in 1998, Houellebecq has been not only the most prominent of French authors, but also the most controversial, not least for his unconventional opinions on the sexual revolution. Often overlooked, however, is how he grants his fictional characters the freedom to contradict his own pet theories, finding fulfilment as they do in the type of sexual liberalism he seems to denounce. Full of such novelistic contradictions, *Plateforme* (not available in English until September next year) is a baffling study of sex tourism and a moral examination of the consequences of globalisation.

A 40-year-old administrator at the Ministry of Culture, Michel, our narrator, is a loser in the sex wars, "more or less resigned to a boring life". He spends sozzled evenings at peep-shows, or alone at home mesmerised by cable TV, but his luck begins to turn after the death of his philandering father, whom he buries with the words "you old bastard". With a sizeable inheritance, he leaves for Thailand on a package holiday, where, in between encounters with Thai prostitutes—"the best lovers in the world"—he meets Valerie, an executive working in the tourist industry.

On returning to Paris, Michel discovers that the bisexual Valerie has a capacity for self-abandonment he believed possible only in the Orient. Generous and maternal, she provides him with a kind of happiness, the nature of which, as is often the case in Houellebecq's fiction, lies in sex free of moral constraint.

The main impediment to the happiness of Michel and Valerie, as it unfolds for well over a third of the novel, is the latter's exhausting work schedule. Hired to transform the El Doreador, a loss-making subsidiary of the tour company Aurore, Valerie struggles to come up with the holiday package that will give her an edge over the global competition. Meanwhile, in the suburbs surrounding the company's air-conditioned tower, social anarchy, analogous to the individualistic anarchy of the market, prevails. As fearful of the streets as they are for their jobs, Aurore's stifled employees are left to wonder "as to the utility of this world being built".

After a trip to a ruined Cuba, Michel believes he has found the solution to Valerie's problems: a package holiday where lonely westerners pay for favours spent in the arms of third-world inhabitants with "nothing to sell but their bodies, and their intact sexuality. It's an ideal exchange." Although the creation of "Aphrodite Clubs" in Thailand is an instant success, no one had reckoned with the puritan fervour of Islamic fundamentalists from neighbouring Malaysia. As often in Houellebecq, the end, like the beginning, is despair.

Such a premise may be uncomfortable, but it possesses its own curious logic. Something of an industrial adventure, a skewed airport novel full of boardroom scenes and exotic locations, *Plateforme* seeks to demythologise the glamour of globalisation, suggesting that if a non-productive west exploits a third-world industrial base, a global division of sexual labour cannot be far behind. To label it "misogynist filth", as has the French editor of a popular travel guide on Thailand, is to misunderstand the novel. Although *Plateforme* is narrated in a deadpan, almost sociological style, which confuses the distinction between fiction and prescription, Houellebecq's intention here is patently satirical, moral even; the novel pushes its themes to the limits of the absurd.

This said, the book has its shortcomings, not least because, as Houellebecq's fame grows, an entire cult of personality, indeed an industry, forms around him, at the expense of a coherent artistic vision. Full of perfunctory, deliberately flat descriptions of Thailand, and often slapdash disquisitions on Islam, prostitution and sexuality, *Plateforme,* with a reproving editor, a rewrite, plus a little more time, might have been a brisker, leaner work. Despite this, it remains an unsettling novel, at odds and yet tuned into the modern world. Few authors can convey the way it feels to be alive today with quite the same demented energy.

Anita Brookner (review date 29 September 2001)

SOURCE: Brookner, Anita. "Sexual Tourism a Go-Go." *Spectator* 287, no. 9034 (29 September 2001): 40-1.

[*In the following review, Brookner finds shortcomings in the ambivalence and underlying complicity of Houellebecq's indictment of global tourism and capitalism in* Plateforme.]

Michel Houellebecq, whose novel *Les Particules élémentaires* (translated as *Atomised*) raised such delighted shock waves in 1998, is no stranger to controversy.

Plateforme has already provoked protests in mainstream French newspapers, not for its obscenity but for certain slighting remarks directed against Islam. Thus Houellebecq ploughs a lonely furrow of political incorrectness which will enrage the incorruptibles and delight his publishers, who have rewarded him with an initial print run of 200,000 copies. Whether they will reap the rewards of their largesse is open to question, since *Plateforme* is an altogether more ambivalent book which may raise expectations that are not entirely fulfilled.

In *Les Particules élémentaires* it was Houellebecq's contention, perfectly valid in itself, that we live in an age of sexual tourism, and that fidelity is a norm left over from prelapsarian times before Philip Larkin's watershed of 1963. Houellebecq, a fairly glum, and by all accounts, indeed his own, an unalluring man, seemed to be at one with his protagonist in undertaking an investigation of this phenomenon on our behalf. In the earlier novel he confined his attention to conditions which were the ostensible setting for innocent group activities, package tours, ecological conventions, health farms, and less overtly straight-forward gatherings; in *Plateforme* he goes further afield, travelling initially to Thailand to examine its reputed sexual amenities, but as observer rather than participant. He crosses the line, in fact, from exploited to exploiter.

It should be said that he is entirely humourless, as he would have to be, but that he writes perfectly correct French and indeed displays a kind of heroism which is not to be deplored. He is, after all, in the grip of a major idea, with which he appears to have come to terms, namely that there are no penalties for indulging in the most extreme forms of sexual licence, that monogamous partnerships have passed into history, and that it is entirely natural to pursue sexual pleasure until such time as age and infirmity take their inevitable toll.

Such paganism would seem to commend itself, and is in any case a well-worn argument. Houellebecq, for all his partisanship, sees it as an almost unavoidable aspect of universal consumerism, and singles out the leisure industry, and notably tourism, as the main agency behind the commodification of what might, in other times, have been seen as simple adventure. Since he has joined the enemy his polemic is considerably muted. 'Michel', the hero or anti-hero of *Plateforme,* has, rather disappointingly, become a bourgeois: he has money, a girlfriend to whom he is devoted, and access to a world of business from which he was initially excluded. He is able to observe the machinations of tour companies, their rivalry, their occasional complicity, and their unceasing efforts to exploit the sexual opportunities offered by the Third World in promoting those so familiar holidays with a difference which will enact the same scenario in selected sites in Asia, in

Africa, in South America, and, it is envisaged, China, to the infinite enrichment of the perpetrators, whose boardroom cerebrations involve the sort of number-crunching which will appeal to readers of a financial bent and serve as an awful warning to such innocents who were, and can no longer be, unaware that such matters are so carefully calibrated.

Thus the earlier idea has become confused. Houellebecq originally had an important point to make. At a time when all authority can be experienced as coercive and a potential threat to one's human rights he took it upon himself to examine the alternative, a life without sanctions, and found it hostile. In *Plateforme,* which is only nominally a fiction, he blames capitalism, in which we are all involved, even—and this is the point—those indigenous peoples who are happy to earn money in exchange for certain intimate services perhaps unavailable in other circumstances. This regime, therefore, is as coercive as any other. Rather more so, in fact, since the threat would seem to come from another direction, from the dispossessed, targeting the tour company executives in their once secure suburban offices, or, more specifically, from religious fundamentalists whose core beliefs are radically opposed to any kind of psychic, let alone physical expansion.

Houellebecq is on more familiar ground when he animadverts against monotheistic religions, which he sees as essentially tyrannical. A cultivated Egyptian, whom 'Michel' encounters in the Sinai desert, congratulates him on being a representative of the Catholic Church which has done so well to diversify into saints and angels, thus avoiding the narrow focus recommended to initiates of religions less eclectic in their forms of worship. Houellebecq does not go so far as to advocate an expansion of the tourist industry into Afghanistan, Iran and Pakistan, but that would appear to be the underlying message. It is when a bomb, detonated by turbaned figures, kills 117 happy hedonists in Thailand that the well-aired diatribe against Islam takes place. A Jordanian acquaintance reassures the injured protagonist that young Muslims are only too eager to exchange their constraints for what they see as the liberty that pertains to capitalism. Thus the tour industry receives an ironic validation.

In its way *Plateforme* is a novel of ideas, even if these ideas are dubious. It would be tempting to draw a wholly redundant moral from all this; surprisingly, none seems to be available. Readers hoping for a sexual odyssey along the lines of *Les Particules élémentaires* will be slightly disappointed. This simply proves that like tourists everywhere they will have read the brochure, i.e. the advance publicity, and have signed up for the tour. Booksellers report a brisk turnover.

Adrian Tahourdin (review date 12 October 2001)

SOURCE: Tahourdin, Adrian. Review of *Plateforme,* by Michel Houellebecq. *Times Literary Supplement,* no. 5141 (12 October 2001): 11.

[*In the following review, Tahourdin commends Houellebecq's bleak prose and penchant for provoking critics but concludes that* Plateforme *does not match the success of* Les Particules élémentaires.]

L'affaire Houellebecq strikes again. Michel Houellebecq is in danger of making a name for himself in the history of publicity. The appearance of his third novel, *Plateforme,* at the end of August was surrounded by as much controversy as its predecessor, *Les Particules élémentaires,* had been. The earlier book was notable for the force with which its author challenged the liberal orthodoxies of the generation of *soixante-huitards* who now make up the Parisian literary and cultural establishment. Houellebecq was denounced as, among other things, a fascist, a crypto-Stalinist and an eugenicist, yet his novel struck a chord with the reading public, and rapidly became a bestseller. His new book, unsurprisingly, sold over 250,000 in its first three weeks.

Houellebecq's publishers Flammarion must have been prepared for difficulties this time; within days of publication, they apologized to the Rector of the Paris Mosque for some offensive remarks in the novel about Islam (the author was unrepentant, and used his now customary ploy of pointing out that his narrator's views are not necessarily his own). The publisher of France's culturally aware *Guide du Routard* threatened to sue over some insulting comments about their guide to Thailand. John Grisham, Frederick Forsyth ("cet imbécile") and Jacques Chirac would also be entitled to take exception to their cameo appearances.

Plateforme describes a year in the life of Michel, a forty-year-old bachelor, who is politically disaffected and a mediocre civil servant in the Culture Ministry in Paris (he doesn't vote). He takes an organized holiday to Thailand, in order to indulge his appetite for young prostitutes, armed with the *Routard* guide to the country. Enraged by its editorial stance against sexual tourism, and its "vulgar elitism", he flings the book out of the window of his coach. Sexual tourism, according to him, is an economic and sociological inevitability, a practical system of exchange between the overworked and loveless inhabitants of the West (in Paris he visits peep shows and SM clubs), and those in the East who are without money but who are in a position to sell sexual favours. Michel's fellow sexual tourists run from strapping young Americans and Antipodeans to single women in their forties, beer-swilling Northern Europeans and whisky-drinking Arabs. Houellebecq is as sharp as ever in his dissection of social groups: the tour party includes retired petit-bourgeois couples who have saved up for the holiday of a lifetime but who have trouble adapting to the local food, a fifty-year-old divorcee and sexual tourist who stopped taking his holidays in Spain *after* Franco's death, and two twentysomething "nanas" who work as "event organizers". While in Thailand, Michel meets Valérie, a high-powered twenty-eight-year-old executive with the travel company. On their return to France, Michel and Valérie become lovers. Valérie is intrigued rather than disturbed by Michel's sexual adventures and allows herself to be persuaded by his contention that, in order to survive in a very competitive market, her company will have to diversify into concepts such as "Eldorador Aphrodite". Their "researches" take them to Cuba and back to Thailand, where Valérie is killed in a graphically described attack on the resort by Islamic fundamentalists.

In common with Houellebecq's two earlier novels (the first, *Extension du domaine de la lutte,* was recently made into a film), *Plateforme* contains a good deal of sex. Asked for the reason why, the author replied "because I write well about it". But the redeeming potential of love is also hinted at, in the finely drawn affair between Michel and Valérie. There is dark humour in the book and, as ever, Houellebecq writes with photographic precision and a clarity of purpose, although when he is developing a theory, the book can read like a sociological tract (there is even a footnoted reference to a journal, *Annals of Tourism Research*).

Plateforme doesn't have the impact of *Les Particules élémentaires,* whose originality and emotional force make it a landmark in French fiction. Houellebecq's view of society, French society in particular, remains bleak (there is an alarming description of one of Paris's satellite towns). His talent to provoke and scandalize is considerable, and is clearly one he takes some pleasure in (it may also partly explain why, at the age of forty-three, he now lives on a remote island off the coast of Ireland). But his (very French) blend of insolence and intellectualizing does not seem to travel well: when *Les Particules* appeared in an English translation last year, as *Atomised,* it failed to create much interest in Britain. The *New York Times* critic called it a "deeply repugnant read". That critic won't be charmed by the new book either, but might have to acknowledge that Houellebecq has a pretty good idea in which direction the world is headed.

Joshua Winter (essay date 6 May 2002)

SOURCE: Winter, Joshua. "France: Into the Void." *New Statesman* 131, no. 4586 (6 May 2002): 25-7.

[*In the following excerpt, Winter examines Houellebecq's notoriety, political perspective, and contemptuous depiction of liberal amorality in* Atomised *and* Plateforme.]

The great chronicler of the moral and cultural emptiness of modern France is Michel Houellebecq, perhaps the most talented and contrary writer in Europe today. Many contemporary French writers play with the idea of nihilism; Houellebecq means it, both in his life and work. In person, Houellebecq, who is in his mid-forties, is a dissolute presence, sickened by a life dedicated to cigarettes, alcohol and trips to bizarre, anarchic sex camps in the Paris suburbs, which he satirises ruthlessly in his marvellous novel *Les Particules élémentaires* (published in Britain two years ago as *Atomised*).

Gerry Feehily, an Irish literary critic based in Paris, met Houellebecq at a party last year. "He was surrounded by all these glamorous publishing women and journalists, but he looked utterly wasted and dishevelled," he told me. "When I spoke to him, he seemed to be shaking; there was this distant, faraway look in his eyes as if he wasn't quite there. But at the same time you could see that he was utterly contemptuous of everything and everyone around him. Sometimes you have the feeling that he really hates France and everything about it."

Atomised tells the story of two brothers, Michel and Bruno, who are born to the same progressive mother, a 1968er in outlook and lifestyle. The brothers are later separated by the fragmentation of their family life; bullied and humiliated at school, they endure a miserable adolescence. They both enter early adulthood as disturbed, isolated figures. "I'd like to believe that the self is an illusion," Bruno tells Michel, "but if it is, it's a pretty painful one." So begins the brothers' journey to find meaning in a world of disappointed aspiration, a journey that takes Bruno into compulsive promiscuity and the sexual *demi-monde* of Paris, and Michel into molecular biology and experiments into the very foundation of what it is to be human.

Houellebecq has thought hard about what it means to live in a post-Christian universe. He believes we are living at the end of an age of reason. What lies ahead is a fall into chaos and *ennui,* as represented by the rise of Islamo-fascism in the east and decadent consumerism in the west. Christian doctrine, he writes, accorded unconditional importance to every human life from conception to death. But today the "agnosticism at the heart of the French republic" has facilitated the "slightly sinister triumph of the determinist world-view", of a world without the possibility of transcendence. But still the value of human life continues to preoccupy the liberal conscience. Which in the "last years of western civilisation contributed to a general mood of depression bordering on masochism".

Houellebecq is a former communist and was once a leading contributor to the progressive literary journal *Perpendiculaire,* from the board of which he was eventually banished after he refused to be held accountable for the racism of his character Bruno. In recent years—even before *Atomised,* which as the *Economist* wrote, was "not so much published as detonated"—he began, like Céline before him, to occupy a position of perpetual opposition, to both left and right, similar to the editorial line of the now defunct *LM* magazine in this country.

More specifically, he has emerged as a combative critic of the revolutionary excesses of the late 1960s, a period which, he believes, laid the foundation for modern lassitude and despair. In *Atomised,* Bruno and Michel are forced to evaluate the codes by which their parents' generation lived—the licentiousness, the irresponsibility, the refusal to conform. Houellebecq—like many younger French novelists, for whom he is the commanding presence, an influence and inspiration—works out of a sense of profound crisis: did we as a nation take a wrong turn? What if our pursuit of sexual satisfaction and freedom was really a kind of imprisonment? Have the costs of living through the revolutionary period of the 1960s been too great to wider society?

With the publication last year of his most recent novel, *Plateforme* (out here in the autumn), Houellebecq has become a figure of even greater controversy and discord in France. *Plateforme* is a study of sex tourism in Thailand and is full of witty, unhinged attacks on liberal-left orthodoxies and on religious fundamentalism (it was published in France before 11 September). From his new home on the south-west coast of Ireland, he continues to detonate missiles of contempt against France, Islam and what he calls the "evils of globalisation". He is an emblematically modern French figure, because he appears to believe in nothing and is opposed to everything. The only respite in his work is a kind of intense erotic abandonment, a wilful surrender to preposterous desires. His novels, though among the most accomplished to have been written in the past 20 years anywhere in the world, share a vision of France that also finds expression in the anti-humanist themes of *Baise-moi* and much of the new French cinema.

"The generation that has grown up since the Second World War, the generation of our parents, was the most optimistic in history," Houellebecq told the writer Andrew Hussey, author of a fine biography of Guy Debord. "They believed in progress, the consumer society, sexual happiness and they were naive and wrong to believe in such things. This generation is different because it knows that pleasure is not the same thing as happiness, that pleasure is the opposite of happiness. That, to me, is an unassailable moral position."

So that, then, is the challenge confronting the political class in France: how to reach a generation that no longer believes in the possibility of progress or indeed of happiness? Small wonder that Le Pen's bootboys are on the march.

Steven Daniell (review date summer-autumn 2002)

SOURCE: Daniell, Steven. Review of *Plateforme,* by Michel Houellebecq. *World Literature Today* 76, nos. 3-4 (summer-autumn 2002): 110.

[*In the following review, Daniell offers a positive assessment of* Plateforme, *which he finds "entertaining and insightful" despite its offensiveness.*]

Michel Houellebecq's third novel, *Plateforme,* looks at a society that is becoming devoid of meaning. As the story unfolds, it becomes apparent that this emptiness threatens not only materialistic Westerners but also the anticapitalist forces desperately trying to forestall globalization, especially in the name of religious or political ideology.

The novel centers around Michel, a forty-year-old exhibits agent for the French Ministry of Culture. In the opening chapter, he must deal with his father's murder by the brother of Aïcha, the father's young Muslim girlfriend. The facts surrounding the murder seem a curiosity at the time; however, the two primary motifs for the text sex and violence, emerge from the crime.

Though Michel was not close to his father, he still needs the break afforded by a tour package to Thailand. During the tour, he meets Valérie, a travel agent with whom he eventually forms intimate social and business relations.

The couple, along with a colleague in the travel industry, develops the idea of replacing some of the company's Eldorador Aventure resorts, which feature nightclubs and nature holidays, with Eldorador Aphrodite resorts, which cater to the sexual adventurer. They persuade a major tour operator to finance the highly profitable scheme, but with the threat of losing their financial backing should the project come under fire. At one of these resorts in Thailand, the sex and the violence, which have remained apart for much of the novel, finally collide starkly and abruptly.

Although the text's rhythm has an American feel to it (Houellebecq has also published research on H. P. Lovecraft), sex and violence play reverse roles. Sexual activity, exclusively for leisure, comes to the forefront and becomes an entertainment staple of the professional classes. These scenes typically range from clinical to erotic, but their sheer quantity rivals the amount of violence seen in much American popular entertainment.

Violence in *Plateforme,* on the contrary, lurks in the background as the domain of Parisian street thugs and Islamic terrorists. Following the incident in the opening chapter, it becomes anonymous and distant. As the story progresses, it grows closer and more extreme. After a street brawl one night leaves seven dead near Valérie's office, Michel asks her whether she could use a gun in self-defense. She replies, "Quand j'étais petite . . . même pas capable de tuer un poulet." Michel's reaction epitomizes the degree to which the increasing violence has devalued human life: "À vrai dire, moi non plus; mais un homme, ça me paraissait nettement plus facile."

Despite Houellebecq's straightforward, almost breezy style, the problems he tackles are hardly simple or trivial. Less controversial issues may appear in the narrative, as when he discusses the state of the art world or the dangers of unfettered materialism. He proves to be especially adept at using dialogue to approach touchier issues such as corporate misconduct, sexual tourism, or Islamic fundamentalism. What appears in these pages will offend or disturb some readers, but the narrative format and writing style both manage to keep the text at once entertaining and insightful.

Michel Houellebecq and Gerry Feehily (interview date 5 August 2002)

SOURCE: Houellebecq, Michel, and Gerry Feehily. "The Man Who Fell to Earth." *New Statesman* 131, no. 4599 (5 August 2002): 36-7.

[*In the following interview, Houellebecq discusses his literary celebrity, his controversial statements about Islam, and the inspirations behind* Plateforme.]

I first met Michel Houellebecq at a party held in Paris, in early September last year, to celebrate the French launch of his third novel, *Plateforme.* A wan, stooped figure wearing a large yellow anorak, baggy jeans and a pair of fluorescent Nike trainers, he wandered in the midst of the black-clad literati of Paris like a stranger to his own fame. Cigarette in hand, he retired to a corner of the room, attended to by a duo of skimpily dressed press agents, with helmet-like haircuts, who collected his empty glasses as he drained them of champagne and who hung on his every word. "I'm not in the right place," he confessed to me, in his soft, faintly lisping voice. "I really should be working. In fact, I'm going right now."

And so he fled the room.

But he was already in trouble. An interview with *Lire,* the literary monthly, had recently appeared, in which, among other things, he described a negative revelation he had experienced on Mount Sinai. "There, where Moses received the Ten Commandments . . . I said to myself that the act of believing in a single God was the act of a cretin, I could find no other word. And the most stupid religion has to be Islam. When you read the

Koran, it's appalling, appalling." This was not the first time that Houellebecq had expressed his contempt for Islam; indeed, his novel, which Heinemann publishes in English as *Platform* in early September, offers a portrait of a group of Muslim militants who are unhinged by hatred of the west.

A Moroccan daily picked up the interview and published an incendiary story about Houellebecq. "This man hates you", said the front-page headline, above a photograph of the author. A few days later, the events of 11 September took place. Shortly afterwards, French Islamic organisations pressed charges of incitement to racial hatred and religious violence against Houellebecq. Concerned by the opprobrium that had descended on his best author, Houellebecq's French editor, Raphaël Sorin, felt it necessary to mollify the Grand Imam of Paris in person. The author himself, jostled and spat at in the streets, cancelled all public engagements and fled to an undisclosed location. To this day, most of his European editors can contact him only by land mail. His lawyers will tackle the charges this autumn.

But it's high summer now, and Houellebecq has resurfaced, briefly, in the bar of the Shelbourne Hotel, Dublin. Head in hands, a glass of red wine in front of him, he talks to me a little about his second novel, *Les Particules élémentaires* (*Atomised*), which recently won the Impac prize for a work of fiction, worth 100,000 euros. Narrated by the first human clone, it tells the tale of two sexually dysfunctional half-brothers, Michel and Bruno, whose family life is destroyed by the excesses of the late 1960s. He wrote most of the novel in Connemara. "It's a very sensitive place," Houellebecq says, "a mixture of sunsets and fields stretching off as far as the eye can see. It was the big reason, I think, why I settled here in Ireland. But maybe Brittany is like that, too . . ." His voice trails off into awkward silence.

Since 1999, Houellebecq has been living in a small island community off the coast of County Cork. It is odd that a writer whose novels and stories are often wilfully obscene, crammed with scenes set in sex clubs, brothels and nudist colonies, should have settled in a country that less than two decades ago continued to hide its single mothers in convents. "But I really feel Ireland is a romantic place," he says. "In terms of light and landscape, for example, it's hardly different from its cinematic image. In the end, I think you make comparisons according to your point of departure. Mine is France. I could have settled in the French countryside, but it's quite crushing there, like all countryside. Visually, to live by the sea, as I do, is a very different sensation. That I don't speak much English is not an impediment."

His relations with his home country are complex. Since *Atomised,* which plausibly argues that late Sixties individualism killed off all hope of love in western society, Houellebecq has set himself on a collision course with left-liberal orthodoxy. A former communist, he now seems to relish confrontation, particularly with liberals who preach tolerance and harmony. Having previously declared that "I love to take the piss out of journalists", he has expressed his admiration for the Pope, his hatred of hippies, and nostalgia for Philippe Pétain, the disgraced leader of the Vichy regime. An incorrigible provocateur, he has yet to enjoy the official consecration of a Goncourt or Médicis prize. "When I finished *Atomised,*" he says, "I just hoped that the critics who had been good to my first book, *Whatever,* would react favourably. Then the interviews started, and the whole thing went a lot further. The book began to be read all over Europe; people were talking about it, they wanted to come to see me, find out my views on all sorts of things. But talking to journalists, quite frankly, is really laborious."

He does not believe, however, that constant media scrutiny has affected his work. That said, he also thinks that writing another novel might be more trouble than it's worth. One cannot help thinking that since *Atomised,* Houellebecq has spread himself too thin. As well as writing *Platform,* he has directed soft-porn films, made a pop album with the Belgian musician Bertrand Burgalat and completed an as yet untranslated travelogue, *Lanzarote,* which includes his own photos of the island's rock formations.

Much of *Platform* was written in Phuket, Thailand, where Houellebecq was surrounded by strip clubs and hostess bars. It tells of the romance between Michel, a melancholic, indolent civil servant at the French ministry of culture, and Valérie, a child-woman executive in the tourist industry. Touring soulless sex clubs, and imprisoned in air-conditioned office blocks, they are looking for a way out. "Frustration is probably the greatest evil," says Houellebecq, "much worse than *ennui,* which is maybe the same. Maybe."

But a way out is found. Houellebecq, having observed that "Thai prostitutes are the best in the world", proposes a chain of sex resorts in the Gulf of Siam where love-hungry Europeans can seek relief. The project succeeds. Valérie's stock options climb high. They retire to one of the resorts they have helped create, but neither has reckoned with the local Muslim fanatics, who supply the novel's devastating climax. "I really think people like Valérie and Michel exist," says Houellebecq. "They are actually very ordinary. All they want is a certain level of comfort, a certain level of pleasure. I like writing about typical people."

Typical or not, Michel, the narrator of *Platform,* has a lucky bag of opinions—on Islam, prostitution and Germans—which sound, after nearly 400 pages, much like Houellebecq's own. Listening to Houellebecq publicly defend his narrator's discovery that "Thai prostitutes are good girls . . . they send money back home to their parents", you get the sense that he can't see much beyond the liberal platitudes of the journalists he despises and longs to offend. His stylised disaffection explains, to a certain extent, his great popularity, particularly among the young. In a sense, he offers the highest expression of a punk attitude of perpetual rebellion, in all its best and worst aspects. He is a captivating writer but often also a foolish one. A novelist with a greater instinct for truth would, for instance, have conceded what *Platform* dutifully overlooks: that a quarter of all Thai prostitutes will die from Aids in the next decade.

But my cassette player has clicked to a stop, and Houellebecq's wine glass is empty. Most of our two hours together has passed in silence. Talking to Houellebecq can be, to paraphrase Nietzsche, a bit like staring into a well: very soon the well starts staring back at you.

"I have to go and see where my wife is," he says. Pulling on a battered leather jacket, he looks into the ashtray, where the mangled fragments of the cigarettes he chews are heaped up. "You know, I often wonder whether we are living in a hologram." Before I ask him whether it's a hologram of his own making, he raises his hands. "Something to think about."

On the way out to the lobby, as he leads me towards the revolving doors, I remember the words of one of his French press agents on that September night in Paris. "Michel lives on his own planet," she said. "He couldn't exist otherwise." As I follow him into the street, a dark-haired woman in a cocktail dress meets us. She raises her glass of wine. "Congratulations, Michel," she says. "You wrote a great book, and you deserve the Impac prize, every penny of it."

Houellebecq takes her hand. A head shorter than she, he looks her up and down and, in faltering English, expresses his thanks. "But you know, I sometimes ask myself, must you deserve something in order to enjoy it?"

With that, he is gone.

Andrew Hussey (review date 19 August 2002)

SOURCE: Hussey, Andrew. "The Pornographer's Manifesto." *New Statesman* 131, no. 4601 (19 August 2002): 34-5.

[*In the following review, Hussey explores the controversy over the pornographic and anti-Islamic elements of* Platform, *contending that Houellebecq's apparent viciousness and intolerance stems from a perverse compassion.*]

Along with Catherine Millet and Michel Houellebecq, one of the bestselling authors in France this past year has been Ovidie, a 21-year-old porn actress. Pierced and dressed in black leather, Ovidie manages to look winsome, cute and sexy all at once ("She makes Catherine Millet look like a bad-tempered primary school teacher," commented one rather overexcited observer). She is a veteran of more than 40 porn films, and describes herself as a feminist, an artist and a philosopher, "*un intello du porno*" ("an intellectual of porn"). In her book, *Porno Manifesto,* Ovidie proudly recalls how she discovered pornography in early adolescence and says that it came to her as a revelation at the same tender age that mere physical events could be the source of so much delight and anguish. Pornography, she believes, is about nothing more than the promise of human happiness. The physical and economic exploitation that are undeniably involved in the sex industry, she says, are wrong only because they are a betrayal of this original, quite innocent trust.

This is also the central premise of **Platform,** Michel Houellebecq's third and most controversial novel, which arrives now in English, in the wake of the literary firestorms that have raged through most of the European countries where it has already been published. Most notably, Houellebecq has been accused of writing pornography as well as defending the most exploitative and despicable forms of sex tourism. A fierce row was already brewing in Paris this time last year when, as the publication date approached, the author was criticised for being misogynistic and racist. Houellebecq was, as ever, indifferent to public opinion. He did not bother to defend himself but spoke out in favour of "sexual communism" and the "democracy of the sex shop", a notion that the sexual market place should be open to all, not only those who succeed with good looks, fame or success.

The row deepened when Houellebecq was challenged on his apparent contempt for Islam (the book's main character rejoices in the massacre of Palestinians on the Gaza Strip). He publicly declared Islam the most stupid and murderous of religions, attracting the hatred of France's large Muslim population and the bafflement of its liberal intellectuals. Houellebecq's wife began to crack up and went missing in Ireland. His publishers started to panic at mention of *fatwas.* Houellebecq himself, scared and genuinely shaken, drank more heavily than ever and gloomily predicted that he would never write again.

But **Platform** is still only a novel, albeit an extraordinarily good one. It tells the story of Michel, a disillusioned and depressed Parisian, whose main pleasures, if they are pleasures at all, are drink and the occasional hand job in the peep-shows of the rue St Denis or the rue de la Gaîté (Houellebecq has written a poem worthy of Larkin about this street). On holiday in Thailand, Michel discovers that paying for sex can be a life-enhancing experience for both participants. The westerner receives real physical gratification, a sensation that has been degraded or lost in our "spectacular society" of commodity fetishism, image and illusion. (Houellebecq is, unsurprisingly, a keen reader of Guy Debord, who originally coined the phrase "society of the spectacle".) The Oriental, in return, without guilt or shame, takes the cash.

Michel's discovery coincides with the beginning of his first real love affair, with Valérie, a beautiful and energetic travel agent who is always ready to indulge Michel in his taste for group sex with random strangers. They return to Paris and plan to set up a company devoted to sex tourism. This indeed is the manifesto, the "platform" of the book's title: that, for the first time in history, as globalised technology and affluence meet, human beings need not be sexually alone and therefore unhappy ever again; utopia is at hand.

Houellebecq does not really believe this, any more than in real life he takes part in the seamlessly choreographed orgies that are a *leitmotif* of the novel. He is a reader of Aldous Huxley and H P Lovecraft and takes from them the idea that utopias are impossible because pleasure, the chief goal of western society, is not really related to happiness. Accordingly, this book is written not in a spirit of irony or mischief or deliberate provocation, but demonstrates a genuine commitment to understanding why, in a post-industrial, post-Christian world where money and technology fulfil all material needs, happiness still seems so far away.

The attacks on Islam are bitter and, naturally, offensive to Muslims. Houellebecq has offered a weak defence of these sections of the book, saying that "it is only a fiction" and that mere narrative logic demands that, when Valérie is killed by extremists, Michel should delight in vengeance against Arabs. However, Houellebecq's real objection to Islam is, I think, that it offers a total challenge to western Enlightenment values. Houellebecq began his career as a kind of Marxist, and the "medieval nostalgia" of Islamic thought is bound to conflict with his way of thinking (this position finds a parallel in the remains of the French Marxist left, for which the term multiculturalism is still a mystery).

The virulence of Houellebecq's dislike comes, in a more complicated way, from his compassion. Like Louis, Ferdinand Céline, the anti-Semitic novelist of the 1930s whom he most resembles both in style and content, Houellebecq has a horror of suffering and violence (he expresses particular distaste for sadomasochistic practices). Céline's anti-Semitism was disgusting in the 1930s and is made more so by history; yet it did not make him a lesser novelist. The same applies to

Houellebecq. One of the most striking and unsettling features of *Platform* is the touching pathos, even tenderness, with which the heterosexual orgies are described, in opposition to the murderous puritanism of Islamic terror. Houellebecq seeks out a symmetry in the most unlikely scenarios: the description of the double penetration of Valérie by a white man and a black man is worthy of the surrealist Hans Bellmer, for example. If this is pornography, it is also of the highest poetic order.

For good or ill, there are few writers in any language who understand the tensions of the present age as well as Houellebecq. Will Self has dismissed him as "a little guy who can't get enough sex", but, as this book makes clear, it is precisely this aspect of his character that makes him so genuinely alienated, and therefore dangerous. This is still the same writer who, when I met him in his council flat in Paris six years ago, giggling, drunk and then all of a sudden very serious, declared himself at war with the world.

Houellebecq was then working on *Les Particules élémentaires* (*Atomised*), the book that catapulted him into the literary stratosphere in London and New York as well as Paris. This was a book which, like Flaubert's *L'Éducation sentimentale,* charted the decline and fall of a generation that had lost all sense of moral purity. (The comparison with Flaubert is not entirely fatuous; the similarity has been observed by several distinguished French critics, and even Julian Barnes concedes the point.) "This book will either make me famous or destroy me," I recall Houellebecq saying at the time. In the event, *Atomised* went on to confirm him as the sharpest and most perceptive chronicler of our era.

Friends who have seen him recently say he talks often of suicide. But it is never clear whether this is to be taken literally or as a metaphor. Now that he really is famous, it remains to be seen whether *Platform*—a subtler, more daring and more politically explicit work even than *Atomised*—fulfils the second part of Houellebecq's slurred prophecy.

Brian Dillon (review date 18 October 2002)

SOURCE: Dillon, Brian. Review of *Platform,* by Michel Houellebecq. *Times Literary Supplement,* no. 5194 (18 October 2002): 24.

[*In the following review, Dillon finds* Platform *to be a tedious, schematic work that is further marred by its English translator.*]

Despite his latest narrator's protest that "I had never known boredom", boredom is the most fascinating thing about Michel Houellebecq's three novels. With *Platform*

he has written a book even more mired in tedium—in a blank, implacable, cosseting dullness: not at all the ache of metaphysical ennui—than his earlier works, *Extension du domaine de la lutte* and *Les Particules élémentaires* (translated, suitably dully, as *Whatever* and *Atomised*). The author no longer seems willing to allow his readers to orient themselves to all this boredom of their own accord; apparently afraid that they will simply switch off, Houellebecq has written a novel at once intriguingly dull and tediously excited about its own significance.

Platform (which was published in France in 2001 and reviewed in the *TLS* of October 12 that year) is mostly narrated by Michel, a minor functionary in the French Ministry of Culture. While "not actively hostile" to art, he concedes that it "cannot change lives. At least not mine." The life in question is grimly circumscribed: "In most circumstances in my life, I have had about as much freedom as a vacuum cleaner." Where the central characters of Houellebecq's earlier books were constantly on the brink of breakdown, Michel's mood is one of utter passivity, weary submission to the rhythms of half-hearted work, alcoholism and meaningless sex. This is introduced with typical laconism: "Usually, when I left the office, I'd take in a peepshow", a habit no more or less engaging than watching television.

The tedium of Michel's existence is interrupted by the murder of his father, then by a holiday in Thailand, where he discovers the consolations of pliant local prostitutes but also the love of a French woman, Valérie. Here Houellebecq begins to insist on the cultural distinction that governs, and ultimately undermines, the rest of the novel. Overwhelmed by the supposed sexual "naturalness" of Valérie and the Thai prostitutes, Michel is incapable of understanding his sexual encounters in anything other than the most banal terms. Far from constituting an eruption of erotic enlightenment, Michel's experience of sex is of a piece with the novel's earlier portrayal of him as by turns rancorous and passive. The sex in *Platform* is not merely repetitive and dull; it is the sexual experience of a very boring man with a sentimentally pornographic imagination: "I smoothly penetrated her . . . thrusting inside her to the rhythm of the waves." The pure kitsch of Michel's ostensible insight—his idiotic distinction between "the natural goodness of Valérie's nature" and the alienated perversion of other Western women—is precisely the point here.

What begins as a portrait of a dulled and clotted imagination is quickly flattened by a narrative schematism that, in its hectic effort to globalize Michel's malaise, undoes the comic force of the novel's early chapters. Michel's entrepreneurial idea for a global sex tourism is swiftly shackled to an unconvincing analysis of all that is morally wrong with West and East alike. A frenzy of pointless action ensues: the new international sex industry attracts the fury of Muslim fundamentalists, and Valérie (like most of Houellebecq's women) meets a gruesome end. An improbable Egyptian pops up to berate Islam, for no reason other than to shore up the novel's shaky narrative and moral structure. As with *Atomised,* Houellebecq has been ill-served by his translator (or editors); the text is peppered with infelicities. As one glaring error has it, "a disappointment letdown": a botched phrase that could equally describe Michel Houellebecq's attempt to expand individual torpor to grandly moral proportions.

Gretchen Rous Besser (review date February 2003)

SOURCE: Besser, Gretchen Rous. Review of *Plateforme,* by Michel Houellebecq. *French Review* 76, no. 3 (February 2003): 640-41.

[*In the following review, Besser praises Houellebecq's provocative depiction of cynicism and amorality in* Plateforme.]

Our favorite iconoclast—the one we love to hate—is back with another pageturner that we can neither admit to savoring nor put down. Not as apocalyptic as his previous *Particules élémentaires* (*FR* 73.4, 763-64), Houellebecq's "novel" [*Plateforme*] is nonetheless provocative to an expected degree. The premise that Western civilization is corrupt, egocentric, and doomed is complemented by an apologetic for instituting sex-for-barter with developing countries. The author's cynical world view comes across most potently in the attitude and actions of his *porte-parole* narrator Michel, whose outlook is summed up in a simple philosophy: "S'il n'y avait pas, de temps à autre, un peu de sexe, en quoi consisterait la vie?" (220-21). Michel voices (the author's?) jaded and subversive aphorisms: "La volonté de puissance existe, et se manifeste sous forme d'*histoire*; elle est en elle-même radicalement improductive" (87); "C'est dans le rapport à autrui qu'on prend conscience de soi; c'est bien ce qui rend le rapport à autrui insupportable" (94); "On peut caractériser la vie comme un processus d'immobilisation, bien visible chez le bouledogue français—si frétillant dans sa jeunesse, si apathique dans son âge mûr" (123); "l'idée d'unicité de la personne humaine n'est qu'une pompeuse absurdité. On se souvient de sa propre vie [. . .] un peu plus que d'un roman qu'on aurait lu par le passé" (189). Michel blasts away at family and spiritual values, idealism, the idea of progress. He attacks American mores, movies, best-sellers, and their pernicious exportation abroad. Variously, he demolishes capitalism, ridicules art, undermines tradition, debunks religion (Islam in particular), and glorifies sex in all its varieties and permutations. He reduces the world's ills—racism, political extremism, economic inequalities—to an intrinsic conflict over young women's vaginas.

During the group trip to Thailand with which the novel opens, Michel meets Wonderwoman, his notion of the Eternal Feminine, in the person of Valérie, who embodies the desiderata that this twenty-first-century Everyman seeks. First, she has a glorious body and a tireless sensuality. An expert and "giving" lover, she is a thoughtful partner, a successful career woman, and an affectionate daughter. What matters most is that her insatiable sex drive—described with pornographic specificity—matches that of her man. They spend a brief moment together in Eden—an earthly paradise of sandy beaches, emerald water, and erotic couplings—before the cataclysm engulfs them.

Valérie's professional colleague Jean-Yves, the third party in this improbable trio, is the kind of ambitious, unhappily-married, sex-deprived workaholic whose wretched existence exemplifies Michel's aversion and justifies his apathy. The three concoct a scheme to capitalize on sexual desire in the West, availability and compliance in the East, by introducing "sexual tourism" to the world. Their experimental adventures constitute part of the book's peep-show appeal.

The action draws on apace with an ever-expanding ripple effect. The back-drops against which the "plot" progresses—self-styled exotic destination resorts, a violence-riddled Parisian suburb—and the many secondary characters who people the story are presented in minute and witty detail. Houellebecq knows how to pique our curiosity, titillate our senses, arouse a self-justificatory ire. Instead of propounding a thesis, he illustrates and vivifies it. His characters live, make love, and suffer on the page.

There is no morality in this author's universe—just greedy, uncaring, self-centered people. Hope is nonexistent. Michel's fate reflects the futility of human effort. "Rien ne survivra de moi, et je ne mérite pas que rien me survive; j'aurai été un individu médiocre, sous tous ses aspects [. . .] On m'oubliera. On m'oubliera vite" (369-70). Whether or not you swallow the author's acidulous pessimism, his views can excite anger, indignation, exasperation, and sorrow. Houellebecq manipulates the power of words like a master. He can charm, fascinate, disgust, and outrage. His books invite dispute and controversy. In our enforced and appreciative silence lies our complicity.

Rod Liddle (review date 28 June 2003)

SOURCE: Liddle, Rod. "Jamais la Politesse." *Spectator* 292, no. 9125 (28 June 2003): 41-2.

[*In the following review, Liddle praises the "transparent beauty" of Houellebecq's prose in* Lanzarote *but criticizes the novella's impact as "slight."*]

'Slight', I think, is the adjective I'm looking for here. I started reading *Lanzarote* as the train pulled out of Waterloo and finished it before Woking. At £9.99 that makes it about as good value, mile for mile, as South West Trains. But, oh, believe me, much more fun.

Houellebecq is celebrated or reviled, depending upon your point of view, as one of those French controversialists who are thrown up every decade or so to discomfort and annoy us. He has been charged, in his homeland, with inciting racial hatred, having allegedly described Islam as a 'stupid' religion—an appraisal he amends in *Lanzarote* to merely 'absurd'. These days he's a virtual recluse, holed up on an island off the coast of Ireland, every bit as puzzled, tormented, unrepentant and probably drunk as the best French novelists are supposed to be. This latest work is terrible value for money and little more than a blueprint for last year's brilliant *Platform*; but all that notwithstanding, you would not wish to miss it.

Because what gets forgotten, when people rail against Houellebecq for being a racist, right-wing pornographer or, for that matter, when they rally to his cause—as I've done in the past—for being uncannily prescient and an acute observer of human behaviour, is the quite astonishing quality of the writing, and the humour.

Lanzarote tells the story of a man who spends a couple of weeks on holiday on the island, in the company of two German lesbians and a lachrymose man called Rudi whom the narrator assumes to be Belgian but is, in fact, Luxembourgish. This misunderstanding of nationalities enables Houellebecq to be spiteful and very, very funny about both Belgium and Luxembourg:

> He [Rudi] spoke of Luxembourg as of a lost Eden, though it's common knowledge that it's a minuscule, mediocre country with no distinguishing characteristics—it's not even a country, more an assortment of dummy companies scattered over parkland, nothing but PO boxes for companies with a taste for tax evasion.

Elsewhere, it is the poor Norwegians who are most decisively abused, but luckily there is ample space across these 87 small pages for Houellebecq to deride also the British, the French, the Greeks and the Italians. He is celebrated for his acid misanthropy, and he rarely disappoints.

It is a deep misanthropy, however, which can be dispelled every now and again by sexual intercourse, the redemptive powers of which permeate each of his previous books and most especially *Platform.* On Lanzarote, the narrator is briefly rescued from a sort of awful, terminal ennui by a lubricious encounter with both of those aforementioned German lesbians. Simultaneously. This despite having informed the woman in the travel agency, when she at first suggested a particular

holiday destination, that 'I don't feel up to fucking'. Au contraire. As is ever the case, he did, in the end, feel 'up to fucking'.

Houellebecq's preoccupation with sex has given his detractors another, very Anglo-Saxon, stick with which to beat him; those who dislike the man attack him for an obsession which they deem to be less shocking than merely passé. But this is to miss the point. At the end of this novella, Rudi—the bereft Luxembourgish holidaymaker—bequeaths the narrator a touching note of goodbye.

> The worst thing about depression is that it makes it virtually impossible even to contemplate the sexual act, even though it might be the only thing which would assuage the terrible feeling of anguish that comes with depression.

Houellebecq is not simply another of those French libertines, like Bataille or Genet or even de Beauvoir. The point is to only connect, although in a rather more physically direct and sometimes peremptory manner than perhaps E. M. Forster originally envisaged.

There is no other writer like him, at the moment, for wit, acuity or the transparent beauty of his prose. His themes are always big and bravely expounded. This time he has kindly attached colour photographs of Lanzarote to his little story. They're neither use nor ornament, but no matter.

FURTHER READING

Criticism

Harris, Michael. "A Look at Causes of Human Unhappiness." *Los Angeles Times* (31 October 2000): E3.
    Harris applauds the honesty, humor, and tenderness of *The Elementary Particles,* though notes that the novel is often one-dimensional and unsubtle.

Karwowski, Michael. "Michel Houellebecq: French Novelist for Our Times." *Contemporary Review* 282, no. 1650 (July 2003): 40-7.
    Karwowski examines the accusations of racism brought against Houellebecq and compliments his consistent tone of impartiality in *Platform.*

Marr, Andrew. "We're All Doomed (Middle-aged French Philosophers Excepted)." *Observer* (21 May 2000): 12.
    Marr admires Houellebecq's ability to make his objectionable subject matter appealing in *Atomised,* noting that the work is "a novel of ideas which comes close to working."

Masson, Sophie. "The Strange Case of Michel Houelle-becq." *Quadrant* 47, no. 6 (June 2003): 52-6.

Masson explores Houellebecq's controversial career, focusing on the reaction to his negative remarks concerning Islam in *Platform*.

Nehring, Cristina. "Love in the Time of Hedonism: Michel Houellebecq's New Novel." *Harper's* 307, no. 1839 (August 2003): 75-81.

Nehring praises the scope of material in *Platform* but notes that Houellebecq examines social issues in "so individual and honest and blithely self-centered a way that it is almost impossible for him to offer a consistent statement about them."

Sturrock, John. "Agitated Neurons." *London Review of Books* 21, no. 2 (21 January 1999): 24-5.

Sturrock examines the controversy surrounding the publication of *Extension du domaine de la lutte* and *Les Particules élémentaires,* concluding that both novels are impressive, if distasteful, commentaries on contemporary life.

Additional coverage of Houellebecq's life and career is contained in the following sources published by the Gale Group: *Contemporary Authors,* **Vol. 185; and** *Literature Resource Center.*

Gita Mehta
1943-

Indian novelist and essayist.

The following entry presents an overview of Mehta's career through 2001.

INTRODUCTION

With her first collection of essays, *Karma Cola: Marketing the Mystic East* (1979), Mehta joined a growing number of critically and popularly acclaimed female Indian authors who write primarily in English. Although the essays in *Karma Cola* function as sarcastic responses to the West's infatuation with India, her novels *Raj* (1989) and *A River Sutra* (1993) seek to create a deeper understanding of Indian history, culture, and mysticism. Mehta's fiction displays a preoccupation with the inherent difficulties behind social interactions, either through examining the cultural disconnects between Great Britain and India during the era of colonial rule or through the myriad social and cultural divisions within traditional Indian society.

BIOGRAPHICAL INFORMATION

Mehta was born in 1943, in Delhi, India. Her father, Biju Patnaik, was a political activist in the Indian Independence movement who was arrested for his activism three weeks after the birth of his daughter. At the age of three, Mehta was sent to be raised in a convent in Kashmir, allowing her mother to travel and campaign for her husband's release. After India regained sovereignty from Great Britain in 1947, Mehta's father was released from prison and resumed his political career. Mehta travelled to England for higher education, earning her university degree at Cambridge University. While at Cambridge, she met and later married Ajai Singh "Sonny" Mehta, with whom she has a son. Having chosen a career in journalism, Mehta has covered a number of significant world events, including the Bangladesh War of 1971 and the first elections in the former Indian princely states. She has also written and directed several television documentaries for the British Broadcasting Corporation (BBC) and the National Broadcasting Company (NBC).

MAJOR WORKS

Mehta's first work, *Karma Cola,* was written as a critical response to the ways that the Western counterculture community has regarded India and Indian

culture. Due to the fascination of spiritualists, hippies, and popular rock musicians The Beatles with Hindu mysticism, large groups of Americans flock to India each year in search of religion, drugs, and enlightenment. Through the essays in *Karma Cola,* Mehta seeks to debunk the notion that all Indians are experts on spiritual matters and to contrast the irony of Western materialism being used to obtain traditionally Eastern religious beliefs. In such essays as "Om Is Where the Art Is" and "Sex and the Single Guru," Mehta humorously and sarcastically exposes the emptiness behind placing one's hopes for the future in the hands of gurus and transcendental meditation. Set in the early- to mid-twentieth century, *Raj* recounts the life of a sheltered Indian princess, Princess Jaya, as she witnesses the end of British imperial rule in India. Her father, once a powerful man in the community, is slowly being forced into obscurity by the strict rules imposed on him by the British Raj—the British government in India. Jaya is eventually sent to marry a prince in a neighboring kingdom, though her husband—like many in India at the time—is obsessed with emulating the British. Her husband's preoccupation with Western values causes him to view anything Eastern as inferior, including his wife. After the era of colonial rule ends in 1947, Jaya is finally able to exert her own independence by registering for a position in the newly formed Indian government. The style and structure of Mehta's second novel, *A River Sutra,* has frequently been compared to Geoffrey Chaucer's *The Canterbury Tales.* The plot is constructed around a series of short sketches—"The Monk's Story," "The Teacher's Story," "The Executive's Story," "The Courtesan's Story," "The Musician's Story," "The Minstrel's Story," and "The Song of the Narmada"—which are brought together as a whole by a nameless narrator who speaks in the first-person. The narrator is a bureaucrat who leaves his government position to manage a small inn along the banks of India's holiest river, the Narmada. The Narmada becomes a recurring motif in each of the stories as well as the narrator's inability to understand the tales of love he hears from his guests. Through these narrative threads, Mehta illuminates the interconnectedness of the diverse range of cultures within India while expounding on the universalities of love. In *Snakes and Ladders: Glimpses of Modern India* (1997), Mehta returns to her critical examination of Indian culture, this time focusing on Indian history since the end of British rule. The essays cover a wide range of subjects from current Indian political thought to the growing influence of American pop culture on Indian youth. Mehta also discusses the duality of India's continuing relationship with Britain and the stagnancy of certain Indian social movements, contrasting them with her father's own passionate activism.

CRITICAL RECEPTION

Since the publication of *Karma Cola,* critics have heralded Mehta as a fresh new voice in Indian literature. Reviewers have consistently praised her wit and insight into Western misconceptions of the East and cross-cultural relations. However, *Raj* has received a mixed critical reaction, with some arguing that the protagonist is overly passive and the narrative is lacking in plot. Others have complained that *Raj* focuses too heavily on historical minutia and fails to create compelling characterizations. *A River Sutra,* conversely, has drawn wide acclaim for its emphasis on the multiculturalism of India and the importance of individuals within a community. The novel has additionally been complimented for Mehta's use of interlocking short stories to cumulatively paint a vivid picture of India's rich spiritual beliefs. Lavinia Greenlaw has remarked that *A River Sutra,* "has a clarity and a dignity that contains these stories of endurance and loss, avoiding any excess of sentiment or pathos." *Snakes and Ladders* has also garnered a favorable critical reception, with reviewers

commending Mehta's insight into current Indian political trends. Michael Gorra has commented that, despite the collection's "disjointed structure," the essays in *Snakes and Ladders* are ultimately "marked by warmth and charm."

PRINCIPAL WORKS

Karma Cola: Marketing the Mystic East (essays) 1979
Raj: A Novel (novel) 1989
A River Sutra (novel) 1993
Snakes and Ladders: Glimpses of Modern India (essays) 1997

CRITICISM

Maurya Simon (review date 9 April 1989)

SOURCE: Simon, Maurya. "A Princess Remembers the Fall of British India." *Los Angeles Times Book Review* (9 April 1989): 10.

[*In the following review, Simon observes that* Raj *is an eloquent and engaging novel, noting that Mehta provides a unique feminine perspective on Indian literature.*]

"Providence," wrote Rudyard Kipling, "created the Maharajahs to offer mankind a spectacle." That spectacle flourished for several millennia within India, prior to the establishment of imperial rule in 1858 by the British Crown. Despite successive waves of foreign invasions and migrations over many centuries, and despite the passing and reformation of dynasties, the institution of Indian kingship (as old as the "Mahabharata" itself) remained constant and ubiquitous throughout the subcontinent until the mid-20th Century.

At the time of the first British colonies, India was ruled by 565 princely states. These states were most remarkable, perhaps, for their multiplicity and diversity. The very palaces and forts of the dynastic rulers varied remarkably, as well, in size, architecture, history and occupation: from a chieftain's well-appointed, tapestried tent to a maharajah's 400-room marble palace housing thousands of servants and retainers, rose-water-filled swimming pools, exotic zoos, squash courts, modern movie theaters and great, gilded durbar halls.

Among the princely rulers were hedonists and ascetics, scholars and sportsmen, tribal chieftains and Oxford graduates, despots and reformers. However, regardless of their wealth, religious background, or aptitude for leadership, most royal leaders of British India initially welcomed imperial rule, for one of the Crown's first acts was to freeze the borders of many kingdoms, thus providing a security and tenure heretofore unknown to the rulers and their predecessors. But there was a stiff price to pay for such security: British paramountcy, a system whereby Indian kings became beholden not to their own rule or people, but to the British Raj, as embodied in the person of the viceroy, and as directly overseen, in each kingdom, by a resident officer.

Suddenly India's powerful kings were demoted to "princes" and "native chiefs," and their vast and ancient domains regarded simply as princely or native states that were subjected to exorbitant taxation by the British Crown. During a 90-year period, India's rulers submitted to a deliberate and gradual erosion of their power, to the threat of divestment and forced abdication of their thrones. Often they were ousted or exiled on the grounds of "princely misconduct" (such as an indiscreet or scandalous sexual liaison), or because they were accused of treason, sedition, or disloyalty to the Crown.

No wonder, then, when the seeds of nationalism began to propagate in the 1920s, many of India's most powerful rulers found themselves in an intractable political dilemma. They felt torn between their often tenuous and ambivalent loyalty to the British Raj and their own loyalty to their traditions and their subjects, who were beginning to demand "home rule" and a more democratic governance.

Gita Mehta's fine novel, *Raj,* accurately documents and compellingly dramatizes the maelstrom of allegiances and conflicting loyalties that beset the Hindu, Muslim and Sikh rulers of princely India. Spanning the era from Queen Victoria's Diamond Jubilee in 1897 to partition and independence in 1947, Mehta chronicles the British Raj's effect both upon the princely states in general, as well as upon the personal life of an Indian princess, Jaya Devi.

Born and reared in the desert kingdom of Balmer, Princess Jaya is guided by conflicting influences throughout her childhood: by her deeply religious mother and by her modern, anti-British father. Contradictory forces direct every aspect of her home life and schooling: Jaya studies Sanskrit and the ancient Rajput laws of sovereignty with the palace guru, womanly demeanor with the purdah ladies in the *zanana* (women's quarters of the palace), current events with her austere and fiercely nationalistic tutor and polo with the British political officer assigned to Balmer.

A series of tragic events leads, eventually, to Jaya's departure from Balmer and to her arrival, as a teenage bride, in the Kingdom of Sirpur. The princess' life here,

too, is contradictory and confusing. Her new husband, Prince Pratap, an Oxford-educated playboy, expects his bride to become Westernized enough to don red nail polish and risqué saris, yet he demands that she conform to his traditional expectations of an appropriately submissive and reticent Hindu wife. Prince Pratap, and his brother the Maharajah Victor, energetically court the favors of the British Raj, while openly indulging their tastes for foreign actresses, Indian prostitutes, for extravagant banquets and lavish balls, for expensive cars and planes.

Early in her marriage, Jaya recognizes the tyranny of the Raj, as it renders her husband and brother-in-law politically impotent and embittered, and as it encourages the excesses of other rulers, whose only permissible act of defiance seems to be to outdo the exhibitionism and materialistic grandeur of English royalty. Jaya's exile from Balmer, and her estrangement from her husband, allow her to gain an objectivity and clarity rare among her friends and associates. Eventually, she comes to see herself, her adopted kingdom and British India as being painfully compromised: All three flounder toward an ideal of self-respect and autonomy, yet each remains dependent upon the good offices of either husband, resident officer or British Crown.

Regardless of her clear political vision, Jaya's personal evolution is clouded by fear and uncertainty of self, by her reluctance to challenge tradition. Nonetheless, her gradual personal transformation is convincing and poignant. Ultimately, as Regent of Sirpur, Jaya learns how to act on her own behalf, even as she acts on behalf of the people she rules. Adroitly, the author parallels the heroine's ascendancy to personal power with the decline of autocracy and British rule.

Many distinguished and capable British authors have depicted and examined life in India under the British Raj (Kipling, Forster, John Masters and Paul Scott, to name but a few), but their views are inescapably British and all too often reflect the prejudices of imperialism. How necessary and instructive it is to hear the story of British colonial rule from descendants of those who were subjugated by it, damaged by its injustices. Doubly refreshing, then, is Mehta's ambitious and successful book, for it allows its readers a fascinating and vivid glimpse into one Indian woman's long moment in history, as she charts her own course and as she witnesses the painful evolution of the most populous fledgling democracy in the world.

Ian Buruma (essay date 18 May 1989)

SOURCE: Buruma, Ian. "Good Night, Sweet Princes." *New York Review of Books* 36, no. 8 (18 May 1989): 9-10, 12.

[*In the following essay, Buruma discusses the British colonial rule of India and its social and cultural effects as portrayed in Mehta's* Raj.]

[In *Raj: A Novel*] Gita Mehta sets the scene well: India, the Roaring Twenties, the Royal Calcutta Turf Club. Jaya, wife of Prince Pratap of Sirpur, is watching the races, dressed in red and indigo, the Sirpur colors. She is joined by her brother-in-law, Maharajah Victor, a gentle man in love with a Hollywood star:

> "The Sirpur colors seem to belong on you, Princess. I often think you are the only one of us who knows who you are."
>
> "But you are the Maharajah, hukam. You are Sirpur."
>
> He looked at her and Jaya was shocked at the unhappiness in his eyes. "Only by birth and the tolerance of the British Crown, not because I believe I am a king. I am acting and actors should be allowed to marry actresses."

That is of course precisely what they were, the rajahs, maharajahs, nawabs, and Nizams of India, actors on a stage set by the British. Effectively emasculated by the Raj, they were useful as vassals to the British Crown, ruling chunks of India, red blotches on the map in a sea of pink, virtually as proxies with British residents watching their every move. Tradition and the mystique of divine kingship lent historical weight to British ideas of "good government." As long as they acted their parts, the Indian princes could spend their lives at play. And some chose very odd plays indeed.

Mehta uses to wonderful effect a celebrated occasion when the Nawab of Junagadh staged a dog wedding, inviting the *crème de la crème* of Indian aristocracy for the occasion: "The marriage of the two dogs, Roshanara; veiled and covered in gems, to Bobby, shivering in his wet silk pajamas, was conducted with all the ceremony that would have accompanied the marriage of a royal princess."

Andrew Robinson, in the latest glossy book for the Indian nostalgia trade, describes the funeral of the Maharajah of Alwar: his impeccably dressed corpse seated stiffly upright in his favorite golden Hispano-Suiza, the rear of which was a copy of the British coronation coach, complete with carriage lamps and gold crowns. Alas, there are no pictures of this occasion. We have to make do instead with Sumio Uchiyama's colorful photos, mostly of the charming Maharajah of Jodhpur (Eton and Oxford) striking traditional poses.

Another noteworthy player, cited by Robinson, was Sayaji Rao, the Gaekwad of Baroda, who trained his parrots to ride silver bicycles and perform dainty dramatic scenes. His granddaughter, Gayatri Devi, remembered one in particular "in which a parrot was run over by a car, examined by a parrot doctor, and finally carried off on a stretcher by parrot bearers. The grand climax of their performance was always a salute fired on a silver cannon."[1]

All this is fun to read of course. The excesses of bored men with unlimited means always are. But Mehta's novel, greatly to her credit, is more than a catalog of bizarre fancies. The story of Jaya is a story of liberation: the liberation of a woman, whose story begins in the opulent seclusion of a palace harem and ends in a court of law, where she registers her name as a political candidate in a newly independent India. But, again to her credit, it is not simply a story of brave, freedom-loving Indians versus arrogant oppressive Brits. It is much more ambivalent than that, for the agents of change, and ultimately of freedom, are often the very same things that oppress and destroy.

Two symbols recur frequently throughout the book: the machine and the bracelet. Glass bangles or glittering gauntlets are forever clinking on Jaya's wrists like manacles, symbols of her young servitude to tradition. Dressed by servants for her marriage to a man she has never even met, she felt "suffocated as the women scratched her body with jeweled gauntlets and heavy anklets." But when the young Englishman she had loved dances with her at a ball, her bangles break in his white glove. And when her maidservants haul bags of contraband salt into a train in defiance of the British monopoly their glass bangles break against the window bars.

The machine is introduced as a destructive force, often in conjunction with money. Thus we learn early on how drought turns Jaya's ancestral country into a wasteland "to be exploited by the machines of a new age without customs or humanity." Thus it is that the palace guru believes that by adopting the machines and institutions of the British, "we would adopt their ways, and in the process lose our souls." Jaya's father is shocked by the idea of investing money in stocks, for moneylending is undignified; it is against the dharma of a Rajput warrior. "Dungra's thick lips, stained red with betel juice, opened in laughter. 'Dignity? Dharma? You live in the past, Jai. Such words have lost their currency. Now the world runs on money.'"

The old world of customs and warriors against the new world of machines and moneylenders; no wonder at least one maharajah is said to have had portraits of Hitler in his study. He was not to know that Hitler, despite his love for Aryan nobility, was hardly interested in saving the Indian soul.

Jaya's attitude toward the machine age is one of sad resignation:

> She thought of her father's mustache falling like a broken wing onto his white tunic as he told the Balmer Raj Guru that machines had ended the dharma of the warrior, and with it the dharma of the king.

For much of her life, inevitably for an Indian woman in the first half of this century, her destiny is controlled by men. They all represent something: her father, the old world Rajput; her husband, the confused, self-hating

Anglicized playboy; her Indian lover, the Bengali babu nationalist; her English friend, the liberal who loves India. These are well-known types, but, as with Jaya, it is their ambivalence that saves them from being cardboard cutouts. For her father may be an old world Rajput, but he also tries to be modern, forcing his wife to break purdah and help the starving villagers during a famine. Osborne, the English friend, may be a liberal who loves India, but he remains loyal to his viceroy, to the point of spying on Jaya's activities when he decides they are against British interests. And the Bengali babu, Arun Roy, is strongly drawn toward the very woman whose power he must destroy.

Sex is of course one of the most fascinating aspects of colonial society, the way sex became mixed up with politics. The early British settlers in India, soldiers and traders, employed by the East India Company, had no qualms about taking Indian mistresses; this was one of the "perks" of living in the tropics. But after the British began to rule India, not as traders but as a kind of superior caste, sex with the natives became a taboo, something upper-caste Hindus understood very well. The taboo was no doubt broken on some occasions, but this degraded the white sahib in Indian as well as British eyes. So even though every encounter between Jaya and Osborne is charged with erotic attraction, nothing happens, nothing can be allowed to happen. Even sex between the sahibs and memsahibs had to be discreet to maintain face in the eyes of the more fastidious natives. Nirad Chaudhuri, for one, was shocked by the sight of white couples carousing on Indian beaches, thereby "bringing disgrace upon the great European tradition of adultery established by all the historic adulteresses from Cleopatra to Madame de Stael."[2]

The penchant among Indian aristocrats for seducing as many white women as they could was degrading in a different way. It was part of their playacting—collecting Hollywood starlets was not so different from collecting Hispano-Suizas. But it was also a kind of racial revenge, though the revenge was not as sweet as it should have been, for it was infused with self-hatred. Mehta catches this well in her description of Jaya as a new bride, still very much the traditional Rajput princess, pining for her absent husband. She asks her older friend and mentor, Lady Modi, otherwise known as Bapsy, why she appears to fill her husband with disgust:

> "Is it the color of our skin? Our hair? Are white women so much more beautiful than we are?"

> "Of course not, darling. It's just that you represent everything the British Empire has taught Pratap and Victor to despise. . . ."

So what should she do about it?

> If you want to attract your husband, Princess, you must make the British envy Pratap, not patronize him. You must make yourself into a woman who is desirable to white men.

This still rings true today, from Bombay to Tokyo, where some women continue to have their eyes fixed to look more Western. Of course this is not for the benefit of Western males, who, in any case, tend to prefer exotic Asian beauty, but to suit their own notion that physically the West is best.

Jaya tries her best to dress like a European flapper, but never becomes the caricature that her cocktail-swilling friend Bapsy is. Nor does she become quite like Bapsy's opposite, Jaya's teacher, Mrs. Roy, a nationalist from Calcutta, dressed in white cotton saris; earnest where Bapsy is frivolous, loyal where Bapsy is fickle, intellectual where Bapsy is shallow. Jaya never becomes like Mrs. Roy, because she remains an aristocrat to the end, even when registering her name as a candidate in India's first independent elections.

Jaya's rebellion is not an intellectual one as Mrs. Roy's is. She wanted to be a dutiful wife, but, rejected by her husband, she ends up hating him and everything he stands for. Refused his love, she gains his power. When she agrees to extricate him from a disastrous affair with an Anglo-Indian demimondaine formerly employed in a Calcutta brothel, she demands that she become regent of his state in the case of his death, which, as so often happens with shiftless playboys in novels, comes rather soon.

Gita Mehta's novel is important because, for once, it deals with the Raj without nostalgia or bitterness. She is at her best when describing the twisted human relations in a colonial society. The first part of the story, Jaya's childhood, interested me less than Jaya's adult life. As a child she is only among Rajputs, with the occasional intrusion of a white man or a Bengali teacher. But it is in the milieu of nationalist radicals, Anglo-Indian mistresses, cynical politicians, decadent maharajahs, and Indian flappers that the novel really comes alive. It is, one feels, a milieu Mehta knows very well: that small, still-existing society in India, where East meets West, a sometimes fruitful, sometimes hilarious, sometimes disastrous encounter. The novel ends with Indira Gandhi's parliamentary bill of 1970, discontinuing privy purses and abolishing the concept of rulership. It was the formal end of princely rule in India. But in few countries is the legacy of history, in spirit and form, so apparent as in India.

The worst legacy of modern colonialism, in India and elsewhere, has been the idea, very much in the foreground of Mehta's novel, that superior race gave Europeans a divine right, even duty, to rule the world. It has left Westerners with a crippling sense of guilt, dangerously affecting their judgment of non-Western affairs. And it has left resentment and a confused sense of inferiority among the former colonial subjects. (The Japanese are a separate case; they tried to outdo the

West by claiming *they* were the divine race destined to rule the world.)

But—and this is one of the strongest themes in Mehta's book—it was the same West, with its machines and institutions, that inspired freedom and democracy, that broke the bangles of feudal bondage. The rhetoric of Indian nationalists was picked up in England, from the Fabians and the London School of Economics. The Bengali babus were in the vanguard of nationalist agitation because—unlike most of their British rulers—they were *au courant* with European ideas; they had read the books people read in London, Oxford, and Cambridge.

They were despised by the British for having done so, for acting above their station, imitating absurdly the ways of a superior race. The British much preferred Indians to remain exotic, hardy warriors, loyal Johnny Pathans and dependable Sikhs, colorful in dress, traditional in behavior. One of the paradoxes of the Raj, deeply confusing to educated Indians, is that the British encouraged emulation on the one hand and hated it on the other. They taught the Indian princes how to play cricket and sent them to English schools, but sniggered at the result: the half-baked Englishman, at home only in places like the Calcutta Turf Club. As Lord Curzon said about the princes at a gathering in 1902:

> Amid the leveling tendency of the age and the inevitable monotony of government conducted upon scientific lines, they keep alive the traditions and customs, they sustain the virility, and they save from extinction the picturesqueness of ancient and noble races.

Note that word picturesque. Above all, India had to be picturesque and, of course, ancient—not so different from the attitude to Asia of the modern Western tourist, or even the well-meaning liberal: ancient and noble culture, not democracy, traditions, and customs, not the modern blight of materialism, machines, money. Under the Raj, the British took care of the money and the machines. And as long as the princes behaved traditionally, that is, as long as they were loyal to the British Crown, like feudal knights to their lords, they could have their champagne parties and golden cars. And it had to be said, those maharajahs threw some damned good parties.

It was the British, more than the Indians, who first attempted to define and preserve traditional India. This irony is often forgotten by writers who see Western colonialism only as an assault on traditional values. No doubt the Raj changed much in India (*pace* those who argue that it was nothing more than a swift ripple in the unchanging and largely inert ocean of Indian history), and all change is a challenge to what existed before. But it is a mistake to pit Western modernity (the machine) too neatly against the fragile glass bangles of Indian tradition. Indeed, some of the picturesque customs of India were of a British make.

Nirad Chaudhuri has pointed out how "the orientalism which became one of the two elements in the modern Indian synthesis, was not the native and traditional Sanskrit learning, but the new learning about the East created by the European orientalists."[3] And in his wonderful essay in *The Invention of Tradition,*[4] Bernard S. Cohn writes how Victorian Englishmen fretted about the Indian "heritage." They decided which monuments ought to be preserved, collected arts and crafts, translated classic texts, and compiled Indian history. "The British rulers," writes Cohn,

> were increasingly defining what was Indian in an official and "objective" sense. Indians had to look like Indians: before 1860 Indian soldiers as well as their European officers wore western-style uniforms; now the dress uniforms of Indians and English included turbans, sashes and tunics thought to be Mughal or Indian.

Injecting nationalist anthropology into politics was a popular idea in nineteenth-century Europe. That was what the Olympic Games were all about: the pageantry of man, each nation in its own uniform, singing its own lusty folk songs, waving its own banners. And this, on an imperial scale, is what the great durbars were about, when the British viceroy, or on one occasion the king-emperor himself, held court in Delhi, like the Mughal emperors before them, to the assembled aristocracy of India. The Indian princes were each issued their own coat of arms, designed by one Robert Taylor, a civil servant and amateur heraldist. Queen Victoria was proclaimed Kaiser-I-Hind in 1876, a brand new title suggested by G. W. Leitner, a professor of Oriental languages.

Cohn gives a hilarious description of the first Imperial Assemblage in Delhi, commemorating Victoria's promotion to empress. Eighty-four thousand Indians and Europeans had pitched their tents over a space of five miles. On January 1, 1877, to the sounds of the "March of Tannhauser," the viceroy Lord Lytton and his wife made their appearance, waving regally from their silver seat perched on top of the largest elephant in India, owned by the Rajah of Benares.

The point of all this is that the British deliberately used picturesque Indian tradition to strengthen their own power, creating a hierarchy of flags and banners, gathered like a great patchwork under the banner of the Kaiser-I-Hind. The diversity of race, religion, and languages of India, demonstrated at these jamborees, made it clear how unity was only possible under the "good government" of the British Crown.

This may not have been entirely a matter of playacting or cynical manipulation. Lord Curzon, like most people of his class and time, truly believed in tradition and customs and ancient and noble races. Certainly Benjamin Disraeli, the architect of British India and the prime mover behind that glorious Imperial Assembly of 1877, did. Hannah Arendt made the persuasive argument that Disraeli dazzled British aristocrats by promoting the myth of his ancient Jewish racial heritage, more ancient and far purer than that of the British aristocracy, which had seen too many infusions of new blood over the years. Race, said Disraeli, was the key to history, and there "is only one thing which makes a race and that is blood," and there is only one aristocracy, the "aristocracy of nature," which consists of "an unmixed race of a first-rate organization."[5] The first-rate organization, in his feverish imagination, was the British Empire and he, as a natural aristocrat, stood at its pinnacle with his beloved queen.

Racial pride, in the new scheme of things, was about all the Indian princes had left. The Rajput warrior, boasting of his ancient bloodlines, dazzled upper-class Englishmen in the same way Disraeli did. This is one reason, apart from the dashed good shooting parties, why the British still looked up to the princes, no matter how absurd their behavior, while despising the Bengali babus.

There was certainly an element of this in the British worship of Ranjitsinhji, Jam Saheb of Nawanagar, a famous cricketer before World War I. (Ranji, sometimes known as "the black prince," makes a brief appearance in Mehta's book, riding to King George's durbar in a solid silver coach.) A. G. Gardener, one of Ranji's British admirers, wrote a celebrated homage to the great cricketer, which is still recited in Indian schools:

> The caste system of our own cricket field as of our own society has only the basis in riches. You cannot be a Runjeet Singh—to give the Jam Saheb the true rendering of his much abused name—unless you have the blood of the lion race in your veins, but you may join the old nobility of England if you have made a brilliant speculation in rubber. . . .

Disraeli would have been amused.

So while the British machine helped to destroy the dharma of the warrior, as Jaya's father lamented, the Raj may actually have helped to strengthen the mythology of warriorhood. The so-called martial races were the Indian corollary of the cold-bath-can-do spirit of the British White Man's Burden. Many Indian princes outdid themselves to fight for the British Empire in both world wars. It was one way for Rajput warriors to retrieve their dharma, even though it quickly became apparent that, as Jaya's father put it, "This is no war for men. It is a war between the mechanisms of slaughter." The salvation of the Hindus, said Swami Vivekananda, who toured the US with great success in the 1890s, lay in three Bs: beef, biceps, and Bhagavad-Gita. It was his answer to the "muscular Christianity" of Dr. Arnold's

England. He said it, it is true, in a moment of despair about British colonial rule. But his response, to match the discipline (a key word of the Raj) and virility of the conqueror, with the same qualities, was typical. To add yet another irony to the history of the Raj, it was a decidedly unmartial Bengali intellectual, Subhas Chandra Bose, who finally gave political expression to militarism.

"Discipline," said a Rajput rajah, showing me around early this year in the Rajastan desert, where Gita Mehta's novel is set, "discipline is the only thing we learnt from the British worth learning, and Indians have lost that. No more discipline."

One hears the same in Singapore and Malaysia: discipline and racial pride, the two prongs of British colonial ideology, are now part of postcolonial propaganda. Social Darwinism, largely discredited in the West, is very much alive in the minds of many Asian leaders. This is the final irony of the empire whose sun never set, that men like Lee Kuan Yew, who fought the British for their countries' independence, now castigate the West for being flabby and decadent, for having forgotten discipline, pride, in short, the old White Man's Burden. The "traditional values" of Singapore, touted as Confucian, are also the values of the Raj. The Darwinist ideas promoted by the likes of Malaysia's prime minister Mahathir would have been warmly applauded by Rudyard Kipling.

Where does this leave the Indian princes, the Rajput descendants of Gita Mehta's heroes? They seem as ambivalent as ever.

> The rajah visitor pointed at the desert villages from his jeep: "Look around, life is just as it was before it was disturbed by the British."
>
> "How was it disturbed?"
>
> He waved his hand dismissively: "Oh, they built electricity, railways, all that."
>
> "Was that a bad thing?"
>
> "It was nothing at all. Look what has been achieved in forty years of independence. Compared to that the Raj was insignificant. They gave us some cars. A few Rolls Royces, here and there. But now we have our own Indian cars. We have airlines, we have nuclear power. Of that we are very, very proud."

And so, a proud man, he returned to his palace, now a tourist hotel, where he received his guests with the courtesy one expects from a Rajput educated like an English gentleman at one of the former princely schools. Some of the lady guests, an Australian painter, a British schoolteacher, a French antique dealer, were dressed up in silk saris. One blond woman had daubed a red spot on her forehead, as though she were a Hindu. On her wrists glittered a mass of glass and silver bangles.

Notes

1. Quoted from Gayatri Devi's memoir: *A Princess Remembers* (1976).

2. *Thy Hand, Great Anarch!* (Addison-Wesley, 1988), p. 167.

3. *The Autobiography of an Unknown Indian* (University of California Press, 1951), p. 447.

4. Eric Hobsbawm and Terence Ranger, eds., *The Invention of Tradition* (Cambridge University Press, 1983).

5. In Hannah Arendt, *Anti-Semitism* (Harcourt Brace Jovanovich, 1968), p. 73.

Yasmin Alibhai (review date 16 June 1989)

SOURCE: Alibhai, Yasmin. "A False Orient." *New Statesman and Society* 2, no. 54 (16 June 1989): 34.

[*In the following review, Alibhai criticizes* Raj *as a meager and bland novel, deficient in characterization and inventiveness.*]

There is a thin novel somewhere in this fat one [*Raj*]. Thin as a gruel that hardly satisfies the appetite it raises, in spite of being served up in an aureate bowl on a table heavy with exquisite silver. The story is the personal odyssey of Jaya, a Rajput princess who moves from a life of seclusion and exclusion in a sumptuous palace, first as a daughter and then the wife of a Maharajah, during the days of British rule, to a life of political commitment and power as she applies to be a candidate in the first free elections in her country. Jaya's story is obviously also meant to symbolize the history of India itself as it moved turbulently from the end of the 19th century to independence in 1949 and the liberation of Indian women as these historical convulsions rocked the social structures of the society.

It doesn't work and the problem may well be the aureate bowl. There is far too much meaningless detail, far too much cloying fascination with the exotic. In an article in the *Observer* a few years ago, Salman Rushdie attacked the kind of Raj Revival Enterprise that had started to flourish in Britain in the eighties. It represented, he said, the recrudescence of an imperial ideology, because the revival was only really interested in creating "a false orient of cruel-lipped princes, dusky slim-hipped maidens, ungodliness of fire and the sword . . . where the natives are surrounded by the branding of human flesh, snakery and widow burning". So why has Gita Mehta, an Indian writer, joined in this exploitative enterprise?

It can, of course, be argued that she is only being historically accurate, that these things did happen. It is clear from the various acknowledgments and references

that much research has gone into the book. Gandhi, Nehru, Curzon, Naidu, Jinnah, Dyer all get a mention, and many others besides. But this is supposed to be a novel and not a boil-in-the-bag history/social anthropology lesson and the imaginative leap that is needed to transform historical realities into fictional realities is rarely made. Unlike the British writers and film makers who have an addiction to the subject, Mehta *does* try to show how the colonials used their power to manipulate people and destroy systems which had evolved through the centuries, but the impact of this is reduced by the overwhelming presence of opulent decadence.

There is hardly any development of character. Jaya ponders in the same idiom, and with the same awareness, as child and adult. At the age of ten, we are required to believe that she "realized with an aching sense of loss that she had ceased to be a child". She never *does* anything solid or memorable. Her power comes to her simply because all those who would have had it conveniently die, one by one. First her father, then her brother, then her despicable husband and finally her son. This may be how the outside world treated Indian women, but does Jaya's internal life have to respond with such lassitude? Writers like Ila Mehta and Mrinal Pande also deal with the powerlessness of Indian women, but their heroines seethe and plot and joust, at least within the safe confines of their brains.

Mehta occasionally gives us a glimpse of what she is capable of writing, a peep behind the purdah. And these are moments when she shows her real feelings. She is angry when she describes how the British reduced the Maharajahs to impotent puppets—"Your empire absorbed our armies, castrated our nobles, confused our scholars, diminished our priests . . ."—and appalled at the humiliation of Jaya at the hands of her husband when he finally rips into her body "until her glass bangles smashed into the jasmine garlands and blood stained the crushed petals". She is afraid when she writes, "Fear opened like a trapdoor beneath the Maharani."

Mehta is also very good when she describes the pain of the west exerting its influence over the east, when Indian sons lose themselves in the arms of French whores and despise their own people. "Are white women more beautiful than we are?" asks Jaya, and is then persuaded to make herself into a woman who is desirable to white men so that her husband will want her. The shadowy figures who come and go also work because they remain ambiguous and escape the verbal overloading that the main characters are burdened with.

But these brief moments do not rescue the book from its superficiality and cliched obsessions. As Rushdie says: "The jewel in the crown is made these days of paste."

Sarah Curtis (review date 7 July 1989)

SOURCE: Curtis, Sarah. "Through the Lattice Chinks." *Times Literary Supplement,* no. 4501 (7 July 1989): 739.

[*In the following review, Curtis praises Mehta's eye for detail in* Raj *but argues that the plot is uninspired and poorly narrated.*]

In *Raj,* Gita Mehta, who was born in India and educated at Bombay and Cambridge Universities, chronicles the last years of the Rajput realms of India, from the turn of the century until 1950 when under the new Indian constitution the rulers of the kingdoms surrendered their powers. She does so through the eyes of Jaya, Princess of Balmer, whose fort and palaces on the edge of the desert have touches of Jaipur, Jaisalmer, Patiala and the other real States mentioned in the book as allies and neighbours. The idea of scanning the disintegration of the Rajputs through the lattice chinks of the zanana from which Mehta's heroine has to emerge is an ambitious and attractive one. The device of a hero born at a historic hour was used by Salman Rushdie in *Midnight's Children,* but there the parallels cease. Unfortunately, Mehta shows neither his narrative skill nor his imaginative gift.

Jaya is caught between conflicting traditions. Her father, the Maharajah Jai Singh, has taught her the traditional four arms of kingship: *Saam*—a king must serve his people's needs; *Daan*—he must provide for their welfare; *Dand*—he must punish injustice; and *Bhed,* he must protect the kingdom with treaties and alliances. He is himself much troubled by *Bhed,* for which he has to appease the rapacious, arrogant British, who tax the loyal princes out of existence and ignore the ancient wisdoms of their land. He sends his heir to England in order to be educated, then killed fighting in the First World War; and yet he hires as his daughter's tutor Mrs Roy, whose brother is a leader of the independence movement.

As disaster after disaster befalls her house, Jaya is contracted in a marriage of convenience to Pratrap, the playboy Prince of ancient Sirpur, more interested in his mistresses than his responsibilities. She responds with a loyalty bred of her upbringing, plays a waiting game and suffers humiliation after humiliation, not least when being shaped into a more sophisticated consort by the strange Lady Modi, a character out of Waugh who is given the odd perceptive line: "You represent", Lady Modi tells her charge, "everything the British Empire has taught Pratrap to despise."

Perhaps Jaya's passivity symbolizes that of mother India; but it has the effect of exposing the mechanics of the plot. The duplicity of the British, the incapacity of the princes to combine to protect their traditions, and the divisions between India's religions, are exhaustively reported. Sometimes a historical character such as Annie Besant or Rabindranath Tagore is inserted into an episode, sometimes there are pages of exposition covering the conferences and events of the year. Like the detail of religious ritual, life in the harem, festival and ceremony, all this is fascinating in its own right but never satisfactorily integrated. Even the satirical accounts of the ludicrous excesses of princely decadence lose their edge because they are set-pieces.

The most interesting character in the book is Jaya's mother, changing from a widow who would have liked to have committed suttee on her husband's funeral pyre to a follower of Gandhi on his salt march. But she does this off-page, and we only hear about it briefly; she is really only a vehicle to represent an aspect of the Indian scene Gita Mehta wanted to project. The English officer of the Raj, with whom Jaya has been half in love since they were both children, serves a similar dual function, as romantic interest and as a symbol of the more acceptable aspects of the British. In the modern Indian tradition, sexuality pervades the book, but we are spared most of the detail.

The trouble is that like most of her characters, Mehta has been over whelmed by conflicting aims. Her serious attention to her theme saves the book from being a mere blockbuster yarn or historical romance; but she shows how difficult it is to combine epic sweep with an exploration of one individual's *dharma.*

Betty Abel (review date October 1989)

SOURCE: Abel, Betty. "Quarterly Fiction Review." *Contemporary Review* 255, no. 1485 (October 1989): 214.

[*In the following excerpt, Abel asserts that* Raj *eloquently illustrates the lives of Indians, particularly Indian women, and their interpersonal relationships with each other and with British colonists in the early to mid-twentieth century.*]

Raj by Gita Mehta, the new rival to Paul Scott, author of *Jewel in the Crown,* is a novel of stature. The plot is as sentimental and ordinary as many other tales of the Indian Continent under British rule: but Gita Mehta brings to this scenario a freshness and depth unusual in a romance of the Orient. Her plot concerns Jaya, a Princess raised in purdah who inevitably falls in love with a handsome young Englishman. Forced to marry a dissolute, unattractive Indian Prince, she later has an affair with a politically radical but heartless Casanova. Nonetheless, Jaya emerges a resolute, politically mature and well-balanced lady, bearing a suspicious resemblance to Indira Ghandi. But there is more to the novel than it seems so trite a plot could bear.

Written by an Indian woman, one moreover who finished her education at Cambridge, the book is marked out by its acceptance of the traditional culture of the Maharajahs which the author can show effortlessly, without self-conscious explanations of the kind which even Paul Scott, being English, needs to deploy in *Jewel in the Crown*. Gita Mehta also understands, without trying, the peculiar chemistry of the Anglo-Indian relationship. She depicts the irresistible attraction of the Western ethic for high-born Indian nationals. The contrasts between the extreme poverty of the masses and the wealth of the Indian elite are shown with exceptional clarity, yet with an innate understanding of the philosophy of the Princes and of the bloodthirsty warrior class in all its medieval arrogance. Simultaneously she knows the meaning of the conservatism of her parents, already an anachronism in the early 1900s, and the choice of a freer democracy for her own generation.

The two alternatives, conveyed by the men in her life, show Mehta the failings of both sides of the Indian struggle, the British and the nationalist. But above all they reveal the inherent contradiction in the English habit of requiring the Princes and professionals to adopt British ideas of democracy and at the same time treating all Indians, whether high or lowly born, as inferior. The women came out of purdah into a different but equally unhappy bondage: it seemed like slavery with a twist, and was just as unacceptable. On the other side, the Nationalists imagined a smooth transition to Western theories of statehood for the inhabitants of an already deeply divided land, full of physical and spiritual contrasts.

The heroine's decision to embrace political life might well be seen as a reflection of Indira Ghandi's life: her ambition was to reconcile the aspirations of Westernized, educated Indians with those of the masses for reasonably stable living conditions. The author's feeling for the innermost desires of all the protagonists makes her contribution to the fiction and history of present-day India an important one.

Lavinia Greenlaw (review date 4 June 1993)

SOURCE: Greenlaw, Lavinia. "A River View." *Times Literary Supplement*, no. 4705 (4 June 1993): 23.

[*In the following review, Greenlaw applauds Mehta for constructing an insightful and flowing narrative in* A River Sutra, *complimenting the novel's skillful use of fables as representations of modern Indian culture.*]

The glossary at the back of *A River Sutra* tells us that *sutra* has two meanings: an aphoristic literary form, and a string or thread. In this book, the two usages are simultaneously employed, as a simple narrative carries the reader through a careful arrangement of interlocking didactic tales. Gita Mehta's skillfully constructed second novel follows the experiences of an Indian bureaucrat who retires to run a government resthouse, in the jungle by the sacred Narmada river. He has become a *vanaprasthi*, "someone who has retired to the forest to reflect". The Narmada is the focus of his meditations, and its many historical and mythological associations mean that he finds life literally flowing past his door; for the river attracts pilgrims and refugees of all kinds. Their stories are brief but intense human dramas that not only explore the desire for enlightenment but also express the complex roots of India's cultural and political heritage.

The bureaucrat's first encounter is with a Jain monk. The son of a diamond merchant, he has forgone a life of luxury in order to seek a greater truth. The pattern of this story is repeated throughout the book: the outcome is apparent from the start but contains a powerful mystery, luring the reader into the tale. Drawing such devices from traditional storytelling, Mehta also seems to be challenging the reader with the idea that the natural focus of interest is not meaning but motivation: as much is revealed in how the characters express themselves as in what they say. The monk casually announces that his father spent 62 million rupees on the ceremony to mark his "departure from the world". Despite his assertion that "Ritual means nothing if you do not know the longing that precedes it", it is the chaotic splendour of this three-day event, with its silver chariots and painted elephants, that holds the bureaucrat's attention.

Repeatedly, the lesson to be drawn from the bureaucrat's encounters seems to be that the knowledge he is seeking will not be found through study and observation, but through experience and, in particular, the experience of desire. "How can you say you have given up the world when you know so little of it?" asks his friend, Tariq Mia, the mullah, who teases him with erotic Sufi songs and, in turn, relates the chilling story of a failed singer turned music-teacher whose ambition for his angelic-voiced pupil leads to the child's death.

Each story contains profound upheaval—a moment when the protagonist is forced to accept a painful revelation or to let go of long-held beliefs: a cynical executive is literally seduced by tribal ritual when he leaves the city to manage a tea garden; a courtesan sees the irrelevance of her ancient art when faced with the conviction of the outlaw, who kidnapped her believing they were married in a former life; and an ascetic rejects the constraints of his austere religious order, to save a young girl from prostitution, acting once more in the secular world.

An interesting fusion of cultural influences evokes a world in which the forces of tradition and change are equally visible: the music teacher takes his pupil to a Calcutta park where the homeless sleep beneath English oaks caught in the red flash of nearby neon light; goatherds graze their flocks next to a Victoria memorial and store their milk in aluminium cans; and the future of the young singer is decided on by a recording studio, then denied by a murderer whose status places him beyond the law. Mehta is gifted at identifying the vivid moments and concise observations that can illuminate such a complex society. Her book about the impact of Western culture on India, *Karma Cola* (1979), was acclaimed for this achievement, and her first novel *Raj* (1989) is packed with historical detail, expressed through the narrative rather than imposed on it.

The voice of *A River Sutra* is quieter and more formal. It has a clarity and a dignity that contains these stories of endurance and loss, avoiding any excess of sentiment or pathos. The harshness of life is inescapable and the value of its lessons paramount. Whenever the bureaucrat is distracted by esoteric abstracts, his assumptions are challenged and he is reminded of the book's epigraph: "Man is the greatest truth. Nothing beyond."

Gita Mehta has a strong sense of dramatic tension and the ability to construct powerful intrigues in the briefest exchange. *A River Sutra* ends with a brilliant narrative twist, revealed just when the bureaucrat, and the reader, have perhaps become a little too sure of their understanding. With gentle humour, Mehta removes the possibility of a definitive answer. This is ultimately a satisfying conclusion, as the bureaucrat's much-patronized servant Chagla shyly asserts: "Nothing is ever lost, sir. That is the beauty of a river view."

William Dalrymple (review date 5 June 1993)

SOURCE: Dalrymple, William. "When the Mocking Had to Stop." *Spectator* 270, no. 8604 (5 June 1993): 38.

[*In the following review, Dalrymple commends Mehta's prose and tone in* A River Sutra, *contending that the separate stories within the novel are varied yet unified in direction.*]

The Hampstead novel this is not. In Gita Mehta's slim new volume [*A River Sutra*] we meet a cast the likes of which has rarely been seen before in the precious pages of English literary fiction. Eat your heart out Anita

Brookner: this book has got ash-smeared ascetics and bejewelled courtesans, shy river-minstrels and enlightenment-seeking suicides, ardent young bandits (seduced—of course—by kidnapped virgins on 'thin cotton quilts' in the jungle), 'charms that give men the strength of elephants in rut' and, most extravagant of all,

> an underground civilisation stretching all the way to the Arabian sea, peopled by a mysterious race, half human, half cobra.

Forget marital infidelity in NW1: in *A River Sutra* top executives do it with *snakes*.

All this comes as something of a surprise from a writer who first made her name—at the end of the flare-flapping, tie-dyed Seventies—by *de*mythologising India. In *Karma Cola: Marketing of the Mystic East,* Gita Mehta had great fun mocking the gullible Westerners who unloaded their purses into the open palms of crooked gurus and bhagwans cruising past in their pink Rolls Royces *en route* for the deposit counter of the nearest Grindlays Bank. Under chapter headings like **'Om Is Where the Art Is'** and **'Sex and the Single Guru',** Mehta lovingly dissected the fraudulent hocus pocus which saw them being so readily lapped up by the credulous hippies wandering India in search of grass and nirvana.

Thirteen years (and a Hindu revival) later, Mehta's tone is very different. This time Hinduism is treated with more reverence: there are no gags in this book about sexy swamis and holy hash. The key question is: has Gita Mehta finally embraced the mumbo-jumbo she so ferociously mocked in *Karma Cola*?

Although at first sight it may seem so, Mehta is far too clever and careful a writer to let herself fall into this trap. She walks a thin line, demonstrating her love for the poetry of Hindu mythology and her admiration for the genuine spirituality of rural India—while always managing to distance herself from anything overtly mystical: she quickly sends up any of her characters who seem in danger of taking the *shakti* too seriously. In *A River Sutra* Mehta has a pretty good crack at having her Karma cake and eating it.

The narrator of *A River Sutra* is an elderly bureaucrat who, on the death of his wife, retires from the red tape of the City and takes a job as the humble manager of a government rest house on the banks of the Narmada. The book develops through a series of self-contained stories and fables told to the rest-house manager by his guests and acquaintances. The stories are united not only by their being told on the banks of the river, but also by their themes, all of which reflect the river's name: Narmada derives from the Sanskrit word for desire. The stories are parables, each bearing a Chaucerian title (**"The Monk's Story," "The Musician's Story"**) and illustrating a different aspect of the destructive nature of love and lust: some also examine the possibility of renunciation.

For all their fantastic subject-matter—demon lovers, naked wanderers, and so on, the fables are beautifully told in a wonderfully stark and simple prose style. The stories sometimes read like modern fairy tales, and in both style and content *A River Sutra* owes a lot to R. K. Narayan, the Indian writer Gita Mehta most admires. She shares Narayan's ability to secrete a powerful and serious message in writing of deceptive naïvety, and as with Narayan it is often only on reflection that the true weight and import of a story dawns on the reader. Indeed the book's brevity and concentrated economy belie the importance of its concerns.

It is only when we move in the territory of courtly India that Mehta's descriptive faculties begin to spin out of control. In the **"Courtesan's Story"** we get pages of this sort of thing:

> [My grandmother] spoke of being rowed to lake palaces under a star-filled sky. Of gossamer nets hanging over beds strewn with jasmine blossoms. Pearls scattered on the sheets. Arched doorways opening to balconies, below which the water lapped softly against the stone foundations.

And so on and on. As many others before her have demonstrated, the courts of the Maharajahs are perilous places for a writer to enter, as they have a tendency to envelop even the finest books on India in a hot mist of purple superlatives. Ruth Prawer Jhabvala is at her most unconvincing when dealing with pearl-hung rajahs; even Paul Scott ran into trouble with an excess of peacock fans.

Yet despite this, *A River Sutra* most resembles an album of courtly Mogul miniatures. While these images lack the solid proportions and carefully calculated perspectives of their Western counterparts, they still have an exquisite charm of their own. In Western art, men are portrayed as men. In Mogul miniatures they are elevated to saints, sufis and heroes, gorgeously attired in bright primary colours, and arranged in compositions which hint at the possibility of the fabulous. So it is with this book. The result is certainly every bit as unexpected and enigmatic as the jewelled images produced in the mysterious *ateliers* of the Great Moguls.

Merle Rubin (review date 2 July 1993)

SOURCE: Rubin, Merle. Review of *A River Sutra,* by Gita Mehta. *Christian Science Monitor* 85, no. 152 (2 July 1993): 10.

[*In the following excerpt, Rubin offers a positive assessment of* A River Sutra, *lauding Mehta's ability to con-nect the novel's individual storylines into a "well-designed whole."*]

Vacation, ideally, is an opportunity for renewal—whether it's a well-earned rest or a stimulating change of pace. The narrator of Gita Mehta's novel *A River Sutra* is an Indian government worker who seeks rest but finds stimulation. Hoping to relax from the hurly-burly of city life, he takes a position as manager of a rest house on the leafy banks of India's holy river, the Narmada.

This peaceful retreat proves to be fertile ground for studying the amazing variety of human behavior. Drawn to the sacred river, a wide array of pilgrims, ascetics, saints, and sinners—even an archaeologist—furnish stories to fascinate, bemuse, and astonish the rest-house manager.

There are stories of people deranged by love, of discouraged people who come to the river in the hope of healing. A young Jain, heir to his family's fortune, tells how he cast off his worldly possessions to follow the harsh, self-denying life of a Jain monk. A Muslim music teacher describes the tragic fate of his most gifted pupil, who had the ability to transport listeners into a state of mystic Sufi rapture. A little girl is rescued by a wandering Hindu ascetic from a life of degradation—with ever more surprising results.

Artists, musicians, outlaws, monks, and mullahs, Hindus, Muslims, Jains, believers, and skeptics—all these diverse individuals and types are presented as tributaries of the great river of Indian culture. Mehta, author of two previous novels, writes with power and simplicity, cleverly weaving the stories into a well-designed whole.

Rahul Jacob (review date 11 July 1993)

SOURCE: Jacob, Rahul. "Down the Stream of Stories." *Los Angeles Times Book Review* (11 July 1993): 3.

[*In the following review, Jacob applauds the graceful and fluid stories in* A River Sutra, *arguing that each story adds dimension to the main focus of the novel.*]

There are a great number of us who are not quite able to believe in religion, yet are unable to embrace atheism, which seems "too final, certain, closed. Itself a kind of belief," as Salman Rushdie observes in *The Satanic Verses,* Caught in the middle, we have more doubts than certainties, more questions than answers. Neglectful of both Mass and mall, we seek a moral dimension to our lives by turning to books for counsel.

The notion of writers as a secular clergy is not a novel one, but Gita Mehta would seem an unlikely candidate for that literary pulpit. It was she, after all, who, in her sometimes excessive satire **Karma Cola,** took—and gave—such delight in skewering the thousands of American and European flower children who traipsed across India in the 1970s in search of enlightenment. They usually met hucksters instead of holy men, and Mehta reveled in the confusion: "They thought we were profound. We knew we were provincial."

In **A River Sutra,** Mehta returns to the same spiritual territory, examining afresh the tendency to disengage from the world rather too quickly. Hers is a humanist interpretation. The novel begins with the words of a 14th-Century Indian poet: "Listen, O brother. Man is the greatest truth. Nothing beyond."

The novel's narrator is a civil servant who gives up an important post to manage a government guest house on the banks of the holy River Narmada. In the Hindu tradition, he is now "a *vanaprasthi,* who has retired to the forest to reflect." He rises before dawn to meditate. At twilight, he watches the river "flickering with tiny flames as if catching fire from the hundreds of clay lamps being floated downstream for the evening devotion."

It turns out, though, that the narrator is at the intersection of a busy human thoroughfare. The power of the river draws all kinds of travelers, who have fantastic, often savage stories to tell. At a bazaar, he meets a gifted musician who is making a pilgrimage to the river Narmada because a broken engagement has left her unable to play a note. Her story also provides the stage for a melodic and accessible discourse on Indian classical music. In another tale, the narrator learns of a music teacher who adopted a blind beggar with a singing talent of which a jealous patron will say, "Such a voice is not human. What will happen to music if this is the standard by which God judges us?" Despite the story's tragic ending, it is apparent that the boy has filled a void in the teacher's life.

Steering cavalierly clear of emotional entanglement, on the other hand, can leave a hole in the heart. An executive at a tea company arrives at the rest house, seeking a riverside temple where he can rid himself of the curse of a tribal woman he has jilted. She has retaliated by capturing his soul between two halves of a coconut during a lunar eclipse. Now he believes he is possessed. The narrator is appalled, but his assistant is sanguine about the young mans predicament: "Without desire, there is no life. Everything will stand still. Become emptiness." These tales, more Grimm than fairy, are deeply unsettling for the narrator. "I suppose all this emotion alarms me," he confesses. "It strikes me as somehow undignified."

By the end, the narrator realizes that "destiny has brought me to the banks of the Narmada to understand the world." The reader feels similarly enlightened. Mehta uses parables, myths, even hymns to weave a book of unusual wisdom, one that gently questions our tendency to quarantine ourselves from the exhilaration and disappointment of attachment. Love and desire are shown to be both noble and barbaric, and not always—indeed, not often—in our control. She suggests that we are never more alive than when we go with the flow of our passions and ambitions; our lives will not be as tidy perhaps, but they will be more fulfilling. On occasion, though, Mehta seems to worry that her readers may not get her drift. She then hammers it home with jarring zealotry.

The structure of the novel is deliberately Indian. The use of a narrator or a *sutradhar* (someone who knits the story together) harks back to the oral tradition of Indian epics. And, instead of the taut, linear narrative of a Western novel, *A River Sutra* (literally a thread) moves like a spinning wheel. Every yarn begins the lazy circle again, another variation on the novel's central themes. Each story ends with a beguiling tug into the next one. The simplicity of Mehta's writing nicely complements the novel's profound concerns. Nor does the wheel stop when you finish the book. It keeps turning, turning, turning for days afterward, assuaging your doubts, questioning your certainties.

Gabriele Annan (review date 15 July 1993)

SOURCE: Annan, Gabriele. "Tales from the Narmada Woods." *New York Review of Books* 40, no. 13 (15 July 1993): 36.

[*In the following review, Annan discusses the depth of emotion in the six varied story stories that comprise* A River Sutra.]

A River Sutra consists of six tales that make up a fictionalized primer on Indian attitudes to religion, love, music, and poetry. An entry in the glossary explains the word *sutra*:

> Literally, a thread or string. Also, a term for literary forms, usually aphoristic in nature.

What this particular *sutra* strings together, though, are not so much aphorisms as parables. They are as easy-to-read, unanalytical, and, in some cases, as violent as the ones in the New Testament—or the tales of Scheherazade, for that matter. This gives them an antique patina in piquant contrast to the jeeps, sound recorders, air conditioning, and relics from a later period of antiquity—like a copy of Goren's *Contract Bridge* moldering in a tea plantation bungalow or the clerk in the guest house who sounds just like the babu in Kipling's *Kim.*

The string part of the narrative is provided by a senior bureaucrat who has chosen to become "a vanaprasthi, someone who has retired to the forest to reflect"—though not to the point of radical asceticism. "I knew I was simply not equipped to wander into the jungle and become a forest hermit," he says. His compromise is to apply for the humble post of managing a government rest house deep in the jungle on the banks of the sacred Narmada River. The parables are brought to him by guests, pilgrims, and fugitives of one kind or another who wash up there, and by his friend Tariq Mia. Tariq Mia is the octogenarian mullah of a Sufi shrine near the rest house. The bureaucrat is a Hindu. Their values don't differ too much, because "Indo-Sufism is based on the concept of mystical love." But the bureaucrat has no gift at all for spiritual insight, so the mullah gets plenty of opportunity to instruct him and the reader at the same time. An idealistic rationalist doctor who runs a six-bed hospital in the nearest little town makes up the trio of ideological positions from which they comment on the six stories that emerge, one by one, from the holy river.

In the first a millionaire playboy leaves the world to become a Jain monk. The second is about a poor Sufi musician who adopts a blind boy with a beautiful voice and trains him as a religious singer. He sings so divinely that he is offered a recording contract, and a rich patron tries to buy him. When his offer is refused, he cuts the boy's throat. In the third story, a sophisticated young tea broker from Calcutta is sexually bewitched by a tribal woman on a tea plantation. He has a breakdown, and is cured only when he submits to a tribal cleansing ritual in the Narmada. The fourth story is the most dramatic: a distinguished courtesan teaches her daughter the high arts of her profession—music, dancing, manners, and grace—while strenuously guarding her virginity. A bandit falls in love with the girl and abducts her. She defies him at first, but eventually his passion wins her over. When he is killed in a police raid she drowns herself in the sacred river.

The fifth story describes another musical education, this time with much technical detail. A great musician has an exceptionally ugly daughter. He trains the little girl to play the *veena*, a stringed instrument, and when she is adolescent he accepts a young man as a pupil on condition that he marry her. The two young people are drawn together by music, and become engaged. But the man breaks his promise and the unhappy girl loses the gift of playing. The last story is about a Naga Baba, a naked ascetic follower of the god Shiva who travels the land with a skull for a begging bowl. He rescues a little girl from a brothel, brings her up, and teaches her to sing, so that she can earn her living as a river minstrel.

This story has a surprising ending which skillfully and disconcertingly jolts one's perspective on the other five: an archaeological expedition complete with crates of scientific equipment and female students in jeans arrives at the rest house. Its leader is Professor V. V. Shankar, "the foremost archaeological authority on the Narmada," and a brisk rationalist. While he is out on an expedition, a river minstrel appears and sings for the bureaucrat. (The lyric of her song fills nearly eight pages, and there are a great many more pages of verse throughout the book.) The professor returns, and the girl bows to touch his feet: he is the Naga Baba, and she the former child prostitute. The bureaucrat is outraged: "Is this your enlightenment?" he says. "Is this why you endured all those penances?" The professor

> gave me an ironic smile. "Don't you know the soul must travel through eighty-four thousand births to become a man?"
>
> He turned and I almost didn't hear him add, "Only then can it reenter the world."

The professor jumps into his jeep and offers the minstrel a lift into town. The bureaucrat is left gazing at the river on which the votive lamps flicker in the moonless night "as the current carried them toward the ocean."

Mehta is telling the West something about Indian spirituality, but I'm not quite sure what it is. Perhaps she is saying that it is to be taken seriously, but not solemnly; that it is what people make it, and possibly not as transcendental as they would like to think. Anyway, she takes for her epigraph a humanistic-sounding invocation from a fourteenth-century Bengali poet:

> *Listen, O brother.*
> *Man is the greatest truth.*
> *Nothing beyond.*

If she doesn't reveal one big truth, she makes up for it with lots of intriguing and enlightening smaller facts: about archaeology, anthropology, mythology, cosmology; about tribal women, and criminals, and adultery among the sophisticated rich in the big cities; about the Indian musical scale and about which is the hardest vow of abstinence to keep: "This may surprise you," says the Jain monk. "Nonviolence. It is very tiring to be worrying all the time that you may be harming some living thing."

In her first book, **Karma Cola,** Mehta mocked Western infatuation with Oriental religion. She is more tolerant and explanatory here, but an undercurrent of impatience surfaces now and then as irony, and relieves the intensity with which she writes about music, poetry, and love. Critics of her previous novel **Raj** complained that it had no heart. At least three of the **River Sutra** stories—**"The Teacher's Story," "The Courtesan's Story,"** and **"The Musician's Story"**—have enough heart to be quite harrowing; though perhaps in the first two the effect is partly due to the violence of their endings.

Still, it is an achievement to have got so much feeling into a book so post-modern and contrived in construction, and so didactic in purpose. The most striking lesson is the importance of learning itself: every relationship in these stories is a pupil-teacher relationship. Even the tribal coolie woman has something to teach the Westernized young executive about the power of sex.

C. N. Ramachandran and A. G. Kahn (essay date 1994)

SOURCE: Ramachandran, C. N., and A. G. Kahn. "Gita Mehta's *A River Sutra*: Two Views." *Literary Criterion* 29, no. 3 (1994): 1-15.

[*In the following essay, Ramachandran and Kahn offer two different critical perspectives on* A River Sutra. *Ramachandran asserts that the multitude of themes and characters in* A River Sutra *act as a mirror of modern India culture—diverse yet bound to the traditions of the past—while Kahn argues that the River Narmada—not the Bureaucrat/narrator—is the main character of the novel.*]

1. C. N. RAMACHANDRAN—MANGALORE UNIVERSITY

A River Sutra is Gita Mehta's third novel, the other two being *Karma Cola* and *Raj.* While the first two novels are in the well-known comic-ironic mode, this novel can be said to be, roughly, in the allegorical mode. Further, one wonders whether *A River Sutra* can be called a novel at all. Having the Western *Don Quixote* and the Indian *Dasakumara Charitha* as its models *A River Sutra* exploits the formal possibilities of the genre to the fullest. It is a framed narrative. It is the story of an I.A.S. Officer, who, after retirement, chooses to be the manager of a Guest House, on the banks of the Narmada river in the Vindhya range. Since at this spot, there are pilgrimage centres of Hindus, Jains, Buddhists and Muslims, the manager constantly comes a cross many pilgrims; and, occasionally, the pilgrims tell him their strange/tragic tales. The novel, after the preamble, begins with **"The Monk's Story,"** and ends with **"The Song of the Narmada."** In all there are seven inset-stories.

Although ancient Indian aestheticians were content to distinguish between *Katha* and *Akhyayika* on the basis of who the narrator is, and didn't explore the narrative further,[1] if we bring together such long narratives as *Kathasaritsagara, Panchatantra, Kadambari* and *Dasakumara Charita,* we can construct an Indian narrative tradition and identify its constituents. To start with, all Indian narratives—be they epics like *Mahabaratha,* fiction such as *Kadambari,* or folk-narratives like *Vethal Panchavimshati*—are framed narratives. In fact, the strategy of 'framing' seems to be essentially oriental, which reached Europe during the Middle Ages through Arabic. Many of Boccaccio's and Chaucer's tales have been traced back to India.[2] Often there is a 'double or triple framing'.[3] Secondly, the narrative mode in the Indian (or Oriental) tradition is non-realistic and fantastic. Thirdly, the framed stories are often variations of certain broad human experiences, no attempt being made to particularise either the characters or incidents in time and space. In fact, almost all narratives can be said to be variations played on a few archetypal patterns of human behaviour.

In a framed narrative, the frame could be passive or dynamic. A passive frame is one which functions only as a mechanical link among the diverse stories (as in *Decameron*). On the other hand, in a dynamic frame, there is constant mediation between the frame and the inset stories; each qualifying and commenting on the other (as in Chaucer's *Canterbury Tales*). Again, a dynamic frame may function as a counterpoint to the inset stories, providing the work multiplicity of point of view or polyphony to use Bakhtin's term[4] (as in Boll's *The Lost Honour of Katherina Bloom.*) Or, the frame may provide a specific spatio-temporal context, as A. K. Ramanujan argues,[5] to the inset story/stories (as in *The Hand Maid's Tale.*)

Generally, frames in Indian narratives are passive; they just serve to bring together assorted stories. Only in the case of *Panchatantra,* the frame has some dynamism in it: the five princes who are told the various stories learn something from each story and at the end their maturation is complete. From this point of view the frame in *A River Sutra* is both functional and dynamic.

The narrator in the frame, the retired bureaucrat, isn't a know-all wise man. Often, he doesn't either understand a tale told him or only partially understands it. After listening to the first tale (**"The Monk's Story"**) he is 'disturbed'; and discusses the meaning of the story with his older friend Tariq Mia. Even Tariq Mia's explanation (that "the human heart has only one secret, the capacity to love" p. 48) is beyond his comprehension. Similarly, after listening to the second story, the frame-narrator is perplexed and angry. He tells the readers: "I was upset by the old Mulla's accusation that I did not understand the World" (p. 92). Sometimes, even Mr. Chagla, his assistant, appears to be more knowledgeable. When Mr. Chagla states, as if he is stating the obvious, that "without desire there is no life", the frame-narrator is baffled. "I stared at him in astonishment", he adds (p. 142).

The point to be noticed here is that the frame-narrator also grows as the novel progresses. In fact, from one point of view, he could be considered the centre around whom and whose process of perception and understanding of men and society, the entire novel revolves. When the novel begins, he is a 'Vana prasthi', and he is determined to be totally detached from the world, from the elevated position of self-assumed wisdom. But at the end, his older friend, Tariq Mia tells him: "Destiny is playing tricks on you. Don't you realize you were brought here to gain the world, not forsake it?" (p. 228) The retired bureaucrat is annoyed and claims that he knows the world well enough. Later, however, he realizes that still he is groping in the dark: "I stared at the flashes of illumination, wondering for the first time what I would do if I ever left the Bungalow" (p. 282).

More importantly, what is to be stressed in the structuring of the novel is its multiple focalisation.[6] Tariq Mia, the friend-philosopher of the main narrator, is also limited in his grasp of men and matters. In fact, there is no single character in the novel whose knowledge of the world is not imperfect. Each tale, narrated from a limited point of view, is later discussed, analysed and commented upon, again in their limited comprehension, by the two frame characters, who share a sort of teacher-pupil relationship. In other words, the novelist here, consciously, seems to adapt the framework of the Upanishads—the pupil sitting close to the teacher and entering into a dialogue with him. In the very beginning of the novel, the writer underscores this point, making her principal narrator say: "Do you know what the word Upanishad means? It means to sit beside and listen. Here I am, sitting, eager to listen." (p. 13)

Now, coming to the framed tales, each of the seven tales is designed as a variation on the single theme of 'attachment.' While the frame-narrator is one who has renounced the world, the first inset-story is of the heir to an international diamond merchant, who also resolves (following the model of Mahavira) to renounce the world, yearning to be free from the world. But, after becoming a Jain Monk, having renounced every possession, he realises he has newer bonds with the world. After narrating his tale, he states, he has to hurry and join his brother monks. "I am too poor to renounce the world twice", he admits (p. 41). And this admission bewilders the principal narrator. The succeeding tales also, similarly, play off the themes of 'attachment-detachment.' Whereas passionate attachment leads to tragic consequences in the **"Teacher's Story"** and **"The Executive's Story," "The Musician's Story"** and **"The Minstrel's Story"** uphold detachment. But again, the last story—**"The Song of the Narmada"**—registers the futility of detachment. The Naga Baba returns to the world as an archaeologist and undertakes Narmada excavations. In other words, each tale either contradicts or qualifies the implications of the earlier tale/s (as in *Canterbury Tales*); and all the inset-tales are qualified by the frame. Consequently, what we get at the end of the novel is a multiple vision of the 'many-coloured dome'—Life.

The vision of life implied by the totality of the text is a paradoxical position of both 'attachment-detachment.' The frame and a few inset-stories mount a serious critique of attachment to the world in the form of wealth, power and sensual indulgence. While the principle narrator is sick of a highly placed bureaucrat's life and voluntarily becomes a 'Vanaprastha', the narrator of the **"Executive's Story"** is even more critical. He observes in his diary that he and his 'estate boys', in their drinking, gambling and wenching, indulged in "Careless self-destruction." Similarly the singer in **"The Musician's Story,"** transforms her unrequited love to the love of divine music.

However, the novel rejects the concept of total detachment as well. At one point, Mr. Chagla gravely states to the frame-narrator: "But, Sir, without desire there is no life. Everything will stand still. Become emptiness. In fact, Sir, be dead" (p. 142). Prof. Shankar alias Naga Baba declares towards the end, dismissing the divinity of the river Narmada: "If anything is sacred about the river, it is the individual experiences of the human beings who have lived here" (p. 267).

Such profound affirmation of life and human experience is reinforced by repeated motifs of love and rebirth. The allusions to the penance of Uma to achieve Shiva's love, to the five arrows of Kama (Panchasayaka) which none can withstand, to the death of Kama (Kamadahana) which makes Kumara's birth possible, to the origins of Veena created by Shiva to immortalize Uma's immortal beauty, to the seven notes of music which are all drawn from Nature—all these allusions indirectly uphold the divinity of love, and conjugal bliss. The lyrics of the great Sufi poet Rumi, quoted here and there appropriately, again strengthen this motif—of love, both human and divine. In fact, the entire novel, *A River Sutra,* is a fascinating mosaic of rich and repetitive images, motifs, and allusions.

What places the novel at the centre of Indian narrative tradition is that each inset story seems to have been selected and elaborated with an awareness of the Indian Rasa theory. For instance, the Monk's story, based on renunciation, has 'Shanta' as its Sthayi, and Karuna as Sanchari rasas. The Teacher's story, centred on greed and jealousy, evokes Bhibhatsa and concommitant Karuna. While the Courtesan's story evokes Sringara and Vira, the Executive's story Adbhuta and Hasya. While Vipralambha Sringara and Karuna are communicated through the Teacher's story, Adbhuta and Karuna dominate the Minstrel's story. It is appropriate from this point of view that the novel's title is partially Indian: the River 'Sutra'.

The all-pervasive central symbol in the novel is the river Narmada. The novel captures her varied moods from varying angles. The river, born in the Vindhyas and flowing westwards, is the meeting point of all the central characters in the climatic moments of their lives. She is the "Delightful one", "forever holy, forever inexhaustible." If sometimes she appears as a bride, flowing to meet her bridegroom, the ocean with all ardour, some other times she has the allurement of a whore. In fact, as Dr. Mitra explains to the bureaucrat, 'narmada' in Sanskrit, also means 'a whore.' What interests Dr. Shankar, the archaeologist, in Narmada is not that it is a 'holy' river but that it is an immortal river. That is, "the Narmada has never changed its course. What we are seeing today is the same river that was seen by the people who lived here a hundred thousand years ago. To me such a sustained record of human presence in the same place—that is immortality" (p. 264). The cave drawings in the vicinity of Narmada are among the "oldest evidence of human life in India." The ancient Alexandrian geographer, Ptolemy, wrote about the Narmada. Vyasa is supposed to have dictated his Mahabharatha on this river bank and Kalidasa's works graphically describe the river and the nearby Vindya range. "It is as if reason and instinct are constantly warring on the banks of the Narmada. I mean, even the war between the Aryans and the pre-Aryans is still unresolved here" (p. 153).

Obviously, Narmada symbolises Life in general, and Indian culture and society in particular. The river, with Shiva and Supaneshwara temples on one side, the Muslim mosque and the tomb of the Sufi poet, Rumi, on the other and many Jain, Buddhist and tribal temples and shrines scattered over its course, symbolises the culture that is both ancient and modern, both monotheistic and theistic, and both Aryan and non-Aryan. In fact, *A River Sutra* could as well have been titled 'Bharath Sutra'.

2. A. G. KAHN—VIKRAM UNIVERSITY, UJJAIN

Gita Mehta blazes a new trail after her *Karma Cola*'s "entertaining account of the consumerist West struggling to gobble up Hinduism and choking itself in process."[7] The enlightenment she tried to pass on to the West must have prompted her to probe deep into the intricacies of Hinduism that needs reinterpretation in a language that the modern world can comprehend. Her *A River Sutra* is, in contrast to her *Karma Cola,* a serious probe not only in the mythology but also in the psychic depths of the conscious/sub-conscious/ unconscious. It was no surprise that scholars tried to vie with one another in examining it at the Sixth International Commonwealth Conference held at Hyderabad (Oct. 93).[8] Another Conference on Indian Writing in English held at Indore (Dec. 93) also evoked interest in the book.[9]

While campaign to "Save Narmada" has already been launched by environmentalists and social activists like Medha Patkar, Baba Amte, Shabana Azmi; interest in Narmada as a river acquires great significance. It would be in the fitness of things to examine first what Gita has to say about Narmada.

I

Shankaracharya's poem on the river is a sublime hymn to Siva's daughter (p. 2, 5). She is Siva's *kripa* [(Grace) p. 272]. *Surasa* [(cleanser) p. 273], Rewa [(dancing deer) p. 274]. She is Delight (p. 274) and at the same is also the evoker of *Narma* (lust) (p. 274). She is twice-born, first of penance and then of love (p. 275). If she evokes desire she also soothes. The serpent of desire is tamed on her banks (p. 6). Though suicide is a sin it is a release from the cycle of rebirth if it is on the banks of Narmada (151-52). Because of its eroding power every pebble assumes the shape of a *lingam* as goes the proverb along her banks *Har kankar ek Shankar* (every pebble is an object of worship). In order to attain Moksha one has to take a dip in the holy Ganges; but mere sight of the river ensures salvation. The devotees call her "Narmade Har!" (Cleanse us, Narmada, the Mother). The novel in this sense is not *A River Sutra* but *A River Stotra* (*Stuti*): An eulogy to the great river.

In addition to the mythical probe that Gita brings to her work she also substantiates it with scientific data. Mr. Shankar, the archaeologist, explains why he loves Narmada:

> I'm afraid I only care for the river's immortality, not its holiness.
>
> > (p. 263)
>
> It has a very fast current, which erodes the river bed, cutting deeper and deeper into the rock. But the Narmada has never changed its course.—To me such a sustained record of human presence in the same place— that is immortality.
>
> > (p. 264)
>
> This river is an unbroken record of the human race. That is why I am here.
>
> > (p. 268)
>
> "You have chosen the wrong place to flee the world, my friend"—"Too many lives converge on these banks."
>
> > (p. 268)

At this juncture we have to remind ourselves that if mythologically Narmada is Siva's daughter; here is a Shankar trying to explain its archaeological significance. By her choice of "Mr. Shankar" Gita Mehta has lent the narrative a subtle nuance.

From the literary point of view the river is not a *sutra* but a *sutradhar.* No, the narrator is not the real *sutradhar.* It is the river that unifies all the episodes into a great human drama. It integrates the tales into a coherence that several scholars fail to notice when they examine it from the narrator's perspective. Not only this, the river integrates Assam with the valleys of Vindhyas, the plains of Malwa. The tribal belief of Assamese folklore integrates Himalayas with the Vindhyas through Narmada—her capacity to cure the "possessed". There might seem an inner contradiction when we find that the two banks have different racial cultures, calendars, histories. Ved Vyas dictated *The Mahabharat* on the banks of this river. People still search for *Abhimanyu,* the elephant in the valleys of the Vindhyas. The Immortal Warrior of Supnaswara gives an indication of the legend. Though we are told that "instincts and reason" (p. 153) are warring here, yet people came here to seek solace and salvation. In this way, the title and the novel have an artistic relationship that establishes itself superbly.

II

If Melville's *Moby Dick* can be regarded as a *whale of books* in context of the Whale it describes, **A River Sutra** has several *sutras* to lead to myriad interpretations. It can be explored in terms of narrative technique, psychological insight in probing the unconscious/subconscious as well as the racial consciousness; sociological, archaeological, mythological explorations could also be fascinating. Equally fascinating would be the philosophy of music as enunciated in two separate tales.

From the narrative point of view the fifteen chapters flow from the origin to its final destination in a natural gush with frequent detours yet returning again and again to the main current: flowing placid sometimes but quite often with gusto.

While the narration by Narrator-1 is removed once from the actual participants, those by Narrator-2 (Tariq Mia) are distanced twice from the actual actors.

This paper, after such lengthy digression, seeks to study the characters under two categories: the fugitives and the steadfast. One must remember the fate of the fugitives in search of peace and serenity in the **Karma Cola,** though in this case Gita Mehta begins a healing touch and grants them the desired enlightenment. The steadfast after their initial convulsions are rooted firmly and chase none; whereas the fugitives escape from some evil/fear to grasp some sheetanchor. The steadfasts are optimistically and confidently adhering to their piece of land. Their vision has reached beyond the horizon and have neither fear nor envy.

It must be noted that the characters are complementary. One can identify the mirror-images; the "other self" which when juxtaposed together can give fullness of character lending them the much desired symmetry.

Person	His/Her Counterpart
Narrator-I	Narrator-2(Tariq Mia)
Ashok (Monk)	Naga Baba
Master Mohan	Old Musician (father)
Nitin Bose	Rahul Singh
(one running away from women and becomes derailed)	(craving for a particular woman and becomes happy)

It is in the union of these opposites that we have a fuller view—the narrator-I who shuns society and abhors all mundane human activities (as mere *Maya*); Tariq Mia has the Sufi's wisdom to recognise "Don't you realize you were brought here to gain the world, not forsake it" (p. 228). Similarly, the Monk in Search of *Nirvana* has yet to reconcile to the idea that Naga Baba could grasp:

Is this your enlightenment? Is this why you endured all these penances?

(p. 281)

The Fugitives

S. No.	Person	Escaping from	The Quest for
1.	Narrator-I	Public life hustle bustle	Peace, Tranquillity of mind.
2.	Ashok (Monk)	Wealth, Luxuries, Carnal pleasures, Power of Money	Nirvana/Freedom, Seeking answers to philosophical questions.
3.	Master Mohan (Teacher)	A cantankerous wife, Fear of failure	Success and fame through the adopted child Imrat.
4.	Nitin Bose (Executive)	Mod Society, Desire of sex/wine, Claustrophobia	Primitive mode of living. Restoration of calm after becoming "possessed".
5.	Rahul Singh (bandit)	Police and the society	1. Vengeance 2. beloved of previous births 3. a home and hearth
6.	Musician's disciple	Ugliness	1. Sublimity as musician 2. beauty in his bride
7.	Naga Baba (Returning as)	Pleasures	Stages of enlightenment mystic power
8.	Mr. Shankar (archaeologist)	Mythology	Rationality, Love for mankind

Don't you know the soul must travel through eighty four thousand births in order to be a man?

(p. 281)

Having earned life as man he does not want to squander it by renouncing. Hence as soon as wisdom dawns on him "Only then can it re-enter the world" (p. 281). Escape does not behove a man—the crown of creation, *Ashraful Makhluqat* (as the Muslims regard man). One cannot attain enlightenment through asceticism but through action—rational and benevolent. It is at this juncture that we discover the significance of the couplet

from Chandidas' love song that acts as the foreword
  to the novel: Listen, O brother.
Man is the greatest truth.
Nothing beyond.

Hence any sect that secludes man is myopic. This is
what Tariq Mia was trying to convince the narrator.

Master Mohan, who failed as musician, tries to see rays
of redemption in the blind disciple he adopted and yet
was deprived of fulfilment of his ambition; the old
father had his shock when his chosen disciple "escapes"
and marries some other girl in place of the ugly
daughter of the maestro. In one case the teacher was the
failure, the disciple a success; in other, the teacher was
a genius but the disciple a mediocre. If in one case
there was a greedy and cantankerous nagging wife, in
another, a patient and tolerant daughter.

The Steadfasts

S. No.	Person	Virtue	Quest
1.	Tariq Mia	Sufi wisdom (p. 86)	× p. 230 p. 270
2.	Courtesan's daughter	faithfulness, sense of honour	× prefers drowning
3.	Uma (Minstrel)	Devotion	Having met the Naga Baba quest comes to an end
4.	Mr. Shankar	Rationality and humaneness	Realised that to love humanity is the essence of all penances.

We see that these steadfasts are no longer goaded by
any quest. Their patience, forbearance has been amply
rewarded banks of a river like Narmada. Her magic
presence radiates the cure that can be an antidote to
snake bite, or malevolent effect of the Saturn (p. 153).

The old musician's daughter, the courtesan's daughter
and the Naga Baba could act as nature and balanced
person only because of the serenity that the river radiates on to people. Ugliness of body was compensated
by nobility of soul. She is trying to become what her
father wants her now to be:

—that I must meditate on the waters of the Narmada,
the symbol of Shiva's penance until I have cured myself
of my attachment to what has passed and can become
again the ragini to every raga.

(p. 225)

I must understand that I am the bride of music, not of a
musician.

(pp. 225-226)

That love, the noblest passion, should drive the bandit
to risk his life to please his beloved is a fact that the
'socialities' will find difficult to swallow. The world
where "drink, shoot, and fuck" (p. 112) reigns supreme;
adoration for a woman might seem ridiculous. But having appreciated the sincerity and warmth of his love,
the Courtesan's daughter forgets her "royal" expecta-

tions. Theirs became a companionship in which "we
could be together for ever, and sometime we set to
search for the warrior but never found him, distracted
by our desire for each other" (p. 185). After her
husband's death instead of returning to society's luxuri-
ous life as a Courtesan, she willingly drowned herself
so that their love could remain untarnished.

The Naga Baba through his penances in the Himalayas
and the deserts had developed capacity to conquer the
limitations of the body. But his real *diksha* began when
he was enjoined by his guru to beg at the houses of
those who were untouchables, unclean or profane. This
discipline to respect the humblest, to hate none, to find
divinity even in the most depraved is initiation to
wisdom. It is during such errand that he rescues a child
from a brothel resulting in a transformation of "chand"
into Uma. The "moonlight" was transformed into "peace
of night" (p. 252).

By the serenity they have attained. We are reminded of
Milton's line: "They also serve who stand and wait."

The three persons who emerge out of the trial and painful experience undergo a process of transmutation. The
stage that the Brahmin is asked to attain through Yoga,
where grief and joy no longer disturb the soul, has been
attained by them. Such alchemy is possible only on the

The message is crystal clear. None can triumph by
negating the MAN. The first step towards enlightenment is to be humble:

you will be a social outcast.
you will be insulted.
you will be hounded.

(p. 37)

But this is only the beginning. One cannot renounce the
world so long as there are teeming millions in agony.
One cannot afford to leave the toiling and suffering
humanity to its fate and achieving Nirvana/Moksha
only for oneself.

Naga Baba's transformation from a fossilised ascetic to
a compassionate person who cares for the child and
after rescuing her from brothel becomes her teacher and
guardian is subtle. The teacher, in this process, himself
learns to be kind and considerate. The enlightenment he
attains enables him to realise that to shun people is not
as challenging as to love and rear man. While the monk
was unwilling to renounce the world twice; Naga Baba
returns to the world he had renounced.

Tariq Mia, the mullah of a small village seems to the
narrator "frozen in time untouched by the events of a
larger world" (p. 270) but this is the stage that Yogis

aspire to. He has "games for older men" (p. 230) because the ignorant is the most certain of his wisdom, "the young believe they understand the world" (p. 230).

Not only these three but even the fugitives do not miss their cup of bliss! The narrator and the executive become wise and more mature, balanced, calm and serene when they are brought to the proximity of primitive life: folk dance, nature's abundant austerity teach them the bliss of solitude.

Taken as a whole the novel is a significant contribution to Indian writing in English—specially to the feminine writing which has all of a sudden in its aggressive stance resorted more to libido than to good sense. In addition, having debunked the conmen of India in **Karma Cola** an attempt to restore the real saints to their pedestal was a necessity long felt. She has done her penance in a dignified manner.

Notes

1. After Kathyayana distinguishes between 'Katha and Akhyayika' *Agni Purana* analyses them in detail. One major difference between the two is that Akhyayika is narrated by the hero while Katha by others. However, Dandi, in the 7th Century argues that there is no difference between the two.

2. See W. F. Bryan and G. Dempster, eds., *Sources and Analogues of Chaucer's "Canterbury Tales"* (Chicago: Univ. of Chicago Press, 1941).

3. For instance, *The Mahabharatha* has two sets of narrators and audiences. First, a sage called Vaishampayana narrates the epic to the king Janamejaya, as it had been narrated earlier by Suta Puranika to an assembly of hermits in the Shaunaka Hermitage. *The Panchatantra,* of course, has many involved stories within stories.

4. Mikhail Bakhtin coins the term 'polyphony', in his long article on Dostoevsky in 1929. Its English translation came out in 1984.

5. A. K. Ramanujan uses the terms 'context sensitive' and 'context free' in his essay, "Is There An Indian Way of Thinking?: An Informal Essay," in *India through Hindu Categories,* ed. Mekim Marriott (StGE Publications, 1990).

6. Gerard Genette's concept in Narrative Discourse (English tr. 1980.)

7. Gita Mehta *Karma Cola,* 1990 (ed.), Minerva: London. (Blurb on this edition).

8. Sixth Commonwealth Conference, Hyderabad (October 93). Four papers were presented. One was presented at Indore.

9. Gita Mehta *A River Sutra,* 1993, Viking (Penguin India), New Delhi, (All quotations are from this edition.)

Marlene Fisher (review date winter 1994)

SOURCE: Fisher, Marlene. Review of *A River Sutra,* by Gita Mehta. *World Literature Today* 68, no. 1 (winter 1994): 214.

[*In the following review, Fisher contrasts the innocence of the narrator with the personalities of the individual characters in* A River Sutra.]

Otherwise nameless, "little brother," as his mullah friend Tariq Mia calls him, is a former senior bureaucrat from Bombay. Following the death of his wife, he has become a *vanaprasthi* of sorts who, so he thought, withdrew from the world by accepting the position of manager of the government rest house on the banks of the Narmada River. Kindly and well-meaning, little brother is the perfect narrator of the stories he hears as he participates vicariously in the passionate lives of those whom he encounters on his daily walks.

The narrator's naïveté and failure to comprehend what he is told act as foil and counterpoint to the lusts and greed and aching desires—to all of the human passions—that had never once consumed his own days. Again and again he asks old Tariq Mia what happened and why: "I was sorry for the young man, but his story made no sense to me"; "I asked what he meant." In response to Professor Shankar's question, "What do you want to know?," he replies, "Why you became an ascetic, why you stopped. What all this means." In fact, the very innocence of little brother, and his puzzled responses to the stories unfolded to him, enhance the tone throughout **A River Sutra** of understatement, of implicit but very real menace, and of the pulsating sense of powers and passions beyond human control.

A River Sutra is a lovely book. Its stories of the monk, the teacher, the executive, the courtesan, the musician, and the minstrel revolve around the character of the Narmada River itself. It is a river whose sources are all the human actions and longings embodied in mythology, archeology, and anthropology. As Professor Shankar, an ascetic who has returned to the world, tells his host at the rest house, the river is sacred because of "the individual experiences of the human beings who have lived here." And when little brother explains that he has retired from the world, his guest tells him that he has "chosen the wrong place" to do so, that "too many lives converge on these banks." So, too, had his friend the mullah admonished him: "Don't you realize you were brought here to gain the world, not forsake it?" Little brother never quite understands.

More than anything else, the Narmada River, that "unbroken record of the human race," harbors love and desire in all their forms. The stories to which the ex-bureaucrat is privy are "only" stories of the human heart: "Listen, O brother. / Man is the greatest truth. / Nothing beyond." These lines that preface *A River Sutra* inform Professor Shankar's revelation to his host: "I have no great truths to share, my friend. I am only a man." Hearing this, little brother is astounded that so much grief and pain led merely to something so obvious. Gita Mehta's tone of quiet irony is sustained to the end. The river flows ceaselessly, and so does human life.

Indira Karamcheti (review date January 1994)

SOURCE: Karamcheti, Indira. "Cover Stories." *Women's Review of Books* 11, no. 4 (January 1994): 20-1.

[*In the following review, Karamcheti compliments Mehta's imagery and cultural romanticism in* A River Sutra *but argues that the stories are superficial and ignore the social and political issues facing modern India.*]

You'd never know it over here, but India is one of the largest makers of movies in the world. The Indian film industry is astonishing for its sheer industriousness, if not for its renown. Yet here in the US, and probably through most of the West, we don't see (and don't really know about) this extraordinary output, this twentieth-century proliferation of Indian self-expression and interpretation of the world. It's not that we're wholly ignorant of it, but, typically, we're familiar with only one name at a time. India's entire fertile film industry has been fetishized in Satyajit Ray, whose works have enormous responsibility for representing "India" and the equally enormous power that comes with it.

Still, relatively more people know about India's film production than about its literary production, which follows a similar trickle-down, or should I say trickle-up, model—"up" at least in the sense that Western markets offer infinitely larger possibilities for profit and prestige (and success in the West translates into increased sales and stardom at home). As with movies, at any given time most of us "over here" are aware of only a few writers from "over there." And when it comes to women writers from India, the numbers shrink even further. Again, it's not that there aren't any; it's just that any given era furnishes only a few names: Sarojini Naidu; Anita Desai, Kamala Markandaya, Santha Rama Rau; Ruth Prawer Jhabvala (by way of Poland and now New York). In more recent times, Bharati Mukherjee's books have been accorded a similar acclaim and a similar, almost exclusive, power to represent immigrant experience, Indian female experience.

Gita Mehta is less well known, although she has now published three books. *Karma Cola* is a witty and sophisticated analysis of contacts between Westerners in search of Eastern enlightenment and Indians becoming Westernized; *Raj,* a less well-received novel labeled "historical," reads more like a generic hybrid between gothic romance and orientalist harem fantasy. Her new book, *A River Sutra,* came out this past summer.

All other things being equal, in many ways this is a satisfying book, full of lovely stories. A frame narrative, along the familiar model of the *Decameron* or the *Canterbury Tales,* links stories around the spine of a single central character and a country inn. A unifying theme is announced by the title word, "sutra," which the thoughtfully included glossary defines as "Literally, a thread or string. Also a term for literary forms, usually aphoristic in nature." So Mehta, using the Narmada river as a narrative structuring device to thread these stories together, at the same time suggests that a philosophical or ethical principle can be pulled, perhaps in aphoristic form, from the river's symbolic presence in the stories. And the first of these suggests that those to follow will be variations played on the theme of love and its power, desire and its cost. The sutra: what we wouldn't do for love.

A widowed bureaucrat retires. Of a philosophical cast of mind, he seeks to contemplate the meaning of his life, and so accepts a position running a government rest house on the banks of the Narmada river, holy both to pilgrims and to the aboriginal Nagas of the region. Born of the god Shiva's sweat, the river first appeared on earth as a beautiful, tempting, changeable virgin. Shiva named her Narmada, the Delightful One. Her holy properties include absolution for attempted suicide, as well as cures for snakebite and madness.

From his vantage point as manager of the Narmada rest house, the retired bureaucrat hears (and we hear with him) six stories, variously titled **"The Monk's Story,"** **"The Teacher's Story,"** **"The Executive's Story,"** **"The Courtesan's Story,"** **"The Musician's Story"** and **"The Minstrel's Story."** They are full of oriental philosophy and extravagance, physical passion and spiritual possession, lust and loot, beauty and booty, renunciation and titillation.

A rich mans renunciation of the world is celebrated with an orgy of spending, of trumpeting elephants, of crowds rioting after gold coins and gems thrown into their midst. An urbanite tea company executive is possessed by the snakelike Rima, an aboriginal tribal woman whose sexual favors he has first enjoyed then rejected, and must undergo an aboriginal rite before the goddess of the Narmada to exorcise her spirit. In an ironic commentary upon the genesis of academic articles, he thereupon writes a piece on tribal practices which he is encouraged to submit to *Asia Review* for publication.

The ferociously ugly daughter of a genius musician father, betrayed by the man she loves, forswears music forever. A child prostitute, rescued from a brothel by an ascetic monk, grows up to become a river minstrel; the ascetic, who has disappeared years before, shows up as, of all things, an academic, the foremost archaeological expert in the country. (One can't help but suspect a serious subtext in this book about academics, a desire to cut them down to size by depicting them as possessed profligates who get converted to ethnography or as naked and raging saints hidden in the potbellied masks of professors.)

Now, as I said, I've got absolutely nothing against all this. I can enjoy a good romantic story full of Sturm und Drang, toil and turmoil, with the best of them. And *A River Sutra* gives me six, count 'em, six, such stories, with all the sensational elements of unimaginable wealth, murder, lust and magic (or sex and hex, as I like to think of them).

What it doesn't give is much reference to any of the disquieting contemporary events, movements, desires, fears, that are currently rending and reshaping India: the growing religious feelings that have led to the razing of a mosque and nationwide riots alienating Hindus and Muslims; the regional identities that encourage talk of creating a separate national homeland for Sikhs; the growth of a middle class, urbanized and Westernized; the push to industrialize, to create a national community and identity through media technologies.

This is not a matter of doing the right thing. Contemporary cultural conflicts are neither more important nor more "truthful" than other stories. An author has no obligation to tell the "truth"—slant, or straight, or in any other direction. Lying is not only the prerogative of the author, but his or her professional practice: it is simply the power to create fictions. In any case, how are we to judge whose India is more authentic, which India more Indian? And, after all, the idea of an India inclined to spiritual dalliance does seem familiar, and thus authentic, to those of us who have read our E. M. Forster and Rudyard Kipling.

But, of course, all other things are not equal. Like it or not, we live in a world where what the West knows, or thinks it knows, about the rest, matters very much to the fate of countries like India. By their myths we shall know them, and by those myths we act upon them too. The myths that *A River Sutra* gives us about India are familiar ones. This is the well-known world of the oriental mystique, compounded equally of poverty, mystery and a spirituality that, by desiring to transport its readers from the particulars of history to a realm of supposedly transcendent "humanity," allows us to choose a romantic, exotic fantasy over another view that may be less familiar, and perhaps less pleasing.

The delicacy, the pleasures, of this book do not, after all, completely satisfy me. It's as if I am trying to enjoy rosewater trifle when what I really want is a spicy, salty and lemony, cashew- and chili-filled *pulihara*. My dissatisfaction is an aesthetic one. That is, it concerns the nature of the reading experience, particularly the aesthetics of reading cross-cultural texts. Without the local habitations and names that an anchor in specific social, political, historical, contexts gives, an anchoring usually provided by the reader's own familiarity with the culture the text is set in, this book reads as too slight, too airy an entertainment, a reinforcement of what is held to be already known rather than an enlargement of mind and spirit with the challenge of the new.

We need, it seems to me, not necessarily other stories to be told, but other ways of telling—or reading—stories and retelling familiar ones that will challenge us to think more and dream less—or, perhaps, to encourage us to construct our dreams on the critical ground of our thinking, and to infuse our thinking with the power of our dreams.

Reading these beguiling tales of the exotic orient, I couldn't help but use what little I know about actual events as a kind of narrative counterpoint, supplementing Mehta's stories with others whose ironic, piquant, or corrective chords would enrich and complicate these too simple, too harmonic melodies. The Narmada is a real river, not a fictional one, and indeed holy, as the book claims. *A River Sutra* becomes even more interesting, evocative, multi-layered when we know something about the Narmada's current role in the national debates about India's industrialization and modernization.

India, financed to some extent by the World Bank, plans a grand total of "30 big, 135 medium and many small dams on the Narmada and its tributaries" (*India Today*, September 30, 1993). The largest of these dams, the massive Sardar Sarovar, with a completion date of 1998-99, has a projected cost of 9,000 crore rupees (a crore equals ten million, so a total of ninety billion rupees), and will displace over one lakh (100,000) of people, many of them tribals or otherwise poor, rural, or nonindustrialized. The building of these dams, the resistance and removal of the people "who have lived for centuries on its banks," as *India Today* puts it—the very ones depicted in *A River Sutra* as a picturesque background frieze of randy peasants filled with folk wisdom—have been at the center of loud, furious and protracted conflict between politicians, industrialists, representatives of the World Bank and global multinational capitalism and environmentalists, as well as tribals and aboriginals and their defenders.

But perhaps the book's silences about India's industrialization and Westernization are themselves the point. Perhaps the omission of these Indian social texts is not so much a way of denying them as a way of demonstrating what is being lost because of them. This seems to me not only valid, but an important and valuable point to make, and one that hits home more effectively through literary representation than through bald polemics.

However, such a point can only be taken if the novelist directs the reader to it, and can count on knowledgeable readers. Readers in India or Indians abroad would probably be able to draw the connection I am making between the two Narmadas and the erasure of Westernization, but it doesn't seem to me that the novel is directed towards them. (Both the actual narrative and a glossary include explanations of all kinds of Indiannesses that would be superfluous for an Indian audience.) As long as the targeted market is a Western one, then the dialogue with Indian social realities will not occur.

This does not make the book meaningless; it just changes what particular meaning is being communicated. It shows that a certain vision and version of India is being sold to that Western market. And how and what exactly is being marketed is worth examining. If the book internally promotes certain myths, as all books do, its own marketing—from its size and shape to the cover art, the blurbs and endorsements, to the various articles, reviews and publicity releases about it—also helps to construct what we think the book is about and what it means.

Book covers, although only one aspect of marketing, shape our understanding of what we read in a subtle but powerfully effective way. The platitude chides, "Never judge a book by its cover." While this may be all very well when it comes to learning not to judge people by the grace or disgrace of their faces, when it comes to books, it's a different story. *Always judge a book by its cover.*

I don't mean this as a prescription for what we ought to do in the future. It's a description of what we do now and always have done when it comes to our reading material.

How do we know that we're reading a "good" book? It comes out first in hardcover before it goes to paperback. A classic? For the Romans, a "classic" author was one who earned enough on his (invariably his) books to merit the imperial tax-collector's interest. Now, a classic author is accorded his (and occasionally her) due by being bound in soft leather and gilt edges. And the opposite of this high culture is revealed by the covers of books intended for the popular markets, such as supermarkets and drugstores: invariably paperback, lurid colors, busy designs, raised lettering and ornate script.

How do we discover gothics and romances, candlelit and silhouetted? How else but by the bodices heaving and panting on the covers? (Where else do we ever see bodices these days?) A western? A mystery? A science fiction story? All of these genres are uncovered by the highly conventional, almost formulaic art work on their covers.

Women's books, as well as books from the Third World, are no exception to this rule. In my years of teaching postcolonial literature (it was called Third World literature when I began), I've been struck not only by the images on the faces of books that draw us into the narratives, but also by the way these images graphically direct our understanding of those stories.

Jorge Amado is an esteemed writer from Latin America who has been taught and read in the US at least since the 1970s. Many of his works use central female characters. *Gabriela, Clove and Cinnamon* works out the gradual civilization of a land, a town and a nation by plotting the relations between men and women in the Brazilian city of Ilheus. The 1988 Avon paperback edition restricts the space given to print, including the title, the author's name, and a quote from a *New York Times* review, to about one-quarter of the cover. The rest contains a stylized, flattened picture of a naked woman, surrounded by large white lilies and other flowers distinguished by their whiteness, in emphatic contrast to the brownness of her body, the darkness of leaves and stems, and the livid yellow of the sky. It's the image that travel agents project of the tropics: love under the sun, romance without responsibility, the antidote for civilization, the gratification of the male body by nature and society. And it's also typical of such graphic images, whether on the covers of books or in commercial travel advertisements, to employ female bodies to convey the notion of a benign, welcoming, and accessible nature.

A more complex example of the same thing can be seen on the cover of Jessica Hagedorn's 1990 novel, *Dogeaters,* a coming-of-age meditation on the corruption of Filipino political economy and sexual politics, seen through several eyes, but primarily those of an adolescent girl. The hardcover's jacket illustration, like Amado's, suggests the profusion, the fertility of the natural world, but here it is somewhat threatening, overwhelming. In fact, what's amazing about this cover is the sheer amount of produce that covers it and the human figures on it: banana bunches hanging from the tree, banana leaves, banana groves, roses, lilies of the valley, one pansy, chillies, at least three different kind of bananas displayed for sale, two kinds of squash, purple grapes, tamarind fruit, custard apple, watermelon, as well as any number of unidentifiable (by me) fruits and vegetables. These natural objects overwhelm and diminish the human beings, as if to suggest that the tropics' fecund, natural forces will defeat human attempts to impose order and reason upon them.

Janice Radway's comment about romance readers' belief in the reality of the fictional world is pertinent and useful here.[1] Even if the events themselves are incredible, says Radway, the physical environment is believed in, so that "anything the readers learn about the fictional universe is automatically coded as 'fact' or 'information' and mentally filed for later use as applicable to the world of day-to-day existence." And a cover is judged as good if it "implicitly confirms the validity of the imaginary universe by giving concrete form to that world *designated* by the book's language." Romances, like postcolonial literature, are often set in exotic, unfamiliar geographic locations; covers, like other, extra-narrative material, can be used to provide "facts" to be filed away for the reader's later use.

I was intrigued enough by this matter of cover art to ask a few people in the publishing world about how a cover design is put together and what they think about its function.[2] I was initially greeted, not with suspicion, but with a kind and gentle puzzlement, of the sort that greets the inquiries of the village idiot about the perfectly obvious. What was there to say about cover art? They told me that there really isn't any codified policy, no business-like strategy about cover art. All insisted on the individuality of the effort, that each cover is tailor-made for each book. Editors and art directors, after reading the books, submit and discuss ideas for the cover, so that the final cover comes out of communal effort. The single determining factor, I was told, is the desire to represent the spirit of the book accurately. Nan A. Talese, who published **A River Sutra** for Doubleday, compared cover art to a poster for the book, translating the linear experience of reading into a holistic image.

But the seemingly straightforward responsibility to keep aesthetic faith with the text in this way becomes immensely complicated by the commercial mechanism of selling books. There are an awful lot of aesthetic needs to satisfy, a lot of tastes to tease and appetites to whet. The cover art not only provokes desire, it also creates the recognition that this is the article that will fill that need. When the needs of the audience conflict with the wishes of the author, the audience will be put first. Indeed, when it comes to creating cover art, it's possible to know too much about the story, to get lost in subtleties that may make no sense without a prior knowledge of the book, and so make no appeal to the potential buyer.

Marge Anderson, Art Director at Pantheon Books, pointed out that there are already graphic traditions, a kind of graphic shorthand the cover designer can rely on. A cover for a novel by an African American might use a painting by Romare Bearden. When it comes to books from the Third World, designers draw on an available vocabulary of "cultural symbolism" such as, I suppose, tropical vegetation and young, beautiful women. But, of course, this is also a delicate balancing act: for both aesthetic and political reasons, the cover needs to get away from exotic stereotypes, to do something a little unpredictable with the recognizable.

Since there just aren't enough books by Indian women to have created a graphic tradition of this kind, the cultural symbolism tends to be a little more obvious. The hardcover version of Bharati Mukherjee's novel *Jasmine* uses an image that reflects a recurring motif in the story: three shards of a broken jug, each painted with an image of Jasmine in India, New York and Iowa, suggest the story's three major settings and the infinite permeability of identity. But the paperback replaces the narrative-specific image with a more generic, more "culturally symbolic" one: a young woman with kohl-rimmed eyes and luscious, lip-gloss-tinged mouth, stares out of an unpainted wooden window frame at the reader, recalling the direct gazes of the women in the Amado and Hagedorn covers. The young girl wears a bright orange blouse, which looks like the *choli* worn under a sari, but the sari itself is missing. The graphic shorthand is clear: confinement and lack of freedom are suggested by her placement behind the window; poverty by the unpainted window frame; sexuality by the challenging gaze, the lack of sari, and the glossy mouth.

On the paperback cover of Gita Mehta's **Raj,** a young, beautiful girl with heavily kohl-lined eyes, a *bindi* and plump, lipsticked mouth again hooks the reader's gaze. But her face is half covered with an ornate, gilded screen, which suggests the confinement of purdah. The image again speaks the Indian woman's lack of freedom, the opulence of the oriental-despot royal families (which contrasts with the extreme poverty of their people) and the secret sexuality of the harem—all of which figure in the narrative itself. Interestingly, one of the reviews quoted on the back cover links these elements to the graphic image of fabric: "Richly decorated and densely worked . . . oversewn like a length of brocade with sex, landscape, polo, politics, tragedy . . ."

A more recent book by an Indian woman writer, which did not receive nearly as much attention as either Mukherjee's or Mehta's work, is Indrani Aikath-Gyaltsen's *Daughters of the House,* a story about man-less women who suddenly need to adjust when one of them brings home a husband. The paperback copy of this book that sells in India has a fairly simple, somewhat stylized drawing of a woman in a sari, standing in the inner courtyard of a house and holding a lotus, certainly an Indian symbol of womanhood, in her hand. The book was later released in hardback in the US: now the jacket has a delicate sixteenth-century painting from South India, of three women with skin of three shades of brown. The painting has lots of breasts, lots of jewelry, and yes, lots of fabric. Its opulence is emphasized by the ornate and copious gilding of the background and title.

All of these covers are intelligent, ingenious and beautiful artifacts—and answers to the complex aesthetic and commercial needs a book cover must address. The cover of *A River Sutra,* designed by Mary Sarah Quinn, has an elegant simplicity and efficiency of expression that seem like genius. The title runs in a broad band of gold like a banner across the top of the cover, balanced by the author's name at the bottom. Against a plain white background, a twisted splash of closely-pleated scarlet silk pours from under the title banner down the page. The twisted, pleated scarlet silk is a wonderfully complicated image: simultaneously evoking the running folds of a river, the sensuous hour-glass of a woman's body and the sinuous curving of a snake—all "true to the voice" of the stories.

Publisher Nan Talese was very emphatic about the individual attention that every book and its cover receives, stressing that her interest was always in conveying the talent of the author. She would be appalled, she told me, at the thought that "we do Third World authors any differently from any others." Given the strong desire to treat each work as unique, and to shun the "ghettoizing" of ethnic, cultural, national identification, it is all the more ironic that the individuality of Mehta's work should be so powerfully expressed by a graphic shorthand for "Indian" and "woman": a rich silk fabric like a scarf and in a woman's shape.

A River Sutra's cover is as delicate and skillful as the narrative itself and, finally, as bound by the West's need to recognize an East that is culturally familiar to it. This does not mean that narrative and graphic art are only stereotypes. To say that would be, indeed, an injustice to the work, the author and the artist. But the new, the unpredictable, that the cover designer aims at, does not seem to be able to get very far away from the predictable, the recognizable. We here in the West seem able to perceive the differences of the East only in the terms that we already know. Yet we are living in a world that is less and less content to be represented in the old, familiar terms—which in most cases were developed as a by-product of imperialism and colonialism. That we are reading Gita Mehta rather than Rudyard Kipling is already something: but surely we should be able to understand something different from Rudyard Kipling in what Gita Mehta says. *A River Sutra* delivers everything its cover promises, but nothing more.

In a way, I'm posing the problem of Modernism, as it touches upon the West's reception of postcolonial texts. I once heard Modernism defined as the famous imperative "Make it new!" and postmodernism as the dictum "Everything old is new again." If so, then in approach-

ing Third World women's texts we have bypassed the new (and thereby skipped the avant-garde) and gone directly to the old, the familiar—merely recycling bits and pieces of existing images and ideas.

How then does newness enter the world? How can these writers increase or modify our knowledge about a part of the world most of us do not know firsthand, but only through the conventionalized terms of art? And the task is not only theirs. How do we, as readers, increase or modify our knowledge? The representational bind, the liberty to do "something a little unpredictable with the recognizable," covers our ability to learn, recognize and allow the new into our understanding. But the representational bind seems to resemble representational bondage. It seems to me that the ability to learn the new is exceedingly slow; like the tailor worm, it can measure only an inch at a time, even if eventually it will measure us for a new suit of clothes. Meantime, we, all of us, authors, readers and publishers alike, continue to recirculate old ideas, old images, old stories in a seemingly closed system, like the recirculated air in multistory office buildings.

I want something bracingly new. And so the lovely, carefully crafted stories in *A River Sutra* do not, finally, satisfy me, because they do not inch very far away from the images of India as we know them, impoverished India, sensual India, meditative, contemplative India. When I was a child, I was told a joke I thought hilarious: "An Indian yogi sat contemplating his navel. He looked, and he looked, and he saw it going round and round and round. Suddenly, he got an idea. He reached down and started to unscrew his navel. He unscrewed and he unscrewed and he unscrewed. And his bottom fell out."

I'm not suggesting that the bottom is about to fall out. But I am saying that it's time for some fresh air.

Notes

1. Janice Radway, *Reading the Romance: Women, Patriarchy, and Popular Literature* (Chapel Hill, NC: University of North Carolina Press, 1984).

2. I would like to express my thanks to Marge Anderson, Art Director for Pantheon; Laurie Brown, Associate Publisher of Vintage Books; and Nan A. Talese of Nan A. Talese/Doubleday for their generosity in talking with me. Their precise articulation of what they do and why was thought-provoking, to say the least. I hope that I've represented their viewpoints accurately and fairly. I am aware that my questions must have struck them as somewhat naive at least some of the time, and their forbearance in not pointing this out to me was and is much appreciated.

Gita Mehta and Wendy Smith (interview date 12 May 1997)

SOURCE: Mehta, Gita, and Wendy Smith. "Gita Mehta: Making India Accessible." *Publishers Weekly* 244, no. 19 (12 May 1997): 53-4.

[*In the following interview, Mehta discusses her writing career, her multinational living arrangements, and the inspirations behind* Snakes and Ladders: Glimpses of Modern India.]

Gita and Sonny Mehta's apartment is an oasis of tranquility in midtown Manhattan. Outside on a chilly March day, Park Avenue traffic is at its mid-afternoon worst, and the chatter of kids exiting from a school next door nearly drowns out the honking horns and screeching brakes. Inside, all distracting sounds seem to be absorbed by the crammed floor-to-ceiling bookshelves, custom-built when the couple moved to New York from London in 1987 when Sonny replaced Robert Gottlieb as Knopf editor-in-chief.

In conversation, Gita Mehta is as voluble as her husband is (famously) taciturn. Formidably well-informed rather than ostentatiously intellectual, she'll jump in one breath from the right kind of water filter to get for a kitchen sink to the currently trendy field of microeconomics. She has the practiced partygoer's ability to focus intently on whomever she's talking to, but she also seems genuinely warm, interested in anyone who crosses her path. She halts her easy flow of discourse only to answer the occasional phone call dealing with various odds and ends that need to be straightened out before her departure in two days for Europe. She's remarkably calm for someone about to embark on a two-month tour of Germany, India and England to promote her new book, a collection of essays entitled ***Snakes and Ladders: Glimpses of Modern India,*** just out from Doubleday/Talese.

This year marks the 50th anniversary of India's independence from the British Empire, an event that indelibly marked Mehta's childhood. Her parents were active in the struggle for liberation; her father was arrested by the English two weeks after her birth in Delhi in 1943, "and I was sent off to boarding school at the age of three, because my mother was racing around trying to get my father out of jail." Even her name recalls those tumultuous times. Gita means song—"as in song of freedom," she explains in ***Snakes and Ladders.*** "It was the 1940s and it seemed freedom was finally at hand."

Although her husband's publishing career has required Mehta to live in the West for most of her adult life, as a writer she is drawn to India by the same powerful current that pulls her back there every winter for a long family visit. Her first book, ***Karma Cola: Marketing the Mystic East*** (1979), took a sardonic look at the Western belief that instant spiritual enlightenment could be acquired by hopping a jet to India and finding the nearest guru.

Raj (1989) covered the 50 years preceding Indian independence in the fictional story of Jaya Singh, daughter and wife of maharajahs who ruled two of India's nominally independent kingdoms. Her second novel, ***A River Sutra*** (1993), blended Indian mythology with piercing depictions of love in its many aspects to show a disenchanted bureaucrat learning about life from the stories of six pilgrims making their way to the banks of India's holiest river.

"You stand on geography as a writer," Mehta says. "Even if you're writing about Superman, you have to invent a planet for him to come from; you can't write in a void. In ***Snakes and Ladders,*** even though it's a series of essays, my hope was that they would have an accretive effect, so that by the time you finish the book and I'm telling you what it is that I love about India, it has become familiar to the reader."

SNAPSHOTS OF A NATION

The content dictated the book's form, she explains. "India is a place where worlds and times are colliding with huge velocity: we're putting satellites into space, and we have bullock carts; there's that constant tension and contradiction of immense sophistication and an almost pre-medieval way of life. I thought the only way I could describe that collision was anecdotally, by taking snapshots, as it were."

Among the essays are a moving portrait of a cooperative bank that enables women to buy themselves out of bonded labor and start their own businesses; a tribute to the "faceless, nameless all-enduring Indian voter" who has continued to believe in democracy despite notorious government corruption and Indira Gandhi's 1975 State of Emergency declaration (under which Mehta's father was again imprisoned); and a delicious evocation of India's colorful pavement booksellers and the kind of reading "uninhibited by literary snobbisms" they promoted.

By saying, in effect, "I am a camera, and the reader can see through my eyes," Mehta felt she created an obligation to reveal something of her personal history as she surveyed her native land. "I thought that readers had to know where I was coming from, so that they could judge whether they felt my position was valid. Just because I'm an Indian doesn't mean I know India. I did not want this to be a book where I play the expert and the reader plays the student; in every book I've written I've been very much against that," she explains.

Karma Cola, in fact, was sparked by Mehta's annoyance at being seen as an automatic India expert. In the late 1970s, Sonny Mehta was at Picador in London and in that capacity visited New York each year to scout American writers for his list. Accompanying him to a Manhattan publishing party, Gita Mehta "was in a sari, as I usually am when it's not the height of winter," she says, alluding to the fact that today she's wearing gray leggings and a black sweater. "Somebody grabbed my arm and said, 'Here's the girl who's going to tell us what karma is all about.' I thought it was astonishing that just because I was dressed this way he thought I could explain this profound philosophical concept. Trying to rise to the occasion and be a wisecracking American, I said, 'Karma isn't what it's cracked up to be.' And Marc Jaffe, who then ran Bantam Books, said, 'Write it.' I thought he was barking mad!"

Nonetheless, she sat down and banged out *Karma Cola* in three weeks. This was 1979, the year of Jonestown, the mass suicide in Guyana by members of a bizarre religious sect. "The subject was, as they say, hot," Mehta recalls. "It was taking the mickey out of [cultish spirituality] at a time when people were really scared about it."

Elaine Markson sold the book to Alice Mayhew at Simon & Schuster, while British agent Deborah Rogers guided it to Jonathan Cape. "I couldn't have asked for a more perfect agent for *Karma Cola* than Elaine, and Alice understood completely what I was trying to say. But I don't have a primary editor—I show my books simultaneously to the British and American publishers—and I really don't go in much for the editorial process. I think it's uniquely American, this intense relationship between the editor and the writer. There's no question that at the level of copyediting Americans are terrific; but there's an alarming passivity in America, where the writer is prepared to share the responsibility for his book. That I do not think is correct. You shouldn't take up public space unless you have something that is really worked out as well as you can do it."

Mehta's distrust of overediting was reinforced by her experience with *Raj,* which took a painful nine years to produce after she signed a contract with S&S. "The problem with *Raj* was that I was being bent all the time to a kind of fictional American shopgirl reader. I think Simon & Schuster's idea was that I would write this blockbuster, which I'm not capable of doing—I'm not good enough to do it!"

She declines, however, to criticize *Raj*'s editor, Michael Korda. "The fault was mine, not the publisher's. I hadn't written a novel before, I didn't know what it was like." On the whole, Mehta was satisfied with the final result, though she feels she rushed the ending and oversimplified complex material.

A LITERARY MARRIAGE

It's hard to imagine this intelligent and self-assured woman being intimidated by any editor. Other writers will undoubtedly find it comforting to know that being married to one of the most powerful people in international publishing doesn't ease authorial insecurities. "It inflames those insecurities," Mehta reflects. "Imagine: you're working on a book, and Gabriel García Márquez comes for a drink—you think, 'Does the world really need me?' And these nightmare sales figures for other writers; I hear Sonny say, 'Well, we've sold 1.2 million copies' of something, and I think, 'Oh my God!' That's why, when I'm really into a book, I go to London [where the Mehtas' son lives]; I can't be an appendage to Sonny's work when I'm writing."

Yet she takes enormous pride in her husband's work at Knopf. "I think his is the unique publishing span: he can do thrillers, he can do blockbusters. He used to publish Jackie Collins in England, and when he came here Jackie said, 'Oh, Sonny, you're going to publish somebody with an unpronounceable name, and he's always going to be one ahead of me [on the best-seller list] in America.'

"When Sonny published *Love in the Time of Cholera* here, he said, 'I'm not going to mention that Márquez got a Nobel Prize so that people are frightened. I'm just going to sell it as a great, great love story.' Sure enough, in hardcover I think they sold nearly 400,000 copies of that book—and Jackie was always one behind Márquez on the best-seller list!"

Her own sales have been more modest, though *Raj* was a best-seller in Europe. Ironically, the book she thought would be the most obscure to Western readers prompted the warmest reaction. "I wrote *A River Sutra* privately; I didn't tell anyone I was doing it, and I genuinely didn't think it would get published outside of India. It astonishes me that that's the one people have responded to most." It just goes to show, she says, "that in the end you have to write for yourself."

Once *A River Sutra* was finished, it didn't seem appropriate for S&S. Lynn Nesbit, who had become Mehta's agent, suggested Nan Talese. "She publishes many writers I admire, so I went with her, and she did a did a wonderful job. Nan is actually the first editor I've had for two books."

Although Mehta intended *Snakes and Ladders* to be a break from a novel that wasn't going well, the switch back to nonfiction was difficult. "Balzac once said, when someone asked him why he wrote fiction, 'Because fact is finite; emotion is infinite.' Going from *A River Sutra* to *Snakes and Ladders* was going from the infinity of emotion to the finiteness of fact. The question is, can you make that finiteness work for the reader, and for yourself? I wrote many essays that I didn't put in the book in the end because they required too much pre-information. I wanted to make modern India accessible to Westerners and to a whole generation of Indians who have no idea what happened 25 years before they were born."

Dividing her time among New York, London and India, Mehta is perhaps uniquely qualified to interpret her homeland for the diverse audience she aspires to. "There's a tremendous richness to living on three continents. The magic of America is the can-doism; it gives me the belief that anything is possible. Each time I finish a book and think I'll never write another, America makes me think, 'Yeah, I'll have another shot.' London's great virtue is that, as the capital of an empire, its libraries have staggering material on India. And because of the British reticence, it's easy to be alone and write there. My heart is in India—it's home—so when I'm there I don't write, I just let it all seep in through my pores."

Her book tour means that Mehta won't be doing any writing for the next few months, though she hopes that *A River Sutra* will prove to be the first volume in a trilogy. She has said that she doesn't really consider herself a writer, quoting Chekhov to the effect that one must write at least seven books before deserving that title. Does she still feel that way? "I feel I'm still an apprentice," she replies. "I may have to write many more than seven books before I'm prepared to say, 'Okay, I think I've got a grip on the craft.'"

Michael Gorra (review date 22 June 1997)

SOURCE: Gorra, Michael. "Character of a Nation." *Washington Post Book World* (22 June 1997): 5.

[*In the following review, Gorra evaluates the strengths and weaknesses of* Snakes and Ladders: Glimpses of Modern India, *noting that the book's weak structure "makes it neither a unified whole nor a collection of fully individual essays."*]

At a dinner party this spring I sat between two novelists from South Asia and listened to them talk about contemporary Indian politics. Was there any chance that the former prime minister, Narasimha Rao, might go to jail on corruption charges? How about the relation between the Hindu fundamentalist Bharatiya Janata Party and the thugs of Bombay's Shiv Sena? Did the Congress Party really think it could bring down the government? The conversation was racily full of India's lifeblood of gossip, and I found to my surprise that I could follow it all. But then I had just finished reading Gita Mehta's *Snakes and Ladders.*

Published to celebrate the 50th anniversary of India's independence from Britain, *Snakes and Ladders* takes its title from a board game in which a roll of the dice determines "how many squares a player may move." Landing at the foot of a ladder lets you climb it. "sometimes moving thirty squares in a single throw." But landing on a snake means you have to slide back down "while your gleeful opponents [streak] past." For Mehta the game provides an apt metaphor for postcolonial India, a country that sometimes seems to have "vaulted over the painful stages experienced by other countries, lifted by ladders we had no right to expect." But at other moments, she adds, "we have been swallowed by the snakes of past nightmares, finding ourselves . . . back at square one."

Mehta's "glimpses of modern India" stand as an attempt to "explain" the country to herself, an explanation that provides a user friendly guide to the many snakes who have stuck their fangs into contemporary Indian politics. She begins with an account of her parents involvement in the Independence movement that echoes Wordsworth—"Bliss was it in that dawn to be alive." But Mehta then shows how the promised land of independence has been weakened by the dominance of the Nehru-Gandhi dynasty. Her analysis seems fair enough; nevertheless it will be familiar to anyone who's read much about the country. What's fresh about it is the deftness with which she weaves personal anecdote into political chronicle. So she describes attending a rally against Indira Gandhi's experiment in totalitarian rule, the "Emergency" of 1975-77, a rally held in Delhi's enormous Friday Mosque. The government cut off the electricity, and the resulting "darkness . . . added a somberness to the occasion . . . allowing us to see the great mosque as it must have been seen by" the Moghul emperors who built it, "its massive lines . . . undiminished by . . . neon." And as for Mrs. Gandhi's claim that Indira was India and India Indira—well, I admire the drop-dead insouciance with which Mehta describes being "bored to tears" by such "overbearing leaders."

India's ladders are more tentatively described. On one level they have to do with such things as the existence of a free press, and the continued functioning, despite massive corruption, of Indian democracy; with the fact as well that the country has become self-sufficient in food. But Mehta is also fascinated by the resilience of her fellow citizens, the ingenuity with which they manage to scrape up a living in the most difficult circumstances; in one of the book's most memorable chapters, she functions as a subcontinental Studs Terkel, interviewing ragpickers at work in Delhi's garbage dumps. And Mehta remains exhilarated by the astonishing scale of India, which beggars that of Western Europe—a country whose "lack of homogeneity" means that "most Indians view most other Indians as foreigners." To Mehta that heterogeneity is a strength, a point that she makes by contrasting India with Japan. For when Japan, that once-closed nation, let in the West, the kimono virtually vanished. India, she writes, has never tried to banish the foreign; and the sari remains.

* * *

Mehta's strongest chapters are not, however, the ones in which she makes such large cultural claims. Instead she's at her best when her subjects seem at their most modest and most personal. I enjoyed the wicked eye with which she describes the visit to India of an American corporate group called the "Young Presidents' Organization," a description that recalls her 1980 *Karma Cola,* a sharply satiric account of the marketing of Indian spirituality in the West. She offers an enchanting essay on her own childhood reading, on "lending libraries . . . that fit into garishly painted tin trunks, small enough to be strapped onto the backs of bicycles." And I think I'll always remember a piece about a filmmaker who raised the money for his movies literally at the grassroots level. He hired a van and a projector, and travelled from village to village, showing classics in the rice fields; *Battleship Potemkin* was the villagers' great favorite.

Parts of *Snakes and Ladders* betray their origins as magazine articles, pieces not only for Britain's *Sunday Times* but for *Vogue* and *House and Garden* as well. The book seems to have a disjointed structure, its chapters loosely stitched together in a way that makes it neither a unified whole nor a collection of fully individual essays. But Gita Mehta's voice is marked by warmth and charm, and this volume serves as a fine reminder as to why India remains, in the words that she lovingly quotes from Mark Twain, "the one land *all* men desire to see, and having seen once, by even a glimpse, would not give that glimpse for the shows of all the rest of the globe combined."

Bharati Mukherjee (review date 8 August 1997)

SOURCE: Mukherjee, Bharati. Review of *Snakes and Ladders: Glimpses of Modern India,* by Gita Mehta. *Times Literary Supplement,* no. 4923 (8 August 1997): 12.

[*In the following review, Mukherjee praises Mehta's insight into Indian social, cultural, and political viewpoints in* Snake and Ladders: Glimpses of Modern India, *drawing particular focus to the nostalgia of Mehta's more personal essays.*]

At the time of the Raj, it was fashionable for British and American writers as diverse as Maud Diver, Rudyard Kipling, E. M. Forster, George Orwell, Beverly

Nichols, John Masters and Katherine Mayo to present the Eastern and the Western thought-processes as opposed. These writers' pronouncements, such as "never the twain shall meet" and "not yet", may have come as a relief to their readers. The enlightenment highway has been designed for a one-way traffic in ideas: from the rational West to the child-like, intuitive East. Even in the 1960s and 70s, when the West's affluent young discovered Hermann Hesse, Carl Jung, Buddhism, Hinduism and the *I Ching,* the traffic remained one way, only this time speeding from the East to the West. The Nirvana-poachers' invasion of industrializing India and the resultant "mythological osmosis" was the subject of Gita Mehta's first work of non-fiction, *Karma Cola.* Now after eighteen years, the novel *Raj* and a collection of short stories, *A River Sutra,* Mehta has returned, in *Snakes and Ladders,* to monitor the progress of the traffic in enlightenment.

Although the game of snakes and ladders may have been invented centuries ago "as a meditation on humanity's progress towards liberation", Mehta remembers that in her childhood "the actual board was suggestive of danger". By using the game as a way of summing up India's fifty-year experiment in sovereignty, Mehta suggests that although the political leaders after Jawaharlal Nehru and Mahatma Gandhi are spending too much time in serpents' bellies, ladders prop themselves against walls for the use of future idealists.

Her epigraph is taken from Goethe, who was tempted to visit India "not for the purpose of discovering something new but in order to view in his way what has been discovered". This establishes Mehta's focus: look for eccentric insights, not exhaustive analysis. Mehta, who lives in New York, but thinks of herself as an Indian, is treated in India by the locals as a *not-quite* or a clueless transient. Her awareness of Indians' limited tolerance of her right to speak to a wide audience about contemporary India gives her observations a touching self-consciousness.

While expatriate Indian scholars are still prospecting the gold of victimology in the exhausted mines of post-colonialism, Mehta discovers a lively population of farmers who prefer watching television to meditating, and describes urban youth in "saris and mini-skirts, anklets and Doc Marten boots, *salwar kameezes* and torn Levi's", who dance Raga-rap and Indi-pop. The most singular achievement of *Snakes and Ladders* is that it celebrates rather than satirizes or trivializes cultural symbiosis.

In thirty-one brief chapters with titles such as **"Who's Afraid of Being Indian?"** and **"Losing It,"** Mehta speed-reads Indian political history, sociology, ecology, communications systems, land-reform movements and middle-class taste in novels and films, and comes up with this original, heartening thesis: "in a world of perpetual motion India remains a perpetual becoming, a vast and protean sea of human improvisations on the great dance of time".

Not all the chapters are equally intriguing. Mehta is at her best when she draws on personal reminiscence instead of serving up a digest of easily available official data. Among the most lively are **"Freedom's Song,"** in which Mehta, defying political correctness, reviews freedom-fighting from the point of view of the child of a privileged, princely family, and **"Reading,"** in which she evokes the indiscriminate range and the intemperate love of reading among the literate, well-off Calcuttans of her generation. In **"Freedom's Song,"** Mehta's late father, who was a prominent politician and industrialist, emerges not as the ambitious, canny politician that many Indian journalists have portrayed, but as a dashing Scarlet Pimpernel who pulls off impossible nationalist feats. Reading Mehta's **"Reading,"** I revisited my own girlhood and the many hours spent in the collected works of second-rate Victorian women novelists, as well as those of Austen, the Brontës, Dickens, Hardy, Bennett and Galsworthy. Colonialism is heinous, of course, but, like Mehta, I find myself unable to apologize for the ecstasy and the imaginative freedom that the colonizers' books gave me.

Beverly Schneller (essay date summer 2001)

SOURCE: Schneller, Beverly. "'Visible and Visitable': The Role of History in Gita Mehta's *Raj* and Rohinton Mistry's *A Fine Balance*." *Journal of Narrative Theory* 31, no. 2 (summer 2001): 233-54.

[*In the following essay, Schneller argues that* Raj *and Rohinton Mistry's* A Fine Balance *both use historical fact as a tool to further their plots and themes, commenting that the "deliberate and deliberative uses of history employed by Mistry and Mehta reveal these works as unique, problematic, and complex."*]

The title of this essay derives from Henry James' comments in his preface to *The Aspern Papers* about the qualities of the novel. He liked to read about a past that was both "visible and visitable," i.e., a past which was alive, relevant, and the creation of its author. Recent post-modern discussion of historiography has also taken a similar approach to the nature of historical narrative and the kinds of meaning historical writing produces. Hayden White, the leader in this debate, argues that there is little difference between historical narrative and the type of prose narrative associated with fictions. As is now well-known, he posits that the historian's point of view towards the material used in historical writing is equivalent to the fiction writer's point of view when

creating a plot for a novel. Whether or not White is right in his analysis is beyond the scope of this essay, but what is of interest in his work is the idea that history is an authorial creation: history is a text shaped by its writer's intention and interpretation of what should be "fact." The implications of White's ideas bear on the name and nature of historical fiction of which *Raj* and *A Fine Balance* are two recent South Asian examples.

Gita Mehta and Rohinton Mistry are writers of popular novels; hers in 1989 and his in 1995. Their subject is the sweep of Indian history; hers before independence from Britain in 1947 and his since. As historical fictions, both Mehta and Mistry are willingly engaged with the burden of the past and participate in what David Cowart has defined as the historians' task of advancing "cultural self-knowledge" typically associated with such "humanistic studies" as history (25). Mehta chooses a female central character, Princess Jaya of Balmer, as the lens through which she transmits her versions of late empire; in contrast, Mistry creates a cast of interrelated characters whose lives offer different but complimentary visions of lower caste Indian life in the 1970s. Neither novel has received much critical attention with most of the existing commentary coming from book reviews in popular periodicals. My purpose in this essay is to compare these two novels in their uses of history; to show how they rely on historical information which they shape to fit their plots; and to discuss how these popular novels perform as history for their readers. To broaden the focus of the essay, I briefly compare how Mehta and Mistry use history in their novels to some recent work by Bapsi Sidwha, a Pakistani novelist, and by Hanif Kureshi, an Indian novelist living in Britain. Because *Raj* and *A Fine Balance* are historical novels of differing types, they provide a window on the ways novelists can incorporate history into their works to teach as well as to delight. Historical novels, in light of Hayden White, may now be considered as kind of historiography and it is as historical novels that *Raj* and *A Fine Balance* need scrutiny.

In the opinion of some book reviewers, Mehta's and Mistry's use of history is problematic. Some have asked the question, "Are we reading history or fiction?" While a few, such as Ian Buruma, identify the challenge facing the South Asian historical novelist. In *The New York Review of Books*, Buruma wrote, "in few countries is the legacy of history, in spirit and form, so apparent as in *India*" (9). For Pico Iyer in *Time*, Mistry has created "the Great Indian novel" (85) while for *The New Yorker*'s anonymous reviewer, *A Fine Balance* is "a novel that can stand with the best of Dickens" (93).[1]

Mehta, praised by Buruma for writing of the Raj "without nostalgia or bitterness" (9) sets Princess Jaya's story across the end of the colonial period including the first elections for the Indian Congress, in which she places her name as a candidate. Mehta's story flirts with the traditions of romance—bad marriage, the loss of a son, the attraction to a British soldier, and the heroine's successful quest for identity in a country where repression of women is culturally enforced. Mistry writes a social commentary illustrating how oppression is not always brought to a country from farther shores. Indians are the villains and the heroes in *A Fine Balance* and what the people do to each other seems as bad if not worse than what happened during the colonial period. Both novelists complicate the easy distinctions between history and fiction in their depictions and interpretations of India's colonial and post-colonial pasts.

Like Forster, Mistry and Mehta make India a character in their novels, and their two novels compare well in other ways, too.[2] Both Mistry and Mehta construct plots which focus on family issues and family loyalty as an extension of nationalism; both write with historical accuracy and use history as an operating principle in their narratives; the scope of both novels is broad as a result. Evolution of the individual in the nation and the evolution of India as a free country provide a common, parallel quest in both works, even if the focus of their histories of India diverge conspicuously. Princess Jaya is a member of the ruling class, who eventually becomes the Maharani of her Indian Kingdom and a politically active woman. She is largely sheltered and protected from the common people until she sees the tide has turned with independence. She finds her own voice and her own mission in the new country. The Hindu tailors, Ishvar and Omprakash Darji, whose lives intersect with those of Dina Dalal and Maneck Kohlah, are of the lower castes. They all become victims of the turbulence caused by the State of Emergency and find their lives changed utterly as a result of their vulnerability in this critical period of Indira Gandhi's rule in the 1970s.

The novelists' styles differ as Mistry follows more in the footsteps of Rushdie's *Midnight's Children* (1980), with its use of the grotesque, the shocking, and the ironic. Mehta's style is more straight forward, using the allegory of the birth of India and the new woman in a recognizable manner. Neither novelist wants to break new ground in literary style, but both seem to want to take the South Asian novel in a direction which differs from those of such contemporaries as Bapsi Sidwha and Hanif Kureishi, as I will discuss a little later in this essay. What we find when we compare *Raj* with *A Fine Balance* are approaches to writing historical fiction in two strains: the first is to use the history as a driving force to develop a character over a span of time and draw out the character from the country of origin as in *Raj*; the other is to adhere to stricter use of history and

make the events the dominate character, to merge function with form and content, to take to heart, as Mistry does, the confluence of "spirit and form" in his fiction.

Because the subject of this piece is the use of history as fiction, I focus on work concerned with the historical elements in both novels. As I describe the novelists' uses of history, then, I consider how reviewers reacted to the use of such material. From their comments, a sort of preference theory of taste emerges, especially concerning *Raj,* which drew more female than male reviewers, who clearly were disturbed at the intrusion of fact into what they wanted to read—a neat romance. Yasmin Alibhai says, for example, "Jaya's story is obviously meant to symbolize the history of India itself as it moved turbulently from the end of the 19th century to independence in 1949 and the liberation of Indian women as these historical convulsions rocked the social structures of society. It doesn't work well and the problem may well be . . . too much meaningless detail, fascination with the exotic" (34). In Alibhai's mind, history and fiction cannot rest peacefully together in a novel, and it seems she faults Mehta for researching the history of the period she creates in *Raj.*

In what follows, I will address such complaints, and in presenting summaries of the novels, I will concentrate on those characters whose lives create the main lines of the plots. Given the scope of the novels, covering decades of Indian life and history, it is necessary to limit summaries to only major characters, though minor characters and sub-plots are also well-developed and integrated into main storylines by Mehta and Mistry. I contend that both novelists have written novels which create the "visitable past" so admired by Henry James through which they created "fictional histories" which give to fiction the power of history's language to describe the past. As Hayden White notes, in historical metafiction, "[e]verything is presented as if it were of the same ontological order . . ." (68); the history is submerged into the fiction and the fiction determines the nature of the history the novelists present. We start with the Raj according to Jaya and Gita Mehta; move on to the new India of Mistry; compare their novels with two of their contemporaries and return to James, via J. Hillis Miller, for a concluding theoretical analysis of the use of history in recent South Asian fiction.

Raj is divided into four parts. "Book One: Balmer" is Jaya's early life; "Book Two: Sirpur" covers her marriage to Prince Pratap; "Book Three: Maharani" portrays her life as the leading woman in the royalty of her kingdom; and "Book Four: Regent" describes her widowhood and her role in leading Sirpur into India and away from its position as an independent kingdom. The last book is also the story of Jaya's activism and her realization that she can continue to serve her country as an elected member of the Indian National Congress.

The novel begins in 1897 and ends in 1949. Princess Jaya finds herself in three interlocking situations in the novel: her parents' home, where she is steeped in Indian culture; in her own home, where she must carry out roles prescribed for her by the British and by the Indians; and in emerging India, the country which has always been her "Home" of homes, through which Jaya Devi experiences personal and cultural freedoms.

Mehta presents detailed descriptions of the cultural and personal transformations which her character experiences and witnesses. As she writes in the preface to the novel, she researched the periods she covers in "exhaustive archives" and a "wide and eccentric span of books" (ix). These are the details it appears that bothered Alibhai, but pleased Buruma, who is careful to praise Mehta for recreating the poshness of the Raj and its various extravagances, including the dog wedding organized by the Nawab of Jungadh. One need only compare Jaya's courtly life with the descriptions of the end of the Raj found in Lawrence James' *Raj: The Making and Unmaking of British India* (1997) to see just how well Mehta shows the wealthy Indians' desire to imitate the British, to play their games, to dress and talk like them, and to spend huge amounts of money keeping up the appearances associated with the "Jewel in the Crown" status India possessed as part of the Empire.

Jaya has been criticized as a flat character by reviewers Rachel Billington and Yasmin Alibhai. Billington, herself a novelist, writes Jaya "must, it seems, unlearn the lessons of thousands of years of Indian history and culture." Further, she complains, "In general, Jaya is a kind of sleep-walker, making her way through remarkable events" (18). Billington and other reviewers miss the point about Jaya, though, and about Mehta's use of history in the novel. As a Maharani, Indian autonomy, even in a diminished state, is better than no native rule at all. Jaya is a presence in the world of colonial India. She is a transcultural woman like many Indian émigrés today, a part of India and a part of another culture, too. As a colonized subject, Jaya's flexibility and quick assumption of a new possibility point to the resilience and the strength of character which was latent in the Indian people. Certain things which happen to Jaya are obvious concessions to Western readers: the attempted suicide by Jaya's widowed mother and Jaya's lessons in how to be a Western woman at the hands of Mrs. Roy, who was hired by Prince Pratap to make Jaya less Indian. For Alibhai, it is Jaya's "mental lassitude" which makes her a poor person; she believes she should "seethe and plot, and joust, at least within the safe confines of her brain" (34). Yet, wanting Jaya to be Gandhi is inappropriate here. Her experiences are limited by history because of her class and her gender; her knowledge of the outside world is minimal and she is a prisoner of the patriarchy of the Raj. When she has the chance, though, she moves ahead and she learns

that her real power is as a symbol for change in a free India. Jaya is not a modern woman or a revolutionary; she is a widow in her early fifties, who is not afraid to try something new for her country. Mehta has, in fact, created a character which is consistent throughout the novel. Jaya has always been in the service of India; the larger historical events simply require she shift her methods but not her focus.

Alibhai contends Mehta is writing an exploitation novel, and though the novel is based on factual events, which yield local color and give depth to the plot, the "nostaligie de l'Empire" remains too strong for the novel to be taken seriously and as a good work of fiction. In particular Alibhai writes: "But this is supposed to be a novel and not a boil-in-bag history/social anthropology lesson and the imaginative leap that is needed to transform historical realities into fictional realities is rarely made" (34). How the "leap" is to be made is left unstated, but one must assume that it involves something more in Alibhai's mind than a well-crafted, accurate portrayal of a character in a specific moment in recorded history. I suspect Alibhai would be equally willing to dismiss Ruth Prawer Jhabvla's 1975 *Heat and Dust,* which is set again the Sepoy Rebellion (1857-8), and gives a similar blend of history and romance. Alibhai seems to believe that history is itself a kind of fiction and one reality fits both nonfiction and fiction. The premise of her critique, which is central to my argument, concerns the kind of history fiction is thought to present. Buruma believes, as do I, that "[Mehta] is at her best when describing the twisted human relations in colonial society" (9).

Princess Jaya's version of India shares some of the same characteristics as Miss Quested's in *A Passage to India* (1924). At first, Jaya and Adele Quested find themselves trying to reconcile India's physical beauty and stunningly rich cultural heritage with its politics, but, in the end the two cannot be reconciled any more than a cross-cultural romance between Princess Jaya and Colonel Osborne or Miss Quested and Dr. Azziz would be possible, probable or desirable for either pair. Both women are looking outside for an India they possess within themselves. Forster, Rushdie, and Mehta blend "dream and reality, revelation and imagination, history and fiction, past and present . . . British culture and Indian culture . . . to [undermine] and continuously [question] the authority of the monologic voice in religion and culture" (Dönnerstag 458-59). Alibhai and Billington want a feminist political novel from Mehta. They are critical, disappointed, and dismissive (though not as dismissive as the *Publisher's Weekly* writer who could not let pass that Mehta, is the "wife of Knopf's Sonny Mehta" (217)). In fact, Mehta uses the popular formula of the romance to enliven, through the eyes of a thoughtful woman whose whole life has been a cautionary tale, the end of the Raj. We experience through Jaya's eyes what it is like to see the old world slip away and the curtain rise on the new.

Jaya is a woman who can assume new roles and transform herself without losing her identity because she is loyal to India and remains so her whole life. There is in **Raj** a female history and a feminist theme after all, as Maharani, then citizen Jaya, never loses her place despite large scale political upheaval and raw violence. Jaya Devi travels around India in the closing pages of the novel, spreading the nationalist message. She wants to insure a peaceful transition from kingdom to part of India for Sirpur. When she registers as an independent candidate for Congress from Sirpur, the election official, hearing her name smiles and says: "The name means victory, madam. May I wish you good luck in your endeavours?" (466). As Osborne and her activist friend, Arun Roy, argue over what the British Empire knew about democracy, Jaya Devi laughs out loud at the absurdity of worrying about the past when the future is so promising (467).

Jaya's optimism is lost on the four characters whose lives are the focus of Rohinton Mistry's *A Fine Balance*. In this novel, the widow, Dina Dalal, refuses her brother's efforts to arrange another marriage for her, and she ekes out a living as a piecemeal seamstress for a woman who operates an export clothing business. Once a woman with close friends and a husband, Dina is alone in Bombay. When her friends from school ask her to let their son rent a room from her while he is in college in Bombay, she is only too glad for the company, though their relationship gets off to an awkward start. She has not had an unrelated man in her home before and Manek Kohlah has never shared a home with anyone other than his parents. Manek is caught by having to live out his parents' dreams for him as a student of engineering, which he eventually abandons.[3] He found the college dorm where he first stayed unnerving in its filth, and he was happy to move in with Dina Aunty.

In a parallel narrative, the reader is introduced to two struggling Hindu leather-workers turned tailors, uncle and nephew, Ishvar and Omprakash (Om) Darji. The two apply for jobs which Dinah has advertised when she finds the work is too much for her alone, and soon they are sewing for her in her apartment and living on an acquaintance's roof. Dina is uneasy about the men as she fears they will try to cut her out of the garment business, so she goes to great pains to see that they do not know where she takes the finished dresses, keeping them as virtual prisoners in her home when she is away delivering and picking up more material and patterns. A third story involves the Beggerman, who operates a large network of street beggars, and who eventually offers Dina and the tailors protection services when she has trouble with her landlord. All in all there are at least five levels or strands of Indian society brought together in *A Fine Balance*: the Himalayan family of Manek, whose father made his fortune in business; Dina and her brother, who are of the middle class; Om and Ishvar, representing the Hindu caste; Manek's school friend, Avinash, who becomes a campus activist and is killed by the police; and the underworld of Beggerman, the hair collector, Rajaram, and the displaced villagers who wander the streets of Bombay helplessly reduced to crime and begging.

Mistry presents the details of the intersecting lives with a microscopic precision that never seems boring or heavy handed. Like Mehta, he offers little personal touches which lend beauty to the narrative, especially in the quilt that Manek, Dina, Om and Ishvar collaborate on as a testimonial of their lives together. When Om and Ishvar find the government housing they were so pleased to have acquired is bulldozed during the State of Emergency, Dina takes them into her house as boarders; they live on her porch. Om and Manek have a predictable attraction to each other. They are both young men with a fire for life moving them; Dina and Ishvar are compelled by a class-consciousness particular to their ages and experiences to try to discourage the two young men from becoming too friendly. Other happy times in the apartment include Ishvar taking over the cooking and Manek's persuading Dina to take care of some stray kittens he found who live outside the kitchen window. In time, the four of them discover a common humanity. They are people who work hard, respect each other, and worry a great about their futures in uncertain times. Ishvar and Dina share the joy of Om's prospective marriage; Dina even feels she has a right to involve herself in the negotiations (540-7). They agree the trip home to the tailors' rural village will yield the promised results.

Chapter Fifteen "Family Planning" is the turning point in the novel. Om and Ishvar have returned home successfully and they are out shopping for Om's wedding and courting clothes when an old friend, Ashraf Chacha, tells them that a family planning clinic has just opened up in the village. Naturally, they all feel uncomfortable with the sterilizations they know go on there. The sinister background the clinic's tents provide is offset by the raucous welcome Om and Ivshar receive when they are recognized in the village (610), but the celebration is seemingly short-lived as the police move in wielding nightsticks and herd Om, Ishvar and others onto the waiting trucks. Ashraf is murdered on the street, Om and Ishvar are sterilized, against their will, and held in the camp for four months until they make their return to Bombay. Because Om spoke out against the family planning initiative and challenged the doctor performing the operations, the young mans testicles were removed, leaving him a eunuch (614-30). When they return, Dina nearly fails to recognize them.

Reduced eventually to begging, Om supports the maimed Ishvar, who lost a leg due to blood poisoning. Dina's life also changes as the State-of-Emergency has ruined Mrs. Gupta's dress trade. She moves in with her brother and becomes a servant to her sister-in-law, Ruby. Manek, who encounters his old friends on the streets pretends not to recognize them when he returns to Bombay for a visit after his military tour has ended, but he does and they know he has, too. The pain is all too much for him: first he loses Avinash, and then his replacement in Om. Manek commits suicide on the train tracks (710). In the end, Om, Ishvar and Dina still find a way to be together: she surreptitiously feeds them from her brother's table and they do a little mending for her. Most of all they keep each others spirits up as their lives go on in a fine balance between life and death, sorrow and happiness, freedom and restraint. While there is pathos in Mistry's novel, the history wards off sentimentality.

A Fine Balance spans eleven years, from 1975 to 1984.[4] The novel, which won four international prizes and was short-listed for four more, is described by reviewers as "ambitious in scope" (Rubin), as a "monumental new novel," of "an heroic canvas" and as "a domestic novel that refuses to remain within its walls" (Mojtabai). None of Mistry's reviewers seem disturbed that he has chosen to write a contemporary historical novel, though A. G. Mojtabai finds herself "loosing touch with Ishvar and Dina" as the novel progress and "interior journies" are not presented (29). In the main, reviewers appear satisfied with Mistry's ability to capture "the real sorrow and inexplicable strength of India" (Iyer) as he treats "India both kindly and harshly" (Ross 239).

Robert L. Ross's essay, "Seeking and Maintaining Balance," is the first U.S.-published critical essay on Mistry's fiction. Ross ponders how much interest Western audiences can be expected to have in Indian politics as he writes in *World Literature Today*:

> Another question arises when considering these two novels (*A Fine Balance* and *Such a Long Journey*; Jowney [1991]): does the exposé of political corruption and tyrany during Indira Gandhi's tenure still hold that much interest? She is long dead . . . The tempest that is Indian politics before, during, and since Mrs. Gandhi's years in power probably fails to intrigue most readers of Mistry's work. It is not the history of the actuality that attracts in Mistry's fiction, but the way he uses these elements . . . he transforms historical situations and the reality of Indian life into a metaphor that shows how the individual reacts to widespread corruption when tangled in its grasp . . . and how people respond to the endless forms of tyranny that government and society inflict.
>
> (240)

While I agree that Mistry integrates the history of India in a way that is relevant to and enhances the theme of *A Fine Balance,* I disagree with Ross's assumption that the incorporation of accurate historical information fails to attract readers. Ross appears to suggest that in Mistry's latest novel, history can be separated from the fiction, which I contend it cannot. The use of history is not limited to images and metaphor as the State-of-Emergency is a violent character in the novel, and as such, needs to be explored.

Indira Gandhi (1917-1984), who was active in the independence movement in the 1930s and 1940s, became a member of the Indian Congress in 1950; party President 1959; Minister of Information in 1964; and Prime Minister in 1964. The State-of-Emergency was declared in June 1975 after she was found guilty of electoral corruption. She enforced censorship, limited civil liberties, and carried out social engineering among the poor. Removed in 1977 when the Congress Party lost the elections, she returned to politics as head of the Indian National Congress in 1978 and as Prime Minister in 1980. In 1984, she was assassinated by her Sikh bodyguards, which led to the retaliatory deaths of 3,000 Sikhs. This assassination is the subject of recent Indian literature, and *A Fine Balance* spans the whole of Gandhi's first term as Prime Minister. Om, Ishvar and the community in which they live mirrors reality and historical situations. Mistry relies on the reader to recognize the validity of his portrayal of the effects of the State-of-Emergency on the Indian poor. As Naomi Jacobs says, when writers use historical or pop-culture figures there is "a concentrated code reference to an elaborate set of associations in the reader's and/or writer's mind" (110). These associations are revealed now.

For Om, Ishvar and the other lower caste characters, the State-of-Emergency leads to arrests, beatings and the destruction of shanty homes in an atmosphere of widespread confusion. The declaration served as a means for Mrs. Gandhi to lash out at her whole country and to punish the easily abused poor. One must read the State-of-Emergency as a Hyrdralike occurrence, in which the tentacles of government reached across the entire subcontinent, destroying lives in its wake. Dina's apartment serves as a safe-haven for Om and Ishvar, who are otherwise homeless at the wrong time. Their caste prohibits them from climbing out of poverty, though they are incredibly diligent and talented tailors. They are judged by their appearances and the outward signs of their caste's poverty, even though they are literate, are saving money from their wages for Om's wedding, paying their bills on time, and generally minding their own business. They are criminalized for being who they are, which is ironic when one recalls that Dina is actually breaking the law by having them work and live in her apartment and the sinister, but oddly likeable hair collector, Rajaram, is a murderer.

Reading the 1999 Human Rights Watch report, *Broken People: Caste Violence against India's 'Untouchables',* underscores the extent of the hardship and the violence the poor of India face and with which Mistry seems well-acquainted. The report's major finding, in the context of its relevance to *A Fine Balance,* is how through "a series of inefficient and corrupt state governments since the early 1970s . . . government officials . . . have acted as agents and turned a blind eye to the killings," displacements, and police-led attacks on rural villagers, called Dalits (Untouchables) (43). Women and those who would dare engage in social activism are routinely singled-out for beatings and other acts of violence, which are termed attacks on modesty. The report describes "the criminalization of social activism" (153-165) and details cases similar to Om's one-man resistance to the vasectomy. Mistry's ability to grasp and portray the lives of the poor, especially how they "languish in makeshift homes on government property" (99) is particularly realistic as Om and Ishvar find themselves mingling with displaced members of Indian society during the State-of-Emergency. *Broken People* elucidates and *A Fine Balance* enlivens the patterns and types of violence and state-sponsored oppression. Started in the 1970s they are still much in evidence, lending credibility to "the fine balance," the thin, delicate balance which is daily life in India.

The State-of-Emergency is Manek Kohlah's nemesis. As a young man who descends into the underworld of Bombay, he fails to survive. A victim of repression in a way that differs from the experience of Om and Ishvar, Manek will not be a hypocrite. His wealth and education would enable him to rise or, to at least do well, but this is irreconcilable with the mass suffering of the Indian people as experienced by his extended family in Bombay. Out of loyalty and in response to their dignity, Manek jumps to his death; his last memory is that of his murdered friend from college, whose parents he had lately met. From the start, Manek is ill-suited to urban Bombay; he is always uncomfortable with what seemed normal to those who had become acculturated to certain levels of squalor and poverty in order to survive. Lacking survival skills, with his head literally in the clouds, Manek is lost in a world without beauty.[5]

Mistry's decision to tell a story of personal courage, resilience, hope and dignity in a destructive world redefines the family by crossing classes and economic barriers. Pamela Dunbar addresses the importance of family in the postcolonial novel when she writes; "The use of [the family] implies a skepticism about the healthy survival of the wider community during a period of historical uncertainty" (103). Readers who know Indian history realize that what Dina, Om and Ishvar have will once again be tested in 1984, the year of the novel's Epilogue, and Mrs. Gandhi's assassination. The balance is once more upset. Gandhi's period as Prime Minister repeatedly tested the character of India and Indians' ability to balance hope and despair.

Both Gita Mehta and Rohinton Mistry illustrate Henry James' concept that a novelist "should regard himself as an historian and his narrative as history" (qtd. in Miller, "History, Narrative" 193). James maintained "fictional histories" bear the same weight of truth as history itself, writing in the Preface to the *Aspern Papers*: "I delight in a palpable imaginable *visitable* past . . . We are divided of course between liking to feel the past strange and liking to feel it familiar; the difficulty is, for intensity, to catch it at the moment when the scales of the balance hang with the right evenness" (197-8).[6] That is, when the fine balance between history and literature is achieved, a lively, realistic history in and as fiction emerges from the story. In the post-modern, and post-colonial novels of Mehta and Mistry, history gives power to the language of fiction. It relies on literary narrative to mix the real with the imaginary. Writers of "fictional histories" bear the "responsibility" of telling the "truth" about the past. It is upon this responsibility that their ethos as novelists and those of their characters rest.

Thus, Mehta and Mistry are in the middle of the debate about historical "truth." In 1946, R. G. Collingwood stated the inevitable dilemma of the historian who was writing about events which he/she did not witness first hand, when he said that if the historian is not present for the event, then "[he] must re-enact the past in his own mind." To write the historical account, he must employ "certain documents or relics of the past" to achieve appropriate levels of "historical thinking," i.e., the mindset which allows "[him] to re-enact in his own mind the experiences about which he wishes to write" (282-3). It seems the same could be said of the historical novelist.

Hayden White, as recently as 1999 in *Figural Realism: Studies in the Mimesis Effect,* claims "historical discourse" is an "interpretation of the past" which literary critics are as capable of assessing as historians (3). Because history writing relies on the same type of narrative linear storytelling, the perceived "opposition between fact and fiction is abolished;" or "the contract" between the real and the imaginary is "dissolved" (66-68). Again, the lines between historical and fictional narrative appear blurry. For literary critics including Cowart in *History and the Contemporary Novel* (1989), historical writing ". . . like imaginative writing, involves the selection of detail, the determination of emphasis, [and] a narrational shaping" (17). These are all properties of fiction writing which in the end affect the validity of the "truth" the reader finds in history. Cowart also maintains that ". . . history makes its greatest contribution when it supplies the creative artist with raw material" (25).

Following from Collingwood to White to Cowart, the reader is left to consider whether the form of the historical novel in any way invalidates the history which one finds in the fiction. As I have already shown, Mehta, through primary research creates her own interpretation of the Raj from the perspective of her female central character. Mistry's use of history is focused more on the situations of the characters he creates which are emblematic of the Indian people. In his work, I find parallels with memoirs and other primary accounts, though unlike Mehta, he does not indicate if he conducted research to develop his story. What the post-modernist view of history as a sibling of fiction suggests is that Mehta's and Mistry's histories of India are as valid as Lawrence James', Siddhartha Dube's or the Human Rights Watch report's authors.

To see more of these "fictional histories" and to highlight how Mistry's and Mehta's use of history differs from their contemporaries, it is helpful to consider, if briefly, two novels by Bapsi Sidwha and one by Hanif Kureishi. Sidwha's *The Crow Eaters* (1981) and *Cracking India* (1988) predate Mistry and Mehta while Kureishi's *The Buddha of Suburbia* was published in 1990 between *Raj* and *A Fine Balance*. Anglo-Indian relations are a common theme in both *The Crow Eaters* and *Raj*; while *Cracking India* has more in common with the brutal realism of *A Fine Balance*.

In *The Crow Eaters* and *The Buddha of Suburbia,* political history is a part of the furniture of setting. Racism is given a slightly larger role by Kureishi; though in the Sidwah novel, the marriage of the youngest son is an allegory for Anglo-Indian relations. When Billy Jungle-walla marries Tanya Easymoney, he allows himself to be as westernized as she already is. Tanya, a beautiful spend thrift, with her "swing of black, bobbed-hair" (201) prefers to dress in British style. Billy is more traditionally raised, and has grown up in the shadow of his handsome, loved brothers. He is eager to gain his father's approval, and after his older brother dies and another becomes a mendicant, Billy assumes his father's store and becomes rich. The tension between Tanya and Billy symbolizes her greedy colonialist mindset; while he represents the wealth of India to her as ready to be plundered.[7]

Another subplot involves Yazdi, the family's second son, and Rosy Watson, an unfortunate Anglo-Indian. Yazdi falls in love with her, and promises to marry her though they are both still school children. He is moved by her accounts of domestic violence perpetrated by her father and stepmother. To get her out of the way in the house, her stepmother arranges for Rosy to be raped in her own home: "They tied her to the bed and brought men into the room . . ." (127), Yazdi tells his father, Freddy. Yazdi, Freddy realizes, does not grasp what Rosy's stepmother has done to her, but as Sidwha knows in creating this situation "Once a girl is raped,

she becomes unmarriageable" (Human Rights Watch 31). For this reason, Freddy sends Yazdi away from Lahore for schooling, and succeeds in keeping Rosy out of the family.

In breaking up his own Romeo and Juliet, Freddy loses Yazdi anyway. By accident, Freddy finds Rosy working in a brothel he and some friends have gone to visit, and to make his point clear and the solidify in his rightness mind of his actions, he has sex with Rosy himself. Perhaps in this way he can make his decision more clear to Yazdi, but it is nevertheless cruel.

The aspects of *The Crow Eaters* that are clearly veri-similar include a rural family moving to the city to prosper; generational conflict; the steadying influence of women in the family; and class-based decision making. Indian history/Pakistani history does not play an essential role in this novel. The characters are affected by internal domestic politics, more so than by the separation of Pakistan from India or by Indian independence. Similarly, the racism of *The Buddha of Suburbia* and the experiences of this novel's main character are part of a fictional situation more than a fictional history.

Karim Amir introduces himself as "an Englishman born and bred" (3) in the first sentence of Kureishi's novel. Karim is the son of an Indian father, Haroon Amir, and an English mother, Margaret. The family lives in South London and tensions between the native British population and the Indian and Pakistani immigrants are always in evidence. Karim's foil is his cousin, Jamilla, a feminist, who sees Karim as selfish and a racetraitor. Although the novel, like *The Crow Eaters* is comic, Karim's inability to see himself as exploited because he is Anglo-Indian and The National Front's attack on people in his circle as well as Jamilla's arranged marriage, adds seriousness and depth to the text.

Karim experiences personal discomfort with his race when he is cast as Mogwli in *The Jungle Bunny Book,* not the dramatic adaptation Kipling wrote, but a play written and directed by a friend of his father's lover. Karim is enjoying the part until he is asked in rehearsal to use a stage-Indian accent, something which his father, who came to England for college in the 1950's, worked hard to eliminate, but Karim does it anyway.

Later in this acting career, Karim is included in a select company in a send up of method acting. He is asked to prepare a real-self sort of part, so the playwright, after seeing what the ensemble creates as characters, can write a play to accommodate them. First, Karim imitates what he sees as hysterical in his uncle, Anwar, whose fasting nearly kills him until Jamilla relents and accepts his choice of husband for her, Changez, a crippled man who loves reading and has no apparent business sense. When challenged by another member of the company,

Tracey, with "Why do you hate yourself, and all black people so much Karim?" (180), Karim is at first confused, then sets out to create Changez for the stage. Like the National Front thugs who cannot tell the difference between Pakistanis and Indians, Karim cannot see the difference between himself as Anglo-Indian and as British; after all, he defined himself as an "Englishman" at the start. As he says, ". . . if I wanted the additional personality bonus of an Indian past, I would have to create it" (213) which he does by siphoning Indian-ness off of Changez.

Karim's closeness to Jamilla is damaged when he fails to appear at a protest march against the National Front which was organized after Changez was mistaken for a Pakistani and beaten up. Jamilla tells Karim the National Front is planning other acts of violence and the protest march will at least let them know they are not welcome. Karim decides "We could not stop it; we could only make our voices heard" (225); but he does not believe in "we" and "our." He is, in fact, so successful in acting the part of Changez as a bumbling woman chaser that he becomes the star of the play, goes on tour to New York and gains a future as an actor on a TV soap opera. For Karim, activism is futile and the road to nowhere. In giving the audience a racist stereotype of an Indian man, he has achieved success. As a man in his twenties, Karim is selfish and more interested in sex than politics. At no point does Kureish break Karim's character with false political sentiments. Karim is shallow and selfish and suffers from the intellectual lassitude Alibhai claimed Jaya Devi possessed. Literary critics, however, have found much to politicize in *The Buddha of Suburbia,* though it makes no effort to be a political novel *per se.*[8]

Cracking India, Sidwha's 1988 novel, compares more favorably to *A Fine Balance.* The narrator is an eight year-old girl, Lenny, who is crippled with polio (like Billy, Changez, Bunny and Om, who are other maimed characters.).[9] She acts as an observer-narrator in keeping with her role as a child. Through her ayah, Lenny crosses paths with a variety of men who wish to be the ayah's suitors, including the "Ice-Candy Man," a vendor of ice treats. In a period of partisan violence, surrounding the Independence movement, the ice-candy man persuades Lenny to betray the hiding place of her Hindu ayah. The ayah is then raped and abducted, appearing in public as the much decorated, rechristened Mumtaz, "wife" of the Ice-Candy Man. Fortunately for the ayah, Lenny's grandmother is a sort of force of nature who arranges for the girl, though damaged, to return to her family.

Lenny's encounters with politics and sectarian violence are suited to her childhood. She listens to dinner conversations about politics, heated debates in the park,

and picks up news she does not really understand in the park with her ayah. Sidwha incorporates the independence movement into the setting, first, then connects it to the most vulnerable member of Lenny's household to give it meaning. The chapters on politics, 15 and 16, in which the ayah is abducted, have the characters saying enough of their views to carry the main ideas of the plot through. How they live their political lives is kept remote from Lenny, who, like Yazdi is witness to something she does not really understand.

Lenny is unaware of the causes of the sectarian violence, the fate of her ayah, or of the cruelty surrounding the marriage of her sometime playmate, a household servant's daughter. The girl's mother really hates the child, and heaps verbal insults and beatings on her. The daughter is unable to physically fight back, but she is willing to provoke her mother and to insult her. At ten years old, she is married to a middle-aged man. For the ceremony, the girl is drugged (Lenny notices she does not seem her usual lively self) presumably by her mother, so she will offer no resistance. Thus, amid all the beauty of the traditional ceremony, a socially sanctioned act of inhumanity occurs. Sidhwa, again, shows her cultural awareness of Indian's women's complicity in acts that are against other women's freedom. While it is true child marriage is a way for parents to protect their daughters from rape by upper class men, the act of the mother in this novel is just vengeful.

Sidwha and Kureishi use historical circumstance as lesser vehicles in creating the settings of their novels. For Sidwha, *Cracking India* moves towards a greater, more direct use of history and contemporary politics, and both Sidwha and Kureishi present an unvarnished view of South Asian culture.

Henry James, R. G. Collingwood, and Hayden White are not far apart on the issue of history and fiction and history as fiction. For James, to be a novelist was to be cultural historian whose duty was to capture the details of the past. For Collingwood and White, the historian is in the same situation, needing to write about the past, which as a human, one is bound to interpret and shape in ways that do or do not conform with taste and cultural preoccupations. Both Mehta and Mistry transform key moments in Indian history into readable fiction and popular history. They are not "Indian historians" but they are invoking the "historical thinking" which Collingwood held was necessary for historical writing. Because history is the operating principle behind both novels, changing the settings of **Raj** and *A Fine Balance* to another time and place, would simply not work. Far from causing readers to move *away* from the fictions because of the historical thinking, as Ross suggests, the deliberate and deliberative uses of history employed by Mistry and Mehta reveal these works as unique, problematic, and complex. *Raj* and *A Fine Balance* make history visitable and visible and as historical novels they are worthy of appreciation having earned a place in the ongoing postmodern debates about truth, meaning and interpretation of the past.

Notes

1. See also Annalisa Oboe, "South African Historical Fiction and Nationalism," and Kavita Mathai, "National Identity in Recent Indian Novels in English."

2. Yoko Fujimoto labels Mistry and other immigrant novelists as "postcolonial transcultural writers" (33).

3. Ragini Ramachandra's essay, "Rohinton Mistry's *Such a Long Journey*: Some First Impressions" enables the reader to quickly compare the plots of his first and second novels. Both share the themes of a younger man disappointing his male elders and of personal loss. Ramachandra glosses over Mistry's use of history in *Such a Long Journey* as "lending a political coloring to the novel apart from investing it with topical interest" (29). Topical interest is not the point in Mistry's treatment of historical events.

4. These years are also addressed in Siddharth Dube's family memoir, *In Land of Poverty: Memoirs of an Indian Family,* especially chapter 7: "The Messiah of the Poor: Indira Gandhi," pp. 99-112. He writes "The campaign of forced sterilization and slum clearance begun by Sanjay Gandhi . . . left her reputation tarnished almost beyond repair, it was inconceivable they were pursued without her concurrence. The campaigns . . . also betrayed Mrs. Gandhi's retrograde attitude to the poor: they were a valuable vote block, they were also the root cause of India's troubles" (106). One and a half million people, mostly in northern Hindu states, were victims of sterilization (107). By the end of the 1970s, the poor felt they would never be able to rise above "the deprivation that [they] had long suffered" (112).

5. Here it is interesting to compare Upamanyu Chatterjee's short story, "The Assassination of Indira Gandhi" with its main character, Bunny Karion, to Mistry's Manek Kohlah. Bunny is a Sikh college student, who against his parents wishes does not follow his religion or wear the beard and turban of his people. He has a drinking problem, and is leading a dissipated life at school in Bombay, when he decides, mostly out of boredom, to just go home. In fact, Bunny is ill with rheumatoid arthritis. As he is recovering from jaundice, Bunny and his family hear of the assassination of Mrs. Gandhi. Bunny feels "in a delirious state, . . . that the world's chaos merely mirrored his own" (207). Less subtle than Mistry or Mehta, Chatterjee drives home the parallels between history and literature. Both Bunny and Manek believe "nothing could claim him" (209), because "(a)mbition was an absurdity, so-much-to-do-and-so-little-time-

to-do-it, how pointless an outlook" (210) in a world full of "mad events" (210). Bunny and Manek give into the State-of-Emergency which is at once a part of their private and public lives.

6. Here, as I will explain later, I draw on J. Hillis Miller's interpretation of Henry James on the relationship of history and fiction.

7. Mrinalini Sinha explains in *Colonial Masculinity* in a succinct way the importance of India to the English economy which makes Tanya's and Billy's marriage a symbolic parallel, see pp. 1-10.

8. See for example, the essays on *The Buddha of Suburbia* in the special section of *Commonwealth Essays and Studies,* ed. with an introduction by James Oubechou. Topics including colonialism, otherness and cultural criticism are addressed by the several authors. Though Kureishi is only 44, he is the subject of a biography by Kenneth C. Kaleta, *Hanif Kureishi: Postcolonial Storyteller.*

9. The defective body of the most native or natural of Indians is overtly suggestive of diseases and injustice in the larger polis; of colonialism and the State-of-Emergency. Rushdie's Salem Sinai is also disfigured with his huge nose and face in the shape of India. The injured bodies here are not open to such parody.

Works Cited

Alibhai, Yasmin. "A False Orient." Rev. of *Raj,* by G. Mehta. *New Statesman and Society* 16 June 1989: 34.

Bayer, Jogamaya. "The Presentation of History in Ruth Prawer Jhabvala's Novel *Heat and Dust.*" Zach and Goodwin 443-447.

Billington, Rachel. "Out of the Purdan into Politics." Rev. of *Raj,* by G. Mehta. *New York Times Book Review* 9 April 1989: 18.

"Briefly Noted—*A Fine Balance.*" *The New Yorker* 3 June 1998: 93.

Buruma, Ian. "Good Night Sweet Princes." Rev. of *Raj,* by G. Mehta. *New York Review of Books* 18 May 1989: 9-12.

Chaterjee, Upamany. "The Assassination of Indira Gandhi." *Mirrorwork.* Ed. Salman Rushdie and Elizabeth West. New York: Owl Books, 1997: 198-210.

Collingwood, R. G. *The Idea of History.* Oxford: Oxford UP, 1946.

Cowart, David. *History and the Contemporary* Novel. Carbondale: Southern Illinois UP, 1989.

Dönnerstag, Jurgen. "Hybrid Forms of Multiculturalism in the Fiction of Salman Rushdie." Zach and Goodwin 455-460.

Dube, Siddharth. *In the Land of Poverty: Memoirs of an Indian Family.* New York: Zed Books, 1998.

Dunbar, Pamel. "Conflict and Continuity: The Family as Emblem of the Postcolonial Society." Zach and Goodwin 103-104.

"Fiction Reprints—*A Fine Balance.*" *Publisher's Weekly,* 22 February 1991: 217.

Fujimoto, Yoko. "Multi-Culturalism and Ethnic Writing in English Canada: A New Development in the National Literary Discourse." Zach and Goodwin 325-330.

Human Rights Watch. *Broken People. Cast Violence against India's 'Untouchables'.* New York: Human Rights Watch, 1999.

"Indira Gandhi." *Cambridge Biographical Dictionary,* 1991.

Ingraham, Janet. "Book Reviews: Fiction." Rev. of *A Fine Balance,* by R. Mistry. *Library Journal* 1 April 1996: 18.

Iyer, Pico. "Down and Really Out." Rev. of *A Fine Balance,* by R. Mistry. *Time* 22 April 1996: 84-5.

Jacobs, Naomi. *The Character of Truth: Historical Figures in Contemporary Fiction.* Carbondale: Southern Illinois UP, 1990.

James, Lawrence. *Raj: The Making and Unmaking of British India.* New York: St. Martin's Press, 1997.

Kaleta, Kenneth C. *Hanif Kureishi: Postcolonial Storyteller* Austin: U of Texas P, 1998.

Kureishi, Hanif. *The Buddha of Suburbia.* New York: Viking, 1990.

Mathai, Kavita. "National Identity in Recent Indian Novels in English." Zach and Goodwin 435-441.

Mehta, Gita. *Raj: A Novel.* 1989. New York: Ballantine Books, 1991.

Miller, J. Hillis. "History, Narrative, and Responsibility: Speech Acts in *The Aspern Papers.*" *Enacting History in Henry James: Narrative, Power, and Ethics.* Ed. Gert Buelens. Cambridge: Cambridge UP, 1997), 193-210.

———. "Narrative and History." *ELH* 41 (1974): 455-473.

Mistry, Rohinton. *A Fine Balance.* 1995. Toronto: McClelland and Stewart, 1997.

Mojtabai, A. G. "An Accidental Family." Rev. of *A Fine Balance* by R. Mistry. *New York Times Book Review,* 23 June 1996: 29.

Oboe, Annalisa. "South African Historical Fiction and Nationalism." Zach and Goodwin 229-237.

Oubechou, James, ed. "*The Buddha of Suburbia.*" Spec. section of *Commonwealth Essays and Studies* 4 (1997): 87-125.

Ramachandra, Ragini. "Rohinton Mistry's *Such a Long Journey*: Some First Impressions." *Literary Criterion* (Bombay) 29.4 (1991): 25-34.

Ross, Robert L. "Seeking and Maintaining Balance: Rohinton Mistry's Fiction." *World Literature Today* 73 (Spring 1999): 239-245.

Rubin, Merle. "Novels of Love and Adversity for Summertime Reading." Rev. of *A Fine Balance,* by R. Mistry. *Christian Science Monitor* 27 June 1996: B1.

Sidwha, Bapsi. *Cracking India.* Minneapolis, MN: Milkweed Editions, 1991. Rpt. of *The Ice-Candy Man.* 1988.

———. *The Crow Eaters.* New York: St. Martin's Press, 1981.

Sinha, Mrinalini. *Colonial Masculinity: The "Manly Englishman" and the "Effeminate Bengali" in the Late Nineteenth Century.* Manchester: Manchester UP, 1995.

White, Hayden. *Figural Realism: Studies in the Mimesis Effect.* Baltimore: Johns Hopkins UP, 1999.

Zach Wolfgang, and Ken L. Goodwin, eds. *Nationalism vs. Internationalism: (Inter)national Dimensions of Literature in English.* Tubingen: Stauffenberg, 1996.

FURTHER READING

Criticism

Chandavarkar, Rajnarayan. "India for the English." *London Review of Books* 12, no. 5 (8 March 1990): 10-11.

> Chandavarkar offers a mixed assessment of *Raj,* asserting that the novel occasionally becomes "ponderous and plodding."

Prose, Francine. "The Sacred and the Profane." *Washington Post Book World* (30 May 1993): 6.

> Prose praises Mehta's evocation of the Indian landscape in *A River Sutra* but argues that the novel often lapses into "portentous philosophizing."

Tharoor, Shashi. "A Passage to Exotic India." *Far Eastern Economic Review* 145, no. 36 (7 September 1989): 82-3.

> Tharoor expresses disappointment with *Raj,* concluding that the work lacks depth, character, and

imagination. Winchester, Simon. "Homespun in India." *Far Eastern Economic Review* 156, no. 46 (18 November 1993): 42.

Winchester stresses the similarities between Mehta's *A River Sutra* and R. K. Narayan's *The Grandmother's Tale*.

Additional coverage of Mehta's life and career is contained in the following sources published by the Gale Group: *Literature of Developing Nations for Students,* **Vol. 2; and** *Literature Resource Center.*

Death of a Salesman

Arthur Miller

American playwright, essayist, novelist, screenwriter, short story writer, nonfiction writer, travel writer, children's writer, and autobiographer.

The following entry presents criticism on Miller's play *Death of a Salesman* (1949) through 2002. For further information on his life and complete works, see *CLC*, Volumes 1, 2, 6, 10, 15, 26, 47, and 78.

INTRODUCTION

With its first production in 1949, *Death of a Salesman* firmly established Miller's reputation as one of the premiere American playwrights. Structured as a modern tragedy, the play depicts the last twenty-four hours in the life of Willy Loman, a sixty-three-year-old traveling salesman, who for thirty-six years has sold his wares all over New England. Miller utilizes Loman's disillusionment with his life and career as a means to measure the enormous gap between the American Dream's promise of eventual success and the devastating reality of one's concrete failure. Both a critical and popular success, *Death of a Salesman* has received a Tony Award, a New York Drama Critics Circle Award, and a Pulitzer Prize as well as being adapted for film and television on several occasions. *Death of a Salesman* is widely recognized as Miller's masterpiece and is frequently listed along side Tennessee Williams's *A Streetcar Named Desire* and Eugene O'Neill's *Long Day's Journey into Night* as one of the canonical works of American drama.

PLOT AND MAJOR CHARACTERS

Death of a Salesman opens with Willy Loman returning to his wife, Linda, at their home in Brooklyn, New York, after an unsuccessful sales trip. The play's structure subverts the traditional linear narrative by intermingling Willy's internal monologues and past recollections with the present action of the plot. After he arrives in Brooklyn, Willy is soon visited by his two grown sons, Biff and Happy (Hap). The eldest son, Biff, a former high school football star, has travelled the country holding a series of aimless jobs. Hap works in a dead-end job at a New York department store and

spends most of his time chasing women and drinking. Willy is extremely critical of his sons' lack of direction and, in turn, Biff and Hap regard him as ineffectual and worry that he is becoming senile in his old age. After talking to Linda about Biff's failure to find a career, Willy recalls his son's success as a football star and is soon reminded of his own marital infidelities with a woman he met on the road. Willy eventually shifts focus to criticizing Hap's spending habits and becomes upset. His neighbor Charlie calms him down and the two men play a game of cards. After Charlie leaves, Willy reminisces about his brother Ben, who left for Africa to mine diamonds and became a great financial success. When Linda finds Willy ranting alone about the past, he leaves the house to take a walk. Concerned about his father's erratic behavior, Biff confronts his mother who accuses him of neglecting his father. When Hap joins the conversation, Linda accuses them both of being ungrateful and of turning their backs on their father. She then reveals that Willy has tried to kill himself on several occasions. When Willy returns, Hap tells him that Biff is going to approach his old boss, Bill Oliver, for a loan to open a sporting-goods store. Although Biff is against the idea, he goes along with the deception to make his father happy.

The next day, Willy finds that he has been fired from his sales job after thirty-six years of service. Upset and on his way to Charlie's office to ask for a job, Willy runs into Charlie's son, Ben, who was a classmate of Biff's. Ben reveals that Biff was irrevocably changed by a surprise visit to Willy during his senior year in high school. Ben comments that, after his abrupt return, Biff became uninterested in college and lost his motivation to better himself. Meanwhile, Biff meets Hap at a restaurant to inform him that he was unable to get the loan from Bill Oliver. However, Biff does admit that he has come to the realization that he has to change his life. When Willy arrives at the restaurant, Biff attempts to tell him the truth about their deception and his failed meeting. Willy leaves his sons and has a flashback to the fateful sales trip when Biff's surprise visit revealed Willy's adulterous affair. Later, back at the family home, Biff confronts Willy about his suicide attempts and informs his father that he will leave in the morning, planning never to return. At that moment, Willy decides to commit suicide, convinced that the settlement on his life insurance policy will provide Biff with the wealth he needs to start a new life. The play concludes with Willy's funeral as the assembled characters reflect on Willy's life and legacy.

MAJOR THEMES

Critics have maintained that much of the enduring universal appeal of *Death of a Salesman* lies in its central theme of the failure of the American Dream. Willy's commitment to false social values—consumerism, ambition, social stature—keeps him from acknowledging the value of human experience—the comforts of personal relationships, family and friends, and love. When Willy realizes that his true value lies in being a good father, he chooses to sacrifice himself in order to give his sons the material wealth he has always desired. In a broader sense, some commentators perceive the play as an indictment of American capitalism and a rejection of materialist values. Competition and responsibility are also prominent themes in *Death of a Salesman*. For example, Willy's tendency to evade responsibility for his behavior and his penchant for blaming others has been passed onto his sons and, as a result, all three men exhibit a poor work ethic and lack of integrity. Willy's inability to discern between reality and fantasy is another recurring motif, particularly as seen through the subjective reality of the play's structure. Miller creates an environment in *Death of a Salesman* where the real time of the play and the internal workings of Willy's mind are brought together. This refusal to separate subjective and objective truths is further reflected in Willy's inability to see his sons for who they really are, which becomes major source of conflict in the play.

CRITICAL RECEPTION

Although *Death of a Salesman* is widely regarded as one of the greatest American plays of the twentieth century, there has been some critical debate over Miller's assertion that the play is, in fact, a modern tragedy. Some reviewers have argued that the work cannot be considered a tragedy in the traditional sense because Willy does not fit the Aristotelian definition of a tragic hero. Others have countered, asserting that Willy attains tragic dimensions by virtue of his intense passion to surpass his earthly limitations. In support of this claim, Robert A. Martin has commented that, "Is there more to the idea of tragedy than transcends the struggle between father and son for forgiveness and dignity?" In addition to these questions of classification, *Death of a Salesman* has also attracted critical notice for its sophisticated critique of the role of capitalism in American society. Commentators have noted that Willy's failure to understand and achieve the American

Dream strongly resonates with modern audiences, contributing significantly to its enduring popularity. *Death of a Salesman* has remained critically and commercially popular since its first performance—a fiftieth-anniversary production in 1999 won a Tony Award for Best Play Revival.

PRINCIPAL WORKS

The Pussycat and the Expert Plumber Who was a Man (radio play) 1941

The Man Who Had All the Luck (play) 1944

Situation Normal (nonfiction) 1944

Focus (novel) 1945

Grandpa and the Statue (radio play) 1945

All My Sons (play) 1947

The Story of Gus (radio play) 1947

Death of a Salesman: Certain Private Conversations in Two Acts and a Requiem (play) 1949

An Enemy of the People [adaptor; from the play by Henrik Ibsen] (play) 1950

The Crucible (play) 1953

A Memory of Two Mondays (play) 1955

A View from the Bridge (play) 1955; revised two-act version, 1956

†*Arthur Miller's Collected Plays, Volume One* (plays) 1957; republished as *Plays: One,* 1988

The Misfits (screenplay) 1961

Jane's Blanket [illustrations by Al Parker] (juvenilia) 1963

After the Fall (play) 1964

Incident at Vichy (play) 1964

I Don't Need You Any More (short stories) 1967

The Price (play) 1968

In Russia [with Inge Morath] (travel writing) 1969

The Creation of the World and Other Business (play) 1972; revised as *Up from Paradise,* 1974

The Archbishop's Ceiling (play) 1977

The Theater Essays of Arthur Miller [edited by Robert A. Martin] (essays) 1978

Chinese Encounters [with Inge Morath] (travel writing) 1979

The American Clock [adaptor; from the nonfiction work *Hard Times* by Studs Terkel] (play) 1980

‡*2 by A.M.* (plays) 1982

Salesman in Beijing [photographs by Inge Morath] (diary) 1984

§*Danger, Memory!: Two Plays* (plays) 1986

Conversations with Arthur Miller [edited by Matthew C. Roudané] (interviews) 1987

Timebends: A Life (autobiography) 1987

Everybody Wins (screenplay) 1990

The Last Yankee (play) 1991; revised two-act version, 1993

The Ride Down Mt. Morgan (play) 1991

Homely Girl: A Life (novella) 1992; also published as *Plain Girl: A Life,* 1995

Broken Glass (play) 1994

Homely Girl: A Life, and Other Stories (novella and short stories) 1995

The Crucible (screenplay) 1996

Mr. Peters' Connections (play) 1998

Echoes Down the Corridor: Collected Essays, 1944-2000 [edited by Steven R. Centola] (essays) 2000

On Politics and the Art of Acting (essays) 2001

Resurrection Blues (play) 2002

*These two works were first performed together in a single production.

†Includes *All My Sons, Death of a Salesman, The Crucible,* and *A View from the Bridge.*

‡This work consists of two one-act plays: *Elegy for a Lady* and *Some Kind of Love Story.*

§This work consists of two one-act plays: *I Can't Remember Anything* and *Clara.*

CRITICISM

Lawrence Rosinger (essay date winter 1987)

SOURCE: Rosinger, Lawrence. "Miller's *Death of a Salesman.*" *Explicator* 45, no. 2 (winter 1987): 55-6.

[*In the following essay, Rosinger discusses the allusions to classical drama and mythology in* Death of a Salesman.]

In commenting on **Death of a Salesman,** Arthur Miller has stated emphatically that modern tragedies need not be bound by Aristotelian principles, especially since the tragedies of our time can revolve about an ordinary person, a Willy Loman, rather than one of high status.[1] It is therefore interesting to note that the vocabulary of **Death of a Salesman** in several instances suggests an older type of drama.

For example, Miller imparts to the salesman's world an element of earlier tragedy when Willy, speaking of his deceased boss, asserts: "That man was a prince, he was a masterful man" (133).[2] The word "prince" (with its ironic hint of royalty) is again stressed in the restaurant scene, when Willy goes to the washroom and Biff says to Miss Forsythe: "you've just seen a prince walk by. A fine, troubled prince. A hardworking, unappreciated prince" (204).

Miller also includes several allusions to classical mythology. In the opening stage direction, he describes Linda as "[m]ost often *jovial*" and Willy as having a "*mercurial* nature" (my emphasis) (131). These unspo-

ken references to gods are supplemented by a passage in which Willy, imagining that Happy and Biff are still in their high school years, declares: "You're both built like Adonises" (146). Again, when recalling Biff's football glory, Willy describes him in these terms: "Like a young god. Hercules—something like that" (171).

A link between Miller and Aristotle appears when Charley goes into Willy's house because he hears Willy shouting. Miller's stage direction declares of Charley at this point: "In all he says . . . there is pity, and, now, trepidation" (152). This seems to be an application of Aristotle's view that "A perfect tragedy . . . should . . . imitate actions which excite pity and fear. . . ."[3] What Miller is telling us here is that Charley is reacting to Willy's situation as one properly reacts to tragedy. The effect is to encourage the audience, in the theater or the study, to do likewise.

It is possible, of course, that the presence of all these items is sheer coincidence, but I do not think so. Their implication is that Willy, "A small man [who] can be just as exhausted as a great man" (163), is in the line of an ancient dramatic tradition.[4] Perhaps, too, there is a quality of ironic humor. One can imagine Miller as amused by classical references in a salesman's story. Yet the words have been chosen with care. A real Willy might actually use "Adonises" or "Hercules" in the sentences assigned to him, just as he and Biff might call someone a "prince." On the other hand, Miller, with appropriate discrimination, confines literary words, such as "jovial," "mercurial," and "trepidation" to the stage directions, i.e., to the area in which the author speaks directly to the actor or reader.

Notes

1. Arthur Miller, introduction, *Arthur Miller's Collected Plays* (New York: Viking, 1957), pp. 31-32.

2. Parenthetical numbers refer to the text of *Death of a Salesman* in Miller's *Collected Plays* (see note 1).

3. From Aristotle's *Poetics,* translated by S. H. Butcher, in *The Reader's Encyclopedia of World Drama,* ed. John Gassner and Edward Quinn (New York: Crowell, 1969), p. 942:1.

4. The play, on one occasion, also echoes Shakespearean comedy. When Willy says to Happy, "The world is an oyster, but you don't crack it open on a mattress!" (152), Miller is recalling Pistol's assertion in *The Merry Wives of Windsor* (II.ii.2-3) that "the world's mine oyster, which I with sword will open."

Leah Hadomi (essay date June 1988)

SOURCE: Hadomi, Leah. "Fantasy and Reality: Dramatic Rhythm in *Death of a Salesman.*" *Modern Drama* 31, no. 2 (June 1988): 157-74.

[*In the following essay, Hadomi provides a stylistic analysis of* Death of a Salesman *through the examina-*

tion of "the ways in which the rhythmic organization of the play is managed in respect of three structural elements in the play: characterization, symbolic clusters, and the plot."]

The subtitle of **Death of a Salesman,** "Certain Private Conversations in Two Acts and a Requiem,"[1] as well as the title originally considered by the playwright, *The Inside of His Head,* already point to the play's thematic essence and major formal characteristic. Thematically, Miller's drama deals with the tension between the private inner world of the protagonist and external reality. Its principal structural characteristic consists of the integration of dramatic realism and expressionism.[2]

The conflicting inner selves that make up Willy Loman's many-sided persona represent his experience of the outer world refracted through the distorting medium of his fantasies. As the action of the play progresses, the connections between Willy's inner world and external reality—which are tenuous enough to begin with—grow increasingly unstable and volatile until he is driven to kill himself, the ultimate act of self-deception in his struggle to impose his fantasies upon a reality that consistently thwarts his ambitions and will.

The shifts in Willy Loman's mind between his dreams and actuality, on the level of his personal existence, and between fantasy and realism on the level of dramatic presentation, are conveyed in structural terms by the patterns in which the play's formal elements unfold to establish the dramatic rhythm of the work. In the analysis of Miller's play that follows, I take my cue from the conceptions of dramatic rhythm as set out by Paul M. Levitt and Kathleen George.[3] In my own consideration of the work, I shall examine the ways in which the rhythmic organization of the play is managed in respect of three structural elements in the play; characterization, symbolic clusters, and the plot.

I

Not only is Willy Loman the chief character of the play but it is primarily from his psychological perspective that the play's dramatic action derives its meaning. The actual events enacted in his presence become the trigger for Willy's recollections and fantasies which constitute the play's imaginary sequences. The significance of each of the play's episodes, as well as the structure of the plot as a whole, depends on the rhythmic alternations between actuality and the protagonist's mental responses to them. His ideal self-image and the reality of his actual behavior and circumstances are the poles of both his inner existence and his dramatic interactions with the other characters of the play. The personalities of each of the *dramatis personae* are connected specifically with a particular feature of Willy's inner self, with a particular stance he has adopted toward his environ-

ment, or with one of the values in which he has educated his sons. Thus the conduct of the play's other characters is in great measure both the effect of his illusory perception of external reality and the cause of his deepening submersion in the world of his fantasies. When reality becomes too painful, Willy retreats into a dream world consisting of his roseate recollections of the past and of fantasies in which he fulfills the aspirations the attainment of which has eluded him in life. Although his memories are based on actual events, these are falsified in his mind by wishful thinking about how they ought to have turned out. Hence in Willy's mind, reality as it is immediately experienced by him merges in his consciousness with his recollection of distant events to form a seamless continuum of past and present time.

The set in Arthur Miller's play furnishes, in the words of Edward Murray, "a flexible medium in which to enact the process of Willy Loman's way of mind."[4] The block of apartment houses and the Loman home provide the static elements of the set. The element of change is furnished by the shifts of the location of action from one part of the stage to another. Its role in Miller's work evokes an instance of Kathleen George's dictum that the polyscenic stage functions according to the same principles as do the other manifestations of dramatic rhythm in pointing to the stable and changing features of the plot.

However, the interplay between fantasy and reality in Willy Loman's mind enacted on stage represents only one aspect of the dramatization of the inner tensions of the protagonist. Willy is torn between his need, on the one hand, to give expression to his innermost longings by establishing a direct and harmonious connection with nature, and by manual labor; on the other, he wishes to maintain his place in society by creating a facade of emulous and combative self-assertiveness, which he tries to reconcile with his obsessive and desperate need to be admired and loved by others. Together these contrary tendencies account for the conflicts both in the ideal conception of himself and in the way he conceives of others, in relation to the idealized image of his own personality. Moreover, Willy's ideal self-image is as fragmented as his real personality. Rather than consisting of a single coherent self, it is compacted of a number of contradictory selves, each of which might alone have formed the core of an integrated personality relatively free of tension, but which together make up an unstable persona that ultimately costs the protagonist his life.

Willy Loman spends much of his time on stage in an ongoing inner dialogue with a number of characters. Some, like Willy's sons and his friend, Charley, belong to the immediate and concrete reality which is being dramatized. Three other figures emerge from Willy's recollection of the past and animate his inner world: his father, his older brother Ben, and old Dave Singleman. All three figures owe their presentation and description in the play to Willy's imagination, whose creation they essentially are. The characters that live through Willy's imagination are both the fruit and inspiration of this inner existence; and, by virtue of Willy Loman's function as the protagonist from whose perspective much of the play's action is seen, these characters furnish the focus of the clash of fantasy and reality in both Willy himself and the other *dramatis personae* of the play.

In Willy's consciousness each of the three men from the past has assumed the status of a personal hero and exemplar whom he aspires to emulate. And together they may make up the ideal end of the continuum between ideality and actuality along which Willy's fluctuations between fantasy and reality take place. Each in his own right also furnishes Willy with a separate "ego ideal" that occupies a distinct place on a descending scale of proximity to the real world.

Connected with Willy's past is the memory of his father, who never assumes substantial form in Willy's mind but nevertheless powerfully informs his fantasy, primarily through his imagined conversations with Ben. Thus, Willy's father, the least accessible and most dimly remembered of the protagonist's exemplars, functions as his "absolute" ego ideal. His brother, Ben, against whose adventurous life and grand mercantile enterprises in far-off places Willy measures his own inadequacy and petty destiny, is his "desiderative" ego ideal. And last, Dave Singleman, the quintessence of the successful salesman and Willy's inspiration and model for feasible achievement, serves the protagonist as his "attainable" ego ideal.

Of these three ideal figures, Willy's father is the most remote from actuality and belongs to the very earliest and vaguest childhood recollections. Though not one of the *dramatis personae,* and spoken of only twice in the course of the play—during Ben's first "visitation" in Act One (pp. 156-57), and then briefly by Willy in Howard's office in Act Two (p. 180)—his spirit dogs Willy and is repeatedly referred to on an auditory level by the sound of flute music, which is first heard as a sort of signature tune when the curtain goes up on the play, and is heard last when the curtain falls on the "Requiem." Hearing his father playing the flute is nearly the only sensory memory Willy has of him—that and his father's "big beard." What we know of the picture in Willy's mind of the man we learn from the description he receives from Ben's apparition. And what emerges from Ben's account is a part-mythic, part-allegorical figure. The image of him drawn by Ben is an emblematic composite of the classic types that are representative of America's heroic age: Willy's father is at once the untamed natural man and the westward-bound pioneer; the artisan, the great inventor, and the successful entrepreneur.

Willy's brother Ben represents an ideal which is closer to reality, that of worldly success, though on a scale so exalted as to be utterly beyond Willy's reach. To Willy's mind Ben is the personification of the great American virtues of self-reliance and initiative by which an enterprising man may attain untold wealth; and it is through Ben that Willy tries to maintain personal connection with the myth of the individual's triumphant march from rags to riches.

In Willy's consciousness Ben mediates between the domains of the ideal and the real. The aura of legend is nearly as strong in his brother as it is in his father. He, too, is a journeyer and adventurer. But what animates him in his rangings appears to be less a hankering for the open road and the "grand outdoors" than the idea of the fortune to be made there. Sentiment plays no part in the tough maxims he tosses out in accounting for his success. Nor does he let family feeling cloud his purpose or divert him from his quest for riches, as is evident from the ease with which he abandons his search for his father to pursue diamond wealth in Africa; or, again, in the offhand manner he receives the news of his mother's death. Even Willy gets short shrift from his older brother. Nevertheless it is Ben's qualities of toughness, unscrupulousness, and implacability in the pursuit of gain that Willy wishes for himself and wants his boys to acquire.

Of Willy Loman's three personal heroes it is Dave Singleman who stands in the most immediate relation to the actuality of Willy's life. Neither the ideal pattern of natural manhood personified by Willy's father, nor the incarnation of freebooting enterprise embodied by his brother, Singleman represents success that is potentially attainable. In Singleman the concept of success is cut down to Willy's size, reduced to an idea more nearly within his scope—that of getting ahead by being "well liked." Success as exemplified in Dave Singleman serves, as well, to sustain in Willy the feeling that, though wanting in the daring and toughness that is his father's legacy to Ben, he too possesses an essential prerequisite for material achievement, and one that he can pass on to his own sons. So, poised in Howard's office between the phantoms of his dead brother and of Biff in his teens, Willy proclaims in an access of confidence: "It's who you know and the smile on your face! It's contacts, Ben, contacts!" (p. 184).

Willy is not content merely to admire these men. He also internalizes their qualities and the ideas they represent, diminishing and trivializing them in the process. Thus the ideas of being in close touch with nature and taking to the open road that are inspired by Willy's memory of his father are diminished in his own life to puttering about in the back yard of his suburban Brooklyn home and making his routine rounds as a traveling salesman; the idea of venturesome private enterprise for high stakes represented by his brother depreciates to drumming merchandise for a commission; and even the example of Singleman's being "remembered and loved and helped by so many different people" (p. 180), over which Willy rhapsodizes to Howard Wagner, is degraded in his own aspirations to the condition of being merely popular and well-liked.

Three of the characters among the principal *dramatis personae* of the play, Biff, Happy and Charley, function in the real world as analogous to the ideal types in Willy's consciousness. Though none of them is a complete substantiation of Willy's ego ideals, there is in each character a dominant trait that identifies him with either Willy's father, or Ben, or Dave Singleman, and that determines Willy's relationship to him.

Biff most closely resembles his grandfather in rejecting the constraints imposed by the middle-class routines of holding down a job and making a living, and in his preference for the life of a drifter out West, working as a hired farm-hand in the outdoors. He has a strong touch of the artist and dreamer in his temperament. He is also the most complex character of the three, the most at odds with himself. In this he closely resembles Willy. Like his father, Biff is torn between rural nostalgia and his need for solid achievement, and is tormented by the knowledge of personal failure. "I've always made a point of not wasting my life," he tells Happy, and then confesses to him, "and everytime I come back here I know that all I've done is to waste my life" (p. 139).

Happy corresponds to Ben, if only in a meager and debased way. He shares his uncle's unscrupulousness and amorality, but has little of his singleness of purpose; and what he has of the last he dedicates to cuckolding his superiors at work and to the pursuit of women in general, activities that make up the only field in which he excels, as Linda recognizes when she sums him up as a "philandering bum" (p. 163). He resembles Ben, too, in the shallowness of his filial emotions. The trite praise he bestows on Linda—"What a woman! They broke the mold when they made her" (p. 169)—is on its own vulgar level as perfunctory and unfeeling as Ben's more elegantly phrased endorsement, "Fine specimen of a lady, Mother" (p. 155). However, some of his traits remind us of Willy, such as his bluster and nursing of injured pride, his insecurity about making good, as well as his philandering.

Charley is Dave Singleman brought down to earth. He has none of Singleman's flamboyance that Willy so rapturously remembers from his younger days. Rather, he is successful salesmanship domesticated. Singleman worked out of a hotel room. Charley maintains an office with a secretary and an accountant. He is stolid but honest and decent, and though not loved like Singleman, he is respected. And, by Willy's own startled admission toward the end, he is Willy Loman's only friend. He is also Willy's perfect foil, a man at peace with what he is and his place in the world.[5]

Excepting Charley, the principal characters of *Death of a Salesman* share the same condition of being torn between the conflicting claims of ideality and actuality; and in this capacity the interrelations among them serve to extend and reinforce the rhythmic articulation of the play on a variety of formal levels. Among the consequences of the inner conflicts and contradictions of Willy Loman and his sons is their uncertainty and confusion concerning their own identities, a circumstance of which each shows himself to be aware at some point in the play. So Biff reveals to his mother, "I just can't take hold, Mom. I can't take hold of some kind of a life" (p. 161); Happy tells Biff, "I don't know what the hell I'm workin' for . . . And still, goddamit, I'm lonely" (p. 139); and Willy confesses to Ben, "I still feel—kind of temporary about myself" (p. 159).[6]

Willy Loman's attitude to the real characters of the play is determined by their relation to the corresponding ideal types in his mind. None of the real characters is an unalloyed embodiment of these exemplars, who have all been debased to varying degrees in their corporeal counterparts. So, for example, Willy's most complex and ambivalent relationship is with Biff, who is associated most closely with Willy's absolute ego ideal.[7] It is of his older son that Willy had always expected the most, and it is Biff's failure to live up to his expectations that grieves him the most. By comparison his relationship with Happy, of whom he expects much less, is straightforward and indifferent. Willy's relationship with Charley, too, is determined by Charley's proximity to the ideal and his own distance therefrom. Because Charley comes closest of anyone Willy knows to the attainable ideal he has set himself but failed to achieve, he treats him with a mixture of respect and envy. The last prevents Willy from accepting Charley's offer of a job, because doing so would be tantamount to an admission of failure, a reason never stated explicitly by Willy but of which Charley is aware, as we learn during Willy's visit to Charley's office in the second act (p. 192):

CHARLEY:

What're you, jealous of me?

WILLY:

I can't work for you, that's all, don't ask me why.

CHARLEY:

(*Angered, takes out more bills*) You been jealous of me all your life, you damned fool! Here, pay your insurance.

By taking money from Charley, instead, in the guise of a loan, Willy is able both to retain his self-esteem and to cling to his self-delusions. In a rare moment of candor Willy privately admits to Charley's virtues and superiority to himself ("a man of few words, and they respect him" [p. 149]), but for the most part he seeks to establish his own pre-eminence by belittling and hectoring him in petty ways, reminding Charley of his ignorance and inadequacy in ordinary matters: domestic repairs, diet, clothing, sports, cards, and so on.

To sum up, therefore, the function of all of the principal characters of the play (apart from Linda) is determined by the operations of Willy's consciousness, suspended between reality and dreams. The measure of their moral significance to Willy is contingent on the degree to which they have taken root in the ideal realm of his consciousness; and the extent to which they have done so is in inverse relation to their actual presence in the dramatic sequences that take place in current time and space. Thus, Willy's father, the absolute ideal figure of the play, assumes the status of a recognizable personality only through the account of him received from the shade of his deceased brother in a scene that unfolds entirely in the mind of the protagonist. Otherwise, he is mentioned only once in the real action of the play, when Willy offhandedly refers to him as a prelude to his pathetic boast to Howard, "We've got quite a little streak of self-reliance in our family" (p. 180). The name of Ben, too, is barely brought up—and then only in passing—in the real dialogue of the play; and it is only in the fantasizing episodes that he takes on palpable shape as a character in the play. And, finally, Dave Singleman, who serves Willy as a tangible, if illusory, example of success potentially within his grasp, comes alive in a present dramatic sequence of the play, even if only through the agency of words rather than action. Significantly, the short eulogy of him that Willy provides, and through which Singleman assumes dramatic life, comes at the moment that Willy is about to be fired and thereby deprived of the last vestige of his hope for the attainable success represented by Singleman.

The dramatic rhythm within and between the characters also finds expression in their attitudes to the opposite sex. Family relations and the role of women function as important compositional elements in the rhythm of the play. When connected to dramatic figures, functioning as Willy's ego-ideals, the women figures are either mentioned briefly or are meaningfully absent. Willy remembers sitting in his mother's lap; Ben remembers his mother as a "Fine specimen of a lady" (p. 155). Ben's wife bore him the legendary number of seven sons, and the third male ideal figure is named "Dave Singleman". The remoteness and idealization of the women figures is paralleled by an abrupt attitude towards the women in the reality of the play—even in the indication of Howard's attitude towards his wife as revealed in the short incident of the tape recorder.

Willy and his sons have an inner conflict in which they fluctuate between loyalty to the mother-woman figure and an attraction to women as sexual objects. Loyalty to the first is linked to stability and integrity in family and social life, whereas the desire for the second represents disintegration of the individual and his role in society. The tension between these two views is seen in Willy, Biff, and Happy but is motivated uniquely in each of them. Willy's affair with the woman in Boston is partly a result of his loneliness but largely a way of boosting his ego. Motivated by a constant craving to be "well liked," he is happy to be "picked" by her. Happy's aggressive promiscuity is one overt aspect of his latent "jungle" life-style. He recognizes that his repeated, almost compulsive affairs with women related to higher executives at his work are an aspect of his "overdeveloped sense of competition" (p. 141). Biff, on the other hand, seems mostly to be pushed to feminine company by his father and brother, who see this as part of his being an admired star. In all three of them sexual attraction is depicted as morally deteriorating and contrary to their relationship to Linda as an idealized wife-mother figure: "They broke the mold when they made her" (p. 169). This inner contradiction is revealed differently in Willy's attitude towards her mending stockings, as an expression of his guilt feelings; in Happy's constant assurance that he longs for a meaningful relation with "Somebody with character; with resistance! Like Mom, y'know?" (p. 140); and in Biff's strong clinging to his mother, expressed as "I don't want my pal looking old" (p. 161) and opposed to his being "too rough with the girls" (p. 151).

The rhythm of the sequence of the two episodes focusing on sexual relations (the Boston woman, and the restaurant scene where the boys pick up two women) is also a formal means serving a thematic idea. The significance of the "Boston woman" is foreshadowed in Act I but only receives full dramatic revelation in the "Restaurant scene" in Act II, when it is reconstructed orally and visually in such a way as to show its significance in the wider context of Willy and Biff's relationship and their recognition of what is true and what is false in their lives. So, whereas in the Boston scene it is the son who fails in social competition by flunking his test in mathematics, in the restaurant scene both father and son appear equally defeated in the economic and social struggle; and while in the Boston episode Biff, appalled by Willy's infidelity, realizes that his talkative, pretentious father is ineffectual (p. 207) and calls him a "phony little fake" (p. 208), in the restaurant scene Biff confesses to his father the pretensions and illusions of his own life too. Thus, sexual infidelity is related to the thematic focus of the play: the conflict between fantasy and reality.

The dramatic rhythm of *Death of a Salesman,* as made manifest in the development of character, takes place through a complex interplay between the function of *dramatis personae* and their interplay with the three levels of Willy's consciousness: first, on the level of ideality; second on the level of Willy's fantasies and dreams; and last, on the level of his perception of concrete reality. It is from these three levels of consciousness that the protagonist's three ego ideals—the absolute, the desiderative, and the attainable—emerge. Taken as a whole, Willy's three levels of consciousness dramatize his attitude to himself, to the "other" and to social reality.

II

The stage itself is a central element of the symbolic system of Miller's play. On the polyscenic set of *Death of a Salesman,* the dialectic processes taking place in the protagonist's mind are accompanied by shifts of location from one part of the stage to another.[8] Additionally, the set combines the elements of stage presentation with those of literary imagery that form symbolic clusters operating within the play's continuum of shifting consciousness between fantasy and reality. The dramatic presentation on stage is thus signalled, punctuated, and reinforced by recurrent visual and auditory effects. So, for example, the visual effects of foliage and trees, and the sound of the flute or of soft music, underscore Willy's rural longings; whereas pulsating music and loud sounds accompany Willy's erotic and savage "jungle" moods.[9]

A number of verbal references of symbolic significance recur throughout the text of Miller's play. These echo and enhance the play's rhythmic design. The significance that attaches itself to them derives from the associations they arouse in the protagonist's consciousness, where they are resolved into two principal symbolic clusters, connected with divergent attitudes that dominate Willy's imaginative life. The first cluster is connected with Willy's deep attachment to nature and nostalgia for the countryside, feelings whose ultimate point of origin is to be traced back to Willy's father. The major references that are included in this cluster are to trees, seeds, and "travel" in its broadest sense. The second cluster is associated with commerce and enterprise of the kind that is personified for Willy by his brother, Ben. The chief symbolic references of this cluster are to "jungle," Ben's watch, and diamonds.

An evident pattern emerges in the way in which the references to trees, wood, branches and leaves bind the domains of fantasy and reality in the play. They are clearly relevant to the ideal figure of Willy's father (a maker of flutes, a musical instrument of wood whose pastoral associations are immediate and altogether obvious), and to Willy's brother Ben (in whose vast tracts of Alaskan timberland Willy almost had a share).

Trees and leaves are the dominant stage effect when Willy's mind turns inward and toward the past, to a time when his longings for a rural existence were more nearly satisfied. As he casts his mind back to a time when his home stood in what was still a landscape setting, the large elm trees that had once grown on his property form an important part of his recollections. In the dramatic present, the elms are gone and all that remains of the rural Brooklyn he had known is his back yard, which by the play's end is the setting of Willy's last effort to reassert control over events by planning a garden in futile defiance of urban encroachment.

For Willy, being truly happy means working with tools—"all I'd need would be a little lumber and some peace of mind" (p. 151), he says, hoping for a better future. Trees are involved in his fantasies of Ben's success in the jungle and in the "timberland in Alaska" (p. 183). Trees color the imagery of Willy's expressions of his inner desperation and need for help, "the woods are burning" (pp. 152, 199). Trees and leaves are thereby involved rhythmically in the linguistic constructs of the play as well as in the visual setting of the stage: the memory of a hammock between the "big trees" (p. 143), of seeds in the garden, of working on the wood ceiling, and the lighting effect of the stage being *"covered with leaves"* (p. 142; see also pp. 151, 200). On the textual level, as well as on the stage, they become signs in the theatrical system indicating the rhythm between fantasy and reality.

Willy's enthusiasm for the outdoors and the countryside is also connected in his mind with the idea of travel and journeying. The idea of travel is inseparable from the images he has of the ideal figures from his past: that of his father driving his wagon and team of horses across the Western states; of Ben globetrotting between continents; and of Dave Singleman traveling in the smoker of the New York, New Haven and Hartford line. His own life, too, is inseparable from travel, and the maintenance of the family car is one of his major concerns. His car is essential to him for his livelihood, and it is also the instrument by which he chooses to bring an end to his life. It is the first thematically significant object to appear in the dramatic text of the play, when it is mentioned in a context that foreshadows the manner of Willy's death (p. 132).

The reference to nature is carried over to the second cluster of images bearing on the theme of commerce and enterprise, but appears now in the menacing guise of the "jungle," poles apart from the idyllic associations aroused by the cluster of rural symbols. Its explicit connection with the theme of enterprise and commerce, as well as its association with the attendant idea of aggressive and unscrupulous competition, is fully developed in the presence of all the principal *dramatis personae* in the scene of Ben's first apparition (pp. 154-60). The specific verbal context in which the reference first occurs is twice repeated almost verbatim by Ben (". . . when I was seventeen I walked into the jungle, and when I was twenty-one I walked out. And by God I was rich": pp. 157, 159-160). On the first occasion that Ben speaks these words he does so at Willy's urging for the benefit of the boys. When he repeats them for the second time, it is at his departure and they are uttered for Willy's ears alone. What happens between the two utterances brings out the thematic significance of the passage as referring to the rule of the jungle that governs the sort of enterprise that Ben represents. And the event that drives this particular moral home is the sparring match between Ben and Biff, in which Ben departs from the rules of fair play and delivers himself of the precept, "Never fight fair with a stranger, boy. You'll never get out of the jungle that way" (p. 158).

By the time Ben's shade departs, Willy seems to have taken Ben's point, when he chimes in with great enthusiasm, "That's just the spirit I want to imbue them with! To walk into the jungle! I was right!" (p. 160). But the truth is that Willy was wrong. Ben's lesson is not about going into jungles, but *coming out* of them, alive and prosperous.

The "watch" and "diamond" references are associated through Ben with the "jungle" reference. Their connection with one another, and their symbolic bearing on commerce, become obvious once their association with the ideas of time and wealth is established, and we recall that these last are proverbially equated in the businessman's adage that time is money.

The watch and diamond references are merged, too, by a specific object in the play: the "watch fob with a diamond in it" that Ben had given to Willy, and Willy had in turn pawned a dozen years earlier to finance Biff's radio correspondence course (p. 160). Thus time and money, the two cherished commodities of business, are in Loman hands turned to loss rather than profit.

Death of a Salesman is rich in ironies on every level. This overall effect is immediately felt in the organization of the stage and the development of the characters, and evolves out of the conflict between dream and actuality that is the theme of Miller's play. In the case of the play's symbols, much of their ironic significance depends on the reversals of their evident or anticipated meaning when they are transposed from the mental domain of the protagonist's dreams and fantasies to objective reality, where events are determined by impersonal forces operating independently of his wishes and will.

III

On the level of plot, the rhythm of *Death of a Salesman* operates not only temporally, by a progression of dramatic action in causal sequence, but perhaps even to a greater extent spatially, as a consequence of the proximate and, at times, nearly simultaneous juxtaposition of real and imagined episodes that are presented on stage in order to be compared. The pattern that emerges from this juxtaposition is that of an alternative of what "is" and what "ought to be," between the reality of Willy Loman's situations in the past and present, and what he would have preferred them to have been. And

to redress his grievances, the protagonist casts about in his memory for persons and events in order to weave agreeable fantasies around them that are surrogate fulfillments of his failed aspirations.

The dramatic progressions of Willy's shifts between dreams and reality are plotted structurally in terms of a rhythmic development whose general design spans the two acts of the play and whose principles can be discerned in the play's major subdivisions. These last, though not explicitly marked out scenes in the text of the play, are the effective equivalent of scenes, since they form identifiable "dramatic segments," as defined by Bernard Beckerman. According to Beckerman, the "substance" of such dramatic units consists of the action that takes place in them; between such activity-defined segments there are what he calls "linkages," by which each segment is tied to the one immediately preceding and following it.[10] In Miller's play, the substance of the acts, as well as the "scenes," consists of the particular dream or reality (and sometimes both) that is being enacted along the temporal vector that marks the path of Willy's career on stage. The linkages between these major units and their subdivisions are the creation of their spatial juxtaposition, on the basis of which the dramatic units are compared. Thus Willy's inner and outer worlds are enacted in scenes that are immediately juxtaposed, sometimes to the point of actually overlapping, and that mirror one another in a pattern of recurrence or reversal. The effect of all this is a spatio-temporal sequence that unfolds as an ironic interplay between fantasy and reality.

Willy Loman's attitude toward the external world can be classified according to the degree in which they approach reality: *fantasy,* in which the protagonist concentrates on fulfilling unrealized wishes concerning the past and the future; *anticipation,* in which he prepares to cope with eventualities in the real world; and *action,* by which he attempts to come to grips with immediate, objective reality. As the plotting of the play progresses, Willy's fantasies gradually assert their sway over his anticipatory and active moods. This occurs in response to his frustration and failure to reinstate his control over his circumstances in the real world. Ultimately his fantasizing comes to dominate his conduct so completely that in his mind suicide becomes an achievement to be equated with success. His conflicts with himself and with the external world are dramatically manipulated on a variety of formal levels within which the rhythms of the plot are developed.

The rhythms of the plot of Miller's play may be analyzed in terms of plot units, as has been schematically set out at the end of this paper. The larger sweep of the dramatic progression is evident in each of the play's acts, in both of which the phases of exposition, complication, crisis, and resolution can be clearly discerned. Taken successively, the two acts follow the same pattern of alternation between fantasy and reality which is characteristic of the overall rhythmic organization of the plot. The first act is dominated by dreams and fantasies; these emerge in the second act under anticipatory and active guises, there to collide with objective reality and shatter. This general progression of dramatic events is supported by ironic juxtapositions that resolve themselves into a broader rhythm of tension and release.

The play starts out in the first act at a late point of attack, *in medias res,* with Willy attempting still to come to terms with reality but chiefly absorbed in recollections of the past. The exposition of the Loman family's past is principally accomplished through the dramatic presentation of the protagonist's fantasies. The exciting force that sets the action of the play into motion is the arrival of Biff, whose homecoming is the occasion for the arousal of Willy's guilt feelings and the onset of his deepening sense of personal failure and his growing realization of defeat. The interplay between the dramatic action of the real characters in the play and that of the episodes of the past which take place in Willy's imagination have the function of setting out and defining the complications in Willy's attitude towards himself and his environment. The enactment of events that take place within Willy's mind tends to suspend the dramatic action of the play until nearly the end of the first act, when the plot begins to gather momentum after the confrontation between the Loman parents and their sons.

The first act can be divided into six "scenes," whose rhythmic pattern is established by the principle of juxtaposition of the protagonist's dramatic present with his inner world. The last comprises a number of distinct attitudes of mind that fall into five general categories which have been defined for *dramatis personae* by Keir Elam, and called "subworlds" by him.[11] According to Elam, there are five possible categories of subworld: the *epistemic,* or the world of a dramatic character's knowledge; the *doxastic,* or the worlds of his beliefs; the *boulomaeic,* or the worlds of his hopes, wishes, and fears; the *oneiric,* or the worlds of his dreams, daydreams, and fantasies; and the *deontic,* or the worlds of his "commands" (defined by Elam as "the states of affairs that he orders to be brought about").[12]

Willy Loman's boulomaeic and oneiric subworlds are expressed dramatically by means of "screen memories" of his inner world.[13] The scenes dramatizing Willy's inner world are juxtaposed with those in which his epistemic, doxastic, and deontic subworlds are enacted.

Between the first and the second acts, the relationships among Willy Loman's subworlds are altered in three principal respects. One such change is quantitative, and has to do with the relative amount of the text in each of the two acts that is devoted to dramatizations of the protagonist's fantasy world as opposed to the world of the "real" action of the play. Fully three-quarters of the text of the first act is given over to Willy's fantasy world—or, more specifically, to the enactment of his doxastic, boulomaeic, and oneiric subworlds. By contrast, a mere eighth of the second act consists of action taking place in the mind of the protagonist, whereas the overwhelming bulk of the same act is devoted to the presentation of Willy's deontic and epistemic subworlds, as he attempts to cope with his actual circumstances.

Another alteration of relationships may be observed in the rhythm of the shifts between the protagonist's inner world and actuality. These shifts in dramatic realm serve as the basis for my proposed division of the two acts of Miller's play into scenes, as set out at the end of this paper. Accordingly, the first act may be subdivided into six scenes, and the second act into twelve. The doubling of the number of scenes in the second half of the play is a function of the accelerated tempo of the protagonist's shifts of perspective, and the mounting disequilibrium in Willy's inner existence as well as the progressive weakening of his ability to distinguish between fantasy and reality.

And finally, as the action of the play progresses from the first to the second act, an alteration takes place in the direction of the shift between the protagonist's imaginary world and reality. In the first act the direction of change is from fantasy to reality; in the second act the direction is reversed.

From the outset of the first act, it is Willy's fantasy subworlds that dominate (i.e., his doxastic, boulomaeic, and oneiric subworlds), and the dramatic action consists largely of the enactment of memories that embody the protagonist's wishes and yearnings. By the end of the act, however, Willy's deontic subworlds takes over, as he and his sons resolve to reassert themselves in the real world by undertaking practical courses of action—Willy by his decision to talk to Howard about improving his situation at work, Happy and Biff by their plan to ask Bill Oliver for a loan to start their own business. In the second act a reversal of direction takes place in which anticipation of change of fortune, and resolution to act, give way to fantasy. The direction of shift from reality to fantasy may be observed in the progression of the scenes of the second act, a synopsis of which I shall now undertake in terms of changing dramatic subworlds. The dominant subworld in scenes 1 and 2 of the second act is deontic. In the first—the breakfast scene—Willy's plans of action in his own and his sons' behalf are revealed in his conversation with Linda. The deontic note struck in the first scene is sustained in the second, taking place in Howard's office, where Willy comes to practical grips with his situation by confronting his employer. Scene 3 dramatizes the effect on Willy of his defeat at the hands of Howard, which causes him to retreat into his boulomaeic and oneiric subworlds through his recollections of his family life in the past and his conversations with Ben; these memories subsume the protagonist's most profound desires and fantasies. In scene 4, set in Charley's office, the dominant mood is epistemic, as Willy obtains a clearer understanding of his real circumstances through his encounter with Charley and his son, Bernard. This consciousness deepens in scenes 5-7, the setting of which is Frank's Chop House. There, fresh from his humiliation and defeat, Willy is made to endure the revelation of the failure of his sons. The consequence is Willy's withdrawal into his fantasy subworlds, as he passes successively through deontic, boulomaeic, and oneiric states of mind. The progression of the enactment of Willy's consciousness is interrupted by scene 8, which is exceptional among the scenes of the second act, being entirely given over to a confrontation between Linda and her sons. However the theme is resumed in scenes 9-12, all of which take place in different parts of the Loman home, the setting of Willy's final withdrawal into his private world. In these closing scenes of the play Willy is torn between his comprehension of his actual situation (specifically in regard to his relationship with his sons and Linda, as presented in scene 10) and his retreat into his fantasy subworlds (scenes 9 and 10).

Stated in the most general terms, therefore, in the second act of Miller's play the direction of movement of the rhythmic shifts of the protagonist's consciousness through the various subworlds is from the deontic to the doxastic and boulomaeic, by way of epistemic. There is additionally an ironic undercurrent to the overt pattern of the shifts in the protagonist's mental attitudes. To the very end Willy persists in regarding his wishes and fantasies as representing attainable goals in the real world. Thus when he takes his life he does so in the belief that his action will obtain the money from his life-insurance policy for Biff (Willy's "diamond" for his son), and that the crowd of mourners that his funeral will attract will vindicate his apparent failure in life. These hopes are treated by him as though they are deontic, but in the Requiem at the end of the play they are shown up to be doxastic and boulomaeic. The focus of the unifying rhythm of **Death of a Salesman** is the theme of the loss of control by the protagonist over the world in which he lives. The various elements that go to make up Miller's play are dramatically presented primarily from inside the protagonist's consciousness, whose shifting perspectives establish the rhythmic progression of the work. Moreover the progression of the play's dramatic rhythm ironically reveals the static nature of the subject to which this essentially dynamic principle is being applied. The variety and mobility taking place between dream and reality—the fixed poles of Willy's shifts of consciousness—are exposed as being equally illusory and meaningless; so that these fundamentally antithetical realms converge to become identical. As the rhythm of the play's dramatic progression unfolds, it reveals Willy's dream (or nightmare, rather) to be the protagonist's single and abiding reality.

ACT I

DRAMATIC PROGRESSION	SCENE	W'S MENTAL REALM	LOCALE OF ACTION	CHARACTERS ON STAGE	PROTAGONIST'S SUBWORLD
EXPOSITION	1 (pp. 131-36)	(A)	LOMAN HOME	W, LINDA	(EPISTEMIC-DOXASTIC)
COMPLICATION	2 (pp. 136-42)	—	LOMAN HOME	BIFF, HAPPY	—
	3 (pp. 142-51)	W(F)	LOMAN HOME	W, BIFF, HAPPY, LINDA, CHARLEY	(DOXASTIC-ONEIRIC)
CRISIS	4 (pp. 152-54)	W(A)	LOMAN HOME	W, HAPPY, CHARLEY	(BOULOMAE)
	5 (pp. 154-60)	W(F)	LOMAN HOME	W, BEN, BIFF, HAPPY, LINDA	(ONEIRIC-BOULOMAEIC)
RESOLUTION	6 (pp. 160-72)	W(A)	LOMAN HOME	W, LINDA BIFF, HAPPY	(BOULOMAE DEONTIC)

ACT II

DRAMATIC PROGRESSION	SCENE	W'S MENTAL REALM	LOCALE OF ACTION	CHARACTERS ON STAGE	PROTAGONIST'S SUBWORLD
EXPOSITION	1 (pp. 173-76)	W(A)	LOMAN HOME	W, LINDA, BIFF	(DEONTIC)
	2 (pp. 177-83)	W(A)	HOWARD'S OFFICE	W, HOWARD	(DEONTIC)
	3 (pp. 183-86)	W(F)	HOWARD'S OFFICE	W, BEN, LINDA, BERNARD, CHARLEY, WOMAN	(BOULOMAEI ONEIRIC)
COMPLICATION	4 (pp. 187-93)	W(A)	CHARLEY'S OFFICE	W, JENNY, BERNARD, CHARLEY	(EPISTEMIC)
	5 (pp. 193-200)	W(A)	FRANK'S CHOP HOUSE	HAPPY, STANLEY, GIRLS, BIFF, W	(EPISTEMIC-DEONTIC)
CRISIS	6 (pp. 200-208)	W(F)	FRANK'S CHOP HOUSE	W, BERNARD, WOMAN, BIFF	(BOULOMAEI DEONTIC)
	7 (p. 209)	W(A)	FRANK'S CHOP HOUSE	W, STANLEY	(BOULOMAEI)
	8 (pp. 210-12)	—	LOMAN HOME	LINDA, BIFF, HAPPY	—
	9 (pp. 212-13)	W(F)	LOMAN HOME	W, BEN	(ONEIRIC-BOULOMAEIC)
RESOLUTION	10 (pp. 213-18)	W(A)	LOMAN HOME	BIFF, HAPPY, LINDA, W	(EPISTEMIC-BOULOMAEIC)
	11 (pp. 218-19)	W(F)	LOMAN HOME	W, BEN	(ONEIRIC-BOULOMAEIC)
	12 (p. 220)	W(A)	—	—	(DEONTIC)

Note: W = Willy: (a) = actuality, and (f) = fantasy

Notes

1. All references to *Death of a Salesman* in this paper are from *Arthur Miller's Collected Plays, Volume I* (New York, 1965), pp. 129-222.

2. See Helen Wickham Koon's Introduction to *Twentieth Century Interpretations of Death of a Salesman,* (Englewood Cliffs, NJ, 1983), p. 13.

3. Paul M. Levitt, *A Structural Approach to the Analysis of Drama* (The Hague and Paris, 1971); Kathleen George *Rhythm in Drama* (Pittsburgh, 1980). Levitt regards rhythm in theater to be the creation of two "change producing elements" which he identifies as "recurrence" and "reversal": recurrences take place in such features as the relationships between characters, and in the repetition of phrases, words, symbols, and motifs; reversals are the result of abrupt changes in the circumstances and situations of the plot; Kathleen George, in her summary of critical opinion concerning rhythm in drama, observes that dramatic rhythm resides essentially in the "alternation between opposites, generally producing a pattern of tension and relaxation" connected with the content of a play and felt by the audience on the level of expectations and their fulfillments; see her Introduction, *Rhythm in Drama,* pp. 13-16, esp. p. 9.

4. *Arthur Miller: Dramatist* (New York, 1967), p. 23.

5. In considering the difference between Charley and Willy, Arthur Miller has observed that, unlike Willy Loman, "Charley is not a fanatic . . . he has learned to live without that frenzy, that ecstasy of spirit which Willy chases to his end"; Miller, Introduction, *Collected Plays,* p. 37.

6. Elizabeth Ann Bettenhausen regards Biff and Happy to be extensions of two different aspects of Willy: "In a sense the two sons simply continue the two sides of Willy: Biff, seeing the fragility and even the illusion of the vicarious identity which depends on being well liked in the business world, chooses to accept the challenge of a different destiny. Happy, on the other hand, is captivated by the challenge of the dream and bound to the possibility of success"; "Forgiving the Idiot in the House: Existential Anxiety in Plays by Arthur Miller and its Implications for Christian Ethics," unpublished Ph.D. dissertation, the University of Iowa, 1972, p. 121.

7. Cf. Sheila Huftel, *Arthur Miller: The Burning Glass* (New York, 1965), p. 108, where she observes that Biff "lives heroic in Willy's mind."

8. About the rhythmic function of the polyscenic stage, see *Rhythm in Drama,* p. 133. Concerning its role in Miller's play, see: Edward Murray, op. cit., and Dennis Welland, *Arthur Miller* (Edinburgh and London, 1961), p. 63.

9. Cf. Helen Marie McMahon, "Arthur Miller's Common Man: The Problem of the Realistic and the Mythic," unpublished Ph.D. dissertation, Purdue University, 1972, pp. 42-45; Enoch Brater, "Miller's Realism and *Death of a Salesman,*" in *Arthur Miller,* ed. R. A. Martin (New York, 1982), pp. 115-26, and esp. 118-122; Brian Parker, "Point of View in Arthur Miller's *Death of a Salesman,*" in *Twentieth Century Interpretations,* pp. 41-55.

10. Bernard Beckerman, *Dynamics of Drama: Theory and Method* (New York, 1970), p. 42. On the "triggers" to the linkages between the scenes of Miller's play, see Franklin Bascom Ashley, "The Theme of Guilt and Responsibility in the Plays of Arthur Miller," unpublished Ph.D. dissertation, the University of South Carolina, 1970.

11. Keir Elam, *The Semiotics of Theatre and Drama* (London, 1980), esp. p. 114: "When characters or spectators hypothesize a state of affairs in WD [i.e., the dramatic world] whether it proves true or false, one can talk of the *subworlds* projected on to it."

12. Ibid., p. 115.

13. "Screen memories" are visual recollections taking a "cinematic" form. See, Otto Fenishel, *The Psychoanalytic Theory of Neurosis* (New York, 1945), pp. 145, 149, 327, 341, 529.

Granger Babcock (essay date fall 1992)

SOURCE: Babcock, Granger. "'What's the Secret?': Willy Loman as Desiring Machine." *American Drama* 2, no. 1 (fall 1992): 59-83.

[*In the following essay, Babcock examines how* Death of a Salesman *presents Willy Loman as a product of capitalist society, noting that the "system of value that the play represents permits no true relationship between men; it permits only isolation through competition."*]

Arthur Miller's **Death of a Salesman** (1949) conveys its critique of American capital in a more complex and subtle manner than critics have thus far recognized. Most criticism of the play, as Sheila Huftel points out, is "governed by the need . . . to know and understand Willy Loman" (103). Unfortunately, much of the energy expended to understand Willy has been too narrowly focused on analyzing the individuated character traits of the protagonist and the attendant issue of tragic stature. The play, in fact, suggests just the opposite—that Willy is not autonomous, self-generated, or self-made (even in "failure"), but that he is completely other to himself; he is more puppet than person, more machine than man, and as such he announces the death, or disappearance, of the subject, the death of the tragic hero, and the birth of "the desiring machine."

Most critics recognize that Arthur Miller intends Willy Loman as a victim of "society." But Willy's construction as a victim is interpreted within the parameters of a self-generated individual and is used as the main reason conservative critics deny *Salesman* tragic status. As a victim, the argument runs, Willy has no understanding of his situation; he is, in the words of Dan Vogel, "too commonplace and limited" (91). Unlike Oedipus, Hamlet, or Lear, Willy is incapable of self-knowledge and is, therefore, not tragic but pathetic: "he cannot summon the intelligence and strength to scrutinize his situation and come to some understanding of it" (Jacobson 247). Even liberal critics like Thomas Adler and Ruby Cohn, who are generally sympathetic towards Willy, tend to judge his character harshly; in their estimation, he is either a "victim of himself and his choices," or he "has achieved neither popularity nor success as a salesman, and has failed as a gardener, carpenter, and father" (Adler 102; Cohn 44). Willy's problem (or part of his problem), then, according to these critics, is that he accepts his fate; he does not possess the vision, volition, capacity, strength, knowledge, or pluck to fight against the cultural forces that shape his life.

The underlying assumption of these arguments is that Willy *can* change his life—with a little hard work, perhaps—but that he *will* not. Behind these judgments is a model: the national subject, or what I will call the masculine unconscious. This model can also be described as the autonomous, active male subject that determines and makes itself, as well as the liberal subject, the rugged individual, or the exceptional American. Whatever linguistic sign the masculine unconscious uses to communicate itself, it is wholly other to the subject, and it is given to the subject by the publicity apparatus of capital. Miller calls this other the "law of success":

> The confusion of some critics viewing *Death of a Salesman* . . . is that they do not see that Willy Loman has broken a law without whose protection life is insupportable, if not incomprehensible to him and to many others; it is a law which says a failure in society and in business has no right to live. Unlike the law against incest, the law of success is not administered by statute or church, but it is very nearly as powerful in its grip upon men.
>
> (*Collected Plays* 35; hereafter referred to as *CP*)

In *Dialectic of Enlightenment* (1947), Max Horkheimer and Theodor Adorno identify the "law of success" as an effect of the "technological rationale" which dominates the cultural and economic institutions of modern industrial nations:

> Through the countless agencies of mass production and its culture the conventionalized modes of behavior are impressed upon the individual as the only natural, respectable, and rational ones. He defines himself as a thing, as a static element, as success or failure.
>
> (28)

That is, under what Horkheimer and Adorno call late capitalism, individual behavior is reduced to a series of "protocols" or stereotypical responses found on the job, on the radio, in the movies, and in the then-emerging television industry. For Adorno, these standardized models of behavior signaled the end of the liberal subject, since "motivation in the old, liberal sense" was being appropriated and "systematically controlled and absorbed by social mechanisms which are directed from above" ("Freudian Theory" 136). In other words, the subject's desire for success (e.g., for material wealth, to "get ahead"), which the subject believes is self-generated, is, in fact, his identification with the rationale of the apparatus, which has programmed individual consumption as spontaneous thought or reason or the assertion of individual will.

Viewed in light of Horkheimer and Adorno's discovery, the operations of Willy Loman's mind reflect this change in subjectivity. Specifically, Willy assumes that his desire is spontaneous, when in fact, as Miller suggests in *Timebends* (1987), it has been "hammered into its strange shape by society, the business life Willy had lived and believed in" (182). Willy's desire does not make him autonomous; it makes him "common" since that desire is what motivates all the men in the play and indeed most men in our culture. In constructing Willy, Miller exposes the liberal subject as a fiction, as part of a structure of value that is an effect of the economy. To dismiss Willy as "pathetic" because he does not have the strength of character to understand his situation or because he has made the wrong choices is to recode the play according to the protocols of the apparatus (i.e., a man is either a success or he is a failure). Willy chooses nothing; he merely follows a blueprint. Like a machine, he operates according to plan. The publicity apparatus tells Willy that if he works hard like Edison, that if he perseveres like Goodrich, that, if he is "well-liked" like Dave Singleman, then he will rise like Charley and become rich and powerful like J. P. Morgan. The blueprint also tells Willy that if he does not become "a success," that if he does not become like a Gene Tunney or a Red Grange, then he is a failure—and that this is his fault. Willy's question to Ben and to Bernard— "What's the secret?"—is therefore by design. Willy cannot see that there is no secret—that success or status is largely determined by extrinsic factors.

Conservative critics do not recognize Willy as an effect of the economy because the critical field in which they operate does not permit this. For them, he is a problem, not a cultural symptom. Critics from the left, such as Raymond Williams, Michael Spindler, and John Orr, while they see Willy as a symptom of capitalist culture, have focused more on Willy's objectification than on his relationship to the apparatus that produced him. Williams, for instance, argues that "Willy Loman is a man who from selling things has passed to selling himself, and has become, in effect, a commodity which like other commodities will at a certain point be discarded by the laws of the economy" (104). While Williams's argument concerning Willy is certainly accurate, given Willy's desire to "make an appearance in the business world" (*CP* 146), I would like to suggest a different way to read Willy, which is more in keeping with the model of subjectivity theorized by Horkheimer and Adorno in *Dialectic of Enlightenment,* and which, I believe, more fully represents the rationalization of consciousness brought about by the symbolic apparatus of late capitalism.

In their book *Anti-Oedipus: Capitalism and Schizophrenia* (1983), Gilles Deleuze and Felix Guattari problematize previous models of subjectivity by eliminating the opposition around which the subject is constructed: "There is no such thing as either man or nature now, only a process that produces the one within the other and couples the machines together. Producing-machines, desiring-machines . . . the self and the non-self, outside and inside, no longer have any meaning whatsoever" (2). According to Deleuze and Guattari, the cognitive subject no longer exists since the subject-object split on which its identity is based has collapsed. The boundary between subject and object collapses, they argue, under the weight of the publicity apparatus of late capitalist cultures, which colonizes the subject from without by pouring its narratives inward. They replace the cognitive model with a quasi-cybernetic model, the desiring machine. The desiring machine runs on information from the outside; its goals, writes Jean-François Lyotard, are "programmed into it" and therefore it cannot "correct in the course of its functioning" (16). The man/machine is programmed to fit the body of capital, to adjust to the demands of efficiency of the larger system. Deleuze and Guattari stress that the identity produced by the system is "a producing/product identity" (7). That is, the machine produces, or in Willy's case reproduces, not only biologically but also ideologically, for the system at the same time that it is produced or constructed by the system.

A more effective way to interpret Deleuze and Guattari's "producing/product identity," especially when we consider Willy Loman and the other men in *Salesman,* is to see it as a producing/consuming identity. The male subject desires to reproduce itself (pass itself on) at the same time it desires to consume success narratives, cheese, Chevrolets, Studebakers, aspirin, women, refrigerators, etc. The male subject reproduces itself by having children and acting as a model for those children. Willy, for instance, wants his sons to learn the law of success embodied by his brother Ben: ". . . when I walked into the jungle, I was seventeen. When I walked out I was twenty-one. And, by God, I was rich" (*CP* 159-60). The male subject consumes by buying products. Listen to Happy:

. . . suppose I get to be merchandise manager? He's a good friend of mine, and he just built a terrific estate on Long Island. And he lived there about two months and sold it, and now he's building another one. He can't enjoy it once it's finished. And I know that's just what I would do. I don't know what the hell I'm workin' for.

(*CP* 139)

Or listen to Howard Wagner talk about his wire recorder: "I tell you . . . I'm gonna take my camera, and my bandsaw, and all my hobbies, and out they go. This is the most fascinating relaxation I've ever found" (*CP* 178). Willy's desire has also been programmed; just listen to Linda tell us why he bought a Hastings refrigerator: "They got the biggest ads of any of them!" (*CP* 148).

The three passages suggest that Miller is aware that (re)production and consumption are programmed. Desire is mediated by an other, by the publicity apparatus of capital. The "subject" merely occupies a circuit or an outlet, or, to use Lyotard's word, a "post," through which messages or units of information pass (15). Willy (or Happy or Howard Wagner) is reduced to the function of a receptacle/transmitter; information travels through him and in him. In this process, memory (the site of the other) becomes a depository for and a transmitter of the masterprograms or "masternarratives" of the system in which the desiring machine operates. The machine's program can thus be viewed as a metanarrative that is used to reinscribe or recode reality into a pattern that the larger system finds acceptable. The metanarrative acts like the unconscious because it is wholly other to the subject and because it works through the subject to structure social life. This operation is seen in Happy's description of the merchandise manager's mindless consumption, in his building of houses which he soon deserts only to build new houses; his desire spins metonymically out of control, seeking difference or fulfillment in what is essentially the same. Neither man understands why he buys things or why he works, yet they both buy and work without question. Presumably they work to "get ahead," to "accomplish something," but in reality they are, like Willy, programmed for the body of capital; it doesn't matter if they get ahead, if they succeed, or even if they become "number-one man." What does matter, however, is that everybody desire to work so that everybody can afford to consume. Desire, to use Sartre's term, has been "massified."

At this point, we turn our attention to Willy Loman and explore how the dreams of capital have programmed his "life." Throughout the play, Willy consumes and then reproduces models and axioms that are part of the masculine unconscious:

Be liked and you will never want.

(*CP* 146)

A man oughta come in with a few words.

(*CP* 149)

I gotta overcome it. I know I gotta overcome it. I'm not dressing to advantage, maybe.

(*CP* 149)

Everybody likes a kidder, but nobody lends him money.

(*CP* 168)

But remember, start big and you'll end up big.

(*CP* 168)

Start off with a couple of your good stories to lighten things up. It's not what you say, it's how you say it—because personality always wins the day.

(*CP* 169)

These axioms (and the model they represent) appear in the text as isolated linguistic events, as the recitations of a lone idiolect, but they are in fact "splinters" or units (traces) of the metanarrative of national subject that speak through the subject. Willy consumes these bits of information just as he consumes aspirins and cheese. Their presence indicates that Willy's subjectivity has been "interpellated" by the ideological apparatus.[1] Another indication of Willy's interpellation are his numerous contradictory statements. Early in the play, for instance, Willy calls Biff a "lazy bum" because Biff does not have a steady job. Three lines later, however, after Linda tells Willy that Biff is "lost," Willy replies incredulously, "Biff Loman is lost. In the greatest country in the world a young man with such—personal attractiveness, gets lost. There's one thing about Biff—he's not lazy" (*CP* 134). Willy then reminds Linda that "Certain men just don't get started till later in life. Like Thomas Edison, I think. Or B. F. Goodrich" (*CP* 135).

In this instance, the masterprogram operates to allegorize the experience of the "subject" by making the subject part of the national narrative of progress; the process is therefore synecdochical (e pluribus unum). The process reveals itself as a fusion or syndesis of narratives, modes of masculinity from different historical periods, that cover over the reality of the present and mystify history. This fusion is first discovered in the practices of late nineteenth-century advertising, where the consumer ideology is bound together with eighteenth- and nineteenth-century conceptions of masculinity. The adjusted or emergent narrative is deposited on the hegemonic narrative, which in turn lends the newer representation its legitimacy or authority.

However, the crucial thing to note about the masterprogram is the way in which Miller suggests it operates through Willy to reinscribe his family history as part of the success narrative of the national subject. Willy desires to be the same as his father or his brother Ben; he desires to be other than he is, to inhabit earlier periods of capital through an other's body, which is essentialized or universal. By banishing *differance,* Willy hopes to construct a stable subjectivity. He no longer wishes to feel "temporary" (*CP* 159) about himself. He no longer wants to be part of the body of capital, which is always (magically) transforming itself, adjusting itself, expanding itself—like the neighborhood in which he lives. The desire to be successful, then, is the desire to connect himself to a transcendental masculinity that erases the reality of his present social position. This erasure is achieved, however, at a cost. The subject is restored to fullness by transforming extrinsic social factors into personal failure. Willy performs this function to empower himself, to restore the independence of the subject, which has been irretrievably lost. In the process, however, he learns to misrecognize himself (and Brooklyn). At the same time, Willy also learns to marginalize other masculinities, the alternative men he might represent, in favor of the dominant models advocated by the culture industry (i.e. Edison, Goodrich, etc.).

As C. W. E. Bigsby notes, "Willy Loman's life is rooted in America's past" (184). More precisely, his identity is rooted in models from two different periods of American capital, which are conflated in his mind. Willy's father represents the unfettered and unalienated labor of mercantile capital. His brother Ben represents the accumulative processes of monopoly capital. Both figures are mythic; that is, both figures embody an heroic past that is disseminated by the symbolic practices of capital and reproduced in individual men. Together, Miller suggests, they represent the (his)tory (not an history) of the (white) race in America. Or, as Irving Jacobson suggests,

> What Willy Loman wants, and what success means in **Death of a Salesman,** is intimately related to his own, and the playwright's, sense of the family. Family dreams extend backward in time to interpret the past, reach forward in time to project images of the future, and pressure reality in the present to conform to memory [ideology] and imagination.

(248)

The flute "melody" that marks the beginning and the ending of the play, and which is heard periodically throughout, is the emblem or signature of Willy's lost father. According to the stage directions, "It is small and fine, telling of grass and trees and the horizon" (*CP* 130). It is, as numerous critics point out, the aural symbol of his "pioneer virtues" (Parker 33). It is the sound of the unalienated commodity, which later returns (transformed) as the mass-produced "golden" pen that Biff steals. It is the sound of the past in the present, the still active residual model which operates to marginalize the present. It represents the desire for opportunity and mobility associated with westward expansion. Willy's father, as Ben tells him, was a small entrepreneur whose life was determined by the structures of a mercantile economy:

> Father was a very great and very wild-hearted man. We would start in Boston, and he'd toss the whole family into the wagon, and then he'd drive the whole team right across the country; through Ohio, and Indiana, Michigan, Illinois, and all the Western states.
>
> *(CP* 157)

Willy's father was a "great inventor" who would "stop in the towns and sell the flutes he'd made on the way" (*CP* 157). "With one gadget," Ben tells Willy, "he made more in a week than a man like you could make in a lifetime" (*CP* 157).

Ben's last statement seems unlikely, and its hyperbole marks a confusion in Willy's mind produced, or mediated, by the other's desire. Willy desires to be like his father because his father is like other successful men, other "great" inventors; his father is a model citizen—he has amassed a fortune. His father is like America's first model citizen, Ben Franklin, who "invented" electricity and the lightning rod. His father is like Thomas A. Edison and B. F. Goodrich, both rich and famous because of their inventions. Nevertheless, given the mercantile economy in which Miller locates Willy's father, it is unlikely that he could have produced a "gadget" that earned him more in a week than Willy earns in his lifetime. This type of event was more common (but still relatively isolated) in the period of capital Ben represents (monopoly capital) when "great" inventors like Edison and Goodrich did earn more money in a week (by producing technology for an emergent industrial economy) than a salesman could earn in thirty-five years. The figure of Willy's father exists simultaneously in Willy's "mind" with the figures of Edison and Goodrich. The simultaneity of the Franklin-Edison-Goodrich-father Loman narrative produces a fusion of the individual stories, which erases the specific history of the individual figures by marginalizing their differences; this fusion, again, is produced by the publicity apparatus of capital. Through the other, that is, Willy plugs himself into the success narrative as he rereads his family history.

A more elaborate example of this type of conflation is found when we examine Ben Loman. On one level, Miller uses the figure of Ben to link the formation of the national subject to the founding of the Republic— that is, Miller clearly chooses the name Ben to remind his readers of Ben Franklin's paradigmatic American masculinity. Ben's continual repetition of the rags to riches story—"Why, boys, when I walked into the jungle, I was seventeen. When I walked out I was twenty-one. And, by God, I was rich" (*CP* 157)—is a deliberate echo of Franklin's *Autobiography,* in which Franklin tells his readers that he walked into Philadelphia with the clothes on his back and within a few years became rich and famous. Notably, Miller conflates the Franklin myth with another version of masculinity from a later stage of American capital, not to differentiate the two, but to suggest that they are both operative, and that the latter version is just a rearticulation of the former. The phrase "acres of diamonds," which Ben continually uses, alludes to a series of lectures and books written by the evangelist Russell Conwell in the 1890s "to spread the gospel of material wealth" (Innes 64-5; Porter 24-7). Conwell's writings, which included *The Safe and Sure Way to Amass a Fortune and Be a Benefactor and Achieve Greatness,* were typical of the "success cult" that dominated American magazine and popular book culture around the turn of the century (Greene 111).

The assumptions about masculinity at the core of Franklin's *Autobiography* are present in Conwell's writings as well. Both writers construct masculinity in very ahistoric ways by insisting that "success" is the result of personal agency or character. Miller uses Ben's speech, which Willy is remembering, to illustrate that language has a history. The traces of Franklin's and Conwell's stories survive as moments of the past in the present, and because they have been decontextualized by the operations of the publicity apparatus, they exist only as ideology within memory (i.e. devoid of their cultural context, they become part of the same moment, the typology of American maleness—not products of specific historical periods and circumstances). These representations do, however, bear the mark of their history and, as such, their difference can only be recognized when their history is restored. The conflation of Franklin and Conwell in Ben's speech is recognized when we try to account for the fact that Ben Loman and Russell Conwell inhabit an America radically different from Franklin's. Ben's ascendancy to what Willy calls "success incarnate" (*CP* 152) takes place in the late 1880s, a period marked by intense imperial expansion and expropriation of native labor and resources. As what Ruby Cohn calls a "ruthless adventurer" (41), Ben represents the accumulative processes of monopoly capital (roughly 1880 to 1910).

Further, the mode of masculinity that Ben represents is radically out of place in the America of the late 1940s (as is Willy's father's "pioneer" masculinity). Willy's desire to be like Ben and like his father manifests itself as a nostalgia that seals him off from the present. As a result, Willy cannot recognize "reality," and he therefore engages in the success fantasy given to him by the other. In addition, Miller also suggests that the nostalgia for previous models or paradigms is constituted by their ability to provide ready-made (read: reductive) interpretations of the world; this operation, however, as Hayden White suggests, is disabling (and therefore destructive) because it prevents individuals and societies from imaginatively confronting the problems of the present (39).

One result of Willy's interpellation is that he cannot see Brooklyn as it is—that is, he is not satisfied with seeing it the way it is; he desires to see it as other, as the old west or the frontier. As he tells Ben, "It's Brooklyn, I know, but we hunt too" (*CP* 158). Willy's desire to see Brooklyn as other is also a symptom of the machine in crisis. The flute melody that represents the fiction of infinite space and unfettered masculine autonomy of the frontier (i.e., the mobility that most Americans expect and desire) is an ideological formation directly at odds with Willy's "reality." Willy can see the "towering, angular shapes" that surround his house "on all sides" (*CP* 130), and he is aware the changes in his neighborhood:

> The way they box us in here. Bricks and windows, windows and bricks. . . . The street is lined with cars. There's not a breath of fresh air in the neighborhood. The grass don't grow anymore, you can't raise a carrot in the backyard. They should've had a law against apartment houses. Remember those two beautiful elm trees out there? When I and Biff hung the swing between them. . . . They should've arrested the builder for cutting those down. They massacred the neighborhood. . . .
>
> (*CP* 134-35)

Yet the cultural processes that allow the "they" to box him in, to massacre the neighborhood, go unrecognized because his models program him for "oversight." In other words, his knowledge of the world is produced by models that act to exclude or screen out disruptive bits of information. Willy's knowledge of his world represents a desire for older modes that reduce his understanding of his social position.

His models also prevent him from seeing the history of his present (ultimately they push his vision inward, which leads to annihilation). His question to Linda that concludes the diatribe about the neighborhood—"How can they whip cheese?"—outlines the contour or boundary of his knowledge about the operations of capital; this question marks the limits of his awareness, outside (or inside) of which he cannot see or transgress. The question represents his limit as a subject. The salesman, ironically, does not understand how products are made. They appear to him, as they sometimes did to Marx, "as autonomous figures endowed with a life of their own" (165). Willy's seemingly trivial question reveals how effective the publicity apparatus (with its fetishization of consumption) is in marginalizing the effects of technological change. As William T. Brucher points out,

Willy's "unexpected, marvellingly innocent question about whipping cheese reveals an ambivalence toward technology livelier and more interesting . . . than a simple dichotomy between farm and factory, past and present" (83-4). Willy's "marvellingly innocent question" reveals a complete ignorance of the cultural processes that affect his life, that cause him to lose his job. Willy's life is, in fact, a denial of the transformative powers of capital. Any recognition of change is subverted by the transcendent (fetishized) models that he worships, which do not record or reflect any change. Celebrity—the lives of B. F. Goodrich and Thomas A. Edison and Dave Singleman—has replaced history. The consumption of technological "progress," as Willy's broken cars, refrigerators, fanbelts, and leaky shower and roof attest, has replaced "real" social relations.

A second result of Willy's interpellation is that he "embues" his sons with the values of the other, what he calls "the spirit of the jungle." These values are mediated through the figure of Ben Loman. "There was the only man I ever met who knew the answers," says Willy (*CP* 155). "There was a man started with the clothes on his back and ended up with diamond mines" (*CP* 152). How does Ben achieve this goal? According to Willy, "The man knew what he wanted and went out and got it. Walked into the jungle, and comes out, the age of twenty one, and he's rich!" (*CP* 152). And this triumph is just what Willy wants for his boys; when Ben comes to visit, Willy brags to him that "That's just the spirit I want to embue them with! To walk into the jungle!" (*CP* 160). He's bringing them up to be "rugged, well-liked, all-around" (*CP* 157). Ben, of course, approves: "Outstanding, manly chaps!" (*CP* 159). Willy's desire is therefore reproduced through and in Biff and Happy; because of Willy's pedagogy, they become carriers of the program. Willy wants them, as Ben advises him, to "Screw on your fists and . . . fight for a fortune . . ." (*CP* 183). He doesn't want them to be "worms," like Bernard (*CP* 151). But as Brian Parker points out, the aggressive practices Ben represents while "admirable in combatting raw nature [become] immoral when turned against one's fellow man" (33).

I suggest above that Ben's aggressiveness represents a brutality that Miller equates with American imperialism. Another way to read Ben's aggressiveness—this time, within the boundaries of the nation—is as competition. Historically, as C. Wright Mills notes, "for men in the era of classical liberalism, competition was never merely an impersonal mechanism regulating the economy of capitalism, or only a guarantee of political freedom. Competition was a means of producing free individuals, a testing field for heroes; in its terms men lived the legend of the self-reliant individual" (11). Whether or not what Mills argues is historically representative, it is safe to assume that in a decentralized economy (an economy without the hierarchy of industrialized structures), individual competition through labor was a way for many to create mobility and wealth. However, as the economy became more centralized and hierarchical, competition, as Willy says, became "maddening" because it did not yield the same results (imagined or otherwise) as it did for men of Willy's father's and Ben's generations.

In Willy's time, in fact, competition has become war-like. After returning from a selling trip, for instance, Willy tells his family he "Knocked 'em cold in Providence, slaughtered 'em in Boston" (*CP* 146). Willy's gift to his sons on his return from this same trip is a punching bag with "Gene Tunney's signature on it." "[I]t's the finest thing for the timing," he tells his apprentices (*CP* 144). Elsewhere, Willy describes business as "murderous" (*CP* 159). When Biff goes to ask Bill Oliver for a loan, Willy's advice is "Knock him dead, boy" (*CP* 170). The violence of Willy's language echoes the ruthlessness of his model, Ben—the same man who attacks Biff: "Never fight fair with a stranger, boy. You'll never get out of the jungle that way" (*CP* 158). Willy's desire to emulate Ben's power thus leads him to bring "the spirit of the jungle" into his home, where it reveals itself as what Sartre calls "counter-finality." His positive intention of providing his boys with a model for success results in the negative legitimation of theft and fantasy.

Miller problematizes Willy's pedagogy by suggesting that even sanctioned expressions of masculinity involve theft. In the scene which follows Ben's fight with Biff, for example, Willy has his sons start to rebuild the front steps because Willy doesn't want Ben to think he is just a salesman; he wants to show Ben that Brooklyn is not Brooklyn ("we hunt too" [*CP* 158]); he wants to show Ben what kind of stock his sons come from: "Why, Biff can fell any one of these trees in no time!" (*CP* 158). Instead of providing the materials to rebuild the front stoop, however, Willy directs his sons to "Go right over where they're building the apartment house and get some sand" (*CP* 158). Charley warns Willy that "if they steal any more from that building the watchman'll put the cops on them" (*CP* 158). Willy responds, addressing Ben, "You shoulda seen the lumber they brought home last week. At least a dozen six-by-tens worth all kinds of money" (*CP* 158). This, of course, is a parody of Ben's logging operations in Alaska, but it also suggests that the individualism that the success ideology sanctions legitimates theft, just as that ideology legitimates the expropriation of foreign land and mineral resources. This is made even clearer in the following lines, when Willy excuses his sons' behavior because, as he says, "I got a couple of fearless characters there" (*CP* 158). Charley counters: "Willy, the jails are full of fearless characters" (*CP* 158), and Ben responds, "And the stock exchange, friend!" (*CP* 158). Again, these lines suggest that Miller recognizes that even legitimized expressions of masculine behavior, practices and beliefs that the American publicity apparatus valorizes, involve theft.

A further example of Miller transforming the success ideology into theft is found in the scene where Biff "borrows" a football from his high school locker room so that he can practice with a "regulation ball" (*CP* 144). Willy, predictably, laughs with Biff at the theft and rewards the action by saying, "Coach'll probably congratulate you on your initiative!" (*CP* 144). Initiative, even in Franklin's day, is one of the key elements of masculine autonomy, and here Miller insists that initiative is a form of theft. Later in the same scene, Biff tells his father, "This Saturday, Pop, this Saturday— just for you, I'm going to break through for a touchdown" (*CP* 145). Happy then reminds Biff that he is "supposed to pass" (*CP* 145). Biff ignores Happy's warning and says, "I'm *taking* one play for Pop (*CP* 145; italics mine). This taking is a pattern that will eventually take over Biff's life, for as Biff tells Willy at the end of the play, "I stole a suit in Kansas City and I was in jail. . . . I stole myself out of every good job since high school!" (*CP* 216). More important for Miller, however, is that this one moment of taking represents a typical moment in the dominant version of American masculinity. Biff's "theft" of the play is another instance of his initiative, another example drawn from the headlines which celebrate individual achievement. For a moment in Willy's mind, Biff is like Red Grange or Gene Tunney. As he tells Charley, "When this game is over . . . you'll be laughing out the other side of your face. They'll be calling him another Red Grange. Twenty-five thousand a year" (*CP* 186). What is lost in Biff's taking, however, is the team. Biff's initiative, and his desire to place himself above the goal of the team, jeopardizes the collective goal of the team—to win the City Championship.

Miller addresses the counter-finality of fantasy in the climax of the play, which is organized around Biff's trip to Bill Oliver's office where he plans to ask Oliver to stake him in a new business venture, "The Loman Brothers," a line of sporting goods. This fiction has been created as a way to deflect Willy's fury at learning that Biff plans to "[s]crew the business world!" and return to the West, because in the West he can do as he pleases. That is, he can swim in the middle of the day and, working as a carpenter, he can whistle on the job; he also tells Happy that "we don't belong in this nuthouse of a city! We belong mixing cement on some open plan . . . "(*CP* 166). At the same time, Biff expresses his hatred of the business world because "They've laughed at Dad for years . . . "(*CP* 166). Willy responds in a characteristic manner: "Go to Filene's, go to the Hub, go to Slattery's, Boston. Call out the name Willy Loman and see what happens!" (*CP* 166). At this point, to quell Willy's anger, optimistic

Happy starts the familiar story ("He's going to see Bill Oliver, Pop" [*CP* 167])—that quickly develops into a success fantasy before the fact: Happy's "feasible idea" is to borrow money from Bill Oliver to start a line of sporting goods (*CP* 167). Of course, Happy's idea is neither feasible nor sensible; it is in fact absurd that Biff believes he can borrow ten thousand dollars from a man he has not seen in fifteen years and from whom he stole merchandise.

At the end of the second act, however, Happy's pipe dream comes apart as Biff begins to insist on the truth; Biff tells Willy that he "was never a salesman for Bill Oliver," that he was a shipping clerk. Willy insists that Biff was a salesman for Oliver, and when Biff tries to correct Willy by asking him to "hold on to the facts," Willy says he's not interested in the facts (*CP* 198-99). What he is interested in is another story, and Willy and Happy begin to work to reimpose the success fantasy they have constructed at the end of the first act, but the fantasy is interrupted by Biff's announcing that he has stolen Bill Oliver's fountain pen.

The final confrontation occurs two scenes later when Biff tells Willy "you're going to hear the truth—what you are and what I am" (*CP* 216). Biff rejects Willy's "phony dream" because

> I ran down eleven flights with a pen in my hand today. And suddenly I stopped. . . . I saw the things that I love in this world. The work and the food and time to sit and smoke. And I looked at the pen and said to myself, what the hell am I grabbing this for? Why am I trying to become what I don't want to be? What am I doing in an office, making a contemptuous, begging fool of myself, when all I want is out there, waiting for me the minute I say I know who I am!
>
> (*CP* 217)

This is an assertion of Biff's desire against Willy's desire and the fantasy that Willy's desire constructs. Because Biff recognizes that his father's dream is false, that his father has been positioned by the law of success to believe in the autonomous male, he is in a position to resist (at least partially) the ideology. Biff does not believe in the version of universal citizenship that Willy believes in. Biff recognizes that he is "a dime a dozen" (*CP* 217), that he will never be B. F. Goodrich or Thomas Edison or Red Grange or J. P. Morgan or Gene Tunney. He attempts to resist the ideology of the success narrative because he doesn't want to be other; he doesn't want to be number one: "I am not a leader of men, Willy, and neither are you. . . . I'm a dollar an hour, Willy. . . . A buck an hour" (*CP* 217). Willy, a believer to the bitter end, insists that he is exceptional: "I am Willy Loman, and you are Biff Loman" (*CP* 217). At this point there is a complete repudiation of the success fantasy: Biff screams, "Pop, I'm nothing! I'm nothing, Pop" (*CP* 217), and he begins to hug his father and cry.

Commenting on this scene, Miller writes that Biff embodies "an opposing system which . . . is in a race for Willy's faith, and it is the system of love which is the opposite of the law of success" (*CP* 36). However, Miller claims that "by the time Willy can perceive [Biff's] love, it can serve only as an ironic comment upon the life he sacrificed for power and for success and its tokens" (*CP* 36). Biff rejects the law that makes men compete with each other and steal from each other in order for them to be successful. Instead, through his characterization of Bernard, Charley, and, (at the end of the play) Biff, Miller seems to offer the possibility of a system where men love each other and try to help one another, rather than exploit one another. His solution to the problem of individualism is moral rather than revolutionary, for as he points out, the "most decent man" in the play "is a capitalist (Charley) whose aims are not different from Willy Loman's" (*CP* 37). The difference between Willy and Charley "is that Charley is not a fanatic": "he has learned how to live without that frenzy, that ecstasy of spirit which Willy chases to the end" (*CP* 37). Likewise, "Bernard . . . works hard, attends to his studies, and attains a worthwhile objective" (*CP* 37). Miller also notes that these people all come from the same social class (*CP* 37), yet Charley and Bernard do not succumb to the frenzy because, in Miller's view, they manage to resist the law of success and can act like decent men. What makes their resistance possible? Miller offers no specific answer. The play suggests that some men are able to do this while others are not; it offers hope, but no specific program: "What theory lies behind this double view? None whatever. It is simply that I knew and know that I feel better when my work is reflecting a balance of the truth as it exists" (*CP* 37).

Nevertheless, because the play is organized around the consciousness of Willy Loman, the play does not reflect the balance that Miller seems to have intended. Because Willy is such a strong presence, he pushes Bernard and Charley to the margins of the play. Willy's is the dominant voice, and it is through this voice that Miller maps the discourse of national identity as it interpellates the "low man." Through this process, Miller attempts to construct a counter discourse by exposing the contradictions within the dominant understanding of the social world. The power of the dominant discourse lies in the ability of its codes and protocols to regulate understanding of the social world; they allow individuals to interpret their experience only in previously elaborated paradigms. In *Salesman,* Miller shows how these codes and protocols are reproduced through memory as they are recirculated and repeated in the texts and representations of the publicity apparatus. The epilogue of the play also suggests that we are free of these representations only in death. When Linda says "We're free. . . . We're free" (*CP* 222), Miller is not just ironically commenting on the paid-up mortgage; he is also suggesting that Willy is free from the law of success only in death.

D. L. Hoeveler suggests that Linda's lines are ironic for another reason. Reading the drama as a "psychomachia," Hoeveler stresses that the *Requiem* functions as a final comment on Willy's dream: "All the characters who had previously functioned as parts of Willy's dream or nightmare are now supposedly free of him. . . . But each of the characters continues to embody the values that Willy demanded of them" (80). These "parts," however, to revise Hoeveler, not only embody the values that Willy demands of them, but also they embody the values of the dominant mode of production and the cultural apparatus which reproduces that mode by reproducing its values. Willy is a part of the body of capital, just as are Happy, Biff, Charley, Bernard, Howard Wagner, and Linda; and as Mark Poster writes, the capitalist mode of production forces human beings not only to become "things . . . in appearance," but also "They undergo . . . a profound interior alteration" (53). They become desiring machines, or as Sartre stresses in *Critique of Dialectical Reason,* they become other to themselves. They embody the values of the Other (the publicity apparatus) that programs them to see others as rivals. The irony of this operation, as Sartre points out, is that in attempting to be different (in attempting to be number-one, to earn the most money, to conquer the world) everyone's desire is the same. Desire, therefore, organizes individuals so that it can isolate them. Sartre calls this formation serial, or unified, alterity.

Ultimately, all the men in the play labor in alterity programmed by the other (or others) as parts of the machine of capital. Their desire and their isolations are expressions of the larger machine. Their "prefabricated being" (being as other-than-itself) is fixated on consumption by the publicity apparatus of capital (Sartre 227). The system of value that the play represents permits no true relationship between men; it permits only isolation through competition. The dissatisfaction of the desiring machine can therefore only express itself through nostalgia, an eternal return to previous models and their (pre)determining goals. The consequence of this interpellation is that solidarity is nullified by the desire of the other, thereby ensuring that men will continue to be exploited by their desire. As Deleuze and Guattari point out, "Desire can never be deceived. . . . It happens that one desires against one's own interests: capitalism profits from this . . ." (257). In the end, then, "attention must be . . . paid" (*CP* 162) to Willy Loman not because he is somehow exceptional (by being an aberration) but because his repression is paradigmatic. Willy has not, as Michael Spindler points out, "seized upon the notion of success as a substitute for genuine identity" (206). Willy, again, seizes nothing; his gods are given to him. Attention must be given to such a man by readers of *Salesman* who would fetishize masculine autonomy, since Miller powerfully suggests that masculine desire is an instrument used by the publicity apparatus of American capital to organize and to regulate social relations and the economy.

Note

1. In the work of Louis Althusser (162-70) *interpellation* denotes the process by which human subjects come to recognize themselves as such by identifying themselves with the subjects referred to by an impersonal "apparatus" of ideological statements: For instance, as the *free* and the *brave* in the phrase "the land of the free and the home of the brave."

Works Cited

Adler, Thomas. *Mirror on the Stage: The Pulitzer Plays as an Approach to American Drama.* West Lafayette: Purdue UP, 1987.

Adorno, Theodor. "Freudian Theory and the Pattern of Fascist Propaganda." *The Essential Frankfurt School Reader.* Ed. Andrew Arato and Eike Gebhardt. New York: Continuum, 1985. 118-37.

Althusser, Louis. *Lenin and Philosophy and Other Essays.* Trans. Ben Brewster. London: NLB, 1971.

Bigsby, C. W. E. *A Critical Introduction to Twentieth-Century American Drama, Vol. 2: Tennessee Williams, Arthur Miller, Edward Albee.* Cambridge: Cambridge UP, 1984.

Brucher, Richard T. "Willy Loman and The Soul of the New Machine: Technology and the Common Man." *Journal of American Studies* 17 (1983): 325-36.

Cohn, Ruby. "The Articulate Victims of Arthur Miller." *Arthur Miller's Death of a Salesman.* Ed. Harold Bloom. New York: Chelsea House, 1988. 39-46.

Deleuze, Gilles, and Felix Guattari. *Anti-Oedipus: Capitalism and Schizophrenia.* Minneapolis: U of Minnesota P, 1983.

Green, Theodore P. *America's Heroes: The Changing Models of Success in American Magazines.* New York: Oxford UP, 1970.

Hoeveler, D. L. "*Death of a Salesman* as Psychomachia." *Arthur Miller's "Death of a Salesman."* Ed. Harold Bloom. New York: Chelsea House, 1988. 77-82.

Horkheimer, Max and Theodor Adorno. *Dialectic of Enlightenment.* 1947. London: Allen Lane, 1973.

Huftel, Sheila. *Arthur Miller: The Burning Glass.* New York: The Citadel Press, 1965.

Innes, Christopher. "The Salesman on the Stage: A Study in the Social Influence of Drama." *Arthur Miller's Death of a Salesman.* Ed. Harold Bloom. New York: Chelsea House, 1988. 59-75.

Jacobson, Irving. "Family Dreams in *Death of a Salesman.*" *American Literature* 47 (1975): 247-58.

Lyotard, Jean-François. *The Postmodern Condition: A Report on Knowledge.* Minneapolis: U of Minnesota P, 1984.

Marx, Karl. *Capital,* vol. 1. New York: Vintage, 1977.

Miller, Arthur. *Arthur Miller's Collected Plays.* New York: Viking, 1957.

———. *Timebends: A Life.* New York: Grove Press, 1987.

Mills, C. Wright. *White Collar: The American Middle Classes.* New York: Oxford UP, 1951.

Orr, John. *Tragic Drama and Modern Society: Studies in the Social and Literary Theory of Drama from 1870 to the Present.* London: Macmillan, 1981.

Parker, Brian. "Point of View in Arthur Miller's *Death of a Salesman.*" *Arthur Miller's Death of a Salesman.* Ed. Harold Bloom. New York: Chelsea House, 1988. 25-38.

Porter, Thomas. "'Acres of Diamonds': *Death of a Salesman.*" *Critical Essays on Arthur Miller.* Ed. James J. Martine. Boston: G. K. Hall, 1979. 24-43.

Poster, Mark. *Sartre's Marxism.* London: Pluto, 1979.

Sartre, Jean-Paul. *Critique of Dialectical Reason.* London: New Left Books, 1976.

Spindler, Michael. *American Literature and Social Change: William Dean Howells to Arthur Miller.* London: Macmillan, 1983.

Vogel, Dan. *The Three Masks of American Tragedy.* Baton Rouge: Louisiana State UP, 1974.

White, Hayden. *Tropics of Discourse: Essays in Cultural Criticism.* Baltimore: Johns Hopkins UP, 1978.

Williams, Raymond. *Modern Tragedy.* London: Verso, 1979.

Steven R. Centola (essay date September 1993)

SOURCE: Centola, Steven R. "Family Values in *Death of a Salesman.*" *CLA Journal* 37, no. 1 (September 1993): 29-41.

[*In the following essay, Centola characterizes* Death of a Salesman *as a modern tragedy, drawing focus to how Willy Loman's core values of family and self exert an indelible force on his relationship with his son Biff.*]

Studies of Arthur Miller's **Death of a Salesman** invariably discuss Willy Loman's self-delusion and moral confusion in relation to Miller's indictment of the competitive, capitalistic society that is responsible for dehumanizing the individual and transforming the once promising agrarian American dream into an urban nightmare.[1] While Miller clearly uses Willy's collapse to attack the false values of a venal American society, the play ultimately captures the audience's attention not because of its blistering attack on social injustice but because of its powerful portrayal of a timeless human dilemma. Simply put, Miller's play tells the story of a man who, on the verge of death, wants desperately to justify his life. As he struggles to fit the jagged pieces of his broken life together, Willy Loman discovers that to assuage his guilt, he must face the consequences of past choices and question the values inherent in the life he has constructed for himself and his family. Willy's painful struggle "to evaluate himself justly"[2] is finally what grips the play's audiences around the world, for everyone, not just people who are culturally or ideologically predisposed to embrace the American dream, can understand the anguish that derives from "being torn away from our chosen image of what and who we are in this world" (**"Tragedy"** [**"Tragedy and the Common Man"**] 5).

One can appreciate the intensity of Willy's struggle only after isolating the things that Willy values and after understanding how the complex interrelationship of opposed loyalties and ideals in Willy's mind motivates every facet of his speech and behavior in the play. By identifying and analyzing Willy Loman's values, we can uncover the intrinsic nature of Willy and Biff's conflict. Discussion of Willy's values specifically clarifies questions pertaining to Willy's infidelity and singular effort both to seek and escape from conscious recognition of the role he played in Biff's failure. Moreover, discussion of Willy's values helps us understand why Willy feels compelled to commit suicide. Ultimately, an analysis of Willy's values even helps to explain why **Death of a Salesman** is a tragedy, for in Willy Loman's drama of frustration, anguish, and alienation, we see a human struggle that is rooted in metaphysical as well as social and psychological concerns.

Throughout the play, Willy exhibits several important personality traits. Thoroughly convinced that "the man who makes an appearance in the business world, the man who creates personal interest, is the man who gets ahead,"[3] Willy is ever conscious of his appearance before others. Quite literally, Willy is probably obsessed with personal appearance because, in his mind, he was convinced himself that since he is destined for success, he must constantly dress the part. However, such fastidiousness also betrays his insecurity, something which often surfaces in his contradictory statements and emotional outbursts—these, of course, being a constant embarrassment for his family as well as a painful reminder to Willy of his ridiculous appearance before others. Beneath the surface optimism, therefore, lurk his frustration and keen sense of failure. That is why he can be spry, amusing, and cheerful one moment and then suddenly become quarrelsome, insulting, and sullen the next. Through Willy's incongruous behavior, Miller makes us sharply aware of the subterranean tensions dividing Willy.

Perhaps just as important as this, though, is the realization that with all of his seemingly absurd antics, and with his humor, quick intelligence, and warmth, Willy becomes likable, if not well liked. Even if we disagree with his actions, we still understand his anguish, share his suffering, and even come to admire him for his relentless pursuit of his impossible dream. With Miller, we come to see Willy as "extraordinary in one sense at least—he is driven to commit what to him is a consummate act of love through which he can hand down his selfhood, his identity. Perversely, perhaps, this has a certain noble claim if only in his having totally believed, and dreamed himself to death."[4]

Willy's quirky speech rhythms, his spontaneous utterance of success-formula platitudes, and his incessant contradictions flesh out his character and reveal his complex and troubled state of mind. More importantly, though, the poverty of his language exposes the conflict in his values that gives rise to all of his troubles in the play. The disparity between the hollowness of Willy's words and the passion with which he utters them underscore the tremendous variance between his deep feelings about and inadequate understanding of fatherhood, salesmanship, and success in one's personal life as well as in the business world in American society. For example, when Willy recites one of his stock phrases—such as "personality always wins the day" (*Salesman* 151)—he is expressing a long-held belief that has taken on the sanctity of a religious doctrine for him. The source of such success formulas may very well be books by Dale Carnegie and Russell Conwell—writers who popularized myths of the self-made man in the early twentieth century.[5] But without attributing such views to any particular influence, we can see that, in Willy's mind, such maxims are weighted with great authority; to him they represent nothing short of magical formulas for instant success. Like so many others in his society, he fails to see the banality in such clichés and is actually using bromidic language to bolster his own faltering self-confidence. By passionately repeating hackneyed phrases, Willy simultaneously tries to assure himself that he has made the right choices and has not wasted his life while he also prevents himself from questioning his conduct and its effect on his relations with others. Ironically, though, his speech says much more to anyone carefully listening.

Without knowing it, Willy cries out for help and denounces the life-lie that has destroyed his family. Even while yearning for success, Willy wants more than material prosperity; he wants to retrieve the love and respect of his family and the self-esteem which he has lost. Yet he goes about striving to achieve these goals in the wrong way because he has deceived himself into thinking that the values of the family he cherishes are inextricably linked with the values of the business world in which he works. He confuses the two and futilely tries to transfer one value system to the other's domain, creating nothing but chaos for himself and pain or embarrassment for everyone around him.

Willy's confusion has much to do with his own feelings of inadequacy as a father. His stubborn denial of these feelings, coupled with his misguided effort to measure his self-worth by the expression of love he thinks he can purchase in his family, only serves to aggravate his condition. Willy unwittingly hastens his own destruction by clinging fiercely to values that perpetually enforce his withdrawal from reality.

This problem is particularly evident in the way Willy approaches the profession of salesmanship. Instead of approaching his profession in the manner of one who understands the demands of the business world, Willy instead convinces himself that his success or failure in business has significance only in that it affects others'—particularly his family's—perception of him. He does not seek wealth for any value it has in itself; financial prosperity is simply the visible sign that he is a good provider for his family.

The confluence of the personal and the professional in Willy's mind is evident as Willy tells Howard Wagner about a time when a salesman could earn a living and appreciate the importance of "respect," "comradeship," "gratitude," "friendship," and "personality" (*Salesman* 180-81)—terms that are repeatedly used by various members of the Loman family. Also significant is the fact that when explaining to his boss how he was introduced to the career of salesmanship, Willy does not use his brother's language or refer to the kinds of survival techniques which Ben undoubtedly would have employed to make his fortune in the jungle. Willy's speech to Howard suggests that Willy chooses to be a salesman because he wants to sell himself, more than any specific product, to others—a point underscored by the obvious omission in the play of any reference to the specific products that Willy carries around in his valises.

The value that Willy attaches to his role as a father is evident throughout the play in numerous passages that reveal his obsession with this image. Soon after the play begins, Willy's concern over his duty to "accomplish something" (*Salesman* 133) is evident. Thinking about the many years which he has spent driving from New York City to New England to sell his products, Willy ruefully wonders why he has worked "a lifetime to pay off [his] house . . . and there's nobody to live in it" (*Salesman* 133). Obviously, Willy feels as though he has invested all of his life in his family and is not getting the kind of return he always expected. This feeling of futility makes him wonder whether he has failed as a father and impels him to explore his past—a psychological journey made effective theatrically by Miller's expressionistic use of lighting, music, and violation of wall-line boundaries. In almost every scene from his past, Willy's dialogue either comments on his role in his sons' development or shows his need to win Ben's approval of how he is rearing Biff and Happy. In scenes where he is congratulating Biff on his initiative for borrowing a regulation football to practice with (*Salesman* 144), or encouraging the boys to steal sand from the apartment house so that he can rebuild the front stoop (*Salesman* 158), or advising his sons to be well liked and make a good appearance in order to get ahead in the world (*Salesman* 146), Willy is unknowingly instilling values in his sons that will have a definite impact on their future development. He also does the same when he counsels Biff to "watch [his] schooling" (*Salesman* 142), tells his sons "Never leave a job till you're finished" (*Salesman* 143), or sentimentally praises America as "full of beautiful towns and fine, upstanding people" (*Salesman* 145). Even in scenes where he is troubled by Biff's stealing, failure of math, and renunciation of his love and authority after discovering his infidelity in Boston, Willy is probing only that part of his past that in some way calls into question his effectiveness as a father.

A look at the memory scenes also helps to explain why Willy values his family more than anything else in his life. Abandoned at an early age by his father, Willy has tried all his life to compensate for this painful loss. When Willy also suffers the sudden disappearance of his older brother, he nearly completely loses his self-confidence and a sense of his own identity as a male. His insecurity about his identity and role as a father is evident in the memory scene where he confesses to Ben that he feels "kind of temporary" (*Salesman* 159) about himself and seeks his brother's assurance that he is doing a good job of bringing up his sons:

W<small>ILLY</small>:

Ben, my boys—can't we talk? They'd go into the jaws of hell for me, see, but I—

B<small>EN</small>:

William, you're being first-rate with your boys. Outstanding, manly chaps!

W<small>ILLY</small>:

(*hanging onto his words*) Oh, Ben, that's good to hear! Because sometimes I'm afraid that I'm not teaching them the right kind of—Ben, how should I teach them?

(*Salesman* 159)

However, although Willy idolizes Ben and treasures his advice and opinions, Willy rarely does what Ben suggests and never imitates his pattern of behavior. In fact, until the end of Act II, when Ben appears entirely as a figment of Willy's imagination in a scene that has nothing to do with any remembered episode from his past, Willy implicitly rejects Ben's lifestyle and approach to business. There can be no doubt that in Willy's mind Ben's image stands for "success incarnate" (*Salesman* 152). Likewise, enshrined in Willy's memory, Ben's cryptic words magically ring "*with a certain vicious audacity*: William, when I walked into the jungle, I was seventeen. When I walked out I was twenty-one. And, by God, I was rich!" (*Salesman* 160). And there is always the tone of remorse in Willy's voice whenever he mentions Ben, for he associates his brother with his own missed opportunity: the Alaska deal which Willy turns down and with it the chance to make a fortune.

Clearly, then, Ben embodies more than just the image of success in Willy's mind; he also represents the road not taken. In other words, he is, in many ways, Willy's alter ego. Ben is the other self which Willy could have become had he chosen to live by a different code of ethics. Therefore, his presence in Willy's mind gives us insight into Willy's character by letting us see not only what Willy values but also what kinds of choices he has made in his life as a result of those values. For while Ben is undoubtedly the embodiment of one kind of American dream to Willy, so too is Dave Singleman representative of another kind—and that is part of Willy's confusion: both men symbolize the American dream, yet in his mind they represent value systems that are diametrically opposed to each other. The memory scenes are important in bringing out this contrast and showing what Willy's perception of Ben reflects about Willy's own conflicting values.

In every memory scene in which Ben appears, his viewpoint is always contrasted with the perspective of another character. This counterbalancing occurs because, while Ben has had a significant impact on Willy's past that continues to remain alive in the present in his imagination, Ben's influence on Willy has actually been no stronger than that which has been exerted upon him by people like Linda and Dave Singleman—the latter actually having the strongest effect, possibly because he exists in Willy's mind only as an idealized image.

The characters' contrasting views, in essence, externalize warring factions within Willy's fractured psyche. Each character represents a different aspect of Willy's personality: Linda most often takes the part of his conscience; Charley generally expresses the voice of reason; and Ben seems to personify Willy's drive toward self-assertion and personal fulfillment. These forces compete against each other, struggling for dominance, but although one might temporarily gain an advantage over the others, no one maintains control indefinitely. All remain active in Willy, leaving him divided, disturbed, and confused.

Linda and Charley are the most conspicuous contrasts to Ben in the memory scenes. They represent that side of Willy that has deliberately chosen not to follow in his brother's footsteps. Yet their views are not remembered as being superior to Ben's, for the image of Ben remains shrouded in mystery and splendor in Willy's memory and serves as a reminder not only of lost opportunity but also of the possibility of transforming dreams into reality. Ben's apparition haunts Willy and prods him to question his choices in life. However, since Willy both wants answers and dreads finding them, tension, not resolution, prevails in these scenes.

Such tension is evident, for example, in the scene where Charley and Ben disagree over Willy's handling of the boys' stealing:

CHARLEY:

> Listen, if they steal any more from that building the watchman'll put the cops on them!

LINDA:

> (*to Willy*) Don't let Biff . . . (*Ben laughs lustily.*)

WILLY:

> You shoulda seen the lumber they brought home last week. At least a dozen six-by-tens worth all kinds a money.

CHARLEY:

> Listen, if that watchman—

WILLY:

> I gave them hell, understand. But I got a couple of fearless characters there.

CHARLEY:

> Willy, the jails are full of fearless characters.

BEN:

> (*clapping Willy on the back, with a laugh at Charley*) And the stock exchange, friend!

> (*Salesman* 158)

Tension is also clearly present when Ben suddenly trips Biff while they are sparring and consequently receives a cold, disapproving stare from Linda (*Salesman* 158). Linda's opposition is even more apparent as she diminishes Ben's influence over Willy during their conversation about the Alaska deal; by reminding Willy of the successful Dave Singleman, she rekindles within him his love of the profession that he associates with family values and the unlimited possibilities inherent

within the American dream (*Salesman* 183-84). Ironically, Linda could actually be said to have hurt Willy by upholding his illusions. Nevertheless, she is instrumental in helping him reject Ben's business ethics, even though Willy does not recognize the value inherent in his choice and foolishly torments himself only with the memory of missed opportunity.

Unlike Willy, Ben functions comfortably in the modern business world. His life history provides confirmation of Howard Wagner's pronouncement that "business is business" (*Salesman* 180), and like Charley, he is a realist who has no illusions about what it takes to be a success. He is a survivor who undoubtedly made a fortune in the jungle through the kinds of ruthless acts which he performs in his sparring session with Biff. He suggests as much when he warns Biff: "Never fight fair with a stranger, boy. You'll never get out of the jungle that way" (*Salesman* 158). Ben's drive for self-fulfillment is undoubtedly predicated upon his denial of any responsibility for others and his repudiation of the values which Willy cherishes and associates with his romanticized view of family life and the past.

In dramatic contrast to the image of this ruthless capitalist stands the idealized figure of Dave Singleman. In Willy's mind, the image of Dave Singleman reflects Willy's unfaltering conviction that personal salvation can be linked with success, that business transactions can be made by people who respect and admire each other. Willy practically worships this legendary salesman who, at the age of eighty-four, "drummed merchandise in thirty-one states" by picking up a phone in his hotel room and calling buyers who remembered and loved him (*Salesman* 180). The legend of Dave Singleman so strongly impresses Willy that he decides that success results from "who you know and the smile on your face! It's contacts . . . being liked" (*Salesman* 184) that guarantee a profitable business. Willy clings to the illusion that he can become another Dave Singleman—in itself an impossible task since no one can become another person, a fact underscored by the name *Single*man, which obviously calls attention to the individual's uniqueness—even though Willy knows he lives in an era when business is "all cut and dried, and there's no chance for bringing friendship to bear—or personality" (*Salesman* 180-81). He fails to see the folly of his dream and ends up passing on not only his dream but also his confusion to Biff and Happy.

Their dilemma not only mirrors Willy's identity crisis but also indicts him for his ineptitude as a father. Moreover, seeing his failure reflected in the lives of his sons further intensifies Willy's guilt and hastens his decline.

Both sons are "*lost*" and "*confused*" (*Salesman* 136). They have inherited their father's powerful dreams but have no true understanding of how to attain them. Biff is more troubled than Happy because he is more conscious of this problem. Biff knows that he does not belong in the business world but still feels obligated to build his future there since that is what his father expects of him. He would prefer to work on a farm, performing manual labor, but he has learned from Willy not to respect such work. In Willy's mind, physical labor is tainted with the suggestion of something demeaning. When Biff suggests that they work as carpenters, Willy reproachfully shouts: "Even your grandfather was better than a carpenter. . . . Go back to the West! Be a carpenter, a cowboy, enjoy yourself!" (*Salesman* 166). With gibes like this in mind, Biff never feels completely satisfied working as a farmhand and tortures himself with guilt over his failure to satisfy Willy's demand that he do something extraordinary with his life.

In the harrowing climactic scene, however, Biff puts an end to his self-deception and tries to force his family to face the truth about him and themselves. He shatters the illusion of his magnificence by firmly telling Willy: "I'm not bringing home any prizes any more, and you're going to stop waiting for me to bring them home!" (*Salesman* 217). Knowing that his days of glory are past and that his dreams have nothing to do with Willy's vision of success for him, Biff embraces his life and stops living a lie. At the play's end, Biff confidently asserts: "I know who I am . . ." (*Salesman* 222). However, while he manages to succeed in his own quest for certitude, he fails to prevent Willy's self-destruction.

Willy commits suicide because he "cannot settle for half but must pursue his dream of himself to the end."[6] He convinces himself that only his death can restore his prominence in his family's eyes and retrieve for him his lost sense of honor. Perhaps without ever being fully conscious of his motives, Willy feels that his sacrifice will purge him of his guilt and make him worthy of Biff's love. When he realizes that he never lost Biff's love, Willy decides that he must die immediately so that he can preserve that love and not jeopardize it with further altercations. In his desperation to perform one extraordinary feat for his son so that he can once and for all verify his greatness and confirm his chosen image of himself in Biff's eyes, Willy turns to what he knows best: selling. He literally fixes a cash value on his life and, in killing himself, tries to complete his biggest sale. Willy thinks that by bequeathing Biff twenty thousand dollars, he will provide conclusive proof of his immutable essence as a good father, a goal that has obsessed him even since the day Biff discovered Willy's infidelity in Boston.

When Biff finds Willy with Miss Francis, Biff is horrified to see the face behind the mask that Willy wears. This sudden revelation of the naked soul in all its weakness and imperfection is more than Biff can bear because he has been trained to elude reality and substitute lies for truth. Beneath Biff's scornful gaze, Willy becomes nothing more than a "liar," a "phony little fake" (*Salesman* 208). Such condemnation leaves Willy feeling disgraced and alienated, so he retreats into the sanctuary of the past in a frantic effort to recapture there what is irretrievably lost in the present: his innocence and chosen identity. He opts for self-deception as a way of maintaining his distorted image of himself—a costly decision that eventually causes his psychological disorientation and death. He goes to his grave, as Biff puts it, without ever knowing "who he was" (*Salesman* 221).

However, Biff is only partially right when he says: Willy "had the wrong dreams. All, all, wrong . . ." (*Salesman* 221). Willy does deny a valuable part of his existence— his aptitude for manual labor—and spends most of his life mistakenly believing that values associated with the family open the door to success in the business world. He also transfers his confusion to his sons. Yet, in spite of his failings, Willy must ultimately be appreciated for valuing so highly the family and his role as a father. Even though he has misconceptions about this role, his inspiring pursuit of his forever elusive identity as the perfect father makes him a tragic figure. That is why Miller writes: "There is a nobility . . . in Willy's struggle. Maybe it comes from his refusal ever to relent, to give up" (*Beijing* [*Salesman in Beijing*] 27). Against all odds, Willy Loman demands that his life have "meaning and significance and honor" (*Beijing* 49).

Of course, in many ways, Willy ultimately fails to fulfill his dream. The Requiem clearly shows that he is not immortalized in death. His funeral is certainly not like the grand one he had imagined, and he still remains misunderstood by his family. But death does not defeat Willy Loman. The Requiem proves that his memory will continue to live on in those who truly mattered to him while he was alive. He might not have won their respect, but he is definitely loved—and perhaps that is all that Willy ever really hoped to achieve. Miller says that what Willy wanted "was to excel, to win out over anonymity and meaninglessness, to love and be loved, and above all, perhaps, to *count*."[7] After considering the importance of family values to Willy Loman, we are decidedly more inclined to say that he does, indeed, *count*—and we can perhaps better understand why his struggle and death make Miller's drama a tragedy of lasting and universal significance.

Notes

1. See, for example, Henry Popkin, "Arthur Miller: The Strange Encounter," *Sewanee Review* 68 (Winter 1960): 48-54; Barry Edward Gross, "Peddler and Pioneer in *Death of a Salesman*," *Modern Drama* 7 (February 1965): 405-10; Thomas E. Porter, *Myth and Modern American Drama* (Detroit: Wayne State

UP, 1969) 127-52; Ronald Hayman, *Arthur Miller* (New York: Frederick Ungar, 1972); Christopher Bigsby, *A Critical Introduction to Twentieth-Century American Drama* (Cambridge: Cambridge UP, 1984) II, 135-248; and Kay Stanton, "Women and the American Dream of *Death of a Salesman*," *Feminist Rereadings of Modern American Drama,* ed. June Schlueter (Madison: Fairleigh Dickinson UP, 1989) 67-102.

2. Arthur Miller, "Tragedy and the Common Man," *The Theater Essays of Arthur Miller,* ed. Robert A. Martin (New York: Penguin Books, 1978) 4. Hereafter cited parenthetically in the text as "Tragedy."

3. Arthur Miller, *Death of a Salesman, Arthur Miller's Collected Plays* (New York: Viking, 1957) I. 146. Hereafter cited parenthetically in the text as *Salesman.*

4. Arthur Miller, *Salesman in Beijing* (New York: Viking, 1984) 190. Hereafter cited parenthetically in the text as *Beijing.*

5. See Dale Carnegie, *How to Win Friends and Influence People* (New York: Simon and Schuster, 1936); and Russell H. Conwell, *Acres of Diamonds* (New York: Harper, 1905). Discussion of these texts and other works which popularized the success myth can be found in Porter, pp. 127-52.

6. Arthur Miller, Introd., *Arthur Miller's Collected Plays* I, 34.

7. Arthur Miller, *Timebends: A Life* (New York: Grove, 1987) 184.

John S. Shockley (essay date summer 1994)

SOURCE: Shockley, John S. "*Death of a Salesman* and American Leadership: Life Imitates Art." *Journal of American Culture* 17, no. 2 (summer 1994): 49-56.

[*In the following essay, Shockley explores the similarities between Willy Loman in* Death of a Salesman *and the life of former U.S. president Ronald Reagan.*]

Death of a Salesman hit the American stage in 1949, catapulting Arthur Miller into the status of the "greats" of American dramatists. While the play was never without its critics, who argued over whether the play could appropriately be called a "tragedy," whether the writing was a bit stilted, and whether Miller's message about American capitalism and the American dream was a bit garbled, it still was an enormously popular play among theater-goers and critics. All of them seemed to find something of the American creed, and of themselves, in the play.[1]

But more than 40 years have passed since the play was written. Should we now view the play as a dated relic of another age, or does it still resonate with the American character? Is the play primarily the personal problem of an aging playwright whose formative years were spent in the Great Depression, and who therefore could never "trust" American capitalism again?[2] If so, do we have little need to understand *Death of a Salesman* or come to terms with it? On the contrary, I shall argue that *Death of a Salesman* still resonates powerfully in American life and culture and that in a fascinating and chilling way life has imitated drama. Willy Loman shares a number of important traits with the most successful American politician of the late twentieth century, Ronald Reagan. To understand American culture and American politics, one must come to grips with the phenomenal success of Ronald Reagan. Arthur Miller's perspective in creating Willy Loman and *Death of a Salesman* can help us do this.

I. The Similarities of Willy Loman and Ronald Reagan

In the first place, both Willy Loman and Ronald Reagan are salesmen. Both understood that a salesman has got to believe in himself and his product before he can sell it to others. Both were selling themselves and the American dream. Ronald Reagan, of course, was a salesman for General Electric, "living well electrically" while touting the corporation's conservative political agenda. But most of all, as he gave "The Speech" to 250,000 GE employees while traveling all over the country, he sold the American dream.[3] And he was selling that both before and after his years as a GE salesman.

After he was dropped by GE, he became a salesman for the conservative ideas of Southern California businessmen, who recognized in him the best spokesman for their ideology that they could find. "A salesman has got to dream, boy. It comes with the territory."[4] So says Charlie, Willy's neighbor, at Willy's funeral. Both Willy and Reagan dreamed the American dream and believed that in America a man could, and should, fulfill himself.

Second, both also had to deny basic points of reality in order to believe in the dream. Willy tried desperately to deny that his sons were failures and that he was failing as a salesman. His son Biff is always about to be a success, about to land a good job. And Willy lies to Linda about the source of his income, telling her the money is coming from sales when in fact Charlie down the street is lending him the money. Throughout the play he is always lying about how important he is and how many "friends" he has. Ronald Reagan, as the son of a failed, alcoholic, shoe salesman, was forced to deny his family's problems from an early age. Ronald Reagan is the adult child of an alcoholic. Yet his father's skills as a raconteur and his mother's encouragement of his acting and entertaining abilities channeled the denials and "stories" into more acceptable outlets than Willy had.

As Willy loved telling jokes to highlight his personality, Reagan loved entertaining others.[5] Denials continued throughout Reagan's life: denying that Hollywood had engaged in a blacklist; denying that the MCA (Music Corporation of America) was involved in bribery and "payola" while Reagan dealt with them as president of the Screen Actors Guild; denying that his tax cuts could be responsible for the mounting federal deficits; denying that his cuts in low-income housing subsidies could be responsible for the rise in homelessness; denying that he sold arms for hostages; and forgetting virtually everything about the Iran-Contra diversion scandal.[6]

To scholars of the Reagan era, one of the most striking features of Reagan the man was his lack of interest in facts, which were often misstated or completely wrong. His view of "facts" was entirely utilitarian, in service to his ideology of the American dream and American foreign policy. Willy too had great difficulty absorbing facts that did not fit the view he wanted to have of himself and his life. The entire play is basically a struggle within Willy's mind between his vision of himself and the painful reality of facts intruding upon his "dream." Perhaps the most painful and poignant moment in the play comes when his son Biff tries to tell Willy that he's not now and will never be the "success" Willy imagines for him. Willy cannot hear him. Actually, in denying basic facts each man was trying to create himself from myth.[7] One was of course more successful at doing this than the other.

Third, Ronald Reagan and Willy Loman also had to fantasize in order to avoid the realities they could not handle and to give themselves the confidence they otherwise would lack. Willy was "well liked" and known all over New England, and at his own funeral his boys would be impressed at how many "friends" would show up (Miller 764, 796). Ronald Reagan moved more than a dozen times during his childhood, and had to learn to survive without close friends. He wanted to play football but was never any good (his eyes were too poor). Yet he was "the Gipper," Notre Dame's great football hero, throughout his political career. His movie career and political career often blended, sometimes consciously as in the above example, and sometimes unconsciously. The "Gipper" was a kind of double fantasy, in that George Gipp himself was a mythical hero based heavily on fantasy. While "Win One for the Gipper," Reagan's favorite movie and political line, probably was said by George Gipp on his death bed, most likely Gipp thought he was talking to his doctor (qtd. in Lippman). In reality, George Gipp was a rather unsavory character who bet on his own games and by today's standards would have been expelled from the sport.[8] But, as with so much of Ronald Reagan and Willy Loman, facts were not allowed to get in the way of the myth. And in another kind of chilling rehearsal for life (politics) imitating art

(the movie), the Reagan movie helped make Gipp into "a teflon hero."

Fourth, while both Willy and Reagan wanted to be well liked, and wanted to have the personalities to "win friends and influence people," neither was successful at forming close personal friendships.[9] In both cases, only their wives stood by them, and in both cases their wives tried to protect them and sustain their husbands' illusions in the face of reality.[10] Each man tried to make sure his "image" presented an air of leadership and success, but both men in fact were more passive than they wanted to appear.[11]

Both men also faced severe problems with their children and denied these problems to themselves and the outside world. Willy's pained relationships with his two sons is one of the basic themes running through *Death of a Salesman*. With Reagan, his relationship with his adopted son Michael (detailed in Michael's autobiography, *On the Outside Looking In*) has been extremely strained. His daughter Patti barely has been on speaking terms with her parents since the publication of her autobiography (thinly disguised as a novel) several years ago (*Home Front*). Both men lacked strong fathers who could nurture them, although their father relationships also contained important differences. In a poignant moment, Willy asks Ben (his older brother) to tell him more about "Dad," who left when Willy was still young, because "I still feel kind of temporary about myself" (Miller 770). Reagan had a much longer relationship with his father, but Reagan's stay in any one place was "kind of temporary." Jack Reagan was also "footloose." He moved constantly, changed jobs, and was usually a failure as a salesman. In addition, Reagan's father's alcoholism was a source of worry and shame. But Ronald Reagan also described his father as "the best raconteur I ever heard," and this surely must have helped Ronald's own skills as a salesman and storyteller.[12]

Fifth, both men had brushes with the uglier side of capitalism, and yet seemed unable to recognize or condemn this brutal side. To Willy it was his older brother Ben, who became a millionaire at a young age and kept admonishing Willy: "Never fight fair with a stranger, boy. You'll never get out of the jungle that way" (Miller 770). Yet Willy constantly wants Ben's approval and is asking him how he managed to be so successful. Willy even views his son Biff's stealing as "initiative."

Reagan was called before a grand jury investigating the seamier side of Hollywood capitalism, the bribery and monopolistic practices of the Music Corporation of America. Its special sweet deals with the Screen Actors Guild while Reagan was president of the Guild and simultaneously getting what looked like kickbacks from MCA nearly resulted in his indictment.[13]

Later, as President, Reagan was surrounded by corruption, influence peddling, indictments, trials and convictions of his aides and associates—Michael Deaver, Lynn Nofziger, John Poindexter—the HUD scandal, the Savings and Loan scandal and the spectacular corruption of some who became multimillionaires during his era. But throughout his administration and throughout *Death of a Salesman* neither Reagan nor Willy ever criticized or condemned any actions by these people. As Willy refused to condemn son Biff's stealing or brother Ben's ruthlessness, neither did Reagan condemn the stealings and illegalities of any of his aides. Neither had a moral code of what were fair and unfair practices, what were proper ways to get rich and what were improper ways. To both, the American creed meant success and riches, but *how* these were obtained neither wanted to examine too closely. Perhaps they did not want to examine this too closely because the truth would have been too painful. To both men America and the American creed seemed to have no place for failure. How one succeeded was therefore not a moral question.

Both the Reagan presidency and *Death of a Salesman* then are dramas about the power of the American dream and the self-deceptions necessary for the kind of American dream believed. These are both potent forces in American politics and culture. But Willy Loman and Ronald Reagan are obviously not identical. Their differences are too important to ignore.

II. The Differences between Willy Loman and Ronald Reagan

From the beginning, Ronald Reagan had physical traits and a personality that made it more likely that he would succeed in America. His personality was a more marketable commodity, both for Hollywood and in politics. He was physically handsome, meticulous about his appearance and successful at entertaining others. His "self-deprecating humor" was in marked contrast to Willy's braggadocio (Cannon 32). Reagan had the ability to inspire others and to make people feel good about themselves. This allowed others to enjoy being around Reagan and gave him the self-confidence Willy wanted but lacked. Yet, like Willy, Reagan was essentially remote from others and could be highly manipulative (229, 218).

As the "good guy" in so many Hollywood movies, Reagan had a clearer sense of the "bad guy" than Willy had. Demonology—the Sandinistas, the Communists, terrorists, etc., abroad and welfare queens and government at home—served Reagan well both in defining himself and explaining the world to others.[14] Willy didn't really know what was happening to him. *Death of a Salesman* is a desperate search to find out what is killing Willy, and Willy never figures it out. The final "Requiem" scene shows that the remaining characters are divided over what the cause was as well. If Willy had had a scapegoat, or a clearer sense of what was killing him, he could have fought back and found a greater reason for living. But Willy never questioned the social, economic or political order. Broader institutional forces are more remote from him, givens in a system where he's searching for fame, success and the American dream.[15] Reagan, however, translated his personal values and dreams into politics and was the defender of the American dream from threats both external and internal.

While both Willy Loman and Ronald Reagan had to confront failure, their responses to their failures were different. Like Willy, Ronald Reagan faced career problems with middle age. He was dumped by Hollywood after a string of B-grade movies. Near the end he was even forced to co-star with a chimpanzee in *Bedtime for Bonzo*. General Electric rescued him from obscurity in Hollywood and honed his speaking skills. But he was dropped on 24-hours' notice by the company when *G.E. Theater* was cancelled, and Reagan was forced to take a salary cut in hosting *Death Valley Days*. By 1964 Reagan was in debt and owed back taxes to the U.S. government.[16] Willy of course was also failing financially and with age. But here the differences in the two men are too important to ignore. Willy had no one to rescue him, save his neighbor Charlie, who in fact did help. But Willy was too proud to give up his salesman's job (or admit that he had been fired) to work for Charlie. Ronald Reagan, however, was quite willing to accept help and funds from anyone, including wealthy admirers of his conservative views:

> A group headed by Justin Dart (Dart Industries; Rexall Drugs; Kraft Foods), Holmes Tutle (a Los Angeles Ford dealer), William French Smith (a wealthy Los Angeles attorney), and A. C. (Cy) Rubel (Chairman of Union Oil Co.) formed the Ronald Reagan Trust Fund to take over his personal finances. . . .
>
> (Dye 71)

Willy didn't have anyone to set up the Willy Loman Trust Fund to take over his personal finances. In addition, Reagan was given a ranch. Willy needed one. This difference allowed Reagan never to lose self-confidence (at least not for long), while Willy's self-worth was collapsing around him (Dye 72).[17]

Other differences follow from ones already mentioned. As Willy's psychological condition deteriorates, he is more obsessed with the meaning of life and his place in history than Ronald Reagan. In his struggle, Willy is engaged in a battle with himself. But that is only because he has to be. Willy is not by nature any more introspective than Ronald Reagan. Reagan seeks love less desperately because he is a more successful salesman. He has enough of what he needs. And while Willy is haunted by his failed relationship with his sons, there is no evidence that Ronald Reagan is. Willy, however, in his own failures, must live more through his sons. Ronald Reagan doesn't need to. These differences thus emphasize that through his more obvious and painful confrontations with failure, Willy has been forced to become more introspective than either Willy or Reagan would have desired. But deep down both men were solipsists. Neither was interested in learning from other people. Neither wanted the real world to intrude upon his fantasy world.

Ronald Reagan, in sum, was what Willy Loman wanted to be: well-liked, at least in a superficial way; entertaining without being a bore; successful; handsome; and not fat. Reagan's attributes allowed him to be rescued by wealthy individuals who realized they could use him for their own purposes, as he used them for his own purposes. But Willy had no Southern California businessmen to come to his rescue when he was washed up, abandoned, aging and unsure of his value to society.

III. ARTHUR MILLER'S VISION OF THE POWER OF THE DREAM

Willy Loman committed suicide. Ronald Reagan became President of the United States. Yet this difference hides greater truths. Each believed in the American dream. That Reagan was elected President twice, and was widely liked by the American people during his tenure, ultimately says more about the American people than about Ronald Reagan. Here Willy Loman and Arthur Miller can help us. That Arthur Miller understood the power of the American dream, and the need of little people to believe in it, helps us later explain the rise and success of Ronald Reagan in American politics when America itself was undergoing a crisis of confidence.

Of course, the American dream has meant different things to different people. Tom Paine ("We have it in our power to begin the world over again"), Franklin Roosevelt and our "rendezvous with destiny" and Martin Luther King ("I have a dream that one day this nation will rise up and live out the true meaning of its creed: 'We hold these truths to be self-evident, that all men are created equal'") all evoke feelings of the New Adam in the New Eden. In this new world the sins, hatreds, unfreedoms and inequalities of other lands can be changed and history can be forgotten.[18]

But Arthur Miller (through Willy Loman) and Ronald Reagan are focusing on an altered dream: the self-reliant individual, Jefferson's yeoman farmer, gradually became the man who could make a lot of money. And to do that, marketing, salesmanship and image became the road to the dream. The defense of heroic individualism became the defense of competition, capitalist exploita-

tion and, in Reagan, also virulent anti-communism. Willy never examines his values and how these values don't fit with his true, more agrarian personality. While Ronald Reagan mouthed the potent cliches of the business ethic as the ultimate form of freedom, he examined the values in hardly any greater depth than Willy. But he did have the advantage, once he entered politics, of being someone who had spent his life, including his professional life, presenting himself as an image, a role to be seen by others.

The rewards of being successful for both men were to be well liked and to be rich. To be rich for both seemed to mean 1) having a place where they can get away from it all—a ranch or "a little place out in the country" and 2) consuming the products of a bountiful business society. To be rich is thus to be "free" in the two senses above, with the added self-confidence of being admired, a model for others.

Willy Loman and Ronald Reagan share this new, salesmanship understanding of the American dream. Miller's purpose, however, is very different from Willy Loman's and Ronald Reagan's. While he wanted to show the power of this dream, he also wanted to show the dangers, the costs and the emptiness of it. In his autobiography, *Timebends,* Miller says that in writing the play he had as a motive "in some far corner of my mind possibly something political; there was the smell in the air of a new American Empire in the making . . . and I wanted to set before the new captains and the so smugly confident kings the corpse of a believer" (184). He does this in many unsubtle ways, including letting us know early on that the Loman family is caught up in mindless consumerism ("whipped cheese"), and that these new products disrupt attempts at meaningful human interaction. Miller shows the power of advertising and consumerism, and the contradictions of attitudes toward products in the Loman family by having Willy call his Chevrolet both "the greatest car ever built" and "that goddamn Chevrolet" in the space of only a few minutes, and in Willy's remark that "Once in my life I would like to own something outright before it's broken!" (Miller 765, 766, 777). But while Willy utters these remarks, he still is completely caught up in the pursuit of the dream.

Miller understood the power of the belief in a New Land, a New Eden, where the normal rules and motives for other countries and other peoples would not apply. Even in its competitive, "get rich" meanings, Miller understood the continuing force of the dream in mobilizing and inspiring people.

"Can we doubt," said Reagan in accepting the Republican nomination for President in 1980, "that only a Divine Providence placed this land, this island of freedom, here as a refuge for all those people in the world who yearn to breathe freely. . . . ?" This is Reagan's belief. But where does this belief lead? Is God a white American, willing to countenance the near genocide of millions of the original Americans and willing to sanction the death and slavery of millions of blacks so that the economic system of white America could grow stronger and be "free"? Reagan's encomium to the American dream can be as soaring and inspirational as it is in part because he never asks or answers these questions, any more than Willy does. Similarly, with American power abroad Ronald Reagan sees only altruism; not imperialism, manifest destiny or messianic causes unwanted by others: "I'd always felt that from our deeds it must be clear to anyone that Americans were a moral people who, starting at the birth of our nation, had always used our power only as a force for good in the world" (qtd. in Wills 3).

Reagan's is a view deeply soothing to a nation questioning its self-confidence after Vietnam, Watergate, stagflation and energy crises. The blinders and the fantasies are not only necessary for the laudatory rhetoric; they also do not prepare anyone for failure. Both Willy and Reagan believed; each was an incurable optimist always wanting to paint a "rosy scenario."[19] And the downside of this view is that there is no place for failure. If in the face of such boundless opportunities ("just check the want ads"), a person does not succeed, there must be something wrong with that person.[20] It is this downside that is so hard for Willy to confront, because he believes so strongly in the American dream. Willy is unable to let go of it, unable to change in the face of reality, and commits suicide in the hope that he is helping his family.

Arthur Miller, through Willy Loman, presages the Reagan prototype through 1) emphasizing the power of the capitalist-consumerist-get-rich-and-be-well-liked dream, and the hold it has on the American people. Miller shows us the power of the myth. 2) He also understood the need for selective perception, fantasy and denial, and the tenuous hold on reality necessary for this strident view of the dream. He prepares us for the Reagan denials, misstatements and lies, and the gap between appearance and reality.[21] To both Willy and Reagan, uttering the cliches of success is virtually the same thing as bringing these cliches into actuality. To both, "saying makes it so," and thus they are an evasion of the truth. Arthur Miller helps us understand that Ronald Reagan succeeded not in spite of but because of all his paradoxes and contradictions. As the defender of the little man's dream, he succeeded because millionaires could use him to champion a dream that benefitted primarily themselves. If he had been truly committed to helping the little Willys of the nation fulfill their dreams, he would have been dumped by his financial backers. Instead, Reagan was the "sincerest claimant to a heritage that never existed . . . —a perfect

blend of an authentic America he grew up in and of that America's own fables about its past."[22] As political analysts have written of Reagan: "He had been in some measure the Wizard of Us, a fabulist presiding over a wondrous Emerald City of the mind. . . . people wanted to believe in it" (Goldman and Mathews 32).[23]

Miller also seems to understand that 3) as pressures on the dream close in, the desire to believe in it will intensify rather than weaken. The American people did not want to hear Jimmy Carter (or John Anderson or Walter Mondale or Bruce Babbitt, etc.) any more than Willy wanted to hear Charlie. A "realist," willing to talk of limits, taxes, sacrifice and mixed motives in a complex world isn't what Willy or the American people wanted to hear. Arthur Miller understood this from of the American psyche and its power.

Surely all writers—political analysts as well as dramatists—recognize the need of people to find meaning in their lives. But Miller understood the particular nature of the American need for meaning. Through giving us Willy Loman, Miller helped us better understand the successful Willy Loman when he appeared on the American stage: Ronald Reagan, the super salesman, everything Willy and our nation of Willys wanted to be. Ronald Reagan understood American fears, hopes, lies, vulnerabilities and the need for optimism better than many political scientists, and he understood the role of the salesman in selling us our dreams better than others did. He had the confidence the rest of us wanted.

But whether we should assess Reagan as critically as son Biff assessed Willy—"He had the wrong dreams. All, all wrong" (Miller 797)—is less clear. After a decade of Reagan and Reaganism we have record budget deficits, record trade deficits, increased dependence upon foreign lenders in the world economy, a crumbling infrastructure and, most poignant and ironic of all, a growing gap between rich and poor. It is now harder, not easier, for the little Willys of society to reach the American dream. To criticize Reagan, we, like Biff, would have to condemn part of ourselves, condemn part of our own dreams, and condemn part of our identity and meaning as Americans. We Americans are a long way from being ready or able to do that. But we should not forget that both Willy Loman and Ronald Reagan embody what ought to be a debate about the essence and direction of America.

Notes

I owe thanks to many people, especially the following: Albert Wertheim of the Indian University Department of English for encouraging my interest in politics and drama; David Olson and Donald McCrone of the University of Washington Political Science Department, along with Norman Walbek of Gustavus Adolphus College, for allowing me to teach courses in politics and drama; and Debbie Wiley of Western Illinois University for preparing the manuscript.

1. For reviews of the play, see Harold Bloom, ed., *Arthur Miller's Death of a Salesman,* 1982. For a review of Arthur Miller in general, see Neil Carson, *Arthur Miller,* 1982. As Carson notes (13) the play ran on Broadway for 742 performances and "transformed Miller's life," elevating him "to a position of prominence where he became exposed to both adulation and criticism of a kind he had not previously experienced."

2. The play is in many ways autobiographical, for Miller's father, Isidore, lost his business and his fortune in the Great Depression and was blamed by his son for an inability to cope with these changes. See the review of Miller's autobiography, *Timebends* (1987), in *The New Republic,* Feb. 8, 1988, 30-34, "All My Sins," by David Denby.

3. These points are mentioned many places, including Lou Cannon, *Reagan,* 1982, 93.

4. Arthur Miller, *Death of a Salesman, The Bedford Introduction to Drama,* Lee Jacobus (ed.), 797. William Heyen, "Arthur Miller's *Death of a Salesman* and the American Dream" in Bloom, *supra* note 1, p. 51, has said, quoting Leslie Fiedler, that American industry produces "not things . . . but dreams disguised as things."

5. Lou Cannon, the journalist who has observed Ronald Reagan the closest over the past three decades, comments in his latest biography of Reagan, "Acting took early hold of him, and never let him go." *President Reagan: The Role of a Lifetime,* 1991, 39.

6. On Reagan denying the Hollywood blacklist, see Victor Navasky, *Naming Names,* 1980 p. 87; for Reagan's relationship with the MCA, see Garry Wills, *Reagan's America,* 1988, chapters 28 and 29. For his confused views on taxes and deficits, see David Stockman, *The Triumph of Politics,* 1986; for the severe cuts in low- and moderate-incoming housing, see Charles Moore and Patricia Hoban-Moore, "Some Lessons from Reagan's HUD: Housing Policy and Public Service," *PS: Political Science and Politics,* Mar. 1990, 13-18; for denying that the diversion of funds took place and for forgetting nearly everything about the Iran-Contra scandal, see *Newsweek,* Apr. 2, 1990, 36 ("A Diminished Ron, a Refurbished Jimmy"). *Newsweek* reports that "Reagan pleaded loss of memory some 150 times in two days of testimony [at the Poindexter trial]—and he had forgotten the conclusion of his own Tower Commission, that funds were diverted to the Contras." In a chilling parallel with the Iran-Contra scandal, Garry Wills reports (325) that as the Justice Department proceeded with the investigation of MCA and the Screen Actors Guild's favorable treatment of them, "Reagan's strategy was to retreat toward constantly expanding areas of forgetfulness." At one point in his grand jury testimony in 1962, Reagan said, "And all of this, including the opinions of myself, is vague at the Guild on everything that took place for all those years all the way back including whether I was present or not" (Wills 323).

7. David Broder, "Reagan Memoir Fails to Tell All," *Minneapolis Star-Tribune,* Nov. 23, 1990, editorial page, comments that "Reagan has devoted most of his eight decades to remaking, not the nation or the world, but himself." Sidney Blumenthal, *Our Long National Daydream: The Political Pageant of the Reagan Era,* 1986, p. xiv, has written, "The essential quality for any actor is to induce in his audience a willing suspension of disbelief . . . [h]e must also suspend disbelief within himself, giving himself over to the role and the scene. Reagan's grip over the nation partly lay in his ability to maintain his grip over himself. Above all, he was a true believer in his role. He used that role to persuade that willing was doing, that saying something made it so." Michael Rogin, *Ronald Reagan, The Movie,* 1987, 3 argues that Ronald Reagan "found out who he was through the roles he played on film."

8. Lippman also reports that after the Notre Dame coach invoked George Gipp's name at half-time, Notre Dame did win 12 to 6, but Army was on the Notre Dame one-yard line as the game ended, and Notre Dame lost the rest of its games that season to finish 5-4 overall. Comments Lippman, "Another few seconds and . . . Ronald Reagan might never have become president."

9. The string of "kiss-and-tell" books from Reagan's closest aides, starting with Michael Deaver and continuing through David Stockman, Larry Speakes and Chief of Staff Don Regan, makes this point painfully clear.

10. Nancy, however, was a greater help to Ronald than Linda was to Willy. As an entertainer herself, she better understood the needs of her husband, but both actively intervened to try to defend their husbands. See Garry Wills, "The Man Who Wasn't There" [a review of Lou Cannon's *President Reagan: The Role of a Lifetime*], *The New York Review of Books,* June 13, 1991, 3-7.

11. Fred Greenstein, "Ronald Reagan—Another Hidden-Hand Ike?" *PS: Political Science and Politics,* Mar. 1990, 7-13 concludes that Reagan was surprisingly passive and remote from the specifics of politics and policy, although he did have strong general beliefs. He quotes Chief of Staff Donald Regan that Reagan's outgoing personality and infectious likability are based on a "natural diffidence."

12. Wills, *supra,* note 6: 15, quoting Reagan's autobiography, *Where's the Rest of Me?* (1965): 14.

13. Wills, *supra* note 6: 322. Wills also concludes (322) that "it seems that Reagan's political career would not have emerged at all if the circumstances of a

1962 investigation had become known at the time; if an indictment of Reagan, seriously considered for months by the Justice Department, had been brought or even publicly threatened; if a civil suit of conspiracy against the MCA had not been settled by a divestiture."

14. One does not appoint master spy and covert operator William Casey as campaign manager unless one has a strong sense of the need for action against "enemies." Michael Rogin, *supra* note 7, argues that demonology was an essential part of Reagan's persona.

15. Helene Wickham Koon, "Introduction," *Twentieth Century Interpretations of Death of a Salesman*, 11, says of Willy that he "accepts the world without question and never seeks to better it, who reacts without thought, who substitutes dreams for knowledge, and who is necessarily self-centered because unanalyzed feelings are his sole touchstone to existence." Willy does, however, protest the surrounding of his house by apartment buildings and the loss of sunlight and space that comes with it. He also protests how things are constantly breaking down. But these protests are completely devoid of meaningful human action. He is apolitical.

16. These events are discussed in Thomas Dye's *Who's Running America? The Reagan Years*, Third Edition, 1983, 69-73 and Garry Wills, *Reagan's America*, 1988, 338-39. Wills, however, states that "Reagan was financially secure by 1962," which seems not to account for the need for his trust fund to be set up by wealthy benefactors.

17. Dye notes other investments for Reagan as well.

18. The first two men are quoted in Ronald Reagan's speech accepting his party's nomination in 1980, which can be found in *Ronald Reagan Talks to America* (1983) 77. But Reagan does not quote Martin Luther King. For contested meanings of the American dream, see David Madden, *American Dream, American Nightmare* (1965), who argues that the American dream comes in an older agrarian and a newer urban form. John Cawelti, *Apostles of the Self-Made Man* (1965), describes three main competing versions: the first came from a more conservative tradition of middle-class Protestantism and stressed piety and honesty; the second stressed more secular qualities of initiative, aggressiveness and competitiveness; the third tied individual fulfillment to social progress more than wealth or status, along the lines of Emerson's self-reliant man. Alfred Ferguson, "The Tragedy of the American Dream," *Thought* (1978) 83-98 explores the "New Adam" in the "New Eden" in greater detail, arguing that the dream now means "it is possible for everyman to be whatever he can imagine himself being" (88). "[T]he wish is father to the fact" (90).

19. William Heyen, *supra* note 4: 49, speaks of Willy Loman as "an incurable yea-sayer, painting everything rosy, prophesizing empire . . . for the Lomans. . . . He is insatiable. He so much needs to believe in his dream." David Stockman, *supra* note 6: 385, recounts a story President Reagan would tell of a boy who is an optimist that gets a roomful of horse manure for a Christmas present: "He's delighted. He digs around the room for hours on end. With all that horse manure, he figured there just had to be a pony in there somewhere!" Stockman uses the term "rosy scenario" to describe President Reagan's constant belief that the nation would "grow" itself out of the deficit problems.

20. John Cawelti, *supra,* note 25, discusses this in more detail. He notes (217) that "positive thinkers like Norman Vincente Peale and Dale Carnegie seem to accept the American business world wholeheartedly. If it has flaws, they are the result of some failure to assume a positive "attitude." Cawelti argues provocatively (217), however, that "positive thinking is . . . a revelation of the failure of the dream," because these books are full of eloquent testimony of anxious, neurotic people and "the failure of the business world to fulfill human needs."

21. To say this is not to say anything as precise as that from Miller we can sense that Ronald Reagan would launch a "war on drugs" while secretly dealing with Manuel Noriega, or condemn "terrorism" while secretly dealing with Iran. Rather, the point is that when these gaps between appearance and truth appear, most Americans will want to believe their leader, especially one who can evoke the symbols of the dream as powerfully as Reagan. If the leader can maintain his self-confidence and affability, even as the truth is (partially) revealed, he will likely survive and be "well liked."

22. Lou Cannon, *Ronald Reagan, supra* note 5: 793, quoting Garry Wills, *supra* note 6.

23. See also Sidney Blumenthal, quoted in footnote 6, *supra.*

Works Cited

Cannon, Lou. *Reagan*. New York: Putnam, 1982.

Dye, Thomas R. *Who's Running America?—The Reagan Years*. Third ed. Englewood Cliffs, NJ: Prentice Hall, 1983.

Goldman, Peter Louis, and Tom Mathews. *The Quest for the Presidency, 1988*. New York: Simon & Schuster, 1989.

Lippman, Theo. "Let Reagan Have Role He Was Born to Play: Rockne." *Minneapolis Star-Tribune,* date unknown (1988) quoting sportswriter Jim Murray.

Miller, Arthur. *Death of a Salesman*. Ed. Lee Jacobus. New York: Bantam Books, 1955.

Wills, Garry. "Mr. Magoo Remembers." *New York Review of Books* 20 Dec. 1990.

H. C. Phelps (essay date summer 1995)

SOURCE: Phelps, H. C. "Miller's *Death of a Salesman.*" *Explicator* 53, no. 4 (summer 1995): 239-40.

[*In the following essay, Phelps examines the uncertainty regarding Biff's love for his father in* Death of a Salesman, *faulting critics for easily accepting Biff's affection as the impetus for Willy's suicide.*]

Curiously, most critics seem to accept at face value the assumption that at the conclusion of Arthur Miller's classic drama ***Death of a Salesman,*** Willy Loman determines to commit suicide because his older son Biff has at last openly and unequivocally declared his "love" for his father (e.g., Aarnes 104; Bigsby 123; Hynes 286; Dukore 39). Yet a close examination of this crucial scene and the subsequent Requiem reveals a far greater degree of ambiguity than has been acknowledged.

Though Willy has obviously contemplated suicide for a long time, he only makes his final, irrevocable decision after the play has reached its undoubted emotional climax, Biff's dramatic declaration to his father: "Pop, I'm nothing! I'm nothing, Pop. Can't you understand that? There's no spite in it anymore. I'm just what I am, that's all." Following this outburst, Biff physically collapses in his father's arms, and Miller carefully comments in his stage direction: "Biff's fury has spent itself, and he breaks down, sobbing, holding on to Willy, who dumbly fumbles for Biff's face." The son's final words to his father in the play are simply: "I'll go in the morning. Put him—put him to bed" (133).

At best, this statement can only be regarded as a tepid and ambiguous expression of concern. Yet Willy's immediate reaction to it is to conclude: "Biff—he likes me!" To which Linda and Happy quickly respond with enthusiastic reinforcement: "He loves you, Willy!" and "Always did, Pop" (133). Their reaction suggests that Biff's feelings are obvious. However, Linda and Happy are repeatedly shown to be among the most deluded, obtuse, and mendacious characters in the play. Earlier, each had made equally enthusiastic and reinforcing— but dangerously inaccurate—comments on the supposed affection of Bill Oliver, Biff's former boss, for his departed employee. When Biff outlined his plan to persuade Oliver to "stake" him to a business venture, he insisted: "He did like me. Always liked me." Linda immediately exclaimed: "He loved you" (64). Earlier, Happy had responded to the plan in a similar fashion: "I bet he'd back you. 'Cause he thought highly of you, Biff" (26). Yet Oliver, when Biff finally sees him in his office, doesn't "remember who [Biff] was or anything" (104).

Even the choice of words of Linda's and Happy's comments in the scene with Willy seems deliberately to echo their earlier remarks, as if Miller is intentionally undermining their credibility in this scene. And if their reactions are as erroneous as they had been earlier with Oliver, it casts Willy's subsequent suicide into a new light. For it is primarily due to their insistence on Biff's love for his father, not to any explicit comment by his son, that Willy decides to take his own life to provide Biff with insurance money for a fresh start.

If Biff does indeed *not* love his father, Willy's suicide must be regarded as just the last in the series of futile, misguided gestures that made up his life. Biff's awareness of this fact, then, would go far to explain his puzzling tension and bitterness at the Requiem, where he argues sullenly with Happy, Charley, and Linda. For perhaps he realizes that to make plain the sad futility of Willy's act would be to rob the ceremony of what little dignity it possesses. Therefore, he remains virtually silent as the other mourners express their eloquent, if contradictory, judgments on Willy's life, insisting only that his father "had the wrong dreams" and "never knew who he was" (138). If the belief that Biff "loves" Willy is only the final, most tragic false perception in a play permeated by such uncertainty, the son's silence on this critical point is both understandable and justified.

Works Cited

Aarnes, William. "Tragic Form and the Possibility of Meaning in *Death of a Salesman.*" *Arthur Miller's Death of a Salesman: Modern Critical Interpretations.* Ed. Harold Bloom. New York: Chelsea House, 1988. 84-110.

Bigsby, C. W. E. "*Death of a Salesman*: In Memoriam." *Modern Critical Interpretations.* Ed. Harold Bloom. 113-128.

Dukore, Bernard F. *Death of a Salesman and The Crucible.* Atlantic Highlands, N. J.: Humanities Press International, 1989

Hynes, Joseph A. "'Attention Must be Paid . . .'" *Death of a Salesman: Text and Criticism.* Ed. Gerald Weales. New York: Viking, 1967. 280-289.

Miller, Arthur. *Death of a Salesman.* New York: Viking Compass Edition, 1958.

Robert A. Martin (essay date fall 1996)

SOURCE: Martin, Robert A. "The Nature of Tragedy in Arthur Miller's *Death of a Salesman.*" *South Atlantic Review* 61, no. 4 (fall 1996): 97-106.

[*In the following essay, Martin explores the elements of classical tragedy in* Death of a Salesman, *arguing that Willy Loman becomes a tragic figure through "his desire and willingness 'to secure one thing—his sense of personal dignity.'"*]

What the performance of a play gives an audience is less a set of ideas, propositions, or abstractions about life and how to live it than what Arthur Miller has called a "felt experience," the imaginative sharing and participation in the lives and actions of imaginary characters. The performance is mythic; our sensibilities are enlivened by imaginary characters and we become engaged in their conflicts. Our thoughts and emotions are never so detached from theirs that we can remain "objective" in our feelings for them and in our judgments of them. If the play touches our humanity, we weep, or we smile; their movements move us, and our thoughts about them are kindled by our feelings toward them. Thus, we are *most* completely engaged in the play, as in any performing art, as it is being performed within a particular space and time. So it may seem, to a degree, presumptuous or meretricious to discuss those ideas of a play, of which the play touches on, without both the writer and reader having directly and immediately experienced the play itself.

Yet many great plays—especially those written by Arthur Miller—are also plays that engage us directly in social, political, and moral questions, in questions that may be posed early in the plays themselves, and which continue to stimulate and engage us. Significantly, these questions may linger, or stimulate us as an audience to ask other related questions, after we have experienced the play. Not only are our feelings stirred by such drama, our ideas about the lives, the social and personal relationships of the characters and their environments, are stirred as well. So Miller does offer us a way to go back to those familiar or less familiar ideas he presents in his plays—by his near-faultless blending of the social, political, moral, and personal questions presented directly or indirectly through his characters.

Miller's great achievement as a playwright allows us to see and understand particular characters or groups of characters as possessing universal, human traits, even as we also see how their lives illuminate, by association, our own lives as individuals and as members of our larger society. In recognizing these larger concerns, we recognize as well that Miller's plays are not exclusively about individuals, but more precisely, are about humanity and human societies with all their contradictions and complications. As an audience we respond to the pointless death of one salesman; but we also respond as members of a society for whom, not the fact, but the *nature* of Willy Loman's life and death simultaneously diminishes and exalts us.

Willy Loman is not a case study to be argued or defended, but a representative character to be "felt" and "experienced." Still, in *Death of a Salesman,* we feel compelled to ask: "Who Is Willy Loman?" for if we do not understand him and do not know who he is, we can hardly understand his death. We may be moved by

Willy; but we also want to know what our responses are about. We have, in other words, an emotional investment in watching and hearing him with his family. How can we come to understand the nature of this experience? If Willy is a pathetic figure, do we feel this to be true—do we know this is true? Or is Willy a tragic figure? Do we feel this and know it to be true? Finally, we ask ourselves, what does this character's death mean in social terms—does it represent more than the death of one obscure salesman? To answer these questions, we must as audience and witnesses enter into our "felt experience" of Willy's life and death, and also, paradoxically, to view from a distance how his life affects our understanding of ourselves, our society, and our shared values.

For several thousand years, philosophers, those early cogent critics, have pondered the meaning of aesthetic experience. Within the realms of playwriting and the theatre, Aristotle's definition of tragedy, as described in *The Poetics,* continues to inform us of what this "felt experience" involves. According to Aristotle:

> Tragedy, then, is an imitation of an action that is serious, complete, and of a certain magnitude; in language embellished with each kind of artistic ornament, the several kinds being found in separate parts of the play; in the form of action, not of narrative; through pity and fear effecting the proper purgation of those emotions.
>
> (Butcher 61)

In assessing **Death of a Salesman,** some critics have found fault with Miller's intention to portray Willy Loman as a tragic figure. Willy has been criticized for being "too little" or "too common" to meet the supposed requirement of Aristotle, i.e., that tragedy can only affect or be affected by noble beings, who are themselves of a "certain nobility or magnitude." But here, it is necessary to note two important points. First, Aristotle's *Poetics* conceives that the prime quality of tragedy is not character, but plot; and second, that Aristotle's opinion about tragedy is based only on the plays he knew—about what necessarily constitutes tragedy. Other philosophers and thinkers—including Miller—have slightly or strongly disagreed with Aristotle's extended definition. But Aristotle's definition of tragedy has retained more followers than detractors, so it is perfectly understandable that classically-oriented critics might object to Willy's qualifications as a figure of tragedy.

Eric Mottram, for one, in his essay, "Arthur Miller: The Development of a Political Dramatist in America," notes that

> If the plot is not to be simply a mocking of the non-passive man, it must show a real chance of heroism and change. This Miller fails to do.
>
> (33)

He further argues that although Miller allows for the common man, such as Willy Loman, to be the agent, in Miller's words, who "thrusts for freedom" that as a tragic protagonist the

> common man is liable to arouse only pity as a poor fool in terror for his life unless he is allowed an understanding that his revolt is towards ends which have a specific chance of attainment.
>
> (33)

It seems reasonable enough to raise the question, does Willy Loman really have an opportunity to develop as a free human being, or are his actions and choices those that proceed from a pitiful and confused character in an impossible situation that leads inexorably to his self-destruction? In short, is Willy, in Mottram's phrase, "a poor fool"? If Willy lacks the ability to engage the circumstances that create a life of disappointment, and if he must die self-defeated, isn't he really just a pathetic character?

It is clear that Willy's life and suicide are perceived by his wife and sons as full of pathos. Although Willy talks grandly of heroic deeds, of great feats of salesmanship, it is evident to everyone (including Willy himself), that his life-long dream of success is flawed. At the age of 63, he confides, ironically, to his imagined image of brother Ben: "I still feel—kind of temporary about myself" (51). He nevertheless keeps searching for the "secret" of success, and pathetically asks Bernard (who was never "well-liked," but who is now a successful lawyer) to help him understand what it is (93). Even Linda, who maintains that "attention, attention must be finally paid to such a person" (56), and who is Willy's strongest defender, recognizes that Willy is fighting an impossible struggle that has left him talking to himself. After his suicide, she confesses that "I can't understand it"—seemingly confirming her previously unspoken opinion of Willy, that he continued to decline emotionally to the point where he cut himself off from her and her sons forever.

Given Willy's self-deluding dream, his suicide, his constant confusion over the right way to live his life, and how to raise his sons ("Because sometimes I'm afraid that I'm not teaching them the right kind of—Ben how should I teach them?"), and given his wife's opinion of him—of a man of "character" (57) but "not the finest character that ever lived" (56), and given his sons' opinions of him—a failure—how can we possibly see Willy as anything other than, as Eric Mottram describes him, a pathetic, pitiable "poor fool in terror"?

We do, however, see more than a pitiable "poor fool" in Willy. Our "felt experience" of Willy's character includes a sense of his idealism and his will to succeed against all odds. Willy is not merely pitiable. Although

his enthusiasm may outstrip the realities of his situations, it also lets us admire his joy of living. A man who is constantly on the edge of pessimism according to his current sales chart, Willy can repeatedly rebound and fill himself with joy, pride, and optimism for the future of his son Biff. A man both of temperament and sensitivity, Willy can be moved to tears by tears, and can be moved beyond mere self-pity. Realizing that Biff loves him, Willy cries out with vibrant enthusiasm: "that boy—that boy is going to be magnificent!" (133).

Numerous critics have suggested that Willy's inability to understand the reality of his competitive salesman's world marks him as merely a pathetic figure, and determines, in effect, his fate. Such criticism implies that Miller fails to give Willy any chance to grow or to free himself from the siren's song of Madison Avenue. But Willy does act freely, not in destroying himself out of a sense of desperation and self-pity, but in sacrificing what is left of his life to provide a more secure future for Biff. Consequently, the small, common man has gained a kind of noble stature in acting heroically in facing death, and in a manner that few of us would have the courage to display. Willy, pragmatically sees his act as one that will immediately benefit Biff through his insurance policy money, and—despite his fear—he acts out his scenario with a strong and passionate determination.

Whether Willy's suicide is seen as a noble act of self-sacrifice by his family is not the point of this play. Willy acts freely—he does *not* have to kill himself. As Miller suggests in **"Tragedy and the Common Man,"** "the morality that the common man chooses, that distinguishes his choice from merely psychological or sociological considerations, implies first the desire and ability to *act*" (5-6). A failure to act freely—even if that free act is an act of sacrifice—conveys to the audience something more than tragedy. But Willy does act freely—and although he acts unwisely, he nevertheless acts heroically, attempting to find in action a solution that evades him in his speech and imagination.

This, however, does not argue that Willy is not, in some ways, a pathetic character. Perhaps *Death of a Salesman* has the rare quality of presenting its protagonist as both a figure of pathos *and* of heroism. If this is so, then *Death of a Salesman* is Miller's finest achievement—for it appears to artfully represent the modern dilemma specifically and generally within the American dream of materialistic success and failure. While graphically portraying the pattern of pathos in Willy Loman, which in Miller's words, means devising a character who "has fought a battle he could not possibly have won" (**"Tragedy and the Common Man"** 7), Miller also creates a character who "is reaching for a token of immortality, a sign that he lived" (Evans 98), and one who acts heroically on his own terms in trying to provide for his son.

And it is even conceivable that Willy's misplaced optimism, his inheritance from nineteenth-century America, is alone enough to classify him as a tragic figure. For whatever else Willy is in his penultimate moment of sacrifice—he is not pessimistic. In an interview with Phillip Gelb, Miller commented that.

> Willy Loman is seeking for a kind of ecstasy in life which the machine civilization deprives people of. He is looking for his selfhood, for his immortal soul, so to speak.
>
> (198)

It is Willy's capacity to act, to act freely, courageously, and with optimism and even ecstasy, that defines him as more of a tragic, rather than pathetic, figure. Despite our dismay at his suicide, we are nevertheless moved by Willy's desire to provide for Biff and regard him as someone who is not, finally, "in terror for his life" (33).

In "Arthur Miller and the Idea of Modern Tragedy," M. W. Steinberg complains that

> Willy Loman does not gain "size" from the situation; . . . his warped values, the illusions concerning the self he projects, reflect those of his society . . . he goes to his death clinging to his illusions. He is a pathetic figure, yet Miller in his essay written at this time says that there is no place for pathos in real tragedy. Pathos, he remarks, is the mode for the pessimist, suitable for the kind of struggle where a man is obviously doomed from the outset. And earlier in the essay Miller postulated that tragedy must be inherently optimistic. In Miller's view of tragedy and his expression of it in his plays, there seems to be some confusion that needs to be examined.
>
> (86-87)

In *Death of a Salesman* there may be, indeed, a suggestion of a seemingly defeated character who may or may not obtain a pyrrhic victory, or even an immortal "thrust for freedom," which, according to Miller in **"Tragedy and the Common Man,"** "is the quality in tragedy which exalts" (5).

Steinberg is not the only critic to describe Willy's play of memory "inside his head" as that of a victim's. In *American Drama since World War II,* Gerald Weales notes briefly that even at the play's beginning, Willy Loman is "past the point of choice" (7). Again, for Weales and Steinberg, Willy appears as a victim whose fate is already sealed. But if this were so, there could be no dramatic conflict possible in the play.

Clearly, Willy is a tragic, if occasionally self-contradictory, figure. That he acts unwisely in confronting Biff and in relating to his family is obvious. But his motives are well-intentioned as he struggles to achieve a victory over those forces that seem to conspire to keep his sons from achieving his own dreams. Willy

does not die heroically; his tragedy is that he dies blindly and alone. To argue that he does not gain size or stature from his struggle is to ignore the courage required for his sacrifice. But Willy's death serves to underscore the point that the capacity to act is considered more noble and heroic than one's limited capacity to live in harmony with a mechanistic society that eventually destroys by entropy. And although Willy is more than, as Steinberg argues, "a victim of his society"—he is a tragic victim in that he believes it is necessary to sacrifice his life in order to provide for his son. Willy has bought into the American Dream of material success and the ever elusive cult of "personality." Indeed, Willy carries with him a host of negative qualities that by themselves would make him a pathetic figure. His natural talents as a carpenter and builder have found limited outlets. His love of nature, his desire to breathe fresh air are all thwarted in his prison-like brick home in Brooklyn. Worse still, his real identity is obscured and crushed by a job that consumes his life and daily happiness.

As P. P. Sharma notes in "Search for Self-Identity in *Death of a Salesman,*" Willy feels "terribly lonely and insecure," which

> is symbolically brought out in the scene when he accidentally switches on the wire recorder and, panic stricken, shouts for Howard's help. Instead of looking within himself, he looks outside to others.
>
> (77)

As Sharma notes, Biff, unlike Willy, "gradually learns to be himself, instead of staying on as a compulsive victim" (78).

Certainly, added to Willy's shortcomings are his lack of self-knowledge and successful business acumen. As an audience, we laugh at Willy's contradictions, his distorted logic, and cringe at his stubbornness. In addition, he both practices and encourages lying, cheating, stealing, violence, day-dreaming, adultery, slander, and contemptuousness. He is the butt of jokes and feels obliged to crack a salesman "right across the face" for calling him a "fat walrus." Nevertheless and notwithstanding, we feel his pathos, and are both moved by and pity his sense of obligation to Biff. Willy Loman is not merely "insecure" and a "compulsive victim," he is absolute and reveals himself as multi-dimensional. As Miller comments in the Introduction to his **Collected Plays,**

> he [Willy] has achieved a very powerful piece of knowledge, which is that he is loved by his son and has been embraced by him and forgiven.
>
> (147)

In other words, Willy is at this point not merely a lost figure drowning in self-pity and pathos. He is a tragic figure, who attains a modern tragic stature, according to

Miller, by his desire and willingness "to secure one thing—his sense of personal dignity" (4). The knowledge that Biff loves him, despite their past differences, allows Willy to achieve a moral victory, which, for Miller, is the stuff of tragedy. Willy regains a faith in himself, just as we in the audience ponder Miller's own conception, the "belief—optimistic if you will, in the perfectibility of man" (**"Tragedy and the Common Man"** 7). The play might also have been titled *Death of a Father.*

Some critics and scholars, however, disagree with Miller's ideas on what constitutes the tragic condition and continue to view Willy as a misguided dream chaser, a character who foolishly throws his life away on the false promises of Madison Avenue, the power of money, and a desire for some imaginary self-aggrandizement. After the play is over, we may be haunted by Willy's suicide and thereby conclude that it represents an act lacking in "good faith," to borrow Jean Paul Sartre's expression. But what elevates this play to the status of tragedy is not only Willy's self-conscious choice to sacrifice his life, that given the nature of our society, we might also make a similar choice. If we fail to empathize with Willy, it may be as Miller suggests in the foreward to his *Theater Essays of Arthur Miller* that "we have lost the art of tragedy for want of a certain level of self-respect, finally, and are in disgrace with ourselves" (xliii). And, as if to underscore his own concerns in *Death of a Salesman,* in his essay **"The Family in Modern Drama,"** Miller has commented that:

> If, for instance, the struggle in *Death of a Salesman* were simply between father and son for recognition and forgiveness it would diminish in importance. But when it extends itself out of the family circle and into society, it broaches those questions of social status, social honor and recognition, which expand its vision and lift it out of the merely particular toward the fate of the generality of men.
>
> (73-74)

Just as Miller sees the stage as "*the* place for ideas, for philosophies, for the most intense discussions of man's fate," he also believes that we can, by contemplating dramatic tragedies, acquire that same knowledge that the tragic figure acquires "pertaining to the right way of living in the world" (**"The Nature of Tragedy"** 9).

How then do Willy Loman's experiences represent those questions that social plays ask? Is there more to the idea of tragedy than transcends the struggle between father and son for forgiveness and dignity? As an audience, our "felt experience" involves our own empathetic feelings toward and about Willy. While we may intellectually identify with him in his existential situation, we may also imaginatively feel, concerning the larger society, that someone might also be led to take "the easy way out." Not only do we pity Willy and his broken dreams, we also fear for ourselves, either at present or in the future, in which the possibility of gaining money through suicide can become a social reality—the final affirmation in a failed life. This is why Willy reflects a social pattern as well as a personal tragedy.

In his new foreword to the Methuen second edition of *The Theatre Essays,* Miller laments the decline of actors and playwrights in the theater as films and television attract them to a different medium. But he ends his lament by stating:

> Embarrassing as it may be to remind ourselves, the theatre does reflect the spirit of a people, and when it lives up to its potential it may even carry them closer to their aspirations. It is the most vulgar of the arts but it is the simplest too. . . . All you need is a human and a board to stand on and something fascinating for him to say and do. With a few right words, sometimes, he can clarify the minds of thousands, still the whirling compass needle of their souls and point it once more toward the stars. . . . Theatre is not going to die, it is as immortal as our dreaming.
>
> (xix-xx)

The tragedy inherent in *Death of a Salesman* is no longer only an American tragedy. It is part of the universal tragedy of love, grief, despair, and betrayal that today characterizes life in most countries of the world. With "a few right words" Miller has again and again expressed in his plays the thoughts and fears of people everywhere. And occasionally he has even pointed that whirling compass needle of their souls toward the stars.

Works Cited

Aristotle. *The Poetics.* Trans. S. H. Butcher. Introduction by Francis Fergusson. New York: Hill and Wang, 1961.

Corrigan, Robert W., ed. *Arthur Miller: Collection of Critical Essays.* Englewood Cliffs, NJ: Prentice, 1969.

Evans, Richard I. *Psychology and Arthur Miller.* New York: Dutton, 1969. Reprinted in *Conversations with Arthur Miller.* Ed. Matthew C. Roudané. Jackson, MS: UP of Mississippi, 1987, 152-72.

Martin, Robert A., ed. *The Theater Essays of Arthur Miller.* New York: Viking, 1978. Reprinted in Penguin edition, 1979, 1985. All references to Miller's essays are to the Viking/Penguin editions.

———. *The Theatre Essays of Arthur Miller.* 2nd edition. London: Methuen, 1994. Contains a new Foreword by Miller and a revised chronology.

Miller, Arthur. "Author's Foreword: Sorting Things Out" in Martin, xli-xliv.

————. *Death of a Salesman*. New York: Penguin, 1986.

————. "The Family in Modern Drama" in Martin, 69-85.

————. Introduction to *The Collected Plays* in Martin, 113-70.

————. "Mortality and Modern Drama." Interview with Phillip Gelb, in Martin, 195-214. Reprinted in *Conversations with Arthur Miller*. Ed. Matthew C. Roudané. Jackson, MS: UP of Mississippi, 1987, 27-34.

————. "The Nature of Tragedy" in Martin, 8-11.

————. Preface to *An Enemy of the People* in Martin, 16-21.

————. "Tragedy and the Common Man" in Martin, 3-7.

Mottram, Eric. "Arthur Miller: The Development of a Political Dramatist in America" in Corrigan, 23-27.

Sharma, P. P. "Search for Self-Identity in *Death of a Salesman*." *The Literary Criterion* 11:2 (1974), 74-79.

Steinberg, M. W. "Arthur Miller and the Idea of Modern Tragedy" in Corrigan, 81-93.

Weales, Gerald. *American Drama since World War II*. New York: Harcourt, 1962.

Frank Ardolino (essay date 1998)

SOURCE: Ardolino, Frank. "Miller's Poetic Use of Demotic English in *Death of a Salesman*." *Studies in American Jewish Literature* 17 (1998): 120-28.

[*In the following essay, Ardolino examines Miller's use of "demotic" language in* Death of a Salesman *and asserts that Miller heightens the tragic elements of the play "by exploiting the sounds and multiple meanings of simple verbal, visual, and numerical images."*]

The level of language of **Death of a Salesman** has long been a subject of critical discussion. Perhaps because Arthur Miller compared his work to ancient Greek tragedy in which poetic or elevated language was a requirement, early critics responded negatively to Miller's demotic English. T. C. Worsley wrote that the play fails in its "attempt to make a poetic approach to everyday life without using poetry . . ." (225). Similarly, John Gassner noted that the play "is well written but is not sustained by incandescent or memorable language . . ." (232). However, later critics have pointed out that Miller does make use of poetic devices. Arthur K. Oberg commented on his patterned speech, striking images, and artful cliches (73, 74, 77), while Marianne Boruch discussed his use of objects as

metaphors. Finally, Lois Gordon described the entire play as a "narrative poem whose overall purpose can be understood only by consideration of its poetic as well as narrative elements" (98-99).

Miller's poetic use of demotic English, the level of language which characters speak and which describes their actions and environment, creates the play's tragic dimension. To achieve the depths of tragedy, Miller expands the ordinarily limited expressive capabilities of demotic English by exploiting the sounds and multiple meanings of simple verbal, visual, and numerical images. Words for ordinary objects, daily activities, geographical places, and conventional relationships also function as puns and homonyms which recall meanings from other contexts and establish new ones. The resulting verbal patterns and images form an interconnected and multileveled network of associated meanings which exist in two temporal perspectives: chronological time and construct in which meaning echo and mirror each other, creating nightmarish repetition and a sense of stasis. The network of demotic language, which generates these two perspectives, forms an image of Willy's demented psyche and tragic fate. Giles Mitchell points out that Willy suffers from a personality disorder, pathological narcissism, which demands "grandiosity, omnipotence and perfection" (391) rather than normal achievement. Willy's madness is like a fatal flaw, which blinds him to his reality and fills him with arrogance or hubris so that he challenges the limits of his humanity. Then, like an offended god who punishes hubris, Willy's psyche drives him to suicide which he insanely believes will result in his apotheosis. Members of the audience respond with pity and fear to Willy's fate, for the psyche, which is ultimately incomprehensible, is a reality in their own lives and Willy's fate might have been theirs. Moreover, Biff's merciful release from Willy's dreams into normal life does not mitigate this response, for Biff's good fortune underlines the psyche's capriciousness.

1

The play's dominant metaphor is the polyvalent image of time. On the one hand, metaphors for chronological time represent physical reality and normal human development from youth to maturity to old age and from one generation to the next. Linda, Charley, and his son Bernard and Frank Wagner and his son Howard live in harmony with chronological time, a condition which Biff achieves after he experiences a profound psychological change. On the other hand, images of stasis represent personality disorders which afflict Willy, Happy, and Biff.

The play's three-part temporal setting—night, the next day, and the following night—indicates the progression of chronological time. But on another level, the temporal setting is an image of containment and stasis which alludes to the play's primary subject, Willy's imprisonment in neurosis and his consequent death. The nighttime settings, along with Willy's ominous cliches, "I'm tired to the death" (13) and "I slept like a dead one," (71) portend his suicide. Moreover, although the daytime setting during act 2, before Willy goes out for the day, Linda mentions a grace period to him (72). The grace period, the time before their insurance premium is due, also alludes to Willy's beliefs that on this day his employer will give him a non-traveling job and that Biff will get a loan to go into business with Happy. The grace period, however, does not give rise to the fulfillment of Willy's desires, but proves to be a mocking prelude to his death.

Much of the play takes place in a psychological construct which Willy creates. An Eden-like paradise which lies at the center of his neurosis, it is characterized by the paradoxical union of reality and his delusory fulfillment of his grandiose dreams of omnipotence. Willy's paradise is identified with the time in which Biff and Happy were growing up in Brooklyn, when they expressed, reflected, and validated his belief in their virtual divinity. Willy ironically incorporated the human concept of progress and the future, time's movement, into his changeless paradise. He believed that Biff, who was already "divine" as a football player, would become more so as a businessman. However, before Biff realized Willy's projected future, he lost faith in Willy's dreams, left the state of mind or paradise Willy had created, and destroyed its coherence. As a result, Willy moved from the condition of stasis to one characterized by a confusion of the present and his fragmented paradise. Willy never experiences the future which is part of normal chronological time because he recognizes only the hyperbolic future which he believes is latent in his paradise. To his destruction, he seeks to actualize it.

Images which Willy uses to express his beliefs in his and his sons' divine power suggest the opposite, powerlessness, or allude to and echo events which undercut his extravagant claims. Confusing divine omnipotence with his sons' good looks and personalities, Willy compares them to Adonis, and implies that their inherent qualities will make them successful businessmen just as the inherent power of gods allow them to achieve without effort:

> That's why I thank Almighty God you're both built like Adonises. Because the man who makes an appearance in the business world, the man who creates personal interest, is the man who gets ahead. Be liked and you will never want . . .
>
> (33)

Willy points to himself as an exemplar of his beliefs, using his name as a manifestation of his omnipotence.

> You take me for instance. I never have to wait in line to see a buyer. . . . "Willy Loman is here!" That's all they have to know, and I go right through.
>
> (33)

Elaborating on name imagery that echoes his own grandiose self-assessment, Willy expresses his belief in Biff's omnipotence and predicts limitless success for his future in business: "And Ben! When he walks into a business office his name will sound out like a bell and all the doors will open to him!" (86). Name imagery, however, also reveals Willy and Biff's failures. In reality, Willy has been working on commission "like a beginner, an unknown" (57). After he overhears Biff tell Linda and Happy that businessmen have laughed at him for years (61), he pathetically asserts his importance by using names:

> They laugh at me, heh? Go to Fileno's, go to the Hub, go to Slattery's, Boston. Call out the name Willy Loman and see what happens! Big Shot!
>
> (62)

Name imagery also reveals Biff's failure to develop a career. When he attempted to meet with Bill Oliver, a businessman, he waited in Oliver's reception room, and "[k]ept sending [his] name in" (104), but it meant nothing to Oliver, and his door remained closed. Moreover, when announcing a name, ringing a bell, and opening a door constitute the dramatic action, it contrasts Willy's belief in his omnipotence with his base behavior. Upon Biff's arrival at Willy's hotel, he asks the telephone operator to ring his room to announce his arrival; when Biff opens the door to Willy's room, he discovers Willy's adultery.

Willy believes that Biff's success as a high school football player is proof of his divinity. As he talks to Ben about him, he points to Biff who stands silently by them like a divine presence. Biff wears his school sweater, symbolic of his athletic career, carries a suitcase, which alludes to Willy and his job as a traveling salesman and to Biff's projected future as a businessman. Happy, like an attendant to a god, carries Biff's regalia, his shoulder guards, gold helmet, and football pants (86). Willy, who believes that Biff, like his gods, fulfills his adage, "Be liked and you will never want" (33), momentarily turns from Ben to remind Biff of his god-like condition and responsibilities: "And that's why when you get out on that field today it's important. Because thousands of people will be rooting for you and loving you" (86).

This iconic image of Biff, however, also alludes to other incidents which occur in reality and prove Willy's beliefs empty. The suitcase suggests Biff's trip to Boston where he discovers his father's betrayal of him and Linda, and his football uniform, which marks the height of his achievement, also points to his failure to graduate from high school. He dropped out and spent the next seventeen years moving from one marginal job to another.

Football imagery not only separates Biff from Willy, but also connects him with Miss Francis and alludes to Willy's having betrayed him. At the Boston hotel, after Willy attempts to deny his relationship with Miss Francis and tells her to leave his room, she turns to Biff and asks, "Are you football or baseball?" "Football," he replies. "That's me too," she says (119-20).

Gardening and building images are also used to express the madness of Willy's paradisiacal state of mind. Willy points out the bucolic aspects of Brooklyn when it was his paradise:

> This time of year it was lilac and wisteria. And then the peonies would come out, and the daffodils. What fragrance in this room!
>
> (17)

Willy continues to use garden imagery to contrast the satisfaction and joy he took in the past when his paradise was intact with the anger he feels toward the urban present when his paradise is fragmented by the increase in traffic and the number of apartment houses (17). As Willy goes on, however, he unwittingly alludes to himself as the destroyer of his garden and of his family in a metaphorical sense: "Remember those two beautiful elm trees out there? . . . They should've arrested the builder for cutting those down . . ." (17). On one level, the two trees are allusions to the Tree of Life and the Tree of Good and Evil, echoes of Willy's Edenic paradise. On another level, the trees allude to Biff, who uses plant imagery to explain his failure to achieve a career—"I just can't take hold, Mom. I can't take hold of some kind of a life" (54)—and to Happy. The builder whom Willy complains about refers to himself, for he has the skills of a carpenter and rebuilds much of his house: "All the cement, the lumber, the reconstruction I put in this house! There ain't a crack to be found in it any more" (74). Willy's house, however, which is a sound structure as a result of his efforts, is a metaphor for his mind, an air-tight prison which confines him in neurosis. Miller reverses the slang use of the word "crack" as "crazy" to suggest that Willy might have escaped his insanity if his house/mind had had a crack in it to allow help to reach him.

Because of his madness, Willy, who literally rebuilds his house, destroys it in the metaphorical sense of progeny or line of descent.

LINDA:

> Well, it [their house] served its purpose.

WILLY:

> What purpose? . . . If only Biff would take this house, and raise a family. . . .
>
> (74)

Ironically, the metaphorical level of language reveals that Charley, who does not have the skills of a carpenter, has successfully built where Willy has failed. Charley's son Bernard matured in harmony with chronological time. He completed his education, became a lawyer, married and had two children. He met mundane expectations, paradoxically only to exceed them. When Willy meets Bernard in Charley's office, he is about to leave for Washington, D.C. To argue a case in the highest arena in his profession, the Supreme Court. The word "supreme," which recalls the "S" on Biff's high school sweater (28) and Willy's belief that Biff would become a superman, mocks Willy's deluded hope and recalls that seventeen years earlier Biff played in a championship football game at prestigious Ebbets Field, but did not go on to a career of any kind. "His life ended after that Ebbets Field game," confides Willy to Bernard (92). He "laid down and died like a hammer hit him!" (93). Ironically, Willy's reference to a hammer, a tool used to build, points to the fact that he, himself, is Biff's destroyer. The image of the hammer mocks Willy who failed as a father by echoing the insulting statement he made to Charley: "A man who can't handle tools is not a man. You're disgusting" (44). It also mocks Biff's failure to become a professional athlete and alludes to Charley and Bernard's professional success: "Great athlete! Between him and his son Bernard they can't hammer a nail! (51)," says Willy contemptuously. Willy's hammering in his garden at night, a negative image of creation, mirrors his tragic reversal of life and death—his belief that he will achieve the future which his neurosis demands by committing suicide.

Like Willy's garden, his Chevy symbolizes his paradise and the particular satisfaction he takes in the mutually reflective relationship he has with his sons. He associates the Chevy with the abundance of nature: "But it's so beautiful up there, Linda, the trees are so thick, and the sun is warm. I opened the windshield [of the Chevy] and just let the warm air bathe over me" (14). The care his son bestowed upon the Chevy represents their past admiration for each other: "Ts. Remember those days? The way Biff used to simonize that car? The dealer refused to believe there was eighty thousand miles on it" (19). "Simonizing" or "waxing," a pun on Willy's waxing euphoric, alludes to the fullness of emotion he experienced in their relationship.

The Chevy, however, is also associated with the personal and professional failures that the Lomans experience in reality. The car is connected through numbers with the great football career Willy believed that Biff would have as a result of his playing quarterback in a championship game at Ebbets field. In response to his friend Charley's skepticism, Willy yells, "Touchdown! Touchdown! Eighty-thousand people! . . . (90), echoing the eighty thousand miles on the car. And when Willy tried to convince Howard to give him a non-traveling job, Willy recalls the year 1928, the model of the Chevy, as the height of his professional success and acceptance in the business world: "[I]n 1928 I had a big year . . . (82)."

Images of geographical expansiveness further reflect Willy's emotional inflation and the inevitable collapse that results from it. In his description of a business trip, Willy evokes and identifies with the grandeur of New England and its history. However, the names of the cities along his route, which is a metaphor for the downward course of his life, are not only images of aggrandizement but of pain that Willy and Biff suffer after their inflated emotions collapse. Providence, the name of Willy's first stop, is presided over by a mayor whose title suggests an eponymous deity. Rather than providing Willy with care and benevolent guidance, however, the mayor of Providence confers a malign fate on him, as the names of the other places on his route attest. "Waterbury, a big clock city" (31), is an image of time which mocks the Loman's and their dreams of success. Moreover, it is also an allusion to Willy's attempt to commit suicide by driving his car into a river (59). Willy's praise of "Boston, the cradle of the Revolution" (31), presages Biff's disillusionment with Willy from him after finding him in a Boston hotel in an adulterous relationship. Portland is the city Willy is unable to reach because of his mental breakdown. Metaphorically, Portland suggests Willy's failure to achieve "port" or fulfillment that he might have expected during the last years of his career. Along with the word "boat," "Portland" alludes to Willy's insane conviction that his dreams will become reality through suicide. Linda, who pities Willy and understands him as a man who has failings, but not as a neurotic, asks Biff to be "sweet' and "loving" to him "[b]ecause he's only a little boat looking for a harbor" (76). The image becomes horrific just prior to his suicide when he psychologically joins Ben, who acts as a Charon figure to bring him to port in the land of the dead.

BEN:

> Time, William, Time! . . .
>
> (*Looking at his watch*) The boat. We'll be late. (*He moves slowly off into the darkness.*)
>
> (135)

Bangor, the name of the last city on Willy's route, onomatopoetically explodes—"bang!"—echoing imagery of emotional inflation and collapse associated with Willy's paradisiacal past. Years after Biff became disillusioned with Willy, he uses imagery of inflation to blame Willy for his failure to achieve a career: ". . . I never got anywhere because you [Willy] blew me so full of hot air I could never stand taking orders from anybody" (131). And he accuses Happy of being a liar: "You big blow, are you the assistant buyer? You're one of the two assistants to the assistant, aren't you?" (131). The group of three which Biff describes forms a deflated parallel to the one Willy once imagined would create a sensation upon entering the Boston stores—Biff and Happy accompanying him, carrying his sample bags: "Oh, won't that be something! Me comin' into the Boston stores with you boys carryin' my bags" (31). In the light of the Loman's lack of success, the bags, suggestive of wind-bags, reflect, finally, the burden of Willy's meretricious beliefs and the unfounded grandiosity that Biff and Happy bore.

Ultimately, images of inflated emotion and collapse cruelly come together in the word "blow," meaning "to treat" as well as "a violent impact," and in the name of the restaurant, "Frank's Chop House." The name "Frank" recalls Frank Wagner, who has been replaced by his heartless son, and "chop", which literally refers to a cut of meat, also means "a sharp blow." In anticipation of getting a loan to establish a sporting goods business, Biff asks Linda to invite Willy to a celebration at Frank's Chop House: "Tell Dad, we want to blow him to a big meal" (74).

Willy expects to make the dinner a dual triumph. He feels sure that his current employer, Howard Wagner, will give him the non-traveling job that he wants. That evening, however, when the three Loman's meet, Willy announces that Howard fired him, and Biff reluctantly tells Willy that Bill Oliver did not give him the loan. When Biff orders drinks that evening, "Scotch all around. Make it doubles" (105), he unwittingly signifies their dual failures.

2

Hidden in Willy's images of a past paradise is an Eve-like temptress, a personification of his neurosis. This ambiguous character, who is a siren on one level and Miss Francis, the woman with whom Willy commits adultery on another, stands in opposition to Linda who is associated with the diurnal rhythms of chronological time and mundane reality. The strength of Willy and Biff's disordered relationship is tested and broken when Willy introduces Miss Francis to him at the Boston hotel. Willy's adultery is obvious, but Willy wants Biff to deny what he sees and understands:

> [N]ow listen pal, she's just a buyer. . . . Now stop crying and do as I say. I gave you an order. Biff, I gave you an order!
>
> (120)

Biff, however, does not comply. Seventeen years later, the word "order" echoes Willy's loss of power over Biff in a conversation in which Willy and Bernard talk about Biff's failure to make up a high school math course.

BERNARD:

Did you tell him [Biff] not to go to summer school?

WILLY:

Me? I begged him to go. I ordered him to go!

(93)

Mathematics, a metaphor for order in mundane reality, and Mr. Birnbaum, its personification, also reveal the damage that Willy does by taking over Biff's life and preventing him from maturing in chronological time. Biff's age, seventeen, and the four points by which he fails math echo and contrast with Ben's achievement. Ben, Willy's dead brother and his image of an ideal business man, was seventeen when he set out to make his fortune. Four years later, he was rich (48). The repetition of "seventeen" and "four" also contrasts Biff's stasis with Bernard's progress in chronological time. Seventeen years after Biff failed math at the age of seventeen, he has no career, but Bernard has become a lawyer. When Willy congratulates him on his success, he alludes to Biff's failure: "I'm—I'm overjoyed to see how you made the grade, Bernard, overjoyed" (92).

Mathematics and Mr. Birnbaum reveal the meretriciousness of Willy's dream. Mr. Birnbaum rejects Willy's conviction that personal attractiveness is more important that actual achievement and refuses to give Biff the four points he needed to pass, thus motivating his trip to Boston. Birnbaum's name comments on the consequences of the trip for both Biff and Willy. As Karl Harshbarger noted, the first syllable in "Birnbaum" is reminiscent of fire and the second one means "tree" in German (58). The whole name echoes Willy's cry of disaster, "the woods are burning" (41, 107). Willy uses the phrase to signify trouble just before he tells Biff and Happy that he was fired. In the circumstances, it is a double pun. At the hotel, Willy, who knows that Biff is knocking on the door of his room, refuses to open it, but The Woman insists: "Maybe the hotel's on fire!" (116). Her exclamation echoes Willy's locution and alludes to imminent disaster for him—Biff's recognition of his duplicity.

After Biff tells Willy why he came to the hotel, he imitates Mr. Birnbaum as he did for his classmates at school:

. . . I got up at the blackboard and imitated him. I crossed my eyes and talked with a lithp. . . . The thquare root of thixthy twee is . . .

(118)

Biff's crossed eyes, which parody Mr. Birnbaum's eyes, are part of a palimpsest of related images and concepts. Without Biff's realizing it, his eyes allude to the remark that The Woman made to Willy just before his arrival: "You are the saddest, self-centerest soul I ever did see-saw . . ." (116). The word "see-saw" presages Biff's seeing and realizing Willy's having betrayed him and Linda. "See-saw," which joins past and present tenses of "to see," also alludes to Willy's disordered experience of time after Biff breaks the bond of their relationship. Moreover, as the image of a child's toy, a see-saw mockingly contrasts Willy's actual position with his dream of divine success. Contrary to ordinary expectations, Willy holds the same job at the end of his career as he did at the beginning of it—working on commission. The movement of the see-saw—its ups and downs in place—contrasts Howard Wagner's rise in the business world with Willy's stasis. At the age of 36, the transposition of Willy's age and the number of years that Willy worked for the Wagners (56), Howard is the head of the company and Willy's superior. Finally, Howard's position contrasts his father Frank's success with Willy's failure. Frank passed on his company to Howard, but Willy has nothing to give his sons.

The math problem, the "thquare root of thixthy twee," is a coded message which reveals Willy's insanity and Biff's participation in it, but they do not recognize its significance. The number "63," Willy's age, identifies him as the focus of the problem. The word "square," an image of an enclosed area, and "root," a plant image, refer to Willy's paradisiacal garden, the two trees representing Biff and Happy which grew there, and the condition of his mind which is imprisoned in insanity, the root of his and his family's problem. Ironically, when Biff concludes his imitation by saying that Birnbaum walked in, drawn by Willy and Biff's laughter, The Woman, whose entrance parallels Mr. Birnbaum's, leaves the bathroom, her hiding place, and enters Willy's room. Biff's eyes are no longer "crossed" and he finally sees who Willy is.

Stocking imagery further unites Willy, The Woman/ Miss Francis, and Linda and Biff in a cycle of betrayal and its recognition. Stockings refer to the nylons Willy gives to Miss Francis, the stock that he sells as a salesman, his status with Biff, and the Loman familial line. During one of Willy's hallucinations, Linda "darns stockings" (36) prior to The Woman's appearance and "mends a pair of her silk stockings" (39) just after her disappearance. When Willy sees Linda at her work, his reaction is intense, for her stockings recall his adultery: "I won't have you mending stockings in this house! Now throw them out! (39). Willy gives stockings to The Woman in exchange for her favors. "And thanks for the stockings, she says to him. "I love a lot of stockings" (39). When Biff surprises Willy and The Woman in his hotel room, she insists on her gift even while

Willy desperately tries to get rid of her: "You had two boxes of size nine sheers for me, and I want them!" (119). Betrayers and the betrayed come together in a "stocking" image when Biff poignantly recognizes Willy's adultery and rejects him: "You—you gave her Mama's stockings!" (121).

"Sheers," the word that Miss Francis uses to refer to silk stockings, also is a pun for "scissors" and suggests cutting, which in turn alludes to Biff's metaphorically cutting the tie that has bound him to Willy. After Biff arrives at home, he burns his sneakers on which he had printed "University of Virginia" (33-34), an act which echoes Willy's utterance of disaster. The act also alludes to the story of Adam and Eve's expulsion from the Garden of Eden for it symbolizes Biff's change from innocence to knowledge, his rejection of Willy's beliefs, and his departure from Willy's paradise. Seventeen years later, at Frank's Chop House, Biff "takes the rolled up hose from his pocket . . ." (115) and shows it to Happy. Another synonym for stocking, the hose is the means by which Willy planned to commit suicide.

Biff's attempt to get the loan from Oliver has not resulted in the recreation of the Loman's mutually reflective relationship, but in Biff's freedom from Willy's domination and movement to psychological health. Earlier images which Willy used to express his vision of Biff's omnipotence—his name's sounding like a bell and opening all doors to him (86)—are echoed in Biff's unwilled insight and ironically compare the experience to the mysteriousness of divine intervention. After Oliver refuses to talk with him, Biff psychologically awakens as if he hears the sound of a bell. For no explainable reason, Biff suddenly realizes the value of his ordinary human life and accepts his identity or name which opens the door to the possibility of his living normally in chronological time.

As a result of Biff's revelation, he and Willy engage in an agon at the Chop House. Biff tries to make Willy see and accept him as an individual, but Willy struggles to return Biff to his former identity as his alter ego. At this point, Willy vacillates between reality and the hallucination of the past when Biff knocked at the door of Willy's hotel room in Boston. In reality, at the restaurant Biff makes a joke of the blow Willy dealt him and offers him acceptance and forgiveness, an act which would have been impossible for him before his revelation. However, Willy, who is about to accept Biff's invitation, turns away from his and responds to The Woman, who pulls him back into the hallucination and asks him to open the hotel room door. An image of guilt and forgiveness, imprisonment and release, the door suggests Willy's betrayal of Linda and Biff and Biff's psychological release from him and his forgiving him. The washroom in Frank's Chop House, which is conflated with the bathroom where the Woman hid, also evokes Linda's washing clothes (33, 47, 85) and her forgiving Willy.

However, Linda's selfless devotion and Biff's filial love are not strong enough to free Willy from his neurosis. Willy does not relinquish his insane dream even after Biff begs him to give it up. Willy imagines that his death will be the means of his and Biff's long-awaited apotheosis as business gods like Ben and Dave Singleman.

Willy's last utterances refer or allude to images of his and Biff's deification and to his own insanity. With great enthusiasm, he asks Ben, "Can you imagine that magnificence [Biff] with twenty thousand dollars in his pocket?" (135). Willy's reference to his life insurance policy echoes Charley's description of J. P. Morgan: "Why must everybody like you? Who liked J. P. Morgan? Was he impressive? In a Turkish bath he'd look like a butcher. But with his pockets on he was very well-liked" (97). Willy carries out his plan to literally put money into Biff's pockets in the demented belief that he will become the equivalent of his gods, businessmen like J. P. Morgan.

Willy completes his vision of the future by translating Biff's love to worship, thus achieving divinity like Dave's in Biff's eyes, and by identifying with Biff whom he believes will become as successful as Ben: "[H]e'll worship me for it!. . . . Oh Ben, I always knew one way or another we were gonna make it, Biff and I!" (135). Finally, Willy sees himself as becoming the embodiment of all success and all time—the eternal in death and the dynamic with Biff in life.

In summary, the imagery which we have discussed, while not exhaustive, exemplifies Miller's poetic use of demotic language. Through his system of associated meanings and dual temporal schemes, Miller infuse the commonplace with tragic significance which mirrors Willy's madness and fate.

Works Cited

Boruch, Marianne. "Miller and Things." *Literary Review* 24.4 (1981): 548-61

Gassner, John. "*Death of a Salesman*: First Impressions, 1949." In Weales. 231-39.

Gordon, Lois. "*Death of a Salesman*: An Appreciation." In Koon. 98-108.

Harshbarger, Karl. *The Burning Jungle: An Analysis of Arthur Miller's Death of a Salesman.* Washington, D. C.: University Press of America, 1979.

Koon, Helene, ed. *Twentieth Century Interpretations of Death of a Salesman.* Princeton, New Jersey: Princeton University Press, 1983.

Miller, Arthur. *Death of a Salesman: Certain Private Conversations in Two Acts and a Requiem.* New York: Penguin, 1949.

Mitchell, Giles. "Living and Dying for the Ideal: A Study of Willy Loman's Narcissism." *The Psychoanalytic Review* 77:3 (Fall 1990): 391-407.

Oberg, Arthur. "*Death of a Salesman* and Arthur Miller's Search for Style." In Weales. 70-78.

Weales, Gerald, ed. *Death of a Salesman: Text and Criticism.* New York: Penguin Books, 1967.

Worsley, T. C. "Poetry without Words." In Weales. 224-27.

Jonathan Witt (essay date June 1998)

SOURCE: Witt, Jonathan. "Song of the Unsung Antihero: How Arthur Miller's *Death of a Salesman* Flatters Us." *Literature & Theology* 12, no. 2 (June 1998): 205-16.

[*In the following essay, Witt investigates the emotional effect that the character of Willy Loman has on theatergoers of* Death of a Salesman, *noting that Loman's conflicting obscurity and fame make him appealing to a wide range of audiences.*]

Many nineteenth and twentieth century writers seek to convey the experience of a lowly character chafing against his obscurity. But how can an author convey such an experience when the very attention of a readership confers upon the character social significance and dignity, even fame? Exactly how obscure can Jude be when he has a four hundred page novel written about him, and written by Thomas Hardy no less? This is a problem I call the audience's paradox, a special form of the observer's paradox. In essence, the audience's paradox is the tension created when a lowly character, chafing against his obscurity, serves as the protagonist of a work of literature and so becomes the centre of the audience's attention, becomes famous.

The paradox is endemic only to post-Enlightenment tragic literature. Pride stands as a pivotal human imperfection in both the Ancient Greek and Judeo-Christian traditions; in contrast, the metaphysics of a debased form of romanticism valorizes pride, both hubris and narcissism, while denigrating humility. In America, the roots of this tendency can be seen at least as early as Walt Whitman. The title of his 'Song of Myself' signals a poem unblushing in its swelling praise of the poem's speaker, and even if we insist that the speaker is not Whitman the man but a cosmic Whitman joined to all humanity by a boundless love, the contempt for humility evinced by the poem is hard to ignore.

Narcissism, in another form, also rears its head in the dark romanticism of Edgar Allen Poe. In both his poetry and his short stories we repeatedly encounter personas who seek narcissistic fulfilment in child brides, a romantic tendency critiqued with savage clarity in Vladimir Nabokov's *Lolita*. And on the other side of the Atlantic, Percy Bysshe Shelley already had created a poetry of unparalleled humourlessness, the need for comic deflation crowded out by the poet's swelling humanism.

But in the next century modern American tragedy would do even more to valorize pride at the expense of humility. Indeed, such literature reinforces the audience's own pride by way of flattery—both by implying in various ways that the audience is superior to the flawed protagonists and, paradoxically, by causing the audience to identify with an artificially elevated protagonist.

Arthur Miller's **Death of a Salesman** starkly illustrates this process, and his stated poetic illuminates for us why this is the case, though we need to distinguish his stated poetic from the poetic actually evidenced in his tragedies. If in creating his greatest drama, Miller actually had followed the advice he offers in **'Tragedy and the Common Man,'** we long ago would have consigned **Death of a Salesman** to the second echelon of American theatre. Fortunately, the sterile poetic we find in **'Tragedy'** merely infects the drama; it does not govern it.

In that oft-reprinted 1949 essay, Miller tells us 'the tragic feeling is evoked in us when we are in the presence of a character who is ready to lay down his life, if need be, to secure . . . his sense of personal dignity'. So far, Miller's poetic seems in harmony with the history of tragedy. And it continues to seem so when he adds, 'From Orestes to Hamlet, Medea to Macbeth, the underlying struggle is that of the individual attempting to gain his "rightful" position in his society.'[1] Do the quotation marks around *rightful* constitute censure of the hero's attitude, or are they an effort to pass on to the reader the attitude of the tragic hero free of Miller's opinion? The ambiguity that Miller adroitly creates here strikes to the heart of tragedy.

Did Oedipus, through his hubris, deserve, even hasten his downfall? Or was he simply a noble man unjustly crushed by amoral fate? Which is the more precise characterization of Oedipus: 'he *commits* a tragic *error*,' or 'he *possesses* a tragic *flaw*'? How should we translate Aristotle's term *hamartia*? Or more to the point, how should we read Sophocles? If we see in Oedipus's tragic flaw an ingrained sin rather than merely an error or a misstep, are we reading into Sophocles' ancient Greek *Weltanschauung* a Renaissance and Christian view of the world? I find the debate invigorating, and yet to insist on an either/or is to miss an ambiguity inherent to tragedy. Oedipus sums up the ambiguity well when the chorus-leader asks him what god incited him to blind himself; Oedipus replies:

> It was Apollo, friends, Apollo.
> He decreed that I should suffer what I suffer;
> But the hand that struck, alas! was my own,
> And not another's.[2]

The ambiguity is deepened rather than rejected by Shakespeare, who needed to reach no further than his own religious tradition for the paradox of man as both free and predestined, simultaneously guilty of choosing sin and doomed to sin by original sin. This paradox resonates through his major tragedies, works in which omen and error, vanity and plain bad luck combine to annihilate the protagonists.

Miller, sensitive to the fate/freedom tension in the great tragedies, is committed to walking the fine line between a facile individualism and a facile fatalism. But then he steps off that line, arguing instead for a definition of tragedy akin to its debased, journalistic meaning, as when a news anchor speaks of a woman *tragically* killed by a drunk driver. This shift is easy to miss. 'The wound from which the inevitable events spiral is the wound of indignity,' Miller writes, 'and its dominant force is indignation. Tragedy, then, is the consequence of a man's total compulsion to evaluate himself justly.'[3] Here, I first took Miller to mean that the tragic hero, for all his pride, ruthlessly searches out the truth about himself, even if it means facing some monstrous ugliness in himself—patricide (Oedipus), incest (Oedipus), vanity (Oedipus, Lear, Macbeth), murderous ambition (Macbeth).

But Miller's subsequent elaboration precludes such an interpretation. He goes on to write that the hero's flaw 'is really nothing—and need be nothing, but his inherent unwillingness to remain passive in the face of what he conceives to be a challenge to his dignity, his image of his rightful status'. Having neutralized the flaw, Miller goes on to exalt it as that quality separating the hero from the common man: 'Only the passive, only those who accept their lot without active retaliation, are "flawless". Most of us are in that category.' When Miller has finished defining it, that category, although supposedly flawless, seems a pretty pathetic place to be. The other category, the category of the flawed but active hero, clearly seems preferable. There the tragic hero battles a world bent on degrading him, and in so doing forces the torpid masses to examine 'everything we have accepted out of fear or insensitivity or ignorance'.[4]

Willy Loman as Prometheus. The world as jealous god.

Or, as Miller explains, 'The tragic hero's destruction in the attempt to evaluate himself justly posits a wrong or an evil in his environment.'[5] Thus, Willy Loman's at-

tempt to reject Biff's view of both of them as 'a dime-a-dozen' is not vanity or egotism, but rather the salesman's noble effort to secure his dignity, his nobility. In other words, it is noble to believe that one is noble. To believe that one is better than others is to be better than others. Vanity is the greatest virtue, humility the greatest sin.

To be humble means, etymologically, to be close to the ground, a condition that Anthony Bloom describes as 'silent and accepting . . . transforming corruption itself into a power of life and a new possibility of creativeness',[6] or what Mikhail Bakhtin could have been speaking of when he described 'the reproductive lower stratum'[7] found in the comedy of grotesque realism. But in Willy Loman's mind being humble, being close to the earth, means being a human doormat for a universe bent on wiping its feet on him, bent on robbing him of his rightful status.

Thankfully, Miller's most famous drama offers us a vision of human pride more complex than a strict adherence to his stated poetic would have allowed. If *Death* prompts us to admire Willy's tenacity, however misdirected, it also forces us to see how his dubious notion of personal dignity, his narrow dedication to being well-liked, has made him grotesque. Such a reading has from the first been well attested to by critics, but a brief analysis of the precise nature of Willy's conception of personal dignity will explain the play's fundamental weakness more probingly than does the conventional wisdom on this matter, which holds that Willy's foolishness robs him of that air of personal dignity fundamental to the great tragic heroes of our tradition.

Christopher Lasch, in *The Culture of Narcissism,* describes 'a way of life that is dying—the culture of competitive individualism, which in its decadence has carried the logic of individualism to the extreme of a war of all against all, the pursuit of happiness to the dead end of a narcissistic preoccupation with the self'.[8] It is in such a world that Willy struggles for both success and love, goals that under the rubric of Willy's personal philosophy are at times synonymous, at times mutually inimical.

Willy's confusion, though by no means unique to our age, is a characteristically modern one. Jürgen Habermas might have been describing Willy Loman and his situation when he spoke on the subject of modernity. Habermas writes that the modernist understands that seemingly settled modes of life often turn out to be mere unstable conventions without rational foundation. Consequently, modern man dares not base his self image on the particular roles and norms he presently fills and fulfils. Instead, he seeks to establish it upon 'the abstract ability to present himself credibly in any situation as someone who can satisfy the requirements of consistency even in the face of incompatible role expectations and in the passage through a sequence of contradictory periods of life'. In short, ego identity supplants role identity.[9] This is Willy Loman in a nutshell. Confused about what direction he should take, early in his adult life he retreated behind the hope that if he could cultivate an impressive manner, he would never want for admiration or material success, regardless of the direction he took.

But the play forcefully dramatizes the distasteful and ultimately unsuccessful result of such a narcissistic tack. When the family discusses Biff's idea to ask his old boss for a loan, Willy repeatedly interrupts his wife and then viciously castigates her for interjecting enthusiastic support for Willy's position, even though she does so at perfectly appropriate moments. Are we to admire Willy's behaviour here, view it as another example of 'his inherent unwillingness to remain passive in the face of what he conceives to be a challenge to his dignity, his image of his rightful status'?[10]

Or consider an earlier scene when Willy, unable to keep his mind on his driving, has returned home prematurely from a sales trip. Here, when he's not shouting at his family, he's conversing enthusiastically with the ghosts of his past. His next door neighbour Charley comes over to see what the racket is all about and lulls Willy into a card game to calm him down

WILLY:

Did you see the ceiling I put up in the living-room?

CHARLEY:

Yeah, that's a piece of work. To put up a ceiling is a mystery to me. How do you do it?

WILLY:

What's the difference?

CHARLEY:

Well, talk about it.

WILLY:

You gonna put up a ceiling?

CHARLEY:

How could I put up a ceiling?

WILLY:

Then what the hell are you bothering me for?

CHARLEY:

You're insulted again.

WILLY:

A man who can't handle tools is not a man. You're disgusting.[11]

Here, as when he repeatedly cuts off his well-meaning wife during his conversations with Biff, Willy is fighting for what he conceives to be his rightful status, fighting, as Happy phrases it at the funeral, 'to be number-one man'.[12] But in his treatment of his wife and Charley we see the ugly, inhuman behaviour to which this personal philosophy leads. This little man is the king of his castle, and he tears down his wife to prove it. He senses that Charley is the better man—the better businessman and the better father—so he ruthlessly belittles him.

For Willy to be happy, 'attention must be paid' as Linda puts it in making a different but not unrelated point. He and his son Biff must not merely be liked, but be 'well-liked'—admired by a throng of cheering fans, so to speak—and not because they earned it, but because 'I am Willy Loman, and you are Biff Loman!'.[13] This philosophy seems warm and humane beside Charley's belief that 'the only thing you got in this world is what you can sell';[14] but the problem with it is that in the economy of attentiveness, demand for attention inevitably outstrips supply. If being well-liked means having a throng of adoring fans, à la Biff when he was captain of the football team, then precious few people will be able to achieve this. For every number-one man, there are many who must settle for sitting in the stands and cheering. When few do settle for the job of cheering for Willy Loman, life for this failed drummer becomes a game of king of the hill in which rather than climbing mountains he climbs sand piles and beats down every one else, if not in fact, then in his imagination.

And so Willy, having failed to succeed through an impressive manner, pretends that he is well liked, that he is the king of his castle, that his carpentry skills place him on a higher plateau than Charley, that his sexual conquest of *The Woman* makes him more of a man. Biff tries and fails to make his father face reality, but only Biff realizes that the phallic pen of egotism, which he clutches at in Oliver's office, is worthless. Only he comes to understand that the pursuit of egotism is as absurd, as irrational, as the theft of the pen itself. Willy Loman's personal philosophy—like the Hastings refrigerator that had 'the biggest ads of any of them!'— just doesn't work. If Arthur Miller the critic misses this point, Arthur Miller the dramatist does not.

And yet the form of Miller's drama suggests that something of Miller the critic did indeed infect Miller the dramatist. Although **Death** forcefully censures the very narcissism Miller applauds in **'Tragedy and the Common Man',** the play nevertheless flatters its audiences. It manages this in two ways.

The more obvious way becomes most apparent in the play's climax. During the course of the play I come to sympathize with Willy Loman, despite his lack of wisdom. But, to paraphrase Sylvan Barnet, Morton Berman, and William Burto's argument, because Willy Loman appears even more foolish than usual in his 'exaltation', it is more difficult for us to identify with him in his death than with a royal figure such as Lear.[15] When Willy exclaims, 'Can you imagine [Biff's] magnificence with twenty thousand dollars in his pocket?' and 'When the mail comes he'll be ahead of Bernard again!',[16] we are effectively protected from participating in his death. His glaring foolishness at the play's climax kills my identification with him precisely when identification is most essential.

There is a similar foolishness in Lear, but it comes early. At the moment of his death we are in sympathy with this wiser, better Lear and so can participate in his ultimate humiliation, death. Miller employs the tragic form to gain some measure of sympathy for his common man, but then he politely shields us from that deepest of poverties, that greatest of indignities, death.

In a less extreme form we have in **Death** the same technique that makes the formulaic horror movie ultimately so reassuring. In such movies, all but one or two characters are obviously victims, idiots who insist on backing into dusty, cobwebbed rooms while a heavy-handed score positively shouts warning. While these obvious victims are dropping like flies, the audience is encouraged to identify principally with the common-sensical hero who is marked from the beginning as a survivor.

Happily, Miller rejects this emotional gimmick through the bulk of the play, drawing us into the foolish Willy Loman's psyche through a variety of experimental techniques and through the ardour of Willy's pursuit of what *The Great Gatsby*'s Nick Carraway called 'the green light, the orgiastic future that year by year recedes before us'.[17] But Miller's brand of humanism finds no value in slaying either the protagonist's or the audience's ego as do the great Classic and Renaissance tragedies. Rather, Miller's humanism values giving man 'his whole due as a personality';[18] and so it values reinforcing the audience's 'sense of personal dignity'.[19] Consequently, Miller chooses not to press Willy into a complete recognition of his littleness and, more significantly, chooses not to press the audience into an identification with a protagonist in his ultimate confrontation with his littleness.

How different this modern-romantic attitude is from that attitude evinced in the great tragedies of Sophocles and Shakespeare. In her essay 'Tragedy and Self Sufficiency', Martha Nussbaum explains that the Athenian valued pity as evidence of a non-hubristic disposition, as acknowledging 'true facts about one's own possibilities'.[20] When audiences feel this pity, they draw near to the sufferer and acknowledge that some-

thing akin to the hero's suffering could happen to them, that both hero and audience live in a world of tragic reversals 'in which the difference between pitier and pitied is a matter far more of luck than of deliberate action'.[21] From such a view fear arises: 'If this happened to the hero, it could happen to anybody,' the pitier reasons. 'And if it could happen to anybody, it could happen to me.' Aristotle went so far as to argue that pity, by definition, demands that the pitier witness in the pitied a pain 'which one may himself expect to endure, or that someone connected with him will'.[22]

The pity evoked in most modern tragedy fails to ruffle us in this way because we can reason that our greater wisdom protects us from the sort of tragedy which befalls a foolish person like Willy Loman. But hardly any such comfort existed for the Athenian who witnessed the fall of Oedipus. Even if our hypothetical Athenian views Oedipus as rash, he sees that fault in a character who is admirable in all other important respects. The doomed king is courageous, honest, intelligent, strong, sympathetic to the plight of his citizens, skillful in combat, in virtually every respect a model man and king. Perhaps Oedipus's rashness is partially to blame for his tragedy, but who is perfect? If fate can trip up and trample under foot such a fine, strong individual, it certainly can trip up and trample an average one.

Shakespeare's great tragedies evoke in me a similar response. Even that murderous usurper, Macbeth, elicits from me a certain measure of Aristotle's brand of pity, for because of Macbeth's many noble qualities I am less tempted than I might be to pity Macbeth condescendingly. In his study of villain-heroes in Elizabethan drama, Clarence Valentine Boyer underscores the fact that Macbeth possesses a highly sensitive nature and a poetic imagination, which together make him capable of extraordinarily deep feeling and cause him to suffer more intensely than anyone else in the play. Not only this, but Macbeth demonstrates extraordinary courage, aspires to extraordinary accomplishments, and both loves deeply and is deeply loved.[23]

Thus, despite his villainy in violently usurping the throne of a good king, we pity Macbeth in his agonizing internal struggle, pity a man who is highly suited to reign but who can reign only through crime, a tragic situation.[24] Finally, we are further spurred to Aristotelian pity by the play's supernatural aura, which, as Boyer puts it, produces 'in us a feeling that there are strange mysterious forces in nature tending to evil, which sweep a man away with them to his destruction once he exposes himself to their power'.[25]

Instead of cultivating and deepening our sense of Aristotelian pity for his protagonist, Miller, in contrast, alienates us from Willy and transfers the recognition to Biff, whose greatest humiliation—the scene in which he waits in Oliver's office for six hours only to find that Oliver, when he arrives, does not even recognize him[26]—appears offstage, preventing me from internalizing Biff's dime-a-dozen status as Biff does. What's more, having been abandoned by the original protagonist, at the conclusion of the play I am tempted to seize upon Biff as a surrogate hero. He possesses a nobility of spirit, a courage in the face of cold reality, that makes him genuinely admirable. But Biff's nobility is not the nobility we feel in an Oedipus gouging out his eyes, in a Macbeth recoiling from his spiritual poverty, or in a Lear weeping himself to death. It is the relatively static nobility of a Tiresias, an Edgar, persons who strike us as basically good from the first, as the salt of the earth. We have experienced no fall and redemption, no death, burial, and resurrection. We have received redemption on the cheap, our facile dignity, typical of the pre-fallen tragic hero, neatly intact.

But *Death of a Salesman* flatters its audience by another, more subtle means, a means that has been overlooked. Earlier I referred to the Hastings refrigerator that Willy bought because it had the biggest ads, and credited Miller with critiquing the personal philosophy that lay behind such a foolish method of choosing a major appliance. Ironically, though, Miller himself has created a very big ad for the dysfunctional Willy Loman and its effect is not altogether unlike the effect of the Hastings refrigerator ad on Willy Loman. For Miller manages to create an audience for a man who does nothing to earn an audience beyond monumentally fouling up his life, manages to make us pay attention to a man we might otherwise have ignored, impresses us with the life of a relatively unimpressive man—in short, gives Willy Loman 'the biggest ads of any of them.' In effect, *Death* brings to the failed salesman's funeral not the handful of kith and kin that his life warranted, but thousands upon thousands of mourners, outdoing even the funeral of the eighty-four year-old salesman Willy so admired. Certainly, the fumbling tenacity with which Willy follows his misguided philosophy ennobles him to a degree, but are we actually ready to insist that this characteristic alone elevates him to a level consistent with his fame?

So here is where we stand: Within the fiction of *Death* we meet Willy Loman, a low man on the totem pole chafing against his obscurity, a man discarded by the sales company for whom he has worked for thirty-five years not because he is loathed but because he is useless. Willy Loman, a man whose highest aspiration in life is to be well-liked, is not even well disliked. He achieves only the status of nuisance. In sum, Willy Loman belongs to that group referred to by Flannery O'Connor's Mrs McIntyre as 'all the extra people in the world'.[27] And even when Loman recognizes his status as an extra person, and takes that most drastic of measures to remedy the situation, he fails. He fails to

impress his son and, we can assume, fails even to make his suicide appear an accident and so garner the $20,000 that supposedly will launch his alter ego, Biff, into a successful business career.

But viewed from the outside, as a character in a play, Willy Loman is not an extra. He is the leading man, the protagonist, the tragic hero, a character who looms large in the audience's imagination. Consequently, his position as dramatic centre tends to misshape our identification with him, a phenomenon overlooked by Miller in his bracing but at times facile attack on the Aristotelian notion that tragic heroes are necessarily persons of rank and importance.

When I insist that a lowly character's position as dramatic centre tends to misshape my identification with that character, some readers will skip over my explicit contention and quarrel with what they perceive as my unstated assumptions, that a work should encourage an audience to identify with its protagonist, or that an audience should strive to achieve such an identification. If, as some advise, I cultivate a rigorous aesthetic distance throughout an engagement, the analytical part of my brain assiduously churning away in Brechtian fashion, the empathetic part remaining dutifully inert, I hardly identify at all. I say 'hardly' because even in a work committed to minimizing identification, such as Brecht's *The Good Woman of Setzuan,* it must prod its audience into some degree of identification before it can alienate them, must draw them in before it can distance them. If one has felt, even briefly, any empathy for the good woman of Setzuan, then one has identified with her.

Or, if I follow an older conventional wisdom and surrender my awareness of the work as a formed object, as a fiction, I become absorbed into the life of the protagonist. But there exists a third alternative to which I suspect most serious auditors aspire. Under this alternative, the reader or viewer, together with Coleridge's ideal poet, brings his or her whole soul into activity,[28] energetically joining the author in the creative process, shuttling between intuition and logic, feeling and thought, empathy and critique, identification and analysis.

But whether critics are advocating a primarily logical, intuitive, or critically imaginative approach to literary engagement, nothing in us, so the unstated assumption goes, need prevent our imaginations from translating the protagonist of dramatic theatre (as opposed to epic or absurdist theatre) off page or stage and into the mind—or recreating him, at least—and then identifying with him.

I disagree.

As we observe Willy Loman playing out his tragedy or, to take other examples, as we follow Rodion Raskolnikov's fall and redemption, or Stephen Dedalus's search for a calling that will exalt him to the sun, or Jude Fawley's struggle against loneliness and obscurity, or Blanche DuBois's search for love and dignity, at some level we are aware of these figures as the centres of their respective worlds, as the focal points of audiences hanging on their every available thought and action. Thus, even when I disappear into a character as small and lowly as Willy Loman, I participate in the romance of the stage. I am caught up in the audience's paradox. Although I feel Willy's obscurity, his insignificance, his failures, these qualities have been transfigured by his role as protagonist. You see, although lowly Willy Loman is oblivious to his status as dramatic centre, I cannot be, am not oblivious to it even in those moments when, slack-jawed, like a boy become his action hero, my identification with him occurs effortlessly.

As Willy Loman, I lead a double life and, in so doing, create a second Willy Loman. I am a second-rate travelling salesman struggling to maintain my dignity. I also am a self among other selves identifying with Willy Loman. The collective imagination of the audience has joined itself to the life playing itself out on the stage. But like a quanta of light fired into the theatre of the subatomic, that collective identification has altered the thing observed.

And here, I speak not of the alterations that inevitably occur when a story moves from author to auditor. Rather, I mean that transformation which only an audience—or better still, an audience among audiences stretched across time—can generate.

Willy Loman is obscure.

Willy Loman is famous.

My mind, the whole of it, right and left, conscious and unconscious, is stuck with the paradox of these opposing realities, two realities inextricably mingled. Certainly, we may posit a Willy Loman who exists in some hypothetical realm as a thoroughly unrenowned failure, stripped of the egotist's supreme fantasy of a rapt audience unto eternity. But that Willy Loman remains stubbornly hypothetical, permanently unknowable, for if we the audience come to know him, he is no longer obscure. Our Willy Loman, for all his failures, for all his obscurity within the world of the fiction, remains to patrons of American theatre a household name.

It would be easy enough to argue that this tension enriches the drama, that Miller, through the magic of the stage, has redeemed life from its stubborn shabbiness. Within the scope of American literature, the work

is canonical. But the work misses entry into the canon of the ages, seems out of place beside such tragedies as *Oedipus, Lear, Hamlet.* This is hardly to damn the work. But under the pressures of that pseudo-democratic spirit which takes the phrase 'all men are created equal' as a refutation of the traditional concept of nobility, Miller's drama participates in that seamier work of Lasch's capitalism, providing not only life and liberty but narcissistic escape for all, even for the common man. For protagonist and audience alike, the movement is away from the ground of reality, a movement that can be compared illuminatingly to the notion of evil propounded by St Basil, and further developed by Augustine, Boethius and Thomas Aquinas—as a movement toward darkness, toward negation.[29] As noted, the modern root of the glorification of such a rebellious impulse can be traced to romanticism.

I do not mean to imply that the movement that began in Germany and moved into the literature of our language principally through Wordsworth and Coleridge is without merit. But like any set of ideas and attitudes, it was and is vulnerable to corruption through excess. Thus, while Goethe gives us glorious Faust and while Whitman gives us an all-embracing cosmic self, modern Americans writers give us *Of Mice and Men*'s Lennie and *Streetcar*'s Blanche DuBois—give us, to put it crudely, idiots and lunatics. If Goethe and Whitman privilege boldness and creativity over humility, realism, and consistency, the heirs of O'Neill and Fitzgerald romanticize narcissism, solipsism, and psychosis even while dramatizing their tragic consequences.

That second generation romantic, Percy Bysshe Shelley, in a long tradition of moral philosophers, insists that love is the secret to living morally, or as Shelley puts it, 'A man, to be greatly good, must imagine intensely and comprehensively; he must put himself in the place of another and of many others; the pains and pleasures of his species must become his own.' He then goes beyond this to declare that literature, far from serving to demoralize, exercises this crucial empathetic faculty.[30] Now, whereas we may agree with Shelley that literature can exercise our powers of empathy, we still can ask how well a particular work actually succeeds in doing this. As for *Death of a Salesman,* how well does its well-attended Willy Loman enlarge our powers of empathy for anyone of flesh and blood? What I have been arguing suggests that our identification with this protagonist does not benefit us as much as it initially might seem. There is a human type, however individuated its members, the beaten and obscure casualty of the rat race, shattered by failure, whom we may encounter again and again in the world beyond page and stage. But we have not been given such a figure in *Death of a Salesman.* Instead, we have been given a synthetic figure sprung from the audience's paradox, an obscure loser paradoxically famous.

Notes

1. A. Miller, 'Tragedy and the Common Man', in *Types of Drama,* sixth edn, eds, S. Barnet, M. Berman and W. Burto (New York: Harper Collins, 1993) pp. 593-4 (p. 593).

2. Sophocles, 'Oedipus the King', in *Types of Drama,* sixth edn, eds, S. Barnet, M. Berman and W. Burto (New York: Harper Collins, 1993) pp. 49-70 (p. 68).

3. 'Tragedy and the Common Man', p. 593.

4. *Ibid.,* p. 593.

5. *Ibid.,* p. 593.

6. A. Bloom, *Beginning to Pray* (New York: Walker, 1986) p. 46.

7. M. Bakhtin, *Rabelais and His World,* trans. H. Iswolsky (London: MIT Press, 1968) p. 21.

8. C. Lasch, *The Culture of Narcissism* (New York: Warner, 1979) p. 21.

9. J. Habermas, *Communication and the Evolution of Society,* 1976, trans. T. McCarthy (Boston: Beacon, 1979) pp. 85-6.

10. 'Tragedy and the Common Man', p. 593.

11. A. Miller, *Death of a Salesman,* 1949 (New York: Penguin, 1976) p. 44.

12. *Ibid.,* p. 139.

13. *Ibid.,* p. 132.

14. *Ibid.,* p. 97.

15. S. Barnet, M. Berman and W. Burto, *Types of Drama,* sixth edn (New York: Harper Collins, 1993) p. 553.

16. *Death of a Salesman,* p. 135.

17. F. Scott Fitzgerald, *The Great Gatsby* (New York: Scribner's, 1925) p. 182.

18. 'Tragedy and the Common Man', p. 594.

19. *Ibid.,* p. 593.

20. M. Nussbaum, 'Tragedy and Self Sufficiency', *Essays on Aristotle's Poetics,* ed. A. O. Rorty (Princeton: Princeton UP, 1992), pp. 261-90 (p. 268).

21. *Ibid.,* p. 267.

22. Aristotle, *Treatise on Rhetoric,* trans. T. Buckley (Amherst: Prometheus Books, 1995) p. 136.

23. C. V. Boyer, *Villain as Hero in Elizabethan Tragedy* (New York: Dutton, 1914) p. 213.

24. *Ibid.,* pp. 203-4.

25. *Ibid.,* p. 208.

26. *Death of a Salesman,* p. 104.

27. F. O'Connor, *The Complete Stories* (New York: Farrar, 1971) p. 226.

28. S. T. Coleridge, *The Oxford Authors: Samuel Taylor Coleridge,* ed. H. J. Jackson (New York: Oxford UP, 1985) p. 480.

29. St Augustine, *City of God,* trans. G. G. Walsh *et al.* (Garden City: Image, 1958) pp. 244-55.

30. P. B. Shelley, 'A Defense of Poetry', *Critical Theory since Plato,* revised edn (New York: Harcourt, 1992) pp. 516-29 (pp. 519-20).

Philip C. Kolin and others (essay date fall 1998)

SOURCE: Kolin, Philip C., and others. "*Death of a Salesman*: A Playwrights' Forum." *Michigan Quarterly Review* 37, no. 4 (fall 1998): 591-623.

[*In the following essay, part of a special issue devoted to Arthur Miller, Kolin gathers reappraisals and interpretations of* Death of a Salesman *from several prestigious playwrights—including Edward Albee, Neil Simon, and Lanford Wilson, among others—on the occasion of the play's fiftieth anniversary.*]

Ever since it premiered on Broadway on 10 February 1949, **Death of a Salesman** has been an indispensable script in the modern theater. Louis Kronenberger described the heightened anticipation New Yorkers felt when the play opened after its tryouts in Philadelphia:

> Whoever you met that had caught the show out of town had clearly seen a masterpiece already, and behaved a little as if he had seen a ghost. Few things in Broadway history can have had so sensational a build-up: fewer still—which is far more wonderful—have been so breathlessly received when they arrived.[1]

Running for 742 Broadway performances, **Salesman** entered the canon of American theater with glory. Eugene O'Neill gave the play his imprimatur: "Miller's bolder than I have been . . . I'm not so sure he hasn't written a great American play."[2] Brooks Atkinson proclaimed in the *New York Times* that "Miller has written a superb drama. . . . It is so simple in style and so inevitable in theme that it scarcely seems like a thing that has been written and acted. For Mr. Miller has looked with compassion into the hearts of some ordinary Americans and quietly transferred their hope and anguish to the theater."[3] Twenty-five years after the premiere, London critic Harold Hobson pronounced **Salesman,** along with *A Streetcar Named Desire* and *Long Day's Journey into Night,* "one of America's three greatest plays."[4] This trinity of plays represented the best American theater offered to an admiring audience of world theatergoers. As Miller himself noted, "I think it is true that wherever there is theater in the world, it has been played."[5]

Miller's accomplishments in *Salesman* were revolutionary for 1949, fundamental for 1999, the play's golden anniversary. His use of time—not flashbacks or interruptions, he is quick and right to point out—was highly experimental, proleptic. According to Miller again, *Salesman* "is one continuous poem."[6] Equally controversial in 1949 was Miller's idea that *Salesman* was a tragedy of the common man. *Salesman* proved that essential tragic ingredients—moral choice, conflict, disruption in family and state, intense loss—were no less viable in the twentieth century than in Sophocles' or Shakespeare's eras. The grumblings of Joseph Wood Krutch over this issue of genre seem short-sighted today in light of the way time has endorsed Miller's views.[7] Perhaps one of the most profound insights on the common man's tragedy came from Miller himself in a 1969 interview: Willy's "uniqueness was bypassed in favor of his total obedience to social stimuli, and he ends up as he does in the play, believing in what he is forced to rebel against."[8] This is as close to hamartia, peripeteia, and tragic fate as it gets. Miller knew full well that "Man is in society but the society is in the man and every individual."[9] Willy's tragedy continues today each time a promised golden parachute fails to open, a job or department is phased out, or a technological advance leads to a personal retrenchment. The tragedy of the Family Loman is replayed as cities decay and their residents' dreams with them.

As the above comments from Miller prove, the playwright is also a perceptive critic—of society and of art, which for Miller are inseparable. Miller's acuity is shared by many of his fellow playwrights as well. To honor the 50th anniversary of *Salesman* on Broadway, I gathered the following encomia, interpretations, reappraisals, and memoirs from some of America's most distinguished playwrights. I encouraged these playwrights to reveal how *Salesman* may have influenced them (Ari Roth contends, "For what writer is immune to the shadow of *Salesman*?"), the American theater, American audiences, and why Miller's play continues to enlighten, to disturb, and to inspire us. Not only are these playwrights' views a valuable text on *Salesman* but, in many instances, they form miniature essays that rightfully take their place in the playwrights' own canon.

Edward Albee

All American playwrights who have been around for a long time seem to have one play above all their others that they're identified with—part of a quick and, very often, superficial journalistic checklist. Say Tennessee Williams and you get *A Streetcar Named Desire*; say Thornton Wilder and you get *Our Town*; say William Inge and you get *Bus Stop*; say Eugene O'Neill and you get *Long Day's Journey into Night*; say me and you get *Who's Afraid of Virginia Woolf?*; say Arthur Miller and you get *Death of a Salesman.*

These "signature" plays are usually very good examples of the playwright's work; certainly they are very popular examples, which may be why they become "signature"; and, sometimes, are the playwright's best, though sometimes it is simply the popularity which tips the balance, leaving in the lurch subtler, quieter, or tougher plays.

No one would question, however, that *Death of a Salesman* is a very fine play—I leave for a hundred years that injured term "great"—and it is certainly one of Arthur Miller's two or three finest, and may well *be* his finest—unless he writes a better one.

Like all of Arthur's plays, *Death of a Salesman* forces us to observe much that we would rather not, consider much that we are less than comfortable with, holds up to us a clear reflection of both our potentialities and our avoidances.

It is a powerful, sad, brutal play, and it has "conscience" written all over it, and probably set a standard for that unpopular word.

Robert Anderson

It makes me feel very old that we are celebrating the fiftieth anniversary of *Death of a Salesman* . . . but also very young, knowing that something that was created fifty years ago has withstood all the "new waves" which have washed over the theater in that time. I remember being at the opening, where strong men wept, bent over in their seats with their heads in their hands, or standing, applauding wildly.

The critic Louis Kronenberger wrote, "The play is so simple, central and terrible, that the run of playwrights will never dare nor care to attempt it." Brooks Atkinson wrote, "*Salesman* is one of the finest dramas in the whole range of American theatre."

So it remains.

What *Salesman* meant to me personally as a fledgling playwright just back from World War II was that it was "there," Arthur Miller was "there" among us, large in stature, large in aspirations. Standing tall.

The night before I was commissioned in the Navy in 1942, I had passed my oral exams for my Ph.D. I think I was passed on the assumption that I would not be coming back. For years I had wanted to be a playwright, but I had studied for my Ph.D. because I am a "belt and suspenders" man and knew that it would be difficult to support myself and my wife as a beginning playwright.

But, miraculously, I had come marching home a playwright. I had won a prize sponsored by the Army and the Navy and The National Theatre conference for the best play written by a serviceman overseas. I had been awarded a Rockefeller Grant, and before my return I had landed one of the great agents, Audrey Wood.

Among the plays I saw soon after my return was Miller's *All My Sons.* It held me riveted. I had studied my Ibsen. So had Miller. His subject was "responsibility," his method the so-called well-made play.

Then, two years later came *Salesman.* As John Gassner wrote, "Miller still has a firm hand on the sequence of events . . ." but he had achieved a poetry, a theater poetry, the whole work magnificently realized in the Elia Kazan production with setting and lighting by Jo Mielziner.

Miller was again writing about family, a subject always close to my heart and concerns. Someone once wrote, "drama should provide the opportunity for the most intense, basic human interrelationships. Is there an arena more intense than the family?"

Though Benedict Nightingale, the English critic, has always expressed his contempt for the American playwright's absorption with family and has wondered when we are going to "cut the umbilical cord," still, with *Death of a Salesman, Long Day's Journey into Night, The Glass Menagerie, Awake and Sing* and others, we have done very well with the "family play."

Salesman struck yet another sensitive area for me. In my teens I had been deeply moved by Charles Lamb's essay, *The Superannuated Man.* The man out of work, diminished, out of the job which had provided the meaningful routine of his life. I had first read this essay during the Depression, when men were throwing themselves out of windows in despair.

My father, at twelve, had found himself an orphan on the streets of New York (1889) working in lumber yards, dressed in cast-off clothes provided by the church. He had then come across an advertisement for free courses in shorthand and typing provided by the Underwood Typewriter Company. He started as a stenographer at five dollars a day and rose to become vice-president of a large copper company. Then in that most terrible year of the stock market crash, 1929, he had been "retired." The only work he could get was as a salesman (insurance), and he found himself waiting in the outer offices of company presidents who, only months before, had been his fellow directors, sitting on boards of prestigious firms.

How contemporary *Salesman* is in this age of downsizing on all levels from laborers to vice presidents (without golden parachutes). The despair, the loss of the feeling of self-worth which overcomes us when we are fired or "retired" from work which has provided us with not only "food on the table" but also a sense of dignity.

This despair, this feeling of worthlessness, is surely a universal experience and will continue to be. And probably fifty years from now, men will be seeing *Salesman,* and, remembering their father or experiencing the shock of recognition of their own lives, will be sitting in some theater, bent over weeping or standing and applauding. For Miller, in portraying the life and death of Willy Loman, has obeyed his own admonition . . . attention has to be paid.

Kenneth Bernard

Nick Carraway in *The Great Gatsby* says, "I see now that this has been a story of the West, after all. . . ." By this he means that *Gatsby* is a story of innocence corrupted, of Westerners possessing "some deficiency in common which made us subtly unadaptable to Eastern life." As Wilson, the desiccated man of the ash heaps, says, "I'm sick . . . I'm all run down . . . I've been here too long. I want to get away. My wife and I want to go West." Arthur Miller's *Death of a Salesman* is of the same paradigmatic order. The opening stage direction makes this clear:

> A melody is heard, played upon a flute . . . telling of grass and trees and the horizon. The curtain rises. Before us is the Salesman's house. We are aware of towering, angular shapes behind it, surrounding it on all sides. . . . As more light appears, we see a solid vault of apartment houses around the fragile-seeming home.

The play ends with the same image:

> Only the music of the flute is left on the darkening stage as over the house the hard towers of the apartment buildings rise into sharp focus.

The grass, trees, music, and horizon are, of course, the elements of the West, the Territory, a *locus amoenus,* imbued with the magical and mythic qualities of virtue, truth, hope, beauty, freedom, and a horizon co-relative with heaven itself, as so many nineteenth-century landscapes give testimony to. "It's beautiful up there," Willy says vaguely to his wife Linda about his life on the road: "the trees are so thick and the sun is warm." Where, exactly, has he been? To what is he referring? Clearly it is the Territory, not the road on which he sells his line.

Willy Loman, *the* (not *a*) Salesman, is another archetypal "Westerner," but in a much abused and debased form, who is unadaptable to eastern life. Instead of a pistol and a horse, he has a sample case and an untrustworthy car. His "territory" is not the open spaces, where a man is a man and his word is better than law, but a series of ash heap settings with layers of corruption, by which Willy has already been compromised (as in his marital infidelities), although he stubbornly clings to other values. His road never goes west. In the East,

Willy is "always in a race with the junkyard," both materially and morally. When, as his wife says proudly, he opens up "unheard of territories," it is for trademark products. He is no explorer of pristine wilderness, engaged in heroic and mythic feats, as was the grandfather in Steinbeck's "A Leader of the People," another defeated "Western" type, or his own heroic older brother Ben, who is associated with epic deeds in Africa and Alaska. In Act II, the hallucinatory Ben says to Willy, "Get out of these cities, they're full of talk and time payments and courts of law." Willy himself says to his son Biff, "Go back to the West! Be a carpenter, a cowboy, enjoy yourself!"

The loss of joy in Willy's world is scarifying, mutilating. Willy's fragile "house" in Brooklyn is a virtual last outpost, "boxed in" as a burial vault, dwarfed and deprived of light and horizon by the towering apartment buildings, which represent the new, angular, and cold urban/commercial order. It is Loman's last stand. The street is lined with cars, there is no fresh air, the grass won't grow, and Willy cannot even grow a carrot in his own back yard, which is what the Territory has been ridiculously reduced to, a place where you "gotta break your neck to see a star. . . ." The builders of the apartment buildings have cut down the beautiful elm trees and "massacred the neighborhood." He remembers when there were lilacs, wisteria, peonies, and daffodils. This downward-spiraling litany continues throughout the play. As Willy puts it more than once, "The woods are burning!" That is to say, the transcendental space within which virtue can be naturally constituted and in which happiness and ideal family are attainable is being destroyed, and what is left are the wizened and morally anemic creatures of the ash heaps, the virtual wasteland that is the estate of modern America, where selling, *anything, anything at all,* is a confirmation of being.

Willy's son Biff, in particular, has absorbed his father's ambivalence. On the one hand, he adores the West, horses, the out-of-doors, working with his hands, and so on. He has also absorbed the common man's Ben Franklin ideal of do-it-yourself expedience, as shown by his numerous correspondence courses. But, on the other hand, he lies, he cheats, and he steals. And just as Willy is regularly called "kid" by his boss, his son Biff, who is thirty-four, says, "I'm mixed up very bad. . . . I'm like a boy." In another incarnation, Biff will be a new type, like Nathanael West's Earl Shoop in *The Day of the Locust,* a displaced urban cowboy, a sometime hustler and pimp, stranded on cement with a far-away look and maybe a barbershop Indian or dying consumptive for a companion, just as Willy, in a later, less tragic, incarnation might well be, say, an Archie Bunker. In total exasperation at one point, Willy's neighbor and friend Charley says to Willy, "When the hell are you going to grow up?" But neither Willy nor Biff *can* grow up in the only world they have. Willy's "massive dreams" will not allow them to grow up. They are ambiguously and delusionally enmeshed in a moral universe that has no currency in their world. Willy's concern with growing carrots, which are good for vision, is a desire somehow to see better, to understand the nature of things, to repair the loss of vision in his old glasses, to stay on the road from which he strays suicidally or on which he absent-mindedly comes close to vehicular homicide. But he does not grow carrots or anything else, although he tries with a flashlight in the dark. He just dies, lamenting a broken life and a broken world.

Whether he is his own victim or society's is something to consider. Most likely he is both. So much of American literature is obsessed with what we have supposedly lost in our transition from wilderness and Territory to a city and suburb, from a pastoral-agricultural society to an industrial-commercial one. The two most produced and studied plays in America, *Death of a Salesman* and Tennessee Williams's *A Streetcar Named Desire,* are both about traveling salesmen, no doubt a telling sign. One of them fails and one succeeds. Williams's Stanley Kowalski is the ultimate mercantile man, with no illusions about America's past, as his "rape" of Blanche reveals. And, as his name implies, he is (like Angelo, the mechanic who doesn't understand Willy's Studebaker) part of the out-of-control population in the stinking apartment houses (read tenements, projects) that Willy complains about. He doesn't worry about things like whipped cheese. He has a firm grip on the corruptions of America, and he will succeed (his child by Stella, Blanche's sister, will unite both an old and new America, for better or worse—for example, a mongrel child comparable to the horrible cultural birthing in Hemingway's "Indian Camp"). The choice between Willy Loman and Stanley Kowalski for national character is not much of a choice. One is a willing victim, the other an unwilling victim, of a fallen world, although there must be reservations in both cases. Even were Willy less corrupt and Stanley more "sensitive," it still would not be much of a choice, although Stanley is far better than Faulkner's equally mercantile Snopses, who similarly represent the new order's "rape" of the old. (The protagonist of Henry James's *The Princess Casamassima,* in a different context, reflects a similar problem of old and new and can only kill himself as a solution.) What is clear is that both Stanley and Willy represent a continuing conflict deep in the American psyche, animating much of our debate about how America and Americans (past, present, and future) should be constituted. It is a debate not likely to be concluded soon, although perhaps temporarily occluded by other concerns.

Miller has a lot of sympathy for Willy. Through Willy's wife he proclaims that "attention must be paid. He's not to be allowed to fall into his grave like an old dog," because he is a "human being." Later, through Willy, he says, "a man is not a piece of fruit!" (read "shit"), and again, "a man has got to add up to something." But how much attention, and why? What *does* Willy add up to? These are important questions. Willy and his sons *contribute* to the very decline Willy bemoans ("personality always wins the day"). And others, like Charley and his son Bernard, who between them can't hammer a nail but who adapt to a corrupting and dehumanizing system ("When a deposit bottle is broken you don't get your nickel back."), are decent and caring people What, we can ask, does this mean? At this nexus, Miller does not seem quite clear. A more contemporary political paradigm about the value of Everyman, about Willy as representative of the downtrodden in an unfair and evil economic system, seems to be imposed on another paradigm, one about the conflict between the values of the West and the East, the Territory and the Community. The latter is historically enduring, reflected in much of our history, politics, and literature. The former, although very likely edifying to many, is a point of view, a *parti pris,* that has little to do with most of the imagery set in motion in the play. A weakness of the preacher-reformer artist is that she lures us to transfer the virtue of her cause to the work at hand. Part of Miller's (and our) moral endorsement of and conferral of tragic status on Willy is the quasi-sanctity of Miller's ideological position—despite the facts he is laying before us of Willy's huge derelictions of character. There is no question that America has come upon hard times, that America, never in a state of grace, has surely fallen away from any possibility of it in its current morass. It is doubtful that paying attention to Willy Loman, in Miller's imposed sense, will help us understand this fall and these hard times. But paying attention to the tragedy of Willy's divided and confused loyalties, his misconceptions and compromises, his pernicious electioneering for false gods, will, I think, help us to understand.

HORTON FOOTE

So much has been written of Arthur Miller's *Death of a Salesman* that it is now as familiar to us as an old and valued friend and seems to have been with us forever. I remember a time though when there was no *Death of a Salesman,* and the year it opened in New York to its dazzling recognition. I saw this celebrated production with Lee J. Cobb and Mildred Dunnock, and later the revival with Dustin Hoffman, and I've read it a number of times as well as read many essays and criticisms of the play.

The real power of the play itself was revealed to me when I was asked by a friend to go and see a production in a small regional theatre in Portsmouth, New Hampshire. Frankly I dreaded going. Hadn't I seen Lee Cobb and Mildred Dunnock both on the stage and

television? Did I want my memory of a wonderful evening in the theater spoiled? Reluctantly, I went. None of the actors were celebrated, but from the very beginning all my reservations about going vanished as the power of the play itself took hold of me and the audience, and made clear to me that the play is graced with an elemental power, with the strength and the enduring truth of a parable, and I was as moved at the end of the play as if I had never seen it or read it before. It's a remarkable piece of work and has deservedly stood the test of time.

JOHN GUARE

In 1952, my father and I went to the movies. Nothing special in that. He and my mother and I, the three of us, our entire family, loved the movies and went a lot. But this night was different. After dinner, out of the blue, my father stood up and said, "Johnny and I are going to the movies. Just the two of us." Where? To the movie version of that play *Death of a Salesman* playing down the street from us at the Colony movie theater on 82nd Street in Jackson Heights in Queens. My mother wasn't invited, which didn't bother her because who wants to see some depressing thing anyway with death in the title especially after seeing *Singin' in the Rain* at the Music Hall earlier in the year which would be our all-time favorite plus we had the new Dumont twelve inch TV so who wanted to go out?

Now I knew all about *Death of a Salesman* because I knew all about the American theater. I was fourteen. We went to Broadway plays all the time like *Annie Get Your Gun, Where's Charley?, Gentlemen Prefer Blondes, Wish You Were Here* which had a real live actual swimming pool right on the stage plus a number one hit song sung by Eddie Fisher. I also knew all about Arthur Miller from *Life* magazine, my main source of information about the world, because I, like Miller, was going to be a playwright, although a funny playwright. That night was really strange because one of the things I knew about him, thanks to all this exciting House Un-American Activities Committee McCarthy stuff, was that for all his success Arthur Miller was probably a Commie, and not only that, so was Frederic March, the star of this movie. I knew everyone who was a Commie in show business not only from the priests and nuns at our church, St. Joan of Arc, who would tell us who to watch out for from *Red Channels,* but also because my father was no less a dignitary than Vice Commander in Charge of Americanism at his American Legion Post: The Elmjack Post #298 which had saluted Hollywood that year for making the kind of movie that should be made, *My Son John,* directed by Leo McCarey. What a story! A wonderful Irish Catholic mother played by Helen Hayes discovered that her beloved Irish Catholic son had become a Communist. After some—but not that much—hand wringing, Helen did the only thing and turned him in to the FBI. Would my family do that to me if I became a Communist? They'd have to. But luckily I would never become a Communist. So why were we going tonight to this leftie *Death of a Salesman*? Hadn't The American Legion in Boston already tried to shut down this movie as Commie propaganda? The Elmjack Post #298 had decided to let the picture open in New York without protest because why give it the attention. The Commies would like that. So why then were the two of us going? Suppose anybody saw us going into the Colony? How would the Vice Commander in Charge of Americanism explain this one— and taking a kid who could be brainwashed. Wait! Had my father secretly become a Communist? Would I have to turn him in? The night became weirdly illicit. My father bought the two tickets. We went in.

Death of a Salesman was kind of boring. The story kept jumping back and forth in time which confused me. Frederic March drove his car back from Boston the way my father drove—all over the road and panicky. Was it March's rotten driving that made my father need to see this movie? March played a guy named Willy who fought with his sons. I didn't have any brothers. Willy had a girlfriend in Boston. Then Willy killed himself to get insurance and everybody went to his funeral. My father had suffered a heart attack two years earlier. I didn't like this movie one bit. We didn't wait for the double feature. We walked home but this time we didn't talk over the jokes from the picture or reenact our favorite bits. "I want to tell you something." My father said that in a low tone of voice you use when you're going to break a secret. I liked being told secrets but not from him. Did he have a girlfriend in Boston?

"I once was a salesman."

"Like the salesman in the movie?"

"No, for Procter & Gamble."

"Ivory soap!" I was very impressed.

This is what he told me.

When World War One, the war to end all wars, was over, my father came back not to New York but to L. A. to start a new life working as a soap salesman in a section called Angel's Flight which was a street on a hill so steep you had to take a cable car to go up and down it.

"You worked for Ivory soap and we could live in L. A. in a place called Angel's Flight. Why aren't we there now?"

My father who worked down at Wall Street and hated it said this in a low slow voice. He tended to mumble anyway so you always had to get close to hear him. "It hadn't worked out." That was it. We walked home in silence.

My mother asked how was the movie? My father said in his bright chipper voice, "The usual Commie propaganda." While he brushed his teeth, I whispered to my mother what my father had told me. "He lived in L. A.?" she said. "He was a salesman for Ivory soap? Then you know more about him than I do."

One thing I did know was that the secret he had just told me was directly connected to the story we had just seen. And seeing that story had somehow made it possible for him to say to me those four terrible words: It. Hadn't. Worked. Out. That night on the walk back from that movie was the only time he ever mentioned that part of his life. If I brought it up later, he'd laugh it off with a song or a joke or a drink. By the time I could've brought it up and pushed it, he had died. But something happened that night. I saw for the first time that a play, a movie that had been a play, something with actors in it, could touch a man as familiar as my father with such mysterious power that it made him a stranger to me and gave him strength to reveal—not a secret—What was it he had told me? Something deeper than a secret. But the play had given him courage to say the most horrible words he could imagine: It. Hadn't. Worked. Out.

T. S. Eliot in his great essay "Tradition and the Individual Talent" writes about the last time the artist was a full-fledged member of the establishment society. In Shakespeare's day, people went to the theater for the same reasons you'd go to the doctor today. Audiences went to the Globe Theater to see their problems acted out. Seeing emotions carried to the extreme helped audiences find the proper limits for their own lives.

Did my father go to see *Death of a Salesman* in this instinctual primal Elizabethan way—although he wouldn't know what the hell that meant if you woke him out of his grave today with all the knowledge in the world. He knew if he saw this story the psychic pain of his life would be—what? forget about healed. Eased. Settle for eased.

Is this what accounts for the universality of Miller's work? His ability to get into people's dreams, to touch their disappointment, to give voice to the American shame of failure, to make that which is most human in us also the very same thing we can least bear to acknowledge? To say Yes, I have been heard. I am not alone. No matter where we are on this planet. Did what my father tell me that night heal him in some way? Did he pay some debt to his only child in this meager confession which haunted him for a lifetime? He never got to that place again. But some debt was paid that night, some dent made that night in the fragile armor we invent to survive, walking home that night in 1952.

A. R. GURNEY

What most intrigues me about *Death of a Salesman*, and indeed about many of Arthur Miller's other plays, is the thematic ambiguities at the core of his work. We all value his solid architecture, his driving moral energy, his sardonic wit, and his ability to seize on subjects which manage to forge disparate audiences into responsive communities all over the world. Yet it would be a mistake to view the playwright simply as a passionate polemicist.

Death of a Salesman, for example, is generally acknowledged to be a major indictment of American capitalism and consumerism. Willy Loman's story dramatizes the heartlessness of a system which seduces and exploits and then casts aside its most devoted supporters. Yet the Bernard subplot embodies almost the opposite position. Here the point would seem to be that if you work hard and play by the rules you can end up arguing a case in front of the Supreme Court, and enjoy a good tennis game on the side. Obviously both plot strands work with and against each other. Willy Loman's story, standing by itself, would be a grim and limited distortion of the American experience; Bernard alone would seem as false as Horatio Alger. Woven together, however, each strand informs and modifies the other, so that at the end we embrace a much more complicated vision of our country and ourselves.

This ability to defy the laws of physics and occupy two places at the same time is what good art can do so compellingly. And it's what makes Miller a major artist. In *The Crucible,* for example, he manages to chronicle the horrors of what happens to a community when pent-up feelings are expressed publicly, while at the same time exploring how *un*expressed feelings can undermine a marriage. In *The Price,* he looks at the price we pay when we cut ourselves off from our roots, juxtaposed with the price we pay when we elect to stay home. In an underestimated recent play of Miller's called *The Ride Down Mount Morgan,* the central character is a bigamist, whose two wives show up in his hospital room after an automobile accident. Talk about two opposing positions occupying the same place at the same time!

In any case, *Death of a Salesman,* for all the power and passion of its politics, and the groundedness of its domestic detail, has at its center this complex sense of ambiguity, which, I believe, will intrigue and move audiences far removed from the particular concerns of this country or century.

DAVID HENRY HWANG

Death of a Salesman is the best play yet written about an American immigrant family. Granted, the Lomans never reveal specifically the country in which Willy was born; they don't speak English with an accent or revel in colorful old-country customs. Nonetheless, the moment I first read the play, I recognized in my bones

an immigrant household, for in Willy's desperate quest to hold onto the American Dream, I heard the voice of my own father. Immigrant patriarchs often embrace American sloganism in order to justify the radical choice they have made, for the pain of uprooting must surely be rewarded with a better life or else it is a fool's choice. Note also the play's obsession with travel: not only is Willy himself a virtual road map of American territories, but his role model Ben ends up in Africa, where he makes his fortune. Ben's advice to Willy is the slogan that has inspired American immigrants for generations: "There's a new continent on your doorstep, William. You could walk out rich. Rich!"

The Loman boys also represent familiar responses of second-and third-generation Americans, who, burdened with a more intimate knowledge of this country, must choose to endorse or reject immigrant romanticism. Happy's need to prove that "Willy Loman did not die in vain" suggests all second-generation Asian Americans currently becoming doctors, lawyers, engineers, and other upwardly-mobile citizens, in part to fulfill the dreams of their parents. On the other hand, Biff's conclusion that "He [Willy] never knew who he was" tells of the loss of identity and cultural confusion often brought on by rapid assimilation.

Though I am virtually certain Willy is an immigrant, I do concede a potential contradiction in the play, when he and Ben discuss their childhoods . . . in South Dakota. Could this be Willy's delusion, his need to be accepted as an American so great that it forces him to invent a false past? Possibly. Or perhaps immigration is so intrinsic a part of the American character, has so shaped the dreams and slogans of this land, that no true examination of the national spirit can escape its pull. All evidence to the contrary, I will always remain convinced that Arthur Miller has written the great American immigrant play. That the Lomans are a typical Asian American household. That *Death of a Salesman* captures, of course, my own family.

ADRIENNE KENNEDY

When I saw *Death of a Salesman* in 1949 I was most struck by the fact that Willy Loman could assess his life and through reflection and memory he could arrive at insights and great conclusions. And in his car after doing this he could die.

He wasn't a character in Shakespeare or Shaw but an ordinary man who nevertheless possessed the right to make such a monumental decision.

I believe it was then I decided, if my memory one day ever presented me with agonizing insights, that I too possessed that right. I found this thought a comfort. And it's why I still love Willy Loman fifty years after.

TONY KUSHNER

I sat behind Arthur Miller at the 1994 Tony Awards, and I stared at the back of his head—far more interesting than anything transpiring on stage. Inside this impressive cranium, inside this dome, I thought to myself, Willy Loman was conceived: for an American playwright, a place comparable in sacrosanctity to the Ark of the Covenant or the Bhodi Tree or the Manger in Bethlehem. I wanted to touch it but I thought its owner might object. The ceremonies ended, and I'd missed my opportunity to make contact with the cradle whence came one of the three postwar pillars—the other two being of course *A Streetcar Named Desire* and *Long Day's Journey into Night*—upon which the stature of serious American playwriting rests. All the wonderful writers who followed the Triad—realists, naturalists, and experimentalists—have at least these three plays in common. Nothing that American theater can point to with pride since the decade which produced these works was not shaped, in some degree, by their influence, in homage or in opposition or, more frequently, both. A salesman, a streetcar, and a journey: three ambient testaments to rootlessness, to American wanderlust and the hazards of nomadism. *Death, Desire* and *Night*: tragedies all, downers embraced by a country of people who like to imagine themselves, perversely, as relentlessly upbeat. Bertolt Brecht in his journal wrote that American theater is written "for people on the move by people who are lost." And that insight before the Big Three had been written or staged!

We think American drama apolitical because the Big Three are family plays. Except of course *Streetcar* is about a family in which a woman who cannot operate within conventional economies is raped. *Journey* is about a family of immigrants haunted by poverty and class. And the Lomans are compelled by the tide of history to return East from a paradisaic pioneer frontier past; the motion of Manifest Destiny has reversed itself, an acid reflux which had carried Gatsby from Chicago to Long Island twenty years before, brings the Lomans to a doomed pursuit of happiness in the place whence happiness, in the previous century, had fled—Happiness having Gone West and never returned, drowned perhaps in the grips of some Pacific undertow.

We think American drama mired in naturalism, lacking formal inventiveness and playfulness, but *Journey* is an extremely artificial play about the theater, full of actors playing actors and the victims of actors. *Streetcar* is great verse drama, as close as we'll ever get, close enough, its characters unforgettable because they speak a language that's as "natural" as any great poetry is—which is to say, not in the least. And *Salesman* has Uncle Ben, whose wealth has made him as alien to the Lomans' struggles and disappointments as the character is, formalistically, to the rest of the play.

I saw *Salesman* when I was six years old, and I never forgot Uncle Ben and his line, "When I went into the jungle I was eighteen years old and when I came out, by God, I was rich!" I don't think I understood the entire story, but in the kaleidoscopic version I subsequently constructed for myself I thought Uncle Ben some sort of great clown who blows open the Loman quotidian bearing tidings of fun, spontaneity, adventure, life,—of which, apparently, menace and real danger were constitutive elements. I didn't, at six, know much about the quotidian. No six year old should know anything about the quotidian. But I think perhaps watching the Loman family love and wound one another, and love and be wounded by the world without, was the first indelible inkling I'd consciously had (lucky child!) of what the Everyday was, that such a monstrous thing existed; and how important it is to despise the Everyday, to live one's life, to the extent one can, resisting it.

Salesman is not only a play about death, though its sadness is overwhelming. It is also about resistance, even unto death. I have never believed that the issue of inexorability ought to be resolved in tragedy. A tragedy in which suffering and death are truly inexorable lacks drama; there needs to be a *what if,* a possible escape, or else the whole thing becomes grimly mechanical, pathetic, not exhilarating, grotesque rather than cathartic. "We're free," Linda keens over her husband's grave. The words in their mortal/mortuary context are heartbreaking, horrible, ironic and deeply true of human beings even in inhuman circumstances. We are free, and that fact is both insufficient, as freedom in isolation always is (which I think is a point of the play), but terribly important and true.

Linda Loman's graveside lament, from that Lake Charles, Louisiana, production in 1962, is what made the biggest impression on my six-year-old sensibilities. This is not surprising, given that my mother, Sylvia Kushner, was playing Linda. She was a wonderful actor, a tragedienne. A professional bassoonist, she was drawn to and felt entirely at home in dark, somber tones, in elegy and minor keys, in sorrow. She was honest on stage, she saved a good deal of her truthfulness, the things she couldn't say in the course of the quotidian, for her music and for the roles she played. She kept the lid on a lot of unhappiness, into which she could tap when she needed to. On stage, grief and rage and pain added years to her looks. As Linda Loman she changed from my beautiful young mother (dressed more dowdily than she ever did in real life) to an old woman in the course of the evening. It was terrifying and wonderful; I was anxious to see her afterwards, to see what she'd look like, if she'd become my mother again. She did change back, but I don't think I ever saw her the same way again. Perhaps having spent several weeks being married to Willy Loman, she never *was* the same.

This was the first time Lake Charles had seen theater-in-the-round, a spatial innovation the advocacy of which caused the more progressive members of the local community theater to split off from the more established Little Theater, to form a company committed to producing plays as controversial as *Salesman* then was. I remember being amazed that I could watch the action and the audience opposite me, all of us watching my mother play Linda Loman, seeing Brenda Bachrack, one of my mother's best friends, crying at the play's genuinely devastating, lonely, cemetery ending. I was very impressed.

The actress who played Willy's floozy in Boston had broken her arm two days before opening and sported a big plaster cast. I thought the cast somehow connected to what made the hotel room scene so sleazy, had something to do with why Biff and Willy were so angry with each other. I didn't know the meaning of the hose the boys find at the beginning of the play but I knew that it was incredibly ominous, and I certainly knew—had I ever really considered death before?—that when Willy leaves at the end of the play, it's a final exit; I knew it broke my mother's heart.

I saw her play several other parts when I was very young, all of them involving the shedding of tears and the venting of rage, none of them Linda, none of the plays *Death of a Salesman.* Since then I've seen maybe half-a-dozen Linda Lomans, only Mildred Dunnock as good as my mother; I've seen Lee J. Cobb's beaten titan and Dustin Hoffman's indestructible rat-terrier. But how do I know *Salesman* is a very great play? Because I knew it when I was six. I didn't know precisely what I'd just seen, but I knew I was in the presence of a great mystery: the sorrow experience brings to innocence, the anger injustice brings to the just. Reading *Salesman* today, I'm still in its presence, I know it still.

KAREN MALPEDE

Everybody's Father

The first, and come to think of it, only time I ever saw *Death of a Salesman* was in a college production at the University of Wisconsin. I remember straining forward in my seat, my knuckles white, gripping the armrests on both sides. The play is so much a part of the American ethos that whether or not one has seen it or read it ever or dozens of times, Miller's sensibility is as if implanted in our heart/brains. My own father was not a salesman, but a certified public accountant. Not a Loman, but the son of Italian immigrants, who had worked his way out of a reactionary Catholic ghetto, married a Jewish woman, moved to fancy suburbs and died at the age of forty-four. He was, I always thought, like Willy, a victim of the American Dream. "Attention must be paid." Miller was a young playwright on the Federal Theater Project. He is the direct descendant of a time in American history when theater felt it had both a right and a duty to speak to the citizens of a democracy about our role as the makers and safeguards of the society in which we live. Miller wants the middle classes to be responsible. He knew that upward mobility and assimilation might sap something finer in the nature of a people of immigrants who suddenly, because they had defeated fascism, could become globally rich and powerful. Rightly so, in *All My Sons* he critiqued the isolationism of the nuclear family. I like the fact that he intertwines personal sexual longings with public ethical dilemmas. I appreciate Miller's honesty, his courage, and his sense of citizenship; his secular Jewish belief that through human action the social world might become a better place, and his conviction that dramatic fiction has a role to play in this worthwhile endeavor. If, as a playwright, I claim Susan Glaspell and Gertrude Stein as mothers, I also lay claim to Miller as one of the great and good fathers of us all.

EMILY MANN

I heard about *Death of a Salesman* when I was a child, eight or nine years old, before I had ever seen a play. My Uncle Phil, my father's oldest brother, was a businessman in what we used to call the "shmatte business," in New York City. He manufactured knit shirts. He was a gruff, perpetually angry man educated only through high school, a man who grew up tough on the streets of Brooklyn. We children were often scared of him.

One night at dinner he told the family about a play he'd seen. This play was called *Death of a Salesman* and he told us it had hit him so hard he couldn't drive home that night to Long Island. He and his wife, Claire, had to take a room in a hotel. I asked my aunt about this years later, and she said, "Oh, yes. Phillie could barely walk out of the theater, so we had to stay over in New York."

Two things hit me as a young girl:

1) My uncle wasn't as tough as I thought he was.

and

2) Theater must be a pretty powerful thing.

MARK MEDOFF

Reading *Death of a Salesman* in my Introduction to Theater class, freshman year, University of Miami, 1958, ranks as a seminal moment in my life. In terms of what the aspiring eighteen-year-old writer learned about the possibilities of structure, it ranks with *The Sound and the Fury, Wuthering Heights,* "The Waste

Land," and *Waiting for Godot.* In terms of the emotional impact of Mr. Miller's play—simple: nothing—nothing!—since has hit me so hard.

JASON MILLIGAN

Arthur Miller's plays have been a major influence on me since the first moment I discovered them. Not just his most famous works, but also his newer, lesser-known plays continue to amaze, fascinate, and challenge me both as an individual and as an artist.

The first Miller play I ever saw was a college production of *Death of a Salesman,* and even though the play was glaringly miscast (a strapping young Hispanic graduate student as Willy Loman), the poetry, power, and passion of Miller's work still shone through, hit me hard, and have stayed with me ever since. Thankfully, I was later able to see Broadway revivals of *Salesman* and many other Miller plays—and I continue to be astounded by the depth of humanity in his writing.

Personally, I have always been fascinated by The Big Moral Questions in life and drama—and that, I believe, is one reason Miller's plays have always resonated so strongly for me. So few writers bother to contemplate the nation's (or world's) moral barometer in their plays anymore, and I believe one reason Miller's plays continue to remain so timely is because they serve a primal function of the theater: to hold a mirror up to our souls, to be the moral conscience of our times. On top of that, Miller has crafted some of the most original, fully-developed characters in American drama. What more could one ask for in a play? You can't. Arthur Miller has already given you everything.

Fifty years and still going strong . . . congratulations to you, Mr. Miller! And thank you for inspiring several generations of playwrights with your vision.

JOYCE CAROL OATES

> He's a man way out there in the blue, riding on a smile and a shoeshine. And when they start not smiling back—that's an earthquake. And then you get yourself a couple of spots on your hat, and you're finished. Nobody dast blame this man. A salesman is got to dream. . . . It comes with the territory.
>
> —Arthur Miller, *Death of a Salesman*

Was it our comforting belief that Willy Loman was "only" a salesman? That *Death of a Salesman* was about—well, an American salesman? And not about all of us?

It's probable that, when I first read this haunting and mysterious play at the age of fourteen or fifteen, I may have thought that Willy Loman was sufficiently "other"—"old." He hardly resembled the men in my family, my father or grandfathers, for he was "in sales" and not a factory worker or small-time farmer, he wasn't a manual laborer but a man of words, speech—what his son Biff bluntly calls "hot air." His occupation, for all its adversities, was "white collar," and his class not the one into which I'd been born; I could not recognize anyone I knew intimately in him, and certainly I could not have recognized myself, nor foreseen a time decades later when it would strike me forcibly that, for all his delusions and intellectual limitations, about which Arthur Miller is unromantically clear-eyed, Willy Loman is all of us. Or, rather, we are Willy Loman, particularly those of us who are writers, poets, dreamers; the yearning soul "way out there in the blue." Dreaming is required of us, even if our dreams are very possibly self-willed delusions. And we recognize our desperate child's voice assuring us, like Willy Loman pep-talking himself at the edge of a lighted stage as at the edge of eternity—"God Almighty, [I'll] be great yet! A star like that, magnificent, can never really fade away!"

Except of course, it can.

It would have been in the early 1950s that I first read *Death of a Salesman,* only a few years after its Broadway premiere and enormous critical and popular success. I would have read it in an anthology of *Best Plays of the Year.* As a young teenager I'd begun avidly devouring drama; apart from Shakespeare, no plays were taught in the schools I attended in upstate New York (in the small city of Lockport and the village of Williamsville, a suburb of Buffalo), and so I read plays with no sense of chronology, in no historic context, no doubt often without much comprehension. Reading late at night when the rest of the household was asleep was an intense activity for me, imbued with mystery, and reading drama was far more enigmatic than reading prose fiction. It seemed to me a challenge that so little was explained in the stage directions; there was no helpful narrative voice; you were obliged to visualize, to "see" the stage in your imagination, the play's characters always in present tense, vividly alive. In drama, people presented themselves primarily in speech, as they do in life. Yet there was an eerie, dreamlike melding of past and present in *Death of a Salesman,* Willy Loman's "present-action" dialogue and his conversations with the ghosts of his past like his revered brother Ben; there was a melting of the barriers between inner and outer worlds that gave to the play its disturbing, poetic quality. (Years later I would learn that Arthur Miller had originally conceived of the play as a monodrama with the title *The Inside of His Head.*)

In the intervening years, Willy Loman has become our quintessential American tragic hero, our domestic Lear, spiraling toward suicide as toward an act of selfless grace, his mad scene on the heath a frantic seed-planting episode by flashlight in the midst of which the once-proud, now disintegrating man confesses, "I've got nobody to talk to." His salesmanship, his family relations, his very life—all have been talk, optimistic and inflated sales-rhetoric; yet, suddenly, the powerful Willy Loman realizes he has nobody to talk *to*; nobody to *listen*. Perhaps the most memorable single remark in the play is the quiet observation that Willy Loman is "liked . . . but not well-liked." In America, this is only B+. It will not be enough.

Nearly fifty years after its composition, *Death of a Salesman* strikes us as the most achingly contemporary of our classic American plays. It has proved to have been a brilliant strategy on the part of the thirty-four-year-old playwright to temper his gifts for social realism with the Expressionistic techniques of experimental drama like Eugene O'Neill's *Strange Interlude* and *The Hairy Ape,* Elmer Rice's *The Adding Machine,* Thornton Wilder's *Our Town,* work by Chekhov, the later Ibsen, Strindberg and Pirandello, for by these methods Willy Loman is raised from the parameters of regionalism and ethnic specificity to the level of the more purely, symbolically "American." Even the claustrophobia of his private familial and sexual obsessions has a universal quality, in the plaintive-poetic language Miller has chosen for him. As we near the twenty-first century, it seems evident that America has become an ever more frantic, self-mesmerized world of salesmanship, image without substance, empty advertising rhetoric and that peculiar product of our consumer culture, "public relations"—a synonym for hypocrisy, deceit, fraud. Where Willy Loman is a salesman, his son Biff is a thief. Yet these are fellow Americans to whom attention must be paid. Arthur Miller has written the tragedy that illuminates the dark side of American success—which is to say, the dark side of us.

OYAMO

On what Arthur Miller's *Death of a Salesman* means to me, an enraged 21st Century Africamerican male:

Salesman means that American theater intellectuals and their scholarly counterparts should rid themselves of their insufferable inferiority complex toward European theater. Enough of this subliminal colonialism! Enough of this snide, elitist derision and aesthetic conformism that attends discussions of American Theater! Had it been left to those blustery, nattering organizers of aesthetic bureaucracies that are clogged with semantic semiotics, we Americans never would have invented jazz. Miller teaches me that the American "Revolution" is not over yet; we won only the military victory; otherwise we are yet colonized. Miller makes me remember that being "black" in America is to be in a state of constant rebellion, and, as such, I exempt myself from the notion of American cultural inferiority.

Salesman is a great 20th century play about universal human suffering which is caused by the pervasive malady of "moral ignorance." Miller had no ancient American (Caucasian) legends and myths upon which to draw when he wrote *Salesman*; he invented his own, as Americans are wont to do. In *Salesman* he gave us an in-depth glimpse at the highly infectious "disease of unrelatedness," American-style alienation and despair in the common man, the Everyman who faces the limitless possibilities of America and dares to dream and fail.

Willy Loman finally failed because he couldn't escape the self-invented myths of his idealized past. Miller purposefully blurred the lines between expressionism, as he learned it from the Germans, and realism. He did this because he wanted us to see the confused "process" of Willy's mind and to reflect perhaps on the confusion of moral values in the modern industrialized Western world. Nations also invent myths about their pasts.

Miller is inventing the American Theater. *Salesman* is an exceptionally strong foundation stone. We can be proud to call him our own. We needn't look overseas for approval of what we do in our American Theater. We needn't aesthetically measure ourselves by 2500 years of someone else's history. Why shoulder Europe's calamity-ridden baggage? America is the world now. Everyone in the world comes here to settle, and they export our culture to their homelands. I think those Europeans who condescend toward us are fearful that we Americans will culturally obliterate them. Well, that may be a justifiable fear, but that's their problem, not ours.

ARI ROTH

So Many Memories

In the contemplative stages of writing this homage, I lost my job. I lost it at Arthur Miller's alma mater which, as it so happens, is my alma mater too. It was a modern-day mugging—no police reports to be filed—a paper decision; a corporate farewell. Following nine years of service, the pro forma phone call—"Thanks for the labor; we've completed our search; you came in second; we'll keep your program; oh, we can help pack your office." I was scheduled to speak at a high school awards ceremony the next week. I'd planned to talk about Miller anyway. For the confluence of an awards ceremony with a 50th anniversary had recalled an earlier commemoration—this one marking the half-century birthday of the University of Michigan's Avery Hopwood Awards, when I received my first literary prize from Mr. Miller himself back in 1981. My dad had taken the Amtrak up from Chicago to watch the ceremony, to bear witness to the leave-taking; this Oedipal movement from one influence to another. I told the high school students of the thrill of meeting Miller that day; of his presenting me with a $400 check for a 13 page play; and then—welcome to the world of Art, kids—of the sting upon reading the contradictory comments from the two national judges; the acerbic dismissal made by playwright-historian Martin Duberman who disagreed with the praise of the other judge (whose name, naturally, escapes me), that my one-act was "imitative of Miller's **The Price**," which, of course, I had yet to read, but which, in turn, of course, I would. And so a connection had been forged; a connection born of common heritage and total coincidence. I embraced and imbibed Miller's influence, bought **The Price** for my mother on her birthday and announced that I was no longer going to be a lawyer but a playwright.

I mythologized Miller way out of proportion, perhaps due to the uniqueness of the man himself: the beguiling convergence of physical attribute, moral authority, and private proclivity. For here was a man whose face, as etched in that 50th Anniversary Hopwood poster lithograph, half-turned, half obscured by shadow, with stern jaw, craggy frown and endlessly sloping forehead, summoned images of a literary Mt. Rushmore. As he strode to the Rackham Auditorium podium that afternoon, I was reminded of his carriage—a tall Jewish man—and how often did one see a tall Jewish man in the Midwest? A lanky Yankee Bronx Jew with the wing span of a Phil Jackson and the rough-hewn hands of a working stiff—the kind of laborer he once had been and would always remain—a maker of things—a builder of furniture; of houses in which actors could live. The texture of work seemed to permeate his being and was one he would lovingly celebrate in **A Memory of Two Mondays**—his tenure as a shipping clerk, where he spent two summers as a teenager during the Depression before taking off in the fall for the University of Michigan. Inspired (and in a hurry) to emulate, I too found work as a shipping clerk in a steel pipe manufacturing plant that very same summer, and then wrote about it, and then submitted it to "the Hopwoods" my senior year.

Miller's work—with its fierce critique of the ravages of a brutally competitive, market-driven economy, his call for a more expansive consciousness imploring that we be responsible not just to ourselves and our families but to our community, to our nation, to the soldiers who fight overseas to defend us and who are just as much blood relation as our own sons—moved me to see him as a kind of theatrical rabbi (albeit, Reform, in the classical sense). Or better yet, a fusion figure, uniting the pulpit, the bench, the lectern, and the spotlight. He had been married to Marilyn after all. And John Proctor had had an affair. A hero could have sin on his hands, lust in his heart, and still wage a moral war. One could indict and not be above the fray but part of the muck. It was, and remains, a populist critique, never a priest's sanctimony.

And so I rally (defensively, perhaps?) whenever Miller is assailed as a moralizing scold, out of step or date. And there are plenty of snipers out there, make no mistake. When our most ambitious playwrights of the moment rush to dismiss, in print, any suggestions of influence that **Salesman** might have on their own grandiose structural designs, I take it as a personal affront. (Does Miller even care? Yet still I scold, "Attention. Attention and respect! Pay up!") For what writer is immune to the shadow of **Salesman**? The personal downfall as social indictment; the elegant movement from objective to subjective; from present to past. Only the cold, ideologically driven could turn his back on the pain of a father and son separated by disappointment.

What I know to be true is this: That **Salesman** was the first play to ever move me to tears. That it was the only show that's caused me to touch a perfect stranger on the arm during intermission. And that it's still the play that comes most readily to mind—to the heart—whenever one fears for one's place; when one loses one's way, or one's job. **Salesman** is there for us in manifold moments. Whenever we falter, when we feel the earthquake, when we bluster or pose or plant seeds in the moonlight. The achievement of **Salesman** is one of exposing vulnerability at every stage of life.

Even as a twelve year old, I knew this in my bones. I wasn't much of a reader growing up, but I bawled when I read my homework assignment in seventh grade. I was at Camp Chi in the Wisconsin Dells with my family for an American Jewish Congress retreat. I went out in a rowboat and began to read the gray and yellow covered paper-back with the picture of a man in a raincoat and a suitcase full of samples under a streetlamp. Floating in a lily-pad covered lagoon, I cried for a man who said to his Uncle Ben, "I have a fine position here, but—well, Dad left when I was such a baby and I never had a chance to talk to him and I still feel kind of temporary about myself." The line rings with the shock of recognition even still. This unfillable void that Willy seeks to stuff with ephemera—this son who can't reach his father, his unutterable longing, expressing love through car wax, despair in a broken fan belt, guilt in a flute that leads a man backwards, forever backwards, to the point of his undoing—to the moment where son unmasks the father and is not made free by the discovery. Somehow I understood all that, floating in a pond in Wisconsin all those years ago. Even though my dad's not in retail, I still saw tons of him in Willy. And now I see much more that is me. With a spot on my hat, I've felt alone in the blue riding on little more than a wing and a prayer, the people not always smiling back.

Remarkable how Miller's lines keep coming back. "A man is not a piece of fruit," I told the high-school assembly, and the weight of that moment in the hall was of a concern not just for one itinerant lecturer, but for a class of humanity that, at least for a moment in time, becomes dispossessed. I told the students of Miller's cautionary words; and of the caution in his example. And that despite the romantic figure he cut, how he went out of his way that Hopwood afternoon in 1981 to urge us not to go into theater ("Your lives will only be filled with pain and misery!"). It was a warning that came with a wink. He knew of the great good to come from work that is difficult, of the catharsis to come from crisis. In *Death of a Salesman,* Miller pays attention and respect to the ways in which we founder, and we are made wiser and more aware for the showing. So moved, we touch a perfect stranger on the arm at intermission; we cry in rowboats in the middle of Wisconsin; we know what links us each to each: a kindred sense of longing and pain. With spots on our hat, our fathers stumbling on the path before us, we, like Biff, are able to find our footing. We regain the road. Thanks to Miller's towering, humble play. Happy birthday, *Salesman.*

Joan M. Schenkar

Death of a Salesman, along with Karel Capek's *R.U.R.* and Eugene O'Neill's *The Hairy Ape,* is centrally lodged in my earliest memory of theater. And that is because I was able to read it—that is, to speak it to myself—in an anthology of literature that must have come down to me from a college-going cousin. Because fewer plays are now being published, fewer children will have the experience of making their own relationship with a play before it is interpreted for them on a stage. I remember *Death of a Salesman* much better for having read it before I saw it.

I was very young when I first looked at the play—perhaps eight or nine years old—and my father was still a kind of traveling salesman himself—so of course the work struck me with the force of a blow, as it continues to do when I read it now. I think it is the only complete tragedy—in loosely classical terms—in the American language and certainly the only one to put a kind of Lear and a kind of Fool in the same body. And it is the only play I can think of to turn a stock figure like "Linda the maltreated wife" into an immensely dignified and personalized chorus of praise for her husband—"attention must be paid"—and get away with it.

Death of a Salesman gives full expression to the dreams and disillusionments of my grandparents' and parents' generation—a purchasable democracy in which being "well-liked" meant, inevitably, being "well-fixed" and success always seemed possible in the antipodes. Because it's such a good play, written to the rhythms of

its subject in language that lasts, it also perfectly exposes What Troubles Us Now—and Willy Loman's obsession with surface instead of substance seems particularly apropos.

Death of a Salesman may be middle-aged, but it is still large-hearted and full-bodied and will, I think, continue to play on the world stage as long as American dreams do.

Neil Simon

I was a young man when *Death of a Salesman* first appeared on Broadway, and as yet had no aspirations to be a playwright. My parents first saw the play and since my father was a salesman himself, one can understand why he was so anxious to see this event that all New York was talking about. My parents were not really theatergoers except for an occasional breezy musical that my father thought a prospective buyer for his garment center wares might get a kick out of. The costly tickets didn't always guarantee a sale for my father, but since his jokes were wearing thin, he could always use some help from professionals.

I remember vividly the night my parents came home from Mr. Miller's play. I never saw my father so excited, so animated, far more stimulated than he had ever been as seen through my teenage view.

"It was so real," he began. "So honest, so truthful. I knew everything this salesman was going through. It felt so much like my own life."

"Well, what was it about?" I asked with enormous curiosity.

"It's about this hard-working salesman and his two lazy sons."

Since my father had two sons, me and my brother, the impact of his insult took a few moments for me to feel the weight of it. I was a teenager in school and my marks did not indicate any reason to be lazy. My brother was in his early twenties and had ideas for his future other than following my father's footsteps into the garment center. He wanted to be a writer and go to Hollywood, an occupation no loftier in my father's mind than becoming a gangster. My brother had girls on his mind which qualified him as being a "bum" in my father's narrow-minded estimation.

When I finally saw *Salesman,* a year or so later, I saw how my father had twisted the story in his mind to fit his own personal scenario, making my brother into the two brothers he saw in the play, and laying the blame for his own lack of accomplishment on his two wastrel sons. Not exactly Willy Loman, who perhaps put too much faith in his older son's ability to become a huge success, thus bailing out Willy's failed dreams by moving the spotlight of responsibility on to his reluctant offspring.

I think many people who saw the play saw it through their own subjective view, that Mr. Miller was telling *their* story and not necessarily the one Mr. Miller had in mind. It made no difference. The play's purpose, as all plays' purpose should be, is to make an impact on the audience's emotions, their psyches, their own sense of being, whether failed or otherwise. No play in my memory ever left such an impact on those who saw it.

I have never gotten *Death of a Salesman* out of my mind and probably never will. In fact, it's the one play that almost kept me from becoming a playwright. It's this play that I measured my own young capabilities against and I knew that that was one mountain too high to climb. Instead, I used it to my own advantage as I made it the one play to *aspire* to. If I only made it two thirds to the summit, I would have achieved more than I ever dreamed of.

JEAN-CLAUDE VAN ITALLIE

Arthur Miller, benevolent patriarch of American playwrights, deserves our homage. His *Death of a Salesman* opened ways to write many of the plays which followed it, both mainstream and experimental.

Salesman was, for its era, radical in form—time shifts back and forth, place changes continually—yet the spirit of Aristotle's unities is preserved. No matter the many unusual theatrical paths we are led down during the action of the play, we feel secure in the hands of the writer. To playwrights experimenting with form, *Salesman* teaches that if you're clear and confident in intention and know how to express that intention, the audience will follow, whatever the shape of your play.

Salesman is classic, however, in its themes, and in the subtle, thorough way Miller explores them. Irreconcilable conflicts between fathers and sons, questions of right and wrong, are raised also in Greek tragedy. But Willy Loman (Low man) is not, like, say Agamemnon in Aeschylus, larger than life.

From *Salesman* we learn that titanic conflicts may be embodied in finely etched contemporary characters somewhat like our imperfect selves, much smaller than gods yet living, in the deepest sense of the word, tragic lives.

Ultimately, as in Chekhov's major plays, I am moved in *Death of a Salesman* by the characters in their hopeless situations, by the playwright's depth of feeling for them, and by the unflagging quality of his attention and his craft.

LANFORD WILSON

This brief tribute was given at the presentation of the Last Frontier Playwright Award to Arthur Miller during the Fourth Annual Theater Conference of the Prince William Sound Community College in Valdez, Alaska, on August 18, 1996.

* * *

I can pinpoint exactly the moment I fell under the spell of the theater. Not "In love with the theater," anyone can fall in love. You have to witness the potential of something to fall under its spell.

Each year the high school freshmen of Ozark, Missouri, travel north the twelve short miles to Springfield to attend a production of Southwest Missouri State University's theater department.

S.M.S.U. is famous for its excellent drama department. In 1951 their major production was Arthur Miller's *Death of a Salesman.*

The curtain rose on Miller's play, the first adult play I had ever seen. The set was stunning. The second story roof of the house was outlined, a thin black line indicating the pitch of the gable, above the room where two brothers slept. Below that was the kitchen of the ground floor.

But the house was dwarfed by giant brick apartment buildings that had arisen on either side. I had lived in Springfield, Missouri, in such an apartment house. My bedroom window looked down on just such an anachronism of a house.

As the Salesman talked (the most natural talk I had ever heard on stage, yet something elevated into speech that was way beyond natural), he remembered when he had moved his family to his house—when the house was new and in a neighborhood of such houses. And as he remembered, I gasped as the sooty apartment buildings faded away, faded into the towering maples of the Salesman's memory. The neighborhood as it had been years ago.

In that moment I realized that in films this effect is merely a cross-fade. But on stage, in this moment, it was a miracle. It was magic. In films it merely takes us to another place. On stage it takes us into the Salesman's mind. It took me to a place where I had never been. I wanted from that moment to be a part of this miraculous medium.

But something else was happening, something larger, and to a fourteen year old, something much more disturbing. Yes: While the Salesman was spinning his beautiful dream, I knew that this clarity and beauty were not going to materialize. This was his idealized dream from the past. The ugly apartment building looming over his house was the reality. There was something in the Salesman that was going to prevent his dream from happening.

I had learned that this was the basis of tragedy, and was thrilled to see that such a story could be told about people, common people, today. But this wasn't all the author was doing. He seemed to be saying that there was something flawed also *in the dream.*

This was something a kid from a middle-class Missouri Republican household had never heard. And I had certainly never known that social criticism and a tragic personal history could be told, simultaneously and compellingly, in a mere *story.*

I came away from the play with my mind reeling. This wasn't the way stories were supposed to work out. Even if something in this guy propelled the Salesman into screwing-up, no author was supposed to say, in the same breath, that the system also had failed the Salesman.

This was my first intimation that the American Dream was—what? An implant, a hoax, an illusion. No mere Night in the Theater was supposed to make me nervous about the ground I stood on.

I realized in that moment that the theater was the only public place where truth could be spoken aloud. No wonder plays, evenings in the theater, entertainments, were censored. No wonder they were banned, no wonder governments were uncertain about this medium above all others. No wonder they wanted to suppress this stuff. No wonder they still want to.

This was the magic of story telling. This was the provocation, the sly galvanization, to political action. No other medium has this power. No wonder I was shocked and compelled by the witchcraft of that night.

And it was all caused, it was all started, by a sleight of hand. It was the first time I had realized that a sleight of hand could *tell* me something rather than hide something from me. The next time I saw this phenomenon was four years later when I saw a regional theater production of *The Crucible.* I wouldn't see it again until I moved to New York City and saw the Off Broadway smash hit production of *A View from the Bridge.*

It is a great privilege to be able to acknowledge, before The Man, my generation's debt to Arthur Miller. And to thank him (I think I thank him, 'cause this stuff ain't easy) for thrilling us, and for showing us the way.

And for setting the standards so high that it will take us all a lifetime to try, in our own way, to repay him for the lesson.

Notes

1. "The Theatre," *Town and Country* 17 (1949), 65.

2. Quoted in Brenda Murphy, *Miller: Death of a Salesman* (Cambridge: Cambridge University Press, 1995), 66.

3. "*Death of a Salesman,* A New Drama by Arthur Miller, Has Premiere at Morosco," *New York Times,* 11 February 1949.

4. "*Streetcar* Bolsters Broadway's British Name," *Christian Science Monitor,* 27 March 1974, F6.

5. Murray Schumach, "Miller Still a *Salesman* for a Changing Theatre," *New York Times,* 26 June 1975, 32.

6. Christian-Albrecht Gollub, "Interview with Arthur Miller," *Michigan Quarterly Review* 16 (1977), 123.

7. "Drama," *Nation* 168 (5 March 1949), 283-84.

8. Richard I. Evans, *Psychology and Arthur Miller* (New York: Dutton, 1969), 91.

9. Robert W. Corrigan, "Interview with Arthur Miller," *Michigan Quarterly Review,* 13; 4 (Fall 1974), 402.

Brenda Murphy (essay date fall 1998)

SOURCE: Murphy, Brenda. "Willy Loman: Icon of Business Culture." *Michigan Quarterly Review* 37, no. 4 (fall 1998): 755-66.

[*In the following essay, Murphy examines the cultural impact of* Death of a Salesman, *focusing on the effect the play has had on the public's perception of salesmen.*]

In 1963, critic and director Esther Merle Jackson wrote a perceptive essay entitled "*Death of a Salesman*: Tragic Myth in the Modern Theatre," in which she argued that [*Death of a Salesman*] is "the most nearly mature myth about human suffering in an industrial age." In *Salesman,* she suggested, Arthur Miller "has formulated a statement about the nature of human crises in the twentieth century which seems, increasingly, to be applicable to the entire fabric of civilized experience." For Jackson, the unique power of this play, as opposed to other significant twentieth-century tragedies, lies in "the critical relationship of its central symbol— the Salesman—to the interpretation of the whole of contemporary life":

> In this image, Miller brings into the theatre a figure who is, in our age, a kind of hero—a ritual representative of an industrial society. It is its intimate associa-

tion with our aspirations which gives to the story of Loman an ambiguous, but highly affecting, substratum of religious, philosophical, political, and social meanings. The appearance of the Salesman Loman as the subject of moral exploration stirs the modern spectator at the alternately joyful and painful periphery of consciousness which is the province of tragedy.[1]

That Esther Jackson was right about *Death of a Salesman*'s mythic relationship to modern culture is clearest from the play's impact on the young. In the fifty years of its life since the premiere, *Salesman* has found its way into university and secondary school curricula throughout the world, and the responses of succeeding generations of students have not diminished in immediacy or intensity. The description of one high school student's experience when he took the part of Biff in his class's staged reading will serve for many:

> Arthur Miller's play *Death of a Salesman* struck me on a very tender nerve. . . . I see many parallels between myself and my father and the Loman family. My father is a salesman. He, too, is much happier with a batch of cement. I feel a strong "can't get near him" feeling with my father. The only way I can get and hold his attention is to tell him of all my accomplishments. We are not close as Willy and Biff are not. I dislike Willy a great deal and this dislike stems from my anger and disappointment in not being close to my father. At the end of this play I was made acutely aware of this anger and disappointment.[2]

The student was so affected by the play that he engaged in a confrontation with his father that was inspired by Biff's confrontation with Willy:

> We talked and talked. For almost half an hour my anger poured from my body into his. When I finished and we had both broken down in tears, I told him everything I had ever wanted to tell him. After my anger had all spewed out, for the first time in my entire life I felt love toward him. *For the first time*!! I feel I have grown up in a very big way. I think I have done in seventeen years what took Biff thirty-four.

> All of this because of a play, a bunch of words printed on paper. How can a play do this? Genius, I say!! *Death of a Salesman* is the greatest piece of literature I've ever read.[3]

The student's aesthetic criterion may not be sophisticated, but it is certainly valid. In many countries, in many languages, in cultures as different from that of the United States as Communist China's and capitalist Japan's, in all kinds of productions, from the most sophisticated efforts of London, Broadway, and Hollywood to a high school classroom reading, *Death of a Salesman* has proved its power to move audiences profoundly. There is no doubt that Arthur Miller has captured something in this play that is vital to human experience in the twentieth century.

The cultural impact of *Death of a Salesman* far exceeds the bounds of those who have encountered it as a theatrical or literary experience, however. Willy Loman and his failure and death have a status as defining cultural phenomena, both inside and outside America's borders, that began to be established in the first year of the play's life. In February 1950, as the original production approached its first anniversary, a newspaper reporter marveled that *Salesman* had "already become a legend in many parts of the world," commenting that "why this play has approached the stature of an American legend in these distant lands defies analysis."[4] In a single year, Arthur Miller had received more than a thousand letters explaining the personal ways in which the play was related to their writers' lives. A number claimed to be the model for Willy, or suggested that Miller record their lives too, because they were so much like Willy's. A number of sermons, both spiritual and secular, had been preached on the text of the play, with ministers, rabbis, and priests explaining its exposure of the emptiness of Willy's dreams of material success, and sales managers using Willy as an object lesson of how not to be a salesman.

In the years immediately following the original production, Willy Loman entered the world's consciousness as the very image of the American traveling salesman, an identity with which the business world was far from comfortable. Writing in the garment industry's own *Women's Wear Daily* shortly after the play's premiere, Thomas R. Dash articulated the conflict between identification with Willy and resistance to him that characterized the typical relationship that people in business were to have with the play. Noting that Willy's was an "individualized tragedy," and that "it does not follow that all salesmen necessarily are discarded to the ashcan after thirty-five years of service for one firm, that they crack mentally and that they dash themselves to pieces on a mad and suicidal ride to the hereafter," he nonetheless had to concede that, "if you have traveled the road and are honest with yourself, you may recognize certain traits of Willy's in your own behavior pattern, both professional and personal." Since the very art of salesmanship "is predicated upon a talent for fictionalizing and romanticizing," Dash suggested, "from the habits formed by this forgivable fantasy and hyperbolic praise of the product, certain illusions of grandeur inevitably creep into the mental fabric of the practitioner. Frequently, as in the case of Willy Loman, these habits percolate into the salesman's personal life." As for Willy's infidelities on the road, Dash wrote, "this writer does not propose to have the wrath of the whole craft descend upon him by making any generalizations . . . let each man probe his own conscience and answer 'True' or 'False.'"[5]

The most immediate and overwhelming response of the business world to the failure and death of Willy Loman was to try to erase it from the public's consciousness. When the first film adaptation of the play was done in 1950, the executives of Columbia Pictures, fearing a public reaction against the movie for its failure to uphold the values of American capitalism, made a short film which they planned to distribute to theaters along with the feature. The short was filmed at the Business School of the City College of New York, and consisted, according to Miller, of "interviews with professors who blithely explained that Willy Loman was entirely atypical, a throwback to the past when salesmen did indeed have some hard problems. But nowadays selling was a fine profession with limitless spiritual compensations as well as financial ones. In fact, they all sounded like Willy Loman with a diploma."⁶ Only when Miller threatened to sue did Columbia withdraw the short film.

By the 1960s, businessmen were nearly desperate to divorce the salesman's identity from that of Willy Loman. Only one in seventeen college students was willing to try selling as a career in 1964.⁷ Business executives blamed this largely on Arthur Miller. "To many novelists, playwrights, sociologists, college students, and many others," wrote Carl Reiser in *Fortune* magazine, the salesman "is aggressively forcing on people goods that they don't want. He is the drummer, with a dubious set of social values—Willy Loman in the Arthur Miller play."⁸ In direct opposition to Willy's image, American business was trying to define a "new salesman" in the 1960s, "a man with a softer touch and greater breadth, a new kind of man to do a new—much more significant—kind of job."⁹ Despite the best efforts of corporate America, however, Willy's image remained the public's clearest vision of the salesman. "To be sure," suggested *Newsweek* in 1964, "the old-style drummer is no longer in the mainstream. But he's still paddling around out there with his smile and shoeshine, his costume a bit more subdued and his supply of jokes, sad to relate, a bit low."¹⁰ *Newsweek*'s article, "The New Breed of Salesman—Not Like Willy," was tellingly illustrated with the familiar Joseph Hirsch drawing of Willy with his sample cases, over the caption: "Willy Loman: An Image Lingers On."

When plans were announced for the CBS television production of *Salesman* in 1966, the Sales Executives Club of New York mobilized itself to prevent further erosion of the salesman's image. Complaining that "Willy Loman has been plaguing our 'selling as a career' efforts for years," the club suggested changes in the script "to improve the image of the salesman depicted in the drama." As had been tried with the Columbia picture, the sales executives suggested a prologue to the play, "alerting viewers that they were about to see the tragedy of a man who went into selling with the wrong ideas, a man who had been improperly trained by today's standards. The prologue would warn that Willy Loman would have been a failure 'in anything else he tackled.'" In case that wasn't enough, an epilogue could be added, called "The Life of the Salesman." The epilogue would indicate that, "with

modern, customer-oriented selling methods, Willy Lomans are ghosts of the past." The Xerox Corporation, which sponsored the telecast, had a golden opportunity, the sales executives thought, "to enlighten the public about what a well-trained modern salesman really does, and dispel the idea that the rewards of a selling career are often disillusionment and death."¹¹ Arthur Miller, the writer of the newspaper report on this effort noted, "could not be reached for comment." It is not hard to imagine what his comment would have been.

In the year following the telecast, an industrial film producer, David R. Hayes, made a film called *Second Chance,* an inspirational film for salesmen that featured football coach Vince Lombardi in a narrative that allowed him to use his "break-'em up football coaching technique on a fictionalized typical salesman." Hayes explained that the reason for scripting the film as a play rather than an inspirational talk was that "we had to undo for the art, science and business of selling . . . what Arthur Miller had done in damage to the field in his stageplay, *Death of a Salesman.* I decided to do it with Miller's own tools—that is, drama."¹² Within two years, the trade film had been sold to 7,000 companies, and had made the fortune of Hayes's industrial film company, Take Ten, Inc. The introduction of dramatic conflict into trade films wrought a major change in the industry, one of Willy Loman's many influences on American business.

Throughout the 1970s, the effort to expunge the image of Willy Loman from the public's view of the salesman continued without much success, despite the continually improving material circumstances of the typical salesman, and the greater security that came from an ever-higher ratio of salary to commission throughout the sales profession. Willy and the play had become an unconscious part of the businessman's vision and vocabulary, as is evident from the titles of articles in business publications. "The Salesman Isn't Dead—He's Different" and "The New Breed of Salesman—Not Like Willy" were succeeded by titles like "Deaths of a Salesman," "The Rebirth of a Salesman," and "The New Life of a Salesman."

With the worsening economy of the 1980s, the cultural resonance of Willy Loman had a new meaning for the generation that had not been born when the play was first produced. Speaking of "underemployed 30-year-olds" who were being forced to "bring their families home to live with bewildered and resentful parents," and middle-aged people "with kids and mortgages who have been out of work for three months," Jeff Faux suggested in 1983 that "Willy Loman could again symbolize a widespread middle-class tragedy—people trapped by expectations of status that no longer fit the cruel realities of the labor market."¹³ Meanwhile, business executives were moving salesmen off salary and back onto commission—just as Howard Wagner had done to Willy—and calling it "Motivating Willy Loman."[14] As one executive put it, "You really should get the carrot as big as possible without making the guy die to reach it . . . Give him salary for the essentials, to help pay the rent and put food on the table, but not much else. Hell, he's supposed to be a salesman."[15]

By this time, Willy Loman had taken on a life of his own, with little or no reference to the play. Edward Spar, the president of a marketing statistics firm, used Willy's putative sales route as an example of sensible county-based marketing for the Association of Public Data Users in 1987. Noting that Willy's territory was simply a matter of convenience and logic, Spar commented that, "if that company existed in reality, Willy's territory wouldn't have changed."[16] Interestingly, the route that Spar gave to Willy was completely imaginary: "Up to Westchester, through Putnam—all the way to Albany, Route 23 over to Pittsfield in Berkshire County, then down to Hartford and back to New York." Although Willy does mention having seen a hammock in Albany, the only indications of his route in the play are his turning back from Yonkers on the night the play begins and his description of his route to the boys when he returns from his trip in the first day-dream scene: Providence, where he met the Mayor, Waterbury, Boston, "a couple of other towns in Mass., and on to Portland and Bangor and straight home,"[17] a not very logical and rather improbable route. To Spar, however, Willy was not a character in a play, but the prototypical salesman with the "New England territory."

Evidence of the extent to which Willy and the American salesman have become identical to the culture at large is everywhere, in the most casual of references. A 1993 *Wall Street Journal* article on the certification, and thus professionalization, of salesmen is entitled, "Willy Loman Might Have Had a Better Self-Image."[18] One on the introduction of portable computers to the sales force is called "What Would Willy Loman Have Done with This?"[19] Neither has any reference to Miller's play. An article on the faltering U.S. balance of trade in *U.S. News and World Report,* called "The Yankee Trader: Death of a Salesman," makes no reference to the play, but carries the familiar Joseph Hirsch image of Willy with his sample cases as an icon on each page of the article.[20] An article opposing advertising for law firms is entitled "Willy Loman Joins the Bar: Death of a Profession?"[21] An article on Fred Friendly's efforts to use television to popularize the U.S. Constitution is called "TV's 'Willy Loman' of the Law."[22] And so on. There is no doubt that, at the end of the twentieth century, Willy Loman, and the Joseph Hirsch image of him, have achieved the status of cultural icon.

The conflict between identification with and resistance to Willy is obvious for members of the sales profession. As Miller has so eloquently put it, "Willy Loman has

broken a law without whose protection life is insupportable if not incomprehensible to him and to many others; it is the law which says that a failure in society and in business has no right to live."[23] Willy has failed in business, and the wages of his sin is death. Having experienced his own father's failure during the Depression, and its personal consequences, Miller knew this business creed intimately when he wrote *Salesman.* The extraordinary thing about the universality and endurance of Willy Loman as cultural icon, however, is that is it not necessary to have experienced Willy's sin and its wages at first hand in order to respond to Willy in the most primal way. This may be because Willy Loman has become the prime site for working out our deepest cultural conflicts and anxieties about the identity and fate of the salesman. And, being Americans, we are all salesmen in one way or another.

The extent to which the American way of life is identified with the salesman, and with Willy, becomes obvious from a cursory look at the numerous obituaries each year that are entitled "Death of a Salesman." This phrase has been used recently to sum up the lives of many successful businessmen, among them Commerce Secretary Ron Brown, who was lauded for his efforts to forge commercial links between the U.S. and China; record promoter Charlie Minor, who was shot by his former girlfriend, stripper Suzette McClure; and Victor Potemkin, known to a generation of New Yorkers for the TV commercials advertising his car dealerships. Less immediately evident is the connection between Willy Loman and counterculture guru and LSD promoter Timothy Leary, or Jerry Rubin, who, noted the *Hartford Courant,* "came to stand for hypocrisy" for the counterculture "when he committed the mortal sin—selling out." As the *Courant* pointed out, however, "Mr. Rubin was always a good salesman who knew how to market a message. Like many others of his generation, he realized that idealism alone doesn't put bread on the table."[24]

There is affection and even respect in identifying Willy Loman with men who are as successful in their fields as Ron Brown and Victor Potemkin. Potemkin, whose death, according to *Automotive News,* was "mourned by the whole automotive community,"[25] might be said to embody Willy's dream of achieving business success and being "well-liked" at the same time. Most often, however, identification with Willy Loman is cultural shorthand for failure, no matter what the field of endeavor. A review of the movie *Cop Land* refers to the local sheriff played by Sylvester Stallone as "a failed American dreamer, a Willy Loman of the police world, a profoundly poignant figure."[26] Failed presidential candidate Phil Gramm is described as "a pathetic self-destroyer like traveling salesman Willy Loman."[27] Political pundit George Will describes President Bill Clinton as "a political Willy Loman" in his unsuccessful attempt to sell his Mideast foreign policy to the American people.[28]

While accepting the iconography of failure that is associated with Willy and his death, business writers often situate themselves in opposition to its implications about the American socio-economic system. Willy Loman didn't have to die, these writers contend. If only he had had better sales training, or better job counseling, or a laptop computer, he would not have failed. The anxiety of having to master new technology, or at worst, of being replaced by it, is displaced by a hopeful rhetoric that suggests technology might be the salesman's salvation. The references to Willy Loman in these articles simultaneously evoke and attempt to dispel the typical salesman's anxiety about losing a job for failing to keep up with technology. "If Only Willy Loman Had Used a Laptop" explains the "competitive edge" that salespeople can get from "having access to product information at the point of sale."[29] Similarly optimistic portrayals of the necessity for updating the salesman's technology are presented in articles like *Business Week*'s "Rebirth of a Salesman: Willy Loman Goes Electronic" and *Advertising Age*'s "Willy Loman Never Had It So Good: New Technologies Enhance the Job of Selling." Upbeat reminders to the sales force that they need to keep up in order to compete have pervaded business journals since the early part of the century. What the evocation of Willy Loman provides is the subliminal suggestion of failure and its consequences should the reader disregard the writer's advice.

Willy Loman appears more substantially in another group of articles that purport to save his successors from his fate by addressing some of the issues that Miller addressed in the play, but within the context of the business environment. "He had the wrong dreams," says Biff of Willy, "All, all wrong." Writing for *Industry Week,* Joseph McKenna asks, "Was Willy Loman in the Wrong Job?" In the article he suggests that the reason Willy Loman "never made a lot of money" was that he "should have been plying another trade—just as many of today's real-life salesmen should be."[30] He goes on to cite an industry consultant who estimates that 55% of those working as sales professionals "don't have the ability to sell" and another 25% are selling the wrong product. This can be remedied through the consultant's method of "job matching," "marrying the appropriate job to the appropriate person with the appropriate skills or correctable weaknesses or both." Similarly, an article on "Career Entrenchment" uses Willy as a case study of the tendency to remain in a job despite one's obvious unfitness for it and suggests ways out of this inappropriate career direction.[31] In "Taking a Lesson from Willy Loman: Brokers Must Move Beyond Sales to Satisfy Risk Manager Demands," readers of *Business Insur-*

ance are advised to "break free of their sales roles" and "act as consultants and partners to risk managers" if they are to avoid Willy's fate.[32] In "The Death of Some Salesmen," Allen Myerson writes that "the old-style career salesman is dead," but that a new force of part-timers is replacing "the likes of Willy Loman," eschewing the old door-to-door methods and replacing them with home parties and demonstrations.

The subliminal message of these articles is clear. To be like Willy is to be a failure. Therefore we will make the job of sales as different as we can from the job as Willy did it. These articles all define the modern, successful salesperson in opposition to a putative Willy Loman. Of course, this is a cultural, not a literary evocation. The fact that Miller's character did not sell door-to-door, nor did he sell insurance, matters little. The point is that he represents the conjunction of traditional sales methods and failure to sell—precisely the formula that the business advisors want to place in opposition to their own ideas. To escape Willy's fate, the salesperson need simply follow this good advice. As one advisor to life insurance salespeople writes in the hopefully entitled "Goodbye, Willy Loman": "as long as we continue to participate in solutions to society's insurance problems and are receptive to change, the challenges that lie before us will be easy to meet . . . if only Willy Loman had known what we do now."[33]

Sometimes the context is darker than this, however. *Death of a Salesman* and Willy Loman are also evoked in cultural commentary that is not selling a quick fix for the individual, but is pointing to significant economic changes and trends that create deep anxiety for some part of the populace. In these cases, *Salesman*'s cultural iconography is a shorthand that reaches the reader's emotions before the analysis begins. In "Ageism and Advertising: It's Time the Ad Industry Got Past Its *Death of a Salesman* View of Employees Over 40," for example, Blake Brodie complains that executives in ad agencies are worried about being seen as surrounding themselves with "older staff," which is "death" in most ad agencies, making it rare to find a creative director who is over thirty-nine or an account executive over forty-five. Associating the anxiety of these relatively youthful executives over the possible loss of their jobs with Willy's predicament—"you can't eat the orange and throw the peel away. A man is not a piece of fruit!"—not only heightens the reader's emotional response but suggests that what might be viewed as an isolated difficulty in a particular "fast-track" yuppie career is part of a pervasive social problem—what the writer is calling "Ageism." Similarly, the mounting fear that one's chosen career could evaporate in the context of the rapidly developing technologies of the business world is expressed in serious articles like *The Economist*'s "Death of a Salesman: Travel Agents," which analyzes the declining profits of travel agents as customers do more of their own travel reservations online, and *Maclean's* "Death of a Car Salesman," which delineates major changes in the tactics of car sales as a result of online buying and the increasing replacement of commissioned agents by salaried sales forces at large car dealerships. These articles are fundamentally optimistic. They endorse the changes in the ways of doing business as better uses of technology that will result in greater efficiency and productivity. But the reference to Willy Loman creates a subtext of anxiety that undermines the positive rhetoric. Older salespeople will not be able to keep up, it reminds the reader. People will lose their jobs. Smaller agencies will be swallowed up by bigger ones. Humanity is losing out to technology.

To read these publications is to discover a mindset that simultaneously loathes Willy Loman and identifies with him. The writers want to put as much distance as possible between themselves and what Willy stands for—failure and death—but they can't help embracing him like a brother. After all, he has enacted their own deepest fears, and the experience has killed him. In Willy Loman, Arthur Miller has supplied to America's business culture—and as Calvin Coolidge reminded us, the business of America *is* business—the site where these deeply conflicted feelings can be engaged with some safety. Much as we try to deny it, Americans need Willy Loman. As long as our socio-economic system survives, Willy Loman will be right there with it, reminding us of our lyrical, fantastic dreams, and our darkest fears.

Notes

1. *CLA Journal* 7 (September 1963), 64.

2. Quoted in Meredith Kopald, "Arthur Miller Wins a Peace Prize: Teaching, Literature, and Therapy," *English Journal* 81 (March 1992), 59.

3. Ibid.

4. Luke P. Carroll, "Birth of a Legend: First Year of *Salesman,*" *New York Tribune* (5 February 1950), section 5, 1.

5. Thomas R. Dash, "'Life' of a Salesman," *Women's Wear Daily* (24 February 1949), 51.

6. *Timebends: A Life* (New York: Grove, 1987), 315.

7. "The New Breed of Salesmen—Not Like Willy," *Newsweek* 64 (5 October 1964), 94.

8. Carl Reiser, "The Salesman Isn't Dead—He's Different," *Fortune* 66 (November 1962), 124.

9. Ibid.

10. "The New Breed," 94.

11. Val Adams, "Willy Loman Irks Fellow Salesmen," *New York Times* (27 March 1966).

12. Morry Roth, "Un-Do *Death of a Salesman*" *Variety* (16 April 1969), 7.

13. "What Now, Willy Loman?" *Mother Jones* (8 November 1983), 52.

14. John A. Byrne, "Motivating Willy Loman," *Forbes* 133 (30 January 1984), 91.

15. Ibid.

16. Martha Farnsworth Riche, "Willy Loman Rides Again," *American Demographics* 10 (March 1988), 8.

17. Arthur Miller, *Death of a Salesman,* Acting Edition (New York: Dramatists Play Service, 1952), 21.

18. 2 April 1993, B1.

19. *The Wall Street Journal* (26 November 1990), B1.

20. 98 (8 April 1985), 64-70.

21. *ABA Journal* 76 (October 1988), 88-92.

22. *The National Law Journal* 9 (6 October 1986), 6.

23. *Arthur Miller's Collected Plays* (New York: Viking, 1957), 35.

24. "Death of a Salesman," *Hartford Courant* (30 November 1994), A18.

25. Jim Henry, "Death of a 'Salesman,'" *Automotive News* (12 June 1995), 3.

26. Brian D. Johnson, "*Cop Land,*" *Maclean's* 110 (25 August 1997), 74.

27. Francis X. Clines, "Downbeat Days for Salesman Gramm," *New York Times* (10 February 1996), 10.

28. George F. Will, "A Political Willy Loman," *Newsweek* (2 March 1998), 92.

29. Jonathan B. Levine and Zachary Schiller, "If Only Willy Loman Had Used a Laptop," *Business Week* (12 October 1987), 137.

30. Joseph F. McKenna, "Was Willy Loman in the Wrong Job?" *Industry Week* 239 (17 September 1990), 11.

31. Kerry D. Carson and Paula Phillips Carson, "Career Entrenchment: A Quiet March toward Occupational Death?" *Academy of Management Executives* 11 (February 1997), 62-75.

32. Sally Roberts, "Taking a Lesson from Willy Loman: Brokers Must Move Beyond Sales to Satisfy Risk Manager Demands," *Business Insurance* 30 (6 May 1996), 49.

33. Alan Press, "Goodbye, Willy Loman," *Best's Review (Life-Health-Insurance)* 90 (September 1989), 70.

Brenda Murphy (essay date 1999)

SOURCE: Murphy, Brenda. "'Personality Wins the Day': *Death of a Salesman* and Popular Sales Advice Literature." *South Atlantic Review* 64, no. 1 (1999): 1-10.

[*In the following essay, Murphy argues that* Death of a Salesman *constructs "a history of the career of the traveling salesman in America."*]

One of the primary characteristics of Willy Loman's character is his penchant for self-contradiction: "Biff is a lazy bum! . . . There's one thing about Biff—he's not lazy" (16). One area where this is evident is Willy's attitude toward business and success. As he tells his boss Howard Wagner, he is aware that in 1948, the "real time" of the play's action, business is "all cut and dried, and there's no chance for bringing friendship to bear—or personality" (81), but he still longs for the days when "there was respect, and comradeship, and gratitude in it" (81). As Brian Dennehy's performance in the 1999 production of *Death of a Salesman* reminds his audience, Willy is a "born" salesman. In the scene between Willy and Howard, he nearly sells Howard on the myth of Dave Singleman before he sabotages his sales pitch by losing his temper. Willy Loman is a very confused man, but his confusion about what it means to be a salesman and what it takes to succeed at the job is as much cultural as personal. In the character of Willy Loman, Arthur Miller has established a metonymic representation of the contradictory beliefs and value-systems that were at the heart of American business culture in the decade after World War II. In his own memory and experience, Willy encompasses three generations of American salesmen, that of his father and his hero Dave Singleman, that of Willy, his brother Ben, and his friend (or brother-in-law) Charley, and that of Willy's sons and his boss, Howard Wagner. In the play, Miller creates a history of the career of the traveling salesman in America through the references to these characters, and in doing so, he suggests the extent to which social and cultural forces have figured in Willy's business failure, and his personal disintegration.

The occupation of traveling salesman began in the United States with the Yankee peddler, in the early nineteenth century. The peddler would buy up cheap, portable manufactured goods in the early industrial centers of the Northeast, pack them in a wagon or peddler's pack, and set off for the rural South or the frontier villages of the West, where he would travel from small town to small town, selling his wares at a high profit. Peddlers were entrepreneurs, operating completely on their own, free to buy and sell whatever they wanted and to travel wherever they liked. Willy Loman's father, born in the mid-nineteenth century, is a peddler, a "very wild-hearted man," according to Ben, who would "toss the whole family in the wagon" and drive right across the country, through Ohio, Indiana, Michigan, Illinois, and all the Western states (49).[1] Miller emphasizes the elder Loman's independence by indicating that he even manufactured the products that he sold, the flutes that he made along the way. According to Ben, he was also a great inventor, who made more in a week with one gadget than a man like Willy could make in a lifetime (49). It is the elder Loman that Miller evokes with the play's flute music, "small and fine, telling of grass and trees and the horizon" (11). It expresses nostalgia for a lost age when the traveling salesman was free and independent, living by his wits and his own hard work.

It is significant that Willy's father traveled west, away from the urban centers of the country, and eventually left his family to go to America's last frontier, Alaska. During Willy's childhood in the 1890s, the Yankee peddler was already an outmoded figure, living on the fringes of society. He had been replaced by a figure who served the interests of the larger manufacturers more efficiently, the drummer. Beginning in the late nineteenth century, the drummer, usually a young man with a pleasant personality, was sent by a large manufacturing firm or wholesaler to greet small retail merchants who came from outlying areas to the industrial centers in order to buy their stock. The drummers would go to hotels, railroad stations, and boat landings, greet the merchants, help them to make their way around the city, and offer them free entertainment in hopes of securing their orders for merchandise. As competition between wholesalers intensified, the drummers were sent on the road with sample cases and catalogs, going out to the merchants rather than waiting for them to come to the city. These were the original "commercial travelers" or "traveling salesmen," and they spent six to nine months a year on the road, living in hotels and sleeping cars.

Dave Singleman, Willy's hero, is Miller's example of the drummer. As Willy tells it, he met Dave Singleman when he was young, in the first decade of the twentieth century. Singleman, a salesman who had drummed merchandise in thirty-one states, was eighty-four years old at the time that Willy met him, and still making his living as a salesman. According to Willy, he could go into twenty or thirty different cities, pick up a phone, and call the buyers, who would give him orders. Willy says that he decided then that he wanted to be a traveling salesman because he wanted to become like Singleman, and be "remembered and loved and helped by so many different people" (81). In the early part of the century, it was character that was considered to be the paramount factor in sales success. Aspiring salesmen were urged to develop the qualities of character that would make customers respect and want to buy from them. A prototype for Dave Singleman, James Fenelon, an eighty-nine year veteran of the traveling sales force in 1916, attributed his success to the fact that "he never used tobacco in any form and that he always acted as a gentleman should" (Geyer 53). His virtue was rewarded when he became ill and the president of the company wrote that "he wanted to keep the dean of the force on the pay roll as long as he lived, even if he never made another trip" (Geyer 53). Willy's generation remembered the time when there was "respect, and comradeship, and gratitude" (81) in business.

In the first two decades of the twentieth century, salesmen were urged to improve sales by improving their character, often as a kind of religious exercise. Self-tests to see whether one had the requisite strength of character for the job were common in popular magazines. One expert suggested a self-examination at the end of each day:

> The salesman should possess the ability to review carefully his work at the close of each day, and decide just where and how he has been weaker than he should have been. There is some reason for the loss of every sale. The salesman may not be at fault, but it is safer for him to assume that he is and to endeavor to put his finger upon his weakness. Such a practice will foster in him the habit of holding himself strictly accountable for errors. He should also at the same time review the essential qualifications of a salesman and decide in which of them he is lacking.

(Jones 170)

The salesman was urged to be thoroughly honest with himself when performing his "task of introspection," for "the salesman can develop only by earnestly striving to discover and eliminate his negative qualities, while at the same time he makes every effort to strengthen his positive ones" (Jones 170-71).

Willy's own career as a salesman begins in the early part of the twentieth century, when it was, as Willy tells his sons, "personality" that was considered the salesman's greatest asset. His job was to make friends with the buyers and merchants, so they would buy what he was selling. The product itself was not all that important. With the growth of mass production, however, the pressure increased on the salesman to move merchandise in order to keep up the volume of production. Consequently, as Willy's generation came into its maturity, married, and raised children during the 1920s, there was a good deal of pressure to sell merchandise, but it was relatively easy to do since the American business economy was enjoying one of its greatest periods of prosperity.

Salesmen at this time debated the best approach to selling merchandise. While there were many like Willy, who put all their faith in personality, friendship, and personal loyalty—"Be liked and you will never want" (33)—there was a new way of thinking about salesmanship. The earlier assumption had been that salesmanship was an essential quality, an innate character trait that could be nurtured and developed, but not created by the aspiring salesman. During the teens and twenties, salesmanship was beginning to be treated as a profession to be learned. The new interest in psychology led experts to think about the psychology of the buyer, and how best to manipulate it, as well as the psychological traits that made for the best salesmen. With mass production and increased competition, buyers and merchants began to think more about profit margins and customer satisfaction than their own personal relation-

ship with the salesman. There was more interest in the quality of the product and the salesman's knowledge about it. Companies began to train their salesmen in the methods of salesmanship and to educate them about the products they were selling. As one writer put it:

> Salesmanship is not trying to persuade people to buy something they do not want. That kind of salesmanship is, indeed, practiced, but not for very long; and no one makes any money out of it. Real salesmanship is demonstrating an article, or whatever it may be, in terms of the person who, it is hoped, will buy it. It is the development of a need, that already exists, into a present want. It is an operation performed first on the intellect and only secondly on the pocketbook of the prospect.

(Hopkins 29)

With the stock market crash in 1929, and the Great Depression that followed it, the competition among salesmen became more and more cutthroat. As Willy tells Ben in one of the day-dream sequences that takes place in 1931, "business is bad, it's murderous" (51). Using all of the tricks that Willy has learned in a lifetime of selling, including seducing the buyer's secretary and bribing her with stockings, Willy is barely able to eke out a living for his family. The salesman was up against an unforgiving business climate that placed the blame for failure squarely on the individual. Business writer J. C. Royle, for example, maintained that all that was needed to increase sales in 1931 was better salesmen: "The sales of the born salesmen have not suffered terribly during the Depression, but the amount of goods handled by the poor salesmen or those who need training has been pitiable." In 1929, he contended, American salesmen did not sell sufficient goods to justify themselves, and "they are urged to do so now under spur of necessity. They are not being asked the impossible either" ("Wanted" 41-2).

During this period, the prevailing idea was still that, as Willy puts it, "the man who makes an appearance in the business world, the man who creates personal interest, is the man who gets ahead" (33). As J. George Frederick suggested in his *1000 Sales Points: The "Vitamin Concentrates" of Modern Salesmanship* (1941), the first element of good salesmanship was to "Polish Off Your Personality." A salesman's personality "must not be rough-hewn. It must feel agreeable and bland to all who contact it, or else it is a handicap. Therefore the first sales fundamental is to present *an acceptable personality*—in neatness, cleanliness, clothes, manner, deportment, expression, etc." (17). Once his own personality was attended to, the salesman could concentrate on the psychological manipulation of the customer.

With most of the younger men in the military, middle-aged salesmen like Willy made an adequate living during World War II, despite the fact that the manufacturing of consumer goods was severely restricted. In the post-war period when the real time of the play takes place, there was a pent-up demand for things like new cars, tires, brand-name liquor, and nylon stockings, which had not been available during the war. The enormous American war industry was being retooled to produce consumer goods, and the advertising business was expanding rapidly as Americans were "educated" into desiring things like vacuum cleaners, television sets, and air conditioners, which had not been manufactured in large quantities before the war. The newly invigorated American business sector seized on the youthful and energetic workforce of young men returning from the military, displacing the women and older men who had been employed during the war. Men like Willy Loman, sixty-three years old in 1948, were being displaced by the younger generation everywhere.

Hap Loman and Howard Wagner represent typical members of this younger generation. Hap is not a salesman, but one of two assistants to the assistant buyer of a large department store. His job is more secure than Willy's, and it carries a regular salary rather than the precarious commission that Willy lives on. Unlike his father, though, Hap does not use his salary to support a family. Instead, he lives a carefree bachelor life, more interested, as Linda tells him, in his apartment and his car and his women than in helping his family, soon to become the ideal consumer of Hugh Hefner's *Playboy*. His final response to his father's death is to proclaim that he is "not licked that easily. I'm staying right in this city, and I'm gonna beat this racket! . . . Willy Loman did not die in vain. He had a good dream. It's the only dream you can have—to come out number-one man" (138-39). Howard Wagner, who has taken over the business that employs Willy after the death of his father Frank, is pragmatic and impersonal in his treatment of the aging salesman. When Willy admits that he can't handle the road anymore, Howard refuses to consider finding him something to do in New York as his father might have done, explaining, "it's a business, kid, and everybody's gotta pull his own weight" (80). When Willy loses control, showing his desperation, Howard fires him, telling him that he is not in a fit state to represent the firm.

The profession of selling underwent a tremendous change after the war. In the late forties, a movement to professionalize the salesman began, promoting sales as a career for college graduates. An important part of this movement was to emphasize the salesman's expertise and downplay his personality. Students were taught in business courses that the salesman's job was to learn everything he could about his product, and about the market, to gather all the data he could and analyze it using the most sophisticated statistical methods—in Willy's words, "today, it's all cut and dried, and there's no chance for bringing friendship to bear—or personal-

ity" (81). A number of books were written about "salesmanship" in the late forties and early fifties, attempting to codify the knowledge that was the fruit of a lifetime of experience for a Willy Loman or a Dave Singleman. Unfortunately for the veteran salesmen, the knowledge was expressed in a new lingo they didn't always understand, and it was based on different values, Howard Wagner's values, where the bottom line was everything

During the forties and fifties, the professional salesman became increasingly driven by things like market studies and demographics. Willy's plea for loyalty and humane treatment—"you can't eat the orange and throw the peel away—a man is not a piece of fruit!" (82)—is irrelevant to Howard's way of thinking. The prevailing view in the post-war business culture was that a salesman's job was not to sell a product—any product—to a buyer because he was liked and trusted by him, but to learn as much as possible about a particular product, identify its market, and bring the product to the buyer, any buyer. The two human beings, salesman and buyer, were becoming the least important elements of the transaction. Willy's complaint that salesmanship was becoming "cut and dried" is meaningless to a man like Howard, who is interested only in the bottom line of profit and loss. That is exactly the way he wants it to be.

A good example of the popular application of the new ideas about salesmanship is Harry Simmons' *How to Sell Like a Star Salesman* (1953). Simmons' description of the first two necessities for salesmanship are "application to the job—keep everlastingly at it" and

> complete knowledge—knowing not only the rules of the game, but the reasons behind the rules and the smart application of the rules to the situation at hand. This also includes every single bit of knowledge about your product that it is possible to acquire; you never know when the smallest fact will develop into a big factor that will turn the tide in your favor.
>
> (Simmons 12)

Simmons' book includes "Twenty-eight pint-size capsules that hold a gallon of helpful sales advice" for the salesman operating in the post-war business environment, several of which speak directly to Willy's failings. For example: "Reach for the order instead of applause. Many a man mistakes sociability for sales ability. He spends his time being a good-time Charley instead of a brass-tacks salesman. And then he complains about business being slow!" and "Tall tales make funny stories, but sound selling talks its way to the cash register! It's just a question of whether you want your sales manager to laugh with you or at you" (Simmons 94). The modern salesman, in Simmons' post-war view, is a serious businessman emphasizing "product information" and "helpmanship"—"helping your customer to buy properly, to use correctly, and to sell efficiently will fill both your pockets with more profits" (Simmons 98).[2]

The successful representatives of Willy's generation in the play, Charley and Ben, are hard-nosed capitalists, who have never allowed themselves to succumb to the sentimentality of the Dave Singleman myth as Willy has. Ben's creed is "never fight fair with a stranger, boy. You'll never get out of the jungle that way" (49). Although Charley is a loyal friend to Willy, he understands that the business world operates by different rules than human relations: "You named him Howard, but you can't sell that. The only thing you got in this world is what you can sell. And the funny thing is that you're a salesman, and you don't know that" (97). Unlike Willy, Charley has been able to adapt to the prevailing business culture. Willy's reaction to his failure in business during the real time of the play is similar to his response to his sense of failure in the other areas of his life. He retreats from present reality into nostalgic daydreams of the past, until he can no longer separate daydream from reality, past from present. His response to Charley's blunt statement of reality is a nostalgic reference to the bromides of the sales literature of the twenties: "I've always felt that if a man was impressive, and well liked, that nothing—" (97).

From the point of view of men like Howard and Charley, Willy's failure in business is a failure to adapt his old-fashioned sales technique—based on the buyer's personal loyalty to the salesman—to the new post-war business climate where salesmanship was based on knowledge of the product and service to the customer. Willy is a dinosaur. Howard fires him because "Business is business," and Charley offers him a job out of charity because he is an old friend, a gesture Willy recognizes and rejects. Through his representation of the three generations of businessmen in the play, however, Miller suggests that Willy's failure is also due to a deep cultural dissonance in the messages he has heard throughout his life. Willy has heard the hard truth from the capitalists, but he has chosen to believe in the Dave Singleman myth, widely reflected in the popular literature of his day, that it was humanity that mattered—whether it was measured in sterling traits of character, as in the early part of the century, or in a pleasing personality, as in the twenties. Despite the fact that Biff has won the chance to play in Ebbets Field through his accomplishments on the football field, Willy really believes, as he tells Ben, that "three great universities are begging for him, and from there the sky's the limit, because it's not what you do, Ben. It's who you know and the smile on your face! . . . that's the wonder, the wonder of this country, that a man can end with diamonds here on the basis of being liked!"

(86). The play's overwhelming message is that this is a lie, and that Willy is a fool to believe it. It is one of the things that destroys him. Willy is not alone, however, as the popular sales literature demonstrates. His belief that innate superiority will win out is the other side of the "strive and thrive" message of the American Protestant success ethic. Willy never ceases to believe that Biff is "magnificent," that he is one of the elect. It is imagining "that magnificence with twenty thousand dollars in his pocket" (135) that Willy goes to his death, destroyed, in one sense, by the salesman's creed of the twenties, from which he has never deviated.

Notes

1. See Barry Gross, "Peddler and Pioneer in *Death of a Salesman*." *Modern Drama* 7 (Feb. 1965): 405-10 for a discussion of these themes.

2. For similar views, see also Paul Ivey and Walter Horvath, *Successful Salesmanship*, 3rd ed., New York: Prentice-Hall, 1953; Melvin S. Hattwick, *The New Psychology of Selling*, New York: McGraw-Hill, 1960.

Works Cited

Frederick, J. George. *1000 Sales Points: The "Vitamin Concentrates" of Modern Salesmanship*. New York: Business Bourse, 1941.

Geyer, O. R. "The Oldest Traveling Salesman." *The American Magazine* 81 (Mar. 1916): 53.

Hopkins, George W. "The Real 'Star Salesman' in Modern Business." *The American Magazine* 93 (Apr. 1922): 28-9, 70.

Jones, John G. *Salesmanship and Sales Management*. New York: Alexander Hamilton Institute, 1919.

Miller, Arthur. *Death of a Salesman*. New York: Viking, 1949.

Simmons, Harry. *How to Sell Like a Star Salesman*. New York: Henry Holt, 1953.

"Wanted: Salesmen." *The Literary Digest* 113 (21 May 1931): 41-2.

Terry Otten (essay date fall 1999)

SOURCE: Otten, Terry. "*Death of a Salesman* at Fifty—Still 'Coming Home to Roost.'" *Texas Studies in Literature and Language* 41, no. 3 (fall 1999): 280-310.

[*In the following essay, Otten addresses the critical debate surrounding the categorization of* Death of a Salesman *as a tragedy, commenting that "the play completes the tragic pattern of the past becoming the present, and it affirms the tragic dictum that there are inevitable consequences to choices."*]

"Tragedy," Eric Bentley has warned, can "easily lure us into talking non-sense" (*Playwright,* 128). If so, *Death of a Salesman* surely doubles the risk. For likely no modern drama has generated more such talk than Miller's classic American play. After only two decades of strenuous debate seemed to have exhausted the subject, critics began to complain about "the pointless academic quibbles" about whether or not *Death of a Salesman* is a "true" tragedy (Weales, *American Drama,* 3). Such topics, wrote Lois Gordon in 1969, "have been explored ad nauseum" (98). Yet thirty years later and a half-century after the play's premiere, the question of its fitness as a tragedy continues to be a central critical concern.

Of course, Miller himself provided much of the impetus for the critical battles by writing his controversial 1949 essay on **"Tragedy and the Common Man"** in defense of Willy Loman as a suitable subject for tragedy, an essay later the same year on **"The Nature of Tragedy,"** and a number of important essays in subsequent years, including the preface **"On Social Plays"** published in the 1955 one-act edition of *A View from the Bridge* and *A Memory of Two Mondays.* Furthermore, the issue was and still is raised one way or the other in many, if not most, interviews, often by Miller himself. Although he admitted in the 1957 introduction to the *Collected Plays* that "I set out not 'to write a tragedy'" and called *Death of a Salesman* "a slippery play" to categorize, he defended it against "some of the attacks upon it as a pseudo-tragedy" (*Theater Essays of Arthur Miller,* 144): "I need not claim that this is a genuine solid-gold tragedy for my opinions on tragedy to be held valid" (146).[1]

By the time he wrote the foreword to his *Theater Essays* (first edited by Robert A. Martin in 1977), Miller admitted, "I have often wished I had never written a word on the subject of tragedy" (*Theater Essays,* lv), and then, "[t]he damage having been done," he went on to argue for the validity of modern tragedy, concluding, "I have not yet seen a convincing explanation of why the tragic mode seems anachronistic now, nor am I about to attempt one" (lv).

The controversy, however, has never really abated among critics, and the topic inevitably continues to surface in interviews. By the time Matthew Roudané interviewed him in November of 1983, Miller seemed less defensive and insistent. Responding to the question of whether or not *Death of a Salesman* was a Sophoclean tragedy, he commented, "I think it does engender tragic feelings, at least in a lot of people. Let's say it's one kind of tragedy. I'm not particularly eager to call it

tragedy or anything else; the label doesn't matter to me" (*Conversations* [*Conversations with Arthur Miller*], 361). And in a recent interview in 1997 he claimed that when people ask him what the play is about, he simply responds, "Well, it's about a salesman and he dies. What can I tell you?" (Mandell).[2]

But undeniably the "damage" *has* been done—one way or the other *Death of a Salesman* still provokes critical wars about the viability of tragedy in the modern age, and particularly in American culture. Even as Miller seems to have moved more into the contemporary literary world in his recent dramas and as more critics have begun to see his canon in postmodern terms alien to the concept of tragedy and traditional approaches to the genre, the question still remains dominant in evaluations of a work that Eugene O'Neill may well have prophesied in response to those who argued that tragedy is foreign to the American experience:

> Supposing someday we should suddenly see with the clear eyes of the soul the true valuation of all our triumphant, brass band materialism, see the cost—and the result in terms of eternal values? What a colossal, ironic, 100 percent American tragedy that would be, what? Tragedy not native to our soil? Why we *are* tragedy the most appalling yet written or unwritten.
>
> (*Selected Letters,* 159)

Miller has always admitted his predilection for tragedy, at times at the cost of obfuscating his plays by defending them as tragedies. The plays "that have lasted," he has insisted, "have shared a kind of tragic vision of man" (*Conversations,* 294). Although "tragedy is still basically the same" and can be traced back to the Bible and "the earliest Western literature, like Greek drama," he told Robert Martin in the late 1960s, "it is unlikely, to say the least, that since so many other kinds of human consciousness have changed that [tragedy] would remain unchanged" (*Conversations,* 200). He acknowledged to Steven Centola in a 1990s interview that his own later plays "may seem more tragic" than his earlier efforts in which "the characters' inability to face themselves gives rise to tragic consequences" (**"Just Looking"** [**"'Just Looking for a Home': A Conversation with Arthur Miller"**] 86-87). This awareness of an evolving form may partly explain why even those critics who share Miller's belief in the "tragic nature" of *Death of a Salesman* often stop short of declaring it (or other of his plays) an unequivocal or conventional tragedy. They instead allude to its "tragic situations," its evocation of "tragic feelings," its "tragic implications" or "tragic rhythms," or other subthemes of the genre.

Nonetheless, Miller has long confessed that classical tragedy and Ibsen's subsequent adaptation of it in the post-Enlightenment period have provided the structural and thematic spine of his work. Looking back over his career in the mid-1980s, he remarked: "I think probably the greatest single discovery I made was the structure of the Greek plays. That really blinded me. It seemed to fit everything that I felt. And then there was Ibsen, who was dealing with the same kind of structural pattern—that is the past meeting the present dilemma" (**Conversations,** 386).³ He recalled that as an undergraduate he read "by chance . . . a Greek tragedy and Ibsen at the same time" and discovered that "something happened x years ago, unbeknownst to the hero, and he's got to grapple with it" (Bigsby, *Arthur Miller,* 49). His devotion to the tragic mode as he perceives it and his varied experiments with tragic form and matter have made him the more vulnerable to critics bent on showing the deficiencies of his works as tragedies or his mere mimicking of an obsolete literary tradition.

Christopher Bigsby may be right in claiming that "the argument over the tragic status of **Death of a Salesman,** finally, is beside the point" ("Introduction," xviii),⁴ but of all Miller plays **Death of a Salesman** has been the lightening rod that has most attracted the unending debates on Miller and tragedy, and any assessment of its endurance and significance after fifty years must engage the question.⁵ Most often paralleled with *Oedipus,* **Death of a Salesman** has also been compared with Shakespearean tragedies (especially *Lear* and *Othello*), Lillo's *The London Merchant,* and various plays by Ibsen, O'Neill, Williams, and others.⁶ Attacks on the play as tragedy have ranged from casual dismissal to vitriolic antagonism. Representative views include Eleanor Clark's early severe condemnation of the play's "pseudo-universality" and "party-line" polemics in her 1949 *Partisan Review* essay. Calling Miller's concept of tragedy "not feasible," Alvin Whitley, among other later critics, admonished Miller to realize "that he is extending the traditional interpretation [of tragedy] to embrace demonstrably different emotional effects" and that "in the basic matter of personal dignity, Willy Loman may have ended where Hamlet unquestionably began" (262). Richard J. Foster labeled Willy a "pathetic bourgeois barbarian" and concluded that the drama was "not a 'tragedy' or great piece of literature" (87-88). Reflecting a common theme among Miller critics, Eric Mottram assaulted Miller's "muddled notions of Greek tragedy and modern psychology" which "lead him to plumb for that old stand-by for the American liberal, 'the individual'" (32). For a more recent indication of dismissive critical commentary regarding Miller's sense of tragedy, one might cite Harold Bloom's rather patronizing remark in his 1991 anthology *Willy Loman:* "All that Loman actually shares with Lear and Oedipus is aging; there is no other likeness whatsoever. Miller has little understanding of Classical or Shakespearean tragedy; he stems entirely from Ibsen" (1).

Because no single concept of modern tragedy has ever attained the status of being *the* standard measure of the genre like Aristotle's *Poetics* in reference to classical tragedy, **Death of a Salesman** is subject to as many interpretations and evaluations as there are definitions. Most modern theories of tragedy severely modify Aristotle whether applied to **Death of a Salesman** or any other modern drama,⁷ but certain elemental subthemes have constituted the targets of critics, among them the loss of community and divine order, the victimization and diminution of the hero, the banality of language, the absence of choice, the protagonist's lack of awareness or epiphany, the irresolution of the ending, and the failure to effect a "catharsis."

Perhaps the most sustained historical study of the development of tragedy generally is Robert Heilman's two-volume exploration of the genre, *Melodrama and Tragedy: Versions of Experience* and *The Iceman, The Arsonist, and The Troubled Agent: Tragedy and Melodrama on the Modern Stage.* Distinguishing between tragedies and what he calls "disaster" plays or serious melodrama, Heilman incorporates the thinking of many theorists, proposing that tragedy includes a "divided" hero driven by counter "imperatives" or "impulses," who chooses between irreconcilable opposites, gains awareness, accepts consequences, and evokes emotions of both defeat and victory (what Heilman calls a "polypathic" rather than "monopathic" response). He differentiates between such plays and "disaster" dramas in which characters are mere victims whose deaths shed little or no light on the nature of human experience. Like all such formulaic criticism, Heilman's at times creates a Procrustean bed of criticism in which some plays of dubious merit are raised in stature as "tragic," and superior dramas receive the more pejorative label of "melodrama." Nonetheless, because his study, in addition to offering a useful survey of dramatic theory and major plays, provides a functional definition that allows for critical discriminations to be made, I shall occasionally use his critical terminology, while keeping in mind Bernard Shaw's admonishment that critics can "become so accustomed to formula that at last they cannot relish or understand a play that has grown naturally, just as they cannot admire the Venus of Milo because she has neither corset nor high-heeled shoes" (54). To be sure, different critics using the very same elements cited by Heilman and others have vociferously declared **Death of a Salesman** both "the great American tragedy" and an exemplum of cheap pathos.⁸ In response to the play's fiftieth anniversary and continued prominence as what many still consider "the great American tragedy," it seems appropriate to look once more at the issues raised in the critical debate as they have been amplified and qualified by different theoretical approaches.

Underlying any consideration of the play's tragic potential is the larger question of whether or not tragedy can exist in an age when "God is dead." Nietzsche warned that it would go hard with tragic poets if God is dead, and writers like Joseph Wood Krutch and George Steiner have long since pronounced the death of tragedy, largely on the grounds that the absence of some identifiable, universal moral law that locates the operation of a transcendent order against which to judge the tragic hero denies the possibility of tragic drama. Miller himself has certainly recognized the problem this poses. When asked if his plays were "modern tragedies," he admitted,

> I changed my mind about it several times. . . . To make direct and arithmetical comparison between any contemporary work and the classic tragedies is impossible because of the function of religion and power, which was taken for granted in an *a priori* consideration of any classic tragedy.
>
> (***Conversations***, 88)

In a seminal discussion on the nature of tragedy with Robert Corrigan, Miller identified society as

> the only thing we've got in modern times that has any parallel to the ancient deities. . . . and what it lacks is sublimity because at bottom, I think, most people . . . have no sense of divinity. . . . and this is what cuts down the tragic vision. It levels.

And he went on to explain, "By society, I don't mean, of course, merely the government. It is the whole way we live, what we want from life and what we do to get it" (***Conversations***, 254). In the same interview he noted that the classic hero

> is working inside a religious cosmology where there is no mistaking a man for God; he is conscious to begin with that he is in the hands of God. . . . We are in the middle of a scrambled egg and mucking about in it, and the difference between the points of contact with the man and his god, so to speak, are fused.
>
> (255)

In effect, in a secular universe the moral center shifts to the individual in relationship to his social environment. As Miller told Robert Martin, "What we've got left is the human half of the old Greek and the old Elizabethan process" in which human beings were measured against the presence of the gods (***Conversations***, 202). As a consequence, Miller concluded,

> if we're going to talk about tragedy at all . . . we've got to find some equivalent to the superhuman schema that had its names in the past, whatever they were. Whether they went under the name of Zeus's laws, or, as in Shakespearean times, reflected a different ideology toward man, they also had lying in the background somewhere an order which was being violated and which the character was seeking to come to some arrangement with.
>
> (***Conversations***, 201)

In ***Death of a Salesman*** society assumes the role of the gods to whom Willy gives allegiance. It constitutes what Heilman calls an "imperative," an obligation to a given, externally located code that compels the tragic hero to act in direct opposition to an opposing imperative or "impulse," which Heilman characterizes as a personal or egocentric need or desire. The dilemma is underscored with irony, though, because unlike the traditional gods of tragedy, Willy's gods provide to be morally indifferent. As Rita Di Giuseppe has written, they have "metamorphosed . . . into the fat gods of consumerism" (115). Miller's depiction of such a secular universe has inevitably led to the protesting cry of some critics who apparently want Miller to provide a transcendent moral force that would belie the realism of his conception.[9] He often frustrates them by contextualizing the play in a realistic, if expressionistic, form that seems too reductive to allow for the grandeur of tragedy; but he encloses within this realism a tragic rhythm that depends upon the integrity of his uncompromised realism. The "discovery of the moral law," he wrote in **"Tragedy and the Common Man,"** is no longer "the discovery of some abstract or metaphysical quantity" but is grounded in the nature of human experience itself (***Theater Essays***, 5).

Eric Bentley offered the much repeated view in his *In Search of Theater* that ***Death of a Salesman*** futilely attempts to align tragedy with social drama, the one conceiving of the hero as responsible for his own fate and the other as the pathetic victim of a severely flawed society.[10] But, as Christopher Bigsby has observed, surely *Oedipus* and *Hamlet* integrate social drama and tragedy ("Introduction," xviii). For Miller, "there are certain duties and social fears that can create a tragic event," specifically when the dialectic develops "between the individual and his social obligations, his social self" (***Conversations***, 346). Miller has described Greek tragedies as "social documents, not little piddling private conversations" written by "a man confronting his society" (***Conversations***, 101). The differences that emerge in modern tragedy when realistically described social forces usurp the role of the gods transfigure tragedy profoundly—but not unrecognizably. Miller has called what emerges "the tragedy of displacement," in which "the tragic dimension" surfaces in the protagonist's struggle for a lost "personal identity" displaced by "the social mask" (***Conversations***, 347). In **"Tragedy and the Common Man"** he attributed "the terror and fear that is classically associated with tragedy" to the "inner dynamic" driven by the "total onslaught of the individual against the seemingly stable cosmos surrounding us" (***Theater Essays***, 4). Not unlike in *Hamlet*, though obviously different from it, the tragic conflict pits one imperative against another: the social imperative of success in direct competition with the personal imperative or "impulse" of finding the authentic self. This transformation of the tragic conflict generates concomitant tensions in the form and focus of the text, between the outer and inner worlds, between Willy as hero and Willy as a psychological case study, between social commentary and personal experience, between the socially accepted view of morality and personal guilt, between suicide and self-sacrifice—in short, between melodramatic documentary and modern tragedy.

Miller himself has sensed the precarious nature of his plays as tragedy, admitting in his essay **"On Social Plays"** that "The debilitation of the tragic drama . . . is commensurate with the fracturing and the aborting of the need of man to maintain a fruitful kind of union with his society" (**Theater Essays,** 62). Furthermore, he has implied that his artistic end in **Death of a Salesman** was closer to Ibsen than to Sophocles. In **Timebends** he confessed that he "wanted to set off before the captains and the so seemingly confident kings the corpse of a believer," to plant "a time bomb under American capitalism" (184); but he knew this differed from the Greek plays which, at the end, "return to confirm the rightness of the laws" (**Theater Essays,** 6). His purpose was political and satirical, for he knew, as Christopher Bigsby has written, that "Willy Loman's American dream is drained of transcendence. It is faith in the supremacy of the material over the spiritual" ("Introduction," xxiii). It is little wonder that Miller threatened a lawsuit when he was asked to permit a twenty-five minute short to be shown before the film version of the play to assure the audience that "nowadays selling was a fine profession with limitless spiritual compensations as well as financial ones"—indeed, it *would* have made the play "*morally* meaningless, a tale told by an idiot signifying nothing" (**Timebends,** 315).

Because Miller both creates a naturalistic, almost Marxist view of American culture in the post-Depression era, some have reduced the drama to social determinism. And the truth is Miller *does* describe Willy as a childlike victim of the cultural values he adopts virtually without question. In Miller's words, he "carried in his pocket the coinage of our day" (**Conversations,** 176) as a "true believer" in the American dream of success. The very embodiment of the myth, he carried an unidentified "product" in his case, "the cipher," in Stephen Barker's reading, "of an empty signifier" (88). And yet Miller grants Willy stature and significance because of, as much as despite, his dogged commitment to a pernicious ideal. One cannot take away Willy's dream without diminishing him, Miller has suggested: "[T]he less capable a man is of walking away from the central conflict of the play, the closer he approaches a tragic existence" (**Theater Essays,** 118). Ironically, like Oedipus, who at every point insists on fulfilling his obligation as king by unwittingly searching for his own father's murderer even though it finally destroys him to do so, Willy unreservedly follows his imperative to its

fatal end, similarly encouraged by all the others around him to abort his quest: Linda, Biff and Happy, Charley, and Bernard all urge him to give up, just as Teiresias, the Chorus, Jocasta, and the shepherd plead with Oedipus to do the same. That Willy does not finally understand the corruptness of the dream exposes his intellectual failure, but he dies in defense of the imperative that consumes him. When in a symposium on the play John Beaufort and David W. Thompson argued that Willy "has no moral values at all," Miller contended that "The trouble with Willy Loman is that he has tremendously powerful ideas. . . . The fact is that he has values" (**Conversations,** 30). As he told the Chinese actors for the 1983 production in Beijing, Willy "hasn't a cynical bone in his body, he is a walking believer, the bearer of a flame. . . . He is forever signaling to a future that he cannot describe and will not live to see, but he is in love with it all the same" (**Salesman,** 49). Even though the imperative devastates him as it does Oedipus, and even though it ironically proves false, Willy "in his fumbling and often ridiculous way . . . is trying to lift up a belief in immense redeeming human possibilities" (49).[11] What matters finally is not so much the validity of the ideal but that Willy offers himself up to affirm it. It motivates him just as the oracle compels Oedipus to fulfill his kingship. However ironically, Willy fulfills his role as salesman with the same determination that compels Oedipus to affirm his kingship.

But it would be absurd to argue Willy's tragic stature on the grounds of his innocent, misguided commitment to the American dream of success, even though his devotion to the code is no less consuming than Oedipus's or Hamlet's commitment to their imperatives. At a deeper level we must ask *why* he invests so totally and self-destructively in support of the dream. For Oedipus or Hamlet, of course, the moral imperative was a given—there was divine order, after all, a divinity that shapes human destiny. For Willy, however, the imperative was not so readily apparent or universally acclaimed. His fierce devotion to it was not for its own sake, but rather it was for Willy a means to an end. In a critically important comment, Miller contended that "Willy is demanding of the market and of his job some real return *psychically*" (**Conversations,** 297-98, emphasis mine). He seeks self-dignity and with it something more, what most defines the counter to the social imperative in the play, to recover the lost love of Biff and preserve the family. Willy does not want simply to fulfill the imperative for the dream's sake, but to express his love through "success." Because his will to succeed consistently frustrates his impulse to love, he suffers the division Heilman ascribes to the tragic hero.[12]

In a reversal of Aristotelian priorities Miller dramatizes, in Browning's phrase, "Action in Character, rather than Character in Action." Or, to put it another way, plot enters character to create "the soul of the action" rather than the narrative or external plot. ***Death of a Salesman*** "removes the ground of the tragic conflict from outer events to inner consciousness," as Easter Merle Jackson has proposed, depicting "a *tragedy of consciousness,* the imitation of a moral crisis in the life of a common man" (68). This shift violates the linear, architectonic movement of classical tragedy by placing the impetus for the action not in the hands of the gods but in Willy's own consciousness. When he announces "I am tired to death" (2), he sets in motion an inexorable internal struggle between past and present. On the verge of neurosis and paranoia because he vacillates hopelessly between two poles, Willy shares an obsessive nature with other tragic figures who skirt madness. But Miller has always insisted that Willy is not insane. His well-known aversion to Frederic March's portrayal in the film version of the play emphasizes the point. "If he was nuts," Miller wrote of Willy in ***Timebends,*** "he would hardly stand as a comment on anything" (325). March, who had been a "first choice for the role on stage," made Willy "simply a mental case," a neurotic, pathological case study, "an idiot" headed for the "looney bin," Miller complained to Christopher Bigsby—but Willy is not "crazy," and the audience recognizes that "This man is obviously going down the chute and he's telling them exactly what they believe" (*Arthur Miller,* 54, 58).

The internalization of the conflict is expressed in the staging of the play. We are on "The Inside of His Head," as Miller first proposed calling the work, on a stage expressive of the dialectical tensions between what Miller refers to as "social time" and "psychic time," city and country, home and workplace, as Willy's "daydreams" project the counter forces operating in his consciousness. On one hand, Miller maintained the dictum of tragedy he learned from the Greeks and Ibsen and coined "the birds coming home to roost" (Bigsby, *Arthur Miller,* 49), initiating the play in the rhythm of ancient tragedy with the appearance of "the *x*-factor" when Willy announces he cannot go on. But from there the play assumes more postmodern traits. As Matthew Roudané has suggested, the text is "Postmodern in texture but gains its theatrical power from ancient echoes, its Hellenic mixture of pity and fear stirring primal emotions" ("*Death of a Salesman,*" 63). Although Elia Kazan recognized from the beginning that Willy creates his own history in the play, only recently have critics begun to appreciate Miller's postmodern view of history, an element increasingly apparent in plays like ***Some Kind of Love Story, Elegy for a Lady,*** and more recent works like ***The Last Yankee, Ride Down Mount Morgan,*** and even ***Mr. Peter's Connections.*** Miller collapses time in ***Death of a Salesman,*** rather than simply showing the past reasserting itself in the present, making past and present coexist so completely that neither we nor Willy can always

distinguish between them. June Schlueter has observed how the extraordinary design "invites a recontextualizing reading of the play and a distinctly postmodern query: To what extent has Willy assumed authorial control of his own history, consciously or unconsciously rewriting and restaging it to suit his emotional needs?" ("Re-memoring Willy's Past," 143). In Miller's use of "re-memory," the text challenges "the historicity of knowledge, the nature of identity, the epistemological status of fictional discourse" (151). Yet for all its postmodern elements, as Roudané has rightly asserted, it "gets its power from ancient echoes." Miller began the play with the conviction that "if I could make [Willy] remember enough he would kill himself" (***Theater Essays,*** 138). The eruption of the past is vital in this sense because it reflects Miller's tragic view of causality, because it is "an acknowledgment," Christopher Bigsby has declared, "that we are responsible for, and a product of, our actions" ("Introduction," xi).[13]

Inspired by seeing *A Streetcar Named Desire,* Miller developed what Brenda Murphy has termed "subjective realism," which she describes as "expressionistic with the illusion of objectivity afforded by realism" (*Miller: Death of a Salesman,* 5). It allowed him to project a concept of time in which "nothing in life comes 'next' but . . . everything exists together at the same time. . . . [Willy] is his past at every moment." As a result the "form seems to be the form of a confession" (***Theater Essays,*** 136). The form thereby conveys the moment of moral consequence when Willy must finally pay the price for his choices—"you've got to retrieve what you've spent and you've got to account for it somehow" (Bigsby, *Arthur Miller,* 201). In fact Miller has employed Biblical language to define the moral significance of the drama, which shows us, "so to speak, the wages of sin" (***Conversations,*** 31). Willy, in a way, confesses despite himself as his memory becomes an unwilled confession. As a divided hero he sins against both imperatives that motivate him. He violates the law of success, Miller has explained, "the law which says that a failure in society and in business has no right to live." But he also sins against "an opposing system which, so to speak, is in a race for Willy's faith, and that is the system of love which is the opposite of the law of success" (***Theater Essays,*** 149). To be true to one set of values necessitates betrayal of the other. That is the tragic dilemma that Miller traced back to Eden, when either way they choose, either by disobeying the injunction not to eat the fruit or denying their impulse toward freedom, Adam and Eve were fated to suffer tragic consequences. Unable to accommodate diametrically opposite demands, Willy must and does make choices in response to the contending codes. He commits adultery in Boston to gain access to buyers, but consequently carries undeniable guilt for breaking "the law of love." In his annotations to the playscript Miller recorded that Willy is in fact "craving to be liberated from his guilt" (qtd. in Rowe, 56).

It is an essential question whether Willy *does* choose and, perhaps more importantly, whether he truly pays a price for his choices. It is difficult not to see his moral viability in light of his pervasive sense of guilt. Even if he fails to make the right moral choices (though no choice can be "right" in relation to the contending poles in the dialectic), he is surely not amoral. The play demands an accounting for his actions. One may contend that Willy lacks intellectual awareness, of course, and is thereby diminished as a tragic hero, but not that he is morally moribund. Few characters in modern drama expose so vividly the presence of a guilty conscience.

When Willy returns "tired to death," Gerald Weales has concluded, he is "past the point of choice" ("Arthur Miller," 172). In a way he is right. The play begins when Willy must finally suffer "the wages of sin" for choices already made, in the same way that Oedipus must confront the consequences of a crime already enacted. But in fact he also makes choices within the time frame of the present. As Miller has insisted, he is unwilling to "remain passive in the face of what he conceives to be a challenge to his dignity" (*Theater Essays,* 4). To this end he chooses not to take Charley's repeated offer of a job, although he already depends on Charley's help and could resolve his immediate financial crisis by accepting the position. Almost without regard to Willy's rejection of the job, Charley ironically explains why when he remarks at the Requiem, "No man only needs a little salary" (110). Willy chooses not to suffer the loss of dignity—to accept would demean him and, perhaps more, would deny the validity of the imperative by which he measures his worth. Most importantly, he chooses the car at the end of the play over the rubber hose, the latter representing both acceptance of defeat and escape from the consequences of failure, the former embodying an act of sacrifice, an ironic affirmation of the failed dream but, nonetheless, a conscious assertion of will. As will be discussed later, suicide by means of the rubber hose constitutes death *from* something, suicide by car death *for* something. Without free will tragedy cannot exist in Miller's view, for tragedy contests the idea that characters are only victims of external powers rather than participants in their own destiny. Just as we can conclude that Willy is morally alive, we must acknowledge that he possesses freedom of choice. He chose to follow the imperative that finally defeats him, and he chooses to die in part to perpetuate the dream. "He brings tragedy down on himself," Raymond Williams has explained in his defense of the play as tragedy, "not by opposing the lie, but by living it" (104).

Willy might be considered a composite tragic hero in that his divided nature and tragic fate are inexplicably bound to his two sons, who represent the poles in the dialectic. Willy's choice to follow the dictates of the cultural ethos most directly affects his family, which provides the locus of the tragic action. The larger community and its unifying myth of universal order are projected in the altar, the palace, and the throne-room in traditional tragedy; but the fragile Loman house, part externally real and part psychically real, houses a fragmented, dysfunctional family, where Willy's adherence to the law of success makes him, as Dan Vogel has noted, a petty "tyrannos" in his own house. But whereas "the family was subsumed by community, by public and even metaphysical-religious repercussions" in Greek drama, William Demastes has reminded us, in the Loman household family matters are disconnected from the larger human society or a spiritually charged cosmos (77). Though Shakespeare's heroes all engage in psychological warfare at some personal level, they all see themselves as primarily agents of the larger community. Oedipus's or Hamlet's "Oedipus Complex" is hardly the "soul of the action" in either text, however much both may be perceived in Freudian terms. But Miller has spoken of family in overtly Freudian terms as, "after all, the nursery of all our neuroses" (*Conversations,* 271), moving tragedy much more into the realm of the psyche and subjective reality as O'Neill tried to do. Some critics, and most notably the psychiatrist Daniel E. Schneider, have read the play as centrally about the Oedipus complex, "an unreal Oedipal bloodbath," in which we witness the search for the father, violent sibling rivalry, castration fear, and crippling guilt over the death of a parent.[14] But while such themes doubtless appear, the rivalry between brothers and their struggles against the father are more important as manifestations of larger mythic forces operating in Willy himself. Biff's association with nature and desire to return to a pastoral world characterized by fecundity and openness parallel Willy's lyrical references to New England, the open windshield and the warm air early in the play and, later in the play, his promise to Linda to someday buy a farm and his desperate attempt to "plant something." Hap's counter-commitment to the idea of success, seen throughout in his unconscionable business dealings and sexual prowess, reaches full expression at the Requiem in his vow to reclaim Willy's dream. But because Willy still naively convinces himself that he will eventually succeed and never doubts the dream Hap embodies, Willy does not need the assurances of his younger son or his forgiveness for not having been a success. It is Biff with whom he must be reconciled for the breech caused by his denial of "the system of love," a denial of his own other self.

Brenda Murphy has noted Miller's evolving conception of Biff. At first seeing the elder son as caught "between hatred for Willy and his own desire for success," the playwright had difficulty "developing a motivation for Biff's hatred" (*Miller: Death of a Salesman*, 9). But especially under Kazan's direction, Miller came to see the work, in Kazan's words, as "a love story—the end of a tragic love between Willy and his son Biff. . . . The whole play is about *love*—Love and Competition" (qtd. in Rowe, 44).[15] When the Chinese actor playing Biff in Beijing wondered why Biff says "I don't know what I want," Miller, in a telling comment, replied,

> You don't say "I don't know what I want," but "I don't know what I'm supposed to want," and this is a key idea. Biff knows very well what he wants, but Willy and his idea of success disapprove of what he wants, and this is the basic reason you have returned here—to somehow resolve this conflict with your father, to get his blessing.
>
> (***Salesman***, 71)

Willy and Biff form a symbiotic relationship. Biff cannot gain freedom from his father's imperative until his father somehow frees him from it—as, tragically speaking, he can do only through death. Similarly, Willy cannot succeed until he can align his love for Biff with the dream he follows. This explains that Biff returns because, as Miller explained to the Beijing actors, he "sometimes feels a painful unrequited love for his father, a sense of something unfinished between them brings feelings of guilt" (***Salesman***, 79). Willy equally feels "unrequited love," which we see in his eagerness for Biff's return, and yet he also suffers "feelings of guilt." Biff has failed to meet Willy's imperative and feels estranged because of it; Willy has violated love for the sake of the dream by which he hoped to express it and feels alienated as well. Inextricably linked, both in Willy's subjective world where he romanticizes Biff in the past to conform to his dream and in the external realm of reality where Biff has markedly failed to succeed, the two return to the crossroads, the place where *x* marks the spot, the hotel room in Boston where the law of success and the law of love collided, inflicting upon father and son a shared guilt that can only be redeemed by the death of the tragic hero.

Like the Greek chorus whose plea for relief unwittingly leads to Oedipus's tragic end, Linda's supplications propel Willy and Biff toward their tragic destiny. As she tells her son, "Biff, his life is in your hands!" (43). Yet from the beginning Linda has provoked intense critical reactions. Many see her as an enabler who "contributes to the truth-illusion matrix" by supporting Willy's "vital lie" (Roudané, "*Death of a Salesman*," 70).[16] Some consider her an even more sinister figure. Guerin Bliquez has called her "the source of the cash-payment fixation" whose acquiescence "in all Willy's weaknesses" makes her a "failure as a wife and mother." Seeing Ben as a rival, Bliquez adds, she emasculates and makes Willy a victim of her "ambition as well as

his own" (384, 386). Calling her "stupid and immoral" for encouraging Willy's self-deceit, Brian Parker accuses Linda of possessing no higher ideal than Willy's dream and finds her "moral sloppiness" manifested in Hap "one degree farther"—"Hap is his mother's son" (54). And Karl Harshbarger makes her an even more malevolent character who coerces Willy "to relate to her as a small boy . . . by not allowing him to communicate his deeper needs to her." sides with Biff against him, and blames him "for his own feelings. She offers him his reward, love and support, only when he becomes dependent on her" (14). He goes so far as to claim that in her "extreme defensiveness" against her own guilt she "must disguise the joy that she, not a man, has been victorious" (28).[17] Linda is also commonly referred to as merely a sentimental sop, a cardboard figure, or "a mouthpiece for Miller's earnestness" (Welland, 50). One critic has named her Jocasta, a "mousy twentieth-century Brooklyn housewife" who, like Oedipus's wife-mother, prevents her husband "from asking the fatal question, 'Who am I?'" (C. Otten, 87).

More recent feminist critics have found Linda a likely target for assaults on Miller, though as early as his 1970 book on Miller, Benjamin Nelson sounded a feminist chord that shows Linda helping "build a doll's house around [Willy] and, consequently, [doing] to Willy what he has been doing to Biff and Happy," making him as well as them "victims of her gingerbread house" (112-13).[18] A number of studies published in the late 1980s deny Linda a significant role in a tragic pattern, depicting her as reflecting a male perspective, which "borrows the methods and espouses the sexual politics of melodrama. . . . If Miller writes tragedy . . . he makes it a male preserve" (Mason, 113). Linda, according to Linda Ben-Zvi, "is the embodiment of society's perception of women" and of Miller's own conception (224), a view shared by Gayle Austin. Employing the feminist theory of Gayle Rubin, Austin laments Miller's reduction of women as "objects to be exchanged" and denial of them "as active subjects in the play" (61, 63). And Kay Stanton concludes that Miller conflates all female characters in the play "in the idea of Woman: all share . . . in their knowing"; and possessing "the potential to reveal masculine inadequacy," they "must be opposed by man" (82).[19] More recently, Linda Kintz has explored Miller's "grammar of space," which projects "a nostalgic view of the universalized masculine protagonist of the *Poetics*," in which conception women like Linda "wait at home, to console and civilize both husband and children, roles that provide a structural, narrative guarantee of masculine agency even in very different historical periods" (106). Tracing antifemale bias to the core of traditional tragedy itself, she raises a serious criticism not only of Linda's role but of the gender-biased nature of tragedy as genre.

These and other feminist attacks on the characterization of Linda and the other women in the play[20] have not gone unchallenged; and relative to seeing the play as tragedy, the issue is important, because Miller conceives of Linda as an essential contributor to the tragic meaning of work. Jan Balakian, for example, has argued that, rather than supporting a sexist view of women, *Death of a Salesman* in "accurately depicting a postwar American culture that subordinates women, . . . cries out for a renewed image of American women" (115). Although the drama realistically portrays America "through the male gaze," it "does not condone the locker-room treatment of women any more than it approves of a dehumanizing capitalism, any more than *A Streetcar Named Desire* approves Stanley Kowalski's brash chauvinism or David Mamet's *Glengarry Glen Ross* approves of sleazy real-estate salesmen" (124). Even if Linda's fierce will and love for Willy cannot save him, Christopher Bigsby had added, "this does not make her a 'useful doormat'" as some feminists have complained ("Introduction," xx).

As Elia Kazan wrote in his directing notes on the play, Linda often appears as if she is ideally "fashioned out of Willy's guilt" and male ego as "Hard-working, sweet, always true, admiring. . . . Dumb, slaving, tender, innocent." In fact, "in life she is much tougher. . . . she has *chosen* Willy! To hell with everyone else. She is terrifyingly tough" (qtd. in Rowe, 47). Certainly Miller did not think of her as a sentimental sop. Kay Stanton has suggested that Miller "seems not to have fully understood" her strength as a "common woman who possesses more tragic nobility than Willy" (96), but at various times Miller has expressed his concern that Linda *not* be sentimentalized, beginning with Mildred Dunnock's original portrayal of the role.[21] He recalled how Kazan forced Dunnock to deliver her long accusatory speech to Bill and Happy in Act II in double time and then doubled the pace of the delivery again in order to straighten "out her spine, and has Linda filled up with outrage and protest rather than self-pity and mere perplexity" (*Timebends,* 189). He also observed how the Linda in the Beijing production, Zhu Lin, at first weakened Linda's character by "exploiting . . . the sentiments" that "will sink them all in a morass of brainless 'feeling' that finally is not feeling at all but an unspecific bath of self-love." Zhu Lin's interpretation reminded him of a Yiddish production in New York in which "the Mother was a lachrymose fount" like mothers "performed by actors of Irish backgrounds" in early film, "always on the verge of tears, too" (*Salesman,* 43).

For Miller, Linda's role was never merely ancillary. And although he acknowledged that she contributes to Willy's death—nothing that "When somebody is destroyed, everybody finally contributes to it" (*Conversations,* 265), he conceived of Linda as "sucked into the same mechanism" as Willy.[22] Though not a "tragic hero," Linda contributes hugely to the tragic vision of the work. She functions in part as a chorus. In the crucial moments when she demands that "Attention must be paid" and when she castigates her sons for abandoning Willy, she both provokes the action and provides a moral commentary on it. Perhaps more, as George Couchman has contributed, she "is conscience itself" to her two sons—"she fixes responsibility for actions, something which, according to the playwright himself, must be done if our theater is to recover the spirit of tragedy" (74). And, Bernard Dukore has added, "Far from demonstrating her stupidity, her comprehension of why [Willy] committed suicide derives from what she, not the audience, was aware of. When she last saw Willy, he was happy because Biff loved him" (28). Her essential recognition, though emotionally rather than intellectually expressed, illuminates the tragic implications of the text.

No mere passive victim, even though she is powerless to prevent Willy's end, Linda is primarily responsible for generating the tragic reunion of Willy and Biff. She can only respond to, not prevent, the fatal encounter she unwittingly prophesies when she tells Biff, with ironic accuracy, that Willy's fate is in his hand; and it is she who tells Biff about the rubber hose, thereby empowering him with the knowledge he needs to confront Willy at the end of the play. The climactic scene occurs at the restaurant when Willy can no longer evade the memory that must return him, like Oedipus, to the crossroads that mark his betrayal. The scene in Howard's office which precedes it would surely be the pivotal moment in the action were this essentially a social or political drama; but rather than being the turning point, it leads directly to it, stripping Willy of his final hope and leaving him without reserves to combat the evidence of his failure as father and husband as well as salesman.[23] Christopher Bigsby has proposed that "There is no crime and hence no culpability (beyond guilt for sexual betrayal), only a baffled man and his sons trying to find their way through a world of images" ("Introduction," xxvi); but the guilt Willy endures goes beyond mere infidelity, and Biff's culpability in abandoning his father both in Boston and at the restaurant adds a moral dimension that exceeds Willy's sexual indiscretions. The restaurant scene, which Miller once stayed up all night to rework during rehearsals (*Timebends,* 189), brilliantly weaves together past and present by simultaneously showing Biff and Hap reenacting Willy's violation of love while Willy concurrently relives it. Again, were this only a social or polemical social play, the scene in Howard's office would constitute the nadir of Willy's hopeless existence, and the restaurant scene would begin the dénouement. But the restaurant scene carries what Miller calls a "metaphysical" dimension, moving the play into the realm of tragedy by dramatizing the usurpation of the present by the past, the place where Willy must reenact rather than excuse or sanitize the past. In true tragic rhythm, every step forward leads back to that defining moment.

Biff's humiliating experience at Oliver's office mirrors Willy's at Howard's, Thomas Porter has noted (142), and links their destinies together as they meet at the restaurant. The scene opens with Hap seducing "Miss Forsyth" with the deception and exaggeration typical of the Lomans, directly establishing a parallel to Willy's sexual infidelity. When Biff arrives, he already has realized his inauthenticity after stealing Oliver's pen and is determined to force Willy and Hap to face the truth about all their self-deceit. Interestingly, Miller changed the early versions of the play, including the initial preproduction script distributed to the production team in 1948. Originally Biff intentionally lies both to Willy *and* Hap about having a lunch meeting with Oliver (Murphy, *Miller: Death of a Salesman*, 6). In the far more meaningful final version, Biff openly rebels against what he has become. Daniel Schneider, in his Freudian interpretation of the scene, calls it "the ultimate act of father-murder . . . [a] very adroitly designed Oedipal murder" in which Biff is "hero of the Oedipal theme" in rebelling against his father (250-51).[24] But while Biff comes in anger against what his father has made of him and does indeed rebel against him, he brings with him a deeper self-hatred and, with it, an understanding of Willy's desperation. Even as Hap competes for the girls unmindful of his father's distress, Biff finds a compassion born of his self-awareness and Willy's agonizing cry that "the woods are burning . . . there's a big blaze going on all around" (83). Biff's consciousness of his own culpability—expressed in his plea to Hap to "help him . . . Help me, help me, I can't bear to look at his face!"—bespeaks of something more than Oedipal revenge on the father. Calling Willy "A fine, troubled prince" (90), he lies about the appointment with Oliver not to conceal his failure, as in the original script, but to alleviate Willy's suffering, even though he finally runs away from Willy in frustration, "*Ready to weep*" (90). Biff wants to be free of the past and free of the imperative of success his father imposes on him, but he cannot achieve these ends without feeling guilt for failing his father, nor can he erase from the past the estrangement that occurred in Boston for which he feels partly responsible. In this modern tragedy, moral as well as psychological forces propel the scene.

As tragic protagonist Willy, above all, must gain some measure of awareness, something now possible when he no longer possesses the capacity to reinvent, glamorize, or excuse the past. The "re-memory" of the experience in the hotel room is driven by guilt left unchecked without recourse to the defensive mechanisms of deceit and denial he has always employed. Consciously trying to fend off responsibility, he told Bernard at Charley's

office that the math teacher, "that son-of-a-bitch," destroyed Biff, but he knows subconsciously Biff "laid down and died like a hammer hit him" because he lost all will when he caught Willy with the secretary (71). Willy's anger at Linda's mending stockings makes apparent his inability to wash his hands of guilt as well. His infidelity, echoed by Biff's prowess as a teenager and Hap's exploitation of his competitors' women, is ironically fused with its opposite. The same sexual exploits which violate "the system of love" Miller alludes to are a means to fulfill the imperative of success, whose ultimate end for Willy is, paradoxically, to secure the family and assert his fatherhood. The merging of Linda's laughter with that of the woman in the hotel represents the fatal union of imperative and impulse in Willy's mind; he is now unable to separate the contending forces that propel him. The sexual encounter with the woman is not the cause of Willy's violation of his love for Linda or his sons but the symptom of a tragic conflict which he has, nonetheless, created. However much Willy struggles to live in denial consciously, he knows subconsciously that he bears responsibility, as his suffering bears witness. The play shifts after the restaurant scene into the future and out of Willy's unconscious, as Willy, having returned to the point of offense, seeks for some means to reconcile the conflicting "laws" that define him. The dénouement inevitably follows the subjective reenactment of the encounter his memory will not let him evade—once again, "the birds come home to roost."

To what degree Willy really understands and accepts responsibility is a matter of unending debate among critics. In his prefatory essay to his *Collected Works,* Miller argued that

> Had Willy been unaware of his separation from values that endure he would have died contentedly polishing his car. . . . But he was agonized by being in a false position, so constantly haunted by the hollowness of all he had put his faith in. . . . That he had not intellectual fluency to verbalize his situation is not the same as saying that he lacked awareness.
>
> (*Theater Essays,* 148)

Nevertheless, in an earlier interview he acknowledged the "danger in pathos, which can destroy any tragedy if it goes too far," and confessed, "I feel that Willy Loman lacks sufficient insight into his situation, which would have made him a greater, more significant figure" (*Conversations,* 26). Miller's detractors, and in some cases defenders, have focused on this issue. Heilman, for example, has written that *Death of a Salesman* is a near-but-not-quite-tragedy because "Willy is always in the first stage of the tragic rhythm—the flight from the truth; but he never comes to the last stage of the tragic rhythm, in which truth breaks through to him" (234). And June Schlueter has argued that although Willy "casts an immense shadow over all of modern drama, he remains a pathetic 'low man'" (Schlueter and Flanagan, 63).[25]

But even granting Willy's limited insight, it would be a mistake to claim that he is ignorant of himself or of his moral offenses. Certainly emotionally, as Lois Gordon contends, "he confronts himself and his world" (103). Roudané persuasively argues that Willy "tragically knows at least part of himself" as is evidenced when he admits to Linda that he looks foolish, that he babbles too much, and that he feels estranged. He "mixes self-disclosure with external fact," as when he sarcastically responds to Hap, "You'll retire me for life on seventy goddam dollars a week?" And his lyric cry, "The woods are burning!" further reflects Willy's "self-knowledge within the marketplace" as "he honestly assesses his overall predicament" when he meets his sons at the restaurant. "Such insights make Willy more than a misfit or an oversimplified Everyman" and "enhance his tragic structure precisely because they reveal to the audience Willy's capacity to distinguish reality from chimera" (*"Death of a Salesman,"* 79). Granting that Willy himself does not comprehend the full meaning of his spiritual crisis or his guilt, Bernard Dukore asks, What if he did fully understand? "The play would then become too explicit and Willy the know-it-all protagonist of a drama with Uplift" (37), devoid of tragic significance and at odds with the play's realistic portrayal.

Miller's commitment to the truthfulness of Willy's character in effect mitigates against his playing the role of the classical tragic hero—he "knows" in the Old Testament sense of experiencing reality, but there is no doubt that his intellectual vision is restricted. When he leaves the restaurant shattered by his painful return to the Boston hotel room, Willy is to a degree freed to act, to choose. Before his mental reenactment he was incapacitated by Howard's final humiliation of him, by his agonizing awareness that Bernard's success reflected on his own failure as father, by Charley's offer of a job that would come at the cost of any self-respect. Now he is galvanized into desperate action. Mobilized by the stinging awareness that he has utterly failed materially and morally, he impulsively tries to plant something, to nature life amid walls of urban apartment houses that symbolize the domination of the nature he loves by the material world created by the selling mythos of American culture to which he is hopelessly tied.

His actions expose his sense of, rather than understanding of, his existential dilemma. In Miller's view of a world without transcendent mythic heroes, Willy alone cannot embody the tragic vision of the play. As part of a composite tragic figure, Biff assumes a dimension of the tragic protagonist Willy is too diminished to satisfy. As a projection of competing forces operating in Wil-

ly's psyche, Biff seeks freedom from the "phony dream" that he nonetheless carries as symbolically part of Willy. Joseph Hynes has expressed dismay that "The only one who gains self-awareness is Biff; but the play is Willy's. . . . the showdown lights up the play's failure as tragedy" (286). But in fact the play does not turn on Willy as a single protagonist. Because Willy is so wedded to the dream, nothing less than his death can free him from it. Biff, however, can acquire freedom from the imperative Willy cannot abandon without self-destruction; but, paradoxically, he can only be freed *by* Willy. Possessing awareness of the corrosive nature of Willy's dream and its devastating effect on his father and himself, Biff pleads with Willy to "take that phony dream and burn it" (106). The *"anagnorosis* is there," declares David Sievers, but "is given . . . to Biff, who is purged of his father's hostility when he comes to see his father for what he is" (396). When he expresses his love for his father in a climactic embrace, he frees Willy to claim his tragic fate, as, paradoxically, Willy's death frees him.

Biff, then, provides the awareness Willy lacks, but he cannot himself resolve the tragic crisis. It may be true that Miller does not adequately develop Biff's character in relation to Willy or fully trace his moral development, although it is clear from the beginning that Biff returns home because he feels a sense of guilt and moral responsibility to heal the breech with his father. Miller himself has stated, "I am sorry the self-realization of the older son, Biff, is not a weightier counterbalance of Willy's character" (*Theater Essays,* 9-10), but his intent is not obscure. Biff is not a counterweight *to* but a counterweight *of* Willy's character. However unwittingly, Willy pays the price to free Biff from the imperative he ironically thinks he dies to defend: "[T]ragedy brings *us* knowledge and enlightenment" as audience, Dukore has wisely remarked, "which it need not do for the tragic hero" (37).

It is hardly surprising that the motivation for Willy's suicide is variously interpreted, for Miller himself substantially altered his earlier depiction of the death. The earlier version of the penultimate scene, Brenda Murphy has noted, occurs not when Biff confronts Willy with the rubber hose but when he confesses for the first time that he lied about the appointment with Oliver (*Miller: Death of a Salesman,* 6). The difference is important because the rubber hose, like the car accidents earlier, reveals Willy's flirtation with surrender to defeat. The car wrecks "were cowardly and escapist," Dan Vogel has rightly claimed, whereas his death at the end of the play is "purposeful, self-sacrificial, and epiphanic" (101). Although it does nothing to achieve Willy's dream, it is not, as June Schlueter has concluded, simply "a deluded death gesture that only compounds the waste of his life" (Schlueter and Flanagan, 65). Miller has identified the cause as Willy's "epiphany" in the penultimate scene when he realizes "He loves me!" and discovers "the resurrected knowledge of his vision with Biff, his seed and hope" (*Salesman,* 170). Having gained "a very powerful piece of knowledge, which is that he is loved by his son and has been embraced by him and forgiven," he can now choose death as fulfillment, not mere escape:

> That he is unable to take the victory thoroughly to his heart, that it closes the circle for him and propels him to his death, is the wage of sin, which was to have committed himself so completely to the counterfeits of dignity and the false coinage embodied in his idea of success that he can prove his existence only by bestowing "power" on his posterity, a power deriving from the sale of his last asset, himself, for the price of his insurance policy.

> (*Theater Essays,* 147)

The point is that Willy, however wrongly, chooses to die in such a way that he believes can restore the equilibrium between the imperative of success and the contesting will to love. "Unwittingly," Miller has written, "he has primed his own son Biff for his revolt against what he himself has done with his life and against what he has come to worship: material success" (*Salesman,* 135).[26] Anything less than death would make Willy's end purely melodramatic. As Kazan recorded, "it is a *deed,* not a feeling" (qtd. in Rowe, 49)—that Willy *chooses* rather than succumbs makes all the difference. In **"The Nature of Tragedy"** (1949), Miller wrote that "When Mr. B., while walking down the street, is struck on the head by a falling piano," we witness "only the pathetic end of Mr. B. . . . the death of Mr. B. does not arouse . . . tragic feeling" and produces no catharsis (*Theater Essays,* 9). Willy's death is neither accidental nor senseless. That he dies *for* something, however misconstrued, rather than *from* debilitating defeat makes his end meaningful—and necessary. His death eliminates Biff's obligation to conform to his father's ideal. Although Christopher Bigsby is right in claiming that it is not "truth" but Willy's "commitment to illusion" that kills him (*Critical Introduction,* 179), the consummate irony is that he frees Biff from the very idea he holds in absolute allegiance. In the final analysis, the dream of success is not Willy's "ultimate concern" but a corruptive means to a higher end. That Willy remains ignorant of the truth that the dream subverts his end to reestablish the love between him and his son does not erase the fact that he dies as the agent of that love.

The effectiveness of the Requiem has been another point of contention among critics: to some it is contrived and extraneous to the rest of the play, to others a necessary commentary on the consequences of the action. Miller has described a distinct breakpoint at the end of the drama. When Willy "dies his consciousness vanishes and there is a space between the requiem and the play. . . . We've left Willy's head now; we're on the earth" (Bigsby, *Arthur Miller,* 59). In his view, crossing the distance between Willy's distorted internal point of view to external reality is essential to the resolution of the play. Without the Requiem there would be only the death of a self-deluded salesman whose end achieves nothing but blind self-annihilation. Willy's "tragedy" would provoke, as George Jean Nathan described it in his famous review of the play, an "experience [like] we suffer in contemplating on the highways a run-over and killed dog, undeniably affecting but without any profound significance" (284). Miller, though, does not portray Willy's death as meaningless, though it is certainly ironic. He has written, "We have abstracted from the Greek drama its air of doom, its physical destruction of the hero, but its victory escapes us. Thus it has become difficult to separate in our minds the ideas of the pathetic and of the tragic" (*Theater Essays,* 59).

In **Death of a Salesman** he attempts to conjoin the pathetic and the tragic in a unique way by uniting the destinies of Biff and Willy. Chester Eisinger has argued that Biff's recognition "provides the contrapuntal release to life that we must see over against Willy's defeat in suicide" (171). But, in a larger sense, Biff's epiphany— that "I know who I am kid" (111)—is not one thing and Willy's death another, not a point/counter-point but an integrated whole. Miller has acknowledged the seeming "rift" in the play between the focus of the dramatic action which falls on Willy and the recognition and moral resolution which fall on Biff. He knew he could not give Willy Biff's insight and be true to Willy's character, which is why he considered the funeral essential to rescue the play from pessimism. Willy's last conversation with Ben keeps his illusion intact,[27] but the Requiem enlarges the vision. You go to a funeral because "You want to think over the life of the departed and it's then, really, that it's nailed down: [Biff] won't accept his life" (Bigsby, *Arthur Miller,* 56). Willy gains emotional awareness of Biff's love and consequently finds self-worth in dying for that love; Biff discovers freeing self-knowledge. His decision to go West may represent, as Nada Zeineddine has suggested, a "metaphorically killing of the father" (178), a last expression of Oedipal rebellion against the father.[28] Biff confidently asserts that Willy "had the wrong dreams. All, all wrong" (111). His rejection of his father's ideal, however, emerges paradoxically from his embrace of his father and his father's ultimate act of love for him.

There is more uncertainty, more lack of resolve, at the end of the play than we ordinarily find in most conventional tragedies. Biff's heading West, Christopher Bigsby has written, "smacks a little of Huck Finn lighting out for the Territory, ahead of the rest. He is moving against history" ("Introduction," xix). And both Bigsby and Gerald Weales have noted the irony that

Biff's return to the West foreshadows the cowboy Gay's fate in *The Misfits,* who is displaced in the dying agrarian society (*Modern American Drama,* 90; "Arthur Miller," 178).[29] Weales also has concluded that "there is no reason to assume that some of the irony" directed to Willy and the other Lomans "does not rub off on Biff" ("Arthur Miller," 169). Nevertheless, Biff most certainly moves "from something and to something." As he developed Biff's character, Miller clearly intended to show that Biff gains independence from, rather than perpetuates, his father's life of illusion. Bernard Dukore has implied that it is good that Miller does not more fully counterbalance Biff's perception against Willy's blindness, because the play "might then become an italicized message." Those who say Biff's vision is "vague, trite and romantic, miss the point" (25). The tragic vision does not depend on being able to predict what will happen to Biff so much as on our awareness that Willy's death dissolves Biff's obligation to meet a spurious ideal, whatever the sequel might say.

Other parts of the Requiem have also been debated vigorously. Charley's "A salesman is got to dream" speech has been variously called out of character and realistic,[30] and Linda's often discussed last words "we're free . . . We're free . . ." (12) have been dismissed as a trite appeal for sympathy and too obvious irony.[31] One might ask what the essential irony is, that Linda thinks they are free when they are not or that they *are* free more than Linda knows—freed from the fear of Willy's death and freed from his illusory ideal. While some, like Ruby Cohn, have accused the Requiem of being "jarringly outside" Willy's mind and devoid of any new insights, it introduces a metaphysical dimension at the end. Rita Di Giuseppe has proposed that Linda's remark about the insurance, "It's the grace period now," gives "the jargon of commerce . . . a metaphysical connotation" (126). And one might add that Miller considered calling the play *A Period of Grace,* as if to emphasize something transcendent that emerges in it.

What we are left with is perhaps a tragedy despite itself—Willy is a victim, but chooses nonetheless; he lacks self-knowledge, but is responsible for his son's self-awareness; his ideal is all wrong, but his commitment to it is aligned with a love he willingly dies for; his death lifts no plague and does not affect the larger community, but it rescues his family from the continuing anxiety of his death and releases Biff from a destructive imperative. Willy is petty, delusional, pathetic; but "Attention, attention must be finally paid to such a person" (43). However circuitously, the play completes the tragic pattern of the past becoming the present, and it affirms the tragic dictum that there are inevitable consequences to choices, that the "the wages of sin" must be paid. Lacking a singular tragic protagonist, it offers a composite figure of father and sons who embody the tragic conflict between the imperative of

success and the "system of love." Leaving society unre deemed, it ends in sacrifice to reclaim the family an restore love. Not "high tragedy" in Aristotelian terms *Death of a Salesman* is something more than melo drama or "low tragedy" in its revelation of tragic vi sion, choice, awareness, and consequence. At fifty year of age, Miller's play is still "coming home to roost."

Notes

1. Miller earlier told Robert Corrigan that he was no "concerned about tragic form" in writing the play "That is after the fact. Just to lay that to rest. The theatre gets too involved in analytical theory" (*Conversations,* 257).

2. He also has described the play as "absurdly simple It is about a salesman and it's his last day on the earth" (*Theater Essays,* 423).

3. Miller also told James J. Martine his often repeated admission that the Greeks and Ibsen were the "two sources for my form—certainly for my ideas of a theatre's purposes" (*Conversations,* 292). He told Olga Carlisle and Rose Styron in a *Paris Review* interview published in 1966 that tragedy "seemed to me the only form there was" when he began writing drama and that he especially admired the Greeks "for their magnificent form, the symmetry. . . . That form has never left me; I suppose it got burned into me" (*Conversations,* 88). He also called himself a "descendent of Ibsen" in an interview with Ronald Hyman: "What he gave me in the beginning was a sense of the past and a sense of the rootedness of everything that happens" (*Conversations,* 189).

4. All citations to *Death of a Salesman* refer to this edition.

5. For a general summary of major opening-night reviews of the play as "tragedy," see especially Murphy, *Miller: Death of a Salesman,* 61-65. Articles and books that directly address the question tend to include summaries of critical opinions on the topic. For an especially useful commentary placing the play against historical definitions of tragedy, see Barker's "The Crisis of Authenticity," particularly his pithy but useful appendix tracing the evolution of theoretical views of tragedy.

6. For more sustained discussions of *Death of a Salesman* and *Oedipus,* see especially Siegel; C. Otten; Bhatia; Bierman, Hart, and Johnson; Jackson.

7. Among those measuring Miller against Aristotle, Rita Di Giuseppe argues most extensively and convincingly that *Death of a Salesman* is a modern Aristotelian tragedy. Her essay might be compared with Stephen Barker's provocative reading of the play in "The Crisis of Authenticity," which treats it as an essentially Nietzschean tragedy.

8. Heilman himself concludes that Willy is "so limited that this is a limitation of the play itself" (*Tragedy*

and Melodrama, 237), a common view of many critics who identify the play with Aristotelian "low tragedy."

9. The theologian-literary critic Tom Driver, for example complains that There being no objective good and evil, and no imperative other than conscience, man himself must be made to bear the full burden of creating his values and living up to them. The immensity of this task is beyond human capacity" (111-12). In fact, Miller's depiction of the moral viability of characters surfaces in their pervasive sense of guilt and the compulsion shared by Willy and Biff to somehow redeem the past. Driver, like Foster and Mottram, among others, seemingly expects Miller to manufacture a god, a metaphysical reality that would somehow resolve the spiritual crisis. But Miller's refusal to identify "an ultimate truth" is more a matter of artistic integrity than a failure of moral vision.

10. John Manders identifies a related unresolved conflict between Marxist and Freudian elements: "If we take the 'psychological' motivation as primary, the 'social' documentation seem gratuitous; if we take the 'social' documentation as primary, the 'psychological' motivation seems gratuitous' (115).

11. In Helene Koon's words, "His principles may be unconscious and built upon fallacies, but he believes in them, practices them, and finally dies for them" (7).

12. Bernard F. Dukore asks the telling question, "does not the desire for love inhere in Willy's occupation, and does not the hope of success link to the family?" (21)

13. In *Modern American Drama 1945-1990* Bigsby has written, "the present cannot be severed from the past nor the individual from his social context: that, after all, is the basis of [Miller's] dramatic method and of his moral faith" (124).

14. Freudian readings appear incidentally in various interpretations of the play as well as being the primary approach of many studies like Schneider's. See especially Field, Hagopian, Harshbarger, and Schlueter and Flanagan.

15. Miller described the play in similar language: "*Death of a Salesman,* really, is a love story between a man and his son" (*Salesman,* 49).

16. Donald Morse also has noted Linda's reinforcement of Willy's "life-lie" (273-77). And William Dillingham, among others, has identified her as a "contributing cause" of the tragedy (344).

17. In his extreme psychological reading Harshbarger argues that Linda dominates Willy and attempts to reduce Biff "to the level of a dependent child" motivated by "a longing for Biff she has always had—a relationship which is symbolized by Biff taking '*her in his arms*'" at the end of the play (28-29).

18. Related to feminist criticism, David Savran attacks the play from a different gender perspective, claiming that "the play eulogizes the contents of the Loman *imaginaire* by its romantization of a self-reliant and staunchly homosocial masculinity and by its corroborative and profound disparagement of women" (36).

19. In a recent article Rhonda Koenig concurs that Miller diminishes female figures, making Linda "a dumb and useful doormat" and reducing all women in the play to either the "wicked slut" or "a combination of good waitress and slipper-bearing retriever" (10, 4).

20. For other feminist interpretations see especially Billman, Canning, Goodman, Hume, and Zeineddine.

21. Even in writing the play Miller was intent on showing Linda's toughness. He even cut the famous "Attention must be paid speech" at one point for fear it made her too sentimental, and he took out of the original dialogue references she made to Biff and Hap as "darling" and "dear" (Murphy, *Miller: Death of a Salesman,* 45).

22. Elsewhere he has commented that "There is a more sinister side to the women characters in my plays. . . . they both receive the benefits of the male's mistakes and protect his mistakes in crazy ways. They are forced to do that. So the females are victims as well" (*Conversations,* 370).

23. Bernard Dukore rightly comments that even if Howard had given Willy a job in the city, it would not eliminate "the elemental source of Willy's discontent, which lies in his relationship with his older son and the world in which they live" (34). One might add that Willy cannot accept Charley's offer of a job for much the same reason. It would not resolve his existential crisis, and Willy's acceptance of it would in fact reduce him to a totally pathetic figure.

24. Field, Eisinger, and Harshburger offer other Freudian analyses. Some critics especially note the Freudian importance of Biff's stealing Oliver's pen, a phallic symbol, thus expressing his assertion of manhood or fear of castration. More simply, the stealing of the pen is another re-enactment of the past, when Biff stole the basketballs, like he stole lumber and the football. His existential self-questioning of his motives for stealing the pen makes him determined to coerce Willy to confront the truth about who he really is.

25. Miller has denied that he intended the name as a pun, claiming he took it from a character in Fritz Lang's early film *The Testament of Mr. Mabuse* (*Timebends,* 177).

26. In the same essay Miller has claimed, "Willy is indeed going toward something through his dying, a meaningful sacrifice, the ultimate irony, and he is filled, not emptied of feeling" (196).

27. Ben represents the most corrupt form of the American dream of success, what Thomas Porter has called "the older version of the Salesman, the ruthless capitalist" whose adventuresome brutality contrasts with Willy's "Dale Carnegie approach to success" (135), most fully idealized in Willy's vision of Dave Singleman. But Ben is also Willy's alter ego, as Sister M. Bettina, SSND, has discussed, "a projection of his brother's personality" whose presence provides "a considerable amount of tragic insight" (83). Willy's dependency on Ben's approval stems from his brother being a substitute father and the sole link to their peddler-father, who sold what he created with his own hands in opposition to Ben, who entered the virulent "jungle" and ripped out the riches. Rita Di Giuseppe has drawn the interesting conclusion that Ben functions "much in the same manner as the 'gods in classical tragedy who hover in the twilight zone uttering prophesies" (117), both the embodiment of the success myth and its arbitrator.

28. Roudané has agreed that Biff "still carries on an Oedipal resistance to his father" at the Requiem (*Death of a Salesman*, 81).

29. In his *Critical Introduction to American Drama* Bigsby has alluded to Gay as "an aging cowboy, as bewildered by the collapse of his world as Willy Loman has been" (185). Other critics, like Eisinger, have similarly contended that Miller sentimentally "romanticizes the rural-agrarian dream" (174).

30. For example, Joseph Hynes has dismissed the speech as "sheer sentimentality" and "untrue" (283), whereas Dennis Welland has claimed that Charley alone understands Willy as salesman "in a wholly unsentimental way" (42). Miller himself considered the speech "objective information . . . it is absolutely real" and presents the obverse of Charley's earlier remark, "'Why must everybody like you. Who liked J. Press, Morgan?' . . . These are two halves of the same thing" (*Conversations*, 351-52). As several critics have noted, Miller's sympathetic portrayal of Charley as successful businessman, father, and neighbor, mitigates against simplistically reading the play as an attack on American capitalism.

31. Joseph Hynes, for example, has described Linda and Charley's words as a "Hallmark Card flourish at the curtain" (284).

Works Cited

Austin, Gayle. "The Exchange of Women and Male Homosexual Desire in Arthur Miller's *Death of a Salesman* and Lillian Hellman's *Another Part of the Forest*." Pp. 59-66 in *Feminist Readings of Modern American Drama*, ed. by June Schlueter. Rutherford, N.J.: Fairleigh Dickinson University Press, 1989.

Balakian, Jan. "Beyond the Male Locker Room: *Death of a Salesman* from a Feminist Perspective." Pp. 115-24 in *Approaches to Teaching Miller's Death of a Salesman,* ed. by Matthew C. Roudané. New York: The Modern Language Association of America, 1995.

Barker, Stephen. "The Crisis of Authenticity: *Death of a Salesman* and the Tragic Muse." Pp. 82-101 in *Approaches to Teaching Miller's Death of a Salesman,* ed. by Matthew C. Roudané. New York: The Modern Language Association of America, 1995.

Bentley, Eric. *The Playwright as Thinker: A Study of Drama in Modern Times.* New York: Meridian Books, 1963.

———. *In Search of Theater.* New York: Vintage Books, 1959.

Ben-Zvi, Linda. "'Home Sweet Home': Deconstructing the Masculine Myth of the Frontier in Modern Drama." Pp. 217-25 *The Frontier Experience and the American Drama,* ed. by David Mogen, Mark Busby, and Paul Bryant. College Station: Texas A&M University Press, 1989.

Bettina, Sister M. "Willy Loman's Brother Ben: Tragic Insight in *Death of a Salesman.*" Pp. 80-83 in *The Merrill Studies in Death of a Salesman.* Comp. by Walter J. Meserve. Columbus, Ohio: Charles E. Merrill, 1972.

Bhatia, Santosh K. *Arthur Miller: Social Drama as Tragedy.* New Delhi: Arnold-Heinemann, 1985.

Bierman, Judah, James Hart, and Stanley Johnson. "Arthur Miller: *Death of a Salesman.*" Pp. 265-71 in *Arthur Miller: Death of a Salesman. Text and Criticism,* ed. by Gerald C. Weales. New York: Viking, 1967.

Bigsby, Christopher, ed. *Arthur Miller and Company.* London: Methuen Drama in association with The Arthur Miller Center for American Studies, 1990.

———, ed. *The Cambridge Companion to Arthur Miller.* Cambridge: Cambridge University Press, 1997.

———. *A Critical Introduction to Twentieth-Century American Drama 2: Tennessee Williams, Arthur Miller, Edward Albee.* Cambridge: Cambridge University Press, 1984.

———. "Introduction" to *Death of a Salesman: Certain Private Conversations in Two Acts and a Requiem.* New York: Penguin Books, 1998.

———. *Modern American Drama, 1945-1980.* New York: Cambridge University Press, 1992.

Billman, Carol. "Women and the Family in American Drama." *Arizona Quarterly* 36.1 (1980): 35-49.

Bliquez, Guerin. "Linda's Role in *Death of a Salesman.*" *Modern Drama* 10 (1968): 383-86.

Bloom, Harold, ed. *Willy Loman.* New York: Chelsea House, 1991.

Canning, Charlotte. "Is This Play about Women? A Feminist Reading of *Death of a Salesman*." Pp. 69-76 in *The Achievement of Arthur Miller: New Essays*, ed. by Steven R. Centola. Dallas: Contemporary Research Associates, 1995.

Centola, Steven R., ed. *The Achievement of Arthur Miller: New Essays*. Dallas: Contemporary Research Associates, 1995.

———. "'Just Looking for a Home': A Conversation with Arthur Miller." *American Drama* 1.1 (1991): 85-94.

Clark, Eleanor. "Old Glamour, New Gloom." *Partisan Review* 16 (1949): 631-35.

Cohn, Ruby. *Dialogue in American Drama*. Bloomington: Indiana University Press, 1971.

Corrigan, Robert W., ed. *Arthur Miller: A Collection of Critical Essays*. Englewood Cliffs, NJ: Prentice-Hall, 1969.

Couchman, Gordon W. "Arthur Miller's Tragedy of Babbitt." Pp. 68-75 in *The Merrill Studies in Death of a Salesman*. Comp. by Walter J. Meserve. Columbus, Ohio: Charles E. Merrill, 1972.

Demastes, William W. "Miller's Use and Modification of the Realistic Tradition." Pp. 74-81 in *Approaches to Teaching Miller's Death of a Salesman*, ed. by Matthew C. Roudané. New York: The Modern Language Association of America, 1995.

Di Giuseppe, Rita. "The Shadow of the Gods: Tragedy and Commitment in *Death of a Salesman*." *Quaderni di lingue e letterature* 14 (1989): 109-28.

Dillingham, William B. "Arthur Miller and the Loss of Conscience." Pp. 339-49 in *Arthur Miller: Death of a Salesman. Text and Criticism*, ed. by Gerald C. Weales. New York: Viking, 1967.

Driver, Tom F. "Strength and Weakness in Arthur Miller." Pp. 105-13 in *The Merrill Studies in Death of a Salesman*. Comp. by Walter J. Meserve. Columbus, Ohio: Charles E. Merrill, 1972.

Dukore, Bernard F. *Death of a Salesman and The Crucible: Text and Performance*. Atlantic Heights, N.J.: Humanities Press, 1989.

Eisinger, Chester E. "Focus on Arthur Miller's *Death of a Salesman*: The Wrong Dream." Pp. 165-74 in *American Dreams, American Nightmares*, ed. by David Madden. Carbondale and Edwardsville: Southern Illinois University Press, 1970.

Field, B. S., Jr. "Hamartia in *Death of a Salesman*." *Twentieth Century Literature* 18 (1972): 19-24.

Foster, Richard J. "Confusion and Tragedy: the Failure of Arthur Miller's *Death of a Salesman*." Pp. 82-88 in *Two Modern American Tragedies: Reviews and Criticism of Death of a Salesman and A Streetcar Named Desire*, ed. by John D. Hurrell. New York: Scribner's, 1961.

Goodman, Charlotte. "The Fox's Clubs: Lillian Hellman, Arthur Miller and Tennessee Williams." Pp. 130-42 in *Modern American Drama: The Female Canon*, ed. by June Schlueter. Rutherford, N.J.: Fairleigh Dickinson University Press, 1990.

Gordon, Lois. "*Death of a Salesman*: An Appreciation." Pp. 98-108 in *Twentieth Century Interpretations of Death of a Salesman*, ed. by Helene Koon. Englewood Cliffs, N.J.: Prentice-Hall, 1983.

Hagopian, John V. "Arthur Miller: The *Salesman*'s Two Cases." *Modern Drama* 6 (1963): 117-25.

Harshbarger, Karl. *The Burning Jungle: An Analysis of Arthur Miller's Death of a Salesman*. Washington, D.C.: University Press of America, 1979.

Heilman, Robert Bechtold. *The Iceman, The Arsonist, and The Troubled Agent: Tragedy and Melodrama on the Modern Stage*. Seattle: University of Washington Press, 1973.

———. *Tragedy and Melodrama: Versions of Experience*. Seattle: University of Washington Press, 1968.

Hume, Beverly. "Linda Loman as 'The Woman' in Miller's *Death of a Salesman*." *NMAL: Notes on Modern American Literature* 9.3 (1985): Item 14.

Hurrell, John D., ed. *Two Modern American Tragedies: Reviews and Criticism of Death of a Salesman and A Streetcar Named Desire*. New York: Scribner's, 1961.

Hynes, Joseph A. "'Attention Must Be Paid. . . .'" Pp. 280-89 in *Arthur Miller: Death of a Salesman. Text and Criticism*, ed. by Gerald C. Weales. New York: Viking, 1967.

Jackson, Esther Merle. "*Death of a Salesman*: Tragic Myth in the Modern Theatre." *CLA Journal* 7 (1963): 63-76.

Kintz, Linda. "The Sociosymbolic Work of Family in *Death of a Salesman*." Pp. 102-14 in *Approaches to Teaching Miller's Death of a Salesman*, ed. by Matthew C. Roudané. New York: The Modern Language Association of America, 1995.

Koenig, Rhoda. "Seduced by *Salesman*'s Patter." *The [London] Sunday Times* 20 Oct. 1996: 10, 4.

Koon, Helene, ed. *Twentieth Century Interpretations of Death of a Salesman*. Englewood Cliffs, N.J.: Prentice-Hall, 1983.

Mandell, Jonathan. "Renaissance Man: At 82 Arthur Miller Is Pleasing a New Generation of Theatergoers." *Newsday* 28 Oct. 1997: B03.

Manders, John. *The Writer and Commitment.* Philadelphia: Dufour Editions, 1962.

Mason, Jeffrey D. "Paper Dolls: Melodrama and Sexual Politics in Arthur Miller's Early Plays." Pp. 103-15 in *Modern American Drama: The Female Canon,* ed. by June Schlueter. Rutherford, N.J.: Fairleigh Dickinson University Press, 1990.

Meserve, Walter J., compiler. *The Merrill Studies in Death of a Salesman.* Columbus, Ohio: Charles E. Merrill, 1972.

Miller, Arthur. *Conversations with Arthur Miller,* ed. by Matthew C. Roudané. Jackson: University Press of Mississippi, 1987.

———. *Death of a Salesman: Certain Private Conversations in Two Acts and a Requiem.* With an introduction by Christopher Bigsby. New York: Penguin, 1998.

———. *Salesman in Beijing.* New York: Viking, 1984.

———. *The Theater Essays of Arthur Miller,* ed. by Robert A. Martin and Steven R. Centola. Revised Edition. New York: Da Capo, 1996.

———. *Timebends: A Life.* New York: Penguin, 1995.

Morse, Donald. "The 'Life Lie' in Three Plays by O'Neill, Williams and Miller." Pp. 273-77 in *Cross-Cultural Studies American, Canadian and European Literature: 1945-1985.* ed. by Mirko Jurak. Ljubljana, Yugoslavia: English Department, Filozofska Fakulteta, Edvard Kardelj University of Ljubljana, 1988.

Mottram, Eric. "Arthur Miller: The Development of a Political Dramatist in America." Pp. 23-47 in *Arthur Miller: A Collection of Critical Essays,* ed. by Robert W. Corrigan. Englewood Cliffs, N.J.: Prentice-Hall, 1969.

Murphy, Brenda. *Miller: Death of a Salesman.* Plays in Production Series. Cambridge: Cambridge University Press, 1995.

Nathan, George Jean. Review of *Death of a Salesman.* Pp. 279-85 in *The Theatre Book of the Year, 1948-49.* New York: Knopf, 1949.

Nelson, Benjamin. *Arthur Miller: Portrait of a Playwright.* New York: David McKay, 1970.

O'Neill, Eugene. *Selected Letters.* Ed. by Travis Bogard and Jackson R. Bryer. New Haven, Conn.: Yale University Press, 1988.

Otten, Charlotte F. "Who Am I? . . . A Re-Investigation of Arthur Miller's *Death of a Salesman.*" Pp. 85-91 in *Twentieth Century Interpretations of Death of a Salesman,* ed. by Helene Koon. Englewood Cliffs, N.J.: Prentice-Hall, 1983.

Parker, Brian. "Point of View in Arthur Miller's *Death of a Salesman.*" Pp. 41-55 in *Twentieth Century Interpretations of Death of a Salesman,* ed. by Helene Koon. Englewood Cliffs, N.J.: Prentice-Hall, 1983.

Porter, Thomas E. *Myth and Modern American Drama.* Detroit: Wayne State University Press, 1969.

Roudané, Matthew C., ed. *Approaches to Teaching Miller's Death of a Salesman.* New York: The Modern Language Association of America, 1995.

———. "*Death of a Salesman* and the Poetics of Arthur Miller." Pp. 60-85 in *Arthur Miller and Company,* ed. by Christopher Bigsby. London: Methuen Drama in association with The Arthur Miller Center for American Studies, 1990.

Rowe, Kenneth Thorpe. *A Theater in Your Head.* New York: Funk & Wagnalls, 1960.

Savran, David. *Communists, Cowboys, and Queers: The Politics of Masculinity in the Work of Arthur Miller and Tennessee Williams.* Minneapolis: University of Minnesota Press, 1992.

Schlueter, June, ed. *Feminist Readings of Modern American Drama.* Rutherford, N.J.: Fairleigh Dickinson University Press, 1989.

———. "Re-membering Willy's Past: Introducing Postmodern Concerns through *Death of a Salesman.*" Pp. 142-54 in *Approaches to Teaching Miller's Death of a Salesman,* ed. by Matthew Roudané. New York: The Modern Language Association of America, 1995.

Schlueter, June, and James K. Flanagan. *Arthur Miller.* New York: Ungar, 1987.

Schneider, Daniel E. *The Psychoanalyst and the Artist.* New York: International Universities Press, 1950.

Shaw, George Bernard. "How to Write a Popular Play." In *Playwrights on Playwriting: The Meaning and Making of Modern Drama from Ibsen to Ionesco,* ed. by Toby Cole. New York: Hill & Wang, 1960.

Siegel, Paul N. "Willy Loman and King Lear." *College English* 17 (1956): 341-45.

Sievers, W. David. "Tennessee Williams and Arthur Miller." *Freud on Broadway: A History of Psychoanalysis and the American Dream.* New York: Hermitage House, 1955.

Stanton, Kay. "Women and the American Dream of *Death of a Salesman,*" pp. 67-102 in *Feminist Readings of Modern American Drama,* ed. by June Schlueter. Rutherford, N.J.: Fairleigh Dickenson University Press, 1989.

Vogel, Dan. *The Three Masks of American Tragedy.* Baton Rouge: Louisiana State University Press, 1974.

Weales, Gerald C. *American Drama since World War II.* New York: Harcourt, Brace & World, 1962.

———, ed. *Arthur Miller: Death of a Salesman. Text and Criticism.* New York: Viking, 1967.

———. "Arthur Miller: Man and His Image." *Tulane Drama Review* 7.1 (1962): 165-80.

Welland, Dennis. *Miller the Playwright.* 3rd ed. New York: Methuen, 1985.

Whitley, Alvin. "Arthur Miller: An Attempt at Modern Tragedy." *Transactions of the Wisconsin Academy of Science, Arts, and Literature* 42 (1953): 257-62.

Williams, Raymond. *Modern Tragedy.* Stanford, Cal.: Stanford University Press, 1966.

Zeineddine, Nada. *Because It Is My Name: Problems of Identity Experienced by Women, Artists, and Breadwinners in the Plays of Henrik Ibsen, Tennessee Williams, and Arthur Miller.* Brauton Devon: Merlin Books, 1991.

Fred Ribkoff (essay date spring 2000)

SOURCE: Ribkoff, Fred. "Shame, Guilt, Empathy, and the Search for Identity in Arthur Miller's *Death of a Salesman.*" *Modern Drama* 43, no. 1 (spring 2000): 48-55.

[*In the following essay, Ribkoff considers the roles of guilt, empathy, shame, and self-identity in* Death of a Salesman.]

Among other things, tragedy dramatizes identity crises. At the root of such crises lie feelings of shame. You might ask: what about guilt? There is no question that guilt plays a major role in tragedy, but tragedy also dramatizes the way in which feelings of shame shape an individual's sense of identity, and thus propel him or her into wrongdoing and guilt. In fact, Bernard Williams examines the relation and distinction between shame and guilt in his study of ancient Greek tragedy and ethics, *Shame and Necessity.* He "claim[s] that if we can come to understand the ethical concepts of the Greeks, we shall recognise them in ourselves."[1] In the process of establishing a kinship between the Greeks and ourselves, Williams provides an excellent foundation upon which to build an argument on the dynamics of shame, guilt, empathy, and the search for identity in Arthur Miller's modern tragedy *Death of a Salesman.* Williams states that

> We can feel both guilt and shame towards the same action. In a moment of cowardice, we let someone down; we feel guilty because we have let them down, ashamed because we have contemptibly fallen short of what we might have hoped of ourselves. . . .
>
> . . . It [guilt] can direct one towards those who have been wronged or damaged, and demand reparation in the name, simply, of what has happened to them. But it cannot by itself help one to understand one's relations to those happenings, or to rebuild the self that has done

these things and the world in which that self has to live. Only shame can do that, because it embodies conceptions of what one is and of how one is related to others.[2]

In order to understand the identity crises of Miller's tragic characters in *Death of a Salesman,* and especially the late, climactic scene in which Biff confronts Willy with the truth, it is necessary to understand shame's relation to guilt and identity. It is the confrontation with feelings of shame that enables Biff to find himself, separate his sense of identity from that of his father, and empathize with his father. Moreover, it is the denial of such feelings that cripples Willy and the rest of the Loman family.

Until Biff stops to examine who he is, while in the process of stealing the fountain pen of his old boss, Bill Oliver, feelings of shame determine his self-perception as well as his conduct. Even before discovering his father with "The Woman" in Boston, Biff's sense of self-worth, like that of his brother Happy, is dependent on his father's conception of success and manhood and on his father's approval. In fact, because Willy is abandoned at the age of three by his father, his elder brother, Ben, becomes the measure of success and manhood for his sons to live up to. Ben is, in Willy's own words, "a great man!" "the only man I ever met who knew the answers."[3] "That's just the way I'm bringing them up, Ben—rugged, well liked, all-around," says Willy while reliving Ben's visit in the past (49). Early in the play, we see Biff through the proud memory of his father. Willy asks Biff, "Bernard is not well liked, is he?" and Biff replies, "He's liked, but he's not well liked" (33). Biff inherits from his father an extremely fragile sense of self-worth dependent on the perceptions of others. "Be liked and you will never want," says the proud father of two sons who are, in his own words, "both built like Adonises" (33). But according to the true Loman heroic creed, it is not good enough simply to be "liked." As Willy points out to Happy earlier, "Charley is . . . liked, but he's not—well liked" (30).

Shame, together with the sense of inadequacy and inferiority manifest in the need to prove oneself to others, is evident in both Loman sons, and of course, in the fatherless father, Willy. The Loman men's shame propels them into wrongdoing and guilt.[4] In Act One, Willy begs Ben to stay "a few days" more, and, in the process of doing so, reveals the degree to which he feels incomplete and inadequate:

Willy:

> (*longingly*) Can't you stay a few days? You're just what I need, Ben, because I—I have a fine position here, but I—well, Dad left when I was such a baby and I never had a chance to talk to him and I still feel— kind of temporary about myself.

(51)

The fact that Willy feels "kind of temporary about" himself is reflected in his inability to complete a thought after he has raised the issue of his identity—the "I." This confession is riddled with dashes—or, in other words, uncomfortable, self-conscious pauses. While in the presence of his god-like brother, Ben, Willy, out of shame, constantly attempts to cover up the sense of failure and inferiority that threatens to expose his sense of inadequacy and weakness every time he is about to say what the "I" really feels.

Willy is driven to commit his greatest wrong by feelings of shame that arise out of his sense of inadequacy as a man. His adulterous affair with "The Woman" in Boston, which haunts both him and his son Biff, is a desperate attempt to confirm and maintain his self-esteem.[5] In the middle of Act One, while reliving the past, Willy confesses to his wife that "people don't seem to take to me" (36), that he "talk[s] too much. A man oughta come in with a few words. One thing about Charley. He's a man of few words, and they respect him" (37). After this confession, "The Woman" appears "*behind a scrim*" as his feelings of guilt for betraying his wife surface in his words to her. Just prior to "The Woman's" first spoken words and interruption, Willy attempts to make sense of his betrayal without mentioning it:

WILLY:

> (*with great feeling*) You're the best there is, Linda, you're a pal, you know that? On the road—on the road I want to grab you sometimes and just kiss the life outa you.
>
> (38)

"*The Woman has come from behind the scrim [. . .] laughing,*" and Willy continues:

> 'Cause I get so lonely—especially when business is bad and there's nobody to talk to. I get the feeling that I'll never sell anything again, that I won't make a living for you, or a business, a business for the boys.
>
> (38)

Willy believes that he turns to another woman out of loneliness for his wife, Linda. But at the root of his loneliness and his need of a woman are feelings of shame he cannot face. He is driven by feelings of inadequacy and failure to seek himself outside of himself, in the eyes of others. "The Woman" makes him feel that he is an important salesman and a powerful man. After she interrupts Willy with the words, "I picked you," Willy immediately asks, "*pleased*," "You picked me?" (38). Again, on the same page, after she says, "And I think you're a wonderful man," Willy asks, "You picked me, heh?" (38). Just prior to leaving, "The Woman" makes a point of saying exactly what Willy wants to hear. "I'll put you right through to the buyers," she says, and, feeling full of masculine power, "*slapping her bottom,*" Willy responds, "Right. Well, bottoms up!" (39).

The father's bravado is the son's shame. At the root of Biff's wrongdoing and feelings of guilt lie shame and feelings of inadequacy and inferiority. But, unlike his father, he faces, and learns from, his shame. Consequently, the play suggests that he can rebuild his sense of self-worth and re-establish his relation to others on healthier grounds. He makes sense of his guilt by confronting the shame buried deep in his sense of identity. Ultimately, the ability to do so enables him to empathize with his father.

Biff's inherited sense of inadequacy and inferiority sends him "running home" (22) in springtime from the outdoor life out West—a life that reflects his own desires and needs. And yet, it is his father's wrong, a shameful act of adultery, coupled with Biff's failure to pass math and go to university to become a football star (as he and his father had hoped), that shatters Biff's already fragile sense of identity and sends him out West in the first place. His own desires and needs cannot hold him still. He is plagued by his father's, and his society's, measure of a person—the mighty dollar, the dream of "building a future" (22). Until Biff discovers his father with "The Woman" in Boston, Willy is as good as a god to him. So, rather than expose his father's shame, which, at some level, he experiences as his own, Biff runs, and attempts to hide, from the collapse of the ideal, invulnerable, infallible image of his father. Thus the source of his sense of identity in shame goes unquestioned. He continues to steal and to move from job to job, not so much because he feels guilty but because he feels ashamed of himself for not living up to an image of success that has already been proven to be a "fake." After he witnesses his father give "The Woman" in Boston "Mama's stockings!" Biff calls his father a "liar!" a "fake!" and a "phony little fake!" (121). He does not, however, reconcile this image of his father with his sense of himself. Not, that is, until he is in the process of stealing a fountain pen belonging his old boss, Bill Oliver. As he says to his father, "I stopped in the middle of that building and I saw—the sky" (132)—the same sky that is obscured from view by the "*towering, angular shapes [. . .] surrounding*" the Loman home "*on all sides*" (11), and which also forms part of the "inspiring" outdoor world Biff has left behind (22). Biff goes to see Oliver in a futile attempt to fit his, if you will, circular self into an "angular" world—a world in the process of crushing both the son and the father, men far more adept at using their hands than at using a pen. Biff reveals to his father that he has taken Oliver's pen, and that he cannot face Oliver again, but Willy accuses him of not "want[ing] to be anything," and Biff, "*now angry at Willy for not crediting his sympathy,*" exclaims, "Don't take it that way! You think it was easy walking into that office after what I'd done to him? A team of horses couldn't have dragged me back to Bill Oliver!" (112-13). There is no question that Biff feels guilty for what he has "done to" Oliver, first, by stealing "that carton of basketballs" (26) years ago, and second, by stealing his fountain pen. On the other hand, he also feels extremely ashamed of himself.

Biff's inherited sense of shame drives him to steal and to perform for his father. The fact that he steals does not, however, bother his father too much. Guilt can be concealed and, perhaps, forgiven and forgotten. Willy suggests as much when he advises Biff to say to Oliver: "You were doing a crossword puzzle and accidentally used his pen!" (112). But Biff's sense of himself is at stake, and he knows it. He knows that he cannot bear to be seen (the classic sign of shame) by Oliver. He can no longer separate his sense of himself from the act of stealing. Biff says to his father: "I stole myself out of every good job since high school!" (131). But, in essence, as Biff now realizes, his self was stolen by his inherited, shame-ridden sense of identity. He never had a chance to see himself outside his father's point of view. Willy feels attacked by Biff's confession that he "stole" himself "out of every good job," and responds: "And whose fault is that?" Biff continues: "And I never got anywhere because you blew me so full of hot air I could never stand taking orders from anybody! That's whose fault it is!" (131).

Biff understands his relation to others, notably his father, only after he literally goes unnoticed and unidentified by someone he thought would recognize him: Bill Oliver. Biff comes to the realization that there is no reason why Oliver should have recognized him, given that he couldn't recognize himself. That is, as Biff says to Happy, "I even believed myself that I'd been a salesman for him! And then he gave me one look and—I realized what a ridiculous lie my whole life has been! We've been talking in a dream for fifteen years. I was a shipping clerk" (104). Unlike his father's true self, which is immersed in shame and guilt, Biff's self surfaces and stays afloat because he learns about his guilt from his shame.

Willy's insistence that Biff is "spiting" him by not going to see Oliver prompts Biff to voice what he sees as the meaning behind his theft and his inability to face his old boss again: "I'm no good, can't you see what I am?" (113). In this case, it is not simply Biff's wrongdoing that makes him identify himself as "no good"; he has now grasped the fact that behind his habit of breaking the law lie feelings of shame. This question, "can't you see what I am?" represents the beginnings of Biff's separation of his own identity from that of his father. By the end of Act Two, Biff is certain, as he says to his brother, that "[t]he man don't know who we are!" At this point he is determined to force his father to "hear the truth—what you are and what I am!" (131, 130). He knows who he thought he was and, thus, why he stole Oliver's pen. As he reveals to his whole family,

> I stopped in the middle of that building and I saw—the sky. I saw the things that I love in this world. The work and the food and time to sit and smoke. And I looked at the pen and said to myself, what the hell am I grabbing this for? Why am I trying to become what I don't want to be? What am I doing in an office, making a contemptuous, begging fool of myself, when all I want is out there, waiting for me the minute I say I know who I am! Why can't I say that, Willy? *He tries to make Willy face him, but Willy pulls away and moves to the left.*
>
> (132)

"Willy," the father who has been transformed from "Dad" into simply a man in his son's eyes, cannot bear to have his dreams, and his heroic vision of his son, himself, and his own brother and father—the vision by which he lives and dies—exposed. Therefore, he *"pulls away"* in shame, before standing his ground and yelling, *"with hatred, threateningly,"* "The door of your life is wide open!" (132). Unlike the scene in the restaurant, in which Biff presents Happy with *"the rolled-up hose"* with which Willy intends to commit suicide and tells his brother that he "can't bear to look at his [father's] face!" out of shame (115), this time Biff does not turn away from his father. He insists on the truth being truly heard by his father. It is only after he realizes that this is an impossibility that *"he pulls away"* (133): "There's no spite in it any more. I'm just what I am, that's all" (133), says the son to his father. He now knows that he is "nothing" only under the umbrella of his father's destructive vision.

By the end of Act Two, Biff has a relatively clear understanding of who he is or, at the very least, who he is not. "I am not a leader of men," he says to his father in a *"fury,"* before *"he breaks down, sobbing"* (132-33). But his father cannot empathize with him because he is incapable of facing his own feelings of guilt and shame. To Willy, Biff's tears symbolize simply his son's love, and not, in any way, the struggle to separate from him. Biff demonstrates that he does in fact love his father, but, at the same time, this love is balanced by the recognition that if there is any chance of saving himself and his father he must leave home for good. The complexity of his feelings for his father goes unrecognized, however. Willy's response to Biff's breakdown is, "Oh, Biff! *Staring wildly*: He cried! Cried to me. *He is choking with his love, and now cries out his promise*: That boy—that boy is going to be magnificent!" (133).

What Biff wants from his father he ends up giving, without getting it back. He wants not only love, but empathy. Moreover, after confronting his own shame and discovering who he is not—that is, not the "boy" his father believes him to be—Biff demonstrates his ability to separate from his father and, consequently, his ability to empathize with him. In his dictionary of psychoanalysis, Charles Rycroft defines empathy as "[t]he capacity to put oneself into the other's shoes. The concept implies that one is both feeling oneself into the object and remaining aware of one's own identity as another person."[6] Biff does exactly this. In tears, he asks his father, "Will you let me go, for Christ's sake? Will you take that phony dream and burn it before something happens?" (133). He is not simply asking for his own freedom from the shame produced by not living up to the dream of success and being "well liked"; he is asking for his father's freedom from shame and guilt as well. He feels for his father and recognizes how "that phony dream" tortures him, at the same time that he retains his own sense of identity. But nothing can save Willy from his inability to accept the failure to live up to his own expectations—not even his son's empathy and forgiveness. Both are powerless in the face of shame.

In "Requiem," the final moments of Miller's tragedy, Biff is alone in his empathic understanding. Even Charley does not understand the meaning of Biff's final words about his father: "He had the wrong dreams. All, all wrong. [. . .] He never knew who he was" (138, intervening dialogue omitted). Happy is *"ready to fight"* after these words, and Charley responds by saying to Biff, "Nobody dast blame this man. You don't understand: Willy was a salesman." But, as Linda suggests prior to this statement by Charley, "He was so wonderful with his hands," and it is this very suggestion that triggers Biff's final words about his father (138). Willy Loman was more himself, relatively free of guilt and shame, when he worked with his hands than at any other time in his life.

Driven by shame, he kills himself in order to preserve his dream of being "well liked" and a successful father and salesman. Of course, the irony is that because of his suicide the odds are very good that neither of his sons will benefit from his sacrifice, and nobody from his world of sales comes to his funeral. Linda's words at the end of the play, and especially the words, "We're free and clear" (139), reveal the degree to which she and her husband lived in denial, in fear of exposing the man who hid in shame behind the idea of being a successful salesman and father. To be "free and clear" is, ultimately, an impossibility for Willy Loman. His vision of success perpetuates crippling feelings of inferiority and inadequacy that drive him to destroy himself.

Unlike Biff, Willy does not confront and come to terms with his shame, and therefore he can never understand his guilt, nor his son's pain and his own responsibility for it. In **"Tragedy and the Common Man,"** Miller states that "In [tragedies], and in them alone, lies the belief—optimistic, if you will, in the perfectibility of man."[7] In *Death of a Salesman,* he suggests, perhaps unintentionally, that the path to "perfection" lies in a confrontation with feelings of shame that enable one to understand guilt and arrive at a clearer sense of identity, as well as to empathize with others.

Notes

1. Bernard Williams, *Shame and Necessity* (Berkeley and Los Angeles: U of California P, 1993), 10.

2. Ibid., 92-94.

3. Arthur Miller, *Death of a Salesman: Certain Private Conversations and a Requiem* (New York: Penguin, 1987), 48, 45. Subsequent references appear parenthetically in the text.

4. In addition to *Shame and Necessity,* Helen Merrell Lynd's *On Shame and the Search for Identity* has been influential in shaping my understanding of the distinction and relation between guilt and shame. Lynd states that "[a] sense of guilt arises from a feeling of wrongdoing, a sense of shame from a feeling of inferiority. Inferiority feelings in shame are rooted in a deeper conflict in the personality than the sense of wrongdoing in guilt." Helen Merrell Lynd, *On Shame and the Search for Identity* (New York: Harcourt, 1967), 22.

5. In *On Shame and the Search for Identity,* Lynd defines shame as "a wound to one's self-esteem, a painful feeling or sense of degradation excited by the consciousness of having done something unworthy of one's previous idea of one's own excellence" (23-24). See note 4.

6. Charles Rycroft, *A Critical Dictionary of Psychoanalysis* (London: Penguin 1988), 42.

7. Arthur Miller, "Tragedy and the Common Man," in *The Theater Essays of Arthur Miller,* ed. Robert A. Martin (New York: Viking, 1978), 7.

Terry W. Thompson (essay date spring 2002)

SOURCE: Thompson, Terry W. "Miller's *Death of a Salesman." Explicator* 60, no. 3 (spring 2002): 162-63.

[*In the following essay, Thompson explores the comparisons between Willy Loman's sons and the mythological figure of Adonis in* Death of a Salesman.]

Early in *Death of a Salesman,* Arthur Miller's most celebrated play, Willy Loman—the financially burdened and emotionally exhausted main character—makes a fleeting reference to a mythological figure who was renowned for his physical beauty. Pronounced during an effusive conversation with his sons, it is an allusion that Willy believes is completely flattering to his two beloved boys, Biff and Happy. However, the reference signifies much more than Willy thinks it does. Like the aging and unenlightened salesman himself, the comparison is superficial and uninformed, tellingly shallow and rather ignorant.

The mythological allusion comes midway through the first act, during one of Willy's rose-tinted recollections of the family's past, when his sons were young and all things were possible. Willy proclaims to the wide-eyed Biff and Happy, "Bernard can get the best marks in school, y'understand, but when he gets out in the business world, y'understand, you are going to be five times ahead of him. That's why I thank Almighty God you're both built like Adonises" (Miller 33). In these lines, Willy not only shows his ignorance of the business world but also demonstrates his sketchy knowledge of the classical myth that he alludes to.

Willy sees his comparison of his two sons with the handsomest of all Greek males (with the possible exception of Narcissus), as a polished, erudite compliment. But sadly, Willy does not know the whole story of Adonis.

The son of Myrrha, a beautiful mortal woman. Adonis grew into "an exceedingly handsome young man, who was loved by the goddess Aphrodite" (Feder 6). This loveliest of all the goddesses—as well as one of the most powerful—tried to educate her young paramour, to guide him with her Olympian intellect and insight. However, the youthful Adonis was invariably headstrong and arrogant, proud and impetuous. A virile, athletic risk-taker by nature, he especially enjoyed the thrill of the chase and the violence of the hunt. On one occasion before he went out hunting, Aphrodite clutched the handsome boy to her immortal breast and sternly warned him, "'Your youth and beauty, and the charms which make [me] love you, have no effect upon lions or bristling boars, or in the eyes and minds of other wild beasts" (Ovid 239). Impulsive and confident, brimming with youthful bravado, Adonis paid her no heed. On the very next hunt, his carelessness brought him to a violent and grisly end: he was gored by a wild boar and expired, "writhing in his own blood" (Ovid 244). After tearing at her breasts with her fingernails, in grief over the tragic death of one so young, so handsome, and so promising, Aphrodite sprinkled Adonis's freshly spilled blood onto the fertile Greek soil where

> within an hour, a flower sprung up, the colour of blood, and in appearance like that of the pomegranate. [. . .] But the enjoyment of this flower is of brief duration: for it is so fragile, its petals so lightly attached, that it quickly falls, shaken from its stem by those same winds that give it its name, anemone.
>
> (Ovid 245)

In essence, Willy Loman's attempt at a flattering mythological allusion turns out to be just as inept as his business advice. It parallels his inability to see deeply

into anything, be it ancient myth, modern commerce, or even the demands of fatherhood. Yet ironically—and totally unperceived by Willy—his allusion actually proves to be a subtle and poignant one: Both of Willy's sons are like bright spring flowers, attractive and beautiful when young, but like the blood-fertilized anemone, their bloom is only temporary. Their young lives, once as promising as that of the handsome Adonis, come to nothing, not because they are killed by a wild animal, but because, like Adonis, they believed that their physical attractiveness and their superficial charm would carry them through lives. Now well into their thirties, when they should be responsible young men out making their careers, supporting families, and living independent lives. Biff and Happy Loman remain as immature, as petty and snickering, as they were in high school, when they spent their time cheating on exams, stealing from neighbors, roughing up girls, and lying at every opportunity. Although they do not die tragically or violently in the play, their youthful promise certainly comes to naught, proving that they are indeed, as their father boasts, just "like Adonises."

Works Cited

Feder, Lillian. *Crowell's Handbook of Classical Literature.* New York: Harper Colophon, 1964

Miller, Arthur. *Death of a Salesman: Certain Private Conversations in Two Acts and a Requiem.* New York: Viking, 1949

Ovid. *The Metamorphoses.* Trans, Mary M. Innes. New York: Penguin, 1955.

Frank Ardolino (essay date August 2002)

SOURCE: Ardolino, Frank. "'I'm Not a Dime a Dozen! I am Willy Loman!': The Significance of Names and Numbers in *Death of a Salesman.*" *Journal of Evolutionary Psychology* (August 2002): 174-84.

[*In the following essay, Ardolino evaluates the role that repeated patterns of letters, names, and numbers play in* Death of a Salesman, *arguing that Miller uses these patterns to "create an expressionistic juxtaposition of the past and present and desire and guilt in Willy's disordered mind."*]

In *Death of a Salesman,* Miller's poetic use of demotic English, the level of language which characters speak and which describes their actions and environment, creates the play's tragic dimension.[1] To achieve the depths of tragedy, Miller expands the ordinarily limited expressive capabilities of demotic English by exploiting the sounds and multiple meanings of simple verbal, visual, and numerical images. Miller's system of onomastic and numerical images and echoes forms a complex network which delineates Willy's insanity and its effects on his family and job.

Much of the play takes place in a psychological construct which Willy creates. An Eden-like paradise which lies at the center of his neurosis, it is characterized by the paradoxical union of reality and his delusory fulfillment of his grandiose dreams of omnipotence. Willy's paradise, which he identifies with the time in which Biff and Happy were growing up in Brooklyn, was also synonymous with his and his sons' exclusive society in which they expressed, reflected, and validated his belief in their virtual divinity. Expressing his enthusiasm for Biff's divine condition, Willy ironically incorporated the concept of progress, time's movement, into his changeless paradise. He believed that Biff, who was already "divine" as a football player, would become more so as a businessman. Before Biff realized Willy's projected future, however, he lost faith in Willy's dreams, left the state of mind or paradise Willy had created, and destroyed its coherence. As a result, Willy moved from the condition of stasis to one created by a confusion of the present and of its fragmented paradise.

Willy never experiences the future which is part of normal chronological time because he recognizes only the future which he believes is latent in his paradise. To his destruction, he seeks to actualize it.

Willy Loman reconstructs the past "not chronologically as in flashback, but *dynamically with the inner logic of his erupting volcanic unconscious*" (Schneider 252.) This "visualized psychoanalytic interpretation woven into reality" (Schneider 253) serves as Miller's principal dramatic method—the simultaneous existence of the past and present in Willy's disordered mind. Miller has said that he was obsessed with "a mode that would open a man's head for a play to take place inside it, evolving through concurrent rather than consecutive actions," which "turned him [Willy] to see present through past and past through present, a form that . . . would be . . . a collecting point for all that his . . . society had poured into him" (*Timebends* 129, 131).

The most difficult aspect of the play is the nature of the scenes, seemingly from the past, which are reconstructed by Willy's disordered mind. It is hard to determine whether Willy is hallucinating or actually recalling a past event. Although it may be impossible to resolve this problem, it is possible to determine the psychological associative processes which dictate why and how Willy experiences these events.

Willy is a salesman who values names, of people, places, and products, and numbers, of salaries and commissions, as the coinage of his personal, commercial, and psychological worlds. Miller uses these names,

even letters, and numbers to create a network of associations which establish a surrealistic pattern of insistent mockery and fatalism repeated in different but related contexts. As a result, the play becomes "a sort of narrative poem":

> Images—car, road, refrigerator, valises, silk stockings, a woman's laughter—through their rhythmic reappearance in the past and present, in different contexts, grow into symbols of his entire life. . . . The imagery is drawn from the hard cold facts of the life . . . Willy Loman, the salesman for the Wagner Company, who lives in a house in Brooklyn. It grows in meaning by association and juxtaposition to metaphorical significance.
>
> (Gordon 98, 107-08)

But this narrative poem is an expressionistic nightmare. The repetition of the names and numbers produce an echo chamber of mockery indicative of Willy's failure to achieve his dreams. He is like a rat in a maze; no matter where he turns he runs into the same indices of defeat. This is a deterministic universe, one that parallels the world of Greek tragedy. Willy can not escape the fate which he in a sense has created through the demented dreams instilled in him by his perversion of the American dream of success (Messenger 199).

Miller suggests that the power of the psyche is comparable to the fate represented by the omnipotent and capricious gods of Greek tragedy. For no apparent reason, Willy's psyche blinds him to the madness of his grandiose dreams of omnipotence and compels him to attempt to replace reality with his own concept of it.[2] In other terms, it drives him to challenge the gods. His delusory fulfillment of his grandiose dreams and the punishment for his hubris come together in his act of suicide. Happy, who is obsessed by sexuality, is a base variation of Willy and a mocking comment on his insane aspirations and death. Characterized by duality and duplicity, Happy lives in unending alternations of assertion and contradiction which result in nothingness. In contrast, Biff's psyche or fate mercifully releases him from Willy's dreams and their effects into the ordered multiplicity and movement of normal life. Biff's good fortune, however, does not explain or justify Willy's tragedy and Happy's meaninglessness. In the face of the incomprehensible and uncontrollable power of the psyche, modern audiences are moved to pity and terror as ancient audiences were moved by the fall of these heroes in Greek tragedy.

Willy points to himself as an exemplar of his beliefs, using his name as a manifestation of his omnipotence: "You take me for instance. I never have to wait in line to see a buyer. . . . 'Willy Loman is here!' That's all they want to know, and I go right through" (33).[3] Elaborating on name imagery that echoes his own self-assessment, Willy expresses his belief in Biff's omnipotence and predicts limitless success for his future in business: "And Ben! when he walks into a business office his name will sound out like a bell and all the doors will open to him!" (86).

But in reality, name imagery reveals Willy and Biff's failures. Willy has been working on commission "like a beginner, an unknown" (57). After he overhears Biff tell Linda and Happy that businessmen have laughed at him for years (61), he pathetically asserts his importance by using names: "They laugh at me, heh? Go to Filene's, go to the Hub, go to Slattery's, Boston. Call out the name Willy Loman and see what happens! Big Shot!" (62). Name imagery further points to Biff's failure to develop a career. When he attempted to meet with Bill Oliver, a businessman, he waited in his reception room, and "[k]ept sending my name in" (104), but it meant nothing to Oliver, and his door remained closed. In sum, when announcing a name, ringing a bell, and opening a door constitute the dramatic action, these actions contrast Willy's belief in his omnipotence with his base reality. Upon Biff's arrival at Willy's hotel, he asks the telephone operator to ring his room to announce his arrival; when Biff opens the door to Willy's room, he discovers Willy's adultery.

The names that appear throughout *Death of a Salesman* can be grouped into three related categories: geographical, personal, and business, the most significant of which often begin with "B," "F," and "S." The geographical names consist primarily of the places Willy travels to as a salesman; the personal include his family, friends, and business associates. Finally, the business category is comprised of the names of the people, stores, and products Willy reveres and intones throughout the play as proof of his value and the signs of the success he envisions for his sons.

Willy uses the names of the places on his business route as images of geographical and temporal expansion to enhance his relationship with his sons. In his description of a business trip, Willy evokes and identifies with the grandeur of New England and its history. The names of the cities along his route, a metaphor for the course of his life, however, are not indicative of his professional success but of the pain that Willy, Biff, and Happy suffer after their inflated emotions collapse.[4] Providence, the name of Willy's first stop, is presided over by a mayor whose title suggests an eponymous deity. Rather than providing Willy with care and benevolent guidance, however, Providence foreshadows and initiates the malign fate which pursues him, as the names of the other places on his route suggest. Waterbury, a "[b]ig clock city" (31), is an image which mocks the Lomans and their dreams of success. Moreover, it is also an allusion to Willy's attempt to commit suicide by driving his car into a river (59). Boston "the cradle of the Revolution" (31), alludes to

Biff's disillusionment with Willy and separation from him after having found him in a Boston hotel in an adulterous relationship.[5] Portland is the city Willy is unable to reach because of his mental breakdown. Metaphorically, Portland suggests Willy's failure to achieve the "port" or fulfillment which he might have expected during the last years of his career. Along with the word *boat*, Portland alludes to Willy's insane conviction that his dreams will become reality through suicide. Linda, who pities Willy and understands him as a man who has failings, but not as a neurotic, asks Biff to be "sweet" and "loving" to him "because he's only a little boat looking for a harbor" (76). The image becomes horrific just prior to his suicide when he psychologically joins Ben who acts as a Charon figure to bring him to port in the land of the dead.

> Time, William, time! . . .
>
> BEN:
>
> > (*looking at his watch*) The boat. We'll be late. (*He moves slowly off into the darkness.*)
>
> > (135)

Bangor, the name of the last city on Willy's route (31), onomatopoetically explodes—"bang!"—recalling imagery of emotional inflation and collapse associated with Willy's dreams. On the one hand, images of cohesion and of expansion respectively reflect the past mutual admiration between him and his sons and Willy's emotional inflation that results from it. Stage directions and rhythmic dialogue bring Willy, Biff, and Happy together like three vaudevillians, as Willy indulges his visions of himself as a master salesman basking in his son's admirations. Willy's mood expands as he tells Biff and Happy about his business trip and promises to take them with him on his next one.

> WILLY:
>
> > This summer, heh?
>
> BIFF AND HAPPY:
>
> > (*together*) Yeah! You bet.
>
> WILLY:
>
> > We'll take our bathing suits.
>
> HAPPY:
>
> > We'll carry your bags, Pop!
>
> WILLY:
>
> > Oh, won't that be something! Me comin' into the Boston stores with you boys carrying my bags, what a sensation!
>
> > (31)

The repetitions of accented "b's" in the words *bet, Boston, boys,* and *bags* unify, energize, and inflate the three Lomans. Willy's vision of Biff and Happy's carrying his bags symbolizes his unity with his sons and their mutual admiration.

A photo from a 1979 National Theatre production of Death of a Salesman *in London, England. Pictured are (from left to right): Stephen Greif as Biff, Warren Mitchell as Willy, Doreen Mantle as Linda, and David Baxt as Happy.*

But years after Biff became disillusioned with Willy, he uses imagery of vain inflation to blame Willy for his failure to achieve a career: ". . . I never got anywhere because you [Willy] blew me so full of hot air I could never stand taking orders from anybody!" (131). And he accuses Happy of being a liar: "You big blow, are you the assistant buyer? You're one of the two assistants to the assistant, aren't you" (131). The group of three which Biff describes forms a deflated parallel to the one Willy once imagined would create a sensation upon entering the Boston stores—Biff and Happy accompanying him, carrying his sample bags. In the light of the Lomans' lack of success, the bags, suggestive of windbags, allude to the burden of Willy's meretricious beliefs and unfounded grandiosity that Biff and Happy bore.

The image of inflated emotion and explosion inherent in *Bangor* is cruelly echoed in the word *blow,* which can mean "to treat" as well as "a violent impact," and in the name of the restaurant "Frank's Chop House."

The name *Frank* recalls Frank Wagner, Willy's former benevolent boss, and *chop,* which refers to a cut of meat, also means "a sharp blow." In anticipation of getting a loan to establish a sporting goods business, Biff asks Linda to invite Willy to a celebration at Frank's Chop House. "Biff came to me this morning, Willy, and he said, 'Tell Dad, we want to blow him to a big meal.' Be there [at Frank's Chop House] at six o'clock, you and your two boys are going to have dinner" (74)[6]. At the restaurant, Biff, who has stolen Bill Oliver's pen and escaped from his office in disgrace, tries to make Willy face the reality of their respective failures. Deeply angered, Willy strikes Biff, a blow which precipitates his subsequent hallucination in which Biff knocks on—or strikes—the door of Willy's hotel room in Boston, initiating the series of events that resulted in Biff's disillusionment.

Willy measures people's worth by their "names"—their popularity and reputation—and by the money they earn and amass. He cherishes and intones sacred names like Dave Singleman, Ben Loman, Bill Oliver, and Frank

Wagner, among others, who "represent aspects of his splintered mind" (Hoeveler 632).

Names beginning with "B" are used to present taunting images of success and failure. Ben, Willy's successful brother, walked into the jungle at seventeen and emerged at twenty-one a wealthy man. Bill Oliver, Biff's past employer and present delusory hope, has a first name which alludes to his monetary success, but he does not lend the money to Biff for his hopeless athletic scheme. Moreover, by its closeness to *Biff* and its equation with *Willy, Bill* mocks their respective failure. Similarly, Willy's reference to B. F. Goodrich, the founder and namesake of a tire manufacturing company, as a businessman who succeeded later in life also ironically alludes to Biff (18). The initials, "B. F.," sound like "Biff," and the last name describes the financial condition that Willy wants for him. In addition, Bernard, Charley's son, has achieved the success that Willy predicted he would never have because he was not well-linked, unlike Biff who was the popular football hero destined for fame and fortune. Willy Loman, the lowman on the economic totem pole, is tormented by the success of Ben, Bernard, and Bill Oliver and by the failure of Biff, which began with his son's flunking math seventeen years ago.

When Biff went to Boston to ask Willy to talk to his math teacher Birnbaum about raising his grade, he saw Willy with The Woman and lost faith in Willy and himself. As Harshbarger has noted, the first syllable in "Birnbaum" is reminiscent of fire and and the second one means "tree" in German (58). The whole name echoes Willy's cry of disaster, "the woods are burning" (41, 107). Willy uses the phrase to signify his growing sense of dread, just before he tells Biff and Happy that he was fired. In the context of the events at the Boston hotel, Birnbaum's name is a double pun. Willy who knows that Biff is knocking on the door of his room, refuses to open it, but The Woman insists: "Maybe the hotel's on fire!" (116). Her exclamation echoes Willy's locution and alludes to imminent disaster for him— Biff's recognition of his duplicity.

The next important letter is "F," found primarily in the names of people, usually *Frank* or a derivative, which convey a conflict between benevolence and protection on the one hand, and dismissal and degradation on the other. The principal benevolent Frank is Frank Wagner, Willy's former employer, who in 1928, according to Willy, made promises to him which his son Howard, whom Willy says he helped name (97), has failed to honor. Other benevolent characters named Frank are Biff's teenaged friend who, under Biff's direction, helps with household chores (34), and the repairman Frank, whom Willy depends upon to repair the cherished Chevrolet (36). At the opposite pole is Miss Francis, Willy's Boston mistress. Finally, there is Frank's Chop House where Willy relives the Boston episode and Happy ignores his father's distress to leave with Miss Forsythe, the "chippy" who parallels Miss Francis.

The third important letter is "S," which appears in the names of important salespeople cut, and in related stores, places, brand names, objects, and qualities which represent concomitantly Willy's dreams of success and his guilt in not fulfilling them cut. Dave Singleman is the eighty-four-year-old salesman who conducted his successful business activities wearing his green velvet slippers, which symbolize the easy success of the David-like single man who conquered the business world (81). The store and place names beginning with "S" include J. H. Simmons, the company for which Miss Francis was the buyer, and the Standish Arms (111), the hotel where Biff witnessed the primal scene of patriarchal betrayal. Also, there are the aspects of Willy's profession, the "smile and a shoeshine" ("Requiem" 138) which Charley says a salesman faces the world with.

A key object with "S" is the silk stockings Willy gave to Miss Francis as a kind of payment for sex, which he guiltily recalls every time he sees Linda mending her stockings. As Boruch has explained, "Willy can't get rid of the ghost of silk stockings, symbol of his infidelity, and cause of Biff's distrust" (554). During one of Willy's hallucinations, Linda "darns stockings" (36) prior to The Woman's appearance and mends "a pair of her silk stockings" (39) just after her disappearance. When Willy sees Linda at her work, his reaction is intense for her stockings recall his adultery: "I won't have you mending stockings in this house! Now throw them out!" When Biff surprises Willy and The Woman in his hotel room, she insists on taking her gift even while Willy desperately tries to get rid of her: "You had two boxes of size nine sheers for me, and I want them!" (119).

Sheers, the word that Miss Francis uses to refer to silk stockings, when spelled *shears* means "scissors" and suggests "to cut," which in turn alludes to Biff's metaphorically cutting the tie that has wrongfully bound him and Willy. He cries out in anguish that Willy has given her "Mama's stockings" (121). After Biff arrives at home, he burns his sneakers on which he had printed "University of Virginia" (94), an act which echoes Willy's utterance of incendiary disaster and symbolizes his change from innocence to knowledge, his rejection of Willy's belief when the "illusion of [Willy's] sexless godhead . . . is shattered" (Schneider 253). Seventeen years later, at Frank's Chop House, Biff "takes the rolled up hose from his pocket" and shows it to Happy (115). Another synonym for stockings, the hose is the means by which Willy planned to commit suicide.

Parallel to the silk stockings is the letter "S" on Biff's football sweater (28), which represents his special or superman status in Willy's eyes. Biff wears the sweater when he discovers his father's adultery in Boston and its "S" is echoed ironically seventeen years later when Willy encounters the now successful and formerly "anemic" and unpopular Bernard, who is going to argue a case before the Supreme Court. The word *Supreme* mocks Willy's deluded prediction about Bernard and recalls that seventeen years earlier Biff played in a championship football game at prestigious Ebbets Field, but did not go on to a career of any kind. "His life ended after that Ebbets Field game," confides Willy to Bernard (92).

2

Numbers, which represent specificity and order in mundane reality, also reveal the damage that Willy does to his family to satisfy his neurotic demands. Like the onomastic images, numbers reveal and comment on Willy and Biff's failures. The numbers used in *Death of a Salesman* denote: 1. diurnal time, the course of a career, and contract stipulations; 2. money, usually in the form of salaries and commissions, earned, sought or expected, and debts; 3. distance, the miles Willy travels in pursuit of his dreams; 4. street designations. The most important numbers are *two* or doubles, *4, 6, 11, 17, 34, 48,* and *63.*

Two's or doubles are an important indication of Willy's inescapable malaise. The play has two acts and takes two days, and Willy lives a dual existence in the past and the present. Willy carries two suitcases (12), emblematic of his business world and the burden of his two sons, who are two years apart (19) and are paralleled by Howard's two children, who are also two years apart (77), and Bernard's two sons (92). Willy mentions the two elm trees which used to be in the backyard but were chopped down, a symbol of destruction of his idyllic plans for his sons (17). There are two sets of brothers, Ben and Willy, and Happy and Biff. Further, Willy gives two pairs of silk stockings to Miss Francis, who is paralleled by the two "chippies" the boys pick up at Frank's where Willy expects to celebrate a dual triumph. He feels sure that Howard will give him the non-traveling job that he wants and that Biff will get the loan from Oliver. When Biff orders drinks that evening, "Scotch all around. Make it doubles," and Stanley, the waiter repeats "doubles," they unwittingly echo the dual failures of Willy and Biff.

Seventeen, Biff's age when he failed math by four points, echoes and contrasts with Ben's achievement. Ben, Willy's dead brother and his image of the ideal Darwinian businessman, was seventeen when he set out to make his fortune. Four years later, he was rich (48). The repetition of *seventeen* and *four* also contrasts Biff's stasis with Bernard's progress in chronological time. Seventeen years after Biff failed math at the age of seventeen, he is professionally in the same place, but Bernard has become a lawyer. When Willy congratulates him on his success, he alludes to Biff's four missed points: "I'm overjoyed to see how you made the grade, Bernard overjoyed" (92).

Thirty-four, the double of *seventeen,* reappears at key moments to mock Willy's pretensions and to signal his tragedy.[7] Biff lost his desire to succeed at the age of

seventeen (92), and now seventeen years later at thirty-four (16), he has returned home to resurrect his life by meeting with Bill Oliver. In anguish after being fired, Willy declares "I put thirty-four years in this firm" (82). Finally, in the "Requiem," Linda says that she does not know why Willy committed suicide because "this is the first time in thirty-five years" (137) they have been free of debt, and she has "made the last payment on the house" (139), which had a twenty-five year mortgage that began when Biff was nine, (73).

Thirty-six and its reverse *sixty-three* also haunt Willy and connect directly with the fateful scene in the Boston hotel. Willy is sixty-three years of age (57), and according to Linda has worked at Wagner's for "thirty-six years this March" (56). Nevertheless, Howard, who is thirty-six (76), unceremoniously fires him. Biff's satiric attack on Mr. Birnbaum initiates the baleful consequences of the trip for both Biff and Willy. After Biff tells Willy why he came to the hotel, he imitates Mr. Birnbaum as he did for his classmates at school: ". . . I got up at the blackboard and imitated him. I crossed my eyes and talked with a lithp . . . The thquare root of thixty twee is . . ." (118).

The math problem, "the thquare root of thixty twee," is a coded message which alludes to Willy's insanity and Biff and Happy's participation in it; however, Willy and Biff do not see its meaning. The number *sixty-three,* Willy's age, identifies him as the focus of the problem. The word *square,* an image of an enclosed area, and *root,* a plant image, refer to Willy's paradisiacal garden and the two trees representing Biff and Happy which grew there, and the condition of his mind which is imprisoned in insanity, the root of his and his family's problems. Biff concludes his imitation by saying, "in the middle of it [Biff's classroom performance] he [Mr. Birnbaum] walked in!" (118). Drawn by Willy and Biff's laughter, The Woman, whose entrance parallels Mr. Birnbaum's, leaves the bathroom, her hiding place, and enters Willy's room. Biff's eyes are no longer "crossed" and he finally sees who Willy is.

The penultimate scene of the second act, which takes place at Frank's Chop House, represents Miller's most effective juxtaposition of the past and the present and the culmination of the onomastic and numerological patterns. Having suffered the dual indignity of being fired by Howard and having to borrow money from Charley, Willy eagerly anticipates meeting his sons at Frank's (six letters) Chop House on 48th Street and 6th Avenue at 6 o'clock. These numbers are portentous. *Forty-eight* is the reverse of the revered Dave Singleman's age at which he was still successful (81). The number may also refer to the two-day duration of the play at the end of which Willy commits suicide. *Six* is also a deadly number, recalling the standard 6'×6' size of graves. Further, Biff failed math, scoring only a "61," in June, the sixth month (93, 118), and when he went to Boston (six letters) he discovered his father's infidelity.

Now Willy confronts his broken son Biff, who waited six hours for Oliver (six letters), and, after being ignored, stole his golden pen, as he once had stolen a carton of basketballs from him, and fled down eleven flights of stairs (104)—11+6=17, the fateful age at which Biff's ambition died and the number of years he has spent wandering aimlessly.

The use of the number *eleven* also suggests the "11th hour," and image of Biff's precarious situation poised between destruction—return to his mutually reflective relationship—and salvation—imminent change in his psychological condition. Biff's description of his anger with both Oliver and himself contains an allusion to his past bondage to Willy's sick dreams: "How the hell did I ever get the idea I was a salesman there? . . . And then he gave me one look and—I realized what a ridiculous lie my whole life has been!" (104). The theft of Bill Oliver's gold fountain pen signals the beginning of Biff's psychological awakening. After he takes the pen, he runs down the eleven flights of stairs, and, in a psychological sense, undoes his past as he descends from inflated dream to fundamental reality: "I stopped in the middle of that building and I saw . . . the things that I love in this world. The work and the food and time to sit and smoke. . . . Why am I trying to become what I don't want to be?" (132). Within the confines of the office building, Biff recognizes and accepts the value of his ordinary life.

Despite his liberating insight, Biff is not able to get Willy to see reality at Frank's Chop House, where a scene of filial denial is enacted which parallels the episode in Boston when Willy denied Biff and Linda in his pursuit of Miss Francis. In a parody of his father's career and values, Happy woos the "strudel" (100) by pretending to be a champagne salesman and by claiming that Biff plays quarterback for the New York Giants, an ironic expansion of Willy's past adulation of him as a stellar high-school quarterback playing the championship game at Ebbets Field. Happy also asserts that his real name is Harold (six letters), which recalls Howard Wagner (six letters each), another son who is disloyal to his father and dismissive of another father. Happy "sells himself" to Miss Forsythe by ordering the champagne just as Willy "scored" with Miss Francis by giving her Linda's silk stockings. Happy denies his father—"that's not my father. He's just a guy" (115)—to go with Miss Forsythe and Letta, names that respectively represent Willy's lack of foresight and his defeat as exemplifies by ominous repetitions.

After his sons leave, Willy ends up hallucinating in the downstairs toilet, which signals his descent into the depths of his madness as he relives the events in Boston when Miss Francis emerged from Willy's bathroom and was seen by Biff. He is helped by the waiter Stanley, whose name recalls the Standish Arms, and he leaves, completely despondent, to search for the fruitless seeds, the image of his faithless sons who have never taken hold in the soil of his own prelapsarian backyard garden, in the hardware store on 6th Avenue, the street of the dead (122).

Miller uses the repeated names, letters, and numbers not only to impart a sense of concrete and specific realism to the dreamlike scenes but also to create an expressionistic juxtaposition of the past and present and desire and guilt in Willy's disordered mind. Everyone can empathize with the tragedy of a little man who persists in trying to gain the elusive success that is all wrong for him and his sons. Willy's dilemma is universal, and Miller's depiction of it is both simple and complex, realistic and surrealistic, and ultimately, sad and nightmarishly fatalistic.

Notes

1. For a discussion of the various ways Arthur Miller uses demotic language, see my article "Miller's Poetic Use of Demotic English in *Death of a Salesman*," *Studies in American Jewish Literature* 17 (1988): 120-28.

2. For an excellent discussion of the nature of Willy's madness, see Giles Mitchell, "Living and Dying for the Ideal: A Study of Willy Loman's Narcissism." *The Psychoanalytic Review* 77 (1990): 391-407.

3. All citations of the play will be from Arthur Miller, *Death of a Salesman* (1949; rpt. Penguin, 1976).

4. Willy uses the cliches of business success to describe to his sons how much he sold in New England— "Knocked 'em cold in Providence, slaughtered 'em in Boston" (33)—but the language conveys the deadly emptiness of his dreams.

5. Boston is also the place from which Ben says their father began his cross country journeys with the family to sell his successful gadgets (49).

6. Tuesday, the day on which dinner takes place (71), may also contain an ironic pun on the number *two.*

7. *Thirty-four* is a key number in Miller's life. As he explains in *Timebends,* he became an overnight success at the age of thirty-four in 1949 with the production and publication of *Death of a Salesman* (184).

Works Cited

Ardolino, Frank. "Miller's Poetic Use of Demotic English in *Death of a Salesman*." *Studies in American Jewish Literature* 17 (1988): 120-28.

Boruch, Marianne. "Miller and Things." *Literary Review* 24 (1981): 548-61.

Gordon, Lois. "*Death of a Salesman*: An Appreciation." In *Twentieth Century Interpretations of Arthur Miller's Death of a Salesman,* ed. Helene Koon. Princeton University Press, 1983. 98-108.

Harshbarger, Karl. *The Burning Jungle: Analysis of Arthur Miller's Death of a Salesman.* Washington, D.C.: University Press of America, 1979.

Hoeveler, Diane. "*Death of a Salesman* as Psychomachia." *Journal of American Culture* 1 (1978): 632-37.

Messenger, Christian. *Sport and the Spirit of Play in Contemporary American Fiction.* N.Y.: Columbia University Press, 1990.

Miller, Arthur. *Death of a Salesman.* 1949; rpt. N.Y.: Penguin, 1976.

————. *Timebends: A Life.* New York: Grove Press, 1987.

Mitchell, Giles. "Living and Dying for the Ideal: A Study of Willy Loman's Narcissism." *The Psychoanalytic Review* 77 (1990): 391-407.

Schneider, Daniel. "Play of Dreams." in *Death of a Salesman: Text and Criticism,* ed. Gerald Weales. New York: Penguin, 1967. 250-58.

FURTHER READING

Criticism

Lahr, John. "Fugitive Mind." *New Yorker* 75, no. 2 (8 March 1999): 93.

> Lahr commends the fiftieth-anniversary production of *Death of a Salesman,* noting that "Miller's reading of the nation's collective unconscious is so accurate that the flaws in this somewhat overpraised production hardly matter."

Meador, Roy. "The Elegy for Willy Loman Lives On." *Biblio* 4, no. 3 (March 1999): 16-17.

> Meader argues that Miller's portrayal of capitalist disillusionment in *Death of a Salesman* has become a prominent part of American social consciousness.

Miller, Arthur, and Colby H. Kullman. "*Death of a Salesman* at Fifty: An Interview with Arthur Miller." *Michigan Quarterly Review* 37, no. 4 (fall 1998): 624-34.

> Miller discusses different productions of *Death of a Salesman* and reflects on the play on the fiftieth anniversary of its first production.

Monet, Cristina. "Smiles and Shoeshines." *Spectator* 283, no. 8923 (14 August 1999): 38.

> Monet compares the fiftieth-anniversary production of *Death of a Salesman* to recent revivals of Eugene O'Neill's *The Iceman Cometh.*

Murphy, Brenda. *Miller: "Death of a Salesman."* Cambridge: Cambridge University Press, 1995, 246 p.

> Murphy constructs a critical history of *Death of a Salesman,* discussing early drafts of the script, the play's impact on the American theatre community, and foreign performances of the play.

Rose, Lloyd. Review of *Death of a Salesman,* by Arthur Miller. *Atlantic* 253 (April 1984): 130-32.

> Rose praises a staging of *Death of a Salesman* staring actor Dustin Hoffman as Willy Loman, lauding the production for its "tremendous, inspired intelligence."

Thompson, Terry W. "The Ironic Hercules Reference in *Death of a Salesman.*" *English Language Notes* 40, no. 4 (June 2003): 73-7.

> Thompson examines the irony behind Willy Loman's allusions to Greek mythology in *Death of a Salesman.*

Weales, Gerald, editor. *Arthur Miller: "Death of a Salesman"—Text and Criticism.* New York: Viking Press, 1967, 426 p.

> Weales presents the full text of *Death of a Salesman* along with critical essays, commentary by Miller, and reviews of the play's first performance.

Additional coverage of Miller's life and career is contained in the following sources published by the Gale Group: *American Writers; American Writers: The Classics,* **Vol. 1;** *Authors and Artists for Young Adults,* **Vol. 15;** *Authors in the News,* **Vol. 1;** *Concise Dictionary of American Literary Biography, 1941-1968; Contemporary American Dramatists; Contemporary Authors,* **Vols. 1-4R;** *Contemporary Authors Bibliographical Series,* **Vol. 3;** *Contemporary Authors New Revision Series,* **Vols. 2, 30, 54, 76;** *Contemporary Dramatists,* **Ed. 5;** *Contemporary Literary Criticism,* **Vols. 1, 2, 6, 10, 15, 26, 47, 78;** *Dictionary of Literary Biography,* **Vols. 7, 266;** *DISCovering Authors; DISCovering Authors: British Edition; DISCovering Authors: Canadian Edition; DISCovering Authors Modules: Dramatists and Most-studied Authors; DISCovering Authors 3.0; Drama Criticism,* **Vol. 1;** *Drama for Students,* **Vols. 1, 3;** *Encyclopedia of World Literature in the 20th Century,* **Ed. 3;** *Literature and Its Times,* **Vols. 1, 4;** *Literature Resource Center; Major 20th-Century Writers,* **Eds. 1, 2;** *Reference Guide to American Literature,* **Ed. 4;** *Twayne's United States Authors; World Literature Criticism;* **and** *Writers for Young Adults Supplement,* **Vol. 1.**

Wole Soyinka
1934-

(Born Akinwande Oluwole Soyinka) Nigerian playwright, poet, novelist, essayist, memoirist, librettist, lecturer, nonfiction writer, editor, and biographer.

The following entry presents an overview of Soyinka's career through 2002. For further information on his life and works, see *CLC,* Volumes 3, 5, 14, 36, and 44.

INTRODUCTION

Recipient of the 1986 Nobel Prize for Literature, Soyinka is often referred to as one of Africa's finest living writers. His plays, novels, and poetry blend elements of traditional Yoruban folk drama and European dramatic form to create both spectacle and penetrating satire. His narrative technique is based on the African cultural tradition where the artist functions as the recorder of the mores and experiences of his society. Soyinka's works reflect this philosophy, serving as a record of twentieth-century Africa's political turmoil and the continent's struggle to reconcile tradition with modernization. Through his nonfiction works and essay collections, Soyinka has established an international reputation as an unflinching commentator on political injustice and knowing provocateur of social criticism.

BIOGRAPHICAL INFORMATION

Soyinka was born in Ìsarà, Nigeria, on July 13, 1934. As a child he became increasingly aware of the pull between African tradition and Western modernization. Aké, his village, was populated mainly with people from the Yoruba tribe and was presided over by the *ogboni,* or tribal elders. Soyinka's grandfather introduced him to the pantheon of Yoruba gods and other figures of tribal folklore. His parents, however, were representatives of colonial influence: his mother was a devout Christian convert, and his father was a headmaster at the village school established by the British. Soyinka published poems and short stories in *Black Orpheus,* a Nigerian literary magazine, before leaving Africa to attend the University of Leeds in England. He returned to Nigeria in 1960, shortly after the country's independence from colonial rule. In 1965 Soyinka was arrested by the Nigerian police, accused of using a gun to force a radio announcer to broadcast incorrect election results. No evidence was ever produced, however, and the PEN writers' organization soon launched a protest campaign, headed by William Styron and Norman Mailer. Soyinka was eventually released after three months. He was next arrested two years later, during Nigeria's civil war for his vocal opposition to the conflict. Soyinka was particularly angered by the Nigerian government's brutal policies toward the Ibo people, who were attempting to form their own country, Biafra. After he traveled to Biafra to establish a peace commission composed of leading intellectuals from both sides for the conflict, the Nigerian police accused Soyinka of helping the Biafrans to buy jet fighters. This time Soyinka was imprisoned for more than two years, although he was never formally charged with a crime. For the majority of his arrest, he was kept in solitary confinement. Although he was denied reading and writing materials, Soyinka created his own ink and began to keep a prison diary, writing on toilet paper and cigarette packages. This diary was published in 1972 as *The Man Died: Prison Notes of Wole Soyinka.* In 1993 Soyinka began a period of self-imposed exile from Nigeria due to General Ibrahim Babangida's refusal to allow a democratic government to take power. Babangida appointed General Sani Abacha as head of the Nigerian state and Soyinka, along with other pro-democracy activists, was charged with treason for his criticism of the military regime. Facing a death sentence, Soyinka left the country in 1994, during which time he traveled and lectured in Europe and the United States. Following the death of Abacha, who held control for five years, the new government, led by General Abdulsalem Abubakar, released numerous political prisoners and promised to hold civilian elections, prompting Soyinka to return to his homeland. Soyinka has held teaching positions at a number of prestigious universities, including the University of Ghana, Cornell University, and Yale University. He also served as the Goldwin Smith professor for African Studies and Theatre Arts at Cornell University from 1988 to 1991. Soyinka has received several awards for his work, such as the Nobel Prize for Literature in 1986 and the Enrico Mattei Award for Humanities in 1986.

MAJOR WORKS

Soyinka's early dramas focus upon the dichotomies of good versus evil and progress versus tradition in African culture. For example, *The Swamp Dwellers* (1958) condemns African superstition by showing religious leaders who exploit the fears of their townspeople for personal gain. Commissioned as part of Nigeria's independence celebration in 1960, *A Dance of the Forests* (1960) warns the newly independent Nigerians that the end of colonial rule does not mean an end to their country's problems. The play features a bickering group of mortals who summon up the egungun—spirits of the dead, revered by the Yoruba people—for a festival. They have presumed the egungun to be noble and wise, but they discover that their ancestors are as petty and spiteful as anyone else. While Soyinka warns against sentimental yearning for Africa's past in *A Dance of the Forests,* he lampoons the indiscriminate embrace of Western modernization in *The Lion and the Jewel* (1959). The plot revolves around Sidi, the village beauty, and the rivalry between her two suitors. The story also follows Baroka, a village chief with many wives, and Lakunle, an enthusiastically Westernized schoolteacher who dreams of molding Sidi into a "civilized" woman. *The Trials of Brother Jero* (1960) was written in response to a request for a play that could be performed in a converted dining hall in Ibadan. Drawing on his observations of the separatist Christian churches of Nigeria, on Ijebu folk narratives, and on theatrical conventions exploited by dramatist Bertolt Brecht, Soyinka constructed a vigorous comedy around the character of a messianic beach prophet. Brother Jero—a trickster figure who sets up a shack on Bar Beach, Lagos, prophesying golden futures in return for

money—belongs to one of the revivalist Christian sects that existed at the time of Nigerian independence. In *Kongi's Harvest* (1965), the demented dictator of the state of Isma, has imprisoned and dethroned the traditional chief, Oba Danlola. To legitimize his seizure of power, Kongi has laid claim to the Oba's spiritual authority through his consecration of the crops at the New Yam Festival.

Stylistically separated from his early farces, Soyinka's later plays rely heavily on classical theatrical devices as a vehicle for Soyinka's potent political and social satires. *The Bacchae of Euripides: A Communion Rite* (1973), an adaptation of the play by Euripides, reinvents the classic tale as a meditation on the nature of personal sacrifice within unjust societies. *Death and the King's Horseman* (1975) combines powerful dramatic verse and characterization with a structure that incorporates contrast and juxtaposition. The play is based on an actual 1945 incident of a colonial officer's intervention to prevent the royal horseman, the Elesin, from committing ritual suicide at his king's funeral, whereupon the Elesin's son would take his father's place in the rite. *A Play of Giants* (1984) is a surreal fantasy about international poetic justice in which an African dictator, on a visit to the United Nations in New York, takes a group of Russian and American delegates hostage. He threatens to release the Soviet-supplied rockets from his embassy arsenal unless an international force is sent to crush the uprising in his own country. *The Beatification of Area Boy: A Lagosian Kaleidoscope* (1995) centers around Sanda, a security guard at a Lagos shopping mall, who ensures that customers are protected when entering and leaving the shop. Despite his position at the mall, the charming Sanda routinely organizes local scams and robberies. It is eventually revealed that Sanda is an ex-revolutionary who had sacrificed his higher education to organize political protests. Soyinka's fictional work expands on the themes expressed in his plays, constructing sweeping narratives of personal and political turmoil in Africa. Soyinka's first novel, *The Interpreters* (1965), is essentially a plotless narrative loosely structured around the informal discussions between five young Nigerian intellectuals. Each has been educated in a foreign country and has returned on the eve of Nigerian independence, hoping to shape Nigeria's destiny. They are hampered by their own confused values, however, as well as by the corruption they encounter in their homeland. *Season of Anomy* (1973), takes the central concerns from *The Interpreters* and selects a new moment at which to consider the choices confronting those working for change. The plot follows a variety of characters including an artist named Ofeyi, a cold-blooded assassin named Isola Demakin, and a harmonious community called Aiyero in a narrative that is thematically linked to the myths of Orpheus and Euridice.

The prose in Soyinka's nonfiction works and essay collections is largely based on his own life and his personal political convictions. *The Man Died: Prison Notes of Wole Soyinka* collects Soyinka's diaries during his imprisonment by Nigerian police for travelling to Biafra to establish a peace commission. He has also composed a trilogy that reflects on his life and the life of his family—*Aké: The Years of Childhood* (1981), *Ìsarà: A Voyage around Essay* (1989), and *Ibadan: The Penkelemes Years: A Memoir, 1946-65* (1994). While *Aké* and *Ibadan* focus on Soyinka's personal life—*Aké* concerns his childhood and *Ibadan* recounts his teen years to his early-twenties—*Ìsarà: A Voyage around Essay* is a biography of Soyinka's father. *Myth, Literature, and the African World* (1976), Soyinka's first essay collection, combines lucid criticism of specific texts with discussions that reveal the scope of Soyinka's acquaintance with literary and theatrical traditions as well as his search for an idiosyncratic perspective. He further explores his interest in the role that politics and literature play in modern Africa in *Art, Dialogue and Outrage: Essays on Literature and Culture* (1988). *The Open Sore of a Continent: A Personal Narrative of the Nigerian Crisis* (1996) reprints a series of vitriolic lectures where Soyinka denounces the Nigerian government under the dictator Sani Abacha and laments the indifference of the West to the present state of Nigerian politics. In *The Burden of Memory, the Muse of Forgiveness* (1999), Soyinka discusses the role of the South African Truth and Reconciliation Commission and questions the nature of objective political truths.

Soyinka has also published several collections of poetry, including *Idanre and Other Poems* (1967), *Ogun Abibiman* (1976), and *Mandela's Earth and Other Poems* (1988). Composed over a period of twenty-four hours, *Idanre* collects a series of mythological poems that feature Yoruba terminology and display subtle manipulations of words, images, and idioms. In *Idanre*, Soyinka draws particular influence from stories associated with the Yoruba mythological figures Ogun, Atunda, Sango, and Oya, and the Idanre Hills. In the twenty-two-page poem *Ogun Abibiman*, Soyinka combines a direct call for African states to take action against the Apartheid movement in South Africa with a mythologized manifesto for the country's liberation. The treatise describes Ogun, Yoruba god of war, joining forces in a violent and mystical union with the legendary Zulu chieftain Shaka. Soyinka published *Samarkand and Other Markets I Have Known* in 2002, a poetry collection that offers reflections on modern politics, his exile from Nigeria, and such writers as Josef Brodsky and Chinua Achebe.

CRITICAL RECEPTION

Soyinka's work has frequently been described as demanding but rewarding to read. Although his plays have been widely praised, they are seldom performed, especially outside of Africa. He has been acknowledged by many critics as Nigeria's finest contemporary dramatist and one of its most distinguished men of letters. While many critics have focused on Soyinka's strengths as a playwright, others have acknowledged his skill as a poet, novelist, and essayist as well. Henry Louis Gates Jr. has written that Soyinka is "a master of the verbal arts. His English is among the finest and most resonant in any literary tradition, fused seamlessly as it is with the resonances and music of the great lyrical, myth-dense, Yoruba tradition." The most significant aspect of Soyinka's work, critics have noted, lies in his approach to literature as a serious agent of social change and his commitment to promoting human rights in Nigeria and other nations. Commentators have maintained that the humor and compassion evident in his writings, as well as his chilling portrayal of the consequences of political greed and oppression, add a universal significance to his portrayals of West African life. His incorporation of Yoruba mythology and ritual in his work has also been a recurring topic of critical interest. His poetry, novels, and nonfiction works have attracted an international readership. Soyinka was the first African to win the Nobel Prize for Literature and he has been applauded by commentators for the versatility and power they have observed in his work.

PRINCIPAL WORKS

The Invention (play) 1955
The Swamp Dwellers (play) 1958
The Lion and the Jewel (play) 1959
A Dance of the Forests (play) 1960
The Trials of Brother Jero (play) 1960
The Republican (play) 1963
The New Republican (play) 1964
Before the Blackout (play) 1965
The Interpreters (novel) 1965
Kongi's Harvest (play) 1965
The Road (play) 1965
The Strong Breed (play) 1966
Idanre and Other Poems (poetry) 1967
Poems from Prison (poetry) 1969; expanded edition published as *A Shuttle in the Crypt,* 1972
Madmen and Specialists (play) 1970
Plays from the Third World: An Anthology [editor] (plays) 1971
The Man Died: Prison Notes of Wole Soyinka (diary) 1972
The Bacchae of Euripides: A Communion Rite [adaptor, from the play by Euripides] (play) 1973
*Collected Plays, Volume One (plays) 1973
Season of Anomy (novel) 1973
Death and the King's Horseman (play) 1975

Myth, Literature, and the African World (essays) 1976
Ogun Abibiman (poetry) 1976
Opera Wonyosi (libretto) 1977
Aké: The Years of Childhood (memoir) 1981
Priority Projects (play) 1982
Requiem for a Futurologist (play) 1983
A Play of Giants (play) 1984
Art, Dialogue and Outrage: Essays on Literature and Culture (essays) 1988
Mandela's Earth and Other Poems (poetry) 1988
Ìsarà: A Voyage around Essay (biography) 1989
Before the Deluge (play) 1991
From Zia with Love (play) 1992
Ibadan: The Penkelemes Years: A Memoir, 1946-65 (memoir) 1994
The Beatification of Area Boy: A Lagosian Kaleidoscope (play) 1995
The Open Sore of a Continent: A Personal Narrative of the Nigerian Crisis (lectures) 1996
Early Poems (poetry) 1997
Arms and the Arts—A Continent's Unequal Dialogue (nonfiction) 1999
The Burden of Memory, the Muse of Forgiveness (nonfiction) 1999
Conversations with Wole Soyinka [edited by Biodun Jeyifo] (interviews) 2001
Samarkand and Other Markets I Have Known (poetry) 2002

*Includes *The Swamp Dwellers, A Dance of the Forests, The Road, The Strong Breed,* and *The Bacchae of Euripides: A Communion Rite.*

CRITICISM

Bruce King (essay date spring 1988)

SOURCE: King, Bruce. "Wole Soyinka and the Nobel Prize for Literature." *Sewanee Review* 96, no. 2 (spring 1988): 339-45.

[*In the following essay, King discusses the development of Soyinka's overall body of work—from* The Interpreters *to* Death and the King's Horseman—*and what Soyinka's receipt of the Nobel Prize for Literature means for African writers.*]

The cultural map of the world is changing radically, and recognition of Soyinka's writings constitutes part of our increased awareness of modern Africa, including its popular music, its contemporary art, and the impressive body of literature that the continent is now producing in response to rapid political, social, and economic changes. One of the best dramatists of our time, Wole Soyinka blends African with European cultural tradi-

tions, the high seriousness of modernist elite literature, and the topicality of African popular theater. He is a modern who writes from an African-centered world view without nostalgia for an idealized past, and his attitude is sophisticated, cosmopolitan, and international in awareness, reference, and relevance. Rather than protesting against the continuing effects of colonialism, he has tried to overcome fragmented, secularized western thought with an integrated vision of life derived from his own Yoruba culture. Unlike European writers who, claiming a dissociation of sensibility in the modern world, turn toward various forms of authority, Soyinka is actively committed to social justice and the preservation of individual freedom, in defiance of the various repressive regimes, black and white, that Africa has produced. Despite the complexity of his writing he has a popular following in Nigeria as a dramatist and as an outspoken, daring public figure, deeply engaged in the main political issues of his country and Africa. His periods of imprisonment, especially the long detention during the Nigerian civil war, make him a symbol for humane values throughout the continent.

Soyinka's writing is probing and energetic; he moves easily between European and Yoruba culture. Although set in such modern Nigerian cities as Lagos and Ibadan, the scenes and situations in his plays and novels seem familiar since they often are influenced by, are adapted from, or imitate well-known works of European literature. Shaped by myth and imagery, the narrative moves back and forth in time. The events are powerful; the language is filled with puns and witty word-play, references, and allusions. Soyinka has an excellent sense of dramatic rhythm and visual theater. Although he is a poet who creates rich layers of images and symbols, his plays resemble those of Ben Jonson and Bertolt Brecht in their energy, knock-about humor, satire, sharply outlined characters, sense of society, unexpected development, and use of popular culture. Besides Yoruba expressions, songs, and myth, he uses a Yorubaized English in his poetry, which, while creating a strange syntax and artificial diction, is in expression highly metaphoric, allusive, and economical.

Soyinka was originally part of a group associated with the University of Ibadan, the Mbari Club, and *Black Orpheus* magazine that included the novelist Chinua Achebe and the poet Christopher Okigbo. In the early 1960s these writers made Nigeria the successor to the Harlem renaissance and the francophonic negritude movement as the torch-bearer of a renaissance of black culture. Blending traditional African arts with those of modern Europe, they shaped a contemporary African culture. Soyinka is the only one of the Mbari group who has continued to develop after the Nigerian civil war. Christopher Okigbo died for Biafra. Achebe, author of *Things Fall Apart* (1958) and *Arrow of God* (1964), has written little since the war; nor have the poets Gabriel Okara and J. P. Clark. Although imprisoned by the federal military government in conditions meant to lead to his death, Soyinka continued to write; denied writing paper, he managed to use scraps of cigarette and toilet paper to smuggle out *Poems from Prison* (1969). His powerful prison diary, *The Man Died* (1972), and other prison poems, *Shuttle in the Crypt* (1972), were published after his release from prison in 1969. The prison writings are quietly angry, broody, detailed in observation of his cell and guards, satirical and personal in their sense of confrontation with the head of the government and yet metaphysical as Soyinka tested his ideas by the reality he faced. A more introspective, imaginative Gulliver found himself imprisoned by the Lilliputians.

Soyinka's energy and his will to survive reflect a cosmology that he developed early and that is central to his writing, often providing an underlying mythical and psychological structure. He uses mythology from his Yoruba culture the way James Joyce and T. S. Eliot use classical and Christian material to bind together writing that otherwise seems fragmented or discontinuous. His novel about alienation of the young university-educated intellectuals from the older corrupt politicians, *The Interpreters* (1965), one of the best novels to come from English-speaking Africa, has no central narrator, narrative, or plot; Soyinka jumps without warning between various scenes and times and the consciousness of different individuals. It is organized by recurring images, symbols, and analogy to Yoruba mythology. The events occurring toward the conclusion of his powerful play *Kongi's Harvest* (1967), a satire on the tyrannies and ideologies of postcolonial Africa, are confusing; and perhaps they can be best explained by the harvest and Ogun myths they embody. Organization by analogy to myths and by recurring images has similarities to the dramatic structures Soyinka studied in Yoruba ritual in which, instead of narrative, the underlying story is represented by significant contrasts and parallels.

At the heart of the vision, used in Soyinka's epic poem *Idanre* (1967) and explained in his difficult *Myth, Literature, and the African World* (1976), is Ogun, god of iron, roads, creativity, and destruction. After the division of an original unity and the creation of the world, man was separated from the gods. Ogun then undertook an epic voyage through the void of unformed matter (like Satan's first journey from hell to earth in *Paradise Lost*) to reach man, thus bridging the gods and man, and the living and dead. Because of this dangerous voyage Ogun became a leader of the Yoruba and settled among them, enjoying palm wine and women until one day, drunk in battle, he savagely destroyed both the enemy and his followers and in remorse withdrew to live by himself. Most of Soyinka's writings bear some analogy to part of this story. The significance of Ogun

is personal and psychological as well as communal and religious. The writer, the prisoner, the actor, the hero must survive an equivalent to Ogun's dangerous journey through the void as part of the process of creation.

The Ogun myth (together with its complementary legend of Sango, the Yoruba king who became god of lightning) enables Soyinka to establish a coherent African cosmology to replace European mythology and Christianity. Such a decentering of an alien vision involves a necessary part of authentic modernization for a Third World writer. Soyinka does not reject foreign culture, as have some African nationalists; nor, as was common in the colonial period, does he judge the validity of African beliefs by their similarities to western and Christian ideas. Instead he places his Yoruba world at the center, seeing European and Indian myths as analogous to African beliefs. The claim that Yoruba tragedy developed out of Ogun ritual and masquerade is similar to claims that Greek tragedy evolved from funeral rites and that medieval and Renaissance drama grew out of the Catholic mass. Hindu notions of reincarnation illustrate Soyinka's concept of history as recurring cycles from which it is difficult to escape. The African agrarian view of life as a seasonal harvest-rebirth cycle also provides the basis of his **"Abiku"** poem, which refers to the Yoruba belief that when a mother often loses her children it is the same child dying and being reborn again and again.

Even as a student Soyinka showed great talent. While at the University of Leeds, he wrote the witty, humorous verse drama *The Lion and the Jewel* (1957). Based on the false eunuch theme of Terence, *Volpone,* and *The Country Wife*, *The Lion and the Jewel* is one of the more charming works of early modern Nigerian literature. Its classical motif of deception in the game of sexual warfare and conquest is ingeniously transposed into a metaphor for the continuing relationship of old Africa to new Africa. The wily old chief who wins the vain maiden from the young, priggish, western-educated suitor has the energy and cunning of those who succeed, but he is also like the "rust" of Soyinka's poem **"Season,"** the rich autumnal maturity that must infuse the new in the cycle of birth, death, and renewal.

On his return to Nigeria, Soyinka's playfulness and sense of humor increasingly were overshadowed by pessimism. In the elaborately symbolic *Dance of the Forests,* performed to celebrate Nigeria's independence in 1960, he mocks negritude claims of an ideal Africa before the coming of the Europeans. He recalls that slavery existed before colonialism and warns that the rulers of the new nation will repeat the past in oppressing and exploiting the people. Soyinka already was integrating music and dance into his plays to make them more Nigerian, closer to Yoruba popular theater. He shifted the action backward and forward through time, creating a puzzling, highly theatrical dramatic form. Such plays embody unexpected revelations that deepen the significance of the events.

Soyinka often includes in his writings an African separatist preacher, since he is fascinated by the power they wield in his community, by their often comic corruption, and by their attempts like his own to syncretize African and western thought. *The Road* (1965), perhaps one of the great plays of our age, portrays a preacher who searches for the meaning of existence, not realizing that it cannot be put into words, whether English or Yoruba. The truth is already experienced by a masquerader in the play who, having been hit by a truck while possessed during the Egungun ceremony, is permanently embodied in a moment of ritualistic immersion in Ogun's transitional voyage. The play is rich in language, humor, social observation, themes, visual symbols, and spectacle. The quest for life's metaphysical significance is dramatized within a context of political violence, police corruption, dangerous roads, and syncretic and chaotic cultural values revealed in varied kinds of English. The mythic structure and even the coherence of the plot are probably overlooked by many readers, but Soyinka's sense of theater holds audiences through the rhythm of events.

The Western Region crisis (1965) in Nigeria developed from an attempt by the ruling conservative northerners to split the Yoruba tribe and impose a minority government. As violence became widespread, Soyinka held up a radio station to call on the government to resign; he was imprisoned, tried, and then freed on a technicality. Within two years he was arrested once more, this time for attempting to create a third force that might prevent the start of a civil war between the federal government and Biafran secessionists. After twenty-seven months in prison, mostly in solitary confinement, he was freed; still opposing the military government, he went into exile for five years, 1970-75. After his release he published the bitter, grotesque play *Madmen and Specialists* (1971), in which war and the use of power are forms of cannibalism and *Season of Anomy* (1973), an allegorical novel about the Nigerian civil war, in which an Orpheus descends into the hell of northern Nigeria (where Soyinka was imprisoned) to bring back his Eurydice and start the process of renewal. Although indicating how an African democratic socialism might be born from the example of one Yoruba village, the novel seems facile and lacks the imaginative depth of Soyinka's best writing. He has long been interested in the *Bacchae* of Euripides. The version [*The Bacchae of Euripides: A Communion Rite*] (1973) that he wrote for the National Theatre in London combines a Marxist and a ritualistic interpretation of the theme and treats Dionysos as similar to Ogun. Since 1977 most of his plays have been political satires, aimed at corrupt politicians, tyrannical governments, and South African rac-

ism; they include *Opera Wonyosi* (1977), a Nigerian adaptation of Brecht's *Threepenny Opera*. A major work is *Aké* (1981), the story of his childhood, with its rich characterizations and observant portraits of the vigorous varied life of a Yoruba community, in which Christianity and animism are near neighbors, often in the same family.

Death and the King's Horseman (1976), which Soyinka directed in New York in 1987, is based on events in Yorubaland during the 1940s when an English district commissioner tried by imprisonment to prevent an Oba from performing a ritualistic suicide which had been demanded of the chief's horseman by tradition. Humiliated by his father's dishonor, the Oba's son commits suicide instead; the father then kills himself in the presence of the district officer. Although based on history, the circumstances have been altered by Soyinka; the events occur during the second world war, an English prince visits during the play's action, and the horseman's son is a western-educated student of medicine. These and other changes create parallels and contrasts between European and Yoruba notions of personal honor, of self-sacrifice for communal purposes, and of the need to face death.

Soyinka affirms what may have been by the 1940s a dying tradition of ritualistic self-sacrifice because it exemplifies the central themes of his own vision, a vision which he claims is based on the African sense of communal well-being. In traditional Yoruba society the preservation of the community is the central concern. Gods are created by the community to be worshiped for the protection and welfare they give in return. There is continuity, based on reciprocality, between the living and their ancestors, the human and the divine, man and nature, sky and earth. If the horseman does not perform his duty as sacrificial messenger to the gods, the community is put at risk.

There is a double focus in the play, almost as if the world of British skepticism and power only superficially impinged on the real world of the Yoruba community. The play is constructed so that the focus moves from themes of cultural conflict to a revelation of the horseman's weakness when he is faced by death. The horseman, despite his imprisonment, can kill himself if he wants. He is reluctant to abandon the fruits of life, the pleasure represented by the young bride he acquires the night he is to die. If he does not die, if his son dies first, the cycle of life, of generations, of seasonal harvest, planting, rebirth, is ruptured. The richness of the play results from this poetic vision, expressed through image, symbol, and allusion, of an organic process threatened by an act of human weakness, which is contrasted to the blindness of the British district officer, who sees only a clash of cultures. The symbols are those of Yoruba mythology; the infusing of the old into the new is like lightning because it is the god San-go's lightning entering the receiving earth. While Soy-inka's play resembles Yoruba ritual, in the way that *Murder in the Cathedral* is analogous to the Catholic mass that it reenacts, the king's horseman is less a victim than someone guilty of lack of will. The real ac-tion involves the psychological struggle of the main character with his beliefs, not the constraints imposed on him. Having suffered from a weakness of will, he sees himself forever shamed and he wonders if the gods have fated him to be the one whose dereliction will destroy his society. Death, as an act of will, affirms his identity and destiny.

Will is at the heart of Soyinka's vision. Tragedy results from will, the will of the hero to challenge the world, to cross the transition between life and death, to be sacrificial messenger, to enter the destructive abyss known by the masquerader and Ogun. Such determina-tion marks Soyinka's own life—his risks in defying governments, his survival after two years in solitary confinement, his political involvement, and his continu-ing creativity. Soyinka's work and life celebrate the hu-man spirit. In this affirmation he resembles writers from eastern Europe who have been awarded Nobel prizes. As a novelist, poet, dramatist, director, theorist, intel-lectual, and citizen, he shows that a unified personality may still be possible in our time.

To see Soyinka's assertion of a Yoruba cosmology as a later, more sophisticated response to colonialism than the negritude idealization of Africa does not limit the achievement to a specific historical moment. Such myth-making should also be seen within the context of claims that a dissociation of sensibility occurred in western Europe during the late Renaissance. The rich layers of imagery, the grounding of myth in ritual and harvest cycles, the creative imitation of literary classics, the organizing of the discontinuous by analogy to myth, and the creation of a private cosmology are all familiar from Eliot and Joyce. Behind the assumption of a crisis in modern culture is a desire to return to a unity of personality in which art, religion, and society are not separate realms. Soyinka is one of the great mythmak-ers of our time; like Yeats, Eliot, Graves, Lawrence, and others, he has created a total vision. A problem with such mythologies is that they are antiscience and therefore essentially romantic and conservative. Soy-inka, however, has made full use of African adaptability: Ogun becomes the god of roads, iron, and of telephone wires and carries the electricity of Sango. Instead of a backward-looking return to the middle ages or to prera-tional blood thought, Soyinka's mythology is part of an active, dynamic, liberating African cultural and political assertion.

The award of the Nobel Prize for Literature to Soyinka also shows that Africa and the Third World will increas-ingly have a place in international modern culture.

Reed Way Dasenbrock (review date summer 1989)

SOURCE: Dasenbrock, Reed Way. Review of *Mande-la's Earth and Other Poems,* by Wole Soyinka. *World Literature Today* 63, no. 3 (summer 1989): 524-25.

[*In the following review, Dasenbrock argues that the poems in* Mandela's Earth and Other Poems *are too responsive to criticism of his earlier poetry and, as a result, the collection seem inauthentic.*]

It should never be said that Wole Soyinka is unrespon-sive to criticism. Attacked by Chinweizu and others as a Eurocentric modernist out of touch with Africa, Soy-inka responded with *Aké: The Years of Childhood,* a memoir that clarified his African roots and cultural al-legiances. Attacked by the same critics for overly dif-ficult and esoteric poetry, Soyinka now responds with *Mandela's Earth,* a new volume of poetry much less enigmatic than his earlier verse and overtly Africanist in its political commitments. However, not all responses are created equal, and though *Aké* is a superb work, possibly Soyinka's greatest achievement, *Mandela's Earth* is not nearly as successful. Soyinka is a great prose writer and dramatist, whether working in an esoteric or exoteric mode, but I have never found his poetry as powerful. *Mandela's Earth,* despite its greater directness, does not make me change my mind.

The volume opens with the sequence that gives it its title, and though the political sentiments expressed there are irreproachable, irreproachable political sentiments do not necessarily make for great poetry. The problem is that Mandela has been in prison for so long that for Soyinka he has become almost completely a symbol and affords nothing concrete for the poet to come to grips with. The only part of the sequence that rises above the tone of unexceptionable sentiments is **"Like Rudolf Hess, the Man Said!,"** which takes off from Pik Botha's statement that "we keep Mandela for the same reason the Allied Powers are holding Rudolf Hess" into a fantasy that Mandela is really Hess or even Men-gele in disguise. Here is the real Soyinka, superb at turning the rhetoric of dictators against themselves in savage and funny ways. However, as if thinking that he might be misunderstood, he retreats from this satire into the tepid pieties of the rest of the sequence.

The lesson to be drawn from the successes and failures of this sequence is a simple one. Soyinka is, as Chin-weizu says in disdain, a modern and individualistic poet, not a voice for a larger collectivity. These poems succeed when Soyinka's individual voice comes through; they fail when he tries to submerge that voice in a larger, public one. Still, this does not justify Chin-weizu's disdain, for the voice that comes through in poems such as **"The Apotheosis of Master Sergeant Doe"** and **"My Tongue Does Not Marry Slogans"** as well as **"Like Rudolf Hess, the Man Said!"** is valuable because it refuses to marry slogans. Soyinka has been an important political voice in contemporary Africa precisely because of his willingness to puncture the shibboleths of those around him.

Nevertheless, there is a sense in which Chinweizu's characterization of Soyinka as essentially a private poet is correct. The best poems in the book are those in the final sequence, **"Dragonfly at My Windowpane,"** especially the poem of that title and the closing piece, **"Cremation of a Wormy Caryatid."** These two poems about moments in nature perceived by Soyinka are clearly modernist in their enigmatic difficulty, though not Euromodernist, since Soyinka alone could have written them. So the final point to be made about *Mandela's Earth* is that Soyinka may have been *too* responsive to criticism. For too much of the collection, it seems as if Soyinka's tongue is trying to marry slogans. A great writer like Soyinka is better off following his own impulse, whether it leads him to write about Mandela or dragonflies and caryatids, than responding to the partial vision of others.

Michael Thorpe (review date autumn 1989)

SOURCE: Thorpe, Michael. Review of *Art, Dialogue, and Outrage: Essays on Literature and Culture,* by Wole Soyinka. *World Literature Today* 63, no. 4 (autumn 1989): 730.

[*In the following review, Thorpe offers a positive assessment of* Art, Dialogue, and Outrage: Essays on Literature and Culture, *calling the work "a rare, vigorous, and cogent writer's apologia."*]

The nineteen essays and addresses—seven previously published—collected in *Art, Dialogue, and Outrage* span some twenty years. Their complexity and multifarious interest are succinctly pointed out in Biodun Jeyifo's excellent introduction by his characterization of Wole Soyinka as both mythopoeist and mythoclast: "variously traditional and modernist, pan-Africanist and liberal-humanist, individualistic and communalistic, gnostic and sceptical, unapologetically idealist and yet on occasion discreetly materialist."

Soyinka himself chose the three-pronged title, and it is the "outrage" that many readers will know least well. Apart from criticizing even such advocates as Moore and Lindfors, in several places Soyinka contests Chinweizu's and others' charges of Eurocentrism, opposing to both the distorted African traditionalism he has dubbed "neo-Tarzanism" and the "Marxystemist," a "creative contextualism" which, "proceeding from its context, enlarges and extends it even as it faithfully explores its initial bearings." Although Chinweizu does

partially close the gap in *Toward the Decolonisation of African Literature,* the present collection includes no response to that book.

Soyinka's eclectic standpoint is reinforced in two hard-hitting pieces on **Death and the King's Horseman,** a drama of "totalist reality." The opposition leveled at here, as in his trenchant dissection of the National Theatre's production of his adaptation of Euripides' *Bacchae* in 1973, is "Euramerican" critical incomprehension, clogged by racist or radical fixations, of his universal aims. By contrast, a lengthy demolition of an article in *Positive Review,* **"The Autistic Hunt: Or, How to Marximise Mediocrity,"** is critical overkill and almost dispensable.

In sum, the volume is a rare, vigorous, and cogent writer's apologia. It is, however, regrettable that, despite "three years' editorial work" by three editors, there are some two typographical (or other) errors per page and no index.

Christopher Hope (review date 11 December 1989)

SOURCE: Hope, Christopher. "Rebels and Dreamers." *New Republic* 201, no. 24 (11 December 1989): 40-2.

[*In the following review, Hope examines how* Ìsarà: A Voyage around Essay *represents a diverse range of literary genres, including memoirs, fairy tales, moral fables, and political studies.*]

When the Nigerian writer Wole Soyinka was awarded the Nobel Prize in 1986, the decision of the Swedish Academy to honor an African writer led to a controversy in Nigeria, and in other parts of Africa, that has not yet abated. Soyinka was attacked by some who espouse what is known as the "Afro-phone" cause; they consider the bestowal of such "European" baubles upon African writers limiting and demeaning at best, and at worst a deliberate attempt imperialistically to undermine the vigor of indigenous African literature. "Afro-centrists," thundered the Nigerian critic Chinweizu at a recent literary gathering, "see the Nobel Prize as a local European prize, whose award to any African is an imperialist act of hegemony . . . a high point of a continuing Western effort to manipulate African culture in a self-stultifying direction that would hold it subordinate to Western culture." Soyinka's acceptance of the prize was seen by those who take this line as an example of "Europhile" tendencies. The sheer ugliness of these terms is a symptom of this often heated and rather unhelpful debate.

Soyinka is no stranger, however, to the charge. He has shown an ability to turn sharply when attacked, and in an interview in 1983 he took the opportunity to respond to his critics with characteristic pungency. He described them as "neo-Tarzanists," and proceeded to revel in the multiplicity of literary sources, European and African, that infuse his own work. Far from hiding the fact that he dealt in "various complimentaries, or singularities, or contradictions," he confessed to embracing them with unabashed enthusiasm. Nowhere is this more emphatically demonstrated than in his new memoir, *Ìsarà: A Voyage around Essay.*

Born in Western Nigeria in 1934, Soyinka studied in England in the 1950s, and his first plays were produced in London. He returned to Nigeria at the time of independence in 1960, and soon established himself as one of the most brilliant of the new generation of African playwrights with works such as *The Lion and the Jewel, A Dance of the Forests,* and *The Trials of Brother Jero.* The *Jero* plays in particular are rich comedies of contemporary Nigerian life. With similar savagery, *Madmen and Specialists* took apart the violent absurdities of the Nigerian civil war in the late 1960s, when a new country called Biafra was born, and brutally snuffed out. Soyinka's other plays have looked searchingly at the last days of colonial life in pre-independence Nigeria. In *Opera Wonyosi* he produced a *Beggar's Opera,* African-style; and in an adaptation of *The Bacchae,* he turned this classic of Euripides to African advantage, and to Nigerian discomfort. Its parallels with the bloodletting during and after the Biafran war were unmistakable. Commenting in 1973 on the public executions held on a Lagos beach, Soyinka rubbed in the point: "The war no longer united people in Stoicism; so they're trying to unite them in bestiality and guilt by the titillation of the power-cravings of the meanest citizen."

Although it was as a dramatist that he first made his name, Soyinka's considerable energies have flowed widely. He has been a teacher, a literary critic, and an editor. Besides his attachment to the theater, where he has worked as writer, actor, director, and producer, Soyinka is also a poet, and his first novel, *The Interpreters,* published in 1965, has become an African classic. The novel traces the lives of a group of young Nigerian intellectuals, whose ambitions and ideals sink slowly in a sea of official corruption. In 1981, with the publication of *Aké: The Years of Childhood,* an autobiography of his first 12 years, he proved himself to be a delicate memoirist.

Soyinka's enthusiasm for political engagement, in African affairs generally and in Nigerian politics specifically, has been as vigorous as his passion for complimentarities and contradictions. He has vividly demonstrated his commitment to African independence and to the destruction of the last vestiges of colonialism, particularly in Southern Africa, that "sore toe" of the continent. At one point he took over as editor of *Transi-*

tion, when that journal was forced to move from Uganda to Accra (a flight forced upon the magazine by the lethal attentions of Idi Amin). He has also served as secretary general of the Union of Writers of African Peoples. But it has been in Nigeria itself that his political beliefs have landed him in trouble more than once. Though he energetically escapes any kind of tribal grouping, Soyinka has consistently celebrated his Yoruba background. His sense of communal customs, beliefs, and values has shaped his writing.

By the sort of fruitful contradiction that distinguishes his work, he expresses his political views with an irrepressible individuality that has not endeared him to the strongmen who come and go in Nigeria. "Heresiarchs of the System," he calls them in his 1971 play *Madmen and Specialists,* those so corrupted by rank and influence as to believe that "the end shall justify the meanness." Soyinka displays himself primarily as a satirist, instinctively uneasy in the presence of power, splendidly disrespectful of the self-love of those who wield it. He has attacked political corruption in Nigeria with angry exhilaration. In fact, it is difficult to think of a writer who has lacerated his own people so fiercely since Karl Kraus pilloried the Viennese with his own loyal hatred.

It is not surprising that Soyinka ran into trouble. He was first arrested in Nigeria on trumped up charges in 1965. Two years later he was detained again by the Nigerian federal authorities during the civil war, and imprisoned for his sympathies for the short-lived secessionist state of Biafra. He was released in 1969. It swiftly became clear that his commitment to freedom in thought and pluralism in politics had not abated. Quite the contrary; if he had been merely a believer in such things on being thrown into jail, Soyinka declared later, then he came out "a fanatic." Prison did nothing to slow him down. In addition to making a free translation of a Yoruba novel while in detention, he also managed to write three plays; and on his release he published a startlingly explicit account of his imprisonment, *The Man Died.* A couple of years later there followed the publication of a major collection of poems, *A Shuttle in the Crypt,* which was marked by his experiences in jail.

In 1972, still uneasy in the political dispensation of the time (Nigeria was to labor under a succession of military dictatorships until 1979), Soyinka left Nigeria for a self-imposed exile in Europe, Africa, and the United States, returning only in 1976 when the regime of General Gowan was overthrown. It was the death of his father during those years in exile that prompted this memoir of the old teacher and his friends in a vanished world. Readers of *Aké* will recall the affectionate portrait of his father, Essay: a kindly but razor-eyed pedagogue, formidable when challenged, serene in contemplation and mighty in combat. Ìsarà is also briefly sketched in that earlier memoir. It was his father's "natal home," and always seemed to be located "several steps into the past," a place of concealed delights, of festivals and surprises, a refuge where the young Wole used to spend New Year's with his teacher father, and his irrepressible mother, known as "wild Christian."

The memoir is constructed from fragments Soyinka discovered in an old tin trunk when he returned to Nigeria some years after his father's death. In the trunk he found "a handful of letters, old journals with marked pages and annotations, notebook jottings . . ." It seems, in all conscience, a meager enough record; but from these fragments Soyinka has constructed a defense against the ruin of time. *Ìsarà* is a number of things: a filial portrait of a beloved father sketched with considerable delicacy and gaiety; a re-creation of a colonial period in its final phases during the late 1930s with the outbreak of the Second World War looming ever closer; an exploration of a generation whose aspirations were governed by their European rulers, the British colonialists, but whose longings and leanings were African.

The passion for memory is more marked than it was in *Aké,* which recounts in fairly straightforward autobiographical fashion the story of Soyinka's boyhood. In the new book, a memory is not simply an involuntary spasm, a way back into the past by which lost time may be reclaimed; it is also a way of staking a claim on the landscape, and a weapon to be wielded against those to whom it never occurred that there was anything to remember. Meditative, somewhat slow in getting started, but taking on a determination not only to recall but to reinvent the town of Ìsarà and people it with characters who might have lived there, this semi-fictional portrait is painted with grace and humor.

Still, within the amiable narrative Soyinka cannot disguise a steady, often profound anger at the unequal struggle of his father's generation against the British. They, the colonizers, were too proud of their ignorance to respond to an Africa that, before they came, had belonged only to itself; even the well-meaning white officials were unable to sense their imminent redundancy. For their part, the inhabitants of Ìsarà are gently satirized; they are full of entrepreneurial dreams, half-baked projects, and the excitable frustrations of those who know, to their regret, that the "real" world exists somewhere else, in London or New York or Berlin. They are respectful, hard-pressed, above all too well-schooled by their European masters to believe in their own, wholly African independence. Yet, as Soyinka shows, it was the modest heroism of his father's generation that made such independence inevitable.

The schizophrenia of a generation of the 1930s caught between Europe and Africa proved very fruitful. It was in many ways an admirable condition, and is chronicled

by Soyinka with burning affection. *Ìsarà* is at once the most relaxed and the most profound of his meditations on the past. His father and his circle of friends and their families each constitute a particular port of memory's call. Because a number of them were educated at Saint Simeon's Seminary in Ilesa, they came to be known as the ex-Ilés; friends who survived their missionary education and who revisit their hometown, "returned to sender," from Lagos and the wider world beyond, for reasons of piety or celebration, for funerals, feasts, and anniversaries. There is Soditan Akinyode, the headteacher; Sipe Efuape, sometime tax inspector and would-be entrepreneur, alias the Resolute Rooster; Osibo, the pharmacist, schooled in the white man's medicine and a fierce opponent of traditional herbalists; and Saaki Akinsanya, militant trade unionist, who is to become, though he does not know it, the future king of Ìsarà.

The degree to which the outside world—with its illustrated brochures of consumer goods, its motor cars and bank bonds, its correspondence schools, depressions, and prodigious wars—dominated and tantalized the people of Ìsarà is strikingly illustrated at the very outset. Soditan Akinyode sits in his father's fiber-cane chair admiring the calligraphy of his American pen-friend, one Wade Cudeback. Cudeback writes of touring America in the wide-eyed prose of the guide book; he is thrilled to be out on the road and bowling along, careful to illuminate and instruct his distant, and unknown, Nigerian correspondent about the wonders on his odyssey: "four provinces of Canada and six states of the United States, a scintillating three thousand five hundred mile trip in my jalopy."

Inspired by such galloping enthusiasm, Soditan dreams of a similar journey in his own country, but he knows that there will be no "jalopy." A bicycle will have to do. Besides the severely practical problems, there is the enormous difficulty of getting a grip on a country that feels like your own but is firmly in the hands of others. Ìsarà also has its wonders, of course: "the battle-contested grounds of the Yoruba kingdoms," sites of the old Fulani Wars, and the ancient kingdom of Oyo. There is the derivation of the Ìsarà praise name itself, a city never taken in battle, Afotamodi, "they whose city ramparts are raised on ammunition." Exotic and fabulous though such places are, they seem somehow to pale by comparison with Cudeback's confident, authorial grip on the names of his native places: the Plains of Abraham, the Magnetic Hill, and the fabulously named city Ashtabula. What matter if the American Indians named Ashtabula and not the white man? All names in America now belong without question to the new settlers. But in Ìsarà and Ilesa the question of naming and knowing seldom arose among students marched across the land of their ancestors by white teachers who never taught their pupils to use their eyes. It is the fate of such histories, Soditan knows, that place names un-looked at fade and disappear.

All the time Europe presses more closely. Mussolini threatens Abyssinia; Hitler is rampant in Europe; the Great Depression affects even the most distant countries. Then the first bombs fall in London, and Nigerians are expected to rally to the British cause, even though some of them have difficulty in distinguishing just who the enemy is supposed to be, caught as they are between two evils, the close British occupier and the distant German invader. "What is our stake," Mrs. Esan, the traveler in woven cloth, demands of the teacher Soditan, "in this quarrel between white people?"

The formidable Mrs. Esan comes to call on teacher Soditan. She is a fierce supporter of local crafts and is scathing about the new imported cloth, "the velvet imposter" that affected Lagosians prefer to the indig-enous product. The introduction of Mrs. Esan into the highly patterned narrative of *Ìsarà* is typical of Soyin-ka's method, which is to create a tightly woven surface of vivid and unexpected patterns not unlike the local Etù cloth so beloved by his character. Apparently minor characters become pivotal in reminding us that beneath the seemingly tranquil surface of small-town life in Nigeria in the faraway 1930s, politics was a passionate, even a bitter, force for change. Mrs. Esan's means of demonstrating this are simple, but devastating. She reads her old teacher a letter from a British administra-tor to a local Nigerian paper:

> You will never find a West African who can invent a big business, such as a steamship line, or a bank, or a railroad. The white man steps in there. The average West African is no more fit to govern his own colonies than the average English member of the Parliament of today is to handle any part of portion of the British Empire. If the African were allowed to try, and we, at the pull of our silly sentimentalists, withdrew the home stiffening, how long would it be before chaos reigned? Five years? One? Six months?

But this is not simply a book about the British in Nigeria, or about racial oppression, or about African independence. Soyinka fastidiously ensures that at no time does it deteriorate into anything expected, conventional, or merely political. *Ìsarà* is an act of filial devotion, a son's informed fiction about a father, ferociously intelligent and quietly heroic. Soditan Akin-yode is really just a lightly fictionalized portrait of Soy-inka's father. Above all, it is a book about the fabulous link forged, at least in the dreamy head of Soditan, between Ìsarà and the longed-for and distant town of Ashtabula. In reality a less than interesting provincial American town, Ashtabula looms large and magnificent in remote contemplation. And long-vanished Ìsarà grows in the imagination of one who sees it, and is both a kingdom of heroes and marvels—as well as a modest town in the Remo district of Nigeria.

Even the breezily informative letters of Cudeback become a tool in the excavation of the sights and sounds of Ìsarà. In an extraordinary passage, the teacher paints pictures of his home using the American's calligraphy. Since Soditan, despite his dreams of travel, is never to leave home—it will be left to his son to make the voy-age around his memories of the old man—he becomes instead the seeing eye of the book, the steady center around which all other characters orbit. Although Cud-eback speaks of foreign wonders, his handwriting reminds Soditan of home: "Each exclamation mark was like the housepost of the *ogboni* shrine. . . . Each D was consistently like the cauliflower ear of Osibi, the pharmacist, while the W was just like an *abetiaja* [a Yoruba dress-cap], or the starched bristling headgear of the Reverend Sisters from Oke Padi hospital."

Ìsarà is, then, many things—a fairy tale, a memoir, a moral fable, and a tribute to a generation educated by the white man, schooled in his ways, but already sens-ing that in Africa his day was almost over. In a final and triumphant chapter these disparate threads are woven together. The new king rides in on his white horse, a regal entry into Ìsarà. Indeed, this final closing section is perhaps the most effective in the book, and il-lustrates Soyinka's dramatic gifts to great advantage. The august and holy personage of Agunrin Odubona, reputed to be over 100 years old, a man whom nobody has heard speak in ten years, the very soul of Ìsarà, sits in judgment on the competing claimants for the throne. And as they talk, the old man bitterly meditates on the fatal collapse of the Nigerian tribal armies before the British invader who, in infernal alliance with the European church, swept all before him in a series of conquests from 1861, with the annexation of Lagos; and then in a succession of wars that continued into the early years of the 20th century.

Ìsarà is, to use the acrimonious terms of the debate about authenticity in African literature, an uncompromis-ingly "Afrophone" book. But in its deceptively leisurely fashion it shows a thoroughly African identity, not by focusing on European deficiencies but by measuring, with grace and with civility, the distance between aspirations for independence and the realities that have followed in Nigeria. In the ex-Ilés of Ìsarà Soyinka celebrates his father's generation, which, whatever the vagaries of the colonial milieu, came slowly but surely into its own. The town springs to life speaking in the accents of men and women who, however small their room for maneuver, hedged in as they were by the decent yet monumental obtuseness of their British governors, exemplify the virtues of ambition, fortitude, and patience. The implication, though Soyinka never needs to state it, is that the generation of Ìsarà sets a standard by which succeeding generations in indepen-dent Nigeria must be measured, and by which they fall short. Even in repose, Wole Soyinka is a discomforting writer.

Reed Way Dasenbrock (review date summer 1990)

SOURCE: Dasenbrock, Reed Way. Review of *Ìsarà: A Voyage around Essay,* by Wole Soyinka. *World Literature Today* 64, no. 3 (summer 1990): 517-18.

[*In the following review, Dasenbrock explores the parallels between* Aké: The Years of Childhood—*the memoir of Soyinka's youth—and* Ìsarà: A Voyage around Essay—*the biography of Soyinka's father.*]

It would seem absurd to call Wole Soyinka, winner of the 1986 Nobel Prize and one of the two or three African writers whose name everyone knows, an underappreciated writer, and indeed on the evidence of his recent verse collection **Mandela's Earth,** one would have to call him an overappreciated poet. Critical assessment of Soyinka has been centered on his plays, however (and, to a lesser extent, on his poetry), and this has meant that he is underappreciated in one respect: as a writer of prose. He is the author of two novels—**The Interpreters** and **Season of Anomy**—as well as three memoirs: **The Man Died, Aké: The Years of Childhood,** and now **Ìsarà. Season of Anomy, Aké,** and **Ìsarà** in particular are achievements as impressive as any of Soyinka's plays.

Ìsarà stands in a particularly close relationship to **Aké,** but it is not in any usual sense a sequel or even a predecessor to that work. The times in which the volumes are set overlap. Soyinka was born in 1934, and **Aké** treats his early childhood, whereas **Ìsarà** ends in 1940 during World War II. Soyinka himself, moreover, is not a character in **Ìsarà** and is not at all an object or agent of narration. This constitutes the major difference between the two memoirs. Though Soyinka assures us that elements in both are fictional, **Aké** seems like a book based directly on childhood memories; **Ìsarà,** in contrast, is an attempt to imagine how the author's father must actually have been as a young man, how—for instance—he must have seemed to his coevals, not to his young son. The work therefore seems to involve more an effort of imagination than of memory, and it may be no more a memoir (or no less a novel) than a work like *A House for Mr Biswas* by V. S. Naipaul. The blurring of genre lines here is fascinating.

Still, the greatest interest of **Ìsarà** for me is in how it thematically continues the project of **Aké,** not how it may generically contrast with it. **Aké** was in large measure a response to those critics such as Chinweizu who have attacked Soyinka as a Euromodernist without African roots, and its dense evocation of the author's childhood worked to show how little there was to that criticism. **Ìsarà** takes the discussion a stage further. Soyinka's father is portrayed throughout the book as a modernizing intellectual of the kind Soyinka is attacked as being; but the climatic action concerns his involve-ment in the struggle over the appointing of a new king for Ìsarà, and a new face of "Teacher Soditan" is shown. Here the modernizing intellectual seems like a traditionalist, for he becomes intensely involved in the struggle despite being told by a friend that such a kingship is outmoded in modern Nigeria. Soyinka's real point—here as elsewhere—is that these are falsely dichotomized choices. If African traditions are to survive, then they must also be transformed. However, as he tells his friend, there is no reason why the kingship of Ìsarà is an outmoded survival if the kingship of England is not. Those pretending to uphold African traditions do them a disservice by insisting that they have no connection to the modern world.

Soyinka's thought and writing here, as always, is rich, supple, and complex. **Ìsarà** is a wonderful book, more intellectually demanding if less evocative than **Aké** and fully worthy of being placed next to it.

C. N. Ramachandran (essay date August 1990)

SOURCE: Ramachandran, C. N. "Structure within Structure: An Analysis of Wole Soyinka's *The Lion and the Jewel.*" *Journal of Commonwealth Literature* 25, no. 1 (August 1990): 199-203.

[*In the following essay, Ramachandran examines stylistic aspects of* The Lion and the Jewel, *noting the effect of the trickster figure and ritual dance on the structure of the play.*]

Although Wole Soyinka's plays have received considerable if not adequate critical attention in India and abroad, the focus has been mostly on his political plays. For instance Michael Etherton discusses Soyinka as a satirist and political thinker in *The Development of African Drama,* and analyses only **Madmen and Specialists, A Dance of the Forests,** and **Opera Wonyosi.**[1] Simon O. Umukoro comments on "the political vision" in Soyinka's plays with particular reference to **A Dance of the Forests** and **Kongi's Harvest.**[2] Lewis Nkosi is interested primarily in tracing Soyinka's political ideology in **A Dance of the Forests** and **The Road.**[3] Consequent upon such undue emphasis placed on the political plays, Soyinka's sheer comic genius and the implicit community values have not been recognized at all. In fact Adrian Roscoe goes to the extent of contending that ". . . the ironic humour of **'Telephone Conversation'** and the mirth of **The Lion and the Jewel** . . . were mere "jeux d'esprit", lighthearted interludes in a career whose underlying mood had grown increasingly dark".[4]

The Lion and the Jewel is a significant work for many reasons. In spirit and structure it is typical of African theatre which, like ancient Indian theatre, weaves music, dance and drama into a rich tapestry in contrast to the main life of western theatre which so often divorces music and dance from drama. Soyinka has himself highlighted this point. Referring to *Shakuntala* he wonders: "Wasn't this closer in many instances to the culture, the literature, the creativity of my own society?"[5] It is not a question of simply adding a few songs and dances to the main text; the totality of poetic drama lies in the rich structure resulting from the different, often inter-locking, elements of dance, music, and drama. "And the whole thing about plays, especially poetic plays", Soyinka points out, "is that there are constant dimensions which are created not even so much in the action as by the metaphor, the metaphorical language".[6] The present paper attempts to analyse the different "dimensions" of *The Lion and the Jewel*. Soyinka's comic genius lies in organizing such diverse structures as counter points to one another within implicit value-structures.

The first broad structure on which others are superimposed in the play is that of the archetypal "Trickster Figure". Jung, who analysed the "Trickster Figure" for the first time, traced it to the carnival of the medieval church: "In picaresque tales, in carnivals and revels, in magic rites and healing, in man's religious fears and exaltations, this phantom of trickster haunts the mythology of all ages, . . ."[7] According to Jung, the "Trickster" is "a forerunner of the saviour, and, like him, God, man, and animal at once. He is both subhuman and superhuman, a bestial and divine being, . . ."[8]

Obviously, the central character in *The Lion and the Jewel*, Baroka the Bale, is the "trickster figure". He is called by everyone "the Old Fox"; and he is a lecher who even at sixty wants to marry a young girl. Lakunle describes him as a "savage thing, degenerate / He would beat a helpless woman if he could . . ."[9] Baroka describes himself as a "sevenhorned devil of strength" (P. 43). He has a huge harem; is given to misuse of authority and corruption; and is wily. Hearing that Sidi has rejected his offer, he pretends to be impotent and baits Sidi who is finally seduced by him. But Baroka also has vitality and zest for life. He is an excellent hunter, generous and open-handed, and the young as well as the old are reported to seek his counsel. In short, Baroka is the "trickster figure" *par excellence,* "God, man, and animal" all at once.

However, there are significant variations on the theme of the "trickster figure". For a start, there are not one but two tricksters in the play. The village belle Sidi too is a trickster who plays—or attempts to play—a practical joke on the Bale. And that reveals the other, more important, variation. The archetypal trickster figure is himself tricked in the end; he falls "victim in his turn to the vengeance of those whom he has injured" as Jung explains.[10] But in *The Lion and the Jewel* the major

trickster, Baroka, is not tricked in turn at all; on the other hand he succeeds in his cunning; and it is the minor trickster, Sidi, who demonstrates the principle of "the biter bit". When at the end Sidi marries Baroka after being deceived by him we ought to feel sorry for her and dislike the Bale. But we don't. How does the playwright manoeuvre us so as to admire the arch trickster?

Partly Soyinka achieves this through his emphasis upon dance. The first communal dance in the play is a re-creation of a real incident concerning a stranger to the village, a photographer. The dancers depict, through elaborate miming and gestures, the photographer coming on his motorcycle which stops suddenly, his attempts at repairing the machine, and his falling into the river while adjusting his camera on Sidi. Lakunle, the school teacher, is forced to play the role of the photographer in the dance; and thus Lakunle is identified with the ridiculous stranger.

It is in this context that one becomes uneasy at a view of the play as a dramatization of "conflict between traditionalism and modernism" as, for instance, Lewis Nkosi does.[11] Soyinka rightly points out: "Not just the teachers, the western critics too; they always follow the line of least resistance and see the clash of cultures. There is no clash of cultures in that play".[12] If we see Lakunle as a symbol of modernity and Baroka of tradition, and conclude that the playwright aligns himself with tradition against modernity, we will be totally missing the import of the play. Lakunle represents not western culture but only hollow westernization, not the real but only the image. The play abundantly establishes that Lakunle is a modern version of Don Quixote, "a book-nourished shrimp". In his wooing of Sidi, he can only use his bookish knowledge: "My Ruth, my Rachel, Esther, Bathsheba / Thou sum of fabled perfections . . ." (p. 18), so rants Lakunle. To him progress means only factories, "newspapers with pictures of seductive girls", ballroom dancing, and cocktail parties. To what extent he is cut off from the earth and life-giving forces is made clear when Sadiku taunts him: "Why don't you do what other men have done. Take a farm for a season. . . . Or will the smell of the wet soil be too much for your delicate nostrils?" (p. 33)

In other words, Lakunle the rival of Baroka represents neither progress nor western culture but only the outward gloss image. Hence the first elaborate dance associates him with the image-man, the photographer. Though Sidi is taken in for a while by her own photographs (as she is by Lakunle), she is too earthy and too full of life to live for long in the world of images. Hence, significantly, she returns the album of her photographs to Lakunle in the end.

From this point of view—that is, from the point of view of differentiating the image from the real—the two elaborate dances with music develop a structure counter to the movement of the "trickster figure". The dances being community dances emphasize the sense of one's belonging to one's community. In the beginning of the first dance we notice that Lakunle is very reluctant to join the others; and he is almost physically dragged by the participants to take up the role of the stranger. But, significantly, Baroka automatically joins the dance and is accepted as such even when he intrudes on the dancers in the middle. He naturally belongs to the community whereas Lakunle is always an outsider.

Even the second dance after the seduction of Sidi is interesting from this point of view. In this dance, called "the dance of virility", the female dancers pursue a masked male and enact the story of Baroka—or, the story of Baroka as they understand it. In this mumming the Baroka-figure is made a comic figure, to be taunted and ridiculed by his wives. But we, as readers or audience, know by now that the Baroka-figure in the dance is only a false image, only a masked figure, not real Baroka. Lakunle appears vastly to enjoy this spectacle in spite of himself. He can never free himself from the "images"—of love, of progress, and of Reality.

Such structures, created by the elaborate dances on the themes of the individual versus community, and the real versus the image, run counter to the movement of the trickster-figure, and make us overlook the darker aspects of the trickster. They create a festive atmosphere in which even the calculated seduction of a simple girl is accepted by us (as Sidi accepts it) as only proper and natural.

In fact, in the play of Soyinka music and dance stand for life-affirming values as they involve an individual's coming out of his ego-centred universe and entering a community-centred universe. Hence the abstract structures created by the dances run always counter to ego-structures involving vain politicians and fanatical religious leaders. In support of this statement we could consider another major play of Soyinka, *Kongi's Harvest*. In this play, whereas all other dances and music are centred on the traditional ruler, Oba Danlola, Sarumi, the next heir, and Segi the courtesan (all normative characters), the dictator Kongi and his retinue are devoid of music and dance. The alternating action in the "First part" brilliantly represents such a contrast: the scene shifts alternatively from Kongi's Retreat to Segi's Club, from solemn counsellors and secretaries deeply involved in devising the right "images" for Kongi to the noisy revellers and music of the club, in short from life-thwarting forces to love and affirmation of life.

Notes

1. Michael Etherton, *The Development of African Drama,* London: Hutchinson University Library of Africa, 1982, pp. 242-85.

2. Simon Obikpeko Umukoro, "The Ogun Hero and Political Vision in Soyinka's Drama", *The Literary Half-Yearly,* Wole Soyinka, 28, 2, 1987, pp. 172-84.

3. Lewis Nkosi, *Tasks and Masks,* Harlow, Essex: Longman Group Ltd., 1981, pp. 173-94.

4. Adrian A. Roscoe, "Soyinka as Poet", in *Readings in Commonwealth Literature,* ed. William Walsh, Oxford: Clarendon Press, 1973, pp. 163-81.

5. Wole Soyinka as quoted by James Gibbs, "Soyinka in Zimbabwe: A Question and Answer Session", *The Literary Half-Yearly,* 28, 2, 1987, p. 68.

6. Soyinka, as quoted by James Gibbs, p. 87.

7. Carl G. Jung, "The Archetypes and the Collective Unconscious", *Collected Works,* Vol. 9, 1, Princeton: Princeton University Press, 1969, p. 260.

8. Jung, p. 263.

9. Wole Soyinka, *The Lion and the Jewel,* in *Collected Plays 2* Oxford: Oxford University Press, 1963, 1974, p. 33. All other quotations from the text refer to this edition.

10. Jung, p. 256.

11. Nkosi, p. 187.

12. Soyinka, as quoted by James Gibbs, "Soyinka in Zimbabwe", p. 79.

Derek Wright (essay date September 1990)

SOURCE: Wright, Derek. "The Festive Year: Wole Soyinka's *Annus Mirabilis.*" *Journal of Modern African Studies* 28, no. 3 (September 1990): 511-19.

[*In the following essay, Wright investigates Soyinka's 1960 Rockefeller Foundation scholarship research project on traditional African festivals and traces the impact of this research on his work, particularly as seen in the play* A Dance of the Forests.]

It was in 1960, the year of independence and therefore a time of celebration and festivities in Nigeria, that Wole Soyinka, after just over five years in Britain (three at the University of Leeds and two at the Royal Court Theatre, London), returned to his native land. This was moreover, according to some sources, a period in which he undertook empirical research into festivities of a different kind, which subsequently supplied a specific input into the ritualism of his early plays.

There has been some critical uncertainty about the precise nature of the Rockefeller Foundation scholarship on which Soyinka returned to Nigeria at the beginning of 1960. On the one hand, there is Gerald Moore's statement that Soyinka was awarded 'a research fellowship in African traditional drama which would enable him to travel widely in Nigeria, studying and recording traditional festivals, rituals and masquerades rich in dramatic content.'[1] The Yoruba theatre historian Joel Adedeji, on the other hand, states very generally that the purpose of the fellowship was to 'make an investigation of the Nigerian dramatic situation and developments'.[2] Bernth Lindfors quotes *The Nigerian Radio Times* of 3 July 1960 as saying that the grant was to enable Soyinka 'to make a survey of Nigerian drama in its modern development', and concludes that he was apparently studying this 'in traditional theatre'.[3]

The vagaries of drama-definition in Nigeria may have contributed something to the confusion (some indigenous theatre critics and historians vigorously exclude 'folk opera' from 'traditional drama', while others are more hospitable), but if the terms of the fellowship covered such a general area as the whole of Nigerian drama in its 'modern development', then they could equally well have applied to the travelling folk theatres of Hubert Ogunde and Kola Ogunmola which had burgeoned during Soyinka's absence abroad in the 1950s. Robert July, who has delved into the archives of the Rockefeller Foundation and drawn upon his own correspondence with the playwright during the period, seems to suggest that Soyinka's festival research, apart from the *egungun* procession of the ancestral dead, was in fact not in Yoruba or even Nigerian material but masquerades and dance troupes of Ghana and Côte d'Ivoire, while much of his Nigerian research was into folk opera and the ceremonies of the Christian *Aladura* church of the Cherubims and Seraphims.[4]

Very little of this research is actually on record, and the relevant files in the University of Ibadan Library, which contain Soyinka's personal correspondence and comments on the future of West African theatre prepared for his Rockefeller sponsors, are not generally available. As a result, the extent of the writer's 1960 festival research and its input into the plays of that period remain imponderable. James Gibbs has concluded, correctly, I think,[5] that there is little evidence of field-work in the paper entitled **'The African Approach to Drama,'** presented at the end of 1960, in which Soyinka referred to a number of West African festivals, including Oshun at Oshogbo.[6] Apart from the *egungun,* most of the material used by Soyinka appears to be derived from academic reading, notably articles by Ulli Beier, Onuora Nzekwu, and K. C. Murray. In his 1986 study, Gibbs speaks of Soyinka's 'acquaintance with numerous Nigerian rites', but this may again refer principally to *egungun* masquerades.[7] They made a brief intrusive appearance in Soyinka's film, *Culture in Transition,*[8] and in his book of critical essays, *Myth, Literature, and the African World* (which is devoted to the metaphysics, not the mechanics, of Ogun rites), he mentions a single harvest play observed in Ihiala in

1961.[9] Beyond these scattered instances, however, evidence of local festival research in this period is thin.

It is also worth noting that some of Soyinka's correspondence with Robert July about West African festivals is dated September 1959, before his return to Nigeria, and that, as Gibbs has pointed out, some sequences of *A Dance of the Forests* were written and performed in Soyinka's 1959 Royal Court Entertainment, before he had undertaken any practical research or contemplated an academic paper on the subject. This makes problematic the degree of direct empirical input into that particular play from Yoruba festival research during the following year. Moreover, when asked in interviews about this period of his life Soyinka has stressed that his principal aim in returning to Nigeria in 1960 was to set up his own theatre company, the 1960 Masks.

In Washington in 1975 Soyinka was rather vague about the nature of his fellowship, and in his replies spoke at length about the folk theatre companies (particularly Duro Ladipo's) but, apart from the random comment that the folk opera developed out of traditional secular masquerades, made no mention of festivals.[10] When asked in a much later interview about his objectives on his return to Nigeria, Soyinka answered that he 'wanted to re-explore Yoruba theatrical forms and be able to establish a drama company which would utilize all the various idioms I'd acquired in my experience both abroad and at home.'[11] None of this gets us any closer to the facts of the fellowship.

* * *

We do, however, know what Soyinka *did* do in 1960 which, in addition to being the year of national independence, was something of a personal *annus mirabilis* for the writer. Soyinka arrived home on the first day of 1960, appropriately marking the dawn of a new year, a new decade, and a new era in his country's history. From that moment on he seems to have moved like a whirling dynamo through the worlds of Nigerian media, theatre, and cultural and academic life. In addition to writing and rehearsing *A Dance of the Forests* with his Masks company (which involved shuttling back and forth between Lagos and Ibadan), and then directing and performing in it at the independence celebrations in October, Soyinka did many other things during that year. He scripted a radio series, **'Broke Time Bar,'** and delivered a series of broadcasts entitled **'Talking through Your Hat'**; wrote and had performed two short plays on radio and two on television, and acted in one of the latter, as well as in an Ibadan stage-production of Brecht's *The Good Woman of Setzuan*; completed the manuscript of *The Trials of Brother Jero,* which had its première performance in Ibadan in the same year; published a number of poems and critical essays, including **'The Future of West African Writing,'** in *The Horn,* and a piece of fake folklore, as a literary spoof, in an English magazine; and commenced the co-editing of *Black Orpheus.*[12] Given even Soyinka's extraordinary industry and versatility, there would seem to have been very little time left over for travelling around festivals.

None of this is meant as mere biographical cavilling. How much festival research Soyinka managed to cram into 1960 alongside these many other activities must remain a matter for conjecture until more information is available. I have not had access to the Ibadan files, and it will be the task of scholars who have been thus privileged to establish the extent and dramatic relevance of this research. My own concern here is with critical readings of the early plays which are based upon the *idea* of relevant and influential empirical research. How many or how few festivals Soyinka observed and recorded is, of course, ultimately of no real importance. No one doubts his intimacy with the *egungun* and other masquerades, or with the Ogun, New Year, and New Yam Festivals that feature in his plays during the 1960s, and this familiarity is, in any case, amply documented in his autobiographical writings.[13] If each of these ritual elements, as they appear in the plays, has the quick of experience—of something learned in living—about them, it is because they were integral to a culture and a worldview imbibed in childhood. But for the same reason, the influence they bring to bear upon Soyinka's art is generally pervasive, permeative, and not easily pinned down to particulars.

I have dwelt at length on the business of Soyinka's 1960 Rockefeller-sponsored research because I suspect that it may have lent encouragement to a certain way of reading the early plays—one that is excessively literal-minded and pedantic—and to an approach which takes little account either of their visionary treatment of ritual features, or of the ironic distance from which they handle much of the traditional material of festivals.

* * *

Perhaps the brief setting of these critical tendencies in their historical context will help to explain how they came about. In the early 1960s, in addition to those western anthropologists and literary critics who tended to relegate African masquerade-theatre to the category of 'pre-drama' or 'quasi-drama',[14] some were only too ready to concede to traditional festivals the full dramatic status that would admit of a fruitful continuity between forms but who regretted that the literary dramatists themselves had not done so, with the result that traditional material had percolated too slowly onto the modern stage. In 1966, which seems to have been the year of expatriate academics giving advice to Nigerian playwrights, three such critics published essays either remarking upon abrupt discontinuities between tradi-

tional and modern forms, or openly exhorting Soyinka, J. P. Clark, and others to look to indigenous forms of dramatic expression for their inspiration.[15]

One of this expatriate troika, Martin Banham, conceded in 1961 that Soyinka had stopped short of 'complete immersion in alien styles', but went on to allege in 1966 that 'in the early plays of the university playwrights there has been a reliance on European theatrical styles, and many of the traditional Nigerian forms of dramatic expression have been ignored if not rejected.'[16] These comments now look remarkably thin when placed beside Soyinka's earliest interview statement, in 1962, about the inevitable incorporation of the traditional masquerade idioms of ritual, dance, and mime into the modern theatre,[17] and in the light of the dramatist's early creative practice: notably, the festive mime of *The Lion and the Jewel,* the spectacular mummery at the end of *A Dance of the Forests,* and the ritual fury of the *egungun* at the climax of *The Road,* all of which plays were written and staged before 1965.

The looked-for cross-currents and continuities were, in fact, visibly present from the beginning, and it is odd that foreign critics who were so concerned about the use of indigenous material should have overlooked its presence in Soyinka's early plays. Nevertheless, such criticisms seem to have had the unfortunate effect of investing those plays with a western bias which was not easily dispelled. In a sensitive and well-meaning review of his 'international drama', Una Maclean was to mistake Soyinka's call for universal standards of criticism for an invitation to read his plays in terms of western styles and sources,[18] and there has, subsequently, been no shortage of western literary debt-collectors (waving scraps of Shakespeare, Synge, O'Neill, and Brecht), and of complaints from Nigerian critics of a too heavy reliance in Soyinka's work upon western notions and forms.[19]

In a belated attempt to redress the balance, and fortified with the idea of a creative input from festival research, some recent Yoruba and other West African commentators have gone to the opposite extreme of regarding traditional festivals and ceremonies as the principal reservoir of Soyinka's drama, to the exclusion of western formalistic influences. This has given some support to a continuing cultural polarisation of Soyinka's plays, which, proceeding on the assumption that if he is not drawing from this piece of Brecht or Synge then he must be borrowing from that festival rite or masquerade, does little justice to the complex interplay in his work between both western and indigenous dramatic forms, on the one hand,[20] and different Yoruba traditions, on the other.

The new school of 'neo-ritualist' critics has ventured to detect some very literal correspondences, at both general and particular levels, between episodes in the early plays and individual ritual practices and religious beliefs. Western commentators must tread warily here, for they cannot pretend to the inside perspective of their African counterparts in these matters. I suspect, however, that the wholesale translation of ritual effects and devices, divorced from their proper festival contexts and applied with scant regard for Soyinka's autonomous dramatic ones, may be as misguided as their earlier neglect or exclusion: to see these things everywhere may be as false to the experience of the plays as not seeing them at all. It has been usefully suggested, for example, that *A Dance of the Forests* owes something to the web-like, centrifugal structure of the annual Obatala festival held at Edi. 'Ropo Sekoni, in a learned and subtle article, searches out in Soyinka's play the latter's multiplicity of episodes and time-dimensions, and patterns of incremental repetition, radiating outwards from monothematic nuclei.[21] Joel Adedeji, on an uncharacteristic excursion into ritual abstractions, discovers in the same play the random elements of mythology, purification, and comedy proper to the festival's paradigm of 'The Play of Moremi'.[22]

Correspondences at this tenuous level of abstraction are perhaps too easily found—so much so that after a while the western critic begins to suspect that the same radial structures may be common to a hundred other festivals, as well as to more than a few African plays—and stand in need of some precise qualifications. For example, there is the very simple and obvious one that the Obatala Festival, after the usual ritual blend of gravity and levity, seriousness and travesty (in which the Passion Play element figures strongly), comes to rest in a prevailing mood of harmony and reconciliation, as befits the peace and serenity of the god himself, not the dark solemnity, discord, and torpor of Soyinka's play. The intellectual refinements of the scholar give short shrift in this instance to the emotional impact and brooding atmospherics of the drama. It is of more particular interest to learn from another critic that Agboreko, the mis-named 'Elder of Sealed Lips' in *A Dance of the Forests,* is the traditional *babalawo,* the high priest of the festival who performs the communal libation to the spirits (via the tree imp Murete) in the manner of his counterparts in the Olokun and Ohuvwe Festivals.[23] As *babalawo,* Agboreko, in the phraseology of the Ghanaian poet Kofi Awooner, 'grasps and unfolds the secret magic of words'.[24]

But such observations profit us little until we notice that the ritual trappings are edged with irony. Agboreko's timid libations are thwarted by capricious gods who are themselves too full of human weaknesses to sustain much human confidence, the sacrifices expiate nothing, and the priest himself is a pompous charlatan, a garrulous windbag whose ponderous proverbs are only spasmodically relevant. It helps to know that the processional dance of the Ondo Ogun Festival is one of the possible models for the Driver's Festival of *The Road,* but only when it is observed that Soyinka has in fact inverted the pattern, so that the interrupted rite which constitutes his play runs not from the dusk of one day to the dawn of another,[25] but between two twilights of the same day, ending with an abrupt finality in the gathering dark and with no hint of renewal, no glimmer of returning light.

I do not know if it has been noticed, but the eponymous anti-hero's direct address to the audience at the opening of *The Trials of Brother Jero* is reminiscent of the Yoruba folk-opera's opening 'glee' in which the gist and moral of the play are given (it is not necessary to go to Brecht or the Greek *parabasis* for these illusion-breaking devices).[26] But, as usual, Soyinka supplies the customary ironic twist: here it is Jero who provides his own (and in his case, highly amoral) prologue. Furthermore, the 'glee' may have its origins in festival, one of its possible models being the ceremonial opening of the *Alarinjo* mask drama, the *ijuba*. Again, if there is a debt here, it is deviously paid. The traditional *ijuba* contains a pledge; a salute by the troupe leader to the lineage from which he drew his inspiration or to the leader from whom he received his training; and, last and least, limited self-praise.[27] As in the other instances, the traditional device is presented in the inverted form of parody. Jero, in a rather crude flashback, invokes the memory of the old prophet to whom he was apprenticed, but only to ridicule and revile him, and then to lavish all of the praise upon himself for his clever deception and betrayal of his old master.

* * *

The neo-ritualist school of criticism overlooks two things. First, there is the historical fact that ceremonies and festivals in modern West African society are no longer sources of power and strength in themselves, and the new dramatic forms dictated by the dynamics of social development cannot be expected to incorporate their features in a dutiful or an uncritically literal-minded manner. Secondly, there is the phenomenon of Soyinka himself, who in his ritual usages, as in all other things, is the most eclectic, idiosyncratic, and supremely inventive of writers. His work is steeped in Yoruba culture, but unfathomably so, to the extent that it has the power to transform it out of all recognition: his are the innovations of the deeply initiated, the improvisations of the maestro who has long dispensed with classical orthodoxies. His use of festival lore is therefore never merely nostalgic or antiquarian but always reinterpretive and interpolative, usually in a highly individual manner, and with an abundance of ironic barbs and twists. In *Kongi's Harvest,* the Festival of the New Yam, which usually signifies renewal and new beginnings, is made to mark the end of an era, and the use of the *egungun* motif in *A Dance of the Forests* completely reverses the customary relationship between the living and the dead: here the ancestors return not to judge but to be judged (or rather, rejudged, in the vain hope that they will receive justice this time around), and instead of being honoured with the customary salute to the lineage (the *orile*), they are chased away.

Soyinka's imagination makes similarly cavalier play in this work around Yoruba ideas of reincarnation. In his ironic readaptation, he reincarnates not the good ancestors who have lived well on earth, as is customary in Yoruba eschatology,[28] but the collaborators with the victims of horrific evil, apparently on the assumption that the former still have some sparks of decency and potential for redemption (though Adenebi proves a hopeless case), and in the hope that the latter will some day find the world ready to receive their goodness. In Soyinka's version it is not the evil-doers who become the wandering, lonely, neglected spirits,[29] but the good who, more in keeping with western Gothic tradition, are so tormented by the memory of their sufferings in their earthly lives that they can find no rest in the spirit world. Soyinka, it would seem, has little interest in reincarnation as a literal phenomenon. When Aroni, in the prologue to *A Dance of the Forests,* reveals that the revenants from the court of Mata Kharibou were in their previous lives 'linked in violence and blood with four of the living generation',[30] the 'blood' refers by association to that shed by violence, not to the literally reincarnated essence or blood of the lineage. The idea of reincarnation has no value in the play except as part of a conglomerate metaphor.

In the giant radial-image complex at the centre of *A Dance of the Forests,* three separate but intricately linked motifs—reincarnation, the *egungun,* and the New Year Festival in which certain *egungun,* like the *Folumo,* are often used for such purposes of purification[31]— converge to focus upon themes common to each of them: the returning dead, the confrontation of the present by the past, the recall of the contemporary world to historical reality and to the abiding truths of the human situation. Ritual, religious, and mythological elements are interesting and important in the plays only with regard to what Soyinka makes of them, notably the ways in which they are pressed as intellectual vehicles into the service of broad imaginative concepts. In the area of ritual the primary interest is not in the features of any particular festival but in the general *idea* of the festival, its imaginative possibilities (for communal celebration, purification, and regeneration), and what it can be made to represent in the troubled transitional period of modern African history.

This does not mean that there are no specifically identifiable ritual features in the plays. Most noticeable among theatrical effects, after the mimes and masques of *The Lion and the Jewel,* are the ritualistic denoue-

ments of *The Road, Kongi's Harvest,* and the later play, *Madmen and Specialists.* In each of these there is that sudden quickening of tempo and whipping up of emotion into frenzied, trance-like states by a rising crescendo of hieratic chanting and drumming which are characteristic of the phenomena of possession and dispossession (or exorcism). There is also, everywhere on the Soyinkan stage but most intensely in the esoteric plays, that sense of a suspension of ordinary reality, and of a deferment of, or removal from, the normal time-order which are hallmarks of the ritual process. The classical unity of time is rigorously adhered to by the outward form of the plays, with the action seldom exceeding a single day and time lapses ruthlessly curtailed, even to the extent of performing without an interval. Within this tight, concentrated pattern, however, the characters move strangely and unpredictably about in—and in and out of—time.

A Dance of the Forests, with its multiple, recurrent action and radial symbolism, is not in fact Aristotelian in shape but has indeed the fluid, free-ranging form of the festival, in which there is always the feeling of events taking place within the context of a larger, cosmic time scale. Yet these are all general drawings upon the ritual heritage, available to any Yoruba artist and not requiring any esoteric knowledge gleaned from specialised research.

Soyinka's plays are not ritual-specific in the sense that their ceremonies can be pinned down to precise forms in contemporary geographic or ethnic settings. The carrier rite in *The Strong Breed,* for example, combines features from different forms of the event as performed both inside and outside of Yorubaland (the riverine setting and ceremonial procedure suggest the Ijaw delta community and its *Amagba* ritual); in Soyinka's version of *The Bacchae* [*The Bacchae of Euripides: A Communion Rite*] it is mixed up with Greek lore and ideas of political revolution. In the New Yam Festival of *Kongi's Harvest,* the vague setting is eclipsed by the only marginally clearer symbolism, and Soyinka seems to be more concerned with the atmospherics of excited preparation than with the event itself.

The 1960 extravaganza, *A Dance of the Forests,* which is assumed by some of the neo-ritualists to be the fruit of that year's festival research, is really, in fact, an extraordinary ritual and mythological concoction, its roots everywhere and nowhere (despairing of derivation, Oyin Ogunba has dubbed it 'a special Wole Soyinka festival').[32] Its intense rituality is at once something more organic and dynamic than the material normally derived from sober academic research: though pervasively and distinctively Yoruba in its cultural origins, it is also a highly personal reinvention. What Soyinka presents, in this and in his other early plays, is not an unmediated, naturalistic reproduction of ritual originals—not a photographic copy from life—but a visionary conception, a reworking of ritual through metaphor into art.

The real miracle at the end of Soyinka's year of wonders is the play itself: a magnificently unstageable, sprawling fantasia of the human cycle of suffering and guilt, patterned into remote but recognisable, familiar but altered ritual forms. It is not necessarily the outcome of that year or of any one learning experience in it. The *Dance* is the fruit of the whole forest: its knowledge is not plucked from any single tree.

Notes

1. Gerald Moore, *Wole Soyinka* (London, 1978 edn.), p. 9.

2. Joel Adedeji, 'A Profile of Nigerian Theatre, 1960-1970', in *Nigeria Magazine* (Lagos), 107-9, 1971, p. 3.

3. Bernth Lindfors, 'The Early Writings of Wole Soyinka', in Lindfors (ed.), *Critical Perspectives on Nigerian Literatures* (Washington, D.C., 1975), p. 184.

4. Robert W. July, 'The Artist's Credo: The Political Philosophy of Wole Soyinka', in *The Journal of Modern African Studies* (Cambridge), 19, 3, September 1981, p. 488.

5. James Gibbs, 'Soyinka's Drama of Essence', in *Utafiti* (Dar es Salaam), 3, 2, 1978, pp. 429, 434-5, and 438.

6. Wole Soyinka, 'The African Approach to Drama', International Symposium on African Culture, Ibadan, 19-24 December 1960.

7. James Gibbs, *Wole Soyinka* (London, 1986), p. 20.

8. Esso World Theatre Production, 1963. Ann Dundon discusses the masquerade sequence in 'Soyinkan Aesthetics in *Culture in Transition*: An Essay on Film', First Ibadan Annual African Literature Conference, 6-10 July 1976, pp. 11-12, kindly supplied by James Gibbs.

9. Wole Soyinka, *Myth, Literature, and the African World* (Cambridge, 1976), p. 38.

10. Wole Soyinka, 'Penthouse Theatre', in Karen L. Morell (ed.), *In Person: Achebe, Awoonor, and Soyinka at the University of Washington* (Washington, D.C., 1975), pp. 94-100.

11. 'Interview: Wole Soyinka' by Jeremy Harding, in *New Statesman* (London), 27 February 1987, p. 22.

12. Details of Soyinka's activities in 1960 can be found in the following: James Gibbs, '"Yapping" and "Pushing": Notes on Wole Soyinka's "Broke Time Bar" Radio Series of the Early Sixties', in *Africa Today* (Denver), 33, 1, 1986, pp. 19-26; Tim Gordon,

'Nigerian Night's Entertainment', review of Brecht's *The Good Woman of Setzuan*, in *Ibadan,* 9, June 1960, p. 20; Bernth Lindfors, 'Wole Soyinka Talking through His Hat' and 'The Early Writings of Wole Soyinka', in Hena Maes-Jelinek (ed.), *Commonwealth Literature and the Modern World* (Brussels, 1975), pp. 115-25 and 165-90; and Bernth Lindfors, 'Egbe's Sworn Enemy—Soyinka's Popular Sport', in Lindfors (ed.), *Early Nigerian Literatures* (New York, 1982), pp. 143-53.

13. For the *egungun,* see Wole Soyinka, *Aké: The Years of Childhood* (London, 1981), pp. 31-5.

14. For example, John Ferguson, 'Nigerian Drama in English', in *Modern Drama* (Toronto), 11, May 1968, p. 10, and Ruth Finnegan, *Oral Literature in Africa* (Oxford, 1970), p. 500.

15. Martin Banham, 'Notes on Nigerian Theatre: 1966', in *BAALE* (Freetown), 4, March 1966, pp. 33-4; Michael Crowder, 'Tradition and Change in Nigerian Literature', in *Tri-Quarterly* (Evanston), 5, 1966, pp. 117 and 124-5; and Molly Mahood, 'Drama in New-Born States', in *Présence africaine* (Paris), 60, 1966, p. 33.

16. Martin Banham, 'A Piece That We May Fairly Call Our Own', in *Ibadan,* 12, June 1961, p. 18, and 'Notes on Nigerian Theatre: 1966', p. 34. This writer concedes in a later article that there is a fusion of traditional Yoruba dramatic forms and universal influences in Soyinka's later plays, but is reluctant to extend this perception to the plays written before 1965. Martin Banham, 'Nigerian Dramatists in English and the Traditional Nigerian Theatre', in William Walsh (ed.), *Readings in Commonwealth Literature* (Oxford, 1973), p. 136.

17. 'Wole Soyinka', in Dennis Duerden and Cosmo Pieterse (eds.), *African Writers Talking* (London, 1972), p. 170.

18. Una Maclean, 'Soyinka's International Drama', in *Black Orpheus* (Lagos), 15, 1964, pp. 46-51.

19. For example, Biodun Jeyifo, *The Truthful Lie: Essays in a Sociology of African Drama* (London, 1985), pp. 26-7. Some echoes of western plays are discussed in detail by James Gibbs, 'Grafting Is an Ancient Art: The Relationship of African and European Elements in the Early Plays of Wole Soyinka', in *World Literature Written in English* (Toronto), 24, Summer 1984, pp. 87-99.

20. This interplay is explored at length by Gibbs, ibid.

21. 'Ropo Sekoni, 'Metaphor as Basis of Form in Soyinka's Drama', in *Research in African Literatures* (Austin, Texas), 14, Spring 1983, pp. 46-50.

22. Joel Adedeji, 'Aesthetics of Soyinka's Theatre', in Dapo Adelugba (ed.), *Before Our Very Eyes* (Ibadan, 1987), pp. 115-18.

23. Austin Asagba, 'Roots of African Drama: Critical Approaches and Elements of Continuity', in *Kunapipi* (Aarhus, Denmark), 8, 3, 1986, p. 95. For the relevant scene in *A Dance of the Forests,* see Wole Soyinka, *Collected Plays,* Vol. 1 (Oxford, 1973), p. 14.

24. Kofi Awoonor, *The Breast of the Earth* (New York, 1975), p. 323.

25. Oyin Ogunba, 'Traditional African Festival Drama', in Ogunba and Abiola Irele (eds.), *Theatre in Africa* (Ibadan, 1978), p. 20.

26. Joel Adedeji, 'The Literature of the Yoruba Opera', in W. L. Ballard (ed.), *Essays on African Literature* (Atlanta, 1973), pp. 59-60.

27. Joel Adedeji, 'Trends in the Content and Form of the Opening Glee in Yoruba Drama', in Lindfors (ed.), *Critical Perspectives on Nigerian Literatures,* pp. 41 and 45, and '"Alarinjo": The Traditional Yoruba Travelling Theatre', in Ogunba and Irele (eds.), op. cit. p. 45.

28. J. O. Awolalu, *Yoruba Beliefs and Sacrificial Rites* (Harlow, 1979), pp. 60 and 65.

29. Ibid. p. 60.

30. Soyinka, *Collected Plays,* Vol. 1, p. 5.

31. Ogunba, 'Traditional African Festival Drama', p. 16.

32. Oyin Ogunba, 'The Traditional Content of the Plays of Wole Soyinka', in *African Literature Today* (London), 5, 1971, p. 106.

Anjali Roy and Viney Kirpal (essay date autumn 1991)

SOURCE: Roy, Anjali, and Viney Kirpal. "Men as Archetypes: Characterization in Soyinka's Novels." *Modern Fiction Studies* 37, no. 3 (autumn 1991): 519-27.

[*In the following essay, Roy and Kirpal discuss how the male characters in* The Interpreters *and* Season of Anomy *function as traditional African male archetypes.*]

Although several articles have been written on the characters of Wole Soyinka's plays, his fictional characters have not been discussed in detail. This leaves a gap in the existing criticism of Soyinka's work, particularly since **The Interpreters** was specially cited for the Nobel Prize for Literature. This paper examines, in depth, the nature of characterization in two Soyinka novels: **The Interpreters** (1965) and **Season of Anomy** (1973), and hopes to fill this lacuna to a great extent.

Any critique of characterization in the African novel not taking into account the traditional African conception of "personality" and "individuality" is, even at its best, limited. Most western analyses of African characters fail for this reason. The majority of western critics underestimate the degree to which African writers are entrenched in the traditional world view and the depth of their conditioning by the traditional perception of man. They do not look up to western models for inspiration but to African oral literatures that, in various ways—realistic as well as stylized—reaffirm traditional images of man.

Originating in a view of personality more communal than individual, traditional standards of characterization are at odds with the western ideal of individualized, growing characters. For instance, the "type" is more of a norm than an aberration in traditional characterization. The modern Nigerian novelist readily adopts traditional type characters: culture heroes like the warrior and the wrestler, stock figures like the trickster and the scapegoat, mythical beings like deities and spirits; whereas fictional criticism, by general consensus, has reserved the "type" for depicting peripheral characters. And although the practice has been shunned by most respected practitioners of modern fiction in the west, Nigerian writers introduce shades of type characterization even in their portrayal of the main characters.

The type characters of oral literature have an inherent advantage over those of fiction. Divested of the particulars of time and place and representatives of certain basic personality types, characters of myth, folktale, and epic transcend their parochial limitations and acquire a universal appeal. It is little wonder that Nigerian novelists should gravitate toward traditional methods of characterization. Also, the versatile nature of the "type" opens up a host of other possibilities. The ideal "types" of heroic poetry are appropriate for tragic and serious treatment;[1] the caricatures of traditional satire can be exploited in ironic depictions; and the quotidian figures of folktale are suitable for making pragmatic comments on life in general.

But more importantly, the "types" are suited to the didactic thrust of the Nigerian novel. The "ideals" can be employed to praise and glorify, the "caricatures" to expose and ridicule. In employing traditional type characterization in the novel, these writers have gained a powerful aesthetic device consistent with their professed didactic intention. But they have also demonstrated the novel's innate capacity to absorb new experiments in form and technique.

"For we must admit," Forster wrote, "that flat people are not in themselves as big achievements as round ones, and also that they are best when they are comic" (50). Wole Soyinka has shown that flatness can encompass tragic depth and profundity and be as noteworthy an achievement as roundness. Forster regards the distinguishing feature of flat characters as their being "constructed round a single idea or quality" (47). The mask, a basic African art form, too, focuses on a single concrete quality. But it does so deliberately, to dispense with minute particulars and to capture the essence of a personality. Annemarie Heywood was right when she described the characters of *The Interpreters* as "masks, voices in an adventure of ideation" (130). But, in her dissatisfaction with the characters' two-dimensional nature and incapacity for development, she overlooked the workings of the "mask" technique. At the root of this method lies a rejection of mimetic realism and an attempt to highlight the "essential" idea. The clamour for complexity and roundness, on the other hand, emanates from a belief in verisimilitude.[2] It is argued that people in real life are far too complicated to be summarized in a single idea. So when Soyinka introduced what the Western critics consider flat characters, he came in for sharp criticism.

Emmanuel Obiechina considers the ancestral masks abounding in African art as representative of basic personality types perceivable by traditional people (29-155). Soyinka's portrayal of his characters in both novels conforms to the same principles. Soyinka depicts his characters as quintessential personality types, as varied and diverse as the masks: the gentle and patient Bandele, the fiery, hot-headed Egbo, the saintly, self-effacing Sekoni, and so on. Ofeyi, the protagonist of *Season of Anomy,* is a development of Egbo with Egbo's aggressiveness much reduced and his sensitivity heightened. Particularized details, although unobtrusively introduced, cease to matter. It is of little consequence that Bandele teaches at the university or that Sagoe works on a newspaper. The writer does not attempt to gain fullness by brushing in added details. Instead, he seeks to drive home his characters' representative status.

The one-dimensional profile of Soyinka's characters emerges from his having frozen them in their fixed, habitual poses. He tends to highlight only one aspect of his characters, giving room to the allegation that they are not fully realized. For example, despite the numerous vignettes of Egbo's past and present, what do they cumulatively add up to except that he is a rebellious, obdurate sensualist? Bandele appears in all his scenes merely to soothe and to appease. In *The Interpreters,* if not in *Season of Anomy,* Soyinka often resorts to the favorite epic device of the recurring epithet. Bandele is always "grave," "patient," and "mild." Egbo either "scowled," "glowered," or looked for someone to provoke. Kola's hand always rests on his brush. The novelist sacrifices gradual, detailed character development for one, bold, striking outline.

The protagonists of traditional African narratives are, invariably, social and professional types rather than specific, particularized individuals (Obiechina 90). Soy-

inka follows the same strategy. His characters are classified through their professional status—the academician (Oguazor), the lawyer (Lasunwon), the bureaucrat (Egbo), the politician (Chief Winsala), the journalist (Sagoe), and the artist (Kola). But one crucial difference alters Soyinka's use of the traditional device. In traditional society, the individual's behavior pattern and individuality were circumscribed by his professional or social status. One could say that the person's identity was inseparable from his professional or social role. But the contemporary Nigerian's profession has ceased to intrude into his private life or lay down the code for his personal behavior. He is, therefore, more of an "individual" in the western sense of the world. Why, then, does Soyinka cling to an anachronistic definition of man? The social definition of characters in Soyinka's novels reveals the novelist's concern with the degeneration and corruption of contemporary Nigerian society. By depicting his characters in their professional capacity, Soyinka is able to map across several cross-sections of Nigerian society and lay bare the sordidness of every sphere of public life in Nigeria today. A fundamental issue in the novel, in fact, is the individual's social responsibility in the nontribal milieu that is raised quite explicitly in the second part of the novel. By dwelling on his characters' social identity, Soyinka is, as it were, applying a tribal yardstick to evaluate contemporary lack of communal responsibility. It leads to the sad discovery that the modern Nigerian has had to pay a heavy price for acquiring an "individual" identity.

O. R. Dathorne in *The Black Mind* defines myth as a story that depicts men as gods (17). In Soyinka we observe a tendency to endow his human heroes with a mythic status. There is a definite identification of the characters in *The Interpreters* with the gods in the Yoruba Pantheon. Ofeyi, the protagonist of *Season of Anomy,* is envisaged as a Black Orpheus. Soyinka's sources range from Yoruba ritual to Greek myth, reflecting the synthesis of diverse, multicultural elements in the writer's mind. But, as Edgar Wright has pointed out, the bicultural writer may borrow a "basic myth of Western culture as universally applicable while at the same time the starting point of the reaching out for a universal humanism is the stable, traditional (but not rigid) regional culture (117-118). In other words, although the novels may span various cultural myths, the outlook remains specifically Yoruba. The vision bringing about a fusion of the human and the divine has its roots in Yoruba theology.

The relationship between the human and the divine, the worshipper and the deity, the *olorisha* and the *orisha* is elucidated by Ulli Beier in his book *The Return of the Gods: The Sacred Art of Susanne Wenger* (44-45). That the human can be comprehended in terms of the divine and the divine represented by the human is inherent in the meaning of the word *olorisha.* One of the translations Ulli Beier offers of the word is "One who is *orisha*." (44) This means that "[t]he worshipper offers his body as a vehicle to *orisha,* he allows the *orisha* 'to mount his head,' to ride him, and he strives to become, for brief moments, the personification of the *orisha*." (44) He further quotes Susanne Wenger, "[t]he final purpose of *orisha* worship is to extend the natural limits of human experience into the sphere of the metaphysical. Man becomes more than man" (45). This, in essence, echoes Soyinka's own views on the human-divine relationship in *Myth, Literature, and the African World* and lies behind his attempt to add a mythical dimension to his human characters (144-145).

A character's relationship with his tutelary deity was frequently drawn upon while portraying character in traditional narrative (Obiechina 95). Soyinka's characters are similarly delineated. A few characters' likenesses to specific Yoruba gods are explicitly stated: Joe Golder's to the animal deity Erinle, Egbo's to the bloodthirsty Ogún. For the others, one learns to make inferences. For example, one instantly spots in Bandele's description—"his mask of infinite patience"—an allusion to the *oriki* praising Obatala:

> He is patient.
> He is silent.
> Without anger he pronounces his judgement.
>
> ("The Creator" 27)

Sekoni, the electrical engineer, is a natural heir to Sango, the Yoruba god of thunder and lightning and therefore of captive power, that is, electricity in a modern context.

The alien reader might miss the significance of these allusions and overlook the ingenuity of the method. But for those with whom the author can assume a familiarity of context, this works as a remarkably economic strategy of characterization. Because the attributes of the gods are already well-known, the author hardly need mention a deity's name to label a character in order to conjure a complete picture.

Given the highly Yoruba reference of Soyinka's work, some amount of obscurity is bound to creep in. But how much of the classical and mythical framework of T. S. Eliot's *The Waste Land* is familiar to the average western reader? (Egudu 55). Obiechina sums up the problem thus: "That kind of overt reference to traditional beliefs is not readily made in the *The Interpreters* because of its modern setting and because its action is enveloped in language of a sophistication that nearly obscures the traditional strands. But unless these strands are unearthed, much useful insight is lost to the reader and much remains obscure" (114-115).

Perhaps, Soyinka resorted to the better-known Greek tale of Orpheus' quest for his lost wife Eurydice in his second novel *Season of Anomy* to overcome the obscurity posed by the deeply Yoruba reference of his earlier work. But his treatment of his Greek sources reveals that in the process of transposing the myth to a different surrounding, he has domesticated or even "Yorubaized" the myth, the Yoruba adaptation of the names being the crudest example (Izevbaye, *Black* 250) Dennis Duerdean has suggested that in his adaptation of the Orpheus figure, Soyinka probably skipped his Greek source to refer to the original Egyptian Isiac mysteries These are closer to home and parallel the rites of the Yoruba god Ogún (98).

In employing the Greek poet-musician, Orpheus, as the symbol of the artist, Soyinka gained a wider reference than he would from his Yoruba counterpart. Yet it is obvious that it is Ogún, the "first" artist, who, is being invoked in Ofeyi's features. There are unmistakable shades of the cult of violence and blood associated with Ogún in the picture of the artist-hero. The emphasis on the need for violence in realizing the artistic quest also points to the Ogún brand of bloodthirsty creativity. When he chooses the Dentist's path of violence, Ofeyi has opted for the traumatic "healing" of the surgeon-god Ogún rather than the gentle "healing" and the mastering of wild energies that Orpheus exemplifies.

The deification of the male characters in the novels was accomplished by mere suggestion and through oblique references to mythical parallels. But in the portrayal of his female characters, Soyinka's indulges in unabashed apotheosis. The female figures in Soyinka's novels—Simi "the sorceress" of *The Interpreters* and Irìyísé, the Eurydice of *Season of Anomy,* or even Taiila, the Indian girl, in the same novel—are all conceived as goddesses and invested with an aura of mystery and beauty. The author breaks into spontaneous homage at the sight of his goddess-like heroines. One of the praise songs or *orikis* in *The Interpreters* describes Simi as "*ayaba osa . . . omo Yemoja*" (Queen of the sea, daughter of Yèmójà) (260). But Simi's light skin, her being a harlot, and her air of ancient mystery bring to mind the image of the Yoruba water-deity, Osun, who is both "the velvet-skin concubine and the ancient woman steeped in magic" (Beier 36). Whether Simi is Olokun, Queen of the Sea, or the river-deity Osun, her association with water is evident.

Irìyísé deification assumes a more direct note. She is accorded immortal status through the process of naming. She is both "Celestial" and "Iridescent." Irìyísé is also more unambiguously identified with regeneration than Simi. Dennis Duerden and D. S. Izevbaye have both perceived in Irìyísé echoes of the earth-goddess rather than of Eurydice after whom she is named (Duerdin 103; Izevbaye 248). This explanation seems quite plausible because Soyinka has modified the Eurydice myth by permitting Irìyísé to re-awaken (unlike her Greek namesake). And considering the primacy of earth cults among the Yoruba, the celebration of the earth-goddess in Soyinka's novel seems natural. Irìyísé's dances symbolically to re-enact the rhythms of the earth, and her solitary confinement later suggests the dormant state of the earth in the "season of anomy." Like Persephone, Irìyísé is imprisoned in the kingdom of the underworld from which she must return at the end of winter. Unlike Eurydice, Irìyísé, as the symbol of regeneration, unwittingly aids the hero in his quest.

In both Simi, the goddess of water, and Irìyísé, the earth-goddess, Soyinka celebrates the female regenerative principle (Interview 57). There are hints of mystical transcendence in Egbo's liaison with Simi. Irìyísé is equally crucial to Ofeyi's quest for regeneration. However, this approach leads Soyinka to concentrate on the symbolical potential of his heroines to the exclusion of their development as actual people.

The utopian framework of *Season of Anomy* permits easy allegorization of character. Their explanatory names—Custodian of the Grain, Trouble Shooter. Spyhole—establish the characters' association with moral qualities and functions. Two major characters, The Dentist and Taiila, exist only as allegorized moral choices for the hero. They stand for the active and introspective alternatives available to the artist Ofeyi—the need for revolutionary action and the tendency toward private inwardness. Again, it is their highly suggestive names that endow these two characters with their defining attributes. The Dentist evokes an image of a violent, surgical operation, whereas Taiila (*taila* means "oil" in Sanskrit) suggests a pallitative of a different kind.

Although it may not be as obvious as it was in *Season of Anomy,* a certain amount of allegorization creeps into *The Interpreters* as well. Individual characters seem to be conceived as embodiments of dispositional traits. Bandele, for instance, emerges as the Conscience of the group as the novel unfolds. As he is seen endlessly exhorting his friends to accept responsibility for their actions, his judiciary function grows clearer. Sekoni epitomizes pure, unmediated Intuition, which finds an outlet in his frenzied canvas "The Wrestler." Sekoni's affinity to Sango, the god of thunder and lightning, also projects him as the manifestation of the Divine Wrath. Egbo shares the temperamental attributes of his patron deity Ogún—an undisguised sensuality and a streak of violence. Allegorization of character, popular with the didactic pedagogue, is of immense help in sharpening the focus on ethical issues. But it diminishes the scope for individualizing characters.

However, allegorization is extremely effective in creating satiric portraits. Directing the satire to (moral) types divests it of personal venom and lends it sharpness. Vice and moral corruption merit a harsher criticism than hypocrisy and affectation. The philistines and the parvenu—the Oguazors, the Lasunwons, the Faseyis, even the Aristotos—may be ridiculed, but they are also tolerated. Each is reduced to a single, ludicrous detail, be it the affected accent of the Professor, the stiff college tie of the lawyer, or the smooth, dishonest face of the Ariosto. But the spiritually depraved are unequivocally condemned. In this respect, *The Interpreters* is more tolerant of vice than *Season of Anomy.* Perhaps in deference to their age, Chief Winsala and Sir Derinola in *The Interpreters* are exposed, nicknamed, but let off lightly. But, in *Season of Anomy,* Soyinka turns absolutely ruthless. The "Hatchet" men of the Cartel—Chief Batoki, Sheikh Zaki Amuri—deserve nothing less than clear, unsparing denunciation.

Soyinka was fascinated by the "carrier" figure in Yoruba Sacrifice. He has examined its role in African society in his play *Death and the King's Horseman.* The "carrier" symbolically bears the burden of the sins and transgressions of the community. Hence his death serves to bring about ritual purgation. The contemporaneity of the novels' setting does not permit direct treatment of the motif, but it can be built into the narrative texture through an allusive and evocative idiom. The "martyr" motif is first introduced in relation to Sekoni by Sagoe, "people like Sekoni end up on the pyre anyway. . . ." (98). The infusion of sacrificial ritual in the description of Sekoni's death leaves no doubt about Sekoni's identification with the "carrier." Sekoni acts as the bearer of the excesses of the decomposing Nigerian society. Yet his death carries a promise of regeneration.

The "carrier" motif is directly established at the very beginning of *Season of Anomy.* At the funeral ceremonies of Aiyéró's founding father, as Irìyísé stands by Ofeyi's side watching the bull-sacrifice, the ivory on Irìyísé's neck seems to blend with the ivory skin of the bulls (16). This ominously foretells her impending sacrifice. Irìyísé becomes the willing sacrifice in Ofeyi's struggle against the dissipation and incontinence of modern Nigeria. But Irìyísé too, like Sekoni, emerges as a symbol of rebirth.

The other famous Yoruba figure that Soyinka employs is that of the "divine trickster," Esu. In *The Interpreters,* the incorrigible journalist Sagoe is obviously modelled after Esu (Priebe 79-86). Sagoe shares with Esu his sparkling wit, cunning, and intelligence. Like Esu, Sagoe is invariably associated with disorder. Whether it be Dehinwa's household or the private party of the Oguazors, Sagoe can be trusted to spark off confusion. We also observe in Sagoe the same undisguised delight in flouting taboos that characterizes Esu. Only Sagoe could get away with hurling out the plastic fruits at the Oguazors. Only Sagoe can convert scatological functions into a consistent philosophy. But more than all this, the strongest resemblance between Sagoe and Esu lies in their satiric intent. The satiric portions in *The Interpreters* rest totally on the exploits of the trickster Sagoe.

Notes

1. James Olney asserts that Chinua Achebe's characters are "ideal" in the Platonic Sense (179).

2. Forster (48-49). For an alternative approach to characterization see D. S. Izevbaye.

Works Cited

Beier, Ulli. *The Return of the Gods: The Sacred Art of Susanne Wenger.* Cambridge: Cambridge UP, 1975.

Dathorne, O. P. *The Black Mind: A History of African Literature.* Minneapolis: U of Minnesota P, 1974.

Duerden, Dennis. *African Art and Literature: The Invisible Present.* London: Heinemann, 1977.

Egudu, R. N. "Criticism of Modern African Literature: The Question of Evaluation." *WLWE: World Literature Written in English* 21 (1982): 54-67.

Forster, E. M. *Aspects of the Novel and Other Writings.* The Abinger Edition of E. M. Forster 12. London: Arnold, 1974. [First Edition: *Aspects of the Novel,* London: Edward Arnold; New York: Harcourt Brace, 1927.]

Gibbs, James, ed. *Critical Perspectives on Wole Soyinka.* Washington: Three Continents, 1980. [Another edition is: London: Heinemann, 1981.]

Heywood, Annemarie. "The Fox's Dance: The Staging of [Wole] Soyinka's Plays." Gibbs 130-138. First published in *African Literature Today* 8 (1976): 42-51.

Izevbaye, D. S. "Naming and the Character of African Fiction." *Research in African Literatures* 12 (1981): 162-184.

———. "Obatala. The Creator." *Yoruba Poetry: An Anthology of Traditional Poems.* Ed. Ulli Beier. Cambridge: Cambridge UP, 1970. 27-28.

———. "Soyinka's Black Orpheus." Gibbs 243-252. First published in *Neo-African Literature and Culture.* Ed. Bernth Lindfors and Ulla Schild. Weisbaden: Heymann, 1976: 147-158.

Obiechina, Emmanuel. *Culture, Tradition, and Society in the West African Novel.* Cambridge: Cambridge UP, 1975.

Olney, James. *Tell Me Africa: An Approach to African Literature.* Princeton: Princeton UP, 1973.

Priebe, Richard. "Soyinka's Brother Jero: Prophet, Politician and Trickster." Gibbs 79-86. First published in *Pan-African Journal* 4 (1971): 431-439.

Soyinka, Wole [Akinwande Oluwole]. *Death and the King's Horseman.* New York: Hill & Wang, 1987. [Other Editions include: Methuen's Modern Plays. London: Eyre Methuen, 1975; New York: W. W. Norton, 1975.]

———. *The Interpreters.* African Writers Series 76. Intro. and notes Eldred Jones. London, Ibadan, Nairobi: Heinemann in association with André Deutsch, 1970. [Other Editions include: London: André Deutsch, 1965; New York: Macmillan, 1965; London: Panther, 1967; African/American Library. Intro. Leslie Lacy. New York: Collier, 1970; Fontana Modern Novels. London: Fontana, 1972; New York: Africana Publishing, 1972.]

———. Interview. *The Illustrated Times of India.* 9-15 Nov. 1986: 56.

———. *Myth, Literature, and the African World.* Cambridge: Cambridge UP, 1976.

———. *Season of Anomy.* London: Rex Collings, 1973. [Other editions include: New York: The Third Press, 1974; London: Arena, 1980; Panafrica Library. Walton-on-Thames, Surrey: Nelson, 1980.]

Wright, Edgar. "The Bilingual, Bicultural African Writer." *The Commonwealth Writer Overseas: Themes of Exile and Expatriation.* Ed. Alastair Niven. Liège: Revue des Langues Vivants et Didier, 1976: 107-119.

Derek Wright (essay date winter 1992)

SOURCE: Wright, Derek. "Soyinka's Smoking Shotgun: The Later Satires." *World Literature Today* 66, no. 1 (winter 1992): 27-34.

[*In the following essay, Wright explores the major themes of Soyinka's later "shotgun" satires, focusing on the political elements in such plays as* A Play of Giants *and* Requiem for a Futurologist.]

Wole Soyinka did not coin the term *shotgun writing*— "you discharge and disappear"—until the 1970s.[1] He had, however, produced occasional subversive satiric sketches throughout the previous decade, and his unpublished one-act Royal Court entertainment *The Invention* (1959), a caustic tour de force on universal racism set in a futuristic South Africa, had been written in the broad satiric tradition of the revue. During the deepening crisis of Nigeria's First Republic, as political murders became more frequent and blatant intimidation by power-addicted local chiefs escalated daily, Soyinka opted increasingly for the direct thrust and immediate corrective impact of the revue sketch performed hot on the heels of the event. In *The New Republican* (1964) and *Before the Blackout* (1965, published in selection in 1971) the targets were various acts of public cowardice and sycophancy performed before both the new time-serving, opportunistic politicians and Nigeria's traditional rulers, portrayed in the sketches either as lecherous rogues or as corrupt feudal chieftains who had betrayed their people throughout history.

Soyinka, however, acknowledged in his preface to *Before the Blackout* the familiar paradox of the satirist: the acute topicality of the material made it libelous in print and dangerously open to political reprisal, but once its targets were dead or dethroned and it ceased to be a threat, it also ceased to be topical. Thus those sketches have worn least well in which Soyinka, working on the assumption that wrongs are only correctable if identifiable, attacked the individual villain rather than the villainy and took little trouble to camouflage his identity. Possible afterthoughts on the short life of close-range satire prompted him, in his prefatory comments, to leave loopholes for updating and contemporary adaptation, and it is significant that the most enduring and most frequently revived of these sketches make no specific contemporary references (notably, the perennially popular *Childe Internationale,* in which a traditional Yoruba father takes in hand his affected been-to wife and his obnoxious daughter, outrageously Americanized by one of the new international schools).[2] The issues raised by this form of satire served as an example, and also as a warning, for Soyinka's later work in the "shotgun" mold, to which he returned in the midseventies.

The year 1975, which brought *Death and the King's Horseman* and Soyinka's return to Nigeria after five years in exile, was something of a watershed in his dramatic career. About this time, whether in response to the exigencies of the worsening political situation or to the pressures of criticism leveled at his work by the Nigerian Left, the dramatist chose to strip from his drama its complex ritual and mythological idiom and informing Yoruba world view in favor of the subversive, agitprop satiric revue, written for performance rather than for publication. This more popular form was adopted for the purpose of urgent political communication with a mass audience, and the works written in it, usually published some years after production and in some case not at all, are theatrical amphibians with one foot in the textual world of Western drama and the other in the improvisational comic folk theater, or *alawada,* of the Yoruba world. Whereas the 1960s revue sketches left occasional loopholes for topical adaptation, this later work was much looser in structure and more openly experimental in approach. "The text of the play was never completely written as it was ever being rewritten and reshaped during rehearsals," Yemi Ogunbiyi has said of Soyinka's production of *Opera Wonyosi* (1977). "Nothing was finally arrived at until the play closed. . . . For him [Soyinka] the text, even his own text, was merely a map with many possible routes."[3] This largely unscripted, hit-and-run kind of street theater, targeting specific political enormities, mounted with minimal publicity, and vanishing before the players could be rounded up by the police of the latest repressive regime, maintained a topical commentary which was best suited to the raw atmosphere of the

marketplace and lorry park. "The cosy, escapist air of formal theatres tends to breed amnesia much too quickly," Soyinka had remarked of his earlier sketches of the 1960s.[4]

Over the next decade the links between Soyinka's theatrical and political involvements were to be particularly close, and the "shotgun" satires, running a constant caustic calypso on public affairs, were a frontline force in the responses to Nigeria's succession of political and economic crises and subsequent scandals and outrages: shrinking oil revenues, plunging foreign exchange, the chronic shortage of books and information, and multiplying ministerial embezzlements and political murders. Sometimes pointedly Nigerian in reference, as in *Before the Blowout* (1978) and *Priority Projects* (1983), and sometimes concerned with evils on the African continent at large, as in *Opera Wonyosi,* the revue satires have in their favor the urgent relevance of their political comment and the spontaneity of the theatrical "happening," with its capacity for surprise, shock, and audience involvement. In their published form, however, they inevitably suffer from a limiting topicality and ephemerality. Performance here has priority, and when the works' virtuoso satiric techniques are allowed to interfere with the dramatic integrity of fully-crafted stage plays, the results are apt to be disappointing: a satiric meanness of characterization, instanced in the mechanical lining up and wheeling on of slight and unsubstantial targets (*Requiem for a Futurologist,* 1985); and a linguistic flatness and general thinness of texture (*A Play of Giants,* 1984), the more noticeable after the verbal richness and somber grandeur of *Death and the King's Horseman.* The invasion of Soyinka's stage drama by the styles and techniques of the opportunistic satiric revue has, I suspect, had much to do with the marked dilution of the substance and quality of his later dramatic writing.

Opera Wonyosi, a ballad opera first performed in 1977 but not published until 1981, is the most substantial and sustained of these satires. With the aid of an eclectic medley of English ballads, Kurt Weill songs, jazz and blues, and the tunes of the 1950s Ibo folk singer Israel Ijemanze, Soyinka transposes the eighteenth-century London of Gay's *Beggars' Opera* and the Victorian Soho of Brecht's *Threepenny Opera* to a bidonville of Bangui, capital of the former Central African Republic, on the eve of the imperial coronation of Jean-Bedel Bokassa, who was to be overthrown two years later when his involvement in the murder of schoolchildren became widely known. The obscenely decadent extravaganza of Bokassa's coronation in one of Africa's poorest countries, which took place in the same week as Soyinka's Ife production, substitutes for the royal jubilee that forms the background to the action in the Gay and Brecht originals and provides Macheath with his royal reprieve at the climax. (Significantly, in Soyinka's African version, the royal pardon which liberates vicious criminals is not extended to political detainees.) The emperor "Boky," or "Folksy Boksy," a crazy caricature of feudal barbarism mixed with servile, sentimental Francophilia, makes one unforgettable appearance in the play, during which he drills and clubs senseless his goon squad before stomping off to "pulp the brains" of the children who have refused to wear his uniforms. The motley collection of rogues and thugs who make up the cast of *Opera Wonyosi,* however, are Nigerian expatriates. These are the "beggarly" racketeers of Chief Anikura (the Peachum of the original); the venal police chief and security expert "Tiger" Brown, on loan to the emperor; the psychopathic Colonel Moses, military adviser to the same; and the thieves, arsonists, drug peddlers, and murderers gathered around the highway robber Macheath. Lest the audience jump to the conclusion that the Nigerian military regime has exported all of its undesirable elements, however, it is made clear at the outset that the expatriate cliques of the Nigerian quarter are meant to serve as a satiric microcosm of the home country during the oil boom of the seventies. In a program note Soyinka insisted that "the genius of race portrayed in this opera is entirely, indisputably and vibrantly Nigerian."

Preferring Gay's ebullient indictment of specific historical vices and corruptions to Brecht's portrayal of universal human depravity, Soyinka uses the wisecracking cynicism of the expatriate scoundrels to draw up a ghastly inventory of Nigerian outrages in the years of the oil dollar or "petro-naira": government-sponsored extortion and assassination; arson and atrocities by a power-drunk soldiery (notoriously, the burning down of Fela Kuti's "Kalakuta Republic"); the public flogging of traffic offenders and execution of felons; murderously punitive industrial conditions in government cement works and levels of state responsibility so low that month-old corpses were left to decompose on public highways; and a general craze for wealth which was epitomized by the wearing of the gaudy *wonyosi,* the absurdly ragged-looking but fantastically expensive lace that was the rage of the tasteless Nigerian nouveaux riches in the 1970s. (Ogunbiyi points out that, accented in a certain way, *opera* in Yoruba can mean "the fool buys.")[5]

Anikura's beggars are, of course, more than what they seem, and their feigned physical deformities are more than distant symbolic allusions to the moral deformation of their country. Among the ragged band are lawyers, professors, doctors, and clergymen whose begging is used by Soyinka as a precise metaphor for the shameless sycophancy to "khaki and brass," the groveling in military gutters by which the professional classes won preferment and promotion during the years of "nairomania" ("Khaki is a man's best friend," runs the refrain of one song). Sycophancy, backed up by

coercion, is the way to a slice of the national cake. In the words of the garrulous Dee-Jay, who replaces Gay's beggarly poet and Brecht's Moritatensänger, "That's what the whole nation is doing—begging for a slice of the action. . . . Here the beggars say, 'Give me a slice of action, or—give me a slice off your throat.'"[6] But Soyinka literalizes his metaphors, and labors them somewhat, by having his mendicant professionals turn professional mendicants. Professor Bamgbapo, who has "bagged" the chairmanships of a number of industrial corporations as well as his university chair by "sucking up to the army boys" ("To beg is to bag," runs the beggars' anthem), has even come to Anikura for "a refresher course" in the form of fieldwork with full-time beggars! (65) Thus the street beggars become synonymous with fawning bureaucrats, and the small crooks actually turn into big ones before our eyes. Anikura, the brain behind the beggars' protection racket (a "beneficent society for the relief of burdened consciences"), is "chairman of highly successful groups of companies," while Polly plays the stock market and, if we can believe it, amalgamates Macheath enterprises with a multinational corporation: "Let's go legitimate like the bigger crooks" (46, 62, 66). However, though the links between legal business practice and crime, and between capitalism and gangsterdom, are certainly present, Soyinka's play is not the assault on capitalism which Brecht meant his to be; instead it is essentially a satire on power. The culprit is the oil-produced wealth that promoted power and the target the criminal lengths to which people were prepared to go to get the money that would buy them power.

Opera Wonyosi is devastating, merciless satire, and the government's prompt intervention to prevent a Lagos production was proof that the play had struck powerfully home. There are odd moments of pure hilarity (Anikura's reference to the American habit of "pleading the Fifth Commandment"), and the dialogue crackles with verbal play ("While Mackie and Brown were ripping the insides of foes" in the civil war, the notorious corpse-stripping "attack traders" were "ripping off both sides"), but the sugar coating on the bitter satiric pill is usually very thin (71, 43). Sometimes the tone is brash, swaggering cynicism in the Brechtian mode, as in Macheath's remark that the stupidity in a Nigerian can be only temporary or feigned because "the smell of money endows the dumbest Nigerian with instant intelligence," or Anikura's comment that fraud by one's fellow countrymen is an infallible alibi for destitution, since everyone knows "that any Nigerian will rob his starving grandmother and push her in the swamp" (54, 4). The latter threatens to have an army of real beggars march on coronation day, not to embarrass tyranny with poverty but to blackmail it into arresting his personal enemy Macheath. At other times the satire is pure vitriolic rage, as in the Bangui equivalent of the Bar Beach Show at Mackie's execution, where schoolchildren are given a holiday to watch the spectacle on television and a deathbed patient from the hospital falls over his wheelchair in righteous bloodlust for a ringside seat and promptly bursts into a gruesome parody of Donald Swann's "Hippopotamus Song": "Blood, blood, glorious blood / Nothing quite like it for offering to God / Banish the gallows / So I can wallow / In the crimson juice of the criminal sod!" (78). Reality here seems always one step ahead of satiric invention, and the unspeakable needs little enhancement from the writer to provoke a sense of outrage.

The terrorizing of civilian populations by megalomaniacal military buffoons and the squalid compliance of the professional classes, cowed by a mendicant mentality, were the painful Nigerian and African realities of the 1970s, and satire targeted at them walks the fine edge between the real and the surreal. Soyinka stated in the playbill to the 1977 Ife production that "the characters in this opera are either strangers or fictitious, for Nigeria is stranger than fiction, and any resemblance to any Nigerian, living or dead, is purely accidental, unintentional and instructive."[7] The repellent historical originals of characters like Boky, more grotesque than any invention, have a way of parodying themselves, but even in the case of the more generalized Nigerian material the preposterous reality keeps breaking through at unexpected moments to dissolve the conventional safe divisions between the stage world and the "real" world. The very closeness of these two worlds made possible a number of surprise effects in performance: Soyinka had the "attack trade" women descend into the audience at the interval to sell their grisly wares, and a coffin, ostensibly containing the real corpse scooped from the roadside the previous day by Tai Solarin, was carried by pallbearers into the auditorium, thus implicating everyone in willful blindness to the daily public obscenity. In one performance the shock tactics of the Theater of the Real were even turned against his own actors: on Soyinka's secret instructions, his orchestra halted the opening number so that Professor Bamgbapo (played by a real-life academic) could be dragged from the chorus and, in front of a university audience, thrashed by a figure looking very much like a real-life Nigerian army officer.

Time has, inevitably, taken the sting from the satire in these topical allusions, which call for constant updating, but Soyinka has been equal to the task. One year on he reassembled his beggarly crew on Nigerian soil to satirize political opportunism at the lifting of the ban on political activities and a contemporaneous national wave of car thefts: in the two sketches of *Before the Blowout,* **"Home to Roost"** and **"Big Game Safari,"** Chief Anikura (now Onikura) returns home to pursue the career of a popular philanthropic politician and smuggles in new and stolen cars to sell at inflated prices or use in his electoral campaign (the cars are the "big game,"

hidden in the jungle and hunted down with metal detectors). In a 1983 revival of the opera itself Soyinka dispensed with Colonel Moses altogether, replacing him with a subtle and slippery academic advisor more suited to the civilian government of the Second Republic. This ability to improvise modifications around basic structures of dialogue, song, and mime to suit changing venues and historical contexts is, along with the amount of audience participation, in the best traditions of the traveling mask theater, the *alarinjo,* which name originated, appropriately, as a term of abuse referring to "rogues, vagabonds and sturdy beggars."[8]

The published text of such works can give only slight indication of their effectiveness in performance, but few critics would single out **Opera Wonyosi** as Soyinka's best work. The musical score has not been widely commended, and even within the loose and highly stylized form of the Brechtian play-with-songs, which attempts no naturalistic blend of lyric and action, the plot creaks with some rather obvious devices. Chief among these is Macheath's invalidation of Anikura's charge against him by having the begging fraternity declared a secret society of the kind banned by the Nigerian military regime: the point is simply to set up the satiric tour de force of the beggar-lawyer Alatako, who succeeds in proving that the government is itself a conspiratorial secret society, a cartel created for mass exploitation and terrorization, implemented always by "unknown soldiers." The extreme length of **Wonyosi** draws attention to its episodic, patchwork structure—neither a full-length play nor a series of revue sketches—and the mechanical tying of the action back to the Gay and Brecht originals proves irksome at times. Mackie's sexual intrigues and betrayals are poorly integrated into the anti-Nigerian satire, and, though Macheath's largely allegorical connection with big business hints cynically at the "moral" of the big fish going free, this is but a faint gesture toward exploding the light opera's conventional happy ending. In accordance with the latter, he turns out to be a lovable rogue whom we feel, in some way, deserves to cheat his fate—an impression quite at odds with that conveyed by the local satire that he is a vicious and evil force rotting society from top to bottom. Macheath, in this version as in the Gay and Brecht models, is a rather artificial villain, something of a satiric dead end, and Soyinka's use of the character has a free rein only when he departs from his originals or takes such liberties with them as to make them say something entirely new.

In his foreword to the play Soyinka envisages his task as "the turning up of the maggot-infested underside of the compost heap" as "a prerequisite of the land's transformation" (iv), and he has said elsewhere that if satire is to have any reformist or revolutionary purpose, the satirist must first arouse "a certain nausea towards a particular situation, to arouse them [people] at all to accept a positive alternative when it is offered to them."[9] For Soyinka, the satirist appears to be a kind of purifying *carrier* who, through ridicule and disgust, clears away the junk of the existing order to make possible the construction of an alternative one; it is the role of another—the reformer—to discover that alternative. He does not take the negative view of satire as a social safety valve, having merely therapeutic or cathartic value, but neither does he see it as offering solutions. *Opera Wonyosi* was criticized, somewhat unfairly, by the Nigerian Left for its failure "to lay bare unambiguously the causal historical and socio-economic network of society" and for its lack of "a solid class perspective."[10] Soyinka has replied to these critics that the satirist's business is not exposition but exposure—in this case of the "decadent, rotted underbelly of a society that has lost its direction" (iii)—and that programs of reform and revolutionary alternatives are the province of the social analyst and ideologist, to whose roles the writer's own distinctive vocation is merely complementary (ii-iii).

Still, there are varying depths and densities of exposure, and if there is in *Wonyosi* surprisingly little penetration, for such a long play, of the forces underlying the crimes and corruptions passingly referred to, then the fault is not that exposure is unaccompanied by analysis but that too much is being exposed for anything to be focused very clearly. In the last third of the play the topical references to guilty parties crowd too thick and fast into the text—some speeches are mere lists of suppressed riots, arson, and lootings—and the result is satiric overkill. The opera takes on too many issues, is too thinly all-embracing, and the overall effect is a diffusion of intensity, a kind of satiric tear-gassing instead of a few carefully aimed bullets, more smoke than shot.

Soyinka has always been more of a crusader than a revolutionary, campaigning for selected causes rather than for the total transformation of society, and in the late seventies he advanced some of these causes by directing the Oyo State Road Safety Corps, bombarding the press with letters on police harassment, censorship, and political corruption, and, in 1980, affiliating himself with the short-lived People's Redemption Party. At the launching of his autobiography *Aké* in 1981 he protested that his "faith in an inevitable revolution" had nothing to do with his own actions but was based squarely in the depredations of the Shagari government.[11] Nevertheless, Soyinka's use of his Guerilla Theater Unit to mobilize opinion against the Shagari government and his attempts during the years of the Second Republic (1979-83) to reach a wider audience by experimenting with the more popular mediums of street theater, Gramophone records, and film have all the makings of revolutionary art. *Rice Unlimited* (1981), in which the actors piled sacks marked "rice" in front of a police-guarded House of Assembly, attacked the running down

of food production during the years of oil mania and the subsequent government racketeering in the sale and resale of imported rice, which made staple foodstuffs unavailable or unaffordable for most of the population. Another unpublished collection of sketches, *Priority Projects* (1983), provocatively performed under the nose of Shagari's personal security guards during a presidential visit to the University of Ife, targeted abortive agricultural and building schemes designed to enrich a ruling party in open connivance with business tycoons, police commissioners, and traditional chiefs. In these sketches the nation which the civil war was fought to keep united is seen as really being two countries: "Mr Country Hide and his brother Seek." The big political brother hides millions of naira, pouring them down bottomless pits of extravagance and corruption (the futile digging and filling in of holes is a prevailing image) while his brother on the street searches in vain for some visible return from the reckless spending. Some of the songs from *Priority Projects* appear on Soyinka's hit record *Unlimited Liability Company* (1983). The scandals of the anarchic Shagari administration—illegal currency exportation, private jets and helicopters, criminals appointed to company directorships, arson and massacre, deportation of political opponents, municipal breakdowns resulting in part-time electricity and mountains of uncollected refuse—are mercilessly exposed in their sharp, instantly graspable pidgin lyrics: "You tief one kobo, dey put you in prison / You tief ten million, na patriotism."[12]

This was candidly experimental theater, rehearsing and performing in the public view on street corners, in markets, and in open spaces on university campuses and casually inviting audience participation. It was also dangerously confrontational in its use of guerrilla tactics to deliver bold and brave satire, and Soyinka himself came under some pressure over his record, which quickly made him a household name across the country (government action was taken against radio and television stations which played it). The writer's last word on the Shagari government was the film *Blues for a Prodigal* (Ewuro Productions, 1984), about the political recruitment of scientists as demolition experts to blow up the opposition. Filming commenced in the dying days of the now thoroughly rotten republic but still had to be shot secretly, with minimal scripting and several switches of location to evade the authorities, and to be processed abroad. "We utilized the guerilla tactics of the travelling theatre," Soyinka said in a recent interview.[13] Ironically, the Lagos print of the film was immediately impounded by the security forces of the new military regime, which thus identified itself with the repressions of its civilian predecessor.

Perhaps as a result of overactivity in revue work and in other mediums, Soyinka published only two full-length dramatic works in the eighties, both, predictably, in the "shotgun" mold. Returning, in *Requiem for a Futurologist,*[14] to the theme of religious charlatanism explored in the two earlier *Jero* plays, he pokes fun at the astrologists and parapsychologists who came to exercise considerable influence over public and political life during the Shagari years (the main target was one of Shagari's toadies, the powerful Dr. Godspower Oyewole). The specific model for the play, fully acknowledged by Soyinka in the introductory material, is Swift's satiric prediction and later announcement, in *The Bickerstaff Letters,* of the death of the astrologer John Partridge, who then had great difficulty convincing people that he was still alive. In Soyinka's vision the rogue-futurologist, the Reverend Dr. Godspeak Igbehodan, is caught in the trap of his more cunning protégé Eleazor Hosannah, who, with a view to superseding his master, predicts his death during a television program. As Eleazor has the Godspeak pedigree, everyone instantly believes the prophecy, and when he publishes Godspeak's obituary, an impatient mob of the faithful lays siege to the master's house, determined to pay their last respects and refusing to be swayed in their resolve by any amount of live appearances.

Eleazor, the archmanipulator and master of disguise, tricks his way back into Godspeak's employment under the semblance of the metaphysician Dr. Semuwe, in which guise he causes the hapless Godspeak to doubt the reality of his own existence and to entertain the possibility that he may, after all, be dead. In this cause Eleazor even bribes the local *egungun* to feign recognition of a fellow spirit in Godspeak's figure at the window (no religion is sacred in this play). As the furious mob prepares to storm the house, the bewildered master reluctantly agrees to play dead and lie in state, and the play ends with Semuwe revealing that "everything is under control," becoming Eleazor again and proclaiming himself the reincarnated Nostradamus, a figure who is the source of much comic disquisition in the course of the play.

There is a limited amount of political satire in *Requiem* in the form of parallels between religious and political opportunism. Regimes, like the prophets they refer to and rely upon, promise what they fail to deliver, and cling to power long after their authority has outrun its legitimacy. It was no accident that in the 1985 published version Godspeak's demise is predicted for New Year's Eve 1983, the date of Shagari's downfall. Though the play was written for the celebration of the twentieth anniversary of the University of Ife, Soyinka withdrew it because even its limited political content had drawn the threat of government interference and censorship, and when the play went on a tour of the university campuses, he made a point of opening each performance with a procession of political parties and different religious faiths. There are also a few sideswipes at favorite local abominations, such as "the highly original driving

habits" that provide a roaring trade for the play's undertaker, and some satire at the expense of the death industry itself, notably the Ghanaian "Master Carpenter" who allows his clients' vulgar fantasies of wealth and status to carry over into the grave in the form of designer coffins shaped like their Cadillacs and television sets. The bulk of the satire, however, is reserved for the human gullibility that invests superstitious faith in the pseudoscience of charlatans. Because of their automatic and absolute belief in astrological predictions, the prophet's followers, who know a walking corpse when they see one, are unable to accept the idea that Eleazor has merely pretended that Godspeak is dead: they therefore believe that the master is really dead and pretending to be alive. Thus is Godspeak boxed, farcically, into a corner from which every protest that he is alive is taken to be one more proof that he is dead. Underlying the verbal and visual humor of this situation, and the fantastically credulous newspaper cuttings cited in the introductory paraphernalia, there is the disturbing picture of a society caught in a spiritual malaise, thirsting after illusion and virtually begging to be deceived. (The play, with its multiple disguises and costume changes, is itself a kind of conjuring trick, depicting a world where all is trickery.) Still, whatever its darker implications, *Requiem* is essentially lighthearted and acutely local satiric comedy, disappointingly slight as a stage play (it evolved out of a much shorter radio play) and with the elaborate joke on the life-death inversion carried on perhaps a little too long. If *Requiem* is really, as Soyinka has bemusingly claimed, part of a "trilogy of transition," following *The Road* and *Death and the King's Horseman,* then it relates to these two towering achievements as the satyr play related to the tragedy in the Greek festival: as satiric postscript and light counterweight.

A Play of Giants, written for a fully equipped theater and with at least one eye on international audiences, is more substantial fare and represents the author's political satire at its most ferocious. Soyinka gathers under the roof of the Bugaran (meaning Ugandan) embassy in New York, and under the transparent anagrams "Kamini," "Kasco," "Gunema," and "Tuboum," a gruesome quartet of real-life African dictators: Amin, Bokassa, Nguema of Equatorial Guinea, and Mobutu of the Congo. In the first part of the play, while ostensibly sitting for a sculpture for a Madame Tussaud's exhibition, these strutting, gibbering psychopaths explain with sadistic relish how their appetites for power are satisfied, their people terrorized, and their barbaric despotisms maintained: by voodoo (Gunema), cannibalism (Tuboum), and an imperium of "pure power" (Kasco). Kamini, who has no talent for analysis, does not have to speak of power: he *is* power, in its most fearsome and ridiculous embodiment, and never ceases to exercise it.

The play is a succession of Kamini's psychopathic explosions, which, like those of the real Amin, arise from willful misconceptions, the paranoid twisting of trivial offenses, and pure, groundless delusions, such as his bizarre notion that the Tussaud statuettes are really life-size statues intended for the United Nations Building across the road from the embassy. When the Chairman of the Bugara Bank informs him of the World Bank's refusal of further loans and explains that he cannot print any more banknotes because the national currency is worth no more than toilet paper, Kamini has his head flushed repeatedly in the toilet bowl; and when the British sculptor, revealing the true destination of his work, utters the unguarded aside that its subject properly belongs in the Chamber of Horrors, Kamini has him beaten up and maimed. The sculptor represents symbolically the obsolete, lame Western view of Amin—that he was not a dangerous threat but a circus freak whose savagery could be contained like a waxworks horror in a museum—and it is ironically apt that when the sculptor next appears, *he* is a museum piece, gagged and "mummified" in bandages from head to foot.

Kamini's anxiety complexes are not entirely gratuitous, however, for defections of Bugaran diplomats are constantly reported and the mounting crises culminate in the news of a coup in his absence. Instantly assuming that the coup has been engineered by the superpowers, Kamini reacts by taking hostage a group of visiting Russian and American delegates and threatening to unleash rockets and grenades from his embassy arsenal upon the United Nations Building unless an international force is sent to Bugara to crush the uprising. In the fantastic apocalyptic finale the rockets go off and the last light fades on the sculptor, quietly working away at what is now a living chamber of horrors. Kamini, who in Soyinka's prefatory words "would rather preside over a necropolis than not preside at all,"[15] turns his embassy into a fortress and then into a tomb, a pyramidal monument to his own barbaric excesses and the sycophantic self-interest of the West. The final sculpted work is, in fact, Soyinka's play, which catches in their frozen manic gestures the most monstrous manifestations of power ever spawned by the African continent.

Soyinka was one of the first to see through Amin's buffoonery, and from 1975 onward he waged a determined campaign in the African press against the dictator's reign of terror, lambasting Western and African governments and intellectuals who either supported Amin or cultivated a convenient deafness to the horror stories that were emerging from Uganda. In the play the latter forces are represented by the Scandinavian journalist Gudrun, mindlessly devoted to the dictator out of some romantically twisted concept of racial purity, and by the black American academic Professor Batey, who, out of misplaced loyalty to notions of black brotherhood and

pan-Africanism, holds up to the black peoples of the world a mass murderer as a model for emulation. Both play and preface make clear that Kamini and his cronies, like their historical counterparts, are originally the postcolonial products of the Western superpowers. Kasco is a Gaullist, Gunema a Franco-worshiper, and Tuboum a Belgian puppet given to fake Africanization schemes. Kamini is placed in power by the British, financed by the Americans, armed by the Russians (until they refuse him an atom bomb to drop on his socialist neighbor), eulogized by the Western press which had unseated his predecessor, and finally deserted by all of them when support for insane African dictators is no longer in their interest. *A Play of Giants* is a surreal fantasia of international poetic justice in which Western support systems catastrophically backfire and the monster runs out of his maker's control: the Russian-supplied weapons are now trained on their own delegations, and the horror comes home to roost in the American sponsor's own back yard.

"I'd rather kill them, but I acknowledge my impotence," Soyinka said of his power-grotesques in an interview at the time of the play's New York production. "All I can do is make fun of them."[16] It is, inevitably, a horrific kind of fun, and they are the more terrifying precisely because their historical originals were once thought to be merely ridiculous comic figures. Soyinka commented in the same 1984 interview that the work was not intended to be "a realistic play," that his "giants" are artificial, composite constructs, endowed with more intelligence, introspection, and eloquence than their originals could muster. Nevertheless, many of their mouthings are reportage material based on original speeches and press statements, and the fantastic virtuoso satirizing of Amin, enough to burst the bounds of any "well-made play," infuses the historical figure's own devilish, manic hysteria into the mood of the play. Soyinka claimed in the interview that the entire rogues' gallery of *A Play of Giants* are "excellent theatrical personalities."[17]

History plus Burlesque does not quite equal Drama, however, and if, as Soyinka remarked, Amin was "the supreme actor," he was a rather obvious, unsubtle one, best suited to broad farce and the 1970s television sketches which made him the constant butt of their satire. The theaters of politics and art are very different. If dramatic effigies of Hitler and Mussolini were put on stage and their mouths stuffed with their speeches and press releases, they would not be much more interesting or authentic as dramatic creations than Soyinka's gruesome foursome. There are odd quirky moments when one of them may spring to life, as in Gunema's chilling, shocking anecdote about his attempt to "taste" the distilled elixir of power by sleeping with the wife of a condemned man and then having them both garrotted. For the rest, they are the vaudeville freaks anticipated by Soyinka's opening circus flourish: "Ladies and Gentlemen, we present . . . a parade of miracle men . . . Giants, Dwarfs, Zombies, the Incredible Anthropophogai, the Original Genus Survivanticus (alive and well in defiance of all scientific explanations)" (*PG* [*A Play of Giants*], x). Cartoon puppets that they are, they burble nonsense and twitch at the behest of every passing sadistic whim and crack of the satiric whip, and the fact that their real-life models were much the same does not make them theatrically viable. Though having just enough distance from contemporary history to work as convincing satiric creations, they are too close to it to succeed as autonomous dramatic ones. The result is that *A Play of Giants,* like so much politically engaged art, is dramatically unengaging.

It is also curiously unpenetrating. In the interview Soyinka expressed the hope that the play would "raise certain intellectual and philosophical questions about power,"[18] and the text tosses a few ideas about. It is suggested that power calls to power, that "vicarious power responds obsequiously to the real thing," and that the "conspiratorial craving for the phenomenon of 'success' . . . cuts across all human occupations," which would explain the professor's admiration of the idiot-tyrant (vi-vii). There is also a hint that the African dictator's power mania is the pathological product of colonialism's long suppression of traditional male authority and the continued taunting of African manhood in the postcolonial world (the Russian diplomat describes Kamini as an "overgrown child"). These suggestions, however, are more in the preface than in the play, which is concerned to deride and debunk, not to analyze. *A Play of Giants* is unflaggingly savage burlesque, but it does not add a great deal to the knowledge of the nature of dictatorship already gleaned from Soyinka's earlier *Kongi's Harvest* (1965) or from *Opera Wonyosi,* and it retains all the usual limitations of its medium. Its claustrophobic set and nervous constricted laughter are, of all these later satires, at the furthest cry from the expansive metaphysical universe of the dramatist's middle period, and for the first time in a Soyinka play there is no music, dance, or mime, indeed not a hint of the visual and aural spectacle of festival theater.

In the late seventies and eighties satire came to constitute Soyinka's characteristic response to Nigeria's and Africa's worsening political crises, and as the bitter-satiric element of his dramatic writing deepened, there was a thinning out of its once rich texture which has not, to date, been repaired. It is perhaps unreasonable at the present time to hope that, after more than a decade's work in this vein, he will return to subjects which, though not necessarily more worthwhile, at least have a greater dramatic viability.

Notes

1. James Gibbs, "Soyinka in Zimbabwe: A Question and Answer Session," *Literary Half-Yearly,* 28:2 (1987), p. 63.

2. This sketch was originally published in Soyinka's *Before the Blackout,* Ibadan, Orisun Acting Editions, 1971. It is now available separately as *Childe Internationale,* Ibadan, Fountain Publications, 1987.

3. Yemi Ogunbiyi, "A Study of Soyinka's *Opera Wonyosi,*" *Nigeria Magazine,* 128-29 (1979), p. 13.

4. Soyinka, preface to *Before the Blackout,* p. 4.

5. Ogunbiyi, p. 3.

6. Wole Soyinka, *Opera Wonyosi,* London, Rex Collings, 1981, p. 1. Further page references are given parenthetically in the text, using the abbreviation *OW* where needed for clarity. For a review, see *WLT* 55:4 (Autumn 1981), p. 718.

7. Quoted in Bernth Lindfors, "Begging Questions in Wole Soyinka's *Opera Wonyosi,*" *Ariel,* 12:3 (1981), p. 31.

8. Joel Adedeji, "'Alarinjo': The Traditional Yoruba Travelling Theatre," in *Theatre in Africa,* Oyin Ogunba and Abiole Irele, eds., Ibadan, Ibadan University Press, 1978, p. 34.

9. Wole Soyinka, "Drama and the Revolutionary Ideal," in *In Person: Achebe, Awoonor, and Soyinka at the University of Washington,* Karen L. Morell, ed., Seattle, Institute of Comparative & Foreign Area Studies/University of Washington, 1975, p. 127.

10. Ogunbiyi, p. 12; Bidun Jeyifo, "Drama and the Social Order: Two Reviews," *Positive Review* (Ile-Ife), 1 (1977), p. 22.

11. Quoted in James Gibbs, "Tear the Painted Masks, Join the Poison Stains: A Preliminary Study of Wole Soyinka's Writings for the Nigerian Press," *Research in African Literatures,* 14:1 (1983), p. 40.

12. *Unlimited Liability Company,* featuring Tunji Oyelana and His Benders with music and lyrics by Wole Soyinka, Ewuro Productions, EWP 001, side 2.

13. Wole Soyinka, interview with Jeremy Harding, *New Statesman,* 27 February 1987, p. 22.

14. Wole Soyinka, *Requiem for a Futurologist,* London, Rex Collings, 1985.

15. Wole Soyinka, *A Play of Giants,* London, Methuen, 1984, p. vii. Further page references are given parenthetically in the text, using the abbreviation *PG* where needed for clarity.

16. Art Borreca, "'Idi Amin Was the Supreme Actor': An Interview with Wole Soyinka," *Theater,* 16:2 (1985), p. 32.

17. Ibid., p. 34.

18. Ibid., p. 36.

Onookome Okome (review date spring 1993)

SOURCE: Okome, Onookome. Review of *From Zia with Love,* by Wole Soyinka. *World Literature Today* 67, no. 2 (spring 1993): 432.

[*In the following review, Okome identifies* From Zia with Love *as one of Soyinka's "power plays," praising the work and commenting that Soyinka has "produced a living text, beautifully structured around the danse macabre and the drama of Nigeria's recent past."*]

Biodun Jeyifo's interview with Wole Soyinka, published in **Six Plays** under Spectrum's logo, has defined clearly a new category of Soyinka's dramatic oeuvre. This new category I wish to refer to as "power plays." The plays within this category deal chiefly with power and politics, the uses and misuses of power, and the politics of power in postcolonial Nigeria and, by extension, Africa. According to this interview, the source of such plays is found in the political *satori* (instant illumination) which Soyinka experienced during the fifties and sixties, a time when many African nations were attaining political self-determination. It was a period of political uncertainty, of gross abuse of power, of ethnic chauvinism, and of blatant corruption. This is the context in which Soyinka wrote **A Dance of the Forest** (1960), **The Republican** (1960), **The New Republican** (1963), **Before the Blackout** (1965), **Kongi's Harvest** (1967), **A Play of Giants** (1984), and now **From Zia with Love.** From the clouds lifting on this morbid political landscape, new techniques of perpetuating mediocrity and the systematic annihilation of the democratic process are being put in place. It is for this reason that these plays are a contestation of our reality, providing the parodic "other" in the discourse of power in contemporary Nigeria.

From Zia with Love is both a painful cry and a warning to those who perpetuate military buffoonery and selfishness in the Nigeria of the present and the very recent past. As is usual with Soyinka, especially since *A Play of Giants,* the main dramatic characters here are based on ousted military leaders—Generals Buhari and Idiagbon—and the event which is dramatized is the most topical in Nigeria's recent history. The central action is the macabre display of arrogance and the unbridled power show that culminated in the killing of several drug peddlers in the mid-eighties following the enactment of a retroactive decree. What is implicit in Soyinka's handling of this "national disgrace," as some have termed it, is not so much the killing of these "cocaine peddlers" as the absolute neglect of human rights which military dictatorships have brought on this country.

The story of **From Zia with Love** is simple enough. A group of megalomaniacs takes over power in Nigeria. This group transforms the nation's complex cultures into a massive cell for everyone, issues draconian decrees, and converts the political system into a fascist outfit. This is only a façade, however, a show purely for public consumption. In "a session in the court of the commandant," with the dramatic dexterity for which he is known, and using music and satire, Soyinka dramatizes the infantility of these "leaders" as they prattle over unserious matters only to issue outrageous decrees. He portrays such characters as laughable, idiotic, and bloodthirsty shadow-chasers. The metaphor of Zia al-Haq, the late Pakistani leader, is clear, representing the misuse of power and the inevitable consequences of such misdeeds.

From the evidence of things seen, Soyinka has produced a living text, beautifully structured around the danse macabre and the drama of Nigeria's recent past. It takes a Soyinka to produce a work such as this. On a very significant level, **From Zia with Love** furthers Soyinka's discourse of power and coloniality. It is fine evidence of Nigeria's political predicament. It is a fine text.

Adebayo Williams (essay date spring 1993)

SOURCE: Williams, Adebayo. "Ritual and the Political Unconscious: The Case of *Death and the King's Horseman.*" *Research in African Literatures* 24, no. 1 (spring 1993): 67-79.

[*In the following essay, Williams explores the function of ritual in* Death and the King's Horseman, *commenting that Soyinka "counterpose[s] the dominant culture of the ancient Oyo kingdom against the equally hegemonic culture of the white invaders."*]

In feudal societies, ritual was part of the cultural dominant. In other words, ritual was part of a complex and insidious apparatus of cultural and political reproduction employed by the dominant groups. It is to be expected, given the superannuation of the feudal mode of production in Western societies, that the phenomenon of ritual itself would have lost much of its power and social efficacy. There is a sense in which this development cannot be divorced from the gains of the Enlightenment and the triumph of rationality. From the eighteenth century, scientific reasoning seemed to have gained ascendancy over the imaginative apprehension of reality. This ascendancy, which also reflected the triumph of the bourgeois world-view in Europe (along with its radical impatience for ancient myths and rituals) received perhaps its classic formulation from Karl Marx. According to him, "all mythology overcomes and dominates and shapes the forces of nature in and through the imagination, hence it disappears as soon as man gains mastery over the forces of nature" (100).

Yet this notwithstanding, it is also obvious that within the context of post-colonial cultural politics, the entire concept of ritual has become a casualty of linguistic imperialism—a Eurocentric, unilinear notion of historical development which negates the other by a forcible evacuation of its space. Thus, in the industrial and scientific age, ritual has acquired the pejorative connotation of a meaningless exercise, a mundane routine. But if any meaningful intellectual encounter between Western societies and the emergent post-colonial cultures of the Third World is to take place, such "emptied" spaces must be recontested with a view to directing people's attention to this profoundly subtle hegemonic assault. To do this is to problematize the very concept of ritual. The first step in this process would be to return ritual to its sacred origins, that is, to see it as an aspect of symbolic thinking which Mircea Eliade regards as sharing the same substance with human existence (*Images* 12). Ritual, then, in the words of Ake Hulkrantz, is a "fixed, usually solemn behaviour that is repeated in certain situations. Anthropologists like to call the latter 'crisis situations,' but there is not always any crisis involved. It would be better to speak of sacred situations in Durkheim's spirit" (136).

For people in pre-industrial societies, rituals served as a vehicle for reestablishing contact with the ontological essence of the tribe. On the sacred nature of rituals, Eliade is again invaluable when he notes that "rituals are given sanctification and rationalization in a culture by being referred to supposedly divine prototypes. Rituals periodically reconfirm the sacredness of their origins and reestablish 'sacred' (as opposed to 'profane') time for the community performing the rituals" (*Myths* 133).

As can be seen from this line of argument, rituals are expressions of human needs and desires; they are also instrumental in satisfying such needs and desires. Since human needs are varied, there will be several prototypes of rituals to take care of them (see Hulkrantz 137). Whatever the form ritual might take, it is clear that human sacrifice is its most severe and extreme form. Several rationales have been advanced to explain the phenomenon of human sacrifice. They range from the need for a reactualization of direct relations between a people and their god to a drive towards the seasonal regeneration of sacred forces. Although the precise function of this undeniably harsh ritual might vary from place to place, it too is a function of social needs.

Many African writers have had recourse to ritual in refuting assumptions about Western cultural superiority. In Chinua Achebe's *Things Fall Apart,* for example, the suicide of Okonkwo is part of a complex ritual of atone-

ment and reassertion of the collective will. In *Arrow of God,* the main crisis is triggered by the imminent repudiation of the sacred ritual of yam-eating. On another level, there is an ideological simulation of ritual suicide in the fate that befalls Clarence, the protagonist in Camara Laye's *The Radiance of the King* and in the horrific mutilations that abound in Yambo Ouologuem's *Bound to Violence.* All these episodes constitute nothing less than the deployment of ritual in a desperate cultural offensive. The mythicization of historical events and prominent figures by some African writers is part of this renewed attempt to discover an authentic African heritage.

But of all these writers, none has been more consistent and unapologetic in the enlistment of ritual for ideological purposes than Wole Soyinka. Soyinka is, by critical consensus, a writer of forbidding depth and complexity. A substantial part of this complexity derives from his deep communion with the cultural paradigms of his people, the Yoruba: their mores, their myths, and above all their rituals. In an insightful appraisal of Soyinka's work, Stanley Macebuh has noted that "for him 'history' has not been so much a record of human action as a demonstration of the manner in which social behaviour so often symbolizes a sometimes voluntary, sometimes unwilling obedience to the subliminal impulse of the ancestral memory" (79). It is not surprising, then, that ritual should play such a crucial role both as an ideological strategy and as a formal category in most of Soyinka's works. A random sample is instructive: the death of Eman, the protagonist of *The Strong Breed*; the killing of the Old Man in *Madmen and Specialists*; the sacrifice of Pentheus in his adaptation of Euripides's *The Bacchae* [*The Bacchae of Euripides: A Communion Rite*]; the mental and physical destruction of Sekoni in *The Interpreters*; and the annihilation of the Professor in *The Road.* All of these incidents have strong ritualistic overtones.

I have analyzed the political implications of Soyinka's penchant for the mythic resolution of actual contradictions as well as the shortcomings of the historicist opposition to this position (Williams "Mythic Imagination"). It is in *Death and the King's Horseman* that we find Soyinka's most explicit deployment of ritual both as an organizing principle and as a surgical instrument for prizing open a people's collective consciousness at a crucial moment of their historical development. The crisis in the play stems from an acute political and psychological threat to the ritual of human sacrifice. This is indeed a critical moment of history, and since the play is a refraction of an actual historical event, it is bound to provide the playwright with an appropriate forum for seminal reflections on a communal impasse. Yet it is important to unravel the deeper ideological necessity behind the ritual in *Death and the King's Horseman,* that is, the actual collective "narrative" of which it is socially symbolic or, to employ the terminology of structural linguistics, the communal "langue" behind the author's "parole." To do this is to inquire into the political reality of the "political unconscious" behind both the social text itself and the playwright's textualization of it in his play.

The idea of a political unconscious as a corollary for the collective consciousness is not a new one. Its hazy outlines can be glimpsed in the works of Sigmund Freud and Carl Jung. In fact, Freud's concept of repression (i.e., the specific mechanism by means of which individuals and societies alike suppress hostile and intolerable truths as a strategy for containing or postponing confrontations with reality) actually foreshadows the theory of the political unconscious.

The political unconscious is inseparable from a theory of culture, for culture, being the material, intellectual, and spiritual totality of a people's way of life, normally sets the pace and the terms for whatever passes into the realm of the political unconscious. But culture itself is always an unstable totality mediated by a whole range of countervailing forces. In a diachronic sense, these forces are often hostile accretions from an earlier cultural mode or developments within the society whose sheer incompatibility with the dominant order might be symptomatic of newer modes struggling to come into existence. Raymond Williams has described these forces as the residual and the emergent.

But the diachronic analysis does not exhaust the possibilities of the countervailing forces. Existing synchronically with the dominant order are tendencies that portend fractures within this order. By virtue of the fact that it is often a reaction to urgent existential dilemmas, the political unconscious is clearly involved with these synchronic forces. Although it is tempting to see the political unconscious as one more instrument for furthering the hegemonic ambitions of the dominant classes, this is not necessarily the case, because the political unconscious has a utopian dimension, enabling it to serve social needs that transcend class barriers. A particular ritual might well serve the political interests of the dominant class, but it can at the same time serve the psychological needs of the dominated class, and in a situation of revolutionary rupture within society, it is possible for the psychological to prevail over the political.

It has been suggested that Freud himself was prevented by a combination of historical and ideological circumstances from realizing the true significance of his great discovery and from pressing it to its logical conclusion. Imprisoned within the self-legitimizing snares of a stable and relatively prosperous bourgeois society, denied the beneficial insight of a major historical rupture within his society, Freud was content with transferring

political and social unease to psychological categories. In other words, Freud himself was a victim of the political unconscious.

In recent times, the most accomplished theorist of the political unconscious is Fredric Jameson, the influential American Marxist scholar. Drawing sustenance from disparate sources including Levi-Strauss, Freud, Foucault, Greimas, Lyotard, and Althusser, Jameson's *The Political Unconscious: Narrative as a Socially Symbolic Act* makes a rigorous case for an overtly political interpretation of all works of art. His thesis is that, since narrative is nothing but a specific mechanism through which the collective consciousness (as expressed through the "parole" of the artist) represses harsh historical contradictions, the overriding task of criticism is to confront the political unconscious of the narrative with the Real.

Two important points emerge from Jameson's approach to the problem. First, he ascribes a collective function to narrative. Appropriating Wittgenstein's seminal insight into the social nature of language, he posits that we cannot imagine a story or indeed its narrator without at the same time imagining the society from which both of them spring. Second, in a direct polemical riposte to conventional Marxists, Jameson avers that the repression of uncomfortable truths is not just a function of the hegemonic classes in human societies, but that it is also adopted by the oppressed as a strategy for survival. In an interesting gloss on this point, William Dowling notes that "for Jameson as a Marxist this is not, of course, some dark, paranoid fantasy: it is the nightmare of history itself as men and women have always lived it, a nightmare that must be repressed as a condition of psychological survival not only the master but also by the slave, not only by the bourgeoisie but also by the proletariat" (118).

Jameson's indebtedness to Levi-Strauss's "The Structural Analysis of Myth" is obvious. In his study of the facial decorations of the Caduveo Indians, Levi-Strauss advances the thesis that the cultural artifact is nothing but the symbolic resolution of a real contradiction, a strategy for containing on the imaginary plane an intolerable concrete dilemma—in this case, the contradictions inherent in a rigidly hierarchical society. Equally obvious is Jameson's indebtedness to Althusser's celebrated definition of ideology as "the imaginary representation of the subject's relationship to his or her real conditions of existence" (132).

For Althusser as for Jameson, ideology is not the monstrous concoction of oppressive classes in oppressive societies; it is a trans-historical and supra-class phenomenon. Ideology is "not just mystification (that is, something that obscures the real relations of things in the world) but essential mystification; one could not imagine a human society without it" (Dowling 83). Althusser's original insight into the dynamics of ideology and Jameson's judicious appropriation of it, constitute a mortal blow to what the latter, in a different context, has dismissed as the "luxury of old-fashioned ideological critique" ("Post-Modernism" 86). Taken together, Althusser and Jameson can be seen to have opened up new frontiers for radical aesthetics and for the possibility of profoundly subtle and sophisticated analyses of an author and his text's insertion within what Althusser has described as the "interpellation" (Resch 534-35).

The political unconscious, then, is the realm of collective day-dreaming or mass fantasy. It is hardly a simple affair, since it involves active struggles on the psychological and political planes. Indeed, it becomes extremely problematic when it involves artistic refractions of what lies within the political unconscious. An artist's relationship with his or her society is often complex, more so if the artist is as politically aware, as culturally conscious, and as intellectually combative as Soyinka. Jameson's cautionary note is instructive. For him, "day-dreaming and wish-fulfilling fantasy are by no means a simple operation, available at any time or place for the taking of a thought. Rather, they involve mechanisms whose inspection may have something further to tell us about the otherwise inconceivable link between desire and history" (*Political Unconscious* 182).

To be sure, Jameson is not without his critics. Some accuse him of confusion and eclectic opportunism both in his theorization of the concept of the political unconscious and in its application of it. According to some of his critics, he often relapses into a theological Marxism by treating arguable hypotheses as "apodictic categories" (Clark 164). Robert Kantor and Joel Weinsheimer make the same point. In perhaps the most sustained statement of these objections, Brom Anderson charges Jameson with "a profoundly apolitical millenarianism" (125). Such objections notwithstanding, the theory of the political unconscious remains a powerful weapon for plotting the dynamics between the surface characteristics of a work of art and its deeper ideological structure.

Within Soyinka's corpus, *Death and the King's Horseman* has achieved the status of a classic. Critics with a formalist bias have hailed its superb characterization, its haunting beauty, and above all its lyrical grandeur, although an oppositional critic such as Biodun Jeyifo has objected to the lyrical beauty of the play on the ideological ground that it seduces us into accepting what he considers to be Soyinka's reactionary worldview in the play. Kyalo Mativo has even gone so far as to observe that "when great form is not in service of great content, it is fraud" (135). I have addressed these objections elsewhere ("Marxian Epistemology" and

"Marxism"), but whatever the case might be, even the objections reinforce the consensus view that the play is possibly the most intensely poetic of all Soyinka's dramatic writings.

Written during a period of exile and existential anguish, the play derives its powerful dynamics from Soyinka's first attempt to grapple directly on the creative level with the "colonial question"—a question that obsessed his literary peers on the continent for over two decades. The playwright's contemptuous dismissal of "hidebound chronologues" notwithstanding, *Death and the King's Horseman* is the creative equivalent of a return of the repressed. In this play, Soyinka manages to capture the power and glory of the ancient Yoruba state in its dying moment. At the same time, he poses a serious intellectual challenge to those who would deny a conquered people their unique mode of apprehending and making sense of reality.

Death and the King's Horseman represents an attempt to confront on a creative level the arrogance and cultural chauvinism of Western imperialism. Soyinka himself has taken umbrage at the "reductionist tendency" that views the dramatic tension in his play as having arisen from "a clash of cultures." According to him, this "prejudicial label . . . presupposes a potential equality *in every given situation* of the alien culture and the indigenous, on the actual soil of the latter" ("Author's Note"). The bitterly polemical tone of this rebuttal illustrates the extent to which Soyinka's threnodic temperament is affronted by mundane cultural equations. Yet by exploring the sacred terror of ritual suicide within the context of the cynicism and cultural dessications of the colonialists, Soyinka is engaged in nothing less than a sublime cultural battle. By counterposing the notion of honor in the ancient Yoruba kingdom (as seen in the tragic career of its principal custodian of culture) against the cynical presumptions and calculations of the colonial officials, Soyinka exposes the absurdity inherent in all assumptions of cultural superiority.

Death and the King's Horseman opens with a grand panorama of the Yoruba market place. Here, Soyinka deploys all his artistic power to paint a picture of grandeur and vitality. According to an old Yoruba saying, "The world is a market place; heaven is home." Apart from its obvious economic importance, the market occupies a signal cultural, political, and spiritual position in the Yoruba cosmos. First, it is a site of political and cultural ferment. Second, it doubles as that numinous zone in which the distinction between the world of the dead and that of the living is abolished. The ancient Yoruba saying captures this crucial contiguity. In most Yoruba towns, the evening market is regarded as the most important, and before the advent of electricity, it was a most eerie sight indeed. Moreover, the market serves as a barometer for the spiritual and psychic health of the community. The most important communal rites are carried out there. It was therefore a stroke of genius to focus on the market place at the beginning of the play. But even here there is a profound irony, for what is going on between the indigenous culture and the alien culture runs counter to the natural logic of the market—a forum for buying and selling. We are confronted with the bizarre phenomenon of a culture that insists upon forcing its hardware on another culture without making a commensurate purchase in return.

The crisis in the play is thus predicated on what is known in economics as a trade imbalance or as a trade deficit between the conqueror's culture and that of the conquered. The praise-singer, in a moving dialogue with Elesin, captures the angst and spiritual anguish of his people:

> Our world was never wrenched from
> Its true course . . . [I]f that world leaves
> its course and smashes on the boulders
> of great void, whose world will
> give us shelter?
>
> (17)

Behind the unease and anguish of this intensely poetic lamentation lie the sympathies of the playwright himself. His very choice of images, "wrench," "boulders," and "void" betrays a starkly apocalyptic mood.

Against this turbulent background one must situate the vexatious dynamics that transform Elesin, an otherwise minor cultural functionary of the ruling class, into a world-historic role as the deliverer of his people. Precisely because his suicide is supposed to compel respect for the integrity and inviolability of a besieged culture, Elesin's routine function takes on a major historical and political burden. For the people, the success or failure of the ritual therefore becomes a matter of life and death. Here is the classic example of a particular ritual that, under historical pressure, transcends its original cultural signification to assume a greater political and spiritual significance.

Yet, if historical circumstances compel a particular ritual to serve purposes more complex than its original ones, how can the same circumstances transform a minor figure into a major historical personage? Indeed, the reverse is often the case. Karl Marx's brilliant comparison of the two Bonapartes comes to mind: "[The French] have not only a caricature of the old Napoleon, they have the old Napoleon himself, caricatured as he must appear in the middle of the nineteenth century" (98). In an interesting gloss on this passage, Terry Eagleton observes: "Bonaparte is not just a parody of Napoleon; he is Napoleon parodying himself. He is the real thing dressed up as false, not just the false thing tricked out as real. What is in question now is not a regressive caricature but a caricaturing regression" (166-67).

So it is with Elesin. And this is the source of the collective and individual tragedy in *Death and the King's Horseman.* Elesin's consciousness has been shaped by the dialectic of his material and political circumstances. If he appears weak, vacillating, self-pitying, self-dramatizing, and self-indulgent, it is because the old Empire has exhausted itself. If he is cynically preoccupied with pleasure and the spoils of office, if he is skeptical about the credibility of his destiny, his attitude is not unrelated to the fact that the hegemony of the empire had long ago been fissured by internal contradictions as well as by the antagonistic logic supplied by the conquering invaders. As evident in the play, the crumbling empire has already been thoroughly infiltrated by the "other" empire and its various fetishes of political authority and cultural power: batons, bands, balls, cells, gramophones, etc. In a rather resentful categorization of the opulence of the Residency, Soyinka comes close to the truth when he describes it as being "redolent of the tawdry decadence of a far-flung but key imperial frontier" (45).

In its dying moment, the empire can only produce an Elesin, a pathetic but ultimately subversive caricature of his illustrious forebears. In the light of this insight, it is difficult to agree with Jeyifo when he asserts that "the play never really dramatises either the force of Elesin's personality or the inevitability of his action" (32). In actuality, there is no force to dramatize; it is absent from Elesin's personality. It is paradoxical that a Marxist critic should slip into the bourgeois notion that history and literature are no more than the study of the acts of great men. A genuinely materialist aesthetics must not be fixated on great personalities; on the contrary, it must strive to relocate personalities within the social and historical forces which engendered them in the first instance. The character of Elesin is an acute reflection of these forces at play.

In this context, it would be utopian to expect him, a critically misendowed man, to surmount the overwhelming historical and social forces ranged against him. To expect such an act is to expect the impossible. That the playwright fails to recognize this fact demonstrates the extent to which his own imagination has been colored by the lingering efficacy of the ideological apparatus of the old Yoruba state. Indeed, in an attempt to resist the mundane forces of concrete history, Soyinka is compelled to look beyond Elesin to his son, Olunde, who is perhaps the most sensitively drawn character in the play. He is the ideological spokesman for the playwright, who is obviously in profound sympathy with the young man's aspirations. Olunde's material and historical circumstances are quite different form his father's. He is armed with immense personal courage and conviction; and his considerable intellect has been honed by a sustained contact with the alien culture in all its contradictions and foibles. He is therefore a perfect match and counterfoil to the arrogance and chauvinism of the colonial administrators. As he tells Mrs. Pilkings: "You forget that I have now spent four years among your people. I discovered that you have no respect for what you do not understand" (50). In another cutting riposte, he exclaims with bitter irony, "You believe that every thing which appears to make sense was learnt from you" (53).

Consumed by his contempt and hatred for the hypocrisy and cant of Western civilization, bewildered by his father's lack of honor, Olunde chooses suicide as a means of redeeming the honor of his society and of expiating what must have seemed to him as his father's abominable cowardice and treachery. But rather than alleviating the burden of the people, Olunde's suicide only compounds their misery. The praise-singer again captures this moment of historic stress:

What the end will be, we are not
gods to tell. But this young shoot has
poured its sap into the parent stalk,
and we know this is not the way
of life. Our world is tumbling in
the void of strangers.

(75)

Yet despite the enormous integrity of Olunde's self-sacrifice, it is difficult to identify the point at which his role as a cultural hero ends and where his role as the rearguard defender of a backward-looking political order prevails. But Soyinka does not leave us in doubt as to his conviction that, if suicide is the ultimate option available to Africa's revolutionary intelligentsia in the struggle for a cultural revalidation of the continent, it must be embraced without flinching.

This position engenders profound ideological difficulties. To start with, it lays itself open to the charge of promoting a cult of romantic suicide. To leftwing critics, Olunde, by terminating his own life, has succumbed to the whims of a reactionary culture and a flagrantly feudalistic ethos. Indeed, for critics of this persuasion, there might be something paradoxically progressive in Elesin's refusal to honor his oath. Jeyifo is precise and uncompromising on this point. According to him, "The notion of honour (and integrity and dignity) for which Soyinka provides a metaphysical rationalisation rests on the patriarchal, feudalist code of the ancient Oyo kingdom, a code built on class entrenchment and class consolidation" (34).

It is necessary at this point to probe further, to "problematize" these various antithetical positions. The first step towards accomplishing this goal will be to counterpose Jameson's doctrine of the political unconscious against Jeyifo's instrumentalist Marxist objection to Soyinka's ideological thrust. As it is, the Elesin ritual is

a projection of a people's collective consciousness. Elesin's suicide is designed to facilitate the smooth transition of the departing king from the world of the living to the world of the dead. Even for departing royalties, solitude might be a terrifying prospect in what Soyinka himself often somberly refers to as the "the abyss of transition." As the Iyaloja, the unwavering matriarch of culture and tradition, explains:

He knows the meaning of a king's passage;
he was not born yesterday. He knows
the peril to the race when our dead
father who goes as intermediary,
waits and waits and knows he is
betrayed. . . . He knows he has condemned our king
 to wander in
the void of evil with beings who are enemies of life.

(71)

In Yoruba culture, a king never "dies." A king wandering "in the void" is therefore an abomination, a serious threat to life and communal well-being. Thus, insofar as Elesin's suicide is conceived to usher the departed king into his new kingdom, it is a crucial ritual of continuity, well-being, and hope; hence, the collective anxiety about the dire consequences of its abortion. Yet as Jameson has contended, a political unconscious always coexists uneasily with even the most apparently innocent manifestations of a people's collective consciousness. The question then becomes: What is the political unconscious behind Elesin's ritual and Soyinka's fabulization of it? In other words, what is the historical contradiction for which the Elesin ritual is supposed to be a symbolic resolution?

On one level, the ritual suicide of Elesin is supposed to take the sting out of the trauma of death by enacting the drama of a privileged carrier who willingly undertakes the journey to the unknown. This act in itself might serve to assuage the people's collective anxiety about being forsaken as a result of the departure of the father of the "tribe." On another level, the ritual might well signify a symbolic conquest of death itself. For in the absence of viable oppositional forces in the community, Death becomes the distinguished scourge and ultimate terror of the ruling class: unconquerable, unanswerable, firm, unsmiling.

The Elesin ritual, then, magically transforms death into an ally of the rulers. In death, the power and grandeur of the rulers remain. The transition of individual kings is thus immaterial: the kingdom remains unassailable. Erich Auerbach regards the poetry of Homer as performing analogous functions for the ancient Greek aristocracy. According to him: ". . . rather than an impression of historical change, Homer evokes the illusion of an unchanging society, a basically stable order, in comparison with which the succession of individuals and changes in personal fortunes appear unimportant" (42).

Similarly, the Elesin ritual is designed to reconcile the people of the ancient Oyo empire to the supremacy, invincibility, and divine nature of what is essentially a feudal society. It is a socially symbolic act insofar as it negotiates the painful reality of death for the ruling class. Hence, the ritual suicide is one of those insidious strategies of survival and containment that Althusser has characterized as an ideological apparatus of the state. It is the political unconscious behind the Elesin ritual in *Death and the King's Horseman.*

Seen from this perspective, Jeyifo's objection is not without merit. *Death and the King's Horseman* does provide metaphysical rationalization for a patriarchal and feudalist code. The play's complicity with this order is obvious in the sense that the playwright accepts the ritual as a communal necessity. But it is not just the dominant classes that fear death. The terror of death is a common denominator in all societies; it is therefore a supra-class phenomenon. Returning to Althusser's definition of ideology, this particular maneuver of the ruling class is an essential mystification, ultimately beneficial to the entire society.

It is this utopian dimension of the Elesin ritual that Soyinka's leftwing critics have failed to comprehend. While recognizing the power and urgency of negative hermeneutics within the Marxist critical enterprise, Jameson argues that the ultimate task of Marxist criticism is to restore the utopian dimension to the work of art, that is, to view the work of art as an expression of some ultimate collective urge while not overlooking "the narrower limits of class privilege which informs its more immediate ideological vocation" (*Political Unconscious* 288). Jameson's conclusion bears quoting at length:

> Such a view dictates an enlarged perspective for any Marxist analysis of culture, which can no longer be content with its demystifying vocation to unmask and to demonstrate the ways in which a cultural artifact fulfils a specific ideological mission, in legitimating a given power structure . . . but [which] must also seek through and beyond this demonstration of the instrumental function of a given cultural object, to project its simultaneously utopian power as the symbolic affirmation of a specific historical and class form of collectivity.
>
> (291)

Jameson's theory has nothing to do with Durkheim's conservative notion of religious and ritual practice as a symbolic affirmation of unity in all collective entities. The failure of Durkheim's theory stems from its fixation on the utopian impulse, a fixation that overlooks the division of all societies into dominant and dominated groups. The obverse of this inadequate approach is any criticism that simply rewrites or allegorizes a work of art in terms of Marx's insight into history as an arena of conflicts between opposing classes.

In the final analysis, what Soyinka accomplished in *Death and the King's Horseman* was to counterpose the dominant culture of the ancient Oyo kingdom against the equally hegemonic culture of the white invaders. His strategy is a brilliant, decolonizing venture. In an age characterized by new forms of cultural domination that result from the economic marginalization of the third world, such an approach might well represent a more pressing project than analyzing the class content of indigenous cultures. In a perceptive critique of Jeyifo's position on *Death and the King's Horseman,* Gareth Griffins and David Moody conclude:

> The issue here is less the correctness of Soyinka's choice of subject or of the revolutionary character of the "class" of his protagonists than the project which the choice of subject and protagonist serve. It seems to us that Soyinka's is a profoundly de-colonising project, and that Jeyifo has lost sight of this in his demand that an alternative (although not actually opposed) project be undertaken by African writers. . . . However, the route forward in Nigeria, as in all post-colonial societies, is in part through a preservation of what Soyinka has called "self-apprehension."
>
> (81)

In *Death and the King's Horseman,* then, the playwright is an unabashed horseman ("Elesin" in the Yoruba language) of a besieged culture, fighting a desperate battle against the cultural "other." In such turbulent circumstances, he could not direct his gaze at the inequities of the traditional hierarchy, lest his resolve be weakened; neither could he bring himself to recognize that the culture he was defending had already succumbed to the alienating necessity of history, lest the rationale for mustering a stiff resistance disappear. This conflict is the political unconscious of the writer himself, and it shows its classic manifestation—Soyinka's prefatory protestations notwithstanding—in this imaginary resolution of a concrete cultural dilemma.

By the same token, his radical critics are also complicit horseman of the cultural and post-colonial "other." For by insisting on the decadent and oppressive nature of the indigenous culture, they are in ideological collusion with that genetic evolutionism and naively unilinear historicism that seeks to justify the cultural, economic, and political atrocities of colonialism as the inevitable consequence of historical "progress." This is the corollary of the teleological fallacy which regards any capitalist formation as an automatic advancement on all indigenous economic formations. It is the cardinal sin of the founding father of Marxism himself. That Karl Marx, despite his initial unease, eventually made his peace with a flagrantly bourgeois notion of historical development shows the extent to which his own sensibility was steeped in the ideological constellations of the nascent capitalist age.

Eagleton has defined succinctly Marx's epistemological impasse. According to him, "In his effort to theorize historical continuities Marx finds the evolutionist problematic closest to hand, but it is clear that it will not do. For you do not escape a naively unilinear historicism merely by reversing its direction" ("Ideology" 73). This lapse of consciousness in all its smug Eurocentric complacency demonstrates how all master narratives, including Marxism, are dogged by a political unconscious which derives from the logic of their own insertion into the historical process. It is the urgent task of all genuinely revolutionary post-colonial discourses to smuggle themselves into this gap in colonial narratives with a view to exploding their internal contradictions. ***Death and the King's Horseman*** fulfils this historic obligation. Whatever its complicity with the indigenous ruling class might be, the importance of Soyinka's classic for a viable post-colonial cultural and political praxis lies in this achievement.

Works Cited

Anderson, Brom. "The Gospel according to Jameson." *Telos* 74 (1987-88): 116-25.

Althusser, Louis. *Lenin and Philosophy and Other Essays*. London: NLB, 1971.

Auerbach, Erich. *Mimesis: The Representation of Reality in Western Literature*. New York: Doubleday, 1957.

Clark, Michael. "Putting Humpty Together Again: Essays toward Integrative Analysis." Rev. of Fredric Jameson, *The Political Unconscious: Narrative as a Socially Symbolic Act* and *Power/Knowledge: Selected Interviews and Other Writings 1972-1977. Poetics Today* 3.1 (1982): 159-70.

Dowling, William C. *Jameson, Althusser, and Marx: An Introduction to the Political Unconscious*. London: Methuen, 1984.

Eagleton, Terry. *Walter Benjamin; Or towards a Revolutionary Criticism*. London: NLB, 1981.

———. "Ideology, Fiction and Narrative." *Social Text* 1 (1979): 32-83.

Eliade, Mircea. *Images and Symbols*. New York: Sheed and Ward, 1969.

———. *Myths, Rites, Symbols: A Mircea Eliade Reader.* Ed. W. C. Beane and W. Doty. New York: Harper and Row, 1976.

Griffiths, Gareth and David Moody. "Of Marx and Missionaries: Soyinka and the Survival of Universalism in Post-Colonial Literary Theory." *After Europe: Critical Theory and Post-Colonial Writing*. Ed. Stephen Slemon and Helen Tiffin. Sidney: Dangaroo, 1989. 74-85.

Hultkrantz, Ake. "Ritual in Native American Religious." *Native Religious Tradition*. Ed. E. H. Wlish and K. Printhipaul. Waterloo: Laurier UP, 1979. 24-38.

Jameson, Fredric. *The Political Unconscious: Narrative as a Socially Symbolic Act*. Ithaca: Cornell UP.

———. "Post-Modernism or the Cultural Logic of Late Capitalism." *New Left Review* 146 (1984): 53-92.

Jeyifo, Biodun. *The Truthful Lie: Essays in a Sociology of African Drama*. London: New Beacon Books, 1985.

Kandor, Robert. Rev. of *The Political Unconscious. Telos* 51 (1982): 206-24.

Macebuh, Stanley. "Poetics and the Mythic Imagination." *Transition* 50 (1976).

Mativo, Kyalo. "Ideology in African Philosophy and Literature." *Ufahumu* 7 (1978): 132-81.

Marx, Karl. *Grundrisse*. London: Basil Blackwell, 1975.

Soyinka, Wole. *Death and the King's Horseman*. London: Methuen, 1975.

Resch, Robert Paul. "Modernism, Postmodernism, and Social Theory: A Comparison of Althusser and Foucault." *Poetics Today* 10.3 (1989): 511-49.

Weinsheimer, Joel. Rev. of Fredric Jameson, *The Political Unconscious: Narrative as A Socially Symbolic Act. Conradiana* 2 (1982): 131-35.

Williams, Adebayo. "The Mythic Imagination and Social Theory: Soyinka and Euripides as Political Thinkers." *Okike* 20 (1982): 36-44.

———. "Marxian Epistemology and the Criticism of African Literature." *Ufahumu* 8.1 (1983): 84-103.

———. "Marxism and the Criticism of African Drama." *ODU* 28 (1985): 103-21.

Williams, Raymond. *Culture*. London: Fontana, 1983.

Adewale Maja-Pearce (review date 24 February 1995)

SOURCE: Maja-Pearce, Adewale. "Soyinka's Faith in the Future." *Times Literary Supplement*, no. 4795 (24 February 1995): 27.

[*In the following review, Maja-Pearce praises Soyinka's honesty and insight in* Ibadan: The Penkelemes Years: A Memoir, 1946-65, *noting that the work "is an act of faith in the possibilities of the future, written with the authority of one who has experienced the worst of those years."*]

In 1965, at the height of the political crisis in the then Western Region of Nigeria, Wole Soyinka entered the state-controlled radio station and forced the bewildered broadcasters—at gun-point—to play a pre-recorded tape announcing the true results of the recent elections, then in the process of being rigged by the government of the day. Whatever else, the future Nobel laureate could hardly be accused of lacking physical courage. He was subsequently charged with armed robbery, and was lucky to be freed on a technicality, but those were the days when Nigerian High Court judges were still able to resist the machinations of a political class determined, in Soyinka's words, "to wallow in the abandoned privileges of the departing colonial masters". Unfortunately, his gesture proved futile. "Who needs the people to vote for us?" declared one of the leading members of the ruling party, whereupon chaos ensued and the Western Region, together with the rest of the country, was plunged into a three-year civil war.

In the foreword to [*Ibadan: The Penkelemes Years: A Memoir, 1946-65*], his second volume of autobiography, Soyinka explains that he had previously resisted the temptation to write a sequel to *Aké: The Years of Childhood* (1982), on the grounds that any "testament after the age of innocence is a lie, or half-truth", but that his eventual change of mind "came from the politics, the unfinished business, of that political entity . . . into which I happen to have been born, its sociology and political pathology", and with it "the agonising, truly lamentable brief memory span that appears to bedevil my society". The immediate reason behind his volte-face was the annulled elections of June 1993, in which the military, after a decade of uninterrupted power, behaved with the same "contempt" and "hubris" as their civilian predecessors thirty years earlier; the fire this time, Soyinka believes, will not only be civil war but the dismemberment of the Nigerian nation.

The seeds of the continuing crisis were already apparent even before the country attained independence from British rule in 1960. As a student in London in the late 1950s, Soyinka had been eager to make contact with members of the various Nigerian official delegations who had come to negotiate the transfer of power from Britain. In each case, as he met the different delegates, he realized that all was not well:

> Flamboyant, egotistical and extravagant, they turned up with or without reason, with baggage and entourage far in excess of their mission, cultivated students who would bring them girls to sleep with, whom they would reward extravagantly. . . . Those politicians wooed student leaders with material gifts and promises, exhorted them to return, not so much for service as to ensure that they were the first in line for the vacated positions of colonial officers. . . .

Shortly after returning home, on the eve of Independence, Soyinka watched a scenario (one he had already anticipated in his early play, *A Dance of the Forests*) played out within the University of Ibadan, which he had joined as a research fellow. A new Chairman of the Governing Council was to be appointed, and a physi-

cian with a Doctor of Science degree from the University of Toronto (the first Nigerian to have reached such exalted heights) was chosen. But quite by chance, a professor from the medical department of that university, on a visit to Nigeria, revealed that the new appointee's DSC was falsely obtained through a secretary in the faculty. An outcry followed, and the man was dismissed, but two years later he was reappointed by the University Visitor, himself a politician of otherwise good standing. As Soyinka wryly comments, "the Visitor and his medical sidekick clearly knew their nationals better than most":

> Anieke's arrival on campus signalled the commencement of defections . . . for the Chairman of the Governing Council had much to offer. He began to receive, first clandestine visits, usually at night, and then, confident visits in broad daylight. As Convocation Day approached, congratulatory telegrams began to arrive at his Lodge, to appear on the pages of newspapers. Petitions on preferments, promotions, pleas for appointments even to political offices. . . .

Elsewhere, Soyinka has characterized the problem of Nigerian society as "the betrayal of vocation for the attractions of power in one form or another", and it is rare indeed to find anyone in public life who occupies their position on merit, or who, having attained their position, evinces even the slightest notion of public service—if only out of a kind of self-interest, including the need to protect their standard of living. More than three decades after Independence, nothing works because nothing is intended to work, and those who do understand the exigencies of the modern state are hounded into prison, exile or an early death. That Soyinka has survived thus far is due in part to the courage that led him to hold up a radio station in a futile attempt to alter the course of Nigerian history; that he still refuses to accept the "denigration of the popular will" by a self-justifying cabal intent only on its own pleasures ought to give hope to those who might otherwise despair that the country will ever reform. *Ibadan: The Penkelemes Years* ("peculiar mess") is an act of faith in the possibilities of the future, written with the authority of one who has experienced the worst of those years.

Henry Louis Gates Jr. (essay date spring 1995)

SOURCE: Gates Jr., Henry Louis. "Wole Soyinka: Mythopoesis and the Agon of Democracy." *Georgia Review* 49, no. 1 (spring 1995): 187-94.

[*In the following essay, Gates explores Soyinka's unique and influential position in African literature, culture, and politics, arguing that Soyinka "bears a relation to the poetics of Africa akin to that which Shakespeare bore to England."*]

This coming June, Wole Soyinka—the first African to receive the Nobel Prize for Literature—will be honored by the International Human Rights Law Group with its Annual Human Rights Award, "in recognition of [his] perseverance for the cause of human rights and democracy in Nigeria, with great eloquence and against great odds. . . . At extreme personal risk," the award letter continues "you have become an international voice for the voiceless and the persecuted in Nigeria, and have remained true to the principles of social justice and public accountability." Soyinka—who has been forced into exile on three occasions since 1986—has, if anything, become an even more vocal exponent of democracy and a public foe against tyranny—not only in Nigeria, but throughout the entire African continent from South Africa to Senegal, from the Ivory Coast to Angola, from Kenya to Zaire.

The uniqueness of Soyinka's role on the African continent cannot be gainsaid. It is a role that he has crafted, or that history has crafted for him, since the earliest stage of his career when, in 1965, he experienced his first imprisonment in Nigeria for protesting a corrupt election. Within two years, he was arrested once again, during the early days of the Nigerian civil war, and held in solitary confinement for the following twenty-seven months. The threat of imprisonment, torture, and death have remained his companions through a succession of oppressive, totalitarian military regimes in a Nigeria as rife with graft and corruption as it is rich in oil. Indeed, Soyinka is one of the few creative writers in the world who could have as justifiably been awarded the Nobel Peace Prize as that for Literature.

The political image of Nigeria—once thought to be destined to play the leadership role among sub-Saharan nations in economic development and in instituting its own form of democracy—has instead become a model of both repression and of the perils of military dictatorship that is very dramatically at odds with its rich cultural heritage, an ancient cultural heritage that embraces traditions evolved by the Hausa, the Igbo, the Yoruba, and several other ethnic groups. Soyinka's work—largely modernistic tragedies with direct formal ties to Euripides, Shakespeare, Synge, Yeats, Brecht, and Lorca—is deeply grounded in Yoruba proverbs and mythology, the densely lyrical and resplendent Yoruba language, and the cryptic mystical poetry of the Ifa Oracle. (In 1994, Soyinka released a recording of Yoruba poetry, accompanied by the Okuta Percussion group.) Indeed, at least since 1961, when he founded the M'bari Writers and Artists Club in Ibadan with the critic Ulli Beier, Soyinka has sought to utilize Yoruba mythology—not as kitsch nor as sentimentality but as fertile grounds for the siting of a vibrant lyrical modernism that is, at once, politically engaged with the local and the immediate even as it unfolds on a mediated plane that speaks directly, simultaneously, and eloquently to the human condition. His plays are no more, or less, "about" Nigeria, let's say, than Shakespeare's *Hamlet* is "about" the politics of the royal court in Denmark. Few artists anywhere, especially those directly engaged politically, are able to achieve this effect in their art.

Since 1986, Soyinka has remained impressively productive, despite the strains of official repression and persecution. He has published two volumes of autobiography, two plays, a book of critical and political essays, a volume of poetry, a recording of poetry, and a collaboration with Tania León on an opera based on an earlier Soyinka play, *A Scourge of Hyacinths.* In July 1994, he was feted in a national celebration of his sixtieth birthday—only two months before the Nigerian military government confiscated first his Nigerian passport, and then his United Nations international passport; the government followed this by banning the publication of a collection of essays written by scholars *about* Soyinka's life and work. It is true, of course, that since 1986 Soyinka has also published dozens of essays addressing immediate political crises in Nigeria. It was these essays and his statements to the Nigerian and international press that led to his being forced into exile late last year. Soyinka can be readily defined as one of Nigeria's (and black Africa's) proto-agonists.

* * *

Soyinka embeds his tragic *agon* in the densely metaphorical world of mythopoesis, structured in a language that is startling for the originality and aptness of its metaphors. We can best see this by analyzing the tragedy that forms the crux of Soyinka's *oeuvre*, **Death and the King's Horseman,** referred to so specifically by the Swedish Academy in its citation honoring Soyinka's works.

In December 1944, Oba Siyenbola Oladigbolu (the Alaafin, or King of Oyo, an ancient Yoruba city in Nigeria) died. He was buried that night. As was the Yoruba tradition, the Horseman of the King, Olokun Esin Jinadu, was expected to commit ritual suicide and lead his Alaafin's favorite horse and dog through the transitional passage to the world of the ancestors. However, the British colonial district officer, Captain J. A. MacKenzie, decided that the custom was savage and intervened in January 1945 to prevent Olokun Esin Jinadu from completing his ritual act, the act for which his entire life had been lived. Faced with the anarchy this unconsummated ritual would work upon the order of the Yoruba world, Olokun Esin Jinadu's son stood as surrogate for his father and sacrificed his own life. The incident, Soyinka told us following a reading, has intrigued him ever since he had first heard of it. It had, he continued, already inspired a play in Yoruba by Duro Lapido called *Oba Waja.*

Soyinka adapted the historical event rather liberally to emphasize the metaphorical and mythical dimensions outside of time, again reflecting implicitly the idea that an event is a sign and that a sign adumbrates something other than itself by contiguity as well as by semblance. The relation that a fiction bears to reality is fundamentally related to the means by which that relation and that fiction are represented. For Soyinka, a text mediates the distance between art and life but in a profoundly ambiguous and metaphorical manner. In that space between the structure of the historical event and the literary event (which is to say, the somehow necessary or probable event), one begins to understand Soyinka's idea of tragedy. The plot of the play, certainly, can indicate what may happen as well as what did happen, and this concern with what a protagonist will probably or necessarily do (rather than what he *did* do) distinguishes Soyinka's universal and poetic art from particular and prosaic Yoruba history. It is his central concern with the philosophical import of human and black experience that so clearly makes him unlike many other black writers. A summary of the play's plot suggests this relation:

The Alaafin of Oyo is dead. To guide the Alaafin's horse through the narrow passage of transition, as tradition demands, the Horseman of the king, Elesin Oba, is required on the night of the king's burial to commit ritual suicide through the sublime agency of his will. The action of the play occurs on the day of his death. Death for the Elesin is not a final contract; it is rather the rite of passage to the larger world of the ancestors, a world linked in the continuous bond of Yoruba metaphysics to that of the living and the unborn. It is a death which the Elesin seems willingly to embrace— but not before he possesses a beautiful market girl, a betrothed virgin whom he encounters as he dances his farewell greeting before the ritual marketplace. Though Iyaloja, the "mother" of the market, protests the Horseman's paradoxical selection, she consents to and arranges this ritualistic union of life and death.

Revolted by the "barbarity" of the custom, British colonial officer Pilkings intervenes to prevent the death at the precise moment of the Horseman's intended transition. Notified by his family, Olunde, the Horseman's eldest heir, has returned from medical school in England intending to bury his father. Confronted with his father's failure of will, the son assumes his hereditary title for the sole purpose of becoming his father's surrogate in death to complete the cosmic restoration of order. In a splendidly poignant climax to the action, the women of the market, led by Iyaloja, unmask the veiled corpse of the son and watch placidly as the Horseman of the king breaks his own neck with his chains, fulfilling his covenant with tradition and the communal will—alas, too late. Two men have died rather than one.

As adapted by Soyinka, this is no mere drama of individual vacillation. Communal order and communal will are the inextricable elements in Elesin's tragedy that not only reflect but amplify his own failure of will. In this sense, Soyinka's drama suggests Greek tragedy much more readily than Elizabethan, and is akin to the mythopoetic tragedies of Synge and Brecht and to Lorca's *Blood Wedding*. Nor is this merely a fable of the evils of colonialism or of white unblinking racism. **Death and the King's Horseman** is a classical work, in which structure and metaphysics are inextricably intertwined.

Structurally, the play is divided into five acts and occurs over almost exactly twenty-four hours. Its basis is communal and ritualistic; its medium is richly metaphorical poetry that, accompanied continuously by music, dance, and mime, creates an air of mystery and wonder. The cumulative effect defines a cosmos comprised at once of nature, of human society, and of the divine. The protagonist's bewilderment and vacillation, blended with his courage and inevitable defeat, signify a crisis, confrontation, and transformation of values—transfixed in a time that oscillates perpetually in an antiphonal moment. The reversal of the *peripeteia* ("situation") and the *anagnorisis* ("recognition") occur at the same time as they do in *Oedipus Rex*.

Soyinka's characterization of his protagonist Elesin is also classically Greek, with the play recording the reciprocal relationship between his character and his fate. Elesin's grand flaw stems not from vice or depravity but from *hamartia* ("an error of judgment"), a sign of his weakness of will. Yet though he is not eminently good or just, Elesin is loved. His will and his character are neither wholly determined nor wholly free; his character is at once noble and prone to error. The nine-member chorus again and again speaks against Elesin's special hubris, his unregenerate will. And his defeat, finally, is great, suffered only after the great attempt. The play's action is as timeless as the child conceived by Elesin on the day of his death. Its plot unfolds in "the seething cauldron of the dark world and psyche," where ambiguity and vacillation play havoc upon the individual.

Although self-sacrifice is a familiar motif in Soyinka's tragedies, the Elesin's sacrifice is not meant to suggest the obliteration of an individual soul but serves rather as an implicit confirmation of an order in which the self exists with all of its integrity yet only as one small part of a larger whole. Elesin Oba, after all, is a conferred title, the importance of which derives from its context within the community and from its ritual function. The Elesin's character is determined in the play—not by any obvious material relationships, however, but rather by the plot itself—as the formal dramatic elements of any tragedy are determined by a silent structuring principle. Great tragic plots always determine the tragic character of their protagonists. To paraphrase Pilking's servant Joseph, the Elesin exists simply to die; he has no choice in the matter, despite the play's repeated reference to the ambiguity inherent in his role. And Pilking's intervention, a kind of self-defense, challenges fundamentally the communal defense of self which this ritual embodies.

Elesin's dilemma is both individual and collective, both social and psychic, all at once. In the same way that Faust's hubristic transgression occurs within his consciousness—occurs, indeed, because of his deification of mind and will—so, too, is Elesin's tragic dilemma enacted internally, within his will. As he ominously suggests early in *Death and the King's Horseman,* "My will has outleapt the conscious act." His hubris is symbolized by his taking of a bride on the morning of his scheduled death in a ritual in which the thanatotic embraces the erotic; he chooses the satisfactions of the self over the exactions of the will. This is Elesin's tragic flaw—and inevitable fall—which results from a convergence of forces at work within the will and without, which conspire to reinforce those subliminal fears that confront all tragic heroes.

Not only is Elesin's Westernized son Olunde's suicide a rejection of the relief of the resolution afforded by the Western philosophical tradition, but it is also a ritual slaying of the father at the crossroads. Olunde's death leaves his father entrapped, penned outside of the rite of passage, for the fleeting moment of transition has passed, making ironic even an act as final as death. Iyaloja, perhaps the most powerful characterization of a woman in African literature, expresses the paradox: "We said, the dew on earth's surface was for you to wash your feet along the slopes of honor. You said No, I shall step in the vomit of cats and the droppings of mice; I shall fight them for the leftovers of the world." In the face of his son's slaying, the Elesin is poignantly left-over, and is a "leftover." There will be no more Elesins, for the unbroken order of this world has now been rent asunder. As Iyaloja remarks acidly, "He is gone at last into the passage but oh, how late it all is. His son will feast on the meat and throw him bones. The passage is clogged with droppings from the King's stallion; he will arrive all stained in dung." To paraphrase the praise singer, the world has finally tilted from its groove.

For centuries the ritual passage of the Horseman had served to retrace an invisible cultural circle, thereby reaffirming the order of this Yoruba world. The ritual dress, the metaphorical language, the Praise-Singer's elegy, the Elesin's dance of death—these remain fundamentally unchanged as memory has recast them from generation to generation. The mixed symbols of semen and blood, implied in the hereditary relationship between succession and authority (and reiterated in the deflowering of the virgin on the day of death) stand as signs of a deeper idea of transition and generation. The role of the Horseman demands not only the acceptance of ambiguity but also its embrace.

Although Elesin's is an individual dilemma—a failure of one human will—the conflict implicit in his role of the king's Horseman is a communal dilemma of preservation of order in the face of change. During the play, at a crucial moment, a traditional proverb is cited which reveals that doubt and ambiguity are not emotions uncharacteristic of the Elesin: "The elder grimly approaches heaven and you ask him to bear your greeting yonder; do you think he makes the journey willingly?" All myth, we know, reconciles two otherwise unreconcilable forces or tensions through the mediation of the mythic structure itself. The *Orestia* is a superb example of this. This trick of "structuration," as it were, is the most characteristic aspect of human mythology.

Soyinka, in his Director's Notes for the playbill of *Death and the King's Horseman,* puts the matter this way: "At the heart of the lyric and the dance of transition in Yoruba tragic art, that core of ambivalence is always implanted. This is how society, even on its own, reveals and demonstrates its capacity for change.

We do not need to know, as the Yoruba historian Samuel Johnson tells us, that at one time the reluctance of an Elesin to accompany a dead Alaafin engendered such a disgrace that the Horseman's family had strangled him themselves, nor that the reluctance of the Elesins had grown as contact with the British increased. We do not need to know these historical facts simply because a single Horseman's ambiguity over his choices is rendered so apparent throughout Soyinka's text. "Conscience"—self-consciousness and introspection, as defined in Hamlet's soliloquy—is also the Horseman's fatal flaw, that which colors "the native hue of resolution . . . with the pale cast of thought."

> Who would fardels bear,
> To grunt and sweat under a weary life,
> But that the dread of something after death,
> The undiscover'd country from whose bourn
> No traveller returns, puzzles the will,
> And makes us rather bear those ills we have,
> Than fly to others that we know not of?
> Thus conscience does make cowards of us all,
> And thus the native hue of resolution
> Is sicklied o'er with the pale cast of thought,
> And enterprises of great pith and moment
> With this regard their currents turn awry,
> And lose the name of action.
>
> (*Hamlet,* III, i.)

As Elesin Oba puts it in a splendid confession near the end of the play, he is committing "the awful treachery of relief" and thinking "the unspeakable blasphemy of seeing the hand of the gods in this alien rupture of his world." This ambiguity of action, reflected in the ambiguity of figurative language and of mythic structure, creates and allows this flexible metaphysical system. Formal and structured, it remains nevertheless fluid and malleable, with a sophisticated and subtle internal logic.

Soyinka embodies perfectly the ambiguity of the Elesin's action in the ambiguity of the play's language. Among all the verbal arts, a play is most obviously an act of language. Soyinka allows the metaphorical and tonal Yoruba language to inform his use of English. Western metaphors for the nature of metaphor, at least since I. A. Richards, are "vehicle" and "tenor," both of which suggest an action of meaning, a transfer through semantic space. But centuries before Richards, the Yoruba defined metaphor as the "horse" of words: "If a word is lost, a metaphor or proverb is used to find it." As do tenor and vehicle, the horse metaphor implies a transfer or carriage of meaning through intention and extension. It is just this aspect of the Yoruba language on which Soyinka relies. The extended use of such densely metaphorical utterances, searching for the lost or hidden meanings of words and events, serves to suggest music, dance, and myth, all aspects of *poiesis* long ago fragmented in Western tragic art.

In Soyinka's tragedies, language and act mesh fundamentally. Enter here a superb example of this in the Praise-Singer's speech near the climax of the play:

> Elesin Oba! I call you by that name only this last time. Remember when I said, if you cannot come, tell my horse. What? I cannot hear you, I said if you cannot come, whisper in the ears of my horse. Is your tongue severed from the roots of Elesin? I can hear no response. I said, if there are boulders you cannot climb, mount my horse's back; this spotless black stallion, he'll bring you over them. Elesin Oba, once you had a tongue that darted like a drummer's stick. I said, if you get lost, my dog will track a path to me. My memory fails me but I think you replied: My feet have found the path, Alafin. I said at last, if evil hands hold you back, just tell my horse there is weight on the hem of your smock. I dare not wait too long. . . .
>
> . . . Oh my companion, if you had followed when you should, we would not say that the horse preceded its rider. If you had followed when it was time, we would not say the dog has raced beyond and left his master behind. If you had raised your will to cut the thread of life at the summons of the drums, we would not say your mere shadow fell across the gateway and took its owner's place at the banquet. But the hunter, laden with a slain buffalo, stayed rooted in the cricket's hole with his toes. What now is left? If there is a dearth of bats, the pigeon must serve us for the offering. Speak the words over your shadow which must now serve in your place.

In this stunning speech, the language of music and the music of language are one. In one sense, the music of the play gives it its force, the reciprocal displacement of the language of music with the music of language. The antiphonal structure of Greek tragedy is also perhaps the most fundamental African aesthetic value and is used as the play's internal structuring mechanism. As in music, the use of repetition—such as the *voudoun* ("voodoo") phrase, "Tell my horse"—serves to create a simultaneity of action. The transitional passage before which Elesin falters is inherent in all black musical forms. Soyinka's dances are darkly lyrical, uniting with the music of the drums and songs of the chorus to usher the audience into a self-contained, hermetic world, an effected reality. Soyinka's greatest achievement is just this: the creation of a compelling world *through* language, *in* language, and *of* language. He has mastered the power of language to create a reality, not merely to reflect reality, and his mastery of spoken language is reinforced by mastery of a second language of music, and a third of dance.

Soyinka is a master of the verbal arts. His English is among the finest and most resonant in any literary tradition, fused seamlessly as it is with the resonances and music of the great lyrical, myth-dense, Yoruba tradition. He bears a relation to the poetics of Africa akin to that which Shakespeare bore to England, Pushkin to Russia, Lorca to Spain, Brecht to Germany, and Joyce to Ireland—he is the point of consciousness of its language. And, within the movement for democracy in Black Africa, he is both its troublesome, insistent conscience and its most eloquent voice.

James Gibbs (review date spring 1995)

SOURCE: Gibbs, James. Review of *Ibadan: The Penkelemes Years: A Memoir, 1946-65,* by Wole Soyinka. *World Literature Today* 69, no. 2 (spring 1995): 420.

[*In the following review, Gibbs commends the insight and wit in* Ibadan: The Penkelemes Years: A Memoir, 1946-65.]

After *Aké,* his volume of childhood memories, was published in 1983, Wole Soyinka maintained that he would not attempt to give an account of his life beyond "the age of innocence." In February 1994 he completed *Ibadan,* with a subtitle that included the word *penkelemes*—a rendition of "peculiar mess"—and the dates 1946 to 1965, which indicated the book would take the author beyond his thirtieth birthday.

In 1946 Soyinka set off for secondary school in Ibadan; by the end of 1965, he had had confrontations with numerous politicians and policemen and was awaiting trial on the charge of holding up the Ibadan radio station. At that point he had fathered four children by three different women and had had, by his own admission, several affairs. So much for innocence.

Soyinka begins his foreword, "*Ibadan* does not pretend to be anything but faction," and he goes on to indicate how he has "fictionalised facts." An example of his method is the creation of "Maren," his protagonist, who, he said in a BBC interview, "is undisguisedly me."

The memoir which follows the foreword is highly selective: Soyinka has dipped his hand into the bulging bag of his life and pulled out just a few of the extraordinary episodes in which he has been involved in. Several seem to have been selected because they reveal his sense of destiny, how close he has come to death, or his tendency to meet "fire with fire."

Each page testifies to the skill of the storyteller, and fascinating tales, told with wit, energy, and a good deal of special pleading, unfold within a loose structure. Context is only vaguely established, and factual information is thrown out in an apparently haphazard manner. Those looking for a chronicle of Soyinka's life will be disappointed, as will those who want explanations of his poetry and plays. This is the tale of a man of action, whose writing and theater work are presented as largely incidental to his battles for Justice. Only by carefully sifting the evidence can the poet be seen in the political activist.

The abuse of power and the ways in which language can be used to attack and transform bullies are recurring and organizing concerns: apparent in the confrontations with "seniors," con men, pickpockets, administrators, leaders, and politicians. Notoriously, Soyinka often acts impetuously and as an individual against injustice, and *Ibadan* does nothing to dent the impression that has been created of, essentially, someone who may act first and think later and is frequently a lone crusader. However, he is not entirely alone: he has "people"—some of whom, such as his parents and wives, he treats very badly—and he needs people. Part of the story he tells is of the creation of a loose alliance of independent spirits who are loyal to him.

The book provides fascinating insights, delightful pen portraits, accurate parodies, and revealing accounts. But there are also elements Soyinka's many admirers will regard as hostages to fortune. For example, "Maren" is variously described as a walking catastrophe, a runt, a troublemaker, a bohemian, and a ne'er-do-well. His self-confidence sometimes becomes arrogance; on occasions, his anger is counterproductive.

Soyinka can certainly be infuriating, and one is constantly balancing his manifest vices against possibly redeeming virtues. It is particularly encouraging that in *Ibadan* he acknowledges faults, mistakes and weaknesses, and it is very refreshing that, after years of coy denials, he admits his role in the radio-station holdup.

Note, however, that continuing a trend in the book, he does not complete the story of the trial: he got off on a technicality and was carried shoulder-high from the court. His political judgment is fallible, but in that instance he certainly succeeded—at a great cost to those around him—in keeping important issues before the Western Region.

All the recent "biographies" Soyinka has written have purposes beyond the obvious concern to capture a period of time and reduce it to writing. Soyinka has suggested that his newest book is relevant because in 1993 and 1994 Nigeria relived some of the nightmares of the sixties. There is at least enough in the parallels to provoke a lively discussion and to show that, despite immediate reactions to the way it opens, there is method in *Ibadan*: it is not a "penkelemes."

Sean O'Brien (review date 10 November 1995)

SOURCE: O'Brien, Sean. "In the House of Horrid Mirth." *Times Literary Supplement*, no. 4832 (10 November 1995): 34.

[*In the following review, O'Brien examines how Soyinka balances comedy and tragedy in* The Beatification of Area Boy.]

At sunrise, Judge, a disbarred and derelict lawyer, wakes as usual on the steps of La Plaza, a Lagos shopping mall. Around him the commercial day of the street stallholders is beginning. Judge is quick to claim credit for a spectacular dawn: "It's a good display, is it not? And to think all I did was breathe against the horizon." Trader, knowing Judge of old, dreads him hanging about during the working day, but can't resist being drawn into debate, pitting his practicality against Judge's deranged metaphysics. When Judge accuses him: "You have the mind of a petty commercial", Trader ripostes: "It feeds me, you know, it feeds me. I'm not complaining." *The Beatification of Area Boy* lines up several such arguments, between the absolutes of law, state and power, and the equally compelling requirements of food, shelter and hope.

The character who connects affairs of state with the everyday lives of the poor is Sanda (Tyrone Huggins), the store security man. Seated at the threshold in his uniform, he explains the world of the street to anxious visitors while running the local Area Boys' protection rackets, from whose depredations he meanwhile purports to spare the wealthy. By these means, we see, he manages to guarantee a life for those he actually protects—the orphaned Boyko and his companions. On his turf they can survive.

The occupation of territory is a major theme in Wole Soyinka's new play. Mama Put, the local caterer, is haunted by memories of homelessness in the Biafran war, and protects her ground and her schoolgirl daughter with the bayonet that soldiers used to kill her brother. The barber jealously guards his chair; the parking attendant his receipts. There is much talk of the expropriation of land for development; indeed, the unnatural brightness of the dawn has been caused by the razing of a settlement of a million people, who are later seen by the cast walking through the city into exile. This sense of sheer numbers does much to account for the anxious, affectionate domesticity created by the occupants of La Plaza's precinct. This place, too, is threatened. In the evening, it will be required for a society wedding. The street will be blocked off and the locals temporarily expelled. The military will make a destructive intervention. Can this fragment of more or less civil society survive the day?

Despite its sombre preoccupations, *The Beatification of Area Boy* is a comedy, played with great warmth by a strong ensemble and distinguished by fine individual performances, in particular from Femi Elufowoju Jr as Trader and Wale Ojo as Judge. Trader is central to what is perhaps the most effective episode, when a customer trying to buy a tie for a job interview turns up on a borrowed bicycle—something not seen in these streets since the oil boom. As Trader points out in a song: "No one on his mettle goes pedalling a bike / Not even with petroleum on an astronomic hike." Somehow the cyclist cannot get the stallholders' attention, least of all Trader's. When he finally dares to ring the bike's bell, Trader is beside himself with delight.

Even a potentially deadly situation is turned into comedy. A policeman tries to protect an injured man from a crowd that plans to necklace him with a petrol-filled tyre, for allegedly making someone's genitals disappear. Sanda's solution involves a locked room and a well-endowed girl.

On this day of changes, though, the resourceful Sanda himself is put to the question when the intended bride comes to inspect the premises. She is Miseyi (Bola Aiyeola), his former girlfriend, from whom we learn that Sanda is not born to the street but a son of the middle classes, who abandoned his studies to serve a revolution which shows no sign of happening.

In this gleefully melodramatic context, the compromised couple can hardly fail to affect each other, and the performance culminates in a spectacular wedding ceremony which is thrown into uproar by Miseyi's change of heart. While the bridegroom is demanding Sanda's public castration, the prospective in-laws discover a quarrel of their own about oil revenues. Here, though, comedy shifts towards romance, first with the reunion of Sanda and Miseyi; second, with the "miraculous" resurrection of Judge (now resplendent in ragged judicial purple) after he is shot by the military.

Imprisoned in the boot of an officer's Mercedes, he has found and donned a bullet-proof vest, believing it to be a waistcoat which will complement his outfit.

Jude Kelly's direction keeps this complex and protean bundle of tales, with its echoes of Brecht and Shaw, rolling at full speed, while accommodating the varied demands of Soyinka's language as it switches from moment to moment in and out of pidgin and standard English and between realism, highly elaborate rhetoric, and the satirical or elegiac songs of the Minstrel and his acoustic guitar. Cast members double as the swaggering brass section from a highlife band (though real drummers would have helped here), and whether in dance or the frequent outbreaks of violence, the ensemble movement is compelling. The occasional periods of stillness, as at the close of the first half, very effectively emphasize the designer Niki Turner's brutalist architecture of tired concrete pillars and bleary glass, against which the characters dramatize their lives.

It is apt that, as part of the nationwide Africa '95 festival, *The Beatification of Area Boy* should be premiered in Leeds, where Soyinka was an undergraduate in the 1950s, and where the study of African and Commonwealth literature received an early impetus. A grim coincidence is the announcement of the death sentence imposed on Ken Saro-Wiwa, the Nigerian author and political activist, whose commitment to the rights of ordinary people has evident parallels to the work which the politically reinvigorated Sanda proposes to undertake at the close of Soyinka's play. Horror, Soyinka has suggested, may be sought at the heart of farce.

James Gibbs (review date summer 1996)

SOURCE: Gibbs, James. Review of *The Beatification of Area Boy,* by Wole Soyinka. *World Literature Today* 70, no. 3 (summer 1996): 750-51.

[*In the following review, Gibbs commends the "musical elements" in* The Beatification of Area Boy *but asserts that the play's conclusion is its "weakest point."*]

The Beatification of Area Boy opened in Leeds, on the day that Ken Saro-Wiwa and eight others were sentenced to death by a tribunal in Port Harcourt. Ten days into the run, the gruesome details of the execution of the Ogoni 9 broke on the world. While hinting at this kind of state violence in his play, Wole Soyinka has, generally, avoided the heavy-handed satire of such earlier works as *A Play of Giants,* creating a text that relies more heavily on music than anything he has written since *Opera Wonyosi.*

The play begins with a "red sky in the morning" that turns out to have been caused by the torching of Maroko, and the refugees from the settlement subsequently invade the stage. The loosely structured "Lagosian kaleidoscope" incorporates, through a variety of conventions, verses from Soyinka's 1983 record *Unlimited Liability Company* and material already worked into sketches as part of a revue, **Before the Deluge.** The result is a protest production for 1995 that draws on earlier work.

At the center of the drama stands Sanda, a security guard employed by the owners of an emporium to ensure that customers are protected when entering and leaving the shop. However, it soon becomes clear that Sanda is the mastermind behind the local "area boys," and that he organizes a variety of robberies and rackets. When an old acquaintance, Miseyi, arrives to do some last-minute shopping in the very street where her wedding is to be celebrated, more of the mystery surrounding the articulate security guard with attitude is cleared away. It transpires that, a true son of the people, Sanda had given up a university course to make a million and lead a revolution.

This Nigerian Robin Hood or Captain Blood carries the main burden of the play, suggesting, in familiar Soyinkan fashion, that the monster of the West African state can be challenged by idealists with charisma and musical gifts: He takes his place within a richly textured drama of street life in which recent history and present corruption rub shoulders, and he is part of a spectacle in which music plays a variety of important roles. Soyinka is prepared to hold back the flow of his drama while the company join in an amusing "Ode to the Bicycle"—it seems bicycles have been rarely seen in Lagos since the oil boom—and the playwright incorporates, in a naturalistic manner, a Minstrel who revealingly attributes some of Soyinka's 1983 lyrics to Sanda! In a telling attack on vanity and aloofness, a soldier sings a Gilbertian number entitled "Don't Touch My Uniform."

Ideally, the production should have opened in Lagos before an audience attuned to its idioms and directly challenged by its vision. But, given the situation in Nigeria, this was clearly impossible, and both the West Yorkshire premiere and the Methuen text remain testimony to the difficulties confronting a committed writer. A professional Nigerian, desperately anxious to contribute to the establishment of democratic processes in his homeland, Soyinka was condemned to speak through Leeds and London.

Given the pressures on composition, the result is, understandably, a bit of a mixture. The transformation at the end of the play, when Sanda heads off into the sunset to raise the political consciousness of the refugees from Maroko, is the weakest point, but the variety of experiences in the supporting characters and the quality of some of the musical elements give the text redeeming strengths.

Makau wa Mutua (review date summer 1996)

SOURCE: Mutua, Makau wa. "Can Nigeria Be One?" *Wilson Quarterly* 20, no. 3 (summer 1996): 91-3.

[*In the following review, Mutua argues that* The Open Sore of a Continent: A Personal Narrative of the Nigerian Crisis *is a powerful nonfiction account of political repression in contemporary Nigeria and Soyinka's "most anguished polemic to date."*]

When Wole Soyinka all but pronounces the death of his native Nigeria, the world should listen. Not only is Soyinka Africa's best-known writer; Nigeria is in many ways the epitome of the modern African state—rich in people and resources, yet devastated by political misrule and ethnic divisiveness.

Born in 1934 and educated in Nigeria and England, Soyinka became in 1986 the first African to win the Nobel Prize in literature. He is best known for such plays as **The Lion and the Jewel** (1959) and **The Trials of Brother Jero** (1961), which combine elements of Yoruba ritual with Western stagecraft. His fictionalized portraits of Nigerian society in transition are both tragic and satirical, with many of his barbs aimed at the villainies of despots. But this nonfictional narrative of political repression in contemporary Nigeria [**The Open Sore of a Continent**] is his most anguished polemic to date. To be sure, Soyinka hopes that Nigeria can be saved from the predations of the present military dictator, General Sani Abacha. But he is at best ambivalent about his country's future. Without saying so, he seems to conclude that Nigeria is doomed.

Soyinka's despair is understandable. Nigeria's political history since independence from Britain in 1960 has been for the most part a nightmarish succession of corrupt and brutal tyrants propped up by the international oil industry. But the real problem, persisting from colonial times to the present, is Nigeria's fragmented ethnic composition. The British attempted to deal with this problem on the eve of their departure. As a condition of independence, they made the three dominant ethnic groups accept a complex power-sharing federal system. Those groups were the Yoruba in the west (20 percent of the total population), the Igbo in the south (17 percent), and the Hausa and Fulani in the north (21 and 9 percent, respectively).

Reasonable as it might have seemed, the design proved flawed. Compared with the oil-rich south and the industrialized west, the predominantly Muslim north is an economic wasteland. Yet the north controls the military and is the most populous region; by 1966, its refusal to share power prompted an Igbo coup, followed by a massacre of Igbos living in the north. The result was the breakaway state of Biafra—reincorporated into Nigeria in 1970 after a four-year civil war that left more than 250,000 civilians dead. Since then, a close-knit syndicate of northern military leaders has jealously held power. It is almost impossible to conceive of any circumstances under which this clique would cede control to civilians from the south or west or, for that matter, to any democratically elected leaders.

Yet rather than rest blame on the flawed federal design, Soyinka argues that the artificiality of Nigeria, and of other modern African states, is no greater than that created in the formation of many nations outside Africa. He suggests that the African nations are passing through a kind of purgatory, waiting to attain the "status of irreversibility—either as paradise or hell." To Soyinka, Nigeria's birthday should have been June 12, 1993, the day when the will of the people, freely expressed through the secret ballot, should have sent the military back to the barracks and ushered in democracy.

Instead, the 1993 election saw the culmination and, finally, the frustration of a devious strategy engineered by General I. B. Babangida, the military ruler since 1985. Through "physical and moneyed thuggery," Babangida made sure that only two parties, and two presidential candidates, would be able to compete for power. At the same time, many suspected that only one outcome would be tolerated by the military: victory by the candidate from the north, Bashir Tofa. Soyinka calls Tofa "a straw figure specifically set up by the perpetuation machinery of I. B. Babangida."

As it turned out, most of Nigeria, including the north, voted for the Yoruba businessman Moshood Abiola. In response, Babangida and a coterie of officers led by fellow northerner Sani Abacha annulled the election, plunging the country into chaos. Abacha then forced Babangida to step down, setting up an interim government that he himself overthrew a few months later. Having declared himself supreme ruler, Abacha has since ruled by ruthlessly suppressing any opponents, real or imagined.

This tale of tin despots with huge egos is enlivened by Soyinka's seductive style. Describing Abacha's phony "transition" program, he writes, "It is a fair assessment of the IQ of Abacha that he actually imagines that this transparent ploy for self-perpetuation would fool the market woman, the roadside mechanic, the student, factory worker, or religious leader of whatever persuasion. Even the village idiot must marvel at such banal attempts to rival a disgraced predecessor."

As persuasive as Soyinka is, however, one might question the faith he invests in the 1993 election. According to one expert observer, Omo Omoruyi, a respected political scientist who was forced to flee for his life after the annulment of the election, the "democratiza-

tion" process was compromised every step of the way by excessive state interference. Why, then, is the election so important in Soyinka's eyes?

The answer, I believe, lies in the ethnicity of the winning candidate. Abiola's presidential ambitions go back at least two decades; after being thwarted once in 1983 he used his enormous wealth to bribe his way back into power. Like a West African Ross Perot, he financed his own party in order to secure a place at the top of its ticket. But Soyinka barely touches upon Abiola's corrupt practices, treating him throughout as a hero. The only explanation is that Abiola, like Soyinka, is a Yoruba.

And therein lies one of the weaknesses of this book. Soyinka is a distinguished champion of democracy. His many writings expose and attack despotic rule, and his activism has forced him into exile, where he has formed an opposition movement called the United Democratic Front of Nigeria. Yet in the passion of his protest, Soyinka reveals his own ethnic bias. His lionizing of a fellow Yoruba, and his belittling of northerners in general (as opposed to the leaders), threaten to undermine his larger purpose.

The Open Sore of a Continent is replete with accounts of brutal acts by the military. But few are as poignant as the persecution of Ken Saro-Wiwa, the writer and defender of one of Nigeria's many minority ethnic groups, the Ogoni. (Together, minority groups comprise 33 percent of the total population.) The Ogoni, who occupy one of the richest oil-producing regions, have suffered the consequences of ecological devastation, seeing their once-lush farmlands turned into an inferno of burning oil swamps. Hence the Movement for the Salvation of the Ogoni People, a civil organization seeking better conditions or, failing that, secession. In 1994, Saro-Wiwa and several other Ogonis were arrested and charged with the murder of four pro-government Ogoni leaders.

In a trial that was universally viewed as a mockery of the most basic human rights and legal guarantees, Saro-Wiwa and his colleagues were convicted and sentenced to die. In November 1995, they were hanged in a show of what Soyinka calls "shabby cruelty." In the case of Saro-Wiwa, a man in his fifties, it took five attempts to kill him. This incident, more than anything else the Abacha regime has done, has relegated it to pariah status in the eyes of the world. Yet the regime cares little for international public opinion as long as the world's largest oil purchasers, including the United States, continue to buy Nigerian oil.

What the death of Saro-Wiwa demonstrates was the determination of the Abacha regime to crush any credible threat to its control of the country's main industry.

The incident further proves that the northern military clique is not about to share power with non-northerners. What, then, are the Yoruba, Igbo, and other minorities supposed to do? How long are they supposed to wait before they receive their due as fellow Nigerians? It seems only a matter of time before a three-state partition becomes the sole viable option. But will the north ever allow separation? These are questions for which Soyinka has no answers. For now, Nigeria seems headed toward the apocalypse. That is why this book is a requiem.

Jeff Thomson (essay date summer 1996)

SOURCE: Thomson, Jeff. "The Politics of the Shuttle: Wole Soyinka's Poetic Space." *Research in African Literatures* 27, no. 2 (summer 1996): 94-101.

[*In the following essay, Thomson surveys Soyinka's political poetry in such works as* A Shuttle in the Crypt, *asserting that "his is a poetry of such personal courage and emotion that one can hardly accuse it of being merely political, yet it is deeply concerned with protest and the reclamation of cultural ground."*]

Robert Bly writes that "the political poem comes out of the deepest privacy" as at the same time he suggests that a poet's imaginative authority derives from an ability to speak for the people, not just to them (qtd. in Lense 18). For a good number of readers, as well as poets and critics, this philosophy borders on anathema. As Carolyn Forché notes,

> We are accustomed to rather easy categories: we distinguish between 'personal' and 'political' poems—the former calling to mind lyrics of love and emotional loss, the latter indicating a public partisanship that is considered divisive, even when necessary.
>
> (31)

This conception of art thrives when love and power, nature and politics are separated by every barrier that can be placed between them; it is tempting to believe that these created distinctions are not just good sense but natural law.

A poet such as Wole Soyinka destroys such easy distinctions. His is a poetry of such personal courage and emotion that one can hardly accuse it of being merely political, yet it is deeply concerned with protest and the reclamation of cultural ground. Soyinka reaches for a new breathing space, for a poetry that allows poets to acknowledge the power of personal resistance and at the same time confront the social and political ramifications of power, especially the abuse of power.

With the exception of a few poems, the entire collection of Soyinka's 1972 *A Shuttle in the Crypt* was written in solitary confinement, punishment for other writings perceived to be sympathetic to the secessionist Biafra party, and all the poems are affected by the reality of that confinement and its accompanying political world. Soyinka's poetic eye witnesses the atrocities of his prison as he attempts personally to transcend their confines and at the same time recapture a lost cultural identity; he seeks personal as well as political salvation through the shuttle, the book's dominant and controlling metaphor.

The shuttle has an elusive double meaning; it is a symbol for both a process of poetic witness and an act of cultural chronicling. In weaving, the shuttle carries the woof or weft (horizontal) threads through the warp (vertical) threads, but Soyinka's metaphor goes far beyond this simple definition. His shuttle is an instrument of personal salvation as well as social reclamation. By making additional use of the shuttle's identity as a type of African bird, Soyinka can tap into the mythology of spiritual freedom, as birds are an archetypal symbol for such freedom: their ability to leave the earth suggests liberty while their closeness to the sky equates them with angels and connects them with the spiritual. As a cultural symbol, the shuttle is both a generative act of writing, as seen in the parallel motion of the pen and the shuttle, and the act of memory which precipitates writing. The shuttle, as Soyinka says in his preface,

> is a unique species of caged animal, a restless bolt of energy, a trapped weaver bird yet charged in repose with unspoken forms and designs. In motion or at rest it is a secretive seed, shrine, kernel, phallus and well of creative mysteries.
>
> (vii-viii)

His poet-shuttle will reestablish the lost role of the tapestry weavers from traditional Yoruba society, reclaiming cultural ground from the priests who disempowered them. Tapestries were elements of storytelling in West African cultures; they were used to tell the histories of the people, their lives and deaths. The weaver women who made the tapestries "wove a spell against this hour / And kept a vigil against dearth and death," as Soyinka says (44).

It is important to note that Soyinka is not a reactionary; he is not attempting to recreate the past. He is, however, attempting to open a new space of poetic response to the horrors of the Nigerian Civil War. The poet who takes on the identity of the shuttle will save himself in the act of writing, but he will also remake the cultural fabric, mark the horror he was witness to, and keep his own vigil over death.

For Soyinka, then, the poet becomes a new type of weaver, a storyteller who gathers the threads and blends them together to save his own sanity and to make a record of the deaths of others. "It was never a mere poetic conceit," he says; "all events, thoughts, dreams, incidental phenomena were, in sheer self-protection perceived and absorbed into the loom-shuttle unity" (vii). The poems of *A Shuttle in the Crypt* are both "a map of the course trodden by the human mind" and an eventual rebirth of the mind and its culture through self-generation and the salvation of poetic memory. His prison becomes a womb, a space of understanding and creation that transcends the attempts of the "mind-butchers" to break down the individual consciousness. It is in *Chimes of Silence,* and especially the poem **"Procession,"** where Soyinka exhaustively explores the ramifications of the duality of the shuttle as the metaphor for both a cultural symbol of witness and accountancy and a personal emblem of the self-sustaining creative process:

> I listened to an enactment of death in the home of death, to the pulse of the shuttle slowing to its final moment of rest, towards that complete in-gathering of being which a shuttle in repose so palpably is.
>
> (vii-viii)

Through his poems Soyinka becomes both bird and loom, capable of both reclaiming the freedom denied him and recording the deaths of others, fighting everything the "mind-butchers" would hope to accomplish by putting him in prison.

In the confines of his cell, Soyinka is given almost nothing to work with mentally:

> My crypt they turned into a cauldron, an inverted bell of faiths whose sonorities are gathered, stirred, skimmed, sieved in the warp and weft of sooty mildew on the walls, of green velvet fungus woven by the rain's cunning fingers.
>
> (33)

He is denied contact with others and must create his world whole cloth out of the fabric of his own mind. In **"Live Burial,"** he defines this world: "Sixteen paces / by seventy-three. They hold / Siege against humanity" (60). The first line break suggests a pacing prisoner, who has counted again and again the confines of his cell and, as Chikwenye Ogunyemi suggests, "the harm that is indicated is not just on himself but on the whole of humanity. Soyinka would agree . . . that a well-balanced society does not need prisons; the operation of a prison is a comment on the society that finds it indispensable" (80). Soyinka's personal besiegement merges with a cultural assault. The whole social group suffers when men (or women) are jailed, caged like animals, and led helplessly to their deaths. Executions cheapen life and allow killing easy access to our psyches. Soyinka, as both prisoner and poet, would put himself in front of this destruction by recording it.

His crypt restricts him in everything but hearing, so unsurprisingly his poems are filled with images of sound—hammering and birdsong, the wails of women, and the echo of disembodied laughter. Through sound, he differentiates between the walls of his prison in **"Bearings,"** the poem that opens *Chimes of Silence.* To the north is the Wailing Wall, so named because

> it overlooks the yard where a voice cried out in agony all of one night and died at dawn, unattended. It is the yard where hymns and prayers rise with a constancy matched only by vigil of crows and vultures.
>
> (32)

To the west is the "Wall of mists, wall of echoes" and to the south is the "Wall of flagellation," named Purgatory by the poet. It is a wall of beating and torture where "Strokes of justice slice a festive air— / It is a day of reckoning" (38). Only the Amber Wall, where above and beyond the prison a young boy reenacts the fall from the Garden of Eden, is defined by sight.

At the center is his cell—"Vault Center"—surprisingly filled with birds:

> Corpse of Vault Center and the lone
> Wood-pigeons breast my ghostly thoughts
>
> On swelling prows of down, plunge
> To grass-roots, soar to fountains of the sun.
>
> (39-40)

For Soyinka, his cell, "This still center of our compass points" (40), is a space filled with birds, symbolic of spirituality and freedom. As the day closes and a "choir of egrets, severs at the day's / recessional, on aisles fading to the infinite," Soyinka is left alone: "a shawl of grey repose / fine moves of air / gathers dusks in me / an oriel window" (40-41). He takes on characteristics of the birds that fill his cell. His vowels and consonants are feather-soft and restful—"The day's sift filters down" (41). He is a bird fluffed up and waiting out the political night which engulfs him.

Yet the next poem, **"Procession,"** moves directly away from the image of birds; it is a meditation on the hanging day of five men. These men are bound for the earth and bound to the earth. The imminence of their deaths connects them to the grave and its associations with the earth:

> Hanging day. A hollow earth
> Echoes footsteps of the grave procession
> Walls in sunspots
> Lean to shadows of the shortening morn
>
> (41)

Note Soyinka's morbid puns: "hollow" for "hallowed" and "grave" meaning both "serious" and "the burial plot." The death of these men will in no way be a holy rite; instead it is a false ceremony that approaches rapidly, as the sundial-like wall suggests.

There is a distance between the poet and the men for several reasons. First, and most obvious, is the distance between the worlds of the living and the dead; the poet will be in the former while the prisoners are soon to occupy the latter. The poet is the recorder of death, as he has already noted in the Preface, and must live on to tell the stories of these men:

> Tread. Drop. Dread. Drop. Dead
>
> What may I tell you? What reveal?
> I who before them peered unseen
> Who stood one legged on the untrodden
> Verge—lest I should not return.
>
> (42)

Soyinka here puts on a mask of naive authority, pretending that he might have nothing to say about the deaths of these men; this is the nature of the pair of rhetorical questions that abruptly follow the executions, questions directed as much to his captors as to a larger audience. This false naivete is a possible hiding place should the jailer find the poems in his cell, but it is also, as I shall examine in a moment, a segue into the large function of these poems as a restorative for the cultural damage the civil war has done. It is a false naivete, though, because he follows the questions with the assertion that he was there and heard the five die. He was on the very verge of death, thus is the only one qualified to tell their story even as he questions the possibility of poetic witness.

Questioning whether one has the qualifications to write what he has seen is a common thread among poets attempting to write the poetry of witness. As Carolyn Forché notes, speaking of Ariel Dorfman but in a passage that might be easily applied to Soyinka:

> The poet claims he cannot find the words to tell the story of people who have been tortured, raped, and murdered. Nevertheless, it is vitally important that the story be told. Who shall tell it?
>
> (37)

Soyinka echoes this reticence again and again:

> What may I tell you of the five
>
> Bell-ringers on the ropes to chimes
> of silence?
>
> (42)

And:

> That I received them?
>
> (42)

And:

> Let no man speak of justice, guilt.
> Far away, blood-stained in their

> Tens of thousands, hands that damned
> These wretches to the pit of triumph
> But here alone the solitary deed.
>
> (42)

The poet as the shuttle—for he completely becomes his image in this section: ". . . I / Wheeled above and flew beneath them" (42)—must find a new way to tell this story, and he does so by developing a personal mythology, framing the poem with a mantle of poetic witness that will replace the standard of the tapestry weavers and cultural gatekeepers.

The second section of **"Procession"** attempts to develop just such a mythology. "Passage," the section opens, suggesting both a movement through space and time, but also the drawing of the shuttle through the loom—Soyinka is beginning his weaving. The first passage is through the land of death, "rich in the rottenness of things" (43). This death is the putrid decomposition of living things, of the body, yet it is "festive" with rebirth, "velvety with mead and maggots." Death gives rise to new life, because it is the natural process of reclamation, but Soyinka's imperative says, "Shade your sight from glare / Of leavings on the mound. The feast is done" (43). Why? I would suggest that for Soyinka this is too easy an answer. If the body is only meat, then the death of the men had no meaning beyond politics. This avenue is pointless for Soyinka. There must be more:

> A coil of cigarette ribbon recreates
> A violet question on the refuse heap
> A headless serpent arched in fire
> In vibrancy of tinsel light, winding
> To futile light, barren knowledge.
>
> (43)

Death asks the most serious of questions and to answer with the simple idea of the organic cycle of rebirth, as the Orobrian serpent in flames represents, leads only to futility. It may be true, it is after all "knowledge," but alone it cannot be enough.

"Passage" again. The moment after death when from "a bean cake hive" ants swarm and break down the world of the dead—"do not these / Hold a vital motion of the earth?" asks Soyinka (43). They are the necessary parasites, but other foragers come after the dead as well—priests. The priests are more insect-like than the insects: they prey on those who live on after burying the dead:

> . . . how well we know them—
> Inheritors of the stricken hearth.
>
> Their hands are closed on emptiness
> And opening, shall give nothing out.
>
> (43)

These priests have nothing to offer. Like the ants, they come in the wake of death, but instead of "a vital motion of the earth," they contribute nothing.

From the priests, Soyinka moves to those whom the priests had dispossessed in the Yoruba culture—the old women of the loom. It is the weaver women who made the tapestries and kept track of the community's individuals. "Through intertwine / Of owlish fingers on the loom, they gave / and wove a spell against this hour / and kept a vigil upon death and dearth" (44). The women's function as cultural protectors was to watch over the people and record their lives and deaths, so that they would not be forgotten and the proper forms of ancestor worship could occur. With the arrival of the priests, the worship of ancestors was displaced with Christian prayer and the community became divided; the priests drew the focus away from the community because Jesus Christ saves only the individual soul. Thus when the deaths of men are not memorialized, the community suffers. A piece of history is lost.

Into this gap steps Soyinka. He claims a position as the new weaver by assuming his new identity as the shuttle, an identity that is both witness to the cultural and personal destruction of the prisons, but also an antidote against it, just as the old women of the looms "wove a spell against [their] hour / And kept a vigil upon death and dearth." With the final "Passage," Soyinka moves through

> . . . a doorless barrier of light
> This is the last we shall revisit
> Passageways of childhood, through rows
> Of broadlooms weaving emerald tapestries
> To wind the effigy of chanting seasons.
>
> (44)

After reliving, in the poem, the world of the weavers, this world of his childhood, he is ready to take over their position. There is a deep need for a new storyteller because the violence and destruction of the Nigerian Civil War has cast a "leathern dark of bats" that "froze the sunlight in the flight / of weaver's hands" (45). The reign of terror and its easy abuse of power has stopped the weaving, stilled the hands of the carriers of cultural wisdom.

To establish his identity as one who exists in communion with the shuttle as a bird, Soyinka must first establish the manner in which a potent bird such as the shuttle could be captured. Thus, he restates the superstition that one can capture a bird's soul by stepping on its shadow as it flies above:

> If you pass under, trap a sky-soul bird
> Your foot upon its shadow as it flies.
>
> (45)

In the second section, this is the first use of a direct address to the reader using the second-person pronoun and it reflects back to Soyinka's rhetorical questions of the first section. The referent of the pronoun is both general readers, those who might now know the superstition, and his captors, those who know. Soyinka is about to turn superstition to his own creative use. It is this creative rebirth that follows directly. He says:

> In the passage of looms, to a hum
> Of water rising in dark wells
> There to play at trap-the-shuttle
> To step on the flight of its shadow soul
> And hold it captive in a home
> Of air and threadwaves, a lamp
> Of dye-fuels hissing in the sun
> Elusive as the thread's design.
>
> (45)

He taunts his captors, suggesting they can only "play" at trap-the-shuttle. His jail is a "home / Of air and threadwaves," not a cell; the duality of his bird-loom shuttle thrives in this place. He is held but not controlled. They may stop his immediate flight but his captivity will spark a new germination, a rebirth of both the lost cultural heritage and personal poetic creativity:

> By footfall on the shade of wings
> On earth, a bird may drop as rain.
> Ghost fires, loom whisper, indigo lines
> On the broad palm of the loom.
>
> (45)

"Indigo lines" and "loom whispers" are obvious references to the poetic process that occurs in prison, hidden and quiet at night. They are a result of, and at the same time are, the bird that drops as rain.

For the poet who will assume the role of shuttle, with its manifestations of both witness and rejuvenation, it is in no way a completely triumphant vision. The reality of prison, obviously, is never far from Soyinka's mind as he writes these poems:

> Mine the bedraggled wings
> Raising a wind's lament to every step
> Floating on lakes to cries of drowning
> Where pebbles bask in twilights of departing
> Mellowed by the sun's last whispers.
>
> (46)

These are poems of pain, dirges and laments, cries of the heart, but they are poems written nonetheless from within Vault Center, written with his sky-soul shadow trapped under the heavy jackboot of his oppressor. The poet has assumed the place of the weavers by keeping a "vigil over dearth and death." He is

> Waiting for the sound that never comes
> To footfalls long receded, echoing

In craters of newly opened space
Listening to a falter of feet
Upon the dark threshold.

(46)

The shuttle waits for the end of the dark times, when the songs and stories of heroism and despair can fill the newly opened space; the shuttle waits to tell what it has heard. Until the footfalls recede, until that free space is newly opened, he will have to listen to the footsteps of men on the dark threshold of their hanging deaths.

The act of remembering and recording the deaths is the vital necessity of the shuttle. In this, Soyinka is like Anna Akhmatova, who in "The Memory of a Poet" (*Poems*) writes:

> In the awful years of the Yezhovian horror, I spent seventeen months standing in line in front of various prisons in Leningrad. One day someone 'recognized me'. Then a woman with blue lips . . . whispered in my ear (everyone there spoke only in whispers):
>
> —Can you describe this?
>
> And I said:
>
> —I can.
>
> Then something like a fleeting smile passed over what had been her face.

(82)

The act of memory becomes vital to the survivors and for the survival of hope, because when people's deaths are lost, their lives are lost. The reality of Soyinka's condition is no more hopeful after he has written; he is still imprisoned, but he has claimed a piece of cultural space where he is capable of memory.

Soyinka writes from the deepest of privacies, a political hell of solitary confinement. As he does, he reaches out to the people, offering what he has witnessed as a testament, both of what he endured and of what others suffered beyond endurance. Soyinka's private self becomes the salvation of a public group; he speaks for the people, not to them. He becomes the shuttle and weaves the story of those things that are too often hidden behind the steel shutter and the tall stone wall.

Works Cited

Akhamatova, Anna. *Poems*. Selected and trans. by Lyn Coffin. New York: Norton, 1983.

Forché, Carolyn. *Against Forgetting: Twentieth-Century Poetry of Witness*. New York: Norton, 1993.

Lense, Edward. "A Voice for the Wild Man: Robert Bly and the Rhetoric of Public Poetry." *AWP Chronicle* 26.2 (1993): 17-20.

Ogunyemi, Chikwenye Okonjo. "The Song of the Caged Bird: Contemporary African Prison Poetry." *Ariel: A Review of International English Literature* 13.4 (1982): 65-84.

Soyinka, Wole. *A Shuttle in the Crypt*. New York: Hill and Wang, 1972.

Peter L. Berger (review date December 1996)

SOURCE: Berger, Peter L. "Out of Africa." *Commentary* 102, no. 6 (December 1996): 70, 72.

[*In the following review, Berger asserts that, despite some stylistic flaws,* The Open Sore of a Continent: A Personal Narrative of the Nigerian Crisis *is both an "useful and moving" work.*]

This book, by the Nigerian playwright who won the Nobel Prize for Literature in 1986, is a cry of the heart. Based on three lectures given by Wole Soyinka at Harvard, **The Open Sore of a Continent** is neither particularly well-organized nor even well-written; but its anguish—or rather, its very great anger—is palpable, and easy to sympathize with.

The greater part of the book consists of a passionate denunciation of the present Nigerian regime, led by Sani Abacha, which came into power after the annulment of the elections of 1993 and the imprisonment of the man who won them. But Nigeria's plunge into autocracy and brutality hardly began with the new military government. Soyinka reflects here on the entire history of his country since independence from Great Britain in 1960, a history which in many ways is paradigmatic of sub-Saharan Africa in general.

As Soyinka tells it, Nigeria exemplifies both the highest hopes and the worst disappointments of African nationhood. The largest African country, with a population exceeding 90 million, it covers a vast territory and harbors rich natural resources, including huge oil reserves. When it emerged from British colonial rule, there was every reason to think it would not only become an economic success but assume the leadership of black Africa.

That was not to be. Like other British ex-colonies, Nigeria was launched with the institutional accouterments of Westminster-style democracy, a judiciary trained in the common-law tradition, and a fair-sized educated middle class. But again in a pattern characteristic of all the new African states, Nigeria's borders, drawn when the European powers were carving up the continent among themselves, bore little relation to the sociological realities on the ground. In particular, Nigeria contains a multiplicity of ethnic groups with little in common, and religiously it is split about evenly between Muslims in the north and Christians in the south, with a strong admixture of indigenous African religions.

Creating a nation out of all this diversity would have been no small task under the best of circumstances. In the event, independent Nigeria has witnessed a seemingly endless cycle of democratic beginnings followed by military dictatorships, pervasive inefficiency and corruption, and persistent ethnic and religious animosity. The bloodiest phase was the civil war occasioned by the attempted secession of eastern Nigeria in 1967 to form the independent state of Biafra. That secession was crushed with great cruelty, as similar secessions have been and are still being crushed in other parts of Africa (Soyinka repeatedly invokes the struggle in southern Sudan).

No more graphic emblem of the current state of affairs in Nigeria can be imagined than the event with which this book concludes: the execution of the civil-rights activist Ken Saro-Wiwa and eight of his colleagues from the Ogoni ethnic group in November 1995. According to Soyinka, the execution was so botched that Saro-Wiwa had to be hanged three or four times before he finally died. His last words on the scaffold are reported to have been: "Why are you people doing this to me? What sort of nation is this?"

"What sort of nation is this?" That is also Soyinka's question. And he goes on to ask an even larger question, one that is imposing itself almost everywhere in the world today: what is a "nation," anyway?

All too often, this question is asked—by Bosnians, Chechens, or Kurds—in the midst of horrendous bloodshed. It is also asked, under more merciful circumstances, by Quebecois and Catalans, and for that matter by Americans pondering the implications of multiculturalism. Although Soyinka poses the question with an admirable sense of urgency, his answer does not get us very far.

Soyinka sharply criticizes the principle, considered virtually sacred by the Organization of African Unity and indeed by almost all African governments, according to which the borders of each presently existing state are inviolable and permanent. He points out that this principle serves the interests of whichever rulers are in control of a given "nation space," and not necessarily the interests of the people who have to endure their rule. "A nation," he writes correctly, "is a collective enterprise; outside of that, it is mostly a gambling space for the opportunism and adventurism of power."

Equally bracing is Soyinka's rejection of a favored piece of conventional wisdom. The chaos into which Nigeria and other African countries have descended has routinely been blamed on their former colonial masters. But, as Soyinka points out, there is more to it than that. The colonial history of Africa does indeed do little credit to the European powers; but in the postcolonial period, the wounds have been largely self-inflicted. "What color," Soyinka asks "are the hands that dehumanize our African peoples today, as they have done for nearly four decades of independence?"

Beyond these assertions, however, Soyinka is not especially helpful in explaining the determining causes of the national debacles of which he writes. Perhaps he comes closest when he observes, "Man is first a cultural being. Before politics, there was clearly culture."

The relation of African cultures to African politics is indeed one of the big puzzles in the world today. Soyinka is hardly alone in ultimately failing to come to grips with it, but he is certainly right to note the lack of congruence between the new political and the old ethnic/cultural maps of the continent, which imposes a formidable handicap on any society seeking to take off into modern economic development. (This handicap, incidentally, was not faced by the successful societies of East Asia.) Other factors at work include the general absence of an idea of private property, especially in the ownership of land; patriarchal and polygamous forms of family life; an ethic of *machismo*, in comparison with which the Latin American version seems positively feminist; and still other features of African culture that may have functioned well in a premodern economy but are clearly dysfunctional under conditions of modernization and urbanization.

Even if we understood more fully the cultural factors that have contributed to the fiasco of African politics, however, we would still be a long way from prescribing remedies. Cultures do not change easily, and they are particularly resistant to deliberate, policy-driven interventions. In Africa, any initiative in this area would almost certainly have to involve religion—now as always a force conducive to swift and radical cultural change. Nigeria, however, seems an unlikely candidate for an experiment of this kind, which perhaps ironically has a greater chance of success in Nelson Mandela's South Africa. Indeed, the outcome of *that* new cultural/political enterprise will carry important lessons not only for Nigeria but for the rest of sub-Saharan Africa.

But I do not mean to criticize Wole Soyinka for the book he did not write. The one he did write is both useful and moving—a "*j'accuse*" that bravely eschews the tactic of blaming all Africa's woes on racism, imperialism, and colonialism; a ringing affirmation of humanity; and an instructive reflection on the moral foundations of nationhood.

Wole Soyinka, Olesegun Ojewuyi, and Shawn-Marie Garrett (interview date spring 1997)

SOURCE: Soyinka, Wole, Olesegun Ojewuyi, and Shawn-Marie Garrett. "A World of Amusement and Pity." *Theater* 28, no. 1 (spring 1997): 61-8.

[*In the following interview, Soyinka discusses multiculturalism, his literary and political interests, and the future of Nigeria.*]

[*Ojewuyi and Garrett*]: *The opening lines of the title song on the album* Ethical Revo-Wetin *go like this: "I love my country, I no go lie, na inside am I go live and die, when e turn me so I twist am so. E push me, I push am. I no go go." How would you write those lines today?*

[Soyinka]: The word "love" is used, I hope you realize, in a dynamic way. In other words, I don't have any, and never have had any, sentimental feelings towards Nigeria as such. I'm not a diehard patriot. I don't wave the flag. So when I say I love my country, I love the earth, I love the soil, I love the people, but it's a strongly conditional love. In other words, you push me, I push you. I believe that nation owes me at least six feet and I'm entitled to that. Preferably, I believe it owes me shelter as well. And by "me," I'm talking about the ordinary citizen. And every individual, every collective, every group interest must ensure that they are not cheated out of anything by that nation. That is the first condition of love.

If a nation is not living up to those expectations, it must expect, as has happened, that its citizens will begin to redefine just what constitutes the object of love, loyalty, identification. Whether they have to die to absolutely belong, to claim those six feet . . . Remember, though, I also give examples of nations which do not, in my view, represent nations, which indulge in grandiose projects at the expense of the citizens. So it's a dynamic relation, a constant questioning.

How do you differentiate between culture and nationhood?

Culture is much, much easier to define than nationhood, even though it is, of course, even more fluid. But for me, culture is the totality of man's productivity, the totality of productive systems—manners, morals, ethics, artifacts, and so on—and each one of these is interwoven, interlinked, with the next. For me, there's no separation, or very little, between the politics of a nation—in other words, the way authority perceives its citizens—and the citizens' expressions through their works, their art, their sense of identity with the totality that makes up a nation. That means culture can also inform, and in fact direct, a nation's political priorities.

In this country, there's a lot of discussion about multiculturalism. Yet frequently the term doesn't seem to live up to the promise of its name. Do you see a way in which theater could play a role in bringing about a true multiculturalism?

First of all, multiculturalism is a fact that cannot be washed away. But the question I think you're asking is this: Is multiculturalism an academic identification, something which sociologists or social anthropologists identify, and does it fail to go beyond that? In other words, is it reflected in the policies of government? Is it reflected in the apportionment of resources? That kind of basic recognition? Well, I'm going to leave you to answer that.

But as for how theater can bring about a genuine multiculturalism, I think it can be effective among the people themselves by bringing to one culture or another a dynamic awareness of the multiple existence of various cultures. This means moving towards not merely tolerance, but towards a real creative/recreative enjoyment of the fact of the multicultural reality. In turn, this may affect the policies of the Ministry of Arts and Culture, or whatever the equivalent is in this country. Certainly it affects the priorities and the awareness of foundations for the arts. But whether theater itself, whether anything, in fact, can bring any government, any political organ, to fruitful relations with the fact of multiple cultures, I do not really know. But definitely among people themselves: those who go to the theater, those to whom theater is taken—in their homes, in their offices, in their ghettos, in their eating places, in the parks—I believe the theater can, not weld together, but at least link together, the consciousness of peoples.

Take a play like ***A Dance in the Forest,*** which I directed in Nigeria. For me, it was an opportunity to send a very strong message. I used the opportunity to introduce, almost in an eclectic manner—but the play lends itself to that—the various cultural groups of the country. I used Ati Logwu dancers, I used acrobats from parts of the north, from the Tiv area. We used Agbor dancers from the midwest. There is also a European element in the play. Now whether, when we look at Nigeria today, that particular approach to that play—or any number of other plays, not just by me but by others—whether this has led to a cultural bonding, well, I'll leave you to take a look at the reality today and decide for yourselves.

Yet once a play—and this is what I think is so marvelous about plays—leaves its original mooring, once it moves out of its cultural background, it becomes something else. You can try and make it as authentic as you like, but there is a kind of symbiotic influence which takes place once you move a play out of its original grounding. I don't care what play it is. Whether it's Shakespeare, Chekhov, J. P. Clark, or Bougando

. . . Even Duro Ladipo's strong, almost pure Yoruba theater: I saw *Oba Koso* in Germany and in the United States, and of course the atmosphere is immediately different. You still enjoy the authentic thing. You know you're being transported to its homeland. But the *metteur en scène*—not necessarily even the director but the person who stages it, who places it on foreign boards—is obliged to do some tinkering which tailors it for its new home. It's unavoidable. So I tend to give outside directors a kind of resigned leeway. When they're directing my plays, all I ask is that they don't trivialize it, or turn it into a piece of exotica.

That's the danger. How can it be avoided?

First of all, a recognition, a really deep recognition, of the universality of art, and art forms, and of the human experience. Understanding that what is on the boards can have correlations within the society in which it is being presented. And artistic integrity, as well as a lack of condescension. When my plays were first done in English-speaking countries, the critical response was not exactly patronizing, not condescending—but nevertheless, it was an ignorant motion towards the grass skirt. If you wanted to present an African subject, there was always a thatched hut and a grass skirt, it was as simplistic as that. But a lot of that has been abandoned now. And the rediscovery of ritual by European and American theaters, particularly in the 60s, has tended to act as leavening between various forms of cultural theater. But ritual can also be trivialized. I've seen some horrendous productions of Jean Genet, whom I insist on calling a ritualist *par excellence*. Often, those who approach his theater don't realize that they are in the provenance of a master ritualist.

What have you observed about European and North American theaters in your recent years of exile?

What happens when a society is sated with prosperity? What happens to a society which believes that all its major conflicts are either resolved or on their way to being resolved? What happens to a society which eventually terminated a devastating and immoral war? I'm talking about the Vietnam War and the defeat of the Americans. That period was very, very political in the theater. And in the period before it, the period of the Black liberation struggle, the theater was filled with highly political plays.

But afterwards? I suppose there is something you might call "war weariness." It settles on people, and they exaggerate the resolutions they believe they have made of various conflicts, and settle down to, shall we say, promoting the good things of life—entertainment, fantasy, and escapism. The audiences turn away with impatience at theater which provokes them towards a new consideration of existing contradictions in society:

"Enough whining, enough agitprop. Let's settle down and enjoy the middle-class prosperity towards which everybody is aspiring." In other words, my observation of American society—and this cuts across most classes, academia especially and the intelligentsia in general—is that your society is moving on towards an even keel, and therefore more general issues are being addressed rather than harsh political issues. As for the underclass, I regret to say that they take refuge in other forms of escape, drugs and so on, rather than provocative arts. This is the observation of an outsider.

What about the role of the mass media in all of this?

The mass media is horrendously guilty of propagating myths in the United States. The mass media has become a victim of its own success, and therefore a kind of social tyrant in the brainwashing of society. And theater is being more and more marginalized. Look at what's happened: the mass media has extended into a kind of contradiction, a kind of personalized, "democratized" media. I know people who've been weaned away from television—I don't imagine this is in large numbers—weaned away from their obsession, their hypnotism by the box, only to transfer their love and loyalty to a different kind of screen. I know of individuals who spend hours—hours!—into the night "surfing," as I believe they call it. And then the individuals we are talking about also fancy themselves as publishers. They feel they are in control now of the information. They can intervene. They can libel to their hearts content. We've been enduring this in our political struggle of recent times. Everybody now is an instant writer, an instant publisher, an instant editor. And so there is a kind of fragmented empowerment, which detracts from the collected social, authentically social, forms of art. People are beginning to live in a virtual reality which attenuates the relevance of theater for many of them.

Having said that, I believe the theater is such a powerful medium, such a human, a human*ized*, medium, that it cannot really be eliminated. No.

In 1984, during the celebration of your 50th birthday, you described yourself as belonging to a "wasted generation." Again in 1994, at the world premiere of **Iku Olokun Esin Akinwumi Isola (Death and the King's Horseman)** *to celebrate your 60th birthday, you declared, "For nearly all of the adult existence of my generation, I have joined hands with others in attempts to disperse the stubborn agents of a depressing eclipse of our future. . . . In these circumstances, I do not find the least cause to celebrate anything, least of all a birthday that represents for me years of frustration and waste." Who are these stubborn agents? Are they limited to the Nigerian landscape, or do you find them in other places, too?*

They're mostly within the Nigerian landscape, simply because that's where I've operated most. The agents, well . . . you know who they are. You find them in the political class. You find them very much these days in the military class. You find them among the collaborators who allow both groups to succeed. You find them among the religious fundamentalists who want to destroy the secular vitality of the nation, who sap its secular, its very healthy, ethos of cohabitation. And who have also destroyed our university system. Those who've enthroned the principle of mediocrity, of bootlicking. Those who've sold autonomous institutions to power. We are a very stupid and open sore of a continent.

You see, when we were students, we couldn't wait to get home. We were the renaissance people who were going to build something which no other people or nation in Africa would be able to boast about. We were eager to demonstrate to the European, the external world, that had held us down, that had colonized us, that they had nothing to show us. Really. That they had nothing. We believed that very passionately. This feeling was very much among those of us who had actually spent some time studying in Europe. We looked at their society: what was it exactly? I found Great Britain filthy. It's only been cleaned up in the last couple of decades. It was *filthy*! It was all slums. Oh, horrendous food! All soggy. They didn't know how to eat, they didn't know how to live. There was no sense of community, the way we understand community at home.

So I studied in England. I appreciated my education. I appreciated the friendships I made. My professors were exemplary. I learned a great deal from them. Libraries were always open, and so on and so forth. But when you talk about life, life in the most profound sense, I found that there was no soul in that place. And many of us felt the same way. So, there we were: eager young people. We just wanted to return home and build, using the cultural confidence we had inherited, which was in us. We had our scientists. We used to meet periodically, those studying physics, or those studying chemistry, engineers and bankers . . . we were the future. And our space was the future space of the world.

Well, you see how it's all turned out. Do you wonder that I feel wasted? I feel wasted simply because I never accepted the status quo, simply because I had a projection, together with others, and I've just seen that projection constantly thwarted.

So you would locate these years of frustration and waste in the totality of your experience as "Ogun-Kongi" Soyinka?

Ogun, I'm afraid, has retreated to Ire Hills. I don't think that the creative hand which is stretched to our people in all directions has been grasped. People do not allow themselves to be pulled up that hill, that

mountain. I think many of us, like Martin Luther King, Jr., have been, in our minds, to the mountain top. But what's the use, giving thought to what could have been, without any sense of fulfillment?

If Ogun has retreated to Ire Hills, what's he doing there?

He's contemplating the world with amusement and pity.

Does he have anything in common with the character of the Professor in **The Road***?*

You ask me now to interpret my own play, which I'm not very fond of doing. Let's just say that the Professor's search for the word is symbolic of both the spiritual and psychic dissatisfaction of many sensitive people with material reality, with the palpable reality of existence. There is always the sense of something hidden, something being withheld. Either you interpret it as the existence of a superior intelligence, which limits what is accessible to humanity, or it can take the form of the peeling away of a veil with which Nature covers herself. And the absolute conviction that life cannot be just what is experienced as it is tasted, smelled. That there is something beyond. It's another form of religion, I suppose. In a way, that's what Professor in his confused and half-mad, half-sane and logical state is about, and what he is constantly groping towards.

With regard to this problem of returning to Nigeria, having been educated in England, what do you think about the discourse of populism versus elitism? Who do you see your theater and your politics speaking to?

I'm very glad you mentioned this so-called elite, because who are the elite? Look at academia: I can point to very, very few people who, by their actions, consciously, have separated themselves from the masses of the people. Intellectuals and artists are some of the most mass-oriented people in the world. This includes painters, sculptors—people who continue in the tradition of the former, the traditional, the indigenous artists in our society. The singers, the theater people. The elite really are the power people. They are the ones who separate themselves, who turn themselves into masters and lord it over the rest. And it is this intense consciousness of the deprivation, of the expropriation of the people, that makes us see intellectuals and artists as allied against the status quo of power.

Very often when people talk of elitism they're talking about stylistics—in literature, for instance. They say, "Oh, who do you expect to understand this? Who are you writing for?" Well, my answer to that always is this: art and creativity is a socialized activity. In other words, you don't pick out just one work of art and say, "Oh, 90 million people can't understand this, therefore it's elitist." This is inaccurate. This is a kind of flagella-tion, either self-flagellation, or external flagellation. You look instead to the entirety of the corpus of artists, and you find that even what appears to be erudite or esoteric is carried forward, reflected in other forms of expres-sion. There is a continuum in artistic processes. And it is a continuum both within the genre and also between the various genres. So I don't get too worried about the elitist tag attached even to some of my own work. I ask people to understand that, as I said, no work exists in isolation.

As another example, I translated a Yoruba classic into English [*The Forest of a Thousand Demons*]. And I know how many aspirins I had to take just to get through my own language. And at the end of that one novel, well, have you seen me dare to tackle another one? The language was Yoruba at its very deepest, and this is the way I believe language *should* be used from time to time, depending upon the burden of the material it's meant to carry.

You told an audience at Wellesley College recently to beware of "fictioning" Africa. What did you mean exactly?

The fictioning of Africa has a long, disreputable history. I've written about the earlier fictioning, the fictioning by the early explores, the missionaries, and throughout antiquity. Herodotus, for example, told some tall tales about the tails he was supposed to have encountered in Africa. But, we haven't encountered them yet and none of their bones have been exhumed. It was also conve-nient for the would-be slavers to demonize Africa. Even before that, during the European Renaissance, the carry-over of bestiaries from Medieval thinking to the con-ceptualization of the African continent lingered into the Renaissance period. And, of course, it was eagerly embraced when it became necessary to justify the slave trade. Modern fictioning, however, is unfortunately be-ing carried out by the apologists for dictatorships on the African continent. The reality of the dictators, the exploiters, creates a totally new genre of fiction, in which we cannot recognize the countries from which some of us have fled. That is the burden of the second round of fictioning.

Do you mean to say that this contemporary "fictioning" is being done by the Africans themselves?

The African-Americans especially. Go back to the time of Idi Amin: who were the greatest fictioners of Idi Amin's reality? People like Roy Innes, ironically chair-man of CORE. He's continued his game with new col-laborators. At that time, if you remember, Idi Amin was the savior of Africa. He was a genial, radical, revolution-ary, benevolent uncle, you know, good-humored. Meanwhile, Idi Amin was butchering his people and eating their livers and throwing the rest of their bodies into the Nile. This deliberate attempt to obscure the hideous actualities of Africa by some of our own kinfolk here is the most painful. I can expect nothing less than fictioning from people who affect a racial superiority towards Africa, who feel that Africans deserve no better than monsters to rule over them—new black monsters in place of the old white monsters. I can understand them. But I find it very, very painful when this tradition is carried on virtually into the new millennium. It's race treachery.

You have predicted that Abacha will be the last dictator Nigeria will ever know. Yet the end of your most recent play, **The Beatification of Area Boy,** *mingles hope and despair in equal measure. What do you see in the future of your theater and Nigeria?*

I am convinced that Abacha is going to be the last dicta-tor. I believe it as passionately as I believed in the 1980s—and this is a belief that I stated in a lecture at the Polytechnic School of London—that apartheid would be wiped out in this very decade. Look at the dynamics of the world today, and look at the dynamics of the African continent. Look at what has just hap-pened recently with the OAU coming out, for a change, to condemn unanimously the takeover in Sierra Leone, to say, "We will not accept this." Who would have predicted that even a year ago? Look now at Abacha in the ridiculous position of having to send troops to restore democracy in Sierra Leone. What is he up to? What does this portend? Is it the "writing on the wall"? Is he procuring favor? Is he trying to buy himself more time? Whatever it is, add it all up together, and you'll see that Abacha is going to be the last dictator of my country.

Now, this doesn't mean that there won't be other at-tempts—there are enough lunatics in the Nigerian army to think that they can get away with something that is already *passé*. But believe me, they will last as long as this Sierra Leone dictator is going to last. You can hold a country for ransom for some time, but that's not re-ally governing or ruling over the country. And it's in that sense that I'm totally convinced that Abacha is go-ing to be the last. The internal dynamics of the nation dictate it. The very process, the very methodology, of the resistance against his regime absolutely guarantee it.

What role does theater have to play in it? We'll continue to stage *The Beatification of Area Boy* with or without Abacha. We do hope to make people question their own self-worth by demonstrating the results of their acquiescence. All over the country, playwrights are be-ing locked up, or prevented from putting their plays on in the national theater—and yet there are still plays be-ing staged.

Israel Eboh was recently arrested and tortured for put-ting on **The Trials of Brother Jero.**

The German expression for it, I believe, is *Sippenhaft,* or "guilt by association." The net goes wider and wider from immediate associates or family, to extended family to extended associates to imagined associates. The number of people who've been interrogated, who've been stopped from leaving, whose passports have been seized at the airport, and sometimes later returned—the paranoia is incredible. That's the nature of the insecurity of dictatorships, the insecurity of power.

But I really hold to this general mobilization of the artistic power that we do have, and believe that theater will play a small, tiny, but significant role in assuring the arrival of this "utopia."

Nadine Gordimer recently criticized Americans and her own country's government for not doing enough to stop the violent suppression of human rights in Nigeria. What can we do?

Ask what you did to bring down apartheid in South Africa, then look at the situation in Nigeria. Look at the existence of 90-day detention laws, infinitely renewable. Look at the reality of minority rule. As grotesque as this proceeding may appear, add up the people shot down in cold blood in Sharpville, in Soweto, quantify this and compare it with the number of people who have been killed in a much shorter period under "Idi Amin" Abacha. Study the reports of Amnesty International, the Human Rights Commission of the Commonwealth, the UN Raporteur, authenticated reports of torture, and of the methods of torture. Ask yourselves: Is the situation there really any different from what was happening in apartheid South Africa? Winnie Mandela survived. She was never gunned down by the apartheid regime. By contrast, Kudirat Abiola, the wife of an imprisoned President-Elect, *was* gunned down. Something so inhuman, so obscene. A violation of the most generous form of decency, of the relationship between power and the government. See if you can determine if the situation in Nigeria today is comparable to that of South Africa under apartheid. If the answer is yes, then obviously the same actions that were taken to bring down apartheid in South Africa must be taken to bring down the regime of "Idi Amin" Abacha.

Abiodun Onadipe (review date April 1997)

SOURCE: Onadipe, Abiodun. Review of *The Open Sore of a Continent: A Personal Narrative of the Nigerian Crisis,* by Wole Soyinka. *Contemporary Review* 270, no. 1575 (April 1997): 211-12.

[*In the following favorable review of* The Open Sore of a Continent: A Personal Narrative of the Nigerian Crisis, *Onadipe maintains that "Soyinka's latest words on Nigeria's enduring political problems will be no less controversial and thought-provoking than any of his earlier literary works."*]

This collection of essays on the Nigerian crisis [*The Open Sore of a Continent*] produces a very angry book in which Wole Soyinka pours his heart out. He pulls no punches and does not dwell on diplomatic or academic niceties. The book marks another significant step in the fecund literary odyssey of this writer. Soyinka's search for equity and perfection in Nigeria, the African continent and even the world appeared to have taken on a sense of urgency following the cancellation of the elections of 1993 by the Nigerian dictator, General Babangida.

Forced into exile for his defiant opposition to the military junta, Wole Soyinka's vitriol and venom are evident and know no limits; the cutting wit of his observations is also very profound in an attempt to rekindle global concern for Nigeria's plight by asking a fundamental question of the international community: are we trying to keep Nigeria a nation or make it one? Soyinka considers Nigeria to be a country of 'many nations'. But sadly he does not say much about the responsibilities of the world towards Nigeria during this period nor does he express views on the sanctions issue.

In a free-ranging, hard-hitting and uncompromising discussion of his central thesis 'when is a nation?', Wole Soyinka calls for the re-examination of the concept of nationhood which, he argues convincingly, transcends geography and encompasses what he sees as an ethical map—a theme he does not limit to the African continent. This debate, which has been exercising academic minds in fields such as international relations, should certainly be enlivened by Soyinka's contribution.

The author's radical, democratic traits are very much in evidence throughout the book. For instance, he continues to urge pro-democracy groups not to relent in their efforts to get the military junta out, as he has been advocating through the clandestine radio station, Radio Kudirat International (renamed after the wife of the detained Chief Abiola), with which Soyinka has been linked since his forced self-exile in 1994.

Bent on keeping alive the realities embodied in the 12 June elections that created 'the miracle birth', Soyinka devotes a lengthy essay to the antecedents of the current crisis, stressing that Nigeria has no future as a nation without fully addressing this issue. He unfairly lays the primary blame for the current crisis squarely on the shoulders of Shehu Shagari, Nigeria's first executive president, and his profligate cronies in government. There are of course many other actors whose actions contributed to this turn of events. The heart of the matter is the visionless and often ruthless leadership that Nigeria has unfortunately been lumbered with, and this predates the Shagari government.

For their roles in the current crisis, Abacha and his former mentor, Babangida, came in for exceptionally critical and scathing comments, not only for betraying Nigerians but for robbing the country of its most-prized possession—nationhood; all because they were bent on massaging the egos of a minority which believes it has the divine right to rule in perpetuity. The pogrom in Ogoniland, which Soyinka characterises as Nigeria's experimentation with ethnic cleansing, can be seen in this light. This has been authorised and sustained by successive military dictators, over and above the call of duty because the offending tribe has 'no idea of Nigeria' and 'no notion of Nigeria'—a fair assessment of these two leaders' repressive time in power.

Though Wole Soyinka maintains that he is no patriot, his love for this 'space', called Nigeria, reveals itself in the deeply felt hurt that seeps through his narrative, written in an informal, disarmingly casual style. This, however, does not compromise the wealth of information at his disposal, especially as it is generously spiced with his personal experiences and delivered in a light-hearted even frivolous way, belying the deadly seriousness of the discussion. Two minor errors need to be pointed out. First, MOSOP is the Movement for the Survival (not Salvation) of the Ogoni People. Second, Shehu Shagari was involved in the Green Revolution and not 'Operation Feed the Nation', which was Obasanjo's agriculture programme.

Arguably the most influential Black writer in the English language, Soyinka's latest words on Nigeria's enduring political problems will be no less controversial and thought-provoking than any of his earlier literary works.

Landeg White (review date 13 June 1997)

SOURCE: White, Landeg. "Walking a Step with Soyinka." *Times Literary Supplement*, no. 4915 (13 June 1997): 27-8.

[*In the following review, White discusses the recurring political motifs in Soyinka's essays and dramas, citing* The Open Sore of a Continent: A Personal Narrative of the Nigerian Crisis *and* Kongi's Harvest *as prime examples.*]

When Ken Saro-Wiwa, the Nigerian, novelist, playwright and President of the Movement for the Salvation of the Ogoni People was hanged on November 10, 1995,

following a rigged and rushed trial, the machinery of execution had rusted from disuse. As he was being led away from the gallows after the third or fourth botched attempt to kill him, he cried out "Why are you people doing this to me? What sort of a nation is this?" It is the question that haunts Wole Soyinka's newest book.

Despair and anger about Africa are commonplace. Writers who address it need a rare eloquence if they are not to lag far behind what is said openly in streets and bars and market places. What can a mere author add to the raging scorn, the inventive scatology, the cackling contempt for corruption and brutality that are the substance of today's "oral traditions"? Or when the people have been bombed or hacked into silence, or herded into refugee columns, criss-crossing borders with their pathetic possessions and their trail of corpses, what role is there for African writers agonizing in their enforced exiles?

Soyinka's title echoes, perhaps unconsciously, an earlier despairing comment on Africa, when the dying Livingstone, himself haemorrhaging, confided to his journal the prayer that someone would abolish the slave trade, "this open sore of the world". It was a plea that played a part in the colonizing experiment, recruiting philanthropy as well as greed and authoritarianism, to the partition of Africa. The boundaries created in that scramble have, with minor adjustments, given birth to, or been aborted as, the independent "nations" that are the object of Soyinka's present enquiries.

I write "enquiries" advisedly, because whatever questions Soyinka puts to his readers, he puts equally urgent questions to himself. If he demands with Ken Saro-Wiwa "What sort of a nation is this?", he asks himself what he is doing as a Nigerian writer, or as a writer from Nigeria. The latest twist in this long saga is that the Nigerian junta, having detained and exiled their Nobel laureate, have charged Soyinka (and eleven others) with the capital offence of high treason.

The Open Sore of a Continent is framed by a personal account of events in Nigeria since the annulled election of June 1993, and is valuable on that account alone. Chief Moshood K. O. Abiola, who won that election, remains in detention, and his senior wife Kudirat has been assassinated. The military junta, which has misruled Nigeria effectively since 1966, has succeeded in convincing some friendly governments that it acted to preserved Nigeria's "unity" against the threat of Yoruba dominance—despite the fact that Chief Abiola is a Muslim and that his Social Democratic Party won a majority of the votes in northern and eastern Nigeria, as well as in the western region where most of the Yoruba people live. Meanwhile, in the defence of that same "unity", the junta has targeted the hapless Ogoni people in their struggle against the depredations of Royal

Dutch/Shell, executing Ken Saro-Wiwa and eight others. It is this taboo issue of ethnic nationalism that Soyinka, a Yoruba, tackles head on.

On Nigeria, his case is simple. The military, and the world outside, should accept the results of the 1993 election. But the larger issues loom. What constitutes nationalism, and what are its territorial implications? Soyinka's pursuit of these questions makes *The Open Sore* a book of significance.

To Africanists of the 1950s, the State was not a problem. Recaptured from colonialism, it could be made the means of raising African living standards to those of the developed world. Some even argued that state formation in Africa had occurred independently of European rule, that colonialism had been no more than an interlude in Africa's long history. Faced with evidence of the widening gap between rich and poor nations, aggravated by the first oil crisis, the argument of the 1970s was that the State should be recaptured from the *petit-bourgeois* nationalists who were looting it for their own ends, and made to serve a revolutionary agenda. The claim of more recent studies, as diverse as Jean-François Bayart's *The Politics of the Belly* and Basil Davidson's *The Black Man's Burden,* is that the State is itself the problem. An alien imposition, owing nothing to African culture or skills, the ex-colonial African State with its constitutional, bureaucratic, educational and linguistic inheritance, is a violation of African history. Its disappearance, with the politics of "state-collapse", need not be bad news.

Kole Omotoso's *Achebe or Soyinka?* contributes to this debate with a fresh accusation. It has to be said that his book is flawed, riddled with inconsistencies and judgments that are patently untrue. He charges Achebe with refusing to write of the "middle" generation of Christian Nigerians whom, Igbo-fashion, he regards as "traitors", preferring pre-colonial heroes or contemporaries. Can Omotoso have read *Things Fall Apart,* with its wholly sympathetic portrait of Mr Brown the missionary, and of Nwoye, Okonkwo's son, alienated by his father's rigour, appalled by the abandoned twins wailing in the forest, and lured irresistibly by the music of evangelism? For all his neo-traditionalism, Achebe is far too fair-minded a writer not to recognize the social and aesthetic reasons for Christianity's success in Africa.

The contrast addressed by the title is the claim, much touted in Nigerian criticism, that Achebe writes "simple and easy to read" narratives which "the people" can understand, while Soyinka's sophisticated obscurity is elitist and neo-colonial and designed to impress foreigners. Omotoso describes this as "premature and superficial", noting that some oral forms, such as divination songs, can also be "obscure". But having rejected one type of xenophobia as a means of contrasting Nigeria's

most distinguished writers, he sets up the equivalent charge that Achebe sees the world as an Igbo and Soyinka as a Yoruba and that neither has anything to say of northerners or of minorities.

Soyinka came to prominence young, and it is true that a few poems in his first volume are cluttered and dense. But what he demonstrated very early, especially in his plays, was a mastery of metaphor, of linked images unfolding until the moment when the drama is consummated and the whole radiates as myth. He has testified generously that he learned this studying Shakespeare with G. Wilson Knight at the University of Leeds. But this is also the main characteristic of the Yoruba *ijala* or praises (not just divination songs) which, with their wit and wordplay, their transcendental toughness and complexity, have always been Soyinka's most immediate inspiration. It is Nigerians educated in the stilted bureaucratic English that passes for a national language who have trouble with this, not the so-called "masses" (nor indeed foreign audiences).

Yet *Achebe or Soyinka?* contains one central argument of troubling importance. The first African writers, says Omotoso, were pan-Africanists. They were concerned with the liberation of the continent rather than of the territories defined by colonial boundaries. When, like Achebe and Soyinka, they turned to themes and images more authentically and explicitly "African", they found their materials in their own backgrounds, making the transition from the pan-African to the local and the ethnic without pausing to consider the new "states" which were coming into existence. "Few African writers", charges Omotoso, "have attempted to understand the kind of pressure that African politicians have had to bear." By the time poets, dramatists and novelists discovered "the State" in the first years of independence, they were already concerned with its failures, writing their satires on incompetence and corruption. At the core of the "literature of disillusionment" were the very ethnic metaphors that were tearing states like Nigeria apart.

One of Omotoso's examples is Soyinka's *Kongi's Harvest* (1967), included in the welcome reissue of his *Collected Plays* (though it is misleading of Oxford University Press to continue calling these "collected" volumes, when they contain nothing more recent than 1973). *Kongi's Harvest* opens with a drum roll, coaxing the audience to rise for the national anthem, and then mocks them by raising the curtain and chanting instead the official praises of the Oba Danlola, the play's hero, currently in detention. From this point on, two rival systems of authority are acted out. Kongi has the trappings of a national flag and anthem, an organizing secretary, Right and Left ears of state, a Five-Year Development Plan, a Carpenters' Brigade of young thugs, a Women's Auxiliary Corps, and a "reformed" fraternity of elders charged with the task of formulating the new philosophy of Kongism. Danlola has the religious authority of an Oba. The land's fertility and the prospects for harvest are vested in him. He is associated with song, dance, warmth and a language rich in symbol—as well as (through his heir) with the city's best nightclub and the new agricultural station. The marvellous thing about the play is the internal consistency of its harvest imagery, culminating in the moment when the year's first yam is presented to Kongi who is supposed to sample it on the people's behalf, but who passes it to an official taster in case it has been poisoned. These images are Yoruba in origin, invested with Soyinka's favourite myth of Ogun, but the play is in English and entirely accessible.

The problem for African writers of the 1960s was not that they ignored the State—how could they when it was banning their works, or detaining them or dispatching them into exile? It was, rather, that everything to do with the colonial and ex-colonial states seemed utterly banal compared with the social and religious hierarchies they had supplanted. The argument of *The Black Man's Burden* is already reflected in the literature of three decades back.

Soyinka denies that **The Open Sore** is a requiem for Nigeria, or that he wishes the federation to collapse into ever-diminishing components. The heart of his book is an extended survey of "national questions" in Europe, the Middle East, North America, Africa and the former Soviet Union. If this sounds absurdly ambitious, the fact remains that he pulls it off. His analysis of the predicaments of Kurds and Rwandans, Bosnian Muslims and French Canadians, Basques and Kuwaitis (not forgetting the "miracle" of Mandela's South Africa), is an intellectual *tour de force,* enriched by his experiences as a traveller and his unfailing gift for language. Who but Soyinka, strolling through the market at Samarkand, would record "It did not require your tragic-romantic recollection of James Elroy Flecker's verse play *Hassan* to make you aware you were plunged into a different culture"? Or, noting the Republic of Ireland's periodic doubts about incorporating Protestants, would characterize the IRA as "a national longing that has nowhere to go"?

Acknowledging, with Omotoso, that for most Nigerians, Pan-African visions have contracted to the exigencies of salvaging the "colonial endowment", Soyinka concludes with a sober and dignified statement of where he stands:

> For the moment, I am able to claim that I accept Nigeria as a duty, that is all. I accept Nigeria as a responsibility, without sentiment. I accept that entity, Nigeria, as a space into which I happen to have been born, and therefore a space within which I am bound to col-

laborate with fellow occupants in the pursuit of justice and ethical life . . . I accept that space as a space of opportunities and responsibilities that must extend beyond its boundaries . . . I accept that space as one that is best kept intact.

In July 1994, Tai Solarin, the septuagenarian educationalist long known as the "conscience of the nation" joined a march for justice organized by Soyinka with the words "Ah Wole, I thought I would come and walk a step or two with you." He died the following morning. Today, as he confronts his would-be executioners, Soyinka has more readers and admirers walking with him than he can possibly know.

David Rieff (review date 16 June 1997)

SOURCE: Rieff, David. Review of *The Open Sore of Continent: A Personal Narrative of the Nigerian Crisis* by Wole Soyinka. *New Republic* 216, no. 24 (16 June 1997): 33-41.

[*In the following review, Rieff chronicles recent Nigerian history and discusses Soyinka's outlook in* The Open Sore of a Continent: A Personal Narrative of the Nigerian Crisis *toward the repressive Nigerian regime and the relative indifference of the West.*]

> Not even God is wise enough.
>
> —Nigerian proverb

I.

The hangmen who, on November 10, 1995, carried out the execution of the Nigerian writer Ken Saro-Wiwa and eight of his colleagues from MOSOP, or the Movement for the Salvation of the Ogoni People, the militant tribal advocacy group that he had helped to found five years earlier, were flown into the southeastern Nigerian city of Port Harcourt, where the doomed men were being held, from the far north of the country. Since hangmen are not in short supply in any region of Nigeria, it can be taken as read that the decision to use outsiders was based on the assumption that as northerners, and as Muslims, they could be relied upon to have not a flicker of sympathy for the Christian southerners whose judicial murder they were to carry out. And they passed this test of loyalty to the dictatorship of General Sani Abacha, himself a northerner. It was only the killings themselves that they bungled.

Saro-Wiwa and his colleagues were arrested in May 1994 on charges of having murdered four Ogoni tribal chiefs who had opposed MOSOP's activities. They were tried by a special tribunal and condemned to death. It was generally assumed, abroad and in Nigeria, that the Abacha regime was divided about what to do with Saro-

Wiwa even after the death sentence, and so it would move slowly. Since the Nigerian army again took control of the country at the end of 1983 (the only respite was a three-month-long return to civilian rule at the end of 1993), each of the generals ruling over Nigeria has been more brutal. Babangida turned out to be worse than Buhari, and Abacha has been the worst of all. Yet even Abacha does not rule on his own.

For the elite whose consent Abacha needs to govern, the execution of Saro-Wiwa posed risks. It was one thing to send forces into Ogoni territory, as the Nigerian state had done in 1993 and 1994; but it was quite another to kill a man who had many friends and supporters abroad. In other cases that had drawn criticism from abroad, the regime had compromised. The other miscarriage of justice that excited interest in the West, the life sentence handed down against General Olusegun Obasanjo, another military leader who had been Nigeria's president, was eventually commuted to a prison term of fifteen years.

To the end, there were rumors in Nigeria that Abacha was trying to cut a deal with Saro-Wiwa, as he had done with many other opponents from within the Nigerian elite. Others believed that the Shell Oil Company, whose despoliation of Ogoniland in the Nigerian southeast had been the focal point of MOSOP's protests, would persuade Abacha to spare Saro-Wiwa's life, if only to spare itself the certain prospect of the renewal of protests and the surprisingly effective boycott that Greenpeace had mounted in 1993. Shell had been coping with other public relations problems, and it did not need more bad publicity.

It turned out that these relatively sanguine assumptions did not take into account what Wole Soyinka rightly identifies in **The Open Sore of a Continent,** his remarkable book on the collapse of Nigeria, as the Abacha regime's determination "to make it impossible for the victims of oil exploration to present a united front in their demands for reparations for their polluted land, a fair share in the resources of their land, and a voice in the control of their own development." Having tried, and failed, to stifle the movement through terror, and having imposed direct military rule on Ogoniland, with a similar lack of success, the regime opted to kill its leader. It hoped that, with Saro-Wiwa dead, MOSOP would wither, and Shell, which had withdrawn under pressure from Ogoniland in 1993, would resume its operations.

For the Abacha regime, the stakes could not have been higher. Oil has always been the lifeblood of the Nigerian state. Nigeria is the world's ninth largest petroleum producer, and Shell is by far the most important petroleum company operating in the country. A typical leaflet issued by Shell, at the height of MOSOP's campaign, was titled Nigeria and Shell: Partners in Progress. In reality, as even Shell officials conceded, the tensions in Ogoniland had hardly been invented by MOSOP. As a Shell "Briefing Note" put it in 1993, people throughout the oil-producing areas believe that they "are not getting a fair share of the oil revenues." The company insisted, though, that this was none of its concern. Saro-Wiwa, it argued, was trying to "internationalize the problem." Shell was simply trying to do its work in what it referred to as "a difficult operating environment, much of it swamps." As for the Ogoni's complaints, they were "Nigerian problems."

Saro-Wiwa claimed repeatedly that the Anglo-Dutch multinational had behaved with particular callousness in the Niger River Delta. He was right. Unfortunately, and this excuses nothing, Shell's conduct was not very different from the conduct of other oil companies in places where they were free to operate more or less as they pleased. Oil companies have earned a particularly bad reputation in this regard, as the recent attempt of Unocal to expand its operations in Myanmar demonstrated once again. Indeed, almost all multinationals involved mainly in the extraction of natural resources in Third World countries exhibit abysmal standards on political and environmental issues. The reason is simple: their only need is for a secure environment in which to mine or to drill. They are not trying to create markets in the countries in which they are operating, and so they do not trouble themselves about the social requirements of a market. All they need is a crude political stability. A terrorist kleptocracy will do nicely.

The notion that these swamps were the Ogoni's homeland, and that Shell's operations were gradually making great areas of it uninhabitable, is never mentioned in the company's brochures and press releases. Saro-Wiwa, a Shell official once wrote, is either "a mild nuisance or a great threat." Although they have never admitted as much publicly, there seems to have been some division within Shell over whether Saro-Wiwa represented a threat or a nuisance. Shell officials monitored Saro-Wiwa's activities with increasing alarm and mounted a campaign in Europe and North America against MOSOP's claims; but how seriously they took MOSOP is unclear.

The Nigerian authorities seemed to have had no such doubts. Shell's drilling operations might have despoiled Ogoniland, but the revenues that the Nigerian federal authorities received from oil-related activities, one-half of which came from Shell's operations (they also generated 90 percent of the country's foreign exchange), were all that stood between the regime and economic collapse. At a time when, as the saying went in Lagos, "this country dey as if e no dey" (this country was as good as dead), the Abacha regime needed desperately to increase oil revenues. It could not tolerate the prospect of seeing the cash impeded by the civic activism of small delta tribes such as the Ogoni.

Even many opponents of the regime found the Ogoni question somewhat distant and mystifying. As Soyinka observes,

> for the majority of Nigerians Ogoni is only some localized problem, remote from the immediate, overall mission or rooting out the military from Nigerian politics, rescuing the nation's wealth from its incontinent hands and terminating, once and for all, its routine murders of innocent citizens on the streets of Lagos and other visible centers of opposition. The massacres in Ogoni are hidden ill-reported. Those that obtain the just publicity of horror, mostly in government-controlled media, are those that are attributed to the Ogoni leadership movements, such as MOSOP.

The news, in 1994, that Ogoniland had been declared a military zone under the direct rule of a federally appointed "Task Force on Internal Security" was greeted indifferently in most parts of Nigeria. And when reports began filtering back to Lagos that in Ogoniland whole villages were uprooted, there was little public outcry. Soyinka saw clearly that, as he puts it, "Ogoniland is the first Nigerian experimentation with 'ethnic cleansing'"; but ordinary Nigerians in Lagos often read about violent incidents whose perpetrators cannot be identified. In 1994, a number of apparently unprovoked attacks on Ogoni villages in which hundreds of people were slaughtered was described by the Nigerian government as the result of "disputes" with other villages. How the attackers got their hands on sophisticated weapons, and why the local Ogoni police were ordered out of the area before the attacks, was never discussed.

What happened in Ogoniland in the early 1990s, once the Nigerian authorities realized that local opposition to the despoliation of the region was growing stronger, was a massive campaign of state terror in which the state-run media would insist that nothing at all was happening, or, if reports of bloodshed could not be suppressed, that government forces were responding to "terrorist" attacks. The Russians tried the same tactic in Chechnya. In Ogoniland, unlike in the Caucasus, the tactic largely worked.

In all likelihood, the attackers were members of the Nigerian armed forces. Still, whatever the army's exactions, nothing that the authorities undertook in the Niger River Delta was effective in suppressing the campaign that Saro-Wiwa had initiated. MOSOP's tactic of singling out Shell and demanding reparations for the environmental damage that the company's operations had done to Ogoniland were gathering strength at the time that Saro-Wiwa was arrested. Shell had declared that its decision to stay out of Ogoniland would remain in force until the civil disturbances ceased. But the trouble showed no sign of diminishing.

The Abacha regime was furious about this development, and it was under no illusion about the threat that an expansion of this kind of tribal activism to other Niger delta tribes posed. MOSOP had to be isolated. Otherwise there loomed the danger that many of the peoples of the delta would revolt against the oil companies. In that sense, Shell's shiny patter about the partnership between the company and the federal state was all too accurate. To Abacha and his cronies, an assault on one was an assault on the other. Small wonder, then, that Lieutenant Colonel Dauda Komo, a protege of Abacha who was then the military governor of Rivers State, the region that encompasses Ogoniland, reportedly had made up his mind that Saro-Wiwa had to die.

The trial was a farce from the start, with witnesses testifying and then recanting their testimony, and the judges doing everything they could to prevent MOSOP's lawyers from mounting a proper defense. The condemned men doubtless knew of the regime's desire to destroy them. In the aftermath of the tribunal, protests against the sentences began to gather in intensity. Before the trial, the Ogoni cause had interested mainly environmental activists, a few committed journalists, and the governments of Denmark, Sweden, Norway and the Netherlands, but now even allies of the Nigerian government such as John Major and Boutros Boutros-Ghali, and notably unsentimental leaders such as the head of the European Union, the Secretary-General of the British Commonwealth, and President Nelson Mandela of South Africa, joined in the appeals to spare Saro-Wiwa's life. The condemned men had at least some reason to hope (though some prescient outsiders such as Soyinka had concluded that their fates were sealed). It seems that none of them realized, on that morning when they were taken from the military camp where they had been held for eighteen months to the Port Harcourt prison, that they were going to their deaths.

They had all faced death before. To be an antigovernment activist in Nigeria in the Abacha era has been an increasingly perilous business. But to stand up, as Saro-Wiwa and his colleagues had done, not only to the Abacha regime, but also to the interests of the Shell Oil Company, was to court extinction. And yet Saro-Wiwa had already had the experience of being jailed and released before. In 1993, he was imprisoned in the same prison in Port Harcourt. In his memoir of that time, *A Month and a Day: A Detention Diary,* he wrote of the "great number of people in Nigeria and abroad [who] had taken steps to save me." So there was at least some reason for Saro-Wiwa and his fellow prisoners to assume that the attention that their cases were receiving in Europe and North America would once again stay the regime's hand. Rumors persist in Lagos to this day that Saro-Wiwa could have made a deal and saved his life. But he laughed when Abacha tried to buy him off, and this slight cost him his life.

Saro-Wiwa was taken out first, and led into a room in which a makeshift scaffold had been erected. A black hood was pulled over his head; a noose was cinched around his neck. But when the chief hangman sprang the lever to drop the trapdoor beneath the prisoner's feet, nothing happened. For minutes, as the bound Saro-Wiwa stood there, the executioners tried to get the lever to operate properly. Then it was decided that Saro-Wiwa would not be killed first. One of the other prisoners would enable the hangmen to assure themselves that the scaffold was working properly.

Saro-Wiwa was led back to the holding cell where his eight comrades—John Kpunien, Barinem Kiobel, Baribo Bera, Saturday Dobue, Daniel Grakao, Monday Eawo, Felix Nwanie and Paul Levura—waited their turn to be murdered. Kpunien was chosen and led into the execution chamber. This time the trapdoor worked. Kpunien's body was removed, and Saro-Wiwa was brought in. But the trapdoor failed. Saro-Wiwa was led to one side, and waited as the henchmen tried to get the thing to do its job, as it had done a few minutes earlier when Kpunien died. At this point, Saro-Wiwa is reported to have screamed: "Why are you people doing this to me? What kind of a nation is this?"

On the fifth try, the Nigerian government's judicial murder of Ken Saro-Wiwa was accomplished.

II.

It is not inaccurate to describe Ken Saro-Wiwa as a Nigerian writer who became the leading advocate of the rights of his people; but he was more than that. From the beginning of his career, he wore many hats. As a writer, he was prolific. He wrote novels, polemics, memoirs, political journalism, plays, poems and children's books. He was born in Bori, on the southern coast of Nigeria, in 1941, the son of an Ogoni chief, J. B. Wiwa, and at different times in his life he did energetic service as a publisher, a businessman, a government official and a television producer. The fame that he enjoyed within Nigeria to the end of his life was due to his having conceived and written "Basi & Co.," Nigeria's most popular television soap opera. As the English writer William Boyd remarks in his affecting preface to *A Month and a Day,* the show "was unashamedly pedagogic. What was wrong with Basi and his chums was wrong with Nigeria: none of them wanted to work, and they all acted as though the world owed them a living. . . . This was soap opera as a form of civic education."

Compared to Wole Soyinka or Chinua Achebe, the major writers of contemporary Nigeria, Saro-Wiwa's writing falls short. He had great energy, and a fertile, impatient imagination, but his literary gifts were more appropriate to the writing of film and television scripts than novels and short stories. Boyd's claim that he was a major writer does his heart credit, but not his head. Saro-Wiwa had only a modest talent. For the most part, his non-fiction is far more powerful than his fiction. Readers with no great knowledge of Nigeria would be most likely to admire, and to profit from, and to be moved by, *A Month and a Day: A Detention Diary,* an account of a period of imprisonment in 1993. It is a cry from the heart of someone who is beginning to realize that he will not prevail. "I had been detained for a month and a day," Saro-Wiwa wrote in the book's conclusion, "during which I had witnessed the efficiency of evil. . . . The genocide of the Ogoni had taken on a new dimension. The manner of it I will narrate in my next book, if I live to tell the tale."

In his lifetime, Saro-Wiwa did write one important novel, *Sozaboy,* whose subtitle is *A Novel in Rotten English.* It appeared in 1985. Told in West African pidgin, *Sozaboy,* or "Soldier Boy," is the, story of a young boy conscripted into the Biafran army during the civil war of 1967-70. It chronicles what Saro-Wiwa saw as the pointless horrors of that conflict with bitter verve and originality. At the end of the book, the young recruit simply flees. His message is clear and unflinching: "And I was thinking how I was prouding myself before to go to soza and call myself Sozaboy. But now if anybody say anything about war or even fight, I will just run and run and run. Believe me yours sincerely." It was advice that Saro-Wiwa was not to take himself.

The plaudits of ordinary Nigerians, especially for "Basi & Co.," were not the main reason that Saro-Wiwa was able to get away with his thinly disguised criticism of his society. His story is a complicated one. Despite his long history of activism on behalf of the Ogoni people—he was agitating for them since his school days—Saro-Wiwa was anything but an anti-establishment figure in Nigeria. Indeed, during the Biafran War of 1967-70, he won favor with an earlier generation of Nigerian military rulers by fiercely opposing the Ibo secessionists. He did so not out of a great belief in Nigerian federalism. As he would later explain in *On a Darkling Plain* (1989), his memoir of his role in the war, the Biafran conflict was not, in his view, about the right to self-determination of the Ibo people and the other southeastern tribes that sided with them, as the secessionists had claimed at the time. The war was, rather, "mostly about the control of the oil resources of the Ogoni and other ethnic groups in the Niger River Delta." Saro-Wiwa was utterly convinced that the choice was between "the Ogoni existing as one of 200 or so ethnic groups in Nigeria or as one of 50 or so ethnic groups in secessionist Biafra." And so "I identified with the federal government."

Most Ogonis had in fact sided with Biafran secession, and viewed the federal troops re-entering the Niger River Delta as occupiers, and so the value of Saro-Wiwa to the Nigerian authorities was substantial. And the rewards that he reaped personally for his anti-Ibo stance were immediate and considerable. Since his murder, this part of Saro-Wiwa's story has tended to be swept under the rug by his allies, as has the fact that, unlike Soyinka, he had not always been a steadfast critic of Nigeria's various despots. Yet to insist upon it does not in any way call into question the authenticity of his ever braver resistance to the authorities in the 1980s. By the early '90s, certainly, all his other activities had receded in importance for him, and he was devoting almost all of his energies to the cause of his own Ogoni people, inside Nigeria through the Movement for the Salvation of the Ogoni People, and in any foreign capital where he could get a hearing.

In the beginning, though, the swift rise of a 27-year-old academic, whose only published work was a pamphlet called *The Ogoni Nationality Today and Tomorrow,* owed more to preferments offered by the authorities during, and in the immediate aftermath of, the Biafran war than to anything else. Saro-Wiwa became a member of the government of the newly created Rivers State, which the Nigerian government had created as part of its decision, taken while the area was still controlled by Biafran forces, to transform southeastern Nigeria administratively, so that there would never again be an Ibo secession. As federal forces pushed their way into Ogoniland, Saro-Wiwa was appointed the civilian administrator of Bonny, an oil port on the Niger River Delta that adjoins Ogoniland. In 1968, after federal troops had regained control of all of Rivers State, he became a minister in the government there. He would remain in the post until 1973, three years after the final crushing of Biafra.

To the end of his life, Saro-Wiwa was unrepentant about his role in the Biafran conflict. The rebel Biafran government of Colonel Odumegwu Ojukwu, as he wrote in *On a Darkling Plain,* and repeated in *A Month and a Day,* was "hostile to the Ogoni . . . people." For this reason, while Saro-Wiwa is now a hero to almost every decent Nigerian in Lagos, Kano, or Abuja, as well as to his many supporters abroad, he was a controversial figure among non-Ogonis in his own region of southeastern Nigeria during his lifetime, and he has remained one after his death. Saro-Wiwa was, in truth, a paradoxical figure, a cosmopolitan ethnic, an ethnic cosmopolitan, a tireless campaigner for human rights who was also a tireless tribalist.

That he had wanted no part of Biafra did not mean that Saro-Wiwa had all that much faith in a unitary Nigeria. It was, in his opinion, simply the least bad alternative. He was, to be sure, a member in good standing of the Nigerian elite, who claimed senior Nigerian employees of Shell among his schoolmates, and who had sent his children to be educated in Britain. (His youngest son died in 1992 while at Eton.) But he always saw himself first and foremost as an Ogoni. The more dangerous he saw the situation of the tribe becoming, the more he threw in his lot with it. "My worry about the Ogoni," he wrote in *A Month and a Day,* "has been an article of faith, conceived of in primary school, nurtured through secondary school, actualized in the Nigerian civil war in 1967-70 and during my tenure as a member of the Rivers State Executive Council, 1968-73."

It is understandable, I guess, that his Ogoni identity impelled him to side with the federal authorities in 1968-71, though it must also be noted that many other Ogonis, probably the majority of them, opted for Biafra. The Biafran secession was itself fought largely over oil. The Ibos, who dominated the Nigerian southeast, felt that its oil should be theirs to control; and when the military coup in 1966 put an end to the first Nigerian republic, which had been a fairly equal federation of regions with three regional governments, and most of the power that the Ibos had exercised in the eastern region was assumed by the federal authorities (the southeast was to be divided into three states), the Ibos opted for independence. In a sense, Saro-Wiwa's view of the Ogoni relationship to the Ibos was the Ibo view of their own relationship to the rest of Nigeria.

Would Biafra have been better or worse for the Ogoni? It is impossible to know what a Biafran state would have looked like. Where Saro-Wiwa was almost certainly right, though, was in perceiving that Ojukwu was no friend of the Ogoni people. Under the circumstances, it was perfectly plausible that he would welcome the new three-state arrangement, since it offered the possibility that in the future the Ogonis rather than the Ibos would play a dominant role in what had become Rivers State.

Saro-Wiwa hoped that the constitutional arrangements that would be created after the war would "take strong cognizance of our desires with regard to the companies prospecting or operating on our soil." Still, long before his arrest in 1994, he was writing that "I realize how pious my hopes were [in the aftermath of the Biafran war], and how much they failed." Having crushed the Biafran secession, the government of General Yakubu Gowon turned out to be no more interested in looking after the cultural or the material interests of numerically insignificant tribes such as the Ogoni than their predecessors had been. There are only half a million Ogonis in a count, of more than 100 million. The central authorities, Saro-Wiwa observed bitterly, might pay lip service to the idea of Nigerian federalism, and to the protection of the rights of ethnic minorities, but their assurances were lies.

Unfortunately for the Ogoni, the aftermath of the Biafran war coincided with the oil boom of the 1970s, with the era of OPEC. The Nigerian authorities were obsessed with exploiting the resource. Within a few years of the end of the civil war, there had occurred a huge increase in exploration and extraction activities in Ogoniland, and it was becoming clear to Saro-Wiwa that the same officials who had found non-Ibo south-easterners such as himself useful during the conflict were now bent on developing the natural resources of Ogoniland, no matter what the human or environmental damage. The tribe's interests no longer mattered in a state besotted by fantasies of wealth and global importance. This was a time when there was much talk within the Nigerian elite of the country acquiring an "African" nuclear bomb and a seat on the Security Council, when the government believed that Nigeria was destined not only to lead Africa, but also to be a beacon for the African diaspora in Europe and North America.

Things looked very different in Ogoniland. As Saro-Wiwa put it in *A Month and a Day,* "the Rivers State itself did not prove to be any better than the Eastern Region in reconciling the interests of its component ethnic groups." All the peoples of the Niger delta had suffered tremendously during the Biafran war. Now the oil that lay beneath their soil was putting their physical survival at risk as surely as the fighting had done. And yet the determination of the federal authorities to exploit the delta was unshakable. As Saro-Wiwa pointed out, by the end of the 1970s oil had become "the be-all and end-all of Nigerian politics and the economy, as well as the central focus of all budgetary ambitions." The new federalist ethos provided a useful cover. Who were the Ogoni to stand in the way of Nigeria's progress? What this post-Biafran "unitarism" really meant, Saro-Wiwa wrote bitterly, was that "the resources of the Ogoni and other ethnic minorities in the Niger River Delta could be more easily purloined while paying lip service to Nigerian federalism and unity."

Oil revenues began to play an important role after the first large strikes were made in the mid-1950s by Shell Oil's corporate predecessor, Shell D'Arcy, which had been given exclusive rights to look for oil in 1937. It was in the 1960s, however, that the real profits began to materialize, once Shell finished a pipeline running from its fields in the Niger River Delta to the Bonny Island terminal near Port Harcourt. When Nigeria became independent, it was widely assumed that it would be one of the great success stories of the continent. Oil would provoke economic development, and the processes of modernization begun under colonialism would accelerate, this time to the benefit of Nigerians rather than foreign companies and Western consumers.

In the aftermath of the Biafran war, royalties from the oil companies became more and more critical to the country's survival. Nigeria was ruled by a succession of military regimes—beginning with General Gowon and including the regime led by General Obasanjo, who, since he has been imprisoned unjustly by General Abacha, is now wrongly regarded as having behaved a great deal better than other Nigerian military leaders—and these regimes had not the faintest idea of how to manage the Nigerian economy. It was a period in Africa when everyone was paying lip service to development. The reality was that neither the Gowon regime in the early 1970s, nor the Murtala-Obasanjo administration that succeeded it, was able to improve the real situation of the Nigerian economy. The only question is whether these rulers were venal or incompetent.

As a result of vastly increased revenues, Nigeria's rulers vastly increased state expenditures. The World Bank's Structural Adjustment Program in Africa is notoriously controversial—as Helmut Schmidt once said, "what is good for the World Bank must not necessarily be good for Africa"—but the Bank's report of 1994, Adjustment in Africa, is utterly convincing when it describes "Nigeria's missed opportunity" during the oil boom of 197-83. As the report points out, the post-1973 increases in the price of oil meant that, for the subsequent decade, Nigeria and Indonesia received extra revenues amounting to about 20 percent of their Gross Domestic Products. The Indonesians used the windfalls ably. Nigeria's rulers squandered it. They directed spending to prestige projects in the cities (where government officials and their cronies lived), grotesquely increasing government consumption, and in many cases stealing outright.

When oil prices buckled in the mid-1980s, the Nigerian economy was totally unprepared. The country's rulers had come to view the oil monies as little more than what Tom Forrest, an economic historian of modern Nigeria, has described as "the opportunity for the large-scale personal acquisition of wealth by those with access to state power." Put more starkly, long before the collapse of the Nigerian economy in the 1980s, the elite was already robbing the state blind. All the while, foreign governments kept insisting that all was well, and putting Nigeria forward as a force for stability in Africa—an ideal regional hegemon, to use the conception favored by the Nixon and Ford administrations. Chinua Achebe's intuition that "Nigeria will die if we keep pretending that she is only slightly indisposed" went unheeded. The corruption, the mismanagement, the repression, the clientelism, and the incompetence of the Nigerian state increased. And the bust was even more dangerous than the boom: the more the economic situation deteriorated, the more the desperation of the satraps to hold on to their power grew.

Saro-Wiwa saw all this clearly. As the crisis deepened, and the situation of the Ogoni became more and more embattled, he came to recognize that his hopes had been in vain. He saw that, from the Biafran War to Abacha's seizure of power, oil on their land had been a catastrophe for Ogoniland. In the immediate aftermath of Nigerian independence, things had been somewhat different. Until the civil war, the practice had been for the authorities to share the oil revenues that they received from foreign companies such as Shell with local administrations on oil-bearing areas. Usually, the federal-local split was fifty-fifty. By 1980, however, only 1.5 percent of the proceeds were going to the people in the areas from which the oil was being extracted. And exploration and drilling were proceeding at a breakneck pace, with not the slightest regard for environmental or safety standards.

Ogoniland was being turned into a disaster area. And Nigerians outside the southeast were not especially perturbed. The previous arrangement, after all, had not favored the majority of Nigerians living in non-oil-producing parts of the country. For them, the despoliation of the Niger River Delta was a matter of passing concern. Economic times were hard, and the oil revenues were almost all that Nigeria could count on. To go back to the old system, in which the small tribes who lived in the oil production areas got a disproportionate share of the revenues, was a very unpopular idea. It was inevitable that, when Saro-Wiwa and his colleagues in MOSOP began to expose what was taking place in Ogoniland, when they carried their case to the National Minorities Council of the United Nations, the Nigerian authorities would respond with fury; but neither Saro-Wiwa nor his foreign supporters seem to have foreseen that there would be little sympathy for the Ogoni there among other Nigerians.

There has been a tendency since Saro-Wiwa's death to overstate the support that he received in Nigeria during his lifetime, and also the commitment that existed outside the country to the Ogoni struggle. Until Saro-Wiwa's arrest, detention, and death, the Ogoni cause stirred little interest, except among a few environmental activists and Anita Roddick, the owner of the Body Shop stores. Saro-Wiwa's trial, the image of the plucky writer with his pipe in his mouth standing up to a corrupt regime bent on murdering him, changed all that. Suddenly there was international outrage. It was fortunate for the Ogoni that they had a leader with Saro-Wiwa's charisma. Many other small tribal peoples, from the Amazon basin to southern Sudan, are uprooted and massacred without ever striking a resonant chord in the small number of rich countries whose public opinion can alter their fate. The real surprise is that the Saro-Wiwa case managed to compel as much attention as it as it did in our tragedy-saturated world.

III.

In *The Open Sore of a Continent,* Wole Soyinka observes that Nigeria has become a state without sense or purpose, except for the enrichment of the murderous kleptocracy that surrounds General Abacha. He ends his book with the suggestion that Saro-Wiwa's murder may sounded the death-knell for Nigeria, that there is nothing left for decent Nigerians to defend any more, that, with the Abacha regime, "we may be witnessing, alas, the end of Nigerian history. It is hard to disagree. A nation that is now being underwritten largely by oil revenues that are put to no constructive purpose, and also now serves as the transit point for 50 percent of the heroin that arrives in the United States, may indeed be irredeemable. Indeed, the Nigerian disaster is so deep and so pervasive that it may well lead, in the very near future, to the breakup of Africa's most populous and (potentially) most rich and most important country.

What is most striking about Soyinka's book is that he no longer finds it possible to lament the end of Nigeria. He ends his book wrathfully. If Saro-Wiwa's death does lead to the end of the Nigerian nation, he writes, it "would be an act of divine justice richly deserved." It is by no means clear, however, that this collapse—Soyinka seems simultaneously to fear it and to look forward to it—will take place. Indeed, there is some evidence, despite intercommunal violence, continued unrest in some parts of the country, and a recent spate of mysterious bombings in Lagos, that in the past year the Abacha regime has solidified its grip on power and broadened its base of support.

Indeed, the most ominous sign that Soyinka may be wrong, that the rulers in Lagos may dodge their just deserts, may be the fate of Soyinka himself. In March 1997, he was condemned to death in absentia by another of General Abacha's tribunals on charges of "levying war" against Nigeria. Unlike Salman Rushdie, of course, Soyinka has all along insisted that the Abacha regime had to be toppled at all costs. Soyinka has not involved himself with antigovernment violence, but he has refused to condemn it. The death of Saro-Wiwa was, for Soyinka, the last straw; and, like Saro-Wiwa, Soyinka demands to know, in his book, "what sort of a nation is this?"

In Lagos, meanwhile, it is business as usual. And business as usual means, well, business. Businessmen who work in Nigeria say that they are finding it easier to conduct their affairs these days. And the political opposition is fragmented. Abacha continues to promise elections and a return to civilian rule, and many Nigerian politicians have chosen to participate in this charade, even though Moshood Abiola, the man who was legally elected president of Nigeria in 1993, continues to rot in jail. Anyway, the chances that a civilian government, of the sort that will stand up to the Nigerian military, might get elected are almost nil.

Nor can Nigeria rely upon what we complacently and inaccurately call "the international community." The aftermath of Saro-Wiwa's execution illustrated this perfectly. There was much talk of imposing serious sanctions against Nigeria, of expelling it from the British Commonwealth, of other steps against it. President Mandela was particularly outspoken. But the South African volte-face has been particularly startling. South African officials account for it privately by insisting that Mandela yielded to pressure from other African leaders who insisted that he tone down his criticisms of the Abacha regime. The administration in Pretoria has its hands full at home. Judging by its behavior during the crises in Liberia, Zaire, Rwanda, Burundi and Nigeria, and by its response to the American proposal to establish an African crisis intervention force, the Mandela government will not take the lead.

The important Western governments have been equally inconstant. As Aryeh Neier pointed out recently, we have a double standard about human rights. In countries of little or no economic or strategic importance, we stand on our principles. But Nigeria is not negligible. Its oil is important, as is the role that it plays in West African security, notably in the Nigerian-led ECOMOG peacekeeping force in Liberia. The Assistant Secretary of State for Human Rights can issue all the reports on abuses in Nigeria that he likes, but when the American ambassador to Abuja has to negotiate a renewal of the Nigerian commitment to ECOMOG, he needs the cooperation of the same regime that his colleagues in Washington have so strenuously condemned.

The dissociation between the rhetoric and the reality of the Clinton administration's policy toward some of the very worst regimes in the world has distorted also its African diplomacy. It is true that American policymakers sometimes have the decency to be troubled by their own inconsistencies; they have not quite attained the cynicism of the Europeans. Still, these scruples did not prevent the United States from cultivating its ties to Mobutu Sese Seko's regime, when Zairean support for Savimbi's forces during the Angolan civil war was important, or, in the aftermath of the cold war, when Western governments needed Zaire to continue allowing the Hutu refugees from Rwanda to remain on Zairean soil. Washington withdrew its support for Mobutu at the last minute, to avoid the embarrassment of backing a loser. (It is not Washington that is to be blamed, though, for the discouraging fact that the alternative to Mobutu Sese Seko is Laurent Kabila.)

The United States could never deal firmly with Nigeria because of the Nigerian government's willingness to lead the African force trying to stabilize the situation in Liberia. Any pressure on the Abacha regime from Washington would have led to the withdrawal of Nigerian troops—a development that Washington, supremely unwilling to commit American troops, has been desperate to avoid. It is impossible to ask Abacha

for favors one day and threaten him the next. There is no reason to think that the Clinton administration will behave any differently when the next group of dissidents are murdered by the Nigerian state. And that day may not be far off. Nineteen other MOSOP members are in jail in Port Harcourt. And now there is a government contract out on Soyinka.

IV.

For Wole Soyinka, the most important lesson of Ken Saro-Wiwa's life and death is the extent to which the last twenty years of Nigerian history has been simply the story of Ogoniland writ large. The really crucial question, though, is whether Nigeria is not Africa writ large. Are the pathologies that Soyinka lays bare in his own country not to be found also in almost all of sub-Saharan Africa? *The Open Sore of a Continent* is an important achievement not least because, without always making the case explicitly (although his brief remarks about the Rwandan genocide are very moving), the fate of Nigeria is, for Soyinka, the fate of Africa. The continent is itself beginning to seem like an open sore.

It must have cost Soyinka a great deal to come to this terrible conclusion. For a man with his anti-colonialist, nationalist, pan-Africanist sympathies to have witnessed the death of so many of his dreams, and to have admitted to his disenchantment so candidly, is remarkable. But if Soyinka is prepared to give up on so much, it is owing not only to his despair over the situation in Nigeria, but also to his commitment to the truth. All writers who turn their attention to politics say that they are committed to the truth. This writer really is. He does not seem to be worried that what he has to say will give aid and comfort to the "wrong" people.

If only the friends of Africa in the West could be as candid. Given the magnitude of the continent's crisis, treating Africa to the same unsentimental analysis that Soyinka has applied to his own country seems long overdue. At the political level, despite the efforts of Randall Robinson at the TransAfrica Institute to rouse support for protests against the Nigerian dictatorship, little of the fervor that accompanied anti-apartheid activism in the United States has proved transferable to abuses in Nigeria, or, for that matter, to what has taken place under Mobutu in Zaire or arap Moi in Kenya.

Consider only the case of Carol Moseley-Braun. The only African American in the U.S. Senate, she has shown herself to be anything but an opponent of the Abacha regime. She has strenuously opposed the Nigeria Democracy Act, which would have imposed American sanctions, and she met in Abuja with General Abacha and his wife (whom she commended for her support and promotion of family values), and she even traveled to Ogoniland in 1996, where she praised Lieutenant Colonel Daud Komo, the regional governor and the Nigerian official most responsible for Saro-Wiwa's murder. Moseley-Braun made at least one of these trips, in the company of her erstwhile fiance and former campaign manager, Kgosie Matthews, who was at one time a lobbyist for the Nigerian government. And so Abacha, Mobutu and Arap Moi all continue to have their defenders in Washington, including a number of important African American political leaders. (And the odd Reaganite, too, such as Steve Symms, the former senator from Idaho, whose firm lobbies for Nigeria, thereby losing one for the Gipper.)

Too many people in Washington wish to ignore the truth about Africa, for reasons of business, solidarity, or—this seems to be the case with the Clinton administration's pronouncements on African affairs—because they fear that thinking gloomy thoughts makes them true. But the truth about Africa is almost unrelievedly awful. As even the most cursory look at the economic indicators reveals, an African revival is not what lies ahead. The urgent task in Africa, all the rosy predictions of the World Bank notwithstanding, is not to engineer recovery, it is to mitigate catastrophe. Officials at the Bank sometimes argue that countries such as South Korea were just as badly off in the 1950s as many African states are today, but with good economic management they became prosperous. Such an argument elides the difference between the economic conditions that obtained half a century ago, when labor was in high demand and the technological skills required for average workers fairly primitive, and the economic conditions today, when there is worldwide overproduction of low-end goods, a vast surplus of labor, and the need for a much more technologically proficient workforce. As in the colonial period, commodities such as oil are almost the only thing Africa has to offer, and many of these are available more cheaply elsewhere.

Africa has almost nothing to offer advanced global capitalism. There are better educated and better disciplined workers willing to work for very low wages all over the world. A collapsing infrastructure makes investment in much of Africa more expensive than in many other regions, no matter how low wage-scales can be forced. Political corruption and political instability further raise the costs for most corporations. And the enormous population increase in Africa means that it is inconceivable that enough jobs can be created for all the people being born. The population of Rwanda was 1.5 million in 1940. Today, even after the genocide, it is over 7 million. The current estimate of the Nigerian population puts it at about 120 million (though census figures are notoriously unreliable). It will double in the next thirty years.

The end of the cold war, moreover, robbed the continent of its strategic urgency, and it is too far away from the borders of the rich countries to pose a threat of mass migration, as Mexico and the Caribbean do for the United States, and the Maghreb does for Western Europe. Africa, in sum, offers many reasons for indifference about Africa. From human rights to the environment, from demography to infrastructure, the news from Africa could hardly be worse. It is no longer a question of the independent African states not having lived up to the expectations of their citizens. (Thirty years ago, General Obasanjo could still insist with a straight face that he fully expected Nigeria to be "among the greatest nations in the world by the year 2000.") It is now a question of survival. Will large parts of sub-Saharan Africa ever exist at more than subsistence level? Will its people ever come to know anything better than Hobbesian horror?

In this dark setting, there is something especially exemplary about Soyinka's analysis. He does not harp upon the incontrovertible fact that the crippling legacy of imperialism, however much it has been used by African politicians and soldiers to cover up their crimes and blunders, remains pervasive. When people in the West consider, say, Zaire, bemoaning its savagery and its corruption, they link these failings to the fact that the Belgians all but cut off higher education to the Zaireans, and to the fact that, at the time of independence, that vast country could boast only a few thousand university graduates with advanced degrees. But Soyinka will brook no excuses for what has happened. He will not allow history to be made into an alibi.

"We have lost thirty years to the sergeants," President Yoweri Museveni of Uganda, one of the few promising political leaders on the continent, has said. He is right. In an era in which the process of economic development by means of free (or freer) market activity is going well in most of the world, does anyone really care to do something for Africa? This is not a matter of aid. Sub-Saharan Africa has received more development aid per capita than any other region of the world over the past quarter of a century. Aid programs—most recently Boutros Boutros-Ghali's proposal for a $25 billion fund for African development—continue to be devised. Will the new assistance be more effective in fostering prosperity than the old assistance?

There will always be bankers and consultants willing to do one more survey, arrange one more loan, organize one more exercise in "capacity, building"; but with no economic remedy and political reform in sight, the international response to the African crisis is likely to be damage control. To a large degree, the expansion of humanitarian aid is a concession to three notions: that Africa does not matter, and so development aid can be decreased; that Africa will be in a shambles, and so monies for disaster relief need to be increased; that Africans cannot look after themselves, and so foreign nongovernmental organizations need to take over certain basic services, whether these involve security, as the South African mercenary organization Executive Outcomes is providing in Sierra Leone, or medical care, as the American evangelical humanitarian group World Vision is providing in Mozambique.

But disaster relief is, by definition, an admission of defeat. It is in no sense a solution, as its best practitioners are the first to admit. But this, I fear, is the point: nobody has any realistic ideas about what to do. There is little in the present climate that the United Nations, which the late Anthony Parsons once described as a "decolonization machine," can do for Africa. The religion of development has not worked, as even most officials now reluctantly concede. Proposals still regularly issue from the United Nations, of course, ranging from U.N. trusteeships for failed states—a solution increasingly in vogue among international relief groups—to the massive payment of reparations by the European Union countries and the United States, an idea floated most recently by the historian Ali Mazrui. So here we are, reduced to the serious discussion of re-colonization and reparation.

As Julius Nyerere has pointed out, without the anchors of the most important African states, above all Nigeria, Zaire, Kenya and South Africa, there can be no progress on the continent. It is all very well to linger over promising developments in the Ivory Coast, or Uganda, or Ghana, but those are small places. Even if they do better than expected economically, and are rewarded by international institutions such as the World Bank and the International Monetary Fund, the collapse of their huge neighbors will swamp them. If Zaire (or as it is now called, Congo) collapses, its neighbors will not be unscathed. The refugees alone will undo whatever progress they have made; and the skewing of resource allocation will see to the rest. And what holds true for Zaire holds true for Nigeria.

Similarly, if the most important countries on the continent remain dictatorships, any prospect of smaller, neighboring countries remaining or becoming democratic seems far-fetched. This is one of the reasons why, to the extent that foreign governments care at all about the fate of Africa, the questions of democracy and human rights will be critical in the coming period. A few years ago Amartya Sen showed in these pages that there has never been a famine in a free society. It seems equally safe to say that without democracy there will never be any recovery in Africa, hard as a democratic Africa is to imagine in present circumstances.

The moral reason is the best reason for caring about the ruin of Africa, and it may be the only reason. If help comes to Africa, it will be offered on grounds of decency, not on grounds of strategy. This, of course, is tantamount to saying that help will not come. The world does not work that way.

Peter Nazareth (review date autumn 1997)

SOURCE: Nazareth, Peter. Review of *The Open Sore of a Continent: A Personal Narrative of the Nigerian Crisis,* by Wole Soyinka. *World Literature Today* 71, no. 4 (autumn 1997): 853.

[*In the following review, Nazareth contends that Soyinka presents a chilling portrayal of contemporary Nigerian politics in* The Open Sore of a Continent: A Personal Narrative of the Nigerian Crisis.]

In March 1997 it was reported in the newspapers that Wole Soyinka had been accused by President Abacha of Nigeria of being a terrorist setting off bombs in Nigeria; Abacha charged him with treason. Soyinka (living outside Nigeria) was reported as saying that this was a death sentence comparable to that imposed on Salman Rushdie. Of course, Soyinka denied the charge.

The Open Sore of a Continent appears to have little to do with literature: it is an expose of the Nigerian crisis and an attack on Abacha. "I do not suggest that the level of intelligence of the military in general is any lower than that of the civil society; no, we have evidence to the contrary," Soyinka says. "I merely propose that it is the dregs who, against all natural laws, appear to rise to the top: Just take a look around and backwards (Sergeant Samuel Doe, Idi Amin, Jean-Bedel Bokassa, and their ilk) and the latest contribution to that company from my own native land, General Idi Sani Abacha!" He presents a chilling portrait:

> Abacha is prepared to reduce Nigeria to rubble as long as he survives to preside over a name—and Abacha is a survivor. He has proved that repeatedly, even in his internal contests with Babangida. Totally lacking in vision, in perspectives, he is a mole trapped in a warren of tunnels.

> At every potential exit he is blinded by the headlights of an oncoming vehicle and freezes. When the light has veered off, he charges to destroy every animate or inanimate object within the path of the vanished beam. Abacha is incapable of the faculty of defining that intrusive light, not even to consider if the light path could actually lead him out of the mindless maze. Abacha has no idea of Nigeria.

The epilogue is an account of the murder of Ken Saro-Wiwa in 1995, an execution carried out in the face of worldwide protests. "What sort of a nation is this?" Soyinka concludes passionately. "We grasp only too painfully what the nation can be, what it deserves to be. If Ken Saro-Wiwa's death-cry does prove, in the end, to have sounded the death-knell of that nation, it would be an act of divine justice richly deserved." After all, we see that Abacha is right: Soyinka has been setting off bombs, except that they are the bombs of words, which is why the book is subtitled "A Personal Narrative of the Nigerian Crisis." The attack on dictatorship in his two plays, **Kongi's Harvest** and **A Play of Giants,** is continued here in nonfiction prose about real life to keep on exposing and thus fighting death-dealers.

Patrick Colm Hogan (essay date winter 1998)

SOURCE: Hogan, Patrick Colm. "Particular Myths, Universal Ethics: Wole Soyinka's *The Swamp Dwellers* in the New Nigeria." *Modern Drama* 41, no. 4 (winter 1998): 584-95.

[*In the following essay, Hogan explores the ethical and mythic aspects of Soyinka's plays, focusing on his early drama* The Swamp Dwellers.]

In *Myth, Literature, and the African World,* Wole Soyinka set out to formulate a theory of African literature in relation to myth. He criticized African writers who based their work on European cosmologies, urging instead greater attention to African systems of belief. In his preface, Soyinka went so far as to say that "There is nothing to choose ultimately between the colonial mentality of . . . West Africa's first black bishop, who grovelled before his white missionary superiors . . . and the new black ideologues who are embarrassed" by African traditions. "Like his religious counterpart, the new ideologue has never stopped to consider whether or not the universal verities of his new doctrine are already contained in, or can be elicited from, the world-view and social structures of his own people"; Soyinka concludes, simply, "they can."[1]

In some ways, the statement is almost commonplace—an assertion of cultural identity of the sort we have come to expect from post-colonization writers, Irish, Indian, African, and so on. And this is, for the most part, how it has been treated. Readers of Soyinka understand him as stressing "the necessity of de-Anglicizing African literature" (to vary Douglas Hyde's famous phrase regarding Irish literature).[2] But this is not by any means all there is to Soyinka's view of literature, nor is it necessarily the most important part. I would distinguish three other elements of Soyinka's theory that are at least as consequential for our understanding of his work. First, Soyinka's view of literature is very much in keeping with that of his teacher, G. Wilson Knight, who "emphasi[zed] . . . the deep ceremonial and mythological properties of dramatic symbolism," as Derek Wright put it.[3] Soyinka's is a fundamentally mythic conception of literary effect. This is not to say that he advocates the rewriting

of mythological or folkloric material per se (as did Yeats, for example). Rather, he advocates the use of myth to structure otherwise realistic plots and to fill out, give weight to, otherwise realistic characters. Myth is important for Soyinka in so far as it increases understanding of or gives dramatic force to real human concerns and conflicts.

The second point is related to this. Soyinka's drama is insistently ethical. Virtually every one of his plays takes up and works through an ethical dilemma. Moreover, it is an ethical dilemma that is not purely personal, but thoroughly social—most often with clear, if frequently indirect, implications for Nigeria's present and future. And this ethical concern is central to his advocacy of literature founded in myth. Indeed, it is central to his advocacy of Yoruba myth in particular. For, in Soyinka's view, Greek mythology, the founding mythology of the West, is inadequate in the *ethical* dimension—specifically, in "the morality of reparation"—that is central to Yoruba myth. Moreover, this ethical dimension has direct consequences for contemporary Nigerian politics: "The saying *orisa l'oba* (the king is a god), embraced at a superficial self-gratifying level, fails to recall today's power-holders to the moral nature of the African deity."[4]

The final point I should like to stress is that, despite his emphasis on African or even Yoruba particularism, Soyinka's concerns are always universalist, and that in two senses. First of all, the mythological prototypes with which he concerns himself are particular manifestations of universal human concerns. Humanists today are inclined to use the phrase "universal verities" with a tone of derision. But, as we have just seen, Soyinka insists that "universal verities" can be found in African culture—and that this is part of the value of drawing on African culture. This is no doubt the reason that he refers to "archetypal protagonists," citing European, Asian, and African instances.[5] Moreover, in his influential essay **"The Fourth Stage,"** included in *Myth* as an appendix, Soyinka makes repeated references to "basic universal impulses," "profound universality," and so forth. He explains tragedy by reference to broad human concerns, linking *King Lear, Oedipus,* and the Yoruba Sango, and so on.[6]

Even more important, however, than this mythopoetic universalism is the ethical universalism that animates Soyinka's use of myth in drama, and which undergirds his political activism as well. Indeed, as we have already seen, Soyinka's interest in Yoruba traditions is motivated not only by anticolonialism, not only by a sense that it is important to draw on African ideas and practices in order to counter European cultural hegemony, but equally by his sense that Yoruba traditions are more thoroughly imbued with ethical principle than are the Hellenic myths of so much European literature. And this Yoruba morality is important precisely because it too is universal. Thus, he writes that, in "Yoruba traditional art . . . [i]t is not the idea (in religious arts) that is transmitted into wood or interpreted in music or movement, but a quintessence of inner being, a symbolic interaction of the many aspects of revelations (*within a universal context*) with their *moral apprehension*" (emphasis added).[7]

As the last point in particular should make clear, Soyinka's universalism in no way implies that Yoruba particularism is unimportant in his work—quite the contrary, in fact. Indeed, in order to comprehend Soyinka's universalism, a critic must carefully relate Soyinka's work to its mythic prototypes, as well as to contemporary social problems. On the other hand, without a recognition of the underlying ethical and mythopoetic universalism, one would likely misunderstand the use of mythic particulars in Soyinka's work. Ngũgĩ wa Thiong'o has perhaps been the most articulate advocate of combining universalism and particularism—or, rather, of recognizing that they are already necessarily combined. For example, in "The Universality of Local Knowledge," he writes that "The universal is contained in the particular just as the particular is contained in the universal. We are all human beings but the fact of our being human does not manifest itself in its abstraction but in the particularity of real living human beings of different climes and races."[8] I take Soyinka's view to be similar (with the difference that Ngũgĩ's universal principles are largely Marxist, while Soyinka's are, again, mythological and ethical). For both, the universal cannot be understood in isolation from the particular, but equally the particular cannot be understood in isolation from the universal.

The Swamp Dwellers provides an excellent illustration of this entire complex of concerns. Though roughly Soyinka's first professional play, it already shows great socio-ethical and mythic sophistication, and it already manifests his universalistic concerns embedded in a specifically Yoruba mythic context. However, despite the fact that it is a finely crafted and highly characteristic—as well as very teachable—play, **The Swamp Dwellers** has received very little critical attention. Moreover, what little attention it has received has tended to be somewhat reductive and even dismissive. For example, Anthony Graham-White finds the blind beggar an "artificial" and "theatrical figure" and the Kadiye a "caricatur[e]" and judges "Soyinka's attitude towards tradition" in the play to be "uncompromisingly hostile."[9] Wright, too, judges the Kadiye "a crude caricature . . . too obviously a fraud . . . to allow for an even contest between tradition and modernity."[10]

The problem here is twofold. First of all, the critics most often fail to understand the Yoruba mythic specificity of the work; second, they usually fail to recognize its ethical universality. Or, when they do recognize the universality, the point tends to remain localized and undeveloped, as when Wright connects the Kadiye with the "universal greed for wealth"[11] or Eldred Durosimi Jones notes "[t]he analogy between the city and the swamp."[12] In this way, too, the play is exemplary. For much criticism of Soyinka seems to me marred by one or the other of these flaws—despite the fact that much of that criticism (including the work of Graham-White, Wright, and Jones) is in other respects insightful, erudite, and sensitive.

In the following pages, then, I should like to reconsider this relatively neglected play, examining it in terms of the ethical and mythic, particularistic and universalistic principles we have been considering—with an emphasis on the particularity of the myth and the universality of the ethics, for I take this to be Soyinka's emphasis. My primary aim is to provide a fuller interpretation of this finely complex play. But, in doing this, I also hope to highlight some fundamental concerns of Soyinka's work that are often passed over or minimized in the criticism.

More exactly, I take it that one of Soyinka's most pervasive themes is the universal tendency of humanity toward corruption, a tendency that often manifests itself in pride or envy or greed (to use the principal markers of corruption in **A Dance of the Forests** [1960]). In Soyinka's view, the impulse toward corruption affects humans at all times and places. But it manifests itself differently, and with different consequences, depending upon the social and political context in which it appears. Indeed, for Soyinka, pride, envy, and greed are not so much private sins as, so to speak, social configurations with important political consequences. Not only do all individuals suffer an impulse toward corruption; all societies have a tendency to institutionalize corruption in a structure of economic and political domination. Many, perhaps most, of Soyinka's plays address this concern. And in each case, his implicit aim is the same: to encourage a recognition of political corruption (with its insidious tendency to recur, in different forms, in every society) and to foster opposition to that corruption—an opposition that has taken form in Soyinka's own life from his work against the destruction of Biafra to his more recent activism for the National Liberation Council of Nigeria.[13]

The City and the Country

Twins, as is well known, are revered among the Yoruba. Linked with the god Ibeji, they are elevated above children of single births. They are a special mark of fertility as well, and the mother of twins is particularly respected. If one twin dies, a small wooden doll is carved in his or her likeness and placed in the family shrine. The twin who has died has a special link with the living twin, and the family prays to the soul of the dead twin to protect the sibling who remains. Because of sanctity, and fear that the second twin might join his or her companion in death, it is taboo to say that one twin has died. Instead, the Yoruba customarily say that "he [or she] has gone to the market."[14]

The Swamp Dwellers begins in the ambience of this myth. Alu has two sons, Awuchike and Igwezu. She worries that one of them has died: "I had another son before the mire drew him into the depths."[15] Her husband, Makuri, protests, "You haven't lost a son yet in the slough." He goes on to explain, "Awuchike got sick of this place and went into the city." But Makuri is insistent: "Awuchike was drowned." Though the brothers are past the age when any taboo would be in effect, nonetheless, in this context, it is a shock to learn of the precise biological relation between them, and in a phrase that reminds us directly of the taboo, the danger of a living twin following his or her sibling into the other world. Alu announces after this exchange, "They are twins. Their close birth would have drawn them together" (83). On hearing this, one wonders if, perhaps, Awuchike is indeed dead, and Makuri is only following the old custom, reasonably substituting "city" for the more standard "market," the two being closely related in any case. Their other son, Igwezu, has just returned home after an eight-month absence. Perhaps Makuri fears that the same fate will befall Igwezu, and thus will not say that Awuchike is dead, but resorts to a variation on the traditional euphemism.

Soon, however, we learn that Makuri "[wi]ll not perform the death rites for a son [he] know[s] to be living." Clearly, for Makuri, this is not mere euphemism. When Alu responds, "If you felt for him like a true father, you'd know he was dead" (84), the audience begins to sense that the death is metaphorical. Shortly after, it becomes clear. Makuri begins to discuss the city: "It ruins them. The city ruins them. What do they seek there except money? . . . There was Gonushi's son for one . . . left his wife and children . . . not a word to anyone." Alu responds, "It was the swamp . . . He went the same way as my son" (87). The point is clear, even outside of Yoruba belief—the city is a swamp, a place of moral degradation, that "kills" those who go there. But reference to Yoruba belief makes it more striking. If Awuchike were physically dead, she would have said, "he has gone to the market," or perhaps "he has gone to the town" or "to the city," where there would be markets every day. In the Yoruba context of beliefs and customs concerning twins, to say that he is dead is to suggest that his fate is worse, that he has undergone a transformation more thorough than that of physical demise. It is, in effect, a spiritual death—and, along with it, a broader, social death, a death of tradition.

The image of the swamp clarifies the point. According to Soyinka, all structured life arises out of chaos—a chaos that continually threatens to overwhelm humanity and perhaps even the gods. For Soyinka, "nothing rescues man (ancestral, living or unborn) from loss of self within this abyss but a titanic resolution of the will"[16]—a resolution of the will that is, in almost every case, tragic in its outcome. For Soyinka, there are three great deities of tragedy: Ogun, god of Iron; Sango, god of lightning; and Obatala, the maker of human forms. Ogun is the great god who bridged chaos, who carved out (with an iron blade) a space for humanity and gods to meet. But in the end, he succumbed to chaos himself—murdering his own people in a drunken frenzy. Sango called down the forces of chaos on himself and ended his own life, abandoned by all and sunk into despair. Once, from wine, Obatala too fell into the abyss; in consequence, he shaped disabled men and women. Since their deformities resulted from his drunkenness, he pronounced the lame, the paralytic, the deaf and mute and blind, his sacred offspring. And he mourns throughout eternity for the suffering caused to them in that one error, that one moment when formless chaos impinged on the god of forms.

The swamp, then, is an image of this chaos, used here to characterize the city. The swamp is natural disorder—the ground always sinking beneath one's feet, leaving one literally and figuratively without a foothold, without a basis for action. The city is artificial disorder—ethical principle or structure replaced by the shifting contingencies, not of physical space, but of economy, and social morality undermined by impulse, by "the bestial human" (as Soyinka terms it in **A Dance of the Forests**),[18] by pride or envy or greed. The point is extended by the further story of Awuchike and Igwezu: the former, far from observing his special obligations, has destroyed his twin—taken his money and his wife, driven him back to a ruined farm and to despair. Igwezu explains, "Awuchike is dead to you and to this house. Let us not raise his ghost" (104). Far from the benevolent twin spirit who may aid his brother in life, Awuchike is a malevolent specter who, like the unholy wanderers in the bush of ghosts, preys upon the living.

THE ETERNITY OF EVIL

Thus far, it might seem that **The Swamp Dwellers** repeats the common motif of the good countryside and the evil city. The idea is re-enforced by the contrast between Igwezu's unfaithful wife, Desala, and his mother, Alu, of whom Makuri says, "There wasn't a woman anywhere more faithful than you, Alu; I never had a moment of worry in the whole of my life" (84). It is also furthered by the implicit identification of Alu with the Yoruba earth goddess Edan—for she conceived the twins when sunk into the earth, and the twins share its colour (86-87).

But the contrast is not that simple (a point noted, in general terms, by most critics of the play). Indeed, it could not be that simple. For the city to be seen as a swamp, and damned, the swamp itself must have the character of malign chaos. The first suggestion of this comes on the same page where Alu compares the city to the swamp, for Makuri points out that Igwezu's crops were "ruined by the floods" (87). Of course, this is not mere natural chance, mere natural chaos. It is itself part of the same development as the city—the result of colonialism, capitalism, industrialization, the shift from tradition to "modernity." For it wasn't only the floods that killed the crops. A few pages later, Makuri explains, "Not a grain was saved, not one tuber in the soil . . . And what the flood left behind was poisoned by the oil in the swamp water" (92). Forty years later, after the cruel alliance of Shell Oil and the Nigerian military in repressing Nigerian democracy, the point is particularly clear: capitalism, industrialization, the city, has already invaded the countryside, here in the form of spillage from the drilling of oil, drilling that would eventually grow to enormous ecological and human waste. (This, rather prescient, point was entirely deliberate on Soyinka's part. As James Gibbs notes, "Soyinka started writing *The Swamp Dwellers* after reading that oil had been found in marketable quantities in the Niger Delta").[19]

But this is not the first suggestion that modernity has already entered into the village. In the opening scene, we see "*a hut on stilts*"; in the hut "*is a barber's swivel chair*" (81). This strange, part comic, part pathetic icon of modernity was a gift to Makuri from Igwezu, when he was in the city. Its significance is made clear in the story of its transportation: "when they were bringing it over the water, it knocked a hole in the bottom of the canoe and nearly sank it"—a virtual liberalization of the idea that traditional practices cannot bear the weight of modernity, but sink under the load. More strikingly, "The carrier got stuck in the swamps and they had to dig him out" (95). This is significant for two reasons. The first should be obvious at this point—modernity, commodities, things acquired for money in the city, are precisely the things that foster pride, envy, and greed, and thus sink one into the swamp of destructive chaos.

More importantly, "carrier" is the term Soyinka uses for the scapegoat figure who takes on all the evil of the village and transports it into the bush. As in *The Strong Breed*, each year one man takes on the task of "carrying" the bestial human out from the town and returning it to the destructive chaos from which it came.[20] But here Soyinka inverts the image, as he did with the twins. Instead of the carrier transporting evil out of the village and into chaos, we find the carrier transporting evil—the evil of modernity—out of chaos into the village.

And yet, that is not all there is to the matter. For the swamp suggested destructive chaos even without the oil, even without the barber's chair. Again, the imagery

indicates this from the beginning. And when the Beggar enters, the point is brought home even more strongly. Employing religious and ethical imagery, the Beggar asks if he can "take a piece of the ground and redeem it from the swamp [. . .] drain the filth away and make the land yield" (92). The suggestion is clear—it is, most importantly, moral "filth" that needs draining, spiritual degradation that requires redemption. Makuri objects that it would be a violation of religious custom. The Beggar explains that he has no desire "to question your faith" (93) and prepares to leave. But just then the representative of that traditional faith can be heard coming toward the hut. We will now understand the nature of the tradition—and, indeed, the nature of the "filth" that might be drained away from the swamp to reclaim the land.

In a place where all able-bodied men and women must engage in productive labour, the Kadiye enters preceded by an obsequious drummer and followed by a fawning servant. In a poor land, "*At least half of the Kadiye's fingers are ringed*"; in a land with little food, he is "*voluminous*" in fat (94). His corruption is obvious immediately—not only from his physical appearance, but from his great interest in Igwezu's material success in the city. In addition, the Beggar, whose religious good faith has already been demonstrated by his acceptance of Makuri's devotion to the swamp, refuses to accept alms from the Kadiye (94). The point is made explicit when Igwezu returns and discusses the Kadiye, explaining that "His thighs are like skinfuls of palm oil" (102), and when he interrogates the Kadiye concerning the animals offered for sacrifice to the divine Serpent (109). The clear implication (recognized by most interpreters of the play) is that he did not sacrifice at all, but ate the offerings himself, deceiving the people out of his own gluttony and greed.

In short, the tendency to corruption is universal. Corruption assumes different forms in the city and in the country. But it arises inevitably in both contexts—and in all others. When asked if he will return to the city, Igwezu asks, "Is it of any earthly use to change one slough for another?" (111). The destructive chaos encroaches everywhere. Always, "the swamp will [. . .] laugh at our endeavours" so that, whatever we may do, "the vapours" of the swamp "will still rise and corrupt the tassels of the corn" (110)—the use of the word "corrupt" is, of course, not accidental.

TRAGEDY, TESTIMONY, AND THE NEW NATION

But where does all this lead? Soyinka is not merely saying that humankind is fallible. His interests are more specific, his worries more pressing and historical. *The Swamp Dwellers* was written at the end of colonialism. It was produced in 1958, the year after Ghana's independence, and two years before Nigerian independence, which could already be anticipated. In this context, it is a play that implicitly introduces the issue of where a new society might proceed, what path the people might choose in new nation. It is, in that sense, a sort of prologue to *A Dance of the Forests,* which takes up the national issue more explicitly and systematically. *Dance,* first performed in connection with the Nigerian Independence Celebrations, ends in uncertainty, wavering between hope and despair for the future. *The Swamp Dwellers,* in contrast, seems far more uncompromisingly grim in its expectations for the future. And this is where the mythological resonances of the play enter. For two of Soyinka's three prime tragic deities are present in the play and suggest its unstated outcome.

The Beggar is blind, one of "the afflicted of the gods" towards whom all are "under the strict injunction of hospitality" (89)—that is because, with his disability, he is beloved of Obatala, linked with him in a special bond. But the tie with the maker of forms goes further. "Obatala" means "lord of the white cloth," for that is Obatala's distinguishing mark.[21] Other gods are preceded by a drummer, announcing them, singing their praise names, glorifying them—like the Kadiye. But the humble and always penitent Obatala refuses such pomp.[22] He is known only by his perfectly white clothing. So too the Beggar: *"He wears a long, tubular gown, white, which comes below his calf"* (88). And the Beggar too is scrupulously penitent, worrying over the purity of his blessings and over the alms he has accepted (91)—like the sins of Obatala, minor crimes in the larger scheme of things. Indeed, Obatala forever eschews palm wine because of his errors in making, which resulted from inebriation—a point stressed by Soyinka.[23] The Beggar too, alone among those in the play, refuses liquor (96).

Most importantly, Obatala is known for two great acts. In the beginning, the earth was covered with water and swamp. All the gods ignored the marshy earth, but Obatala went to the supreme god, Olorun (also called Olodumare),[24] and volunteered to drain the marsh and make solid land that could support life. Olorun agreed, and Obatala descended from heaven and made land. But there were as yet no people to live there. So Obatala took up his second great task. He reached into the wet clay and shaped the human form, into which Olorun breathed life.[25] So, too, the Beggar focuses on the "miles" of swamp before the sea, where, as Makuri warns him, "you'll not find a human soul" (89), and he wishes, like Obatala, to "redeem [. . .] the swamp [. . .] to drain the filth away and make the land yield" (92). He is prevented only because Makuri and the Kadiye, deviating from the principles of Olorun himself, and thus from the highest source of tradition and of universal ethics, forbid it. Moreover, like Obatala, the maker of forms from clay, the Beggar wishes "to knead

[the soil] between my fingers" (89), to take "this soil [. . .] to scoop it up in [his] hands [. . .] cleaving ridges under the flood and making little balls of mud" for sheltering seeds (111). At one point, the Beggar even goes so far as to identify the soil formed by his hands with new human life, saying, "I shall [. . .] work the land. [. . .] I feel I can make it yield in my hands like an obedient child" (101).

Igwezu at first appears ambiguous. There are hints of a connection with Ogun. He is the only one in the play to hold a blade, and that immediately links him with the god of war, of weapons, and of iron. But other links are stronger. In some stories, including those discussed by Soyinka, Obatala is presented as a friend of the impetuous god/king Sango. And thus the devotion of the Beggar to Igwezu might suggest a connection between Igwezu and the god of lightning. Sango was a great and powerful king. But—perhaps through his own pride and cruelty, perhaps through the fickleness of his people, and of all people; in any case, because of some intrusion of chaos into ethical and social order—he was abandoned by the people, denounced by the chiefs. He was dethroned and replaced in the kingship by his brother.[26] He fled from the city to the countryside. But even his wife abandoned him. In the end, he was left alone with one loyal slave. He told the slave to wait, that he would return, and wandered off into the forest. After a time, the slave sought him out and found that Sango had hanged himself. The slave returned to the city and bore testimony to what had happened.[27]

This is Igwezu. Replaced in the city by his brother, abandoned by his wife, repudiated by the priest, he flees into the wilderness. The Beggar volunteers to be his loyal bondsman, calls him "master" (111), says that he will remain with him to the end, share his suffering. When Igwezu walks off, the Beggar explains that he will fulfill the function of Sango's one loyal companion: "I shall be here to give account" (112). That line ends the play. We can only conclude that, like Sango, Igwezu has gone off to hang himself, for "Only the innocent and the dotards" can live in this world of human corruption (112).

The ending of the play expresses a virtually complete hopelessness. Yes, the Beggar is a saint—but what possibility is there for ordinary humanity in following Obatala? There is no indication that he will ever be able to do anything other than bear witness, that he will ever be allowed to drain the swamp—if the Kadiye does not prevent it, the oil company will. He is like Forest Head in *A Dance of the Forests*: "Yet I must persist, knowing that nothing is ever altered. My secret is my eternal burden—to pierce the encrustations of soul-deadening habit, and bare the mirror of original nakedness—knowing full well, it is all futility."[28]

Moreover, this is not a purely personal suffering, hopelessness of the individual soul trapped between corruption and corruption, suffocating in the vapours of the swamp. It is also social, even national. In *A Dance of the Forests,* the future of the nation is uncertain. Perhaps it will improve. But here, Soyinka holds out no hope of better times, no possibility of improvement. Indeed, the Beggar has already borne witness to this impossibility, has already provided the testimony about the "rebirth" of the land—an allegory for the "rebirth" of the nation, only two years distant for Nigeria.

The Beggar explains that he grew up in a land with no hope of new life springing from the soil, a land in which "Our season is one long continuous drought." But suddenly it began to rain; the rain continued, and leaves grew, shoots of grains sprouted and "hope began to spring in the heart of everyone" (98). They set to work on the land, hoeing and planting. But when the harvest appeared, it was consumed by locusts. This land is Africa, or Nigeria. The drought, which kept all the people poor—so that "the land had lain barren for generations [. . .] the fields had yielded no grain for the lifetime of the eldest in the village"—was the period of colonial domination, which had begun a century before. The momentary hope is independence, with its expectation of universal freedom and prosperity: "This was the closest that we had ever felt to one another. This was the moment that the village became a clan, and the clan a household," the moment of national pride, the brief sense that anything is possible now that we control our own destiny. But the expectations of freedom are always quickly disappointed. The indigenous elite, moneyed collaborators (like Awuchike), the fake village heads, with their positions secured for the last 100 years by British guns, all the exploiters of the people descend on the spoils, leaving nothing for the mass of men and women: "The feast was not meant for us." The image of locusts is apt: "They [. . .] squatted on the land. It only took an hour or two, and the village returned to normal" (98-99).

As I have already mentioned, Soyinka is not always so determinedly pessimistic. Sometimes he is, at least, uncertain. *A Dance of the Forests* ends with similar images. Referring to the night's events, Demoke alludes to Sango in an obscure phrase, saying, "It was the same lightning that seared us through the head." Agboreko asks, "Does that mean something wise, child?" but there is no answer. On the other hand, perhaps Sango will be the despair that leads to suicide. But perhaps he will be the lightning that destroys enemies. Agboreko asks another question: "Of the future, did you learn anything?" This time, the Old Man answers, "When the crops have been gathered . . ." He is alluding to an earlier statement made by Agboreko himself, "When the crops have been gathered it will be time enough for the winnowing of the grains."[29] Thus, in *A Dance,* the

harvest time has not yet arrived. Perhaps it will be plentiful. Perhaps there will be a feast for all. Perhaps this time the locusts will not descend. It is a brief moment of hope, however slight and equivocal.

But in *The Swamp Dwellers,* it seems unambiguous that Sango enters at the end as a figure of despair. And it is entirely clear not only that one harvest was destroyed by parasites, but that there will be no other harvests in the years ahead, that there will never be a feast. The implications for Nigeria's future are grim, but perhaps no more so than the implications for humanity as a whole. For, again, the corruption is general, the swamp ubiquitous (though sometimes it appears to be a city, and sometimes a drought, and sometimes a plague of locusts). And the mythic prototypes, however narrowly Yoruba, are universal as well, and universally tragic.

Notes

1. Wole Soyinka, preface to *Myth, Literature, and the African World* (Cambridge, 1976), xii.

2. See Douglas Hyde, "The Necessity for De-Anglicising Ireland," in Charles Gavan Duffy, George Sigerson, and Douglas Hyde, *The Revival of Irish Literature* (London, 1894), 117-61.

3. Derek Wright, *Wole Soyinka Revisited* (New York, 1993), 6.

4. Soyinka, *Myth,* 14-15. See note 1.

5. Ibid., 3.

6. Soyinka, "The Fourth Stage," appendix to *Myth,* 142, 147, 154.

7. Ibid., 141.

8. Ngũgĩ wa Thiong'o, "The Universality of Local Knowledge," in *Moving the Centre: The Struggle for Cultural Freedoms* (London, 1993), 26.

9. Anthony Graham-White, *The Drama of Black Africa* (New York, 1974), 126-27.

10. Wright, 47. See note 3.

11. Ibid., 45.

12. Eldred Durosimi Jones, *The Writing of Wole Soyinka,* rev. ed. (London, 1983), 33.

13. See, for example, Wole Soyinka, "Nigeria Waits," *The Nation* (4 December 1995), 692-93.

14. George E. Simpson, *Yoruba Religion and Medicine in Ibadan* (Ibadan, Nigeria, 1980), 44.

15. Wole Soyinka, *The Swamp Dwellers,* in *Collected Plays 1* (Oxford, 1973), 83. Subsequent references appear parenthetically in the text.

16. Soyinka, "Fourth Stage," 149. See note 6.

17. Soyinka, *Myth,* 1.

18. Wole Soyinka, *A Dance of the Forests,* in *Collected Plays 1,* 5.

19. James Gibbs, *Wole Soyinka* (New York, 1986), 39.

20. See Wole Soyinka, *The Strong Breed,* in *Collected Plays 1,* 113-46.

21. Harold Courlander, *Tales of Yoruba Gods and Heroes* (New York, 1973), 16.

22. Ibid., 83.

23. Soyinka. "Fourth Stage," 15, 159.

24. For the full story, see Courlander, 15-23. See note 21.

25. See Soyinka, *Myth,* 15.

26. Rev. Samuel Johnson, *The History of the Yorubas: From the Earliest Times to the Beginning of the British Protectorate,* ed. Dr. O. Johnson (London, 1921), 148.

27. A. B. Ellis, *The Yoruba-Speaking Peoples of the Slave Coast of West Africa* (1894; reprint, Oosterhout, Netherlands, 1970), 50-51.

28. Soyinka, *A Dance,* 71. See note 18.

29. Ibid., 74, 72.

Olufemi Vaughan (review date December 1998)

SOURCE: Vaughan, Olufemi. Review of *The Open Sore of a Continent: A Personal Narrative of the Nigerian Crisis,* by Wole Soyinka. *Journal of Modern African Studies* 36, no. 4 (December 1998): 702-04.

[*In the following review, Vaughan argues that* The Open Sore of a Continent: A Personal Narrative of the Nigerian Crisis *is both a courageous critique of the Nigerian government as well as a celebration of the spirit of the Nigerian people.*]

The Open Sore of a Continent is Wole Soyinka's personal narrative of Nigeria's on-going crisis. It is a courageous critique of the growing abuse of power by authoritarian regimes in one of Africa's largest and most powerful countries. It also celebrates the indefatigable spirit of the Nigerian people, and their long struggle for democracy.

The book leads the reader through the perverse world of Nigerian power politics, dominated by a daunting array of military cliques, regional politicians, communal powerbrokers, civil servants and contractors. These issues are analysed in their appropriate historical context, marked by the politicisation and fragmentation of the military, its domination of the extractive agencies of the state, and the marginalisation of the mass of Nigerians. The product of a flawed colonial legacy, deep structural imbalances intensified by the decolonisation process, and corrupt postcolonial regimes, Nigeria's military only further undermined the corporate interests of Nigeria's diverse communities.

There is, however, resistance. One of its most spirited manifestations has been the Movement for the Survival of the Ogoni People's (MOSOP) struggle against environmental degradation, political repression and economic exploitation. Although their struggle against the military regimes of General Babangida and General Abacha ended tragically, with the execution of MOSOP leader, writer Ken Saro Wiwa and his eight compatriots in 1995, their martyrdom is now a rallying point for the ongoing struggles against the excessive concentration of power and resources. This courageous popular resistance, Soyinka contends, was also epitomised by the alliance of Nigerians of diverse cultural backgrounds—dashing the myth of an irreversible North-South divide—to expose and subvert General Babangida's cynical transition programme to democracy. The people's mandate was subsequently annulled by a regime bent on imposing the wishes of a small minority at all costs. For Soyinka this brazen act effectively annulled the Nigerian 'nation' as we know it.

Soyinka wants the reader to understand just how Nigeria got to this impasse. This is achieved through detailed narratives of the last two decades. Five particularly important themes or episodes stand out. First, it is symptomatic of the crisis of governance that the leaders of failed regimes (Gowon, Buhari, Idiagbon, Ojukwu, Shagari, Dikko, etc.) are quickly rehabilitated by their successors—successors distinguished only by their ever-greater capacity for violence, corruption and the plunder of national resources. A second point emerges from the tenure of Sunday Adewusi as Second Republic police boss in Oyo state. This case is not only a sad reminder of the general crisis in Nigerian law enforcement, but more importantly, an illustration of the cynicism of the holders of state power.

Soyinka's third narrative centres on the Buhari regime. Going beyond the junta's well-known human rights abuses, he provides compelling evidence of its efforts to further entrench the domination of the upper North by marginalising Southern leaders, while promoting the political class of the emirate states. Fourth, Soyinka provides a succinct account of the crisis of legitimacy in Nigeria's Second Republic. This is analysed through the rampant 'kleptomania' of the Shagari years, as well as the violent popular reaction to the massive rigging of the 1983 elections. Finally, in his narrative of the Babangida years, Soyinka dissects the regime's *raison d'être,* its cynical transition programme to democracy. This was a colossal failure, where cynical manipulation, massive corruption, and state terror derailed an expensive attempt to impose 'democracy' from above.

Soyinka's detractors may suggest that this book is limited by an excessively instrumentalist perspective, unduly blaming the delegitimisation of the Nigerian state on the Northern political class. Soyinka attempts to address this point by arguing that the balance of power among dominant ethno-regional political classes is an integral factor in the struggle for popular democracy. This is the crux of what Soyinka refers to as the 'national question'. The pre-existing structural framework has sustained the power of the major ethno-regional political classes—including Soyinka's own Yoruba elite—since decolonisation. He insists, however, that any enduring political system, capable of confronting the pressures of ethnicity, religion, region and class, must recognise the right of all Nigerians to full citizenship.

Thus, as a true Nigerian patriot, Soyinka cautions against a retreat to ethnic enclaves. While he recognises the appeal of reconstructed communal pasts, Soyinka suggests that history is not on the side of those who advance such projects. Constructing political consciousness on the basis of essentialised cultures and ideologies, though integral to the Nigerian political process, can only further fractionalise an already divided democratic opposition. The important lesson of the annulled presidential election of 12 June 1993 thus lies in the struggle to forge progressive alliances across ethno-regional lines.

The Open Sore of a Continent is both a courageous leap of faith and a sobering account of all that has gone wrong with Nigeria's troubled nation-state project. Above all, it pays tribute to the ever-renewed struggle of the Nigerian masses for effective citizenship—the construction of civil society, the expansion of the political space and the defence of human dignity. These are the critical demands that Nigerian progressive must seek to fulfill.

David Caute (review date 23 January 1999)

SOURCE: Caute, David. "Guilt-Edged Comforts." *Spectator* 282, no. 8894 (23 January 1999): 34-5.

[*In the following review, Caute delineates the role of memory in* The Burden of Memory, the Muse of Forgiveness.]

Among the most thriving branches to have sprouted from the fecund trunk of historical studies is the one called Memory. History, of course, is about remembering, but the study of the collective memory—normally

patriotic and piously self-justifying in holy texts, poems, museums and memorials—has recently gained impetus from an increasingly fashionable political project: to force a defeated opponent not merely to surrender his pennant but to crap on it in the same motion.

This is done with the most saintly of smiles: it's called Truth and Reconciliation. The victors of Versailles post-1918 and Nuremberg post-1945 had not thought of it: Germans were required to hand over material reparations, cede provinces and offer certain necks to the hangman. They were not, however, required to vow love for their conquerors on the scaffold and adjust their collective memory to affirm their own guilt. More recently, the Federal German Republic brought leading apparatchiks of the defunct GDR to trial without requiring them to denounce Marx, Engels and Lenin. Our SAS snatch-squads in former Yugoslavia deliver 'war criminals' to the Hague in anticipation of the normal self-justifying defence.

But another agenda has been surfacing during the half-century since Hitler put an end to himself without a hint of contrition. The collective memories of defeated tribes (whether nations or regimes) must be wrenched from the usual pieties of self-congratulation, the normal bitterness attendant on defeat ('We were sold down the river'), into a marvellous sacrament of self-loathing and guilt. Young Germans must be 'educated' in the sins of their fathers. They must 'never forget' the Holocaust. Young Russians must 'never forget' Stalinism and the gulag archipelago. No child anywhere must ever be allowed to 'forget' what we, not he, remember. Japan must apologise (and pay up). Prominent thugs of the apartheid regime must bare their breasts with a sufficient display of conversion to satisfy the saint of the hour, Desmond Tutu. The ritual is meant to convey a healing, moral symbiosis—but where consent is withheld, as in the case of ex-President Botha, well, gentlemen, what a shame that he should force us to produce the thumbscrews.

Clearly Germans have become addicted to the culture of guilt. Should the Regierunsviertel, the administrative quarter of Germany's restored capital, Berlin, wear the hair shirt of repentance by refurbishing two Nazi landmarks, Schacht's Reichsbank and Goering's Air Ministry, as the new Foreign Office and Finance Ministry? Is it possible to preserve a spirit of collective atonement by forcing passing citizens not to look at architectural eyesores? Should Berlin build a Holocaust Monument, a version of Jerusalem's Yad Vashem, or a Holocaust Museum? The debate rages.

It so happens (as Wole Soyinka points out [in *The Burden of Memory, the Muse of Forgiveness*]) that the dominant nations, the great moralisers of the 20th century, were up to their elbows in the slave trade for

300 years. So where is their own *mea culpa*? As a boy I witnessed the self-righteousness of the British officer class and its wives in occupied Germany (BAOR) as they bartered small packets of coffee and a few cigarettes for cut glass and fine china. No one challenged my parents' generation about the African slave trade or asked why it was a crime to conquer non-Aryans as *Untermenschen* (Hitler) but merely common sense to conquer Africans as 'savages' (Montgomery). The Japanese have now apologised and set up a compensation fund for Korean 'comfort women', but what about the millions of African women who 'comforted' unwelcome visitors from Britain, France, Holland, Germany, Spain and Portugal? Soyinka notes that the *fin de millénaire* fever of atonement does not extend to African demands for reparations.

He's right, of course, as usual. But could we slave traders, he asks, compensate the heirs of the victims even if we found the will to do so? Who would we hand over the Slave Fund to? The Emperor Bokassa? Idi Amin? Nelson Mandela is a Good Man, but not necessarily a competent accountant. Soyinka reminds us that postcolonial black Africa has not lacked its own gallery of genocidal criminals: Macias Nguema of Equitorial Guinea, the voodoo tyrant; Master-Sergeant Doe of Liberia; the cannibal Field Marshal Idi Amin Dada of Uganda (still alive, apparently, in Saudi Arabia); most colourful of all, Emperor-for-Life Jean Bedel Bokassa. And who should administer the Slave Fund in Rwanda: the Tutsi survivors of Hutu massacres or the other way round?

Soyinka once proposed to a gathering of World Bank executives that the slaving nations should simply annul the debts of the African world. But would this benefit people or governments, most particularly improvident governments? One could also return the looted art treasures of the Continent, now secured in European museums. In an interesting essay on 'negritude' and the parting of the ways between francophone and anglophone African literature, Soyinka quotes Aimé Césaire's eloquent plea on behalf of

> Those who invented neither gunpowder nor
> compass,
> Those who never knew how to conquer
> steam or electricity,
> Those who explored neither seas nor sky,
> But those without whom the earth would not
> be earth . . .

But, Soyinka asks, how can one negotiate reparations in any form when dealing with an internal slave-master like Mobutu Sese Seko or Sanni Abacha? How could one ensure that material reparations reached the 'people' and did not, like so much ongoing 'aid', fall straight into the hands of internal élites no less rapacious than their colonial forebears?

The Burden of Memory is based on Soyinka's lectures at the W. E. B. du Bois Institute at Harvard where he has been a Fellow during his years of heroically outspoken exile from Nigerian fascism. Since giving these lectures, he has seen his native land delivered from the tyranny of Sanni Abacha, 'the midget lord of the nation that launched a campaign for slavery reparations'. A lucid rage seizes Soyinka whenever he contemplates a Nigeria 'criss-crossed today by the sycophantic trails of slime along which crawl the erstwhile majesties of obis, obas and emirs in homage to the new slave masters in military uniform'. More than 20 years ago, he was imprisoned by the baby-faced General Gowon; in Nigeria one does indeed 'imprison Voltaire'—to quote de Gaulle on Sartre—even when the Voltaire is the first black African to have been awarded the Nobel Prize for Literature. For Wole Soyinka, himself almost overloaded by memory, the ongoing tragedy of Nigerian politics will remain unfinished business.

Stephen Howe (review date 5 February 1999)

SOURCE: Howe, Stephen. "Africa Dreaming." *New Statesman* 128, no. 4422 (5 February 1999): 48-9.

[*In the following review, Howe examines the parallels between* The Burden of Memory, the Muse of Forgiveness *and Antjie Krog's* Country of My Skull.]

South Africa and Nigeria are, actually or potentially, the twin giants of the African continent, even if their appallingly bloody recent histories threw up seemingly impassable barriers against a more hopeful future. South Africa seems to have come through those barriers, in a transformation that is routinely, and not foolishly, called miraculous—though it would indeed be foolish to understate its fragility or ambiguity. Nigeria, still under military rule after several failed or deliberately aborted transitions to democracy, has its future hanging in the balance.

A key element, perhaps the most truly magical one, in South Africa's "miracle" has been the work of the Truth and Reconciliation Commission (TRC). Headed by Archbishop Desmond Tutu, one of the most remarkable moral figures of our times, it was charged by the new government with compiling the fullest possible picture of past human rights abuses; to establish the truth of that terrible recent past, and through doing so prevent its perpetuation. Truth and reconciliation were seen as inseparably linked; neither was possible without the other.

Country of My Skull is an observer's account of the TRC's hearings and the events around them by a South African radio reporter and important Afrikaans poet.

Simultaneously, Wole Soyinka—Nigeria's (and perhaps Africa's) greatest writer, but also its most famous political dissident—has pondered the wider meanings of the TRC and asks what lessons it may carry for his own country and indeed for the whole continent. Krog's and Soyinka's books, composed thousands of miles apart though equally impassioned, are thus yoked together with surprising intimacy.

Krog's account is compelling, well written and moving. But it is open to some sharp criticisms—and they've not been lacking in responses to the book within South Africa. In placing herself, her reactions and mood swings so much at the centre of the story as she follows the appalling testimony of the victims, is Krog not displaying a distasteful narcissism? Doesn't her "postmodern" scepticism about the notion of historical truth, interspersing her documentary account with fictionalised autobiographical passages, involve a kind of intellectual frivolity when set against the weight of pain the commission documents? And her confrontations with her own prejudices, including the admission that she cannot "read" the emotions and body language of her fellow black citizens as easily as the whites, might be thought either admirably honest or disconcertingly self-indulgent.

Krog's book should ideally be read alongside the TRC report itself (available in its entirety online at http://www.truth.org.za). The report, not just a dry summation, allows victims, survivors and perpetrators to speak for themselves. It includes the commissioners' own reflections on what makes people become oppressors, or on the links between masculinity and violence.

Soyinka's latest non-fiction book is less impressive, and seemingly less carefully crafted, than its immediate predecessor on the Nigerian crisis, *The Open Sore of a Continent* (1996). Indeed its two halves—the first more directly political, musing on the ideas of reconciliation, reparations, forgiveness, truth and memory in the aftermath of tyranny; the second a more literary reflection on the legacy of the "*négritude*" poets—are only loosely articulated, with the South African example the connecting thread. The text veers between acute insights and portentous generalisations.

Soyinka arouses passions, especially among his fellow Nigerians, as strong as those he expresses himself. The pro-government Nigerian press has recently been filled with unpleasant and, if even a quarter true, damaging stories about Soyinka's behaviour. That's only to be expected, and could easily be dismissed were it not that some of the same accusations are repeated by more independent-minded critics, and are circulating widely among the global Nigerian Internet community.

Soyinka brings to his political writings the same taste for polemic and satire that make his plays so compelling. He is a forceful, scathingly funny critic of his literary and political opponents; but he is not a discriminating or magnanimous one. He may not be the "tribalist" that some enemies have called him but he can refer, gratuitously, to people's ethnic origins, and his justified pride in the cultural achievements of his own Yoruba tradition sometimes shades towards chauvinism. And he couldn't be called a consistent political thinker. In some places he warns solemnly and movingly against the desire for revenge that so often follows the fall of dictatorship and which South Africa has so far impressively avoided. It is clear, though, that Soyinka himself cannot resist the impulse to vengeance.

Wole Soyinka aspires, it seems, to become Nigeria's Vaclav Havel: a philosopher-president overseeing the country's passage back to democracy. He certainly has the intellectual standing and courage for the role. It remains to be seen whether he can achieve the generosity of spirit—the capacity to bring people together—of a Havel, Nelson Mandela or Tutu. Despite being a country of such potential wealth and creativity, Nigeria remains mired in autocracy, corruption and factional violence. Soyinka may be too volatile, too much the angry old man, to attain the required qualities to lead the country back to democratic health.

James Gibbs (review date summer 2000)

SOURCE: Gibbs, James. Review of *The Burden of Memory, the Muse of Forgiveness,* by Wole Soyinka. *World Literature Today* 74, no. 3 (summer 2000): 573.

[*In the following negative review, Gibbs identifies a series of inaccuracies in* The Burden of Memory, the Muse of Forgiveness *and faults the collection for its "carelessness."*]

During April 1997, Wole Soyinka delivered the Stewart-Macmillan lectures at the Du Bois Institute of Harvard University under the titles **"Reparations, Truth, and Reconciliation," "L. S. Senghor and Negritude—J'accuse, mais je pardonne,"** and **"Negritude and the Gods of Equity."** By the time the papers were being gathered for publication [in *The Burden of Memory, the Muse of Forgiveness*], major developments had taken place: for example, Moshood Abiola and Sani Abacha had died. Nevertheless, Soyinka decided "to leave the lectures as delivered—that is to keep such references in the 'active sense' in which they were made."

The lectures were initially prepared at a time when Soyinka was involved in an intense campaign against tyranny in his homeland. But, as the titles of the individual lectures suggest, he stood back from immediate issues, returning to a debate he had initiated as a "brash, creative youth" with the high priest of *négritude*, Léopold Senghor. He also responded to events in post-apartheid South Africa, referring to the work of Senghor's "contemporary kindred spirit," Desmond Tutu. The Nobel laureate quotes his own observation, "A tiger does not proclaim his tigritude," without adding the tag: "he pounces." The pounce is, however, implied and draws attention to the aggression of tigers and the recognition that informs Soyinka's thinking: a call to forgiveness is an inadequate response to violence.

The eloquently titled volume has been in the public domain since January 1999, long enough to have divided readers and reviewers. Anthony Daniels describes Soyinka's "attempts at angry eloquence [as] merely flatulent," while Mpalive Msiskia asserts that the book will "delight the student of literature for the beauty of its prose and its combination of cultural and textual criticism." He also thinks it will "greatly enrich the student of international politics and African history." Caryl Phillips goes some way with this, considering the "analysis of the 20th Century problem of memory and forgiveness in the African world . . . both timely and important," but finds Soyinka incapable of "formulating a strategy for reparations." More damagingly, Robin Cohen observes that Soyinka misunderstood "fundamentally the working of the Truth and Reconciliation Commission."

Disappointingly, the opportunity to follow up an impressive performance at Harvard with a distinguished text was not taken. Carelessness emerges in the (near) homophones: Gandhi comes out as "Ghandi," Sani as "Sanni," Du Bois as "Dubois," and the Ku Klux Klan as (once) "the Klu Klux Klan." More seriously, inaccurate observations about, for example, the number of Ghanaians executed and the operation of French colonial policy create a feeling of distrust which affects the reader's reaction to the bold assertions Soyinka makes on a wide range of topics. This feeling is compounded by the inadequacy of academic support and the absence of evidence of close reading of recent texts or events. The Soyinka who emerges from this volume is a characteristically trenchant critic—he has attitude—but he is much better on literary than political matters, much better on the platform than on the page.

Elizabeth Heger Boyle (review date October-December 2000)

SOURCE: Boyle, Elizabeth Heger. "Gesture without Motion? Poetry and Politics in Africa." *Human Rights Review* 2, no. 1 (October-December 2000): 134-39.

[*In the following review of* The Burden of Memory, the Muse of Forgiveness, *Boyle investigates the importance of symbolism in Soyinka's work, Soyinka's perception of the relationship between different African groups and Soyinka's attitude toward South Africa's Truth and Reconciliation Commission.*]

Can symbolic gestures organized around notions of human rights have any real impact on power relations in the global system? Specifically, did the South African Truth and Reconciliation Commission (the "Truth Commission") serve any useful function or did it simply placate the "have nots" in South African society? These are some of the core issues in Wole Soyinka's most recent book, *The Burden of Memory, the Muse of Forgiveness*. Soyinka suggests that memory can foster a shared future for divergent cultures and bring globally dispersed black races together. But some memories are better than others according to Soyinka, and the Truth Commission failed both in creating an honest memory of South African history and in providing reparations that would permit the country to enjoy a shared future.

Recent theoretical development in the social sciences provide a backdrop to Soyinka's ideas. Like Soyinka, sociological institutionalists imagine that the international system of sovereign states and ideas of international law are constructed out of a common and universalistic world cultural frame, in other words, a sense of natural law.[1] Unlike Soyinka, institutionalists would emphasize that truth commissions (as well as legal systems in general) are created to reflect these higher Platonic ideals.[2] From the institutionalist perspective, the South African Truth and Reconciliation Commission's failure to right individual wrongs is not surprising nor does it signify failure for the overall project. The Truth Commission linked the voices of victims to the ideals of the international system. Although the victims received minimal immediate compensation for their suffering, their voices have become part of the universal principles that shape action in the international system and serve as a source of identity for individuals and nation-states. In a very profound way, the victims who appeared before the Truth Commission may have empowered other would-be victims.

The Burden of Memory, the Muse of Forgiveness grapples with many themes, from the effectiveness of the South African Truth and Reconciliation Commission to the proper topics of African poetry. The chapters in the book are derived from three lectures that Soyinka gave at the W. E. B. Du Bois Institute at Harvard University. Soyinka's brilliance is particularly evident in the book when he discusses literature. Soyinka won a Nobel Prize for Literature in 1986, and his vivid description and contextual explanations of "Negritude" poetry is inspiring. In the last two chapters of the book, **"L. S. Senghor and Negritude—J'accuse, mais, je pardonne"** and **"Negritude and the Gods of Equity,"** Soyinka suggests that Negritude poetry can provide a shared space where Africans around the world come together spiritually, understand their shared history, and fashion a shared future.

Soyinka's thoughts on the importance of symbols in international society frame this article. Within this frame, I discuss his ideas on shared identities among black races and the relationship of modern individuals to history. I then discuss his perspective on the South African Truth and Reconciliation Commission, developing the contrast with sociological institutionalism.

MEMORY AND UNITY THROUGH SYMBOLS

The power of memory is beautifully illustrated in the final pages of *The Burden of Memory, the Muse of Forgiveness* in which Soyinka relates an African legend. In 1230, in pre-enslavement, pre-islamic[3] Africa, a war was fought between Soundiata Keita and Soumare Kante, the king of Soso. In a famous battle, Soumare is defeated by Soundiata. As one of the spoils of war, Soundiata attains a little musical instrument called the Sosso-Bala. Legend says that the Sosso-Bala was inspired by genies and endowed with supernatural power. Soundiata entrusted the instrument to his personal poet/storyteller, Bala Fasseke Kouyate. For nearly eight hundred years, the family of Bala Fasseke has held the Sosso-Bala in trust for the descendents of Soundiata Keita. During those eight centuries, the instrument never left the family of Bala Fasseke until very recently, when it was taken to France as part of the ninetieth birthday celebration of the French/ Senegalese poet and politician, Léopold Sédar Senghor. The Sosso-Bala had inspired much of Senghor's poetry, and the rare presence of the Sosso-Bala was to provide the climax of a three-day celebration. Soyinka describes the crowd waiting in great anticipation. But the crowning moment was anti-climatic: a musician carried the instrument—a lightweight xylophone made of unpolished wood laid over an array of irregular sized gourds—in under his armpit. The sound was nothing extraordinary, just a crisp, aged tonality.

Soyinka writes:

> Yet there, right before us, lay eight centuries of history, poetry, of pride, inspiration, and sacred heritage. A simple, unassuming xylophone that was, however, born out of conflict, of a bloody struggle for power and the travails of nation-building, yet innocuous in its appearance, at once an embodiment of history, yet insulated from it. . . .
>
> (p. 191)

As the musician began to play the instrument, the voice of a female storyteller and a choir created a harmony that enfolded the entire gathering in a "mantle of humanity" that "excluded none, neither the colonizers nor the colonized, neither the slavers nor the enslaved, the disdainers or the disdained" (p. 193).

For Soyinka, the story of the Sosso-Bala provides a glimpse into the possibilities of global harmony and humanized vision, despite a history of bloodshed, exploitation and despair. And Soyinka knows about despair—and hope. Exiled from his native Nigeria by the Sani Abacha regime, he campaigned to keep international pressure on efforts to restore democracy there. With Abacha's unexpected death earlier this year, Soyinka was able to return to his home country.

NEGRITUDE POETRY AND AFRICAN IDENTITY

In the chapter devoted to Senghor, Soyinka describes the tensions which brought African-Francophone and African-American poets together but which also set them apart. In both the United States and the French colonies, Africans have the status of "citizens." Despite the equality of status, equality in fact among Africans and Europeans has never been achieved under either system because of discrimination. Nevertheless, the French and American systems contrast with the British system, where no such pretense of equal status was ever entertained. Thus, despite language differences, the similar political structure of the U.S. and France created a shared sense of identity for African poets in those countries.

On the other hand, the history of African-Francophones and African-Americans is very different, and that difference influences the nature of their forward-looking strategies. Soyinka contrasts Martin Luther King with Senghor to illustrate this point. While both King and Senghor advocated nonviolent means of change, King was a self-described extremist who felled his adversaries by adopting the moral high ground on precisely those fields—law and religion—that his adversaries held dear. Soyinka is less sympathetic to Senghor's strategy of forgiveness, which he sees as playing into the French elite condescension toward Africans:

> [Senghor is] Father Confessor who seizes the poetic privilege of presuming the confession of his sinners, treats their mea culpas as already intoned, then grants them absolution.
>
> (p. 113)

Ultimately, Soyinka grasps the common ground between King and Senghor—the desire to create a bridge to other cultures and a "tool for the retrieval of dispersed black races anywhere in the world," and this goal is the theme of his third and final chapter. The shared history uncovered in the process of creating this bridge is like the Sosso-Bala: although it includes imperfections and is occasionally mundane, it nevertheless offers an important source of identity and understanding.

RECONCILIATION IN SOUTH AFRICA?

Given Soyinka's insight into the symbolic importance of the mundane Sosso-Bala, his failure to recognize the symbolic importance of the South African Truth and

Reconciliation Commission in the first chapter of the book is surprising. The Truth Commission emerged out of the complex negotiations between political parties in South Africa in the early 1990s. It rested on an historical foundation that limited its design and abilities.[4] The two broad purposes of the Truth Commission were to acknowledge and deal with past human rights abuses and to bring closure to the past.[5]

Soyinka highlights three fundamental concerns with the Truth Commission. First, self-confessed criminals were not remorseful. Soyinka and others have noted that some victims were re-traumatized by perpetrators who disclosed their conduct coldly, with arrogance, and without apology. This behavior is sobering and disturbing; but it does not indicate a failure of the entire project. In fact, the stories of the cold-hearted confessions have spread around the globe, illuminating yet again the illegitimacy of the former regime. Indeed, if the ability to evoke remorse was the basis for determining justice, very few modern criminal justice systems would measure up. The value of the Truth Commission lay in its ability to create a sacred space where South Africans in particular, and the international community in general, could express their shared revulsion for those who perpetuated the former exclusionary regime. In other words, the Truth Commission's value should be measured in whether it successfully delegitimated the conduct of the criminals, not whether it reformed them.

Soyinka's second concern is that the Truth Commission is unlikely to have any deterrent effect on other despotic regimes in Africa because it was not sufficiently punitive. That is indisputable, but once again, it does not undermine the overall value of the Truth Commission. Soyinka himself points out that the 1979 bloody coup in Ghana, in which six military officers were publicly executed (as baying students yelled, "Kill! Kill! Blood! Blood! More blood!" [p. 16]) was similarly unsuccessful as a deterrent. Those who exercise power with impunity do not identify with fallen regimes—whether the latter regimes are felled in bloody coups or chastised in formal legal proceedings. Again, the important goal of the South African Truth and Reconciliation Commission was to showcase the humanity of the new regime (in a manner consistent with the strategies of Martin Luther King) and to pointedly exclude those who did not share the same vision. The power of its symbolism was concretely demonstrated within South Africa when ANC's rivals, especially the Inkatha Freedom Party, felt compelled to participate in its proceedings. If corrupt leaders refuse to be moved, they solidify their status as outcasts in the international community, a status that has real consequences in terms of international censure.

Soyinka's final concern—that truth was not accompanied by reparation in South Africa—is the most compelling.[6] Here he returns to his tendency to view the world in broad terms and to appreciate the importance of symbols in creating change. He links reparations in South Africa to African mobilization for reparations generally. In the period since Soyinka's speeches were delivered, the request for reparations has been somewhat successful. For example, a bill currently pending in the U.S. Congress would make U.S. support to the International Monetary Fund contingent on limited loan forgiveness to "heavily indebted poor countries" (H.R. 1305, Debt Forgiveness Act of 1999). While there is still much to be done in this regard, the reparations movement does have a voice in the international system and demonstrates how symbols that draw distinctions between justice and injustice can have real consequences.

THE ROLE OF SYMBOLS IN GLOBAL SOCIETY

The implicit goal of the South African Truth and Reconciliation Commission was to define the future of South African society in terms of general human rights principles.[7] Because the Truth Commission was more a reflection than an instrument of these principles, it was from the beginning unlikely to have great direct influence on social conditions in Africa. This "decoupling" between symbol (international discourse) and action (the actual implementation of policy) in South Africa and elsewhere has generated much controversy and consternation.[8] The essence of decoupling is supporting an ideal but failing to carry out the ideal in day-to-day business and activities. Why does decoupling occur and to what extent does it undermine the overall international project of promoting human rights?

There are at least two explanations for why symbol and action were decoupled in the case of the South African Truth and Reconciliation Commission. First, conflicts that can be evaded at the discursive level must be dealt with concretely when a bureaucracy (such as the Truth Commission) tries to implement an ideal. For example, the members of the Truth Commission felt they had to remain impassive even during the cold-hearted recitations of wrongs alluded to earlier, because if they appeared biased the National Party would withdraw its support from the proceedings. Concrete conflicts, such as these, force a decoupling between the perfect ideal of what the Truth Commission ought to have done and what in fact it reasonably could do. Further, the ambiguity of its goals also increased the likelihood that the Truth Commission would have difficulty linking symbol and action. While very concrete and measurable requests must be rejected outright or adopted—they leave little room for purely ceremonial adoption—moral requests or outcomes that are difficult to assess are more likely to receive formal support but be informally ignored. Because the existence of the Truth Commission was highly negotiated, more specificity in its goals was never a realistic option.

This "decoupling" between symbol and action on the Truth Commission is reasonably taken by Soyinka and others to indicate the ineffectiveness of the Commission. But there is reason to be more optimistic. Despite the practical constraints and limitations of the local reality, the South African Truth and Reconciliation Commission illuminated and empowered perspectives that had been silenced under apartheid. The Truth Commission, while itself derived from the principle of human rights, also fed back into the international system to increase the legitimacy of the human rights message and to make that principle accessible to more individuals.[9] Other truth commissions established after South Africa's can learn concrete lessons from the South African experience while enjoying greater legitimacy (and hence power to make changes) because they follow a model pre-established in South Africa and other countries.

The South African Truth and Reconciliation Commission is part of symbolic rites of passage that make it impossible for South Africa to return to the apartheid system. Such actions at the national level reinforce the legitimacy of the human rights ideals promoted by the international system. Soyinka is correct to be skeptical, in part because the international system that fuels truth commissions and similar reforms is hegemonic and Western in its orientation. Nevertheless, the international system puts real weight behind symbolic action, and in that way empowers an extraordinary range of formerly powerful, but also formerly powerless, individuals. Like the Sosso-Bala, in Soyinka's story truth commissions, in South Africa and elsewhere, have the potential to be profound, but even when mundane, provide a source of identity and shared understanding around the world.

Notes

1. John W. Meyer et al., "World Society and the Nation-State," *American Journal of Sociology* 103, (1997): 144-181; Elizabeth Heger Boyle and John W. Meyer, "Modern Law as a Secularized and Global Model: Implications for the Sociology of Law," *Soziale Welt* 49 (1998): 213-232; for a review of literature on the power of norms in international relations, see Martha Finnemore and Kathryn Sikkink, "International Norm Dynamics and Political Change," *International Organizations* 52 [1998]: 887-917.

2. Whether these ideals truly exist is an open question (e.g., see the debate between Bryan Turner, "Outline of a Theory of Human Rights," *Sociology* 27 (1993): 489-512, and Malcolm Waters, "Human Rights and the Universalisation of Interests: Towards a Social Constructionist Approach," *Sociology* 30 (1996): 593-600.

3. Soyinka chooses to not capitalize the names of religions to protest the failure of most individuals to capitalize the names of traditional African religions.

4. Peter Parker, "The Politics of Indemnities, Truth Telling and Reconciliation in South Africa: Ending Apartheid without Forgetting," *Human Rights Law Journal* 17 (1996): 1-13.

5. Peter Bouckaert, "The Negotiated Revolution: South Africa's Transition to a Multiracial Democracy," *Stanford Journal of International Law* 33 (1997): 375-410; Paul Lansing and Julie C. King, "South Africa's Truth and Reconciliation Commission: The Conflict Between Individual Justice and National Healing in the Post-Apartheid Age," *Arizona Journal of International and Comparative Law* 15 (1998): 753-787.

6. Peter A. Schey, Dinah L. Shelton, and Naomi Roht-Arriaza, "Addressing Human Rights Abuses: Truth Commissions and the Value of Amnesty," *Whittier Law Review* 19 (1997): 325-343.

7. Jeremy Sarkin, "The Development of a Human Rights Culture in South Africa," *Human Rights Quarterly* 20 (1998): 628-665.

8. Margaret Keck and Kathryn Sikkink, *Activists without Borders: Transnational Advocacy* (Ithaca: Cornell, 1998); Susan Silbey, "'Let Them Eat Cake': Globalization, Postmodern Colonialism, and the Possibilities of Justice," *Law & Society Review* 31 (1997): 207-228.

9. Jeremy Sarkin, "The Necessity and Challenges of Establishing a Truth and Reconciliation Commission in Rwanda," *Human Rights Quarterly* 21 (1999): 767-823.

Andrea J. Nouryeh (essay date winter 2001)

SOURCE: Nouryeh, Andrea J. "Soyinka's Euripides: Postcolonial Resistance or Avant-Garde Adaptation?" *Research in African Literatures* 32, no. 4 (winter 2001): 160-71.

[*In the following essay, Nouryeh explores how* The Bacchae of Euripides: A Communion Rite, *Soyinka's adaptation of the play by Euripides, significantly alters the role that gender politics played in the original text and concludes that Soyinka's version acts as "problematized example of a decolonized canonical work."*]

After encountering Isidore Okpewho's essay "Soyinka, Euripides, and the Anxiety of Empire" (in *RAL* 30.4: 32-55), I was challenged not only to read Euripides's *The Bacchae* through the lens of Soyinka's adaptation but further to read Soyinka's *The Bacchae of Euripides* as a reaction to the source text through the lens of Okpewho's critical eyes. This kind of comparative reading entails unraveling a dense web of intertextuality inherent in a dramaturgical approach to contemporary theatrical adaptations of classical plays. First, there are my own—multiple readings of at least five translation/adaptations of *The Bacchae* over a 35-year period. Second, there are Soyinka's essays about Yoruba myths and cosmology; his connection to and interpretation of the god Ogun and his significance to Yoruba society; his critique of, as well as insistence upon, the community's need of the carrier and scapegoating rituals of purification for the New Year among the Yoruba, Ijo, and Onitsha that surface in such plays as *The Strong Breed* and *Death and the King's Horseman.* In addition there is the fact that Soyinka mastered English and European drama under the tutelage of G. Wilson Knight and with the encouragement of the Royal Court Theater managed to have a young playwright's dream fulfilled: full-scale productions of *The Swamp Dwellers* and *The Invention* within a year of his graduation; and *The Lion and the Jewel* and *The Road* in London in 1966. Complicating this reading further is the fact that *The Bacchae of Euripides* was commissioned by the National Theatre, a politically savvy move since Soyinka had proven his "prowess" as an anglophone African playwright whose theater met Eurocentric standards but relied on Afrocentric aesthetics and sensibility and, therefore, his adaptation would enhance the theater's experimental agenda. Finally, as a dramaturg I have explored Soyinka's adaptation of *The Bacchae* as it would be seen in production more than as a literary appropriation of Euripides's play that reflects the playwright's Nigerian roots. It is a series of physical as well as verbal responses to its source text where Soyinka's choice of setting and stage directions, inserted bits of stage business, alteration of the make-up and role of the chorus are as dependent upon contemporary performance modes and uses of space as upon his desire to create a play that is as relevant to its current audience as it was for a Greek audience in the fifth century BCE.

Okpewho concludes the following: "While Soyinka may be a broad-based humanist who explores the common ties that bind the human race, he is primarily a nativist in the sense of seeing his indigenous culture as the starting point of any such universalist gestures" (51). He convincingly shows why Soyinka found a soulmate in Euripides and then used the adaptation as a way to elucidate the political, social, and economic climate of fifth-century imperialistic Athens that Euripides himself may have had to underplay. He also points out intercultural penetrations where Ogun and Dionysos merge and at the same time are differentiated, a fact that is substantiated by Soyinka's use of oriki praise songs and passages from his poem **"Idanre."** Finally, Okpewho makes a very powerful argument about Soyinka's "parochializing strategies" or "counter-hegemonic moves" that center his adaptation in Yoruba culture and politics (38). These are readily seen in the charnel house image of skeletal remains reminiscent of the gladiatorial spectacle of mass executions that took place on Bar Beach during the aftermath of the Biafran civil war.

They are also prevalent in the attitudes of both rulers, Pentheus and Kadmos, who could be echoing the sentiments of Nigeria's military leaders from whom Soyinka had fled. In responding to his essay, I cannot but agree with this conclusion that Soyinka's syncretism is grounded in a challenge to the dictatorial excesses of the government in his homeland as well as to the hegemonic position of the British academy. Certainly the playwright's substitution of Ogun for Dionysos is more than a personal choice; it serves as a corrective for "what he sees as an error in Euripides's portrait of chthonic essence" (Okpewho 52), and thus becomes a way to resist the colonial insistence upon cultural superiority that was reified in the university educations offered to Soyinka and his contemporaries at Ibadan and Ife before independence.

My challenge to Okpewho centers around his suggestion that "Soyinka's effort [is] a translation of culture, not of text" (32). I would have to qualify this either by suggesting that we add an "s" to "culture" or reexamine Soyinka's **The Bacchae of Euripides** with the question "Whose culture is it being translated into?" Okpewho illustrates that the adaptation is certainly not a real challenge to the cultural context to which Euripides was responding in his play. The very fact that Soyinka adapts Euripides's *The Bacchae* is testimony to the high regard in which he holds the original text and its author. I would then argue that if the play is, as Okpewho suggests, a challenge to the Western academic canon in which Euripides has found a literary home, why is it rife with popular culture elements from England the United States rather than those of Nigeria? It is not that I question his assumption that Soyinka's challenges to the "inadequacies" in the canonical text become a way to promote African values and outlook of race that African society and leadership have abdicated (Okpewho 52). Rather, I believe the adaptation is syncretistic; both Soyinka's personal and distinctly African worldview and contemporary London theatergoers' expectations drive the verbal and physical choices. As a result, it is my contention that Soyinka's text is a problematized example of a decolonized canonical work. Further, I would argue that in substituting Ogun for Dionysos, the playwright is compelled to transform the ending into a communion rite that creates a conundrum: while the transformation of Pentheus's head into a fountain of blood transubstantiated into wine is a depiction of the renewal of life and unification of the community that his sacrifice made possible, it is bought with a disquieting negation of Agave's voice as a grieving mother.

My departure from Okpewho's conclusions is predicated on some facts about theatrical production and theater institutions that he does not take into account. Soyinka was commissioned to adopt Euripides's play by the National Theatre, an organization that had been under the leadership of Sir Laurence Olivier until 1973 and was under the direction of Sir Peter Hall at that time. Hall was noted for his experimental work with Peter Brook at the Royal Shakespeare Company where the implications of Artaud's theater of cruelty had been explored in production and where Shakespearean revivals mirrored the concepts expressed in Jan Kott's *Shakespeare: Our Contemporary*. As a result, Soyinka's audience was to be a self-selecting group of middle-and upperclass Britons who had enjoyed this new and exhilarating approach to the canon. The context in which Soyinka found himself was an England that had changed significantly since he had studied and worked there prior to Nigerian independence. Since the 1960s, the country had been undergoing a painful redefinition of identity. Youth subcultures like the rockers, punks, and Teddy Boys emerged from the working classes and their challenges to the class structure and propriety of the privileged proliferated the London scene. With the repeal of the laws prohibiting homosexuality and the rise of feminism, cultural hegemony was giving way to egalitarianism. In addition, the aftermath of the collapse of empire had already begun to have serious economic and social ramifications. Even the "Oxbridge" hold on intellectual matters—and subsequently the canon—was undermined at the University of Birmingham where cultural studies was shifting the focus of cultural enquiry from that which was deemed "highbrow" to the popular.

With these facts in mind, I would argue that Soyinka was writing for a specific English audience at the behest of a substantial British theatrical institution and, therefore, like all theater professionals, was looking for ways to contemporize the play in order to ensure that he was creating a theatrical experience that would have currency for the patrons. In 1970 Michael Spears's study, *Dionysos and the City,* published by Oxford University Press, claimed that Dionysos was a metaphor for the contemporary theater of the late 1960s. Spears pointed to the use of the nudity, audience participation, performance strategies inspired by Artaud, as well as the development of the rock musical that focused upon the "tribal rites" of the youth subcultures. Two figures in contemporary performance become the embodiment of Dionysos for Spears: "the black militant, violently releasing dark and repressed forces both in society and within the psyche, and the rock musician with his female devotees and his orgiastic cult of collective emotion" (Maduakor 251). Richard Schechner's adaptation of Euripides's *The Bacchae* into *Dionysos in 1969* for the Performance Group is one such example. It makes perfect sense to see the fact that Soyinka was drawn to Euripides's play and that the National might wish to "get on the bandwagon" with a contemporary *Bacchae* of their own as a serendipitous confluence.

A desire to create a viable adaptation of the play for a 1970s British audience cannot be ignored as a major contributing factor in Soyinka's aesthetic choices, choices that often mirror Spears's observations. It certainly explains the inclusion of certain popular entertainment modes in his adaptation, aspects of Soyinka's text that Okpewho omits from his discussion. These include the musical hall or vaudeville turns that characterize the scenes between Tiresias and Kadmos: the risqué dialogue centering on the Freudian slip where fawn skin has become foreskin, the satirical costume parade in which the ivy wreath that Kadmos has woven can be worn either "trad or trendy" (24), and the sight gags that include the collapsible thyrsus that Kadmos cannot lean on or keep "erect" and the two-step that the two pals use to start for Kithaeron and which is repeated when Pentheus is led off to watch the revels. With the Slave Leader and chorus, Dionysos worship is transformed into a cross between the ecstasy of an audience at a rock concert who are enthralled by the star they have come to see and hear and the ecstasy that a gospel preacher's rhetorical style elicits from the singers and congregants. If the National Theatre audience was not immediately familiar with any of these popular forms, they had been introduced to them through documentaries and other forms of media. To carry this one step further, it is not hard to see the dressing of Pentheus in women's garb rather than armor, under the hypnotic spell of Dionysos, as analogous to the kind of nightclub stunt where a mesmerist embarrasses his unwitting subject while the audience gets voyeuristic pleasure out of the absurd behavior that the "victim" is made to perform. One could argue that the pageants that Soyinka includes, the wedding scene from Herodotus about Hippoclides and Agaristha and the wedding scene at Cana from the New Testament, are like Elizabethan masques and that the rites of May and its Maypole used to stage the moment when Agave shows off "her kill" are equally important importations from English popular or folk culture. Robert Baker-White does an extensive study in his article "The Politics of Ritual in Wole Soyinka's *The Bacchae of Euripides*" of how many of these various anachronisms in Soyinka's play are essentially tropes of Western popularist forms of contemporary ritual (380). They all depend upon the same kind of group solidarity that results from communal scapegoating or audience participation that Dionysos and Ogun worship seem to require. Given Soyinka's knowledge of Western drama and his use of performance texts from English history, his use of this correlation between popular entertainment and nonhierarchical ritual performance should be seen as a deliberate attempt to provide contemporary examples of the ritualistic experience.

What complicates the evaluation of Soyinka's adaptation of *The Bacchae* is the fact that he uses translations of the play rather than the original. Unlike postcolonial adaptations and translation of Shakespeare, which if performed in front of British audiences must contend with the sanctity of the Bard's text and its Elizabeth context, an adaptation of a classical Greek text has more flexibility. After all, there is no definitive version in English that is known by an audience. Thus an equally valid and new translation is possible for each age. It is interesting to note that Soyinka has never chosen to adapt plays from the English canon but rather has chosen those that challenge the status quo like Brecht's *Three Penny Opera* and currently Jarry's *Ubu Roi*. This speaks somewhat to my contention that the playwright might be less interested in contesting the canon than in working with plays from an established literary and theatrical tradition that challenge rather than reaffirm ideologies of their times and which speak to the specific conditions in Nigeria that he wishes to comment upon.

One problem with the translations that Soyinka relied upon for his **Bacchae** is that they are texts to be read rather than performed. As a result, they insert stage directions that would not have appeared in the original and refer the reader to theatrical conventions that are necessarily forfeited whenever a Greek tragedy is staged in contemporary theaters. One example is Dionysos's smiling mask and meek, effeminate gait. Okpewho contends that Soyinka's Dionysos is more ruggedly masculine because he reflects Ogun and that he does not smile because of his kinship to Pentheus as well as the solemnity of the scapegoating ritual into which he will force his cousin (42). Beyond the fact that Arrowsmith's description of Dionysos illustrates the manner in which the god would be depicted as the embodiment of the masculine and feminine sides of human beings and the benevolence that he delivers to his worshipers, the translator provides this for students of the classics to understand how the actor might have played the role. Yet neither the translator nor Okpewho suggests what seems obvious to a theater historian: that these choices would make Dionysos's physical presence distinct from his cousin Pentheus's in an ampitheater seating at least 10,000. Since he and Pentheus would necessarily look almost exactly alike once Pentheus entered wearing the garb of a Bacchante and a blond curly wig—a twinning effect important to Euripides's explicit underscoring of the irrational and impulsive nature that is a crucial aspect of both characters—use of specific mask as well as effeminacy in gesture would ensure some visible differentiation.

Another example of a literary imposition on the classical text is revealed in the description of the placement of Semele's tomb covered in grape ivy. Okpewho looks to Dodd's rather than Arrowsmith's description of the grave as being on the stage, with smoke rising and with vine-shoots trailing over the fence that surrounds it (41). Yet Dodd's description presumes a proscenium stage. This is despite the fact that in the posthumous production of Euripides's play the tomb was probably set at the altar of Dionysos in the center of the orchestra floor—a symbol of the festival for which the plays were initially staged—to signify Dionysos's connection to harvest and the requisite death and decay out of which nature is renewed. Okpewho's suggestion that in the original play death overshadows the vines is premised upon a literary description that is faulty. Soyinka's placement of the tomb on the stage with the palace and threshing floor to emphasize the harvest is in keeping with the original spiritual connection that an Athenian audience would make between Semele's tomb and the promise of Dionysian plenty. While this certainly enhances the promise of life's renewal over the revenge theme that is central to Soyinka's adaptation, it is another example of how the playwright has updated Euripides's play for a contemporary audience. I would conclude that these as well as many others of Soyinka's choices for the stage setting as well as the physical description of his characters are no different from those of any theater director who struggles to find physical attributes that suit his or her contemporary production concept. Soyinka, therefore, seems to be challenging the English and classicist reading of Euripides's text from the 1950s and 1960s that may obscure certain aspects of the original rather than the parent text itself.

While it is true that Soyinka emphasizes the issues of slavery, the inclusiveness of Dionysos worship that breaks down class barriers, and the promise of freedom and potential for revolution that the god symbolized, this is not peculiar to a postcolonial agenda. In fact, it seems that the playwright is acknowledging an entire century of Western thought about Greek tragedy. As a student of drama, Soyinka surely read Nietzsche's interpretation of the Dionysian rites in *The Birth of Tragedy*:

> Not only does the bond between man and man come to be forged once more by the magic of the Dionysian rites but nature itself long alienated or subjugated, rises again to celebrate the reconciliation with her prodigal son, man. The earth offers its gifts voluntarily, and the savage beasts of mountain and desert approach in peace. The chariot of Dionysos is bedecked with flowers and garlands; panthers and tigers stride beneath his yoke. . . . Now the slave emerges as a freeman; all the hostile walls which either necessity or despotism has created between men are shattered.
>
> (Maduakor 250)

With this quote in mind, I find it difficult to see most of Soyinka's adaptive strategies as anything but a tribute to the spirit of the parent text as seen by modern critics and interpreters. Forays into contemporary translations by Paul Roche or Michael Cacoyannis would illustrate that Soyinka shares a perspective on the play that is characteristic of a late twentieth-century sensibility:

emphasis upon Athens as an imperialistic power that mistreated its slaves, upon Pentheus as an unyielding and misguided dictator, upon the need for justice which is balance and order that benefits the whole society rather than justice as a self-serving exercise of power, upon the promise of freedom and equality that is inherent in the cult of Dionysos.

Most convincing to me is Okpewho's argument that Soyinka's conflation of Ogun with Dionysos illustrates his taking ownership of the myth and using it for his own ends. I see this in the same light as the Japanese productions of Greek drama by Tadashi Suzuki and of Shakespeare's *Macbeth* and *The Tempest* by Yukio Ninagawa that depend upon Kabuki and Noh drama conventions and characterizations, though Soyinka continues to write in English and wrote *The Bacchae of Euripides* for an English audience. Since Dionysos is no longer a deity with a following, there are a host of correlative god-figures and their requisite rituals that could be used to breathe life into the characterization. For Soyinka this is Ogun, a deity who still is worshiped among Yoruba people and is singularly important to the playwright himself. That this is a parochialism is certain but it does not preclude an English audience from comprehending the deity's essential nature. However, it is at the heart of why Soyinka must alter the play's final scenes. His deity must be vindicated in the denouement as the Promethean friend to humans rather than the impetuous, intemperate, adolescent boy god. By altering the character of Dionysos into Ogun, Soyinka removes the central axis of Euripides's play: that the young Pentheus and his half-mortal cousin Dionysos are two sides of the same coin. The impulsiveness and cruel, unmeasured power that the young King Pentheus exercises in concert with his inability to recognize the sensuousness and irrationality of Dionysos within himself are the qualities that unleash the same uncontrolled forces of will in the god. Clearly, Soyinka rejects this mirror image as well as its implications in the original play because it does not fit with his vision of Dionysos as Ogun. I suspect it is these alterations that are at the heart of Okpewho's thesis that Soyinka used the opportunity of the commission from the National Theatre to "assert his nativist instincts" (51) as a means of "debunking the claims and assumptions of ethical superiority of the colonialists" (Olaniyan 56).

In his introduction to the published version of the script, Soyinka states that Euripides's play deserves a more fitting ending (x). I would argue that like Soyinka not many contemporary playgoers and readers of *The Bacchae* find the play's ending satisfying. The message is confusing and certainly the reasons behind Dionysos's actions are hard to accept. He is cruel and without empathy and all that has been accomplished is the satisfaction of his need for vengeance. As Okpewho points out, the promise of restoration and renewal

"hangs unfulfilled, because the scapegoat appears to have died a death that, contrary to the logic of the ritual, promises nothing whatsoever to his community" (48). Although we may have found justice in Pentheus's sacrifice, we are horrified by the description of his death and therefore are left feeling immense sympathy for Kadmos and Agave who are subsequently unfairly punished even further.

Given his focus on Ogun, it is not surprising that Soyinka dealt with his dissatisfaction by rewriting the "uneven" and "crude" play's last scenes as a corrective (Morell 102). Taking issue with he manner in which the play trails off in dejection and mourning, Soyinka allows the dismemberment of Pentheus to have spiritual meaning for the community rather than merely illustrate the consequences of repressing the riotous forces that lie within each man and woman. The poetry of the play's last scene underscores a new kind of fecundity— blood as nourishment for the Kithaeron, a king's blood that will unite men and women, slaves and freemen with their masters. Thus Pentheus really dies like Christ for the good of humankind; his head becomes a fountain of blood turned into wine, a "barbaric banquet" (Soyinka x) reminiscent of the Catholic Mass. This ritual allows each celebrant to be unified with each other and with their god. It is an ending that links the Greek Dionysos with Ogun and Jesus and links Dionysian rites and Christian rituals with carrier and scapegoat purifications for the New Year in Nigeria. Although Soyinka justifies this choice as a way to underscore the play's totality—"a celebration of life, bloody and tumultuous, an extravagant rite of the human and social psyche" (x)—he has created a ritual that has no antecedent in Europe or Nigeria. Perhaps this is a fitting humanistic intercultural move on the playwright's part. It is a far better purification rite than the Eleusian Mystery rite that it supplants in the context of the play and is a ritual ending that seems to be all-inclusive, both for the celebrants and for the audience. But is it successful and does it accomplish all that Soyinka intends?

There is a formal integrity enhanced by themes with which the playwright has wrestled in earlier dramas that frames the two renewal rituals depicted in the play. At the outside of the action, the Slave Leader reflects upon the unfairness of the Mysteries of Eleusis. He questions the reason for appointing an Old Slave to serve as scapegoat, be paraded through the streets, and be flogged to death. He asks, "Why us?" to which the Herdsman replies, "Why not?" (4). We hear these lines again at the play's denouement. Kadmos, the former king, asks in his grief about the sacrifice of his grandson Pentheus, "Why us?" to which Agave, now resigned to the fact that she killed her son, replies, "Why not?" (97). The echo of these lines resonates with important political and philosophical questions about the power dynamics in scapegoating rituals that are critiqued in Soyinka's *The Strong Breed.* Tiresias had known that Thebes could not afford to sacrifice another slave, so he had volunteered to imitate the purification rite in order to avoid revolt. However, it is not until the moment of Agave's recognition of what she has done to Pentheus and her need to prepare his body for burial that Tiresias realizes that Pentheus's death was necessary, that the "life sustaining earth" demanded it (96). The state-sanctioned rituals that they had been performing and in which he had taken part were empty tokens; they did not get at the heart of Thebes's worst sins because the victims were seen as dispensable and the community, particularly its leaders, had not suffered any substantial loss. This scene works rather well within Soyinka's vision about individual sacrifice for the good of the community that was part of traditional culture among the Yoruba, Ijo, and Ibo people, but it does not address the unfair use of Agave as the god's agent of her son's death.

Soyinka's omission of any justification for Agave's tragedy as well as his depiction of her ready acquiescence to the necessity of her son's sacrifice at her own hands is difficult enough to comprehend. In his introduction. Soyinka explains this as requisite for the appropriate resolution of the ritual: her final understanding is symbolic of the community's "recognition and acceptance of those cosmic forces for which the chorus is custodian and vessel in the potency of ritual enactment" and is crucial to the release of Nature's beneficence (x). Even if one accepts this explanation, the final picture of the play—Agave, under the impaled head of Pentheus, lifting her head back from the ladder which she has flattened herself against and hugged, in order "to let a jet [of blood/win] flush full in her face and flush her mouth" (97)—is more than grotesquely unnatural. The curtain descends upon a conflation of a mother's volitional cannibalization of her son as well as an intimation of her incestuous desire that the ejaculating phallic image—Pentheus's head as the top of a huge thyrsus and displayed in a Maypole dance only moments before—suggests (Okpewho 49). I would argue that this final image of her willing participation in the communion rite, and her complicity in her own oppression, undermines the very positive renewal for the community that this ritual is supposed to represent.

It is here that I take issue with Soyinka's adaptation as a corrective to Euripides's dramaturgy. Euripides wrote plays that used the subjugation of women as a rhetorical strategy for critiquing Athenian policies. He was keenly aware of the mistreatment of foreign women, the limited freedoms of wives, the threat of rape or concubinage in case of war. None of this sensibility is in Soyinka's version. In the parent text, Dionysos is hell-bent upon revenge not only because his paternity is in question but because his mother's memory has been besmirched and her relationship with Zeus has bee[n] denied. His aunts had refused to believe that Semel[e] had been impregnated by the god and destroyed b[y] Hera's jealousy and had insisted that she was [a] promiscuous woman whose lying caused Zeus t[o] destroy her and her bastard child. This is the centra[l] reason that Dionysos strikes them and all the women i[n] Thebes with the frenzy of his Maenads, a frenzy tha[t] sends them out of their homes, abandoning all of thei[r] duties as wives and mothers in order to join in the bac[-] chanals in the mountains. Dionysos is thus capable o[f] using them to exact revenge upon the men, particularl[y] Pentheus, who refuse to acknowledge him as a god an[d] to punish his aunts for betraying his mother's memor[y] Soyinka eliminates all of this from the prologue of hi[s] version. In fact, it is Pentheus alone who slanders Se[-] mele: He claims Dionysos still lives? Some nerve!

> A likely story for a brat who got roasted
> Right in his mother's womb, blasted by the bolts
> Of Zeus. The slut! Slandered Zeus by proclaiming
> The bastard's divine paternity. That myth he instantly
> Exploded in her womb, a fiery warning against all
>   profanity.
> You'd think my own relations would have learnt
> From that family history but no! Ino and Autonoe
> My own mother Agave are principals at the obsceni-
>   ties!
> I'll teach them myself. I have woven
> Iron nets to trap them. I'll bring an end
> To the cunning subversion. . . .

(28)

Not only does this underscore Pentheus's outrage at th[e] sexuality that Dionysos unleashes but it places th[e] young king in the position of being the only one wh[o] refuses to believe in the existence, let alone the deity of his cousin and submit to his rites. Thus he become[s] the only obstacle for Dionysos worship and its promis[e] of freedom, equality, and plenty for the community While this speech helps solidify the reasons Pentheu[s] must be the "sacrificial lamb," it does not help provid[e] any explanations for why Agave must also suffer.

In Euripides's version Agave's recognition of her ac[-] tions in the heat of a frenzy that the god imposed upo[n] her is tragic but has some kind of logic. She i[s] devastated by the loss of her son and is mortified by he[r] own culpability. Her grief is palpable and her dejectio[n] feels real. This is the grief of Hecuba and Adromach[e] in *The Women of Troy,* magnified by the fact that Agave not at outside enemy, is herself the murderer. In Soyin[-] ka's version Agave audibly grieves and then calmly begins to retrieve his head to prepare him for burial. I[n] contrast, once she learns that she is her son's murdere[r] she becomes quiet, submissive, and resigned. Her onl[y] verbal response is a soft sigh, "A-ah" (96). Perhaps thi[s] is a sign of shock or perhaps this is a sign of intens[e] anguish, but Soyinka does not give clues in the script t[o] the actor or reader. Although there is time for her to as-similate the truth about her complicity in Pentheus's dismemberment and how this sacrifice has been neces-sitated by the needs of a troubled Thebes, her answer, "Why not?" to her father's cry, "Why us?" (97) seems hardly a plausible reaction as she reaches for her son's head, which she had triumphantly placed upon the wall only moments earlier as a trophy of women's strength and hunting prowess. If this moment echoes in any way the *Mater Dolorosa* or *Piela,* as seen by some critics of the play (Okpewho 11), it is a distorted and perverse reference. Mary is not implicated in Christ's crucifixion and she wept over her son's body when she was helped to take him down from the cross.

While the final image of Agave as a celebrant at the moment that the curtain descends is essential for the union of the once-divided community to be complete, it is an image that silences any outrage that women might express at the notion that a god, or any man, would use a woman as the tool of her own child's destruction for no reason and expect her to bear it without any sign of resistance or despair. Even the women who sacrificed their children during the Middle Passage did so know-ingly and to prevent them from living in slavery, but they did this with heavy hearts. Mothers whose sons die in a war or a hunt that was meant to ensure the good of the community audibly mourn when they are presented with the bodies. When they often accept posthumous medals of honor give in their sons memories, they often do so with dignity but rarely without visible sadness. What would they do if they had been the ones who had mistakenly shot them? Soyinka's play assumes that no woman in the audience would be alienated by the case with which Agave gives in to necessity and joins her community in celebration.

In assessing Soyinka's ending of the play, it is hard to reconcile the notion that any woman capable of bring-ing forth and nurturing life could be so misused by a deity whom she worshiped of her own volition because she recognized his connection to the forces of birth and death as well as the promise of renewal. It is equally difficult to accept that she would willingly take part in a ritual that culminates in the feasting upon her child's body, an act that is supposed to erase the social divi-sions that give one group power over another. Okpewho sees Soyinka's denial of revenge as a fitting impetus for Pentheus's sacrifice in favor of the king's death to serve as the means for purification and subsequent rebirth as a fitting way to restore the "sacral logic of the play" (49). I, on the other hand, see that the playwright's final "master-stroke of representation of the sort of 'prodi-gious, barbaric banquet' befitting the 'ecstasy' Dionysos promised Tiresias and Thebes" (Okpewho 49) is paradoxically both an image of unification for the on-stage witnesses and the audience as well as a stimulus for further estrangement.

This problematic spectacle of Pentheus's head spouting blood from all orifices like a severed yet still ejaculat-ing phallus that is subsequently illuminated with the glow of the god's presence is exactly the kind of final disquieting image called for in Artaud's *Theater and Its Double.* Even Soyinka's introduction suggests an aesthetic that has shock value because of its violent imagery: "The more than hinted-at cannibalism cor-responds to the periodic needs of humans to swill, gorge and copulate on a scale as huge as Nature's on her monstrous cycle of regeneration" (xi). It is only a brief step from this description to lines spoken by the Marquis de Sade about Nature's indifference to human-kind's excesses in Peter Weiss's *The Persecution and Assassination of Jean-Paul Marat as Performed by the Inmates of the Asylum of Charenton under the Direction of the Marquis de Sade,* a 1964 production that introduced the London public to workshop experiments with Artaudian techniques used by Peter Brook and Charles Marowitz in staging the play for the Royal Shakespeare Company:

> Any animal plant or man who dies
> adds to Nature's compost heap
> becomes the manure without which
> nothing could grow nothing could be created
> Death is simply part of the process
> Every death even the cruelest death
> drowns in the total indifference of Nature
> Nature herself would watch unmoved
> if we destroyed the entire human race
>   [rising]
> I hate Nature
> this passionless spectator this unbreakable iceberg-
>   face
> that can bear everything
> this goads us to greater and greater acts
>   [breathing heavily]
> Haven't we always beaten down those weaker than
>   ourselves
> Haven't we torn at their throats
> with continuous villainy and lust
> Haven't we experimented in our laboratories
> before applying the final solution. . . .
>
>   (23-24)

Reflecting on the image of the dismemberment of Damien, the man who unsuccessfully attempted to as-sassinate Louis XV, which completes de Sade's monologue, one cannot help seeing its analogous relationship to the messenger's description of Pen-theus's death on Kithaeron in Euripides's *The Bacchae.* Thus, it is not hard to situate the theatrical choices for Soyinka's ending of **The Bacchae of Euripides** within a theatrical context of the early 1970s where massive quantities of stage blood were utilized to graphically depict beheadings, maimings, and other tortures found in Elizabethan and Jacobean tragedies that had reso-nances for a world that had not yet made its peace with the atrocities of World War II or the Vietnam conflict. I conclude that rather than neatly resolving the need for community solidarity that reflects a traditional use of scapegoating rituals as part of a New Yam Festival, Soyinka's play potential alienates its audience or arouses in them a set of deeply disturbing emotions, the goal of Artaudian cruelty. This may not have been the playwright's intention but, in the end, the substitution of a real ritual with a splashy image created by Western theater technology makes highly problematic the claim that Soyinka is "using a Yoruba god to correct what he sees as an error in Euripides's portrait of a chthonic essence" (Okpewho 52).

Works Cited

Arrowsmith, William, trans. *The Bacchae. The Complete Greek Tragedies. Vol. 4: Euripides.* Ed. David Grene and Richmond Lattimore. Chicago: U of Chicago P. 1959.

Baker-White, Robert. "The Politics of Ritual in Wole Soyinka's *The Bacchae of Euripides*." *Comparative Drama* 27.3 (1993): 333-98.

Cacoyannis, Michael, trans. *The Bacchae.* New York: New American Library, 1982.

Dodds, E. R., ed. *Euripides, Bacchae.* 2nd ed. Oxford: Clarendon, 1960.

Kott, Jan. *Shakespeare: Our Contemporary.* New York: Norton, 1974.

Maduakor, Obi. *Wole Soyinka: An Introduction to His Writing.* New York: Garland, 1986.

Morell, Karen L., ed. *In Person: Achebe, Awoonor, and Soyinka at the University of Washington.* Scattle: African Studies Publications, 1975.

Okpewho, Isidore. "Soyinka, Euripides, and the Anxiety of Empire." *Research in African Literatures* 30.4 (1999): 32-55.

Olaniyan, Tejumola. *Scars of Conquest. Masks of Resistance: The Invention of Cultural Identities in African, African American and Caribbean Drama.* New York: Oxford UP, 1995.

Roche, Paul, trans. *Three Plays of Euripides: Alcestis, Mediea. The Bacchae.* New York: Norton, 1974.

Soyinka, Wole. *The Bacchae of Euripides: A Communion Rite.* New York: Norton, 1974.

Spears, Monroe. *Dionysus and the City.* Oxford: Oxford UP, 1970.

Weiss, Peter. *The Persecution and Assassination of Jean Paul Marat as Performed by the Inmates of the Asylum of Chgarenton under the Direction of the Marquis de Sade.* New York: Atheneum, 1966.

Alan Jacobs (essay date November-December 2001)

SOURCE: Jacobs, Alan. "Wole Soyinka's Outrage: The Divided Soul of Nigeria's Nobel Laureate." *Books & Culture* 7, no. 6 (November-December 2001): 28-31.

[*In the following essay, Jacobs provides a critical overview of Soyinka's life and work, praising Soyinka' "comprehensive genius" and asserting that he regard Soyinka as one of the greatest living writers.*]

1

Like many teachers of literature, I am sometimes asked to name the Greatest Living Writer. (I can hear the capital letters in the voices of those who ask.) Invariably I name two candidates: the Polish-Lithuanian poet Czeslaw Milosz and the Nigerian playwright Wole Soyinka. These names are usually greeted by puzzlement for, though both have won the Nobel Prize for Literature—Milosz in 1980 and Soyinka in 1986—and both have been on *The McNeil-Lehrer Newshour,* neither has entered the American public consciousness in a potent way. Milosz is more likely to be familiar, though, and apparently my interlocutors think him a more plausible choice; my claim for Soyinka almost always earns skeptical looks.

I imagine that this skepticism derives from the still common picture of Africa as the dark continent, full of illiterate savages (a picture that the Western media do little to dispel); and also from the suspicion that any African Nobel laureate must be the beneficiary of multicultural affirmative action. But if anything, Soyinka is a more comprehensive genius even than Milosz. Here is a writer of spectacular literary gifts; he is an acclaimed lyric and satirical poet, a brilliant novelist of ideas, a memoirist both nostalgic and harrowing, and almost certainly the greatest religious dramatist of our time. The assumption that he has come to our attention only because of academic politics is profoundly unjust—though perhaps understandable, considering the number of mediocre talents who have assumed recent prominence for just such reasons.

That assumption also carries a heavy load of irony given the distance between the triviality of American academic politics—what Henry Louis Gates, Jr. has aptly called our "marionette theater of the political"—and the *real* political crises which have continually afflicted Soyinka and his work. Soyinka's 1996 book on the political collapse of his native Nigeria. **The Open Sore of a Continent,** teaches us how absurdly misbegotten our whole literary-political conversation tends to be. Through this book, and through the shape his career has assumed, Soyinka brings compelling messages to our warring parties. To the traditionalists who deplore "the politicization of literary discourse." Soyinka serves as a living reminder that writers in some parts of the world don't get to *choose* whether their work will be political; that is a privilege enjoyed by those who happen to be born into stable and relatively peaceable societies. Others have politics thrust upon them. But Soyinka also tells our Young Turks that their cardinal principle—Everything is Political—is true only in an utterly trivial sense. To adapt a famous phrase from George Orwell, if everything is political, some things are a hell of a lot more political than others.

Whichever side of this dispute one tends to be on, or even if one isn't on either side, Soyinka's story is worth paying attention to, because his career has been virtually detailed by the collapse of his native country into political tyranny and social chaos. Soyinka has not eagerly thrown his energies into protest and polemic in the way that, for instance, Aleksandr Solzhenitsyn did in the days of the Soviet empire; unlike Solzhenitsyn, he is no *natural* polemicist. However, Soyinka has also been unable to follow the route of Solzhenitsyn's older contemporary Boris Pasternak, which was to combat political tyranny by ignoring it, by cultivating a realm of personal feeling impervious to the corrosive solvent of Politics. (As Czeslaw Milosz writes of Pasternak, "confronted by argument, he replied with his sacred dance.") Soyinka has felt called upon to respond to the collapse of Nigeria, and as a result his career has taken a very different direction than it once promised to do. It is hard to question his choice; it is equally hard to celebrate it, for it has led a fecund and celebratory poetic mind into an abyss of outrage.

Soyinka's homeland has suffered from the same consequences of colonialism that have afflicted almost every modern African state. The area now called Nigeria is occupied by many peoples, the most prominent among then being the Hausa, the Yoruba, and the Ibo. The boundaries of the country do not reflect the distribution of these ethnic populations; there are Ibo people in Cameroon, Yoruba in Benin, Hausa in Niger. The physical shape of Nigeria is an administrative fiction deriving from the way the colonial powers parceled out the "dark continent" in the nineteenth century. (Somalia alone among African countries is ethnically homogeneous.) So when the British granted independence to Nigeria in 1960, this most populous of African nations had some considerable work to do to make itself *into* a real nation, as opposed to a collection of adversarial ethnicities. These problems have been exacerbated by almost continually increasing tensions between Christians and Muslims in the country.

No wonder, then, that civic rule has been the exception rather than the norm in Nigeria's history, and that civilian governments have served only at the behest of the military, who have been quick to take over and impose martial law whenever they have sensed the coming of chaos, or genuine democracy—for them the two amount to more or less the same thing. And with martial law has always come strict censorship of all the media, which makes it difficult for even the most apolitical writer to avoid politics. Besides, respect for intellectuals is so great in most African cultures that writers can scarcely resist the pleas of their people for help.

2

Wole Soyinka's people, in the ethnic sense, are the Yoruba, and there is no culture in the world more fascinating. The Yoruba are traditionally among the greatest sculptors in Africa, and their labyrinthine mythology is so coherent and compelling that even the selling of many Yoruba people into slavery could not eradicate it: especially in places where great numbers of Yoruba were transported (most notably Brazil and Hain) it survived by adapting itself, syncretistically, to certain Catholic traditions. The chief Yoruba gods (the *orisa*) became conflated with the popular saints; the results can be seen even today in religions, or cults, like Santeria. The notorious Haitian practice of voodoo is largely, an evil corruption of Yoruba medicine, which typically seeks to confuse the evil spirits who cause illness and draw them from the ill person into a doll or effigy, which is then beaten or destroyed. This form of medical treatment is crucial to one of Soyinka's earliest and most accessibly powerful plays, *The Strong Breed* (1959).

Perhaps not surprisingly, the Yoruba have long practiced the arts of drama, and Soyinka is an heir of that tradition. It is really inaccurate to say that Yoruba drama is religious, because even to make such a statement one must employ a vocabulary which distinguishes between religion and other forms of culture in a way alien to Africa. For the Yoruba, as for almost all Africans, every aspect of culture is religious through and through—it simply *is* worship or celebration or healing or teaching—and religion is thoroughly cultural. In Africa, the notion of "the aesthetic" as a distinct category of experience is unthinkable. No Yoruba arts can be identified as part of the human realm as distinct from that of the gods and spirits. In part this is because of the animism of Yoruba culture, but such a complete integration of religion and culture does not require animism. It seems to have characterized ancient Israel, for instance: the poetry of the Israelites is inseparable from their covenantal relationship with Yahweh. Similarly, Westerners seem to have difficulty understanding why Muslims insist upon the universal application of *sharia,* or islamic law, and tend to think that Muslims don't know how to respect the appropriate cultural boundaries. Yoruba drama arises from what one might call such a "total culture."

Soyinka, though, was raised in a Christian home. His mother's brand and intensity of piety may be guessed at from this: in his memoirs he refers to her almost exclusively as "Wild Christian." But it seems that his chief interest in the doctrines and practices of Christianity derives from their similarities to Yoruba traditions. Biblical themes always echo in his work, especially early in his career: the story of the Prodigal Son in *The Swamp Dwellers* (about 1958), the Passion (with staggering force) in *The Strong Breed*. But, as in his fascinating adaptation of Euripides's *The Bacchae* [*The Bacchae of Euripides: A Communion Rite*] (1973), so do the themes of classical tragedy. It is clear that Soyinka has been interested in the primordial mythic truths that lie behind the doctrines and practices of particular religions: he shares the Jungian view that all religions are concretized and particularized versions of universal experiences. Moreover, he seems to espouse the Feuerbachian projection theory of religion as he says in his critical book *Myth, Literature, and the African World* (1976), "myths arise from man's attempt to externalise and communicate his inner intuitions," and more recently he has written, in oracular tones. "THE WILL of man is placed beyond surrender. . . . ORISA reveals Destiny as—SELF-DESTINATION."

These universalistic and syncretistic tendencies are more easily reconcilable with Yoruba than with Christian or Muslim beliefs, as Soyinka observes in the essay **"Reparations, Truth, and Reconciliation,"** one of a series of lectures given at Harvard University in 1997 and published as *The Burden of Memory, the Muse of Forgiveness* (1999):

> Just what is *African,* for a start, about any section of that continent that arrogantly considers any change of faith an apostasy, punishable even by death? What is *African* about religious intolerance and deadly fanaticism? The spirituality of the black continent, as attested, for instance, in the religion of the *orisa*, abhors such principles of coercion or exclusion, and recognizes all manifestations of spiritual urgings as attributes of the complex disposition of the godhead. *Tolerance* is synonymous with the spirituality of the black continent, *intolerance* is anathema!

Soyinka's imagination is thus secondarily and derivatively Christian at best, despite his upbringing and his long-term fascination with Christian doctrine. And as we shall see, he has sought to exorcise that fascination in rather frightening ways.

When, as a young man, he came to study in England at the University of Leeds, it is not at all surprising that Soyinka fell under the influence of the controversial Shakespearean scholar G. Wilson Knight. For Knight's career was devoted chiefly to the contention that Shakespeare's plays, however "secular" they might appear, were really Christian (in a mythie or archetypal sort of way) through and through. It must have seemed perfectly natural to Soyinka, coming from his Yoruba world, that such would be the case, indeed it must have

been hard for him to think of drama in any other term. No wonder he ultimately decided to adapt *The Bacchae*: the Euripedean original, so obviously shaped b and angrily responsive to the Athenian worship of D onysos, was a clear picture of what he had alway understood drama to be. Soyinka's version, a turbulen tragic fantasy half-Greek and half-African, is one of th most striking and provocative plays of our time, and i its exploration of irreconcilable worldviews often seem a veiled commentary on the troubles of modern Africa

3

Soyinka's plays are often said to be about the moder "clash of cultures" in Africa between Western an African traditional ways, but this is a phrase for whic Soyinka has a singular contempt. In an "Author's Note to what may well be his greatest play, the tragedy *Deat and the King's Horseman* (1975), which is based on historical event, he complains that "the bane of theme of this genre is that they are no sooner employe creatively than they acquire the facile tag of 'clash o cultures,' a prejudicial label which, quite apart from it frequent misapplication, presupposes a potential equal ity in every given situation of the alien culture and th indigenous, on the actual soil of the latter."

One might think that Soyinka is here reminding us tha the British came to Africa with technologies and force that traditional African cultures could not hope to resis in other words, that he is reminding us of his people' status as victims. That would be a misreading. The Brit ish did indeed bring superior physical force to Nigeria but Soyinka is more concerned to point out that th spiritual and cultural forces upon which the Yorub relied were far more impressive. Now, Soyinka is neve shy about offering potent critiques of his culture, an not just in its modern manifestations; from those earl plays, *The Swamp Dwellers* and *The Strong Breed,* w can see a fierce indictment of how power corrupts eve at the level of the village, where leaders pervert thei people's traditions and manipulate them for their ow gain. But those traditions themselves, Soyinka is alway eager to say, have enormous power, and when rightl used and respectfully employed can overcome th humiliations inflicted upon the Yoruba by Britis imperialism. This is indeed the central theme of *Deat and the King's Horseman,* where tradition finds a wa to rescue the dignity of a people even when the colonia power seems to have things well under control.

In Nigeria during World War II, a king has died. Ob Elesin, the king's horseman and a lesser king himsel ("Oba" means "king" or "chief"), is expected, at th end of the month of ceremonies marking the king' passing, to follow his master into the spirit world of th ancestors. In other words, he is to commit ritual suicide It is his greatest wish to do so, and in the villag marketplace, surrounded by people who love an respect him, he awaits the appointed time.

All is prepared. Listen! [*A steady drum-beat from the distance.*] Yes. It is nearly time. The King's dog has been killed. The King's favourite horse is about to follow his master. My brother chiefs know their task and perform it well. . . . My faithful drummers, do me your last service. This is where I have chosen to do my leave-taking, in this heart of life, this hive which contains the swarm of the world in its small compass. . . . Just then I felt my spirit's eagerness. . . . But wait a while my spirit. Wait. Wait for the coming of the courier of the King.

But Simon Pilkings, the district officer in this British colonial outpost, intervenes to prevent the suicide, which violates British law and which he considers to be a barbaric custom. And his intervention succeeds in part because at the crucial moment Elesin hesitates, and thereby cooperates with Pilkings in bringing shame upon himself, his people, and his king (who is by Elesin's cowardice "condemned to wander in the void of evil with beings who are the enemies of life"). Elesin's son Olunde—who had been in England studying medicine and returned when he heard of the death of the king—explains this to Simon Pilkings's wife Jane before he knows that the interference has succeeded. When she suggests that Elesin "is entitled to whatever protection is available to him"—that is, available from her husband as instrument of the colonial Law—Olunde quickly replies.

How can I make you understand? He *has* protection. No one can undertake what he does tonight without the deepest protection the mind can conceive. What can you offer him in place of his peace of mind? In place of the honour and veneration of his own people?

And it is Olunde—the one who Elesin feared would in England forget or repudiate the old tribal ways—who finds a way to rescue his people and his king from the shame brought by Elesin.

In his preface Soyinka is determined to insist that the colonial situation of the play be seen as a catalyst for an exploration of what is permanent in Yoruba society; the play is about "transition," the transition from this world to the world of the spirits and the ancestors, and as such cannot be reduced to a single historical moment. The colonial era simply troubles the waters, it cannot dam the river of Yoruba tradition. "The confrontation in the play," Soyinka writes, "is largely metaphysical, contained in the human vehicle which is Elesin and the universe of the Yoruba mind—the world of the living, the dead, and the unborn." Simon Pilkings thinks he holds the power in this situation, that he participates in a story which his people are writing and of which they are the protagonists; but Soyinka reveals him as merely a plot device, a means by which "the universe of the Yoruba mind" is explored.

This potent tragedy marked a return to Soyinka's early themes and concerns, arresting a drift toward political satire that had begun some years before. One sees this

tendency in his two wickedly funny plays about the shyster preacher and self-proclaimed prophet Brother Jereboam (*The Trials of Brother Jero* [1960] and *Jero's Metamorphosis* [1968]), who ultimately becomes the "general" of a Nigerian version of the Salvation Army, sending his "troops" out into a dangerous world while he remains secure in his office. Lingering just below the surface of these plays is a commentary on the ambitions and absurdities of Nigeria's hyperactive military. The Jero plays were followed by Soyinka's darkest, bitterest play, *Madmen and Specialists* (1970), which reveals his disgust at the crisis of Biafra in 1969.

Biafra was the new country proclaimed by leaders of the Ibo people of eastern Nigeria; but their attempt to secede from Nigeria ended when they were beaten and starved into submission. Soyinka's sympathy for the Biafran rebels led to his arrest and lengthy detainment, an experience chronicled in his searing memoir, *The Man Died* (1972).

Madmen and Specialists emphasizes the ways that the lust for power, and not just power itself, corrupts gifted men and turns them into tyrants who cannot abide dissent or even questioning. One can easily see why after writing this play and *The Man Died,* Soyinka would produce *Death and the King's Horseman,* with its passionate commitment to the maintenance of a great spiritual tradition that cannot be extinguished or even derailed by the traumas of political history. But as passionately as Soyinka expresses that commitment, what speaks still louder than the brilliance of the play is that in the quarter-century since it appeared Soyinka has severely curtailed his theatrical writing. (And most of the plays he has written are topical political satires, like the *The Beautification of Area Boy.*) It is hard to imagine a greater loss for modern drama.

4

This is not to say that Soyinka has fallen silent. But since the '70s he has largely forsaken the communal and necessarily collaborative work of the theater for political commentary and memoir; and for a time early in the 1990s he was a government official. Perhaps the most remarkable product of this period is not the properly celebrated memoir *Aké: The Years of Childhood* (1981), but rather its successor, *Ìsarà: A Voyage around Essay* (1989). "Essay" is Soyinka's father, the schoolteacher S. A. Soyinka, and this novelistic attempt to imagine and describe Essay's youth and young manhood is a moving act of filial devotion, a tribute to a wry, dignified man and his colorful circle of friends.

Interestingly, the narrative revolves around the successful attempt by Essay and his friends to influence a matter of *local* politics, the selection of the Odemo (or chief) of the town of Ìsarà. The frustrations of trying to shape a nation must have made such local concerns seem less painful and more rewarding. But in any case, we see in all the works of this period Soyinka's continued determination to follow E. M. Forster's famous advice: "Only connect!" Connection is Soyinka's constant goal, his natural tendency as a writer; but it is immensely sad to see him cut at least some of his ties to the theater in order to participate in a political realm from which he seems to find little real hope of connection.

Soyinka's experience as a minister in the Nigerian government ended badly, as he probably knew it would. In 1994, after the national police told him that they could not protect him from others who wanted to kill him, he took the hint and left Nigeria covertly. During his exile over the next four years, he launched rhetorical missiles at the dictator General Sani Abacha and his corrupt regime.

The Open Sore of a Continent is a product of that period—not so much a book as a collection of projectiles. Only rarely do Soyinka's literary gifts shine through, but some of the great dramatist's flair for characterization is evident in this comparison of Abacha with his predecessor, General Ibrahim Babangida:

> Babangida's love of power was visualized in actual terms: power over Nigeria, over the nation's impressive size, its potential, over the nation's powerful status within the community of nations. The potency of Nigeria, in short, was an augmentation of his own sense of personal power. It corrupted him thoroughly, and all the more disastrously because he had come to identify that Nigeria and her resources with his own person and personal wealth. Not so Abacha. Abacha is prepared to reduce Nigeria to rubble as long as he survives to preside over a name—and Abacha is a survivor. . . . Totally lacking in vision, in perspectives, he is a mole trapped in a warren of tunnels. At every potential exit he is blinded by the headlights of an oncoming vehicle and freezes. When the light has veered off, he charges to destroy every animate or inanimate object within the path of the vanished beam. Abacha is incapable of the faculty of defining that intrusive light, [or] even to consider if the light path could actually lead him out of the mindless maze.

But prose so vivid is rare in this book. Mostly, it is the wrathful detailing of the indignities Abacha and his henchmen inflicted on Nigeria, a detailing interrupted only by the repeated mastication of what have become for Soyinka the fundamental questions: in Africa, is the concept of "nation" viable? Does "Nigeria" exist? Has it existed? Can it exist? Soyinka is not quite ready to abandon the project of nationhood, but he is not far from it.

In 1988 Soyinka published a collection of essays titled *Art, Dialogue, and Outrage* (an expanded second edition appeared in 1993), and there, as in *The Open Sore of a Continent,* outrage is certainly the chief not sounded. One is tempted to ask what, exactly, Soyink *wants,* since everything seems to make him so angry What, for instance, is a plausible alternative to th almost-bankrupt project of the Nigerian nation-state What artistic practices does he find healthy and proper

I think the answer to these questions is pretty clear: th Soyinka who speaks in these works is concerned, a was T. S. Eliot, with the "dissociation of sensibility, with the fragmenting of a culture and thus of the mind that inhabit it. He wants unity and wholeness. And thi can only be achieved within the context of a particula ethnic tradition; that is, for him, within the Yoruba tradition. Furthermore, the Yoruba tradition can only flouris again if its competitors are, forcibly if necessary extracted from the cultural space of Nigeria. Olunde' victory over Simon Pilkings was local and temporary greater victories call for more drastic measures.

In a scathing essay titled **"Neo-Tarzanism: The Poet ics of Pseudo-Tradition,"** first published in *Transition* magazine in 1975, Soyinka responds to critics who have thought him insufficiently African in his allegiances by gleefully trumping their best cards. He makes a proposi tion:

> That the very existence and practice [in Africa] of nontraditional religions be declared retrogressive and colonialist. So let us . . . ban these religions from our continent altogether. This is a serious proposition as [my critics] will discover when they find the energy and determination to launch a movement for the eradication of islam and christianity from the black continent. I cannot alas find the will to place myself at the forefront of such a movement but I shall readily play John the Baptist to their anti-christ.

This is followed immediately by an ironic reflection on how even an "anti-Christian" statement finds itsel drawing on "the metaphors of Christian religious history": such is the "endemic effect of great religions." I is hard to be sure if Soyinka really believes wholeheartedly in this "proposition," or rather has been driven to it by his critics' accusations; still, that he chose not only to write the essay in the mid-'70s but also retrieved it to serve as the concluding piece in *Art, Dialogue, and Outrage* seems, to me, telling. Even if one takes Soyinka's proposition as a bit of Swiftian satire—even if, in other words, he recognizes the practical impossibility of "banning" Christianity and Islam from Africa altogether—there is no doubt that such an outcome constitutes an ideal for him.

If this radical excision of the alien faiths, this intolerance in the name of tolerance, and a consequent restoration of Yoruba cultural purity, are the only ways in which Soyinka's anger can be soothed, then outrage will continue to be his portion. And that is not only because Christianity and Islam are now too deeply implicated in Nigeria for their removal, but also because all such dreams of cultural purity, of "unified sensibility," are illusory and deceitful. No human culture ever has been or ever could be whole and pure and undefiled by external "contamination." And such laboratory purity, if achieved, would be lifeless: as Mikhail Bakhtin repeatedly insisted, it is at the boundaries of culture, languages, and faiths that the real excitement happens; the most dynamic cultures are those called to respond to the strange, the other, the different in their midst. Soyinka's plays amply testify to this: it is Olunde's *response* to Pilkings's colonial paternalism that energizes **Death and the King's Horseman**; it is the *competing* understandings of sacrifice in the Yoruba and the Christian traditions that give **The Strong Breed** its peculiar power. Soyinka's desire to eliminate cultural and religious otherness from Nigeria is not only regrettable as an example of what some people call "the new tribalism"; it would mean death to the very Yoruba tradition he wants to save.

5

Whenever modern cultures reach a certain stage of political development they seem to turn toward their artists and intellectuals for guidance and leadership: one thinks also of Václav Havel in the Czech Republic, and Mario Vargas Llosa in Peru. (Earlier examples from Africa include the first president of Kenya, Jomo Kenyatta, who was an anthropologist, and the first president of Senegal. Léopold Senghor, who was a poet.) None of these men seems fully comfortable with his political role. But this is work that they know they must do, a call they cannot refuse.

Soyinka continues to proclaim the continuity of Yoruba tradition and its ability to survive the traumas of history; but he plays the role of political actor too. In October 1998, several months after the death of Abacha, Soyinka returned from exile. Less than a week after his arrival he gave a blistering speech to a university crowd, excoriating Abacha (whom he compared to Hitler) and expressing hope that Nigeria was at last on the way to democratic rule. (Three years later, under the elected leadership of President Olusegun Obasanjo, a former general, the country has so far maintained a shaky commitment to reform.)

But if Soyinka's condemnation of dictatorship and his hope for reform alike appeal to a notion of shared humanity, why should anyone pay attention? His contempt for "the colonizing hordes," whether "Eurochristian" or "Arab-islamic," knows no bounds, but he is equally contemptuous when he turns his gaze on his fellow Africans. Wherever he turns he sees folly, hypocrisy, "mendacity, ineptitude, corruption, and sadism." He is a humanist disgusted by humanity.

This descent into bitterness is not pleasant to record; would that it were arrested and the direction of Soyinka's thought reversed. But there is something inevitable about such bitterness, I think, for ethically earnest intellectuals living in the various post-Christian worlds. The moralistic humanism which is Soyinka's chief weapon against the dictators arose in Western culture in the eighteenth and nineteenth centuries as a substitute for a Christianity which was then thought to be dying. But, it turns out, belief in a common humanity seems to require the support of Christian doctrine and cannot be sustained without an appeal to the *imago dei* and Christ's universal offer of salvation. And when humanism collapses, as it must, what is left but Sani Abacha's will to power or Soyinka's retreat into tribalism?

Indeed, the two choices may be one: I cited earlier Soyinka's own prophetic claim that "THE WILL of man is placed beyond surrender." The Yoruba tradition is rich and potent; while often cruel, it is in many ways beautiful; but it lacks the resources necessary to wage the battle for "the rights of man as a universal principle" that Soyinka now finds himself called upon to wage. Thus the last movement of a brilliant literary career may necessarily echo with rage and wrath.

Yaw Adu-Gyamfi (essay date fall 2002)

SOURCE: Adu-Gyamfi, Yaw. "Orality in Writing: Its Cultural and Political Significance in Wole Soyinka's *Ogun Abibiman*." *Research in African Literatures* 33, no. 3 (fall 2002): 104-24.

[*In the following essay, Adu-Gyamfi evaluates Soyinka's use of African oral traditions in* Ogun Abibiman, *noting that the collection's vocabulary "reflects a highly conscious sense of African oral poetics."*]

In "New Trends in Modern African Poetry," Tanure Ojaide observes that "poetry in African is [. . .] currently enjoying an unprecedented creative outburst and popularity" (4). This popularity, according to him, seems to arise from "some aesthetic strength hitherto unrealized in written African poetry which has successfully adapted oral poetry technique into the written form" (4). Though written in English, the poetry carries the African sensibility, culture, and worldview, as well as the rhythms, structures, and techniques of oral tradition, resulting in what Wole Soyinka calls "double writing," or interweaving of various ethnic, geographic, personal, and peculiar African oral features into the European-derived written form (**"Neo-Tarzanism"** 319). Such oral features include ceremonial chants, tonal lyricism, poetry of the primal drum and flute, proverbs, riddles, myths, songs, folktales, the antiphonal call-and-response styles, and the rhythmic, repetitive, digressive, and formulaic modes of language use.

This use of African oral tradition is abundantly evident in the works of major African writers. To the Nigerian poet Christopher Okigbo, the artist's vocation is a priestly office charged with maintaining the culture of his/her society as a whole. *Heavensgate, Distances,* and *Limits,* make this claim evident. Like Okigbo, Ghanaian poet Kofi Awoonor is preoccupied with African folk traditions, as well as the damaging effects of the European presence in Africa. As suggested by the title of his collection *Rediscovery and Other Poems,* the poetry is chiefly concerned with the plight of a contemporary Africa uprooted from its traditional past by contact with an uncomprehending Europe and the poet's attempts to regain this past.

Use of traditional African oral discourse is also discernible in the poetry of Southern Africa, especially poetry against apartheid. David B. Copland's analysis of Basotho *sefela* (songs of the inveterate travelers) elucidates the oral content of this poetry, and it shows that *sefela* springs from traditional praise poems common throughout Southern Africa (qtd. in White 7). Nor is the oral emphasis restricted to Western and Southern Africa. In East Africa, the two major poets, Jared Angira and Okot p'Bitek, use oral textual features to reflect African culture. Okot p'Bitek's *Song of Lawino,* for instance, relies heavily on traditional oral literature in its use of Acoli proverbs and songs. The most obvious markers of orality in the text are the acknowledged borrowings, indented quotations, that Lawino uses to illustrate *kit Acoli* in many respects.

That a new literary orientation exists in contemporary African Literature cannot be doubted. Though the long list of African writers using and expanding features of oral discourse is enormous, I focus on Wole Soyinka's *Ogun Abibiman* because not much work on orality in Soyinka's poetry has been done. Moreover, Wole Soyinka has often been accused of relying too heavily on European models in his writing. Although he does not deny his use of such models, because he advocates literary eclecticism, he has consistently argued for the African basis of his poetry in essays such as **"Neo-Tarzanism," "The Writer in a Modern African State,"** and **"The Choice and Use of the English Language."** Surrounded by controversy over its African or European sources, Soyinka's work becomes viable for a study such as this, which situates African literature within a new trend.

In discussing orality in Soyinka's *Ogun Abibiman,* I suggest that even Soyinka's use of neometaphysical strains, double- and triple-barreled neologisms, cadences of sprung rhythm, and complex punctuation and language, which many think are derived from European forms, have their basis in Ifa divination and African *apae* (appellation or praise) poetry as well. As Soyinka argues in **"Neo-Tarzanism,"** the language of his poetry

is not that of the common African oral poems, which "being easiest to translate, have found their way into anthologies and school texts; it is not merely those lyrics which because they are favorites at festivals of the Arts haunted by ethnologists [. . .] supply the readiest source material for [. . .] academics" (313). Instead, it is the kind that, like the sculpture, dance, and music of Africa, integrates various media of expression "into the moulding of the sensibility which tries today to carve new forms out of the alien words, expressing not only the itemised experience, but reflecting the unified conceptualization of the experience" (327). Soyinka calls this strategy "selective eclecticism" (329) and argues that the "[t]raditional poetry [he uses] is [. . .] also to be found in the very [. . .] unique temper of world comprehension that permeates language for the truly immersed" (313). There was as much neometaphysical strain and "sprung rhythm" in traditional African poetry, he adds, as in the poetry of Hopkins and the others he was alleged to have copied (319).

Concentrating on *Ogun Abibiman,* its theme of Black nationalism, of Africa's liberation struggles, and its relations to traditional African war poetics, I argue that Soyinka uses *Ogun Abibiman* to highlight his position, taken in *Myth, Literature, and the African World,* that African literature can be expressed through traditional African categories. He demonstrates, as Stuart Sim points out, "that 'the self-apprehension' of the African world in terms of concepts and categories can be embodied in properly African cultural forms, forms which can be considered to have artistic merit" (376). In view of this remark, the fact that critics have not paid much attention to African cultural forms in Soyinka's *Ogun Abibiman* comes as a surprise. To date, criticism on the poem, such as W. B. Last's "*Ogun Abibiman*" and Omolara Ogundipe-Leslie's 'A Comment on *Ogun Abibiman,*'" has thematized the poem's contemporary links with Africa's liberation struggles in Southern Africa. Very little or no attention has been paid to the poem's relations to oral African war poetry; yet it is to such poetry that the postcolonial Soyinka returns, rewriting it for a sociopolitical purpose.

African war poetics comprise the unique discursive practices that operated as war strategies in precolonial Africa, especially in Zulu *izibongo* (Finnegan, *World Treasury* 120-34); Yoruba *oriki* and war poetry (Beier 38-41, 120; Finnegan 152-54); Galla *gheraera* from Ethiopia (Trask 113); *gabay* war songs from Somalia (Finnegan 101); Dinka war/hunting poetry (Deng 202); *imigubo* and *imihubo* war poetry of the Ngoni of Malawi (Finnegan, *Oral Poetry* 201); Ashanti war poetry from Ghana (Nketia, *Drumming* 107-12, 147); Shona *detembo rehondo* from Zimbabwe (Hodza and Fortune 32, 339-44); Swahili *tenzi,* the long religious poems dealing with the heroic deeds of Muslim heroes; the *Lianja Epic,* the long prose narrative of the Nkundo of Zaire; and the *Sunjata Epic* of Somalia and Sene-gambia, which narrates the exploits of the hero Sunjata.

This precolonial African war poetics characteristically included making reference to the presence of, and the human dependence on, gods, spirits, supernatural forces, and ancestors in times of war or national emergencies; using an engaged poetic voice to stir up public senti-ments against an imminent danger to the community; stressing the virtues of group strength, heroism, and patriotism; resorting to particular oral generic modes, like the victory ritual of song and celebration, drum poetry, dancing, and chanting, which together give the discourse a public, sociopolitical character; and using special technical features, like detailed descriptions of war objects and a dramatization of war situations. These descriptions, usually couched in short verse form (to fit the urgency of a war situation) and punctuated with emphatic repetition, puns, proverbs, parallelism, appel-lations, alliteration, and animal and plant imagery, represented compressed ways of expressing imminent victory. These traditional devices, repressed for decades in anglophone African poetry as a consequence of colonialism, are the discursive strategies that Soyinka redeploys in *Ogun Abibiman.* They are used as coun-tercolonial discourse against the imposed European knowledges, values, disciplines, and institutions that were part of the imperial state apparatus during the colonial period.

The title words "Ogun" (Yoruba god) and "Abibiman," an Akan word Soyinka defines as "the Black [Abibi] Nation [man]; the land of the Black Peoples; the Black World; that which pertains to, the matter, the affair of, Black peoples" (*Ogun Abibiman* 23), were initially oral signifiers limited to particular ethnic groups, the Yorubas of Nigeria and Akans of Ghana, respectively. But in carrying forward these references through a writ-ten form, Soyinka broadens their conceptual reference to give the text a more pan-African character. Ogun, the god of iron, war, lightning, creation, and transition, the-matizes traditional African war poetics; he embodies action, primal energy, and destruction, on one hand, and passivity, regeneration, and resolution of conflicts, on the other. Soyinka succinctly alludes to this multiple nature of the god in his essay **"And after the Narcis-sist?"**:

> Ogun is the antithesis of cowardice and Philistinism, yet within him is contained also the complement of the creative essence, a bloodthirsty destructiveness. Mixed up with the gestative inhibition of his nature [is] the destructive explosion of an incalculable energy. Contradictory as they are, it is necessary to experience these aspects of the god as a single comprehended es-sence.
>
> (14)

The complementary nature of Ogun is here emphasized, but Soyinka does not mince words in making the reader aware that the many sides of Ogun consolidate into one complex whole, which is nevertheless expressed as a two-sided phenomenon to reflect in both singular and plural dimensions the creative and the destructive propensities embodied in Ogun. Explicating this nature of Ogun elsewhere, Soyinka reconstructs it as "the paradoxical truth of destructiveness and creativeness in acting man" (*Myth* 150). Thus the ambivalent nature of Ogun is expanded into an effective means of presenting not just the philosophical concept of complementary pairs, but also the reality of both the destructive and creative potential inherent in human beings. Soyinka also parallels Ogun's complementary nature to the "banked loop of the 'Mobius Strip'" (*Idanre* 83) to emphasize the multiform nature of the god. Soyinka explains the Mobius Strip as

> a mathe-magical ring, infinite in self-recreation into independent but linked rings and therefore the freest conceivable (to me) symbol of human or divine (e. g. Yoruba, Olympian) relationships. A symbol of opti-mism, also, as it gives the illusion of a "kink" in the circle and a possible centrifugal escape from the eternal cycle of [the] evil history of man [. . .] for the Mobius Strip is a very simple figure of aesthetic and scientific truths and contradictions.
>
> (88)

As Richard Priebe observes, "the 'Mobius Strip' there becomes a symbol of the poet's reinterpretation of the myth of Ogun—in fact a metonym for the god" (125).

By adopting the Mobius Strip as the Ogunian image, Soyinka represents the complementary nature of Ogun within a circular pattern: Ogun thus becomes, among other things, a philosophical concept of existence, involving alternating circles of creativeness and destructiveness, each unit of the duality made a condi-tion of the other. In their mythographic analyses of Soyinka's poetry, Afam Ebeogu has traced this underly-ing pattern of death and rebirth in Soyinka's mythic references, while Donatus Nwoga concludes that "the wisdom which he [Soyinka] finds [in Yoruba tradition], and what [. . .] emerges from his poems and gives significance to them, is recognition of the cyclic nature of death and resurrection, of destruction and new creation" (183). Hence in Soyinka's poetic reconstruc-tion of Ogun, the Yoruba deity is not just a god but an embodiment of complex nodes of concepts and catego-ries.

The name *Abibiman* (Africa) also thrusts up several cultural, geographical, and political assumptions. Abibi-man is of course Africa, but Soyinka's definition of it names all Black peoples, including diasporic Africans, as citizens by right of color. Unlike the name Africa that encompasses an enormous assortment of peoples, including White Africans, the name Abibiman endows its principal morpheme, Abibi, with the privilege of ownership; non-Black Africans are excluded from the referential implications of the word. Also, translated into a colonial language, for example English, Abibi means black. As is well known, black in the White World has negative connotations. But in adopting an indigenous name for black, Soyinka moves away from the colonial definition of the word black to one that has more positive connotations, somewhat similar to a Negritudist redefinition of the word. The term is invested with a sense of Black pride, which indeed constitutes a bold cultural and political venture for a people whose inter- and intracontinental affairs are still dominated by neocolonial forces and colonial languages. Soyinka's naming therefore can be described in terms of what Elleke Boehmer calls double cleaving: "a cleaving from, moving away from colonial definitions, transgressing the boundaries of colonial discourse, and in order to effect this, cleaving to, borrowing, taking over, or appropriating the ideological, linguistic, and textual forms of [African oral traditions]" (105-06). What this double cleaving creates is a hybridity that, by proliferating differences, contests and reverses degrading stereotypes about the word Black into positive significations.

The positive implications of the name are, however, not without some problems. Although the name is a catch-all word for all Blacks, establishing cultural homogeneity among a wide variety of cultural groups, its constitutive implications are so broad that very little room is left for needed specification of individual parts. Such a construction, to use Arun Mukherjee's formulation, homogenizes and creates a native devoid of gender, class, and ethnicity. The logic of the name is also fraught with exclusivist and essentialist viewpoints about Africa that exclude non-Black Africans who, either by right of birth or naturalization, qualify as Africans. Exclusivism and essentialism, as Edward Said argues, reconstitute difference as identity, conferring identities by demarcating "we"/"they" (us/them) oppositions—the same dichotomizing and essentializing discourse of which the colonizer is accused. Said argues especially against the self-indulgence of celebrating one's own identity, since according to him identity does not imply "an ontologically given and externally determined stability, or uniqueness, or irreducible character, or privileged status as something total and complete in and of itself" (407). In effect, no one ethnic group today can claim, if it ever could, to be pure. We are all *métissage*.

However, the problems of homogeneity and essentialism in Soyinka's definition of Abibiman wither in light of the apparently converse argument in which his definition is to be understood in terms of the ideology of Black Consciousness. Steve Biko, one of the outstanding leaders of the Black Consciousness movement, defines it as follows:

> Briefly defined [. . .] Black Consciousness is in essence the realization by the black [person] of the need to rally together with his [kind] around the cause of their oppression—the blackness of their skin—and to operate as a group in order to rid themselves of the shackles that bind them to perpetual servitude. [. . .] It seeks to infuse the black community with a new-found pride in themselves, their efforts, their value systems, their culture, their religion and their outlook on life.
>
> (qtd. in Ngara 133)

As Emmanuel Ngara explains, Black consciousness "neither idealizes blackness nor posits a theory of racial superiority. Its argument is that white racism is the major political force in South Africa and that Africans, Indians and coloureds are branded 'non-whites' and are therefore oppressed by reason of their colour" (133). Among other things, this ideology gives a sense of the oppression of all Blacks; it evokes Pan-Africanist ideas, the oneness of all Blacks. This solidarity is symbolized in the title *Ogun Abibiman,* and in lines such as "Ogun treads the earth of Shaka" (24); "Rogbodiyan! Rogbodiyan! / Bayete Ba ba! Bayete" (11), which all suggest (through the mixture of Akan/Yoruba, Zulu/Yoruba words and the movement from one geographical area to another) the unity of the Black race and the abrogation of geographical and linguistic borders among Blacks.

Ogun Abibiman's foreword celebrates Mozambique's Samora Machel's declaration of war against the then-White-ruled Rhodesia (now Zimbabwe), and appraises this event as a prelude to "the definitive probe towards an ultimate goal, a summation of the continent's liberation struggle against the bastion of inhumanity—apartheid South Africa." In *Mandela's Earth,* Soyinka's next poetry collection, he reversed this praise however when Machel retreated from his declaration by compromising with the South African government in signing the Nkomati accord, the nonaggression pact between the two countries, which pledged that the two governments would not give material aid or bases to any group threatening the security of the other. Mozambique complied by expelling thousands of African National Congress (ANC) members who had escaped the atrocities of apartheid. Soyinka bitterly condemns this act in **"Apologia (Nkomati),"** the last of the "Mandela's Earth" section, arguing that such capitulation "betray[s] our being" (25).

Though the preface to *Ogun Abibiman* gives prominence to the nationalist efforts of living beings like Machel, the actual poem, twenty-four pages long, does not. Rather, it is preoccupied with ancestral warrior spirits, like Ogun and Shaka, preparing and leading the offensive against Rhodesia and South Africa. This belief in the involvement of gods and ancestral spirits in the affairs of the living is perhaps the poem's most outstanding feature that signals Soyinka's use of traditional African war discourse.

Soyinka calls this involvement of spirits in the affairs of the living the "principle of complementarity," which he defines as the simultaneous interaction between the supernatural and the material world. He goes so far as to caution postcolonial writers of African descent that "to ignore this [principle] and pursue the alternative route of negation is, for whatever motives, an attempt to perpetuate the external subjugation of the black continent" (*Myth* 19). Stephen Slemon represents this simultaneous interaction as a positive aspect of counter-colonial discourse. He sees it not just as an intrinsic part of the everyday reality of most postcolonial societies, but most importantly as a way of rereading and rewriting colonial discourse. According to Slemon, the strategy is adopted to create or recreate postcolonial local identities in order to effect not only difference but resistance to the totalizing systems of the "massive imperial centre" (11), and to confound the values and discursive structures constituted by colonial discourse.

Consequently, the opening lines of the first section of Soyinka's poem have Ogun reawakening to the task of leading his people to battle to destroy White racist power in Southern Africa. His appearance is felt in the whole of *Abibiman*:

> No longer are the forests green; storms
> Assail the palm, the egret and the snail.
> Bared, the dark heart of a hidden nursery
> Of embers flares aglow, a landmass writhes
> From end to end, bathed and steeped
> In stern tonalities.
>
>   (1)

His whirling, incalculable energy causes storms, "earthquakes," "a flood unseasonal" (1), and agitates the whole cosmos, penetrating even into the womb of the earth to cause the "earth [to] / Ring in unaccustomed accents" (2). Present with Ogun are ancestral spirits whom Soyinka refers to as "[a] horde of martyrs [who] burst upon our present— / [marching], beside the living" (2). Though alluding to the coming of Ogun and the heroic dead to accompany the living to battle, this section also suggests the particular mode in which the traditional African experiences ancestral spirits. It shows how all of *Abibiman* feels Ogun's energy, and how the god's indomitable will is felt in the Black soul. As Soyinka pointed out during a question-and-answer session at the African Studies Association Conference in Los Angeles, November 1979, the belief in the involvement of gods and the heroic dead in the affairs of the living is common to many societies, but unique to Africa in this one respect: "the way it is permanently affective in the consciousness and activity of the living" (qtd. in Katrak 43). Indeed, this belief constitutes a different way of understanding life for the majority of traditional Africans, and informs "[their] sense of strife, of conflict and resolution" (43).

Ogun, who is also the god of Harvest, as Soyinka makes us aware in *Idanre* (86), is represented as abandoning his agricultural functions and devoting himself solely to the forging of a weapon that will bring inevitable victory to his people:

> Rust and silence fill the thatch
> Of Ogun's farmstead.
> . . .
> A planting season [is] lost. [. . .   Rust
> Possesses cutlass and hoe. But listen. . . . !
>
> Carillons in the distance. A festal
> Anvil wreathed in peals, split by a fervid
> Tongue of ore in whiteglow.
> The Blacksmith's forearm lifts,
> And dances. . . .
> Its swathes are not of peace.
>
> Who dare restrain this novel form, this dread
> Conversion of the slumbering ore. . . .
>
>   (3-4)

This allusion to Ogun forging a weapon recalls a far worse situation in Yoruba mythology. Yoruba myth has it that there came a time when the contemporaneous experience of the living and the nonliving, or of the mortals and gods, was upset due to rebellion on the part of mortals. This "disruption in the cosmic principle of complementarity," as Soyinka calls it (*Myth* 22), resulted in a long isolation of the gods from mortals that brought about an "immense chaotic growth which had sealed off reunion [between mortals and the gods]" (144). The gods tried, but failed to demolish this impassable barrier, until Ogun, "armed with the first technical instrument which he had forged from the ore of mountain-womb" (28-29), "not only dared to look into transitional essence, but triumphantly bridged it with knowledge, with art, with vision and the mystic creativity of science—a total and profound hubristic assertiveness that is beyond any parallel in Yoruba experience" (157). He thus earned the appellation "the first creative energy, the first challenger and conqueror of transition" (145). Ogun once again forging a weapon from "slumbering ore" in *Ogun Abibiman* serves an inspirational purpose, which stems from the basic philosophy that no problem is as big as the one the disruption in the cosmic principle caused. If Ogun was able to forge a weapon to conquer the abyss of transition, it follows logically that he would be able to forge another one to tackle the oppression of Blacks in Southern Africa. This analogy not only replaces fear with hope in the people of Abibiman, but more importantly it banishes all thoughts of cowardice and the slightest expectation of disappointment.

Witness Soyinka's imagining of the victory ritual of song and celebration, accompanied with drumming, dancing, and chanting, that develops into a "burgeoning [. . .] convergence of wills" as the "chimes of re-creation recalls [the people] / To an origin, a oneness":

The singer's tongue is loosened
The drummer's armpits
flex for a lyrical contention

. . .

Now self-acclaiming,
Spurs the Cause to the season of enthronement.

(4)

Unlike the Homeric lyre, which provides an instrumental accompaniment to singing or to the poetic words of the individual poet, drumming in this social context involves not just the stirring of group sentiment to enhance the public and sociopolitical character of the business at hand, but the sending of a special poetic message that exists in its own right. This is the tradition of the famous "talking drum" that is popular in Ghana and Nigeria, especially among the Akan and Yoruba, where it is used to perform poetry in honor of a king or god, to transmit state history on state occasions, convey external danger in times of war, or, as Kwabena Nketia points out, to communicate "the presence of a divinity [. . .] or some particular [divine] character participating in [an] event" (*Drumming* 229). In the case of **Ogun Abibiman,** the honoring of the divine presence seems the most probable purpose for the drumming, since it is Ogun's presence that sparks the excitement at this point in the poem. As a language whose words are not spoken or sung by mouth but played out loud to help transmit message in a sort of telegraphic code, drum language serves as an effective and strategic countercolonial discourse: on one hand, it shuts off the colonizers from the fuller meaning and significance of what is communicated; on the other, it invites its intended African audience to listen and respond accordingly to the message of the talking drum. Reference to the "drummer's [. . .] lyrical contention" introduces not just a different poetic discourse, but another poetic voice besides that of the posited poet/speaker. The former, however, is suppressed, and comes to life only through the readers' or audience's imaginative evocation of the music and poetry of the primal drum. Unlike Kobina Eyi Acquah's *Music for a Dream Dance* or Edward Kamau Brathwaite's *Arrivants* where drum poetry is directly reproduced in the written text, **Ogun Abibiman** just makes reference to drum poetry to mirror its occurrence in the text. To the reader who is not familiar with the Yoruba language and the special ways in which it communicates to people, this evocation of drum poetry will seem puzzling or incomplete. But as Ulli Beier explains in the introduction to his book *Yoruba Poetry,* Yoruba poetic language is full of allusions and incomplete phrases that readers are left to complete in their own minds. The assumption behind such linguistic and poetic practice is that readers, upon encountering this episode of the drummer's lyrical contention (as a reference to drum poetry), will recall and incorporate the commonly known poetry of the talking drum into the text. By incorporating this discourse of the primal drum, Soy-

inka demonstrates that he is in search of participants as much as listeners, people who, by encountering a reference to the celebrative voice of the drummer, will reproduce complete versions into the text from memory. Hence the poem is couched in an artistic frame that envisions potential audience participation in order to energize and lift the text from the printed page into a dynamic experience.

As a further means of enhancing the dramatic experience, the poet, as "acolyte to [Ogun]" (4), assumes the role of the public poetic voice, arguing that war is the only just, hopeful, and logical thing to embark on because all attempts, like dialogue, sanctions, and diplomacy, aimed at attaining a peaceful solution to the Southern Africa problem, have not only failed but worsened the situation:

Sanctions followed Dialogue, games
Of time-pleading.
And Sharpeville followed Dialogue
And Dialogue
Chased its tail, a dogged dog
Dodging the febrile barks
Of protest—
Always from beyond the fence.
Sharpeville
Bared its teeth, and that
Proved no sleeping dog
Though the kind world let it lie.

(6)

The repetition of and pun on "dogs," a word-play Obi Maduakor mistakenly describes as "amateurish" (77), appear funny but not playful. The word-play evokes the dissimilar meanings of, and attitudes toward, notable remarks dealing with dogs in both the African and colonial worlds. The Western proverb "Let sleeping dogs lie," which enjoins people to leave things as they are, undisturbed, expresses a satisfaction with the status quo, and clashes with its opposed meaning in the African context: "Sharpeville / Bared its teeth, and that / Proved no sleeping dog. . . . / Ogun is the tale that wags the dog / All dogs, and all have had their day" (6). The African phrase dealing with Ogun's connection with the dog essentially means there is no place for "sleeping dogs" because Ogun shakes them out of their slumber. It is creatively representative of oral folk culture, stressing the belief that the current situation requires action.

Of significance is the fact that although Soyinka uses an African proverb to abrogate a Western one, he reinforces the African one with another English proverb in the subsequent line: "All dogs, and all have had their day" (6), derived from "every dog shall have its day." Since proverbs are a distillation of generations of experience reflecting particular worldviews, and therefore must be understood in the broader context of cultural transmission, it is useful to note that by reinforcing or merging an African proverb with a Western one, Soyinka uses selective appropriation to forge a new linguistic and cultural relationship, a sharing of meanings, experiences, and visions where none existed before.

Soyinka's point, that war is the only way to ensure the liberation of Blacks in Southern Africa, can be understood better from some observations that the great African thinker and scientist, Cheikh Anta Diop, makes about the issue in a 1970 interview with *Afriscope*. Expressing a contemporary African reaction against dialogue, especially the Organization of African Unity's (OAU's) official policy of dialogue with South Africa, Diop argues that South Africa is not seeking dialogue, but time, the necessary time to develop her nuclear arsenal that will consequently pose the threat of extermination to Blacks who oppose White rule in Southern Africa (255). Technologically speaking, South Africa was at this time very close to the thermonuclear stage, which situation for Soyinka argued for an intensification of the liberation struggle: to move away from dialogue and other "games / Of time-pleading" to the ultimate—what he calls a steel event, or armed struggle.

Though the sense of literature as engagement, revolt, and rehabilitation of an oppressed, colonized race characterize *Ogun Abibiman,* significant words that Soyinka uses to reflect this sense of engagement are paradoxical. As Ngara points out, two principles run through the entire poem, and these are symbolized by the subtitle of part one: "Steel Usurps the Forests; Silence Dethrones Dialogue":

> Steel refers to arms of war, to Africa's acceptance of an armed liberation struggle; while the dethroning of dialogue by silence signifies the rejection of the policy of dialogue with South Africa which had been advocated by some members of the Organization of African Unity (OAU). Silence also lends weight to the tense atmosphere created in this part of the poem, an atmosphere which symbolizes a moment in African history charged with tension and emotion, indicating Africa's preparedness for the final onslaught.
>
> (97)

Silence, often defined as utter stillness, not speaking, voicelessness, here reveals itself paradoxically as resistance, as tension. In effect, silence here speaks louder than words; it becomes what Tzvetan Todorov would consider *comportement verbal* in *The Poetics of Prose*—the idea that the very act of not speaking "speaks." In particular, Soyinka relates silence to dedication to a cause, the objective of freedom, to which "in vow of silence," Ogun and the people of Abibiman have committed themselves until the "task is done" (2).

Soyinka's description of this critical moment of political commitment to a future in which apartheid in South Africa is overcome involves an intricate tapestry of African-heritage poetry down the centuries, as well as the politics of the gaze, which is a crucial sign of colonial control and resistance. Black soldiers, described in terms of appellations and animal imagery symbolizing action, strength, beauty, and grace, glance at their objective with a determination that causes other anticolonial representations of the politics of the gaze to pale into insignificance:

> In time of race, no beauty slights the duiker's
> In time of strength, the elephant stands alone
> In time of hunt, the lion's grace is holy
> In time of flight, the egret mocks the envious
> In time of strife, none vies with Him
> Of seven paths, Ogun, who to right a wrong
> Emptied reservoirs of blood in heaven
> Yet raged with thirst—I read
> His savage beauty on black brows,
> In depths of molten bronze aflame
> Beyond their eyes' fixated distances
> And tremble!
>
> (7)

This passage is influenced by appellation poetry, particularly its stylistic features, analysis of which sheds light on Soyinka's poetic style and his choice and use of language. Akosua Anyidoho, in "Linguistic Parallels in Traditional Akan Appellation Poetry," lists the major stylistic aspects of appellation poetry as the frequent reference to praise names, parallelism of structure, and the formation of compound words. All these aspects are present in Soyinka's poem. The most obvious is the frequent recurrence of praise reference names: personal names, epithets, appellations, and names of animals and birds, some representing the totems of the person being adored. Indeed the high frequency of names in the short passage above—duiker, elephant, lion, egret, He of seven paths, Ogun, heaven, etc.—may appear excessive until its significance is grasped in the oral context. As Kwesi Yankah points out, the purpose is to "individuate and depict the referent as deserving the attention of society among a paradigm of peers and co-equals" (382). Citing Ogun's actions in heaven is particularly significant because it magnifies and elevates his status by suggesting that he has the power to make blood flow copiously even in heaven.

Parallel structures are likewise used in *Ogun Abibiman* to emphasize the heroic characteristics of Ogun. The selection of syntactically equivalent structures ultimately leads to the climax where Ogun is proclaimed the unconquerable warrior. And just as in appellation poetry the lexical items are restricted to the semantic field of war-related vocabulary, so they are in the passage written by Soyinka. Even the actions of the animals and birds are a type of warfare, all intended to stress the might of the referent.

Perhaps the most significant features of appellation poetry are its sound systems and tonal structure that enable artists to form compounds out of phrase and clauses. This device, as Anyidoho explains, "entails agglutinating the words in the phrase or clause, deleting the subject and attaching a nominal prefix to the new word whenever necessary" (76). F. Dolphyne's *The Akan (Twi-Fante) Language: Its Sound System and Tonal Structure* explains the device in detail. D. P. Kunene's *Heroic Poetry of the Basotho,* and M. Damane and P. Sanders's *Lithoko-Sotho Praise-Poems* also illustrate a similar device in Zulu poetry. An example from Akan appellation poetry is "*Ahu-abↄ-birim*" (fierce conqueror), compounded from the clause "*Ohu a ↄbↄ birim,*" meaning "he sees it and panics." These compounds, derived from phrases and clauses, are all neologisms used to reflect major characteristics of the referent, such as his/her/its might, movements, and conduct. Examples of compounding abound in the second section of ***Ogun Abibiman***: "Breeze-that-cools-Bayete's-blood" (10), "blood-streams" (12), and "life-usurper's fortress" (15). Major consequences of this compounding device are that it produces double and triple compounds; creates obscurities, new meanings, and heightened intensity; and results in syntactic jugglery and scrambling of word order. These are the same characteristics in Soyinka's poetry that Chinweizu, Madubuike, and Jemie, co-authors of *Toward the Decolonization of African Literature,* see as an imitation of European literary mannerisms parroting the "toughness" for readers of neometaphysical poets like Gerard Manley Hopkins. What they claim is a Western poetic tradition of complexity for its own sake they find in Soyinka's poetry too, and they see it as not just evidence of neo-colonialism, but the outcome of what they called "unsuccessful mimesis: The Hopkins Disease" (viii). Consequently, they write off Soyinka's poetry, asserting that it is anti-African because of its lack of African values, especially the "classic simplicity and terseness" (185) of African traditional poetry.

Undoubtedly, these observations are in part accurate. Soyinka himself does not deny the central charges of "wilful obscurity," syntactic disjunction, and the subtle rhythmic texture of his poetry (**"Neo-Tarzanism"** 327). In his explanation, however, Soyinka has always maintained that these characteristics of his poetry reflect positive Afrocentric literary values, rather than the neocolonial mimicry the Chinweizu group has attributed to him. In Soyinka's **"The Choice and Use of the English Language,"** the complexities are seen as reflecting an authentic African cultural and visionary experience:

> Coming from a people (the Yoruba) whose love of language for its own sake, for its very maneuverability is probably unmatched on the continent and maybe even in the world, I testify to this capacity of the tool to, literally, possess the user.

(3)

Soyinka regards his use of language as an offspring of African oral tradition, revealing the complex nature of the African character, which many European scholars had hitherto misrepresented as a boring being of idyllic goodness and simplicity. Soyinka's explanation is not to say that the "classic simplicity" the Chinweizu group talk about and his complex language are antithetical, for both are forms of oral literature, and their difference does underline the varied linguistic range of African oral literature.

From Soyinka's explanation, one can surmise that he relies on what Oluwole Adejare sees as "mortised strands," a situation where "the writer incorporates texts from several sources in the production of his own" (128), to the point where the boundaries of the mortised strands may become difficult to distinguish. Moreover, the mortised strands acquire a new semiotic framework that elicits new meanings. Adejare's book outlines instances in other works by Soyinka where he relies on this strategy. Critics, however, have been quick to identify the European sources rather than the African ones, a misunderstanding that most critics from Africa and the Black diaspora are also guilty of. The problem with Black critics, however, is not insufficient attention, but their internalizing of a Western frame of reference to the point where identification of Western sources occurs before that of African poetics.

Titled "Shaka!," the second section of ***Ogun Abibiman*** features a shift in focus from preoccupation with the gods' involvement in the affairs of the living to that of the famous Zulu King, Shaka, an ancestral warlord. Shaka, described by Soyinka as "Africa's most renowned nation builder" and as a "military and socio-organizational genius" (23), epitomizes ancestor-warriors who, though they have transcended mortality to become god-like heroes, are traditionally believed to participate in the military affairs of the living. The involvement of Shaka in Abibiman's independence struggle is also crucial in a countercolonial way: his presence reinforces the nationalist and postcolonial argument of an unbroken chain of resistance to colonial rule. Edward Said explains:

> The question of dating the resistance to imperialism in subject territories is crucial to both sides [the colonizer and the colonized] in how imperialism is seen. [. . .] To the colonizer, the Natives 'were really happy until roused by troublemakers,' but for the liberation/nationalist fighter[s], leading the struggle against the European power, legitimacy [. . .] depend[s] on their asserting an unbroken continuity leading to the first warriors who stood against the intrusive white man.

(197)

Soyinka's appeal to the past is therefore not just an evocation of precolonial culture, but also his disagreement with a colonial history that teachers that those who started the resistance to colonialism invented their nationalism in colonial schools, not by emulating the resistance of their ancestors. Thus, although Shaka generally epitomizes precolonial ancestors, put in this context of dating anticolonial resistance, he particularly epitomizes historical personalities such as Yaa Asantewaa, the Ashanti Queen-mother who led one of the most stubborn and effective military resistance efforts against the British colonial presence in Africa.

Shaka's military invincibility and his past achievements are the theme here. Soyinka alludes to how Shaka accomplished the seemingly impossible task of turning a petty Zulu chieftaincy, to any of the borders of which one could walk in less than an hour, into a kingdom that encompassed the whole of South-Eastern Africa, extending from the great Kei river in the Cape to the Zambezi, and from the Indian Ocean to the farthest confines of Bechuanaland. E. A. Ritter observes that "from a rabble of 500 men, [Shaka] increased his army to 50,000 warriors whose discipline exceeded that of the Roman legions at their best" (345). These achievements are appraised in the following lines of *Ogun Abibiman*:

> Shaka, King and general
> Fought battles, invented rare techniques, created
> Order from chaos, coloured the sights of men
> In self-transcending visions, sought
> Man's renewal in the fount of knowledge.
> From shards of tribe and bandit mores, Shaka
> Raised the city of man in commonweal.
>
> (15)

This recounting of Shaka's achievements is designed to inspire confidence in the people of Abibiman. The most important inspiration, however, comes from the fact that as a warrior, Shaka never lost a battle. Zulu war and royal heroic poetry capture this feat in what may be described as traditional Africa's poetic equivalent of the Homeric epithet: "the ever-ready-to-meet-any-challenge" (Finnegan, *World Treasury* 121), which epithet usually is used with other Zulu war songs in Shaka's honor, especially this: "He has annihilated the enemies! / Where shall he now make war? / He has vanquished all the Kings! / Where shall he make war?" (Finnegan 134). Because Shaka and Ogun are set on the same course of action—to annihilate the enemy in Southern Africa—Soyinka uses expressions which seem to merge the two spirits: "Shaka, roused, / Defines his being anew in Ogun's embrace" (9); "I feel and know [Ogun's] tread as mine" (10); "Our histories meet, the forests merge / With the savannah" (11). All that this merging of identities means in the oral context is that these two spirits, god and heroic dead, both invincible in war, approve of war, and have come to lead Africa against the colonial regimes in Southern Africa. The choral battle song in Yoruba, which portrays Ogun and Shaka shaking hands, symbolizes both this leadership role and the two leaders' approval of war:

> Ròbòdiyàn! Ròbòdiyàn!
> Ogún re lé e Shákà

> Ròbòdiyàn
> Ogún gbo wó o Shákà
> O di ròbòdiyàn
>
> (9)

Soyinka's English version reads:

> Turmoil on turmoil!
> Ogun treads the earth of Shaka
> Turmoil on the loose
> Ogun shakes the hand of Shaka
> All is in turmoil.
>
> (24)

But the translation is not very useful since its semiotic significance must be decoded from the original form. The switching from the English to the Yoruba choral song in this and other parts of the poem is significant in that the tonal structure of the Yoruba language has a powerful effect on the melodic structure of the poem. And as the persona of Acquah's "Ol Man River" points out, "there are some things / Which can only be said in song / Only in the mother tongue" (29). The Yoruba choral song, therefore, becomes Soyinka's major means of revealing phonetic tone as a traditional textual characteristic of his poetry.

In the Yoruba version, the power of assonance in conveying meaning is very strong. The constant repetition of the "o" sound that is variantly produced in high, medium, and low tones, together with the tireless alliteration and repetition of the consonants "g," "b," "d," gives the poem an energy of tone that helps to intensify the ritualistic atmosphere of frenzy. The use of parallelism is also more effective in the Yoruba. The "re lé e" and "gbo wó o" elements in the second and fourth lines combine with the repetitions of "Ogun" and "Shaka" in both lines to give a racier tone to the chant, which in turn heightens its musical quality. Although the "re lé e" and "gbo wó o" elements sound differently, they contain two syllables that have the same tonal pattern. As well, they are semantically related. Levin has called this phenomenon in which there is parallelism on both the phonological and semantic levels "true coupling," which he argues is a mark of good poetry (qtd. in Anyidoho 75). Throughout this section of the poem, much emphasis is put on choral verse chants that appear in the context of a leader-and-chorus song as well as what Finnegan describes as "the convention [of uttering] certain set war cries [. . .] at the time of the actual charge" (*Oral Literature* 211). The poet/speaker as leader of the chorus speaks a eulogy to Shaka with the chorus responding with refrains and war cries such as "Sigidi! Sigidi! / Sigidi Baba! Bayete!" (11); "Ròbòdiyàn! Ròbòdiyàn! / Bayete Baba! Bayete" (11); "Bayete Baba! Bayete!" (12); "Shaka! Shaka! / Bayete Baba! Bayete!" (12); "amaZulu / Shaka! Shaka! / Bayete Baba! Bayete!" 12-13). After each refrain and war cry, the poet as speaker/Shaka continues the telling with a fresh theme.

Molara Ogundipe-Leslie likens Shaka's speech following the Yoruba choric acclaim of turmoil to "a royal monologue in the best Shakespearean tradition" (198), and describes his performance as "strikingly Elizabethan both in language and in the exploration of character and motivation" (199). While Ogundipe-Leslie's analysis points to parallels with and even the use of the Western literary tradition, another perspective on the speech, especially its peculiar uses of animal imagery and references to African warrior and hunting traditions, would stress the use of oral literary heritage. To give but one example, Shaka's mention that he is the "dread that takes bull elephants by storm . . . / And brings them low on trembling knee" (9) immediately portrays him as a master hunter and warrior in a manner familiar to African praise discourse. As Nketia points out, an individual achieves special status as a hunter or warrior if he or she is able to kill a number of wild elephants (*Music* 47). Here as elsewhere, Soyinka relies on semantic ties of similarities between two discourses, Shakespearean or Elizabethan royal monologue and African warrior and hunter poetic traditions, to forge a synthesis from his traditional African and Western literary discourses.

The point of Shaka's argument, however, is not one of "aggrandizement," as W. B. Last suggests (196), to draw awareness to his status as a superb warrior, but the communication of the resolution that he will allow nothing to stand in his way. This idea is especially conveyed, albeit obscurely, in the Zulu word *Sigidi*, which Soyinka partially glosses as "The song of the spear-blade as it bites: I have eaten!" (24). The metaphorical relationship between this Zulu word and the warrior's vow that nothing will stand in his way is aptly described by the popular *imigubo* war song from the Ngoni of Malawi: "All [those] who oppose us / Quickly our spears / Shall pierce their breasts" (Finnegan, *Oral Poetry* 210). What appears as boasting therefore signifies not vain boasting but a recounting of a warrior's former achievements as a pledge or an oath from which s/he cannot withdraw.

Another important animal metaphor in Shaka's speech that marks it as traditional African oral discourse is his comparison of white and black soldiers to termites and black soldier ants respectively:

> The termite is no match
> For the black soldier ant, yet termites gnawed
> The houseposts of our kraals even while
> We made the stranger welcome
> . . .
> The task must gain completion, our fount
> Of being cleansed from termites' spittle.
>
> (12-13)

Soyinka's metaphor emphasizes the strength of the African soldier and it recalls similar ones in traditional African war poems, like the drum "call" of the Ashanti army, and the 142-line *oriki* (Yoruba praise poem) in honor of Ibikunle, a one-time *Balogun* (warlord) of the Ibadan army. In the latter poem, Ibikunle's formidable strength and his fearlessness in battle are likened to "a lone elephant that rocks the jungle / . . . [and] the whole world to its foundation" (Finnegan, *World Treasury* 153-54). And in the Ashanti drum call, the large numbers in the Ashanti army, an element the warriors boast of as their source of strength, is described as "locusts in myriads" to reflect the group's strength in "thick numbers" (Nketia, *Drumming* 111-12). Soyinka's animal imagery also belittles the strength of the enemy so as to boost the confidence of the Black soldier. Although the speaker does recognize the extent of the danger posed by the enemy's presence because of his insidious refusal to fight in the way of warriors, this recognition serves only as the better reason for a fearless determination and rigid resolve to annihilate the enemy.

Reference to imminent danger posed by an enemy is itself a common theme used in traditional African war poetry to both mobilize people for, and justify, an impending war. The first stanza of this Shona *detembo rehondo* (war poem) deals with such a theme:

> Cowards remain behind, . . .
> Those who have my love, and those denied it,
> Must not fight shy today!
> . . .
> No longer is anywhere safe from death.
>
> (Hodza and Fortune 32)

Here, as in *Ogun Abibiman,* the seriousness of approaching danger generates a sufficient spirit of unity and patriotism to make the poet call on all Blacks, those he loves and those he hates, to come together to combat the enemy fearlessly.

The last section of *Ogun Abibiman,* titled "Sigidi," deals with Soyinka's positive evaluation of Abibiman's decision to embark upon a military campaign in Southern Africa. Though the section has features of the earlier two sections—alliteration, parallelism, praise-names and chants, for example—its major features are the use of rhetorical questions and the engaged poetic voice. The poet maintains that the purpose of the war is not vengeance, not hate, not a show of brute force, but justice, hope, and an oppressed peoples' need for self-fulfillment and self-realization:

> If then we claim—the poet is now given
> Tongue to celebrate, if dancers
> Soar above the branches, and weird tunes
> Startle a quiescent world—Vengeance
> Is not the god we celebrate, nor hate, . . .
> . . .
> Our songs acclaim
> Cessation of a long despair, extol the ends
> Of sacrifice born in our will, not weakness.
> We celebrate the end of that compliant
> Innocence of our millineal trees.
>
> (20)

Although critics, especially Obi Maduakor, see this portion as the section's central message, I think there is more to this final section than critics to date have asserted. It deals with the nature of sorrow songs as well as gives Soyinka's response to some of the specific derogatory remarks that he anticipates the neo-colonial world will pass about Abibiman's decision to engage in an "*mfekane*" (19)—"a crushing total war" (24).

Soyinka observes that the colonial world, "whose rhetoric is sightless violence" (19), is likely to forget all too soon about the cesspools of violence in Guernica, Lidice, and Sharpeville, and rather condemn the Oguns, Shakas, and their African warriors as a primitive horde of blood-thirsty anarchists, models of Yeats's rough beast that unleashes disorder, chaos, and a blood-dimmed tide on a peaceful world. Soyinka, however, counters this view with an allusion to Yeats's "Easter 1916," which contextualizes certain types of violence, like liberation struggles, as positive, and as something capable of giving birth to a terrible beauty:

> When, safely distanced, throned in saintly
> Censure, the prophet's voice possesses you—
> Mere anarchy is loosed upon the world et cetera
> Remember too, the awesome beauty at the door of
> birth
>
> (21)

Thus, by evoking the fundamental ambivalence of Yeats's concept of violence, especially when poems like "The Second Coming" are interpreted together with "Easter 1916," "Meditations in Time of Civil War," and others in *The Tower* (1928), Soyinka is able to subvert the one-sided way of looking at the armed nationalist struggle in Southern Africa, and to argue on the contrary that the *mfekane* in Southern Africa is a creative war bound to yield positive results, like the "cessation of a long despair" (21) of Blacks in Southern Africa. In addition, peace will return to the streets of Sharpeville and Soweto (20), and relief will come to the "[black] midwives with / The dark wine . . . / Ministering to history, delivering the missing / Chapter of the text" (21).

The image of midwives with dark wine ministering to history recalls the poem **"Black Singer"** (*Idanre* 36) in which the persona, a female symbolizing the people and history of Africa, pours out in her song "the dark-some wine" of her people's history of slavery, suffering, abuses, and sorrow. These songs reflect things so deep that they can be said only in song, songs like the lament of the Akan *nnwonkoro*, the *asafo* songs of Fanti and Ashanti warriors, songs of oral sages, of South African freedom fighters, and the music of the *atentenben*, which, according to Kofi Anyidoho, is above all "the instrument of the dirge, of quiet reflection, [and] of mournful meditation" on the Black history of pain (14). As Soyinka rightly observes, these sorrow songs constitute the "missing / Chapter of the text," meaning that the reader is asked, either through mnemonic experience or participatory role, to incorporate these songs into the text to make it complete. In a way, the full completion of the text depends on the drawing of

all these voices into one coherent discourse, and the challenge, therefore, is to fulfill the poet's quest for wholeness by including all the oral and auditory components that will confirm the text's validity as a shared dramatic experience.

Just as in **"Black Singer"** the singer's task is an arduous one, serving two important functions—first, as a "votive vase" to bring relief to Black people everywhere and, second, as a symbol of the fusion point where the "hurt of sirens" merges into the rhythm of song to produce the necessary motivation for action—in *Ogun Abibiman,* the midwives' song brings both relief and motivation for action:

> Now is the hour of song, the hour
> Of ecstasy on dancer's feet.
> The drummer's
> Exhortations fortify the heart.
> The clans are massed from hill to hill
> . . .
>
>   a throb
> Of feet to the ancient cry of—*Sigidi*!
>
> (22)

These functions of relief and motivation are perhaps the true essence of sorrow songs. Though they underscore unspeakable pain and express the deepest miseries of a people, paradoxically they are meant to express hope and freedom in spite of pain and misery.

W. E. B. Du Bois in "Of Sorrow Songs" defines for us this central paradox of sorrow songs:

> Through all the sorrow of the Sorrow Songs there breathes a hope—a faith in the ultimate justice of things. The minor cadences of despair change often to triumph and calm confidence. Sometimes it is faith in life, sometimes faith in death, sometimes assurance of boundless justice in some fair world beyond. But whichever it is, the meaning is always clear: that sometime, somewhere, men will judge men by their souls and not by their skins.
>
> (261)

Ultimately, it is this sense of hope, of mountains made low, of the ultimate realization of the magnificent Pan-African ideal that *Ogun Abibiman* is all about. Soyinka's sketch of this moment of hope, as Black soldiers march to war, drumming, dancing, chanting, and celebrating the consequent ascendancy of Ogun, is captured in an emphatic repetition of the appellations and politics of the gaze that conclude the first section. The rest, of course, is history! Though *Ogun Abibiman* is about war, Soyinka's vocabulary expressing that theme reflects a highly conscious sense of African oral poetics. In its closeness to its African roots, the poem reflects a recreation in English of the sound and syntax of African derived oral tradition, a process J. M. Coetzee calls transfer, meaning "the rendering of foreign speech in an English stylistically marked to remind the reader of the foreign original" (117). At significant moments in the poem, he not only switches to but emphasizes the oral sources of his discourse, which calls for responsive listening, and forces one to acknowledge not only orality in writing, but also aurality in reading. Within the context of postcolonial studies, this style requires critics to shift the ontology of deriving meaning in Soyinka's poetry from its location in a fixed written text to a larger discursive context that includes orality. Of necessity, critics will have to expand their critical perspectives on Soyinka to reflect how his use of traditional modes transcends national boundaries to produce a committed Pan Africanism and a genuine Black-centered consciousness.

Works Cited

Acquah, Kobina Eyi. *Music for a Dream Dance*. Accra: Asempa, 1989.

Anyidoho, Kofi. "Introduction." Acquah 9-18.

Adejare, Oluwole. *Language and Style in Soyinka: A Systematic Textlinguistic Study of a Literary Idiolect.* Ibadan: Heinemann, 1992.

Anyidoho, Akosua. "Linguistic Parallels in Traditional Akan Appellation Poetry." *Research in African Literatures* 22.1 (1991): 67-82.

Beier, Ulli. *Yoruba Poetry*. New York: Cambridge UP, 1970.

Boehmer, Elleke. *Colonial and Postcolonial Literature.* New York: Oxford UP, 1995.

Chinweizu et al. *Toward the Decolonization of African Literature.* Enugu: Fourth Dimension, 1980.

Coetzee, J. M. *While Writing: On the Culture of Letters in South Africa.* New Haven: Yale UP, 1988.

Copland, B. David. *In the Time of Cannibals: The Word Music of South Africa's Basotho Migrants.* Chicago: U of Chicago P, 1995.

Damane, M., and P. Sanders. *Lithoko-Sotho Praise-Poems.* Oxford: Clarendon, 1974.

Deng, M. Francis. *The Dinka and their Songs.* Oxford: Clarendon, 1937.

Diop, Cheikh Anta. "Interviews with Carlos Moore (for *Afriscope*)." *Great African Thinkers*. Ed. Ivan Sertima. New Brunswick: Transaction Books, 1986. 249-83.

Dolphyne, F. *The Akan (Twi-Fante) Language: Its Sound System and Tonal Structure* Accra: Ghana UP, 1988.

Du Bois, W. E. B. "Of Sorrow Songs." *The Souls of Black Folk*. Chicago: McClurg, 1940.

Ebeogu, Afam. "From *Idanre* to *Ogun Abibiman*: An Exploration of Soyinka's Use of Ogun Images." *The Journal of Commonwealth Literature* 15 (1980): 84-89.

Finnegan, Ruth. *A World Treasury of Oral Poetry.* Bloomington: Indiana UP, 1978.

———. *Oral Poetry in Africa*. Oxford: Clarendon, 1970.

Gibbs, James, Ed. *Critical Perspectives on Wole Soyinka.* London: Heinemann, 1980.

Hodza, A. C., and G. Fortune. *Shona Praise Poetry.* Oxford: Clarendon, 1979.

Katrak, Ketu. *Wole Soyinka and Modern Tragedy.* New York: Greenwood, 1986.

Kunene, D. P. *Heroic Poetry of the Basotho.* Oxford: Clarendon, 1974.

Last, B. W. "*Ogun Abibiman.*" *World Literature Written in English* 20.2 (1981): 191-200.

Maduakor, Obi. *Wole Soyinka: An Introduction to His Writing*. New York: Garland, 1986.

Mukherjee, Arun. *Towards an Aesthetics of Opposition: Essays on Literature, Criticism, and Cultural Imperialism.* Toronto: Williams-Wallace, 1988.

Ngara, Emmanuel. *Ideology and Form in African Poetry.* Nairobi: Heinemann, 1990.

Nketia, Kwabena J. H. *The Music of Africa.* New York: Norton, 1974.

———. *Drumming in Akan Communities of Ghana.* Legon: U of Ghana P. 1963.

Nwoga, Donatus. "Poetry as Revelation: Wole Soyinka." Gibbs 173-85.

Ogundipe-Leslie, Omolara. "A Comment on *Ogun Abibiman.*" *Critical Perspectives on Wole Soyinka.* Ed. James Gibbs. Washington, DC: Three Continents P, 1980. 198-99.

Ojaide, Tanure. "New Trends in Modern African Poetry." *Research in African Literatures* 26.1 (1995): 4-19.

Priebe, Richard. *Myth, Realism, and the West African Writer.* Trenton: Africa World P, 1988.

Ritter, E. A. *Shaka Zulu: The Rise of the Zulu Empire.* New York: Putnam's, 1957.

Said, Edward. *Culture and Imperialism*. London: Chatto and Windus, 1993.

Sim, Stuart. ed. *The A-Z Guide to Modern Literary and Cultural Theorists.* London: Prentice Hall, 1995.

Slemon, Stephen. "Monuments of Empire: Allegory Counter Discourse/Post-Colonial Writing." *Kunapipi* 9.3 (1987): 1-16.

Soyinka, Wole. "And after the Narcissist?" *African Forum* 1. 4 (1966): 53-64.

———. *Idanre and Other Poems*. London: Methuen, 1967.

―――. *Mandela's Earth and Other Poems.* New York: Random House, 1988.

―――. *Ogun Abibiman.* London: Rex Collings, 1976.

―――. *Myth, Literature, and the African World.* Cambridge: Cambridge UP, 1976.

―――. "Neo-Tarzanism: The Poetics of Pseudo-Tradition." *Art, Dialogue, and Outrage.* Ibadan: New Horn, 1988. 315-29.

―――. "The Choice and Use of Language." *Cultural Events in Africa* 75 (1971): 3-6.

―――. "The Writer in a Modern African State." *Art, Dialogue, and Outrage.* Ibadan: New Horn, 1988. 15-20.

Todorov, Tzvetan. *The Conquest of America.* Trans. Richard Howard. New York: Harper and Row, 1984.

Trask, Willard. *The Unwritten Song.* Vol. 1. New York: Macmillan, 1966.

White, Landeg. "Going to De Beers." *Times Literary Supplement* 3 June 1995: 7-8.

Yankah, Kojo. "To Praise or Not to Praise the King: The Akan Apae in the Context of Referential Poetry." *Research in African Literatures* 14. 3 (1983): 381-400.

Yeats, William Butler. *Yeats's Poems.* Ed. Norman Jeffares. London: Macmillan, 1989.

FURTHER READING

Criticism

Benson, Peter. Review of *Ìsarà: A Voyage around Essay,* by Wole Soyinka. *Literary Review* 33, no. 3 (spring 1990): 397-98.

Benson argues that Soyinka creates a skillful portrayal of African cultural identity in *Ìsarà: A Voyage around Essay.*

Gurnah, Abdulrazak. "The Fiction of Wole Soyinka." In *Wole Soyinka: An Appraisal,* edited by Adewale Maja-Pearce, pp. 61-80. Oxford: Heinemann, 1994.

Gurnah examines Soyinka's major thematic concerns in *The Interpreters* and *Season of Anomy.*

Msiska, Mpalive-Hangson. "Redemptive Tragedies." In *Wole Soyinka,* pp. 53-77. Plymouth, U.K.: Northcote House, 1998.

Msiska traces the recurring themes of corruption, the abuse of power, and redemption in Soyinka's body of work.

Ojaide, Tanure. "Two Worlds: Influences on the Poetry of Wole Soyinka." *Black American Literature Forum* 22, no. 4 (winter 1988): 767-76.

Ojaide investigates the major influences behind Soyinka's verse in such volumes as *Idanre and Other Poems,* noting that analysis "reveals the admixture of indigenous and foreign qualities in [his] poems."

Soyinka, Wole, and Maya Jaggi. *Guardian* (2 November 2002): 12-13.

Soyinka discusses the political climate in Nigeria, his writing career, and his poetry collection *Samarkand and Other Markets I Have Known.*

Additional coverage of Soyinka's life and career is contained in the following sources published by the Gale Group: *African Writers; Black Literature Criticism,* **Ed. 3;** *Black Writers,* **Eds. 2, 3;** *Concise Dictionary of World Literary Biography,* **Vol. 3;** *Contemporary Authors,* **Vols. 13-16R;** *Contemporary Authors New Revision Series,* **Vols. 27, 39, 82;** *Contemporary Dramatists,* **Ed. 5;** *Contemporary Literary Criticism,* **Vols. 3, 5, 14, 36, 44;** *Contemporary Novelists,* **Ed. 7;** *Contemporary Poets,* **Ed. 7;** *Dictionary of Literary Biography,* **Vol. 125;** *DISCovering Authors; DISCovering Authors: British Edition; DISCovering Authors: Canadian Edition; DISCovering Authors Modules: Dramatists, Most-studied Authors, and Multicultural; DISCovering Authors 3.0; Drama Criticism,* **Vol. 2;** *Drama for Students,* **Vol. 10;** *Literature Resource Center; Major 20th-Century Writers,* **Eds. 1, 2;** *Reference Guide to English Literature,* **Ed. 2;** *Twayne's World Authors; World Literature and Its Times,* **Vol. 2; and** *World Literature Criticism.*

How to Use This Index

CMW = *St. James Guide to Crime & Mystery Writers*
CN = *Contemporary Novelists*
CP = *Contemporary Poets*
CPW = *Contemporary Popular Writers*
CSW = *Contemporary Southern Writers*
CWD = *Contemporary Women Dramatists*
CWP = *Contemporary Women Poets*
CWRI = *St. James Guide to Children's Writers*
CWW = *Contemporary World Writers*
DA = *DISCovering Authors*
DA3 = *DISCovering Authors 3.0*
DAB = *DISCovering Authors: British Edition*
DAC = *DISCovering Authors: Canadian Edition*
DAM = *DISCovering Authors: Modules*
   DRAM: *Dramatists Module;* **MST:** *Most-studied Authors Module;*
   MULT: *Multicultural Authors Module;* **NOV:** *Novelists Module;*
   POET: *Poets Module;* **POP:** *Popular Fiction and Genre Authors Module*
DFS = *Drama for Students*
DLB = *Dictionary of Literary Biography*
DLBD = *Dictionary of Literary Biography Documentary Series*
DLBY = *Dictionary of Literary Biography Yearbook*
DNFS = *Literature of Developing Nations for Students*
EFS = *Epics for Students*
EXPN = *Exploring Novels*
EXPP = *Exploring Poetry*
EXPS = *Exploring Short Stories*
EW = *European Writers*
FANT = *St. James Guide to Fantasy Writers*
FW = *Feminist Writers*
GFL = *Guide to French Literature,* Beginnings to 1789, 1798 to the Present
GLL = *Gay and Lesbian Literature*
HGG = *St. James Guide to Horror, Ghost & Gothic Writers*
HW = *Hispanic Writers*
IDFW = *International Dictionary of Films and Filmmakers: Writers and Production Artists*
IDTP = *International Dictionary of Theatre: Playwrights*
LAIT = *Literature and Its Times*
LAW = *Latin American Writers*
JRDA = *Junior DISCovering Authors*
MAICYA = *Major Authors and Illustrators for Children and Young Adults*
MAICYAS = *Major Authors and Illustrators for Children and Young Adults Supplement*
MAWW = *Modern American Women Writers*
MJW = *Modern Japanese Writers*
MTCW = *Major 20th-Century Writers*
NCFS = *Nonfiction Classics for Students*
NFS = *Novels for Students*
PAB = *Poets: American and British*
PFS = *Poetry for Students*
RGAL = *Reference Guide to American Literature*
RGEL = *Reference Guide to English Literature*
RGSF = *Reference Guide to Short Fiction*
RGWL = *Reference Guide to World Literature*
RHW = *Twentieth-Century Romance and Historical Writers*
SAAS = *Something about the Author Autobiography Series*
SATA = *Something about the Author*
SFW = *St. James Guide to Science Fiction Writers*
SSFS = *Short Stories for Students*
TCWW = *Twentieth-Century Western Writers*
WLIT = *World Literature and Its Times*
WP = *World Poets*
YABC = *Yesterday's Authors of Books for Children*
YAW = *St. James Guide to Young Adult Writers*

Literary Criticism Series
Cumulative Author Index

Allen, Sidney H.
See Hartmann, Sadakichi
Allen, Woody 1935- .... **CLC 16, 52**
See also AAYA 10, 51; CA 33-36R; CANR
27, 38, 63; DAM POP; DLB 44; MTCW
1
Allende, Isabel 1942- ... **CLC 39, 57, 97, 170;**
HLC 1; WLCS
See also AAYA 18; CA 125; 130; CANR
51, 74; CDWLB 3; CWW 2; DA3; DAM
MULT, NOV; DLB 145; DNFS 1; EWL
3; FW; HW 1, 2; INT CA-130; LAIT 5;
LAWS 1; LMFS 2; MTCW 1, 2; NCFS 1;
NFS 6; RGSF 2; RGWL 3; SSFS 11, 16;
WLIT 1
Alleyn, Ellen
See Rossetti, Christina (Georgina)
Alleyne, Carla D. .... **CLC 65**
Allingham, Margery (Louise)
1904-1966 .... **CLC 19**
See also CA 5-8R; 25-28R; CANR 4, 58;
CMW 4; DLB 77; MSW; MTCW 1, 2
Allingham, William 1824-1889 ...... **NCLC 25**
See also DLB 35; RGEL 2
Allison, Dorothy E. 1949- .... **CLC 78, 153**
See also AAYA 53; CA 140; CANR 66, 107;
CSW; DA3; FW; MTCW 1; NFS 11;
RGAL 4
Alloula, Malek .... **CLC 65**
Allston, Washington 1779-1843 .... **NCLC 2**
See also DLB 1, 235
Almedingen, E. M. .... **CLC 12**
See Almedingen, Martha Edith von
See also SATA 3
Almedingen, Martha Edith von 1898-1971
See Almedingen, E. M.
See also CA 1-4R; CANR 1
Almodovar, Pedro 1949(?)- .... **CLC 114;**
HLCS 1
See also CA 133; CANR 72; HW 2
Almqvist, Carl Jonas Love
1793-1866 .... **NCLC 42**
Alonso, Damaso 1898-1990 .... **CLC 14**
See also CA 110; 131; 130; CANR 72; DLB
108; EWL 3; HW 1, 2
Alov
See Gogol, Nikolai (Vasilyevich)
Alta 1942- .... **CLC 19**
See also CA 57-60
Alter, Robert B(ernard) 1935- .... **CLC 34**
See also CA 49-52; CANR 1, 47, 100
Alther, Lisa 1944- .... **CLC 7, 41**
See also BPFB 1; CA 65-68; CAAS 30;
CANR 12, 30, 51; CN 7; CSW; GLL 2;
MTCW 1
Althusser, L.
See Althusser, Louis
Althusser, Louis 1918-1990 .... **CLC 106**
See also CA 131; 132; CANR 102; DLB
242
Altman, Robert 1925- .... **CLC 16, 116**
See also CA 73-76; CANR 43
Alurista .... **HLCS 1**
See Urista, Alberto H.
See also DLB 82
Alvarez, A(lfred) 1929- .... **CLC 5, 13**
See also CA 1-4R; CANR 3, 33, 63, 101;
CN 7; CP 7; DLB 14, 40
Alvarez, Alejandro Rodriguez 1903-1965
See Casona, Alejandro
See also CA 131; 93-96; HW 1
Alvarez, Julia 1950- .... **CLC 93; HLCS 1**
See also AAYA 25; AMWS 7; CA 147;
CANR 69, 101; DA3; DLB 282; LATS 1;
MTCW 1; NFS 5, 9; SATA 129; WLIT 1
Alvaro, Corrado 1896-1956 .... **TCLC 60**
See also CA 163; DLB 264; EWL 3

Amado, Jorge 1912-2001 ... **CLC 13, 40, 106;**
HLC 1
See also CA 77-80; 201; CANR 35, 74;
DAM MULT, NOV; DLB 113; EWL 3;
HW 2; LAW; LAWS 1; MTCW 1, 2;
RGWL 2, 3; TWA; WLIT 1
Ambler, Eric 1909-1998 .... **CLC 4, 6, 9**
See also BRWS 4; CA 9-12R; 171; CANR
7, 38, 74; CMW 4; CN 7; DLB 77; MSW;
MTCW 1, 2; TEA
Ambrose, Stephen E(dward)
1936-2002 .... **CLC 145**
See also AAYA 44; CA 1-4R; 209; CANR
3, 43, 57, 83, 105; NCFS 2; SATA 40,
138
Amichai, Yehuda 1924-2000 .. **CLC 9, 22, 57,**
116; PC 38
See also CA 85-88; 189; CANR 46, 60, 99;
CWW 2; EWL 3; MTCW 1
Amichai, Yehudah
See Amichai, Yehuda
Amiel, Henri Frederic 1821-1881 .... **NCLC 4**
See also DLB 217
Amis, Kingsley (William)
1922-1995 ...... **CLC 1, 2, 3, 5, 8, 13, 40,**
44, 129
See also AITN 2; BPFB 1; BRWS 2; CA
9-12R; 150; CANR 8, 28, 54; CDBLB
1945-1960; CN 7; CP 7; DA; DA3; DAB;
DAC; DAM MST, NOV; DLB 15, 27,
100, 139; DLBY 1996; EWL 3; HGG;
INT CANR-8; MTCW 1, 2; RGEL 2;
RGSF 2; SFW 4
Amis, Martin (Louis) 1949- .... **CLC 4, 9, 38,**
62, 101
See also BEST 90:3; BRWS 4; CA 65-68;
CANR 8, 27, 54, 73, 95; CN 7; DA3;
DLB 14, 194; EWL 3; INT CANR-27;
MTCW 1
Ammianus Marcellinus c. 330-c.
395 .... **CMLC 60**
See also AW 2; DLB 211
Ammons, A(rchie) R(andolph)
1926-2001 ...... **CLC 2, 3, 5, 8, 9, 25, 57,**
108; PC 16
See also AITN 1; AMWS 7; CA 9-12R;
193; CANR 6, 36, 51, 73, 107; CP 7;
CSW; DAM POET; DLB 5, 165; EWL 3;
MTCW 1, 2; RGAL 4
Amo, Tauraatua i
See Adams, Henry (Brooks)
Amory, Thomas 1691(?)-1788 .... **LC 48**
See also DLB 39
Anand, Mulk Raj 1905- .... **CLC 23, 93**
See also CA 65-68; CANR 32, 64; CN 7;
DAM NOV; EWL 3; MTCW 1, 2; RGSF
2
Anatol
See Schnitzler, Arthur
Anaximander c. 611B.C.-c.
546B.C. .... **CMLC 22**
Anaya, Rudolfo A(lfonso) 1937- ...... **CLC 23,**
148; HLC 1
See also AAYA 20; BYA 13; CA 45-48;
CAAS 4; CANR 1, 32, 51; CN 7; DAM
MULT, NOV; DLB 82, 206, 278; HW 1;
LAIT 4; MTCW 1, 2; NFS 12; RGAL 4;
RGSF 2; WLIT 1
Andersen, Hans Christian
1805-1875 .... **NCLC 7, 79; SSC 6, 56;**
WLC
See also CLR 6; DA; DA3; DAB; DAC;
DAM MST, POP; EW 6; MAICYA 1, 2;
RGSF 2; RGWL 2, 3; SATA 100; TWA;
WCH; YABC 1
Anderson, C. Farley
See Mencken, H(enry) L(ouis); Nathan,
George Jean

Anderson, Jessica (Margaret) Queale
1916- .... **CLC 37**
See also CA 9-12R; CANR 4, 62; CN 7
Anderson, Jon (Victor) 1940- .... **CLC 9**
See also CA 25-28R; CANR 20; DAM
POET
Anderson, Lindsay (Gordon)
1923-1994 .... **CLC 20**
See also CA 125; 128; 146; CANR 77
Anderson, Maxwell 1888-1959 .... **TCLC 2**
See also CA 105; 152; DAM DRAM; DFS
16; DLB 7, 228; MTCW 2; RGAL 4
Anderson, Poul (William)
1926-2001 .... **CLC 15**
See also AAYA 5, 34; BPFB 1; BYA 6, 8,
9; CA 1-4R; 181; 199; CAAE 181; CAAS
2; CANR 2, 15, 34, 64, 110; CLR 58;
DLB 8; FANT; INT CANR-15; MTCW 1,
2; SATA 90; SATA-Brief 39; SATA-Essay
106; SCFW 2; SFW 4; SUFW 1, 2
Anderson, Robert (Woodruff)
1917- .... **CLC 23**
See also AITN 1; CA 21-24R; CANR 32;
DAM DRAM; DLB 7; LAIT 5
Anderson, Roberta Joan
See Mitchell, Joni
Anderson, Sherwood 1876-1941 .. **SSC 1, 46;**
TCLC 1, 10, 24, 123; WLC
See also AAYA 30; AMW; BPFB 1; CA
104; 121; CANR 61; CDALB 1917-1929;
DA; DA3; DAB; DAC; DAM MST, NOV;
DLB 4, 9, 86; DLBD 1; EWL 3; EXPS;
GLL 2; MTCW 1, 2; NFS 4; RGAL 4;
RGSF 2; SSFS 4, 10, 11; TUS
Andier, Pierre
See Desnos, Robert
Andouard
See Giraudoux, Jean(-Hippolyte)
Andrade, Carlos Drummond de ..... **CLC 18**
See Drummond de Andrade, Carlos
See also EWL 3; RGWL 2, 3
Andrade, Mario de .... **TCLC 43**
See de Andrade, Mario
See also EWL 3; LAW; RGWL 2, 3; WLIT
1
Andreae, Johann V(alentin)
1586-1654 .... **LC 32**
See also DLB 164
Andreas Capellanus fl. c. 1185- .... **CMLC 45**
See also DLB 208
Andreas-Salome, Lou 1861-1937 ... **TCLC 56**
See also CA 178; DLB 66
Andreev, Leonid
See Andreyev, Leonid (Nikolaevich)
See also EWL 3
Andress, Lesley
See Sanders, Lawrence
Andrewes, Lancelot 1555-1626 .... **LC 5**
See also DLB 151, 172
Andrews, Cicily Fairfield
See West, Rebecca
Andrews, Elton V.
See Pohl, Frederik
Andreyev, Leonid (Nikolaevich)
1871-1919 .... **TCLC 3**
See Andreev, Leonid
See also CA 104; 185
Andric, Ivo 1892-1975 .... **CLC 8; SSC 36;**
TCLC 135
See also CA 81-84; 57-60; CANR 43, 60;
CDWLB 4; DLB 147; EW 11; EWL 3;
MTCW 1; RGSF 2; RGWL 2, 3
Androvar
See Prado (Calvo), Pedro
Angelique, Pierre
See Bataille, Georges
Angell, Roger 1920- .... **CLC 26**
See also CA 57-60; CANR 13, 44, 70; DLB
171, 185

Beer, Johann 1655-1700 .... **LC 5**
  See also DLB 168
Beer, Patricia 1924- .... **CLC 58**
  See also CA 61-64; 183; CANR 13, 46; CP
  7; CWP; DLB 40; FW
Beerbohm, Max
  See Beerbohm, (Henry) Max(imilian)
Beerbohm, (Henry) Max(imilian)
  1872-1956 .... **TCLC 1, 24**
  See also BRWS 2; CA 104; 154; CANR 79;
  DLB 34, 100; FANT
Beer-Hofmann, Richard
  1866-1945 .... **TCLC 60**
  See also CA 160; DLB 81
Beg, Shemus
  See Stephens, James
Begiebing, Robert J(ohn) 1946- .... **CLC 70**
  See also CA 122; CANR 40, 88
Behan, Brendan 1923-1964 ...... **CLC 1, 8, 11,
  15, 79**
  See also BRWS 2; CA 73-76; CANR 33;
  CBD; CDBLB 1945-1960; DAM DRAM;
  DFS 7; DLB 13, 233; EWL 3; MTCW 1,
  2
Behn, Aphra 1640(?)-1689 .. **DC 4; LC 1, 30,
  42; PC 13; WLC**
  See also BRWS 3; DA; DA3; DAB; DAC;
  DAM DRAM, MST, NOV, POET; DFS
  16; DLB 39, 80, 131; FW; TEA; WLIT 3
Behrman, S(amuel) N(athaniel)
  1893-1973 .... **CLC 40**
  See also CA 13-16; 45-48; CAD; CAP 1;
  DLB 7, 44; IDFW 3; RGAL 4
Belasco, David 1853-1931 .... **TCLC 3**
  See also CA 104; 168; DLB 7; RGAL 4
Belcheva, Elisaveta Lyubomirova
  1893-1991 .... **CLC 10**
  See Bagryana, Elisaveta
Beldone, Phil "Cheech"
  See Ellison, Harlan (Jay)
Beleno
  See Azuela, Mariano
Belinski, Vissarion Grigoryevich
  1811-1848 .... **NCLC 5**
  See also DLB 198
Belitt, Ben 1911- .... **CLC 22**
  See also CA 13-16R; CAAS 4; CANR 7,
  77; CP 7; DLB 5
Bell, Gertrude (Margaret Lowthian)
  1868-1926 .... **TCLC 67**
  See also CA 167; CANR 110; DLB 174
Bell, J. Freeman
  See Zangwill, Israel
Bell, James Madison 1826-1902 .... **BLC 1;
  TCLC 43**
  See also BW 1; CA 122; 124; DAM MULT;
  DLB 50
Bell, Madison Smartt 1957- ...... **CLC 41, 102**
  See also AMWS 10; BPFB 1; CA 111, 183;
  CAAE 183; CANR 28, 54, 73; CN 7;
  CSW; DLB 218, 278; MTCW 1
Bell, Marvin (Hartley) 1937- .... **CLC 8, 31**
  See also CA 21-24R; CAAS 14; CANR 59,
  102; CP 7; DAM POET; DLB 5; MTCW
  1
Bell, W. L. D.
  See Mencken, H(enry) L(ouis)
Bellamy, Atwood C.
  See Mencken, H(enry) L(ouis)
Bellamy, Edward 1850-1898 ...... **NCLC 4, 86**
  See also DLB 12; NFS 15; RGAL 4; SFW
  4
Belli, Gioconda 1949- .... **HLCS 1**
  See also CA 152; CWW 2; EWL 3; RGWL
  3
Bellin, Edward J.
  See Kuttner, Henry

**Belloc, (Joseph) Hilaire (Pierre Sebastien
  Rene Swanton)** 1870-1953 .... **PC 24;
  TCLC 7, 18**
  See also CA 106; 152; CWRI 5; DAM
  POET; DLB 19, 100, 141, 174; EWL 3;
  MTCW 1; SATA 112; WCH; YABC 1
Belloc, Joseph Peter Rene Hilaire
  See Belloc, (Joseph) Hilaire (Pierre Sebas-
  tien Rene Swanton)
Belloc, Joseph Pierre Hilaire
  See Belloc, (Joseph) Hilaire (Pierre Sebas-
  tien Rene Swanton)
Belloc, M. A.
  See Lowndes, Marie Adelaide (Belloc)
Belloc-Lowndes, Mrs.
  See Lowndes, Marie Adelaide (Belloc)
Bellow, Saul 1915- . **CLC 1, 2, 3, 6, 8, 10, 13,
  15, 25, 33, 34, 63, 79; SSC 14; WLC**
  See also AITN 2; AMW; AMWR 2; BEST
  89:3; BPFB 1; CA 5-8R; CABS 1; CANR
  29, 53, 95; CDALB 1941-1968; CN 7;
  DA; DA3; DAB; DAC; DAM MST, NOV,
  POP; DLB 2, 28; DLBD 3; DLBY 1982;
  EWL 3; MTCW 1, 2; NFS 4, 14; RGAL
  4; RGSF 2; SSFS 12; TUS
Belser, Reimond Karel Maria de 1929-
  See Ruyslinck, Ward
  See also CA 152
Bely, Andrey .... **PC 11; TCLC 7**
  See Bugayev, Boris Nikolayevich
  See also EW 9; EWL 3; MTCW 1
Belyi, Andrei
  See Bugayev, Boris Nikolayevich
  See also RGWL 2, 3
Bembo, Pietro 1470-1547 .... **LC 79**
  See also RGWL 2, 3
Benary, Margot
  See Benary-Isbert, Margot
Benary-Isbert, Margot 1889-1979 .... **CLC 12**
  See also CA 5-8R; 89-92; CANR 4, 72;
  CLR 12; MAICYA 1, 2; SATA 2; SATA-
  Obit 21
Benavente (y Martinez), Jacinto
  1866-1954 .... **HLCS 1; TCLC 3**
  See also CA 106; 131; CANR 81; DAM
  DRAM, MULT; EWL 3; GLL 2; HW 1,
  2; MTCW 1, 2
Benchley, Peter (Bradford) 1940- .. **CLC 4, 8**
  See also AAYA 14; AITN 2; BPFB 1; CA
  17-20R; CANR 12, 35, 66, 115; CPW;
  DAM NOV, POP; HGG; MTCW 1, 2;
  SATA 3, 89
Benchley, Robert (Charles)
  1889-1945 .... **TCLC 1, 55**
  See also CA 105; 153; DLB 11; RGAL 4
Benda, Julien 1867-1956 .... **TCLC 60**
  See also CA 120; 154; GFL 1789 to the
  Present
Benedict, Ruth (Fulton)
  1887-1948 .... **TCLC 60**
  See also CA 158; DLB 246
Benedikt, Michael 1935- .... **CLC 4, 14**
  See also CA 13-16R; CANR 7; CP 7; DLB
  5
Benet, Juan 1927-1993 .... **CLC 28**
  See also CA 143; EWL 3
Benet, Stephen Vincent 1898-1943 ... **SSC 10;
  TCLC 7**
  See also AMWS 11; CA 104; 152; DA3;
  DAM POET; DLB 4, 48, 102, 249, 284;
  DLBY 1997; EWL 3; HGG; MTCW 1;
  RGAL 4; RGSF 2; SUFW; WP; YABC 1
Benet, William Rose 1886-1950 ..... **TCLC 28**
  See also CA 118; 152; DAM POET; DLB
  45; RGAL 4
Benford, Gregory (Albert) 1941- ..... **CLC 52**
  See also BPFB 1; CA 69-72, 175; CAAE
  175; CAAS 27; CANR 12, 24, 49, 95;
  CSW; DLBY 1982; SCFW 2; SFW 4

Bengtsson, Frans (Gunnar)
  1894-1954 .... **TCLC 48**
  See also CA 170; EWL 3
Benjamin, David
  See Slavitt, David R(ytman)
Benjamin, Lois
  See Gould, Lois
Benjamin, Walter 1892-1940 .... **TCLC 39**
  See also CA 164; DLB 242; EW 11; EWL
  3
Benn, Gottfried 1886-1956 .. **PC 35; TCLC 3**
  See also CA 106; 153; DLB 56; EWL 3;
  RGWL 2, 3
Bennett, Alan 1934- .... **CLC 45, 77**
  See also BRWS 8; CA 103; CANR 35, 55,
  106; CBD; CD 5; DAB; DAM MST;
  MTCW 1, 2
Bennett, (Enoch) Arnold
  1867-1931 .... **TCLC 5, 20**
  See also BRW 6; CA 106; 155; CDBLB
  1890-1914; DLB 10, 34, 98, 135; EWL 3;
  MTCW 2
Bennett, Elizabeth
  See Mitchell, Margaret (Munnerlyn)
Bennett, George Harold 1930-
  See Bennett, Hal
  See also BW 1; CA 97-100; CANR 87
Bennett, Gwendolyn B. 1902-1981 .... **HR 2**
  See also BW 1; CA 125; DLB 51; WP
Bennett, Hal .... **CLC 5**
  See Bennett, George Harold
  See also DLB 33
Bennett, Jay 1912- .... **CLC 35**
  See also AAYA 10; CA 69-72; CANR 11,
  42, 79; JRDA; SAAS 4; SATA 41, 87;
  SATA-Brief 27; WYA; YAW
Bennett, Louise (Simone) 1919- .... **BLC 1;
  CLC 28**
  See also BW 2, 3; CA 151; CDWLB 3; CP
  7; DAM MULT; DLB 117; EWL 3
Benson, A. C. 1862-1925 .... **TCLC 123**
  See also DLB 98
Benson, E(dward) F(rederic)
  1867-1940 .... **TCLC 27**
  See also CA 114; 157; DLB 135, 153;
  HGG; SUFW 1
Benson, Jackson J. 1930- .... **CLC 34**
  See also CA 25-28R; DLB 111
Benson, Sally 1900-1972 .... **CLC 17**
  See also CA 19-20; 37-40R; CAP 1; SATA
  1, 35; SATA-Obit 27
Benson, Stella 1892-1933 .... **TCLC 17**
  See also CA 117; 154, 155; DLB 36, 162;
  FANT; TEA
Bentham, Jeremy 1748-1832 .... **NCLC 38**
  See also DLB 107, 158, 252
Bentley, E(dmund) C(lerihew)
  1875-1956 .... **TCLC 12**
  See also CA 108; DLB 70; MSW
Bentley, Eric (Russell) 1916- .... **CLC 24**
  See also CA 5-8R; CAD; CANR 6, 67;
  CBD; CD 5; INT CANR-6
ben Uzair, Salem
  See Horne, Richard Henry Hengist
Beranger, Pierre Jean de
  1780-1857 .... **NCLC 34**
Berdyaev, Nicolas
  See Berdyaev, Nikolai (Aleksandrovich)
Berdyaev, Nikolai (Aleksandrovich)
  1874-1948 .... **TCLC 67**
  See also CA 120; 157
Berdyayev, Nikolai (Aleksandrovich)
  See Berdyaev, Nikolai (Aleksandrovich)
Berendt, John (Lawrence) 1939- ...... **CLC 86**
  See also CA 146; CANR 75, 93; DA3;
  MTCW 1

Bontemps, Arna(ud Wendell)
1902-1973 ..... **BLC 1; CLC 1, 18; HR 2**
See also BW 1; CA 1-4R; 41-44R; CANR 4, 35; CLR 6; CWRI 5; DA3; DLB MULT, NOV, POET; DLB 48, 51; JRDA; MAICYA 1, 2; MTCW 1, 2; SATA 2, 44; SATA-Obit 24; WCH; WP

Booth, Martin 1944- .... **CLC 13**
See also CA 93-96; CAAE 188; CAAS 2; CANR 92

Booth, Philip 1925- .... **CLC 23**
See also CA 5-8R; CANR 5, 88; CP 7; DLBY 1982

Booth, Wayne C(layson) 1921- ...... **CLC 24**
See also CA 1-4R; CAAS 5; CANR 3, 43, 117; DLB 67

Borchert, Wolfgang 1921-1947 .... **TCLC 5**
See also CA 104; 188; DLB 69, 124; EWL 3

Borel, Petrus 1809-1859 .... **NCLC 41**
See also DLB 119; GFL 1789 to the Present

Borges, Jorge Luis 1899-1986 ... **CLC 1, 2, 3, 4, 6, 8, 9, 10, 13, 19, 44, 48, 83; HLC 1; PC 22, 32; SSC 4, 41; TCLC 109; WLC**
See also AAYA 26; BPFB 1; CA 21-24R; CANR 19, 33, 75, 105; CDWLB 3; DA; DA3; DAB; DAC; DAM MST, MULT; DLB 113, 283; DLBY 1986; DNFS 1, 2; EWL 3; HW 1, 2; LAW; LMFS 2; MSW; MTCW 1, 2; RGSF 2; RGWL 2, 3; SFW 4; SSFS 17; TWA; WLIT 1

Borowski, Tadeusz 1922-1951 .... **SSC 48; TCLC 9**
See also CA 106; 154; CDWLB 4; DLB 215; EWL 3; RGSF 2; RGWL 3; SSFS 13

Borrow, George (Henry)
1803-1881 .... **NCLC 9**
See also DLB 21, 55, 166

Bosch (Gavino), Juan 1909-2001 ..... **HLCS 1**
See also CA 151; 204; DAM MST, MULT; DLB 145; HW 1, 2

Bosman, Herman Charles
1905-1951 .... **TCLC 49**
See Malan, Herman
See also CA 160; DLB 225; RGSF 2

Bosschere, Jean de 1878(?)-1953 ... **TCLC 19**
See also CA 115; 186

Boswell, James 1740-1795 ... **LC 4, 50; WLC**
See also BRW 3; CDBLB 1660-1789; DA; DAB; DAC; DAM MST; DLB 104, 142; TEA; WLIT 3

Bottomley, Gordon 1874-1948 ..... **TCLC 107**
See also CA 120; 192; DLB 10

Bottoms, David 1949- .... **CLC 53**
See also CA 105; CANR 22; CSW; DLB 120; DLBY 1983

Boucicault, Dion 1820-1890 .... **NCLC 41**

Boucolon, Maryse
See Conde, Maryse

Bourget, Paul (Charles Joseph)
1852-1935 .... **TCLC 12**
See also CA 107; 196; DLB 123; GFL 1789 to the Present

Bourjaily, Vance (Nye) 1922- .... **CLC 8, 62**
See also CA 1-4R; CAAS 1; CANR 2, 72; CN 7; DLB 2, 143

Bourne, Randolph S(illiman)
1886-1918 .... **TCLC 16**
See also AMW; CA 117; 155; DLB 63

Bova, Ben(jamin William) 1932- ...... **CLC 45**
See also AAYA 16; CA 5-8R; CAAS 18; CANR 11, 56, 94, 111; CLR 3; DLBY 1981; INT CANR-11; MAICYA 1, 2; MTCW 1; SATA 6, 68, 133; SFW 4

Bowen, Elizabeth (Dorothea Cole)
1899-1973 . **CLC 1, 3, 6, 11, 15, 22, 118; SSC 3, 28**
See also BRWS 2; CA 17-18; 41-44R; CANR 35, 105; CAP 2; CDBLB 1945-1960; DA3; DAM NOV; DLB 15, 162; EWL 3; EXPS; FW; HGG; MTCW 1, 2; NFS 13; RGSF 2; SSFS 5; SUFW 1; TEA; WLIT 4

Bowering, George 1935- .... **CLC 15, 47**
See also CA 21-24R; CAAS 16; CANR 10; CP 7; DLB 53

Bowering, Marilyn R(uthe) 1949- .... **CLC 32**
See also CA 101; CANR 49; CP 7; CWP

Bowers, Edgar 1924-2000 .... **CLC 9**
See also CA 5-8R; 188; CANR 24; CP 7; CSW; DLB 5

Bowers, Mrs. J. Milton 1842-1914
See Bierce, Ambrose (Gwinett)

Bowie, David .... **CLC 17**
See Jones, David Robert

Bowles, Jane (Sydney) 1917-1973 ..... **CLC 3, 68**
See Bowles, Jane Auer
See also CA 19-20; 41-44R; CAP 2

Bowles, Jane Auer
See Bowles, Jane (Sydney)
See also EWL 3

Bowles, Paul (Frederick) 1910-1999 . **CLC 1, 2, 19, 53; SSC 3**
See also AMWS 4; CA 1-4R; 186; CAAS 1; CANR 1, 19, 50, 75; CN 7; DA3; DLB 5, 6, 218; EWL 3; MTCW 1, 2; RGAL 4; SSFS 17

Bowles, William Lisle 1762-1850 . **NCLC 103**
See also DLB 93

Box, Edgar
See Vidal, Gore
See also GLL 1

Boyd, James 1888-1944 .... **TCLC 115**
See also CA 186; DLB 9; DLBD 16; RGAL 4; RHW

Boyd, Nancy
See Millay, Edna St. Vincent
See also GLL 1

Boyd, Thomas (Alexander)
1898-1935 .... **TCLC 111**
See also CA 111; 183; DLB 9; DLBD 16

Boyd, William 1952- .... **CLC 28, 53, 70**
See also CA 114; 120; CANR 51, 71; CN 7; DLB 231

Boyle, Kay 1902-1992 .... **CLC 1, 5, 19, 58, 121; SSC 5**
See also CA 13-16R; 140; CAAS 1; CANR 29, 61, 110; DLB 4, 9, 48, 86; DLBY 1993; EWL 3; MTCW 1, 2; RGAL 4; RGSF 2; SSFS 10, 13, 14

Boyle, Mark
See Kienzle, William X(avier)

Boyle, Patrick 1905-1982 .... **CLC 19**
See also CA 127

Boyle, T. C.
See Boyle, T(homas) Coraghessan
See also AMWS 8

Boyle, T(homas) Coraghessan
1948- .... **CLC 36, 55, 90; SSC 16**
See Boyle, T. C.
See also AAYA 47; BEST 90:4; BPFB 1; CA 120; CANR 44, 76, 89; CN 7; CPW; DA3; DAM POP; DLB 218, 278; DLBY 1986; EWL 3; MTCW 2; SSFS 13

Boz
See Dickens, Charles (John Huffam)

Brackenridge, Hugh Henry
1748-1816 .... **NCLC 7**
See also DLB 11, 37; RGAL 4

Bradbury, Edward P.
See Moorcock, Michael (John)
See also MTCW 2

Bradbury, Malcolm (Stanley)
1932-2000 .... **CLC 32, 61**
See also CA 1-4R; CANR 1, 33, 91, 98; CN 7; DA3; DAM NOV; DLB 14, 207; EWL 3; MTCW 1, 2

Bradbury, Ray (Douglas) 1920- .... **CLC 1, 3, 10, 15, 42, 98; SSC 29, 53; WLC**
See also AAYA 15; AITN 1, 2; AMWS 4; BPFB 1; BYA 4, 5, 11; CA 1-4R; CANR 2, 30, 75; CDALB 1968-1988; CN 7; CPW; DA; DA3; DAB; DAC; DAM MST, NOV, POP; DLB 2, 8; EXPN; EXPS; HGG; LAIT 3, 5; LATS 1; LMFS 2; MTCW 1, 2; NFS 1; RGAL 4; RGSF 2; SATA 11, 64, 123; SCFW 2; SFW 4; SSFS 1; SUFW 1, 2; TUS; YAW

Braddon, Mary Elizabeth
1837-1915 .... **TCLC 111**
See also BRWS 8; CA 108; 179; CMW 4; DLB 18, 70, 156; HGG

Bradford, Gamaliel 1863-1932 .... **TCLC 36**
See also CA 160; DLB 17

Bradford, William 1590-1657 .... **LC 64**
See also DLB 24, 30; RGAL 4

Bradley, David (Henry), Jr. 1950- .... **BLC 1; CLC 23, 118**
See also BW 1, 3; CA 104; CANR 26, 81; CN 7; DAM MULT; DLB 33

Bradley, John Ed(mund, Jr.) 1958- . **CLC 55**
See also CA 139; CANR 99; CN 7; CSW

Bradley, Marion Zimmer
1930-1999 .... **CLC 30**
See Chapman, Lee; Dexter, John; Gardner, Miriam; Ives, Morgan; Rivers, Elfrida
See also AAYA 40; BPFB 1; CA 57-60; 185; CAAS 10; CANR 7, 31, 51, 75, 107; CPW; DA3; DAM POP; DLB 8; FANT; FW; MTCW 1, 2; SATA 90, 139; SATA-Obit 116; SFW 4; SUFW 2; YAW

Bradshaw, John 1933- .... **CLC 70**
See also CA 138; CANR 61

Bradstreet, Anne 1612(?)-1672 ...... **LC 4, 30; PC 10**
See also AMWS 1; CDALB 1640-1865; DA; DA3; DAC; DAM MST, POET; DLB 24; EXPP; FW; PFS 6; RGAL 4; TUS; WP

Brady, Joan 1939- .... **CLC 86**
See also CA 141

Bragg, Melvyn 1939- .... **CLC 10**
See also BEST 89:3; CA 57-60; CANR 10, 48, 89; CN 7; DLB 14, 271; RHW

Brahe, Tycho 1546-1601 .... **LC 45**

Braine, John (Gerard) 1922-1986 . **CLC 1, 3, 41**
See also CA 1-4R; 120; CANR 1, 33; CD-BLB 1945-1960; DLB 15; DLBY 1986; EWL 3; MTCW 1

Braithwaite, William Stanley (Beaumont)
1878-1962 .... **BLC 1; HR 2**
See also BW 1; CA 125; DAM MULT; DLB 50, 54

Bramah, Ernest 1868-1942 .... **TCLC 72**
See also CA 156; CMW 4; DLB 70; FANT

Brammer, William 1930(?)-1978 ...... **CLC 31**
See also CA 77-80

Brancati, Vitaliano 1907-1954 .... **TCLC 12**
See also CA 109; DLB 264; EWL 3

Brancato, Robin F(idler) 1936- .... **CLC 35**
See also AAYA 9; BYA 6; CA 69-72; CANR 11, 45; CLR 32; JRDA; MAICYA 2; MAICYAS 1; SAAS 9; SATA 97; WYA; YAW

Brand, Max
See Faust, Frederick (Schiller)
See also BPFB 1; TCWW 2

Brand, Millen 1906-1980 .... **CLC 7**
See also CA 21-24R; 97-100; CANR 72

Caldwell, (Janet Miriam) Taylor (Holland)
1900-1985 .... **CLC 2, 28, 39**
See also BPFB 1; CA 5-8R; 116; CANR 5;
DA3; DAM NOV, POP; DLBD 17; RHW

Calhoun, John Caldwell
1782-1850 .... **NCLC 15**
See also DLB 3, 248

Calisher, Hortense 1911- ..... **CLC 2, 4, 8, 38,
134; SSC 15**
See also CA 1-4R; CANR 1, 22, 117; CN
7; DAM NOV; DLB 2, 218; INT
CANR-22; MTCW 1, 2; RGAL 4; RGSF
2

Callaghan, Morley Edward
1903-1990 .... **CLC 3, 14, 41, 65**
See also CA 9-12R; 132; CANR 33, 73;
DAC; DAM MST; DLB 68; EWL 3;
MTCW 1, 2; RGEL 2; RGSF 2

Callimachus c. 305B.C.-c.
240B.C. .... **CMLC 18**
See also AW 1; DLB 176; RGWL 2, 3

Calvin, Jean
See Calvin, John
See also GFL Beginnings to 1789

Calvin, John 1509-1564 .... **LC 37**
See also Calvin, Jean

Calvino, Italo 1923-1985 .... **CLC 5, 8, 11, 22,
33, 39, 73; SSC 3, 48**
See also CA 85-88; 116; CANR 23, 61;
DAM NOV; DLB 196; EW 13; EWL 3;
MTCW 1, 2; RGSF 2; RGWL 2, 3; SFW
4; SSFS 12

Camara Laye
See Laye, Camara
See also EWL 3

Camden, William 1551-1623 .... **LC 77**
See also DLB 172

Cameron, Carey 1952- .... **CLC 59**
See also CA 135

Cameron, Peter 1959- .... **CLC 44**
See also AMWS 12; CA 125; CANR 50,
117; DLB 234; GLL 2

Camoens, Luis Vaz de 1524(?)-1580
See Camoes, Luis de
See also EW 2

Camoes, Luis de 1524(?)-1580 . **HLCS 1; LC
62; PC 31**
See Camoens, Luis Vaz de
See also RGWL 2, 3

Campana, Dino 1885-1932 .... **TCLC 20**
See also CA 117; DLB 114; EWL 3

Campanella, Tommaso 1568-1639 .... **LC 32**
See also RGWL 2, 3

Campbell, John W(ood, Jr.)
1910-1971 .... **CLC 32**
See also CA 21-22; 29-32R; CANR 34;
CAP 2; DLB 8; MTCW 1; SCFW; SFW 4

Campbell, Joseph 1904-1987 .... **CLC 69**
See also AAYA 3; BEST 89:2; CA 1-4R;
124; CANR 3, 28, 61, 107; DA3; MTCW
1, 2

Campbell, Maria 1940- .... **CLC 85; NNAL**
See also CA 102; CANR 54; CCA 1; DAC

Campbell, Paul N. 1923-
See hooks, bell
See also CA 21-24R

Campbell, (John) Ramsey 1946- ..... **CLC 42;
SSC 19**
See also AAYA 51; CA 57-60; CANR 7,
102; DLB 261; HGG; INT CANR-7;
SUFW 1, 2

Campbell, (Ignatius) Roy (Dunnachie)
1901-1957 .... **TCLC 5**
See also AFW; CA 104; 155; DLB 20, 225;
EWL 3; MTCW 2; RGEL 2

Campbell, Thomas 1777-1844 .... **NCLC 19**
See also DLB 93, 144; RGEL 2

Campbell, Wilfred .... **TCLC 9**
See Campbell, William

Campbell, William 1858(?)-1918
See Campbell, Wilfred
See also CA 106; DLB 92

Campion, Jane 1954- .... **CLC 95**
See also AAYA 33; CA 138; CANR 87

Campion, Thomas 1567-1620 .... **LC 78**
See also CDBLB Before 1660; DAM POET;
DLB 58, 172; RGEL 2

Camus, Albert 1913-1960 ...... **CLC 1, 2, 4, 9,
11, 14, 32, 63, 69, 124; DC 2; SSC 9;
WLC**
See also AAYA 36; AFW; BPFB 1; CA 89-
92; DA; DA3; DAB; DAC; DAM DRAM,
MST, NOV; DLB 72; EW 13; EWL 3;
EXPN; EXPS; GFL 1789 to the Present;
LATS 1; LMFS 2; MTCW 1, 2; NFS 6,
16; RGSF 2; RGWL 2, 3; SSFS 4; TWA

Canby, Vincent 1924-2000 .... **CLC 13**
See also CA 81-84; 191

Cancale
See Desnos, Robert

Canetti, Elias 1905-1994 .. **CLC 3, 14, 25, 75,
86**
See also CA 21-24R; 146; CANR 23, 61,
79; CDWLB 2; CWW 2; DA3; DLB 85,
124; EW 12; EWL 3; MTCW 1, 2; RGWL
2, 3; TWA

Canfield, Dorothea F.
See Fisher, Dorothy (Frances) Canfield

Canfield, Dorothea Frances
See Fisher, Dorothy (Frances) Canfield

Canfield, Dorothy
See Fisher, Dorothy (Frances) Canfield

Canin, Ethan 1960- .... **CLC 55**
See also CA 131; 135

Cankar, Ivan 1876-1918 .... **TCLC 105**
See also CDWLB 4; DLB 147; EWL 3

Cannon, Curt
See Hunter, Evan

Cao, Lan 1961- .... **CLC 109**
See also CA 165

Cape, Judith
See Page, P(atricia) K(athleen)
See also CCA 1

Capek, Karel 1890-1938 .... **DC 1; SSC 36;
TCLC 6, 37; WLC**
See also CA 104; 140; CDWLB 4; DA;
DA3; DAB; DAC; DAM DRAM, MST,
NOV; DFS 7, 11; DLB 215; EW 10; EWL
3; MTCW 1; RGSF 2; RGWL 2, 3; SCFW
2; SFW 4

Capote, Truman 1924-1984 . **CLC 1, 3, 8, 13,
19, 34, 38, 58; SSC 2, 47; WLC**
See also AMWS 3; BPFB 1; CA 5-8R; 113;
CANR 18, 62; CDALB 1941-1968; CPW;
DA; DA3; DAB; DAC; DAM MST, NOV,
POP; DLB 2, 185, 227; DLBY 1980,
1984; EWL 3; EXPS; GLL 1; LAIT 3;
MTCW 1, 2; NCFS 2; RGAL 4; RGSF 2;
SATA 91; SSFS 2; TUS

Capra, Frank 1897-1991 .... **CLC 16**
See also AAYA 52; CA 61-64; 135

Caputo, Philip 1941- .... **CLC 32**
See also CA 73-76; CANR 40; YAW

Caragiale, Ion Luca 1852-1912 ...... **TCLC 76**
See also CA 157

Card, Orson Scott 1951- .... **CLC 44, 47, 50**
See also AAYA 11, 42; BPFB 1; BYA 5, 8;
CA 102; CANR 27, 47, 73, 102, 106;
CPW; DA3; DAM POP; FANT; INT
CANR-27; MTCW 1, 2; NFS 5; SATA
83, 127; SCFW 2; SFW 4; SUFW 2; YAW

Cardenal, Ernesto 1925- .... **CLC 31, 161;
HLC 1; PC 22**
See also CA 49-52; CANR 2, 32, 66; CWW
2; DAM MULT, POET; EWL 3; HW 1, 2;
LAWS 1; MTCW 1, 2; RGWL 2, 3

Cardozo, Benjamin N(athan)
1870-1938 .... **TCLC 65**
See also CA 117; 164

Carducci, Giosue (Alessandro Giuseppe)
1835-1907 .... **PC 46; TCLC 32**
See also CA 163; EW 7; RGWL 2, 3

Carew, Thomas 1595(?)-1640 . **LC 13; PC 29**
See also BRW 2; DLB 126; PAB; RGEL 2

Carey, Ernestine Gilbreth 1908- .... **CLC 17**
See also CA 5-8R; CANR 71; SATA 2

Carey, Peter 1943- .... **CLC 40, 55, 96**
See also CA 123; 127; CANR 53, 76, 117;
CN 7; EWL 3; INT CA-127; MTCW 1, 2;
RGSF 2; SATA 94

Carleton, William 1794-1869 .... **NCLC 3**
See also DLB 159; RGEL 2; RGSF 2

Carlisle, Henry (Coffin) 1926- .... **CLC 33**
See also CA 13-16R; CANR 15, 85

Carlsen, Chris
See Holdstock, Robert P.

Carlson, Ron(ald F.) 1947- .... **CLC 54**
See also CA 105; CAAE 189; CANR 27;
DLB 244

Carlyle, Thomas 1795-1881 ..... **NCLC 22, 70**
See also BRW 4; CDBLB 1789-1832; DA;
DAB; DAC; DAM MST; DLB 55, 144,
254; RGEL 2; TEA

Carman, (William) Bliss 1861-1929 ... **PC 34;
TCLC 7**
See also CA 104; 152; DAC; DLB 92;
RGEL 2

Carnegie, Dale 1888-1955 .... **TCLC 53**

Carossa, Hans 1878-1956 .... **TCLC 48**
See also CA 170; DLB 66; EWL 3

Carpenter, Don(ald Richard)
1931-1995 .... **CLC 41**
See also CA 45-48; 149; CANR 1, 71

Carpenter, Edward 1844-1929 .... **TCLC 88**
See also CA 163; GLL 1

Carpenter, John (Howard) 1948- ... **CLC 161**
See also AAYA 2; CA 134; SATA 58

Carpenter, Johnny
See Carpenter, John (Howard)

Carpentier (y Valmont), Alejo
1904-1980 . **CLC 8, 11, 38, 110; HLC 1;
SSC 35**
See also CA 65-68; 97-100; CANR 11, 70;
CDWLB 3; DAM MULT; DLB 113; EWL
3; HW 1, 2; LAW; LMFS 2; RGSF 2;
RGWL 2, 3; WLIT 1

Carr, Caleb 1955(?)- .... **CLC 86**
See also CA 147; CANR 73; DA3

Carr, Emily 1871-1945 .... **TCLC 32**
See also CA 159; DLB 68; FW; GLL 2

Carr, John Dickson 1906-1977 .... **CLC 3**
See Fairbairn, Roger
See also CA 49-52; 69-72; CANR 3, 33,
60; CMW 4; MSW; MTCW 1, 2

Carr, Philippa
See Hibbert, Eleanor Alice Burford

Carr, Virginia Spencer 1929- .... **CLC 34**
See also CA 61-64; DLB 111

Carrere, Emmanuel 1957- .... **CLC 89**
See also CA 200

Carrier, Roch 1937- .... **CLC 13, 78**
See also CA 130; CANR 61; CCA 1; DAC;
DAM MST; DLB 53; SATA 105

Carroll, James Dennis
See Carroll, Jim

Carroll, James P. 1943(?)- .... **CLC 38**
See also CA 81-84; CANR 73; MTCW 1

Carroll, Jim 1951- .... **CLC 35, 143**
See Carroll, James Dennis
See also AAYA 17; CA 45-48; CANR 42,
115

Carroll, Lewis ... **NCLC 2, 53; PC 18; WLC**
See Dodgson, Charles L(utwidge)
See also AAYA 39; BRW 5; BYA 5, 13; CD-
BLB 1832-1890; CLR 2, 18; DLB 18,

Challans, Mary 1905-1983
See Renault, Mary
See also CA 81-84; 111; CANR 74; DA3;
MTCW 2; SATA 23; SATA-Obit 36; TEA

Challis, George
See Faust, Frederick (Schiller)
See also TCWW 2

Chambers, Aidan 1934- .... **CLC 35**
See also AAYA 27; CA 25-28R; CANR 12,
31, 58, 116; JRDA; MAICYA 1, 2; SAAS
12; SATA 1, 69, 108; WYA; YAW

Chambers, James 1948-
See Cliff, Jimmy
See also CA 124

Chambers, Jessie
See Lawrence, D(avid) H(erbert Richards)
See also GLL 1

Chambers, Robert W(illiam)
1865-1933 .... **TCLC 41**
See also CA 165; DLB 202; HGG; SATA
107; SUFW 1

Chambers, (David) Whittaker
1901-1961 .... **TCLC 129**
See also CA 89-92

Chamisso, Adelbert von
1781-1838 .... **NCLC 82**
See also DLB 90; RGWL 2, 3; SUFW 1

Chance, James T.
See Carpenter, John (Howard)

Chance, John T.
See Carpenter, John (Howard)

Chandler, Raymond (Thornton)
1888-1959 .... **SSC 23; TCLC 1, 7**
See also AAYA 25; AMWS 4; BPFB 1; CA
104; 129; CANR 60, 107; CDALB 1929-
1941; CMW 4; DA3; DLB 226, 253;
DLBD 6; EWL 3; MSW; MTCW 1, 2;
NFS 17; RGAL 4; TUS

Chang, Diana 1934- .... **AAL**
See also CWP; EXPP

Chang, Eileen 1921-1995 .... **AAL; SSC 28**
See Chang Ai-Ling
See also CA 166; CWW 2

Chang, Jung 1952- .... **CLC 71**
See also CA 142

Chang Ai-Ling
See Chang, Eileen
See also EWL 3

Channing, William Ellery
1780-1842 .... **NCLC 17**
See also DLB 1, 59, 235; RGAL 4

Chao, Patricia 1955- .... **CLC 119**
See also CA 163

Chaplin, Charles Spencer
1889-1977 .... **CLC 16**
See Chaplin, Charlie
See also CA 81-84; 73-76

Chaplin, Charlie
See Chaplin, Charles Spencer
See also DLB 44

Chapman, George 1559(?)-1634 . **DC 19; LC
22**
See also BRW 1; DAM DRAM; DLB 62,
121; LMFS 1; RGEL 2

Chapman, Graham 1941-1989 .... **CLC 21**
See Monty Python
See also CA 116; 129; CANR 35, 95

Chapman, John Jay 1862-1933 .... **TCLC 7**
See also CA 104; 191

Chapman, Lee
See Bradley, Marion Zimmer
See also GLL 1

Chapman, Walker
See Silverberg, Robert

Chappell, Fred (Davis) 1936- .... **CLC 40, 78,
162**
See also CA 5-8R; CAAE 198; CAAS 4;
CANR 8, 33, 67, 110; CN 7; CP 7; CSW;
DLB 6, 105; HGG

Char, Rene(-Emile) 1907-1988 .... **CLC 9, 11,
14, 55**
See also CA 13-16R; 124; CANR 32; DAM
POET; DLB 258; EWL 3; GFL 1789 to
the Present; MTCW 1, 2; RGWL 2, 3

Charby, Jay
See Ellison, Harlan (Jay)

Chardin, Pierre Teilhard de
See Teilhard de Chardin, (Marie Joseph)
Pierre

Chariton fl. 1st cent. (?)- .... **CMLC 49**

Charlemagne 742-814 .... **CMLC 37**

Charles I 1600-1649 .... **LC 13**

Charriere, Isabelle de 1740-1805 .. **NCLC 66**

Chartier, Emile-Auguste
See Alain

Charyn, Jerome 1937- .... **CLC 5, 8, 18**
See also CA 5-8R; CAAS 1; CANR 7, 61,
101; CMW 4; CN 7; DLBY 1983; MTCW
1

Chase, Adam
See Marlowe, Stephen

Chase, Mary (Coyle) 1907-1981 .... **DC 1**
See also CA 77-80; 105; CAD; CWD; DFS
11; DLB 228; SATA 17; SATA-Obit 29

Chase, Mary Ellen 1887-1973 .... **CLC 2;
TCLC 124**
See also CA 13-16; 41-44R; CAP 1; SATA
10

Chase, Nicholas
See Hyde, Anthony
See also CCA 1

Chateaubriand, Francois Rene de
1768-1848 .... **NCLC 3**
See also DLB 119; EW 5; GFL 1789 to the
Present; RGWL 2, 3; TWA

Chatterje, Sarat Chandra 1876-1936(?)
See Chatterji, Saratchandra
See also CA 109

Chatterji, Bankim Chandra
1838-1894 .... **NCLC 19**

Chatterji, Saratchandra .... **TCLC 13**
See Chatterje, Sarat Chandra
See also CA 186; EWL 3

Chatterton, Thomas 1752-1770 .... **LC 3, 54**
See also DAM POET; DLB 109; RGEL 2

Chatwin, (Charles) Bruce
1940-1989 .... **CLC 28, 57, 59**
See also AAYA 4; BEST 90:1; BRWS 4;
CA 85-88; 127; CPW; DAM POP; DLB
194, 204; EWL 3

Chaucer, Daniel
See Ford, Ford Madox
See also RHW

Chaucer, Geoffrey 1340(?)-1400 .. **LC 17, 56;
PC 19; WLCS**
See also BRW 1; BRWC 1; BRWR 2; CD-
BLB Before 1660; DA; DA3; DAB;
DAC; DAM MST, POET; DLB 146;
LAIT 1; PAB; PFS 14; RGEL 2; TEA;
WLIT 3; WP

Chavez, Denise (Elia) 1948- .... **HLC 1**
See also CA 131; CANR 56, 81; DAM
MULT; DLB 122; FW; HW 1, 2; MTCW
2

Chaviaras, Strates 1935-
See Haviaras, Stratis
See also CA 105

Chayefsky, Paddy .... **CLC 23**
See Chayefsky, Sidney
See also CAD; DLB 7, 44; DLBY 1981;
RGAL 4

Chayefsky, Sidney 1923-1981
See Chayefsky, Paddy
See also CA 9-12R; 104; CANR 18; DAM
DRAM

Chedid, Andree 1920- .... **CLC 47**
See also CA 145; CANR 95; EWL 3

Cheever, John 1912-1982 ..... **CLC 3, 7, 8, 11,
15, 25, 64; SSC 1, 38, 57; WLC**
See also AMWS 1; BPFB 1; CA 5-8R; 106;
CABS 1; CANR 5, 27, 76; CDALB 1941-
1968; CPW; DA; DA3; DAB; DAC;
DAM MST, NOV, POP; DLB 2, 102, 227;
DLBY 1980, 1982; EWL 3; EXPS; INT
CANR-5; MTCW 1, 2; RGAL 4; RGSF
2; SSFS 2, 14; TUS

Cheever, Susan 1943- .... **CLC 18, 48**
See also CA 103; CANR 27, 51, 92; DLBY
1982; INT CANR-27

Chekhonte, Antosha
See Chekhov, Anton (Pavlovich)

Chekhov, Anton (Pavlovich)
1860-1904 ...... **DC 9; SSC 2, 28, 41, 51;
TCLC 3, 10, 31, 55, 96; WLC**
See also BYA 14; CA 104; 124; DA; DA3;
DAB; DAC; DAM DRAM, MST; DFS 1,
5, 10, 12; DLB 277; EW 7; EWL 3;
EXPS; LAIT 3; LATS 1; RGSF 2; RGWL
2, 3; SATA 90; SSFS 5, 13, 14; TWA

Cheney, Lynne V. 1941- .... **CLC 70**
See also CA 89-92; CANR 58, 117

Chernyshevsky, Nikolai Gavrilovich
See Chernyshevsky, Nikolay Gavrilovich
See also DLB 238

Chernyshevsky, Nikolay Gavrilovich
1828-1889 .... **NCLC 1**
See Chernyshevsky, Nikolai Gavrilovich

Cherry, Carolyn Janice 1942-
See Cherryh, C. J.
See also CA 65-68; CANR 10

Cherryh, C. J. .... **CLC 35**
See Cherry, Carolyn Janice
See also AAYA 24; BPFB 1; DLBY 1980;
FANT; SATA 93; SCFW 2; SFW 4; YAW

Chesnutt, Charles W(addell)
1858-1932 .... **BLC 1; SSC 7, 54; TCLC
5, 39**
See also AFAW 1, 2; BW 1, 3; CA 106;
125; CANR 76; DAM MULT; DLB 12,
50, 78; EWL 3; MTCW 1, 2; RGAL 4;
RGSF 2; SSFS 11

Chester, Alfred 1929(?)-1971 .... **CLC 49**
See also CA 196; 33-36R; DLB 130

Chesterton, G(ilbert) K(eith)
1874-1936 . **PC 28; SSC 1, 46; TCLC 1,
6, 64**
See also BRW 6; CA 104; 132; CANR 73;
CDBLB 1914-1945; CMW 4; DAM NOV,
POET; DLB 10, 19, 34, 70, 98, 149, 178;
EWL 3; FANT; MSW; MTCW 1, 2;
RGEL 2; RGSF 2; SATA 27; SUFW 1

Chiang, Pin-chin 1904-1986
See Ding Ling
See also CA 118

Chief Joseph 1840-1904 .... **NNAL**
See also CA 152; DA3; DAM MULT

Chief Seattle 1786(?)-1866 .... **NNAL**
See also DA3; DAM MULT

Ch'ien, Chung-shu 1910-1998 .... **CLC 22**
See also CA 130; CANR 73; MTCW 1, 2

Chikamatsu Monzaemon 1653-1724 ... **LC 66**
See also RGWL 2, 3

Child, L. Maria
See Child, Lydia Maria

Child, Lydia Maria 1802-1880 .. **NCLC 6, 73**
See also DLB 1, 74, 243; RGAL 4; SATA
67

Child, Mrs.
See Child, Lydia Maria

Child, Philip 1898-1978 .... **CLC 19, 68**
See also CA 13-14; CAP 1; DLB 68; RHW;
SATA 47

Childers, (Robert) Erskine
1870-1922 .... **TCLC 65**
See also CA 113; 153; DLB 70

Clerihew, E.
See Bentley, E(dmund) C(lerihew)

Clerk, N. W.
See Lewis, C(live) S(taples)

Cliff, Jimmy .... **CLC 21**
See Chambers, James
See also CA 193

Cliff, Michelle 1946- .... **BLCS; CLC 120**
See also BW 2; CA 116; CANR 39, 72; CD-
WLB 3; DLB 157; FW; GLL 2

Clifford, Lady Anne 1590-1676 .... **LC 76**
See also DLB 151

Clifton, (Thelma) Lucille 1936- .... **BLC 1;
CLC 19, 66, 162; PC 17**
See also AFAW 2; BW 2, 3; CA 49-52;
CANR 2, 24, 42, 76, 97; CLR 5; CP 7;
CSW; CWP; CWRI 5; DA3; DAM MULT,
POET; DLB 5, 41; EXPP; MAICYA 1, 2;
MTCW 1, 2; PFS 1, 14; SATA 20, 69,
128; WP

Clinton, Dirk
See Silverberg, Robert

Clough, Arthur Hugh 1819-1861 ... **NCLC 27**
See also BRW 5; DLB 32; RGEL 2

Clutha, Janet Paterson Frame 1924-
See Frame, Janet
See also CA 1-4R; CANR 2, 36, 76; MTCW
1, 2; SATA 119

Clyne, Terence
See Blatty, William Peter

Cobalt, Martin
See Mayne, William (James Carter)

Cobb, Irvin S(hrewsbury)
1876-1944 .... **TCLC 77**
See also CA 175; DLB 11, 25, 86

Cobbett, William 1763-1835 .... **NCLC 49**
See also DLB 43, 107, 158; RGEL 2

Coburn, D(onald) L(ee) 1938- .... **CLC 10**
See also CA 89-92

Cocteau, Jean (Maurice Eugene Clement)
1889-1963 ...... **CLC 1, 8, 15, 16, 43; DC
17; TCLC 119; WLC**
See also CA 25-28; CANR 40; CAP 2; DA;
DA3; DAB; DAC; DAM DRAM, MST,
NOV; DLB 65, 258; EW 10; EWL 3; GFL
1789 to the Present; MTCW 1, 2; RGWL
2, 3; TWA

Codrescu, Andrei 1946- .... **CLC 46, 121**
See also CA 33-36R; CAAS 19; CANR 13,
34, 53, 76; DA3; DAM POET; MTCW 2

Coe, Max
See Bourne, Randolph S(illiman)

Coe, Tucker
See Westlake, Donald E(dwin)

Coen, Ethan 1958- .... **CLC 108**
See also CA 126; CANR 85

Coen, Joel 1955- .... **CLC 108**
See also CA 126; CANR 119

The Coen Brothers
See Coen, Ethan; Coen, Joel

Coetzee, J(ohn) M(ichael) 1940- ...... **CLC 23,
33, 66, 117, 161, 162**
See also AAYA 37; AFW; BRWS 6; CA 77-
80; CANR 41, 54, 74, 114; CN 7; DA3;
DAM NOV; DLB 225; EWL 3; LMFS 2;
MTCW 1, 2; WLIT 2

Coffey, Brian
See Koontz, Dean R(ay)

Coffin, Robert P(eter) Tristram
1892-1955 .... **TCLC 95**
See also CA 123; 169; DLB 45

Cohan, George M(ichael)
1878-1942 .... **TCLC 60**
See also CA 157; DLB 249; RGAL 4

Cohen, Arthur A(llen) 1928-1986 ...... **CLC 7,
31**
See also CA 1-4R; 120; CANR 1, 17, 42;
DLB 28

Cohen, Leonard (Norman) 1934- ...... **CLC 3,
38**
See also CA 21-24R; CANR 14, 69; CN 7;
CP 7; DAC; DAM MST; DLB 53; EWL
3; MTCW 1

Cohen, Matt(hew) 1942-1999 .... **CLC 19**
See also CA 61-64; 187; CAAS 18; CANR
40; CN 7; DAC; DLB 53

Cohen-Solal, Annie 19(?)- .... **CLC 50**

Colegate, Isabel 1931- .... **CLC 36**
See also CA 17-20R; CANR 8, 22, 74; CN
7; DLB 14, 231; INT CANR-22; MTCW
1

Coleman, Emmett
See Reed, Ishmael

Coleridge, Hartley 1796-1849 .... **NCLC 90**
See also DLB 96

Coleridge, M. E.
See Coleridge, Mary E(lizabeth)

Coleridge, Mary E(lizabeth)
1861-1907 .... **TCLC 73**
See also CA 116; 166; DLB 19, 98

Coleridge, Samuel Taylor
1772-1834 ...... **NCLC 9, 54, 99, 111; PC
11, 39; WLC**
See also BRW 4; BRWR 2; BYA 4; CD-
BLB 1789-1832; DA; DA3; DAB; DAC;
DAM MST, POET; DLB 93, 107; EXPP;
LATS 1; LMFS 1; PAB; PFS 4, 5; RGEL
2; TEA; WLIT 3; WP

Coleridge, Sara 1802-1852 .... **NCLC 31**
See also DLB 199

Coles, Don 1928- .... **CLC 46**
See also CA 115; CANR 38; CP 7

Coles, Robert (Martin) 1929- .... **CLC 108**
See also CA 45-48; CANR 3, 32, 66, 70;
INT CANR-32; SATA 23

Colette, (Sidonie-Gabrielle)
1873-1954 .... **SSC 10; TCLC 1, 5, 16**
See Willy, Colette
See also CA 104; 131; DA3; DAM NOV;
DLB 65; EW 9; EWL 3; GFL 1789 to the
Present; MTCW 1, 2; RGWL 2, 3; TWA

Collett, (Jacobine) Camilla (Wergeland)
1813-1895 .... **NCLC 22**

Collier, Christopher 1930- .... **CLC 30**
See also AAYA 13; BYA 2; CA 33-36R;
CANR 13, 33, 102; JRDA; MAICYA 1,
2; SATA 16, 70; WYA; YAW 1

Collier, James Lincoln 1928- .... **CLC 30**
See also AAYA 13; BYA 2; CA 9-12R;
CANR 4, 33, 60, 102; CLR 3; DAM POP;
JRDA; MAICYA 1, 2; SAAS 21; SATA 8,
70; WYA; YAW 1

Collier, Jeremy 1650-1726 .... **LC 6**

Collier, John 1901-1980 . **SSC 19; TCLC 127**
See also CA 65-68; 97-100; CANR 10;
DLB 77, 255; FANT; SUFW 1

Collier, Mary 1690-1762 .... **LC 86**
See also DLB 95

Collingwood, R(obin) G(eorge)
1889(?)-1943 .... **TCLC 67**
See also CA 117; 155; DLB 262

Collins, Hunt
See Hunter, Evan

Collins, Linda 1931- .... **CLC 44**
See also CA 125

Collins, Tom
See Furphy, Joseph
See also RGEL 2

Collins, (William) Wilkie
1824-1889 .... **NCLC 1, 18, 93**
See also BRWS 6; CDBLB 1832-1890;
CMW 4; DLB 18, 70, 159; MSW; RGEL
2; RGSF 2; SUFW 1; WLIT 4

Collins, William 1721-1759 .... **LC 4, 40**
See also BRW 3; DAM POET; DLB 109;
RGEL 2

Collodi, Carlo .... **NCLC 54**
See Lorenzini, Carlo
See also CLR 5; WCH

Colman, George
See Glassco, John

Colonna, Vittoria 1492-1547 .... **LC 71**
See also RGWL 2, 3

Colt, Winchester Remington
See Hubbard, L(afayette) Ron(ald)

Colter, Cyrus J. 1910-2002 .... **CLC 58**
See also BW 1; CA 65-68; 205; CANR 10,
66; CN 7; DLB 33

Colton, James
See Hansen, Joseph
See also GLL 1

Colum, Padraic 1881-1972 .... **CLC 28**
See also BYA 4; CA 73-76; 33-36R; CANR
35; CLR 36; CWRI 5; DLB 19; MAICYA
1, 2; MTCW 1; RGEL 2; SATA 15; WCH

Colvin, James
See Moorcock, Michael (John)

Colwin, Laurie (E.) 1944-1992 .... **CLC 5, 13,
23, 84**
See also CA 89-92; 139; CANR 20, 46;
DLB 218; DLBY 1980; MTCW 1

Comfort, Alex(ander) 1920-2000 .... **CLC 7**
See also CA 1-4R; 190; CANR 1, 45; CP 7;
DAM POP; MTCW 1

Comfort, Montgomery
See Campbell, (John) Ramsey

Compton-Burnett, I(vy)
1892(?)-1969 .... **CLC 1, 3, 10, 15, 34**
See also BRW 7; CA 1-4R; 25-28R; CANR
4; DAM NOV; DLB 36; EWL 3; MTCW
1; RGEL 2

Comstock, Anthony 1844-1915 ...... **TCLC 13**
See also CA 110; 169

Comte, Auguste 1798-1857 .... **NCLC 54**

Conan Doyle, Arthur
See Doyle, Sir Arthur Conan
See also BPFB 1; BYA 4, 5, 11

Conde (Abellan), Carmen
1901-1996 .... **HLCS 1**
See also CA 177; DLB 108; EWL 3; HW 2

Conde, Maryse 1937- ..... **BLCS; CLC 52, 92**
See also BW 2, 3; CA 110; CAAE 190;
CANR 30, 53, 76; CWW 2; DAM MULT;
EWL 3; MTCW 1

Condillac, Etienne Bonnot de
1714-1780 .... **LC 26**

Condon, Richard (Thomas)
1915-1996 .... **CLC 4, 6, 8, 10, 45, 100**
See also BEST 90:3; BPFB 1; CA 1-4R;
151; CAAS 1; CANR 2, 23; CMW 4; CN
7; DAM NOV; INT CANR-23; MTCW 1,
2

Confucius 551B.C.-479B.C. .... **CMLC 19;
WLCS**
See also DA; DA3; DAB; DAC; DAM
MST

Congreve, William 1670-1729 ... **DC 2; LC 5,
21; WLC**
See also BRW 2; CDBLB 1660-1789; DA;
DAB; DAC; DAM DRAM, MST, POET;
DFS 15; DLB 39, 84; RGEL 2; WLIT 3

Conley, Robert J(ackson) 1940- .... **NNAL**
See also CA 41-44R; CANR 15, 34, 45, 96;
DAM MULT

Connell, Evan S(helby), Jr. 1924- . **CLC 4, 6,
45**
See also AAYA 7; CA 1-4R; CAAS 2;
CANR 2, 39, 76, 97; CN 7; DAM NOV;
DLB 2; DLBY 1981; MTCW 1, 2

Connelly, Marc(us Cook) 1890-1980 . **CLC 7**
See also CA 85-88; 102; CANR 30; DFS
12; DLB 7; DLBY 1980; RGAL 4; SATA-
Obit 25

DLBD 2; DLBY 1984, 1997; EWL 3; MTCW 1, 2; RGAL 4

Crabbe, George 1754-1832 .... **NCLC 26, 121**
See also BRW 3; DLB 93; RGEL 2

Crace, Jim 1946- .... **CLC 157; SSC 61**
See also CA 128; 135; CANR 55, 70; CN 7; DLB 231; INT CA-135

Craddock, Charles Egbert
See Murfree, Mary Noailles

Craig, A. A.
See Anderson, Poul (William)

Craik, Mrs.
See Craik, Dinah Maria (Mulock)
See also RGEL 2

Craik, Dinah Maria (Mulock)
1826-1887 .... **NCLC 38**
See Craik, Mrs.; Mulock, Dinah Maria
See also DLB 35, 163; MAICYA 1, 2; SATA 34

Cram, Ralph Adams 1863-1942 ..... **TCLC 45**
See also CA 160

Cranch, Christopher Pearse
1813-1892 .... **NCLC 115**
See also DLB 1, 42, 243

Crane, (Harold) Hart 1899-1932 .... **PC 3; TCLC 2, 5, 80; WLC**
See also AMW; AMWR 2; CA 104; 127; CDALB 1917-1929; DA; DA3; DAB; DAC; DAM MST, POET; DLB 4, 48; EWL 3; MTCW 1, 2; RGAL 4; TUS

Crane, R(onald) S(almon)
1886-1967 .... **CLC 27**
See also CA 85-88; DLB 63

Crane, Stephen (Townley)
1871-1900 ...... **SSC 7, 56; TCLC 11, 17, 32; WLC**
See also AAYA 21; AMW; AMWC 1; BPFB 1; BYA 3; CA 109; 140; CANR 84; CDALB 1865-1917; DA; DA3; DAB; DAC; DAM MST, NOV, POET; DLB 12, 54, 78; EXPN; EXPS; LAIT 2; LMFS 2; NFS 4; PFS 9; RGAL 4; RGSF 2; SSFS 4; TUS; WYA; YABC 2

Cranshaw, Stanley
See Fisher, Dorothy (Frances) Canfield

Crase, Douglas 1944- .... **CLC 58**
See also CA 106

Crashaw, Richard 1612(?)-1649 .... **LC 24**
See also BRW 2; DLB 126; PAB; RGEL 2

Cratinus c. 519B.C.-c. 422B.C. ..... **CMLC 54**
See also LMFS 1

Craven, Margaret 1901-1980 .... **CLC 17**
See also BYA 2; CA 103; CCA 1; DAC; LAIT 5

Crawford, F(rancis) Marion
1854-1909 .... **TCLC 10**
See also CA 107; 168; DLB 71; HGG; RGAL 4; SUFW 1

Crawford, Isabella Valancy
1850-1887 .... **NCLC 12, 127**
See also DLB 92; RGEL 2

Crayon, Geoffrey
See Irving, Washington

Creasey, John 1908-1973 .... **CLC 11**
See Marric, J. J.
See also CA 5-8R; 41-44R; CANR 8, 59; CMW 4; DLB 77; MTCW 1

Crebillon, Claude Prosper Jolyot de (fils)
1707-1777 .... **LC 1, 28**
See also GFL Beginnings to 1789

Credo
See Creasey, John

Credo, Alvaro J. de
See Prado (Calvo), Pedro

Creeley, Robert (White) 1926- .. **CLC 1, 2, 4, 8, 11, 15, 36, 78**
See also AMWS 4; CA 1-4R; CAAS 10; CANR 23, 43, 89; CP 7; DA3; DAM

POET; DLB 5, 16, 169; DLBD 17; EWL 3; MTCW 1, 2; RGAL 4; WP

Crevecoeur, Hector St. John de
See Crevecoeur, Michel Guillaume Jean de
See also ANW

Crevecoeur, Michel Guillaume Jean de
1735-1813 .... **NCLC 105**
See Crevecoeur, Hector St. John de
See also AMWS 1; DLB 37

Crevel, Rene 1900-1935 .... **TCLC 112**
See also GLL 2

Crews, Harry (Eugene) 1935- ..... **CLC 6, 23, 49**
See also AITN 1; AMWS 11; BPFB 1; CA 25-28R; CANR 20, 57; CN 7; CSW; DA3; DLB 6, 143, 185; MTCW 1, 2; RGAL 4

Crichton, (John) Michael 1942- .... **CLC 2, 6, 54, 90**
See also AAYA 10, 49; AITN 2; BPFB 1; CA 25-28R; CANR 13, 40, 54, 76; CMW 4; CN 7; CPW; DA3; DAM NOV, POP; DLBY 1981; INT CANR-13; JRDA; MTCW 1, 2; SATA 9, 88; SFW 4; YAW

Crispin, Edmund .... **CLC 22**
See Montgomery, (Robert) Bruce
See also DLB 87; MSW

Cristofer, Michael 1945(?)- .... **CLC 28**
See also CA 110; 152; CAD; CD 5; DAM DRAM; DFS 15; DLB 7

Criton
See Alain

Croce, Benedetto 1866-1952 .... **TCLC 37**
See also CA 120; 155; EW 8; EWL 3

Crockett, David 1786-1836 .... **NCLC 8**
See also DLB 3, 11, 183, 248

Crockett, Davy
See Crockett, David

Crofts, Freeman Wills 1879-1957 .. **TCLC 55**
See also CA 115; 195; CMW 4; DLB 77; MSW

Croker, John Wilson 1780-1857 .... **NCLC 10**
See also DLB 110

Crommelynck, Fernand 1885-1970 .. **CLC 75**
See also CA 189; 89-92; EWL 3

Cromwell, Oliver 1599-1658 .... **LC 43**

Cronenberg, David 1943- .... **CLC 143**
See also CA 138; CCA 1

Cronin, A(rchibald) J(oseph)
1896-1981 .... **CLC 32**
See also BPFB 1; CA 1-4R; 102; CANR 5; DLB 191; SATA 47; SATA-Obit 25

Cross, Amanda
See Heilbrun, Carolyn G(old)
See also BPFB 1; CMW; CPW; MSW

Crothers, Rachel 1878-1958 .... **TCLC 19**
See also CA 113; 194; CAD; CWD; DLB 7, 266; RGAL 4

Croves, Hal
See Traven, B.

Crow Dog, Mary (Ellen) (?)- .... **CLC 93**
See Brave Bird, Mary
See also CA 154

Crowfield, Christopher
See Stowe, Harriet (Elizabeth) Beecher

Crowley, Aleister .... **TCLC 7**
See Crowley, Edward Alexander
See also GLL 1

Crowley, Edward Alexander 1875-1947
See Crowley, Aleister
See also CA 104; HGG

Crowley, John 1942- .... **CLC 57**
See also BPFB 1; CA 61-64; CANR 43, 98; DLBY 1982; SATA 65, 140; SFW 4; SUFW 2

Crud
See Crumb, R(obert)

Crumarums
See Crumb, R(obert)

Crumb, R(obert) 1943- .... **CLC 17**
See also CA 106; CANR 107

Crumbum
See Crumb, R(obert)

Crumski
See Crumb, R(obert)

Crum the Bum
See Crumb, R(obert)

Crunk
See Crumb, R(obert)

Crustt
See Crumb, R(obert)

Crutchfield, Les
See Trumbo, Dalton

Cruz, Victor Hernandez 1949- ... **HLC 1; PC 37**
See also BW 2; CA 65-68; CAAS 17; CANR 14, 32, 74; CP 7; DAM MULT, POET; DLB 41; DNFS 1; EXPP; HW 1, 2; MTCW 1; PFS 16; WP

Cryer, Gretchen (Kiger) 1935- .... **CLC 21**
See also CA 114; 123

Csath, Geza 1887-1919 .... **TCLC 13**
See also CA 111

Cudlip, David R(ockwell) 1933- .... **CLC 34**
See also CA 177

Cullen, Countee 1903-1946 .... **BLC 1; HR 2; PC 20; TCLC 4, 37; WLCS**
See also AFAW 2; AMWS 4; BW 1; CA 108; 124; CDALB 1917-1929; DA; DA3; DAC; DAM MST, MULT, POET; DLB 4, 48, 51; EWL 3; EXPP; LMFS 2; MTCW 1, 2; PFS 3; RGAL 4; SATA 18; WP

Culleton, Beatrice 1949- .... **NNAL**
See also CA 120; CANR 83; DAC

Cum, R.
See Crumb, R(obert)

Cummings, Bruce F(rederick) 1889-1919
See Barbellion, W. N. P.
See also CA 123

Cummings, E(dward) E(stlin)
1894-1962 .. **CLC 1, 3, 8, 12, 15, 68; PC 5; TCLC 137; WLC**
See also AAYA 41; AMW; CA 73-76; CANR 31; CDALB 1929-1941; DA; DA3; DAB; DAC; DAM MST, POET; DLB 4, 48; EWL 3; EXPP; MTCW 1, 2; PAB; PFS 1, 3, 12, 13; RGAL 4; TUS; WP

Cunha, Euclides (Rodrigues Pimenta) da
1866-1909 .... **TCLC 24**
See also CA 123; LAW; WLIT 1

Cunningham, E. V.
See Fast, Howard (Melvin)

Cunningham, J(ames) V(incent)
1911-1985 .... **CLC 3, 31**
See also CA 1-4R; 115; CANR 1, 72; DLB 5

Cunningham, Julia (Woolfolk)
1916- .... **CLC 12**
See also CA 9-12R; CANR 4, 19, 36; CWRI 5; JRDA; MAICYA 1, 2; SAAS 2; SATA 1, 26, 132

Cunningham, Michael 1952- .... **CLC 34**
See also CA 136; CANR 96; GLL 2

Cunninghame Graham, R. B.
See Cunninghame Graham, Robert (Gallnigad) Bontine

Cunninghame Graham, Robert (Gallnigad) Bontine 1852-1936 .... **TCLC 19**
See Graham, R(obert) B(ontine) Cunninghame
See also CA 119; 184

Curnow, (Thomas) Allen (Monro)
1911-2001 .... **PC 48**
See also CA 69-72; 202; CANR 48, 99; CP 7; EWL 3; RGEL 2

Currie, Ellen 19(?)- .... **CLC 44**
Curtin, Philip
   See Lowndes, Marie Adelaide (Belloc)
Curtin, Phillip
   See Lowndes, Marie Adelaide (Belloc)
Curtis, Price
   See Ellison, Harlan (Jay)
Cusanus, Nicolaus 1401-1464 .... **LC 80**
   See Nicholas of Cusa
Cutrate, Joe
   See Spiegelman, Art
Cynewulf c. 770- .... **CMLC 23**
   See also DLB 146; RGEL 2
Cyrano de Bergerac, Savinien de
   1619-1655 .... **LC 65**
   See also DLB 268; GFL Beginnings to
   1789; RGWL 2, 3
Cyril of Alexandria c. 375-c. 430 . **CMLC 59**
Czaczkes, Shmuel Yosef Halevi
   See Agnon, S(hmuel) Y(osef Halevi)
Dabrowska, Maria (Szumska)
   1889-1965 .... **CLC 15**
   See also CA 106; CDWLB 4; DLB 215;
   EWL 3
Dabydeen, David 1955- .... **CLC 34**
   See also BW 1; CA 125; CANR 56, 92; CN
   7; CP 7
Dacey, Philip 1939- .... **CLC 51**
   See also CA 37-40R; CAAS 17; CANR 14,
   32, 64; CP 7; DLB 105
Dagerman, Stig (Halvard)
   1923-1954 .... **TCLC 17**
   See also CA 117; 155; DLB 259; EWL 3
D'Aguiar, Fred 1960- .... **CLC 145**
   See also CA 148; CANR 83, 101; CP 7;
   DLB 157; EWL 3
Dahl, Roald 1916-1990 .... **CLC 1, 6, 18, 79**
   See also AAYA 15; BPFB 1; BRWS 4; BYA
   5; CA 1-4R; 133; CANR 6, 32, 37, 62;
   CLR 1, 7, 41; CPW; DA3; DAB; DAC;
   DAM MST, NOV, POP; DLB 139, 255;
   HGG; JRDA; MAICYA 1, 2; MTCW 1,
   2; RGSF 2; SATA 1, 26, 73; SATA-Obit
   65; SSFS 4; TEA; YAW
Dahlberg, Edward 1900-1977 .. **CLC 1, 7, 14**
   See also CA 9-12R; 69-72; CANR 31, 62;
   DLB 48; MTCW 1; RGAL 4
Daitch, Susan 1954- .... **CLC 103**
   See also CA 161
Dale, Colin .... **TCLC 18**
   See Lawrence, T(homas) E(dward)
Dale, George E.
   See Asimov, Isaac
Dalton, Roque 1935-1975(?) ..... **HLCS 1; PC 36**
   See also CA 176; DLB 283; HW 2
Daly, Elizabeth 1878-1967 .... **CLC 52**
   See also CA 23-24; 25-28R; CANR 60;
   CAP 2; CMW 4
Daly, Mary 1928- .... **CLC 173**
   See also CA 25-28R; CANR 30, 62; FW;
   GLL 1; MTCW 1
Daly, Maureen 1921- .... **CLC 17**
   See also AAYA 5; BYA 6; CANR 37, 83,
   108; JRDA; MAICYA 1, 2; SAAS 1;
   SATA 2, 129; WYA; YAW
Damas, Leon-Gontran 1912-1978 .... **CLC 84**
   See also BW 1; CA 125; 73-76; EWL 3
Dana, Richard Henry Sr.
   1787-1879 .... **NCLC 53**
Daniel, Samuel 1562(?)-1619 .... **LC 24**
   See also DLB 62; RGEL 2
Daniels, Brett
   See Adler, Renata
Dannay, Frederic 1905-1982 .... **CLC 11**
   See Queen, Ellery
   See also CA 1-4R; 107; CANR 1, 39; CMW
   4; DAM POP; DLB 137; MTCW 1

D'Annunzio, Gabriele 1863-1938 ... **TCLC 6, 40**
   See also CA 104; 155; EW 8; EWL 3;
   RGWL 2, 3; TWA
Danois, N. le
   See Gourmont, Remy(-Marie-Charles) de
Dante 1265-1321 .... **CMLC 3, 18, 39; PC 21; WLCS**
   See also DA; DA3; DAB; DAC; DAM
   MST, POET; EFS 1; EW 1; LAIT 1;
   RGWL 2, 3; TWA; WP
d'Antibes, Germain
   See Simenon, Georges (Jacques Christian)
Danticat, Edwidge 1969- .... **CLC 94, 139**
   See also AAYA 29; CA 152; CAAE 192;
   CANR 73; DNFS 1; EXPS; LATS 1;
   MTCW 1; SSFS 1; YAW
Danvers, Dennis 1947- .... **CLC 70**
Danziger, Paula 1944- .... **CLC 21**
   See also AAYA 4, 36; BYA 6, 7, 14; CA
   112; 115; CANR 37; CLR 20; JRDA;
   MAICYA 1, 2; SATA 36, 63, 102; SATA-
   Brief 30; WYA; YAW
Da Ponte, Lorenzo 1749-1838 .... **NCLC 50**
Dario, Ruben 1867-1916 .... **HLC 1; PC 15; TCLC 4**
   See also CA 131; CANR 81; DAM MULT;
   EWL 3; HW 1, 2; LAW; MTCW 1, 2;
   RGWL 2, 3
Darley, George 1795-1846 .... **NCLC 2**
   See also DLB 96; RGEL 2
Darrow, Clarence (Seward)
   1857-1938 .... **TCLC 81**
   See also CA 164
Darwin, Charles 1809-1882 .... **NCLC 57**
   See also BRWS 7; DLB 57, 166; LATS 1;
   RGEL 2; TEA; WLIT 4
Darwin, Erasmus 1731-1802 .... **NCLC 106**
   See also DLB 93; RGEL 2
Daryush, Elizabeth 1887-1977 ...... **CLC 6, 19**
   See also CA 49-52; CANR 3, 81; DLB 20
Das, Kamala 1934- .... **PC 43**
   See also CA 101; CANR 27, 59; CP 7;
   CWP; FW
Dasgupta, Surendranath
   1887-1952 .... **TCLC 81**
   See also CA 157
Dashwood, Edmee Elizabeth Monica de la
   Pasture 1890-1943
   See Delafield, E. M.
   See also CA 119; 154
da Silva, Antonio Jose
   1705-1739 .... **NCLC 114**
Daudet, (Louis Marie) Alphonse
   1840-1897 .... **NCLC 1**
   See also DLB 123; GFL 1789 to the Present;
   RGSF 2
Daumal, Rene 1908-1944 .... **TCLC 14**
   See also CA 114; EWL 3
Davenant, William 1606-1668 .... **LC 13**
   See also DLB 58, 126; RGEL 2
Davenport, Guy (Mattison, Jr.)
   1927- .... **CLC 6, 14, 38; SSC 16**
   See also CA 33-36R; CANR 23, 73; CN 7;
   CSW; DLB 130
David, Robert
   See Nezval, Vitezslav
Davidson, Avram (James) 1923-1993
   See Queen, Ellery
   See also CA 101; 171; CANR 26; DLB 8;
   FANT; SFW 4; SUFW 1, 2
Davidson, Donald (Grady)
   1893-1968 .... **CLC 2, 13, 19**
   See also CA 5-8R; 25-28R; CANR 4, 84;
   DLB 45
Davidson, Hugh
   See Hamilton, Edmond
Davidson, John 1857-1909 .... **TCLC 24**
   See also CA 118; DLB 19; RGEL 2

Davidson, Sara 1943- .... **CLC 9**
   See also CA 81-84; CANR 44, 68; DLB
   185
Davie, Donald (Alfred) 1922-1995 .... **CLC 5, 8, 10, 31; PC 29**
   See also BRWS 6; CA 1-4R; 149; CAAS 3;
   CANR 1, 44; CP 7; DLB 27; MTCW 1;
   RGEL 2
Davie, Elspeth 1919-1995 .... **SSC 52**
   See also CA 120; 126; 150; DLB 139
Davies, Ray(mond Douglas) 1944- ... **CLC 21**
   See also CA 116; 146; CANR 92
Davies, Rhys 1901-1978 .... **CLC 23**
   See also CA 9-12R; 81-84; CANR 4; DLB
   139, 191
Davies, (William) Robertson
   1913-1995 .... **CLC 2, 7, 13, 25, 42, 75, 91; WLC**
   See Marchbanks, Samuel
   See also BEST 89:2; BPFB 1; CA 33-36R;
   150; CANR 17, 42, 103; CN 7; CPW;
   DA; DA3; DAB; DAC; DAM MST, NOV,
   POP; DLB 68; EWL 3; HGG; INT CANR-
   17; MTCW 1, 2; RGEL 2; TWA
Davies, Sir John 1569-1626 .... **LC 85**
   See also DLB 172
Davies, Walter C.
   See Kornbluth, C(yril) M.
Davies, William Henry 1871-1940 ... **TCLC 5**
   See also CA 104; 179; DLB 19, 174; EWL
   3; RGEL 2
Da Vinci, Leonardo 1452-1519 ..... **LC 12, 57, 60**
   See also AAYA 40
Davis, Angela (Yvonne) 1944- .... **CLC 77**
   See also BW 2, 3; CA 57-60; CANR 10,
   81; CSW; DA3; DAM MULT; FW
Davis, B. Lynch
   See Bioy Casares, Adolfo; Borges, Jorge
   Luis
Davis, Frank Marshall 1905-1987 ...... **BLC 1**
   See also BW 2, 3; CA 125; 123; CANR 42,
   80; DAM MULT; DLB 51
Davis, Gordon
   See Hunt, E(verette) Howard, (Jr.)
Davis, H(arold) L(enoir) 1896-1960 . **CLC 49**
   See also ANW; CA 178; 89-92; DLB 9,
   206; SATA 114
Davis, Rebecca (Blaine) Harding
   1831-1910 .... **SSC 38; TCLC 6**
   See also CA 104; 179; DLB 74, 239; FW;
   NFS 14; RGAL 4; TUS
Davis, Richard Harding
   1864-1916 .... **TCLC 24**
   See also CA 114; 179; DLB 12, 23, 78, 79,
   189; DLBD 13; RGAL 4
Davison, Frank Dalby 1893-1970 ..... **CLC 15**
   See also CA 116; DLB 260
Davison, Lawrence H.
   See Lawrence, D(avid) H(erbert Richards)
Davison, Peter (Hubert) 1928- .... **CLC 28**
   See also CA 9-12R; CAAS 4; CANR 3, 43,
   84; CP 7; DLB 5
Davys, Mary 1674-1732 .... **LC 1, 46**
   See also DLB 39
Dawson, (Guy) Fielding (Lewis)
   1930-2002 .... **CLC 6**
   See also CA 85-88; 202; CANR 108; DLB
   130; DLBY 2002
Dawson, Peter
   See Faust, Frederick (Schiller)
   See also TCWW 2, 2
Day, Clarence (Shepard, Jr.)
   1874-1935 .... **TCLC 25**
   See also CA 108; 199; DLB 11
Day, John 1574(?)-1640(?) .... **LC 70**
   See also DLB 62, 170; RGEL 2
Day, Thomas 1748-1789 .... **LC 1**
   See also DLB 39; YABC 1

Doeblin, Alfred 1878-1957 .... **TCLC 13**
See Doblin, Alfred
See also CA 110; 141; DLB 66

Doerr, Harriet 1910- .... **CLC 34**
See also CA 117; 122; CANR 47; INT CA-122; LATS 1

Domecq, H(onorio Bustos)
See Bioy Casares, Adolfo

Domecq, H(onorio) Bustos
See Bioy Casares, Adolfo; Borges, Jorge Luis

Domini, Rey
See Lorde, Audre (Geraldine)
See also GLL 1

Dominique
See Proust, (Valentin-Louis-George-Eugene-)Marcel

Don, A
See Stephen, Sir Leslie

Donaldson, Stephen R(eeder)
1947- .... **CLC 46, 138**
See also AAYA 36; BPFB 1; CA 89-92; CANR 13, 55, 99; CPW; DAM POP; FANT; INT CANR-13; SATA 121; SFW 4; SUFW 1, 2

Donleavy, J(ames) P(atrick) 1926- .... **CLC 1, 4, 6, 10, 45**
See also AITN 2; BPFB 1; CA 9-12R; CANR 24, 49, 62, 80; CBD; CD 5; CN 7; DLB 6, 173; INT CANR-24; MTCW 1, 2; RGAL 4

Donnadieu, Marguerite
See Duras, Marguerite
See also CWW 2

Donne, John 1572-1631 ... **LC 10, 24, 91; PC 1, 43; WLC**
See also BRW 1; BRWC 1; BRWR 2; CD-BLB Before 1660; DA; DAB; DAC; DAM MST, POET; DLB 121, 151; EXPP; PAB; PFS 2, 11; RGEL 2; TEA; WLIT 3; WP

Donnell, David 1939(?)- .... **CLC 34**
See also CA 197

Donoghue, P. S.
See Hunt, E(verette) Howard, (Jr.)

Donoso (Yanez), Jose 1924-1996 ... **CLC 4, 8, 11, 32, 99; HLC 1; SSC 34; TCLC 133**
See also CA 81-84; 155; CANR 32, 73; CD-WLB 3; DAM MULT; DLB 113; EWL 3; HW 1, 2; LAW; LAWS 1; MTCW 1, 2; RGSF 2; WLIT 1

Donovan, John 1928-1992 .... **CLC 35**
See also AAYA 20; CA 97-100; 137; CLR 3; MAICYA 1, 2; SATA 72; SATA-Brief 29; YAW

Don Roberto
See Cunninghame Graham, Robert (Gallnigad) Bontine

Doolittle, Hilda 1886-1961 . **CLC 3, 8, 14, 31, 34, 73; PC 5; WLC**
See H. D.
See also AMWS 1; CA 97-100; CANR 35; DA; DAC; DAM MST, POET; DLB 4, 45; EWL 3; FW; GLL 1; LMFS 2; MAWW; MTCW 1, 2; PFS 6; RGAL 4

Doppo, Kunikida .... **TCLC 99**
See Kunikida Doppo

Dorfman, Ariel 1942- .... **CLC 48, 77; HLC 1**
See also CA 124; 130; CANR 67, 70; CWW 2; DAM MULT; DFS 4; EWL 3; HW 1, 2; INT CA-130; WLIT 1

Dorn, Edward (Merton)
1929-1999 .... **CLC 10, 18**
See also CA 93-96; 187; CANR 42, 79; CP 7; DLB 5; INT 93-96; WP

Dor-Ner, Zvi .... **CLC 70**

Dorris, Michael (Anthony)
1945-1997 .... **CLC 109; NNAL**
See also AAYA 20; BEST 90:1; BYA 12; CA 102; 157; CANR 19, 46, 75; CLR 58; DA3; DAM MULT, NOV; DLB 175; LAIT 5; MTCW 2; NFS 3; RGAL 4; SATA 75; SATA-Obit 94; TCWW 2; YAW

Dorris, Michael A.
See Dorris, Michael (Anthony)

Dorsan, Luc
See Simenon, Georges (Jacques Christian)

Dorsange, Jean
See Simenon, Georges (Jacques Christian)

Dos Passos, John (Roderigo)
1896-1970 ... **CLC 1, 4, 8, 11, 15, 25, 34, 82; WLC**
See also AMW; BPFB 1; CA 1-4R; 29-32R; CANR 3; CDALB 1929-1941; DA; DA3; DAB; DAC; DAM MST, NOV; DLB 4, 9; DLBD 1, 15, 274; DLBY 1996; EWL 3; MTCW 1, 2; NFS 14; RGAL 4; TUS

Dossage, Jean
See Simenon, Georges (Jacques Christian)

Dostoevsky, Fedor Mikhailovich
1821-1881 .. **NCLC 2, 7, 21, 33, 43, 119; SSC 2, 33, 44; WLC**
See Dostoevsky, Fyodor
See also AAYA 40; DA; DA3; DAB; DAC; DAM MST, NOV; EW 7; EXPN; NFS 3, 8; RGSF 2; RGWL 2, 3; SSFS 8; TWA

Dostoevsky, Fyodor
See Dostoevsky, Fedor Mikhailovich
See also DLB 238; LATS 1; LMFS 1, 2

Doty, M. R.
See Doty, Mark (Alan)

Doty, Mark
See Doty, Mark (Alan)

Doty, Mark (Alan) 1953(?)- .... **CLC 176**
See also AMWS 11; CA 161, 183; CAAE 183; CANR 110

Doty, Mark A.
See Doty, Mark (Alan)

Doughty, Charles M(ontagu)
1843-1926 .... **TCLC 27**
See also CA 115; 178; DLB 19, 57, 174

Douglas, Ellen .... **CLC 73**
See Haxton, Josephine Ayres; Williamson, Ellen Douglas
See also CN 7; CSW

Douglas, Gavin 1475(?)-1522 .... **LC 20**
See also DLB 132; RGEL 2

Douglas, George
See Brown, George Douglas
See also RGEL 2

Douglas, Keith (Castellain)
1920-1944 .... **TCLC 40**
See also BRW 7; CA 160; DLB 27; EWL 3; PAB; RGEL 2

Douglas, Leonard
See Bradbury, Ray (Douglas)

Douglas, Michael
See Crichton, (John) Michael

Douglas, (George) Norman
1868-1952 .... **TCLC 68**
See also BRW 6; CA 119; 157; DLB 34, 195; RGEL 2

Douglas, William
See Brown, George Douglas

Douglass, Frederick 1817(?)-1895 ..... **BLC 1; NCLC 7, 55; WLC**
See also AAYA 48; AFAW 1, 2; AMWC 1; AMWS 3; CDALB 1640-1865; DA; DA3; DAC; DAM MST, MULT; DLB 1, 43, 50, 79, 243; FW; LAIT 2; NCFS 2; RGAL 4; SATA 29

Dourado, (Waldomiro Freitas) Autran
1926- .... **CLC 23, 60**
See also CA 25-28R; 179; CANR 34, 81; DLB 145; HW 2

Dourado, Waldomiro Autran
See Dourado, (Waldomiro Freitas) Autran
See also CA 179

Dove, Rita (Frances) 1952- . **BLCS; CLC 50, 81; PC 6**
See also AAYA 46; AMWS 4; BW 2; CA 109; CAAS 19; CANR 27, 42, 68, 76, 97; CDALBS; CP 7; CSW; CWP; DA3; DAM MULT, POET; DLB 120; EWL 3; EXPP; MTCW 1; PFS 1, 15; RGAL 4

Doveglion
See Villa, Jose Garcia

Dowell, Coleman 1925-1985 .... **CLC 60**
See also CA 25-28R; 117; CANR 10; DLB 130; GLL 2

Dowson, Ernest (Christopher)
1867-1900 .... **TCLC 4**
See also CA 105; 150; DLB 19, 135; RGEL 2

Doyle, A. Conan
See Doyle, Sir Arthur Conan

Doyle, Sir Arthur Conan
1859-1930 .... **SSC 12; TCLC 7; WLC**
See Conan Doyle, Arthur
See also AAYA 14; BRWS 2; CA 104; 122; CDBLB 1890-1914; CMW 4; DA; DA3; DAB; DAC; DAM MST, NOV; DLB 18, 70, 156, 178; EXPS; HGG; LAIT 2; MSW; MTCW 1, 2; RGEL 2; RGSF 2; RHW; SATA 24; SCFW 2; SFW 4; SSFS 2; TEA; WCH; WLIT 4; WYA; YAW

Doyle, Conan
See Doyle, Sir Arthur Conan

Doyle, John
See Graves, Robert (von Ranke)

Doyle, Roddy 1958(?)- .... **CLC 81, 178**
See also AAYA 14; BRWS 5; CA 143; CANR 73; CN 7; DA3; DLB 194

Doyle, Sir A. Conan
See Doyle, Sir Arthur Conan

Dr. A
See Asimov, Isaac; Silverstein, Alvin; Silverstein, Virginia B(arbara Opshelor)

Drabble, Margaret 1939- ...... **CLC 2, 3, 5, 8, 10, 22, 53, 129**
See also BRWS 4; CA 13-16R; CANR 18, 35, 63, 112; CDBLB 1960 to Present; CN 7; CPW; DA3; DAB; DAC; DAM MST, NOV, POP; DLB 14, 155, 231; EWL 3; FW; MTCW 1, 2; RGEL 2; SATA 48; TEA

Drakulic, Slavenka 1949- .... **CLC 173**
See also CA 144; CANR 92

Drakulic-Ilic, Slavenka
See Drakulic, Slavenka

Drapier, M. B.
See Swift, Jonathan

Drayham, James
See Mencken, H(enry) L(ouis)

Drayton, Michael 1563-1631 .... **LC 8**
See also DAM POET; DLB 121; RGEL 2

Dreadstone, Carl
See Campbell, (John) Ramsey

Dreiser, Theodore (Herman Albert)
1871-1945 .... **SSC 30; TCLC 10, 18, 35, 83; WLC**
See also AMW; AMWR 2; CA 106; 132; CDALB 1865-1917; DA; DA3; DAC; DAM MST, NOV; DLB 9, 12, 102, 137; DLBD 1; EWL 3; LAIT 2; LMFS 2; MTCW 1, 2; NFS 17; RGAL 4; TUS

Drexler, Rosalyn 1926- .... **CLC 2, 6**
See also CA 81-84; CAD; CANR 68; CD 5; CWD

Dreyer, Carl Theodor 1889-1968 ...... **CLC 16**
See also CA 116

Drieu la Rochelle, Pierre(-Eugene)
1893-1945 .... **TCLC 21**
See also CA 117; DLB 72; EWL 3; GFL
1789 to the Present

Drinkwater, John 1882-1937 .... **TCLC 57**
See also CA 109; 149; DLB 10, 19, 149;
RGEL 2

Drop Shot
See Cable, George Washington

Droste-Hulshoff, Annette Freiin von
1797-1848 .... **NCLC 3**
See also CDWLB 2; DLB 133; RGSF 2;
RGWL 2, 3

Drummond, Walter
See Silverberg, Robert

Drummond, William Henry
1854-1907 .... **TCLC 25**
See also CA 160; DLB 92

Drummond de Andrade, Carlos
1902-1987 .... **CLC 18; TCLC 139**
See Andrade, Carlos Drummond de
See also CA 132; 123; LAW

Drummond of Hawthornden, William
1585-1649 .... **LC 83**
See also DLB 121, 213; RGEL 2

Drury, Allen (Stuart) 1918-1998 .... **CLC 37**
See also CA 57-60; 170; CANR 18, 52; CN
7; INT CANR-18

Dryden, John 1631-1700 ..... **DC 3; LC 3, 21;
PC 25; WLC**
See also BRW 2; CDBLB 1660-1789; DA;
DAB; DAC; DAM DRAM, MST, POET;
DLB 80, 101, 131; EXPP; IDTP; LMFS
1; RGEL 2; TEA; WLIT 3

du Bellay, Joachim 1524-1560 .... **LC 92**
See also GFL Beginnings to 1789; RGWL
2, 3

Duberman, Martin (Bauml) 1930- ..... **CLC 8**
See also CA 1-4R; CAD; CANR 2, 63; CD
5

Dubie, Norman (Evans) 1945- .... **CLC 36**
See also CA 69-72; CANR 12, 115; CP 7;
DLB 120; PFS 12

Du Bois, W(illiam) E(dward) B(urghardt)
1868-1963 ..... **BLC 1; CLC 1, 2, 13, 64,
96; HR 2; WLC**
See also AAYA 40; AFAW 1, 2; AMWC 1;
AMWS 2; BW 1, 3; CA 85-88; CANR
34, 82; CDALB 1865-1917; DA; DA3;
DAC; DAM MST, MULT, NOV; DLB 47,
50, 91, 246, 284; EWL 3; EXPP; LAIT
2; LMFS 2; MTCW 1, 2; NCFS 1; PFS 13;
RGAL 4; SATA 42

Dubus, Andre 1936-1999 ..... **CLC 13, 36, 97;
SSC 15**
See also AMWS 7; CA 21-24R; 177; CANR
17; CN 7; CSW; DLB 130; INT CANR-
17; RGAL 4; SSFS 10

Duca Minimo
See D'Annunzio, Gabriele

Ducharme, Rejean 1941- .... **CLC 74**
See also CA 165; DLB 60

Duchen, Claire .... **CLC 65**

Duclos, Charles Pinot- 1704-1772 .... **LC 1**
See also GFL Beginnings to 1789

Dudek, Louis 1918- .... **CLC 11, 19**
See also CA 45-48; CAAS 14; CANR 1;
CP 7; DLB 88

Duerrenmatt, Friedrich 1921-1990 ... **CLC 1,
4, 8, 11, 15, 43, 102**
See Durrenmatt, Friedrich
See also CA 17-20R; CANR 33; CMW 4;
DAM DRAM; DLB 69, 124; MTCW 1, 2

Duffy, Bruce 1953(?)- .... **CLC 50**
See also CA 172

Duffy, Maureen 1933- .... **CLC 37**
See also CA 25-28R; CANR 33, 68; CBD;
CN 7; CP 7; CWD; CWP; DFS 15; DLB
14; FW; MTCW 1

Du Fu
See Tu Fu
See also RGWL 2, 3

Dugan, Alan 1923- .... **CLC 2, 6**
See also CA 81-84; CANR 119; CP 7; DLB
5; PFS 10

du Gard, Roger Martin
See Martin du Gard, Roger

Duhamel, Georges 1884-1966 .... **CLC 8**
See also CA 81-84; 25-28R; CANR 35;
DLB 65; EWL 3; GFL 1789 to the
Present; MTCW 1

Dujardin, Edouard (Emile Louis)
1861-1949 .... **TCLC 13**
See also CA 109; DLB 123

Duke, Raoul
See Thompson, Hunter S(tockton)

Dulles, John Foster 1888-1959 .... **TCLC 72**
See also CA 115; 149

Dumas, Alexandre (pere)
1802-1870 .... **NCLC 11, 71; WLC**
See also AAYA 22; BYA 3; DA; DA3;
DAB; DAC; DAM MST, NOV; DLB 119,
192; EW 6; GFL 1789 to the Present;
LAIT 1, 2; NFS 14; RGWL 2, 3; SATA
18; TWA; WCH

Dumas, Alexandre (fils) 1824-1895 ...... **DC 1;
NCLC 9**
See also DLB 192; GFL 1789 to the Present;
RGWL 2, 3

Dumas, Claudine
See Malzberg, Barry N(athaniel)

Dumas, Henry L. 1934-1968 .... **CLC 6, 62**
See also BW 1; CA 85-88; DLB 41; RGAL
4

du Maurier, Daphne 1907-1989 .. **CLC 6, 11,
59; SSC 18**
See also AAYA 37; BPFB 1; BRWS 3; CA
5-8R; 128; CANR 6, 55; CMW 4; CPW;
DA3; DAB; DAC; DAM MST, POP;
DLB 191; HGG; LAIT 3; MSW; MTCW
1, 2; NFS 12; RGEL 2; RGSF 2; RHW;
SATA 27; SATA-Obit 60; SSFS 14, 16;
TEA

Du Maurier, George 1834-1896 ..... **NCLC 86**
See also DLB 153, 178; RGEL 2

Dunbar, Paul Laurence 1872-1906 ... **BLC 1;
PC 5; SSC 8; TCLC 2, 12; WLC**
See also AFAW 1, 2; AMWS 2; BW 1, 3;
CA 104; 124; CANR 79; CDALB 1865-
1917; DA; DA3; DAC; DAM MST,
MULT, POET; DLB 50, 54, 78; EXPP;
RGAL 4; SATA 34

Dunbar, William 1460(?)-1520(?) .... **LC 20**
See also BRWS 8; DLB 132, 146; RGEL 2

Dunbar-Nelson, Alice .... **HR 2**
See Nelson, Alice Ruth Moore Dunbar

Duncan, Dora Angela
See Duncan, Isadora

Duncan, Isadora 1877(?)-1927 .... **TCLC 68**
See also CA 118; 149

Duncan, Lois 1934- .... **CLC 26**
See also AAYA 4, 34; BYA 6, 8; CA 1-4R;
CANR 2, 23, 36, 111; CLR 29; JRDA;
MAICYA 1, 2; MAICYAS 1; SAAS 2;
SATA 1, 36, 75, 133, 141; WYA; YAW

Duncan, Robert (Edward)
1919-1988 .... **CLC 1, 2, 4, 7, 15, 41, 55;
PC 2**
See also BG 2; CA 9-12R; 124; CANR 28,
62; DAM POET; DLB 5, 16, 193; EWL
3; MTCW 1, 2; PFS 13; RGAL 4; WP

Duncan, Sara Jeannette
1861-1922 .... **TCLC 60**
See also CA 157; DLB 92

Dunlap, William 1766-1839 .... **NCLC 2**
See also DLB 30, 37, 59; RGAL 4

Dunn, Douglas (Eaglesham) 1942- .... **CLC 6,
40**
See also CA 45-48; CANR 2, 33; CP 7;
DLB 40; MTCW 1

Dunn, Katherine (Karen) 1945- .... **CLC 71**
See also CA 33-36R; CANR 72; HGG;
MTCW 1

Dunn, Stephen (Elliott) 1939- .... **CLC 36**
See also AMWS 11; CA 33-36R; CANR
12, 48, 53, 105; CP 7; DLB 105

Dunne, Finley Peter 1867-1936 ...... **TCLC 28**
See also CA 108; 178; DLB 11, 23; RGAL
4

Dunne, John Gregory 1932- .... **CLC 28**
See also CA 25-28R; CANR 14, 50; CN 7;
DLBY 1980

Dunsany, Lord .... **TCLC 2, 59**
See Dunsany, Edward John Moreton Drax
Plunkett
See also DLB 77, 153, 156, 255; FANT;
IDTP; RGEL 2; SFW 4; SUFW 1

**Dunsany, Edward John Moreton Drax
Plunkett** 1878-1957
See Dunsany, Lord
See also CA 104; 148; DLB 10; MTCW 1

Duns Scotus, John 1266(?)-1308 ... **CMLC 59**
See also DLB 115

du Perry, Jean
See Simenon, Georges (Jacques Christian)

Durang, Christopher (Ferdinand)
1949- .... **CLC 27, 38**
See also CA 105; CAD; CANR 50, 76; CD
5; MTCW 1

Duras, Marguerite 1914-1996 . **CLC 3, 6, 11,
20, 34, 40, 68, 100; SSC 40**
See Donnadieu, Marguerite
See also BPFB 1; CA 25-28R; 151; CANR
50; CWW 2; DLB 83; EWL 3; GFL 1789
to the Present; IDFW 4; MTCW 1, 2;
RGWL 2, 3; TWA

Durban, (Rosa) Pam 1947- .... **CLC 39**
See also CA 123; CANR 98; CSW

Durcan, Paul 1944- .... **CLC 43, 70**
See also CA 134; CP 7; DAM POET; EWL
3

Durkheim, Emile 1858-1917 .... **TCLC 55**

Durrell, Lawrence (George)
1912-1990 ..... **CLC 1, 4, 6, 8, 13, 27, 41**
See also BPFB 1; BRWS 1; CA 9-12R; 132;
CANR 40, 77; CDBLB 1945-1960; DAM
NOV; DLB 15, 27, 204; DLBY 1990;
EWL 3; MTCW 1, 2; RGEL 2; SFW 4;
TEA

Durrenmatt, Friedrich
See Duerrenmatt, Friedrich
See also CDWLB 2; EW 13; EWL 3;
RGWL 2, 3

Dutt, Michael Madhusudan
1824-1873 .... **NCLC 118**

Dutt, Toru 1856-1877 .... **NCLC 29**
See also DLB 240

Dwight, Timothy 1752-1817 .... **NCLC 13**
See also DLB 37; RGAL 4

Dworkin, Andrea 1946- .... **CLC 43, 123**
See also CA 77-80; CAAS 21; CANR 16,
39, 76, 96; FW; GLL 1; INT CANR-16;
MTCW 1, 2

Dwyer, Deanna
See Koontz, Dean R(ay)

Dwyer, K. R.
See Koontz, Dean R(ay)

Dybek, Stuart 1942- .... **CLC 114; SSC 55**
See also CA 97-100; CANR 39; DLB 130

Dye, Richard
See De Voto, Bernard (Augustine)

Dyer, Geoff 1958- .... **CLC 149**
See also CA 125; CANR 88

Dyer, George 1755-1841 .... **NCLC 129**
See also DLB 93

Dylan, Bob 1941- .... **CLC 3, 4, 6, 12, 77; PC 37**
See also CA 41-44R; CANR 108; CP 7; DLB 16

Dyson, John 1943- .... **CLC 70**
See also CA 144

Dzyubin, Eduard Georgievich 1895-1934
See Bagritsky, Eduard
See also CA 170

E. V. L.
See Lucas, E(dward) V(errall)

Eagleton, Terence (Francis) 1943- .. **CLC 63, 132**
See also CA 57-60; CANR 7, 23, 68, 115; DLB 242; LMFS 2; MTCW 1, 2

Eagleton, Terry
See Eagleton, Terence (Francis)

Early, Jack
See Scoppettone, Sandra
See also GLL 1

East, Michael
See West, Morris L(anglo)

Eastaway, Edward
See Thomas, (Philip) Edward

Eastlake, William (Derry)
1917-1997 .... **CLC 8**
See also CA 5-8R; 158; CAAS 1; CANR 5, 63; CN 7; DLB 6, 206; INT CANR-5; TCWW 2

Eastman, Charles A(lexander)
1858-1939 .... **NNAL; TCLC 55**
See also CA 179; CANR 91; DAM MULT; DLB 175; YABC 1

Eaton, Edith Maude 1865-1914 .... **AAL**
See Far, Sui Sin
See also CA 154; DLB 221; FW

Eaton, Winnifred 1875-1954 .... **AAL**
See also DLB 221; RGAL 4

Eberhart, Richard (Ghormley)
1904- .... **CLC 3, 11, 19, 56**
See also AMW; CA 1-4R; CANR 2; CDALB 1941-1968; CP 7; DAM POET; DLB 48; MTCW 1; RGAL 4

Eberstadt, Fernanda 1960- .... **CLC 39**
See also CA 136; CANR 69

Echegaray (y Eizaguirre), Jose (Maria Waldo) 1832-1916 .... **HLCS 1; TCLC 4**
See also CA 104; CANR 32; EWL 3; HW 1; MTCW 1

Echeverria, (Jose) Esteban (Antonino)
1805-1851 .... **NCLC 18**
See also LAW

Echo
See Proust, (Valentin-Louis-George-Eugene-)Marcel

Eckert, Allan W. 1931- .... **CLC 17**
See also AAYA 18; BYA 2; CA 13-16R; CANR 14, 45; INT CANR-14; MAICYA 2; MAICYAS 1; SAAS 21; SATA 29, 91; SATA-Brief 27

Eckhart, Meister 1260(?)-1327(?) ... **CMLC 9**
See also DLB 115; LMFS 1

Eckmar, F. R.
See de Hartog, Jan

Eco, Umberto 1932- .... **CLC 28, 60, 142**
See also BEST 90:1; BPFB 1; CA 77-80; CANR 12, 33, 55, 110; CPW; CWW 2; DA3; DAM NOV, POP; DLB 196, 242; EWL 3; MSW; MTCW 1, 2; RGWL 3

Eddison, E(ric) R(ucker)
1882-1945 .... **TCLC 15**
See also CA 109; 156; DLB 255; FANT; SFW 4; SUFW 1

Eddy, Mary (Ann Morse) Baker
1821-1910 .... **TCLC 71**
See also CA 113; 174

Edel, (Joseph) Leon 1907-1997 .. **CLC 29, 34**
See also CA 1-4R; 161; CANR 1, 22, 112; DLB 103; INT CANR-22

Eden, Emily 1797-1869 .... **NCLC 10**

Edgar, David 1948- .... **CLC 42**
See also CA 57-60; CANR 12, 61, 112; CBD; CD 5; DAM DRAM; DFS 15; DLB 13, 233; MTCW 1

Edgerton, Clyde (Carlyle) 1944- ...... **CLC 39**
See also AAYA 17; CA 118; 134; CANR 64; CSW; DLB 278; INT 134; YAW

Edgeworth, Maria 1768-1849 ... **NCLC 1, 51**
See also BRWS 3; DLB 116, 159, 163; FW; RGEL 2; SATA 21; TEA; WLIT 3

Edmonds, Paul
See Kuttner, Henry

Edmonds, Walter D(umaux)
1903-1998 .... **CLC 35**
See also BYA 2; CA 5-8R; CANR 2; CWRI 5; DLB 9; LAIT 1; MAICYA 1, 2; RHW; SAAS 4; SATA 1, 27; SATA-Obit 99

Edmondson, Wallace
See Ellison, Harlan (Jay)

Edson, Russell 1935- .... **CLC 13**
See also CA 33-36R; CANR 115; DLB 244; WP

Edwards, Bronwen Elizabeth
See Rose, Wendy

Edwards, G(erald) B(asil)
1899-1976 .... **CLC 25**
See also CA 201; 110

Edwards, Gus 1939- .... **CLC 43**
See also CA 108; INT 108

Edwards, Jonathan 1703-1758 .... **LC 7, 54**
See also AMW; DA; DAC; DAM MST; DLB 24, 270; RGAL 4; TUS

Edwards, Sarah Pierpont 1710-1758 .. **LC 87**
See also DLB 200

Efron, Marina Ivanovna Tsvetaeva
See Tsvetaeva (Efron), Marina (Ivanovna)

Egoyan, Atom 1960- .... **CLC 151**
See also CA 157

Ehle, John (Marsden, Jr.) 1925- ...... **CLC 27**
See also CA 9-12R; CSW

Ehrenbourg, Ilya (Grigoryevich)
See Ehrenburg, Ilya (Grigoryevich)

Ehrenburg, Ilya (Grigoryevich)
1891-1967 .... **CLC 18, 34, 62**
See Erenburg, Il'ia Grigor'evich
See also CA 102; 25-28R; EWL 3

Ehrenburg, Ilyo (Grigoryevich)
See Ehrenburg, Ilya (Grigoryevich)

Ehrenreich, Barbara 1941- .... **CLC 110**
See also BEST 90:4; CA 73-76; CANR 16, 37, 62, 117; DLB 246; FW; MTCW 1, 2

Eich, Gunter
See Eich, Gunter
See also RGWL 2, 3

Eich, Gunter 1907-1972 .... **CLC 15**
See Eich, Gunter
See also CA 111; 93-96; DLB 69, 124; EWL 3

Eichendorff, Joseph 1788-1857 .... **NCLC 8**
See also DLB 90; RGWL 2, 3

Eigner, Larry .... **CLC 9**
See Eigner, Laurence (Joel)
See also CAAS 23; DLB 5; WP

Eigner, Laurence (Joel) 1927-1996
See Eigner, Larry
See also CA 9-12R; 151; CANR 6, 84; CP 7; DLB 193

Einhard c. 770-840 .... **CMLC 50**
See also DLB 148

Einstein, Albert 1879-1955 .... **TCLC 65**
See also CA 121; 133; MTCW 1, 2

Eiseley, Loren
See Eiseley, Loren Corey
See also DLB 275

Eiseley, Loren Corey 1907-1977 .... **CLC 7**
See Eiseley, Loren
See also AAYA 5; ANW; CA 1-4R; 73-76; CANR 6; DLBD 17

Eisenstadt, Jill 1963- .... **CLC 50**
See also CA 140

Eisenstein, Sergei (Mikhailovich)
1898-1948 .... **TCLC 57**
See also CA 114; 149

Eisner, Simon
See Kornbluth, C(yril) M.

Ekeloef, (Bengt) Gunnar
1907-1968 .... **CLC 27; PC 23**
See Ekelof, (Bengt) Gunnar
See also CA 123; 25-28R; DAM POET

Ekelof, (Bengt) Gunnar 1907-1968
See Ekeloef, (Bengt) Gunnar
See also DLB 259; EW 12; EWL 3

Ekelund, Vilhelm 1880-1949 .... **TCLC 75**
See also CA 189; EWL 3

Ekwensi, C. O. D.
See Ekwensi, Cyprian (Odiatu Duaka)

Ekwensi, Cyprian (Odiatu Duaka)
1921- .... **BLC 1; CLC 4**
See also AFW; BW 2, 3; CA 29-32R; CANR 18, 42, 74; CDWLB 3; CN 7; CWRI 5; DAM MULT; DLB 117; EWL 3; MTCW 1, 2; RGEL 2; SATA 66; WLIT 2

Elaine .... **TCLC 18**
See Leverson, Ada Esther

El Crummo
See Crumb, R(obert)

Elder, Lonne III 1931-1996 ..... **BLC 1; DC 8**
See also BW 1, 3; CA 81-84; 152; CAD; CANR 25; DAM MULT; DLB 7, 38, 44

Eleanor of Aquitaine 1122-1204 ... **CMLC 39**

Elia
See Lamb, Charles

Eliade, Mircea 1907-1986 .... **CLC 19**
See also CA 65-68; 119; CANR 30, 62; CD-WLB 4; DLB 220; EWL 3; MTCW 1; RGWL 3; SFW 4

Eliot, A. D.
See Jewett, (Theodora) Sarah Orne

Eliot, Alice
See Jewett, (Theodora) Sarah Orne

Eliot, Dan
See Silverberg, Robert

Eliot, George 1819-1880 ...... **NCLC 4, 13, 23, 41, 49, 89, 118; PC 20; WLC**
See also BRW 5; BRWC 1; BRWR 2; CD-BLB 1832-1890; CN 7; CPW; DA; DA3; DAB; DAC; DAM MST, NOV; DLB 21, 35, 55; LATS 1; LMFS 1; NFS 17; RGEL 2; RGSF 2; SSFS 8; TEA; WLIT 3

Eliot, John 1604-1690 .... **LC 5**
See also DLB 24

Eliot, T(homas) S(tearns)
1888-1965 ... **CLC 1, 2, 3, 6, 9, 10, 13, 15, 24, 34, 41, 55, 57, 113; PC 5, 31; WLC**
See also AAYA 28; AMW; AMWC 1; AMWR 1; BRW 7; BRWR 2; CA 5-8R; 25-28R; CANR 41; CDALB 1929-1941; DA; DA3; DAB; DAC; DAM DRAM, MST, POET; DFS 4, 13; DLB 7, 10, 45, 63, 245; DLBY 1988; EWL 3; EXPP; LAIT 3; LATS 1; LMFS 2; MTCW 1, 2; PAB; PFS 1, 7; RGAL 4; RGEL 2; TUS; WLIT 4; WP

Elizabeth 1866-1941 .... **TCLC 41**

Elkin, Stanley L(awrence)
1930-1995 .. **CLC 4, 6, 9, 14, 27, 51, 91; SSC 12**
See also AMWS 6; BPFB 1; CA 9-12R; 148; CANR 8, 46; CN 7; CPW; DAM

Evan, Evin
See Faust, Frederick (Schiller)
Evans, Caradoc 1878-1945 ... **SSC 43; TCLC 85**
See also DLB 162
Evans, Evan
See Faust, Frederick (Schiller)
See also TCWW 2
Evans, Marian
See Eliot, George
Evans, Mary Ann
See Eliot, George
Evarts, Esther
See Benson, Sally
Everett, Percival
See Everett, Percival L.
See also CSW
Everett, Percival L. 1956- .... **CLC 57**
See Everett, Percival
See also BW 2; CA 129; CANR 94
Everson, R(onald) G(ilmour)
1903-1992 .... **CLC 27**
See also CA 17-20R; DLB 88
Everson, William (Oliver)
1912-1994 .... **CLC 1, 5, 14**
See also BG 2; CA 9-12R; 145; CANR 20;
DLB 5, 16, 212; MTCW 1
Evtushenko, Evgenii Aleksandrovich
See Yevtushenko, Yevgeny (Alexandrovich)
See also RGWL 2, 3
Ewart, Gavin (Buchanan)
1916-1995 .... **CLC 13, 46**
See also BRWS 7; CA 89-92; 150; CANR
17, 46; CP 7; DLB 40; MTCW 1
Ewers, Hanns Heinz 1871-1943 ..... **TCLC 12**
See also CA 109; 149
Ewing, Frederick R.
See Sturgeon, Theodore (Hamilton)
Exley, Frederick (Earl) 1929-1992 .... **CLC 6, 11**
See also AITN 2; BPFB 1; CA 81-84; 138;
CANR 117; DLB 143; DLBY 1981
Eynhardt, Guillermo
See Quiroga, Horacio (Sylvestre)
Ezekiel, Nissim 1924- .... **CLC 61**
See also CA 61-64; CP 7; EWL 3
Ezekiel, Tish O'Dowd 1943- .... **CLC 34**
See also CA 129
Fadeev, Aleksandr Aleksandrovich
See Bulgya, Alexander Alexandrovich
See also DLB 272
Fadeev, Alexandr Alexandrovich
See Bulgya, Alexander Alexandrovich
See also EWL 3
Fadeyev, A.
See Bulgya, Alexander Alexandrovich
Fadeyev, Alexander .... **TCLC 53**
See Bulgya, Alexander Alexandrovich
Fagen, Donald 1948- .... **CLC 26**
Fainzilberg, Ilya Arnoldovich 1897-1937
See Ilf, Ilya
See also CA 120; 165
Fair, Ronald L. 1932- .... **CLC 18**
See also BW 1; CA 69-72; CANR 25; DLB 33
Fairbairn, Roger
See Carr, John Dickson
Fairbairns, Zoe (Ann) 1948- .... **CLC 32**
See also CA 103; CANR 21, 85; CN 7
Fairfield, Flora
See Alcott, Louisa May
Fairman, Paul W. 1916-1977
See Queen, Ellery
See also CA 114; SFW 4
Falco, Gian
See Papini, Giovanni
Falconer, James
See Kirkup, James

Falconer, Kenneth
See Kornbluth, C(yril) M.
Falkland, Samuel
See Heijermans, Herman
Fallaci, Oriana 1930- .... **CLC 11, 110**
See also CA 77-80; CANR 15, 58; FW;
MTCW 1
Faludi, Susan 1959- .... **CLC 140**
See also CA 138; FW; MTCW 1; NCFS 3
Faludy, George 1913- .... **CLC 42**
See also CA 21-24R
Faludy, Gyoergy
See Faludy, George
Fanon, Frantz 1925-1961 .... **BLC 2; CLC 74**
See also BW 1; CA 116; 89-92; DAM
MULT; LMFS 2; WLIT 2
Fanshawe, Ann 1625-1680 .... **LC 11**
Fante, John (Thomas) 1911-1983 ..... **CLC 60**
See also AMWS 11; CA 69-72; 109; CANR
23, 104; DLB 130; DLBY 1983
Far, Sui Sin .... **SSC 62**
See Eaton, Edith Maude
See also SSFS 4
Farah, Nuruddin 1945- ...... **BLC 2; CLC 53, 137**
See also AFW; BW 2, 3; CA 106; CANR
81; CDWLB 3; CN 7; DAM MULT; DLB
125; EWL 3; WLIT 2
Fargue, Leon-Paul 1876(?)-1947 .... **TCLC 11**
See also CA 109; CANR 107; DLB 258;
EWL 3
Farigoule, Louis
See Romains, Jules
Farina, Richard 1936(?)-1966 .... **CLC 9**
See also CA 81-84; 25-28R
Farley, Walter (Lorimer)
1915-1989 .... **CLC 17**
See also BYA 14; CA 17-20R; CANR 8,
29, 84; DLB 22; JRDA; MAICYA 1, 2;
SATA 2, 43, 132; YAW
Farmer, Philip Jose 1918- .... **CLC 1, 19**
See also AAYA 28; BPFB 1; CA 1-4R;
CANR 4, 35, 111; DLB 8; MTCW 1;
SATA 93; SCFW 2; SFW 4
Farquhar, George 1677-1707 .... **LC 21**
See also BRW 2; DAM DRAM; DLB 84;
RGEL 2
Farrell, J(ames) G(ordon)
1935-1979 .... **CLC 6**
See also CA 73-76; 89-92; CANR 36; DLB
14, 271; MTCW 1; RGEL 2; RHW; WLIT 4
Farrell, James T(homas) 1904-1979 . **CLC 1, 4, 8, 11, 66; SSC 28**
See also AMW; BPFB 1; CA 5-8R; 89-92;
CANR 9, 61; DLB 4, 9, 86; DLBD 2;
EWL 3; MTCW 1, 2; RGAL 4
Farrell, Warren (Thomas) 1943- ...... **CLC 70**
See also CA 146; CANR 120
Farren, Richard J.
See Betjeman, John
Farren, Richard M.
See Betjeman, John
Fassbinder, Rainer Werner
1946-1982 .... **CLC 20**
See also CA 93-96; 106; CANR 31
Fast, Howard (Melvin) 1914-2003 .. **CLC 23, 131**
See also AAYA 16; BPFB 1; CA 1-4R; 181;
CAAE 181; CAAS 18; CANR 1, 33, 54,
75, 98; CMW 4; CN 7; CPW; DAM NOV;
DLB 9; INT CANR-33; LATS 1; MTCW
1; RHW; SATA 7; SATA-Essay 107;
TCWW 2; YAW
Faulcon, Robert
See Holdstock, Robert P.

Faulkner, William (Cuthbert)
1897-1962 .... **CLC 1, 3, 6, 8, 9, 11, 14, 18, 28, 52, 68; SSC 1, 35, 42; WLC**
See also AAYA 7; AMW; AMWR 1; BPFB
1; BYA 5; CA 81-84; CANR 33; CDALB
1929-1941; DA; DA3; DAB; DAC; DAM
MST, NOV; DLB 9, 11, 44, 102; DLBD
2; DLBY 1986, 1997; EWL 3; EXPN;
EXPS; LAIT 2; LATS 1; LMFS 2; MTCW
1, 2; NFS 4, 8, 13; RGAL 4; RGSF 2;
SSFS 2, 5, 6, 12; TUS
Fauset, Jessie Redmon
1882(?)-1961 .. **BLC 2; CLC 19, 54; HR 2**
See also AFAW 2; BW 1; CA 109; CANR
83; DAM MULT; DLB 51; FW; LMFS 2;
MAWW
Faust, Frederick (Schiller)
1892-1944(?) .... **TCLC 49**
See Austin, Frank; Brand, Max; Challis,
George; Dawson, Peter; Dexter, Martin;
Evans, Evan; Frederick, John; Frost, Fred-
erick; Manning, David; Silver, Nicholas
See also CA 108; 152; DAM POP; DLB
256; TUS
Faust, Irvin 1924- .... **CLC 8**
See also CA 33-36R; CANR 28, 67; CN 7;
DLB 2, 28, 218, 278; DLBY 1980
Faustino, Domingo 1811-1888 ...... **NCLC 123**
Fawkes, Guy
See Benchley, Robert (Charles)
Fearing, Kenneth (Flexner)
1902-1961 .... **CLC 51**
See also CA 93-96; CANR 59; CMW 4;
DLB 9; RGAL 4
Fecamps, Elise
See Creasey, John
Federman, Raymond 1928- .... **CLC 6, 47**
See also CA 17-20R; CAAE 208; CAAS 8;
CANR 10, 43, 83, 108; CN 7; DLBY 1980
Federspiel, J(uerg) F. 1931- .... **CLC 42**
See also CA 146
Feiffer, Jules (Ralph) 1929- ...... **CLC 2, 8, 64**
See also AAYA 3; CA 17-20R; CAD; CANR
30, 59; CD 5; DAM DRAM; DLB 7, 44;
INT CANR-30; MTCW 1; SATA 8, 61,
111
Feige, Hermann Albert Otto Maximilian
See Traven, B.
Feinberg, David B. 1956-1994 .... **CLC 59**
See also CA 135; 147
Feinstein, Elaine 1930- .... **CLC 36**
See also CA 69-72; CAAS 1; CANR 31,
68; CN 7; CP 7; CWP; DLB 14, 40;
MTCW 1
Feke, Gilbert David .... **CLC 65**
Feldman, Irving (Mordecai) 1928- ..... **CLC 7**
See also CA 1-4R; CANR 1; CP 7; DLB
169
Felix-Tchicaya, Gerald
See Tchicaya, Gerald Felix
Fellini, Federico 1920-1993 .... **CLC 16, 85**
See also CA 65-68; 143; CANR 33
Felltham, Owen 1602(?)-1668 .... **LC 92**
See also DLB 126, 151
Felsen, Henry Gregor 1916-1995 ..... **CLC 17**
See also CA 1-4R; 180; CANR 1; SAAS 2;
SATA 1
Felski, Rita .... **CLC 65**
Fenno, Jack
See Calisher, Hortense
Fenollosa, Ernest (Francisco)
1853-1908 .... **TCLC 91**
Fenton, James Martin 1949- .... **CLC 32**
See also CA 102; CANR 108; CP 7; DLB
40; PFS 11

4; CPW; DA3; DAM NOV, POP; DLB
87; DLBY 1981; INT CANR-33; MTCW
1

Fontane, Theodor 1819-1898 .... NCLC 26
See also CDWLB 2; DLB 129; EW 6;
RGWL 2, 3; TWA

Fontenot, Chester .... CLC 65

Fonvizin, Denis Ivanovich
1744(?)-1792 .... LC 81
See also DLB 150; RGWL 2, 3

Foote, Horton 1916- .... CLC 51, 91
See also CA 73-76; CAD; CANR 34, 51,
110; CD 5; CSW; DA3; DAM DRAM;
DLB 26, 266; EWL 3; INT CANR-34

Foote, Mary Hallock 1847-1938 .. TCLC 108
See also DLB 186, 188, 202, 221

Foote, Shelby 1916- .... CLC 75
See also AAYA 40; CA 5-8R; CANR 3, 45,
74; CN 7; CPW; CSW; DA3; DAM NOV,
POP; DLB 2, 17; MTCW 2; RHW

Forbes, Cosmo
See Lewton, Val

Forbes, Esther 1891-1967 .... CLC 12
See also AAYA 17; BYA 2; CA 13-14; 25-
28R; CAP 1; CLR 27; DLB 22; JRDA;
MAICYA 1, 2; RHW; SATA 2, 100; YAW

Forche, Carolyn (Louise) 1950- .... CLC 25,
83, 86; PC 10
See also CA 109; 117; CANR 50, 74; CP 7;
CWP; DA3; DAM POET; DLB 5, 193;
INT CA-117; MTCW 1; RGAL 4

Ford, Elbur
See Hibbert, Eleanor Alice Burford

Ford, Ford Madox 1873-1939 ... TCLC 1, 15,
39, 57
See Chaucer, Daniel
See also BRW 6; CA 104; 132; CANR 74;
CDBLB 1914-1945; DA3; DAM NOV;
DLB 34, 98, 162; EWL 3; MTCW 1, 2;
RGEL 2; TEA

Ford, Henry 1863-1947 .... TCLC 73
See also CA 115; 148

Ford, Jack
See Ford, John

Ford, John 1586-1639 .... DC 8; LC 68
See also BRW 2; CDBLB Before 1660;
DA3; DAM DRAM; DFS 7; DLB 58;
IDTP; RGEL 2

Ford, John 1895-1973 .... CLC 16
See also CA 187; 45-48

Ford, Richard 1944- .... CLC 46, 99
See also AMWS 5; CA 69-72; CANR 11,
47, 86; CN 7; CSW; DLB 227; EWL 3;
MTCW 1; RGAL 4; RGSF 2

Ford, Webster
See Masters, Edgar Lee

Foreman, Richard 1937- .... CLC 50
See also CA 65-68; CAD; CANR 32, 63;
CD 5

Forester, C(ecil) S(cott) 1899-1966 ... CLC 35
See also CA 73-76; 25-28R; CANR 83;
DLB 191; RGEL 2; RHW; SATA 13

Forez
See Mauriac, Francois (Charles)

Forman, James
See Forman, James D(ouglas)

Forman, James D(ouglas) 1932- .... CLC 21
See also AAYA 17; CA 9-12R; CANR 4,
19, 42; JRDA; MAICYA 1, 2; SATA 8,
70; YAW

Forman, Milos 1932- .... CLC 164
See also CA 109

Fornes, Maria Irene 1930- . CLC 39, 61; DC
10; HLCS 1
See also CA 25-28R; CAD; CANR 28, 81;
CD 5; CWD; DLB 7; HW 1, 2; INT
CANR-28; MTCW 1; RGAL 4

Forrest, Leon (Richard)
1937-1997 .... BLCS; CLC 4
See also AFAW 2; BW 2; CA 89-92; 162;
CAAS 7; CANR 25, 52, 87; CN 7; DLB
33

Forster, E(dward) M(organ)
1879-1970 ...... CLC 1, 2, 3, 4, 9, 10, 13,
15, 22, 45, 77; SSC 27; TCLC 125;
WLC
See also AAYA 2, 37; BRW 6; BRWR 2;
CA 13-14; 25-28R; CANR 45; CAP 1;
CDBLB 1914-1945; DA; DA3; DAB;
DAC; DAM MST, NOV; DLB 34, 98,
162, 178, 195; DLBD 10; EWL 3; EXPN;
LAIT 3; LMFS 1; MTCW 1, 2; NCFS 1;
NFS 3, 10, 11; RGEL 2; RGSF 2; SATA
57; SUFW 1; TEA; WLIT 4

Forster, John 1812-1876 .... NCLC 11
See also DLB 144, 184

Forster, Margaret 1938- .... CLC 149
See also CA 133; CANR 62, 115; CN 7;
DLB 155, 271

Forsyth, Frederick 1938- .... CLC 2, 5, 36
See also BEST 89:4; CA 85-88; CANR 38,
62, 115; CMW 4; CN 7; CPW; DAM
NOV, POP; DLB 87; MTCW 1, 2

Forten, Charlotte L. 1837-1914 .... BLC 2;
TCLC 16
See Grimke, Charlotte L(ottie) Forten
See also DLB 50, 239

Fortinbras
See Grieg, (Johan) Nordahl (Brun)

Foscolo, Ugo 1778-1827 .... NCLC 8, 97
See also EW 5

Fosse, Bob .... CLC 20
See Fosse, Robert Louis

Fosse, Robert Louis 1927-1987
See Fosse, Bob
See also CA 110; 123

Foster, Hannah Webster
1758-1840 .... NCLC 99
See also DLB 37, 200; RGAL 4

Foster, Stephen Collins
1826-1864 .... NCLC 26
See also RGAL 4

Foucault, Michel 1926-1984 . CLC 31, 34, 69
See also CA 105; 113; CANR 34; DLB 242;
EW 13; EWL 3; GFL 1789 to the Present;
GLL 1; LMFS 2; MTCW 1, 2; TWA

**Fouque, Friedrich (Heinrich Karl) de la
Motte** 1777-1843 .... NCLC 2
See also DLB 90; RGWL 2, 3; SUFW 1

Fourier, Charles 1772-1837 .... NCLC 51

Fournier, Henri-Alban 1886-1914
See Alain-Fournier
See also CA 104; 179

Fournier, Pierre 1916- .... CLC 11
See Gascar, Pierre
See also CA 89-92; CANR 16, 40

Fowles, John (Robert) 1926- . CLC 1, 2, 3, 4,
6, 9, 10, 15, 33, 87; SSC 33
See also BPFB 1; BRWS 1; CA 5-8R;
CANR 25, 71, 134; CDBLB 1960 to
Present; CN 7; DA3; DAB; DAC; DAM
MST; DLB 14, 139, 207; EWL 3; HGG;
MTCW 1, 2; RGEL 2; RHW; SATA 22;
TEA; WLIT 4

Fox, Paula 1923- .... CLC 2, 8, 121
See also AAYA 3, 37; BYA 3, 8; CA 73-76;
CANR 20, 36, 62, 105; CLR 1, 44; DLB
52; JRDA; MAICYA 1, 2; MTCW 1; NFS
12; SATA 17, 60, 120; WYA; YAW

Fox, William Price (Jr.) 1926- .... CLC 22
See also CA 17-20R; CAAS 19; CANR 11;
CSW; DLB 2; DLBY 1981

Foxe, John 1517(?)-1587 .... LC 14
See also DLB 132

Frame, Janet .. CLC 2, 3, 6, 22, 66, 96; SSC
29
See Clutha, Janet Paterson Frame
See also CN 7; CWP; EWL 3; RGEL 2;
RGSF 2; TWA

France, Anatole .... TCLC 9
See Thibault, Jacques Anatole Francois
See also DLB 123; EWL 3; GFL 1789 to
the Present; MTCW 1; RGWL 2, 3;
SUFW 1

Francis, Claude .... CLC 50
See also CA 192

Francis, Dick 1920- .... CLC 2, 22, 42, 102
See also AAYA 5, 21; BEST 89:3; BPFB 1;
CA 5-8R; CANR 9, 42, 68, 100; CDBLB
1960 to Present; CMW 4; CN 7; DA3;
DAM POP; DLB 87; INT CANR-9;
MSW; MTCW 1, 2

Francis, Robert (Churchill)
1901-1987 .... CLC 15; PC 34
See also AMWS 9; CA 1-4R; 123; CANR
1; EXPP; PFS 12

Francis, Lord Jeffrey
See Jeffrey, Francis
See also DLB 107

Frank, Anne(lies Marie)
1929-1945 .... TCLC 17; WLC
See also AAYA 12; BYA 1; CA 113; 133;
CANR 68; DA; DA3; DAB; DAC; DAM
MST; LAIT 4; MAICYA 2; MAICYAS 1;
MTCW 1, 2; NCFS 2; SATA 87; SATA-
Brief 42; WYA; YAW

Frank, Bruno 1887-1945 .... TCLC 81
See also CA 189; DLB 118; EWL 3

Frank, Elizabeth 1945- .... CLC 39
See also CA 121; 126; CANR 78; INT 126

Frankl, Viktor E(mil) 1905-1997 ...... CLC 93
See also CA 65-68; 161

Franklin, Benjamin
See Hasek, Jaroslav (Matej Frantisek)

Franklin, Benjamin 1706-1790 .... LC 25;
WLCS
See also AMW; CDALB 1640-1865; DA;
DA3; DAB; DAC; DAM MST; DLB 24,
43, 73, 183; LAIT 1; RGAL 4; TUS

**Franklin, (Stella Maria Sarah) Miles
(Lampe)** 1879-1954 .... TCLC 7
See also CA 104; 164; DLB 230; FW;
MTCW 2; RGEL 2; TWA

Fraser, Antonia (Pakenham) 1932- . CLC 32,
107
See also CA 85-88; CANR 44, 65, 119;
CMW; DLB 276; MTCW 1, 2; SATA-
Brief 32

Fraser, George MacDonald 1925- ...... CLC 7
See also AAYA 48; CA 45-48, 180; CAAE
180; CANR 2, 48, 74; MTCW 1; RHW

Fraser, Sylvia 1935- .... CLC 64
See also CA 45-48; CANR 1, 16, 60; CCA
1

Frayn, Michael 1933- . CLC 3, 7, 31, 47, 176
See also BRWS 7; CA 5-8R; CANR 30, 69,
114; CBD; CD 5; CN 7; DAM DRAM,
NOV; DLB 13, 14, 194, 245; FANT;
MTCW 1, 2; SFW 4

Fraze, Candida (Merrill) 1945- .... CLC 50
See also CA 126

Frazer, Andrew
See Marlowe, Stephen

Frazer, J(ames) G(eorge)
1854-1941 .... TCLC 32
See also BRWS 3; CA 118

Frazer, Robert Caine
See Creasey, John

Frazer, Sir James George
See Frazer, J(ames) G(eorge)

Frazier, Charles 1950- .... CLC 109
See also AAYA 34; CA 161; CSW

Glowacki, Aleksander
    See Prus, Boleslaw
Gluck, Louise (Elisabeth) 1943- .. **CLC 7, 22, 44, 81, 160; PC 16**
    See also AMWS 5; CA 33-36R; CANR 40, 69, 108; CP 7; CWP; DA3; DAM POET; DLB 5; MTCW 2; PFS 5, 15; RGAL 4
Glyn, Elinor 1864-1943 .... **TCLC 72**
    See also DLB 153; RHW
Gobineau, Joseph-Arthur
    1816-1882 .... **NCLC 17**
    See also DLB 123; GFL 1789 to the Present
Godard, Jean-Luc 1930- .... **CLC 20**
    See also CA 93-96
Godden, (Margaret) Rumer
    1907-1998 .... **CLC 53**
    See also AAYA 6; BPFB 2; BYA 2, 5; CA 5-8R; 172; CANR 4, 27, 36, 55, 80; CLR 20; CN 7; CWRI 5; DLB 161; MAICYA 1, 2; RHW; SAAS 12; SATA 3, 36; SATA-Obit 109; TEA
Godoy Alcayaga, Lucila 1899-1957 .. **HLC 2; PC 32; TCLC 2**
    See Mistral, Gabriela
    See also BW 2; CA 104; 131; CANR 81; DAM MULT; DNFS; HW 1, 2; MTCW 1, 2
Godwin, Gail (Kathleen) 1937- ..... **CLC 5, 8, 22, 31, 69, 125**
    See also BPFB 2; CA 29-32R; CANR 15, 43, 69; CN 7; CPW; CSW; DA3; DAM POP; DLB 6, 234; INT CANR-15; MTCW 1, 2
Godwin, William 1756-1836 .... **NCLC 14**
    See also CDBLB 1789-1832; CMW 4; DLB 39, 104, 142, 158, 163, 262; HGG; RGEL 2
Goebbels, Josef
    See Goebbels, (Paul) Joseph
Goebbels, (Paul) Joseph
    1897-1945 .... **TCLC 68**
    See also CA 115; 148
Goebbels, Joseph Paul
    See Goebbels, (Paul) Joseph
Goethe, Johann Wolfgang von
    1749-1832 .... **DC 20; NCLC 4, 22, 34, 90; PC 5; SSC 38; WLC**
    See also CDWLB 2; DA; DA3; DAB; DAC; DAM DRAM, MST, POET; DLB 94; EW 5; LATS 1; LMFS 1; RGWL 2, 3; TWA
Gogarty, Oliver St. John
    1878-1957 .... **TCLC 15**
    See also CA 109; 150; DLB 15, 19; RGEL 2
Gogol, Nikolai (Vasilyevich)
    1809-1852 .... **DC 1; NCLC 5, 15, 31; SSC 4, 29, 52; WLC**
    See also DA; DAB; DAC; DAM DRAM, MST; DFS 12; DLB 198; EW 6; EXPS; RGSF 2; RGWL 2, 3; SSFS 7; TWA
Goines, Donald 1937(?)-1974 ... **BLC 2; CLC 80**
    See also AITN 1; BW 1, 3; CA 124; 114; CANR 82; CMW 4; DA3; DAM MULT, POP; DLB 33
Gold, Herbert 1924- ... **CLC 4, 7, 14, 42, 152**
    See also CA 9-12R; CANR 17, 45; CN 7; DLB 2; DLBY 1981
Goldbarth, Albert 1948- .... **CLC 5, 38**
    See also AMWS 12; CA 53-56; CANR 6, 40; CP 7; DLB 120
Goldberg, Anatol 1910-1982 .... **CLC 34**
    See also CA 131; 117
Goldemberg, Isaac 1945- .... **CLC 52**
    See also CA 69-72; CAAS 12; CANR 11, 32; EWL 3; HW 1; WLIT 1

Golding, William (Gerald)
    1911-1993 ..... **CLC 1, 2, 3, 8, 10, 17, 27, 58, 81; WLC**
    See also AAYA 5, 44; BPFB 2; BRWR 1; BRWS 1; BYA 2; CA 5-8R; 141; CANR 13, 33, 54; CDBLB 1945-1960; DA; DA3; DAB; DAC; DAM MST, NOV; DLB 15, 100, 255; EWL 3; EXPN; HGG; LAIT 4; MTCW 1, 2; NFS 2; RGEL 2; RHW; SFW 4; TEA; WLIT 4; YAW
Goldman, Emma 1869-1940 .... **TCLC 13**
    See also CA 110; 150; DLB 221; FW; RGAL 4; TUS
Goldman, Francisco 1954- .... **CLC 76**
    See also CA 162
Goldman, William (W.) 1931- ...... **CLC 1, 48**
    See also BPFB 2; CA 9-12R; CANR 29, 69, 106; CN 7; DLB 44; FANT; IDFW 3, 4
Goldmann, Lucien 1913-1970 .... **CLC 24**
    See also CA 25-28; CAP 2
Goldoni, Carlo 1707-1793 .... **LC 4**
    See also DAM DRAM; EW 4; RGWL 2, 3
Goldsberry, Steven 1949- .... **CLC 34**
    See also CA 131
Goldsmith, Oliver 1730-1774 .... **DC 8; LC 2, 48; WLC**
    See also BRW 3; CDBLB 1660-1789; DA; DAB; DAC; DAM DRAM, MST, NOV, POET; DFS 1; DLB 39, 89, 104, 109, 142; IDTP; RGEL 2; SATA 26; TEA; WLIT 3
Goldsmith, Peter
    See Priestley, J(ohn) B(oynton)
Gombrowicz, Witold 1904-1969 .... **CLC 4, 7, 11, 49**
    See also CA 19-20; 25-28R; CANR 105; CAP 2; CDWLB 4; DAM DRAM; DLB 215; EW 12; EWL 3; RGWL 2, 3; TWA
Gomez de Avellaneda, Gertrudis
    1814-1873 .... **NCLC 111**
    See also LAW
Gomez de la Serna, Ramon
    1888-1963 .... **CLC 9**
    See also CA 153; 116; CANR 79; EWL 3; HW 1, 2
Goncharov, Ivan Alexandrovich
    1812-1891 .... **NCLC 1, 63**
    See also DLB 238; EW 6; RGWL 2, 3
Goncourt, Edmond (Louis Antoine Huot) de
    1822-1896 .... **NCLC 7**
    See also DLB 123; EW 7; GFL 1789 to the Present; RGWL 2, 3
Goncourt, Jules (Alfred Huot) de
    1830-1870 .... **NCLC 7**
    See also DLB 123; EW 7; GFL 1789 to the Present; RGWL 2, 3
Gongora (y Argote), Luis de
    1561-1627 .... **LC 72**
    See also RGWL 2, 3
Gontier, Fernande 19(?)- .... **CLC 50**
Gonzalez Martinez, Enrique
    1871-1952 .... **TCLC 72**
    See also CA 166; CANR 81; EWL 3; HW 1, 2
Goodison, Lorna 1947- .... **PC 36**
    See also CA 142; CANR 88; CP 7; CWP; DLB 157; EWL 3
Goodman, Paul 1911-1972 ..... **CLC 1, 2, 4, 7**
    See also CA 19-20; 37-40R; CAD; CANR 34; CAP 2; DLB 130, 246; MTCW 1; RGAL 4
Gordimer, Nadine 1923- ...... **CLC 3, 5, 7, 10, 18, 33, 51, 70, 123, 160, 161; SSC 17; WLCS**
    See also AAYA 39; AFW; BRWS 2; CA 5-8R; CANR 3, 28, 56, 88; CN 7; DA; DA3; DAB; DAC; DAM MST, NOV; DLB 225; EWL 3; EXPS; INT CANR-28;

    LATS 1; MTCW 1, 2; NFS 4; RGEL 2; RGSF 2; SSFS 2, 14; TWA; WLIT 2;
Gordon, Adam Lindsay
    1833-1870 .... **NCLC 21**
    See also DLB 230
Gordon, Caroline 1895-1981 . **CLC 6, 13, 29, 83; SSC 15**
    See also AMW; CA 11-12; 103; CANR 36; CAP 1; DLB 4, 9, 102; DLBD 17; DLBY 1981; EWL 3; MTCW 1, 2; RGAL 4; RGSF 2
Gordon, Charles William 1860-1937
    See Connor, Ralph
    See also CA 109
Gordon, Mary (Catherine) 1949- .... **CLC 13, 22, 128; SSC 59**
    See also AMWS 4; BPFB 2; CA 102; CANR 44, 92; CN 7; DLB 6; DLBY 1981; FW; INT CA-102; MTCW 1
Gordon, N. J.
    See Bosman, Herman Charles
Gordon, Sol 1923- .... **CLC 26**
    See also CA 53-56; CANR 4; SATA 11
Gordone, Charles 1925-1995 .. **CLC 1, 4; DC 8**
    See also BW 1, 3; CA 93-96; 180; 150; CAAE 180; CAD; CANR 55; DAM DRAM; DLB 7; INT 93-96; MTCW 1
Gore, Catherine 1800-1861 .... **NCLC 65**
    See also DLB 116; RGEL 2
Gorenko, Anna Andreevna
    See Akhmatova, Anna
Gorky, Maxim .... **SSC 28; TCLC 8; WLC**
    See Peshkov, Alexei Maximovich
    See also DAB; DFS 9; EW 8; EWL 3; MTCW 2; TWA
Goryan, Sirak
    See Saroyan, William
Gosse, Edmund (William)
    1849-1928 .... **TCLC 28**
    See also CA 117; DLB 57, 144, 184; RGEL 2
Gotlieb, Phyllis Fay (Bloom) 1926- .. **CLC 18**
    See also CA 13-16R; CANR 7; DLB 88, 251; SFW 4
Gottesman, S. D.
    See Kornbluth, C(yril) M.; Pohl, Frederik
Gottfried von Strassburg fl. c.
    1170-1215 .... **CMLC 10**
    See also CDWLB 2; DLB 138; EW 1; RGWL 2, 3
Gotthelf, Jeremias 1797-1854 .... **NCLC 117**
    See also DLB 133; RGWL 2, 3
Gottschalk, Laura Riding
    See Jackson, Laura (Riding)
Gould, Lois 1932(?)-2002 .... **CLC 4, 10**
    See also CA 77-80; 208; CANR 29; MTCW 1
Gould, Stephen Jay 1941-2002 .... **CLC 163**
    See also AAYA 26; BEST 90:2; CA 77-80; 205; CANR 10, 27, 56, 75; CPW; INT CANR-27; MTCW 1, 2
Gourmont, Remy(-Marie-Charles) de
    1858-1915 .... **TCLC 17**
    See also CA 109; 150; GFL 1789 to the Present; MTCW 2
Govier, Katherine 1948- .... **CLC 51**
    See also CA 101; CANR 18, 40; CCA 1
Gower, John c. 1330-1408 .... **LC 76**
    See also BRW 1; DLB 146; RGEL 2
Goyen, (Charles) William
    1915-1983 .... **CLC 5, 8, 14, 40**
    See also AITN 2; CA 5-8R; 110; CANR 6, 71; DLB 2, 218; DLBY 1983; EWL 3; INT CANR-6

Hayden, Robert E(arl) 1913-1980 ..... **BLC 2;**
CLC 5, 9, 14, 37; PC 6
See also AFAW 1, 2; AMWS 2; BW 1, 3;
CA 69-72; 97-100; CABS 2; CANR 24,
75, 82; CDALB 1941-1968; DA; DAC;
DAM MST, MULT, POET; DLB 5, 76;
EWL 3; EXPP; MTCW 1, 2; PFS 1;
RGAL 4; SATA 19; SATA-Obit 26; WP

Hayek, F(riedrich) A(ugust von)
1899-1992 .... **TCLC 109**
See also CA 93-96; 137; CANR 20; MTCW
1, 2

Hayford, J(oseph) E(phraim) Casely
See Casely-Hayford, J(oseph) E(phraim)

Hayman, Ronald 1932- .... **CLC 44**
See also CA 25-28R; CANR 18, 50, 88; CD
5; DLB 155

Hayne, Paul Hamilton 1830-1886 . **NCLC 94**
See also DLB 3, 64, 79, 248; RGAL 4

Hays, Mary 1760-1843 .... **NCLC 114**
See also DLB 142, 158; RGEL 2

Haywood, Eliza (Fowler)
1693(?)-1756 .... **LC 1, 44**
See also DLB 39; RGEL 2

Hazlitt, William 1778-1830 ...... **NCLC 29, 82**
See also BRW 4; DLB 110, 158; RGEL 2;
TEA

Hazzard, Shirley 1931- .... **CLC 18**
See also CA 9-12R; CANR 4, 70; CN 7;
DLBY 1982; MTCW 1

Head, Bessie 1937-1986 ...... **BLC 2; CLC 25,**
67; SSC 52
See also AFW; BW 2, 3; CA 29-32R; 119;
CANR 25, 82; CDWLB 3; DA3; DAM
MULT; DLB 117, 225; EWL 3; EXPS;
FW; MTCW 1, 2; RGSF 2; SSFS 5, 13;
WLIT 2

Headon, (Nicky) Topper 1956(?)- ..... **CLC 30**

Heaney, Seamus (Justin) 1939- ..... **CLC 5, 7,**
14, 25, 37, 74, 91, 171; PC 18; WLCS
See also BRWR 1; BRWS 2; CA 85-88;
CANR 25, 48, 75, 91; CDBLB 1960 to
Present; CP 7; DA3; DAB; DAM POET;
DLB 40; DLBY 1995; EWL 3; EXPP;
MTCW 1, 2; PAB; PFS 2, 5, 8, 17; RGEL
2; TEA; WLIT 4

Hearn, (Patricio) Lafcadio (Tessima Carlos)
1850-1904 .... **TCLC 9**
See also CA 105; 166; DLB 12, 78, 189;
HGG; RGAL 4

Hearne, Vicki 1946-2001 .... **CLC 56**
See also CA 139; 201

Hearon, Shelby 1931- .... **CLC 63**
See also AITN 2; AMWS 8; CA 25-28R;
CANR 18, 48, 103; CSW

Heat-Moon, William Least .... **CLC 29**
See Trogdon, William (Lewis)
See also AAYA 9

Hebbel, Friedrich 1813-1863 . **DC 21; NCLC**
43
See also CDWLB 2; DAM DRAM; DLB
129; EW 6; RGWL 2, 3

Hebert, Anne 1916-2000 ...... **CLC 4, 13, 29**
See also CA 85-88; 187; CANR 69; CCA
1; CWP; CWW 2; DA3; DAC; DAM
MST, POET; DLB 68; EWL 3; GFL 1789
to the Present; MTCW 1, 2

Hecht, Anthony (Evan) 1923- ...... **CLC 8, 13,**
19
See also AMWS 10; CA 9-12R; CANR 6,
108; CP 7; DAM POET; DLB 5, 169;
EWL 3; PFS 6; WP

Hecht, Ben 1894-1964 ..... **CLC 8; TCLC 101**
See also CA 85-88; DFS 9; DLB 7, 9, 25,
26, 28, 86; FANT; IDFW 3, 4; RGAL 4

Hedayat, Sadeq 1903-1951 .... **TCLC 21**
See also CA 120; EWL 3; RGSF 2

Hegel, Georg Wilhelm Friedrich
1770-1831 .... **NCLC 46**
See also DLB 90; TWA

Heidegger, Martin 1889-1976 .... **CLC 24**
See also CA 81-84; 65-68; CANR 34;
MTCW 1, 2

Heidenstam, (Carl Gustaf) Verner von
1859-1940 .... **TCLC 5**
See also CA 104

Heidi Louise
See Erdrich, Louise

Heifner, Jack 1946- .... **CLC 11**
See also CA 105; CANR 47

Heijermans, Herman 1864-1924 .... **TCLC 24**
See also CA 123; EWL 3

Heilbrun, Carolyn G(old) 1926- ... **CLC 25,**
173
See Cross, Amanda
See also CA 45-48; CANR 1, 28, 58, 94;
FW

Hein, Christoph 1944- .... **CLC 154**
See also CA 158; CANR 108; CDWLB 2;
CWW 2; DLB 124

Heine, Heinrich 1797-1856 .... **NCLC 4, 54;**
PC 25
See also CDWLB 2; DLB 90; EW 5; RGWL
2, 3; TWA

Heinemann, Larry (Curtiss) 1944- .. **CLC 50**
See also CA 110; CAAS 21; CANR 31, 81;
DLBD 9; INT CANR-31

Heiney, Donald (William) 1921-1993
See Harris, MacDonald
See also CA 1-4R; 142; CANR 3, 58; FANT

Heinlein, Robert A(nson) 1907-1988 . **CLC 1,**
3, 8, 14, 26, 55; SSC 55
See also AAYA 17; BPFB 2; BYA 4, 13;
CA 1-4R; 125; CANR 1, 20, 53; CLR 75;
CPW; DA3; DAM POP; DLB 8; EXPS;
JRDA; LAIT 5; LMFS 2; MAICYA 1, 2;
MTCW 1, 2; RGAL 4; SATA 9, 69;
SATA-Obit 56; SCFW; SFW 4; SSFS 7;
YAW

Helforth, John
See Doolittle, Hilda

Heliodorus fl. 3rd cent. - .... **CMLC 52**

Hellenhofferu, Vojtech Kapristian z
See Hasek, Jaroslav (Matej Frantisek)

Heller, Joseph 1923-1999 . **CLC 1, 3, 5, 8, 11,**
36, 63; TCLC 131; WLC
See also AAYA 24; AITN 1; AMWS 4;
BPFB 2; BYA 1; CA 5-8R; 187; CABS 1;
CANR 8, 42, 66; CN 7; CPW; DA; DA3;
DAB; DAC; DAM MST, NOV, POP;
DLB 2, 28, 227; DLBY 1980, 2002; EWL
3; EXPN; INT CANR-8; LAIT 4; MTCW
1, 2; NFS 1; RGAL 4; TUS; YAW

Hellman, Lillian (Florence)
1906-1984 .. **CLC 2, 4, 8, 14, 18, 34, 44,**
52; DC 1; TCLC 119
See also AAYA 47; AITN 1, 2; AMWS 1;
CA 13-16R; 112; CAD; CANR 33; CWD;
DA3; DAM DRAM; DFS 1, 3, 14; DLB
7, 228; DLBY 1984; EWL 3; FW; LAIT
3; MAWW; MTCW 1, 2; RGAL 4; TUS

Helprin, Mark 1947- .... **CLC 7, 10, 22, 32**
See also CA 81-84; CANR 47, 64;
CDALBS; CPW; DA3; DAM NOV, POP;
DLBY 1985; FANT; MTCW 1, 2; SUFW
2

Helvetius, Claude-Adrien 1715-1771 .. **LC 26**

Helyar, Jane Penelope Josephine 1933-
See Poole, Josephine
See also CA 21-24R; CANR 10, 26; CWRI
5; SATA 82; SATA-Essay 138

Hemans, Felicia 1793-1835 ...... **NCLC 29, 71**
See also DLB 96; RGEL 2

Hemingway, Ernest (Miller)
1899-1961 .... **CLC 1, 3, 6, 8, 10, 13, 19,**
30, 34, 39, 41, 44, 50, 61, 80; SSC 1, 25,
36, 40, 63; TCLC 115; WLC
See also AAYA 19; AMW; AMWC 1;
AMWR 1; BPFB 2; BYA 2, 3, 13; CA
77-80; CANR 34; CDALB 1917-1929;
DA; DA3; DAB; DAC; DAM MST, NOV,
DLB 4, 9, 102, 210; DLBD 1, 15, 16;
DLBY 1981, 1987, 1996, 1998; EWL 3;
EXPN; EXPS; LAIT 3, 4; LATS 1;
MTCW 1, 2; NFS 1, 5, 6, 14; RGAL 4;
RGSF 2; SSFS 17; TUS; WYA

Hempel, Amy 1951- .... **CLC 39**
See also CA 118; 137; CANR 70; DA3;
DLB 218; EXPS; MTCW 2; SSFS 2

Henderson, F. C.
See Mencken, H(enry) L(ouis)

Henderson, Sylvia
See Ashton-Warner, Sylvia (Constance)

Henderson, Zenna (Chlarson)
1917-1983 .... **SSC 29**
See also CA 1-4R; 133; CANR 1, 84; DLB
8; SATA 5; SFW 4

Henkin, Joshua .... **CLC 119**
See also CA 161

Henley, Beth .... **CLC 23; DC 6, 14**
See Henley, Elizabeth Becker
See also CABS 3; CAD; CD 5; CSW;
CWD; DFS 2; DLBY 1986; FW

Henley, Elizabeth Becker 1952-
See Henley, Beth
See also CA 107; CANR 32, 73; DA3;
DAM DRAM, MST; MTCW 1, 2

Henley, William Ernest 1849-1903 .. **TCLC 8**
See also CA 105; DLB 19; RGEL 2

Hennissart, Martha
See Lathen, Emma
See also CA 85-88; CANR 64

Henry VIII 1491-1547 .... **LC 10**
See also DLB 132

Henry, O. ..... **SSC 5, 49; TCLC 1, 19; WLC**
See Porter, William Sydney
See also AAYA 41; AMWS 2; EXPS; RGAL
4; RGSF 2; SSFS 2

Henry, Patrick 1736-1799 .... **LC 25**
See also LAIT 1

Henryson, Robert 1430(?)-1506(?) ...... **LC 20**
See also BRWS 7; DLB 146; RGEL 2

Henschke, Alfred
See Klabund

Henson, Lance 1944- .... **NNAL**
See also CA 146; DLB 175

Hentoff, Nat(han Irving) 1925- .... **CLC 26**
See also AAYA 4, 42; BYA 6; CA 1-4R;
CAAS 6; CANR 5, 25, 77, 114; CLR 1,
52; INT CANR-25; JRDA; MAICYA 1,
2; SATA 42, 69, 133; SATA-Brief 27;
WYA; YAW

Heppenstall, (John) Rayner
1911-1981 .... **CLC 10**
See also CA 1-4R; 103; CANR 29; EWL 3

Heraclitus c. 540B.C.-c. 450B.C. ... **CMLC 22**
See also DLB 176

Herbert, Frank (Patrick)
1920-1986 .... **CLC 12, 23, 35, 44, 85**
See also AAYA 21; BPFB 2; BYA 4, 14;
CA 53-56; 118; CANR 5, 43; CDALBS;
CPW; DAM POP; DLB 8; INT CANR-5;
LAIT 5; MTCW 1, 2; NFS 17; SATA 9,
37; SATA-Obit 47; SCFW 2; SFW 4;
YAW

Herbert, George 1593-1633 ...... **LC 24; PC 4**
See also BRW 2; BRWR 2; CDBLB Before
1660; DAB; DAM POET; DLB 126;
EXPP; RGEL 2; TEA; WP

Herbert, Zbigniew 1924-1998 ..... **CLC 9, 43; PC 50**
See also CA 89-92; 169; CANR 36, 74; CD-WLB 4; CWW 2; DAM POET; DLB 232; EWL 3; MTCW 1

Herbst, Josephine (Frey) 1897-1969 .... **CLC 34**
See also CA 5-8R; 25-28R; DLB 9

Herder, Johann Gottfried von 1744-1803 .... **NCLC 8**
See also DLB 97; EW 4; TWA

Heredia, Jose Maria 1803-1839 .... **HLCS 2**
See also LAW

Hergesheimer, Joseph 1880-1954 ... **TCLC 11**
See also CA 109; 194; DLB 102, 9; RGAL 4

Herlihy, James Leo 1927-1993 .... **CLC 6**
See also CA 1-4R; 143; CAD; CANR 2

Herman, William
See Bierce, Ambrose (Gwinett)

Hermogenes fl. c. 175- .... **CMLC 6**

Hernandez, Jose 1834-1886 .... **NCLC 17**
See also LAW; RGWL 2, 3; WLIT 1

Herodotus c. 484B.C.-c. 420B.C. .. **CMLC 17**
See also AW 1; CDWLB 1; DLB 176; RGWL 2, 3; TWA

Herrick, Robert 1591-1674 .... **LC 13; PC 9**
See also BRW 2; DA; DAB; DAC; DAM MST, POP; DLB 126; EXPP; PFS 13; RGAL 4; RGEL 2; TEA; WP

Herring, Guilles
See Somerville, Edith Oenone

Herriot, James 1916-1995 .... **CLC 12**
See Wight, James Alfred
See also AAYA 1; BPFB 2; CA 148; CANR 40; CLR 80; CPW; DAM POP; LAIT 3; MAICYA 2; MAICYAS 1; MTCW 2; SATA 86, 135; TEA; YAW

Herris, Violet
See Hunt, Violet

Herrmann, Dorothy 1941- .... **CLC 44**
See also CA 107

Herrmann, Taffy
See Herrmann, Dorothy

Hersey, John (Richard) 1914-1993 .... **CLC 1, 2, 7, 9, 40, 81, 97**
See also AAYA 29; BPFB 2; CA 17-20R; 140; CANR 33; CDALBS; CPW; DAM POP; DLB 6, 185, 278; MTCW 1, 2; SATA 25; SATA-Obit 76; TUS

Herzen, Aleksandr Ivanovich 1812-1870 .... **NCLC 10, 61**
See Herzen, Alexander

Herzen, Alexander
See Herzen, Aleksandr Ivanovich
See also DLB 277

Herzl, Theodor 1860-1904 .... **TCLC 36**
See also CA 168

Herzog, Werner 1942- .... **CLC 16**
See also CA 89-92

Hesiod c. 8th cent. B.C.- .... **CMLC 5**
See also AW 1; DLB 176; RGWL 2, 3

Hesse, Hermann 1877-1962 ... **CLC 1, 2, 3, 6, 11, 17, 25, 69; SSC 9, 49; WLC**
See also AAYA 43; BPFB 2; CA 17-18; CAP 2; CDWLB 2; DA; DA3; DAB; DAC; DAM MST, NOV; DLB 66; EW 9; EWL 3; EXPN; LAIT 1; MTCW 1, 2; NFS 6, 15; RGWL 2, 3; SATA 50; TWA

Hewes, Cady
See De Voto, Bernard (Augustine)

Heyen, William 1940- .... **CLC 13, 18**
See also CA 33-36R; CAAS 9; CANR 98; CP 7; DLB 5

Heyerdahl, Thor 1914-2002 .... **CLC 26**
See also CA 5-8R; 207; CANR 5, 22, 66; 73; LAIT 4; MTCW 1, 2; SATA 2, 52

Heym, Georg (Theodor Franz Arthur) 1887-1912 .... **TCLC 9**
See also CA 106; 181

Heym, Stefan 1913-2001 .... **CLC 41**
See also CA 9-12R; 203; CANR 4; CWW 2; DLB 69; EWL 3

Heyse, Paul (Johann Ludwig von) 1830-1914 .... **TCLC 8**
See also CA 104; 209; DLB 129

Heyward, (Edwin) DuBose 1885-1940 .... **HR 2; TCLC 59**
See also CA 108; 157; DLB 7, 9, 45, 249; SATA 21

Heywood, John 1497(?)-1580(?) .... **LC 65**
See also DLB 136; RGEL 2

Hibbert, Eleanor Alice Burford 1906-1993 .... **CLC 7**
See Holt, Victoria
See also BEST 90:4; CA 17-20R; 140; CANR 9, 28, 59; CMW 4; CPW; DAM POP; MTCW 2; RHW; SATA 2; SATA-Obit 74

Hichens, Robert (Smythe) 1864-1950 .... **TCLC 64**
See also CA 162; DLB 153; HGG; RHW; SUFW

Higgins, George V(incent) 1939-1999 .... **CLC 4, 7, 10, 18**
See also BPFB 2; CA 77-80; 186; CAAS 5; CANR 17, 51, 89, 96; CMW 4; CN 7; DLB 2; DLBY 1981, 1998; INT CANR-17; MSW; MTCW 1

Higginson, Thomas Wentworth 1823-1911 .... **TCLC 36**
See also CA 162; DLB 1, 64, 243

Higgonet, Margaret ed. .... **CLC 65**

Highet, Helen
See MacInnes, Helen (Clark)

Highsmith, (Mary) Patricia 1921-1995 .... **CLC 2, 4, 14, 42, 102**
See Morgan, Claire
See also AAYA 48; BRWS 5; CA 1-4R; 147; CANR 1, 20, 48, 62, 108; CMW 4; CPW; DA3; DAM NOV, POP; MSW; MTCW 1, 2

Highwater, Jamake (Mamake) 1942(?)-2001 .... **CLC 12**
See also AAYA 7; BPFB 2; BYA 4; CA 65-68; 199; CAAS 7; CANR 10, 34, 84; CLR 17; CWRI 5; DLB 52; DLBY 1985; JRDA; MAICYA 1, 2; SATA 32, 69; SATA-Brief 30

Highway, Tomson 1951- ...... **CLC 92; NNAL**
See also CA 151; CANR 75; CCA 1; CD 5; DAC; DAM MULT; DFS 2; MTCW 2

Hijuelos, Oscar 1951- .... **CLC 65; HLC 1**
See also AAYA 25; AMWS 8; BEST 90:1; CA 123; CANR 50, 75; CPW; DA3; DAM MULT, POP; DLB 145; HW 1, 2; MTCW 2; NFS 17; RGAL 4; WLIT 1

Hikmet, Nazim 1902(?)-1963 .... **CLC 40**
See also CA 141; 93-96; EWL 3

Hildegard von Bingen 1098-1179 . **CMLC 20**
See also DLB 148

Hildesheimer, Wolfgang 1916-1991 .. **CLC 49**
See also CA 101; 135; DLB 69, 124; EWL 3

Hill, Geoffrey (William) 1932- ...... **CLC 5, 8, 18, 45**
See also BRWS 5; CA 81-84; CANR 21, 89; CDBLB 1960 to Present; CP 7; DAM POET; DLB 40; EWL 3; MTCW 1; RGEL 2

Hill, George Roy 1921- .... **CLC 26**
See also CA 110; 122

Hill, John
See Koontz, Dean R(ay)

Hill, Susan (Elizabeth) 1942- ..... **CLC 4, 113**
See also CA 33-36R; CANR 29, 69; CN 7; DAB; DAM MST, NOV; DLB 14, 139; HGG; MTCW 1; RHW

Hillard, Asa G. III .... **CLC 70**

Hillerman, Tony 1925- .... **CLC 62, 170**
See also AAYA 40; BEST 89:1; BPFB 2; CA 29-32R; CANR 21, 42, 65, 97; CMW 4; CPW; DA3; DAM POP; DLB 206; MSW; RGAL 4; SATA 6; TCWW 2; YAW

Hillesum, Etty 1914-1943 .... **TCLC 49**
See also CA 137

Hilliard, Noel (Harvey) 1929-1996 ... **CLC 15**
See also CA 9-12R; CANR 7, 69; CN 7

Hillis, Rick 1956- .... **CLC 66**
See also CA 134

Hilton, James 1900-1954 .... **TCLC 21**
See also CA 108; 169; DLB 34, 77; FANT; SATA 34

Hilton, Walter (?)-1396 .... **CMLC 58**
See also DLB 146; RGEL 2

Himes, Chester (Bomar) 1909-1984 .. **BLC 2; CLC 2, 4, 7, 18, 58, 108; TCLC 139**
See also AFAW 2; BPFB 2; BW 2; CA 25-28R; 114; CANR 22, 89; CMW 4; DAM MULT; DLB 2, 76, 143, 226; EWL 3; MSW; MTCW 1, 2; RGAL 4

Hinde, Thomas .... **CLC 6, 11**
See Chitty, Thomas Willes
See also EWL 3

Hine, (William) Daryl 1936- .... **CLC 15**
See also CA 1-4R; CAAS 15; CANR 1, 20; CP 7; DLB 60

Hinkson, Katharine Tynan
See Tynan, Katharine

Hinojosa(-Smith), Rolando (R.) 1929- .... **HLC 1**
See Hinojosa-Smith, Rolando
See also CA 131; CAAS 16; CANR 62; DAM MULT; DLB 82; HW 1, 2; MTCW 2; RGAL 4

Hinton, S(usan) E(loise) 1950- .. **CLC 30, 111**
See also AAYA 2, 33; BPFB 2; BYA 2, 3; CA 81-84; CANR 32, 62, 92; CDALBS; CLR 3, 23; CPW; DA; DA3; DAB; DAC; DAM MST, NOV; JRDA; LAIT 5; MAICYA 1, 2; MTCW 1, 2; NFS 5, 9, 15, 16; SATA 19, 58, 115; WYA; YAW

Hippius, Zinaida .... **TCLC 9**
See Gippius, Zinaida (Nikolaevna)
See also EWL 3

Hiraoka, Kimitake 1925-1970
See Mishima, Yukio
See also CA 97-100; 29-32R; DA3; DAM DRAM; GLL 1; MTCW 1, 2

Hirsch, E(ric) D(onald), Jr. 1928- .... **CLC 79**
See also CA 25-28R; CANR 27, 51; DLB 67; INT CANR-27; MTCW 1

Hirsch, Edward 1950- .... **CLC 31, 50**
See also CA 104; CANR 20, 42, 102; CP 7; DLB 120

Hitchcock, Alfred (Joseph) 1899-1980 .... **CLC 16**
See also AAYA 22; CA 159; 97-100; SATA 27; SATA-Obit 24

Hitchens, Christopher (Eric) 1949- .... **CLC 157**
See also CA 152; CANR 89

Hitler, Adolf 1889-1945 .... **TCLC 53**
See also CA 117; 147

Hoagland, Edward 1932- .... **CLC 28**
See also ANW; CA 1-4R; CANR 2, 31, 57, 107; CN 7; DLB 6; SATA 51; TCWW 2

Hoban, Russell (Conwell) 1925- ... **CLC 7, 25**
See also BPFB 2; CA 5-8R; CANR 23, 37, 66, 114; CLR 3, 69; CN 7; CWRI 5; DAM NOV; DLB 52; FANT; MAICYA 1, 2; MTCW 1, 2; SATA 1, 40, 78, 136; SFW 4; SUFW 2

Horovitz, Israel (Arthur) 1939- .... **CLC 56**
See also CA 33-36R; CAD; CANR 46, 59;
CD 5; DAM DRAM; DLB 7

Horton, George Moses
1797(?)-1883(?) .... **NCLC 87**
See also DLB 50

Horvath, odon von 1901-1938
See von Horvath, Odon
See also EWL 3

Horvath, Oedoen von -1938
See von Horvath, Odon

Horwitz, Julius 1920-1986 .... **CLC 14**
See also CA 9-12R; 119; CANR 12

Hospital, Janette Turner 1942- .... **CLC 42, 145**
See also CA 108; CANR 48; CN 7; DLBY 2002; RGSF 2

Hostos, E. M. de
See Hostos (y Bonilla), Eugenio Maria de

Hostos, Eugenio M. de
See Hostos (y Bonilla), Eugenio Maria de

Hostos, Eugenio Maria
See Hostos (y Bonilla), Eugenio Maria de

Hostos (y Bonilla), Eugenio Maria de
1839-1903 .... **TCLC 24**
See also CA 123; 131; HW 1

Houdini
See Lovecraft, H(oward) P(hillips)

Houellebecq, Michel 1958- .... **CLC 179**

Hougan, Carolyn 1943- .... **CLC 34**
See also CA 139

Household, Geoffrey (Edward West)
1900-1988 .... **CLC 11**
See also CA 77-80; 126; CANR 58; CMW 4; DLB 87; SATA 14; SATA-Obit 59

Housman, A(lfred) E(dward)
1859-1936 .... **PC 2, 43; TCLC 1, 10; WLCS**
See also BRW 6; CA 104; 125; DA; DA3; DAB; DAC; DAM MST, POET; DLB 19, 284; EWL 3; EXPP; MTCW 1, 2; PAB; PFS 4, 7; RGEL 2; TEA; WP

Housman, Laurence 1865-1959 .... **TCLC 7**
See also CA 106; 155; DLB 10; FANT; RGEL 2; SATA 25

Houston, Jeanne (Toyo) Wakatsuki
1934- .... **AAL**
See also AAYA 49; CA 103; CAAS 16; CANR 29; LAIT 4; SATA 78

Howard, Elizabeth Jane 1923- ..... **CLC 7, 29**
See also CA 5-8R; CANR 8, 62; CN 7

Howard, Maureen 1930- .... **CLC 5, 14, 46, 151**
See also CA 53-56; CANR 31, 75; CN 7; DLBY 1983; INT CANR-31; MTCW 1, 2

Howard, Richard 1929- .... **CLC 7, 10, 47**
See also AITN 1; CA 85-88; CANR 25, 80; CP 7; DLB 5; INT CANR-25

Howard, Robert E(rvin)
1906-1936 .... **TCLC 8**
See also BPFB 2; BYA 5; CA 105; 157; FANT; SUFW 1

Howard, Warren F.
See Pohl, Frederik

Howe, Fanny (Quincy) 1940- .... **CLC 47**
See also CA 117; CAAE 187; CAAS 27; CANR 70, 116; CP 7; CWP; SATA-Brief 52

Howe, Irving 1920-1993 .... **CLC 85**
See also AMWS 6; CA 9-12R; 141; CANR 21, 50; DLB 67; EWL 3; MTCW 1, 2

Howe, Julia Ward 1819-1910 .... **TCLC 21**
See also CA 117; 191; DLB 1, 189, 235; FW

Howe, Susan 1937- .... **CLC 72, 152**
See also AMWS 4; CA 160; CP 7; CWP; DLB 120; FW; RGAL 4

Howe, Tina 1937- .... **CLC 48**
See also CA 109; CAD; CD 5; CWD

Howell, James 1594(?)-1666 .... **LC 13**
See also DLB 151

Howells, W. D.
See Howells, William Dean

Howells, William D.
See Howells, William Dean

Howells, William Dean 1837-1920 ... **SSC 36; TCLC 7, 17, 41**
See also AMW; CA 104; 134; CDALB 1865-1917; DLB 12, 64, 74, 79, 189; LMFS 1; MTCW 2; RGAL 4; TUS

Howes, Barbara 1914-1996 .... **CLC 15**
See also CA 9-12R; 151; CAAS 3; CANR 53; CP 7; SATA 5

Hrabal, Bohumil 1914-1997 .... **CLC 13, 67**
See also CA 106; 156; CAAS 12; CANR 57; CWW 2; DLB 232; EWL 3; RGSF 2

Hrotsvit of Gandersheim c. 935-c. 1000 .... **CMLC 29**
See also DLB 148

Hsi, Chu 1130-1200 .... **CMLC 42**

Hsun, Lu
See Lu Hsun

Hubbard, L(afayette) Ron(ald)
1911-1986 .... **CLC 43**
See also CA 77-80; 118; CANR 52; CPW; DA3; DAM POP; FANT; MTCW 2; SFW 4

Huch, Ricarda (Octavia)
1864-1947 .... **TCLC 13**
See also CA 111; 189; DLB 66; EWL 3

Huddle, David 1942- .... **CLC 49**
See also CA 57-60; CAAS 20; CANR 89; DLB 130

Hudson, Jeffrey
See Crichton, (John) Michael

Hudson, W(illiam) H(enry)
1841-1922 .... **TCLC 29**
See also CA 115; 190; DLB 98, 153, 174; RGEL 2; SATA 35

Hueffer, Ford Madox
See Ford, Ford Madox

Hughart, Barry 1934- .... **CLC 39**
See also CA 137; FANT; SFW 4; SUFW 2

Hughes, Colin
See Creasey, John

Hughes, David (John) 1930- .... **CLC 48**
See also CA 116; 129; CN 7; DLB 14

Hughes, Edward James
See Hughes, Ted
See also DA3; DAM MST, POET

Hughes, (James Mercer) Langston
1902-1967 ..... **BLC 2; CLC 1, 5, 10, 15, 35, 44, 108; DC 3; HR 2; PC 1; SSC 6; WLC**
See also AAYA 12; AFAW 1, 2; AMWR 1; AMWS 1; BW 1, 3; CA 1-4R; 25-28R; CANR 1, 34, 82; CDALB 1929-1941; CLR 17; DA; DA3; DAB; DAC; DAM DRAM, MST, MULT, POET; DFS 6; DLB 4, 7, 48, 51, 86, 228; EWL 3; EXPP; EXPS; JRDA; LAIT 3; LMFS 2; MAI-CYA 1, 2; MTCW 1, 2; PAB; PFS 1, 3, 6, 10, 15; RGAL 4; RGSF 2; SATA 4, 33; SSFS 4, 7; TUS; WCH; WP; YAW

Hughes, Richard (Arthur Warren)
1900-1976 .... **CLC 1, 11**
See also CA 5-8R; 65-68; CANR 4; DAM NOV; DLB 15, 161; EWL 3; MTCW 1; RGEL 2; SATA 8; SATA-Obit 25

Hughes, Ted 1930-1998 . **CLC 2, 4, 9, 14, 37, 119; PC 7**
See Hughes, Edward James
See also BRWR 2; BRWS 1; CA 1-4R; 171; CANR 1, 33, 66, 108; CLR 3; CP 7; DAB; DAC; DLB 40, 161; EWL 3; EXPP; MAICYA 1, 2; MTCW 1, 2; PAB; PFS 4; RGEL 2; SATA 49; SATA-Brief 27; SATA-Obit 107; TEA; YAW

Hugo, Richard
See Huch, Ricarda (Octavia)

Hugo, Richard F(ranklin)
1923-1982 .... **CLC 6, 18, 32**
See also AMWS 6; CA 49-52; 108; CANR 3; DAM POET; DLB 5, 206; EWL 3; PFS 17; RGAL 4

Hugo, Victor (Marie) 1802-1885 .... **NCLC 3, 10, 21; PC 17; WLC**
See also AAYA 28; DA; DA3; DAB; DAC; DAM DRAM, MST, NOV, POET; DLB 119, 192, 217; EFS 2; EW 6; EXPN; GFL 1789 to the Present; LAIT 1, 2; NFS 5; RGWL 2, 3; SATA 47; TWA

Huidobro, Vicente
See Huidobro Fernandez, Vicente Garcia
See also DLB 283; EWL 3; LAW

Huidobro Fernandez, Vicente Garcia
1893-1948 .... **TCLC 31**
See Huidobro, Vicente
See also CA 131; HW 1

Hulme, Keri 1947- .... **CLC 39, 130**
See also CA 125; CANR 69; CN 7; CP 7; CWP; EWL 3; FW; INT 125

Hulme, T(homas) E(rnest)
1883-1917 .... **TCLC 21**
See also BRWS 6; CA 117; 203; DLB 19

Hume, David 1711-1776 .... **LC 7, 56**
See also BRWS 3; DLB 104, 252; LMFS 1; TEA

Humphrey, William 1924-1997 .... **CLC 45**
See also AMWS 9; CA 77-80; 160; CANR 68; CN 7; CSW; DLB 6, 212, 234, 278; TCWW 2

Humphreys, Emyr Owen 1919- .... **CLC 47**
See also CA 5-8R; CANR 3, 24; CN 7; DLB 15

Humphreys, Josephine 1945- ..... **CLC 34, 57**
See also CA 121; 127; CANR 97; CSW; INT 127

Huneker, James Gibbons
1860-1921 .... **TCLC 65**
See also CA 193; DLB 71; RGAL 4

Hungerford, Hesba Fay
See Brinsmead, H(esba) F(ay)

Hungerford, Pixie
See Brinsmead, H(esba) F(ay)

Hunt, E(verette) Howard, (Jr.)
1918- .... **CLC 3**
See also AITN 1; CA 45-48; CANR 2, 47, 103; CMW 4

Hunt, Francesca
See Holland, Isabelle (Christian)

Hunt, Howard
See Hunt, E(verette) Howard, (Jr.)

Hunt, Kyle
See Creasey, John

Hunt, (James Henry) Leigh
1784-1859 .... **NCLC 1, 70**
See also DAM POET; DLB 96, 110, 144; RGEL 2; TEA

Hunt, Marsha 1946- .... **CLC 70**
See also BW 2, 3; CA 143; CANR 79

Hunt, Violet 1866(?)-1942 .... **TCLC 53**
See also CA 184; DLB 162, 197

Hunter, E. Waldo
See Sturgeon, Theodore (Hamilton)

Hunter, Evan 1926- .... **CLC 11, 31**
See McBain, Ed
See also AAYA 39; BPFB 2; CA 5-8R; CANR 5, 38, 62, 97; CMW 4; CN 7; CPW; DAM POP; DLBY 1982; INT CANR-5; MSW; MTCW 1; SATA 25; SFW 4

Hunter, Kristin 1931-
See Lattany, Kristin (Elaine Eggleston) Hunter

Hunter, Mary
See Austin, Mary (Hunter)

Judd, Cyril
  See Kornbluth, C(yril) M.; Pohl, Frederik
Juenger, Ernst 1895-1998 .... **CLC 125**
  See Junger, Ernst
  See also CA 101; 167; CANR 21, 47, 106;
    DLB 56
Julian of Norwich 1342(?)-1416(?) . **LC 6, 52**
  See also DLB 146; LMFS 1
Julius Caesar 100B.C.-44B.C.
  See Caesar, Julius
  See also CDWLB 1; DLB 211
Junger, Ernst
  See Juenger, Ernst
  See also CDWLB 2; EWL 3; RGWL 2, 3
Junger, Sebastian 1962- .... **CLC 109**
  See also AAYA 28; CA 165
Juniper, Alex
  See Hospital, Janette Turner
Junius
  See Luxemburg, Rosa
Just, Ward (Swift) 1935- .... **CLC 4, 27**
  See also CA 25-28R; CANR 32, 87; CN 7;
    INT CANR-32
Justice, Donald (Rodney) 1925- .. **CLC 6, 19,
    102**
  See also AMWS 7; CA 5-8R; CANR 26,
    54, 74; CP 7; CSW; DAM POET; DLBY
    1983; EWL 3; INT CANR-26; MTCW 2;
    PFS 14
Juvenal c. 60-c. 130 .... **CMLC 8**
  See also AW 2; CDWLB 1; DLB 211;
    RGWL 2, 3
Juvenis
  See Bourne, Randolph S(illiman)
K., Alice
  See Knapp, Caroline
Kabakov, Sasha .... **CLC 59**
Kacew, Romain 1914-1980
  See Gary, Romain
  See also CA 108; 102
Kadare, Ismail 1936- .... **CLC 52**
  See also CA 161; EWL 3; RGWL 3
Kadohata, Cynthia .... **CLC 59, 122**
  See also CA 140
Kafka, Franz 1883-1924 ... **SSC 5, 29, 35, 60;
    TCLC 2, 6, 13, 29, 47, 53, 112; WLC**
  See also AAYA 31; BPFB 2; CA 105; 126;
    CDWLB 2; DA; DA3; DAB; DAC; DAM
    MST, NOV; DLB 81; EW 9; EWL 3;
    EXPS; LATS 1; LMFS 2; MTCW 1, 2;
    NFS 7; RGSF 2; RGWL 2, 3; SFW 4;
    SSFS 3, 7, 12; TWA
Kahanovitsch, Pinkhes
  See Der Nister
Kahn, Roger 1927- .... **CLC 30**
  See also CA 25-28R; CANR 44, 69; DLB
    171; SATA 37
Kain, Saul
  See Sassoon, Siegfried (Lorraine)
Kaiser, Georg 1878-1945 .... **TCLC 9**
  See also CA 106; 190; CDWLB 2; DLB
    124; EWL 3; LMFS 2; RGWL 2, 3
Kaledin, Sergei .... **CLC 59**
Kaletski, Alexander 1946- .... **CLC 39**
  See also CA 118; 143
Kalidasa fl. c. 400-455 .... **CMLC 9; PC 22**
  See also RGWL 2, 3
Kallman, Chester (Simon)
  1921-1975 .... **CLC 2**
  See also CA 45-48; 53-56; CANR 3
Kaminsky, Melvin 1926-
  See Brooks, Mel
  See also CA 65-68; CANR 16
Kaminsky, Stuart M(elvin) 1934- ..... **CLC 59**
  See also CA 73-76; CANR 29, 53, 89;
    CMW 4
Kandinsky, Wassily 1866-1944 .... **TCLC 92**
  See also CA 118; 155

Kane, Francis
  See Robbins, Harold
Kane, Henry 1918-
  See Queen, Ellery
  See also CA 156; CMW 4
Kane, Paul
  See Simon, Paul (Frederick)
Kanin, Garson 1912-1999 .... **CLC 22**
  See also AITN 1; CA 5-8R; 177; CAD;
    CANR 7, 78; DLB 7; IDFW 3, 4
Kaniuk, Yoram 1930- .... **CLC 19**
  See also CA 134
Kant, Immanuel 1724-1804 ..... **NCLC 27, 67**
  See also DLB 94
Kantor, MacKinlay 1904-1977 .... **CLC 7**
  See also CA 61-64; 73-76; CANR 60, 63;
    DLB 9, 102; MTCW 2; RHW; TCWW 2
Kanze Motokiyo
  See Zeami
Kaplan, David Michael 1946- .... **CLC 50**
  See also CA 187
Kaplan, James 1951- .... **CLC 59**
  See also CA 135
Karadzic, Vuk Stefanovic
  1787-1864 .... **NCLC 115**
  See also CDWLB 4; DLB 147
Karageorge, Michael
  See Anderson, Poul (William)
Karamzin, Nikolai Mikhailovich
  1766-1826 .... **NCLC 3**
  See also DLB 150; RGSF 2
Karapanou, Margarita 1946- .... **CLC 13**
  See also CA 101
Karinthy, Frigyes 1887-1938 .... **TCLC 47**
  See also CA 170; DLB 215; EWL 3
Karl, Frederick R(obert) 1927- .... **CLC 34**
  See also CA 5-8R; CANR 3, 44
Kastel, Warren
  See Silverberg, Robert
Kataev, Evgeny Petrovich 1903-1942
  See Petrov, Evgeny
  See also CA 120
Kataphusin
  See Ruskin, John
Katz, Steve 1935- .... **CLC 47**
  See also CA 25-28R; CAAS 14, 64; CANR
    12; CN 7; DLBY 1983
Kauffman, Janet 1945- .... **CLC 42**
  See also CA 117; CANR 43, 84; DLB 218;
    DLBY 1986
Kaufman, Bob (Garnell) 1925-1986 . **CLC 49**
  See also BG 3; BW 1; CA 41-44R; 118;
    CANR 22; DLB 16, 41
Kaufman, George S. 1889-1961 ...... **CLC 38;
    DC 17**
  See also CA 108; 93-96; DAM DRAM;
    DFS 1, 10; DLB 7; INT CA-108; MTCW
    2; RGAL 4; TUS
Kaufman, Sue .... **CLC 3, 8**
  See Barondess, Sue K(aufman)
Kavafis, Konstantinos Petrou 1863-1933
  See Cavafy, C(onstantine) P(eter)
  See also CA 104
Kavan, Anna 1901-1968 .... **CLC 5, 13, 82**
  See also BRWS 7; CA 5-8R; CANR 6, 57;
    DLB 255; MTCW 1; RGEL 2; SFW 4
Kavanagh, Dan
  See Barnes, Julian (Patrick)
Kavanagh, Julie 1952- .... **CLC 119**
  See also CA 163
Kavanagh, Patrick (Joseph)
  1904-1967 .... **CLC 22; PC 33**
  See also BRWS 7; CA 123; 25-28R; DLB
    15, 20; EWL 3; MTCW 1; RGEL 2

Kawabata, Yasunari 1899-1972 ..... **CLC 2, 5,
    9, 18, 107; SSC 17**
  See Kawabata Yasunari
  See also CA 93-96; 33-36R; CANR 88;
    DAM MULT; MJW; MTCW 2; RGSF 2;
    RGWL 2, 3
Kawabata Yasunari
  See Kawabata, Yasunari
  See also DLB 180; EWL 3
Kaye, M(ary) M(argaret) 1909- .... **CLC 28**
  See also CA 89-92; CANR 24, 60, 102;
    MTCW 1, 2; RHW; SATA 62
Kaye, Mollie
  See Kaye, M(ary) M(argaret)
Kaye-Smith, Sheila 1887-1956 .... **TCLC 20**
  See also CA 118; 203; DLB 36
Kaymor, Patrice Maguilene
  See Senghor, Leopold Sedar
Kazakov, Yuri Pavlovich 1927-1982 . **SSC 43**
  See Kazakov, Yury
  See also CA 5-8R; CANR 36; MTCW 1;
    RGSF 2
Kazakov, Yury
  See Kazakov, Yuri Pavlovich
  See also EWL 3
Kazan, Elia 1909- .... **CLC 6, 16, 63**
  See also CA 21-24R; CANR 32, 78
Kazantzakis, Nikos 1883(?)-1957 .... **TCLC 2,
    5, 33**
  See also BPFB 2; CA 105; 132; DA3; EW
    9; EWL 3; MTCW 1, 2; RGWL 2, 3
Kazin, Alfred 1915-1998 ..... **CLC 34, 38, 119**
  See also AMWS 8; CA 1-4R; CAAS 7;
    CANR 1, 45, 79; DLB 67; EWL 3
Keane, Mary Nesta (Skrine) 1904-1996
  See Keane, Molly
  See also CA 108; 114; 151; CN 7; RHW
Keane, Molly .... **CLC 31**
  See Keane, Mary Nesta (Skrine)
  See also INT 114
Keates, Jonathan 1946(?)- .... **CLC 34**
  See also CA 163
Keaton, Buster 1895-1966 .... **CLC 20**
  See also CA 194
Keats, John 1795-1821 ...... **NCLC 8, 73, 121;
    PC 1; WLC**
  See also BRW 4; BRWR 1; CDBLB 1789-
    1832; DA; DA3; DAB; DAC; DAM MST,
    POET; DLB 96, 110; EXPP; LMFS 1;
    PAB; PFS 1, 2, 3, 9, 16; RGEL 2; TEA;
    WLIT 3; WP
Keble, John 1792-1866 .... **NCLC 87**
  See also DLB 32, 55; RGEL 2
Keene, Donald 1922- .... **CLC 34**
  See also CA 1-4R; CANR 5, 119
Keillor, Garrison .... **CLC 40, 115**
  See Keillor, Gary (Edward)
  See also AAYA 2; BEST 89:3; BPFB 2;
    DLBY 1987; EWL 3; SATA 58; TUS
Keillor, Gary (Edward) 1942-
  See Keillor, Garrison
  See also CA 111; 117; CANR 36, 59; CPW;
    DA3; DAM POP; MTCW 1, 2
Keith, Carlos
  See Lewton, Val
Keith, Michael
  See Hubbard, L(afayette) Ron(ald)
Keller, Gottfried 1819-1890 .... **NCLC 2; SSC
    26**
  See also CDWLB 2; DLB 129; EW; RGSF
    2; RGWL 2, 3
Keller, Nora Okja 1965- .... **CLC 109**
  See also CA 187
Kellerman, Jonathan 1949- .... **CLC 44**
  See also AAYA 35; BEST 90:1; CA 106;
    CANR 29, 51; CMW 4; CPW; DA3;
    DAM POP; INT CANR-29

Kinnell, Galway 1927- ..... **CLC 1, 2, 3, 5, 13, 29, 129; PC 26**
See also AMWS 3; CA 9-12R; CANR 10, 34, 66, 116; CP 7; DLB 5; DLBY 1987; EWL 3; INT CANR-34; MTCW 1, 2; PAB; PFS 9; RGAL 4; WP

Kinsella, Thomas 1928- .... **CLC 4, 19, 138**
See also BRWS 5; CA 17-20R; CANR 15; CP 7; DLB 27; EWL 3; MTCW 1, 2; RGEL 2; TEA

Kinsella, W(illiam) P(atrick) 1935- . **CLC 27, 43, 166**
See also AAYA 7; BPFB 2; CA 97-100; CAAS 7; CANR 21, 35, 66, 75; CN 7; CPW; DAC; DAM NOV, POP; FANT; INT CANR-21; LAIT 5; MTCW 1, 2; NFS 15; RGSF 2

Kinsey, Alfred C(harles)
1894-1956 .... **TCLC 91**
See also CA 115; 170; MTCW 2

Kipling, (Joseph) Rudyard 1865-1936 . **PC 3; SSC 5, 54; TCLC 8, 17; WLC**
See also AAYA 32; BRW 6; BRWC 1; BYA 4; CA 105; 120; CANR 33; CDBLB 1890-1914; CLR 39, 65; CWRI 5; DA; DA3; DAB; DAC; DAM MST, POET; DLB 19, 34, 141, 156; EWL 3; EXPS; FANT; LAIT 3; LMFS 1; MAICYA 1, 2; MTCW 1, 2; RGEL 2; RGSF 2; SATA 100; SFW 4; SSFS 8; SUFW 1; TEA; WCH; WLIT 4; YABC 2

Kirk, Russell (Amos) 1918-1994 .. **TCLC 119**
See also AITN 1; CA 1-4R; 145; CAAS 9; CANR 1, 20, 60; HGG; INT CANR-20; MTCW 1, 2

Kirkland, Caroline M. 1801-1864 . **NCLC 85**
See also DLB 3, 73, 74, 250, 254; DLBD 13

Kirkup, James 1918- .... **CLC 1**
See also CA 1-4R; CAAS 4; CANR 2; CP 7; DLB 27; SATA 12

Kirkwood, James 1930(?)-1989 .... **CLC 9**
See also AITN 2; CA 1-4R; 128; CANR 6, 40; GLL 2

Kirsch, Sarah 1935- .... **CLC 176**
See also CA 178; CWW 2; DLB 75; EWL 3

Kirshner, Sidney
See Kingsley, Sidney

Kis, Danilo 1935-1989 .... **CLC 57**
See also CA 109; 118; 129; CANR 61; CDWLB 4; DLB 181; EWL 3; MTCW 1; RGSF 2; RGWL 2, 3

Kissinger, Henry A(lfred) 1923- ..... **CLC 137**
See also CA 1-4R; CANR 2, 33, 66, 109; MTCW 1

Kivi, Aleksis 1834-1872 .... **NCLC 30**

Kizer, Carolyn (Ashley) 1925- .. **CLC 15, 39, 80**
See also CA 65-68; CAAS 5; CANR 24, 70; CP 7; CWP; DAM POET; DLB 5, 169; EWL 3; MTCW 2

Klabund 1890-1928 .... **TCLC 44**
See also CA 162; DLB 66

Klappert, Peter 1942- .... **CLC 57**
See also CA 33-36R; CSW; DLB 5

Klein, A(braham) M(oses)
1909-1972 .... **CLC 19**
See also CA 101; 37-40R; DAB; DAC; DAM MST; DLB 68; EWL 3; RGEL 2

Klein, Joe
See Klein, Joseph

Klein, Joseph 1946- .... **CLC 154**
See also CA 85-88; CANR 55

Klein, Norma 1938-1989 .... **CLC 30**
See also AAYA 2, 35; BPFB 2; BYA 6, 7, 8; CA 41-44R; 128; CANR 15, 37; CLR 2, 19; INT CANR-15; JRDA; MAICYA 1, 2; SAAS 1; SATA 7, 57; WYA; YAW

Klein, T(heodore) E(ibon) D(onald)
1947- .... **CLC 34**
See also CA 119; CANR 44, 75; HGG

Kleist, Heinrich von 1777-1811 ...... **NCLC 2, 37; SSC 22**
See also CDWLB 2; DAM DRAM; DLB 90; EW 5; RGSF 2; RGWL 2, 3

Klima, Ivan 1931- .... **CLC 56, 172**
See also CA 25-28R; CANR 17, 50, 91; CDWLB 4; CWW 2; DAM NOV; DLB 232; EWL 3; RGWL 3

Klimentev, Andrei Platonovich
See Klimentov, Andrei Platonovich

Klimentov, Andrei Platonovich
1899-1951 .... **SSC 42; TCLC 14**
See Platonov, Andrei Platonovich; Platonov, Andrey Platonovich
See also CA 108

Klinger, Friedrich Maximilian von
1752-1831 .... **NCLC 1**
See also DLB 94

Klingsor the Magician
See Hartmann, Sadakichi

Klopstock, Friedrich Gottlieb
1724-1803 .... **NCLC 11**
See also DLB 97; EW 4; RGWL 2, 3

Kluge, Alexander 1932- .... **SSC 61**
See also CA 81-84; DLB 75

Knapp, Caroline 1959-2002 .... **CLC 99**
See also CA 154; 207

Knebel, Fletcher 1911-1993 .... **CLC 14**
See also AITN 1; CA 1-4R; 140; CAAS 3; CANR 1, 36; SATA 36; SATA-Obit 75

Knickerbocker, Diedrich
See Irving, Washington

Knight, Etheridge 1931-1991 ... **BLC 2; CLC 40; PC 14**
See also BW 1, 3; CA 21-24R; 133; CANR 23, 82; DAM POET; DLB 41; MTCW 2; RGAL 4

Knight, Sarah Kemble 1666-1727 .... **LC 7**
See also DLB 24, 200

Knister, Raymond 1899-1932 .... **TCLC 56**
See also CA 186; DLB 68; RGEL 2

Knowles, John 1926-2001 ... **CLC 1, 4, 10, 26**
See also AAYA 10; AMWS 12; BPFB 2; BYA 3; CA 17-20R; 203; CANR 40, 74, 76; CDALB 1968-1988; CN 7; DA; DAC; DAM MST, NOV; DLB 6; EXPN; MTCW 1, 2; NFS 2; RGAL 4; SATA 8, 89; SATA-Obit 134; YAW

Knox, Calvin M.
See Silverberg, Robert

Knox, John c. 1505-1572 .... **LC 37**
See also DLB 132

Knye, Cassandra
See Disch, Thomas M(ichael)

Koch, C(hristopher) J(ohn) 1932- .... **CLC 42**
See also CA 127; CANR 84; CN 7

Koch, Christopher
See Koch, C(hristopher) J(ohn)

Koch, Kenneth (Jay) 1925-2002 .... **CLC 5, 8, 44**
See also CA 1-4R; 207; CAD; CANR 6, 36, 57, 97; CD 5; CP 7; DAM POET; DLB 5; INT CANR-36; MTCW 2; SATA 65; WP

Kochanowski, Jan 1530-1584 .... **LC 10**
See also RGWL 2, 3

Kock, Charles Paul de 1794-1871 . **NCLC 16**

Koda Rohan
See Koda Shigeyuki

Koda Rohan
See Koda Shigeyuki
See also DLB 180

Koda Shigeyuki 1867-1947 .... **TCLC 22**
See Koda Rohan
See also CA 121; 183

Koestler, Arthur 1905-1983 ... **CLC 1, 3, 6, 8, 15, 33**
See also BRWS 1; CA 1-4R; 109; CANR 1, 33; CDBLB 1945-1960; DLBY 1983; EWL 3; MTCW 1, 2; RGEL 2

Kogawa, Joy Nozomi 1935- ...... **CLC 78, 129**
See also AAYA 47; CA 101; CANR 19, 62; CN 7; CWP; DAC; DAM MST, MULT; FW; MTCW 2; NFS 3; SATA 99

Kohout, Pavel 1928- .... **CLC 13**
See also CA 45-48; CANR 3

Koizumi, Yakumo
See Hearn, (Patricio) Lafcadio (Tessima Carlos)

Kolmar, Gertrud 1894-1943 .... **TCLC 40**
See also CA 167; EWL 3

Komunyakaa, Yusef 1947- .. **BLCS; CLC 86, 94**
See also AFAW 2; CA 147; CANR 83; CP 7; CSW; DLB 120; EWL 3; PFS 5; RGAL 4

Konrad, George
See Konrad, Gyorgy
See also CWW 2

Konrad, Gyorgy 1933- .... **CLC 4, 10, 73**
See Konrad, George
See also CA 85-88; CANR 97; CDWLB 4; CWW 2; DLB 232; EWL 3

Konwicki, Tadeusz 1926- .... **CLC 8, 28, 54, 117**
See also CA 101; CAAS 9; CANR 39, 59; CWW 2; DLB 232; EWL 3; IDFW 3; MTCW 1

Koontz, Dean R(ay) 1945- .... **CLC 78**
See also AAYA 9, 31; BEST 89:3, 90:2; CA 108; CANR 19, 36, 52, 95; CMW 4; CPW; DA3; DAM NOV, POP; HGG; MTCW 1; SATA 92; SFW 4; SUFW 2; YAW

Kopernik, Mikolaj
See Copernicus, Nicolaus

Kopit, Arthur (Lee) 1937- ...... **CLC 1, 18, 33**
See also AITN 1; CA 81-84; CABS 3; CD 5; DAM DRAM; DFS 7, 14; DLB 7; MTCW 1; RGAL 4

Kopitar, Jernej (Bartholomaus)
1780-1844 .... **NCLC 117**

Kops, Bernard 1926- .... **CLC 4**
See also CA 5-8R; CANR 84; CBD; CN 7; CP 7; DLB 13

Kornbluth, C(yril) M. 1923-1958 .... **TCLC 8**
See also CA 105; 160; DLB 8; SFW 4

Korolenko, V. G.
See Korolenko, Vladimir Galaktionovich

Korolenko, Vladimir
See Korolenko, Vladimir Galaktionovich

Korolenko, Vladimir G.
See Korolenko, Vladimir Galaktionovich

Korolenko, Vladimir Galaktionovich
1853-1921 .... **TCLC 22**
See also CA 121; DLB 277

Korzybski, Alfred (Habdank Skarbek)
1879-1950 .... **TCLC 61**
See also CA 123; 160

Kosinski, Jerzy (Nikodem)
1933-1991 .... **CLC 1, 2, 3, 6, 10, 15, 53, 70**
See also AMWS 7; BPFB 2; CA 17-20R; 134; CANR 9, 46; DA3; DAM NOV; DLB 2; DLBY 1982; EWL 3; HGG; MTCW 1, 2; NFS 12; RGAL 4; TUS

Kostelanetz, Richard (Cory) 1940- .. **CLC 28**
See also CA 13-16R; CAAS 8; CANR 38, 77; CN 7; CP 7

Kostrowitzki, Wilhelm Apollinaris de
1880-1918
See Apollinaire, Guillaume
See also CA 104

Kotlowitz, Robert 1924- .... **CLC 4**
See also CA 33-36R; CANR 36

Kotzebue, August (Friedrich Ferdinand) von
1761-1819 .... **NCLC 25**
See also DLB 94

Kotzwinkle, William 1938- ..... **CLC 5, 14, 35**
See also BPFB 2; CA 45-48; CANR 3, 44,
84; CLR 6; DLB 173; FANT; MAICYA
1, 2; SATA 24, 70; SFW 4; SUFW 2;
YAW

Kowna, Stancy
See Szymborska, Wislawa

Kozol, Jonathan 1936- .... **CLC 17**
See also AAYA 46; CA 61-64; CANR 16,
45, 96

Kozoll, Michael 1940(?)- .... **CLC 35**

Kramer, Kathryn 19(?)- .... **CLC 34**

Kramer, Larry 1935- .... **CLC 42; DC 8**
See also CA 124; 126; CANR 60; DAM
POP; DLB 249; GLL 1

Krasicki, Ignacy 1735-1801 .... **NCLC 8**

Krasinski, Zygmunt 1812-1859 .... **NCLC 4**
See also RGWL 2, 3

Kraus, Karl 1874-1936 .... **TCLC 5**
See also CA 104; DLB 118; EWL 3

Kreve (Mickevicius), Vincas
1882-1954 .... **TCLC 27**
See also CA 170; DLB 220; EWL 3

Kristeva, Julia 1941- .... **CLC 77, 140**
See also CA 154; CANR 99; DLB 242;
EWL 3; FW; LMFS 2

Kristofferson, Kris 1936- .... **CLC 26**
See also CA 104

Krizanc, John 1956- .... **CLC 57**
See also CA 187

Krleza, Miroslav 1893-1981 .... **CLC 8, 114**
See also CA 97-100; 105; CANR 50; CD-
WLB 4; DLB 147; EW 11; RGWL 2, 3

Kroetsch, Robert 1927- .. **CLC 5, 23, 57, 132**
See also CA 17-20R; CANR 8, 38; CCA 1;
CN 7; CP 7; DAC; DAM POET; DLB 53;
MTCW 1

Kroetz, Franz
See Kroetz, Franz Xaver

Kroetz, Franz Xaver 1946- .... **CLC 41**
See also CA 130; EWL 3

Kroker, Arthur (W.) 1945- .... **CLC 77**
See also CA 161

Kropotkin, Peter (Aleksieevich)
1842-1921 .... **TCLC 36**
See Kropotkin, Petr Alekseevich
See also CA 119

Kropotkin, Petr Alekseevich
See Kropotkin, Peter (Aleksieevich)
See also DLB 277

Krotkov, Yuri 1917-1981 .... **CLC 19**
See also CA 102

Krumb
See Crumb, R(obert)

Krumgold, Joseph (Quincy)
1908-1980 .... **CLC 12**
See also BYA 1, 2; CA 9-12R; 101; CANR
7; MAICYA 1, 2; SATA 1, 48; SATA-Obit
23; YAW

Krumwitz
See Crumb, R(obert)

Krutch, Joseph Wood 1893-1970 ..... **CLC 24**
See also ANW; CA 1-4R; 25-28R; CANR
4; DLB 63, 206, 275

Krutzch, Gus
See Eliot, T(homas) S(tearns)

Krylov, Ivan Andreevich
1768(?)-1844 .... **NCLC 1**
See also DLB 150

Kubin, Alfred (Leopold Isidor)
1877-1959 .... **TCLC 23**
See also CA 112; 149; CANR 104; DLB 81

Kubrick, Stanley 1928-1999 .... **CLC 16;**
TCLC 112
See also AAYA 30; CA 81-84; 177; CANR
33; DLB 26

Kueng, Hans 1928-
See Kung, Hans
See also CA 53-56; CANR 66; MTCW 1, 2

Kumin, Maxine (Winokur) 1925- ..... **CLC 5,**
13, 28, 164; PC 15
See also AITN 2; AMWS 4; ANW; CA
1-4R; CAAS 8; CANR 1, 21, 69, 115; CP
7; CWP; DA3; DAM POET; DLB 5;
EWL 3; EXPP; MTCW 1, 2; PAB; SATA
12

Kundera, Milan 1929- . **CLC 4, 9, 19, 32, 68,**
115, 135; SSC 24
See also AAYA 2; BPFB 2; CA 85-88;
CANR 19, 52, 74; CDWLB 4; CWW 2;
DA3; DAM NOV; DLB 232; EW 13;
EWL 3; MTCW 1, 2; RGSF 2; RGWL 3;
SSFS 10

Kunene, Mazisi (Raymond) 1930- ... **CLC 85**
See also BW 1, 3; CA 125; CANR 81; CP
7; DLB 117

Kung, Hans .... **CLC 130**
See Kueng, Hans

Kunikida Doppo 1869(?)-1908
See Doppo, Kunikida
See also DLB 180; EWL 3

Kunitz, Stanley (Jasspon) 1905- .. **CLC 6, 11,**
14, 148; PC 19
See also AMWS 3; CA 41-44R; CANR 26,
57, 98; CP 7; DA3; DLB 48; INT CANR-
26; MTCW 1, 2; PFS 11; RGAL 4

Kunze, Reiner 1933- .... **CLC 10**
See also CA 93-96; CWW 2; DLB 75; EWL
3

Kuprin, Aleksander Ivanovich
1870-1938 .... **TCLC 5**
See Kuprin, Alexandr Ivanovich
See also CA 104; 182

Kuprin, Alexandr Ivanovich
See Kuprin, Aleksander Ivanovich
See also EWL 3

Kureishi, Hanif 1954(?)- .... **CLC 64, 135**
See also CA 139; CANR 113; CBD; CD 5;
CN 7; DLB 194, 245; GLL 2; IDFW 4;
WLIT 4

Kurosawa, Akira 1910-1998 ..... **CLC 16, 119**
See also AAYA 11; CA 101; 170; CANR
46; DAM MULT

Kushner, Tony 1957(?)- .... **CLC 81; DC 10**
See also AMWS 9; CA 144; CAD; CANR
74; CD 5; DA3; DAM DRAM; DFS 5;
DLB 228; EWL 3; GLL 1; LAIT 5;
MTCW 2; RGAL 4

Kuttner, Henry 1915-1958 .... **TCLC 10**
See also CA 107; 157; DLB 8; FANT;
SCFW 2; SFW 4

Kutty, Madhavi
See Das, Kamala

Kuzma, Greg 1944- .... **CLC 7**
See also CA 33-36R; CANR 70

Kuzmin, Mikhail 1872(?)-1936 ...... **TCLC 40**
See also CA 170; EWL 3

Kyd, Thomas 1558-1594 .... **DC 3; LC 22**
See also BRW 1; DAM DRAM; DLB 62;
IDTP; LMFS 1; RGEL 2; TEA; WLIT 3

Kyprianos, Iossif
See Samarakis, Antonis

L. S.
See Stephen, Sir Leslie

Labrunie, Gerard
See Nerval, Gerard de

La Bruyere, Jean de 1645-1696 .... **LC 17**
See also DLB 268; EW 3; GFL Beginnings
to 1789

Lacan, Jacques (Marie Emile)
1901-1981 .... **CLC 75**
See also CA 121; 104; EWL 3; TWA

Laclos, Pierre Ambroise Francois
1741-1803 .... **NCLC 4, 87**
See also EW 4; GFL Beginnings to 1789;
RGWL 2, 3

Lacolere, Francois
See Aragon, Louis

La Colere, Francois
See Aragon, Louis

La Deshabilleuse
See Simenon, Georges (Jacques Christian)

Lady Gregory
See Gregory, Lady Isabella Augusta (Persse)

Lady of Quality, A
See Bagnold, Enid

La Fayette, Marie-(Madelaine Pioche de la
Vergne) 1634-1693 .... **LC 2**
See Lafayette, Marie-Madeleine
See also GFL Beginnings to 1789; RGWL
2, 3

Lafayette, Marie-Madeleine
See La Fayette, Marie-(Madelaine Pioche
de la Vergne)
See also DLB 268

Lafayette, Rene
See Hubbard, L(afayette) Ron(ald)

La Flesche, Francis 1857(?)-1932 ...... **NNAL**
See also CA 144; CANR 83; DLB 175

La Fontaine, Jean de 1621-1695 .... **LC 50**
See also DLB 268; EW 3; GFL Beginnings
to 1789; MAICYA 1, 2; RGWL 2, 3;
SATA 18

Laforgue, Jules 1860-1887 . **NCLC 5, 53; PC**
14; SSC 20
See also DLB 217; EW 7; GFL 1789 to the
Present; RGWL 2, 3

Layamon
See Layamon
See also DLB 146

Lagerkvist, Paer (Fabian)
1891-1974 .... **CLC 7, 10, 13, 54**
See Lagerkvist, Par
See also CA 85-88; 49-52; DA3; DAM
DRAM, NOV; MTCW 1, 2; TWA

Lagerkvist, Par .... **SSC 12**
See Lagerkvist, Paer (Fabian)
See also DLB 259; EW 10; EWL 3; MTCW
2; RGSF 2; RGWL 2, 3

Lagerloef, Selma (Ottiliana Lovisa)
1858-1940 .... **TCLC 4, 36**
See Lagerlof, Selma (Ottiliana Lovisa)
See also CA 108; MTCW 2; SATA 15

Lagerlof, Selma (Ottiliana Lovisa)
See Lagerloef, Selma (Ottiliana Lovisa)
See also CLR 7; SATA 15

La Guma, (Justin) Alex(ander)
1925-1985 .... **BLCS; CLC 19**
See also AFW; BW 1, 3; CA 49-52; 118;
CANR 25, 81; CDWLB 3; DAM NOV;
DLB 117, 225; EWL 3; MTCW 1, 2;
WLIT 2

Laidlaw, A. K.
See Grieve, C(hristopher) M(urray)

Lainez, Manuel Mujica
See Mujica Lainez, Manuel
See also HW 1

Laing, R(onald) D(avid) 1927-1989 . **CLC 95**
See also CA 107; 129; CANR 34; MTCW 1

Lamartine, Alphonse (Marie Louis Prat) de
1790-1869 .... **NCLC 11; PC 16**
See also DAM POET; DLB 217; GFL 1789
to the Present; RGWL 2, 3

Lamb, Charles 1775-1834 ..... **NCLC 10, 113;**
WLC
See also BRW 4; CDBLB 1789-1832; DA;
DAB; DAC; DAM MST; DLB 93, 107,
163; RGEL 2; SATA 17; TEA

Lamb, Lady Caroline 1785-1828 ... **NCLC 38**
　　See also DLB 116
Lamb, Mary Ann 1764-1847 .... **NCLC 125**
　　See also DLB 163; SATA 17
Lame Deer 1903(?)-1976 .... **NNAL**
　　See also CA 69-72
Lamming, George (William) 1927- ... **BLC 2;**
　　CLC 2, 4, 66, 144
　　See also BW 2, 3; CA 85-88; CANR 26,
　　76; CDWLB 3; CN 7; DAM MULT; DLB
　　125; EWL 3; MTCW 1, 2; NFS 15; RGEL
　　2
L'Amour, Louis (Dearborn)
　　1908-1988 .... **CLC 25, 55**
　　See Burns, Tex; Mayo, Jim
　　See also AAYA 16; AITN 2; BEST 89:2;
　　BPFB 2; CA 1-4R; 125; CANR 3, 25, 40;
　　CPW; DA3; DAM NOV, POP; DLB 206;
　　DLBY 1980; MTCW 1, 2; RGAL 4
Lampedusa, Giuseppe (Tomasi) di
　　.. **TCLC 13**
　　See Tomasi di Lampedusa, Giuseppe
　　See also CA 164; EW 11; MTCW 2; RGWL
　　2, 3
Lampman, Archibald 1861-1899 ... **NCLC 25**
　　See also DLB 92; RGEL 2; TWA
Lancaster, Bruce 1896-1963 .... **CLC 36**
　　See also CA 9-10; CANR 70; CAP 1; SATA
　　9
Lanchester, John 1962- .... **CLC 99**
　　See also CA 194; DLB 267
Landau, Mark Alexandrovich
　　See Aldanov, Mark (Alexandrovich)
Landau-Aldanov, Mark Alexandrovich
　　See Aldanov, Mark (Alexandrovich)
Landis, Jerry
　　See Simon, Paul (Frederick)
Landis, John 1950- .... **CLC 26**
　　See also CA 112; 122
Landolfi, Tommaso 1908-1979 .... **CLC 11, 49**
　　See also CA 127; 117; DLB 177; EWL 3
Landon, Letitia Elizabeth
　　1802-1838 .... **NCLC 15**
　　See also DLB 96
Landor, Walter Savage
　　1775-1864 .... **NCLC 14**
　　See also BRW 4; DLB 93, 107; RGEL 2
Landwirth, Heinz 1927-
　　See Lind, Jakov
　　See also CA 9-12R; CANR 7
Lane, Patrick 1939- .... **CLC 25**
　　See also CA 97-100; CANR 54; CP 7; DAM
　　POET; DLB 53; INT 97-100
Lang, Andrew 1844-1912 .... **TCLC 16**
　　See also CA 114; 137; CANR 85; DLB 98,
　　141, 184; FANT; MAICYA 1, 2; RGEL 2;
　　SATA 16; WCH
Lang, Fritz 1890-1976 .... **CLC 20, 103**
　　See also CA 77-80; 69-72; CANR 30
Lange, John
　　See Crichton, (John) Michael
Langer, Elinor 1939- .... **CLC 34**
　　See also CA 121
Langland, William 1332(?)-1400(?) ..... **LC 19**
　　See also BRW 1; DA; DAB; DAC; DAM
　　MST, POET; DLB 146; RGEL 2; TEA;
　　WLIT 3
Langstaff, Launcelot
　　See Irving, Washington
Lanier, Sidney 1842-1881 . **NCLC 6, 118; PC**
　　50
　　See also AMWS 1; DAM POET; DLB 64;
　　DLBD 13; EXPP; MAICYA 1; PFS 14;
　　RGAL 4; SATA 18
Lanyer, Aemilia 1569-1645 ...... **LC 10, 30, 83**
　　See also DLB 121
Lao-Tzu
　　See Lao Tzu

Lao Tzu c. 6th cent. B.C.-3rd cent.
　　B.C. .... **CMLC 7**
Lapine, James (Elliot) 1949- .... **CLC 39**
　　See also CA 123; 130; CANR 54; INT 130
Larbaud, Valery (Nicolas)
　　1881-1957 .... **TCLC 9**
　　See also CA 106; 152; EWL 3; GFL 1789
　　to the Present
Lardner, Ring
　　See Lardner, Ring(gold) W(ilmer)
　　See also BPFB 2; CDALB 1917-1929; DLB
　　11, 25, 86, 171; DLBD 16; RGAL 4;
　　RGSF 2
Lardner, Ring W., Jr.
　　See Lardner, Ring(gold) W(ilmer)
Lardner, Ring(gold) W(ilmer)
　　1885-1933 .... **SSC 32; TCLC 2, 14**
　　See Lardner, Ring
　　See also AMW; CA 104; 131; MTCW 1, 2;
　　TUS
Laredo, Betty
　　See Codrescu, Andrei
Larkin, Maia
　　See Wojciechowska, Maia (Teresa)
Larkin, Philip (Arthur) 1922-1985 ... **CLC 3,**
　　5, 8, 9, 13, 18, 33, 39, 64; PC 21
　　See also BRWS 1; CA 5-8R; 117; CANR
　　24, 62; CDBLB 1960 to Present; DA3;
　　DAB; DAM MST, POET; DLB 27; EWL
　　3; MTCW 1, 2; PFS 3, 4, 12; RGEL 2
La Roche, Sophie von
　　1730-1807 .... **NCLC 121**
　　See also DLB 94
Larra (y Sanchez de Castro), Mariano Jose
　　de 1809-1837 .... **NCLC 17**
Larsen, Eric 1941- .... **CLC 55**
　　See also CA 132
Larsen, Nella 1893(?)-1963 .... **BLC 2; CLC**
　　37; HR 3
　　See also AFAW 1, 2; BW 1; CA 125; CANR
　　83; DAM MULT; DLB 51; FW; LATS 1;
　　LMFS 2
Larson, Charles R(aymond) 1938- ... **CLC 31**
　　See also CA 53-56; CANR 4
Larson, Jonathan 1961-1996 .... **CLC 99**
　　See also AAYA 28; CA 156
Las Casas, Bartolome de
　　1474-1566 .... **HLCS; LC 31**
　　See Casas, Bartolome de las
　　See also LAW
Lasch, Christopher 1932-1994 .... **CLC 102**
　　See also CA 73-76; 144; CANR 25, 118;
　　DLB 246; MTCW 1, 2
Lasker-Schueler, Else 1869-1945 ... **TCLC 57**
　　See Lasker-Schuler, Else
　　See also CA 183; DLB 66, 124
Lasker-Schuler, Else
　　See Lasker-Schueler, Else
　　See also EWL 3
Laski, Harold J(oseph) 1893-1950 . **TCLC 79**
　　See also CA 188
Latham, Jean Lee 1902-1995 .... **CLC 12**
　　See also AITN 1; BYA 1; CA 5-8R; CANR
　　7, 84; CLR 50; MAICYA 1, 2; SATA 2,
　　68; YAW
Latham, Mavis
　　See Clark, Mavis Thorpe
Lathen, Emma .... **CLC 2**
　　See Hennissart, Martha; Latsis, Mary J(ane)
　　See also BPFB 2; CMW 4
Lathrop, Francis
　　See Leiber, Fritz (Reuter, Jr.)
Latsis, Mary J(ane) 1927(?)-1997
　　See Lathen, Emma
　　See also CA 85-88; 162; CMW 4
Lattany, Kristin
　　See Lattany, Kristin (Elaine Eggleston)
　　Hunter

Lattany, Kristin (Elaine Eggleston) Hunter
　　1931- .... **CLC 35**
　　See also AITN 1; BW 1; BYA 3; CA 13-
　　16R; CANR 13, 108; CLR 3; CN 7; DLB
　　33; INT CANR-13; MAICYA 1, 2; SAAS
　　10; SATA 12, 132; YAW
Lattimore, Richmond (Alexander)
　　1906-1984 .... **CLC 3**
　　See also CA 1-4R; 112; CANR 1
Laughlin, James 1914-1997 .... **CLC 49**
　　See also CA 21-24R; 162; CAAS 22; CANR
　　9, 47; CP 7; DLB 48; DLBY 1996, 1997
Laurence, (Jean) Margaret (Wemyss)
　　1926-1987 . **CLC 3, 6, 13, 50, 62; SSC 7**
　　See also BYA 13; CA 5-8R; 121; CANR
　　33; DAC; DAM MST; DLB 53; EWL 3;
　　FW; MTCW 1, 2; NFS 11; RGEL 2;
　　RGSF 2; SATA-Obit 50; TCWW 2
Laurent, Antoine 1952- .... **CLC 50**
Lauscher, Hermann
　　See Hesse, Hermann
Lautreamont 1846-1870 .. **NCLC 12; SSC 14**
　　See Lautreamont, Isidore Lucien Ducasse
　　See also GFL 1789 to the Present; RGWL
　　2, 3
Lautreamont, Isidore Lucien Ducasse
　　See Lautreamont
　　See also DLB 217
Laverty, Donald
　　See Blish, James (Benjamin)
Lavin, Mary 1912-1996 . **CLC 4, 18, 99; SSC**
　　4
　　See also CA 9-12R; 151; CANR 33; CN 7;
　　DLB 15; FW; MTCW 1; RGEL 2; RGSF
　　2
Lavond, Paul Dennis
　　See Kornbluth, C(yril) M.; Pohl, Frederik
Lawler, Raymond Evenor 1922- .... **CLC 58**
　　See also CA 103; CD 5; RGEL 2
Lawrence, D(avid) H(erbert Richards)
　　1885-1930 ... **SSC 4, 19; TCLC 2, 9, 16,**
　　33, 48, 61, 93; WLC
　　See Chambers, Jessie
　　See also BPFB 2; BRW 7; BRWR 2; CA
　　104; 121; CDBLB 1914-1945; DA; DA3;
　　DAB; DAC; DAM MST, NOV, POET;
　　DLB 10, 19, 36, 98, 162, 195; EWL 3;
　　EXPP; EXPS; LAIT 2, 3; MTCW 1, 2;
　　PFS 6; RGEL 2; RGSF 2; SSFS 2, 6;
　　TEA; WLIT 4; WP
Lawrence, T(homas) E(dward)
　　1888-1935 .... **TCLC 18**
　　See Dale, Colin
　　See also BRWS 2; CA 115; 167; DLB 195
Lawrence of Arabia
　　See Lawrence, T(homas) E(dward)
Lawson, Henry (Archibald Hertzberg)
　　1867-1922 .... **SSC 18; TCLC 27**
　　See also CA 120; 181; DLB 230; RGEL 2;
　　RGSF 2
Lawton, Dennis
　　See Faust, Frederick (Schiller)
Laxness, Halldor .... **CLC 25**
　　See Gudjonsson, Halldor Kiljan
　　See also EW 12; EWL 3; RGWL 2, 3
Layamon fl. c. 1200- .... **CMLC 10**
　　See Layamon
　　See also RGEL 2
Laye, Camara 1928-1980 ..... **BLC 2; CLC 4,**
　　38
　　See Camara Laye
　　See also AFW; BW 1; CA 85-88; 97-100;
　　CANR 25; DAM MULT; MTCW 1, 2;
　　WLIT 2
Layton, Irving (Peter) 1912- .... **CLC 2, 15,**
　　164
　　See also CA 1-4R; CANR 2, 33, 43, 66; CP
　　7; DAC; DAM MST, POET; DLB 88;
　　EWL 3; MTCW 1, 2; PFS 12; RGEL 2

Mazer, Norma Fox 1931- .... **CLC 26**
See also AAYA 5, 36; BYA 1, 8; CA 69-72; CANR 12, 32, 66; CLR 23; JRDA; MAI-CYA 1, 2; SAAS 1; SATA 24, 67, 105; WYA; YAW

Mazzini, Guiseppe 1805-1872 .... **NCLC 34**

McAlmon, Robert (Menzies)
1895-1956 .... **TCLC 97**
See also CA 107; 168; DLB 4, 45; DLBD 15; GLL 1

McAuley, James Phillip 1917-1976 .. **CLC 45**
See also CA 97-100; DLB 260; RGEL 2

McBain, Ed
See Hunter, Evan
See also MSW

McBrien, William (Augustine)
1930- .... **CLC 44**
See also CA 107; CANR 90

McCabe, Patrick 1955- .... **CLC 133**
See also CA 130; CANR 50, 90; CN 7; DLB 194

McCaffrey, Anne (Inez) 1926- .... **CLC 17**
See also AAYA 6, 34; AITN 2; BEST 89:2; BPFB 2; BYA 5; CA 25-28R; CANR 15, 35, 55, 96; CLR 49; CPW; DA3; DAM NOV, POP; DLB 8; JRDA; MAICYA 1, 2; MTCW 1, 2; SAAS 11; SATA 8, 70, 116; SFW 4; SUFW 2; WYA; YAW

McCall, Nathan 1955(?)- .... **CLC 86**
See also BW 3; CA 146; CANR 88

McCann, Arthur
See Campbell, John W(ood, Jr.)

McCann, Edson
See Pohl, Frederik

McCarthy, Charles, Jr. 1933-
See McCarthy, Cormac
See also CANR 42, 69, 101; CN 7; CPW; CSW; DA3; DAM POP; MTCW 2

McCarthy, Cormac .... **CLC 4, 57, 59, 101**
See McCarthy, Charles, Jr.
See also AAYA 41; AMWS 8; BPFB 2; CA 13-16R; CANR 10; DLB 6, 143, 256; EWL 3; LATS 1; TCWW 2

McCarthy, Mary (Therese)
1912-1989 .. **CLC 1, 3, 5, 14, 24, 39, 59; SSC 24**
See also AMW; BPFB 2; CA 5-8R; 129; CANR 16, 50, 64; DA3; DLB 2; DLBY 1981; EWL 3; FW; INT CANR-16; MAWW; MTCW 1, 2; RGAL 4; TUS

McCartney, (James) Paul 1942- . **CLC 12, 35**
See also CA 146; CANR 111

McCauley, Stephen (D.) 1955- .... **CLC 50**
See also CA 141

McClaren, Peter .... **CLC 70**

McClure, Michael (Thomas) 1932- ... **CLC 6, 10**
See also BG 3; CA 21-24R; CAD; CANR 17, 46, 77; CD 5; CP 7; DLB 16; WP

McCorkle, Jill (Collins) 1958- .... **CLC 51**
See also CA 121; CANR 113; CSW; DLB 234; DLBY 1987

McCourt, Frank 1930- .... **CLC 109**
See also AMWS 12; CA 157; CANR 97; NCFS 1

McCourt, James 1941- .... **CLC 5**
See also CA 57-60; CANR 98

McCourt, Malachy 1931- .... **CLC 119**
See also SATA 126

McCoy, Horace (Stanley)
1897-1955 .... **TCLC 28**
See also CA 108; 155; CMW 4; DLB 9

McCrae, John 1872-1918 .... **TCLC 12**
See also CA 109; DLB 92; PFS 5

McCreigh, James
See Pohl, Frederik

McCullers, (Lula) Carson (Smith)
1917-1967 .... **CLC 1, 4, 10, 12, 48, 100; SSC 9, 24; WLC**
See also AAYA 21; AMW; BPFB 2; CA 5-8R; 25-28R; CABS 1, 3; CANR 18; CDALB 1941-1968; DA; DA3; DAB; DAC; DAM MST, NOV; DFS 5; DLB 2, 7, 173, 228; EWL 3; EXPS; FW; GLL 1; LAIT 3, 4; MAWW; MTCW 1, 2; NFS 6, 13; RGAL 4; RGSF 2; SATA 27; SSFS 5; TUS; YAW

McCulloch, John Tyler
See Burroughs, Edgar Rice

McCullough, Colleen 1938(?)- .. **CLC 27, 107**
See also AAYA 36; BPFB 2; CA 81-84; CANR 17, 46, 67, 98; CPW; DA3; DAM NOV, POP; MTCW 1, 2; RHW

McCunn, Ruthanne Lum 1946- .... **AAL**
See also CA 119; CANR 43, 96; LAIT 2; SATA 63

McDermott, Alice 1953- .... **CLC 90**
See also CA 109; CANR 40, 90

McElroy, Joseph 1930- .... **CLC 5, 47**
See also CA 17-20R; CN 7

McEwan, Ian (Russell) 1948- .... **CLC 13, 66, 169**
See also BEST 90:4; BRWS 4; CA 61-64; CANR 14, 41, 69, 87; CN 7; DAM NOV; DLB 14, 194; HGG; MTCW 1, 2; RGSF 2; SUFW 2; TEA

McFadden, David 1940- .... **CLC 48**
See also CA 104; CP 7; DLB 60; INT 104

McFarland, Dennis 1950- .... **CLC 65**
See also CA 165; CANR 110

McGahern, John 1934- ... **CLC 5, 9, 48, 156; SSC 17**
See also CA 17-20R; CANR 29, 68, 113; CN 7; DLB 14, 231; MTCW 1

McGinley, Patrick (Anthony) 1937- . **CLC 41**
See also CA 120; 127; CANR 56; INT 127

McGinley, Phyllis 1905-1978 .... **CLC 14**
See also CA 9-12R; 77-80; CANR 19; CWRI 5; DLB 11, 48; PFS 9, 13; SATA 2, 44; SATA-Obit 24

McGinniss, Joe 1942- .... **CLC 32**
See also AITN 2; BEST 89:2; CA 25-28R; CANR 26, 70; CPW; DLB 185; INT CANR-26

McGivern, Maureen Daly
See Daly, Maureen

McGrath, Patrick 1950- .... **CLC 55**
See also CA 136; CANR 65; CN 7; DLB 231; HGG; SUFW 2

McGrath, Thomas (Matthew)
1916-1990 .... **CLC 28, 59**
See also AMWS 10; CA 9-12R; 132; CANR 6, 33, 95; DAM POET; MTCW 1; SATA 41; SATA-Obit 66

McGuane, Thomas (Francis III)
1939- .... **CLC 3, 7, 18, 45, 127**
See also AITN 2; BPFB 2; CA 49-52; CANR 5, 24, 49, 94; CN 7; DLB 2, 212; DLBY 1980; EWL 3; INT CANR-24; MTCW 1; TCWW 2

McGuckian, Medbh 1950- .... **CLC 48, 174; PC 27**
See also BRWS 5; CA 143; CP 7; CWP; DAM POET; DLB 40

McHale, Tom 1942(?)-1982 .... **CLC 3, 5**
See also AITN 1; CA 77-80; 106

McIlvanney, William 1936- .... **CLC 42**
See also CA 25-28R; CANR 61; CMW 4; DLB 14, 207

McIlwraith, Maureen Mollie Hunter
See Hunter, Mollie
See also SATA 2

McInerney, Jay 1955- .... **CLC 34, 112**
See also AAYA 18; BPFB 2; CA 116; 123; CANR 45, 68, 116; CN 7; DA3; DAM POP; INT 123; MTCW 2

McIntyre, Vonda N(eel) 1948- .... **CLC 18**
See also CA 81-84; CANR 17, 34, 69; MTCW 1; SFW 4; YAW

McKay, Claude .... **BLC 3; HR 3; PC 2; TCLC 7, 41; WLC**
See McKay, Festus Claudius
See also AFAW 1, 2; AMWS 10; DAB; DLB 4, 45, 51, 117; EWL 3; EXPP; GLL 2; LAIT 3; LMFS 2; PAB; PFS 4; RGAL 4; WP

McKay, Festus Claudius 1889-1948
See McKay, Claude
See also BW 1, 3; CA 104; 124; CANR 73; DA; DAC; DAM MST, MULT, NOV, POET; MTCW 1, 2; TUS

McKuen, Rod 1933- .... **CLC 1, 3**
See also AITN 1; CA 41-44R; CANR 40

McLoughlin, R. B.
See Mencken, H(enry) L(ouis)

McLuhan, (Herbert) Marshall
1911-1980 .... **CLC 37, 83**
See also CA 9-12R; 102; CANR 12, 34, 61; DLB 88; INT CANR-12; MTCW 1, 2

McManus, Declan Patrick Aloysius
See Costello, Elvis

McMillan, Terry (L.) 1951- . **BLCS; CLC 50, 61, 112**
See also AAYA 21; BPFB 2; BW 2, 3; CA 140; CANR 60, 104; CPW; DA3; DAM MULT, NOV, POP; MTCW 2; RGAL 4; YAW

McMurtry, Larry (Jeff) 1936- .. **CLC 2, 3, 7, 11, 27, 44, 127**
See also AAYA 15; AITN 2; AMWS 5; BEST 89:2; BPFB 2; CA 5-8R; CANR 19, 43, 64, 103; CDALB 1968-1988; CN 7; CPW; CSW; DA3; DAM NOV, POP; DLB 2, 143, 256; DLBY 1980, 1987; EWL 3; MTCW 1, 2; RGAL 4; TCWW 2

McNally, T. M. 1961- .... **CLC 82**

McNally, Terrence 1939- .... **CLC 4, 7, 41, 91**
See also CA 45-48; CAD; CANR 2, 56, 116; CD 5; DA3; DAM DRAM; DFS 16; DLB 7, 249; EWL 3; GLL 1; MTCW 2

McNamer, Deirdre 1950- .... **CLC 70**

McNeal, Tom .... **CLC 119**

McNeile, Herman Cyril 1888-1937
See Sapper
See also CA 184; CMW 4; DLB 77

McNickle, (William) D'Arcy
1904-1977 .... **CLC 89; NNAL**
See also CA 9-12R; 85-88; CANR 5, 45; DAM MULT; DLB 175, 212; RGAL 4; SATA-Obit 22

McPhee, John (Angus) 1931- .... **CLC 36**
See also AMWS 3; ANW; BEST 90:1; CA 65-68; CANR 20, 46, 64, 69; CPW; DLB 185, 275; MTCW 1, 2; TUS

McPherson, James Alan 1943- . **BLCS; CLC 19, 77**
See also BW 1, 3; CA 25-28R; CAAS 17; CANR 24, 74; CN 7; CSW; DLB 38, 244; EWL 3; MTCW 1, 2; RGAL 4; RGSF 2

McPherson, William (Alexander)
1933- .... **CLC 34**
See also CA 69-72; CANR 28; INT CANR-28

McTaggart, J. McT. Ellis
See McTaggart, John McTaggart Ellis

McTaggart, John McTaggart Ellis
1866-1925 .... **TCLC 105**
See also CA 120; DLB 262

Mead, George Herbert 1863-1931 . **TCLC 89**
See also CA 212; DLB 270

Niven, Laurence Van Cott 1938-
See Niven, Larry
See also CA 21-24R; CAAE 207; CAAS 12; CANR 14, 44, 66, 113; CPW; DAM POP; MTCW 1, 2; SATA 95; SFW 4

Nixon, Agnes Eckhardt 1927- .... **CLC 21**
See also CA 110

Nizan, Paul 1905-1940 .... **TCLC 40**
See also CA 161; DLB 72; EWL 3; GFL 1789 to the Present

Nkosi, Lewis 1936- .... **BLC 3; CLC 45**
See also BW 1, 3; CA 65-68; CANR 27, 81; CBD; CD 5; DAM MULT; DLB 157, 225

Nodier, (Jean) Charles (Emmanuel)
1780-1844 .... **NCLC 19**
See also DLB 119; GFL 1789 to the Present

Noguchi, Yone 1875-1947 .... **TCLC 80**

Nolan, Christopher 1965- .... **CLC 58**
See also CA 111; CANR 88

Noon, Jeff 1957- .... **CLC 91**
See also CA 148; CANR 83; DLB 267; SFW 4

Norden, Charles
See Durrell, Lawrence (George)

Nordhoff, Charles Bernard
1887-1947 .... **TCLC 23**
See also CA 108; 211; DLB 9; LAIT 1; RHW 1; SATA 23

Norfolk, Lawrence 1963- .... **CLC 76**
See also CA 144; CANR 85; CN 7; DLB 267

Norman, Marsha 1947- .... **CLC 28; DC 8**
See also CA 105; CABS 3; CAD; CANR 41; CD 5; CSW; CWD; DAM DRAM; DFS 2; DLB 266; DLBY 1984; FW

Normyx
See Douglas, (George) Norman

Norris, (Benjamin) Frank(lin, Jr.)
1870-1902 .... **SSC 28; TCLC 24**
See also AMW; BPFB 2; CA 110; 160; CDALB 1865-1917; DLB 12, 71, 186; LMFS 2; NFS 12; RGAL 4; TCWW 2; TUS

Norris, Leslie 1921- .... **CLC 14**
See also CA 11-12; CANR 14, 117; CAP 1; CP 7; DLB 27, 256

North, Andrew
See Norton, Andre

North, Anthony
See Koontz, Dean R(ay)

North, Captain George
See Stevenson, Robert Louis (Balfour)

North, Captain George
See Stevenson, Robert Louis (Balfour)

North, Milou
See Erdrich, Louise

Northrup, B. A.
See Hubbard, L(afayette) Ron(ald)

North Staffs
See Hulme, T(homas) E(rnest)

Northup, Solomon 1808-1863 ...... **NCLC 105**

Norton, Alice Mary
See Norton, Andre
See also MAICYA 1; SATA 1, 43

Norton, Andre 1912- .... **CLC 12**
See Norton, Alice Mary
See also AAYA 14; BPFB 2; BYA 4, 10, 12; CA 1-4R; CANR 68; CLR 50; DLB 8, 52; JRDA; MAICYA 2; MTCW 1; SATA 91; SUFW 1, 2; YAW

Norton, Caroline 1808-1877 .... **NCLC 47**
See also DLB 21, 159, 199

Norway, Nevil Shute 1899-1960
See Shute, Nevil
See also CA 102; 93-96; CANR 85; MTCW 2

Norwid, Cyprian Kamil
1821-1883 .... **NCLC 17**
See also RGWL 3

Nosille, Nabrah
See Ellison, Harlan (Jay)

Nossack, Hans Erich 1901-1978 .... **CLC 6**
See also CA 93-96; 85-88; DLB 69; EWL 3

Nostradamus 1503-1566 .... **LC 27**

Nosu, Chuji
See Ozu, Yasujiro

Notenburg, Eleanora (Genrikhovna) von
See Guro, Elena

Nova, Craig 1945- .... **CLC 7, 31**
See also CA 45-48; CANR 2, 53

Novak, Joseph
See Kosinski, Jerzy (Nikodem)

Novalis 1772-1801 .... **NCLC 13**
See also CDWLB 2; DLB 90; EW 5; RGWL 2, 3

Novick, Peter 1934- .... **CLC 164**
See also CA 188

Novis, Emile
See Weil, Simone (Adolphine)

Nowlan, Alden (Albert) 1933-1983 ... **CLC 15**
See also CA 9-12R; CANR 5; DAC; DAM MST; DLB 53; PFS 12

Noyes, Alfred 1880-1958 ...... **PC 27; TCLC 7**
See also CA 104; 188; DLB 20; EXPP; FANT; PFS 4; RGEL 2

Nugent, Richard Bruce 1906(?)-1987 ... **HR 3**
See also BW 1; CA 125; DLB 51; GLL 2

Nunn, Kem .... **CLC 34**
See also CA 159

Nwapa, Flora (Nwanzuruaha)
1931-1993 .... **BLCS; CLC 133**
See also BW 2; CA 143; CANR 83; CD-WLB 3; CWRI 5; DLB 125; EWL 3; WLIT 2

Nye, Robert 1939- .... **CLC 13, 42**
See also CA 33-36R; CANR 29, 67, 107; CN 7; CP 7; CWRI 5; DAM NOV; DLB 14, 271; FANT; HGG; MTCW 1; RHW; SATA 6

Nyro, Laura 1947-1997 .... **CLC 17**
See also CA 194

Oates, Joyce Carol 1938- .. **CLC 1, 2, 3, 6, 9, 11, 15, 19, 33, 52, 108, 134; SSC 6; WLC**
See also AAYA 15, 52; AITN 1; AMWS 2; BEST 89:2; BPFB 2; BYA 11; CA 5-8R; CANR 25, 45, 74, 113, 113; CDALB 1968-1988; CN 7; CP 7; CPW; CWP; DA; DA3; DAB; DAC; DAM MST, NOV, POP; DLB 2, 5, 130; DLBY 1981; EWL 3; EXPS; FW; HGG; INT CANR-25; LAIT 4; MAWW; MTCW 1, 2; NFS 8; RGAL 4; RGSF 2; SSFS 17; SUFW 2; TUS

O'Brian, E. G.
See Clarke, Arthur C(harles)

O'Brian, Patrick 1914-2000 .... **CLC 152**
See also CA 144; 187; CANR 74; CPW; MTCW 2; RHW

O'Brien, Darcy 1939-1998 .... **CLC 11**
See also CA 21-24R; 167; CANR 8, 59

O'Brien, Edna 1936- ..... **CLC 3, 5, 8, 13, 36, 65, 116; SSC 10**
See also BRWS 5; CA 1-4R; CANR 6, 41, 65, 102; CDBLB 1960 to Present; CN 7; DA3; DAM NOV; DLB 14, 231; EWL 3; FW; MTCW 1, 2; RGSF 2; WLIT 4

O'Brien, Fitz-James 1828-1862 ..... **NCLC 21**
See also DLB 74; RGAL 4; SUFW

O'Brien, Flann .... **CLC 1, 4, 5, 7, 10, 47**
See O Nuallain, Brian
See also BRWS 2; DLB 231; EWL 3; RGEL 2

O'Brien, Richard 1942- .... **CLC 17**
See also CA 124

O'Brien, (William) Tim(othy) 1946- . **CLC 7, 19, 40, 103**
See also AAYA 16; AMWS 5; CA 85-88; CANR 40, 58; CDALBS; CN 7; CPW; DA3; DAM POP; DLB 152; DLBD 9; DLBY 1980; MTCW 2; RGAL 4; SSFS 5, 15

Obstfelder, Sigbjoern 1866-1900 .... **TCLC 23**
See also CA 123

O'Casey, Sean 1880-1964 .... **CLC 1, 5, 9, 11, 15, 88; DC 12; WLCS**
See also BRW 7; CA 89-92; CANR 62; CBD; CDBLB 1914-1945; DA3; DAB; DAC; DAM DRAM, MST; DLB 10; EWL 3; MTCW 1, 2; RGEL 2; TEA; WLIT 4

O'Cathasaigh, Sean
See O'Casey, Sean

Occom, Samson 1723-1792 .... **LC 60; NNAL**
See also DLB 175

Ochs, Phil(ip David) 1940-1976 .... **CLC 17**
See also CA 185; 65-68

O'Connor, Edwin (Greene)
1918-1968 .... **CLC 14**
See also CA 93-96; 25-28R

O'Connor, (Mary) Flannery
1925-1964 .... **CLC 1, 2, 3, 6, 10, 13, 15, 21, 66, 104; SSC 1, 23, 61; TCLC 132; WLC**
See also AAYA 7; AMW; AMWR 2; BPFB 3; CA 1-4R; CANR 3, 41; CDALB 1941-1968; DA; DA3; DAB; DAC; DAM MST, NOV; DLB 2, 152; DLBD 12; DLBY 1980; EWL 3; EXPS; LAIT 5; MAWW; MTCW 1, 2; NFS 3; RGAL 4; RGSF 2; SSFS 2, 7, 10; TUS

O'Connor, Frank .... **CLC 23; SSC 5**
See O'Donovan, Michael Francis
See also DLB 162; EWL 3; RGSF 2; SSFS 5

O'Dell, Scott 1898-1989 .... **CLC 30**
See also AAYA 3, 44; BPFB 3; BYA 1, 2, 3, 5; CA 61-64; 129; CANR 12, 30, 112; CLR 1, 16; DLB 52; JRDA; MAICYA 1, 2; SATA 12, 60, 134; WYA; YAW

Odets, Clifford 1906-1963 ..... **CLC 2, 28, 98; DC 6**
See also AMWS 2; CA 85-88; CAD; CANR 62; DAM DRAM; DFS 2, 26; EWL 3; MTCW 1, 2; RGAL 4; TUS

O'Doherty, Brian 1928- .... **CLC 76**
See also CA 105; CANR 108

O'Donnell, K. M.
See Malzberg, Barry N(athaniel)

O'Donnell, Lawrence
See Kuttner, Henry

O'Donovan, Michael Francis
1903-1966 .... **CLC 14**
See O'Connor, Frank
See also CA 93-96; CANR 84

Oe, Kenzaburo 1935- .. **CLC 10, 36, 86; SSC 20**
See Oe Kenzaburo
See also CA 97-100; CANR 36, 50, 74; CWW 2; DA3; DAM NOV; DLB 182; DLBY 1994; EWL 3; LATS 1; MJW; MTCW 1, 2; RGSF 2; RGWL 2, 3

Oe Kenzaburo
See Oe, Kenzaburo
See also EWL 3

O'Faolain, Julia 1932- .... **CLC 6, 19, 47, 108**
See also CA 81-84; CAAS 2; CANR 12, 61; CN 7; DLB 14, 231; FW; MTCW 1; RHW

O'Faolain, Sean 1900-1991 ...... **CLC 1, 7, 14, 32, 70; SSC 13**
See also CA 61-64; 134; CANR 12, 66; DLB 15, 162; MTCW 1, 2; RGEL 2; RGSF 2

Price, (Edward) Reynolds 1933- ... **CLC 3, 6, 13, 43, 50, 63; SSC 22**
See also AMWS 6; CA 1-4R; CANR 1, 37, 57, 87; CN 7; CSW; DAM NOV; DLB 2, 218, 278; EWL 3; INT CANR-37

Price, Richard 1949- .... **CLC 6, 12**
See also CA 49-52; CANR 3; DLBY 1981

Prichard, Katharine Susannah
1883-1969 .... **CLC 46**
See also CA 11-12; CANR 33; CAP 1; DLB 260; MTCW 1; RGEL 2; RGSF 2; SATA 66

Priestley, J(ohn) B(oynton)
1894-1984 .... **CLC 2, 5, 9, 34**
See also BRW 7; CA 9-12R; 113; CANR 33; CDBLB 1914-1945; DA3; DAM DRAM, NOV; DLB 10, 34, 77, 100, 139; DLBY 1984; EWL 3; MTCW 1, 2; RGEL 2; SFW 4

Prince 1958(?)- .... **CLC 35**

Prince, F(rank) T(empleton) 1912- .. **CLC 22**
See also CA 101; CANR 43, 79; CP 7; DLB 20

Prince Kropotkin
See Kropotkin, Peter (Aleksieevich)

Prior, Matthew 1664-1721 .... **LC 4**
See also DLB 95; RGEL 2

Prishvin, Mikhail 1873-1954 .... **TCLC 75**
See Prishvin, Mikhail Mikhailovich

Prishvin, Mikhail Mikhailovich
See Prishvin, Mikhail
See also DLB 272; EWL 3

Pritchard, William H(arrison)
1932- .... **CLC 34**
See also CA 65-68; CANR 23, 95; DLB 111

Pritchett, V(ictor) S(awdon)
1900-1997 ... **CLC 5, 13, 15, 41; SSC 14**
See also BPFB 3; BRWS 3; CA 61-64; 157; CANR 31, 63; CN 7; DA3; DAM NOV; DLB 15, 139; EWL 3; MTCW 1, 2; RGEL 2; RGSF 2; TEA

Private 19022
See Manning, Frederic

Probst, Mark 1925- .... **CLC 59**
See also CA 130

Prokosch, Frederic 1908-1989 ...... **CLC 4, 48**
See also CA 73-76; 128; CANR 82; DLB 48; MTCW 2

Propertius, Sextus c. 50B.C.-c.
16B.C. .... **CMLC 32**
See also AW 2; CDWLB 1; DLB 211; RGWL 2, 3

Prophet, The
See Dreiser, Theodore (Herman Albert)

Prose, Francine 1947- .... **CLC 45**
See also CA 109; 112; CANR 46, 95; DLB 234; SATA 101

Proudhon
See Cunha, Euclides (Rodrigues Pimenta) da

Proulx, Annie
See Proulx, E(dna) Annie

Proulx, E(dna) Annie 1935- ...... **CLC 81, 158**
See also AMWS 7; BPFB 3; CA 145; CANR 65, 110; CN 7; CPW 1; DA3; DAM POP; MTCW 2

Proust,
(Valentin-Louis-George-Eugene-)Marcel
1871-1922 .... **TCLC 7, 13, 33; WLC**
See also BPFB 3; CA 104; 120; CANR 110; DA; DA3; DAB; DAC; DAM MST, NOV; DLB 65; EW 8; EWL 3; GFL 1789 to the Present; MTCW 1, 2; RGWL 2, 3; TWA

Prowler, Harley
See Masters, Edgar Lee

Prus, Boleslaw 1845-1912 .... **TCLC 48**
See also RGWL 2, 3

Pryor, Richard (Franklin Lenox Thomas)
1940- .... **CLC 26**
See also CA 122; 152

Przybyszewski, Stanislaw
1868-1927 .... **TCLC 36**
See also CA 160; DLB 66; EWL 3

Pteleon
See Grieve, C(hristopher) M(urray)
See also DAM POET

Puckett, Lute
See Masters, Edgar Lee

Puig, Manuel 1932-1990 .... **CLC 3, 5, 10, 28, 65, 133; HLC 2**
See also BPFB 3; CA 45-48; CANR 2, 32, 63; CDWLB 3; DA3; DAM MULT; DLB 113; DNFS 1; EWL 3; GLL 1; HW 1, 2; LAW; MTCW 1, 2; RGWL 2, 3; TWA; WLIT 1

Pulitzer, Joseph 1847-1911 .... **TCLC 76**
See also CA 114; DLB 23

Purchas, Samuel 1577(?)-1626 .... **LC 70**
See also DLB 151

Purdy, A(lfred) W(ellington)
1918-2000 .... **CLC 3, 6, 14, 50**
See also CA 81-84; 189; CAAS 17; CANR 42, 66; CP 7; DAC; DAM MST, POET; DLB 88; PFS 5; RGEL 2

Purdy, James (Amos) 1923- .... **CLC 2, 4, 10, 28, 52**
See also AMWS 7; CA 33-36R; CAAS 1; CANR 19, 51; CN 7; DLB 2, 218; EWL 3; INT CANR-19; MTCW 1; RGAL 4

Pure, Simon
See Swinnerton, Frank Arthur

Pushkin, Aleksandr Sergeevich
See Pushkin, Alexander (Sergeyevich)
See also DLB 205

Pushkin, Alexander (Sergeyevich)
1799-1837 .... **NCLC 3, 27, 83; PC 10; SSC 27, 55; WLC**
See Pushkin, Aleksandr Sergeevich
See also DA; DA3; DAB; DAC; DAM DRAM, MST, POET; EW 5; EXPS; RGSF 2; RGWL 2, 3; SATA 61; SSFS 9; TWA

P'u Sung-ling 1640-1715 .... **LC 49; SSC 31**

Putnam, Arthur Lee
See Alger, Horatio, Jr.

Puzo, Mario 1920-1999 .... **CLC 1, 2, 6, 36, 107**
See also BPFB 3; CA 65-68; 185; CANR 4, 42, 65, 99; CN 7; CPW; DA3; DAM NOV, POP; DLB 6; MTCW 1, 2; NFS 16; RGAL 4

Pygge, Edward
See Barnes, Julian (Patrick)

Pyle, Ernest Taylor 1900-1945
See Pyle, Ernie
See also CA 115; 160

Pyle, Ernie .... **TCLC 75**
See Pyle, Ernest Taylor
See also DLB 29; MTCW 2

Pyle, Howard 1853-1911 .... **TCLC 81**
See also BYA 2, 4; CA 109; 137; CLR 22; DLB 42, 188; DLBD 13; LAIT 1; MAI-CYA 1, 2; SATA 16, 100; WCH; YAW

Pym, Barbara (Mary Crampton)
1913-1980 .... **CLC 13, 19, 37, 111**
See also BPFB 3; BRWS 2; CA 13-14; 97-100; CANR 13, 34; CAP 1; DLB 14, 207; DLBY 1987; EWL 3; MTCW 1, 2; RGEL 2; TEA

Pynchon, Thomas (Ruggles, Jr.)
1937- ...... **CLC 2, 3, 6, 9, 11, 18, 33, 62, 72, 123; SSC 14; WLC**
See also AMWS 2; BEST 90:2; BPFB 3; CA 17-20R; CANR 22, 46, 73; CN 7; CPW 1; DA; DA3; DAB; DAC; DAM MST, NOV, POP; DLB 2, 173; EWL 3; MTCW 1, 2; RGAL 4; SFW 4; TUS

Pythagoras c. 582B.C.-c. 507B.C. . **CMLC 22**
See also DLB 176

Q
See Quiller-Couch, Sir Arthur (Thomas)

Qian, Chongzhu
See Ch'ien, Chung-shu

Qian Zhongshu
See Ch'ien, Chung-shu

Qroll
See Dagerman, Stig (Halvard)

Quarrington, Paul (Lewis) 1953- ..... **CLC 65**
See also CA 129; CANR 62, 95

Quasimodo, Salvatore 1901-1968 .... **CLC 10; PC 47**
See also CA 13-16; 25-28R; CAP 1; DLB 114; EW 12; EWL 3; MTCW 1; RGWL 2, 3

Quatermass, Martin
See Carpenter, John (Howard)

Quay, Stephen 1947- .... **CLC 95**
See also CA 189

Quay, Timothy 1947- .... **CLC 95**
See also CA 189

Queen, Ellery .... **CLC 3, 11**
See Dannay, Frederic; Davidson, Avram (James); Deming, Richard; Fairman, Paul W.; Flora, Fletcher; Hoch, Edward D(entinger); Kane, Henry; Lee, Manfred B(ennington); Marlowe, Stephen; Powell, (Oval) Talmage; Sheldon, Walter J(ames); Sturgeon, Theodore (Hamilton); Tracy, Don(ald Fiske); Vance, John Holbrook
See also BPFB 3; CMW 4; MSW; RGAL 4

Queen, Ellery, Jr.
See Dannay, Frederic; Lee, Manfred B(ennington)

Queneau, Raymond 1903-1976 ..... **CLC 2, 5, 10, 42**
See also CA 77-80; 69-72; CANR 32; DLB 72, 258; EW 12; EWL 3; GFL 1789 to the Present; MTCW 1, 2; RGWL 2, 3

Quevedo, Francisco de 1580-1645 .... **LC 23**

Quiller-Couch, Sir Arthur (Thomas)
1863-1944 .... **TCLC 53**
See also CA 118; 166; DLB 135, 153, 190; HGG; RGEL 2; SUFW 1

Quin, Ann (Marie) 1936-1973 .... **CLC 6**
See also CA 9-12R; 45-48; DLB 14, 231

Quincey, Thomas de
See De Quincey, Thomas

Quinn, Martin
See Smith, Martin Cruz

Quinn, Peter 1947- .... **CLC 91**
See also CA 197

Quinn, Simon
See Smith, Martin Cruz

Quintana, Leroy V. 1944- ...... **HLC 2; PC 36**
See also CA 131; CANR 65; DAM MULT; DLB 82; HW 1, 2

Quiroga, Horacio (Sylvestre)
1878-1937 .... **HLC 2; TCLC 20**
See also CA 117; 131; DAM MULT; EWL 3; HW 1; LAW; MTCW 1; RGSF 2; WLIT 1

Quoirez, Francoise 1935- .... **CLC 9**
See Sagan, Francoise
See also CA 49-52; CANR 6, 39, 73; CWW 2; MTCW 1, 2; TWA

Raabe, Wilhelm (Karl) 1831-1910 . **TCLC 45**
See also CA 167; DLB 129

Rabe, David (William) 1940- .. **CLC 4, 8, 33; DC 16**
See also CA 85-88; CABS 3; CAD; CANR 59; CD 5; DAM DRAM; DFS 3, 8, 13; DLB 7, 228; EWL 3

DAM MST, NOV; DLB 56; EWL 3;
EXPN; LAIT 3; MTCW 1, 2; NFS 4;
RGWL 2, 3

Remington, Frederic 1861-1909 ..... **TCLC 89**
See also CA 108; 169; DLB 12, 186, 188;
SATA 41

Remizov, A.
See Remizov, Aleksei (Mikhailovich)

Remizov, A. M.
See Remizov, Aleksei (Mikhailovich)

Remizov, Aleksei (Mikhailovich)
1877-1957 .... **TCLC 27**
See Remizov, Alexey Mikhaylovich
See also CA 125; 133

Remizov, Alexey Mikhaylovich
See Remizov, Aleksei (Mikhailovich)
See also EWL 3

Renan, Joseph Ernest 1823-1892 .. **NCLC 26**
See also GFL 1789 to the Present

Renard, Jules(-Pierre) 1864-1910 .. **TCLC 17**
See also CA 117; 202; GFL 1789 to the
Present

Renault, Mary .... **CLC 3, 11, 17**
See Challans, Mary
See also BPFB 3; BYA 2; DLBY 1983;
EWL 3; GLL 1; LAIT 1; MTCW 2; RGEL
2; RHW

Rendell, Ruth (Barbara) 1930- .. **CLC 28, 48**
See Vine, Barbara
See also BPFB 3; CA 109; CANR 32, 52,
74; CN 7; CPW; DAM POP; DLB 87,
276; INT CANR-32; MSW; MTCW 1, 2

Renoir, Jean 1894-1979 .... **CLC 20**
See also CA 129; 85-88

Resnais, Alain 1922- .... **CLC 16**

Revard, Carter (Curtis) 1931- .... **NNAL**
See also CA 144; CANR 81; PFS 5

Reverdy, Pierre 1889-1960 .... **CLC 53**
See also CA 97-100; 89-92; DLB 258; EWL
3; GFL 1789 to the Present

Rexroth, Kenneth 1905-1982 .... **CLC 1, 2, 6,
11, 22, 49, 112; PC 20**
See also BG 3; CA 5-8R; 107; CANR 14,
34, 63; CDALB 1941-1968; DAM POET;
DLB 16, 48, 165, 212; DLBY 1982; EWL
3; INT CANR-14; MTCW 1, 2; RGAL 4

Reyes, Alfonso 1889-1959 .... **HLCS 2; TCLC
33**
See also CA 131; EWL 3; HW 1; LAW

Reyes y Basoalto, Ricardo Eliecer Neftali
See Neruda, Pablo

Reymont, Wladyslaw (Stanislaw)
1868(?)-1925 .... **TCLC 5**
See also CA 104; EWL 3

Reynolds, Jonathan 1942- .... **CLC 6, 38**
See also CA 65-68; CANR 28

Reynolds, Joshua 1723-1792 .... **LC 15**
See also DLB 104

Reynolds, Michael S(hane)
1937-2000 .... **CLC 44**
See also CA 65-68; 189; CANR 9, 89, 97

Reznikoff, Charles 1894-1976 .... **CLC 9**
See also CA 33-36; 61-64; CAP 2; DLB 28,
45; WP

Rezzori (d'Arezzo), Gregor von
1914-1998 .... **CLC 25**
See also CA 122; 136; 167

Rhine, Richard
See Silverstein, Alvin; Silverstein, Virginia
B(arbara Opshelor)

Rhodes, Eugene Manlove
1869-1934 .... **TCLC 53**
See also CA 198; DLB 256

R'hoone, Lord
See Balzac, Honore de

Rhys, Jean 1894(?)-1979 ...... **CLC 2, 4, 6, 14,
19, 51, 124; SSC 21**
See also BRWS 2; CA 25-28R; 85-88;
CANR 35, 62; CDBLB 1945-1960; CD-

WLB 3; DA3; DAM NOV; DLB 36, 117,
162; DNFS 2; EWL 3; LATS 1; MTCW
1, 2; RGEL 2; RGSF 2; RHW; TEA

Ribeiro, Darcy 1922-1997 .... **CLC 34**
See also CA 33-36R; 156; EWL 3

Ribeiro, Joao Ubaldo (Osorio Pimentel)
1941- .... **CLC 10, 67**
See also CA 81-84; EWL 3

Ribman, Ronald (Burt) 1932- .... **CLC 7**
See also CA 21-24R; CAD; CANR 46, 80;
CD 5

Ricci, Nino 1959- .... **CLC 70**
See also CA 137; CCA 1

Rice, Anne 1941- .... **CLC 41, 128**
See Rampling, Anne
See also AAYA 9, 53; AMWS 7; BEST
89:2; BPFB 3; CA 65-68; CANR 12, 36,
53, 74, 100; CN 7; CPW; CSW; DA3;
DAM POP; GLL 2; HGG; MTCW 2;
SUFW 2; YAW

Rice, Elmer (Leopold) 1892-1967 ...... **CLC 7,
49**
See Reizenstein, Elmer Leopold
See also CA 21-22; 25-28R; CAP 2; DAM
DRAM; DFS 12; DLB 4, 7; MTCW 1, 2;
RGAL 4

Rice, Tim(othy Miles Bindon)
1944- .... **CLC 21**
See also CA 103; CANR 46; DFS 7

Rich, Adrienne (Cecile) 1929- ... **CLC 3, 6, 7,
11, 18, 36, 73, 76, 125; PC 5**
See also AMWR 2; AMWS 1; CA 9-12R;
CANR 20, 53, 74; CDALBS; CP 7; CSW;
CWP; DA3; DAM POET; DLB 5, 67;
EWL 3; EXPP; FW; MAWW; MTCW 1,
2; PAB; PFS 15; RGAL 4; WP

Rich, Barbara
See Graves, Robert (von Ranke)

Rich, Robert
See Trumbo, Dalton

Richard, Keith .... **CLC 17**
See Richards, Keith

Richards, David Adams 1950- .... **CLC 59**
See also CA 93-96; CANR 60, 110; DAC;
DLB 53

Richards, I(vor) A(rmstrong)
1893-1979 .... **CLC 14, 24**
See also BRWS 2; CA 41-44R; 89-92;
CANR 34, 74; DLB 27; EWL 3; MTCW
2; RGEL 2

Richards, Keith 1943-
See Richard, Keith
See also CA 107; CANR 77

Richardson, Anne
See Roiphe, Anne (Richardson)

Richardson, Dorothy Miller
1873-1957 .... **TCLC 3**
See also CA 104; 192; DLB 36; EWL 3;
FW; RGEL 2

**Richardson (Robertson), Ethel Florence
Lindesay** 1870-1946
See Richardson, Henry Handel
See also CA 105; 190; DLB 230; RHW

Richardson, Henry Handel .... **TCLC 4**
See Richardson (Robertson), Ethel Florence
Lindesay
See also DLB 197; EWL 3; RGEL 2; RGSF
2

Richardson, John 1796-1852 .... **NCLC 55**
See also CCA 1; DAC; DLB 99

Richardson, Samuel 1689-1761 ...... **LC 1, 44;
WLC**
See also BRW 3; CDBLB 1660-1789; DA;
DAB; DAC; DAM MST, NOV; DLB 39;
RGEL 2; TEA; WLIT 3

Richardson, Willis 1889-1977 .... **HR 3**
See also BW 1; CA 124; DLB 51; SATA 60

Richler, Mordecai 1931-2001 .... **CLC 3, 5, 9,
13, 18, 46, 70**
See also AITN 1; CA 65-68; 201; CANR
31, 62, 111; CCA 1; CLR 17; CWRI 5;
DAC; DAM MST, NOV; DLB 53; EWL
3; MAICYA 1, 2; MTCW 1, 2; RGEL 2;
SATA 44, 98; SATA-Brief 27; TWA

Richter, Conrad (Michael)
1890-1968 .... **CLC 30**
See also AAYA 21; BYA 2; CA 5-8R; 25-
28R; CANR 23; DLB 9, 212; LAIT 1;
MTCW 1, 2; RGAL 4; SATA 3; TCWW
2; TUS; YAW

Ricostranza, Tom
See Ellis, Trey

Riddell, Charlotte 1832-1906 .... **TCLC 40**
See Riddell, Mrs. J. H.
See also CA 165; DLB 156

Riddell, Mrs. J. H.
See Riddell, Charlotte
See also HGG; SUFW

Ridge, John Rollin 1827-1867 ...... **NCLC 82;
NNAL**
See also CA 144; DAM MULT; DLB 175

Ridgeway, Jason
See Marlowe, Stephen

Ridgway, Keith 1965- .... **CLC 119**
See also CA 172

Riding, Laura .... **CLC 3, 7**
See Jackson, Laura (Riding)
See also RGAL 4

Riefenstahl, Berta Helene Amalia 1902-
See Riefenstahl, Leni
See also CA 108

Riefenstahl, Leni .... **CLC 16**
See Riefenstahl, Berta Helene Amalia

Riffe, Ernest
See Bergman, (Ernst) Ingmar

Riggs, (Rolla) Lynn
1899-1954 .... **NNAL; TCLC 56**
See also CA 144; DAM MULT; DLB 175

Riis, Jacob A(ugust) 1849-1914 ..... **TCLC 80**
See also CA 113; 168; DLB 23

Riley, James Whitcomb 1849-1916 .... **PC 48;
TCLC 51**
See also CA 118; 137; DAM POET; MAI-
CYA 1, 2; RGAL 4; SATA 17

Riley, Tex
See Creasey, John

Rilke, Rainer Maria 1875-1926 .... **PC 2;
TCLC 1, 6, 19**
See also CA 104; 132; CANR 62, 99; CD-
WLB 2; DA3; DAM POET; DLB 81; EW
9; EWL 3; MTCW 1, 2; RGWL 2, 3;
TWA; WP

Rimbaud, (Jean Nicolas) Arthur
1854-1891 .... **NCLC 4, 35, 82; PC 3;
WLC**
See also DA; DA3; DAB; DAC; DAM
MST, POET; DLB 217; EW 7; GFL 1789
to the Present; LMFS 2; RGWL 2, 3;
TWA; WP

Rinehart, Mary Roberts
1876-1958 .... **TCLC 52**
See also BPFB 3; CA 108; 166; RGAL 4;
RHW

Ringmaster, The
See Mencken, H(enry) L(ouis)

Ringwood, Gwen(dolyn Margaret) Pharis
1910-1984 .... **CLC 48**
See also CA 148; 112; DLB 88

Rio, Michel 1945(?)- .... **CLC 43**
See also CA 201

Ritsos, Giannes
See Ritsos, Yannis

Ritsos, Yannis 1909-1990 .... **CLC 6, 13, 31**
See also CA 77-80; 133; CANR 39, 61; EW
12; EWL 3; MTCW 1; RGWL 2, 3

Sjowall, Maj
See Sjoewall, Maj
See also BPFB 3; CMW 4; MSW

Skelton, John 1460(?)-1529 ..... **LC 71; PC 25**
See also BRW 1; DLB 136; RGEL 2

Skelton, Robin 1925-1997 .... **CLC 13**
See Zuk, Georges
See also AITN 2; CA 5-8R; 160; CAAS 5;
CANR 28, 89; CCA 1; CP 7; DLB 27, 53

Skolimowski, Jerzy 1938- .... **CLC 20**
See also CA 128

Skram, Amalie (Bertha)
1847-1905 .... **TCLC 25**
See also CA 165

Skvorecky, Josef (Vaclav) 1924- ...... **CLC 15,
39, 69, 152**
See also CA 61-64; CAAS 1; CANR 10,
34, 63, 108; CDWLB 4; DA3; DAC;
DAM NOV; DLB 232; EWL 3; MTCW
1, 2

Slade, Bernard .... **CLC 11, 46**
See Newbound, Bernard Slade
See also CAAS 9; CCA 1; DLB 53

Slaughter, Carolyn 1946- .... **CLC 56**
See also CA 85-88; CANR 85; CN 7

Slaughter, Frank G(ill) 1908-2001 ... **CLC 29**
See also AITN 2; CA 5-8R; 197; CANR 5,
85; INT CANR-5; RHW

Slavitt, David R(ytman) 1935- ..... **CLC 5, 14**
See also CA 21-24R; CAAS 3; CANR 41,
83; CP 7; DLB 5, 6

Slesinger, Tess 1905-1945 .... **TCLC 10**
See also CA 107; 199; DLB 102

Slessor, Kenneth 1901-1971 .... **CLC 14**
See also CA 102; 89-92; DLB 260; RGEL
2

Slowacki, Juliusz 1809-1849 .... **NCLC 15**
See also RGWL 3

Smart, Christopher 1722-1771 . **LC 3; PC 13**
See also DAM POET; DLB 109; RGEL 2

Smart, Elizabeth 1913-1986 .... **CLC 54**
See also CA 81-84; 118; DLB 88

Smiley, Jane (Graves) 1949- ..... **CLC 53, 76,
144**
See also AMWS 6; BPFB 3; CA 104;
CANR 30, 50, 74, 96; CN 7; CPW 1;
DA3; DAM POP; DLB 227, 234; EWL 3;
INT CANR-30

Smith, A(rthur) J(ames) M(arshall)
1902-1980 .... **CLC 15**
See also CA 1-4R; 102; CANR 4; DAC;
DLB 88; RGEL 2

Smith, Adam 1723(?)-1790 .... **LC 36**
See also DLB 104, 252; RGEL 2

Smith, Alexander 1829-1867 .... **NCLC 59**
See also DLB 32, 55

Smith, Anna Deavere 1950- .... **CLC 86**
See also CA 133; CANR 103; CD 5; DFS 2

Smith, Betty (Wehner) 1904-1972 .... **CLC 19**
See also BPFB 3; BYA 3; CA 5-8R; 33-
36R; DLBY 1982; LAIT 3; RGAL 4;
SATA 6

Smith, Charlotte (Turner)
1749-1806 .... **NCLC 23, 115**
See also DLB 39, 109; RGEL 2; TEA

Smith, Clark Ashton 1893-1961 .... **CLC 43**
See also CA 143; CANR 81; FANT; HGG;
MTCW 2; SCFW 2; SFW 4; SUFW

Smith, Dave .... **CLC 22, 42**
See Smith, David (Jeddie)
See also CAAS 7; DLB 5

Smith, David (Jeddie) 1942-
See Smith, Dave
See also CA 49-52; CANR 1, 59, 120; CP
7; CSW; DAM POET

Smith, Florence Margaret 1902-1971
See Smith, Stevie
See also CA 17-18; 29-32R; CANR 35;
CAP 2; DAM POET; MTCW 1, 2; TEA

Smith, Iain Crichton 1928-1998 .... **CLC 64**
See also CA 21-24R; 171; CN 7; CP 7; DLB
40, 139; RGSF 2

Smith, John 1580(?)-1631 .... **LC 9**
See also DLB 24, 30; TUS

Smith, Johnston
See Crane, Stephen (Townley)

Smith, Joseph, Jr. 1805-1844 .... **NCLC 53**

Smith, Lee 1944- .... **CLC 25, 73**
See also CA 114; 119; CANR 46, 118;
CSW; DLB 143; DLBY 1983; EWL 3;
INT CA-119; RGAL 4

Smith, Martin
See Smith, Martin Cruz

Smith, Martin Cruz 1942- .. **CLC 25; NNAL**
See also BEST 89:4; BPFB 3; CA 85-88;
CANR 6, 23, 43, 65, 119; CMW 4; CPW;
DAM MULT, POP; HGG; INT CANR-
23; MTCW 2; RGAL 4

Smith, Patti 1946- .... **CLC 12**
See also CA 93-96; CANR 63

Smith, Pauline (Urmson)
1882-1959 .... **TCLC 25**
See also DLB 225; EWL 3

Smith, Rosamond
See Oates, Joyce Carol

Smith, Sheila Kaye
See Kaye-Smith, Sheila

Smith, Stevie .... **CLC 3, 8, 25, 44; PC 12**
See Smith, Florence Margaret
See also BRWS 2; DLB 20; EWL 3; MTCW
2; PAB; PFS 3; RGEL 2

Smith, Wilbur (Addison) 1933- .... **CLC 33**
See also CA 13-16R; CANR 7, 46, 66;
CPW; MTCW 1, 2

Smith, William Jay 1918- .... **CLC 6**
See also CA 5-8R; CANR 44, 106; CP 7;
CSW; CWRI 5; DLB 5; MAICYA 1, 2;
SAAS 22; SATA 2, 68

Smith, Woodrow Wilson
See Kuttner, Henry

Smith, Zadie 1976- .... **CLC 158**
See also AAYA 50; CA 193

Smolenskin, Peretz 1842-1885 .... **NCLC 30**

Smollett, Tobias (George) 1721-1771 ... **LC 2,
46**
See also BRW 3; CDBLB 1660-1789; DLB
39, 104; RGEL 2; TEA

Snodgrass, W(illiam) D(e Witt)
1926- .... **CLC 2, 6, 10, 18, 68**
See also AMWS 6; CA 1-4R; CANR 6, 36,
65, 85; CP 7; DAM POET; DLB 5;
MTCW 1, 2; RGAL 4

Snorri Sturluson 1179-1241 .... **CMLC 56**
See also RGWL 2, 3

Snow, C(harles) P(ercy) 1905-1980 ... **CLC 1,
4, 6, 9, 13, 19**
See also BRW 7; CA 5-8R; 101; CANR 28;
CDBLB 1945-1960; DAM NOV; DLB 15,
77; DLBD 17; EWL 3; MTCW 1, 2;
RGEL 2; TEA

Snow, Frances Compton
See Adams, Henry (Brooks)

Snyder, Gary (Sherman) 1930- . **CLC 1, 2, 5,
9, 32, 120; PC 21**
See also AMWS 8; ANW; BG 3; CA 17-
20R; CANR 30, 60; CP 7; DA3; DAM
POET; DLB 5, 16, 165, 212, 237, 275;
EWL 3; MTCW 2; PFS 9; RGAL 4; WP

Snyder, Zilpha Keatley 1927- .... **CLC 17**
See also AAYA 15; BYA 1; CA 9-12R;
CANR 38; CLR 31; JRDA; MAICYA 1,
2; SAAS 2; SATA 1, 28, 75, 110; SATA-
Essay 112; YAW

Soares, Bernardo
See Pessoa, Fernando (Antonio Nogueira)

Sobh, A.
See Shamlu, Ahmad

Sobol, Joshua 1939- .... **CLC 60**
See Sobol, Yehoshua
See also CA 200; CWW 2

Sobol, Yehoshua 1939-
See Sobol, Joshua
See also CWW 2

Socrates 470B.C.-399B.C. .... **CMLC 27**

Soderberg, Hjalmar 1869-1941 ...... **TCLC 39**
See also DLB 259; EWL 3; RGSF 2

Soderbergh, Steven 1963- .... **CLC 154**
See also AAYA 43

Sodergran, Edith (Irene) 1892-1923
See Soedergran, Edith (Irene)
See also CA 202; DLB 259; EW 11; EWL
3; RGWL 2, 3

Soedergran, Edith (Irene)
1892-1923 .... **TCLC 31**
See Sodergran, Edith (Irene)

Softly, Edgar
See Lovecraft, H(oward) P(hillips)

Softly, Edward
See Lovecraft, H(oward) P(hillips)

Sokolov, Alexander V(sevolodovich) 1943-
See Sokolov, Sasha
See also CA 73-76

Sokolov, Raymond 1941- .... **CLC 7**
See also CA 85-88

Sokolov, Sasha .... **CLC 59**
See Sokolov, Alexander V(sevolodovich)
See also CWW 2; DLB 285; EWL 3; RGWL
2, 3

Sokolov, Sasha .... **CLC 59**

Solo, Jay
See Ellison, Harlan (Jay)

Sologub, Fyodor .... **TCLC 9**
See Teternikov, Fyodor Kuzmich
See also EWL 3

Solomons, Ikey Esquir
See Thackeray, William Makepeace

Solomos, Dionysios 1798-1857 .... **NCLC 15**

Solwoska, Mara
See French, Marilyn

Solzhenitsyn, Aleksandr I(sayevich)
1918- .. **CLC 1, 2, 4, 7, 9, 10, 18, 26, 34,
78, 134; SSC 32; WLC**
See Solzhenitsyn, Aleksandr Isaevich
See also AAYA 49; AITN 1; BPFB 3; CA
69-72; CANR 40, 65, 116; DA; DA3;
DAB; DAC; DAM MST, NOV; EW 13;
EXPS; LAIT 4; MTCW 1, 2; NFS 6;
RGSF 2; RGWL 2, 3; SSFS 9; TWA

Solzhenitsyn, Aleksandr Isaevich
See Solzhenitsyn, Aleksandr I(sayevich)
See also EWL 3

Somers, Jane
See Lessing, Doris (May)

Somerville, Edith Oenone
1858-1949 .... **SSC 56; TCLC 51**
See also CA 196; DLB 135; RGEL 2; RGSF
2

Somerville & Ross
See Martin, Violet Florence; Somerville,
Edith Oenone

Sommer, Scott 1951- .... **CLC 25**
See also CA 106

Sondheim, Stephen (Joshua) 1930- . **CLC 30,
39, 147**
See also AAYA 11; CA 103; CANR 47, 67;
DAM DRAM; LAIT 4

Sone, Monica 1919- .... **AAL**

Song, Cathy 1955- .... **AAL; PC 21**
See also CA 154; CANR 118; CWP; DLB
169; EXPP; FW; PFS 5

Sontag, Susan 1933- .... **CLC 1, 2, 10, 13, 31,
105**
See also AMWS 3; CA 17-20R; CANR 25,
51, 74, 97; CN 7; CPW; DA3; DAM POP;
DLB 2, 67; EWL 3; MAWW; MTCW 1,
2; RGAL 4; RHW; SSFS 10

Tomalin, Claire 1933- .... **CLC 166**
　　See also CA 89-92; CANR 52, 88; DLB
　　155
Tomasi di Lampedusa, Giuseppe 1896-1957
　　See Lampedusa, Giuseppe (Tomasi) di
　　See also CA 111; DLB 177; EWL 3
Tomlin, Lily .... **CLC 17**
　　See Tomlin, Mary Jean
Tomlin, Mary Jean 1939(?)-
　　See Tomlin, Lily
　　See also CA 117
Tomline, F. Latour
　　See Gilbert, W(illiam) S(chwenck)
Tomlinson, (Alfred) Charles 1927- .... **CLC 2,**
　　4, 6, 13, 45; PC 17
　　See also CA 5-8R; CANR 33; CP 7; DAM
　　POET; DLB 40
Tomlinson, H(enry) M(ajor)
　　1873-1958 .... **TCLC 71**
　　See also CA 118; 161; DLB 36, 100, 195
Tonson, Jacob fl. 1655(?)-1736 .... **LC 86**
　　See also DLB 170
Toole, John Kennedy 1937-1969 ..... **CLC 19,**
　　64
　　See also BPFB 3; CA 104; DLBY 1981;
　　MTCW 2
Toomer, Eugene
　　See Toomer, Jean
Toomer, Eugene Pinchback
　　See Toomer, Jean
Toomer, Jean 1894-1967 .. **BLC 3; CLC 1, 4,**
　　13, 22; HR 3; PC 7; SSC 1, 45; WLCS
　　See also AFAW 1, 2; AMWS 3, 9; BW 1;
　　CA 85-88; CDALB 1917-1929; DA3;
　　DAM MULT; DLB 45, 51; EWL 3; EXPP;
　　EXPS; LMFS 2; MTCW 1, 2; NFS 11;
　　RGAL 4; RGSF 2; SSFS 5
Toomer, Nathan Jean
　　See Toomer, Jean
Toomer, Nathan Pinchback
　　See Toomer, Jean
Torley, Luke
　　See Blish, James (Benjamin)
Tornimparte, Alessandra
　　See Ginzburg, Natalia
Torre, Raoul della
　　See Mencken, H(enry) L(ouis)
Torrence, Ridgely 1874-1950 .... **TCLC 97**
　　See also DLB 54, 249
Torrey, E(dwin) Fuller 1937- .... **CLC 34**
　　See also CA 119; CANR 71
Torsvan, Ben Traven
　　See Traven, B.
Torsvan, Benno Traven
　　See Traven, B.
Torsvan, Berick Traven
　　See Traven, B.
Torsvan, Berwick Traven
　　See Traven, B.
Torsvan, Bruno Traven
　　See Traven, B.
Torsvan, Traven
　　See Traven, B.
Tourneur, Cyril 1575(?)-1626 .... **LC 66**
　　See also BRW 2; DAM DRAM; DLB 58;
　　RGEL 2
Tournier, Michel (Edouard) 1924- .... **CLC 6,**
　　23, 36, 95
　　See also CA 49-52; CANR 3, 36, 74; DLB
　　83; EWL 3; GFL 1789 to the Present;
　　MTCW 1, 2; SATA 23
Tournimparte, Alessandra
　　See Ginzburg, Natalia
Towers, Ivar
　　See Kornbluth, C(yril) M.
Towne, Robert (Burton) 1936(?)- ..... **CLC 87**
　　See also CA 108; DLB 44; IDFW 3, 4

Townsend, Sue .... **CLC 61**
　　See Townsend, Susan Lilian
　　See also AAYA 28; CA 119; 127; CANR
　　65, 107; CBD; CD 5; CPW; CWD; DAB;
　　DAC; DAM MST; DLB 271; INT 127;
　　SATA 55, 93; SATA-Brief 48; YAW
Townsend, Susan Lilian 1946-
　　See Townsend, Sue
Townshend, Pete
　　See Townshend, Peter (Dennis Blandford)
Townshend, Peter (Dennis Blandford)
　　1945- .... **CLC 17, 42**
　　See also CA 107
Tozzi, Federigo 1883-1920 .... **TCLC 31**
　　See also CA 160; CANR 110; DLB 264;
　　EWL 3
Tracy, Don(ald Fiske) 1905-1970(?)
　　See Queen, Ellery
　　See also CA 1-4R; 176; CANR 2
Trafford, F. G.
　　See Riddell, Charlotte
Traill, Catharine Parr 1802-1899 .. **NCLC 31**
　　See also DLB 99
Trakl, Georg 1887-1914 .... **PC 20; TCLC 5**
　　See also CA 104; 165; EW 10; EWL 3;
　　LMFS 2; MTCW 2; RGWL 2, 3
Tranquilli, Secondino
　　See Silone, Ignazio
Transtroemer, Tomas Gosta
　　See Transtromer, Tomas (Goesta)
Transtromer, Tomas
　　See Transtromer, Tomas (Goesta)
Transtromer, Tomas (Goesta)
　　1931- .... **CLC 52, 65**
　　See also CA 117; 129; CAAS 17; CANR
　　115; DAM POET; DLB 257; EWL 3
Transtromer, Tomas Gosta
　　See Transtromer, Tomas (Goesta)
Traven, B. 1882(?)-1969 .... **CLC 8, 11**
　　See also CA 19-20; 25-28R; CAP 2; DLB
　　9, 56; EWL 3; MTCW 1; RGAL 4
Trediakovsky, Vasilii Kirillovich
　　1703-1769 .... **LC 68**
　　See also DLB 150
Treitel, Jonathan 1959- .... **CLC 70**
　　See also CA 210; DLB 267
Trelawny, Edward John
　　1792-1881 .... **NCLC 85**
　　See also DLB 110, 116, 144
Tremain, Rose 1943- .... **CLC 42**
　　See also CA 97-100; CANR 44, 95; CN 7;
　　DLB 14, 271; RGSF 2; RHW
Tremblay, Michel 1942- .... **CLC 29, 102**
　　See also CA 116; 128; CCA 1; CWW 2;
　　DAC; DAM MST; DLB 60; EWL 3; GLL
　　1; MTCW 1, 2
Trevanian .... **CLC 29**
　　See Whitaker, Rod(ney)
Trevor, Glen
　　See Hilton, James
Trevor, William .. **CLC 7, 9, 14, 25, 71, 116;**
　　SSC 21, 58
　　See Cox, William Trevor
　　See also BRWS 4; CBD; CD 5; CN 7; DLB
　　14, 139; EWL 3; LATS 1; MTCW 2;
　　RGEL 2; RGSF 2; SSFS 10
Trifonov, Iurii (Valentinovich)
　　See Trifonov, Yuri (Valentinovich)
　　See also RGWL 2, 3
Trifonov, Yuri (Valentinovich)
　　1925-1981 .... **CLC 45**
　　See Trifonov, Iurii (Valentinovich); Tri-
　　fonov, Yury Valentinovich
　　See also CA 126; 103; MTCW 1
Trifonov, Yury Valentinovich
　　See Trifonov, Yuri (Valentinovich)
　　See also EWL 3

Trilling, Diana (Rubin) 1905-1996 . **CLC 129**
　　See also CA 5-8R; 154; CANR 10, 46; INT
　　CANR-10; MTCW 1, 2
Trilling, Lionel 1905-1975 .... **CLC 9, 11, 24**
　　See also AMWS 3; CA 9-12R; 61-64;
　　CANR 10, 105; DLB 28, 63; EWL 3; INT
　　CANR-10; MTCW 1, 2; RGAL 4; TUS
Trimball, W. H.
　　See Mencken, H(enry) L(ouis)
Tristan
　　See Gomez de la Serna, Ramon
Tristram
　　See Housman, A(lfred) E(dward)
Trogdon, William (Lewis) 1939-
　　See Heat-Moon, William Least
　　See also CA 115; 119; CANR 47, 89; CPW;
　　INT CA-119
Trollope, Anthony 1815-1882 .... **NCLC 6, 33,**
　　101; SSC 28; WLC
　　See also BRW 5; CDBLB 1832-1890; DA;
　　DA3; DAB; DAC; DAM MST, NOV;
　　DLB 21, 57, 159; RGEL 2; RGSF 2;
　　SATA 22
Trollope, Frances 1779-1863 .... **NCLC 30**
　　See also DLB 21, 166
Trotsky, Leon 1879-1940 .... **TCLC 22**
　　See also CA 118; 167
Trotter (Cockburn), Catharine
　　1679-1749 .... **LC 8**
　　See also DLB 84, 252
Trotter, Wilfred 1872-1939 .... **TCLC 97**
Trout, Kilgore
　　See Farmer, Philip Jose
Trow, George W. S. 1943- .... **CLC 52**
　　See also CA 126; CANR 91
Troyat, Henri 1911- .... **CLC 23**
　　See also CA 45-48; CANR 2, 33, 67, 117;
　　GFL 1789 to the Present; MTCW 1
Trudeau, G(arretson) B(eekman) 1948-
　　See Trudeau, Garry B.
　　See also CA 81-84; CANR 31; SATA 35
Trudeau, Garry B. .... **CLC 12**
　　See Trudeau, G(arretson) B(eekman)
　　See also AAYA 10; AITN 2
Truffaut, Francois 1932-1984 ... **CLC 20, 101**
　　See also CA 81-84; 113; CANR 34
Trumbo, Dalton 1905-1976 .... **CLC 19**
　　See also CA 21-24R; 69-72; CANR 10;
　　DLB 26; IDFW 3, 4; YAW
Trumbull, John 1750-1831 .... **NCLC 30**
　　See also DLB 31; RGAL 4
Trundlett, Helen B.
　　See Eliot, T(homas) S(tearns)
Truth, Sojourner 1797(?)-1883 .... **NCLC 94**
　　See also DLB 239; FW; LAIT 2
Tryon, Thomas 1926-1991 .... **CLC 3, 11**
　　See also AITN 1; BPFB 3; CA 29-32R; 135;
　　CANR 32, 77; CPW; DA3; DAM POP;
　　HGG; MTCW 1
Tryon, Tom
　　See Tryon, Thomas
Ts'ao Hsueh-ch'in 1715(?)-1763 .... **LC 1**
Tsushima, Shuji 1909-1948
　　See Dazai Osamu
　　See also CA 107
Tsvetaeva (Efron), Marina (Ivanovna)
　　1892-1941 .... **PC 14; TCLC 7, 35**
　　See also CA 104; 128; CANR 73; EW 11;
　　MTCW 1, 2; RGWL 2, 3
Tuck, Lily 1938- .... **CLC 70**
　　See also CA 139; CANR 90
Tu Fu 712-770 .... **PC 9**
　　See Du Fu
　　See also DAM MULT; TWA; WP
Tunis, John R(oberts) 1889-1975 ..... **CLC 12**
　　See also BYA 1; CA 61-64; CANR 62; DLB
　　22, 171; JRDA; MAICYA 1, 2; SATA 37;
　　SATA-Brief 30; YAW

Van Doren, Carl (Clinton)
1885-1950 .... **TCLC 18**
See also CA 111; 168
Van Doren, Mark 1894-1972 .... **CLC 6, 10**
See also CA 1-4R; 37-40R; CANR 3; DLB
45, 284; MTCW 1, 2; RGAL 4
Van Druten, John (William)
1901-1957 .... **TCLC 2**
See also CA 104; 161; DLB 10; RGAL 4
Van Duyn, Mona (Jane) 1921- ...... **CLC 3, 7, 63, 116**
See also CA 9-12R; CANR 7, 38, 60, 116;
CP 7; CWP; DAM POET; DLB 5
Van Dyne, Edith
See Baum, L(yman) Frank
van Itallie, Jean-Claude 1936- .... **CLC 3**
See also CA 45-48; CAAS 2; CAD; CANR
1, 48; CD 5; DLB 7
Van Loot, Cornelius Obenchain
See Roberts, Kenneth (Lewis)
van Ostaijen, Paul 1896-1928 .... **TCLC 33**
See also CA 163
Van Peebles, Melvin 1932- .... **CLC 2, 20**
See also BW 2, 3; CA 85-88; CANR 27,
67, 82; DAM MULT
van Schendel, Arthur(-Francois-Emile)
1874-1946 .... **TCLC 56**
See also EWL 3
Vansittart, Peter 1920- .... **CLC 42**
See also CA 1-4R; CANR 3, 49, 90; CN 7;
RHW
Van Vechten, Carl 1880-1964 ... **CLC 33; HR 3**
See also AMWS 2; CA 183; 89-92; DLB 4,
9, 51; RGAL 4
van Vogt, A(lfred) E(lton) 1912-2000 . **CLC 1**
See also BPFB 3; BYA 13, 14; CA 21-24R;
190; CANR 28; DLB 8, 251; SATA 14;
SATA-Obit 124; SCFW; SFW 4
Vara, Madeleine
See Jackson, Laura (Riding)
Varda, Agnes 1928- .... **CLC 16**
See also CA 116; 122
Vargas Llosa, (Jorge) Mario (Pedro)
1939- .... **CLC 3, 6, 9, 10, 15, 31, 42, 85; HLC 2**
See Llosa, (Jorge) Mario (Pedro) Vargas
See also BPFB 3; CA 73-76; CANR 18, 32,
42, 67, 116; CDWLB 3; DA; DA3; DAB;
DAC; DAM MST, MULT, NOV; DLB
145; DNFS 2; EWL 3; HW 1, 2; LAIT 5;
LATS 1; LAW; LAWS 1; MTCW 1, 2;
RGWL 2; SSFS 14; TWA; WLIT 1
Vasiliu, George
See Bacovia, George
Vasiliu, Gheorghe
See Bacovia, George
See also CA 123; 189
Vassa, Gustavus
See Equiano, Olaudah
Vassilikos, Vassilis 1933- .... **CLC 4, 8**
See also CA 81-84; CANR 75; EWL 3
Vaughan, Henry 1621-1695 .... **LC 27**
See also BRW 2; DLB 131; PAB; RGEL 2
Vaughn, Stephanie .... **CLC 62**
Vazov, Ivan (Minchov) 1850-1921 . **TCLC 25**
See also CA 121; 167; CDWLB 4; DLB
147
Veblen, Thorstein B(unde)
1857-1929 .... **TCLC 31**
See also AMWS 1; CA 115; 165; DLB 246
Vega, Lope de 1562-1635 .... **HLCS 2; LC 23**
See also EW 2; RGWL 2, 3
Vendler, Helen (Hennessy) 1933- ... **CLC 138**
See also CA 41-44R; CANR 25, 72; MTCW
1, 2
Venison, Alfred
See Pound, Ezra (Weston Loomis)

Verdi, Marie de
See Mencken, H(enry) L(ouis)
Verdu, Matilde
See Cela, Camilo Jose
Verga, Giovanni (Carmelo)
1840-1922 .... **SSC 21; TCLC 3**
See also CA 104; 123; CANR 101; EW 7;
EWL 3; RGSF 2; RGWL 2, 3
Vergil 70B.C.-19B.C. ... **CMLC 9, 40; PC 12; WLCS**
See Virgil
See also AW 2; DA; DA3; DAB; DAC;
DAM MST, POET; EFS 1; LMFS 1
Verhaeren, Emile (Adolphe Gustave)
1855-1916 .... **TCLC 12**
See also CA 109; EWL 3; GFL 1789 to the
Present
Verlaine, Paul (Marie) 1844-1896 .. **NCLC 2, 51; PC 2, 32**
See also DAM POET; DLB 217; EW 7;
GFL 1789 to the Present; LMFS 2; RGWL
2, 3; TWA
Verne, Jules (Gabriel) 1828-1905 ... **TCLC 6, 52**
See also AAYA 16; BYA 4; CA 110; 131;
CLR 88; DA3; DLB 123; GFL 1789 to
the Present; JRDA; LAIT 2; LMFS 2;
MAICYA 1, 2; RGWL 2, 3; SATA 21;
SCFW; SFW 4; TWA; WCH
Verus, Marcus Annius
See Aurelius, Marcus
Very, Jones 1813-1880 .... **NCLC 9**
See also DLB 1, 243; RGAL 4
Vesaas, Tarjei 1897-1970 .... **CLC 48**
See also CA 190; 29-32R; EW 11; EWL 3;
RGWL 3
Vialis, Gaston
See Simenon, Georges (Jacques Christian)
Vian, Boris 1920-1959(?) .... **TCLC 9**
See also CA 106; 164; CANR 111; DLB
72; EWL 3; GFL 1789 to the Present;
MTCW 2; RGWL 2, 3
Viaud, (Louis Marie) Julien 1850-1923
See Loti, Pierre
See also CA 107
Vicar, Henry
See Felsen, Henry Gregor
Vicker, Angus
See Felsen, Henry Gregor
Vidal, Gore 1925- ...... **CLC 2, 4, 6, 8, 10, 22, 33, 72, 142**
See Box, Edgar
See also AITN 1; AMWS 4; BEST 90:2;
BPFB 3; CA 5-8R; CAD; CANR 13, 45,
65, 100; CD 5; CDALBS; CN 7; CPW;
DA3; DAM NOV, POP; DFS 2; DLB 6,
152; EWL 3; INT CANR-13; MTCW 1,
2; RGAL 4; RHW; TUS
Viereck, Peter (Robert Edwin)
1916- .... **CLC 4; PC 27**
See also CA 1-4R; CANR 1, 47; CP 7; DLB
5; PFS 9, 14
Vigny, Alfred (Victor) de
1797-1863 .... **NCLC 7, 102; PC 26**
See also DAM POET; DLB 119, 192, 217;
EW 5; GFL 1789 to the Present; RGWL
2, 3
Vilakazi, Benedict Wallet
1906-1947 .... **TCLC 37**
See also CA 168
Villa, Jose Garcia 1914-1997 .... **AAL; PC 22**
See also CA 25-28R; CANR 12, 118; EWL
3; EXPP
Villa, Jose Garcia 1914-1997
See Villa, Jose Garcia
Villarreal, Jose Antonio 1924- .... **HLC 2**
See also CA 133; CANR 93; DAM MULT;
DLB 82; HW 1; LAIT 4; RGAL 4

Villaurrutia, Xavier 1903-1950 ...... **TCLC 80**
See also CA 192; EWL 3; HW 1; LAW
Villaverde, Cirilo 1812-1894 .... **NCLC 121**
See also LAW
Villehardouin, Geoffroi de
1150(?)-1218(?) .... **CMLC 38**
**Villiers de l'Isle Adam, Jean Marie Mathias
Philippe Auguste** 1838-1889 ... **NCLC 3; SSC 14**
See also DLB 123, 192; GFL 1789 to the
Present; RGSF 2
Villon, Francois 1431-1463(?) . **LC 62; PC 13**
See also DLB 208; EW 2; RGWL 2, 3;
TWA
Vine, Barbara .... **CLC 50**
See Rendell, Ruth (Barbara)
See also BEST 90:4
Vinge, Joan (Carol) D(ennison)
1948- .... **CLC 30; SSC 24**
See also AAYA 32; BPFB 3; CA 93-96;
CANR 72; SATA 36, 113; SFW 4; YAW
Viola, Herman J(oseph) 1938- .... **CLC 70**
See also CA 61-64; CANR 8, 23, 48, 91;
SATA 126
Violis, G.
See Simenon, Georges (Jacques Christian)
Viramontes, Helena Maria 1954- .... **HLCS 2**
See also CA 159; DLB 122; HW 2
Virgil
See Vergil
See also CDWLB 1; DLB 211; LAIT 1;
RGWL 2, 3; WP
Visconti, Luchino 1906-1976 .... **CLC 16**
See also CA 81-84; 65-68; CANR 39
Vittorini, Elio 1908-1966 .... **CLC 6, 9, 14**
See also CA 133; 25-28R; DLB 264; EW
12; EWL 3; RGWL 2, 3
Vivekananda, Swami 1863-1902 .... **TCLC 88**
Vizenor, Gerald Robert 1934- .... **CLC 103; NNAL**
See also CA 13-16R; CAAE 205; CAAS
22; CANR 5, 21, 44, 67; DAM MULT;
DLB 175, 227; MTCW 2; TCWW 2
Vizinczey, Stephen 1933- .... **CLC 40**
See also CA 128; CCA 1; INT 128
Vliet, R(ussell) G(ordon)
1929-1984 .... **CLC 22**
See also CA 37-40R; 112; CANR 18
Vogau, Boris Andreyevich 1894-1937(?)
See Pilnyak, Boris
See also CA 123
Vogel, Paula A(nne) 1951- ... **CLC 76; DC 19**
See also CA 108; CAD; CANR 119; CD 5;
CWD; DFS 14; RGAL 4
Voigt, Cynthia 1942- .... **CLC 30**
See also AAYA 3, 30; BYA 1, 3, 6, 7, 8;
CA 106; CANR 18, 37, 40, 94; CLR 13,
48; INT CANR-18; JRDA; LAIT 5; MAI-
CYA 1, 2; MAICYAS 1; SATA 48, 79,
116; SATA-Brief 33; WYA; YAW
Voigt, Ellen Bryant 1943- .... **CLC 54**
See also CA 69-72; CANR 11, 29, 55, 115;
CP 7; CSW; CWP; DLB 120
Voinovich, Vladimir (Nikolaevich)
1932- .... **CLC 10, 49, 147**
See also CA 81-84; CAAS 12; CANR 33,
67; MTCW 1
Vollmann, William T. 1959- .... **CLC 89**
See also CA 134; CANR 67, 116; CPW;
DA3; DAM NOV, POP; MTCW 2
Voloshinov, V. N.
See Bakhtin, Mikhail Mikhailovich
Voltaire 1694-1778 .... **LC 14, 79; SSC 12; WLC**
See also BYA 13; DA; DA3; DAB; DAC;
DAM DRAM, MST; EW 4; GFL Begin-
nings to 1789; LATS 1; LMFS 1; NFS 7;
RGWL 2, 3; TWA

von Aschendrof, Baron Ignatz
See Ford, Ford Madox
von Chamisso, Adelbert
See Chamisso, Adelbert von
von Daeniken, Erich 1935- .... **CLC 30**
See also AITN 1; CA 37-40R; CANR 17, 44
von Daniken, Erich
See von Daeniken, Erich
von Hartmann, Eduard
1842-1906 .... **TCLC 96**
von Hayek, Friedrich August
See Hayek, F(riedrich) A(ugust von)
von Heidenstam, (Carl Gustaf) Verner
See Heidenstam, (Carl Gustaf) Verner von
von Heyse, Paul (Johann Ludwig)
See Heyse, Paul (Johann Ludwig von)
von Hofmannsthal, Hugo
See Hofmannsthal, Hugo von
von Horvath, Odon
See von Horvath, Odon
von Horvath, Odon
See von Horvath, Odon
von Horvath, Odon 1901-1938 .... **TCLC 45**
See von Horvath, Oedoen
See also CA 118; 194; DLB 85, 124; RGWL 2, 3
von Horvath, Oedoen
See von Horvath, Odon
See also CA 184
von Kleist, Heinrich
See Kleist, Heinrich von
von Liliencron, (Friedrich Adolf Axel) Detlev
See Liliencron, (Friedrich Adolf Axel) Detlev von
Vonnegut, Kurt, Jr. 1922- . **CLC 1, 2, 3, 4, 5, 8, 12, 22, 40, 60, 111; SSC 8; WLC**
See also AAYA 6, 44; AITN 1; AMWS 2; BEST 90:4; BPFB 3; BYA 3, 14; CA 1-4R; CANR 1, 25, 49, 75, 92; CDALB 1968-1988; CN 7; CPW 1; DA; DA3; DAB; DAC; DAM MST, NOV, POP; DLB 2, 8, 152; DLBD 3; DLBY 1980; EWL 3; EXPN; EXPS; LAIT 4; LMFS 2; MTCW 1, 2; NFS 3; RGAL 4; SCFW; SFW 4; SSFS 5; TUS; YAW
Von Rachen, Kurt
See Hubbard, L(afayette) Ron(ald)
von Rezzori (d'Arezzo), Gregor
See Rezzori (d'Arezzo), Gregor von
von Sternberg, Josef
See Sternberg, Josef von
Vorster, Gordon 1924- .... **CLC 34**
See also CA 133
Vosce, Trudie
See Ozick, Cynthia
Voznesensky, Andrei (Andreievich)
1933- .... **CLC 1, 15, 57**
See Voznesensky, Andrey
See also CA 89-92; CANR 37; CWW 2; DAM POET; MTCW 1
Voznesensky, Andrey
See Voznesensky, Andrei (Andreievich)
See also EWL 3
Wace, Robert c. 1100-c. 1175 .... **CMLC 55**
See also DLB 146
Waddington, Miriam 1917- .... **CLC 28**
See also CA 21-24R; CANR 12, 30; CCA 1; CP 7; DLB 68
Wagman, Fredrica 1937- .... **CLC 7**
See also CA 97-100; INT 97-100
Wagner, Linda W.
See Wagner-Martin, Linda (C.)
Wagner, Linda Welshimer
See Wagner-Martin, Linda (C.)
Wagner, Richard 1813-1883 ..... **NCLC 9, 119**
See also DLB 129; EW 6

Wagner-Martin, Linda (C.) 1936- .... **CLC 50**
See also CA 159
Wagoner, David (Russell) 1926- .... **CLC 3, 5, 15; PC 33**
See also AMWS 9; CA 1-4R; CAAS 3; CANR 2, 71; CN 7; CP 7; DLB 5, 256; SATA 14; TCWW 2
Wah, Fred(erick James) 1939- .... **CLC 44**
See also CA 107; 141; CP 7; DLB 60
Wahloo, Per 1926-1975 .... **CLC 7**
See also BPFB 3; CA 61-64; CANR 73; CMW 4; MSW
Wahloo, Peter
See Wahloo, Per
Wain, John (Barrington) 1925-1994 . **CLC 2, 11, 15, 46**
See also CA 5-8R; 145; CAAS 4; CANR 23, 54; CDBLB 1960 to Present; DLB 15, 27, 139, 155; EWL 3; MTCW 1, 2
Wajda, Andrzej 1926- .... **CLC 16**
See also CA 102
Wakefield, Dan 1932- .... **CLC 7**
See also CA 21-24R; CAAE 211; CAAS 7; CN 7
Wakefield, Herbert Russell
1888-1965 .... **TCLC 120**
See also CA 5-8R; CANR 77; HGG; SUFW
Wakoski, Diane 1937- ...... **CLC 2, 4, 7, 9, 11, 40; PC 15**
See also CA 13-16R; CAAS 1; CANR 9, 60, 106; CP 7; CWP; DAM POET; DLB 5; INT CANR-9; MTCW 2
Wakoski-Sherbell, Diane
See Wakoski, Diane
Walcott, Derek (Alton) 1930- ... **BLC 3; CLC 2, 4, 9, 14, 25, 42, 67, 76, 160; DC 7; PC 46**
See also BW 2; CA 89-92; CANR 26, 47, 75, 80; CBD; CD 5; CDWLB 3; CP 7; DA3; DAB; DAC; DAM MST, MULT, POET; DLB 117; DLBY 1981; DNFS 1; EFS 1; EWL 3; LMFS 2; MTCW 1, 2; PFS 6; RGEL 2; TWA
Waldman, Anne (Lesley) 1945- .... **CLC 7**
See also BG 3; CA 37-40R; CAAS 17; CANR 34, 69, 116; CP 7; CWP; DLB 16
Waldo, E. Hunter
See Sturgeon, Theodore (Hamilton)
Waldo, Edward Hamilton
See Sturgeon, Theodore (Hamilton)
Walker, Alice (Malsenior) 1944- .... **BLC 3; CLC 5, 6, 9, 19, 27, 46, 58, 103, 167; PC 30; SSC 5; WLCS**
See also AAYA 3, 33; AFAW 1, 2; AMWS 3; BEST 89:4; BPFB 3; BW 2, 3; CA 37-40R; CANR 9, 27, 49, 66, 82; CDALB 1968-1988; CN 7; CPW; CSW; DA; DA3; DAB; DAC; DAM MST, MULT, NOV, POET, POP; DLB 6, 33, 143; EWL 3; EXPN; EXPS; FW; INT CANR-27; LAIT 3; MAWW; MTCW 1, 2; NFS 5; RGAL 4; RGSF 2; SATA 31; SSFS 2, 11; TUS; YAW
Walker, David Harry 1911-1992 ...... **CLC 14**
See also CA 1-4R; 137; CANR 1; CWRI 5; SATA 8; SATA-Obit 71
Walker, Edward Joseph 1934-
See Walker, Ted
See also CA 21-24R; CANR 12, 28, 53; CP 7
Walker, George F. 1947- .... **CLC 44, 61**
See also CA 103; CANR 21, 43, 59; CD 5; DAB; DAC; DAM MST; DLB 60
Walker, Joseph A. 1935- .... **CLC 19**
See also BW 1, 3; CA 89-92; CAD; CANR 26; CD 5; DAM DRAM, MST; DFS 12; DLB 38

Walker, Margaret (Abigail)
1915-1998 .... **BLC; CLC 1, 6; PC 20; TCLC 129**
See also AFAW 1, 2; BW 2, 3; CA 73-76; 172; CANR 26, 54, 76; CN 7; CP 7; CSW; DAM MULT; DLB 76, 152; EXPP; FW; MTCW 1, 2; RGAL 4; RHW
Walker, Ted .... **CLC 13**
See Walker, Edward Joseph
See also DLB 40
Wallace, David Foster 1962- ..... **CLC 50, 114**
See also AAYA 50; AMWS 10; CA 132; CANR 59; DA3; MTCW 2
Wallace, Dexter
See Masters, Edgar Lee
Wallace, (Richard Horatio) Edgar
1875-1932 .... **TCLC 57**
See also CA 115; CMW 4; DLB 70; MSW; RGEL 2
Wallace, Irving 1916-1990 .... **CLC 7, 13**
See also AITN 1; BPFB 3; CA 1-4R; 132; CAAS 1; CANR 1, 27; CPW; DAM NOV, POP; INT CANR-27; MTCW 1, 2
Wallant, Edward Lewis 1926-1962 ... **CLC 5, 10**
See also CA 1-4R; CANR 22; DLB 2, 28, 143; EWL 3; MTCW 1, 2; RGAL 4
Wallas, Graham 1858-1932 .... **TCLC 91**
Waller, Edmund 1606-1687 .... **LC 86**
See also BRW 2; DAM POET; DLB 126; PAB; RGEL 2
Walley, Byron
See Card, Orson Scott
Walpole, Horace 1717-1797 .... **LC 2, 49**
See also BRW 3; DLB 39, 104, 213; HGG; LMFS 1; RGEL 2; SUFW 1; TEA
Walpole, Hugh (Seymour)
1884-1941 .... **TCLC 5**
See also CA 104; 165; DLB 34; HGG; MTCW 2; RGEL 2; RHW
Walrond, Eric (Derwent) 1898-1966 .... **HR 3**
See also BW 1; CA 125; DLB 51
Walser, Martin 1927- .... **CLC 27**
See also CA 57-60; CANR 8, 46; CWW 2; DLB 75, 124; EWL 3
Walser, Robert 1878-1956 ..... **SSC 20; TCLC 18**
See also CA 118; 165; CANR 100; DLB 66; EWL 3
Walsh, Gillian Paton
See Paton Walsh, Gillian
Walsh, Jill Paton .... **CLC 35**
See Paton Walsh, Gillian
See also CLR 2, 65; WYA
Walter, Villiam Christian
See Andersen, Hans Christian
Walters, Anna L(ee) 1946- .... **NNAL**
See also CA 73-76
Walther von der Vogelweide c.
1170-1228 .... **CMLC 56**
Walton, Izaak 1593-1683 .... **LC 72**
See also BRW 2; CDBLB Before 1660; DLB 151, 213; RGEL 2
Wambaugh, Joseph (Aloysius), Jr.
1937- .... **CLC 3, 18**
See also AITN 1; BEST 89:3; BPFB 3; CA 33-36R; CANR 42, 65, 115; CMW 4; CPW 1; DA3; DAM NOV, POP; DLB 6; DLBY 1983; MSW; MTCW 1, 2
Wang Wei 699(?)-761(?) .... **PC 18**
See also TWA
Ward, Arthur Henry Sarsfield 1883-1959
See Rohmer, Sax
See also CA 108; 173; CMW 4; HGG
Ward, Douglas Turner 1930- .... **CLC 19**
See also BW 1; CA 81-84; CAD; CANR 27; CD 5; DLB 7, 38
Ward, E. D.
See Lucas, E(dward) V(errall)

Whittemore, (Edward) Reed, Jr.
1919- .... **CLC 4**
See also CA 9-12R; CAAS 8; CANR 4,
119; CP 7; DLB 5

Whittier, John Greenleaf
1807-1892 .... **NCLC 8, 59**
See also AMWS 1; DLB 1, 243; RGAL 4

Whittlebot, Hernia
See Coward, Noel (Peirce)

Wicker, Thomas Grey 1926-
See Wicker, Tom
See also CA 65-68; CANR 21, 46

Wicker, Tom .... **CLC 7**
See Wicker, Thomas Grey

Wideman, John Edgar 1941- ... **BLC 3; CLC
5, 34, 36, 67, 122; SSC 62**
See also AFAW 1, 2; AMWS 10; BPFB 4;
BW 2, 3; CA 85-88; CANR 14, 42, 67,
109; CN 7; DAM MULT; DLB 33, 143;
MTCW 2; RGAL 4; RGSF 2; SSFS 6, 12

Wiebe, Rudy (Henry) 1934- .. **CLC 6, 11, 14,
138**
See also CA 37-40R; CANR 42, 67; CN 7;
DAC; DAM MST; DLB 60; RHW

Wieland, Christoph Martin
1733-1813 .... **NCLC 17**
See also DLB 97; EW 4; LMFS 1; RGWL
2, 3

Wiene, Robert 1881-1938 .... **TCLC 56**

Wieners, John 1934- .... **CLC 7**
See also BG 3; CA 13-16R; CP 7; DLB 16;
WP

Wiesel, Elie(zer) 1928- .... **CLC 3, 5, 11, 37,
165; WLCS**
See also AAYA 7; AITN 1; CA 5-8R; CAAS
4; CANR 8, 40, 65; CDALBS; DA; DA3;
DAB; DAC; DAM MST, NOV; DLB 83;
DLBY 1987; EWL 3; INT CANR-8;
LAIT 4; MTCW 1, 2; NCFS 4; NFS 4;
RGWL 3; SATA 56; YAW

Wiggins, Marianne 1947- .... **CLC 57**
See also BEST 89:3; CA 130; CANR 60

Wiggs, Susan .... **CLC 70**
See also CA 201

Wight, James Alfred 1916-1995
See Herriot, James
See also CA 77-80; SATA 55; SATA-Brief
44

Wilbur, Richard (Purdy) 1921- ..... **CLC 3, 6,
9, 14, 53, 110**
See also AMWS 3; CA 1-4R; CABS 2;
CANR 2, 29, 76, 93; CDALBS; CP 7;
DA; DAB; DAC; DAM MST, POET;
DLB 5, 169; EWL 3; EXPP; INT CANR-
29; MTCW 1, 2; PAB; PFS 11, 12, 16;
RGAL 4; SATA 9, 108; WP

Wild, Peter 1940- .... **CLC 14**
See also CA 37-40R; CP 7; DLB 5

Wilde, Oscar (Fingal O'Flahertie Wills)
1854(?)-1900 ..... **DC 17; SSC 11; TCLC
1, 8, 23, 41; WLC**
See also AAYA 49; BRW 5; BRWC 1;
BRWR 2; CA 104; 119; CANR 112; CD-
BLB 1890-1914; DA; DA3; DAB; DAC;
DAM DRAM, MST, NOV; DFS 4, 8, 9;
DLB 10, 19, 34, 57, 141, 156, 190; EXPS;
FANT; LATS 1; RGEL 2; RGSF 2; SATA
24; SSFS 7; SUFW; TEA; WCH; WLIT 4

Wilder, Billy .... **CLC 20**
See Wilder, Samuel
See also DLB 26

Wilder, Samuel 1906-2002
See Wilder, Billy
See also CA 89-92; 205

Wilder, Stephen
See Marlowe, Stephen

Wilder, Thornton (Niven)
1897-1975 .. **CLC 1, 5, 6, 10, 15, 35, 82;
DC 1; WLC**
See also AAYA 29; AITN 2; AMW; CA 13-
16R; 61-64; CAD; CANR 40; CDALBS;
DA; DA3; DAB; DAC; DAM DRAM,
MST, NOV; DFS 1, 4, 16; DLB 4, 7, 9,
228; DLBY 1997; EWL 3; LAIT 3;
MTCW 1, 2; RGAL 4; RHW; WYAS 1

Wilding, Michael 1942- ...... **CLC 73; SSC 50**
See also CA 104; CANR 24, 49, 106; CN
7; RGSF 2

Wiley, Richard 1944- .... **CLC 44**
See also CA 121; 129; CANR 71

Wilhelm, Kate .... **CLC 7**
See Wilhelm, Katie (Gertrude)
See also AAYA 20; CAAS 5; DLB 8; INT
CANR-17; SCFW 2

Wilhelm, Katie (Gertrude) 1928-
See Wilhelm, Kate
See also CA 37-40R; CANR 17, 36, 60, 94;
MTCW 1; SFW 4

Wilkins, Mary
See Freeman, Mary E(leanor) Wilkins

Willard, Nancy 1936- .... **CLC 7, 37**
See also BYA 5; CA 89-92; CANR 10, 39,
68, 107; CLR 5; CWP; CWRI 5; DLB 5,
52; FANT; MAICYA 1, 2; MTCW 1;
SATA 37, 71, 127; SATA-Brief 30; SUFW
2

William of Malmesbury c. 1090B.C.-c.
1140B.C. .... **CMLC 57**

William of Ockham 1290-1349 ..... **CMLC 32**

Williams, Ben Ames 1889-1953 ..... **TCLC 89**
See also CA 183; DLB 102

Williams, C(harles) K(enneth)
1936- .... **CLC 33, 56, 148**
See also CA 37-40R; CAAS 26; CANR 57,
106; CP 7; DAM POET; DLB 5

Williams, Charles
See Collier, James Lincoln

Williams, Charles (Walter Stansby)
1886-1945 .... **TCLC 1, 11**
See also CA 104; 163; DLB 100, 153, 255;
FANT; RGEL 2; SUFW 1

Williams, Ella Gwendolen Rees
See Rhys, Jean

Williams, (George) Emlyn
1905-1987 .... **CLC 15**
See also CA 104; 123; CANR 36; DAM
DRAM; DLB 10, 77; IDTP; MTCW 1

Williams, Hank 1923-1953 .... **TCLC 81**
See Williams, Hiram King

Williams, Hiram Hank
See Williams, Hank

Williams, Hiram King
See Williams, Hank
See also CA 188

Williams, Hugo (Mordaunt) 1942- ... **CLC 42**
See also CA 17-20R; CANR 45, 119; CP 7;
DLB 40

Williams, J. Walker
See Wodehouse, P(elham) G(renville)

Williams, John A(lfred) 1925- . **BLC 3; CLC
5, 13**
See also AFAW 2; BW 2, 3; CA 53-56;
CAAE 195; CAAS 3; CANR 6, 26, 51,
118; CN 7; CSW; DAM MULT; DLB 2,
33; EWL 3; INT CANR-6; RGAL 4; SFW
4

Williams, Jonathan (Chamberlain)
1929- .... **CLC 13**
See also CA 9-12R; CAAS 12; CANR 8,
108; CP 7; DLB 5

Williams, Joy 1944- .... **CLC 31**
See also CA 41-44R; CANR 22, 48, 97

Williams, Norman 1952- .... **CLC 39**
See also CA 118

Williams, Sherley Anne 1944-1999 ... **BLC 3;
CLC 89**
See also AFAW 2; BW 2, 3; CA 73-76; 185;
CANR 25, 82; DAM MULT, POET; DLB
41; INT CANR-25; SATA 78; SATA-Obit
116

Williams, Shirley
See Williams, Sherley Anne

Williams, Tennessee 1911-1983 . **CLC 1, 2, 5,
7, 8, 11, 15, 19, 30, 39, 45, 71, 111; DC
4; WLC**
See also AAYA 31; AITN 1, 2; AMW;
AMWC 1; CA 5-8R; 108; CABS 3; CAD;
CANR 31; CDALB 1941-1968; DA;
DA3; DAB; DAC; DAM DRAM, MST;
DFS 17; DLB 7; DLBD 4; DLBY 1983;
EWL 3; GLL 1; LAIT 4; LATS 1; MTCW
1, 2; RGAL 4; TUS

Williams, Thomas (Alonzo)
1926-1990 .... **CLC 14**
See also CA 1-4R; 132; CANR 2

Williams, William C.
See Williams, William Carlos

Williams, William Carlos
1883-1963 .... **CLC 1, 2, 5, 9, 13, 22, 42,
67; PC 7; SSC 31**
See also AAYA 46; AMW; AMWR 1; CA
89-92; CANR 34; CDALB 1917-1929;
DA; DA3; DAB; DAC; DAM MST,
POET; DLB 4, 16, 54, 86; EWL 3; EXPP;
MTCW 1, 2; NCFS 4; PAB; PFS 1, 6, 11;
RGAL 4; RGSF 2; TUS; WP

Williamson, David (Keith) 1942- ... **CLC 56**
See also CA 103; CANR 41; CD 5

Williamson, Ellen Douglas 1905-1984
See Douglas, Ellen
See also CA 17-20R; 114; CANR 39

Williamson, Jack .... **CLC 29**
See Williamson, John Stewart
See also CAAS 8; DLB 8; SCFW 2

Williamson, John Stewart 1908-
See Williamson, Jack
See also CA 17-20R; CANR 23, 70; SFW 4

Willie, Frederick
See Lovecraft, H(oward) P(hillips)

Willingham, Calder (Baynard, Jr.)
1922-1995 .... **CLC 5, 51**
See also CA 5-8R; 147; CANR 3; CSW;
DLB 2, 44; IDFW 3, 4; MTCW 1

Willis, Charles
See Clarke, Arthur C(harles)

Willy
See Colette, (Sidonie-Gabrielle)

Willy, Colette
See Colette, (Sidonie-Gabrielle)
See also GLL 1

Wilmot, John 1647-1680 .... **LC 75**
See Rochester
See also BRW 2; DLB 131; PAB

Wilson, A(ndrew) N(orman) 1950- .. **CLC 33**
See also BRWS 6; CA 112; 122; CN 7;
DLB 14, 155, 194; MTCW 2

Wilson, Angus (Frank Johnstone)
1913-1991 . **CLC 2, 3, 5, 25, 34; SSC 21**
See also BRWS 1; CA 5-8R; 134; CANR
21; DLB 15, 139, 155; EWL 3; MTCW 1,
2; RGEL 2; RGSF 2

Wilson, August 1945- ... **BLC 3; CLC 39, 50,
63, 118; DC 2; WLCS**
See also AAYA 16; AFAW 2; AMWS 8; BW
2, 3; CA 115; 122; CAD; CANR 42, 54,
76; CD 5; DA; DA3; DAB; DAC; DAM
DRAM, MST, MULT; DFS 3, 7, 15, 17;
DLB 228; EWL 3; LAIT 4; LATS 1;
MTCW 1, 2; RGAL 4

Wilson, Brian 1942- .... **CLC 12**

Wilson, Colin 1931- .... **CLC 3, 14**
See also CA 1-4R; CAAS 5; CANR 1, 22,
33, 77; CMW 4; CN 7; DLB 14, 194;
HGG; MTCW 1; SFW 4

Wright, Frank Lloyd 1867-1959 .... **TCLC 95**
  See also AAYA 33; CA 174
Wright, Jack R.
  See Harris, Mark
Wright, James (Arlington)
  1927-1980 .... **CLC 3, 5, 10, 28; PC 36**
  See also AITN 2; AMWS 3; CA 49-52; 97-100; CANR 4, 34, 64; CDALBS; DAM POET; DLB 5, 169; EWL 3; EXPP; MTCW 1, 2; PFS 7, 8; RGAL 4; TUS; WP
Wright, Judith (Arundell)
  1915-2000 .... **CLC 11, 53; PC 14**
  See also CA 13-16R; 188; CANR 31, 76, 93; CP 7; CWP; DLB 260; EWL 3; MTCW 1, 2; PFS 8; RGEL 2; SATA 14; SATA-Obit 121
Wright, L(aurali) R. 1939- .... **CLC 44**
  See also CA 138; CMW 4
Wright, Richard (Nathaniel)
  1908-1960 ... **BLC 3; CLC 1, 3, 4, 9, 14, 21, 48, 74; SSC 2; TCLC 136; WLC**
  See also AAYA 5, 42; AFAW 1, 2; AMW; BPFB 3; BW 1; BYA 2; CA 108; CANR 64; CDALB 1929-1941; DA; DA3; DAB; DAC; DAM MST, MULT, NOV; DLB 76, 102; DLBD 2; EWL 3; EXPN; LAIT 3, 4; MTCW 1, 2; NCFS 1; NFS 1, 7; RGAL 4; RGSF 2; SSFS 3, 9, 15; TUS; YAW
Wright, Richard B(ruce) 1937- .... **CLC 6**
  See also CA 85-88; CANR 120; DLB 53
Wright, Rick 1945- .... **CLC 35**
Wright, Rowland
  See Wells, Carolyn
Wright, Stephen 1946- .... **CLC 33**
Wright, Willard Huntington 1888-1939
  See Van Dine, S. S.
  See also CA 115; 189; CMW 4; DLBD 16
Wright, William 1930- .... **CLC 44**
  See also CA 53-56; CANR 7, 23
Wroth, Lady Mary 1587-1653(?) .... **LC 30; PC 38**
  See also DLB 121
Wu Ch'eng-en 1500(?)-1582(?) .... **LC 7**
Wu Ching-tzu 1701-1754 .... **LC 2**
Wulfstan c. 10th cent. -1023 .... **CMLC 59**
Wurlitzer, Rudolph 1938(?)- .... **CLC 2, 4, 15**
  See also CA 85-88; CN 7; DLB 173
Wyatt, Sir Thomas c. 1503-1542 . **LC 70; PC 27**
  See also BRW 1; DLB 132; EXPP; RGEL 2; TEA
Wycherley, William 1640-1716 .... **LC 8, 21**
  See also BRW 2; CDBLB 1660-1789; DAM DRAM; DLB 80; RGEL 2
Wylie, Elinor (Morton Hoyt)
  1885-1928 .... **PC 23; TCLC 8**
  See also AMWS 1; CA 105; 162; DLB 9, 45; EXPP; RGAL 4
Wylie, Philip (Gordon) 1902-1971 ... **CLC 43**
  See also CA 21-22; 33-36R; CAP 2; DLB 9; SFW 4
Wyndham, John .... **CLC 19**
  See Harris, John (Wyndham Parkes Lucas) Beynon
  See also DLB 255; SCFW 2
Wyss, Johann David Von
  1743-1818 .... **NCLC 10**
  See also JRDA; MAICYA 1, 2; SATA 29; SATA-Brief 27
Xenophon c. 430B.C.-c. 354B.C. ... **CMLC 17**
  See also AW 1; DLB 176; RGWL 2, 3
Xingjian, Gao 1940-
  See Gao Xingjian
  See also CA 193; RGWL 3
Yakamochi 718-785 .... **CMLC 45; PC 48**
Yakumo Koizumi
  See Hearn, (Patricio) Lafcadio (Tessima Carlos)

Yamada, Mitsuye (May) 1923- .... **PC 44**
  See also CA 77-80
Yamamoto, Hisaye 1921- .... **AAL; SSC 34**
  See also DAM MULT; LAIT 4; SSFS 14
Yamauchi, Wakako 1924- .... **AAL**
Yanez, Jose Donoso
  See Donoso (Yanez), Jose
Yanovsky, Basile S.
  See Yanovsky, V(assily) S(emenovich)
Yanovsky, V(assily) S(emenovich)
  1906-1989 .... **CLC 2, 18**
  See also CA 97-100; 129
Yates, Richard 1926-1992 .... **CLC 7, 8, 23**
  See also AMWS 11; CA 5-8R; 139; CANR 10, 43; DLB 2, 234; DLBY 1981, 1992; INT CANR-10
Yeats, W. B.
  See Yeats, William Butler
Yeats, William Butler 1865-1939 .... **PC 20; TCLC 1, 11, 18, 31, 93, 116; WLC**
  See also AAYA 48; BRW 6; BRWR 1; CA 104; 127; CANR 45; CDBLB 1890-1914; DA; DA3; DAB; DAC; DAM DRAM, MST, POET; DLB 10, 19, 98, 156; EWL 3; EXPP; MTCW 1, 2; NCFS 3; PAB; PFS 1, 2, 5, 7, 13, 15; RGEL 2; TEA; WLIT 4; WP
Yehoshua, A(braham) B. 1936- .. **CLC 13, 31**
  See also CA 33-36R; CANR 43, 90; EWL 3; RGSF 2; RGWL 3
Yellow Bird
  See Ridge, John Rollin
Yep, Laurence Michael 1948- .... **CLC 35**
  See also AAYA 5, 31; BYA 7; CA 49-52; CANR 1, 46, 92; CLR 3, 17, 54; DLB 52; FANT; JRDA; MAICYA 1, 2; MAICYAS 1; SATA 7, 69, 123; WYA; YAW
Yerby, Frank G(arvin) 1916-1991 ..... **BLC 3; CLC 1, 7, 22**
  See also BPFB 3; BW 1, 3; CA 9-12R; 136; CANR 16, 52; DAM MULT; DLB 76; INT CANR-16; MTCW 1; RGAL 4; RHW
Yesenin, Sergei Alexandrovich
  See Esenin, Sergei (Alexandrovich)
Yesenin, Sergey
  See Esenin, Sergei (Alexandrovich)
  See also EWL 3
Yevtushenko, Yevgeny (Alexandrovich)
  1933- ...... **CLC 1, 3, 13, 26, 51, 126; PC 40**
  See Evtushenko, Evgenii Aleksandrovich
  See also CA 81-84; CANR 33, 54; CWW 2; DAM POET; EWL 3; MTCW 1
Yezierska, Anzia 1885(?)-1970 .... **CLC 46**
  See also CA 126; 89-92; DLB 28, 221; FW; MTCW 1; RGAL 4; SSFS 15
Yglesias, Helen 1915- .... **CLC 7, 22**
  See also CA 37-40R; CAAS 20; CANR 15, 65, 95; CN 7; INT CANR-15; MTCW 1
Yokomitsu, Riichi 1898-1947 .... **TCLC 47**
  See also CA 170; EWL 3
Yonge, Charlotte (Mary)
  1823-1901 .... **TCLC 48**
  See also CA 109; 163; DLB 18, 163; RGEL 2; SATA 17; WCH
York, Jeremy
  See Creasey, John
York, Simon
  See Heinlein, Robert A(nson)
Yorke, Henry Vincent 1905-1974 ..... **CLC 13**
  See Green, Henry
  See also CA 85-88; 49-52
Yosano Akiko 1878-1942 .... **PC 11; TCLC 59**
  See also CA 161; EWL 3; RGWL 3
Yoshimoto, Banana .... **CLC 84**
  See Yoshimoto, Mahoko
  See also AAYA 50; NFS 7

Yoshimoto, Mahoko 1964-
  See Yoshimoto, Banana
  See also CA 144; CANR 98; SSFS 16
Young, Al(bert James) 1939- ... **BLC 3; CLC 19**
  See also BW 2, 3; CA 29-32R; CANR 26, 65, 109; CN 7; CP 7; DAM MULT; DLB 33
Young, Andrew (John) 1885-1971 ...... **CLC 5**
  See also CA 5-8R; CANR 7, 29; RGEL 2
Young, Collier
  See Bloch, Robert (Albert)
Young, Edward 1683-1765 .... **LC 3, 40**
  See also DLB 95; RGEL 2
Young, Marguerite (Vivian)
  1909-1995 .... **CLC 82**
  See also CA 13-16; 150; CAP 1; CN 7
Young, Neil 1945- .... **CLC 17**
  See also CA 110; CCA 1
Young Bear, Ray A. 1950- ... **CLC 94; NNAL**
  See also CA 146; DAM MULT; DLB 175
Yourcenar, Marguerite 1903-1987 ... **CLC 19, 38, 50, 87**
  See also BPFB 3; CA 69-72; CANR 23, 60, 93; DAM NOV; DLB 72; DLBY 1988; EW 12; EWL 3; GFL 1789 to the Present; GLL 1; MTCW 1, 2; RGWL 2, 3
Yuan, Chu 340(?)B.C.-278(?)B.C. . **CMLC 36**
Yurick, Sol 1925- .... **CLC 6**
  See also CA 13-16R; CANR 25; CN 7
Zabolotsky, Nikolai Alekseevich
  1903-1958 .... **TCLC 52**
  See Zabolotsky, Nikolay Alekseevich
  See also CA 116; 164
Zabolotsky, Nikolay Alekseevich
  See Zabolotsky, Nikolai Alekseevich
  See also EWL 3
Zagajewski, Adam 1945- .... **PC 27**
  See also CA 186; DLB 232; EWL 3
Zalygin, Sergei -2000 .... **CLC 59**
Zamiatin, Evgenii
  See Zamyatin, Evgeny Ivanovich
  See also RGSF 2; RGWL 2, 3
Zamiatin, Evgenii Ivanovich
  See Zamyatin, Evgeny Ivanovich
  See also DLB 272
Zamiatin, Yevgenii
  See Zamyatin, Evgeny Ivanovich
Zamora, Bernice (B. Ortiz) 1938- .. **CLC 89; HLC 2**
  See also CA 151; CANR 80; DAM MULT; DLB 82; HW 1, 2
Zamyatin, Evgeny Ivanovich
  1884-1937 .... **TCLC 8, 37**
  See Zamiatin, Evgenii; Zamiatin, Evgenii Ivanovich; Zamyatin, Yevgeny Ivanovich
  See also CA 105; 166; EW 10; SFW 4
Zamyatin, Yevgeny Ivanovich
  See Zamyatin, Evgeny Ivanovich
  See also EWL 3
Zangwill, Israel 1864-1926 ... **SSC 44; TCLC 16**
  See also CA 109; 167; CMW 4; DLB 10, 135, 197; RGEL 2
Zappa, Francis Vincent, Jr. 1940-1993
  See Zappa, Frank
  See also CA 108; 143; CANR 57
Zappa, Frank .... **CLC 17**
  See Zappa, Francis Vincent, Jr.
Zaturenska, Marya 1902-1982 ..... **CLC 6, 11**
  See also CA 13-16R; 105; CANR 22
Zeami 1363-1443 .... **DC 7; LC 86**
  See also DLB 203; RGWL 2, 3
Zelazny, Roger (Joseph) 1937-1995 . **CLC 21**
  See also AAYA 7; BPFB 3; CA 21-24R; 148; CANR 26, 60; CN 7; DLB 8; FANT; MTCW 1, 2; SATA 57; SATA-Brief 39; SCFW 4; SFW 4; SUFW 1, 2

Literary Criticism Series
Cumulative Topic Index

This index lists all topic entries in Gale's *Classical and Medieval Literature Criticism* (CMLC), *Contemporary Literary Criticism* (CLC), *Drama Criticism* (DC), *Literature Criticism from 1400 to 1800* (LC), *Nineteenth-Century Literature Criticism* (NCLC), *Short Story Criticism* (SSC), and *Twentieth-Century Literary Criticism* (TCLC). The index also lists topic entries in the Gale Critical Companion Collection, which includes the following publications: *The Beat Generation* (BG), and *Harlem Renaissance* (HR).

Topic Index

CLC Cumulative Nationality Index

Nationality Index

Nationality Index

CLC-179 Title Index

ISBN 0-7876-6752-8